Phaidon Press Limited
Regent's Wharf
All Saints Street
London N1 9PA

www.phaidon.com

First published in English 2005
Reprinted 2005, 2006 (three times)
© 2005 Phaidon Press Limited

ISBN 0 7148 4467 5 (UK edition)

First published in Italian by Editoriale
Domus as *Il cucchiaio d'argento* 1950.
Eighth edition (revised, expanded and
redesigned) 1997.
© Editoriale Domus

A CIP catalogue record for this book is
available from the British Library.

The Publishers would like to thank
Lagostina, Paderno and Wedgwood for
having kindly provided some of the
china, pots, pans and tools illustrated
in this book.   -

Designed by Italo Lupi with Marina del
Cinque and Alessandra Beluffi

Photography by Jason Lowe

Drawings by Francesca Bazzurro

The Publishers would also like to thank
Hilary Bird, Tessa Clark, Linda Doeser,
Clelia d'Onofrio, Carmen Figini, Trish
Hilferty and Tom Norrington-Davies for
their contributions to the book.

Printed in Italy

13th February 2009
54050000169938

THE

SILVER

SPOON

SAUCES, MARINADES AND FLAVOURED BUTTERS	45
ANTIPASTI, APPETIZERS AND PIZZAS	91
FIRST COURSES	201
EGGS AND FRITTATA	351
VEGETABLES	397
FISH, CRUSTACEANS AND SHELLFISH	587
MEAT AND OFFAL	735

CONTENTS

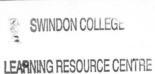

7 | EATING IS A SERIOUS MATTER
17 | COOKING TERMS
36 | TOOLS AND EQUIPMENT

875 | POULTRY
947 | GAME
987 | CHEESE
1001 | DESSERTS AND BAKING
1121 | MENUS BY CELEBRATED CHEFS

1201 | LIST OF RECIPES
1218 | INDEX

EATING IS A SERIOUS MATTER

Eating is a serious matter in Italy. Cooking and food are among the finest expressions of Italian culture, vividly portraying the country's history and traditions. Like all other arts, cookery is based on measures and proportions, on the balance and fusion of different elements. It blends ancient traditions with contemporary innovation and evolves constantly, even in the twenty-first century, as a result of its position at the centre of Italian family life. At home with family or friends, for a special occasion, in a fancy restaurant or in a humble trattoria, or even when preparing a simple everyday meal, for Italians, cooking is synonymous with good food, good wine and good company. Whether rustic or sophisticated, Italian cooking is traditionally based on excellent, fresh, seasonal ingredients. This is one of the main reasons why Italian food varies so much from region to region and even from village to village. In the north, where cattle and dairy farming are prevalent, we find a cuisine based on butter, meat and Parmigiano, while travelling towards the south we encounter olive oil (extra vergine, of course), ripe tomatoes, gorgeous aubergines and fresh fish. Italian cookery is based on Italy's rural traditions and depends very much on the vast variety of the country's agricultural produce. Yet even if nowadays you can find almost any kind of food at any time of the year, Italians still follow the rhythm of the seasons and will wait until spring to enjoy asparagus, or the summer for a fresh Insalata caprese. But as soon as the temperature falls in the autumn, everyone is ready for a warming plate of Braised Beef with Barolo. In Italian families, special occasions are still celebrated at home with a five-course meal (antipasto, first course, main course with vegetables, cheese and dessert). But, when eating everyday, a one-meal dish such as lasagne, pizza or ribollita will satisfy even the most demanding of appetites. The country's infinite variety of dishes allows Italians to create an excellent and healthy meal whether they choose to spend their entire day cooking, putting together a stunning Brodetto Marchigiano (a fish soup made using several varieties of fish and shellfish), or if, instead, they go home and make a simple but authentic dish of Spaghetti aglio olio e peperoncino, with its four ingredients never missing from any Italian kitchen. Authentic Italian dishes are very often based on just a few, humble ingredients. What makes them so tasty and delicious is that, over the centuries, Italians have discovered exactly how to achieve the perfect mix of flavours. It sometimes seems that

Italians learn to cook before they learn to talk and their skills are handed down from one generation to the next. The perfection of Italian cookery has been achieved through centuries of testing in family kitchens, with millions of dishes served to the most discerning of critics. *The Silver Spoon* is the result of a labour of love, with only the very best recipes from Italian families and cooks within its covers. This is the one cookery book every Italian passes on to their children, teaching them the skills of their parents and grandparents, and allowing them to understand what Italian cooking is really about. It shows them how to prepare a healthy and delicious meal by, firstly, choosing the right ingredients and then by following a variety of recipes that may be either simple or complicated, but always explained in the clearest and simplest of ways. For these reasons *The Silver Spoon* is the most successful cookery book in Italy, the book that has its place in every family kitchen, the one that many brides have received as a wedding gift. Conceived by Editoriale Domus, publisher of *Domus*, the Italian design and architectural magazine famously directed by Gio Ponti, the first edition came out in 1950 with the title *Il cucchiaio d'argento* (the silver spoon). This name stems from an English phrase that symbolizes plenty, wealth and good fortune: to be born with a silver spoon in your mouth describes how someone has been born with a fortunate heritage … just like the culinary heritage *The Silver Spoon* gives to its readers. From its very first appearance, the book immediately made its mark on the world of gastronomy, and from that point onwards it has never been out of print, quickly becoming the classic volume of Italian cooking and the leading authority in Italy. To compile *Il cucchiaio d'argento*, cookery experts were commissioned by Editoriale Domus to collect hundreds of traditional recipes from throughout the Italian regions, showing every regional speciality. During the more than 50 years in which the book has been in print, it has been constantly updated, with various successive editions, each one adapting the recipes and techniques to our modern lifestyle without losing the principles of authentic Italian cuisine. The result is an extraordinary cookbook containing over 2,000 recipes. Now translated for the first time into English, *The Silver Spoon* can transform every English-speaking reader into an experienced Italian cook, teaching them the thousands of secrets of how to cook a truly authentic Italian meal.

OUR SPOON

As we started working on the English-language edition of *Il cucchiaio d'argento*, it quickly became obvious that it was not enough to simply translate the recipes without any adaptation as there is a fundamental difference between the Italian approach to cooking and that of the English-speaking countries. English-language cookbooks tend to contain far more detailed explanations than their Italian counterparts. We have moved the original Italian recipes much nearer to what is expected by English-speaking readers but we have also been careful to retain the Italian character of the book. Also, when a recipe indicates ingredients that are not readily available outside Italy, we have tried to suggest alternative and more commonly found ingredients alongside the originals. In this way, we have made as many of the recipes as possible available to everyone. To make the book easy to use, we have also included imperial measurements - though in the same way as for all recipes books, the user should, of course, only follow one or the other set of measurements. To preserve the authenticity of the Italian edition, we have included all of the recipes that feature in *Il cucchiaio d'argento*, even if some of them seem unfamiliar to an English-speaking audience. In this way, the book remains an authentic Italian cookbook and includes all of the dishes that Italians like to prepare and eat. *The Silver*

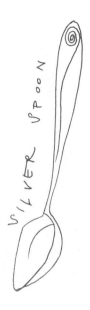

SILVER SPOON

Spoon is organised in chapters by course, with each course using a different colour in the design of its pages. The recipes are listed according to the alphabetical order of their original Italian titles, though each recipe also has an English translation of its name alongside. In the final section of the book there is a collection of menus comprising signature dishes by 14 celebrated Italian cooks, together with a further 9 menus from some of the very best Italian restaurants and chefs throughout the world. There is a comprehensive index that allows the reader to look up specific ingredients, to find the recipes in which that ingredient is used and, of course, it also includes the names of the recipes both in English and Italian. For this English edition we have commissioned 200 new images from the distinguished food photographer, Jason Lowe. An expert cook prepared each dish using only natural, authentic ingredients and, as soon as the food was ready, it was photographed on pure white crockery or in the pan in which it was cooked. In this way, we have ensured that the food looks both as delicious and natural as possible, with all the little imperfections that make home cooked recipes so appealing. Illuminated only using natural daylight, the photography in *The Silver Spoon* conjures up the flavours and aromas of the authentic cuisine of Italy.

GUIDE TO USING
THE SILVER SPOON

This book contains over 2,000 recipes; some are traditional and regional Italian dishes, while others are more contemporary additions. For this latest edition, the ingredients and cooking times of some recipes have been updated in the light of changing tastes and lifestyles. Others have been left virtually untouched to retain their unique characteristics. The majority can be easily adapted to suit your personal requirements. Most of the recipes are designed for four servings. (The number of servings for each recipe is usually specified.) This is a convenient quantity and can be usually be halved or doubled to accommodate smaller groups or for entertaining guests. Some recipes, such as roasts, work better in slightly larger quantities and may serve six or eight. Other recipes - antipasti, salads and sauces, for example - do not list the number of servings, as quantities may be varied without compromising the results. Both metric and imperial measurements have been used throughout. Use one system, not a mix of the two, as they are not interchangeable. Where no quantity is specified these ingredients should be used according to personal taste.

NOTES ABOUT COOKING

Like most specialist fields, cookery has its own vocabulary. Many foreign terms, often French and, in the case of *The Silver Spoon*, Italian, are frequently used – blanquette and al dente, for example. We have included a glossary of common terms, particularly those used in this book. This chapter also includes a guide to tools and equipment.

WHERE TO FIND WHAT YOU WANT

SAUCES, MARINADES AND FLAVOURED BUTTERS

Recipes for both hot and cold classics, such as béchamel and mayonnaise, are included here.

→ Marinades may be used to flavour and tenderize a wide range of ingredients before cooking. Leave ingredients to marinate in a cool place rather than the refrigerator for up to 2 hours. If marinating for longer, place the mixture in the refrigerator. In both cases, it is sensible to cover the dish.

→ Flavoured butters may be used for cooking, but are more often added when the dish is served. Note that quantities can sometimes seem excessive, but there is always a reason for the amount specified.

ANTIPASTI, APPETIZERS AND PIZZAS

Antipasti and appetizers are designed to stimulate the taste buds and are served in small quantities to leave plenty of room for the dishes that will follow. This chapter also includes recipes for pizzas, although nowadays these tend to be served as a main dish.

FIRST COURSES

This chapter is divided into the traditional Italian classifications of 'in broth' and 'dry'. 'In broth' includes recipes for a wide range of soups; 'dry' includes fresh and dried pasta, rice, risottos, polenta and gnocchi.

EGGS AND FRITTATA

The recipes are arranged according to the different ways of cooking eggs.

VEGETABLES

Vegetables have always played an important role in the Mediterranean diet. Over 30 sub-sections describe the basic preparation and cooking techniques of individual vegetables, followed by a collection of mouthwatering recipes.

FISH, CRUSTACEANS AND SHELLFISH

Italy is rightfully famous for its fish and seafood dishes and this chapter is packed with recipes for more than 40 different kinds. It is divided into sub-sections, covering sea fish, freshwater fish, crustaceans and shellfish, and also includes general advice on preparation and cooking techniques. Where particular types of fish may be difficult to obtain outside southern Europe, more readily available varieties have been suggested. Also included are a collection of recipes for fish soups and for cooking frogs and snails.

MEAT AND OFFAL

This chapter is sub-divided into sections covering all the different types of meat eaten in Italy. The introductions to the main sub-sections offer a helpful guide to the different cuts of meat and the techniques most suitable for cooking them.

→ The chapter concludes with a wide range of offal recipes. Both familiar and less familiar types are included. This chapter also includes a selection of recipes for Italian sausages.

POULTRY

Chicken is very popular in Italy. This chapter also includes recipes and information on all other farmed birds and is one of the few places where the English-language edition differs from the Italian. Even though rabbit is now widely farmed, we still classify it as furred game and the recipes for rabbit appear within Game. Quail recipes are also included within Game.

GAME

This chapter includes both furred and feathered game and, given Italian enthusiasm for hunting, it is not surprising that the recipes are simply fabulous. Much of what is classified as game is now widely available farmed.

CHEESE

Italy is rightly proud of the more than 400 different types of cheese it produces, many of them protected by DOC controls. The introduction to this chapter provides advice on choosing, using and storing cheese, plus a guide to tasty combinations with cheese.

DESSERTS AND BAKING

Home-made desserts are not widespread in Italy as people tend to buy them at the local pasticceria. But don't let this put you off. The many fabulous recipes included here are joined by basic recipes for a range of pastry doughs for those who really love baking.

MENUS BY CELEBRATED CHEFS

This chapter features menus by some of the most famous chefs in Italy from the past five decades. This edition has the additional bonus of including menus by a galaxy of international chefs, working in countries as far apart as the United Kingdom, the United States, Australia and New Zealand.

LIST OF RECIPES AND INDEX

The book concludes with a complete list of recipes arranged by chapter and a comprehensive index.

15

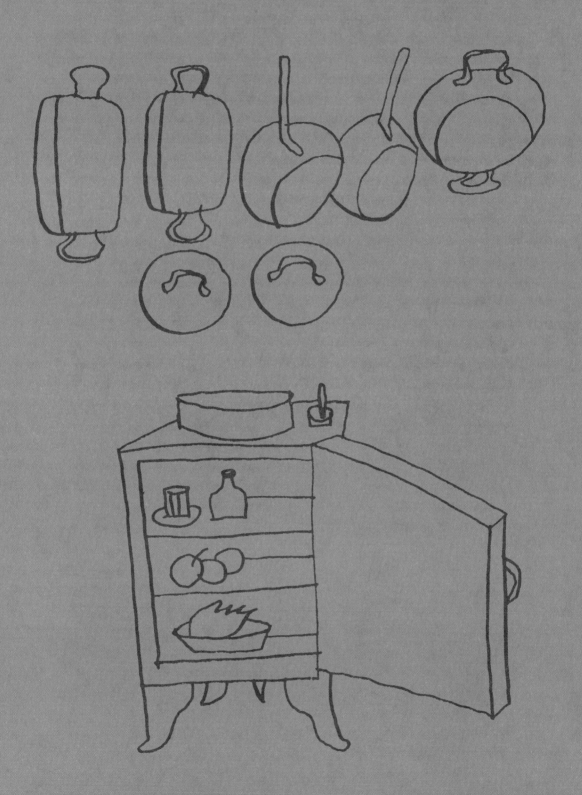

COOKING TERMS →

COOKING TERMS

To poach, to soften and to deglaze – these verbs describe a way of cooking an egg, a method of making a mixture more delicate and how to dilute cooking juices. Busecca, carpione and fricassée are the words for tripe in Milan, spiced water and vinegar for marinating fried meat and vegetables and a sauce made of eggs and lemon juice for cooking meat and vegetables. Pie, blini and soubise mean a pastry case with a savoury or sweet filling, a small pancake and an onion sauce. These are some of the more than 200 entries that make up this short dictionary of cookery terms and idioms which you frequently read in cookery books and magazines and which we all use, often without knowing precisely what they mean.

VINEGAR

ACETO BALSAMICO

Vinegar made from cooked and concentrated wine must from Trebbiano grapes. It is matured for at least 10 years and some-times much longer, and can be made only in a designated area surrounding the city of Modena. It is quite expensive but has a unique mellow flavour.

ACIDULATE

To add vinegar or lemon juice to water (or another liquid) for immers-ing some vegetables, such as globe artichokes, to prevent them from turning black before cooking.

ADD WHILE COLD

To add an ingredient to a liquid or sauce before heating. For exam-ple, meat is put in cold water when the flavour of the stock is more important than that of the meat.

COOKING TERMS

ADD WHILE HOT

To add an ingredient to a hot or boiling liquid or sauce. For example, meat is put in hot water when the flavour of the meat is more important than that of the stock.

AGRODOLCE

This dressing made with herbs, wine vinegar, sugar, onion and garlic is served with fish, game and vegetables, particularly onions and aubergines.

AÏOLI

This garlic-flavoured mayonnaise was originally called ailloli, and is a speciality of the south of France, where it is usually served with fish.

À LA MAÎTRE D'HÔTEL

A dish served with butter flavoured with chopped parsley and a little lemon juice. It is usually chilled in a roll, then sliced and served on meat or fish.

À LA TARTARE

Lean minced steak served raw, mixed with egg yolk, lemon juice, pickles, olive oil, herbs and spices.

AL DENTE

The point during cooking at which pasta and rice become tender but are still firm to the bite and should, therefore, be removed from the heat and drained. Vegetables cooked al dente are tastier and retain more nutrients.

ALL'INGLESE

Meaning 'in the English style' this, perhaps rather unflatteringly, describes food cooked and seasoned in a very simple way, such as vegetables boiled and served with melted butter or plain boiled rice seasoned with just a drop of oil.

AMARETTI

Sweet biscuits flavoured with almond or apricot kernels, these are served with creamy desserts such as mousse and other desserts (see page 1031).

APFELSTRUDEL

Among the various Austrian strudels – filled, wafer-thin pastry rolls – this is perhaps the most popular. It consists of a thin sheet of pastry that is filled with apples, sugar, sultanas, cinnamon, dried fruit and nuts, then rolled up and baked. It is often served warm.

ARRABBIATA

Literally 'angry', meaning hot, this is a method of cooking chops, rabbit and chicken in a frying pan with plenty of spices. It is also used to describe penne or other pasta covered with a tomato and hot chilli sauce.

ARROWROOT

A powdered American root used for thickening sauces. It is similar to cornflour but has the advantage of producing a transparent sauce.

A'SCAPECE

This is a typically Neapolitan mixture of aubergines, courgettes and other vegetables which are fried, and then left to marinate in vinegar and chopped garlic. It keeps for a long time in the refrigerator.

ASPIC

This is a French term meaning meat, fish or vegetables in gelatine prepared in a steel or copper mould with characteristic decoration.

ASSIETTE

A French term for a dish of mixed cold meats.

AU GRATIN

When a dish is sprinkled with grated cheese or topped with béchamel sauce, dotted with butter and sprinkled with breadcrumbs, then cooked in the oven until golden, it is said to be au gratin.

BAKE IN A PARCEL

To wrap food in foil, baking parchment or greaseproof paper and bake in the oven. This method requires very little oil or fat and is excellent for meat, fish and vegetables as it retains the cooking juices.

BARD

To wrap a roast or a breast of poultry or game with slices of pancetta or bacon, pancetta fat or bacon fat, or ham partly to flavour the meat and partly to protect it from fierce heat which might otherwise dry

it out. Three-quarters of the way through the cooking time the barding is removed so that the covered area may brown like the rest.

BATTUTO

Onion, carrot, celery and garlic chopped with a sharp heavy knife form the basis of many Italian dishes. It is sometimes sautéed with pancetta, pancetta fat or pork-back fat as a base for minestrones and meat dishes.

BED

A base of vegetables, salad leaves or other ingredients on which a dish is served.

BEURRE MANIÉ

A paste made from equal quantities of plain flour and butter used to thicken sauces. It is added in small pieces at a time and the sauce is stirred until the beurre manié is completely incorporated before another piece is added.

BLANCH

To partially cook fruit or vegetables briefly in boiling water to make them softer or easier to peel.

BLANQUETTE

Veal, chicken or lamb is cooked without browning. It is typical of French cuisine.

BLEND

To combine ingredients, by hand or with an electric mixer, until creamy and fully incorporated.

21

BLINI

Pancakes made of flour, milk, butter, eggs and a little salt, cooked in the oven and served hot. In traditional Russian cuisine they are often served with caviar, smoked salmon and soured cream.

BOIL

To cook meat, vegetables etc. for a specified time in water or stock.

BOLOGNESE

Meaning from the city of Bologna, this term describes a series of typical Emilian dishes that are part of classic Italian cuisine, such ragù (meat sauce), tagliatelle, tortellini and lasagne.

BONE

To remove the bones from fish or meat.

BORTSCH

Also sometimes spelt borsch, this thick meat and vegetable soup, served with soured cream, is made with beetroot which gives it its characteristic red colour. It is an eastern European speciality and is very popular in Russia.

BOTTARGA

Salted, pressed grey mullet (or tuna) roe is prepared like a salami. Slices, drizzled with olive oil and lemon juice or spread on toast, make a tasty antipasto. Crumbled and lightly heated in oil, it makes a pleasant sauce for spaghetti. It is a Sardinian speciality.

BOUILLABAISSE

A French fish soup or stew which always includes spiny lobster and scorpion fish and never contains mussels. Among its many ingredients are saffron, garlic, tomatoes and dried orange rind. It is a typical Provençal dish associated with the port of Marseille.

BOUQUET GARNI

Fresh herbs tied together so that they may be easily removed from stock or other dishes after cooking. The Italian bouquet garni consists of flat-leaf parsley, basil, thyme and bay leaves. However it may vary and include celery, sage and other herbs.

BRAISE

To cook slowly in a covered pan or casserole on a low heat with a small quantity of liquid, usually specified in the recipe. Braising is mainly used for red meats, poultry and game.

BREADCRUMB

To coat meat, fish or vegetables in breadcrumbs – after dipping them in beaten egg –.before frying.

BRESAOLA

Slices of raw beef fillet are salted and air-dried, rather like prosciutto. It is speciality from Valtellina and may also be made with horse meat.

BRODETTO

Adriatic fish soup. There are many regional variations, but the most classic is from Romagna.

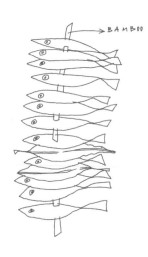

BAMBOO

BROWN IN A PAN

To cook vegetables over a low heat in butter or oil until they go a light golden colour. This is particularly common with thinly sliced onion or garlic cloves. Meat or vegetables may also be cooked in oil or butter in a frying pan over a high heat until a rich, even brown in colour during the first or final stage of cooking.

BROWN IN THE OVEN

To make the top of a dish cooked in the oven, such as lasagne, become golden brown in colour. To brown meat and fish, just add oil, butter or a mixture of the two. Pastry is brushed with beaten egg yolk so that it turns golden brown.

BRUNCH

More substantial than breakfast and less filling than lunch, this meal is eaten in Britain and the United States, mainly on holidays and at weekends, between eleven o'clock and midday. Nowadays, it has been adopted in Europe too.

BRUSCHETTA

Meaning lightly toasted, this consists of a slice of home-made bread, lightly toasted, rubbed with garlic, seasoned with salt and drizzled with olive oil. Chopped tomato, oregano and wild fennel may be added.

BUSECCA

Milanese tripe with kidney beans.

CACCIATORE

Meaning 'in the style of a hunter', this is a method of cooking chicken, hare and rabbit, combined with mushrooms, onions, white wine, herbs and spices. There are many regional variations.

CACCIUCCO

This Tyrrhenian fish soup, almost a stew, exists in many versions, but the most classic is from Livorno.

CAGNONE

Boiled rice, seasoned with chopped garlic and sage, fried in butter and served with Parmesan cheese.

CANAPÉS

Slices of bread, often toasted or fried in butter, topped with a variety of ingredients, such as flavoured butter, cheese, caviar, smoked salmon, anchovies, hard-boiled eggs, ham, tapenade and so on. They are served as an antipasto or with pre-dinner drinks.

CANDY OR CRYSTALLIZE

To immerse fruit in a sugar syrup several times until the sugar is absorbed. The fruit loses most of its water content, becomes thicker and can be stored for a long time. Candying is, however, a long and laborious process.

CAPONATA

This famous Sicilian dish is, according to some, Catalan in origin. Diced vegetables, mainly aubergines, cooked in sweet and sour sauce, are served warm, cold or as an antipasto.

CARAMELIZE

To melt sugar by heating it with a little water and using it to cover fresh fruit, to prepare a brittle or praline or to decorate moulds.

CARPIONE

This pan-fried mixture of olive oil, chopped onion, sage, celery and carrot combined with water and vinegar, is poured piping hot on to vegetables and freshwater fish.

CHANTILLY

Both a savoury and sweet version of this sauce exist. The savoury sauce is based on mayonnaise and whipped cream, while the sweet version is based on whipped cream and sugar. It takes its name from a château in France.

CHATEAUBRIAND

This describes steaks of about 300–400 g/11–14 oz in weight and about 2.5 cm/1 inch thick, cut from the heart of the fillet and grilled, roasted or pan-fried. They may be served with various sauces, including sweet and sour sauce and flavoured butters. According to some, the name derives from the beef-rearing farms of Chateaubriand but others think it derives from the writer René de Chateaubriand.

CHITARRA

A utensil, traditionally from Abruzzo, used to make macaroni alla chitarra, which resembles square spaghetti. It is a wooden frame with stretched metal wires on which fresh pasta is placed and cut and its name derives from its similarity to a guitar.

CHOP

To cut vegetables, herbs, bacon and other ingredients into small pieces using a heavy knife.

CLARIFY

This is a procedure for making meat stock clearer by adding beaten egg white about 30 minutes before cooking is complete, simmering the stock, then straining it. Butter may also be clarified. For instructions on how to clarify butter, see page 88.

CLEAN

To immerse brains, sweetbreads, kidneys or game in fresh water with a little lemon juice or vinegar, in order to reduce their odour and strong flavour; to immerse shell-fish in water in order to remove sand and other impurities; and also to gut fish or draw feathered game.

COCOTTE

A thick, round porcelain, terracotta or metal vessel. It absorbs heat well, transmitting it evenly to the food.

COMPOSTA

Various fruits – both fresh and dried – are cooked over a low heat in syrup, with vanilla, cinnamon, lemon rind and other flavourings. It is served cold.

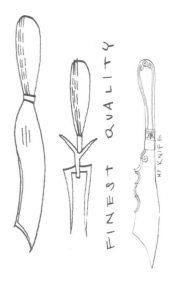

COOK OVER A LOW HEAT

Dishes, such as stews, which require long cooking times to tenderize ingredients, are cooked over a low heat, that is, with the heat turned down to its lowest setting.

COOK UNTIL SOFTENED

To cook vegetables gently over a low heat. Typically, onion is cooked in butter or oil until soft – that is, until it has lost its moisture content and becomes translucent.

COVER

To seal a saucepan or dish with a lid or foil, either to shorten the cooking time or to slow down evaporation and therefore prevent the ingredients from drying up.

COVER WITH A THIN LAYER

To pour on, or brush a dish with, a thin layer of cream, gelatine or sauce.

CROISSANT

A sweet or savoury crescent-shaped, flaky pastry. It is ideal for breakfast and may be filled with cream, jam, cheese, ham, etc.

CRUSH

To grind ingredients, such as peppercorns, whole spices and garlic, to help release their aroma. This is traditionally done in a mortar with a pestle. A spice grinder may also be used, and if you don't have a pestle and mortar you can use the end of a rolling pin or two spoons.

CURDLE

When the egg in a sauce coagulates rather than mixes in smoothly, it is said to curdle. This may happen with mayonnaise and egg custards.

CURRIED

A dish cooked with curry powder or curry spices, an Indian or South-east Asian mixture of such spices as turmeric, pepper, cumin and ginger. Curry sauce is an excellent accompaniment to dishes including rice, chicken, mutton, lamb, eggs and many vegetables.

CUT INTO PORTIONS

To cut poultry or game birds into serving pieces using poultry shears or a very sharp knife.

DECORATE

To decorate single plates or serving dishes of sweet ingredients with fruit, sifted sugar and/or cocoa powder, swirls of cream or other finishes to make them look attractive and to achieve a balance between the various shapes and colours.

DEEP–FRY

To cook in plenty of hot oil or fat over high heat. Olive or vegetable oils may be used for deep-frying, although olive oil has a lower smoke point than oils such as groundnut . Margarine and butter are not suitable as they tend to burn. Lard may not be advisable for dietary reasons.

COOKING TERMS

DEGLAZE

To loosen sediment and dissolve the cooking juices produced in roasting tins and frying pans with water, wine or stock to make a gravy or sauce.

DICE

To cut vegetables, meat or other ingredients into small, even cubes.

DILUTE

To make a thick sauce or seasoning thinner.

DISSOLVE

To mix a dry ingredient, such as sugar, in a liquid until it forms a solution.

DOUBLE BOILER

This is for a cooking method whereby delicate ingredients are cooked in a container over a pan of barely simmering water. It is used for delicate sauces to melt chocolate and to heat or reheat dishes without changing their flavour and consistency.

DRIPPING

The cooking juices which collect on the base of a roasting tin. When diluted with water, stock or wine and heated, it may be used as a sauce and poured on meat or served separately in a sauce boat.

DUST WITH FLOUR

Meat, vegetables and fish are often dusted – lightly coated – with flour before frying. Baking tins, work surfaces and pastry dough are also dusted with flour to stop the pastry sticking to the rolling pin.

EMULSIFY

To mix two liquids of different densities, such as oil and vinegar or lemon juice, by whisking them together. The resulting mixture is unstable and the ingredients will separate again after a while.

EVAPORATE

To dry off an added liquid, such as stock, wine or liqueur, to give dishes extra flavour.

FILL

Layers of a cake are alternated with, and puffs are filled with, custard, chocolate, cream or jam.

FILLET

To remove fillets of raw or cooked fish from the bones. A very sharp, flexible knife is required for raw fish.

FLAMBÉ

From the French flamber, this means to pour an alcoholic liquid, such as brandy, on a dish after cooking and then ignite it to burn off the alcohol and keep the aroma.

FLAVOUR

To give additional flavour and aroma to food by adding herbs, such as parsley, rosemary, sage or thyme, and/or vegetables, such as carrots, onions and celery.

FRATTAU BREAD

This Sardinian bread, also known as music paper, is a thin round of dough made with water, durum wheat flour and salt, cooked for a few minutes over a low heat. It is called frattau bread when it is boiled in water and served with a poached egg, tomato sauce and cheese on top.

FRICASSÉE

A sauce consisting of eggs and lemon poured on to veal, lamb, rabbit or chicken. When heated, it thickens and takes on a creamy consistency. The dish must be removed from the heat as soon as it is ready, otherwise the sauce thickens excessively and develops an unpleasant flavour.

FRUIT SALAD

Mixed, thinly sliced or diced fresh or cooked fruit, sprinkled with lemon juice, orange juice, sugar and, sometimes, liqueur. Fruit salads vary according to the season. In the winter there is a limited choice and they may be enriched with dried fruit and nuts – raisins, walnuts, figs, etc. In the summer, they may be served with ice cream.

FRY LIGHTLY

To cook a mixture, such as chopped vegetables, in oil or butter over a low heat without browning.

GALANTINE

A boned boiling fowl or chicken filled with a mixture of diced meat, hard-boiled eggs, ham, truffle and other ingredients. It is sewn up and poached. Galantine is served cold, thinly sliced, and is often set in aspic.

GARNISH

To decorate single plates or serving dishes of savoury ingredients with cut vegetables, herb sprigs, lemon slices or other garnishes to make them look attractive and to achieve a visual balance between the various shapes and colours and to enhance the flavour of the ingredients.

GAZPACHO

A famous, chilled Spanish soup made from chopped raw tomatoes, onion, cucumbers, peppers and breadcrumbs. It is partly puréed, drizzled with olive oil and vinegar and served ice-cold.

GIARDINIERA

A mixture of vegetables, mainly baby onions, carrots, cauliflower, peppers and cucumbers, preserved in vinegar. It is similar to the French 'a la jardinière', meaning garden vegetables.

GIUDIA

A method of frying globe artichokes popular among the Jewish community in Rome, from which the name derives. Whole artichokes are deep-fried in a pan of hot oil. They open like flowers and turn a beautiful copper colour when they are cooked.

GLAZE

To glaze a roast means to spread shiny, clear cooking juices over the meat. To glaze vegetables means to cook them in lightly sugared liquid which makes them shiny.

GREASE

To brush a baking tin, roasting tin, mould or baking parchment with oil or melted butter or to smear it with butter in order to prevent the mixture from sticking during cooking, roasting or baking. Unsalted butter is better as it is less likely to burn than salted butter.

GRILL

To cook meat, fish or vegetables on a grill or in a griddle pan. You can also grill over glowing charcoal on a barbecue.

HANG

To leave meat for a length of time after butchering so that it becomes tender and succulent. The process still continues when the meat is frozen, although very much more slowly. As a rule, fish should not be hung.

HEAP

This is the classic way of arranging flour on the work surface before mixing. Sift the flour into a small pyramid, make a hollow in the centre and break the eggs into it or add other ingredients, according to the instructions of each recipe.

ICE

Cakes and biscuits are iced by covering the surface with a shiny sugar layer, which may be coloured to taste with chocolate or food dyes. There are a number of different types of icing. For recipes, see pages 1015 to 1016.

INFUSE

To leave ingredients to soak in a liquid or spice mix, such as wine, liqueur or seasoning, for a specified period.

JULIENNE

Vegetables cut into very thin batons, which absorb oil, lemon juice or mayonnaise well. This technique is used for preparing raw salads and other vegetable dishes.

KNEAD

To mix solid and liquid ingredients by 'working them' for varying lengths of time by hand, with a spatula or with an electric mixer fitted with dough hooks. Pasta and yeast doughs are kneaded vigorously, whereas pastry dough is kneaded lightly.

KNÖDEL

A large dumpling, 8–10 cm/ 3–4 inches in diameter, made from breadcrumbs soaked in milk and kneaded with herbs, spices and various other ingredients, such as eggs and sausage meat. They are served in clear soup or alone as a first course.

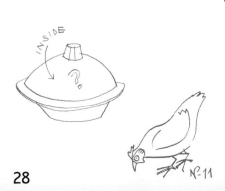

LARD

To make small incisions in a piece of meat and insert pieces of pancetta or bacon fat, pancetta, bacon or ham. The fat melts during cooking and tenderizes and seasons the dish.

LINE

To cover the inside of a tin or mould with pastry, slices of pancetta or bacon, or vegetables to prepare it for a filling.

MARINATE

To place meat, game or fish in an aromatic mixture, usually based on olive oil, lemon juice, vinegar, wine, spices and herbs, in order to flavour and tenderize it.

MEAT OR VEGETABLE EXTRACT

This is similar to a stock cube. It is a meat or vegetable concentrate in the form of a thick liquid or granules. It is sold in jars and used to flavour stocks, gravies and sauces.

MILANESE

Meaning 'from the city of Milan', this is a cooking method in which meat or vegetables are dipped in beaten egg and then coated with breadcrumbs before frying. Milanese chops fried in butter are particularly famous.

MINCE

To grind ingredients, such as beef for hamburgers, very finely using a mincer or food processor.

MOCETTA

A speciality from Valle d'Aosta, this is a type of raw 'ham' made from the thigh of an ibex, chamois or goat. It is preserved in brine with herbs and air-dried. It is served as an antipasto.

MOUSSAKA

A famous Greek dish, similar to Italian Parmesan aubergines, with alternate layers of aubergine, minced beef or lamb sauce, local cheeses, tomato sauce, etc.

MOUSSE

A soft, frothy preparation which sets in the refrigerator. It may be savoury, flavoured with ham, tuna, goose liver, salmon, etc., or sweet, flavoured with chocolate, vanilla, etc.

MUESLI

A mixture of oat and barley flakes, dried fruit, nuts, wheat germ, honey, etc. served with milk or yogurt. It is the most popular breakfast in Switzerland and today is widespread in many other countries.

MUGNAIA

This is the Italian translation of the French phrase 'a la meunière', literally meaning 'in the style of the miller's wife'. Fillets of fish are dusted with flour and browned in butter. This method is particularly recommended for sole, but also works well with other white fish.

MUSTARD

This condiment is made from mustard seeds mixed with vinegar, pepper and other spices. Cremona mustard is an Italian speciality of candied fruit immersed in a syrup of honey, mustard and wine. It may be mild or strong, and is eaten with roast and boiled meat and mature cheeses. Venetian mustard is similar to Cremona mustard, and Mantuan mostarda is made from sliced apple. For salad dressings and flavouring stews, Dijon mustard is usually the preferred type.

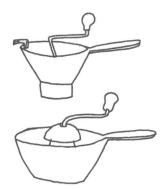

OLLA PODRIDA

This very popular Spanish hotpot consists of mixed boiled meats, including chorizo, as well as chickpeas.

PAELLA

This is the national dish of Spain. There are a huge number of regional variations and it even varies from town to town. The classic version, the Valencian paella, is made with rice, chicken, shellfish, vegetables, spices and saffron, and cooked in a big iron frying pan also called a paella.

PANCETTA

Cured pork taken from the belly of the pig, like streaky bacon, but cured differently. It may be smoked or unsmoked, natural or rolled, and flavoured with spices. It is used in pasta sauces, kebabs and to add flavour to many other dishes. If pancetta is not available, use bacon.

PANSOTTI

Genoese ravioli, with a rich filling of mixed herbs and vegetables, such as borage and Swiss chard. Pansotti are served with walnut sauce.

PARFAIT

A French word meaning 'perfect', this describes a soft, frothy chilled dessert made from cream and eggs and flavoured with vanilla or other flavourings.

PARMENTIER

A number of potato-based dishes take their name from the man who popularized the potato in France.

PARMIGIANA, ALLA

Aubergines in Parmesan are famous. They are first fried, then baked au gratin in the oven. This method is also suitable for other vegetables.

PARMIGIANO, AL

This describes cooked pasta, rice or vegetables seasoned with melted butter and grated Parmesan cheese.

PASSATA

Bottled strained tomatoes which are less concentrated than tomato purée.

PÂTÉ

A mixture of finely chopped cooked meat or fish, usually smoked, mixed with butter and left to set for a few hours in the refrigerator. It is served as an antipasto to be spread on toast. Probably the most famous is goose liver pâté, but chicken liver pâté is also immensely popular.

PIE

A farmhouse pie made with beef, game, chicken or fruit, arranged in layers in a pastry case, topped with another sheet of pastry and baked in the oven. It is a traditional British and American dish.

PILAF

Long-grain rice is boiled in a small quantity of water or stock, dried in the oven and seasoned in various ways. It can be used in a variety of recipes.

PILLOTTO

A cooking method involving a grill or a spit. When the meat is half-cooked, a piece of bacon fat is wrapped in a sheet of thick paper, slipped on to a toasting fork and passed over the flame. The paper catches fire and the heat causes the fat to drip and spread out over the meat.

PINZIMONIO

A dressing consisting of olive oil, salt, lemon juice or vinegar and pepper. It is used as a dip for raw vegetables cut into strips.

POACH

To cook eggs by breaking them into boiling water and cooking them for a few minutes. Fish, meat and poultry may also be poached in gently simmering water or stock.

POTACCHIO

Chicken, rabbit or lamb stewed in tomato sauce.

POT—AU—FEU

French mixed boiled meat of various kinds with pulses, cooked in the same pan and served together.

POUND

To soften the texture of ingredients using various utensils, such as a meat mallet. For example, dried cod, octopus and some cuts of meat are softened by pounding in order to break up their fibres.

PRE—SALÉ

The meat from flocks of sheep allowed to graze on salt marshes. It has a very pleasant flavour.

PROSCIUTTO

This is the Italian word for any kind of ham, including cooked ham. However, in Britain it is used to refer exclusively to raw, dry-cured ham, usually from Parma. Other fine versions of prosciutto are produced in Veneto and San Daniele.

PUNTARELLE

A type of thinly sliced catalogna – Italian dandelion – dressed with oil, vinegar, salt, garlic and anchovies. It is typical of Roman cuisine.

PURÉE

To reduce a solid or semi-solid substance or mixture to a semi-liquid or smooth cream using a food processor or blender.

RED WINE

QUENELLE

A French dish consisting of small meat or fish dumplings poached in simmering water and served with sauce or au gratin. The word also describes the oval shape made with a spoon that can be used when serving soft desserts.

QUICHE

A tart originally made in Alsace-Lorraine. The quiche Lorraine is the most famous – a pastry case filled with bacon and beaten eggs.

RACLETTE

A cheese from Valais in Switzerland, the word raclette also describes the way it is served. A half-wheel is heated with an open flame and half- melted flakes are scraped from the middle and served immediately with boiled potatoes and gherkins.

RAGÙ

Interestingly, the name derives from the French ragoût, but this is the quintessential Italian pasta sauce. It is either made with minced meat (Bolognese) or by prolonged stewing of a piece of meat with tomatoes, oil and spices, as is the custom in southern Italy.

REDUCE

To make a liquid, such as a stock or sauce, thicker and more concentrated by heating it for longer.

RIBOLLITA

This Tuscan peasant soup has today now become a delicacy of classic Italian cuisine. It is based on Tuscan cabbage (cavolo nero) and beans. It is cooked, then left to stand until the next day, when it is put back on the heat – the name, which literally means 'reboiled', derives from this. For the recipe of this dish, see page 246.

ROAST

To cook meat, fish or vegetables in the oven, on a spit or in a pan (pot roast), after initially browning over a high heat.

ROLL OUT

To roll out pastry or other dough on a flat surface to an even thickness. You should always roll in only one direction, occasionally turning the dough a quarter turn.

SALMÍ

This is a way of preparing game, particularly hare, that is similar to the French civet and English jugged. The meat is cut into pieces, marinated for a couple of days in wine with plenty of spices and, finally, stewed.

SALMORIGLIO

This sauce made of olive oil, lemon juice, parsley, oregano and salted water is prepared in Calabria and Sicily to season slices of barbecued swordfish.

SALT

To sprinkle sliced aubergines, cucumbers and, sometimes, courgettes with salt to draw out their juices. This was once essential with aubergines which used to have very bitter juices, but contemporary varieties are much milder.

SANDWICH

Two slices of buttered bread filled with ham, salami, cheese, salad, etc. It takes its name from John Montagu, 4th Earl of Sandwich, an inveterate card player who had sandwiches brought to the gaming table in order to avoid interrupting play. The club sandwich is a multi-layered sandwich with three slices of bread, sometimes toasted. Open or Danish sandwiches consist of a single slice of bread, often rye bread, with a topping. Filled rolls or baguettes are known by a variety of different names, such as submarines, poor boys or torpedoes.

SASHIMI

A typical Japanese dish in which fillets of raw fish are sliced according to strict rules, and served with wasabi, Japanese horseradish.

SAUTÉ

To cook meat, fish or vegetables in a frying pan or sauté pan with oil or butter until the ingredients browned and cooked through. Pasta and risotto may also be sautéed.

SCHIDIONATA

Birds and small chickens cooked on a spit.

SEASON

To enrich the taste of a dish by adding salt, pepper and other condiments, such as paprika.

SHRED

To cut ingredients, such as cabbage and lettuce, into very thin strips.

SIFT

Flour, caster sugar, cocoa powder and other dry ingredients may be shaken through a sieve before mixing with oil, melted butter or milk to prevent lumps from forming.

SIMMER

To bring a liquid to just below boiling point or to turn down the heat under a liquid that has reached boiling point so that the surface of the liquid barely ripples. For example, the court-bouillon in which fish is poached and the water in a double boiler should barely simmer.

SINGE

To pass chickens, pigeons and game quickly over a flame to remove any feathers or quills remaining on the skin.

SKIM

To remove the scum or froth that forms on the surface of some liquids, such as stock, during boiling. A skimmer or a slotted spoon is the most suitable tool.

SKIM THE FAT

To remove the excess fat which sometimes forms on the surface of stock. The easiest way is to chill the stock in the refrigerator and then remove the solid layer of fat that will set on the surface.

SLASH

When whole fish is to be grilled or baked, two or three diagonal slashes may be made on both sides to make it easier for the heat – and flavourings – to penetrate. The surface of risen yeast dough, particularly for breads, is slashed so that it rises well during baking.

SMETANA

A yogurt-like product made with soured cream which Eastern Europeans use copiously even in their beetroot soup (bortsch).

SNIP

To make small cuts in ingredients for a variety of purposes. For example, the edges of steaks are often snipped so that they do not pucker. Chives are often snipped with kitchen scissors rather than chopped with a knife, as this is quicker, easier and doesn't bruise them.

SOAK

To soften and rehydrate some foods, such as sheets of gelatine, dried fruit and dried mushrooms, in water or other liquid so that they regain volume and freshness.

SOFTEN

To make a food softer, for example, by taking the butter out of the refrigerator and leaving it at room temperature for 30 minutes so that it can be spread more easily, or beaten.

SOUBISE

A sauce based on mashed or puréed onions, invented by the Prince de Soubise, an amateur gourmet.

SOFT BUTTER

SPATCHCOCK

A preparation method used particularly for chickens and poussins, in which they are cut along the back, opened out, pounded, marinated in oil, lemon and pepper and cooked under the grill or on the barbecue.

SPECK

A smoked pork ham that is a typical, very tasty speciality from Alto Adige in Italy, Germany and Scandinavia.

SPRINKLE

Sprinkling ingredients with a small quantity of wine, liqueur or juice during cooking is better than drowning them by pouring all the liquid in at once. This also refers to sprinkling small quantities of sauce or cooking juices on the surface of various dishes.

STEW

To cook meat or fish on a low heat with a little liquid in a covered pan.

STIR IN

To mix a liquid or semi-liquid ingredient with a dry ingredient. This is usually carried out in several stages to obtain an even mixture – liquid is added to dry ingredients or vice versa, a little at a time, and the rest is added only when the mixture is smooth and even.

STIR IN BUTTER OR CREAM

To give an even and velvety texture to a dish by stirring in butter or cream when it has finished cooking. A classical example is risotto. For recipes, see pages 328 to 339.

STOCK CUBES AND POWDER

Seasoning made of meat extract and monosodium glutamate which brings out the flavour and aroma of foods. It is used for stocks and soups and to flavour sauces, gravies, meat and vegetables.

STUFATO

A large piece of beef cooked, slowly over a low heat, without browning, in a covered pan over a low heat with wine, herbs and spices.

STUFF

To put a savoury mixture inside the main roast or baked ingredient, such as turkey or fish, or vegetable 'shells' such as tomatoes.

STUFFING

Any filling for chicken, turkey, pigeon, pheasant or fish. It consists of many finely chopped ingredients, which vary according to the recipe, mixed with breadcrumbs, moistened with milk and bound with egg.

SUPPLÌ

Rice croquettes stuffed with a little minced meat or, more commonly, a piece of mozzarella cheese. The melted mozzarella stretches into thin threads resembling telephone wires when you bite into it, hence its name supplì al telefono. Supplì are very popular in Rome and central Italy.

SUSHI

Morsels of rice garnished with wasabi, Japanese horseradish, and a fillet of raw fish.

TABASCO SAUCE

Made from vinegar, herbs, hot chilli, salt and sugar, this sauce takes its name from a Mexican state where chilli cultivation predominates. It should be used sparingly. The most famous brand of Tabasco is made in Louisiana.

TAHINI

A mixture of sesame seeds, lemon juice and water, this is one of the most typical hors d'oeuvres of Arabian cuisine and is widely used in Middle Eastern cooking.

TARAMASALATA

A type of pâté or dip made with smoked grey mullet roe, olive oil, bread, milk, egg yolk, olives and other ingredients. Nowadays, smoked cod's roe is more often used. It is spread on bread, particularly pitta bread, and is one of the most popular hors d'oeuvres in Turkey and Greece.

TATIN, TARTE

A French apple pie in which slices of apple are arranged like the rays of the sun, sprinkled with plenty of sugar and covered with puff pastry. When the pie dish is turned out, the apples look as if they are covered with a caramel 'mirror'.

TEMPURA

A typical Japanese dish in which fish or vegetables are dipped in a light batter and fried in soya or other seed oils.

THICKEN

To make a sauce thicker by adding flour, cornflour, beurre manié (see page 88), egg yolk or double cream, and heating for a few minutes.

TOFU

A cake with a cheese-like texture made from a milky substance derived from soya beans. It has very little flavour, but is rich in protein and quickly absorbs the flavours of other ingredients. It is popular in China and Japan and is now widely available. It is also known as beancurd.

TRIFOLATO

Various types of ingredients cooked in a frying pan with olive oil or butter and garlic and/or onion. Parsley is added at the end.

UMIDO

This is usually meat stewed or braised in tomato sauce and flavoured with olive oil, parsley, other herbs and spices. This method of cooking may be used with meat, fish, chicken and rabbit.

UNLEAVENED BREAD

Bread made without yeast or other raising agents.

VICHYSSOISE

A leek and potato soup that is served chilled. The name is French, as was its inventor, but the dish comes from North America (see page 224).

VINAIGRETTE

The classic salad dressing – olive oil, wine vinegar and salt – whisked together to an even mixture.

WHISK/BEAT

Cream, egg whites, butter and sauces are whisked or beaten with a hand-held or electric whisk to increase their volume and make them frothy. Flavourings may be beaten into softened butter.

WORCESTERSHIRE SAUCE

A sweet and sour condiment for seasoning meat, fish and vegetables. An English speciality that is essential for the cocktail Bloody Mary.

TOOLS
AND EQUIPMENT

Large kitchens are making a comeback in suburban homes around large cities. The once revolutionary kitchenette, which solved several space problems, is today considered a bit cramped even for the increasing population of singles, who are very often amateur gourmets anyway. In any case, whatever the size of your kitchen, it is advisable to purchase equipment in stages and buy accessories and electrical appliances according to real needs and changing habits. It is also important for all utensils to be ready for use and always to hand. Otherwise, you might just as well not have them.

POTS AND PANS

COPPER

This is ideal for saucepans, as copper is an excellent conductor of heat and ensures even heat distribution. However, copper pans are heavy, they dent easily, require a high level of maintenance and are expensive.

STAINLESS STEEL

Hygienic and robust, but mediocre conductors of heat, stainless steel saucepans are not recommended for dry dishes which tend to stick to the base. On the other hand, they are excellent for boiling meat and cooking pasta. Some of the best manufacturers make steel pans with a copper base, which improves heat distribution. Enamelled steel pans have rather fallen into disuse, partly because they chip rather easily and also because they are not dishwasher safe.

ALUMINIUM

Light and good heat conductors, aluminium pans are, however, porous and not very hygienic. Decades ago aluminium was considered a cheap material, but today it is more appreciated thanks to modern manufacturing techniques which make it smoother, more resistant to chipping and easier to clean. Thick aluminium pans are often found in professional kitchens. It is best to use uncoated metal for boiling. For other cooking methods, aluminium with a non-stick coating is recommended because it allows cooking without fat. This coating is delicate and it is advisable to use wooden or plastic utensils to avoid scratching it. The secret of any pan, whether it is made of steel or aluminium, is its thickness. The thicker the metal on the base, the better it is at transmitting heat and therefore cooking ingredients quickly and evenly.

SPECIAL PANS AND DISHES

The starting point for correctly preparing a dish is a sound knowledge of cooking methods and an understanding that each foodstuff often requires its own method and a pan or dish made of the appropriate material. The best way to meet these requirements – as learned from the experience of cookery professionals – is to have a range of pots, pans, casseroles and dishes made from a variety of materials. As well as metal ones, pans and dishes made from earthenware, porcelain and ovenproof glass are suitable for some cooking techniques. Without excluding the ever-versatile steel pans, other equipment is also of great help in the kitchen. For example, the classic non-stick cast-iron frying pan is an incomparable natural controller of the temperature of oil. Oil, in fact, should never reach smoking point, which is bad for your health and also when it could catch fire. A fish kettle is a long oval pan with a removable rack and lid, designed for cooking whole fish. Rhomboid fish kettles are also available for cooking large flat fish, such as turbot, but are rarely found in domestic kitchens. The choice of specialist equipment is vast, since fish kettles and other pans are available in a variety of materials, from copper to steel and aluminium. The price varies considerably too. A tall, narrow pan for cooking asparagus is also useful, as well as oval pans of various sizes for pot roasts and poultry. A cast-iron griddle pan can be used to cook vegetables and small slices of meat without additional fat, an important consideration in these health-conscious days.

A small frying pan for eggs, omelettes and crêpes is also essential. Ideally, it should be made of heavy cast iron, but it is more practical if it has a non-stick coating. A double boiler with a set of nested copper or ceramic bowls is also invaluable. No less useful are stainless steel baskets used for steaming. Alternatively, to give an exotic touch to the kitchen, why not buy a classic set of Chinese stackable bamboo steaming baskets? Lastly comes the pressure cooker. It is purely a matter of choice – some people cannot live without one, while others rule it out right from the start. It certainly can be useful for people with limited time.

The shapes of cooking vessels are important and are not simply dictated by the whim of their designers. They are linked with various cooking techniques and designed for correct heat diffusion. One example is the sauté pan, made with high, flared sides and a strong long handle that is easy to grip. It is ideal for cooking dishes, such as creams and zabaglione, which have to be stirred frequently. Another example is the flat shape of some frying pans designed for cooking meat and vegetables or omelettes and crêpes, which must be turned over and cooked on both sides.

A WORKING KITCHEN

SMALL APPLIANCES

Knives, chopping boards, ladles and can openers are utensils that everyone is familiar with. However, when choosing small electrical appliances it is easy to make mistakes, attracted by promises of convenience. Be wary of appliances that promise lots of functions – kneading, grating, puréeing, mincing, etc. Bear in mind that it is necessary to take them apart and wash, dry and replace the components each time you use them. When possible, choose appliances with specific purposes that match your needs and place them on the work surface or hook them on to the wall under the wall units so that they are readily available.

POWER SOCKETS

Have a suitable number of power sockets installed, away from the sink for safety reasons. It is best to connect appliances used every day, such as a coffee machine, citrus juicer, toaster, microwave oven, etc., to specific sockets. Others, such as an electric grill, bread machine, electric carving knife or a deep-fryer, may be connected only when needed. Electrical appliances do not always save time. For example, if you use a deep-fryer only occasionally, remember that it has to be emptied each time and thoroughly cleaned. A traditional iron frying pan may well be more practical. A food processor takes up a lot of room and unless you use it frequently, you may be better off with hand-held food mill.

GOOD ORGANIZATION

The practicality of a kitchen depends to a great extent on the space available. For example, a sink unit under the window may be pleasant, but often means having no space for a draining board. The most useful unit is one with two sinks. An extractor fan or cooker hood that recirculates the air is not very effective against odours. It is better to have one connected to the outside. Storage located under the work surface is especially practical if it can be pulled out, like drawers, so that you can see the contents at a glance. The most frequently used objects should be placed in the wall units, arranged in lines on shelves or hung on hooks to avoid opening and closing drawers and cupboard doors.

POTS
AND PANS

01   20-cm/8-inch diameter pan
02   24-cm/91/2-inch diameter pan
03   24-cm/91/2-inch diameter colander
04   28-cm/11-inch diameter lid
05   28-cm/11-inch diameter pan
06   20-cm/8-inch diameter pan
07   24-cm/91/2-inch diameter pan
08   26 x 18-cm/101/4 x 7-inch ovenproof glass dish
09   23 x 30-cm/9 x 12-inch ovenproof glass casserole

10   20-cm/8-inch diameter cast iron casserole

11   40 x 16-cm/16 x 61/4-inch fish kettle

12   24-cm/91/2-inch diameter ring mould

13   26-cm/101/4-inch diameter cake tin

14   rectangular cake tin

15   28-cm/11-inch diameter quiche tin

16   22-cm/83/4-inch diameter frying pan

17   28-cm/11-inch diameter frying pan

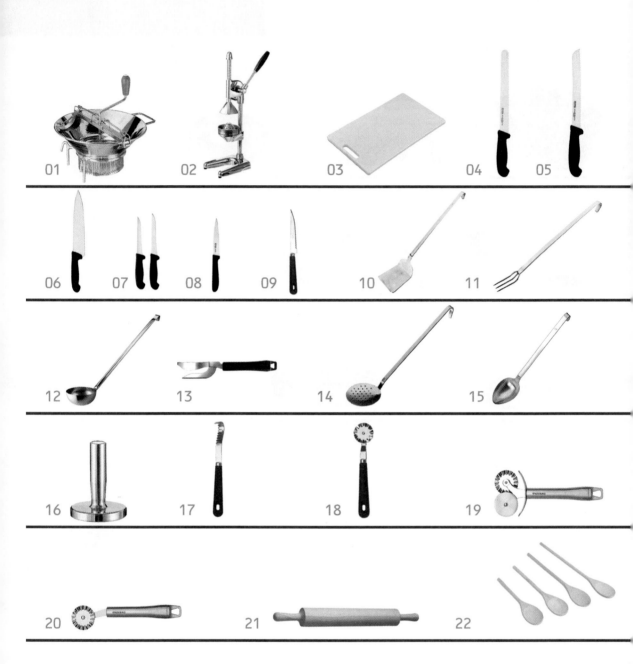

UTENSILS

01	food mill	11	long-handled fork
02	citrus juicer	12	ladle
03	chopping board	13	fish slice
04	bread knife	14	slotted spoon
05	carving knife	15	large spoon
06	kitchen knife	16	meat mallet
07	steak knife	17	butter curler
08	paring knife	18	pastry wheel
09	vegetable knife	19	ravioli cutter
10	spatula	20	pastry roller

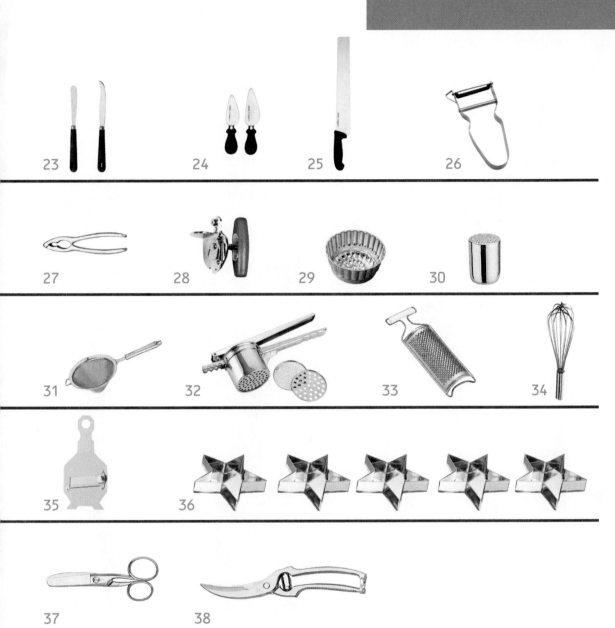

21	rolling pin	31	conical sieve
22	wooden spoons	32	potato masher
23	butter knife	33	grater
24	cheese slice	34	whisk
25	cheese knife	35	truffle shaver
26	potato peeler	36	various small biscuit cutters
27	nutcrackers	37	kitchen scissors
28	can opener	38	poultry shears
29	fluted mould		
30	sugar shaker		

INSIDE ?

PICKLE JARS

LITTLE SPOON

+ SOUP
& SAUCE

POT

ELEGANTLY DECORATED DISH

BUTTER!

44

SAUCES →

MARINADES →

FLAVOURED BUTTERS →

SAUCES

This subject is without doubt a delicate one. Hot, cold, sweet or spicy…with sauces there are no half-measures: they can enhance the flavour of a dish or completely smother it with disastrous consequences. Nevertheless, it is almost impossible to do without them. Almost since the dawn of time, people have striven to add flavour to food. Indeed, there are foods which, without an appropriate sauce, would be inedible or, at least, would not be eaten with any enthusiasm. Just think about pasta. Try to imagine spaghetti without a fragrant fresh tomato sauce, trenette without the subtle aroma of pesto or baked lasagne without the delicate texture of a béchamel. All sauces need careful preparation: the various ingredients react chemically with each other and even the best cook cannot break the laws of nature. It is worth pointing out that almost all sauces are derived from a few basic recipes. These recipes were subsequently developed and transformed by professional chefs or amateur enthusiasts. Anyone who wants to develop their culinary skills must start by getting to know the basic sauces and learning how to make them perfectly. Only later can you move on to more complicated sauces and, perhaps, even invent your own. Before tackling the various traditional, new, revised, lightened recipes, here are a few tips and suggestions: as the quality of a sauce lies in its fragrance, lightness and aroma, all the ingredients must be extremely fresh as well as top quality. Butter, for example, where required, should be the finest available and, in Italy, is always unsalted unless otherwise stated. Pans should be heavy-based to ensure even cooking. To keep a sauce hot until you are ready to serve, it is best to sit the pan in another pan full of hot water. To prevent a skin from forming on the surface, sprinkle a little diced butter or a few tablespoonfuls of liquid on the surface and don't stir in until serving. Finally, remember not to overdo sauces: they need to be used with discretion. This means their flavour must complement the food with which they are served not smother it.

MARINADES

When you want to spice up a meat or game dish and tenderize it, a marinade will produce the best results. One of the most common ingredients is red or white wine, depending on the desired result: one gives a strong flavour to the mixture and the other brings out the taste of the meat.

FLAVOURED BUTTERS

Also known as compound butters or by their French name, beurres composés, these are made by mixing another ingredient with butter to give it a strong flavour: herbs, mustard, anchovies, tuna, etc. Flavoured butters may be used to add extra zest to steaks, fish and omelettes and may also be spread on canapés.

HOT SAUCES

BAGNA CAUDA

Bring a saucepan of water to the boil, then lower the heat and simmer. Heat the olive oil with the butter in a smaller saucepan without letting them brown. Add the garlic and place the saucepan in the simmering water. Chop the anchovies, add them to the oil mixture and mash with a wooden spoon until they have disintegrated and the sauce is smooth. Just before serving, add the truffle. Pour the bagna cauda into a fondue pot or dish and serve. For poached cardoons or raw vegetables.

BAGNA CAUDA

Serves 4

5 tablespoons olive oil

80 g/3 oz butter

2 garlic cloves, finely chopped

100 g/3½ oz salted anchovies, heads removed, cleaned and filleted (see page 596), soaked in cold water for 10 minutes and drained

1 small white truffle, very thinly sliced

BÉCHAMEL SAUCE (BASIC RECIPE)

BESCIAMELLA

Serves 4

50 g/2 oz butter
50 g/2 oz plain flour
500 ml/ 18 fl oz milk
pinch of freshly grated nutmeg (optional)
salt and pepper

Melt the butter in a saucepan over a medium heat. Whisk in the flour. Pour in all the milk, whisking constantly until it starts to boil. Season with salt, lower the heat, cover and simmer gently, stirring occasionally, for at least 20 minutes. Béchamel sauce should not taste floury. Remove the saucepan from the heat. Taste and add more salt if necessary and season with pepper and/or nutmeg. If the sauce is too thick, add a little more milk. If too runny, return to the heat and add a knob of butter mixed with an equal quantity of plain flour. Making this delicious sauce, considered a basic sauce because of the numerous variations to which it has given rise, is an essential skill for anyone keen to cook. For a richer béchamel sauce, replace half the milk with the same amount of double cream; for a lighter béchamel sauce, add half milk and half water. For gratins, soufflés or stuffings.

MUSHROOM BÉCHAMEL

BESCIAMELLA AI FUNGHI

Serves 4

25 g/1 oz butter
150 g/5 oz cultivated mushrooms, thinly sliced
1 quantity Béchamel Sauce (see above)
3 tablespoons double cream
salt and pepper

Melt the butter in a saucepan. Add the mushrooms, cover and cook over a low heat for about 10 minutes until they release all their liquid. Remove the lid, increase the heat and boil off the liquid. Season with salt. Heat the béchamel sauce and stir in the mushrooms. Season with pepper to taste and gently fold in the cream.
For short pasta, veal escalopes or poached eggs.

MAÎTRE D'HÔTEL BÉCHAMEL

BESCIAMELLA MAÎTRE D'HÔTEL

Serves 4

½ quantity Béchamel Sauce (see above)
1 tablespoon chopped fresh parsley
juice of 1 lemon, strained
40 g/1½ oz butter

Add 4–5 tablespoons warm water to the béchamel sauce and stir well. Bring just to the boil and stir in the parsley and lemon juice. Remove the saucepan from the heat and stir in the butter.
For poached eggs, fish or sautéed vegetables.

BÉCHAMEL WITH CREAM

BESCIAMELLA ALLA PANNA

Serves 4

1 quantity Béchamel Sauce (see above)
250 ml/8 fl oz single cream

As soon as the béchamel has finished cooking, remove the saucepan from the heat and stir in the cream, mixing well. Made like this, the sauce is more delicate.
For gratins.

PAPRIKA BÉCHAMEL

BESCIAMELLA ALLA PAPRICA

Melt the butter in a saucepan. Add the onion and cook over a low heat, stirring occasionally, until softened and translucent but not browned. Whisk in the flour. Pour in all the milk, whisking constantly until it starts to boil. Season with salt, lower the heat, cover and simmer gently, stirring occasionally, for at least 20 minutes. A few minutes before removing the saucepan from the heat, stir in the paprika.
For meat, fish or boiled vegetables.

Serves 4
50 g/2 oz butter
1 baby onion, chopped
50 g/2 oz plain flour
500 ml/ 18 fl oz milk
1 tablespoon hot paprika
salt

MUSTARD BÉCHAMEL

BESCIAMELLA ALLA SENAPE

Mix the mustard powder with a little warm water to a paste. Add to the béchamel sauce and stir in the butter.
For fish, poultry or grilled meat.

Serves 4
1 teaspoon mustard powder
$^1/_2$ quantity Béchamel Sauce (see opposite)
20 g/ $^3/_4$ oz butter

YOGURT BÉCHAMEL

BESCIAMELLA ALLO YOGURT

When the béchamel sauce is ready, add the cream and simmer, stirring constantly, for 15 minutes. Remove the saucepan from the heat and leave to cool slightly. Stir in the yogurt and lemon juice, then stir in the mustard. Season with salt if necessary.
For broiled fish or poached chicken.

Serves 4
1 quantity Béchamel Sauce (see opposite)
100 ml/3$^1/_2$ fl oz double cream
150 ml/$^1/_4$ pint low-fat plain yogurt
juice of 1 lemon, strained
2 teaspoons mild mustard
salt

MORNAY SAUCE

BESCIAMELLA MORNAY

Beat the egg yolk with the cream in a small bowl. When the béchamel sauce is ready, remove the saucepan from the heat and stir in the Gruyère and Parmesan, then stir in the egg yolk mixture.Season to taste with salt and pepper. Pour into a sauce boat.
For poached eggs, fish, vegetables or gratins.

Serves 4
1 egg yolk
100 ml/3$^1/_2$ fl oz double cream
1 quantity Béchamel Sauce (see opposite)
25 g/1 oz Gruyère cheese, freshly grated
25 g/1 oz Parmesan cheese, freshly grated
salt and pepper

SOUBISE SAUCE

BESCIAMELLA SOUBISE

Serves 4

500g /1 lb 2 oz white onions, thinly sliced

50 g/2 oz butter

1 quantity Béchamel Sauce (see page 50)

250 ml /3 fl oz double cream

salt

Parboil the onions for 5 minutes, then drain well and leave to cool. Melt the butter in a saucepan and add the onions, a pinch of salt and a few tablespoons of warm water. Cover and cook over a low heat for about 1 hour until mushy, but not brown. Stir the onion purée into the béchamel sauce. Add the cream and heat through, stirring, over a medium heat.

For poached eggs or boiled vegetables.

BOLOGNESE MEAT SAUCE

RAGÙ ALLA BOLOGNESE

Serves 4

40 g/1 1/2 oz butter

2 tablespoons olive oil

1 onion, chopped

1 celery stick, chopped

1 carrot, chopped

250 g/9 oz minced steak

1 tablespoon concentrated tomato purée

salt and pepper

Heat the butter and olive oil in a small saucepan and add the onion, celery, carrot and ground steak. Season with salt and pepper to taste. Mix well and cook over a low heat for a few minutes until the vegetables have softened and the meat starts to brown. Mix the tomato purée with a little water to dilute it and add to the saucepan. Cover and cook over a very low heat for 1 1/2 hours, adding a little hot water if the sauce seems to be drying out. This ragù (meat sauce) may be made with mixed meats and flavoured with mushrooms.

For timbales or tagliatelle.

WHITE MEAT SAUCE

RAGÙ BIANCO

Serves 4–6

2 tablespoons olive oil

50 g/2 oz butter

1 onion, finely chopped

1 celery stick, finely chopped

1 carrot, finely chopped

50 g/2 oz pancetta or bacon, diced

400 g/14 oz mixed minced beef and pork

100 ml/3 1/2 fl oz white wine

200 ml/7 fl oz Chicken Stock (see page 209)

2–3 tablespoonsdouble cream (optional)

salt

Heat the olive oil and butter in a shallow saucepan. Add the onion, celery, carrot and pancetta or bacon and cook over a low heat for 5 minutes until softened. Increase the heat to high, add the meat and mix well. Cook, stirring frequently, until browned. Add the wine and cook until it has evaporated. Season to taste with salt and add a ladleful of the stock. Lower the heat and cook for 1 1/2 hours, adding more stock as the sauce dries out. Finally, stir in the cream to give a more mellow flavor.

For all types of pasta.

CHICKEN LIVER SAUCE

Melt the butter in a frying pan. Add the chicken livers and cook, stirring frequently, for 4 minutes. Be careful not to overcook the livers or they will become tough. Add the wine and cook over a low heat until evaporated. Season with salt and stir in the cream. Remove the pan from the heat and season with pepper.

For timbales, pasta, as an omelette filling, on escalopes or with a vegetable soufflé.

RAGÙ CON FEGATINI

Serves 4

65 g/2¹/₂ oz butter

250 g/9 oz chicken livers, trimmed and chopped

2–3 tablespoons dry white wine

3 tablespoons double cream

salt and pepper

SPINACH SAUCE

Put the spinach in a large saucepan with just the water clinging to its leaves after washing and cook for 5 minutes. Drain, squeeze out as much liquid as possible, then purée in a food processor. Melt the butter in another saucepan and pour in the milk and spinach purée. Season with salt. Cook over a medium heat, stirring the mixture occasionally, until thickened. If the sauce remains runny, stir in the flour and cook for 10 minutes. Remove the saucepan from the heat and add more salt, if necessary, and white pepper to taste. If this sauce is served with pasta, such as farfalle or pennette lisce, hand around plenty of grated Parmesan cheese.

For short pasta or poached eggs.

SALSA AGLI SPINACI

Serves 4

800 g/1³/₄ lb spinach

40 g/1¹/₂ oz butter

250 ml/8 fl oz milk

1 tablespoon plain flour (optional)

salt and white pepper

LEEK SAUCE

Melt the butter in a saucepan. Add the leeks and cook over a low heat, stirring occasionally, for about 5 minutes until softened but not browned. Sprinkle in the flour and gradually stir in the boiling stock. Cook for a further 10 minutes. Remove the saucepan from the heat and push the leek mixture through a sieve into a clean saucepan. Reheat the sauce gently, then stir in the lemon juice, cream and chopped parsley. Season with salt and white pepper to taste.

For chops.

SALSA AI PORRI

Serves 4

25 g/1 oz butter

2 leeks, trimmed and thinly sliced

25 g/1 oz plain flour

500 ml/18 fl oz boiling Chicken or Vegetable Stock (see page 209)

juice of ¹/₂ lemon, strained

100 ml/3¹/₂ fl oz double cream

1 tablespoon chopped fresh parsley

salt and white pepper

BUTTER SAUCE

SALSA AL BURRO

Serves 4

¹/₂ white onion, finely chopped

100 ml/3¹/₂ fl oz white wine vinegar

50 g/2 oz butter, softened and cut into small pieces

1–2 tablespoons chopped fresh parsley

salt and pepper

Put the onion and vinegar in a small saucepan. Set over a medium heat and cook until the liquid has reduced by one-third. Process the mixture in a food processor, then pour back into the saucepan. Place the saucepan only partially over the heat so that the sauce is heated very slowly. Add the softened butter, a piece at a time, stirring constantly. The sauce will increase in volume and become white and creamy. Stir in the parsley and season with salt and pepper to taste.

For poached fish.

CURRY SAUCE

SALSA AL CURRY

Serves 4

50 g/2 oz butter

¹/₄ onion, chopped

2 tablespoons curry powder

1 tablespoon plain flour

salt and pepper

Melt the butter in a saucepan. Add the onion and cook over a low heat, stirring occasionally, for about 5 minutes until softened. Mix the curry powder with a little hot water to make a paste. Sprinkle the flour into the saucepan and stir well, then stir in the curry paste. Cook over a low heat for 30 minutes, gradually adding more water as it is absorbed. Season with salt and pepper.

For vegetables, eggs or poultry.

ONION SAUCE

SALSA ALLE CIPOLLINE

Serves 4

80 g/3 oz butter

4 baby onions, finely chopped

2 egg yolks

6 fresh basil leaves, chopped

salt and pepper

Melt the butter in a saucepan over a low heat. Add the onions and cook, stirring occasionally, for 15 minutes. Remove the saucepan from the heat and process the mixture in a food processor to a purée. Scrape the purée into a bowl and stir in the egg yolks, mixing gently. Stir in the basil and season to taste with salt and pepper.

For grilled fish or würstel (northern Italian sausage rather like a frankfurter).

APPLE SAUCE

SALSA ALLE MELE

Serves 4

2 russet apples, peeled, cored and thinly sliced

25 g/1 oz butter

juice of 1 lemon, strained

3 tablespoons double cream

1 tablespoon grated horseradish

salt and pepper

Pour water into a saucepan to a depth of 2 cm/³/₄ inch. Add the apples, cover and cook over a medium heat, stirring occasionally with a wooden spoon, for about 15 minutes until very soft. Gently stir in the butter, lemon juice and cream and season with salt and pepper. Finally, stir in the grated horseradish, then serve.

For pork, goose or duck.

SAFFRON SAUCE

Pour the fish stock into a saucepan and heat gently. Place the saffron in a bowl and add about 5 tablespoons of the hot stock. Set aside. Melt the butter in another saucepan. Add the flour, a pinch of salt and the saffron mixture. Stir carefully, then gradually stir in the remaining hot stock. Cover and simmer for 15 minutes. Remove the saucepan from the heat, taste and add more salt if necessary. Garnish with extra saffron threads.

For poached or roasted fish.

SALSA ALLO ZAFFERANO

Serves 4

300 ml/¹/₂ pint Fish Stock (see page 208)

1 teaspoon saffron threads, plus extra to garnish

80 g/3 oz butter

3 tablespoons plain flour

salt

MARSALA SAUCE

Melt the butter in a saucepan and stir in the flour. Cook, stirring constantly, until lightly browned. Stir in the stock, a little at a time, and bring to the boil, stirring constantly. Lower the heat and continue cooking until reduced by half. Season to taste with salt and pepper. Pour in the Marsala, bring to the boil and turn off the heat so that the wine's aroma is not lost. If using, stir in the black truffle.

For smoked ham, kidneys or sautéed chicken fillets.

SALSA AL MARSALA

Serves 4

80 g/3 oz butter

25 g/1 oz plain flour

300 ml/¹/₂ pint Chicken Stock (see page 209)

3 tablespoons Marsala

1 black truffle (optional), thinly sliced

salt and pepper

BÉARNAISE SAUCE (BASIC RECIPE)

Pour the vinegar into a stainless steel saucepan. Add the shallots, tarragon and a pinch of salt. Set over a medium heat until the liquid has reduced by more than half. Strain and leave to cool slightly. Lightly beat the eggs yolks with 1 teaspoon water. Stir the egg yolk mixture into the cooled vinegar, then add the lemon juice. Pour the mixture into the top of a double boiler or a heatproof bowl. Set over a saucepan of barely simmering water and whisk constantly until increased in volume. Add the melted butter and whisk until thickened. Season with the cayenne pepper.

For all kinds of grilled or spit-roasted meat and steamed vegetables, such as asparagus spears, French beans or courgettes.

SALSA BEARNESE (RICETTA BASE)

Serves 4

100 ml/3¹/₂ fl oz white wine vinegar

4 shallots, chopped

2 tablespoons fresh tarragon leaves

3 egg yolks

1 tablespoon lemon juice, strained

200 g/7 oz butter, melted

pinch of cayenne pepper

salt

EASY BÉARNAISE SAUCE

SALSA BEARNESE SEMPLIFICATA

Serves 4

2 egg yolks
2 tablespoons double cream
1 tablespoon white wine vinegar
pinch of cayenne pepper
80 g/3 oz butter, cut into pieces
1 tablespoon chopped fresh tarragon
1 tablespoon chopped fresh flat-leaf parsley
salt

Mix together the egg yolks, cream, vinegar, cayenne pepper and a pinch of salt in the top of a double boiler or a heatproof bowl. Set over barely simmering water and heat gently, whisking constantly. When the sauce starts to thicken, add the butter, a few pieces at a time, whisking constantly. Stir in the tarragon and parsley and remove the saucepan from the heat.
For all grilled or spit-roasted meat.

CHINESE SAUCE

SALSA CINESE

Serves 4

200 ml/7 fl oz white wine vinegar
25 g/1 oz sugar
pepper

Pour the vinegar into a saucepan and add the sugar and a pinch of pepper. Bring to the boil and simmer for 15 minutes. Serve while still very hot.
For rice or poached chicken.

ANCHOVY SAUCE

SALSA D'ACCIUGHE

Serves 4

250 g/9 oz salted anchovies
200 ml/7 fl oz olive oil
1 garlic clove

Place the anchovies flat on a board, skin side up. Press along the backbones with your thumb, then turn them over and remove the bones. Rinse the fish and then chop. Heat the oil in a saucepan. Add the garlic and cook until it has turned brown, then remove and discard. Add the anchovies and cook, mashing with a wooden spoon until they have completely disintegrated.
For poached eggs, hot boiled vegetables or pasta.

MARCHAND DE VIN SAUCE

SALSA DEL VINAIO

Serves 4

2 shallots, finely chopped
250 ml/8 fl oz red wine
pinch of chopped fresh thyme
$1/2$ bay leaf, crumbled
60 g/$2^{1}/_{2}$ oz butter, softened and cut into pieces
juice of $1/2$ lemon, strained
salt and pepper

Put the shallots in a saucepan and add the wine, thyme and bay leaf and season with salt and pepper. Cook over a low heat until the liquid has reduced by about half. Remove the saucepan from the heat, strain and whisk in the butter, one piece at a time. When the mixture is thick and frothy, whisk in the lemon juice. Pour into a sauce boat and serve.
For red meat or grills.

BRAIN SAUCE

Fill a large saucepan two-thirds full with water, add the bay leaf and bring to the boil. Drain the brain, add to the saucepan and cook for about 10 minutes. Drain the brain, place in a bowl and crush carefully with a wooden spoon. Shell and halve the eggs and scoop out the yolks into the bowl. Stir the mixture, drizzling in sufficient olive oil to obtain a pouring consistency. Stir in the onion, parsley and capers and season with salt and lemon juice to taste.
For boiled meat.

SALSA DI CERVELLA

Serves 4

1 bay leaf

1 small lamb's brain, membranes

and blood vessels removed

and soaked in cold water for 1 hour

2 eggs, hard-boiled

olive oil, for drizzling

1 baby onion, chopped

1 fresh parsley sprig, chopped

1 tablespoon capers, drained, rinsed and chopped

juice of 1 lemon, strained

salt

WALNUT SAUCE

Place the walnuts in a bowl and pour in boiling water to cover. Leave to stand for 3 minutes, then drain. When the nuts are cool enough to handle, rub off the skins. Chop the nuts and put in a bowl with the olive oil and cream. Season with salt and white pepper. Mix to an even sauce.
For fresh fettuccine or boiled turnips.

SALSA DI NOCI

Serves 4

250 g/9 oz shelled walnuts

4 tablespoons olive oil

2 tablespoons double cream

salt and white pepper

RED PEPPER SAUCE

Blanch the peppers in salted, boiling water for a few minutes, then drain. Peel off the skins, halve and remove the seeds and membranes. Chop coarsely, then process in a food processor to a purée. Pour the vinegar into a saucepan, add the garlic and heat for a few minutes. Strain the vinegar into the food processor and add the oil. Process until smooth.
For steamed fish or bollito misto (mixed boiled meats).

SALSA DI PEPERONI

Serves 4

2 large red peppers

2 tablespoons white wine vinegar

2 garlic cloves, chopped

3 tablespoons olive oil

salt

TOMATO SAUCE

Put the tomatoes with their can juice, if using canned tomatoes, into a saucepan and add the sugar, garlic and a pinch of salt. Cover and cook over a very low heat for about 30 minutes without stirring. Mash the tomatoes with a wooden spoon and, if using canned tomatoes, cook for a further 15 minutes. Remove the saucepan from the heat and leave to cool. Stir in the olive oil and basil.
For spaghetti or escalopes.

SALSA DI POMODORO

Serves 4

250 g/9 oz canned tomatoes or fresh tomatoes, peeled

pinch of sugar

2 garlic cloves

2 tablespoons olive oil

10 fresh basil leaves, torn

salt

QUICK TOMATO SAUCE

SALSA DI POMODORO VELOCE

Serves 4

6 plum tomatoes

4 tablespoons olive oil

2 garlic cloves

1 fresh parsley sprig

salt

Blanch the tomatoes in boiling water for a few seconds, then peel, seed and dice. Place in a small saucepan and add the olive oil, garlic, parsley and a pinch of salt. Cook, uncovered, over a medium heat for 10 minutes. Remove and discard the garlic and parsley. Taste and add more salt if necessary. Pour the sauce directly on to drained pasta while still hot. Do not sprinkle with grated Parmesan cheese. If you like a stronger flavour, thicken the sauce over a high heat for the last 5 minutes of the cooking time, making sure it does not stick to the saucepan.
For short or long pasta.

HORSERADISH SAUCE

SALSA DI RAFANO O CREN

Serves 4

25 g/1 oz butter

25 g/1 oz plain flour

150 m/¹/₄ pint Meat Stock (see page 208)

1 tablespoon grated horseradish

pinch of sugar

Melt the butter in a small saucepan. Stir in the flour and cook, stirring constantly, until the flour turns brown. Stir in the stock. Add the grated horseradish and sugar and cook, stirring frequently, for 10 minutes.
For poached meat.

NORMANDY SAUCE

SALSA NORMANNA

Serves 4

25 g/1 oz butter

25 g/1 oz plain flour

pinch of freshly grated nutmeg

3 tablespoons white wine

100 ml/3¹/₂ fl oz double cream

1 tablespoon lemon juice, strained

salt and pepper

Melt the butter in a saucepan and stir in the flour, nutmeg and a pinch each of salt and pepper. Mix well, then pour in the wine, cream and lemon juice. Cook over a low heat, stirring constantly, until fairly thick.
For lamb chops.

HOLLANDAISE SAUCE

SALSA OLANDESE

Serves 4

3 egg yolks

200 g/7 oz butter, softened and cut into pieces

juice of ¹/₂ lemon, strained

Beat the egg yolks with 3 tablespoons water in a heat-proof bowl. Set the bowl over a saucepan of barely simmering water and whisk well. Whisk in the butter, one piece at a time, and continue whisking for about 15 minutes until the sauce is thick and frothy. Remove from the heat and stir in the lemon juice.
For grilled or poached turbot or salmon.

PIQUANT SAUCE

SALSA PICCANTE

Serves 4

3 hard-boiled egg yolks

1 tablespoon white wine vinegar

1 tablespoon mild or hot mustard

pinch of sugar

300 g/11 oz tomatoes, peeled and diced

2 raw egg yolks

25 g/1 oz butter

salt and pepper

Mash the hard-boiled egg yolks in a saucepan, then stir in the vinegar, mustard, sugar and tomatoes and season with salt and pepper. Set the saucepan over a low heat to warm through, then move it slightly off the heat and stir in the raw egg yolks until combined. Remove the saucepan from the heat and beat in the butter.

For boiled rice.

ROYAL SAUCE

SALSA REALE

Serves 4

2 white bread slices, crusts removed

hot milk, for soaking

25 g/1 oz butter

1 baby onion, finely chopped

1 carrot, finely chopped

2 tablespoons finely chopped fresh flat-leaf parsley

2 tablespoons plain flour

200 ml/7 fl oz Chicken or Vegetable Stock (see page 209)

200 ml/7 fl oz white wine

Tear the bread into pieces, place in a bowl and pour in enough hot milk to cover. Set aside to soak. Melt the butter in a saucepan. Add the onion, carrot and parsley and cook over a low heat, stirring occasionally, for about 5 minutes until the onion has softened. Sprinkle in the flour and stir in the stock and wine. Cook for about 30 minutes. Remove the saucepan from the heat and pour the mixture into a food processor. Process, then squeeze out the bread and add to the sauce. Process again and reheat the sauce before serving.

For short pasta or boiled rice.

ESPAGNOLE SAUCE

SALSA SPAGNOLA

Serves 4

25 g/1 oz butter

80 g/3 oz prosciutto, diced

1 carrot, chopped

1 onion, chopped

fresh flat-leaf parsley sprig

6 black peppercorns

1 clove

1 quantity Vegetable Stock (see page 209)

salt

Melt the butter in a saucepan. Add the prosciutto, carrot, onion, parsley, peppercorns and clove and cook over a medium heat, stirring occasionally, for about 5 minutes. Add the stock and season with salt to taste. Cook for about 45 minutes, then push through a sieve into a bowl or sauce boat. This sauce should be served hot, so reheat it in a double boiler if necessary.

For pasticcio (baked pasta pie) or fresh pasta.

SPECIAL SAUCE

Preheat the oven to 180°C/350°F/Gas Mark 4. Tie the beef into a neat round with kitchen string if this has not already been done. Scatter the butter over the base of an oval roasting tin. Place the meat on top, cover with the onion slices and roast for about 1 hour until the cooking juices are thick and dark. Season with salt and white pepper halfway through the cooking time. Remove the tin from the oven and place the meat on a plate. Place the roasting tin on the hob over a low heat, add the brandy and cook until evaporated. Stir in the cream, a tablespoonful at a time, making sure the sauce does not become too runny. Mix well to combine the flavours and serve with tagliatelle. The meat can be served cold with Mayonnaise (see page 65).

For fresh tagliatelle.

SALSA SPECIALE

Serves 4

750 g/1 lb 10 oz topside of beef

100 g/3½ oz butter, diced

1 large white onion, very thinly sliced

50 ml/2 fl oz brandy

100 ml/3½ fl oz double cream

salt and white pepper

SPICY SAUCE

Melt the butter in a saucepan. Add the onion and cook over a low heat, stirring occasionally, for about 10 minutes until lightly browned. Add the brandy and cook until the liquid is reduced by half. Add the tomatoes and simmer for 5 minutes. Add the chervil, cayenne pepper and Worcestershire sauce. Mix well and pour into a sauce boat.

For grilled steak.

SALSA SUPERPICCANTE

Serves 4

50 g/2 oz butter

1 baby onion, finely chopped

200 ml/7 fl oz brandy

2 tomatoes, peeled, seeded and finely chopped

1 tablespoon chopped fresh chervil

pinch of cayenne pepper

generous dash of Worcestershire sauce

VELOUTÉ SAUCE (BASIC RECIPE)

Melt the butter in a saucepan over a low heat. Sprinkle in the flour and stir until the mixture becomes golden brown and smooth. Gradually stir in the stock, a little at a time. Bring to the boil and cook, stirring frequently, for about 15 minutes. Season with salt and pepper to taste.

For lasagne or meatballs.

SALSA VELLUTATA (RICETTA BASE)

Serves 4

40 g/1½ oz butter

40 g/1½ oz plain flour

500 ml/18 fl oz Meat, Fish or Vegetable Stock

(see pages 208–209)

salt and pepper

SAUCE AURORE

Place the tomatoes in a food processor and process to a purée. Add the purée to the velouté sauce and cook until thickened. Season to taste with salt and pepper.

For grilled fish, poached chicken or poached eggs.

SALSA VELLUTATA AURORA

Serves 4

400 g/14 oz tomatoes, peeled, seeded

and coarsely chopped

1 quantity Velouté Sauce (see above)

salt and pepper

SUGO AGLI SCAMPI E CAPPESANTE

Serves 4

5 tablespoons olive oil

4 shallots, chopped

2 salted anchovies, heads removed,
cleaned and filleted (see page 596), soaked in
cold water for 10 minutes, drained and chopped

4 scallops, shelled and chopped

1 tablespoon brandy

250 g/8 fl oz passata

200 g/7 oz langoustines or Dublin Bay prawns, peeled

100 ml/3¹/₂ fl oz white wine

2 tablespoons chopped fresh flat-leaf parsley

salt and pepper

SEAFOOD SAUCE

Heat 2 tablespoons of the olive oil in a saucepan. Add the shallots and cook over a low heat, stirring occasionally, for 3–5 minutes until softened and translucent. Add the anchovies and cook, mashing with a wooden spoon until they have completely disintegrated. Add the scallops and cook for 1 minute, then sprinkle with brandy and cook until evaporated. Pour in the passata and cook over a medium heat for about 10 minutes, then season with salt and pepper to taste. Meanwhile, heat the remaining olive oil in a frying pan. Add the langoustines or prawns and cook for 2–3 minutes. Sprinkle with the white wine and cook until evaporated, then add the parsley and season with salt. Cook over a low heat for 5 minutes. Tip the langoustine or prawn mixture into the tomato mixture and stir to mix.

For fresh taglierini, ricotta and spinach ravioli or tagliatelle.

SUGO AL TONNO

Serves 4

250 g/9 oz canned tomatoes

1 garlic clove

120 g/4 oz canned tuna in oil, drained

2 tablespoons olive oil

1 salted anchovy, head removed, cleaned and filleted
(see page 596), soaked in cold water for 10 minutes,
drained and finely chopped

salt

TUNA SAUCE

Tip the tomatoes and their can juice into a saucepan, add the garlic and a pinch of salt and bring to the boil over a medium heat. Cook for 15 minutes, then lower the heat, mash the tomatoes with a wooden spoon and cook until the liquid has reduced slightly. Remove the saucepan from the heat. Remove and discard the garlic. Flake the tuna with a fork and stir into the tomato sauce. Add the olive oil and anchovy and spoon over very hot spaghetti. For spaghetti.

COLD SAUCES

AÏOLI

AÏOLI

Serves 4

2 egg yolks

3 garlic cloves, finely chopped

100 ml/3¹/₂ fl oz olive oil

lemon juice, strained, to taste

salt and pepper

Beat the egg yolks with the garlic in a bowl. Gradually add the olive oil, as if making mayonnaise. Season with salt, pepper and a few drops of lemon juice to taste. This sauce can also be made in a food processor (see basic recipe for Mayonnaise, opposite).

For fish.

REDCURRANT AND APPLE CHUTNEY

CHUTNEY AL RIBES E MELE

Serves 4

50 g/2 oz sultanas

400 g/14 oz green apples, peeled, cored and diced

250 g/9 oz redcurrants

100 g/3¹/₂ oz chopped walnuts

100 ml/3¹/₂ fl oz white wine vinegar

100 ml/3¹/₂ fl oz orange juice

100 g/3¹/₂ oz sugar

2 cloves

5-cm/2-inch cinnamon stick

Place the sultanas in a bowl, add hot water to cover and set aside to soak for 15 minutes, then drain. Place all the ingredients in a large saucepan and bring to a boil over a low heat, stirring occasionally. Simmer, uncovered, for at least 30 minutes until the mixture has the consistency of jam. Pour into a bowl and leave to cool. Discard the cloves and cinnamon stick. This sauce is widely eaten in India. It can be stored in a screw-top jar in the refrigerator for a few days.

For grilled meat.

ONION CHUTNEY

Put the sultanas, onions, sugar, tomato purée, bay leaf, green peppercorns and cayenne pepper in a large saucepan. Pour in 250 ml/8 fl oz water and the vinegar. Cover and cook for 2 hours. Remove the lid and cook for 1 hour more to reduce. For game or curries.

CHUTNEY DI CIPOLLINE

Serves 4

120 g/4 oz sultanas, soaked in warm water
for 15 minutes and drained
500 g/1 lb 2 oz baby onions
75 g/2³/₄ oz sugar
3 tablespoons concentrated tomato purée
1 bay leaf
10 green peppercorns
pinch of cayenne pepper
250 ml/8 fl oz white wine vinegar

MAYONNAISE (BASIC RECIPE)

Mayonnaise is probably the best loved and most frequently eaten sauce in the world. It is almost always bought ready made and there are several good brands available. However, it is useful to know how to make it by hand or in a food processor and it is worth savouring the delicacy of home-made mayonnaise every now and again. Both techniques are described here. Always make sure that the oil and eggs are at room temperature; if they are too cold, the mayonnaise may not bind. Add the oil a drop at a time and do the same with the lemon juice or vinegar. If the mayonnaise separates, whisk a fresh egg yolk in another bowl and gradually whisk in the separated mixture a drop at a time. To make mayonnaise by hand, put the egg yolks in a bowl and season with a pinch each of salt and pepper. Add the oil, a drop at a time, beating constantly with a small whisk or wooden spoon. As soon as the mixture thickens, whisk in a drop of lemon juice or vinegar. Continue adding the oil and lemon juice or vinegar alternately, beating constantly, until all the ingredients are used. To make mayonnaise in a food processor, place an egg yolk and a whole egg in the food processor, season with salt and pepper and add 2 tablespoons of the oil and a drop of the lemon juice or vinegar. Process for a few seconds at maximum speed. When the ingredients are thoroughly mixed, add the remaining oil and lemon juice or vinegar and process for 1 minute. For both methods, taste and adjust the seasoning if necessary. Pour the mayonnaise into a sauce boat and store in the refrigerator.

For boiled or roasted meat, raw or cooked vegetables or as a garnish.

MAIONESE (RICETTA BASE)

Serves 4

2 egg yolks or 1 egg yolk and 1 egg (see method)
about 200 ml/7 fl oz sunflower oil
2 tablespoons lemon juice or white wine vinegar
salt and pepper

CURRY AND CREAM MAYONNAISE

Gently stir the cream into the mayonnaise and season with the curry powder. Mix well. Pour into a sauce boat and serve.
For seafood and chicken salads or hard-boiled eggs.

MAIONESE AL CURRY E PANNA

Serves 4

3 tablespoons single cream

1 quantity Mayonnaise (see page 65)

1 teaspoon curry powder

GORGONZOLA MAYONNAISE

Make the mayonnaise with vinegar instead of lemon juice and beat the mustard into the egg yolks before adding the oil. Cream the Gorgonzola in a bowl and beat into the mayonnaise, a little at a time. Season to taste with salt if necessary. Pour into a sauce boat.
For cold meat.

MAIONESE AL GORGONZOLA

Serves 4

1 quantity Mayonnaise (see page 65)

1 teaspoon Dijon mustard

100 g/3½ oz Gorgonzola cheese, crumbled

salt (optional)

WHIPPED CREAM MAYONNAISE

Stir the mustard into the mayonnaise, then fold in the whipped cream. Serve in a sauce boat.
For fish or shellfish.

MAIONESE ALLA PANNA MONTATA

Serves 4

1 teaspoon Dijon mustard

1 quantity Mayonnaise (see page 65)

3 tablespoons double cream, whipped

AVOCADO MAYONNAISE

Stir the cream, ketchup, lime juice, Worcestershire sauce and a dash of Tabasco into the mayonnaise and season with salt to taste. Peel and halve the avocado and remove the stone. Cut into wedges, then slice thinly. Add to the mayonnaise and mix gently. Spoon into a sauce boat and garnish with slices of lime.
For prawns, chicken and rice or poached eggs.

MAIONESE ALL'AVOCADO

Serves 4

3 tablespoons double cream

2 tablespoons tomato ketchup

2 tablespoons lime juice, strained

2 tablespoons Worcestershire sauce

dash of Tabasco sauce

1 quantity Mayonnaise (see page 65)

1 avocado

salt

lime slices, to garnish

HERB MAYONNAISE

Cook the spinach in a little salted, boiling water for 5 minutes, then drain and leave to cool. When cool, place the spinach, tarragon and watercress in a food processor and process to a purée. Stir the purée into the mayonnaise until the mixture is an even green colour. Season with salt to taste.
For poached fish or hard-boiled eggs.

MAIONESE ALLE ERBE

Serves 4

200 g/7 oz spinach

1 fresh tarragon sprig

½ bunch of watercress

1 quantity Mayonnaise (see page 65)

salt

HORSERADISH MAYONNAISE

MAIONESE AL RAFANO

Serves 4

1 tablespoon grated horseradish
1 quantity Mayonnaise (see page 65)

Stir the horseradish into the mayonnaise, mixing well.
For cold meat.

ANDALUSIAN MAYONNAISE

MAIONESE ANDALUSA

Serves 4

4 tablespoons tomato purée
1 quantity Mayonnaise (see page 65)
1 green pepper, halved, seeded and finely chopped
¼ dried red chilli, crumbled

Stir the tomato purée into the mayonnaise, 1 tablespoon at a time.
Stir in the green pepper and chilli.
For raw vegetables.

MALTESE MAYONNAISE

MAIONESE MALTESE

Serves 4

1 blood orange
1 quantity Mayonnaise (see page 65 and method)
salt

Using a small, sharp knife, peel the orange, avoiding the bitter white pith. Blanch the orange rind in a small saucepan of boiling water for 1 minute, then drain and refresh under cold running water. Chop finely. Squeeze the orange and strain the juice. Prepare the mayonnaise, but do not add lemon juice or vinegar. Stir in the orange rind, then beat in the juice. Season with salt if necessary. For asparagus, artichokes or poached chicken.

PESTO

PESTO

Serves 4

25 fresh basil leaves
100 ml/3½ fl oz extra virgin olive oil
40 g/1½ oz pine nuts
25 g/1 oz Parmesan cheese, freshly grated
25 g/1 oz pecorino cheese, freshly grated
salt

Put the basil leaves in a food processor with the olive oil, pine nuts and a pinch of salt. Process briefly at medium speed. Add the grated cheeses and process again.
For asparagus, egg dishes, spaghetti or gnocchi.

RÉMOULADE SAUCE

RÉMOULADE

Serves 4

1 garlic clove
1 egg yolk
about 150 ml/¼ pint olive oil
1 teaspoon white wine vinegar
1 fresh flat-leaf parsley sprig, very finely chopped
salt

Rub the garlic around the inside of the bowl you are going to use to make the sauce. Put the egg yolk in the bowl, season with a pinch of salt and gradually beat in the olive oil, a drop at a time. The exact amount of oil depends on how much the egg absorbs. When the sauce has reached the desired consistency, beat in the vinegar and parsley. Season with salt to taste.
For poached fish.

PINE NUT SAUCE

Drain the anchovy and pat dry with kitchen paper. Shell and halve the egg, then scoop out the yolk. Finely chop together the anchovy, egg yolk, pine nuts, capers, olives, bread, parsley and garlic. Put the mixture in a bowl and drizzle with olive oil, stirring constantly, as if making mayonnaise. Season to taste with salt and pepper. Serve in a sauce boat.
For poached fish.

SALSA AI PINOLI

Serves 4

1 salted anchovy, head removed, cleaned and filleted (see page 596), soaked in cold water for 10 minutes and drained
1 egg, hard-boiled
50 g/2 oz pine nuts
20 g/³/₄ oz capers, drained and rinsed
4 stoned green olives
1 white bread slice, crusts removed
1 fresh flat-leaf parsley sprig • ¹/₂ garlic clove
olive oil, for drizzling
salt and pepper

GORGONZOLA SAUCE

Cream the Gorgonzola in a bowl, then gradually beat in the cream or milk. When the mixture has a creamy consistency, season with salt and pepper and add the grated horseradish. Mix well and serve.
For canapés or raw vegetables.

SALSA AL GORGONZOLA

Serves 4

300 g/11 oz mild Gorgonzola cheese, crumbled
2 tablespoons single cream or 100 ml/3¹/₂ fl oz milk
1 tablespoon grated horseradish
salt and pepper

BALSAMIC VINEGAR SAUCE

Put the capers, parsley, boiled potato and a pinch of salt in a food processor and process to a purée. Scrape into a bowl and gradually beat in the olive oil to make a thick sauce. Stir in the balsamic vinegar.
For short pasta or spaghetti.

SALSA ALL'ACETO BALSAMICO

Serves 4

25 g/1 oz capers, drained and rinsed
¹/₂ bunch of fresh flat-leaf parsley, coarsely chopped
1 potato, boiled and coarsely chopped
about 150 ml/¹/₄ pint olive oil
1 tablespoon balsamic vinegar
salt

PAPRIKA SAUCE

Shell and halve the eggs, then scoop out the yolks into a bowl. Mash well with a fork and stir in the mustard. Add a pinch each of salt and pepper and stir in the paprika. Stir in the cream and lemon juice. Mix well and serve.
For celeriac or rice salad.

SALSA ALLA PAPRICA

Serves 4

2 eggs, hard-boiled
1 tablespoon Dijon mustard
¹/₂ teaspoon paprika
100 ml/3¹/₂ fl oz single cream
1 tablespoon lemon juice
salt and pepper

RICOTTA SAUCE

SALSA ALLA RICOTTA

Serves 4

250 g/9 oz ricotta cheese

4 tablespoons mascarpone cheese • 2 tablespoons milk

1 egg yolk • 4 walnuts, peeled and chopped

1–2 tablespoons chopped fresh chives

salt and pepper

Place the ricotta in a bowl and stir in the mascarpone and milk. Season to taste with salt and pepper. Stir in the egg yolk and add the walnuts and chives. Mix well, then taste and adjust the seasoning if necessary.

For short pasta or canapés.

YOGURT SAUCE

SALSA ALLO YOGURT

Serves 4

4 gherkins, drained and very finely chopped

4 fresh mint leaves, very finely chopped

150 ml/¼ pint natural yogurt

dash of olive oil (optional) • salt

Stir the gherkins and mint into the yogurt and season to taste with salt and a dash of olive oil if you like.

For griddled and barbecued meat or baked potatoes.

GRAPEFRUIT SAUCE

SALSA AL POMPELMO

Serves 4

200 g/7 oz mascarpone cheese

juice of 1 grapefruit, strained

1 tablespoon chopped fresh chervil

salt and pepper

Beat the mascarpone in a bowl with a small whisk until light and smooth. Gradually whisk in the grapefruit juice. Season with salt and pepper and stir in the chervil. Mix gently and pour into a sauce boat.

For roast pork.

BLACK TRUFFLE SAUCE

SALSA AL TARTUFO NERO

Serves 4

2 fresh black truffles • 3 salted anchovies, heads removed, cleaned and filleted (see page 596), soaked in cold water for 10 minutes, drained and finely chopped • about 150 ml/¼ pint light olive oil

dash of lemon juice

Clean the truffles with a small damp brush. Grate into a bowl and add the anchovies. Stir in the olive oil to make a fairly runny sauce. (Use a light, delicately flavoured oil so that the truffle flavour dominates.) Just before serving, sprinkle with a dash of lemon juice.

For tagliolini or poached chicken.

BARBECUE SAUCE

SALSA BARBECUE

Serves 4

2 tablespoons mustard

3 tablespoons milk • 175 ml/6 fl oz olive oil

5 tablespoons mixed pickles, such as capers, gherkins, onions and carrots, chopped

2 tablespoons chopped fresh flat-leaf parsley

juice of ½ lemon, strained • salt and pepper

Mix together the mustard and milk in a bowl. Gradually whisk in the olive oil a drop at a time. When the sauce has thickened, season to taste with salt and pepper, then stir in the pickles, parsley and lemon juice. Mix well and pour into a sauce boat.

For grilled meat or fish.

COCKTAIL SAUCE

SALSA COCKTAIL

Serves 4

3 tablespoons tomato ketchup

1 tablespoon Worcestershire sauce

1 teaspoon brandy

1 teaspoon sherry

250 ml/8 fl oz double cream

salt and white pepper

Mix together the tomato ketchup, Worcestershire sauce, brandy and sherry in a bowl. Lightly whisk the cream, then gently fold into the other ingredients. Season with a little salt and white pepper. Stir shellfish into this sauce and place in a dish lined with lettuce leaves.

For spiny lobster, langoustines, Dublin Bay prawns or shrimp.

CAPER SAUCE

SALSA DI CAPPERI

Serves 4

3 tablespoons capers, drained

150 ml/¼ pint olive oil or to taste

juice of ½ lemon, strained

Place the capers in a bowl, add cold water to cover and set aside to soak for 15 minutes. Drain well and chop finely. Transfer the capers to a sauce boat and stir in the olive oil and lemon juice. Taste and, if necessary, add more olive oil or lemon juice.

For breaded veal chops.

MINT SAUCE

SALSA DI MENTA

Serves 4

10–15 fresh mint leaves, chopped

1 tablespoon sugar

4 tablespoons white wine vinegar

Put the mint in a bowl and pour on 3 tablespoons boiling water. Leave to infuse and cool slightly. Stir in the sugar and vinegar and mix well. Leave the sauce to stand for at least 30 minutes before serving.

For boiled courgettes.

WHIPPED CREAM AND RADISH SAUCE

SALSA DI PANNA MONTATA E RAVANELLI

Serves 4

3 bunches of radishes, trimmed

1 teaspoon Bordeaux mustard

lemon juice, to taste

250 ml/8 fl oz double cream, stiffly whipped

salt

Place the radishes in a bowl, add cold water to cover and set aside to soak for about 30 minutes. Drain, then process briefly in a food processor to chop finely. Do not over-process into a purée. Transfer to a bowl and add a little salt. Stir in the mustard and a few drops of lemon juice. Gently fold in the whipped cream, 1 tablespoon at a time, taking care not to knock out the air.

For fish or cold meat.

GRIBICHE SAUCE

Shell and halve the eggs, then scoop out the yolks into a bowl and mash well with a wooden spoon. Finely chop the egg whites and set aside. Add the mustard and vinegar to the egg yolks and season with salt and pepper. Gradually beat in the olive oil a drop at a time. Stir in the tarragon, parsley and capers. Stir gently. Just before serving, stir in the reserved egg whites.
For deep-fried langoustines or Dublin Bay prawns or poached eggs.

SALSA GRIBICHE
Serves 4
3 eggs, hard-boiled
1 teaspoon Dijon mustard
2 tablespoons white wine vinegar
200–250 ml/7–8 fl oz olive oil
1 tablespoon chopped fresh tarragon
1 tablespoon chopped fresh flat-leaf parsley
50 g/2 oz capers, drained,
rinsed and finely chopped
salt and pepper

MEDITERRANEAN SAUCE

Mix together the mustard and milk in a bowl. Gradually whisk in the olive oil a drop at a time. When the mixture has the desired consistency, season with salt and pepper to taste. Add a drop of lemon juice, then stir in the tomato purée until the mixture takes on an even, slightly pink colour. Taste and adjust the seasoning if necessary. Serve in sauce boat.
For fish, poultry or cold meat.

SALSA MEDITERRANEA
Serves 4
1 tablespoon Dijon mustard
2 tablespoons milk
200 ml/7 fl oz olive oil
lemon juice, to taste
1 tablespoon concentrated tomato purée
salt and pepper

RUSSIAN GARLIC SAUCE

Crush the garlic with a little salt in a bowl using a large spoon. (A garlic press may also be used.) Stir in the warm stock, leave to cool and then pour into a sauce boat.
For grilled meat.

SALSA RUSSA ALL'AGLIO
Serves 4
4-5 garlic cloves, halved
100 ml/3½ fl oz warm Chicken Stock (see page 209)
salt

TARTARE SAUCE

Nowadays, in order to save time, this sauce is usually made by adding pickled onions, parsley and vinegar to mayonnaise. However, the genuine recipe is somewhat different. Shell and halve the hard-boiled eggs, then scoop the yolks into a bowl. Add the raw yolk and mash together until smooth and even. Season with a little salt and pepper, and stir in the onions and parsley. Gradually whisk in the olive oil, a drop at a time. When the sauce has begun to thicken, whisk in a little of the vinegar. Continue adding the olive oil and vinegar alternately, whisking constantly. If a stronger flavour is required, add some tarragon.
For cold meat or poached fish.

SALSA TARTARA
Serves 4
3 eggs, hard-boiled
1 egg yolk
2 baby white onions, finely chopped
2–3 tablespoons chopped fresh flat-leaf parsley
200 ml/7 fl oz olive oil
4 tablespoons white wine vinegar
1 tablespoon chopped fresh tarragon (optional)
salt and pepper

TUNA SAUCE

SALSA TONNATA

Serves 4

100 g/3¹/₂ oz canned tuna in oil, drained

50 g/2 oz capers, drained and rinsed

2 salted anchovies, heads removed, cleaned and

filleted (see page 596)

1 hard-boiled egg yolk

200 ml/7 fl oz olive oil

juice of ¹/₂ lemon, strained

salt and pepper

Finely chop the tuna, capers and anchovies and place in a food processor. Crumble in the egg yolk and season with salt and pepper. Add a few tablespoons of the olive oil and process for a few seconds. Add the remaining oil and process briefly again. If the sauce is too thick, add a little more oil. Pour into a sauce boat, add the lemon juice, mix well and leave to stand for 10 minutes before serving.

For poached meat or fish.

GREEN SAUCE

SALSA VERDE

Serves 4

1 small potato

2 eggs, hard-boiled

2 salted anchovies, heads removed, cleaned and

filleted (see page 596), soaked in cold water for

10 minutes and drained

1 fresh flat-leaf parsley sprig, leaves only

¹/₂ garlic clove

1 gherkin, drained

200 ml/7 fl oz olive oil

2 tablespoons white wine vinegar

salt and pepper

Cook the potato in lightly salted, boiling water for 15 minutes or until tender. Drain and peel. While still hot, put in a bowl and mash well with a fork. Shell and halve the eggs, then scoop the yolks into the bowl and mix with the mashed potato. Drain the anchovies, pat dry and chop finely with the parsley, garlic and gherkin. Add to the potato and mix well. Gradually beat in the olive oil, a drop at a time. Season with salt and pepper and stir in the vinegar.

For boiled meat or cold, poached fish.

TAPÉNADE

TAPÉNADE

Serves 4

100 g/3¹/₂ oz salted anchovies, heads removed,

cleaned and filleted (see page 596), soaked in

cold water for 10 minutes and drained

200 g/7 oz stoned black olives

150 g/5 oz capers, drained and rinsed

100 g/3¹/₂ oz canned tuna in oil, drained

1 teaspoon Dijon mustard

olive oil, for drizzling

50 ml/2 fl oz brandy

2 tablespoons lemon juice, strained

pinch of fresh thyme

¹/₂ garlic clove, finely chopped

pepper

Drain the anchovies, pat dry and chop with the olives, capers and tuna. Place in a bowl and stir in the mustard. Drizzle in olive oil to taste, stirring constantly. Add the brandy, lemon juice, thyme and garlic. Season lightly with pepper. (The fairly strong taste of this Provençal sauce may be made less intense by omitting the pepper.) Some people prefer to mix all the ingredients with Mayonnaise (see page 65). The result is equally pleasant. Store in the refrigerator.

For boiled meat, hard-boiled eggs or fish.

VINAIGRETTE

Serves 4

2 tablespoons white wine vinegar

6 tablespoons olive oil

salt

VINAIGRETTE

Whisk a generous pinch of salt into the vinegar in a bowl. Add the olive oil and whisk well. To make the dressing even tastier, you can add a little anchovy paste, 1 tablespoon natural yogurt or 1 teaspoon Dijon mustard.
For all salads.

FONDI DI COTTURA | BASES FOR SAUCES

I ROUX

50 g/2 oz butter

50 g/2 oz plain flour

500 ml/18 fl oz Meat or Vegetable Stock (see page 209)

salt and pepper

ROUX

The word roux is French and means reddish. In cooking, it refers to a mixture of butter and flour cooked for a varying length of time according to what is required. Roux are divided into white (briefly cooked), blond (cooked a little longer) and brown (cooked thoroughly). It is not possible to give precise cooking times as you can only check the progress of the roux by looking at it. Roux are used to thicken soups and sauces, and in both cases the dish becomes tastier. Melt the butter in a saucepan and, as soon as it turns golden brown, sprinkle in the flour, stirring constantly to prevent lumps from forming. Gradually stir in the stock. Cook, stirring occasionally, for about 20 minutes. Season with salt and pepper to taste. If a runnier roux is needed, use only 25 g/1 oz each of the flour and butter but the same amount of stock.

I FONDI

STOCKS

These are generally meat, fish and vegetable stocks which are added to roux to make various sauces. To make a classic meat stock, cook a few beef and veal bones in olive oil and butter, add water and continue cooking for several hours until the liquid thickens. A quicker method is to use the dripping from any roasted meat mixed with a little stock or water. To ensure a smooth sauce without lumps use cold stock if the roux is hot and add hot stock if the roux is cold.
For more stock recipes see pages 208–209.

MARINADES

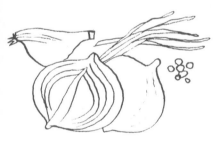

BRANDY MARINADE

Mix together the brandy, olive oil, thyme and bay leaf and season with salt and pepper. Marinate meat for a few hours. For white meat.

MARINATA AL BRANDY

3 tablespoons brandy

4 tablespoons olive oil

1 fresh thyme sprig

1 bay leaf

salt and pepper

JUNIPER MARINADE

Pour the wine into a large bowl, add the onion and juniper berries and season with salt and pepper. Marinate meat for 5–12 hours, stirring frequently. For white meat.

MARINATA AL GINEPRO

1 litre/1³/₄ pints red wine

1 onion, sliced

8–10 juniper berries, crushed

salt and pepper

VINEGAR MARINADE

MARINATA ALL'ACETO

200 ml/7 fl oz white wine vinegar
200 ml/7 fl oz olive oil
juice of 1 lemon, strained
2 teaspoons finely chopped fresh rosemary
1 tablespoon finely chopped fresh flat-leaf parsley
pinch of dried oregano
salt and pepper

Mix together the vinegar, olive oil and lemon juice in a large bowl. Add the rosemary, parsley and oregano and season with salt and pepper. Marinate fish for a couple of hours before cooking. For fish.

YOGURT MARINADE

MARINATA ALLO YOGURT

1 onion, coarsely chopped
500 ml/18 fl oz low-fat natural yogurt
salt and pepper

Place the onion in a food processor and process to a purée, then push through a sieve into a bowl. Add the yogurt and season with salt and pepper. Marinate meat for 3–4 hours. For lamb or kid.

WHITE WINE MARINADE

MARINATA AL VINO BIANCO

1 onion, sliced
1 litre/1³/₄ pints dry white wine
250 ml/8 fl oz olive oil
juice of 1 lemon, strained
salt and pepper

Place the onion in a bowl, add the wine, olive oil and lemon juice and season with salt and pepper. Marinate fish for 2 hours.
For fish.

RED WINE MARINADE

MARINATA AL VINO ROSSO

2 carrots, thinly sliced
2 red onions, thinly sliced
2 garlic cloves, thinly sliced
4 fresh thyme sprigs
6 bay leaves
6 black peppercorns
1 litre/1³/₄ pints red wine
400 ml/14 fl oz olive oil
600 ml/1 pint red wine vinegar
salt

Mix together the carrots, onions and garlic and arrange half the mixture in a layer on the base of a large bowl. Add half the thyme and half the bay leaves, then place meat on top. Cover with the remaining sliced vegetables, thyme and bay leaves and sprinkle with the peppercorns and salt. Mix together the wine, olive oil and vinegar in a jug, then pour into the bowl. Marinate for at least 12 hours.
For red meat or game.

HERB MARINADE

MARINATA AROMATICA

1 onion, sliced
3 tablespoons chopped fresh flat-leaf parsley
1 tablespoon chopped fresh thyme
2 bay leaves, torn into pieces
2 garlic cloves, thinly sliced
5 tablespoons olive oil
2 teaspoons lemon juice, strained
salt and pepper

Season meat with salt and pepper and cover with the onion, parsley, thyme, bay leaves and garlic. Mix together the olive oil and lemon juice and pour over the meat. Marinate in a cool place for about 2 hours.
For sliced meat or chicken breasts.

COOKED MARINADE

MARINATA COTTA

5 tablespoons olive oil
2 carrots, chopped
2 onions, chopped
1 celery stick, chopped
1 litre/1³/₄ pints red wine
400 ml/14 fl oz red wine vinegar
2 teaspoons chopped fresh thyme
6 black peppercorns
salt

Heat the olive oil in a large saucepan. Add the carrots, onions and celery and cook over a low heat, stirring occasionally, for about 10 minutes until lightly browned. Add the wine, vinegar, thyme and peppercorns and season with salt. Simmer over a low heat for 30 minutes. Leave to cool before using to marinate meat for about 24 hours.
For red meat or game.

SPICY MARINADE

MARINATA PICCANTE

400 ml/14 fl oz olive oil
3 tablespoons Worcestershire sauce
juice of 1 lemon, strained
dash of Tabasco sauce
salt

Pour the olive oil into a large bowl, add the Worcestershire sauce, lemon juice and a dash of Tabasco and season with salt. Whisk well to mix. Marinate meat for 2 hours.
For red or white meat.

QUICK LEMON MARINADE

MARINATA VELOCE AL LIMONE

400 ml/14 fl oz olive oil
juice of 1 lemon, strained
2 fresh flat-leaf parsley sprigs, leaves only
1 small shallot, chopped
1 fresh thyme sprig, leaves only
1 bay leaf
salt and pepper

Mix together the olive oil, lemon juice, parsley, shallot, thyme and bay leaf in a bowl and season with salt and pepper. Marinate meat or fish for 30 minutes.
For fish or steak.

FLAVOURED BUTTERS

BURRO AGLI SPINACI

100 g/3¹/₂ oz spinach
100 g/3¹/₂ oz butter, softened
salt

SPINACH BUTTER

Cook the spinach in just the water clinging to its leaves after washing for 5 minutes until tender. Drain well, squeezing out as much liquid as possible, and chop finely. Cream the butter in a bowl, then beat in the spinach and season with salt.
For roast meat.

BURRO AI FUNGHI

130 g/4¹/₂ oz butter, softened, plus extra for frying
100 g/3¹/₂ oz mushrooms, sliced
1 tablespoon chopped fresh flat-leaf parsley
salt and pepper

MUSHROOM BUTTER

Melt 25 g/1 oz of the butter in a saucepan. Add the mushrooms, season with salt and pepper and cook over a medium heat, stirring occasionally, for about 5 minutes until tender. Transfer to a food processor and process to a purée, then leave to cool. Cream the remaining butter in a bowl, then beat in the mushrooms and parsley.
For canapés, crostini or grilled meat.

SHRIMP BUTTER

Cream the butter in a bowl, then beat in the shrimp or prawns and season with salt and pepper.
For canapés or crostini.

BURRO AI GAMBERETTI

100 g/3½ oz butter, softened

100 g/3½ oz peeled, cooked shrimp

or small prawns, finely chopped

salt and white pepper

BASIL BUTTER

Place the butter in the top of a double boiler or in a heatproof bowl and melt over barely simmering water. Remove the saucepan from the heat, whisk in the basil and lemon juice and season with salt and pepper.
For fish or shellfish.

BURRO AL BASILICO

100 g/3½ oz butter, diced

1 large bunch of fresh basil, leaves torn into pieces

2–3 tablespoons lemon juice, strained

salt and pepper

CAVIAR BUTTER

Gently stir the caviar to a cream in a bowl, then mix with the butter. Stir the mixture until soft.
For canapés.

BURRO AL CAVIALE

25 g/1 oz caviar

100 g/3½ oz butter, softened

CURRY BUTTER

Cream the butter in a bowl and beat in the curry powder, mixing well.
For crostini or hamburgers.

BURRO AL CURRY

100 g/3½ oz butter, softened

pinch of curry powder

FENNEL BUTTER

Blanch the garlic in a small saucepan of boiling water for about 1 minute, then drain, peel and mash well with a fork. Cream the butter in a bowl and beat in the garlic. Grind the fennel seeds in a mortar with a pestle or in a spice grinder and beat into the butter. Beat in the lemon juice and a pinch of white pepper.
For meat or grilled fish.

BURRO AL FINOCCHIO

1 garlic clove

100 g/3½ oz butter, softened

2 teaspoons fennel seeds

juice of ½ lemon, strained

white pepper

BUTTER WITH CHEESE AND ALMONDS

Cream the cheese in a bowl and beat in the almonds. Add the butter and mix well.
For crostini.

BURRO AL FORMAGGIO E MANDORLE

100 g/3½ oz strong soft cheese

10 blanched almonds, chopped

100 g/3½ oz butter, softened

GORGONZOLA BUTTER

Beat together the butter and Gorgonzola in a bowl until smooth and even. Beat in the parsley.
For grilled meat.

BURRO AL GORGONZOLA

100 g/3¹/₂ oz butter, softened
70 g/2 ³/₄ oz Gorgonzola cheese, crumbled
1 fresh flat-leaf parsley sprig, chopped

BUTTER WITH DRIED SALTED ROE

Pour the wine into a saucepan, add the roe and cook until tender. Remove from the heat and leave to cool, then drain. Cream the butter in a bowl, then crumble in the roe and beat well. Beat in the mustard.
For crostini.

BURRO ALLA BOTTARGA

100 ml/3¹/₂ fl oz dry white wine
80 g/3 oz pressed dried grey mullet or tuna roe, sliced
100 g/3¹/₂ oz butter, softened
¹/₂ teaspoon Dijon mustard

BURGUNDY BUTTER

Cream the butter in a bowl, then beat in the shallot, garlic and parsley. Season with salt and pepper and mix gently.
For snails or steak.

BURRO ALLA BOURGUIGNONNE

100 g/3¹/₂ oz butter, softened
1 shallot, finely chopped
¹/₂ garlic clove, finely chopped
1 fresh flat-leaf parsley sprig, finely chopped
salt and pepper

ANCHOVY BUTTER

Cream the butter in a bowl. Beat in the anchovies, then beat in the anchovy paste.
For grilled meat.

BURRO ALL'ACCIUGA

100 g/3¹/₂ oz butter, softened
50 g/2 oz salted anchovies, heads removed, cleaned and filleted (see page 596) and finely chopped • 1 teaspoon anchovy paste

GARLIC BUTTER

Blanch the garlic in boiling water for about 1 minute, then drain, peel and mash. Cream the butter in a bowl, then beat in the mashed garlic. Mix carefully.
For warm garlic bread or steaks.

BURRO ALL'AGLIO

100 g/3¹/₂ oz garlic cloves
100 g/3¹/₂ oz butter, softened

MAÎTRE D'HÔTEL BUTTER

Cream the butter in a bowl, then beat in the parsley, some salt, very little pepper and a few drops of lemon juice. Make into a roll and wrap in foil. Chill in the refrigerator until set. Cut into slices to serve.
For steaks, escalopes or poached fish.

BURRO ALLA MAÎTRE D'HÔTEL

100 g/3¹/₂ oz butter, softened
1 tablespoon chopped fresh flat-leaf parsley
lemon juice, strained, to taste
salt and pepper

← Grilled steak with anchovy butter

85

BUTTER SAUCE

Put the butter in a small saucepan and melt over a low heat. As soon as it begins to colour, add the lemon juice, a pinch of salt and a pinch of pepper. For poached fish or boiled vegetables.

BURRO ALLA MUGNAIA
100 g/3¹/₂ oz butter
2 tablespoons lemon juice, strained
salt and pepper

LOBSTER BUTTER

Break off the lobster's head, then twist off and reserve the claws. Remove and discard the stomach sac. Cut open the shell along the belly and push apart to remove the meat in one piece. Remove the dark vein along the back with the point of a knife. Finely chop the meat, coral and tomalley. Crack open the claws, pick out the meat and chop finely. Cream the butter in a bowl, then stir in the lobster meat, coral and tomalley. Lightly season with salt.
For canapés.

BURRO ALLA POLPA D'ARAGOSTA
1 small boiled lobster
100 g/3¹/₂ oz butter, softened
salt

SAGE BUTTER

Melt the butter in a small saucepan over a low heat. As soon as it starts to colour, add the sage leaves and season with salt. When the leaves are crisp, remove the saucepan from the heat and serve the butter immediately.
For boiled rice, grilled meat or ravioli.

BURRO ALLA SALVIA
100 g/3¹/₂ oz butter
15 fresh sage leaves
salt

MUSTARD BUTTER

Cream the butter in a bowl, then beat in the mustard and a pinch of salt. Mix until the colour is even.
For canapés.

BURRO ALLA SENAPE
100 g/3¹/₂ oz butter
1 teaspoon Dijon mustard
salt

SARDINE BUTTER

Skin the sardines and remove the bones. Mash or work through a food mill. Cream the butter in a bowl, then beat in the sardines. Season with a pinch of white pepper.
For canapés or toast.

BURRO ALLE SARDINE
4 canned sardines in oil, drained
100 g/3¹/₂ oz butter, softened
white pepper

Ravioli with sage butter

BURRO AL RAFANO

100 g/3¹/₂ oz butter, softened

50 g/2 oz horseradish, grated

salt

HORSERADISH BUTTER

Cream the butter in a bowl, then beat in the horseradish. Season with salt.

For canapés or roast meat.

BURRO AL SALMONE AFFUMICATO

100 g/3¹/₂ oz butter, softened

50 g/2 oz smoked salmon, finely chopped

SMOKED SALMON BUTTER

Cream the butter in a bowl, then gently stir in the salmon.

For canapés or crostini.

BURRO AL TONNO

100 g/3¹/₂ oz butter, softened

50 g/2 oz canned tuna in oil, drained and flaked

TUNA BUTTER

Cream the butter in a bowl, then gently stir in the tuna.

For white bread canapés or milk rolls.

BURRO CHIARIFICATO

1 kg/2¹/₄ lb butter

CLARIFIED BUTTER

Put the butter in the top of a double boiler or a heatproof bowl and set over barely simmering water. Heat for 1 hour. At this point, the water content of the butter will have evaporated and the casein will be deposited on the bottom in a hazelnut-colour layer. Line a strainer with muslin and pour the liquid through. Pour the clarified butter into a screw-top jar, close the lid and store in the refrigerator. If used instead of normal butter, halve the quantity.

BURRO FUSO

100 g/3¹/₂ oz butter

salt and pepper

dash of lemon juice, strained (optional)

MELTED BUTTER

Put the butter in the top of a double boiler or in a heatproof bowl and set over a saucepan of barely simmering water to melt. When slightly frothy, add salt and pepper, stir and pour into a sauce boat. To accentuate the taste of the butter, add a dash of lemon juice if you like.

BURRO 'INFARINATO'

butter

plain flour

BEURRE MANIÉ

This butter is used to thicken sauces, so exact quantities cannot be specified as they will vary according to the amount of sauce. As a general guide, blend together 20–25 g/³/₄–1 oz butter with 3–4 tablespoons flour and add to the cooking juices in small pieces, stirring well. The butter should melt without the liquid boiling.

SOFT BUTTER

→ Smoked salmon butter on canapés →

ANTIPASTI →

APPETIZERS →

PIZZAS →

ANTIPASTI

Classic Italian antipasti are based on cold meats, such as ham, salami, bresaola (dried salted beef), coppa (rolled and cured pork shoulder in a sausage casing in northern Italy or brawn made from pig's head in central Italy) and culatello (cured pork rump), served with pickles or vegetables preserved in oil, such as baby artichokes, mushrooms, gherkins and pickled onions. A more international selection consists of bowls of prawns, shells full of fish, and shellfish (spiny lobsters, spider crabs and oysters), salmon and smoked sturgeon. Another alternative – by far the most expensive – is caviar served on a bed of ice. Finally, something lighter is required for the summer, such as the traditional combination of prosciutto and melon, or prosciutto and figs. Antipasti served with pre-dinner drinks before sitting at the table are completely different. Practicality and good sense indicate a choice of small assorted hot and cold morsels that can be picked up with the fingers and finished off in one or two bites – canapés, various kinds of puffs and pizzette (mini pizzas). In any case, antipasti must be served and enjoyed in sensibly limited quantities, so that your guests will be able to do justice to the courses which follow. Antipasti based on vegetables, even if they also contain eggs, tuna, anchovies or cheese, should comply with the following rules for serving wine. In general serve light white wines, suitable for the beginning of a meal. When eggs are a major component, a soft white wine like Soave, dry Albana, Castel del Monte Bianco or Cirò Bianco should be served. If the flavour of tuna or anchovies dominates, choose a structured wine such as Gavi, Sylvaner, Pinot Bianco or Chardonnay. When vegetables are combined with grated cheese, choose light wines but if the dish contains a lot of cheese, some red wines are also fine, so long as they are not full-bodied and not aged. It's not usually recommended to serve any wine with artichokes because of their tannin content but partnering them with highly aromatic white wines, such as dry Malvasia, aromatic Traminer or dry Moscato, is something of a taste sensation. Cold meats are the most classic Italian antipasto, and if you want the right wine to go with them, it is best to choose a traditional one from among those typical of their origin. The ideal partner for smoked cold meats is a rosé or a light red wine. Sparkling wine is normally served with appetizers like barquettes, tartlets, vol-au-vents, etc.

APPETIZERS

Puffs, crêpes, tartlets, assorted small vol-au-vents, game terrines, crusty pies, mousses and anything else which is served at the beginning of a meal are considered appetizers and are normally served only on formal occasions. Their deliberate abundance is intended to give an idea of the richness of the menu to follow.

PIZZAS

If there is a dish that is simultaneously a food, a symbol and a ritual, that dish is the pizza. As a food it could hardly be more complete, as a symbol it could hardly be clearer, and as a ritual it could hardly be more enjoyable. When Italians say pizza, it is taken for granted that they are referring to the Neapolitan pizza, topped with mozzarella cheese and tomato. Pizzas are included in this section of the book because, although they are generally thought of as a dish in themselves, they make great antipasti too when cut into small pieces or baked as miniatures, known in Italian as pizzette. Not quite so famous, but deeply rooted in its region of origin, is the Ligurian version of pizza, better known as focaccia. The surface of the different types is sprinkled with oil, onions, vegetables and anchovies.

ITALIAN ANTIPASTI

ANTIPASTI

Prosciutto, cooked and smoked hams; regional salamis, small cacciatore sausages, coppa (cured pork shoulder) and soppressata (smoky pork salami); bresaola (dried salted fillet of beef); and mortadella (Bologna sausage). Any of these served with fruit, including exotic fruit, make delicious antipasti.

PROSCIUTTO AND FIGS

Whether they are green or black, the figs must be ripe; they are served peeled and cut into star shapes for a decorative effect. A mild type of prosciutto is best for this dish.

PROSCIUTTO AND PINEAPPLE

A pleasant combination as a result of the sweet-savoury contrast. The pineapple must be fresh, peeled and cut into slices.

PROSCIUTTO AND MELON

This is truly the best-loved antipasto among Italians. It has also been very successfully exported abroad. The melon is served cut into wedges which are left attached to the rind at one end or, more simply, completely rindless. Melon may be combined either with mild or strongly flavoured prosciutto.

COOKED HAM AND KIWI FRUIT

A delicate, pleasant combination in terms of both flavour and colour. The peeled kiwi fruits are thinly sliced.

BRESAOLA WITH OIL AND LEMON

An hour before serving, the bresaola is cut into wafer-thin slices and dressed with a drizzle of olive oil, lemon juice to taste, salt and pepper.

BRESAOLA AND GRAPEFRUIT

Wrap single segments of completely peeled grapefruit in small slices of bresaola and fasten with a cocktail stick. Together they have a pleasant fresh taste.

TOMATO BRUSCHETTA

Toast the slices of bread on both sides under the grill or on a barbecue. Rub them with garlic while they still hot and put back under the grill for a moment. Arrange the tomatoes on the bread. Season with salt and pepper and drizzle with olive oil.

BRUSCHETTA AL POMODORO

Serves 4

8 country bread slices

4 garlic cloves

6–8 ripe plum tomatoes, diced

extra virgin olive oil, for drizzling

salt and pepper

PIEDMONTESE TARTARE

Place the veal in a bowl and drizzle with olive oil and lemon juice. Add the mustard, season with salt and pepper and mix well. Set aside for about 2 hours to allow the flavours to infuse. When serving, arrange the meat in a dome in the middle of a platter and garnish with the mushrooms and shavings of truffle.

CARNE CRUDA ALLA PIEMONTESE

Serves 4

300g/11 oz veal, minced

olive oil, for drizzling

lemon juice, strained, to taste

$1/4$–$1/2$ teaspoon Dijon mustard

200 g/7 oz mushrooms, thinly sliced

1 white truffle, thinly shaved

salt and pepper

SEMOLINA BASKETS

Bring the milk to the boil in a saucepan over a low heat and sprinkle in the semolina, whisking constantly to prevent lumps from forming. Simmer for 10 minutes, stirring constantly. Season with salt and remove the pan from the heat. Stir in 50 g/2 oz of the butter, the eggs and lemon rind. Dampen a work surface with a little water and pour the semolina on to it in a layer about 2 cm/³/₄ inch thick. Leave to cool. When the semolina has set, stamp out rounds using a damp biscuit cutter or the rim of a glass. Use a smaller cutter or glass to stamp out the centre of half of the rounds to make rings. Discard the centres. Place the rings on top of the complete rounds to form 'baskets'. Place on a baking sheet and brush with a little milk. Preheat the oven to 180°C/350°F/Gas Mark 4. Heat the remaining butter in a frying pan. Add the onion and sage leaves and cook over a low heat, stirring occasionally, for about 5 minutes until the onion has softened. Add the chicken livers and cook, stirring constantly, for 3–5 minutes until lightly browned and tender. Pour in the Marsala and cook until it has evaporated. Sprinkle in the flour, stir in the tomato purée and the hot stock and season with salt and pepper. Cook until reduced and thickened, then remove from the heat and use the mixture to fill the baskets. Heat through for a few minutes in the oven.

CESTINI DI SEMOLINO

Serves 6

1 litre/1³/₄ pints milk, plus extra for brushing

250 g/9 oz semolina

70 g/2³/₄ oz butter

2 eggs, lightly beaten

grated rind of 1 lemon

¹/₂ onion, chopped

4 fresh sage leaves

200 g/7 oz chicken livers, trimmed and chopped

4 tablespoons dry Marsala

1 teaspoon plain flour

1 tablespoon tomato purée

2 tablespoons hot Chicken Stock (see page 209)

salt and pepper

HAM MOULDS

Slice the carrot into eight rounds and then cut each one into a decorative flower shape. Cut the gherkins into thin slices, then cut into 16 small leaf shapes. Melt the butter in a small saucepan. Stir in the flour, then gradually stir in the stock. Bring to the boil, stirring constantly, then simmer for 10 minutes, stirring. Season to taste with salt, pepper and nutmeg. Remove the pan from the heat and leave to cool. Process the ham in a food processor, then stir into the sauce. Chill in the refrigerator for 30 minutes. Prepare the gelatine according to the instructions on the packet. Add the Marsala and heat for longer than the packet instructions state in order to reduce the mixture. Rinse eight individual moulds in cold water, dry and pour 1 tablespoon of the gelatine mixture into each. Put a carrot 'flower' on the base of each mould with two gherkin 'leaves' alongside. Return to the refrigerator and chill until set. Once set, add another tablespoon of the gelatine mixture to each mould and return to the refrigerator. Meanwhile, stir the ham mixture until light and frothy. Whisk the cream until soft peaks form, then fold into the ham mixture. Divide this mousse among the moulds and return to the refrigerator to set. To serve, turn each mould out on to a separate lettuce leaf and arrange on a platter.

CUPOLETTE DI PROSCIUTTO

Serves 6–8

1 carrot

2–3 gherkins, drained

25 g/1 oz butter

1 tablespoon plain flour

200 ml/7 fl oz Chicken Stock (see page 209)

pinch of freshly grated nutmeg

500 g/1 lb 2 oz lean cooked ham, chopped

25 g/1 oz gelatine

1 tablespoon Marsala

100 ml/3½ fl oz double cream

salt and pepper

8 lettuce leaves, to serve

VINE LEAF PARCELS

Blanch the vine leaves in boiling water for 3 minutes. Drain and spread out on a tea towel. Tear the bread into pieces and place in a bowl with the milk. Set aside to soak. Melt 25 g/1 oz of the butter in a saucepan. Add the onions and cook over a low heat, stirring occasionally, for about 10 minutes until golden. Stir in the prosciutto. Melt half the remaining butter in a small frying pan. Add the veal and cook, stirring occasionally, until golden brown all over. Put the onion and prosciutto mixture and the veal in a food processor. Squeeze out the bread and add to the food processor with the egg and nutmeg. Season with salt and pepper and process to a purée. Place 1 tablespoon of the purée in the middle of each vine leaf and wrap into a parcel. Melt the remaining butter in a saucepan and add the parcels. When hot, sprinkle with the wine and cook until it has evaporated. Pour in 500 ml/18 fl oz water and cook for 40 minutes until the liquid has almost completely evaporated. Drizzle with the lemon juice and serve.

FAGOTTINI DI FOGLIE DI VITE

Serves 6

24 vine leaves

50 g/2 oz bread slices, crusts removed

100 ml/3½ fl oz milk

80 g/3 oz butter

2 onions, chopped

50 g/2 oz prosciutto, chopped

200 g/7 oz veal, chopped

1 egg

pinch of freshly grated nutmeg

100 ml/3½ fl oz dry white wine

juice of 1 lemon, strained

salt and pepper

tomato bruschetta

97

FAGOTTINI DI MORTADELLA

Serves 4

100 g/3¹/₂ oz ricotta cheese

1 yellow pepper, halved, seeded and finely chopped

4 shelled walnuts, chopped

4 thick slices mortadella, quartered

salt

MORTADELLA PARCELS

Place the ricotta in a bowl and stir until smooth. Add the yellow pepper and walnuts and season with salt. Spoon a little of the ricotta mixture on to the point of each mortadella triangle and roll up. Place the parcels in the refrigerator until ready to serve.

INVOLTINI DI INSALATA RUSSA

Serves 4

4 fairly thick slices of cooked ham

1 quantity Russian Salad (see page 116)

8 pickled pearl onions, drained

lettuce leaves, to serve

RUSSIAN SALAD ROULADES

Place the slices of ham flat on a work surface. Spread a heaped tablespoon of Russian salad on each one. Roll up and insert a pickled pearl onion at each end of the rolls. Place the roulades on a bed of lettuce leaves arranged in the shape of a fan on a serving platter.

LESSO DI MANZO IN CARPIONE

Serves 4

500 g/1 lb 2 oz boiled beef, chopped

3 tablespoons olive oil

1 onion, sliced

4 fresh sage leaves

1 fresh rosemary sprig

150 ml/¹/₄ pint white wine vinegar

175 ml/6 fl oz white wine

salt

SOUSED BOILED BEEF

Place the beef in a heatproof dish and set aside. Heat the olive oil in a saucepan. Add the onion and cook over a low heat, stirring occasionally, for about 10 minutes until golden brown. Add the sage leaves, rosemary, vinegar and a pinch salt. Simmer over a low heat until the vinegar has evaporated. Pour in the wine diluted with a little water and cook for a few minutes. Pour the hot mixture over the beef and leave to steep in a cool place for several hours.

LESSO DI MANZO IN TORTINO

Serves 4

olive oil, for brushing

500 g/1 lb 2 oz boiled beef, chopped

3 eggs

juice of 1 lemon, strained

salt and pepper

BOILED BEEF TORTINO

Brush a flameproof glass or earthenware dish with olive oil and add the beef. Beat the eggs with the lemon juice and salt and pepper to taste. Place the dish over a low heat, pour in the egg mixture and mix quickly so that the beef is coated. Cook for 2 minutes, then remove from the heat and serve hot.

SWEET–AND–SOUR TONGUE

Cook the tongue in boiling water for 1 hour or until tender. Peel off the skin while it is still hot and cut into the tongue slices. Dust lightly with flour. Heat the olive oil and butter in a frying pan. Add the tongue slices and cook for 5 minutes on each side. Drain the sultanas and add them to the pan with the pine nuts. Cook over a low heat for 15 minutes. Mix together the chocolate, vinegar, sugar, flour and a pinch of salt in a bowl. Add 5 tablespoons hot water and stir until the chocolate has melted and the sugar has dissolved. Pour the mixture into the pan and bring to the boil. If there doesn't seem to be enough sauce, add a little more hot water. Season with salt to taste and serve.

LINGUA IN DOLCEFORTE

Serves 6

1 calf's tongue, trimmed,

soaked in cold water overnight and drained

1 tablespoon plain flour, plus extra for dusting

2 tablespoons olive oil

25 g/1 oz butter

50 g/2 oz sultanas, soaked in warm water

for 10 minutes

25g/1 oz pine nuts

25 g/1 oz dark chocolate, grated or finely chopped

6 tablespoons white wine vinegar

40g/1$^1/_2$ oz sugar

salt

NERVETTI WITH ONIONS

Place the calf's feet in a large saucepan with one onion, the celery and carrot. Pour in water to cover and add a pinch of salt. Bring to the boil, then lower the heat and simmer for about 2 hours. Drain well, cut the meat off the bones while it is still hot, then cut it into strips (nervetti). Place in a dish. Thinly slice the remaining onion and mix with the meat. Drizzle with olive oil and season with salt and pepper. Set aside for at least 30 minutes to steep.

NERVETTI E CIPOLLE

Serves 4

2 calf's feet, blanched and central bones removed

2 onions

1 celery stick

1 carrot

olive oil, for drizzling

salt and pepper

SPICY QUAILS' EGGS

Bring a pan of water to the boil, add the eggs and cook for 8 minutes. Drain, refresh under cold water, then shell. Cut them in half. Stack several lettuce leaves on top of each other, roll up and cut into slices to make thin strips. Repeat with the remaining lettuce. Make a bed of lettuce strips on a serving platter. Place half the quails' eggs on top, in groups of four arranged like flower petals. Gently stir the cream into the mayonnaise, then stir in the orange juice. Season with salt and white pepper to taste. Pour into a sauce boat and serve with the salad.

OVETTI DI QUAGLIA PICCANTI

Serves 4

16 quails' eggs

200 g/7 oz round lettuce

2 tablespoons double cream, whipped

250 ml/8 fl oz Mayonnaise (see page 65)

4 tablespoons orange juice, strained

salt and white pepper

ROSEMARY AND CHEESE ROLLS

PANINI AL ROSMARINO E FORMAGGIO

Serves 6

100 ml/3¹/₂ fl oz milk

40 g/1¹/₂ oz butter

15 g/¹/₂ oz dried yeast

300 g/11 oz plain flour, plus extra for dusting

vegetable oil, for greasing

2¹/₂ tablespoons finely chopped fresh rosemary

70 g/2³/₄ oz mild provolone cheese, grated

3 tablespoons double cream

25 g/1 oz smoked pancetta, cut into strips

salt

Pour the milk into a small saucepan, add the butter and set over a low heat. When the butter has melted, remove the pan from the heat, stir well and set aside to cool to lukewarm. Sprinkle the yeast over the milk mixture and set aside for about 10 minutes until frothy. Sift the flour and a pinch of salt into a bowl and make a well in the centre. Stir the yeast mixture, pour into the well and, using your fingers, gradually incorporate the dry ingredients. Knead thoroughly, then shape into a ball. Oil a clean bowl, place the dough in it and cover with oiled cling film. Set aside in a warm place until doubled in volume. Turn out on to a lightly floured surface and knead again, gradually kneading in the rosemary. Divide the mixture into six pieces and shape into balls. Place on a baking sheet and leave to rise for about 1 hour. Preheat the oven to 180°C/350°F/Gas Mark 4. Flatten the rolls slightly with your hand and bake for 15 minutes. Meanwhile, prepare the filling. Heat the provolone, cream and pancetta in a small pan over a low heat. When the rolls are cooked, remove them from the oven and increase the oven temperature to 200°C/400°F/Gas Mark 6. Cut off the tops of the rolls and hollow out the soft crumb without breaking the crust. Fill the hollows with the cheese mixture and replace the tops. Reheat in the oven for a few minutes.

PINEAPPLE KEBABS

SPIEDINI ALL'ANANAS

Serves 4

200 g/7 oz red peppers, halved and seeded

4 onions

200 g/7 oz prosciutto in a single piece, cut into 2-cm/³/₄-inch cubes

200 g/7 oz fresh pineapple, cut into 2-cm/³/₄-inch cubes

200 /7 oz fontina cheese, cut into 2-cm/³/₄-inch cubes

16 fresh basil leaves

olive oil, for frying

50–80 g/2–3 oz breadcrumbs

1 egg • plain flour, for dusting

salt and pepper

watercress, to serve

Parboil the red peppers and onions in boiling water for a few minutes. Drain and leave to cool. Cut the peppers and onions into 2-cm/³/₄-inch cubes and thread the pieces of pepper, onion, prosciutto, pineapple and fontina and the basil leaves alternately on to skewers. Heat the olive oil in a large frying pan. Spread out the breadcrumbs on a shallow plate. Beat the egg with salt and pepper in a bowl. Lightly dust the kebabs with flour, shaking off any excess. Dip them into the egg and drain off any excess, then quickly roll in the breadcrumbs several times to coat. Fry in hot olive oil and drain on kitchen paper. Serve on a bed of watercress.

SAGE APPETIZER

STUZZICHINI DI SALVIA

Serves 4

1 egg

30 fresh sage leaves

25 g/1 oz fine white breadcrumbs

olive oil, for frying

salt

mild provolone cheese, diced

Beat the egg with a pinch of salt in a bowl. Add the sage leaves, making sure that they are immersed, and set aside for 2 minutes. Drain the leaves well and dip in the breadcrumbs to coat. Heat plenty of olive oil in a frying pan, add the sage leaves and cook until golden brown. Drain on kitchen paper and serve with the provolone.

SCHERRER'S TARTARE

TARTARA ALLA SCHERRER

Serves 4

4 herring fillets, diced

1 green apple, diced

1 gherkin, drained and diced

1 shallot, finely chopped

6 fresh chives, finely chopped

2 tablespoons olive oil

80 g/3 oz butter

8 wholemeal bread slices

pepper

Combine the herring fillets, apple, gherkin, shallot and chives in a bowl, stir in the olive oil and season with pepper. Melt a knob of the butter in a frying pan. Add one or two slices of bread and fry on both sides until golden. Remove from the pan and drain on kitchen paper. Fry the remaining slices of bread, adding more butter as necessary. Arrange the fried bread on a serving dish, top with the herring mixture and serve. Scherrer, the owner of a Hamburg restaurant with the same name, created the original recipe.

TRUFFLE, CHICKEN AND LAMB'S LETTUCE

TARTUFO, POLLO E SONGINO

Serves 4

4 tablespoons olive oil, plus extra for drizzling

400 g/14 oz skinless chicken breast fillets

200 g/7 oz lamb's lettuce

1 small black truffle, thinly shaved

salt and pepper

For the dressing

1 tablespoon anchovy paste

olive oil, for drizzling

juice of 1 lemon, strained

Heat the olive oil in a frying pan. Add the chicken and cook over a medium heat, turning occasionally, for 15 minutes until golden brown all over. Remove from the pan and cut into thin strips. Make a bed of lamb's lettuce on a serving platter. Drizzle with olive oil, season with salt and pepper and toss gently. Place the chicken strips on the lettuce and sprinkle with the truffle shavings. For the dressing, place the anchovy paste in a bowl, mash with a fork and gradually drizzle olive oil in to make a smooth paste. Stir in the lemon juice. Drizzle the dressing over the chicken and truffles and serve without tossing.

FISH
ANTIPASTI

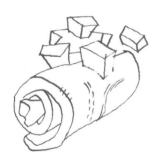

FISH
FILLET

FRESH ANCHOVIES WITH LEMON

Rinse the anchovies and pat dry with kitchen paper. Arrange the fillets in a non-metallic dish or soup plate, sprinkle with salt and pour in the lemon juice or vinegar. Leave to marinate in a cool place for 24 hours. Drain the anchovies, arrange on a serving dish and sprinkle with the parsley and onion slices. Drizzle with olive oil and serve immediately.

ACCIUGHE AL LIMONE

Serves 4

16 fresh anchovies, heads removed, cleaned and filleted (see page 596)

120 ml/4 fl oz lemon juice, strained, or white wine vinegar

3 tablespoons chopped fresh flat-leaf parsley

2 baby onions, thinly sliced

olive oil, for drizzling

salt

PRAWN BITES

BOCCONCINI DI GAMBERETTI

Serves 4

1 onion, coarsely chopped

250 g/9 oz raw prawns, peeled and deveined

5 fresh flat-leaf parsley sprigs, coarsely chopped

250 g/9 oz plain flour • 100 ml/3¹/₂ fl oz milk

1 egg • olive oil, for frying

salt and pepper

Put the onion, prawns and parsley in a food processor, season with salt and process for 1 minute. Add the flour, milk, egg and 100 ml/3¹/₂ fl oz water. Process again until combined. Season with salt and pepper to taste. Heat plenty of olive oil in a frying pan. Add the prawn mixture, a tablespoonful at a time, and cook until golden brown. Remove with a slotted spoon, drain on kitchen paper and serve hot or cold.

CHERRY TOMATO AND CRAB BITES

BOCCONCINI DI POMODORI E GRANCHIO

Serves 4

12 red cherry tomatoes

250 g/9 oz white crab meat, drained if canned

3 tablespoons Mayonnaise (see page 65)

salt and pepper

12 black olives, to garnish

Cut the tops off the tomatoes and scoop out some of the pulp. Sprinkle the insides with salt and place them upside down on kitchen paper to drain. Mix the crab meat with the mayonnaise in a bowl and season with salt and pepper. Fill the tomatoes with the crab mixture and garnish with the olives.

TUNA BITES

BOCCONCINI DI TONNO

Serves 4

2 eggs, hard-boiled

200 g/7 oz canned tuna in oil, drained and flaked

100 g/3¹/₂ oz ricotta cheese

20 g/³/₄ oz capers, drained

2 tablespoons finely chopped fresh basil

rind of 1 lemon, grated

2 tablespoons lemon juice, strained

25 g/1 oz butter, softened • salt and pepper

rocket, to serve

Shell and chop the eggs. Push the eggs, tuna and ricotta through a sieve into a bowl. Stir in the capers, basil, lemon rind, lemon juice and butter and season to taste with salt and pepper. Shape the mixture into balls and chill in the refrigerator until ready to serve. Just before serving, arrange a bed of rocket on a platter and place the tuna bites on top.

STUFFED SQUID

CALAMARI RIPIENI

Serves 4

500 ml/18 fl oz dry white wine

2 bay leaves • 8 squid, cleaned

300 g/11 oz cooked, peeled prawns

1 garlic clove, chopped

2 tablespoons chopped fresh flat-leaf parsley

juice of 2 lemons, strained

100 ml/3 ¹/₂ fl oz olive oil, plus extra for drizzling

salt and pepper

Pour 1 litre/1³/₄ pints water into a large saucepan and add the white wine, bay leaves and a pinch of salt. Bring to the boil, add the squid and simmer for 20 minutes. Drain and leave to cool. Place the prawns, garlic, 1 tablespoon of the parsley and 2 tablespoons of the lemon juice in a bowl, drizzle generously with olive oil and season with pepper. Mix well. Stuff the squid sacs with the prawn mixture and arrange on a serving dish. Whisk together the olive oil, the remaining lemon juice and the remaining parsley. Season with salt and pepper and pour the dressing over the squid.

FISH CARPACCIO

Place the fish in the freezer or refrigerator for 1–2 hours to firm up. Using a very sharp knife, cut the swordfish and salmon into thin slices. Arrange on a serving dish and keep in the refrigerator until ready to serve. Put the olive oil, garlic, brandy, parsley and thyme in a food processor and season with salt and pepper. Process to mix well. Just before serving, sprinkle the carpaccio with the dressing.

CARPACCIO DI PESCE

Serves 4

250-g/9-oz swordfish fillet

250-g/9-oz salmon fillet • 100 ml/3^1/$_2$ fl oz olive oil

1 garlic clove, finely chopped

1 tablespoon brandy

^{1}/$_2$ bunch of fresh flat-leaf parsley, coarsely chopped

1 teaspoon fresh thyme leaves • salt and pepper

BABY SQUID IN BASKETS

Discard any mussels that do not close immediately when sharply tapped. Put the mussels in a frying pan with 2 tablespoons of the olive oil, the wine, parsley, garlic and a pinch of pepper. Set over a high heat for 3–5 minutes until the shells open. Remove the pan from the heat and discard any mussels that have not opened. Strain the mussels, reserving the cooking liquid, and remove them from their shells. Strain the cooking liquid through a muslin-lined strainer. Preheat the oven to 220°C/425°F/Gas Mark 7. Grease eight individual ramekins with butter. Roll out the pastry on a lightly floured surface and line the ramekins. Place in the refrigerator until required. Heat the remaining olive oil in another frying pan. Add the prawns and cook, stirring frequently, for 3–5 minutes. Add the squid and mussels and simmer gently. Whisk together the egg yolks, reserved mussel cooking liquid, grated Parmesan and shallot in a bowl and season with salt and pepper. Add the seafood mixture, stir well and divide among the ramekins. Place on a baking sheet and bake for 15–20 minutes until set and golden. Serve warm.

CESTINI DI CALAMARETTI

Serves 6–8

150 g/5 oz live mussels, scrubbed and beards removed

4 tablespoons olive oil

3 tablespoons dry white wine

2 tablespoons chopped fresh flat-leaf parsley

1 garlic clove, finely chopped

butter, for greasing

250 g/9 oz ready-made puff pastry dough,

thawed if frozen

plain flour, for dusting

100 g/3^1/$_2$ oz raw prawns, peeled and deveined

200 g/7 oz baby squid, cleaned, blanched and chopped

2 egg yolks

100 g/3^1/$_2$ oz Parmesan cheese, freshly grated

1 shallot, chopped

salt and pepper

LANGOUSTINE COCKTAIL

Bring a pan of lightly salted water to the boil. Add the langoustines or prawns, onion and carrot and cook for 2–5 minutes until tender. Drain well and peel the langoustines or prawns. Mix together the mayonnaise, cream, Worcestershire sauce and ketchup in a bowl. Sprinkle with gin and whisky, season with salt to taste and stir. Line four serving dishes with the most tender lettuce leaves. Divide the langoustines or prawns among them and spoon over the sauce. Chill in the refrigerator until ready to serve.

COCKTAIL DI SCAMPI

Serves 4

800 g/1^3/$_4$ lb langoustines or Dublin Bay prawns

1 onion, chopped • 1 carrot, chopped

300 ml/^{1}/$_2$ pint Mayonnaise (see page 65)

200 ml/7 fl oz single cream

1 teaspoon Worcestershire sauce

1 teaspoon tomato ketchup

1 teaspoon gin, or to taste

1 teaspoon whisky, or to taste

1 lettuce • salt

SMOKED TROUT IN PINK CREAM

DELIZIE DI TROTA IN CREMA ROSA

Serves 4

80 g/3 oz butter

400 g/14 oz smoked trout fillets, skinned and coarsely chopped

1 tablespoon brandy, or to taste

2 tablespoons olive oil

$1/2$ onion, chopped

1 red pepper, halved, seeded and chopped

100 g/$3^{1}/_{2}$ oz tomato purée

100 ml/$3^{1}/_{2}$ fl oz double cream

salt and pepper

Melt the butter in a double boiler or a heatproof bowl set over a pan of barely simmering water, then remove from the heat. Meanwhile, place the trout in a food processor and process to purée. Scrape into a bowl, stir in the melted butter and brandy and season with salt and pepper. Divide the mixture among four individual moulds and put in the refrigerator for a few hours to set. Heat the olive oil in a frying pan. Add the onion and red pepper and cook over a low heat, stirring occasionally, for 5 minutes until softened. Add the tomato purée, season with salt and pepper and cook for 15 minutes. Remove the pan from the heat and leave to cool slightly. Spoon the vegetable mixture into a food processor and process to a purée. Scrape into a bowl and stir in the cream. To serve, pour 2 tablespoons of the pink cream into the middle of each of four plates and turn out the moulds on top.

SPIDER CRAB AU GRATIN

GRANCEOLA GRATINATA

Serves 4

4 live or freshly cooked spider crabs

40 g/$1^{1}/_{2}$ oz butter, plus extra for greasing

3 tablespoons brandy

2 egg yolks

$1/2$ quantity Béchamel Sauce (see page 50)

50 g/2 oz Gruyère cheese, grated

salt

If using live spider crabs, plunge them into a large pan of salted, boiling water, cover and cook for about 15 minutes. Drain and leave to cool. When the crabs are cold, remove the claws and legs. Using a small strong knife, force the shells apart, inserting it under the tail flaps. Remove and discard the gills and stomach sacs. Extract the white meat and pinkish-red corals, if present, from the bodies, then crack the claws and legs and pick out the meat. Wash and dry the crab shells to use as serving dishes, then grease with butter. (You can also use individual gratin dishes.) Preheat the oven to 180°C/350°F/Gas Mark 4. Stir the corals and brandy together in a bowl. Stir the crab meat, egg yolks and brandy mixture into the béchamel sauce and spoon into the crab shells or dishes. Sprinkle with the grated Gruyère and dot with the butter. Place on a baking sheet and bake for 15–20 minutes until golden and bubbling.

CRAB AND LANGOUSTINE CUPS

Wash the grapefruit well and cut in half. Cut around the flesh and scoop it out without damaging the 'shells'. Chop the flesh and reserve the shells to use as serving dishes. Grate the carrots into a bowl and immediately stir in the lemon juice. Cook the langoustines or prawns in a pan of lightly salted, boiling water for 2–5 minutes until tender. Drain, peel and chop. Stir the langoustines or prawns, crab meat, olives and 4 tablespoons of the grapefruit flesh into the carrot mixture. Season to taste with salt and pepper. Divide the mixture among the grapefruit shells and chill in the refrigerator until ready to serve.

GRANCHI E SCAMPI IN COPPETTE

Serves 4

2 grapefruit

3 small carrots

juice of 1 lemon, strained

12 langoustines or Dublin Bay prawns

120 g/4 oz canned crab meat, drained

4 tablespoons black olives, stoned

salt and pepper

BABY OCTOPUS AND GREEN BEAN SALAD

Cook the beans in lightly salted, boiling water until just tender, then drain and put in a salad bowl. Bring a pan of water to the boil and add the octopuses. Cook for 1 minute, then drain and halve the larger ones, leaving the smaller ones whole. Pour the vinegar into a small saucepan and add the basil, marjoram, parsley, garlic and chilli. Bring to the boil and cook for a few minutes until reduced. Remove from the heat and strain into a bowl. Flake the tuna and sprinkle it over the beans, then add the octopuses. Drizzle olive oil over the salad, then spoon over the spiced vinegar and season with salt and pepper. Chill in the refrigerator for 2 hours before serving.

INSALATA DI MOSCARDINI E FAGIOLINI

Serves 6

1 kg/2¼ lb green beans, trimmed

400 g/14 oz baby octopuses, cleaned and skinned

175 ml/6 fl oz red-wine vinegar

2 tablespoons chopped fresh basil

2 tablespoons chopped fresh marjoram

1 tablespoon chopped fresh flat-leaf parsley

1 garlic clove, chopped

1 fresh chilli

150 g/5 oz canned tuna in oil, drained

olive oil, for drizzling

salt and pepper

WHITEBAIT SALAD

Wash the fish carefully and thoroughly. Parboil for a few minutes in salted water. Drain carefully and leave to cool. Mix together the olive oil and lemon juice in a bowl and season with salt and white pepper. Pour the dressing over the whitebait and toss. Leave to stand for 10 minutes before serving.

INSALATA DI BIANCHETTI

Serves 4

500 g/1 lb 2 oz whitebait

4 tablespoons olive oil

juice of ½ lemon, strained

salt and white pepper

OCTOPUS AND ROCKET SALAD

Put a little water in a saucepan and add the wine and peppercorns. Bring to the boil, add the sea salt and immerse the octopus. Cook for 1 hour or until the thickest tentacles can be pricked with a fork. Remove the pan from the heat and leave the octopus to cool in the water for at least 20 minutes. Meanwhile, mix together the rocket, pine nuts and apple. Drain the octopus, pull off and discard the skin and chop the flesh. Add to the rocket mixture. Whisk together the olive oil and lemon juice in a jug, season with salt and pepper and pour over the salad.

INSALATA DI POLPO E RUCOLA

Serves 6

100 ml/3 1/2 fl oz dry white wine

6 black peppercorns

1 teaspoon coarse sea salt

800-g/1 3/4-lb octopus, cleaned and tenderized

2 bunches of rocket, chopped

4 tablespoons pine nuts

1/2 apple, peeled, cored and diced

120 ml/4 fl oz olive oil

juice of 1 lemon, strained

salt and pepper

LANGOUSTINE AND FIG SALAD

Bring a pan of lightly salted water to the boil. Add the langoustines or prawns and cook for 2–5 minutes until tender. Drain and peel, then set aside. Place the tomatoes in a food processor with the lemon juice, grapefruit juice and Tabasco, season with salt and pepper and process to a purée. Pour the sauce into a bowl and gradually whisk in the olive oil. Using a melon baller or teaspoon, scoop out about 40 small balls of melon flesh. Using a dampened knife cut each fig into four wedges. To serve, divide the rocket among four serving plates, placing it in the centre, and arrange the figs, langoustines or prawns and melon balls around like sun rays. Spoon over the sauce and serve.

INSALATA DI SCAMPI E FICHI

Serves 4

500 g/1 lb 2 oz langoustines or Dublin Bay prawns

4 plum tomatoes, peeled, seeded and coarsely chopped

juice of 1/2 lemon, strained

juice of 1/2 grapefruit, strained

dash of Tabasco sauce

4 tablespoons olive oil

1 melon, halved and seeded

4 fresh figs, peeled

1 bunch of rocket

salt and pepper

MEDITERRANEAN PRAWNS WITH ROCKET

Arrange the rocket on a serving dish. Peel and devein the prawns, reserving any roe for the garnish. Put the prawns in the top of a steamer and cook over a medium heat for 4 minutes. Meanwhile, whisk together the lemon juice and olive oil and season with salt. Arrange the prawns on the bed of rocket, garnish with the reserved roe and drizzle with the lemon dressing. Serve immediately while the prawns are still warm.

MANZZANCOLLE ALLA RUCOLA

Serves 4

200 g/7 oz rocket

800 g/1 3/4 lb raw Mediterranean prawns

juice of 1 lemon, strained

100 ml/3 1/2 fl oz olive oil

salt

OYSTERS

Just before serving open the oysters. Protect the hand holding the oyster with a tea towel and insert an oyster knife or small strong knife into the hinged edge, then twist to prise the shells apart. Slide the blade along the inside of the upper shell to sever the muscle and lift off the shell. Taking care not to spill the juices, slide the blade under the oyster to sever the lower muscle. Arrange the oysters on the half-shells on a bed of crushed ice. They may be eaten as they are, with a dash of lemon juice or with thin slices of lightly buttered toast.

OSTRICHE

Serves 4

24 oysters

crushed ice, to serve

lemon (optional)

buttered toast (optional)

RAW SOLE WITH CHILLI

Place the sole fillets in a serving dish. Mix together the passata, onion, lemon juice, orange juice, Worcestershire sauce, chilli powder and a pinch of salt in a bowl. Pour this mixture over the fish and set aside in the refrigerator to marinate for at least 4 hours. Remove the dish from the refrigerator 10 minutes before serving.

SOGLIOLETTE CRUDE AL PEPERONCINO

Serves 4

1 kg/2¼ lb sole fillets, skinned

2 tablespoons passata

2 tablespoons chopped onion

2 tablespoons lemon juice, strained

1 tablespoon orange juice, strained

dash of Worcestershire sauce

pinch of chilli powder

salt

VEGETABLE ANTIPASTI

CAPONATA IN AGRODOLCE

Serves 4

800 g/1³/₄ lb aubergines, diced

120 ml/4 fl oz olive oil

1 celery stick, chopped

1 onion, thinly sliced

300 g/11 oz ripe tomatoes, peeled and diced

1¹/₂ teaspoons sugar

100 ml/3¹/₂ fl oz white wine vinegar

1 tablespoon pine nuts

100 g/3¹/₂ oz stoned green olives

25 g/1 oz capers

1 tablespoon sultanas, soaked in hot water

for 10 minutes and drained

salt and pepper

fresh basil leaves, to garnish

SWEET–AND–SOUR CAPONATA

Put the aubergines in a colander, sprinkle with salt and leave to stand for 30 minutes. Rinse and pat dry with kitchen paper. Heat 5 tablespoons of the oil in a large frying pan. Add the aubergines and cook over a medium heat, stirring frequently, until golden brown all over. Meanwhile, heat the remaining olive oil in another pan. Add the celery, onion and tomatoes and cook over a low heat for 10–15 minutes until thickened and pulpy. Season with salt and pepper to taste. Stir in the sugar, vinegar, pine nuts, olives, capers and sultanas and bring to the boil over a low heat. Add the aubergines and simmer for 10 minutes. Serve the caponata hot or warm, sprinkled with small basil leaves.

ARTICHOKES JARDINIÈRE

CARCIOFI ALLA GIARDINIERA

Serves 4

Half-fill a bowl with cold water and add the lemon juice. Working on one artichoke at a time, break off the stems and cut off the coarse outer leaves. Trim off the top 2 cm/³/₄ inch. Scoop out and discard the chokes, then cut the artichokes into wedges. Drop them in the acidulated water to prevent discoloration. Pour 600 ml/1 pint water into a saucepan and add the olive oil, clove, bay leaf, onion, peppercorns and sea salt. Drain the artichokes, add them to the pan and bring to the boil. Cook over a medium heat until most of the liquid has evaporated and the artichokes are tender. Drain, reserving 2–3 tablespoons of the cooking liquid. Discard the clove, bay leaf and peppercorns. Line a wide, shallow salad bowl with lettuce leaves. Arrange the artichoke wedges on top. Whisk together the reserved cooking liquid and the anchovy paste in a jug, then pour the sauce over the artichokes. Add the olives to the bowl and sprinkle the salad with the chopped eggs.

juice of 1 lemon, strained

8 globe artichokes

4 tablespoons olive oil

1 clove

1 bay leaf

¹/₂ onion, thinly sliced

6 black peppercorns

1 teaspoon coarse sea salt

1 lettuce

¹/₂ teaspoon anchovy paste

100 g/3¹/₂ oz stoned black olives

2 eggs, hard-boiled and finely chopped

STUFFED ARTICHOKES JARDINIÈRE

CARCIOFI GIARDINIERA SAPORITI

Serves 4

Beat the egg with the grapefruit juice in a bowl and season with salt and pepper. Add the Parmesan, breadcrumbs, capers and anchovies and mix well. Set aside. Half-fill a bowl with cold water and add the lemon juice. Working on one artichoke at a time, break off the stems and cut off the coarse outer leaves. Trim off the top 2 cm/³/₄ inch. Scoop out and discard the chokes. Drop the artichokes in the acidulated water to prevent discoloration. Half-fill a large saucepan with water, stir in the flour and a pinch of salt. Drain the artichokes, add them to the pan and bring to the boil. Lower the heat and simmer for about 15 minutes until tender. Preheat the oven to 200°C/400°F/Gas Mark 6. Drain the artichokes and stuff with the Parmesan and anchovy mixture. Arrange the artichokes in an ovenproof dish and drizzle with olive oil. Bake for 20 minutes and serve warm.

1 egg

juice of ¹/₂ grapefruit, strained

50 g/2 oz Parmesan cheese, freshly grated

2 tablespoons breadcrumbs

1 tablespoon capers

2 salted anchovies, heads removed, cleaned and filleted (see page 596), soaked in cold water for 10 minutes, drained and finely chopped

juice of 1 lemon, strained

8 globe artichokes

1 tablespoon plain flour

olive oil, for drizzling

salt and pepper

CIPOLLE GRATINATE

Serves 4

4 large onions, peeled

butter, for greasing

150 g/5 oz cooked ham, chopped

4 tablespoons passata

4 tablespoons Parmesan cheese, freshly grated

1/2 quantity Béchamel Sauce (see page 50)

salt and pepper

STUFFED ONION GRATIN

Bring a large pan of salted water to the boil. Add the whole onions and parboil for a few minutes. Drain well, cut in half horizontally and gently scoop out the middles to leave eight 'shells'. Preheat the oven to 180°C/350°F/Gas Mark 4 and grease an ovenproof dish with butter. Chop the scooped-out onion and mix with the ham and passata in a bowl. Season with salt and pepper. Stuff the onion shells with this mixture. Arrange them in the prepared dish. Stir the Parmesan into the béchamel sauce and season with salt and pepper to taste. Pour the sauce over the stuffed onions and bake until golden brown and bubbling. Serve immediately.

CIPOLLINE ALLA SENAPE ARANCIONE

Serves 4

16 baby onions

2 teaspoons olive oil, plus extra for drizzling

600 ml/1 pint dry white wine

25 g/1 oz butter

2 carrots, chopped

2 tablespoons plain flour

2 tablespoons mustard

200 g/7 oz bacon, diced

50 ml/2 fl oz double cream

salt and pepper

ONIONS IN ORANGE MUSTARD

Preheat the oven to 180°C/350°F/Gas Mark 4. Place the onions in a high-sided roasting tin and drizzle with a little olive oil. Pour in 400 ml/14 fl oz of the white wine and season with salt and pepper. Bake for about 30 minutes until the liquid has almost completely evaporated. Melt the butter in a frying pan. Add the carrots and cook over a low heat, stirring occasionally, for 5 minutes. Sprinkle with the flour and stir in, then add the mustard and season with salt and pepper. Cook, stirring frequently, until thickened. Heat the olive oil in another frying pan. Add the bacon and cook, stirring occasionally, for 4–5 minutes. Sprinkle with the remaining wine and cook until it has evaporated. Stir in the cream, then pour the mixture into the pan of carrots and stir well. Transfer the onions to a serving dish and pour the sauce on top.

CUORICINI DI SPINACI

Serves 6

500 g/1 lb 2 oz spinach

1 quantity Béchamel Sauce (see page 50)

pinch of freshly grated nutmeg

2 egg yolks

50 g/2 oz plain flour

50 g/2 oz breadcrumbs

2 eggs

6 tablespoons olive oil

salt and pepper

SPINACH HEARTS

Cook the spinach in lightly salted, boiling water for about 5 minutes until tender. Drain, squeezing out as much liquid as possible, then chop and leave to cool slightly. Season the béchamel sauce with the nutmeg and salt and pepper to taste, then stir in the spinach and beat in the egg yolks. Spread out the mixture on a work surface and leave to cool completely. Spread out the flour on a plate, spread out the breadcrumbs on another plate and beat the whole eggs in a shallow dish. Heat the olive oil in a large frying pan. When the spinach mixture is cold, stamp out shapes using a heart-shaped biscuit cutter. Dip them first in the flour, then in the beaten eggs and, finally, in the breadcrumbs. Cook in the hot oil, in batches if necessary, until golden brown all over. Drain on kitchen paper and serve warm.

MUSHROOM SALAD

Thinly slice the mushrooms and sprinkle with the lemon juice. Mix the mushrooms with the prawns in a serving bowl. Season with salt and pepper, drizzle with oil and garnish with parsley.

FUNGHI IN INSALATA
Serves 4
300 g/11 oz Caesar's mushrooms
or other wild mushrooms
juice of 1 lemon, strained
400 g/14 oz cooked prawns, peeled and deveined
olive oil, for drizzling • salt and pepper
fresh flat-leaf parsley, chopped, to garnish

CHICORY WITH HAM

Put the diced fontina and mozzarella in a bowl, add the milk and set aside to soften for 1 hour. Bring a large pan of salted water to the boil. Add the chicory heads and simmer for 15 minutes, then drain well. Preheat the oven to 200°C/400°F/Gas Mark 6. Grease an ovenproof dish with butter. Wrap each head of chicory in a slice of prosciutto and arrange in the prepared dish. Tip the cheese and milk mixture into a frying pan and heat gently, stirring, to make a thick, smooth cream. Season with salt and pepper. Remove the pan from the heat, stir in the egg yolks and pour the sauce over the prosciutto-wrapped chicory. Sprinkle with the Parmesan, dot with the butter and bake for 10 minutes.

INDIVIA AL PROSCIUTTO
Serves 4
150 g/5 oz fontina cheese, diced
150 g/5 oz mozzarella cheese, diced
250 ml/8 fl oz milk
4 chicory heads
25 g/1 oz butter, plus extra for greasing
4 prosciutto slices
2 egg yolks, lightly beaten
50 g/2 oz Parmesan cheese, freshly grated
salt and pepper

CAULIFLOWER SALAD (1)

Cook the cauliflower florets in boiling water until al dente. Drain, leave to cool, then place in a salad bowl. Mash the anchovy fillets in the lemon juice in a bowl and add the olive oil, garlic and tuna. Season with salt, mix and use to dress the cauliflower.

INSALATA DI CAVOLFIORE (1)
Serves 4
1 cauliflower, cut into florets
6 canned anchovy fillets, drained
juice of 1 lemon, strained
6 tablespoons olive oil • 1/2 garlic clove, chopped
150 g/5 oz canned tuna in oil, drained and flaked
salt

CAULIFLOWER SALAD (2)

Cook the cauliflower florets in salted, boiling water until al dente. Drain, leave to cool, then place in a salad bowl. Mix together the olive oil and vinegar in a bowl, add the parsley and tarragon and season with salt and pepper. Use to dress the cauliflower and leave to stand for 1 hour. Serve separately with mayonnaise with a little mustard.

INSALATA DI CAVOLFIORE (2)
Serves 4
1 cauliflower, cut into florets
6 tablespoons olive oil
3 tablespoons white wine vinegar
1 tablespoon chopped fresh flat-leaf parsley
2 teaspoons chopped fresh tarragon
salt and pepper • mustard mayonnaise, to serve

115

CUCUMBER AND PRAWN SALAD

INSALATA DI CETRIOLI E GAMBERI

Serves 4

4 cucumbers, peeled and cut into thin batons

400 g/14 oz cooked prawns, peeled and deveined

100 ml/3¹/₂ fl oz double cream

juice of 1 lemon, strained

1 teaspoon paprika

2 tablespoons chopped fresh flat-leaf parsley

salt

Place the cucumbers and prawns in a salad bowl. Mix together the cream and lemon juice in a bowl, stir in the paprika and season with salt. Pour the dressing over the salad, sprinkle with parsley and toss well. If you do not like the flavour of cucumber, substitute boiled courgettes.

RUSSIAN SALAD

INSALATA RUSSA

Serves 4

100 g/3¹/₂ oz shelled peas

100 g/3¹/₂ oz green beans

6 cauliflower florets

2 potatoes

2 carrots

3 cornichons or small gherkins, drained and diced

1 cooked beetroot, diced

1 egg, hard-boiled, shelled and diced

1 quantity Mayonnaise (see page 65)

Cook the peas, beans, cauliflower, potatoes and carrots in separate pans of boiling water until al dente. Drain well and chop them, apart from the peas. Put all the vegetables in a salad bowl with the cornichons or gherkins, beetroot and egg. Stir in enough mayonnaise to form a soft mixture. Chill in the refrigerator for 2–3 hours. Shortly before serving, arrange the Russian salad in a dome in the middle of a dish and garnish to taste.

STUFFED AUBERGINES

MELANZANE RIPIENE

Serves 4

4 aubergines

3 tablespoons olive oil, plus extra for brushing

1 onion, chopped

1 celery stick, chopped

3 red or green peppers, halved, seeded and chopped

4 ripe tomatoes, diced

2 eggs, lightly beaten

3 tablespoons Parmesan cheese, freshly grated

salt and pepper

Halve the aubergines lengthways and scoop out the flesh without piercing the 'shells'. Chop the flesh and reserve the shells. Heat the oil in a large frying pan. Add the onion and cook over a low heat, stirring occasionally, for 5 minutes until soft. Add the chopped aubergine flesh, celery, peppers and toma-toes, season with salt and pepper and cook over a low heat for 15 minutes. Meanwhile, preheat the oven to 180°C/350°F/Gas Mark 4. Brush an ovenproof dish with olive oil. Remove the pan from the heat and stir in the eggs. Fill the aubergine shells with the mixture and place in the prepared dish. Sprinkle with the Parmesan and bake until golden and bubbling. Remove from the oven and leave to cool. Serve cold.

ROLLED PEPPERS

Place the peppers on a baking sheet under a preheated grill. Grill, turning frequently, until charred and blackened. Transfer to a plastic bag, tie the top and leave to cool. Peel off the pepper skins, rinse gently under cold running water and pat dry. Halve and seed the peppers, then cut the flesh into two or three large slices. Place the tuna, olives, tomato, chilli and basil in a food processor and process to a purée. Add enough lemon juice to make a soft mixture and add the olive oil. Spread each slice of pepper with the tuna sauce and roll up. Keep in a cool place before serving.

PEPERONI ARROTOLATI

Serves 4

4 large red or green peppers

300 g/11 oz canned tuna in oil, drained

10 stoned black olives, coarsely chopped

1 tomato, peeled, seeded and coarsely chopped

1 fresh red chilli, seeded and coarsely chopped

12 fresh basil leaves

3–4 tablespoons lemon juice, strained

1 tablespoon olive oil

TOMATO FLOWERS

Cut off the tops of the tomatoes and scoop out the seeds. Sprinkle with salt and place upside down on kitchen paper to drain. Meanwhile, shell the eggs and halve lengthways. Scoop out the yolks without breaking the whites. Place the tuna, olives, egg yolks, mayonnaise and mustard in a food processor and process to a purée. Season with salt to taste. Spoon the mixture into eight of the egg-white halves, doming it on top. Arrange rocket leaves in the tomatoes so that they look like a whorl of petals, and place the filled egg halves in the middle. Garnish with mayonnaise and arrange on a serving dish. Chop the remaining egg whites and sprinkle them around the tomato flowers. Serve cold.

POMODORI FIORITI

Serves 4

4 large tomatoes, about the same size

6 eggs, hard-boiled

100 g/3¹/₂ oz canned tuna, drained and flaked

1 tablespoon stoned green olives, coarsely chopped

1 tablespoon Mayonnaise (see page 65), plus extra to garnish

1 teaspoon Dijon mustard

1 bunch of rocket

salt

STUFFED PORCINI MUSHROOMS

Preheat the oven to 160°C/325°F/Gas Mark 3. Line a roasting tin with baking parchment. Remove the mushroom caps, reserving the stems. Place the caps in the roasting tin and bake for 5 minutes. Remove from the oven and increase the temperature to 180°C/350°F/Gas Mark 4. Transfer the mushroom caps to a plate, discard the baking parchment and brush the roasting tin with oil. Slice the stems. Chop the anchovy fillets. Heat 1 tablespoon of the olive oil in a frying pan. Add the onion, parsley, garlic and anchovies and cook over a low heat, stirring occasionally, for 5 minutes. Add the mushroom stems, cook for 3–4 minutes more, then season with salt and pepper. Remove the pan from the heat. Squeeze out the bread and stir it into the pan with the egg and remaining olive oil. Place the mushroom caps in the roasting tin gill sides uppermost and fill with the mixture. Sprinkle with the breadcrumbs and bake for 20 minutes.

PORCINI RIPIENI

Serves 4

8 porcini mushrooms

2 tablespoons olive oil, plus extra for brushing

2 salted anchovies, heads removed, cleaned and filleted (see page 596), soaked in cold water for 10 minutes and drained

1 onion, thinly sliced

1 tablespoon fresh flat-leaf parsley

1 garlic clove, chopped

2 bread slices, crusts removed, soaked in cold water for 10 minutes

1 egg, lightly beaten

4 tablespoons breadcrumbs

salt and pepper

SACCHETTI DELL'ORTOLANO

Serves 4

4 yellow peppers

2 tablespoons olive oil, plus extra for brushing

4 aubergines, diced

1 garlic clove

1 tablespoon concentrated tomato purée

1 tablespoon capers

6 fresh basil leaves, chopped

6 black olives

150 g/5 oz mozzarella cheese, diced

salt and pepper

4 fresh basil leaves, to garnish

GREENGROCER'S BAG

Place the peppers on a baking sheet under a preheated grill. Grill, turning frequently, until charred and blackened. Transfer to a plastic bag, tie the top and leave to cool. Peel off the pepper skins, cut off the tops and remove the seeds and membranes without piercing the 'shells'. Preheat the oven to 180°C/350°F/Gas Mark 4. Brush an ovenproof dish with oil. Heat the olive oil in a frying pan. Add the aubergines and garlic and cook over a low heat for 5 minutes until golden brown. Mix the tomato purée with 1 teaspoon hot water and add to the pan with the capers, chopped basil leaves and olives. Cook for a few more minutes. Remove and discard the garlic and season with salt and pepper. Remove the pan from the heat and add the mozzarella. Fill the peppers with the mixture and place in the prepared dish. Bake for 10 minutes. Garnish each pepper with a basil leaf and serve warm.

STRUDEL DELL'ORTO

Serves 8

300 g/11 oz petits pois, shelled

300 g/11 oz green beans, halved

300 g/11 oz asparagus spears

300 g/11 oz artichoke hearts, quartered

200 g/7 oz carrots, chopped

200 g/7 oz potatoes, chopped

150 g/5 oz butter

1 garlic clove

4 tablespoons single cream

250 g/9 oz ready-made puff pastry dough, thawed if frozen

plain flour, for dusting

1 egg yolk, lightly beaten

salt and pepper

VEGETABLE–GARDEN STRUDEL

Preheat the oven to 180°C/350°F/Gas Mark 4. Cook the petit pois, beans, asparagus, artichoke hearts, carrots and potatoes in separate pans of boiling water until al dente. Drain well. Heat 100 g/3$\frac{1}{2}$ oz of the butter with the garlic in a large frying pan. Remove and discard the garlic, add all the vegetables and cook, stirring frequently, for 5 minutes. Season with salt and pepper to taste. Remove the pan from the heat and stir in the cream. Roll out the pastry into a fairly thin rectangle on a lightly floured surface. Melt the remaining butter and brush it over the surface of the pastry. Scatter the vegetables over the pastry and roll up gently, crimping the edges to seal. Brush the strudel with the egg yolk, place on a baking sheet and bake for about 30 minutes until golden. Leave to stand for 10 minutes before serving.

PEPPER PIE

Heat the butter and olive oil in a frying pan. Add the onion and cook over a low heat, stirring occasionally, for 10 minutes until golden brown. Add the peppers and potatoes. Cook over a low heat for 15 minutes. Preheat the oven to 200°C/400°F/Gas Mark 6. Grease an ovenproof dish with butter. Chop the anchovies and put them with the eggs, basil and marjoram in a food processor and process to a purée. Transfer to a bowl, season with salt and add the onion and pepper mixture. Mix well, then spoon into the prepared dish and bake for 20 minutes. Turn out on to a warm platter and serve warm.

TORTINO DI PEPERONI

Serves 4

25 g/1 oz butter, plus extra for greasing

2 tablespoons olive oil

1 onion, chopped

1 each red, yellow and green peppers,

halved, seeded and sliced

3 potatoes, diced

2 salted anchovies, heads removed, cleaned and

filleted (see page 596), soaked in cold water for

10 minutes and drained

2 eggs

1 tablespoon chopped fresh basil

1 tablespoon chopped fresh marjoram

salt

COURGETTE PIE

Preheat the oven to 200°C/400°F/Gas Mark 6. Grease a roasting tin with butter. Spread out 3 tablespoons of the flour and the Parmesan in separate shallow plates. Beat 1 egg in a bowl. Dip the courgette slices first in the flour, then in the egg and finally in the Parmesan. Heat the olive oil in a frying pan. Add the courgette slices and cook over a medium heat until golden brown and crisp. Drain on kitchen paper and arrange on the base of the prepared roasting tin. Separate the remaining eggs. Place the butter, fontina, Gruyère, the remaining flour and the milk in a frying pan over a low heat. Melt, stirring constantly. Season with the nutmeg, salt and pepper. Remove the pan from the heat and add the salami and egg yolks, one at a time. Whisk the egg whites until stiff, then fold into the sauce. Pour the sauce over the courgettes and bake until the top of the pie is golden brown. Serve hot.

TORTINO DI ZUCCHINE

Serves 4

50 g/2 oz butter, plus extra for greasing

5 tablespoons plain flour, for dusting

3 tablespoons Parmesan cheese, freshly grated

4 eggs

4 courgettes, trimmed and sliced into rounds

4 tablespoons olive oil

150 g/5 oz fontina cheese, diced

150 g/5 oz Gruyère cheese, diced

200 ml/7 fl oz milk

pinch of freshly grated nutmeg

100 g/3 ½ oz salami, diced

salt and pepper

UOVA NEL NIDO

Serves 4

2 salted anchovies, heads removed, cleaned and filleted (see page 596), soaked in water for 10 minutes and drained

40 g/1 1/2 oz pine nuts

7 tablespoons olive oil

25 g/1 oz butter

8 artichoke hearts

dash of tomato ketchup

dash of Worcestershire sauce

4 eggs, hard-boiled

salt and pepper

fresh flat-leaf parsley, chopped, to garnish

NEST EGGS

Place the chopped anchovy fillets in a food processor with the pine nuts, 6 tablespoons of the olive oil and the butter and process to a purée. Heat the remaining olive oil in a frying pan, add the purée and artichoke hearts and cook, stirring gently, for a few minutes. Season with ketchup, Worcestershire sauce, salt and pepper and cook for 10 minutes. Meanwhile, shell the eggs and cut in half. Arrange the artichoke hearts on a serving dish, put an egg half in the middle of each heart and sprinkle with cooking juices. Garnish with the parsley.

ZUCCHINE RIPIENE

Serves 4

olive oil, for brushing and drizzling

4 courgettes, halved lengthways

100 g/3 1/2 oz canned tuna in oil, drained and flaked

2 eggs

2 tablespoons Parmesan cheese, freshly grated

2 tablespoons breadcrumbs

1 sprig fresh flat-leaf parsley, chopped

1 tablespoon white wine

salt and pepper

STUFFED COURGETTES

Preheat the oven to 180°C/350°F/Gas Mark 4. Brush a roasting tin with oil. Scoop out most of the courgette flesh with a teaspoon without piercing the 'shells'. Reserve the shells. Place the flesh in a bowl with the tuna, eggs, half the Parmesan, 1 tablespoon of the breadcrumbs and the parsley and season with salt and pepper to taste. Drizzle with olive oil, mix well and spoon into the courgette shells. Arrange the courgettes in the prepared tin and sprinkle with the remaining Parmesan, remaining breadcrumbs and the wine. Bake for about 30 minutes. Serve hot or warm.

CANAPÉS

Canapés consist of square slices of bread, crusts removed, that are cut into halves or quarters or into small triangles. They may be left as they are, lightly toasted or quickly fried in butter to give extra flavour. Ingredients such as hard-boiled eggs, anchovies, ham and cheese are arranged on top according to taste and with careful consideration of how flavours and colours combine.

CHICKEN LIVER CANAPÉS

Melt the butter in a frying pan. Add the chicken livers and cook over a medium heat, stirring frequently, until browned. Sprinkle with the brandy and cook until it has evaporated. Chop the anchovy fillets, add to the pan and season with salt, if necessary, and pepper. Stir for 1 minute, then remove the pan from the heat. Lightly toast the bread slices on both sides, cut in half and spread with the liver mixture. Serve cold or warm.

CANAPÉ AI FEGATINI

Serves 4

50 g/2 oz butter

300 g/11 oz chicken livers, trimmed and

coarsely chopped

50ml/2 fl oz brandy

3 salted anchovies, heads removed, cleaned and

filleted (see page 596)

4 white bread slices, crusts removed

salt and pepper

CHEESE CANAPÉS

CANAPÉ AL FORMAGGIO

Serves 4

3 small fresh goats' cheeses, at room temperature

100 g/3½ oz mature Gorgonzola cheese

4 wholemeal bread slices

fresh chives, chopped, to garnish

Put the cheeses into a bowl and mash well with a fork. Cut the bread slices in half and spread with the cheese mixture. Sprinkle with chives to garnish and store in a cool place until ready to serve.

NIÇOISE CANAPÉS

CANAPÉ ALLA NIZZARDA

Serves 4

2 eggs, hard-boiled

4 ripe tomatoes, sliced, outer slices discarded

olive oil, for drizzling

4 white bread slices, crusts removed

butter, for spreading

salt

100 g/3½ oz stoned black olives, sliced

Shell the eggs, slice thinly, preferably with an egg slicer, and sprinkle with salt. Place the tomatoes in a shallow dish and drizzle with olive oil. Spread the bread with butter and cut in half. Place two slices of tomato, slightly overlapping, on each half-slice of bread and put a slice of egg between them. Garnish with the olives.

LOBSTER CANAPÉS

CANAPÉ ALL'ARAGOSTA

Serves 4

½ quantity Mayonnaise (see page 65)

1 tablespoon brandy

1–2 teaspoons tomato ketchup

4 wholemeal bread slices, crusts removed

1 small cooked lobster tail, shelled and sliced into 8 pieces

8 small fresh thyme sprigs, to garnish

Mix together the mayonnaise, brandy and ketchup in a bowl. Cut the slices of bread in half and spread with the mayonnaise mixture. Place a slice of lobster in the middle of each and garnish with a sprig of thyme.

HOT CANAPÉS WITH MOZZARELLA

CANAPÉ CALDI CON LE OVOLINE

Serves 4

4 salted anchovies, heads removed, cleaned and filleted (see page 596)

4 white bread slices, crusts removed

8 small buffalo milk mozzarella cheeses, halved

2 tomatoes, sliced

fresh flat-leaf parsley, chopped, to garnish

Preheat the oven to 220°C/425°F/Gas Mark 7. Cut the slices of bread in half. Place half a mozzarella cheese and an anchovy fillet on each. Arrange tomato slices all round. Place the canapés on a baking sheet and bake for a few minutes until the cheese has melted. Sprinkle with parsley and serve.

AVOCADO AND TOMATO CANAPÉS

CANAPÉ DI AVOCADO E POMODORI

Serves 4

¹/₂ quantity Mayonnaise (see page 65)

1 tablespoon chopped fresh flat-leaf parsley

dash of Worcestershire sauce

4 white bread slices, crusts removed

¹/₂ avocado

juice of 1 lemon, strained

8 cherry tomatoes

Mix 2 tablespoons of the mayonnaise with the parsley and Worcestershire sauce. Cut the bread in half and spread with the remaining mayonnaise. Peel, halve and stone the avocado, then cut into slices crossways. Sprinkle with the lemon juice to prevent discoloration. Cut a cross in each tomato without cutting all the way through and open it out like a star. Put a tomato in the middle of each piece of bread and garnish with the parsley, mayonnaise and avocado.

CARROT CANAPÉS

CANAPÉ DI CAROTE

Serves 4

1 carrot

¹/₂ green apple, cored

juice of ¹/₂ lemon, strained

4 white bread slices, crusts removed

2 tablespoons chopped fresh flat-leaf parsley

50 g/2 oz pickles, chopped

¹/₂ quantity Mayonnaise (see page 65)

Cut the carrot and apple into thin batons, mix together and sprinkle with the lemon juice to prevent the apple from going brown. Cut the bread in half. Mix together the parsley, pickles and mayonnaise, then spread the mixture on the bread. Place a little carrot and apple in the middle of each half-slice.

HAM CANAPÉS

CANAPÉ DI PROSCIUTTO

Serves 4

50 g/2 oz butter

100 g/3¹/₂ oz lean cooked ham, very finely chopped

4 white bread slices, crusts removed

8 baby artichokes in oil, drained, to garnish

Cream the butter, then beat in the ham. Cut the bread in half and spread with the ham mixture. Garnish by placing a baby artichoke, opened out like a small rose, in the middle of each half-slice.

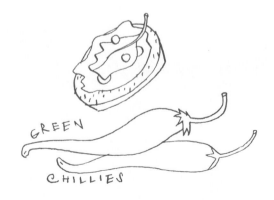

GREEN CHILLIES

CROSTINI

Crostini are synonymous with tastiness. There is an extensive choice of bases: home-made breads of all types are ideal, but you can also use baguettes, focaccia – plain and flavoured – soda bread, sourdough loaves, breads made with polenta, rice, millet or buckwheat and rye bread. Chicken and game livers are the classic toppings, but you can also spread crostini with chopped meat flavoured with herbs, mature cheeses and game mousses.

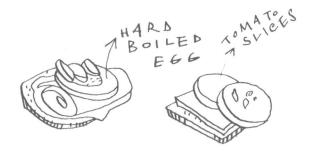

TUSCAN ANCHOVY CROSTINI

Place the anchovies skin side uppermost and press along the backbones with your thumb. Remove the bones. Place the fillets in the base of a dish. Squeeze out the white bread and mix with the parsley, onion, garlic, capers and chilli, then beat in the olive oil and vinegar. Pour this sauce over the anchovies and leave to stand for a day. Just before serving, toast the rye bread, spread with butter and top with the anchovy mixture.

CROSTINI ALLA TOSCANA

Serves 4–6

200 g/7 oz salted anchovies, heads removed, cleaned and filleted (see page 596), soaked in cold water for 10 minutes and drained

1 white bread slice, crusts removed, soaked in cold water for 10 minutes

2 tablespoons chopped fresh flat-leaf parsley

1/2 small onion, chopped

1 garlic clove, chopped

50 g/2 oz capers, chopped

1 fresh red chilli, seeded and chopped

6 tablespoons olive oil

3 tablespoons white-wine vinegar

4–6 rye bread slices

butter, for spreading

CHICKEN LIVER CROSTINI

CROSTINI CON FEGATINI DI POLLO

Serves 4–6

2 tablespoons olive oil

1 carrot, chopped

¹/₂ onion, chopped

1 celery stick, chopped

6 chicken livers, trimmed

3 tablespoons red wine vinegar

100 ml/3¹/₂ fl oz dry white wine

2 egg yolks

juice of 1 lemon, strained

4–6 wholemeal bread slices, lightly toasted

salt and pepper

1 tablespoon capers, to garnish

Heat the olive oil in a frying pan. Add the carrot, onion and celery and cook over a low heat, stirring occasionally, for 5 minutes. Dip the chicken livers into the vinegar, pat dry with kitchen paper and add to pan. Pour in the wine and season with salt and pepper. Cook, stirring frequently, until browned. Remove the chicken livers from the pan and chop finely, then return them to the pan and cook for a further 2 minutes. Beat together the egg yolks and lemon juice in a bowl. Remove the pan from the heat and stir in the egg yolk mixture. Spread on slices of lightly toasted bread and garnish with the capers. Serve immediately.

CHICKEN LIVER AND PROSCIUTTO CROSTINI

CROSTINI CON FEGATINI DI POLLO E PROSCIUTTO

Serves 4–6

3 tablespoons olive oil

40 g/1¹/₂ oz butter

130 g/4¹/₂ oz prosciutto

1 onion, chopped

about 6 tablespoons warm milk or Meat Stock (see page 208)

150 g/5 oz chicken livers, trimmed and chopped

2 fresh sage leaves

4–6 country-style bread slices, lightly toasted

8 fresh rosemary sprigs

Heat the olive oil and half the butter in a saucepan. Add the prosciutto and onion and cook over a very low heat, stirring occasionally, for 30 minutes, gradually adding the milk or stock to keep the mixture moist. Add the chicken livers and sage leaves and bring to the boil. Boil for 3 minutes, stirring constantly. Remove the pan from the heat, mince the mixture with a mincer or in a food processor and return to the pan. Bring to the boil, adding a little more milk or stock if necessary. Stir in the remaining butter and cook for a further 3 minutes. Cut the toasted bread in half and spread with the liver mixture. Arrange criss-cross sprigs of rosemary on the base of a serving dish and lay the crostini on top.

MUSHROOM AND CAPER CROSTINI

CROSTINI CON FUNGHI E CAPPERI

Serves 4–6

3 tablespoons olive oil

300 g/11 oz porcini mushrooms, chopped

1¹/₂ teaspoons chopped fresh marjoram

1 garlic clove, chopped

about 6 tablespoons Meat Stock (see page 208)

1 tablespoon capers

1 tablespoon chopped fresh flat-leaf parsley

1 loaf of country-style bread, sliced and lightly toasted

salt and pepper

Heat the oil in a frying pan. Add the mushrooms, marjoram and garlic and cook, stirring frequently, over a medium heat for 20 minutes, gradually adding the stock. Add the capers and parsley and season with salt and pepper. Increase the heat and boil off the liquid. Spread the mixture on slices of lightly toasted bread and serve.

CROSTINI CON FUNGHI IN GUAZZETTO

Serves 4–6

2 garlic cloves

2 tablespoons olive oil

2 Italian sausages, chopped

1 tablespoon chopped fresh flat-leaf parsley

200 ml/7 fl oz dry white wine

300 g/11 oz mixed wild and cultivated mushrooms, coarsely chopped

150 g/5 oz tomatoes, peeled and chopped

about 6 tablespoons Meat Stock (see page 208)

4–6 Tuscan or wholemeal bread slices, toasted

salt and pepper

fresh mint leaves, to garnish

CROSTINI WITH MUSHROOMS IN A LIGHT SAUCE

Chop one garlic clove. Heat the oil in a frying pan. Add the sausages, chopped garlic and parsley and cook over a low heat, stirring occasionally, for 5 minutes. Pour in the wine and cook until evaporated. Add the mushrooms and cook for a few minutes, then add the tomatoes. Cook, gradually adding the stock, until cooked through and tender. Season with salt and pepper to taste. Lightly toast the bread on both sides. Rub with the remaining garlic and spread the mushroom mixture on top. Garnish with the mint leaves and serve immediately.

CROSTINI CON POMPELMO

Serves 4–6

15 g/½ oz butter, plus extra for greasing

juice of 2 grapefruit, strained

1 tablespoon Gruyère cheese, grated

150 g/5 oz mild Gouda cheese, grated

2 tablespoons double cream

1 egg yolk, lightly beaten

4–6 white bread slices, crusts removed

salt and pepper

GRAPEFRUIT CROSTINI

Preheat the oven to 180°C/350°F/Gas Mark 4. Grease a baking sheet with butter. Pour the grapefruit juice into a small saucepan and add the butter, Gruyère and Gouda. Sprinkle with salt and pepper. Stir in the cream and cook over a low heat, stirring constantly, for 10 minutes. Remove the pan from the heat and stir in the egg yolk. Return to the heat and cook, stirring until smooth; do not allow the mixture to boil Spread the slices of bread with the mixture and place on the prepared baking sheet. Bake for a few minutes until lightly browned. Serve hot.

CROSTINI CON SALSICCIA

Serves 4–6

3 Italian sausages, skinned

150 g/5 oz stracchino cheese, such as taleggio or robiola, crumbled

1 tablespoon fennel seeds

4–6 country-style bread slices

salt

SAUSAGE CROSTINI

Preheat the oven to 180°C/350°F/Gas Mark 4. Crumble the sausages into a bowl and mix in the cheese and fennel seeds. Season with salt to taste and stir well. Spread the mixture on the slices of bread, place on a baking sheet and bake for 15 minutes. Arrange on a platter and serve immediately while still very hot.

SWEET–AND–SOUR CROSTINI

CROSTINI IN AGRODOLCE
Serves 4–6

50 g/2 oz sultanas, soaked in hot water for 10 minutes and drained
80 g/3 oz capers, coarsely chopped
25 g/1 oz pine nuts, coarsely chopped
50 g/2 oz prosciutto, finely chopped
25 g/1 oz butter
1 teaspoon sugar
1½ teaspoons plain flour
juice of 1 small orange, strained
3 tablespoons white wine vinegar
1 baguette, sliced diagonally
salt and pepper

Coarsely chop the sultanas. Mix together the sultanas, capers, pine nuts and prosciutto in a bowl. Put the butter, sugar and flour in a small saucepan and stir over a low heat. When the mixture starts to froth, pour in the orange juice and vinegar and cook for a few minutes more. Pour the sauce over the prosciutto mixture, season with salt and pepper to taste and mix gently. Lightly toast the bread on both sides and spread with plenty of the prosciutto mixture. Arrange on a serving dish and serve warm. These crostini are also good served cold. They have an unusual flavour, but are really worth tasting.

SEAFOOD CROSTINI

CROSTINI MARINARI
Serves 6

250 g/9 oz small squid, cleaned
250 g/9 oz cooked prawns, peeled and deveined
1 egg, lightly beaten
1 garlic clove, chopped
1 sprig fresh flat-leaf parsley, chopped
2 tablespoons fresh breadcrumbs
olive oil, for drizzling
1 baguette, sliced diagonally
salt and pepper

Preheat the oven to 180°C/350°F/Gas Mark 4. Coarsely chop the squid and prawns and place in a bowl. Mix in the egg, garlic, parsley and breadcrumbs. Drizzle with olive oil and season with salt and pepper. Thickly spread the mixture on the slices of bread, place on a baking sheet and bake for 15 minutes. Serve immediately.

MOUNTAIN CROSTINI WITH SPECK AND APPLE CREAM

CROSTINI MONTANARI CON SPECK E CREMA DI MELE
Serves 6

5-cm/2-inch piece of horseradish, grated
1 green apple, peeled, cored and chopped
juice of ½ lemon, strained
100 ml/3½ fl oz low-fat natural yogurt
100 ml/3½ fl oz double cream
1 baguette, sliced diagonally
200 g/7 oz speck or smoked ham, sliced
salt and pepper

Mix together the horseradish and apple in a bowl and sprinkle with the lemon juice. Stir in the yogurt, then add the cream and season with salt and pepper to taste. Spread the mixture on the slices of bread, top with a slice of speck or ham and serve.

TARTINES

Tartines are always served cold and must have a distinctive flavour. They are closely related to ordinary canapés and crostini (which are also served hot), so it's worth following a few rules to distinguish them. First, tartines must be small and not overloaded. As far as shape is concerned, you can let your imagination run riot: stars, hearts, ovals, diamonds, squares or small triangles. You can use almost any kind of bread, apart from rye bread, which would crumble. For all kinds of bread, the crusts must be removed. The surface of the bread should almost always be lightly buttered to prevent the tartines from becoming soggy. Remove the butter from the refrigerator at least 1 hour before using so that it is easy to spread. Tartines prepared in advance may be stored, covered with foil.

PRAWN BUTTER TARTINES

Reserve eight prawns and chop the remainder. Cream the butter in a bowl, then beat in the chopped prawns, parsley, marjoram and basil and season with salt and pepper. Spread the mixture on the squares of bread and place on a serving dish. Garnish each one with a whole prawn, a small leaf of rocket and a few capers.

TARTINE AL BURRO DI GAMBERETTI
Serves 4

400 g/14 oz cooked prawns, peeled and deveined

200 g/7 oz butter, at room temperature

1 tablespoon chopped fresh flat-leaf parsley

2 teaspoons chopped fresh marjoram

4 fresh basil leaves, chopped

2 white bread slices, crusts removed,

cut into small squares

salt and pepper

small rocket leaves, to garnish

capers

CAVIAR TARTINES

TARTINE AL CAVIALE

Serves 4

2 lemons, sliced

25 ml/1 fl oz vodka

40–50 g/1½-2 oz butter, at room temperature

pinch of paprika

4–6 white bread slices

200 g/7 oz caviar

salt

Place the lemon slices in a soup plate and sprinkle with the vodka. Beat the butter with the paprika and a pinch of salt in a bowl. Stamp out rounds from the slices of bread using a biscuit cutter or glass and spread with the paprika butter. Place a slice of drained lemon on each with a teaspoonful of caviar on top.

CUCUMBER TARTINES

TARTINE AL CETRIOLO

Serves 4

2 cucumbers, peeled

50 g/2 oz cream cheese

dash of lemon juice, strained

1 teaspoon chopped fresh flat-leaf parsley

½ wholemeal loaf, cut diagonally and crusts removed

salt and pepper

Halve one cucumber lengthways, then cut into very thin semi-circular slices. Place in a colander, sprinkle with salt and leave to drain. Chop the other cucumber and stir it into the cream cheese. Add a dash of lemon juice and the parsley and season with salt and pepper. Cut the slices of bread into squares and spread with the mixture. Arrange the cucumber slices on top as if they were fish scales. Serve cold.

WATERCRESS TARTINES

TARTINE AL CRESCIONE

Serves 4

4 eggs, hard-boiled

4 tablespoons Mayonnaise (see page 65)

juice of 1 lemon, strained

1 bunch of watercress, coarsely chopped

4–8 white bread slices, crusts removed

salt and pepper

Shell and chop the eggs, then mix with the mayonnaise and lemon juice. Season with salt and pepper and stir in the watercress. Cut the slices of bread in half and spread with the mixture. Chill in the refrigerator until ready to serve.

CHEESE AND BRANDY TARTINES

TARTINE AL FORMAGGIO E BRANDY

Serves 4

200 g/7 oz robiola cheese, crumbled

100 ml/3½ fl oz brandy

5 walnuts, chopped

1 tablespoon pine nuts, finely chopped

4–8 white bread slices

pepper

walnut halves, to garnish

Cream the cheese in a bowl, then beat in the brandy, walnuts and pine nuts and season with pepper. Stamp out rounds from the bread using a biscuit cutter or glass and spread with the cheese mixture. Garnish each round with a walnut half. The robiola may be replaced with Gorgonzola or Roquefort.

RUSTIC TARTINES

Cream the cheeses in a bowl, then beat in the olives, chillies and tuna. Season with salt to taste. Stamp out rounds from the slices of bread using a biscuit cutter or glass and spread with the mixture. Garnish with the pickled pearl onions.

TARTINE ALLA CAMPAGNOLA

Serves 4

5 small fresh goats' cheeses

12 green olives, stoned and sliced

4 pickled chillies, seeded and chopped

about 50 g/2 oz canned tuna in oil,

drained and flaked

4–8 white bread slices

salt

pickled pearl onions, to garnish

GRAPPA AND PEAR TARTINES

Beat the mascarpone with the fromage frais in a bowl, then beat in the grappa. Peel, halve, core and cut the pear into quarters. Cut each quarter in half and sprinkle with the lemon juice. Cut each slice of fontina into four triangles. Spread the bread with the mascarpone mixture and top each with a wedge of pear and a triangle of fontina.

TARTINE ALLA GRAPPA CON LE PERE

Serves 4

200 g/7 oz mascarpone cheese

200 ml/7 fl oz fromage frais

1 tablespoon grappa

1 pear

juice of $^1/_2$ lemon, strained

2 slices fontina cheese

2–4 white bread slices,

crusts removed, cut into squares

PIZZAIOLA TARTINES

Sprinkle the insides of the tomatoes with salt and place upside down on kitchen paper to drain for 5 minutes, then chop. Mix together the tomatoes, spring onions, olives and parsley in a bowl, season with salt and pepper and drizzle with olive oil. Stir well to mix. Stamp out rounds from the bread with a biscuit cutter or glass and toast lightly on both sides. Spread the toast with butter and then with the tomato mixture. Top with a slice of mozzarella and sprinkle with oregano.

TARTINE ALLA PIZZAIOLA

Serves 4

2 firm ripe tomatoes, halved and seeded

2 spring onions, chopped

6 green olives, stoned and chopped

1 tablespoon very finely chopped

fresh flat-leaf parsley

olive oil, for drizzling

4–6 white bread slices

40–50 g/1$^1/_2$–2 oz butter, at room temperature

250 g/9 oz buffalo milk mozzarella, thinly sliced

salt and pepper

fresh oregano, chopped, to garnish

AVOCADO TARTINES

Peel, halve and stone the avocados, then chop the flesh. Place in a food processor with the cream cheese, lemon flesh and juice, Worcestershire sauce and chives and season with salt and pepper. Process until smooth. Spread the bread with the avocado mixture and top each piece with a tomato half. Garnish with the basil leaves.

TARTINE ALL'AVOCADO

Serves 4

2 avocados

150 g/5 oz cream cheese

1/2 lemon, peeled and chopped

juice of 1/2 lemon, strained

dash of Worcestershire sauce

1 tablespoon chopped fresh chives

4–6 white bread slices,
crusts removed, cut into squares

10 cherry tomatoes, halved

salt and pepper

fresh basil leaves, to garnish

ROQUEFORT TARTINES

Beat the cheeses together in a bowl with a fork. Beat in the cream, season with salt and pepper and beat with a small whisk until soft and creamy. Cut the slices of the bread in half and spread with the cream cheese mixture. Garnish each piece with one white grape and one black grape.

TARTINE AL ROQUEFORT

Serves 4

100 g/3 1/2 oz Roquefort cheese, crumbled

100 g/3 1/2 oz cream cheese

2 tablespoons double cream

4–6 wholemeal bread slices, crusts removed

salt and pepper

white and black grapes, to garnish

TUNA TARTINES

Shell and coarsely chop the egg. Place the tuna, capers and onions in a food processor and process to a purée. Cream the butter in a bowl. Push the hard-boiled egg through a sieve into the bowl and beat in with the tuna purée. Beat in lemon juice to taste, season with salt and drizzle with olive oil. Beat well until combined. Cut the slices of bread in half and spread with the mixture using a damp knife or palette knife. Garnish each tartine with olive rings and a few strips of pickled pepper.

TARTINE AL TONNO

Serves 4

1 egg, hard-boiled

80 g/3 oz canned tuna in oil, drained and flaked

1 1/2 teaspoons capers

25 g/1 oz pickled pearl onions, drained

25 g/1 oz butter, at room temperature

juice of 1 lemon, strained

olive oil, for drizzling

4–6 white bread slices, crusts removed

salt

To garnish

80 g/3 oz green olives, stoned and sliced

1 pickled pepper, cut into strips

TWO—COLOUR OMELETTE TARTINES

TARTINE BICOLORE DI FRITTATINE

Serves 4

2 eggs

3 fresh chives, finely chopped

1 sprig fresh flat-leaf parsley, finely chopped

1 tablespoon olive oil

4–8 white bread slices, crusts removed

black olive paste, for spreading

salt and pepper

Beat the eggs with the chives and parsley in a bowl and season with salt and pepper. Heat a little of the olive oil in a small omelette pan. Pour in one-third of the egg mixture, tilt the pan to coat and cook over a medium heat until the underside is set and the omelette is crisp. Slide out on to a plate and make two more omelettes in the same way. Cut into 5-mm/$\frac{1}{4}$-inch wide strips. Lightly spread the bread with olive paste and place strips of omelette diagonally on top.

ANCHOVY AND EGG SAUCE TARTINES

TARTINE CON ACCIUGHE IN SALSA

Serves 4

1 egg, hard-boiled

1 tablespoon white wine vinegar

2 tablespoons olive oil

2 tablespoons chopped fresh flat-leaf parsley

2–4 white bread slices, crusts removed

50 g/2 oz canned anchovy fillets, drained

salt and pepper

pickled pearl onions, halved, to garnish

Shell and halve the egg, then scoop the yolk out into a bowl. Stir in the vinegar, olive oil and parsley and season with salt and pepper. Cut the slices of bread into triangles and toast lightly on both sides. Spread with a little of the egg mixture, arrange two anchovy fillets on top and garnish with the pickled pearl onion halves.

CRAB AND APPLE TARTINES

TARTINE DI GRANCHIO ALLE MELE

Serves 4

120 g/4 oz canned crab meat, drained

2 tablespoons Mayonnaise (see page 65)

1 green apple

juice of 1 lemon, strained

4–6 white bread slices, crusts removed

1 tablespoon chopped fresh flat-leaf parsley

salt and pepper

Flake the crab meat in a bowl with a fork, then stir in the mayonnaise and season with salt and pepper. Peel, core and finely dice the apple and sprinkle with a little of the lemon juice. Add the apple to the crab meat and stir in the remaining lemon juice. Cut the slices of bread in half and spread with the crab mixture. Sprinkle with the parsley. Store in the refrigerator until ready to serve.

JELLIED TONGUE TARTINES

TARTINE GELATINATE ALLA LINGUA

Serves 4

1 sachet (about 11 g/$\frac{1}{3}$ oz) powdered gelatine

or 7 g/$\frac{1}{8}$ oz leaf gelatine

4 gherkins, drained

1 small round loaf, thinly sliced and crusts removed

200 g/7 oz foie gras pâté

16 slices cooked pickled tongue

Prepare the gelatine according to the instructions on the packet and leave to cool. Slice each gherkin lengthways into four. Spread the bread with plenty of foie gras pâté, place a small slice of tongue on top of each piece and garnish with a gherkin slice. Dip a pastry brush in the gelatine and gently brush the tartines with several layers until evenly coated. Chill in the refrigerator for 2 hours until set.

JELLIED MUSTARD TARTINES

Prepare the gelatine according to the instructions on the packet and leave to cool. Shell and slice the eggs, preferably with an egg slicer. Cut the slices of bread in half. Cream the butter in a bowl, then beat in the mustard. Spread each half-slice with the mustard cream, place a slice of egg on top and arrange two anchovy fillets on opposite sides. Dip a pastry brush in the gelatine and gently brush the tartines with several layers. Chill in the refrigerator for 2 hours until set.

TARTINE GELATINATE ALLA SENAPE

Serves 4

1 sachet (about 11 g/^{1}/$_3$ oz) powdered gelatine

or 7 g/^{1}/$_8$ oz leaf gelatine

3 eggs, hard-boiled

8 wholemeal bread slices, crusts removed

80 g/3 oz butter, at room temperature

2 tablespoons Dijon mustard

32 canned anchovy fillets, drained

JELLIED RUSSIAN SALAD TARTINES

Prepare the gelatine according to the instructions on the packet and leave to cool. Shell and slice the eggs, preferably with an egg slicer. Lightly butter the slices of bread and spread with a layer of Russian salad. Place a slice of egg on top and put a prawn in the middle. Dip a pastry brush in the gelatine and gently brush several layers over the tartines. Chill in the refrigerator for 2 hours until set.

TARTINE GELATINATE
ALL'INSALATA RUSSA

Serves 4

1 sachet (about 11 g/^{1}/$_3$ oz) powdered gelatine

or 7 g/^{1}/$_8$ oz leaf gelatine

3 eggs, hard-boiled

80 g/3 oz butter, at room temperature

16 slices wholemeal bread

300 g/11 oz Russian Salad (see page 116)

16 cooked prawns, peeled and deveined

BARQUETTES AND TARTLETS

APPETIZERS

When you are serving aperitifs or cocktails, these delightful, little morsels – mostly served hot – are the perfect accompaniment. Their delicious, mellow flavour comes from their pastry cases, which contain varying amounts of butter and hold the filling. They are made from pâte brisée, which is used to line boat-shaped tins for barquettes, and round tins in the case of tartlets. They are baked, left to cool, then filled in a variety ways just before serving so that the pastry does not become soggy. Unfilled barquettes and tartlets may be stored in bags in the freezer. Thaw at room temperature before use.

PASTA BRISÉE

Makes 35–50 barquettes or tartlets

250 g/9 oz plain flour, plus extra for dusting

175 g/6 oz butter, softened and diced

1 egg, lightly beaten

salt

PÂTE BRISÉE

Sift the flour and a pinch of salt into a mound on the work surface and add the diced butter. Rub in the butter with your fingertips until the mixture resembles breadcrumbs. Shape into a mound, make a well in the centre and pour in the beaten egg and 2 tablespoons water. Knead lightly by hand (your hands should be cold – if necessary hold them under cold running water) or using a metal palette knife. Wrap the pastry in cling film, flatten gently with a rolling pin and chill in the refrigerator for 1 hour. Preheat the oven to 180°C/350°F/Gas Mark 4. Divide the pastry into several pieces, roll out on a lightly floured surface and use to line boat-shaped, oval or round tartlet tins. Line with baking parchment or grease-proof paper and fill with baking beans. Bake for 15–20 minutes. Remove the tins from the oven, remove the beans and parchment or paper and leave to cool before filling. The quantity of pastry given here is also enough for two 23-cm/9-inch round pies. Halve or double the quantity according to your requirements.

PRAWN BARQUETTES

Put the onion, celery, carrot and parsley in a saucepan, pour in water to cover, bring to the boil and add a pinch of salt. Add the prawns and cook for 3–4 minutes, then drain, reserving the cooking liquid. Return the cooking liquid to the pan, add the potatoes and cook for 10–15 minutes until tender. Drain and mash with 25 g/1 oz of the butter and as much hot milk as required. Heat the remaining butter in a small saucepan, add the tomatoes and cook over a low heat for 3–4 minutes until tender. Remove the pan from the heat and season to taste with salt. Peel and devein the prawns. To serve, divide the mashed potato among the pastry cases and arrange the prawns and tomatoes on top. Heat in a preheated oven, 200°C/400°F/Gas Mark 6, for a few minutes before serving.

BARCHETTE AI GAMBERETTI

Makes 35–50 barquettes

¹/₄ onion

1 celery stick

1 carrot

1 fresh flat-leaf parsley sprig

35–50 raw small prawns

3 potatoes, diced

40 g/1¹/₂ oz butter

about 150 ml/¹/₄ pint hot milk

2 tomatoes, diced

35–50 Pâte Brisée barquette cases (see opposite)

salt

FOUR–CHEESE BARQUETTES

Cook the pasta in salted, boiling water for 8–10 minutes until al dente. Drain and stir in the butter and all the cheeses. To serve, fill the pastry cases with a little of the pasta mixture and cover with 1–2 tablespoons of the béchamel sauce. Place on a baking sheet and bake in a preheated oven, 200°C/400°F/Gas Mark 6, until golden and bubbling.

BARCHETTE AI QUATTRO FORMAGGI

Makes 35–50 barquettes

150 g/5 oz ditalini pasta

50 g/2 oz butter

50 g/2 oz fontina cheese, grated

50 g/2 oz Emmenthal cheese, grated

50 g/2 oz caciotta cheese, grated

50 g/2 oz mozzarella cheese, finely chopped

35–50 Pâte Brisée barquette cases (see opposite)

1 quantity Béchamel Sauce (see page 50)

salt

ANCHOVY BARQUETTES

Heat the oil in a small saucepan. Add the garlic and onion and cook over a low heat, stirring occasionally, for 5 minutes until softened. Stir in the tomato purée, cook for a few minutes more and then remove from the heat. Stir in the capers and anchovies. To serve, fill the pastry cases with the mixture and garnish with the olives.

BARCHETTE DI ACCIUGHE

Makes 35–50 barquettes

1 tablespoon olive oil

1 garlic clove, finely chopped

1 onion, finely chopped

2 tablespoons concentrated tomato purée

2 tablespoons capers

6 canned anchovy fillets, drained and chopped

35–50 Pâte Brisée barquette cases (see opposite)

stoned black olives, quartered, to garnish

141

CRAB BARQUETTES

Melt the butter in a frying pan. Add the pancetta and onion and cook over a low heat, stirring occasionally, until the onion is soft. Remove the pan from the heat. Beat the eggs with the Parmesan and cream in a bowl and season with salt and pepper. Stir the crab meat, pancetta and onion into the egg mixture. To serve, spoon the mixture into the pastry cases. Place on a baking sheet and bake in a preheated oven, 200°C/400°F/Gas Mark 6, for about 10 minutes or until the filling has set.

BARCHETTE DI POLPA DI GRANCHIO

Makes 35–50 barquettes

25 g/1 oz butter

25 g/1 oz pancetta, diced

1/2 onion, finely chopped

2 eggs

25 g/1 oz Parmesan cheese, freshly grated

2 tablespoons double cream

100 g/3 1/2 oz white crab meat, drained if canned

35–50 Pâte Brisée barquette cases (see page 140)

salt and pepper

CHEESE TARTLETS

Melt the butter in a saucepan. Add the leek and cook over a low heat, stirring occasionally, for about 5 minutes until softened. Add the petits pois, season with salt and pepper and cook, stirring occasionally, for about 20 minutes. Beat the eggs with the milk, nutmeg and a pinch of salt in a bowl. To serve, spoon the leek and petits pois mixture into the pastry cases, cover with 1 tablespoon of the egg mixture and top with a few cubes of Roquefort. Place on a baking sheet and bake in a preheated oven, 200°C/400°F/Gas Mark 6, for about 10 minutes.

TARTELETTE AL FORMAGGIO

Makes 35–50 tartlets

25 g/1 oz butter

1 leek, trimmed and thinly sliced

150 g/5 oz shelled petits pois

2 eggs

100 ml/3 1/2 fl oz milk

pinch of freshly grated nutmeg

200 g/7 oz Roquefort cheese, diced

35–50 Pâte Brisée tartlet cases (see page 140)

salt and pepper

GORGONZOLA TARTLETS

Beat together the mascarpone and Gorgonzola in a bowl, then stir in the parsley and season with salt and pepper. To serve, spoon the cheese mixture into a piping bag fitted with a star nozzle and fill the pastry cases with the mixture. Garnish each tartlet with a walnut half and a pistachio.

TARTELETTE AL GORGONZOLA

Makes 35–50 tartlets

200 g/7 oz mascarpone cheese

100 g/3 1/2 oz Gorgonzola cheese

1 tablespoon chopped fresh flat-leaf parsley

35–50 Pâte Brisée tartlet cases (see page 140)

salt and pepper

To garnish

walnut halves

pistachio nuts

TARTELETTE DI AVOCADO

Makes 35–50 tartlets

25 cherry tomatoes, halved and seeded

2 ripe avocados

1 teaspoon lemon juice, strained

300 ml/½ pint fromage frais

2 tablespoons double cream

35–50 Pâte Brisée tartlet cases (see page 140)

salt and pepper

35–50 fresh basil leaves

AVOCADO TARTLETS

Sprinkle the insides of the tomatoes with salt and place upside down on kitchen paper to drain. Peel, halve and stone the avocados. Chop the flesh, place in a food processor with the lemon juice and process to a purée. Beat together the fromage frais and cream in a bowl, then stir in the avocado purée and season with salt and pepper to taste. To serve, fill the pastry cases with the avocado mixture. Top each with a tomato half and garnish with a basil leaf.

TARTELETTE DI POLLO

Makes 35–50 tartlets

300 g/11 oz skinless, boneless chicken breasts

2 eggs, hard-boiled

2 tablespoons Mayonnaise (see page 65)

1 tablespoon double cream, whipped

35–50 Pâte Brisée tartlet cases (see page 140)

salt

cornichons or small gherkins, drained and thinly sliced, to garnish

CHICKEN TARTLETS

Place the chicken breasts in a saucepan, add water to cover and bring to the boil. Lower the heat, cover and simmer gently for about 20 minutes until cooked through. Drain and leave to cool, then chop coarsely and mince with a mincer or in a food processor. Shell and halve the eggs, then scoop out the yolks and mix with the chicken. Stir in the mayonnaise and cream and season with salt to taste. To serve, fill the pastry cases with the chicken mixture and garnish with the cornichons or gherkins.

SAVOURY PUFFS

The puffs made according to the recipe for Savoury Choux Paste on page 1011 may also be filled with cream cheese, fish, vegetables, etc. If more flavour is required, you can also add a pinch of salt or pepper or even 2 tablespoons grated cheese. It is best to keep the puffs small so that they are easier to eat at cocktail parties or stand-up buffets. Puffs are always served warm or hot and arranged on serving dishes in concentric circles or piled up in pyramids. If they are to accompany aperitifs, allow four per person. If they are large, two is sufficient.

BIGNÉ AI FUNGHI

Serves 4

25 g/1 oz butter

1 tablespoon olive oil

300 g/11 oz mushrooms, coarsely chopped

175 ml/6 fl oz double cream

50 g/2 oz Emmenthal cheese, grated

8 large puffs (see page 1011)

salt and pepper

MUSHROOM PUFFS

Heat the butter and oil in a frying pan. Add the mushrooms and cook for about 7 minutes until tender. Stir in the cream and grated cheese, season with salt and pepper and remove the pan from the heat. Make a slit in the top of each puff and stuff with plenty of the mushroom mixture. Place on a baking sheet and bake in a preheated oven, 200°C/400°F/Gas Mark 6, for a few minutes to warm through, then serve.

BIGNÉ ALLA CREMA DI FORMAGGIO

Serves 4

150 ml/¹/₄ pint double cream

100 g/3¹/₂ oz Gorgonzola cheese, diced

100 g/3¹/₂ oz fontina cheese, diced

100 g/3¹/₂ oz provolone cheese, diced

1 tablespoon chopped celery leaves

pinch of freshly grated nutmeg

16 small puffs (see page 1011)

salt and white pepper

CREAMY CHEESE PUFFS

Divide the cream equally among three saucepans. Add the Gorgonzola to one pan, the fontina to another and the provolone to the third. In turn, melt the cheeses into the cream over a low heat, stirring constantly. Season with salt before removing each pan from the heat. Stir the celery leaves into the Gorgonzola mixture, a pinch of white pepper into the fontina and the nutmeg into the provolone mixture. Make a slit in the puffs and fill with the three cheese mixtures. Serve piled into a pyramid.

SALMON PUFFS

BIGNÉ AL SALMONE

Serves 4

1 quantity Béchamel Sauce (see page 50)

pinch of freshly grated nutmeg

3 tablespoons double cream

300 g/11 oz ricotta cheese

80 g/3 oz smoked salmon, chopped

1 tablespoon chopped fresh flat-leaf parsley

8 large puffs (see page 1011)

4 tablespoons Parmesan cheese, freshly grated

salt and pepper

Preheat the oven to 200°C/400°F/Gas Mark 6. Season the béchamel sauce with a little nutmeg. Beat together the cream and ricotta in a bowl, stir in the salmon and parsley and season with salt and pepper. Spoon the mixture into a piping bag. Make a slit in the puffs and fill with the salmon mixture. Place the filled puffs in an ovenproof dish, sprinkle with the Parmesan and spoon the béchamel sauce over them. Bake for 10 minutes and serve.

BACON FRITTERS

FRITTELLE AL BACON

Serves 4

25 g/1 oz butter

3 bacon rashers

1^1/$_2$ teaspoons chopped fresh flat-leaf parsley

^{1}/$_2$–1 teaspoon Dijon mustard

1 quantity Savoury Choux Paste (see page 1011)

vegetable oil, for deep-frying

pepper

Melt the butter in a frying pan. Add the bacon rashers and cook until crisp. Remove from the pan and chop. Mix the bacon with the parsley, a pinch of pepper and mustard to taste in a bowl. Stir the bacon mixture into the choux paste, then shape into small balls. Heat the vegetable oil to 180–190°C/350–375°F or until a cube of day-old bread browns in 30 seconds. Add the paste balls and deep-fry for a few minutes until puffed up and golden brown. Drain on kitchen paper and serve hot.

TOMATO FRITTERS

SGONFIOTTI DI POMODORI

Serves 4

20 cherry tomatoes

150 g/5 oz mozzarella cheese, diced

8 fresh basil leaves, chopped

2 anchovy fillets in oil, drained and chopped

vegetable oil, for deep-frying

1 quantity Savoury Choux Paste (see page 1011)

salt

Slice off the tops (stalk end) of the tomatoes with a small sharp knife and remove the seeds. Sprinkle the insides with salt and place upside down on kitchen paper to drain. Meanwhile, mix together the mozzarella, basil and anchovies in a bowl. Heat the vegetable oil to 180–190°C/350–375°F or until a cube of day-old bread browns in 30 seconds. Fill the tomatoes with the cheese mixture, then dip them, one at a time, in the choux paste. Deep-fry in the hot oil until puffed up and golden brown. Drain on kitchen paper and serve hot.

BOUCHÉES
AND PUFF PASTRY

These small puff or rough puff pastry cases containing a variety of fillings are among the most delectable antipasti. (They make great desserts too.) They can be shaped like tartlets, bowls or simple rectangles, but the classic shape is the vol-au-vent, which the French make very small and call bouchées since they may be eaten in a single bite. The extremely light pastry is a little difficult and time consuming to make and ready-made pastry is almost always used. There are some excellent brands of frozen pastry and they are all sufficiently light. Bouchées and puffs are almost always served hot so that the pastry, which is based on butter, and the filling melt in the mouth. Therefore, keep them warm in a low oven until ready to serve.

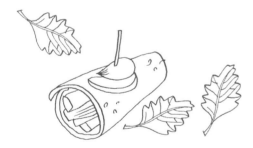

RICOTTA MORSELS

Mix the ham with 1 tablespoon of the ricotta in a bowl and set aside. Make a soft Pâte Brisée (see page 140) with the remaining ricotta, the butter, flour and a pinch of salt, and leave to stand for 1 hour. Preheat the oven to 180°C/350°F/Gas Mark 4. Line a baking sheet with baking parchment. Roll out the dough on a lightly floured work surface into a fairly thin sheet. Stamp out rounds using a biscuit cutter or a glass. Spoon a little of the ham mixture in the middle of each round, fold in half and crimp the edges to seal. Brush with the egg yolk and place on the prepared baking sheet. Bake for 20 minutes. Serve warm or cold. These morsels have a subtle flavour and are ideal as elegant appetizers.

BOCCONCINI DI RICOTTA

Serves 6

100 g/3¹/₂ oz cooked ham, chopped

100 g/3¹/₂ oz ricotta cheese

100 g/3¹/₂ oz butter

100 g/3¹/₂ oz plain flour, plus extra for dusting

1 egg yolk, lightly beaten

salt

COUNTRY BOUCHÉES

BOCCONCINI RUSTICI

Serves 6

25 g/1 oz butter

350 g/12 oz chicken livers, trimmed and coarsely chopped • 3 fresh sage leaves

1 fresh marjoram sprig, leaves only

2 tablespoons plain flour, plus extra for dusting

2 tablespoons Marsala

100 ml/3¹/₂ fl oz double cream

250 g/9 oz ready-made puff pastry dough, thawed if frozen

18 ready-to-eat prunes • 1 egg yolk, lightly beaten

salt and pepper

Melt the butter in a frying pan. Add the chicken livers, sage and marjoram and cook over a medium heat, stirring frequently, for a few minutes until lightly browned. Sprinkle in the flour and stir well. Pour in the Marsala and cook until it has evaporated. Lower the heat, stir in the cream, season with salt and pepper and cook, stirring occasionally, for about 10 minutes. Preheat the oven to 200°C/400°F/Gas Mark 6. Meanwhile, roll out the pastry on a lightly floured surface and cut into 18 squares. Place a little of the chicken liver mixture in the middle of each square and top with a prune. Brush the sides of the squares with egg yolk, fold over and press to seal. Place on a baking sheet and bake for about 20 minutes until golden brown, then serve.

PARISIAN BRIOCHES

BRIOCHES ALLA PARIGINA

Serves 6

50 g/2 oz butter • 150 g/5 oz smoked pancetta, diced

150 g/5 oz cooked ham, diced

150 g/5 oz Gruyère cheese, diced

4 würstel or frankfurters, chopped

300 ml/¹/₂ pint double cream

50 ml/2 fl oz brandy • 18 small brioches

salt and pepper

Preheat the oven to 180°C/350°F/Gas Mark 4. Melt the butter in a saucepan, add the pancetta, ham, Gruyère and sausages and mix well. Add the cream and brandy and cook, stirring frequently, until the mixture has thickened. Remove the pan from the heat and season with salt and pepper to taste. Slice the brioches horizontally just over halfway up and set the tops aside. Carefully pull out some of the soft crumb and fill the hollows with the pancetta mixture. Replace the tops. Arrange the brioches on a baking sheet and bake forabout 10 minutes.Serve warm.

COUNTRY BONBONS

CARAMELLE RUSTICHE

Serves 6–8

25 g/1 oz breadcrumbs

4 tablespoons milk

25 g/1 oz butter

300 g/11 oz minced meat, such as beef or veal

150 g/5 oz mortadella, finely chopped

1 tablespoon chopped fresh flat-leaf parsley

40 g/1¹/₂ oz Parmesan cheese, freshly grated

2 eggs, lightly beaten

250 g/9 oz ready-made puff pastry dough, thawed if frozen

plain flour, for dusting

1 egg yolk

salt and pepper

Preheat the oven to 200°C/400°F/Gas Mark 6. Line a baking sheet with baking parchment. Put the breadcrumbs in a bowl, add 3 tablespoons of the milk and set aside to soak. Melt the butter in a frying pan. Add the meat and cook over a medium heat, stirring frequently, for about 5 minutes until lightly browned. Remove from the heat and tip into a bowl. Squeeze out the breadcrumbs and add to the bowl with the mortadella, parsley and Parmesan. Stir in the beaten eggs and season with salt and pepper. When everything is thoroughly combined, shape the mixture into 30 small balls. Roll out the pastry on a lightly floured surface to a fairly thin sheet and cut out 30 squares with a fluted pastry wheel. Place a ball of the meat mixture in the middle of each square, then roll up and twist the ends like a toffee wrapper. Lightly beat the egg yolk with the remaining milk, then brush over the bonbons. Place on the prepared baking sheet and bake for about 20 minutes.

RADICCHIO BUNDLES

Preheat the oven to 200°C/400°F/Gas Mark 6. Grease a baking sheet with butter. Melt the butter in a saucepan. Add the radicchio and cook over a low heat, stirring occasionally, for a few minutes until soft. Season with salt and pepper and remove from the heat. Roll out the pastry on a lightly floured surface into a thin sheet and stamp out rounds with a biscuit cutter or a glass. Put a little radicchio in the middle of each round and place two slices of cheese and one slice of truffle on top. Brush the edges of the pastry with egg yolk and gather into bundles. Brush with egg yolk, place on the prepared baking sheet and bake for about 10 minutes until golden brown.

FAGOTTINI DI RADICCHIO

Serves 6

25 g/1 oz butter, plus extra for greasing

2 heads of radicchio, coarsely chopped

250 g/9 oz ready-made puff

pastry dough, thawed if frozen

plain flour, for dusting

80 g/3 oz quartirolo or taleggio cheese, thinly sliced

1 small white truffle, thinly sliced

1 egg yolk, lightly beaten

salt and pepper

SMALL CHEESE CRACKERS

Preheat the oven to 180°C/350°F/Gas Mark 4. Cook the potatoes in lightly salted, boiling water for 15–20 minutes or until tender. Drain, peel and mash with a potato masher, then stir in the flour and half the butter. Knead the mixture well and roll out on a lightly floured surface to 5 mm/$\frac{1}{4}$ inch thick. Mix together the Gorgonzola, the remaining butter and the walnuts in a bowl. Cut the potato dough into small triangles and cover half of them with slices of cheese cut to shape. Spread with the Gorgonzola mixture, cover with another potato dough triangle and crimp the edges well. Place on a baking sheet and brush the tops with egg yolk. Bake for 15 minutes, then remove from the oven, brush with more egg yolk and sprinkle with finely chopped walnuts to garnish. Return to the oven for 2 minutes, then serve.

GALLETTINE AL FORMAGGIO

Serves 6–8

1 kg/2$\frac{1}{4}$ lb potatoes

150 g/5 oz plain flour, plus extra for dusting

100 g/3$\frac{1}{2}$ oz butter, softened

80 g/3 oz Gorgonzola cheese, crumbled

50 g/2 oz shelled walnuts, chopped

5 Italian sottilette or thin Gruyère cheese slices

1 egg yolk, lightly beaten

salt

finely chopped walnuts, to garnish

ROMAN CRESCENTS

Sift the flour with a pinch of salt into a mound on a work surface. Make a well in the centre and add the butter, egg yolks and 1 teaspoon water. Using your fingers, gradually incorporate the flour, adding more water if necessary. Knead lightly, then form into a ball and leave to rest for 1 hour. Roll out the dough on a lightly floured surface to a thin sheet, then stamp out rounds with a biscuit cutter or a glass. Heat the vegetable oil to 180–190°C/350–375°F or until a cube of day-old bread browns in 30 seconds. Meanwhile, mix together the ham, sage, provolone, Parmesan and whole egg in a bowl and season with salt and pepper. Spoon a little of the mixture into the middle of each round, fold over and crimp the edges to seal. Brush the crescents with the egg white and deep-fry in the oil until golden brown. Drain on kitchen paper and serve hot.

MEZZELUNE ALLA ROMANA

Serves 6

300 g/11 oz plain flour, plus extra for dusting

50 g/2 oz butter, softened

2 egg yolks

vegetable oil, for deep-frying

100 g/3$\frac{1}{2}$ oz cooked ham, chopped

10 fresh sage leaves, chopped

100 g/3$\frac{1}{2}$ oz mature provolone cheese, diced

2$\frac{1}{2}$ tablespoons Parmesan cheese, freshly grated

1 egg, lightly beaten

1 egg white, lightly beaten

salt and pepper

PICONCINI FROM MARCHE

Sift the flour with a pinch of salt into a mound on a work surface. Make a well in the centre and add the egg, butter and 2 tablespoons of the milk. Using your fingers, gradually incorporate the flour, adding more milk if necessary. Knead lightly, form into a ball and set aside to rest in the refrigerator for 20 minutes. Preheat the oven to 180°C/350°F/Gas Mark 4. Line a baking sheet with baking parchment. Roll out the pastry on a lightly floured surface to a fairly thin sheet and stamp out 5-cm/2-inch rounds with a biscuit cutter or a glass. To make the filling, beat the eggs with a pinch salt in a soup plate, then stir in the Parmesan. If the mixture is too runny, add more grated Parmesan. Put a teaspoonful of filling on each round, fold over and crimp the edges. Gently pinch the middle of each piconcino with a pair of scissors and brush with milk. Place on the prepared baking sheet and bake for about 20 minutes. Serve warm with aperitifs.

PICONCINI MARCHIGIANI

Serves 6–8

300 g/11 oz plain flour, plus extra for dusting

1 egg

100 g/3¹/₂ oz butter, softened and diced

2–3 tablespoons milk, plus extra for brushing

salt

For the filling

2 eggs

150 g/5 oz Parmesan cheese, freshly grated

salt

CURRIED CHICKEN PUFFS

Preheat the oven to 200°C/400°F/Gas Mark 6. Roll out the pastry on a lightly floured surface and stamp out 12 rounds with a biscuit cutter or a glass. Place on a baking sheet and bake for 15–20 minutes until puffed up and golden. Transfer to a wire rack to cool. Place the chicken meat in a processor and process until very finely chopped. Transfer to a bowl and season to taste with curry powder. Stir in the béchamel sauce and egg yolks and season with salt and pepper to taste. When ready to serve, sandwich the chicken mixture between pairs of pastry rounds. Place on a baking sheet and heat through in a preheated oven, 180°C/350°F/Gas Mark 4, for 10 minutes.

SFOGLIATINE AL POLLO E CURRY

Serves 6

250 g/9 oz puff pastry dough, thawed if frozen

plain flour, for dusting

200 g/7 oz cooked chicken meat, coarsely chopped

curry powder, to taste

250 ml/8 fl oz Béchamel Sauce (see page 50)

2 egg yolks, lightly beaten

salt and pepper

SFOGLIATINE CON FUNGHI

Serves 6

25 g/1 oz butter, plus extra for greasing

300 g/11 oz mushrooms

juice of 1 lemon, strained

250 g/9 oz puff pastry dough, thawed if frozen

plain flour, for dusting

6 cooked ham slices, halved

40 g/1½ oz pine nuts

150 g/5 oz fontina cheese, sliced

1 egg yolk, lightly beaten

salt and pepper

MUSHROOM PUFFS

Preheat the oven to 200°C/400°F/Gas Mark 6. Lightly grease a baking sheet with butter. Slice the mushrooms and sprinkle with the lemon juice. Melt the butter in a frying pan. Add the mushrooms and cook over a medium heat, stirring frequently, for about 7 minutes until tender. (If all the liquid evaporates, add 1 tablespoon warm water.) Roll out the pastry on a lightly floured surface to 3 mm/⅛ inch thick. Stamp out 10-cm/4-inch rounds with a biscuit cutter or a glass. Spread out the half-slices of ham and put a few slices of mushroom, a few pine nuts, a strip of fontina and a pinch of salt and pepper on each. Fold in the sides to enclose the other ingredients, and lay a ham bundle in the middle of each pastry round. Fold the pastry over and crimp the edges to seal. Arrange the puffs on the prepared baking sheet, brush with the egg yolk and bake for about 15 minutes or until golden brown.

SFOGLIATINE CON RAFANO E WÜRSTEL

Serves 6

6 würstel or frankfurters

1 quantity Horseradish Butter (see page 88)

12 puff pastry rounds

(see Curried Chicken Puffs, page 153)

HORSERADISH AND SAUSAGE PUFFS

Cook the sausages in gently simmering water for about 8 minutes. Drain, leave to cool, then skin and chop very finely. Mix together the sausage meat and horseradish butter. When ready to serve, sandwich the sausage mixture between pairs of pastry rounds. Arrange on a dish and serve cold. Highly recommended with aperitifs.

SFOGLIATINE CON SCAMPI AL CURRY

Serves 6

200 g/7 oz langoustines or Dublin Bay prawns

½ onion, sliced

20 g/¾ oz butter

1 teaspoon plain flour

¼ teaspoon curry powder

1 egg yolk

12 puff pastry rounds

(see Curried Chicken Puffs, page 153)

salt

CURRIED LANGOUSTINE PUFFS

Bring a large pan of lightly salted water to the boil. Add the langoustines or prawns and onion and cook for 2–5 minutes. Drain, reserving the cooking liquid, and peel the langoustines or prawns. Mix together the butter and flour in a saucepan over a low heat and gradually stir in the reserved cooking liquid. Simmer, stirring constantly, for 15 minutes. Season with salt and stir in the langoustines or prawns, curry powder and egg yolk. Remove the pan from the heat. When ready to serve, sandwich the mixture between pairs of pastry rounds. Place on a baking sheet and heat through in a preheated oven, 180°C/350°F/Gas Mark 4, for 5 minutes.

CRÊPES

There are dozens of different types of crêpes, both sweet and savoury. They offer lots of scope and are equally suitable for solving the problem of how to start an elegant dinner party or what to serve as a fun snack. Crêpes are easy, but quite time-consuming, to make. Therefore it is a good idea to make a few more than you think you will need and keep them in the refrigerator to fill when required. A small, heavy-based non-stick crêpe pan is generally the most successful and popular utensil for cooking crêpes. Electric hotplates with a non-stick coating have been on the market for several years. A ladleful of batter is poured on to the hotplate and, once the underside is cooked, the crêpe is flipped over with a spatula to cook the other side. Whichever way you cook them, crêpes should always be fairly thin.

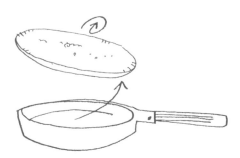

CRÊPE BATTER (BASIC RECIPE)

Sift the flour into a bowl, add the eggs and 3–4 tablespoons of the milk and mix well. Gradually stir in the remaining milk to make a fairly runny batter. Melt the butter in a double boiler in a heat-proof bowl over a pan of simmering water, leave to cool almost completely, then add to the batter. Season with salt, beat again for a few minutes with a small whisk, then leave to stand for at least 1 hour. Brush the base of a crêpe pan with oil and heat, then pour in 2 tablespoons of the batter. Turn and tilt the pan so that the batter covers the base evenly. Cook for 3–4 minutes until the underside is set and golden brown, then flip over with a spatula and cook the other side for about 2 minutes until golden. Slide the crêpe out of the pan on to a plate. Make more crêpes in the same way until all the batter is used. If sweet crêpes are required, replace the salt with sugar.

PASTELLA PER CRÊPES (RICETTA BASE)
Makes 12
100 g/3^1/$_2$ oz plain flour
2 eggs
250 ml/8 fl oz milk
25 g/1 oz butter
vegetable oil, for brushing
salt

ASPARAGUS CRÊPES

CRÊPES AGLI ASPARAGI

Makes 12

800 g/1¾ lb asparagus, trimmed

50 g/2 oz butter, plus extra for greasing

12 crêpes (see page 155)

150 ml/¼ pint double cream

50 g/2 oz Parmesan cheese, freshly grated

salt

Cook the asparagus in lightly salted, boiling water for 15 minutes. Drain and chop coarsely. Melt half the butter in a large frying pan, add the asparagus and cook over a low heat, stirring occasionally, for 5 minutes. Preheat the oven to 200°C/400°F/Gas Mark 6 and grease an ovenproof dish with butter. Brush the crêpes with some of the cream, sprinkle half with the Parmesan, place the asparagus on top and roll up. Arrange in a single layer in the prepared dish, pour in the remaining cream, dot with the remaining butter and sprinkle with the remaining Parmesan. Bake for about 10 minutes until golden and bubbling. Remove from the oven and cut each roll into three or four sections before serving.

MUSHROOM CRÊPES

CRÊPES AI FUNGHI

Makes 12

50 g/2 oz butter, plus extra for greasing

100 g/3½ oz mushrooms, thinly sliced

1 tablespoon chopped fresh flat-leaf parsley

50 ml/2 fl oz brandy

1 quantity Béchamel Sauce (see page 50)

12 crêpes (see page 155)

3 tablespoons Parmesan cheese, freshly grated

salt and pepper

Preheat the oven to 200°C/400°F/Gas Mark 6. Grease an ovenproof dish with butter. Melt half the butter in a frying pan. Add the mushrooms and cook over a low heat, stirring occasionally, for 5 minutes. Add the parsley, season with salt and pepper, sprinkle with the brandy and cook for a further 3–4 minutes until the liquid has evaporated. Spread 1 tablespoon of the béchamel sauce on each crêpe, top with 1 tablespoon of the mushrooms and roll up. Arrange in a single layer in the prepared dish, pour the remaining béchamel sauce over them, sprinkle with the Parmesan and dot with the remaining butter. Bake for 10–15 minutes.

ANCHOVY CRÊPES

CRÊPES ALLE ACCIUGHE

Makes 12

12 crêpes (see page 155)

16 canned anchovy fillets, drained

100 g/3½ oz butter, softened

Keep the crêpes warm or reheat stored crêpes. Finely chop four of the anchovy fillets. Cream the butter in a bowl, then beat in the chopped anchovies. Gently spread the mixture over the crêpes and put a whole anchovy fillet in the middle of each. Roll up and serve.

HAM AND FONTINA CRÊPES

CRÊPES AL PROSCIUTTO E FONTINA

Makes 12

25 g/1 oz butter, plus extra for greasing

12 crêpes (see page 155)

200 g/7 oz cooked ham, chopped

100 g/3½ oz fontina cheese, diced

1 quantity Béchamel Sauce (see page 50)

3 tablespoons Parmesan cheese, freshly grated

pinch of freshly grated nutmeg

Preheat the oven to 200°C/400°F/Gas Mark 6. Grease an ovenproof dish with butter. Sprinkle the crêpes with the ham and fontina. Roll up and arrange in a single layer in the prepared dish. Pour the béchamel sauce over them, sprinkle with the Parmesan and nutmeg and dot with the butter. Bake for about 10 minutes until golden and bubbling. Serve the crêpes whole or halved diagonally.

PÂTÉS
AND TERRINES

When the assistant at the delicatessen cuts a chunk off that soft block covered in gelatine and lays the slices of 'pâté' that we requested on a tray, assuring us that it is the very best quality, we are all using the term wrongly, even though this misuse has now become standard: we should, in fact, say mousse. The French word pâté really means something quite different. First, it is always covered in pastry which is cooked together with the filling, which may consist of a mashed or chopped mixture of meat, vegetables, fish or pulses. It is also usually served hot as an hors d'oeuvre or as the main course of a formal dinner. Terrines are part of the pâté family. Here, the filling, which is partly minced and partly cut into strips or slices, is arranged in an earthenware container lined with strips of bacon so that when it is sliced it reveals a decorative mosaic pattern. To cook, the terrine is covered and placed in a water bath or bain-marie before being baked in the oven. It is then left to cool, chilled in the refrigerator, turned out and thinly sliced.

Serves 4

4 sheets leaf gelatine
250 g/9 oz fresh pineapple, coarsely chopped
juice of ½ lemon, strained
4 tablespoons milk
350 ml/12 fl oz double cream, whipped
prosciutto slices, to serve

PINEAPPLE BAVAROIS

Soak the sheets of gelatine in cold water for 5 minutes to soften. Place the pineapple in a food processor and process at maximum speed to a purée. Scrape into a bowl and stir in the lemon juice. Squeeze out the gelatine and place in a small saucepan with the milk and heat gently until the gelatine dissolves. Remove from the heat and leave to cool slightly, then add the pineapple. Leave to cool completely, then fold in the cream. Rinse out a mould with cold water and drain. Spoon the mixture into the mould and chill in the refrigerator for 6–7 hours. To serve, turn out on to a serving dish. Serve with slices of prosciutto.

FLORENTINE MOULD

Heat the oil in a frying pan. Add the onion and cook over a low heat, stirring occasionally, for 5 minutes until soft. Add the steak, increase the heat to high and cook, stirring frequently, until browned. Sprinkle with the brandy and cook until it has evaporated, then season with salt and pepper and remove the pan from the heat. Leave to cool, then mince very finely with a mincer or in a food processor. Scrape into a bowl and beat in 100 g/3½ oz of the butter, then chill in the refrigerator. Cook the carrots and peas in salted, boiling water until tender, then remove with a slotted spoon and add the chicken breast to the pan. Poach for 15 minutes or until cooked through and tender. Drain the chicken, chop and mix with the remaining butter, the truffle pâté, if using, and the Marsala. Stir until thoroughly combined, then season with salt and pepper to taste. Gently stir in the peas, carrots and ham. Grease a 2-litre/3½-pint mould with butter. (In Florence, a dome-shaped zuccotto mould is used.) Spoon in the steak pâté and smooth the surface with the back of a damp tablespoon. Spoon the chicken mixture on top. Tap the mould on the work surface several times to release any air pockets. Cover with cling film and chill in the refrigerator for 4–5 hours. Remove from the refrigerator about 10 minutes before serving to bring back to room temperature. Turn out on to a dish and garnish with parsley sprigs and rose-cut radishes.

GRAN ZUCCOTTO DI PÂTÉ

Serves 10–12

2 tablespoons olive oil

1 onion, thinly sliced

600 g/1 lb 5 oz lean steak, finely chopped

25 ml 1 fl oz brandy

200 g/7 oz butter, softened, plus extra for greasing

100 g/3½ oz carrots, diced

100 g/3½ oz shelled peas

1 skinless, boneless chicken breast

30 g/1 oz truffle pâté (optional)

100 ml/3½ fl oz Marsala

150 g/5 oz cooked ham

in a single piece, finely chopped

salt and pepper

To garnish

fresh flat-leaf parsley sprigs

rose-cut radishes

GORGONZOLA MOUSSE

Put the three cheeses and the butter in a food processor and process to a soft, even cream. Line a tart tin with cling film. Spoon in the mixture, smooth the surface and cover with more cling film. Chill in the refrigerator for about 3 hours. Turn out on to a serving dish and garnish with the walnut halves arranged in a circle. Serve with raw carrots.

MOUSSE DI GORGONZOLA

Serves 6–8

200 g/7 oz Gorgonzola cheese, crumbled

300 g/11 oz stracchino cheese,

such as taleggio, diced

100 g/3½ oz robiola cheese, diced

100 g/3½ oz butter, softened

walnut halves, to garnish

raw carrots, to serve

PIGEON MOUSSE WITH TRUFFLE VINAIGRETTE

MOUSSE DI PICCIONE CON VINAIGRETTE AL TARTUFO

Serves 10–12

175 ml/6 fl oz Armagnac brandy

1 teaspoon sugar

2 pigeons, boned and livers reserved

100 g/3½ oz goose liver, sliced

100 g/3½ oz chicken livers, trimmed

135 ml/4½ fl oz olive oil

200 ml/7 fl oz double cream, whipped

3 shallots, finely chopped

1 sprig fresh flat-leaf parsley, finely chopped

100 ml/3½ fl oz white wine vinegar

2 teaspoons truffle pâté

1 tablespoon Dijon mustard

salt and pepper

crackers, to serve

Pour the Armagnac into a bowl and stir in the sugar and salt and pepper to taste. Chop the pigeon meat and add to the bowl with the pigeon livers, goose liver and chicken livers. Set aside to marinate for 12 hours. Heat 3 tablespoons of the oil in a large frying pan. Drain all the meat, reserving the marinade, and add to the pan. Cook over a medium heat, stirring frequently and gradually adding the reserved marinade. Season with salt and pepper to taste, remove the pan from the heat and leave to cool. Mince all the meat with a mincer or in a food processor and place in a bowl. Gently fold in the whipped cream, cover and chill in the refrigerator for 12 hours. Meanwhile, mix together the shallots, parsley, the remaining olive oil, the vinegar, truffle pâté and mustard. Store in the refrigerator until required. To serve, scoop almond-shaped balls from the pigeon mousse, using two dessertspoons, and put two on each individual plate. Sprinkle with the vinaigrette and serve with crackers.

MEADOW FLOWER MOUSSE

MOUSSE DI PRATOLINE

Serves 6

30 edible flowers, such as violas, marjoram, heartsease, tansy or meadowsweet

80 g/3 oz mascarpone cheese

1 tablespoon milk

dash of lemon juice, strained

salt and white pepper

toasted bread, to serve

Wash the flowers, pat dry, set eight aside for the garnish and chop the remainder. Beat the mascarpone with the milk and lemon juice in a bowl, then stir in the chopped flowers and season with salt and pepper to taste. Shape into a dome on a serving dish and garnish with the whole flowers. Serve with toasted bread.

HAM AND KIWI FRUIT MOUSSE

MOUSSE DI PROSCIUTTO E KIWI

Serves 6–8

400 g/14 oz cooked ham, diced

120 g/4 oz robiola cheese, diced

50 g/2 oz butter, softened

salt and pepper

3 kiwi fruits, peeled and sliced, to garnish

Put the ham, cheese and butter in a food processor and season with salt and pepper. Process until smooth. Line a mould with cling film, spoon in the ham mousse and smooth the surface. Cover with more cling film and chill in the refrigerator for 3 hours. Turn out and garnish with kiwi fruit.

SALMON MOUSSE WITH PRAWN CREAM

Preheat the oven to 160°C/325°F/Gas Mark 3. Grease a ring mould with butter. Skin and chop the salmon fillets and place in a bowl. Put the skin, any trimmings, the bones and head in a large saucepan. Add water to cover, bring to the boil, then lower the heat and simmer for 30 minutes. Whisk the egg whites in a grease-free bowl until stiff. Stiffly whip the cream in another bowl. Fold the egg whites, then the cream into the chopped salmon and season with salt and pepper. Pour the mixture into the ring mould and place in a roasting tin. Pour in boiling water to come about halfway up the side of the mould and bake for 45–50 minutes. Meanwhile, strain the salmon stock into a bowl. Make the prawn cream. Peel and devein the prawns and finely chop the shells. Heat half the butter in a frying pan, add the shells and cook, stirring frequently, for a few minutes. Sprinkle with the brandy and cook until it has evaporated, then season with salt and pepper. Mix the remaining butter and the flour to a paste and add to the pan, stirring. Stir in as much of the hot salmon stock as required to make a slightly runny sauce. Strain into a bowl and add the prawns. Turn out the mousse and pour the prawn cream in the middle. Serve immediately.

MOUSSE DI SALMONE CON CREMA
Serves 6–8
butter, for greasing
600 g/1 lb 5 oz salmon, cleaned and filleted, bones and head reserved
2 egg whites
250 ml/8 fl oz double cream
salt and white pepper

For the prawn cream
18 cooked prawns
50 g/2 oz butter
50 ml/2 fl oz brandy
1 tablespoon plain flour
salt and pepper

COLD TOMATO MOUSSE

Sprinkle the insides of the tomatoes with salt and place upside down on kitchen paper to drain for 10 minutes. Place the tomatoes in a food processor and process to a purée. Scrape into a large bowl, add the chives and garlic and mix well. Gently stir in the mayonnaise, then the yogurt, then the cream and season with salt and pepper to taste. Spoon into individual dishes and chill in the refrigerator. Serve garnished with the basil leaves.

MOUSSE FREDDA DI POMODORI
Serves 6
8 ripe tomatoes, peeled and seeded
1 tablespoon chopped fresh chives
1 garlic clove, chopped
1 quantity Mayonnaise (see page 65)
150 ml/¹/₄ pint low-fat natural yogurt
100 ml/3¹/₂ fl oz double cream
salt and pepper
fresh basil leaves, to garnish

PÂTÉ AI FEGATINI

Serves 6

150 g/5 oz butter

400 g/14 oz chicken livers, trimmed

1/2 onion, chopped

5 fresh thyme leaves

2 tablespoons Marsala

1 tablespoon brandy

2 tablespoons double cream, whipped

salt and pepper

CHICKEN LIVER PÂTÉ

Melt 100 g/3½ oz of the butter in a heatproof bowl over a pan of barely simmering water. Remove from the heat and set aside to cool. Melt the remaining butter in a frying pan. Add the chicken livers, onion and thyme and cook over a medium heat, stirring frequently, for 2 minutes. Sprinkle with the Marsala, season with salt and pepper and cook for 3 minutes. Remove the pan from the heat, chop the chicken livers and place in a bowl. Stir in the cooled melted butter, then add the brandy and fold in the cream. Chill in the refrigerator for 6 hours.

PÂTÉ DELICATO DI POLLO

Serves 8

120 g/4 oz butter, softened

200 g/7 oz skinless, boneless chicken breast, sliced

300 g/11 oz cooked ham

1 small potato

200 ml/7 fl oz double cream

100 ml/3½ fl oz Béchamel Sauce (see page 50)

25 ml/1 fl oz brandy

25 g/1 oz powdered gelatine

1 egg, hard-boiled

1 fresh flat-leaf parsley sprig, leaves only

salt and pepper

DELICATE CHICKEN PÂTÉ

Chill a rectangular mould in the freezer. Melt 25 g/1 oz of the butter in a frying pan. Add the chicken and cook over a medium heat, stirring occasionally, for 8–10 minutes until cooked. Remove from the pan and chop together with 200 g/7 oz of the ham, then place in a bowl. Cook the potato in a pan of lightly salted, boiling water for 10 minutes until tender, then drain, peel and mash. Add the potato to the chicken and ham mixture, then gently stir in the remaining butter, the cream and béchamel sauce and season with salt and pepper. Sprinkle with 1 tablespoon of the brandy and mix, then set aside. Meanwhile, prepare the gelatine according to the packet instructions and add the remaining brandy. Spoon a little gelatine into the chilled mould and turn so that it coats the sides and base. Put in the refrigerator to set. Using a heart-shaped cutter, stamp out small hearts from the remaining ham. Shell and slice the egg, preferably with an egg slicer. Arrange the ham hearts on the base of the mould alternating with slices of egg and the parsley leaves. Spoon in another layer of gelatine and brush some over the sides. Return to the refrigerator for at least 30 minutes. When the gelatine has set, spoon in the chicken mixture, pressing it down gently with the palm of your hand. Spoon the remaining gelatine on top. Chill in the refrigerator for at least 5 hours until set. Turn out on to a serving dish and serve immediately.

DELICATE CALF'S LIVER PÂTÉ

PÂTÉ DELICATO DI VITELLO

Serves 6–8

350 g/12 oz calf's liver, sliced

plain flour, for dusting

120 g/4 oz butter

100 ml/3¹/₂ fl oz Marsala

100 g/3¹/₂ oz prosciutto, chopped

1 egg yolk

salt and pepper

fresh sage leaves, to garnish

toast triangles, to serve

Lightly dust the liver with flour. Melt 25 g/1 oz of the butter in a frying pan, add the liver and cook over a high heat, stirring frequently, for 5 minutes. Pour in the Marsala and cook for about 7 minutes until it has evaporated. Season with salt and pepper to taste and remove from the heat. Chop the liver and dice the remaining butter. Place them in a food processor with the pan juices, prosciutto and egg yolk and process until smooth. Line a rectangular mould with cling film, spoon in the pâté and chill in the refrigerator for at least 5 hours until set. Turn out, slice thinly and garnish with the sage. Serve with toast triangles.

SMOKED SALMON PÂTÉ

PÂTÉ DI SALMONE

Serves 6–8

25 g/1 oz butter, melted, plus extra for greasing

3 potatoes

200 g/7 oz smoked salmon, chopped

3 tablespoons stoned black olives, coarsely chopped

2 canned anchovy fillets in oil, drained and chopped

salt and pepper

cornichons or small gherkins, drained, to garnish

Grease a mould with butter. Cook the potatoes in lightly salted, boiling water for 15 minutes or until tender. Drain, peel and mash with a potato masher. Put the salmon, olives, melted butter and anchovies in a food processor, season with salt and pepper and process to a purée. Stir the purée into the mashed potatoes. Spoon the mixture into the prepared mould, smooth the surface and chill in the refrigerator for 6 hours. Turn out and garnish with cornichons or gherkins.

TUNA PÂTÉ

PÂTÉ DI TONNO

Serves 6

100 g/3¹/₂ oz canned anchovy fillets in oil, drained

300 g/11 oz canned tuna in oil, drained

juice of 1 lemon, strained

150 g/5 oz butter, softened

olive oil, for brushing

salt and pepper

To garnish

2 smoked salmon slices, cut into strips

Italian mixed pickled vegetables (sottaceti)

Put the anchovies and tuna in a food processor and process to a purée. Scrape into a bowl, stir in the lemon juice, then the butter. Season with salt and pepper and mix well. Brush a mould with olive oil, spoon in the mixture and smooth the surface. Chill in the refrigerator for at least 3 hours. Just before serving, turn out on to a serving dish and garnish with strips of smoked salmon and Italian pickles.

TERRINA D'ANATRA

Serves 8–10

butter, for greasing

1 duck, boned, liver reserved

250 g/9 oz lardons

100 g/3¹/₂ oz prosciutto, cut into strips

100 ml/3¹/₂ fl oz brandy

150 g/5 oz minced veal

150 g/5 oz minced pork loin

2 eggs, lightly beaten

salt and pepper

DUCK TERRINE

Grease a terrine or loaf tin with butter. Chop the duck meat and put into a large bowl. Cut 100 g/3¹/₂ oz of the lardons into strips and add to the bowl with the prosciutto. Sprinkle with the brandy, season with salt and pepper and mix well. Cover and set aside for 2 hours. Preheat the oven to 160°C/325°F/Gas Mark 3. Chop 100 g/3¹/₂ oz of the remaining lardons with the duck liver and mix with the veal and pork. Season with salt and pepper and stir in the eggs. Combine with the duck meat mixture and spoon into the prepared dish, pressing down well. Lay the remaining lardons on top. Cover with a lid or foil, place in a roasting tin and add boiling water to come about halfway up the sides. Bake for 2 hours. Remove from the oven and uncover. Place a sheet of foil on the surface, put a weight on top and chill in the refrigerator for 24 hours. Before turning the terrine out, remove any fat that has formed on the surface.

MOULDS
AND SOUFFLÉS

Both moulds and soufflés are important antipasti, make elegant second courses and can be served as unusual and delicious accompaniments. For example, serving a succulent veal roast with a soufflé is a sure sign of a certain culinary sophistication. It is not at all true that moulds and soufflés are difficult to make. All you have to do is carefully follow the method in each recipe and, above all, allow yourself enough time to do so. The difference between the two dishes lies in their consistency: a mould is firmer and a soufflé is lighter and airier. In practice, a soufflé is a mixture that puffs up during cooking until it is higher than the rim of the dish. The basic element for the success of both is eggs. For example, in vegetable moulds the eggs help to keep the mixture together. However, you should never add an extra egg to be 'on the safe side', as the mixture may become too tough during cooking and acquire an unpleasant flavour. A mould is cooked when you can push a wooden cocktail stick into it and it comes out dry. After cooking, in general leave to stand for 5 minutes, then turn out on to a dish and serve. In soufflés, on the other hand, whisked egg whites carry out the main task. The incorporated air bubbles increase the volume of the mixture and make it softer, and at the same time almost 'elastic'. Soufflés are made by mixing the chopped or mashed main ingredient (cheese, ham or fish) with a firm béchamel sauce, egg yolks and stiffly whisked egg whites. Two important warnings: fill the dish only two-thirds full so that the soufflé puffs up and rises over the rim; and do not open the oven door during cooking. Serve the soufflé in the dish it is cooked in.

FLAN DI TONNO CON SALSA AI PORRI

Serves 4

butter, for greasing

200 g/7 oz canned tuna in spring water, drained

4 eggs, separated • salt and pepper

fresh flat-leaf parsley, chopped, to garnish

For the sauce

25 g/1 oz butter

2 tablespoons double cream

4 leeks, trimmed and sliced

salt and pepper

TUNA MOULD WITH LEEK SAUCE

Preheat the oven to 180°C/350°F/Gas Mark 4 and grease a tart tin with butter. Place half the tuna and the egg yolks in a food processor, process to a purée and scrape into a bowl. Stiffly whisk the egg whites, then fold them into the tuna mixture. Finely chop the remaining tuna, season with salt and pepper and fold in. Pour the mixture into the prepared tin, place in a roasting tin and pour in boiling water to come about halfway up the side. Bake for about 45 minutes. For the sauce, heat the butter and cream in a saucepan, add the leeks and cook over a low heat for 20 minutes. Season with salt and pepper. Turn out the mould and top with the leek sauce. Garnish with parsley and serve immediately.

SFORMATINI DI PORRI

Serves 6

butter, for greasing

1 kg/2¼ lb leeks, trimmed • 50 g/2 oz pine nuts

50 g/2 oz Parmesan cheese, freshly grated

2 eggs, separated

salt

For the béchamel sauce

25 g/1 oz butter • 25 g/1 oz plain flour

200 ml/7 fl oz milk • 50 ml/2 fl oz double cream

pinch of freshly grated nutmeg

LEEK MOULDS

First make the béchamel sauce (see page 50) with the ingredients listed, then leave to cool. Preheat the oven to 180°C/350°F/Gas Mark 4 and grease six individual tart tins with butter. Meanwhile, cook the leeks in salted, boiling water for 10 minutes until tender. Drain, pass through a food mill into a bowl and add the pine nuts. Stir the mixture into the cold béchamel sauce, then stir in the Parmesan and egg yolks and season with salt. Stiffly whisk the egg whites and fold in. Pour the mixture into the prepared tins and bake for 30 minutes. Remove the tins from the oven and leave to stand for a few minutes, then turn out on to a serving dish.

SFORMATINI DI ZUCCHINE

Serves 4

25 g/1 oz butter, plus extra for greasing

250 g/9 oz courgettes, sliced

1 tablespoon olive oil • 1 shallot, finely chopped

2 eggs, lightly beaten

2 tablespoons Parmesan cheese, freshly grated

salt and pepper

For the béchamel sauce

25 g/1 oz butter

20 g/¾ oz plain flour • 200 ml/7 fl oz milk

pinch of freshly grated nutmeg

COURGETTE MOULDS

Preheat the oven to 180°C/350°F/Gas Mark 4 and grease four dariole moulds with butter. Cook the courgettes in salted, boiling water for 10 minutes until tender. Drain and mash with a fork. Heat the oil and butter in a frying pan, add the shallot and cook over a low heat, stirring occasionally, for 4–5 minutes until softened. Stir in the courgettes and season with salt and pepper. Cook for a few minutes more until all the liquid has evaporated, then remove from the heat. Make the béchamel sauce (see page 50) with the ingredients listed, then stir in the courgette mixture, eggs and Parmesan. Divide the mixture among the moulds, then place in a roasting tin and add boiling water to come about halfway up the sides. Bake for 30–35 minutes. Leave to stand for 5 minutes, then turn out the moulds and serve.

TWO-COLOUR MOULD

Cook the spinach, in just the water clinging to the leaves after washing, for 5 minutes until tender. Drain, squeezing out as much liquid as possible, and chop. Melt half the butter in a small saucepan, stir in half the flour, then gradually stir in half the milk. Bring to the boil, stirring constantly. Cook, stirring, until thickened, then remove from the heat, stir in the thyme and season with salt and pepper. Beat in two egg yolks, one at a time, then add the spinach, Emmenthal and potato flour. Leave to cool, then stiffly whisk one egg white and fold in. Preheat the oven to 180°C/350°F/Gas Mark 4 and grease a tart tin with butter. Cook the carrots in salted, boiling water for 10 minutes until tender. Drain and pass through a food mill into a saucepan. Stir in the remaining butter, flour and milk and cook over a low heat, stirring constantly, until thickened. Remove from the heat, stir in the Parmesan and nutmeg and season with salt and pepper. Leave to cool slightly, then beat in the remaining egg yolks. Stiffly whisk the remaining egg whites and fold in. Spread 3 tablespoons of the spinach mixture on the base of the prepared tin, pour the carrot mixture on top and cover with the remaining spinach. Place in a roasting tin, add boiling water to come about halfway up the side and bake for about 1 hour. Remove the tin from the oven, leave to stand for 5 minutes, then turn out on to a serving dish. This dish may also be served as a first course.

SFORMATO BICOLORE

Serves 4

800 g/1³/₄ lb spinach

50 g/2 oz butter, plus extra for greasing

50 g/2 oz plain flour

500 ml/18 fl oz milk

¹/₂ teaspoon chopped fresh thyme

4 eggs, separated

40 g/1¹/₂ oz Emmenthal cheese, grated

1 teaspoon potato flour

350 g/12 oz baby carrots

40 g/1¹/₂ oz Parmesan cheese, freshly grated

pinch of freshly grated nutmeg

salt and pepper

ARTICHOKE HEART MOULD

Preheat the oven to 180°C/350°F/Gas Mark 4. Grease a tart tin with butter, then sprinkle in the breadcrumbs, turning the tin to coat. Tip out any excess. Bring a pan of salted water to the boil and add the lemon juice. Break off the artichoke stems, strip off all the leaves, remove the chokes and add the hearts to the pan. Cook for 15 minutes, then drain, chop and leave to cool slightly. Lightly beat the eggs and Parmesan in a bowl and stir in the artichoke hearts. Stir the mixture into the béchamel sauce and season with salt and pepper. Pour into the prepared tin and bake for about 45 minutes. Remove from the oven, leave to stand for 5 minutes, then turn out on to a dish and serve.

SFORMATO DI CARCIOFI

Serves 4

butter, for greasing

40 g/1¹/₂ oz fresh breadcrumbs

juice of ¹/₂ lemon, strained

6 globe artichokes

2 eggs, lightly beaten

40 g/1¹/₂ oz Parmesan cheese, freshly grated

1 quantity Béchamel Sauce (see page 50)

salt and pepper

CARROT MOULD

SFORMATO DI CAROTE

Serves 4

butter, for greasing

1.2 kg/2½ lb baby carrots

300 ml/½ pint Béchamel Sauce (see page 50)

100 g/3½ oz Emmenthal cheese, grated

40 g/1½ oz Parmesan cheese, freshly grated

3 eggs, lightly beaten

pinch of freshly grated nutmeg

salt and pepper

Preheat the oven to 180°C/350°F/Gas Mark 4. Grease a tart tin with butter. Steam the carrots for 8–10 minutes until tender. Set four or five carrots aside and pass the remainder through a food mill. Slice some of the reserved carrots lengthways into strips and arrange in a star shape on the base of the tin. Slice the remaining reserved carrots into rounds and arrange in rows around the sides of the tin. Pour the carrot purée into a pan and set over a low heat to dry out. Remove from the heat, stir in the béchamel sauce, Emmenthal, Parmesan, eggs and nutmeg and season with salt and pepper. Pour the mixture into the tart tin without disturbing the garnish. Place in a roasting tin and add boiling water to come about halfway up the side. Bake for 45–50 minutes. Leave to stand for 5 minutes, then turn out on to a serving dish.

CARROT AND FENNEL MOULD

SFORMATO DI CAROTE E FINOCCHI

Serves 6

40 g/1½ oz butter, plus extra for greasing

500 g/1 lb 2 oz carrots

6 small fennel bulbs, quartered

200 ml/7 fl oz milk

4 tablespoons Parmesan cheese, freshly grated

½ quantity Béchamel Sauce (see page 50)

2 eggs, separated

Preheat the oven to 180°C/350°F/Gas Mark 4. Grease a tart tin with butter. Cook the carrots in salted, boiling water for 10 minutes until tender, then drain. Meanwhile, cook the fennel in salted, boiling water for 10–15 minutes until tender, then drain. Melt half the butter in a frying pan, add the carrots and cook over a low heat, stirring occasionally, for 5 minutes. Add half the milk and cook until it has been absorbed. Process the carrot mixture in a food processor to a purée. Melt the remaining butter in a frying pan, add the fennel and cook over a low heat, stirring occasionally, for 5 minutes. Add the remaining milk and cook until it has been absorbed. Process the fennel mixture in a food processor to a purée. Stir the Parmesan into the béchamel sauce and divide the mixture in half. Stir the carrot purée into one bowl of sauce and the fennel purée into the other. Beat one egg yolk into each bowl. Stiffly whisk the egg whites and fold half into each mixture. Pour the mixtures in alternate layers into the prepared tin. Place the tin in a roasting tin and add boiling water to come about halfway up the side. Bake for 40–50 minutes. Leave to stand for 10 minutes, then turn out on to a serving dish. This mould may also be served as an original first course instead of risotto or pasta.

CAULIFLOWER MOULD

Preheat the oven to 180°C/350°F/Gas Mark 4. Grease a tart tin with butter. Cook the cauliflower in salted, boiling water for 8–10 minutes until tender, then drain well. Melt the butter in a frying pan, add the cauliflower and cook over a low heat, stirring occasionally, for 5 minutes until lightly browned. Season with salt and pepper, pour in the milk and cook until it has been absorbed. Remove the pan from the heat and push the mixture through a sieve. Beat the eggs into the béchamel sauce, one at a time, then stir in the Gruyère and puréed cauliflower. Pour into the prepared tin, place in a roasting tin and add boiling water to come about halfway up the side. Bake for 1 hour. Leave to stand for a few minutes, then turn out on to a serving dish.

SFORMATO DI CAVOLFIORE

Serves 6

25 g/1 oz butter, plus extra for greasing

1.2 kg/2½ lb cauliflower, cut into florets

5 tablespoons milk

3 eggs

1 quantity Béchamel Sauce (see page 50)

80 g/3 oz Gruyère cheese, grated

salt and pepper

CHICORY MOULD

Preheat the oven to 180°C/350°F/Gas Mark 4. Grease a tart tin with butter. Cook the chicory in salted, boiling water for 10 minutes until tender. Drain, squeezing out as much liquid as possible, and chop coarsely. Melt the butter in a frying pan, add the chicory and cook over a low heat, stirring occasionally, for 5 minutes, then remove from the heat. Lightly beat the eggs with a pinch of salt, then stir into the chicory. Stir the chicory mixture into the béchamel sauce and pour into the prepared tin. Place in a roasting tin, add boiling water to come about halfway up the side and bake for 45–50 minutes. Leave to stand for 5 minutes, then turn out on to a serving dish.

SFORMATO DI CICORIA

Serves 4

25 g/1 oz butter, plus extra for greasing

1 kg/2¼ lb chicory

2 eggs

300 ml/½ pint Béchamel Sauce (see page 50)

salt

FENNEL MOULD

Preheat the oven to 180°C/350°F/Gas Mark 4. Grease a tart tin with butter. Melt the butter in a frying pan, add the fennel and cook over a low heat, stirring occasionally, for 5 minutes. Season with salt and pepper, pour in the milk and cook until it has been absorbed. Transfer the fennel to a bowl, leave to cool, then mash with a fork. Beat the eggs with the Parmesan and stir into the fennel. Stir the fennel mixture into the béchamel sauce and pour into the prepared tin. Place in a roasting tin, add boiling water to come about halfway up the side and bake for 45 minutes. Leave to stand for 5 minutes, then turn out and serve hot.

SFORMATO DI FINOCCHI

Serves 6

25 g/1 oz butter, plus extra for greasing

1.5 kg/3¼ lb fennel bulbs, cut into wedges

200 ml/7 fl oz milk

3 eggs

50 g/2 oz Parmesan cheese, freshly grated

300 ml/½ pint Béchamel Sauce (see page 50)

salt and pepper

Serves 6

50 g/2 oz butter, plus extra for greasing

40 g/1½ oz breadcrumbs

750 g/1 lb 10 oz shelled peas

150 ml/¼ pint Chicken Stock (see page 209)

pinch of ground cinnamon

1 tablespoon plain flour

2 amaretti, crumbled

2 tablespoons double cream

3 eggs, separated

salt

PEA AND AMARETTI MOULD

Preheat the oven to 180°C/350°F/Gas Mark 4. Grease a tart tin with butter, sprinkle with the breadcrumbs and turn the tin to coat. Tip out any excess. Melt half the butter in a saucepan, add the peas and cook over a low heat, stirring occasionally, for 5 minutes. Add the stock and cinnamon and simmer for 5 minutes or until the peas are tender. Drain and pass through a food mill. Melt the remaining butter in a pan. Pour in the pea purée, sprinkle with the flour and cook over a low heat, stirring constantly. Add the amaretti, cream and egg yolks and season to taste with salt. Remove from the heat and leave to cool. Stiffly whisk the egg whites and fold in. Pour into the prepared tin and bake for about 45 minutes then serve.

Serves 6

25 g/1 oz butter, plus extra for greasing

2 bunches of celery, chopped

1 quantity Béchamel Sauce (see page 50)

50 g/2 oz Parmesan cheese, freshly grated

150 g/5 oz cooked ham, chopped

3 eggs, separated

salt

CELERY AND HAM MOULD

Preheat the oven to 180°C/350°F/Gas Mark 4. Grease a tart tin with butter. Cook the celery in salted, boiling water for 15 minutes, then drain. Melt the butter in a saucepan, add the celery and cook over a low heat, stirring frequently and breaking up the pieces with a spoon, for 5 minutes. Stir into the béchamel sauce with the Parmesan and ham. Beat in the egg yolks, one at a time. Stiffly whisk the egg whites and fold in. Pour into the prepared tin and bake for 45–50 minutes. Leave to stand for 5 minutes, then turn out on to a serving dish.

Serves 6

25 g/1 oz butter, plus extra for greasing

40 g/1½ oz breadcrumbs

1 kg/2¼ lb spinach

50 g/2 oz Italian salami, diced

50 g/2 oz fontina cheese, diced

1 quantity Béchamel Sauce (see page 50)

3 eggs, separated

salt and pepper

SPINACH MOULD

Preheat the oven to 180°C/350°F/Gas Mark 4. Grease a ring mould with butter, sprinkle with the breadcrumbs and turn the mould to coat. Tip out any excess. Cook the spinach, in just the water clinging to the leaves after washing, for 5 minutes. Drain, squeezing out as much liquid as possible, and chop. Melt the butter in a pan, add the spinach and cook over a low heat, stirring occasionally, for 4–5 minutes. Stir the spinach, salami and fontina into the béchamel sauce and season with salt and pepper to taste. Beat in the egg yolks, one at a time. Stiffly whisk the egg whites and fold in. Pour the mixture into the mould, place in a roasting tin and add boiling water to reach about halfway up the side. Bake for 45–50 minutes. Leave to stand for 5 minutes, then turn out on to a serving dish and serve. Mushroom Trifolati (see page 486) or small meatballs may be served in the middle of the ring.

SEA TROUT MOULD

Preheat the oven to 180°C/350°F/Gas Mark 4. Grease six dariole moulds or ramekins with butter. For the stock, put the fish heads, onion, carrot, leek and a pinch of salt in a saucepan, pour in 1 litre/1³/₄ pints water, bring to the boil and simmer for 5 minutes. Strain into a clean pan, set over a high heat and cook until reduced by half. Remove from the heat and leave to cool. Coarsely chop the fish fillets, place in a food processor, season with salt and pepper and process to a purée. Add the egg yolks, potato flour and all but 1 tablespoon of the cream. Pour the mixture into the prepared moulds, place in a roasting tin and add boiling water to come about halfway up the sides. Bake for about 25 minutes. Leave to stand for 5 minutes before turning out. For the vegetables, melt the butter in a saucepan, add the carrots, celery, leeks and courgettes and cook over a low heat, stirring occasionally, for 5 minutes. Remove from the heat and keep warm. For the sauce, stir the potato flour into the cooled fish stock. Bring to the boil over a low heat, stirring constantly. Add the saffron and reserved cream, bring back to the boil and season with salt and pepper to taste. Add the wine and simmer gently for a few minutes. Remove from the heat, stir in the butter and spoon a thin layer of the sauce on to a warm serving dish. Arrange a layer of vegetables on the dish and turn out the sea trout moulds on top. Sprinkle with the parsley and garnish with the tomato. Serve immediately with the remaining sauce handed separately.

SFORMATO DI TROTA SALMONATA

Serves 6

butter, for greasing

1-kg/2¹/₄-lb sea trout, filleted and skinned

2 egg yolks

1 tablespoon potato flour

250 ml/8 fl oz double cream

2 tablespoons chopped fresh flat-leaf parsley

salt and pepper

1 tomato, peeled and diced, to garnish

For the stock

a few white fish heads, gills removed

1 onion • 1 carrot • 1 leek

salt

For the vegetables

25 g/1 oz butter

2 carrots, cut into thin strips

2 celery sticks, cut into thin strips

2 leeks, cut into thin strips

2 courgettes, cut into thin strips

For the sauce

1 tablespoon potato flour

pinch of saffron threads

100 ml/3¹/₂ fl oz dry white wine

25 g/1 oz butter

CLAM AND MUSSEL MOULD

Preheat the oven to 180°C/350°F/Gas Mark 4. Grease a tart tin with butter. Place the shellfish in a pan, add 250 ml/8 fl oz water and cook over a high heat until the shells open. Remove the shellfish, discarding any that remain closed, and strain the cooking liquid through a muslin-lined strainer. Make the velouté sauce with the shellfish cooking liquid, season with salt and pepper and leave to cool slightly. Remove the mussels and clams from the shells and chop. Stir the egg yolks, poached fish and shellfish into the sauce. Stiffly whisk the egg whites and fold in. Pour the mixture into the prepared tin and bake for 40 minutes. Leave to stand for 5 minutes, then turn out on to a dish and serve.

SFORMATO DI VONGOLE E COZZE

Serves 6

butter, for greasing

500 g/1 lb 2 oz clams, scrubbed

500 g/1 lb 2 oz mussels, scrubbed and beards removed

1 quantity Velouté Sauce (see page 61 and method)

4 eggs, separated

100 g/3¹/₂ oz poached white fish fillet, flaked

salt and pepper

PUMPKIN MOULD

SFORMATO DI ZUCCA

Serves 4

25 g/1 oz butter, plus extra for greasing

1 onion, sliced

1 kg/2¼ lb pumpkin, peeled, seeded and diced

1 quantity Béchamel Sauce (see page 50)

50 g/2 oz Parmesan cheese, grated

2 egg yolks

40 g/1½ oz pine nuts

salt and pepper

Preheat the oven to 160°C/325°F/Gas Mark 3. Grease a tart tin with butter. Melt the butter in a saucepan. Add the onion and cook over a low heat, stirring occasionally, for 5 minutes until softened. Add the pumpkin and 150 ml/¼ pint water and cook, stirring and mashing occasionally, until the pumpkin is very soft. Remove from the heat, stir in the béchamel sauce, Parmesan, egg yolks and pine nuts and season with salt and pepper. Pour the mixture into the prepared tin and bake for 1 hour. Increase the oven temperature to 180°C/350°F/Gas Mark 4 and bake for a further 10 minutes. Leave to cool in the tin, then turn out. This mould is excellent served with spinach sautéed in butter.

CHESTNUT SOUFFLÉ

SOUFFLÉ DI CASTAGNE

Serves 4

50 g/2 oz butter, plus extra for greasing

600 g/1 lb 5 oz chestnuts, shelled

150 ml/¼ pint Meat Stock (see page 208)

2 egg whites

salt

Preheat the oven to 200°C/400°F/Gas Mark 6. Grease a soufflé dish with butter. Parboil the chestnuts in a pan of salted water, then drain and rub off the skins. Pass the nuts through a food mill into a saucepan. Pour in the stock, add the butter and season with salt. Place on a low heat and stir until the purée is fairly dry, then remove from the heat and leave to cool. Stiffly whisk the egg whites and fold into the mixture. Spoon into the prepared dish and bake for about 20 minutes, then lower the temperature to 180°C/350°F/Gas Mark 4 and bake for 5 minutes more. Serve immediately.

ONION SOUFFLÉ

SOUFFLÉ DI CIPOLLE

Serves 6

25 g/1 oz butter, plus extra for greasing

300 g/11 oz small onions, finely chopped

250 ml/8 fl oz hot Meat Stock (see page 208)

50 ml/2 fl oz brandy

pinch of sugar (optional)

100 g/3½ oz Emmenthal cheese, grated

4 eggs, separated

250 ml/8 fl oz Béchamel Sauce (see page 50)

pinch of grated nutmeg

salt and pepper

Melt the butter in a saucepan, add the onions and cook over a low heat, stirring occasionally, for 10 minutes until lightly browned. Pour in the stock and simmer for 1 hour. Preheat the oven to 200°C/400°F/Gas Mark 6. Grease a soufflé dish with butter. Season the onions with salt and pepper and add the brandy with a pinch of sugar if the mixture tastes a little sour. Cook until the liquid has evaporated, then stir in the Emmenthal and remove from the heat. Stir the egg yolks into the béchamel sauce, one at a time, then stir in the onions and nutmeg and season with salt. Stiffly whisk the egg whites and fold in. Spoon the mixture into the prepared dish and bake for 20 minutes. Lower the oven temperature to 180°C/350°F/Gas Mark 4 and bake for 5 minutes more. Serve immediately.

FRENCH BEAN SOUFFLÉ

SOUFFLÉ DI FAGIOLINI

Serves 4

butter, for greasing

800 g/1³/₄ lb French beans, trimmed

2 tablespoons Parmesan cheese, freshly grated

4 eggs, separated

For the béchamel sauce

80 g/3 oz butter

80 g/3 oz plain flour • 500 ml/18 fl oz milk

salt and pepper

Preheat the oven to 200°C/400°F/Gas Mark 6. Grease a soufflé dish with butter. Cook the beans in boiling water for 5 minutes until al dente. Drain and pass through a food mill. Make the béchamel sauce (see page 50) with the ingredients listed and season with salt and pepper. Stir in the beans, remove from the heat and stir in the grated cheese. Leave to cool slightly, then beat in the egg yolks, one at a time. Stiffly whisk the egg whites and fold in. Spoon into the prepared dish and bake for about 20 minutes. Lower the oven temperature to 180°C/350°F/Gas Mark 4 and bake for 5 minutes more. Serve immediately.

CHEESE SOUFFLÉ

SOUFFLÉ DI FORMAGGIO

Serves 4

butter, for greasing

40 g/1¹/₂ oz breadcrumbs

1 quantity Béchamel Sauce (see page 50)

150 g/5 oz Emmenthal cheese, thinly sliced into strips

3 eggs, separated

salt

Preheat the oven to 200°C/400°F/Gas Mark 6. Grease a soufflé dish with butter, sprinkle with the breadcrumbs and turn to coat. Tip out any excess. Pour the béchamel sauce into the top of a double boiler or into a heatproof bowl set over a pan of barely simmering water, add the Emmenthal and stir until melted. Season with salt and leave to cool. Beat in the egg yolks, one at a time. Stiffly whisk the egg whites and fold in. Spoon into the prepared dish and bake for 20 minutes. Lower the oven temperature to 180°C/350°F/Gas Mark 4 and bake for 5 minutes more. Serve immediately.

MUSHROOM SOUFFLÉ

SOUFFLÉ DI FUNGHI

Serves 4

25 g/1 oz butter, plus extra for greasing

40 g/1¹/₂ oz breadcrumbs

3 tablespoons olive oil

1 onion, chopped • 1 garlic clove, chopped

1 salted anchovy, head removed, cleaned and filleted (see page 596)

750 g/1 lb 10 oz mushrooms, preferably porcini, thinly sliced

3–4 tablespoons Meat Stock (see page 208)

2 tablespoons chopped fresh flat-leaf parsley

150 g/5 oz fontina cheese

1 quantity Béchamel Sauce (see page 50)

3 eggs, separated

salt and pepper

Preheat the oven to 200°C/400°F/Gas Mark 6. Grease a soufflé dish with butter, sprinkle with the breadcrumbs and turn to coat. Tip out any excess. Heat the olive oil and butter in a small saucepan, add the onion, garlic and anchovy and cook over a low heat, stirring occasionally, for 5 minutes. Add the mushrooms, season with salt and pepper and cook, stirring occasionally, for 30 minutes. Add a little stock if the mixture seems to be drying out. Towards the end of the cooking time increase the heat and add the parsley. Dice about three-quarters of the fontina and slice the remainder. Stir the diced cheese into the béchamel sauce, then beat in the egg yolks, one at a time. Stiffly whisk the egg whites and fold in. Spoon half the mixture into the prepared dish, add the mushrooms with their cooking juices and cover with the remaining soufflé mixture and the sliced fontina. Bake for 20 minutes, then lower the oven temperature to 180°C/350°F/ Gas Mark 4 and bake for 5 minutes more. Serve immediately.

CRAB SOUFFLÉ

Preheat the oven to 200°C/400°F/Gas Mark 6. Grease a soufflé dish with butter. Melt the butter in a pan, add the pepper and cook over a low heat, stirring occasionally, until softened. Transfer to a food processor and process to a purée. Sprinkle the crab meat with the vermouth and set aside. Beat the egg yolks into the velouté sauce, one at a time, then stir in the crab meat and red pepper purée. Season with salt and pepper. Stiffly whisk the egg whites and fold in. Spoon into the prepared dish and bake for about 20 minutes, then lower the oven temperature to 180°C/350°F/Gas Mark 4 and bake for 5 minutes more. Serve immediately.

SOUFFLÉ DI GRANCHIO

Serves 4

25 g/1 oz butter, plus extra for greasing

1 red pepper, halved, seeded and diced

200 g/7 oz crab meat, drained and flaked

1 tablespoon vermouth

4 eggs, separated

1 quantity Velouté Sauce (see page 61)

salt and pepper

SPICY CORN SOUFFLÉ

Preheat the oven to 200°C/400°F/Gas Mark 6. Grease a soufflé dish with butter. Melt the butter in a small saucepan over a low heat, stir in the flour and gradually stir in the milk. Cook, stirring constantly, until the mixture is thickened and smooth, then remove from the heat, stir in the Emmenthal and leave to cool slightly. Beat in the egg yolks, one at a time, then stir in the corn, pepper, chilli and paprika and season with salt and pepper. Stiffly whisk the egg whites and fold in. Spoon into the prepared dish and bake for 20 minutes, then lower the oven temperature to 180°C/350°F/Gas Mark 4 and bake for 5 minutes more. Serve immediately.

SOUFFLÉ DI MAIS PICCANTE

Serves 4

25 g/1 oz butter, plus extra for greasing

2 tablespoons plain flour

100 ml/3½ fl oz milk

300 g/11 oz Emmenthal cheese, grated

3 eggs, separated

350 g/12 oz canned sweetcorn, drained

½ red pepper, seeded and chopped

½ fresh chilli, seeded and chopped

pinch of paprika

salt and pepper

POTATO SOUFFLÉ

Cook the potatoes in salted, boiling water for 20 minutes until tender, then drain and mash with a potato masher. Place in a saucepan and stir in the butter and cream over a low heat. Cook, stirring constantly, for 15 minutes, then remove from the heat, stir in the nutmeg and season with salt and pepper. Leave to cool slightly. Preheat the oven to 200°C/400°F/Gas Mark 6. Grease a soufflé dish with butter, sprinkle with the breadcrumbs and turn to coat. Tip out any excess. Beat the egg yolks into the potato mixture, one at a time, then stir in the ham and Parmesan. Stiffly whisk the egg whites and fold in. Spoon into the prepared dish and bake for 20 minutes, then lower the oven temperature to 180°C/350°F/Gas Mark 4 and bake for 5 minutes more. Serve immediately.

SOUFFLÉ DI PATATE

Serves 6

800 g/1¾ lb potatoes

80 g/3 oz butter, plus extra for greasing

200 ml/7 fl oz double cream

pinch of freshly grated nutmeg

40 g/1½ oz breadcrumbs

4 eggs, separated

150 g/5 oz cooked ham, diced

4 tablespoons Parmesan cheese, freshly grated

salt and pepper

TOMATO SOUFFLÉ

SOUFFLÉ DI POMODORI

Serves 6

20 g/³/₄ oz butter, plus extra for greasing

¹/₂ onion, thinly sliced

300 g/11 oz tomatoes, peeled and chopped

4 fresh basil leaves, chopped

25 g/1 oz Parmesan cheese, freshly grated

25 g/1 oz Gruyère cheese, freshly grated

1 quantity Béchamel Sauce (see page 50)

4 eggs, separated

salt and pepper

Melt the butter in a pan, add the onion and cook over a low heat, stirring occasionally, for 10 minutes until golden brown. Add the tomatoes and basil and season with salt and pepper. Increase the heat and cook for 10–15 minutes until thickened and pulpy. Preheat the oven to 200°C/400°F/Gas Mark 6. Grease a soufflé dish with butter. Stir the tomato sauce, Parmesan and Gruyère into the béchamel sauce and season with salt and pepper. Beat in the egg yolks, one at a time. Stiffly whisk the egg whites and fold in. Spoon into the prepared dish and bake for 20 minutes. Lower the oven temperature to 180°C/350°F/Gas Mark 4 and bake for 5 minutes more. Serve immediately.

HAM SOUFFLÉ

SOUFFLÉ DI PROSCIUTTO

Serves 4

80 g/3 oz butter, plus extra for greasing

65 g/2¹/₂ oz plain flour

250 ml/8 fl oz milk

40 g/1¹/₂ oz breadcrumbs

2 eggs, separated

100 g/3¹/₂ oz Parmesan cheese, freshly grated

100 g/3¹/₂ oz cooked ham, coarsely chopped

salt

Melt the butter in a saucepan, stir in the flour and cook, stirring constantly, for 3–4 minutes until lightly browned. Gradually stir in the milk, add a pinch of salt and cook, stirring, until the mixture comes away from the sides of the pan. Remove from the heat and leave to cool. Preheat the oven to 200°C/400°F/Gas Mark 6. Grease a soufflé dish with butter, sprinkle with the breadcrumbs and turn to coat. Tip out any excess. Beat the egg yolks into the cooled sauce, one at a time, then stir in the Parmesan and ham. Stiffly whisk the egg whites and fold in. Spoon the mixture into the prepared dish and bake for 20 minutes, then lower the oven temperature to 180°C/350°F/Gas Mark 4 and bake for 5 minutes more. Serve immediately.

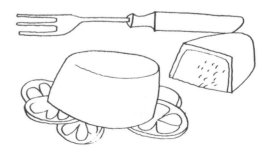

SAVOURY TARTS, QUICHES AND PIES

At one time, savoury tarts and pies were eaten only as snacks, at picnics or stand-up buffets. Today they increasingly replace the appetizer at elegant luncheons. They almost always have a pastry casing or base, which may be made of puff pastry, rough puff pastry or Pâte Brisée (see page 140). In most cases, savoury Italian tarts are filled with vegetables mixed with béchamel sauce, ricotta, eggs and soft and hard cheeses. Although mostly round, tarts may also be baked in square or rectangular tins so that they can be cut more easily into squares and served with aperitifs. At the table they are served warm and whole, on wooden, wickerwork or rough pottery plates. Some are also good served cold.

ASPARAGUS QUICHE

Cook the asparagus in salted, boiling water for about 20 minutes until tender. Drain well and chop the spears, leaving the tips whole. Preheat the oven to 160°C/325°F/Gas Mark 3. Dust a quiche tin with flour. Roll out the pastry on a lightly floured surface to a round and line the prepared tin. Prick the base all over with a fork, line with baking parchment, fill with baking beans and bake blind for 15 minutes. Remove the beans and parchment, then spoon the asparagus over the base of the pastry case and sprinkle with the Gruyère. Increase the oven temperature to 200°C/400°F/Gas Mark 6. Beat together the eggs, cream, milk and nutmeg in a bowl, season with salt and pepper and carefully pour into the pastry case. Bake for about 20 minutes and serve hot.

QUICHE AGLI ASPARAGI

Serves 6

250 g/9 oz asparagus spears, trimmed

plain flour, for dusting

200 g/7 oz puff pastry dough, thawed if frozen

100 g/3¹/₂ oz Gruyère cheese, freshly grated

3 eggs

150 ml/¹/₄ pint double cream

150 ml/¹/₄ pint milk

pinch of freshly grated nutmeg

salt and pepper

Serves 6

plain flour, for dusting

200 g/7 oz Pâte Brisée

(see page 140), thawed if frozen

3 smoked salmon slices, chopped

150 g/5 oz Gruyère cheese, grated

4 eggs

250 ml/8 fl oz double cream

salt and pepper

SMOKED SALMON QUICHE

Preheat the oven to 160°C/325°F/Gas Mark 3. Dust a quiche tin with flour. Roll out the pâte brisée on a lightly floured surface to a round and line the prepared tin. Prick the base all over with a fork, line with baking parchment, fill with baking beans and bake blind for 15 minutes. Remove the beans and parchment, scatter the salmon over the base of the pastry case and sprinkle with the Gruyère. Increase the oven temperature to 180°C/350°F/Gas Mark 4. Beat together the eggs and cream in a bowl, season with salt and pepper and pour over the salmon. Bake for 45 minutes.

Serves 6

plain flour, for dusting

300 g/11 oz puff pastry dough, thawed if frozen

150 g/5 oz bacon, diced

3 eggs

250–300 ml/8–10 fl oz double cream

pinch of freshly grated nutmeg

salt and pepper

QUICHE LORRAINE

Preheat the oven to 160°C/325°F/Gas Mark 3. Dust a quiche tin with flour. Roll out the pastry on a lightly floured surface to a round and line the prepared tin. Prick the base all over with a fork, line with baking parchment, fill with baking beans and bake blind for 15 minutes. Meanwhile, cook the bacon in a small non-stick frying pan, stirring frequently, for 5–8 minutes until golden brown but not crisp. Drain on kitchen paper. Beat together the eggs, cream and nutmeg in a bowl and season with salt and pepper. Remove the beans and parchment from the pastry case. Increase the oven temperature to 180°C/350°F/Gas Mark 4. Scatter the bacon over the base of the pastry case, pour the cream mixture over it and bake for about 30 minutes. Serve hot or warm in slices.

MUSHROOM TART
WITH WALNUT CREAM

For the walnut cream, tear the bread into pieces, place in a bowl, add the milk and set aside to soak. Melt the butter in a small frying pan, add the shallot and cook over a low heat, stirring occasionally, for about 5 minutes until softened. Squeeze out the bread, put it in a food processor with the egg, ham, walnuts and shallot and process until smooth. Scrape into a bowl, season with salt and pepper and chill in the refrigerator for 45 minutes. Meanwhile, parboil the mushrooms in salted water for 5 minutes. Drain, pat dry and slice thickly. Preheat the oven to 160°C/325°F/Gas Mark 3. Sprinkle a tart or quiche tin with flour. Roll out the pastry on a lightly floured surface, and line the prepared tin. Line with baking parchment, fill with baking beans and bake blind for 10 minutes. Melt the butter in a small frying pan, add the garlic and cook for 2–3 minutes. Remove the garlic. Remove the walnut mixture from the refrigerator and stir in the cream. Remove the beans and parchment from the pastry case and increase the oven temperature to 200°C/400°F/Gas Mark 6. Pour the walnut cream into the pastry case, arrange the mushrooms on top like sunrays, brush the rim with the garlic-flavoured butter and bake for 30 minutes.

SFOGLIA DI FUNGHI ALLA CREMA DI NOCI

Serves 6–8

1.2 kg/2½ lb mixed mushrooms, such as porcini, honey fungus and button mushrooms

plain flour, for dusting

300 g/11 oz puff pastry dough, thawed if frozen

15 g/½ oz butter

1 garlic clove, halved

For the walnut cream

25 g/1 oz bread (1 thick slice), crusts removed

3 tablespoons milk

25 g/1 oz butter

1 shallot, thinly sliced

1 egg

50 g/2 oz cooked ham, chopped

100 g/3½ oz shelled walnuts, chopped

120 ml/4 fl oz double cream

salt and pepper

BROCCOLI TART

Preheat the oven to 180°C/350°F/Gas Mark 4. Line a tart or quiche tin with baking parchment. Parboil the broccoli in salted water for about 5 minutes. Drain and chop, leaving the florets whole. Melt the butter in a pan, add the broccoli and a little salt and cook over a low heat, stirring occasionally, for 5 minutes. Remove from the heat. Roll out the pastry on a lightly floured surface and line the prepared tin, trimming the edges. Prick the base all over with a fork. Mix half the fontina with the nutmeg and sprinkle evenly over the pastry base. Arrange the broccoli on top. Mix the remaining fontina with the béchamel sauce and pour over the broccoli. Roll the pastry edges over and brush with the egg yolk. Bake for about 40 minutes.

TORTA AI BROCCOLETTI

Serves 4–6

500 g/1 lb 2 oz sprouting broccoli, cut into florets

25 g/1 oz butter

300 g/11 oz puff pastry dough, thawed if frozen

plain flour, for dusting

250 g/9 oz mild fontina cheese, grated

pinch of freshly grated nutmeg

1 quantity Béchamel Sauce (see page 50)

1 egg yolk, lightly beaten

salt

SEAFOOD TART

TORTA ALLA MARINARA

Serves 6

butter, for greasing

plain flour, for dusting

200 g/7 oz Pâte Brisée (see page 140), thawed if frozen

4 tablespoons chopped fresh flat-leaf parsley

2 tablespoons olive oil

1 garlic clove

200 g/7 oz shelled clams

200 g/7 oz ricotta cheese

2 eggs, lightly beaten

3 tablespoons double cream

200 g/7 oz small cooked prawns, peeled

salt and pepper

Preheat the oven to 160°C/325°F/Gas Mark 3. Grease a tart or quiche tin with butter and dust with flour. Sprinkle the pâte brisée with 2 tablespoons of the parsley and roll out on a lightly floured surface, then line the prepared tin. Trim the edges and reserve the trimmings. Prick the base all over with a fork, then line with baking parchment and fill with baking beans. Bake blind for 15 minutes, then leave to cool. Remove the parchment and beans. Heat the olive oil in a saucepan, add the garlic and clams, plus a drop of water if necessary, and cook for 3–4 minutes. Remove and discard the garlic, add the remaining parsley and remove from the heat. Combine the ricotta and eggs in a bowl, season with salt and pepper, then stir in the cream, clams and prawns. Spoon the filling into the pastry case, spreading it out evenly. Roll out the trimmings, cut into thin strips, brush the ends with water and arrange in a lattice over the top of the tart. Bake for 40 minutes.

ROCKET AND TALEGGIO PIE

TORTA ALLA RUCOLA E TALEGGIO

Serves 6

200 g/7 oz plain flour, plus extra for dusting

1 tablespoon poppy seeds

1 tablespoon chopped fresh marjoram

100 g/3 1/2 oz butter, chilled and diced, plus extra for greasing

For the filling

200 g/7 oz rocket

300 g/11 oz cream cheese

200 g/7 oz Taleggio cheese, diced

2 tablespoons breadcrumbs

2 eggs

salt and pepper

Sift the flour with a pinch of salt into a mound on a work surface, sprinkle with the poppy seeds and marjoram and rub in the butter with your fingertips. Add enough cold water to make a soft pastry, then shape into a ball, cover with cling film and leave to rest for 1 hour. Preheat the oven to 180°C/350°F/Gas Mark 4. Grease a tart or quiche tin with butter. Parboil the rocket for a few minutes in salted water, then drain, squeezing out as much liquid as possible. Put the rocket in a food processor with both cheeses, the breadcrumbs and eggs. Process at low speed, then season with salt and pepper. Roll out the pastry on a lightly floured surface, and line the prepared tin, trim the edges and reserve the trimmings. Fill with the rocket and cheese mixture and roll the pastry edges over slightly. Roll out the trimmings, cut into thin strips, brush the ends with water and arrange in a lattice over the top of the pie. Bake for about 40 minutes.

COD AND MUSHROOM TART

Pour 500 ml/18 fl oz water and the wine into a saucepan. Stud the onion with the cloves, add to the pan and bring to the boil. Add the fish and cook over a low heat for about 20 minutes. Remove the cod with a fish slice and boil the stock to reduce slightly, then set aside. Sprinkle the cod with the marjoram, thyme and parsley, and season with pepper. Melt the butter in a frying pan, add the mushrooms and cook over a low heat, stirring occasionally, for about 10 minutes. Remove from the heat and set aside. Preheat the oven to 160°C/325°F/Gas Mark 3. Grease a tart or quiche tin with butter. Make the béchamel sauce using half milk and half fish stock, then stir in the mushrooms, Gruyère, cream and eggs and season with salt and pepper. Roll out the pâte brisée on a lightly floured surface and line the prepared tin. Prick the base all over with a fork, line with baking parchment and fill with baking beans. Bake blind for 15 minutes, then remove from the oven and increase the temperature to 180°C/350°F/Gas Mark 4. Remove the parchment and beans. Chop the fish and sprinkle evenly over the pastry case. Cover with the béchamel sauce mixture and return to the oven for 40 minutes. Serve warm.

TORTA DELICATA DI MERLUZZO
AGLI CHAMPIGNON

Serves 6

500 ml/18 fl oz dry white wine

1 large onion, halved

2 cloves

6 cod fillets, skinned

1 tablespoon chopped fresh marjoram

2 teaspoons chopped fresh thyme

1 fresh flat-leaf parsley sprig, leaves only

25 g/1 oz butter, plus extra for greasing

1 kg/2¼ lb mushrooms, thinly sliced

1 quantity Béchamel Sauce

(see page 50 and method)

100 g/3½ oz Gruyère cheese, grated

2 tablespoons double cream

2 eggs, lightly beaten

250 g/9 oz Pâte Brisée

(see page 140), thawed if frozen

salt and pepper

SAVOURY CABBAGE PIE

Sift the flour into a bowl, add 150 g/5 oz of the butter and rub in with your fingertips. Stir in 3–4 tablespoons water to make a firm pastry. Set aside for 1 hour. Cook the carrots and cauliflower in separate pans of lightly salted, boiling water for 10 minutes until tender, then drain. Cut the cauliflower into florets. Melt 40 g/1½ oz of the remaining butter in a pan, add the cauliflower and cook, stirring frequently, for 5 minutes, then season with salt and remove from the pan. Melt the remaining butter in the pan, add the cabbage and cook, stirring frequently, for 5 minutes until softened, season with salt and remove from the heat. Preheat the oven to 200°C/400°F/Gas Mark 6. Grease a large pie dish with butter. Divide the pastry into two pieces, one larger than the other. Roll out the large piece on a lightly floured surface and line the prepared dish. Shell the eggs and slice, preferably with an egg slicer. Make a layer of egg slices in the base of the dish, cover with a layer of cauliflower florets, then a layer of fontina, then a layer of cabbage and carrots. Continue making layers until all the ingredients are used. Roll out the remaining pastry, cover the pie, trim and crimp the edges to seal. Cut a hole in the centre of the lid and prick the surface with a fork. Bake for 30 minutes and serve hot.

TORTA DI CAVOLI

Serves 6–8

250 g/9 oz wholemeal flour, plus extra for dusting

250 g/9 oz butter, plus extra for greasing

3 carrots, sliced

1 medium cauliflower

½ white cabbage, shredded

4 eggs, hard-boiled

150 g/5 oz fontina cheese, sliced

salt

OLD—FASHIONED ONION TART

TORTA DI CIPOLLE ALL'ANTICA

Serves 6

50 g/2 oz butter, plus extra for greasing

plain flour, for dusting

150 g/5 oz sultanas

250 ml/8 fl oz dry white wine

200 g/7 oz Pâte Brisée

(see page 140), thawed if frozen

1 kg/2¼ lb onions, thinly sliced

marrow from 2 beef bones, diced

pinch of sugar

salt and pepper

Preheat the oven to 160°C/325°F/Gas Mark 3. Grease a tart or quiche tin with butter and sprinkle with flour, tipping the tin to coat. Put the sultanas in a bowl, pour in the wine and set aside to soak. Roll out the pâte brisée on a lightly floured surface and line the prepared tin, trimming the edges. Reserve the trimmings. Prick the base all over with a fork. Line with baking parchment, fill with baking beans and bake blind for 15 minutes. Remove the pastry case and increase the oven temperature to 180°C/350°F/Gas Mark 4. Meanwhile, melt the butter in a frying pan, add the onions and cook over a low heat, stirring occasionally, for 10 minutes until golden brown. Stir in the beef marrow, the sultanas with the wine and a pinch of sugar, season with salt and pepper and cook until the wine has evaporated. Remove the parchment and beans from the pastry case, pour in the onion mixture and spread evenly. Roll out the trimmings, cut into thin strips, brush the ends with water and arrange in a lattice over the top of the tart. Bake for 30 minutes. Serve warm, cut into slices.

WILD GREENS AND ARTICHOKE PIE

TORTA DI ERBETTE E CARCIOFI

Serves 6

500 g/1 lb 2 oz plain flour, plus extra for dusting

6 tablespoons olive oil

2 white bread slices, crusts removed

120 ml/4 fl oz pint milk

500 g/1 lb 2 oz leafy green vegetables,

such as Swiss chard, spinach and turnip tops

juice of 1 lemon, strained

12 globe artichokes

butter, for greasing

1 onion, thinly sliced

100 g/3½ oz pecorino cheese, freshly grated

50 g/2 oz Parmesan cheese, freshly grated

1 tablespoon chopped fresh marjoram

salt and pepper

Sift the flour with a pinch of salt into a mound on a work surface, then add 4 tablespoons of the olive oil and just enough water to knead to a soft pastry. Set aside in the refrigerator to rest for 30 minutes. Tear the bread into pieces, place in a bowl and pour in the milk. Set aside to soak. Cook the greens in salted, boiling water for 5—10 minutes until tender, then drain, squeezing out as much liquid as possible, and chop. Half-fill a bowl with water and add the lemon juice. Remove and discard the outer leaves from the artichokes, cut off the top 5 cm/2 inches of the remaining leaves and remove the chokes. Drop into the acidulated water and set aside for about 10 minutes. Preheat the oven to 200°C/ 400°F/Gas Mark 6 and grease a tart or quiche tin with butter. Drain the artichokes, chop and put in a saucepan with the onion and the remaining oil. Cook over a low heat for 10 minutes until softened. Squeeze out the bread and add to the pan with the greens and cheeses. Mix well, season with salt and pepper and sprinkle with the marjoram. Roll out the pastry on a lightly floured surface into two rounds, one larger than the other. Place the larger one in the prepared tin, spoon in the vegetable mixture, cover with the second pastry round and crimp the edges to seal. Prick with a fork in a spiral pattern and bake for about 40 minutes. This pie may be served hot, warm or cold.

CHICKEN AND CHERVIL TART

Preheat the oven to 160°C/325°F/Gas Mark 3. Grease a tart or quiche tin with butter. Melt half the butter in a pan, add the onion and cook over a low heat, stirring occasionally, for 5 minutes until softened. Pour in 500 ml/18 fl oz water and the wine, bring to the boil and add the chicken. Bring back to the boil, then remove the chicken and onion with a slotted spoon and boil the liquid until reduced. Heat the remaining butter in another pan, add the chervil and cook, stirring frequently, for a few minutes. Stir in the flour, the reduced cooking liquid and the milk, season with salt and pepper and bring to the boil, stirring constantly. Turn off the heat and stir in the chicken, onion, Gruyère and cream. Roll out the pâte brisée on a lightly floured surface to a round and line the prepared tin. Prick the base all over with a fork, line with baking parchment and fill with baking beans. Bake blind for 15 minutes. Remove the beans and parchment, spoon in the filling, roll the pastry edges inwards slightly and prick with a fork. Increase the oven temperature to 180°C/350°F/Gas Mark 4 and bake for about 40 minutes. Serve warm.

TORTA DI POLLO AL CERFOGLIO
Serves 6

50 g/2 oz butter, plus extra for greasing
50 g/2 oz onion, thinly sliced
500 ml/18 fl oz white wine
500 g/1 lb 2 oz skinless,
boneless chicken breasts, diced
2 bunches of fresh chervil, chopped
50 g/2 oz plain flour, plus extra for dusting
750 ml/1¼ pints milk
100 g/3½ oz Gruyère cheese, grated
100 ml/3½ fl oz double cream
200 g/7 oz Pâte Brisée
(see page 140), thawed if frozen
salt and pepper

LEEK TART

Preheat the oven to 160°C/325°F/Gas Mark 3. Grease a tart or quiche tin with butter. Melt the butter in a saucepan, add the leeks and cook over a low heat, stirring occasionally, for 5 minutes until softened. Sprinkle with the Parmesan and season with salt and pepper, then remove from the heat. Beat together the milk, cream, eggs, flour, Emmenthal and nutmeg in a bowl. Stir in the leeks and set aside. Roll out the pâte brisée on a lightly floured surface to a round and line the prepared tin. Prick the base all over with a fork, line with baking parchment and fill with baking beans. Bake blind for 15 minutes. Remove the beans and parchment, spoon in the filling and bake for about 40 minutes. Serve warm.

TORTA DI PORRI
Serves 6

50 g/1 oz butter, plus extra for greasing
800 g/1¾ lb leeks, trimmed and thinly sliced
1 tablespoon Parmesan cheese, freshly grated
200 ml/7 fl oz milk
150 ml/¼ pint double cream
3 eggs, lightly beaten
1 teaspoon plain flour, plus extra for dusting
65 g/2½ oz Emmenthal cheese, grated
pinch of freshly grated nutmeg
200 g/7 oz Pâte Brisée
(see page 140), thawed if frozen
salt and pepper

Serves 6

50 g/2 oz butter, plus extra for greasing

2 bunches of fresh tarragon, finely chopped

50 g/2 oz plain flour, plus extra for dusting

750 ml/1¼ pints milk

200 g/7 oz cooked ham, diced

100 g/3½ oz Gruyère cheese, grated

100 ml/3½ fl oz double cream

200 g/7 oz Pâte Brisée

(see page 140), thawed if frozen

salt and pepper

HAM AND TARRAGON TART

Preheat the oven to 160°C/325°F/Gas Mark 3. Grease a tart or quiche tin with butter. Melt the butter in a saucepan, add the tarragon and cook over a low heat, stirring frequently, for a few minutes. Stir in the flour, then gradually stir in the milk and season with salt and pepper. Bring to the boil, stirring constantly, then remove from the heat. Add the ham, Gruyère and cream and set aside. Roll out the pâte brisée into a round on a lightly floured surface and line the prepared tin. Prick the base all over with a fork, line with baking parchment and fill with baking beans. Bake blind for 15 minutes. Remove the beans and parchment, spoon in the ham and tarragon mixture, roll the pastry edge inwards slightly and prick with a fork. Increase the oven temperature to 180°C/350°F/Gas Mark 4 and bake for 30 minutes. Leave to cool slightly, then serve.

Serves 6

40 g/1½ oz butter, plus extra for greasing

4 salmon fillets

1 kg/2¼ lb spinach

50 g/2 oz plain flour, plus extra for dusting

500 ml/18 fl oz milk

pinch of freshly grated nutmeg

2 teaspoons chopped fresh thyme

100 g/3½ oz Gruyère cheese, grated

100 ml/3½ fl oz double cream

200 g/7 oz Pâte Brisée

(see page 140), thawed if frozen

salt and pepper

SPINACH AND
SALMON TART

Preheat the oven to 160°C/325°F/Gas Mark 3. Grease a tart or quiche tin with butter. Place the salmon in a saucepan, add water to cover and a pinch of salt and bring just to the boil. Lower the heat and poach for 10 minutes. Meanwhile, cook the spinach, in just the water clinging to the leaves after washing, for 5 minutes, then drain well, squeezing out as much liquid as possible, and chop. Drain the salmon, reserving 300 ml/½ pint of the cooking liquid, and flake. Melt the butter in a saucepan, stir in the flour, milk, reserved cooking liquid, nutmeg and thyme and season with salt and pepper. Remove from the heat and stir in the Gruyère, cream, spinach and salmon. Roll out the pâte brisée into a round on a lightly floured surface and line the prepared tin. Prick the base all over with a fork, line with baking parchment and fill with baking beans. Bake blind for 15 minutes. Remove the beans and parchment, spoon in the spinach and salmon mixture, roll over the pastry edges slightly and prick with a fork. Increase the oven temperature to 180°C/350°F/Gas Mark 4 and bake for 30 minutes. Serve warm.

RUSTIC VEGETABLE PIE

Cook the spinach, chard, salad leaves, courgettes and leeks in salted, boiling water for 5–10 minutes until tender. Drain, squeeze out as much liquid as possible and chop coarsely. Beat the eggs with the pecorino, add the vegetables and 6 tablespoons of the oil and season with salt and pepper. Mix well and leave to stand. Preheat the oven to 200°C/400°F/Gas Mark 6 and line a rectangular pie dish with baking parchment. Sift the flour with a pinch of salt into a mound on a work surface. Make a well in the centre, add the remaining oil and 275 ml/9 fl oz warm water and gradually incorporate the flour using your fingers. Knead well, then roll out on a lightly floured surface into two rectangles, one larger than the other. Line the pie dish with the larger sheet and spoon in the vegetable mixture. Cover with the smaller sheet of pastry, trim and crimp the edges to seal. Make a hole in the centre. Bake for 30 minutes. This pie, called 'scarpazza' in Tuscany, may be served warm or cold.

TORTA DI VERDURE DELLA LUNIGIANA

Serves 6–8

500 g/1 lb 2 oz spinach

500 g/1 lb 2 oz Swiss chard

500 g/1 lb 2 oz wild salad leaves,

such as borage, rocket and dandelion

2 courgettes, sliced

2 leeks, trimmed and sliced

2 eggs

50 g/2 oz pecorino cheese, grated

150 ml/¼ pint olive oil

300 g/11 oz plain flour, plus extra for dusting

salt and pepper

PUMPKIN PIE

Preheat the oven to 180°C/350°F/Gas Mark 4. Grease a pie dish with butter. Place the mushrooms in a bowl, add warm water to cover and set aside to soak for 20 minutes. Place the pumpkin in an ovenproof dish, drizzle with the oil and bake for 20 minutes, then push through a sieve. Increase the oven temperature to 200°C/400°F/Gas Mark 6. Drain and chop the mushrooms. Melt the butter in a small saucepan, add the onion and mushrooms and cook over a low heat, stirring occasionally, for 5 minutes. Add the pumpkin purée and cook, stirring constantly, for 10 minutes. Remove the pan from the heat and stir in the Parmesan, egg and egg yolk and season with salt and pepper. Divide the pastry in half and roll out one piece to a round on a lightly floured surface. Line the prepared dish, cover the base with the Gruyère and spoon in the pumpkin mixture. Roll out the remaining pastry into a round and cover the pie. Trim and crimp the edges together to seal, prick all over with a fork and bake for 1 hour.

TORTA DI ZUCCA

Serves 6–8

50 g/2 oz butter, plus extra for greasing

20 g/¾ oz dried mushrooms

1 kg/2¼ lb pumpkin, peeled, seeded and sliced

2 tablespoons olive oil

1 onion, thinly sliced into rings

4 tablespoons Parmesan cheese, freshly grated

1 egg

1 egg yolk

300 g/11 oz puff pastry dough, thawed if frozen

plain flour, for dusting

50 g/2 oz Gruyère cheese, sliced

salt and pepper

EASTER PIE

TORTA PASQUALINA

Serves 12

butter, for greasing

600 g/1 lb 5 oz Swiss chard

10 eggs

300 g/11 oz ricotta cheese

2 tablespoons Parmesan cheese, freshly grated

2 tablespoons breadcrumbs

200 ml/7 fl oz double cream

1 tablespoon chopped fresh marjoram

400 g/14 oz puff pastry dough, thawed if frozen

plain flour, for dusting

olive oil, for brushing

salt and pepper

Preheat the oven to 200°C/400°F/Gas Mark 6. Grease a large pie dish with butter. Cook the chard in salted, boiling water for 10 minutes until tender, then drain and chop. Beat together four of the eggs. Push the ricotta through a sieve into a bowl, add the beaten eggs, Parmesan, breadcrumbs and cream and season with salt and pepper. Stir in the chard and marjoram. Roll out half the pastry on a lightly floured surface into two thin sheets. Line the prepared dish with a sheet of pastry, letting the edges overhang, and brush with oil. Place the second sheet on top and pour in half the chard mixture. Make six small hollows in the chard mixture and break an egg into each. Season with salt and pepper, cover with the remaining chard mixture and smooth the surface with a damp knife. Roll out the remaining pastry into two thin sheets. Place one on the filling and brush with oil, then top with the second and crimp carefully around the sides to seal. Prick the surface with a fork. Bake for about 1 hour. Easter pie may be served hot or cold.

FARMHOUSE RAINBOW PIE

TORTA RUSTICA ARCOBALENO

Serves 8–10

300 g/11 oz plain flour, plus extra for dusting

200 ml/7 fl oz dry white wine

1 tablespoon olive oil

500 g/1 lb 2 oz spinach

25 g/1 oz butter, plus extra for greasing

100 ml/3¹/₂ fl oz double cream

4 tablespoons Parmesan cheese, freshly grated

1 tablespoon chopped fresh thyme

2 red peppers

2 yellow peppers

200 g/7 oz cooked ham, thinly sliced

200 g/7 oz fontina cheese, thinly sliced

1 egg yolk, lightly beaten

salt and pepper

Sift the flour with a pinch of salt into a mound on a work surface. Make a well in the centre and pour in the wine and oil, then gradually incorporate the flour with your fingers, adding enough water to make a smooth pastry. Knead lightly, form into a ball and place in the refrigerator to rest for 30 minutes. Cook the spinach, in just the water clinging to the leaves after washing, for 5 minutes, then drain, squeezing out as much liquid as possible, and chop. Melt the butter in a frying pan, add the spinach and cook, stirring frequently, for 5 minutes, then season with salt and pepper and stir in the cream, Parmesan and thyme. Place the peppers on a baking sheet and set under a preheated grill, turning frequently, until the skins are charred and blistered. Transfer to a plastic bag and tie the top. When cool enough to handle, peel off the skins, halve and seed the peppers and cut into large slices. Preheat the oven to 180°C/350°F/Gas Mark 4. Grease a large pie dish with butter. Divide the pastry in half. Roll out one piece on a lightly floured surface and line the prepared dish. Arrange a layer of ham on the base, cover with a layer of the spinach mixture, then a layer of red pepper and a layer of fontina. Repeat the layers, using yellow pepper instead of the red. Continue making layers until all the ingredients are used, gently pressing each one down. Roll out the remaining pastry, cover the pie, trim and crimp the edges to seal. Prick with a fork and brush with the egg yolk. Bake for 1 hour, then serve hot or cold.

TORTA RUSTICA ZIA MARIA

Serves 6–8

300 g/11 oz plain flour

3 eggs

1 tablespoon sugar

100 g/3¹/₂ oz butter, softened

3–4 tablespoons milk

2 tablespoons Parmesan cheese, freshly grated

200 g/7 oz mozzarella cheese, diced

150 g/5 oz cooked ham, cut into strips

100 g/3¹/₂ oz mortadella, cut into strips

¹/₂ quantity Béchamel Sauce (see page 50)

AUNT MARIA'S FARMHOUSE PIE

Preheat the oven to 180°C/350°F/Gas Mark 4. Sift the flour into a mound on a work surface, make a well in the centre and add one of the eggs, the sugar, butter and half the milk. Gradually incorporate the flour with your fingertips, adding more milk if necessary to make a soft pastry. Knead lightly. Beat the remaining eggs in a bowl, then add the Parmesan, mozzarella, ham and mortadella and mix well. Set a small piece of pastry aside, roll out the remainder on a lightly floured surface and line a pie dish. Spoon in the filling, level the surface and cover with a thin layer of béchamel sauce. Roll out the remaining pastry, cut into thin strips, brush the ends with water and arrange in a lattice over the top of the pie. Brush with milk and bake for 45 minutes. Serve warm.

VOL–AU–VENT

The famous French chef and pastry cook Antonin Carême (1784–1833) not only invented pièces montées, table centre-pieces, but also created the fragile and delicious vol-au-vent. An extremely fine puff pastry he put in the oven one day started to rise with the heat and puffed up so wonderfully that one of his assistants drew his attention to it by calling out, 'It is flying in the wind' hence 'vol-au-vent'. The experts say that a classic vol-au-vent should be 15 cm/6 inches in diameter, but both bigger and smaller ones are now made. Nowadays, most people buy vol-au-vent cases ready made or order them from bakeries, so it's probably sensible to consider how different-sized ones are used. The small or extremely small ones, just over 3 cm/1¹/₄ inches in diameter, that can be eaten in one bite, are suitable for filling with ragù (meat sauce), creamed mushrooms or peas and for serving at stand-up buffets with aperitifs. Medium-size ones, 6 cm/2¹/₂ inches, filled with chicken giblets, brains with butter or asparagus and mushrooms, are an alternative first course instead of pasta or risotto. The biggest ones, 15–20 cm/6–8 inches, filled with tortellini, raviolini or maccheroncini, are suitable for formal dinners because of their impressive appearance.

VALLE D'AOSTA VOL–AU–VENTS

Place the fontina in a bowl, pour in half the milk and leave to soak for 4–5 hours. Preheat the oven to 150°C/300°F/Gas Mark 2. Drain the cheese, place in the top of a double boiler or a heatproof bowl set over a pan of barely simmering water, pour in the remaining milk and melt the cheese, stirring constantly. Stir in the egg yolks, one at a time, and season with salt and pepper to taste. Pour the cheese sauce into the vol-au-vent cases, place them on a baking sheet, and warm through in the oven for a few minutes before serving.

VOL–AU–VENT ALLA VALDOSTANA

Serves 4

300 g/11 oz fontina cheese, thinly sliced

400 ml/14 fl oz milk

2 egg yolks

8 medium vol-au-vent cases

salt and pepper

CHICKEN VOL−AU−VENTS

VOL−AU−VENT AL POLLO

Serves 4

2 tablespoons olive oil

1 onion, thinly sliced

100 g/3¹/₂ oz leeks, white part only, thinly sliced

200 g/7 oz skinless, boneless chicken breast, diced

40 g/1¹/₂ oz blanched almonds, chopped

1¹/₂ teaspoons plain flour

100 ml/3¹/₂ fl oz dry white wine

250 ml/8 fl oz Chicken Stock (see page 209)

1 tablespoon chopped fresh flat-leaf parsley

8 medium vol-au-vent cases

salt and pepper

Preheat the oven to 150°C/300°F/Gas Mark 2. Heat the oil in a frying pan and cook the onion and leeks over a low heat, stirring occasionally, for 5 minutes until softened. Add the chicken and almonds, sprinkle with the flour, pour in the wine and cook until the liquid has evaporated. Stir in the stock, season with salt and pepper and cook until the sauce is fairly thick. Remove the pan from the heat and stir in the parsley. Fill the vol-au-vent cases with the mixture, place on a baking sheet and warm through in the oven for a few minutes.

HAM VOL−AU−VENTS

VOL−AU−VENT AL PROSCIUTTO

Serves 4

25 g/1 oz butter

1 onion, chopped

100 g/3¹/₂ oz prosciutto, diced

100 g/3¹/₂ oz shelled petits pois

150 ml/¹/₄ pint Meat Stock (see page 208)

100 g/3¹/₂ oz cooked ham, diced

3 tablespoons double cream

1 egg yolk, lightly beaten

8 medium vol-au-vent cases

salt and pepper

Preheat the oven to 150°C/300°F/Gas Mark 2. Line a baking sheet with foil. Melt the butter in a small pan, add the onion and cook over a low heat, stirring occasionally, for 5 minutes until softened. Add the prosciutto, petits pois and stock and cook for about 10 minutes until the liquid has evaporated. Season with salt and pepper, remove from the heat and stir in the cooked ham, cream and egg yolk. Mix well, then return to the heat for a few minutes. Fill the vol-au-vent cases with the mixture, place on a baking sheet and warm through in the oven for 5 minutes.

PRAWN VOL−AU−VENTS

VOL−AU−VENT CON GLI SCAMPI

Serves 4

25 g/1 oz butter

¹/₂ onion, thinly sliced

pinch of curry powder

1 teaspoon plain flour

200 ml/7 fl oz milk

1 teaspoon tomato purée

1 egg, lightly beaten

juice of 1 lemon, strained

200 g/7 oz cooked prawns, peeled and deveined

12 small vol-au-vent cases

salt and pepper

Preheat the oven to 150°C/300°F/Gas Mark 2. Heat the butter in a saucepan, add the onion and cook over a low heat, stirring occasionally, for 5 minutes until softened and translucent. Stir in the curry powder and flour, then gradually stir in the milk. Stir the tomato purée with ¹/₂ teaspoon lukewarm water and stir into the pan. Season with salt and pepper and cook until thickened. Quickly stir in the egg, lemon juice and prawns and immediately remove the pan from the heat. Fill the vol-au-vent cases with the mixture, place on a baking sheet and heat through in the oven for 5 minutes.

PIZZAS

Yes – pizza really was a completely Italian idea which the whole world has copied. Truly the word pizza is used in every corner of the globe. All Italians take it for granted that the term refers to the Neapolitan pizza. The ingredients for the base are flour, fresh yeast, water and salt. (If fresh yeast is not available, use half the quantity of dried yeast and follow the packet instructions for dissolving it.) The topping in the case of a classic pizza is oil, tomato and mozzarella cheese. However, infinite variations are possible, using, for example, fish, a variety of cheeses, eggs and vegetables. Pizzas may be served as a first course, a snack, for dinner and as a dessert. They may vary in size from pizzette (mini pizzas), served with aperitifs, to normal and gigantic pizzas. Pizzas need fizzy drinks to stimulate the digestion. Beer is fine, but those who prefer wine may choose a sparkling white, preferably light, young and fruity.

PIZZA DOUGH (BASIC RECIPE)

Sift the flour and salt into a mound on a work surface and make a well in the centre. Mash the yeast in the water with a fork until very smooth and pour into the well. Incorporate the flour with your fingers to make a soft dough. Knead well, pulling and stretching until it becomes smooth and elastic. Shape into a ball, cut a cross in the top, place in a bowl and cover. Leave to rise in a warm place for about 3 hours until almost doubled in size. Flatten the dough with the palm of your hand and roll out on a lightly floured surface to a round about 5 mm/¹/₄ inch thick. Brush a baking sheet with oil or line it with baking parchment. Put the dough round on it and press out until it covers the area. Make sure the rim is thicker than the centre. Scatter with the topping ingredients, leaving a 2-cm/³/₄-inch margin around the edge.

IMPASTO PER LA PIZZA
(RICETTA BASE)

Serves 4

250 g/9 oz plain flour,
preferably Italian type 00, plus extra for dusting
³/₄ teaspoon salt
15 g/¹/₂ oz fresh yeast
120 ml/4 fl oz lukewarm water
olive oil, for brushing (optional)

CALZONE

CALZONE

Serves 2

olive oil, for brushing

1 quantity Pizza Dough (see page 193)

plain flour, for dusting

50 g/2 oz mozzarella cheese, diced

25 g/1 oz Italian salami, diced

25 g/1 oz cooked ham, diced

1 egg, lightly beaten

25 g/1 oz ricotta cheese, crumbled

salt and pepper

Preheat the oven to 220°C/425°F/Gas Mark 7. Brush a baking sheet with oil or line with baking parchment. Knead the dough for 1 minute. Roll out on a lightly floured surface into two rounds. Mix together the mozzarella, salami, ham and egg, then season with salt and pepper and add the ricotta. Scatter the mixture on one side of each dough round and fold the rounds in half. Crimp the edges to seal. Place on the baking sheet and bake for about 15 minutes.

MUSHROOM PIZZA

PIZZA AI FUNGHI

Serves 4

3 tablespoons olive oil, plus extra for brushing

1 garlic clove, chopped

350 g/12 oz mushrooms, sliced

2 tablespoons chopped fresh flat-leaf parsley

1 quantity Pizza Dough (see page 193)

plain flour, for dusting

salt and pepper

Heat the oil in a frying pan, add the garlic and mushrooms and cook over a low heat, stirring frequently, for 5 minutes. Season with salt and pepper, sprinkle with the parsley and simmer over a very low heat for about 30 minutes. Preheat the oven to 220°C/425°F/Gas Mark 7 and brush a baking sheet with oil or line it with baking parchment. Roll out the dough on a lightly floured surface, then press it out on the baking sheet. Scatter the mushrooms on top and bake for 20 minutes.

PIZZA NAPOLETANA

PIZZA ALLA NAPOLETANA

Serves 4

olive oil, for brushing and drizzling

1 quantity Pizza Dough (see page 193)

plain flour, for dusting

5–6 tomatoes, peeled and chopped

150/5 oz mozzarella cheese, sliced

pinch of dried oregano

8 canned anchovy fillets, drained

salt

Preheat the oven to 220°C/425°F/Gas Mark 7. Brush a baking sheet with oil or line with baking parchment. Roll out the dough on a lightly floured surface, then press it out on the baking sheet. Scatter the tomato flesh evenly on top and drizzle with oil poured around, once, in a circle. Bake for about 18 minutes. Add the mozzarella, oregano and anchovies, season with salt and drizzle with oil if necessary. Bake for a further 7–8 minutes until crisp.

FISHERMAN'S PIZZA

PIZZA ALLA PESCATORA

Serves 4

300 g/11 oz baby octopuses, cleaned and skinned

2 tablespoons olive oil,

plus extra for brushing and drizzling

300 g/11 oz raw prawns

300 g/11 oz clams, scrubbed

300 g/11 oz mussels,

scrubbed and beards removed

1 onion, thinly sliced

4 garlic cloves, thinly sliced

1 fresh chilli, seeded and chopped

1 tablespoon chopped fresh flat-leaf parsley

1 quantity Pizza Dough (see page 193)

plain flour, for dusting

300 g/11 oz cherry tomatoes, peeled and quartered

salt

Cook the octopuses in salted, boiling water until tender, then drain well. Preheat the oven to 220°C/425°F/Gas Mark 7. Brush a baking sheet with oil and line with baking parchment. Parboil the prawns for 2–3 minutes, then drain, peel and devein them. Discard any clams or mussels with broken shells or that do not shut immediately when sharply tapped. Place them in a dry frying pan and set over a high heat for 5 minutes until they open. Discard any that remain closed. Remove the clams and mussels from their shells. Heat the oil in a frying pan, add the onion, garlic and chilli and cook over a low heat, stirring occasionally, for 5 minutes, then add the octopuses, mussels, clams and prawns. Season with salt and cook, stirring frequently, for 5 minutes. Remove from the heat and add the parsley. Roll out the dough on a lightly floured surface, then press it out on the baking sheet. Scatter the tomatoes on top, drizzle with oil and bake for about 15 minutes. Arrange the seafood on top and return the pizza to the oven for a further 7–8 minutes (no longer or the seafood will become tough).

POTATO PIZZA

PIZZA ALLE PATATE

Serves 4

3 large potatoes

olive oil, for brushing and drizzling

1 quantity Pizza Dough (see page 193)

plain flour, for dusting

200 g/7 oz pancetta, diced

100 g/3½ oz Taleggio cheese, diced

50 g/2 oz Parmesan cheese, shaved

2 teaspoons chopped fresh rosemary

salt and pepper

Cook the potatoes in salted, boiling water for 20 minutes until tender. Drain, peel and thinly slice. Preheat the oven to 220°C/425°F/Gas Mark 7. Brush a baking sheet with oil or line with baking parchment. Roll out the dough on a lightly floured surface, then press out on the baking sheet. Arrange the slices of potatoes on top and drizzle with oil. Bake for about 15 minutes, then scatter with the pancetta, cheeses and rosemary and season with salt and pepper. Drizzle with oil and bake for a further 7–8 minutes. Serve hot.

'WHITE' PIZZA

PIZZA BIANCA

Serves 4

olive oil for brushing and drizzling

1 quantity Pizza Dough (see page 193)

plain flour, for dusting

150 g/5 oz mozzarella cheese, sliced

150 g/5 oz Taleggio cheese, diced

pinch of dried oregano • salt and pepper

Preheat the oven to 220°C/425°F/Gas Mark 7. Brush a baking sheet with oil or line with baking parchment. Roll out the dough on a lightly floured surface, then press out on the baking sheet. Arrange the mozzarella and Taleggio on top, sprinkle with oregano, season with salt and pepper and drizzle with oil. Bake for about 20 minutes.

SAUSAGE PIZZA

PIZZA CON LE SALSICCE

Serves 4

olive oil, for brushing and drizzling
200 g/7 oz Italian sausages, skinned and crumbled
50 g/2 oz pecorino cheese, freshly grated
1 quantity Pizza Dough (see page 193)
plain flour, for dusting
4 tomatoes, peeled and chopped
100 g/3¹/₂ oz smoked pancetta, sliced
1 teaspoon chopped fresh rosemary
6 fresh basil leaves, torn
salt and pepper

Preheat the oven to 220°C/425°F/Gas Mark 7. Brush a baking sheet with oil or line with baking parchment. Mix together the sausages and pecorino in a bowl and season with salt and pepper. Roll out the dough on a lightly floured surface, then press it out on the baking sheet. Scatter the tomatoes on top and drizzle with oil. Bake for 20 minutes. Scatter with the sausage mixture and top with the pancetta. Sprinkle with the rosemary and basil, drizzle with oil and bake for a further 7–8 minutes.

CHICORY PIZZA

PIZZA D'INDIVIA

Serves

2 tablespoons oil, plus extra for brushing
1 onion, chopped
1 garlic clove, chopped
100 g/3¹/₂ oz tomatoes, peeled and chopped
4 chicory heads, trimmed and separated into leaves
2 tablespoons double cream
1 quantity Pizza Dough (see page 193)
plain flour, for dusting
100 g/3¹/₂ oz prosciutto, sliced
salt

Heat the oil in a pan, add the onion and garlic and cook over a low heat, stirring occasionally, for 5 minutes until soft. Add the tomatoes and chicory, cover and cook for 10 minutes. Sprinkle with salt and continue cooking for a further 20 minutes, adding a little hot water if the mixture seems to be drying out. Meanwhile, preheat the oven to 220°C/425°F/Gas Mark 7. Brush a baking sheet with oil or line with baking parchment. When the chicory is very soft, stir in the cream and cook until thickened, then remove from the heat. Roll out the dough on a lightly floured surface, then press it out on the baking sheet. Spread the chicory mixture on top and bake for 20 minutes. Remove the pizza from the oven, lay the slices of prosciutto on top and serve immediately.

MARGHERITA PIZZA

PIZZA MARGHERITA

Serves 4

olive oil, for brushing and drizzling
1 quantity Pizza Dough (see page 193)
plain flour, for dusting
5–6 tomatoes, peeled and chopped
150 g/5 oz mozzarella cheese, sliced
6 fresh basil leaves, torn
salt and pepper

Preheat the oven to 220°C/425°F/Gas Mark 7. Brush a baking sheet with oil or line with baking parchment. Roll out the dough on a lightly floured surface, then press it out on the baking sheet. Scatter the tomatoes on top and drizzle with oil. Bake for 15–20 minutes. Add the mozzarella slices and basil, season with salt and pepper and drizzle with oil. Bake for a further 7–8 minutes.

FOUR SEASONS PIZZA

Preheat the oven to 220°C/425°F/Gas Mark 7. Brush a baking sheet with oil or line with baking parchment. Cut the anchovy fillets in half lengthways. Discard any mussels with broken shells or that do not shut immediately when sharply tapped. Place in a dry frying pan and set over a high heat for 5 minutes until they open. Remove the mussels from their shells. Roll out the dough on a lightly floured surface, then press it out on the baking sheet. Scatter thetomatoes on top and mark out a cross using the back of a knife. Arrange the anchovy fillets and green olives in one quarter, the mussels in another, the ham and mozzarella in the third, and the artichokes and black olives in the fourth. Season with salt and pepper, drizzle with oil and bake for 15–20 minutes.

PIZZA QUATTRO STAGIONI

Serves 4

olive oil, for brushing and drizzling

4 salted anchovies, heads removed, cleaned and filleted (see page 596), soaked in cold water for 10 minutes and drained

100 g/3¹/₂ oz mussels, scrubbed and beards removed

1 quantity Pizza Dough (see page 193)

plain flour, for dusting

4 tomatoes, peeled and chopped

50 g/2 oz green olives

50 g/2 oz cooked ham, diced

50 g/2 oz mozzarella cheese, diced

4 baby artichokes in oil, drained and halved

50 g/2 oz black olives

salt and pepper

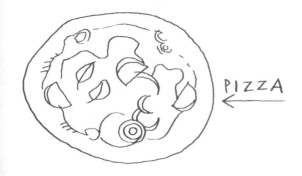

PIZZA ←

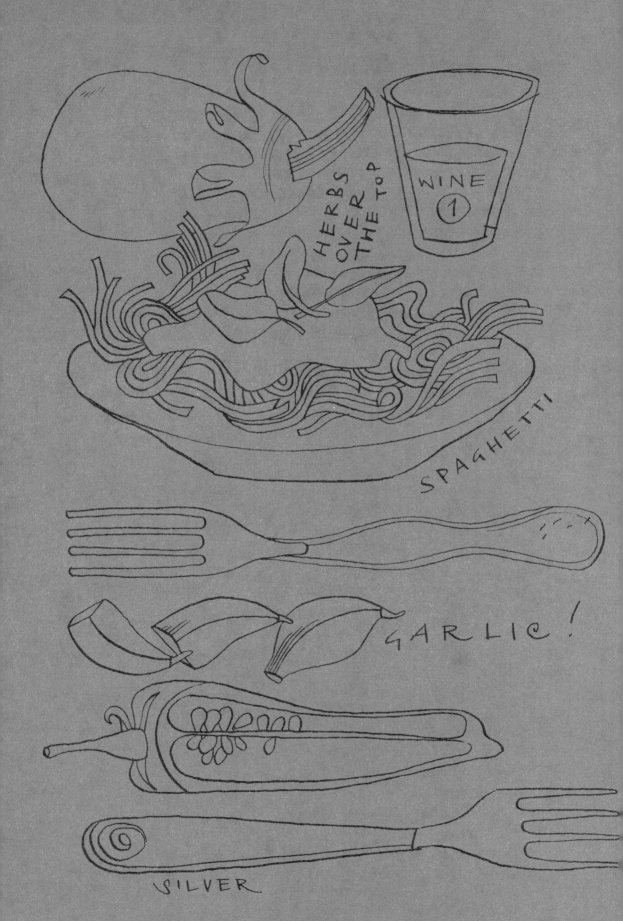

HERBS OVER THE TOP

WINE ①

SPAGHETTI

GARLIC!

SILVER

FIRST
COURSES →

FIRST COURSES

The traditional Italian classification of first courses is minestre in brodo, literally soups in broth, and minestre asciutte, literally dry soups. Besides various kinds of soups, the first group also includes mashes and purées. The second group includes fresh and dried pasta, rice, risottos, polenta and gnocchi. This method of classification can lead to confusion among those readers who are approaching the world of Italian cuisine for the first time, particularly in the case of pasta, which is defined as a 'dry soup'. It therefore seemed simpler and clearer to call this chapter First Courses and divide it into two parts: In Broth and Dry. For those new to Italian cooking, it should also be pointed out that first and second courses are considered of equal importance and size, unlike their British namesakes.

IN BROTH

Soup was once common on Italian dinner tables, but then the habit of serving soup almost died out. Soup tureens were left forgotten in sideboards or occasionally exhibited as original centrepieces or collectors' items. The rediscovery of some ancient cereals, such as farro, together with a trend towards a vegetarian diet and the return of soups to the menus of some young restaurateurs who looked to the past for inspiration, has brought the whole soup family back into fashion. The recipes in this section include classic recipes from both Italy and elsewhere as well as traditional and contemporary dishes. The recipes are divided according to type: broths, cream soups, various soups, minestrones and thick soups.

DRY

Dry first courses are always present on Italian dinner tables. Pasta is definitely the most popular dish in Italy, but the word 'pasta' does nothing to describe the number of different varieties that this family contains. Basic fresh pasta is made with eggs and plain flour (preferably Italian type 00). Lasagna is probably the best known; comprising thin sheets of pasta dough, lasagne can be layered within a traditional oven-baked dish or, when they are rolled up, instantly transformed into cannelloni. Fresh pasta can also be cut

into thinner strips: tagliatelle, delicate ribbons which are excellent accompaniments to rich sauces; smaller tagliolini e tagliatelline, suitable for more delicate sauces; and fettucine, larger and thicker shapes, perfect with meat, sausage, mushroom and tomato sauces. In addition to fresh pasta with eggs, others are made with different types of flour. Orecchiette, made with a mixture of flour and semolina, are the most typical pasta shapes from Puglia. Made by hand, orecchiette are shaped like small shells, with a rough outer surface created by the light press of the maker's thumb. Orecchiette are the ideal accompaniment to vegetable sauces. Next come the many different types of filled pasta - ravioli, tortelli, tortellini and tortelloni, each with a different shape and size. These can be stuffed with meat, fish, vegetables or cheese and are perfect either with basic sauces such as butter and sage or more complicated ones, chosen specifically to accompany the flavour of their stuffing. Dried pasta is simpler in its composition: durum wheat flour and water are combined to create the numerous shapes that accompany all different kinds of sauces. First of all comes spaghetti; loved throughout the world, these long strings are the ideal accompaniment for tomato, vegetable, fish and clam sauces. Bucatini, the pasta chosen for an authentic pasta all'amatriciana, are long tubes. Linguine, which are flat, 3 mm wide and around 26 cm long, are common in Liguria, and bavette and trenette are similar to linguine. All three are perfect served with herbs or fish sauce. Among the different types of short pasta, macaroni and penne are probably the most popular. The term 'macaroni' includes a lot of different varieties, such as rigatoni and tortiglioni, but all macaroni and penne are cylindrical and can either be smooth (lisce) or have a coarser 'striped' (rigate) texture. (Pasta shapes such as these, which have a central channel, allow the sauce to be retained.) Farfalle, small rectangles pinched in the centre to form the shape of a butterfly, are ideal for tomato, pea, light and cream sauces, while fusilli, with their twisted corkscrew shape, are good for tasty Mediterranean sauces based on vegetables. The recipes here have been selected mainly for their short preparation times and lightness, but the great and more substantial traditional dishes have not been overlooked. This collection of dry first courses is divided into gnocchi, fresh pasta, dried pasta, polenta, rice, rice salads, risottos and timbales.

BROTHS

FIRST COURSES IN BROTHS

The way in which plain water is transformed from a taste-less, colourless and odourless liquid into broth is almost magical. It becomes fine, fragrant and tasty, thanks to the qualities given to it by meat, salt, herbs and spices. Broths may be made from meat (dark, thick or clear), fish and vegetables (single or mixed). There are some basic rules about the stocks used for broths.

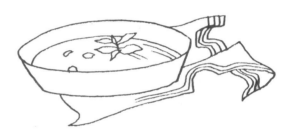

QUANTITIES AND COOKING TIMES

THE SAUCEPAN

Pans should be made of aluminium or stainless steel to prevent them from tainting the flavour of the broth.

WATER

4 litres per 1 kg/7 pints per 2¼ lb beef or veal; 3.5 litres per 1.5 kg/6 pints per 3¼ lb chicken.

SALT

¼ teaspoon per 1 litre/1¾ pints water. Otherwise you risk an unpleasantly salty stock; taste and adjust the seasoning at the end of cooking.

HERBS AND VEGETABLES

The water must be brought to the boil gradually and the vegetables and herbs should be added in the right proportions. For every 1 kg/2¼ lb meat: 100 g/3½ oz carrots, 100 g/3½ oz onions, 100 g/3½ oz leeks and 1 celery stick. Parsley is optional and some people like to stick a clove into the onion to add a slight hint of spice.

DARK

This is the classic meat stock. The most suitable cuts of beef are the shoulder and rump. For veal stock, on the other hand, use the neck and the shank. A good butcher will advise you.

CONCENTRATED STOCK OR CONSOMMÉ

The original version dates back to a long and complicated nineteenth-century recipe. Today a more modern recipe ensures excellent results.

CLEAR OR DELICATE

Chicken stock. Some people strengthen the flavour by adding a piece of beef to the pan, but this section includes the classic recipe (see page 209) without beef. Ideal for tortellini.

FISH

Fish stock has a delicate flavour. Recommended fish are cod and skate. Cod stock is delicious for rice and parsley soup. An excellent fatless stock may be made from the shells of seafood, including prawns, plus the heads and tails of various white fish. It is suitable for sauces and soups.

VEGETABLE

Meat is completely replaced by more or less the same quantity of various types of vegetables. The most suitable are carrots, turnips (they give a lot of flavour), onions, leeks and cherry tomatoes. As far as potatoes are concerned, add no more than two. Vegetable stock is excellent for a large number of thin soups and is also pleasant as a simple drink.

STOCK AND BOUILLON CUBES AND POWDERS

These can be used to make almost any type of stock (beef, chicken, vegetable or fish) in a few minutes. They are useful time-savers, but you should check the salt content. Some brands have a much better flavour than others.

RICOTTA DUMPLINGS IN BROTH

BOMBOLINE DI RICOTTA IN BRODO

Serves 4

250 g/9 oz ricotta cheese

1 egg

65 g/2¹/₂ oz plain flour, plus extra for coating

pinch of freshly grated nutmeg

1 litre/1³/₄ pints Meat Stock (see page 208)

3 tablespoons olive oil

salt and pepper

Parmesan cheese, freshly grated

Beat the ricotta with a wooden spoon until smooth, then stir in the egg, flour and nutmeg and season with salt and pepper. Shape the mixture into small dumplings the size of hazelnuts. Coat the dumplings lightly in flour. Meanwhile, bring the stock to the boil over a low heat. Heat the oil in a frying pan, add the dumplings and cook until golden brown all over. Drain on kitchen paper. Put the dumplings into a soup tureen and ladle in the stock. Serve with Parmesan.

WATERCRESS BROTH

BRODO AL CRESCIONE

Serves 4

1 bunch of watercress

1 litre /1³/₄ pints Chicken Stock (see page 209)

1 celery stick, chopped

1 fresh flat-leaf parsley sprig, chopped

salt and pepper

toast, to serve

Set 12 watercress leaves aside and finely chop the remainder. Gradually bring the stock to the boil and add the watercress, celery and parsley. Cook over a low heat, stirring constantly, for a few minutes. Strain the broth and season with salt and pepper to taste. Place the reserved watercress leaves on the base of bowls or soup plates and ladle the broth over them. Serve with slices of toast.

SPICED WINE BROTH

BRODO AL VINO AROMATIZZATO

Serves 4

1 litre/1³/₄ pints Meat Stock (see page 208)

2 cloves

200 ml/7 fl oz dry white wine

3 egg yolks

pinch of ground cinnamon

pinch of freshly grated nutmeg

Place the pan of stock over a low heat, add the cloves and bring to the boil. Heat the wine in another pan. Whisk the egg yolks in a soup tureen, then pour in the stock and warm wine and stir in the cinnamon and nutmeg. Serve immediately.

SMALL CHEESE GNOCCHI IN CLEAR BROTH

BRODO CON GNOCCHETTI DI FORMAGGIO

Serves 4

40 g/1¹/₂ oz butter, softened

1 egg, separated

1¹/₂ tablespoons Parmesan cheese, freshly grated, plus extra for serving

1 tablespoon plain flour

1.5 litres/2¹/₂ pints Meat or Chicken Stock (see pages 208–209)

salt

Cream the butter in a bowl, then stir in the egg yolk, Parmesan and flour. Mix well. Beat the egg white in another bowl, then add to the mixture with a pinch of salt. Bring the stock to the boil. Add the cheese mixture, 1 teaspoon at a time. When the gnocchi float to the surface, they are cooked. Ladle into a soup tureen and serve with plenty of Parmesan.

BREAD GNOCCHI IN BROTH

For the stock, place all the vegetables in a saucepan, pour in 1.5 litres/2½ pints water, season with salt and bring to the boil. Lower the heat and simmer for 45 minutes. Meanwhile, prepare the gnocchi. Mix together the breadcrumbs, Parmesan, eggs and half the chive in a bowl and season with salt and pepper. The mixture should be medium-thick so, if necessary, add more breadcrumbs. Shape the mixture into 1-cm/½-inch rolls. Cut into short lengths and flatten the middles slightly with your finger. Strain the stock into a clean pan and return to the heat. (The vegetables can be eaten cold as a salad or baked au gratin in the oven.) Add the gnocchi to the stock. When they float to the surface they are ready. Ladle into a soup tureen, sprinkle with the remaining chive and serve with Parmesan.

BRODO CON GNOCCHETTI DI PANE

Serves 4

For the stock

1 leek, trimmed and chopped

1 onion, chopped

2 celery sticks, chopped

2 carrots, chopped

salt

For the gnocchi

120 g/4 oz breadcrumbs

50 g/2 oz Parmesan cheese, freshly grated, plus extra for serving

2 eggs • 1 small fresh chive, chopped

salt and pepper

BROTH À LA ROYALE

This is a basic recipe for various different royales – soup garnishes – each named according to the type of cream of vegetable soup chosen (pea, asparagus, carrot, etc.). Beat the eggs with salt and pepper to taste. Add 200 ml/7 fl oz of the stock, a little at a time, followed by the cream of vegetable soup chosen. Grease a heatproof dish or several small moulds with plenty of butter. Pour in the mixture, place in a large shallow pan, pour in boiling water to come about halfway up the sides and cook over a low heat for 12–15 minutes until the mixture sets, making sure the water barely simmers. Remove from the heat, leave to cool, then turn out the royale and cut into squares. Heat the remaining stock, then ladle into a soup tureen and garnish with the royales.

BRODO CON ROYALE

Serves 4

2 eggs

1 litre/1¾ pints Vegetable Stock (see page 209)

cream of vegetable soup (for recipes, see pages 212–224)

butter, for greasing

salt and pepper

HOME–MADE BROTH À LA ROYALE

Beat the eggs, then beat in the flour and Parmesan and season with salt and a little pepper. Stir in just enough milk to give the texture of cream. Grease several small moulds with butter and pour in the mixture. Place in a large shallow pan, pour in boiling water to come about halfway up the sides and cook for 12–15 minutes until the mixture sets, making sure the water barely simmers. Remove from the heat, leave to cool, then turn out and cut into cubes. Heat the remaining stock in a saucepan, then ladle into a soup tureen and add the royales.

BRODO CON ROYALE ALLA CASALINGA

Serves 4

4 eggs

1 tablespoon plain flour

2 tablespoons Parmesan cheese, freshly grated

3–5 tablespoons milk

butter, for greasing

1 litre/1¾ pints Vegetable Stock (see page 209)

salt and pepper

BROTH WITH CRÊPE STRIPS

BRODO CON TAGLIOLINI DI CRÊPES

Serves 4

120 g/4 oz plain flour
1 egg
1 egg yolk
200 ml/7 fl oz milk
50 g/2 oz butter
1 litre /1³/₄ pints Chicken Stock (see opposite)
salt

Combine the flour, egg and egg yolk in a bowl and gradually stir in the milk – the batter should be quite thin. Melt 25 g/1 oz of the butter, stir into the batter with a pinch of salt and set aside for 1 hour. Heat a knob of the butter in a small frying pan and pour in 1 tablespoon of the batter. Cook for 4–5 minutes until the underside is browned, then flip over and cook for a further 2 minutes until the second side is browned. Slide out on to a plate and continue making crêpes in the same way, adding more butter as required, until the batter is used up. Meanwhile, heat the stock in a large saucepan. Cut the crêpes into thin strips, divide among individual soup bowls and ladle the hot stock over them.

MEAT STOCK

BRODO DI CARNE

Serves 4

800 g /1³/₄ lb lean beef, cut into cubes
600 g /1 lb 5 oz veal, cut into cubes
1 onion, coarsely chopped
50 g/2 oz carrots, coarsely chopped
100 g/3¹/₂ oz leeks, trimmed and coarsely chopped
1 celery stick, coarsely chopped
salt

Place the meat in a large saucepan, add cold water to cover and bring to the boil, bearing in mind that slow cooking and gentle simmering are essential for successful stock. Skim off any scum that rises to the surface and add the onion, carrots, leeks and celery and season with salt. Lower the heat and simmer for about 3¹/₂ hours. Remove from the heat, strain into a bowl, leave to cool, then chill in the refrigerator. When the fat has solidified on the surface carefully remove and discard. The stock may be used for soups, risottos and making gravy.

FISH STOCK (1)

BRODO DI PESCE (1)

Serves 4–6

1 fresh flat-leaf parsley sprig
1 fresh thyme sprig
1 onion, chopped
1 carrot, sliced
1 celery stick, sliced
1 tablespoon black peppercorns, lightly crushed
1 kg/ 2¹/₄ lb white fish or white fish bones and heads, gills removed
salt

Pour 2 litres/3 pints water into a large saucepan, add the herbs, onion, carrot, celery and peppercorns and season with salt. Gradually bring to the boil, then lower the heat and simmer for 30 minutes. Remove from the heat, leave to cool, then add the fish (the water should just cover). Return to the heat, bring just to the boil, then lower the heat and simmer for 20 minutes. Remove from the heat and leave the fish to cool in the stock for a stronger flavour. Strain the stock and use for a rice soup or Seafood Risotto (see page 328). If using only bones and heads, add to the pan with the herbs and vegetables and simmer for 30 minutes. Leave to cool slightly, then strain.

FISH STOCK (2)

Pour 2 litres/3½ pints water into a saucepan and add the vegetables, parsley and wine. Season with salt and pepper and bring just to the boil. Lower the heat and simmer for 30 minutes. Add the skate and simmer for 20 minutes. Remove the fish and strain the stock into a bowl, pressing down well on the vegetables with a spoon. If a very clear stock is required, dampen and squeeze out a square of muslin and use as a filter in the strainer.

BRODO DI PESCE (2)

Serves 4–6

1 onion

1 cherry tomato

1 celery stick

fresh flat-leaf parsley

5 tablespoons dry white wine

1 kg/2¼ lb skate wings

salt and pepper

CHICKEN STOCK

It is best to use a boiling fowl, if you can find one, as it produces a more delicate flavour than a chicken and is less likely to be intensively raised. Place the bird and vegetables in a large saucepan and add a pinch of salt and water to cover. Bring to the boil over a medium-high heat, then lower the heat and simmer for at least 2 hours, occasionally skimming off any scum that rises to the surface. Strain through a wire mesh strainer into a bowl, leave to cool, then chill in the refrigerator. When the fat has solidified on the surface, remove and discard it. Chicken stock may be served as a broth with small gnocchi, julienne vegetables or small omelettes cut into thin strips.

BRODO DI POLLO

Serves 4–6

1 chicken or boiling fowl, skinned and trimmed of visible fat

1 onion

1 carrot

1 celery stick

salt

VEGETABLE STOCK

Place all the vegetables in a large saucepan, pour in 1.5 litres/2½ pints water, add a pinch of salt and bring to the boil. Lower the heat and simmer gently for about 20 minutes. Remove from the heat and leave to cool slightly, then strain into a bowl pressing down well on the vegetables with a spoon.

BRODO DI VERDURE

Serves 4–6

2 potatoes, coarsely chopped

2 onions, coarsely chopped

2 leeks, trimmed and coarsely chopped

2 carrots, coarsely chopped

2 turnips, coarsely chopped

1 celery stick, coarsely chopped

3 cherry tomatoes, coarsely chopped

salt

AROMATIC COLD BROTH

BRODO FREDDO AROMATICO

Serves 4

750 ml/1¼ pints Meat Stock (see page 208)

4 fresh basil leaves, chopped

1 fresh chervil sprig, chopped

1 fresh flat-leaf parsley sprig, chopped

4 mint leaves, chopped

2 teaspoons chopped fresh thyme

salt

Prepare a fairly thick meat stock, leave to cool, then strain through a fine strainer into a saucepan to remove the fat. Bring to the boil over a low heat. Place all the herbs in a soup tureen, remove the stock from the heat and ladle it over them. Season lightly with salt and leave to infuse for at least 2 hours, then serve.

CONSOMMÉ

CONSOMMÉ

Serves 4

300 g/11 oz minced beef

1 leek, trimmed and chopped

1 carrot, chopped

1 celery stick, chopped

2 egg whites

2.5 litres/4¼ pints Meat Stock (see page 208)

4 tablespoons dry sherry (optional)

Put the beef, vegetables and egg whites into a saucepan. Pour in the stock and mix well. Gradually bring to the boil, stirring constantly. Lower the heat and simmer for about 1 hour. Strain through a muslin-lined strainer into a bowl, then ladle into soup bowls. If you want to add extra fragrance, stir 1 tablespoon dry sherry into each bowl.

CONCENTRATED FISH STOCK

FUMETTO DI PESCE

2 tablespoons olive oil or 25 g/1 oz butter

1 carrot, chopped

1 celery stick, chopped

1 small onion, chopped

6 black peppercorns, lightly crushed

1 kg/2¼ lb white fish heads, gills removed, and bones

salt

Heat the oil or butter in a saucepan, add the vegetables and cook over a low heat, stirring occasionally, for 5 minutes. Season with salt and add the peppercorns. Pour in 1 litre/1¾ pints warm water, add the fish bones and heads, cover and bring to the boil. Skim off any scum that rises to the surface. Lower the heat and simmer for about 45 minutes until the liquid has reduced by half. Remove from the heat, leave to cool slightly, then strain. Concentrated fish stock is used to enhance the taste of poached fish, seafood risottos and fish sauces and soups.

ASPIC

Put the bones, calf's foot, minced beef, leek, carrots, celery and egg whites into a large saucepan. Pour in the stock and bring to the boil, stirring occasionally and skimming off any scum that rises to the surface. Lower the heat and simmer for about 2 hours, then season with salt to taste. Strain into a bowl and leave to cool. If the mixture is not completely translucent, return to the heat, add a beaten egg white and boil for 5 minutes. Strain again and leave to cool. Chill in the refrigerator. Aspic does not have to set completely: a jelly-like consistency is adequate. Just before serving, place in appropriate bowls. Although it has fallen out of fashion, aspic makes an elegant start to a meal.

GELATINA

Makes 1 litre/1³/₄ pints of aspic

500 g/1 lb 2 oz beef bones

250 g/9 oz veal shin or knuckle bones

1 calf's foot

300 g/11 oz minced beef

1 leek, trimmed and chopped

2 carrots, chopped

1 celery stick, chopped

2 egg whites, lightly beaten

2.5 litres/4¹/₄ pints Meat Stock (see page 208)

salt

CREAM SOUPS

Cream soups are light, delicate and easy to prepare. They are always delightful served to mark the start of an elegant and sophisticated dinner. They may be made from vegetables, pulses or puréed meat. To give them the right consistency, just add béchamel sauce or a few tablespoonfuls of mashed potato. To make them more velvety, add a little cream, perhaps mixed with one or two egg yolks. For a little more flavour, try adding a few curls of extremely fresh butter just before serving. Cream soups are classically served with small triangles of bread fried in butter. If they are served in individual soup plates, the surface may be decorated with a swirl of whipped cream (particularly good with Cream of Lettuce Soup), a hard-boiled quail's egg (with Cream of Tomato Soup) or balls of carrot fried in butter (with Cream of Bean Soup). Nowadays, the food processor has made their preparation very quick and easy. Cream soups have one great advantage above all – they may be prepared the day before and warmed up just before serving.

CREAM OF PORCINI SOUP

Put the chicken, carrot, celery and onion in a large saucepan, pour in 2 litres/3½ pints water, add a pinch of salt and bring to the boil. Lower the heat and simmer for 40 minutes until the chicken is tender. Meanwhile, melt half the butter in a frying pan, add the porcini and cook, stirring frequently, for about 7 minutes. Sprinkle with the brandy and cook until it has evaporated. Season with salt and pepper and remove from the heat. Lift the chicken out of the pan and strain the stock. Cut off the breast fillets, slice and set aside. Remove the remaining meat from the bones and place in a food processor with a ladleful of the stock and two-thirds of the porcini. Process to a purée. Melt the remaining butter in a saucepan, add the leeks and cook over a low heat, stirring occasionally, for 5 minutes. Stir in the flour and gradually stir in the stock. Bring to the boil, stirring constantly, then lower the heat and simmer for 10 minutes. Stir in the purée and cook for a further 5 minutes, then pour in the cream. Pour into a soup tureen and garnish with the sliced breast fillets and remaining porcini.

CREMA AI PORCINI

Serves 4

½ chicken
1 carrot
1 celery stick
1 onion
50 g/2 oz butter
350 g/12 oz porcini, sliced
50 ml/2 fl oz brandy
2 leeks, trimmed and finely chopped
25 g/1 oz plain flour
100 ml /3½ fl oz double cream
salt and pepper

CREAM OF JERUSALEM ARTICHOKE SOUP

Heat the olive oil in a saucepan, add the onion and cook over a low heat, stirring occasionally, for 5 minutes until softened. Add the Jerusalem artichokes and cook for 3–4 minutes, then pour in the stock and bring to the boil. Cover and cook over a low heat for 30 minutes. Transfer the mixture to a food processor and process until smooth. Season with salt to taste. Stir in the cream and reheat if necessary. Pour into a soup tureen, sprinkle with the parsley and serve.

CREMA AI TOPINAMBUR

Serves 4

2 tablespoons olive oil
1 onion, thinly sliced
400 g/14 oz Jerusalem artichokes, chopped
³/₄ quantity Meat Stock (see page 208)
200 ml/7 fl oz double cream
1 fresh flat-leaf parsley sprig, chopped
salt

CREAM OF TRUFFLE SOUP

CREMA AL TARTUFO

Serves 4

3 tablespoons olive oil

2 leeks, trimmed and chopped

500 g/1 lb 2 oz potatoes, sliced

³/₄ quantity Vegetable Stock (see page 209)

300 ml/¹/₂ pint milk

120 ml/4 fl oz double cream

12 bread slices, crusts removed

100 g/3 ¹/₂ oz fontina cheese, sliced

salt

1 black truffle, shaved, to garnish

Heat the oil in a saucepan, add the leeks and cook over a low heat, stirring occasionally, for 5 minutes until softened. Add the potatoes and cook for a further 5 minutes until lightly browned, then pour in the stock and milk. Season with salt, cover and cook over a medium heat for 45 minutes. Transfer to a food processor and process to a purée, add the cream and process again. Return to the pan and keep warm over a very low heat. Toast the bread on one side under a preheated grill, then turn over, top with the slices of fontina and grill until the cheese melts. Taste the soup and adjust the seasoning if necessary. If it requires thickening, place it on the heat for a little longer. Ladle into individual soup plates and garnish with the truffle. Serve with the fontina toast.

CREAM OF ASPARAGUS SOUP

CREMA DI ASPARAGI

Serves 4

600 g/1 lb 5 oz green asparagus, spears trimmed

50 g/2 oz butter

1 onion, thinly sliced

2 tablespoons plain flour

100 ml/3¹/₂ fl oz white wine

1 litre/1³/₄ pints Vegetable Stock (see page 209)

2–3 tablespoons double cream

salt and pepper

Cut off and reserve the asparagus tips and chop the stems. Melt the butter in a saucepan, add the onion and cook over a low heat, stirring occasionally, for 5 minutes until softened. Add the asparagus stems and cook for a few minutes, then sprinkle with the flour, stir well and pour in the wine and stock. Season with salt and pepper and cook over a low heat, stirring frequently, for 30 minutes. Transfer to a food processor and process to a purée. Bring 350 ml/12 fl oz water to the boil in a pan and parboil the asparagus tips for 2 minutes. Pour the purée into a clean saucepan and reheat. Drain the asparagus tips and add to the soup with the cream. Serve in individual soup plates.

CREAM OF ARTICHOKE SOUP

CREMA DI CARCIOFI

Serves 4

2 tablespoons lemon juice, strained

6 globe artichokes

65 g/2¹/₂ oz butter

1 onion, thinly sliced

1 celery stick, chopped

200 g/7 oz potatoes, cut into wedges

1.5 litres/2¹/₂ pints Chicken Stock (see page 209)

1 egg yolk

salt and pepper

Parmesan cheese, freshly grated, to serve

Half-fill a bowl with water and stir in the lemon juice. Working on one artichoke at a time, break off the stems, cut off all the leaves and remove the chokes. Drop the hearts into the acidulated water. Melt 45 g/1¹/₂ oz of the butter in a saucepan, add the onion and celery and cook over a low heat, stirring occasionally, for 5 minutes until softened. Drain the artichoke hearts, add to the pan with the potatoes and cook for 5 minutes. Pour in the stock, season with salt and pepper to taste, cover and simmer for about 40 minutes. Transfer to a food processor and process to a purée. Pour into a clean pan, taste and adjust the seasoning if necessary and reheat. Beat the egg yolk with the remaining butter. Remove the soup from the heat and stir in the egg yolk mixture to thicken. Serve in individual soup plates with plenty of Parmesan.

CREAM OF CARROT SOUP

Put the carrots and garlic in a saucepan, pour in water to cover and add a pinch of salt. Bring to the boil over a medium heat and cook until almost all the liquid is absorbed. Transfer to a food processor and process to a purée. Pour the mixture back into the saucepan. Warm the milk in another saucepan, then stir it into the carrot purée with the stock and mix well. Cook for 10 minutes until fairly thick. Taste and adjust the seasoning. Ladle the soup into individual flameproof soup plates. Sprinkle with the fontina, nutmeg and a pinch of pepper. Put the plates under a preheated grill to melt the cheese, then serve.

CREMA DI CAROTE

Serves 4

800 g/1³/₄ lb carrots, chopped

1 garlic clove

500 ml/18 fl oz milk

400 ml/14 fl oz Meat Stock (see page 208)

40 g/1¹/₂ oz fontina cheese, grated

pinch of freshly grated nutmeg

salt and pepper

CREAM OF CARROT AND MUSSEL SOUP

Dice two carrots and slice the remainder. Melt 25 g/1 oz of the butter in a saucepan, add the diced carrots, a pinch of salt and a pinch of sugar and cook over a low heat, stirring occasionally, for 5 minutes. Remove from the heat and set aside. Melt the remaining butter in another pan, add the sliced carrots, a pinch of salt and a pinch of sugar and cook over a low heat, stirring occasionally, for 5 minutes. Pour in the stock and simmer for about 20 minutes. Transfer to a food processor and process to a purée. Discard any mussels with broken shells or that do not shut immediately when sharply tapped. Heat the mussels in a frying pan with the wine and garlic for 5 minutes until they open. Discard any that remain closed. Remove the mussels from their shells. Reheat the carrot purée, then pour into a soup tureen and add the diced carrots and the mussels. Sprinkle with the parsley and serve immediately.

CREMA DI CAROTE CON LE COZZE

Serves 4

675 g/1¹/₂ lb carrots

65 g/2¹/₂ oz butter

2 pinches of sugar

1 litre/1³/₄ pints Chicken Stock (see page 209)

32 mussels, scrubbed and beards removed

200 ml/7 fl oz white wine

¹/₂ garlic clove

1 tablespoon chopped fresh flat-leaf parsley

salt

CREAM OF CAULIFLOWER SOUP WITH MUSSELS

Melt the butter in a saucepan, add the shallot and cook over a low heat, stirring occasionally, for 5 minutes. Add the parsley and lemon juice. Discard any mussels with broken shells or that do not shut immediately when sharply tapped. Add the mussels to the pan and cook for about 5 minutes until the shells open. Strain the mussels, reserving the cooking liquid. Discard any mussels that remain closed and remove the rest from their shells. Strain the cooking liquid into a saucepan, add 1 litre/1³/₄ pints water and bring to the boil. Add the cauliflower florets and cook for 15 minutes. Transfer the mixture to a food processor and process to a purée. Pour into a clean pan, add the cream and mussels and season with salt and pepper. Reheat for 5 minutes, pour into a soup tureen and serve with croûtons.

CREMA DI CAVOLFIORE CON LE COZZE

Serves 4

25 g/1 oz butter

1 shallot, thinly sliced

2 tablespoons chopped fresh flat-leaf parsley

juice of 1 lemon, strained

1 kg/2¹/₄ lb mussels, scrubbed and beards removed

1 small cauliflower, cut into florets

100 ml/3¹/₂ fl oz double cream

salt and pepper

croûtons, to serve

CREAM OF CHICKPEAS AU GRATIN

Place the chickpeas in a saucepan with 1.5 litres/2¹/₂ pints cold water and the onion. Bring to the boil, cover and cook over a medium heat for 2 hours. Transfer the mixture to a food processor and process to a purée. Heat the oil in a pan, add the garlic and rosemary and cook for a few minutes, then season with salt and pepper. Remove and discard the garlic and rosemary and pour the flavoured oil on to the chickpea purée. Ladle into individual flameproof soup plates, place the toast on top, sprinkle with the fontina and melt the cheese under a preheated grill.

CREMA DI CECI AL GRATIN

Serves 4

200 g/7 oz chickpeas, soaked overnight in cold water to cover and drained

1 onion, sliced

2 tablespoons olive oil

1 garlic clove

1 fresh rosemary sprig

4 bread slices, toasted

50 g/2 oz fontina cheese, grated

salt and pepper

CREAM OF BEAN SOUP

Put the beans, potatoes, onion and carrot into a saucepan, add 1.5 litres/2¹/₂ pints water, bring to the boil and simmer for 20 minutes. Transfer to a food processor and process to a purée. Season with salt and pepper and pour into a saucepan. Add the milk, butter, basil and Parmesan and bring back to the boil for 1 minute. Pour into a soup tureen and serve with croûtons.

CREMA DI FAVE

Serves 4

500 g/1 lb 2 oz shelled broad beans

3 potatoes, sliced

1 onion, sliced

1 carrot, sliced

3 tablespoons milk

25 g/1 oz butter

1 tablespoon chopped fresh basil

1 tablespoon Parmesan cheese, freshly grated

salt and pepper

croûtons, to serve

217

CREAM OF FENNEL SOUP WITH SMOKED SALMON

CREMA DI FINOCCHI
AL SALMONE AFFUMICATO

Serves 4

25 g/1 oz butter
3 fennel bulbs, sliced
1 tablespoon double cream
80 g/3 oz smoked salmon, chopped
pinch of dill
salt and pepper

Melt the butter in a saucepan, add the fennel and 5 tablespoons water and cook over a low heat for about 20 minutes. Stir in another 5 tablespoons water, transfer the mixture to a food processor and process to a purée. Pour into a soup tureen, stir in the cream and season with salt and pepper to taste. Add the salmon and dill and serve.

CREAM OF PRAWN AND BEAN SOUP

CREMA DI GAMBERETTI E FAGIOLI

Serves 4

200 g/7 oz fresh cannellini beans
80 g/3 oz butter
1 shallot, chopped
200 g/7 oz raw prawns, peeled and deveined
100 ml/3½ fl oz dry white wine
1 litre/1¾ pints Vegetable Stock (see page 209)
50 g/2 oz plain flour
5 tablespoons double cream
1 fresh thyme sprig, leaves only
salt and pepper

Cook the beans in boiling water until tender, then drain and pass through a food mill. Melt 25 g/1 oz of the butter in a pan, add the shallot and cook over a low heat, stirring occasionally, for 5 minutes. Add the prawns and cook for 2 minutes, then add the wine and cook until it has evaporated. Season with salt and pepper, transfer to a food processor and process to a purée. Bring the stock to a boil in a saucepan. Melt the remaining butter in another pan and stir in the flour. Pour in the bean purée, gradually stir in the boiling stock and cook over a low heat for about 15 minutes. Add the cream and thyme to the prawn purée, then pour into the bean mixture. Pour into a soup tureen and serve.

CREAM OF PRAWN AND TOMATO SOUP

CREMA DI GAMBERI E POMODORI

Serves 4

1 litre/1¾ pints Vegetable Stock (see page 209)
1 kg/2¼ lb large prawns
40 g/1½ oz butter
40 g/1½ oz plain flour
5 ripe tomatoes, peeled, seeded and chopped
2 teaspoons curry powder
salt

Bring the stock to the boil in a saucepan, add the prawns and cook for 3 minutes. Drain, reserving the stock. Peel and devein the prawns, set 10 aside for the garnish and finely chop the remainder. Strain the stock. Melt the butter in a pan, stir in the flour and cook, stirring constantly, for 2–4 minutes, then gradually stir in the stock. Bring to the boil, stirring constantly, lower the heat and simmer, stirring constantly, for 10 minutes. Add the chopped prawns. Process the tomatoes in a food processor to a purée, add the curry powder, process briefly again and add to the soup. Bring to the boil for a few minutes and season with salt to taste. Pour into a soup tureen, garnish with the reserved prawns and serve.

CREAM OF CHICORY SOUP

Bring the stock to the boil in a saucepan. Melt 25 g/1 oz of the butter in another pan, add the peas, cover and cook over a low heat for 5 minutes. Season with salt, pour in the stock and cook for about 20 minutes. Meanwhile, melt the remaining butter in another saucepan, stir in the flour and gradually stir in the milk. Cook, stirring constantly, until thickened, then season with salt and pepper. Add the chicory, cover and cook over a low heat for 15 minutes. Transfer to a food processor and process to a purée. Pour into a soup tureen and sprinkle with the parsley. Serve with Parmesan.

CREMA DI INDIVIA BELGA

Serves 4

500 ml/18 fl oz Meat Stock (see page 208)

80 g/3 oz butter

100 g/3$^1/_2$ oz shelled peas

50 g/2 oz plain flour

500 ml/18 fl oz milk

500 g/1 lb 2 oz chicory, chopped

1 tablespoon chopped fresh flat-leaf parsley

salt and pepper

Parmesan cheese, freshly grated, to serve

CREAM OF LETTUCE SOUP

Bring the milk and stock to the boil, season with salt, add the lettuces and cook for 5 minutes. Transfer to a food processor and process to a purée, then pour into a clean pan. Melt the butter in another pan, stir in the flour and cook, stirring constantly, for 3–5 minutes, then stir into the purée and season with salt and pepper to taste. Simmer for 15 minutes. Lightly beat the egg yolk with the Parmesan in a soup tureen, then gradually ladle in the soup, stirring constantly.

CREMA DI LATTUGA

Serves 4

500 ml/18 fl oz milk

500 ml/18 fl oz Meat Stock (see page 208)

3 lettuces, coarsely shredded

25 g/1 oz butter

2 tablespoons plain flour

1 egg yolk

1 tablespoon Parmesan cheese, freshly grated

salt and pepper

CREAM OF DRIED PULSES SOUP

Put the pulses in a saucepan with the carrot, celery, onion and potatoes, add water to cover and bring to the boil. Lower the heat and simmer until tender. Transfer to a food processor and process to a purée. Add the cream and process briefly again, then season with salt and pepper to taste. Pour into a soup tureen and serve with the grated Parmesan.

CREMA DI LEGUMI

Serves 4

300 g/11 oz mixed dried pulses, such as beans, lentils and peas, soaked overnight in cold water and drained

1 carrot, chopped

1 celery stick, chopped

1 onion, chopped

2 potatoes, sliced

2 tablespoons double cream

salt and pepper

Parmesan cheese, freshly grated to serve

CREAM OF POTATO SOUP

CREMA DI PATATE

Serves 4

1 litre/1¾ pints Vegetable Stock (see page 209)

50 g/2 oz butter

2 leeks, trimmed and chopped

600 g/1 lb 5 oz potatoes, diced

4 bread slices, crusts removed, diced

100 ml/3½ fl oz double cream

salt

croûtons, to serve

Bring the stock to the boil. Melt 25 g/1 oz of the butter in another pan, add the leeks and cook over a low heat, stirring occasionally, for 5 minutes until softened. Add the potatoes and cook for a few minutes, then pour in the stock, season with salt to taste and cook over a medium heat for about 20 minutes. Meanwhile, melt the remaining butter in a frying pan, add the bread cubes and cook, stirring frequently, until golden brown all over. Drain on kitchen paper. Transfer the potato mixture to a food processor and process to a purée. Return to the pan and bring back to the boil, then stir in the cream. Pour into a soup tureen and serve with the croûtons.

CREAM OF PEA AND POTATO SOUP

CREMA DI PISELLI E PATATE

Serves 4

2 tablespoons olive oil

600 g/1 lb 5 oz shelled peas

3 potatoes, diced

2 leeks, trimmed and chopped

2 tablespoons natural yogurt

6 fresh mint leaves

4 thin bread slices, crusts removed, toasted

juice of ½ lemon, strained

salt

Heat the oil in a saucepan, add the peas, potatoes and leeks and cook for 1 minute. Pour in 1 litre/1¾ pints water and cook for 20 minutes until the vegetables are tender. Reserve 1 tablespoon of the peas. Transfer the rest of the mixture to a food processor and process to a purée, then return to the pan and reheat. Add the reserved peas and season with salt to taste. Stir in the yogurt, add the mint leaves and pour into a soup tureen. Serve with the slices of toast sprinkled with the lemon juice.

CREAM OF TOMATO SOUP

CREMA DI POMODORO

Serves 4

25 g/1 oz butter

1 onion, thinly sliced

1 kg/2¼ lb plum tomatoes, peeled, seeded and sliced

2 potatoes, diced

100 ml/3½ fl oz double cream

salt and pepper

Parmesan cheese, freshly grated, to serve

croûtons, to serve

Melt the butter in a saucepan, add the onion and cook over a low heat, stirring occasionally, for 5 minutes until softened. Add the tomatoes and cook for 15 minutes. Season with salt and pepper to taste, pour in 750 ml/1¼ pints water, add the potatoes and bring to the boil. Lower the heat and simmer for 1 hour. Transfer to a food processor and process to a purée, then pour into a saucepan. Reheat, then stir in the cream. Pour into a soup tureen and serve with Parmesan and croûtons.

CREAM OF LEEK SOUP

Heat the oil in saucepan, add the leeks and cook over a low heat, stirring occasionally, for 5 minutes. Stir together the tomato purée and milk, add to the pan and heat gently. Transfer to a food processor and process to a purée. Melt the butter in a saucepan, stir in the flour, then gradually stir in the stock. Cook, stirring constantly, for 20 minutes, then add the leek purée and cook over a very low heat for a further 15 minutes. Season lightly with salt. Beat together the egg yolk, cream and Parmesan in a bowl, then whisk into the soup. Pour the soup into a soup tureen and serve.

CREMA DI PORRI

Serves 4

3 tablespoons olive oil

6 leeks, white parts only thinly sliced

1 tablespoon tomato purée

175 ml/6 fl oz milk

25 g/1 oz butter

40 g/1½ oz plain flour

1 litre/1¾ pints Vegetable Stock (see page 209)

1 egg yolk

2 tablespoons double cream

4 tablespoons Parmesan cheese, freshly grated

salt and pepper

CREAM OF CELERY SOUP

Bring the stock to the boil. Heat the butter and oil in another pan, add the onion and celery and cook, stirring occasionally, for 4 minutes. Pour in the stock, add the potatoes, cover and simmer for 40 minutes. Transfer to a food processor and process to a purée, then pour into a pan and reheat. Meanwhile, heat the milk to simmering point. Remove the soup from the heat, stir in the hot milk and season with salt. Pour into a soup tureen and serve with Parmesan.

CREMA DI SEDANO

Serves 4

1 litre/1¾ pints Meat Stock (see page 208)

25 g/1 oz butter

1 tablespoon olive oil

1 onion, chopped

400 g/14 oz celery, chopped

3 potatoes, diced

5 tablespoons milk

salt

Parmesan cheese, freshly grated, to serve

CREAM OF SPINACH SOUP

Bring the stock to the boil. Melt the butter in another pan, add the onions and cook over a low heat, stirring occasionally, for 5 minutes until softened. Stir in the flour and cook, stirring constantly, for 2 minutes, then gradually stir in the hot stock. Add the spinach and simmer for about 20 minutes. Stir in the lemon juice, then transfer to a food processor and process to a purée. Pour into a saucepan, season with salt and pepper to taste, stir in the cream and simmer briefly. Remove from the heat, cover and leave to stand for 5 minutes. Pour into individual soup plates and garnish with a swirl of cream sprinkled with a pinch of hot paprika.

CREMA DI SPINACI

Serves 4

1 litre/1¾ Meat Stock (see page 208)

40 g/1½ oz butter

2 onions, finely chopped

40 g/1½ oz plain flour

500 g/1 lb 2 oz frozen chopped spinach, thawed

3 tablespoons lemon juice, strained

2 tablespoons double cream, plus extra to garnish

salt and pepper

hot paprika, to garnish

CREAM OF PUMPKIN SOUP AU GRATIN

CREMA DI ZUCCA GRATINATA

Serves 4

1 litre/1³/₄ pints milk

3 potatoes, cut into wedges

500 g/1 lb 2 oz peeled, seeded and chopped pumpkin

1 fresh sage leaf

100 ml/3¹/₂ fl oz double cream

4 country-style bread slices

2 tablespoons Parmesan cheese, freshly grated

salt and pepper

Pour the milk and 350 ml/12 fl oz water into a saucepan and bring to the boil. Add the potatoes, pumpkin and sage, season with salt and pepper and bring back to the boil. Lower the heat to medium and cook for 40 minutes. Remove the sage leaf, transfer the mixture to a food processor and process to a purée. Pour into a saucepan, stir in the cream, season with salt and pepper to taste and reheat for a few minutes. Pour into individual flameproof soup plates. Top with a slice of bread, sprinkle with the Parmesan and melt the cheese under a preheated grill.

CREAM OF COURGETTE SOUP

CREMA DI ZUCCHINE

Serves 4

25 g/1 oz butter

800 g/1³/₄ lb courgettes, sliced

1 onion, thinly sliced

1 garlic clove, crushed

500 ml/18 fl oz Chicken Stock (see page 209)

500 ml/18 fl oz milk

1 fresh flat-leaf parsley sprig, chopped

salt and pepper

Melt the butter in a pan, add the courgettes, onion and garlic and cook over a low heat for 15 minutes. Pour in the stock and cook for a further 15 minutes. Transfer to a food processor and process to a purée, then pour into a pan. Heat the milk to simmering point in another pan, then stir it into the purée and season with salt and pepper to taste. Reheat to simmering point, pour into a soup tureen, sprinkle with the parsley and serve.

COLD CUCUMBER CREAM SOUP

CREMA FREDDA DI CETRIOLI

Serves 4

500 ml/18 fl oz Meat Stock (see page 208)

3 tablespoons olive oil

1 onion, chopped

250 g/9 oz cucumbers, chopped

250 g/9 oz potatoes, diced

25 g/1 oz lettuce, chopped

6 fresh mint leaves, plus extra to garnish

50 ml/2 fl oz double cream

salt and pepper

Bring the stock to the boil. Heat the oil in another pan, add the onion and cook over a low heat, stirring occasionally, for 5 minutes until softened. Add the cucumbers, potatoes, lettuce and mint and cook for a further 5 minutes. Season with salt and pepper to taste, pour in the hot stock and cook for about 15 minutes. Transfer to a food processor and process to a purée. Pour into a saucepan and reheat. Stir in the cream and heat for 5 minutes more. Remove from the heat, leave to cool to room temperature, then chill in the refrigerator for several hours. To serve, pour into a soup tureen and garnish with mint leaves.

VELVETY LENTIL SOUP

VELLUTATA DI LENTICCHIE

Serves 4

200 g/7 oz green lentils,
soaked in cold water for 3 hours and drained
100 g/3 ½ oz red lentils,
soaked in cold water for 3 hours and drained
2 baby onions, halved
1 garlic clove, crushed
1 fresh thyme sprig
200 ml/7 fl oz double cream
pinch of freshly grated nutmeg
salt and pepper

Put the lentils, onions, garlic and thyme in a saucepan, pour in 1 litre/1¾ pints water, bring to the boil, then cover and cook over a medium heat, stirring occasionally, for 30–40 minutes. Remove the thyme. Reserve 3 tablespoons of the lentils, then transfer the mixture to a food processor and process to a purée. Pour into a soup tureen and whisk in the cream. Season with the nutmeg and salt and pepper, stir in the reserved lentils and serve.

GREEN CREAM SOUP

CREMA VERDE

Serves 4

25 g/1 oz butter
2 leeks, white part only, thinly sliced
3 potatoes, diced
1 litre/1¾ pints Vegetable Stock (see page 209)
250 g/9 oz watercress, chopped
pinch of freshly grated nutmeg
150 ml/¼ pint double cream
salt and pepper
buttered toasted croûtons, to serve

Melt the butter in a saucepan, add the leeks and cook over a low heat, stirring occasionally, for 5 minutes until softened. Add the potatoes, pour in the stock and cook over a low heat for 10 minutes. Add the watercress and nutmeg, season with salt and pepper and cook for a further 10 minutes. Transfer to a food processor and process to a purée. Pour into a pan, stir in the cream and reheat briefly. Serve with toasted croûtons lightly spread with butter.

VICHYSSOISE

VICHYSSOISE

Serves 4

2 celery hearts, chopped
2 leeks, white parts only, chopped
2 potatoes, diced
1 litre/1¾ pints Chicken Stock (see page 209)
200 ml/7 fl oz double cream
salt and pepper
fresh flat-leaf parsley, chopped, to garnish

Put the celery hearts, leeks and potatoes in a saucepan, pour in the stock, season with salt and pepper to taste and bring to the boil. Lower the heat and simmer for about 45 minutes. Transfer to a food processor and process to a purée. Pour into a pan, stir in the cream and reheat. Pour into individual soup plates, leave to cool, then chill in the refrigerator. Serve garnished with parsley.

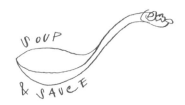

VARIOUS SOUPS

The soups in this section range from simple, thin soups suitable for dinner – clear broths with a few star-, ring- or seed-shaped pasta specks – to substantial rice, pasta, tapioca and semolina soups. These are often enriched with liver, vegetables or pulses and served with grated cheese as a final touch. Soups may be made from home-made meat stock or stock cubes or bouillon powder, be thick or thin and be served hot, warm or even cold.

FARFALLINE WITH PESTO

Heat the oil in a saucepan, add the onion, carrots and potatoes and cook over a low heat, stirring occasionally, for 5 minutes. Add 1.5 litres/2¹/₂ pints water, bring to the boil and simmer for 20 minutes. Add the pesto and beans and cook for 10 minutes until tender. Add the pasta and cook until al dente. Remove the pan from the heat and sprinkle the soup with the Parmesan, stir well and leave to stand for a few minutes before ladling into a soup tureen and serving. This is a fresh aromatic soup. Salt is not required because the pesto gives it a strong flavour, but you can season to taste if you like. If you wish to use fresh pesto, see page 68.

FARFALLINE AL PESTO
Serves 4
3 tablespoons olive oil
1 onion, chopped
2 carrots, chopped
2 potatoes, diced
140 g/4³/₄ oz bottled pesto
100 g/3¹/₂ oz French beans, trimmed
185 g/6¹/₂ oz farfalline pasta
25 g/1 oz Parmesan cheese, freshly grated
salt

GAZPACHO

GAZPACHO

Serves 4

150 g/5 oz white bread slices, crusts removed

800 g/1¾ lb tomatoes

2 red peppers, halved and seeded

2 cucumbers

1 garlic clove

2 spring onions

3–4 tablespoons olive oil

juice of 1 lemon, strained

ice cubes

salt and pepper

Tear the bread into pieces, place in a bowl, add water to cover and leave to soak. Coarsely chop half the tomatoes, 1 red pepper, 1 cucumber and the garlic and place in a food processor. Add the bread and process to a purée. Pour into a large bowl and add up to 1 litre/1¾ pints water to obtain the desired consistency. Chill in the refrigerator. Meanwhile, cut the remaining red pepper into strips and slice the remaining cucumber, the remaining tomatoes and the spring onions and place in separate bowls. Whisk together the olive oil and lemon juice. Just before serving, season the soup with salt and pepper and stir in the oil and lemon juice dressing. Pour into a soup tureen, add a few ice cubes and serve with the bowls of raw vegetables.

SIMPLE GAZPACHO

GAZPACHO SEMPLICE

Serves 4

1 large cucumber, peeled and thinly sliced

1.5 kg/3¼ lb tomatoes, peeled and seeded

2 spring onions, finely chopped

6 fresh basil leaves, finely chopped

1 tablespoon chopped fresh flat-leaf parsley

3 tablespoons olive oil

juice of 1 lemon, strained

ice cubes

salt and pepper

Put the cucumber in a colander, sprinkle with salt and set aside to drain for 20 minutes. Put the tomatoes in a food processor and process to a purée, then scrape into a bowl. Rinse the cucumber and pat dry with kitchen paper, then add to the tomato purée along with the spring onions, parsley and basil. Season with salt and pepper to taste. Beat the oil with the lemon juice and stir into the soup. Chill in the refrigerator for a few hours, then ladle into a soup tureen and add a few ice cubes.

LENTIL AND SQUID SOUP

LENTICCHIE E CALAMERETTI

Serves 4

200 g/7 oz lentils, soaked in cold water for 3 hours and drained

500 g/1 lb 2 oz small squid, cleaned and chopped

250 g/9 oz leafy green vegetables, such as Swiss chard or beetroot tops, coarsely chopped

pinch of chilli powder

salt

Put the lentils into a saucepan, add 1.5 litres/2½ pints water and bring to the boil. Add the squid, lower the heat, cover and simmer for 30 minutes. Add the green vegetables, cover the pan again and cook for a further 30 minutes. Add the chilli powder and season with salt to taste, then ladle into a soup tureen.

MESC–IUÀ

Put the cannellini beans, chickpeas and farro into a saucepan, add 1.5 litres/ 2¹/₂ pints water, bring to the boil, then lower the heat and simmer for about 3 hours. Ladle into a soup tureen, drizzle with oil and season with salt and pepper. This is one of the most ancient Ligurian soups and is very common in La Spezia. It seems to date back to the time of the Saracens.

MESC–IUÀ

Serves 4

200 g/7 oz dried cannellini beans, soaked in cold water overnight and drained

200 g/7 oz dried chickpeas, soaked in cold water overnight and drained

100 g/3¹/₂ oz pearl farro, soaked in cold water overnight and drained

olive oil, for drizzling

salt and pepper

COURGETTE FLOWER SOUP

Bring the stock to the boil. Heat the butter and olive oil in another pan, add the onion, carrot and celery and cook over a low heat, stirring occasionally, for 10 minutes. Add the courgettes and courgette flowers and cook for 2 minutes, then pour in the hot stock. Bring to the boil, add the pasta and cook until al dente. Season with salt and pepper to taste, ladle into a soup tureen and serve with Parmesan.

MINESTRA AI FIORI DI ZUCCHINE

Serves 4

1 litre/1³/₄ pints Meat Stock (see page 208)

25 g/1 oz butter

1 tablespoon olive oil

1 onion, chopped

1 carrot, chopped

1 celery stick, chopped

4 courgettes, finely diced

300 g/11 oz courgette flowers, cut into strips

120 g/4 oz soup pasta, such as ditalini

salt and pepper

Parmesan cheese, freshly grated, to serve

WHEAT GERM SOUP

Soak the wheat germ and beans in the stock overnight. Pour into a saucepan, add 1 litre/1³/₄ pints water and bring to the boil over a low heat. Heat the oil in another saucepan, add the onion, celery and tomatoes and cook over a low heat, stirring occasionally, for 5 minutes. Add a ladleful of the boiling stock, then pour the mixture into the pan of beans. Simmer for about 2 hours until the beans are tender. Season with salt and pepper and stir in the basil. Leave the soup to stand in a warm place for 10 minutes before ladling into a soup tureen and serving.

MINESTRA AL GERME DI GRANO

Serves 4

100 g/3¹/₂ oz wheat germ

50 g/2 oz dried toscanelli or cannellini beans

1 litre/1³/₄ pints Meat Stock (see page 208)

2 tablespoons olive oil

1 onion, chopped

1 celery stick, chopped

2 ripe tomatoes, chopped

1 bunch of fresh basil, chopped

salt and pepper

HERB SOUP

Bring the stock to the boil. Melt the butter in another pan, add the onion and potatoes and cook over a low heat, stirring occasionally, for about 5 minutes until the onion is translucent and the potatoes are soft. Sprinkle with the oregano, season with salt and pepper to taste and cook for a further 10 minutes. Pour in the boiling stock and simmer for about 20 minutes until the potatoes have almost disintegrated. Stir in the basil and parsley, then ladle into a soup tureen and serve.

MINESTRA AROMATICA

Serves 4

1.5 litres/2¹/₂ pints Meat Stock (see page 208)

25 g/1 oz butter • 1 onion, thinly sliced

800 g/1³/₄ lb potatoes, diced

1 teaspoon dried oregano

10 fresh basil leaves, chopped

1 tablespoon chopped fresh flat-leaf parsley

salt and pepper

CORN SOUP

Bring the stock to the boil. Melt the butter in another pan, add the onion and cook over a low heat, stirring occasionally, for 5 minutes until translucent. Add the sweetcorn and courgettes, cook for 2 minutes, then add the mushrooms and courgette flowers and cook for a few minutes more. Pour in the hot stock and simmer for about 20 minutes. Season lightly with salt, ladle into a soup tureen, add the chilli and serve.

MINESTRA CON IL MAIS

Serves 4

1.5 litres/2¹/₂ pints Chicken Stock (see page 209)

40 g/1¹/₂ oz butter • 1 onion, thinly sliced

250 g/9 oz canned sweetcorn, drained

150 g/5 oz courgettes, coarsely chopped

150 g/5 oz mushrooms, sliced

16 courgette flowers, cut into strips

¹/₂ fresh chilli, seeded and finely chopped

salt

LEEK SOUP

Put the leeks, carrot, celery and olive oil in a saucepan and add 2 tablespoons water. Cook over a low heat for about 5 minutes. Add 1.5 litres/2¹/₂ pints water, increase the heat to medium and bring to the boil. Stir in the rice and a pinch of salt and bring back to the boil. Lower the heat to medium-low and cook, stirringocca-sionally, for about 20 minutes until the rice is tender. Ladle into a soup tureen and serve with plenty of Parmesan.

MINESTRA CON I PORRI

Serves 4

4 leeks, white parts only, sliced

1 carrot, chopped • 1 celery stick, chopped

2 tablespoons olive oil

165 g/5¹/₂ oz long-grain rice

salt

Parmesan cheese, freshly grated, to serve

SOUP WITH MEATBALLS

Tear the bread into pieces, place in a bowl and add 3 tablespoons water. Set aside to soak. Mix together the veal, egg yolk and Parmesan in another bowl. Squeeze out the bread, add to the veal mixture with the ham and season with salt and pepper. Bring the stock to the boil. Shape the veal mixture into small balls, add to the stock and simmer over a medium heat for 15 minutes. Ladle into a soup tureen and serve. Leftover boiled or roast meat may be used to make the meatballs.

MINESTRA CON NOCCIOLINE DI CARNE

Serves 4

1 bread slice, crusts removed

150 g/5 oz minced veal

1 egg yolk

50 g/2 oz Parmesan cheese, freshly grated

1 slice cooked ham, chopped

1.5 litres/2¹/₂ pints Meat Stock (see page 208)

salt and pepper

BARLEY AND PULSE SOUP

MINESTRA CON ORZO E LEGUMI

Serves 4

2 litres/3¹/₂ pints Meat Stock (see page 208)

4 tablespoons olive oil

1 onion, chopped

1 garlic clove, chopped

100 g/3¹/₂ oz dried borlotti beans, soaked in cold water overnight and drained

50 g/2 oz dried green soya beans, soaked in cold water overnight and drained

50 g/2 oz dried chickpeas, soaked in cold water overnight and drained

50 g/2 oz lentils

100 g/3¹/₂ oz barley

salt and pepper

Bring the stock to the boil. Heat 3 tablespoons of the olive oil in another pan, add the onion and garlic and cook over a low heat, stirring occasionally, for 10 minutes until lightly browned. Add the beans, chickpeas, lentils and barley and cook for a few minutes. Pour in the stock, bring to the boil and boil vigorously for 15 minutes. Lower the heat to medium and cook for 1¹/₂ hours. Season with salt and pepper and stir in the remaining oil, then ladle into a soup tureen and serve.

WHITEBAIT SOUP

MINESTRA DI BIANCHETTI

Serves 4

100 g/3¹/₂ oz whitebait

1.5 litres/2¹/₂ pints Fish Stock (see page 208)

100 g/3¹/₂ oz capelli d'angelo pasta

1 tablespoon extra virgin olive oil

salt and pepper

Rinse the whitebait. Bring the stock to the boil and add the whitebait and 'angel-hair' pasta. Cook for just under 2 minutes. Stir in the olive oil, season with salt and pepper, ladle into a soup tureen and serve immediately.

CHICKPEA AND SPINACH SOUP

MINESTRA DI CECI E SPINACI

Serves 4

1.5 litres/2¹/₂ pints Meat Stock (see page 208)

3 tablespoons olive oil, plus extra for drizzling

1 onion, chopped

1 carrot, chopped

1 celery stick, chopped

250 g/9 oz spinach, chopped

150 g/5 oz canned or cooked chickpeas, drained

100 g/3¹/₂ oz soup pasta

salt and pepper

Bring the stock to the boil in a saucepan. Heat the oil in another pan, add the onion, carrot and celery and cook over a low heat, stirring occasionally, for 5 minutes until softened. Add the spinach, season with salt and cook for a few minutes more. Add the chickpeas and stock and simmer for 30 minutes. Add the pasta and cook until al dente. Season with pepper, ladle into a soup tureen, drizzle with olive oil and serve.

SWISS CHARD AND LENTIL SOUP

Bring the stock to the boil. Heat the oil in another pan, add the onion, garlic, celery and carrot and cook over a low heat, stirring occasionally, for 10 minutes until lightly browned. Stir in the Swiss chard and cook for 2–3 minutes, then add the lentils and tomato purée and stir well. Pour in the stock, bring back to the boil and add the rice. Cook for 15 minutes or until the rice is tender. Season with salt and pepper, ladle into a soup tureen, drizzle with olive oil and serve with Parmesan.

MINESTRA DI COSTE E LENTICCHIE

Serves 4–6

1.5 litres/2¹/₂ pints Meat Stock (see page 208)

3 tablespoons olive oil, plus extra for drizzling

1 onion, finely chopped

1 garlic clove,

finely chopped

1 celery stick, finely chopped

1 carrot, finely chopped

350 g/12 oz Swiss chard, coarsely chopped

150 g/5 oz lentils, soaked in cold water

for 3 hours and drained

2 tablespoons tomato purée

100 g/3¹/₂ oz long-grain rice

salt and pepper

Parmesan cheese, freshly grated, to serve

FARRO AND LEEK SOUP

Heat the oil in saucepan, add the leeks and cook over a low heat, stirring occasionally, for 10 minutes until golden brown. Add the farro, pour in the stock, season with salt and simmer over a low heat for 1¹/₂ hours or until the farro is tender. Season with pepper, ladle into a soup tureen and sprinkle with the Parmesan.

MINESTRA DI FARRO E PORRI

Serves 4

2 tablespoons olive oil

2 leeks, white parts only sliced

300 g/11 oz pearl farro

1.5 litres/2¹/₂ pints Meat Stock (see page 208)

2 tablespoons Parmesan cheese, freshly grated

salt and pepper

MILLET SOUP

Pour 1.5 litres/2¹/₂ pints water into a saucepan, add the onion, carrot and celery and bring to the boil. Stir in the millet flour, season with salt and pepper and cook over a medium heat for about 1 hour. Ladle into a soup tureen, stir in the olive oil and sprinkle with the parsley.

MINESTRA DI MIGLIO

Serves 4

1 onion, chopped

1 carrot, chopped

1 celery stick, chopped

100 g/3¹/₂ oz toasted millet flour

2 tablespoons extra virgin olive oil

1 fresh flat-leaf parsley sprig, chopped

salt and pepper

MINESTRA DI ORTICHE

Serves 4

600 g/1 lb 5 oz fresh nettles

1.5 litres/2¹/₂ pints Meat Stock (see page 208)

3 tablespoons olive oil

50 g/2 oz pancetta, diced

1 garlic clove, chopped

2 ripe tomatoes, peeled, seeded and chopped

150 g/5 oz long-grain rice

salt

NETTLE SOUP

Wearing a pair of gloves, remove all the nettle leaves and strings that cling to the stems. Wash and drain well and chop coarsely. Bring the stock to the boil. Heat the oil in another pan, add the pancetta and garlic and cook for 5 minutes. Add the tomatoes and cook for a further 10 minutes, then season with salt and stir in the nettles. Cook for a few minutes more, then pour in the stock, bring back to the boil and add the rice. Cook for 15–20 minutes until the rice is tender. Ladle into a soup tureen and serve immediately.

MINESTRA DI ORZO E POLLO

Serves 4

2 chicken quarters

2 onions, chopped

1 carrot, chopped

1 celery stick, chopped

120 g/4 oz barley

25 g/1 oz butter

100 ml/3¹/₂ fl oz dry white wine

¹/₂ teaspoon ground cumin

salt and pepper

BARLEY AND CHICKEN SOUP

Put the chicken, one of the onions, the carrot and celery in a saucepan, add 2 litres/3¹/₂ pints water and bring to the boil. Lower the heat and simmer for 1 hour, skimming the surface occasionally. Meanwhile, cook the barley in salted, boiling water for 30 minutes, then drain well. Melt the butter in a frying pan, add the barley and the remaining onion and cook over a low heat, stirring occasionally, for 5 minutes. Sprinkle with the wine and cook until it has evaporated. When the chicken is cooked through, lift it out of the stock with a slotted spoon. Remove and discard the skin and cut the meat off the bones. Return the meat to the stock, add the barley mixture and cook for a further 10 minutes. Stir in the cumin and season with salt and pepper to taste. Ladle into a soup tureen and serve.

MINESTRA DI OVOLI

Serves 4

40 g/1¹/₂ oz butter

300 g/11 oz Caesar's mushrooms, sliced

1.5 litres/2¹/₂ pints Meat Stock (see page 208)

1 egg

1 tablespoon Parmesan cheese, freshly grated

salt

CAESAR'S MUSHROOM SOUP

Melt the butter in a saucepan, add the mushrooms and season with salt, then cover and cook over a high heat for about 15 minutes until a thick, yellowish sauce has formed. Meanwhile, bring the stock to the boil in another saucepan. Pour the stock into the pan of mushrooms and simmer over a low heat for 15 minutes. Beat the egg with the Parmesan, then stir into the soup. Ladle into a soup tureen and serve immediately.

LEEK AND POTATO SOUP

Put the leeks, potatoes, onion and a pinch of salt into a saucepan, pour in 150 ml/5 fl oz water and cook for about 10 minutes. Add 500 ml/18 fl oz warm water, cover and cook over a low heat for 30 minutes. Ladle half the soup into a food processor and process to a purée, then return to the saucepan. Cook over a low heat for a further 20 minutes. Drizzle with olive oil, sprinkle with the parsley and serve with Parmesan.

MINESTRA DI PORRI E PATATE

Serves 4

600 g/1 lb 5 oz leeks, white parts only sliced

3 potatoes, diced • 1 onion, sliced

olive oil, for drizzling

1 fresh flat-leaf parsley sprig, chopped

salt

Parmesan cheese, freshly grated, to serve

FLEMISH SOUP

Put the chicory, chicken, mushrooms, carrot, potato, celery and leeks into a saucepan, add 1.5 litres/2½ pints water and bring to the boil. Cover and simmer over a low heat for 1 hour. Season with salt to taste. Beat the egg yolk with the cream in a soup tureen, ladle in the soup, stirring, and serve.

MINESTRA FIAMMINGA

Serves 4

4 chicory heads, thinly sliced

200-g/7-oz skinless, boneless chicken breast, cut into thin strips

200 g/7 oz button mushrooms, thinly sliced

1 carrot, cut into thin batons • 1 potato, cut into thin batons • 1 celery stick, cut into thin batons

2 leeks, trimmed and thinly sliced

1 egg yolk • 200 ml/7 fl oz double cream • salt

THREE-COLOUR SOUP

Beat the eggs with the Parmesan and a pinch of salt. Heat a little of the olive oil in a small omelette pan, add a little of the egg mixture and tilt the pan to coat the base. Cook over a low heat, drawing the cooked egg towards the centre to allow the raw egg to flow underneath. When the underside is set, slide the omelette out of the pan. Make one or two more omelettes in the same way, adding more oil as necessary. Roll up the omelettes and cut into strips. Cook the peas in salted, boiling water for 8–10 minutes until tender, then drain. Bring the stock to the boil. Put the tongue, omelette strips and peas in a soup tureen. Pour in the stock and serve immediately.

MINESTRA TRICOLORE

Serves 4

2 eggs

25 g/1 oz Parmesan cheese, freshly grated

1 tablespoon olive oil

80 g/3 oz shelled peas

1 litre/1¾ pints Meat Stock (see page 208)

100 g/3 ½ oz pickled tongue, cut into strips

salt

GREEN SOUP

Cook the Swiss chard in salted, boiling water until tender, then drain and leave to cool. Squeeze out as much liquid as possible and shred. Mix together the chard, Parmesan, eggs, a pinch of salt and a ladleful of stock. Bring the remaining stock to the boil, then whisk in the chard mixture. Simmer gently for 5 minutes, then ladle into a soup tureen. Serve with Parmesan.

MINESTRA VERDE

Serves 4

400 g/14 oz Swiss chard

40 g/1½ oz Parmesan cheese, freshly grated, plus extra for serving • 3 eggs, lightly beaten

1.5 litres/2½ pints Meat Stock (see page 208)

salt

BREAD SOUP

PANCOTTO

Serves 4

4 tablespoons olive oil, plus extra for drizzling
3 ripe tomatoes, peeled, seeded and chopped
1 garlic clove, chopped
400 g/14 oz day-old bread, crusts removed, diced
25 g/1 oz Parmesan cheese, freshly grated
salt and pepper

Heat the oil in a saucepan, add the tomatoes and garlic and cook over a low heat, stirring frequently, for 10 minutes. Pour in 250 ml/8 fl oz boiling water, add the bread and mix well. Pour in 1 litre/1³/₄ pints water and season with salt. Cook over a medium heat until the soup is fairly thick. Remove from the heat and leave to stand for a few minutes. Drizzle with oil and stir, then ladle into a soup tureen, sprinkle with Parmesan, season with pepper and serve.

BREAD SOUP WITH TOMATO

PAPPA AL POMODORO

Serves 4

1 tablespoon olive oil
300 g/11 oz ripe tomatoes, peeled, seeded and coarsely chopped
1 garlic clove, chopped
1 celery stick, chopped
2 day-old country-style bread slices, cubed
6 fresh basil leaves, chopped
25 g/1 oz Parmesan cheese, freshly grated
salt and pepper

Put the olive oil, tomatoes, garlic, celery and a pinch each of salt and pepper into a saucepan, add 1.2 litres/2 pints water and bring to the boil. Lower the heat and simmer for about 1 hour. Remove the pan from the heat and leave to stand. About 30 minutes before serving, stir in the bread and simmer the soup over a low heat. Ladle into a soup tureen, sprinkle with the basil and Parmesan and serve.

PASSATELLI

PASSATELLI

Serves 4

100 g/3¹/₂ oz breadcrumbs
100 g/3¹/₂ oz Parmesan cheese, freshly grated, plus extra to serve
25 g/1 oz butter, melted
pinch of freshly grated nutmeg
3 eggs, lightly beaten
1 litre/1³/₄ pints Meat Stock (see page 208)
salt

Mix together the breadcrumbs, Parmesan, melted butter, nutmeg, eggs and a large pinch of salt in a bowl. The mixture should be fairly firm; if it is too soft, add more breadcrumbs. Bring the stock to the boil in a saucepan. Hold a potato masher with fairly large holes over the saucepan and press the breadcrumb mixture through it to form short, worm-shaped dumplings. Serve with Parmesan.

PASTA AND CHICKPEAS

Put the chickpeas in a saucepan, add 2 litres/3½ pints water and bring to the boil. Lower the heat, cover and cook for about 1½ hours. Remove about 3 ladlefuls of the chickpeas, place in a food processor and process to a purée. Scrape the purée into the saucepan, re-cover and cook for a further 1½ hours. Heat the olive oil in a frying pan, add the garlic, rosemary and tomatoes and cook, stirring occasionally, for 10 minutes. Stir the tomato mixture into the chickpeas and season with salt. Add the tagliatelle and cook until al dente. Season with pepper, ladle into a soup tureen, drizzle with oil and sprinkle with the Parmesan.

PASTA E CECI ALLA TOSCANA

Serves 4

200 g/7 oz dried chickpeas, soaked
in cold water overnight and drained

1 tablespoon olive oil, plus extra for drizzling

1 garlic clove, crushed

1 fresh rosemary sprig, chopped

250 g/9 oz tomatoes, peeled and chopped

150 g/5 oz fresh tagliatelle, cut into short lengths

25 g/1 oz Parmesan cheese, freshly grated

salt and pepper

PASTA AND WHITE BEAN

Put the beans into a saucepan, add cold water to cover and bring to the boil. Lower the heat and simmer for about 2 hours. Transfer half the beans to a food processor and process to a purée. Heat the oil in a saucepan, add the sage leaves and garlic and cook for a few minutes. Pour in the bean purée and 1.5 litres/2½ pints water, season with salt and pepper and stir in the passata. Finally, add the whole beans. Bring to the boil, add the pasta and cook for 10 minutes or until al dente, then ladle into a soup tureen. This is excellent hot, cold or even warm.

PASTA E FAGIOLI

Serves 4

400 g/14 oz dried white beans, soaked
in cold water overnight and drained

3 tablespoons olive oil

4 sage leaves

1 garlic clove, crushed

3 tablespoons passata

80 g/3 oz maltagliati pasta

salt and pepper

PASTA, POTATOES AND CELERY

Heat the olive oil in saucepan, add the carrot and celery hearts and cook over a low heat, stirring occasionally, for 5 minutes. Stir in the pancetta, add the potatoes and pour in 1 litre/1¾ pints hot water. Cover and simmer for 30 minutes. Stir in the tomato purée, season with salt and pepper and add more water if necessary. Add the pasta and cook until al dente. Ladle into a soup tureen and serve with Parmesan.

PASTA, PATATE E SEDANO

Serves 4

3 tablespoons olive oil

1 carrot, chopped

2 celery hearts, chopped

50 g/2 oz pancetta, diced

1 kg/2¼ lb potatoes, diced

1 tablespoon concentrated tomato purée

200 g/7 oz ditalini pasta

salt and pepper

Parmesan cheese, freshly grated, to serve

PORRIDGE

PORRIDGE

Serves 4

100 g/3¹⁄₂ oz oat flakes • salt

sugar (optional)

cold milk or single cream, to serve

Bring 500 ml/18 fl oz water to the boil. Add a pinch of salt, sprinkle in the oat flakes and stir until thickened. Simmer for 15 minutes. Serve hot with milk or single cream handed separately. Porridge may be sweetened with sugar.

POT–AU–FEU

POT–AU–FEU

Serves 6

4 potatoes

800 g/1³⁄₄ lb lean beef

500 g/1 lb 2 oz veal

1 marrowbone

2 turnips, chopped • 1 leek, chopped

3 carrots, chopped

1 onion, chopped

1 celery stick, chopped • 1 garlic clove, chopped

salt

Cook the potatoes in lightly salted, boiling water for 20 minutes until tender. Meanwhile, put the beef and veal into a large saucepan and add plenty of water to cover and a pinch of salt. Wrap the marrowbone in muslin, add to the pan and bring to the boil. Skim off any scum that rises to the surface, then add the chopped vegetables and the garlic. Simmer over a low heat for 3¹⁄₂ hours. Meanwhile, peel and dice the potatoes. Remove the meat and vegetables from the pan and arrange on a warm serving dish. Add the potatoes to the soup, heat through briefly, then ladle into a soup tureen. Serve the two dishes at the same time.

QUADRUCCI WITH VEGETABLES

QUADRUCCI CON VERDURE

Serves 4

1.5 litres/2¹⁄₂ pints Meat Stock (see page 208)

3 tablespoons olive oil

1 onion, chopped • 1 carrot, chopped

1 celery stick, chopped

200 g/7 oz potatoes, diced

200 g/7 oz turnips, diced

150 g/5 oz quadrucci pasta

salt and pepper

Bring the stock to the boil. Heat the oil in another pan, add the onion, carrot and celery and cook over a low heat, stirring occasionally, for 10 minutes until lightly browned. Add the potatoes and turnips, mix well and pour in the stock. Bring back to the boil, then lower the heat and cook for about 45 minutes. Add the pasta and cook for a further 8 minutes until al dente. Season with salt and pepper to taste. Ladle into a soup tureen and serve.

RICE AND PEAS

RISI E BISI

Serves 4

1.2 litres/2 pints Meat Stock (see page208)

3 tablespoons olive oil • 50 g/2 oz butter

1 onion, chopped

1 garlic clove • 1 celery stick, chopped

250 g/9 oz shelled peas

200 g/7 oz risotto rice

25 g/1 oz Parmesan cheese, freshly grated

salt

Bring the stock to the boil. Heat the oil and half the butter in another pan, add the onion, garlic and celery and cook over a low heat, stirring occasionally, for 5 minutes. Remove and discard the garlic. Add the peas followed by the rice. Stir for about 1 minute, then stir in a ladleful of the stock. Cook, adding the stock a ladleful at a time, for about 20 minutes until the rice is tender and all the stock has been used. Season with salt to taste, stir in the remaining butter and the Parmesan, ladle into a soup tureen and serve.

RICE AND POTATOES

RISO E PATATE

Serves 4

25 g/1 oz butter

1 onion, chopped

50 g/2 oz prosciutto, diced

200 g/7 oz risotto rice

300 g/11 oz potatoes, diced

1.5 litres/2¹/₂ pints Meat Stock (see page 208)

1 fresh flat-leaf parsley sprig, chopped

salt

Melt the butter in a saucepan, add the onion and prosciutto and cook over a low heat, stirring occasionally, for 10 minutes until lightly browned. Add the rice and stir well to coat with the butter. Season with salt, add the potatoes and stir in a ladleful of the stock. Cook, adding the stock a ladleful at a time, for about 20 minutes until the rice is tender and all the stock has been used. Ladle into a soup tureen, sprinkle with the parsley and serve.

SEMOLINA

SEMOLINO

Serves 4

1.5 litres/2¹/₂ pints Meat Stock (see page 208)

80 g/3 oz semolina

25 g/1 oz butter

2 egg yolks, lightly beaten

Parmesan cheese, freshly grated, to serve

Bring the stock to the boil and sprinkle in the semolina, stirring constantly. Cook for 10 minutes, then stir in the butter and remove the pan from the heat. Ladle into a soup tureen and stir in the egg yolks. Serve with Parmesan. You can make this soup thicker or thinner according to taste.

STRACCIATELLA

STRACCIATELLA

Serves 4

25 g/1 oz breadcrumbs

40 g/1¹/₂ oz Parmesan cheese, freshly grated

3 eggs, lightly beaten

1.5 litres/2¹/₂ pints Meat Stock (see page 208)

1¹/₂ teaspoons chopped fresh flat-leaf parsley

salt

Mix together the breadcrumbs, Parmesan, eggs and a pinch of salt in a bowl. Heat the stock, add a ladleful to the egg mixture and mix until smooth. Bring the stock to the boil and add the egg mixture, which will float up to the surface in a clump. Break up slightly with the prongs of a fork. Ladle the soup into a tureen, sprinkle with the parsley and serve.

TAPIOCA

TAPIOCA

Serves 4

1.5 litres/2¹/₂ pints Meat Stock (see page 208)

100 g/3¹/₂ oz tapioca

25 g/1 oz Parmesan cheese, freshly grated

double cream, whipped (optional)

lettuce (optional)

salt

Bring the stock to the boil and pour in the tapioca, stirring constantly. Add a pinch of salt and cook, stirring constantly, for about 10 minutes. Ladle into a soup tureen and serve with Parmesan. If you like, stir in a few tablespoonfuls of cream before serving. Another alternative is to add lettuce: cut 3–4 lettuce leaves into strips, soften with a knob of butter over a low heat for a few minutes and add to the tapioca halfway through cooking.

MINESTRONES

Cream soups, soups and now minestrones – a true crescendo. Fresh garden vegetables and herbs go into a minestrone, along with pasta, rice and pulses (according to taste) and the essential butter, bacon fat, oil or lard. For a lighter version, the oil or butter may be added when the soup has been cooked. In the case of lard or bacon fat, which are necessarily added at the beginning to give flavour to the ingredients, it is advisable to limit their frying time. Almost every Italian region has its own exclusive recipe and this chapter lists the most famous. Hot minestrone is a pleasant winter dish, and the cold version is a true delicacy, provided it is not served straight from the refrigerator.

GENOESE PESTO MINESTRONE

Put the dried mushrooms in a bowl, add hot water to cover and set aside to soak for 20 minutes, then drain and chop. Put the mushrooms, broad beans, cabbage, French beans, tomatoes, courgettes, aubergine and a pinch of salt into a saucepan, pour in 2 litres/3¹/₂ pints water and the olive oil and bring to the boil. Lower the heat and simmer for 2 hours. Add the rice or pasta and cook until al dente. Remove from the heat and stir in the pesto. Ladle into a soup tureen and serve very hot with Parmesan. This minestrone is also good cold. In this case do not add oil during cooking, and leave to cool to room temperature. Just before serving, drizzle with a little oil.

MINESTRONE ALLA GENOVESE COL PESTO

Serves 4–6

15 g/¹/₂ oz dried mushrooms

100 g/3¹/₂ oz shelled broad beans

¹/₂ cabbage, shredded

200 g/7 oz French beans, cut into short lengths

3 tomatoes, chopped

3 courgettes, chopped

1 aubergine, chopped

3 tablespoons olive oil

80 g/3 oz long-grain rice or short pasta

Pesto (see page 68), to taste

salt

Parmesan cheese, freshly grated, to serve

MILANESE MINESTRONE

Finely chop the lardons with the garlic and onion. When the mixture is quite fine, add the parsley and celery and chop. Put the mixture into a saucepan, add the tomatoes, carrots, potatoes, courgettes and oil and pour in 2 litres/3½ pints water. Season with salt and bring to the boil over a high heat. Lower the heat and cook for at least 2 hours. Add the peas and cabbage, simmer for 15 minutes, then add the rice and simmer, stirring occasionally, for a further 18 minutes until it is tender. Stir in the herbs, ladle into a soup tureen and serve with plenty of Parmesan. This minestrone should be fairly thick. It is excellent hot, but it is also good served warm or cold in the summer.

MINESTRONE ALLA MILANESE

Serves 4–6

40 g/1½ oz lardons

½ garlic clove

½ onion

1 fresh flat-leaf parsley sprig

1 celery stick

3 tomatoes, peeled, seeded and diced

2 carrots, chopped • 3 potatoes, chopped

2 courgettes, chopped

2 tablespoons olive oil

200 g/7 oz shelled peas

½ Savoy cabbage, shredded

100 g/3½ oz fresh shelled borlotti beans

100 g/3½ oz long-grain rice

4 fresh sage leaves, chopped

6 fresh basil leaves, chopped

salt

Parmesan cheese, freshly grated, to serve

MINESTRONE NAPOLETANA

Place the pepper under a preheated grill and cook, turning frequently, until the skin is charred and blistered. Place in a plastic bag and tie the top. When cool enough to handle, peel off the skin, halve and seed the pepper and dice the flesh. Finely chop the pancetta with the onion, carrot and garlic. Heat the oil, add the pancetta mixture and cook over a low heat for a few minutes until lightly browned. Add the tomatoes and cook for about 10 minutes. Add 2 litres/3½ pints water and season with salt and pepper. Bring to the boil, add the potatoes and beans and simmer for 1 hour. Add the courgettes, peas, cabbage, escarole, aubergines and yellow pepper. Simmer for a further 30 minutes. Add the pasta and cook for 10 minutes until al dente. Season with salt if necessary. Ladle the minestrone into a soup tureen, sprinkle with the basil and serve with provolone.

MINESTRONE ALLA NAPOLETANA

Serves 4–6

1 yellow pepper

50 g/2 oz pancetta

½ onion

½ carrot

½ garlic clove

2 tablespoons olive oil

3 tomatoes, peeled, seeded and chopped

1 fresh flat-leaf parsley sprig, chopped

2 potatoes, diced

100 g/3½ oz shelled broad beans

2 courgettes, sliced

100 g/3½ oz shelled peas

¼ cabbage, coarsely shredded

1 escarole head, cut into strips

2 aubergines, diced

100 g/3½ oz cannolicchi pasta

2 teaspoons chopped fresh basil

salt and pepper

provolone cheese, freshly grated, to serve

MINESTRONES

MINESTRONE ALLA PUGLIESE

Serves 4–6

900 g/2 lb turnip tops

2 onions, chopped

5 tablespoons olive oil

pinch of chilli powder

150 g/5 oz tortiglioni pasta

25 g/1 oz pecorino cheese, freshly grated

salt and pepper

PUGLIAN MINESTRONE

If possible choose turnip tops in flower since they are tastier. Cook in salted, boiling water for about 10 minutes, then separate the stems from the flowers. Chop the stems and put in a saucepan with the onions, 3 tablespoons of the olive oil, the chilli powder and a pinch of pepper. Cook over a low heat, stirring frequently, for 5 minutes, then pour in 1.5 litres/2½ pints hot water and simmer for 1¾ hours. Stir in the pasta, then stir in the turnip flowers and cook until the pasta is al dente. Remove the pan from the heat, stir in the pecorino and leave to stand for a few minutes. Season with a little more pepper and chilli powder, stir in the remaining oil, ladle into a soup tureen and serve.

MINESTRONE ALLA RUSSA

Serves 4–6

40 g/1½ oz butter

1 white onion, finely chopped

2 garlic cloves, finely chopped

500 g/1 lb 2 oz raw beetroot, diced

1 celery heart, chopped

3 tomatoes, peeled, seeded and chopped

pinch of sugar

2 tablespoons white wine vinegar

1.5 litres/2½ pints Meat Stock (see page 208)

400 g/14 oz potatoes, cut into wedges

400 g/14 oz white cabbage, shredded

500 g/1 lb 2 oz boiled beef, diced

2 tablespoons chopped fresh flat-leaf parsley

salt

250 ml/8 fl oz soured cream, to serve

BORSCH

Melt the butter in a large saucepan, add the onion and garlic and cook over a low heat, stirring occasionally, for 5 minutes until soft. Add the beetroot, celery, half the tomatoes, sugar, a pinch of salt and 175 ml/6 fl oz of the stock and cook over a medium heat for 30 minutes. Meanwhile, cook the potatoes and cabbage in the remaining stock in another saucepan for about 20 minutes, but do not let the potatoes overcook. Add the remaining tomatoes, the beef and the beetroot mixture, stir and simmer for a further 10 minutes. Season with salt if necessary, sprinkle with the parsley and remove the pan from the heat. Pour the minestrone into a soup tureen and serve with sour cream. This Russian version of minestrone is immediately recognizable owing to the red colour of the beetroot. There are other versions, but this is the most common.

TUSCAN MINESTRONE

Put the beans, rosemary and bay leaf into a saucepan, add cold water to cover, bring to the boil and simmer for about 2 hours. Remove and discard the herbs, then transfer half the beans to a food processor and process to a purée. Scrape the purée back into the saucepan. Heat the oil in another saucepan, add the onion, celery, carrot and parsley and cook over a low heat, stirring occasionally, for 5 minutes. Add the escarole, tomato, courgette and leek and cook for a further 10 minutes. Stir the vegetable mixture into the beans, season with salt and pepper to taste and add more hot water if necessary. Bring to the boil, add the rice and cook for 15–20 minutes until tender. Ladle into a soup tureen and serve with Parmesan.

MINESTRONE ALLA TOSCANA

Serves 4–6

100 g/3¹/₂ oz toscanelli or cannellini beans, soaked overnight in cold water and drained

1 fresh rosemary sprig • 1 bay leaf

4 tablespoons olive oil

1 onion, chopped • 1 celery stick, chopped

1 carrot, chopped

1 tablespoon chopped fresh flat-leaf parsley

1 escarole head, chopped

1 tomato, peeled, seeded and chopped

1 courgette, chopped

1 leek, white part only chopped

80 g/3 oz long-grain rice • salt and pepper

Parmesan cheese, freshly grated, to serve

FARRO AND BEAN MINESTRONE

Heat the olive oil in a saucepan, add the onion, carrot, celery and garlic and cook over a low heat, stirring occasionally, for 5 minutes. Sprinkle with the wine and cook until it has evaporated. Add the tomatoes and sage leaves and simmer, stirring occasionally, for 15 minutes. Add the beans and 1 litre/1³/₄ pints water, bring to the boil, then lower the heat and simmer for 1 hour. Transfer to a food processor and process to a purée. Pour into a clean pan, bring to the boil, season with salt and pepper to taste and add the farro. Lower the heat and simmer for 1¹/₂ hours. Ladle into a soup tureen, drizzle with olive oil and serve.

MINESTRONE DI FARRO E FAGIOLI

Serves 4

2 tablespoons olive oil, plus extra for drizzling

1 onion, chopped • 1 carrot, chopped

1 celery stick, chopped • 1 garlic clove, chopped

100 ml/3¹/₂ fl oz white wine

2 tomatoes, peeled and chopped

2 fresh sage leaves

150 g/5 oz dried white beans, soaked in cold water overnight and drained

200 g/7 oz pearl farro, soaked in cold water overnight and drained

salt and pepper

WINTER MINESTRONE

Put the potatoes, carrots, turnip, leeks, cabbage, celery and chard stalks into a saucepan, pour in 1.5 litres/2¹/₂ pints water, add a pinch of salt and bring to the boil. Lower the heat and simmer for 1 hour. Season with salt. Transfer 2 ladlefuls of the mixture to a food processor, process to a purée and return to the pan. Mix well and cook for a few minutes more. Stir in the parsley and oil, ladle into a soup tureen and serve.

MINESTRONE D'INVERNO

Serves 4

2 potatoes, chopped • 2 carrots, chopped

1 turnip, chopped • 2 leeks, trimmed and chopped

1 small Savoy cabbage, shredded

1 celery stick, chopped

bunch of Swiss chard stalks, chopped

1 tablespoon chopped fresh flat-leaf parsley

1 tablespoon olive oil

salt

SEASONAL MINESTRONE

Put the mushrooms in a bowl, pour in warm water to cover and set aside to soak for 20 minutes, then drain. Cook the broad beans in lightly salted, boiling water for 10 minutes, then add the potatoes, French beans, courgettes and mushrooms. Stir in 3 tablespoons of the oil and cook a further 15 minutes until the vegetables are tender. Add the pasta and cook for 15 minutes. Meanwhile, heat the remaining oil with the garlic in a small saucepan, add the tomatoes and tomato purée, season with salt and pepper and cook over a low heat, stirring occasionally, for 10–15 minutes. Stir the tomato mixture into the soup and serve.

MINESTRONE DI STAGIONE

Serves 4

20 g/³/₄ oz dried mushrooms

200 g/7 oz shelled broad beans

2 potatoes, sliced

200 g/7 oz French beans, chopped

200 g/7 oz courgettes, sliced

5 tablespoons olive oil

100 g/3¹/₂ oz ditalini pasta

1 garlic clove, chopped

3 tomatoes, peeled and chopped

1 teaspoon concentrated tomato purée

salt and pepper

SAVOY CABBAGE AND RICE MINESTRONE

Heat 1 tablespoon of the oil in a saucepan with 100 ml/3¹/₂ fl oz water, add the leeks, prosciutto and rosemary and cook over a low heat for 10 minutes until the leeks have softened. Add the tomatoes, season with salt and pepper and cook for a further 10 minutes. Stir in the cabbage, add 1 litre /1³/₄ pints warm water, increase the heat to medium and simmer for 15 minutes. Bring to the boil, add the rice and stir and cook for about 18 minutes until tender. Ladle into a soup tureen, stir in the remaining oil and the Parmesan and serve.

MINESTRONE DI VERZA E RISO

Serves 4–6

4 tablespoons olive oil

2 leeks, trimmed and chopped

1 thick prosciutto slice, chopped

1 fresh rosemary sprig

2 tomatoes, peeled, seeded and coarsely chopped

600 g/1 lb 5 oz Savoy cabbage, cut into strips

100 g/3¹/₂ oz long-grain rice

1 tablespoon Parmesan cheese, freshly grated

salt and pepper

THICK SOUPS

The distinctive characteristic of most Italian thick soups is the immersion of one or more slices of bread in the stock with no additional pasta or rice. Other typical ingredients include pulses, fish and vegetables. Thick soups are tasty and aromatic and are often cooked au gratin in the oven. Onion Soup (see page 249) is particularly delicious and famous, while Pavian Soup (see page 248), served with an egg lying on golden fried bread, is especially attractive.

RIBOLLITA

RIBOLLITA

Serves 4

3 tablespoons olive oil, plus extra for drizzling

1 carrot, chopped

1 onion, chopped

1 celery stick, chopped

3 fresh or canned tomatoes, peeled

1 fresh thyme sprig

2 potatoes, coarsely diced

675 g/1¹/₂ lb cavolo nero

(Tuscan cabbage), shredded

150 g/5 oz fresh white beans,

or 80 g/3 oz dried white beans,

soaked in cold water overnight and drained

4 country-style bread slices

salt and pepper

This soup is called ribollita (reboiled) because it was originally made using the previous day's leftover vegetable soup heated in an earthenware pot with thinly sliced onion, black pepper and olive oil sprinkled on the surface. It was taken off the heat and served when the onion had turned golden brown. Today, however, it is normally made as follows. Heat the oil in a saucepan, add the carrot, onion and celery and cook over a low heat, stirring occasionally, for 5 minutes until softened. Add the tomatoes, thyme and potatoes and cook for a few minutes, then add the cavolo nero and beans. Pour in 2 litres/3¹/₂ pints water and season with salt. Bring to the boil, lower the heat, cover and simmer for about 2 hours. Preheat the oven to 180°C/350°F/Gas Mark 4. Place the bread on the base of a large earthenware casserole and ladle in the soup. Cook in the oven for about 10 minutes. Sprinkle with pepper and drizzle with oil.

PAVIAN SOUP

ZUPPA ALLA PAVESE

Serves 4

750 ml/1¼ pints Meat Stock (see page 208)

25 g/1 oz butter

8 bread slices, crusts removed

4 eggs

4 tablespoons Parmesan cheese, freshly grated

salt

Preheat the oven to 200°C/400°F/Gas Mark 6. Bring the stock to the boil. Meanwhile, melt the butter in a frying pan, add the bread, in batches, and fry until golden on both sides. Drain on kitchen paper. Place the fried bread on the base of four ovenproof soup bowls. Break an egg on top of each, ladle in the boiling stock and sprinkle with the Parmesan. Place the bowls on a baking sheet in the oven for a few minutes until the cheese melts. Alternatively, you can serve the soup immediately after adding the cheese. This soup is substantial, but delicate at the same time.

BARLEY SOUP AL VERDE

ZUPPA CON ORZO AL VERDE

Serves 4

1.5 litres/2½ pints Meat Stock (see page 208)

3 tablespoons olive oil

1 onion, chopped

1 fresh sage leaf

100 g/3½ oz Savoy cabbage, cut into strips

250 g/9 oz spinach, chopped

120 g/4 oz pearl barley

25 g/1 oz Parmesan cheese, freshly grated

salt

croûtons, to serve

Bring the stock to the boil. Heat the oil in another pan, add the onion and sage leaf and cook over a low heat, stirring occasionally, for 5 minutes. Stir in the cabbage and spinach and cook for a few minutes more. Pour in the hot stock, cover and cook on a medium heat for 15 minutes. Add the barley, season with salt and cook for a further 30 minutes. Remove from the heat, ladle into a soup tureen, sprinkle with the Parmesan and serve with croûtons.

BARLEY AND PEA SOUP

ZUPPA CON ORZO E PISELLI

Serves 4

500 ml/18 fl oz milk

200 g/7 oz barley

150 g/5 oz shelled fresh peas or frozen peas

pinch of chilli powder

salt and pepper

Bring the milk and 1 litre/1¾ pints water to the boil. Add the barley and peas, season with salt, pepper and chilli powder to taste and cook over a low heat for about 30 minutes, stirring occasionally. Ladle into a soup tureen. This is a very simple soup, but is nutritious and tasty. It may be enriched by adding diced chicken breast.

CABBAGE SOUP

Heat the oil in a saucepan, add the onion, carrot and celery and cook over a low heat, stirring occasionally, for 10 minutes until lightly browned. Add both kinds of cabbage, season with salt and cook for 10 minutes. Pour in 1.5 litres/2½ pints water and bring to the boil. Lower the heat, cover and simmer for 1 hour. If the soup is too watery, remove the lid and cook for a few minutes more. Preheat the oven to 200°C/400°F/Gas Mark 6. Toast the bread on both sides under a preheated grill and place in four ovenproof soup bowls. Ladle the soup over it, sprinkle with the Parmesan and place on a baking sheet in the oven for a few minutes until the cheese melts.

ZUPPA DI CAVOLI

Serves 4

3 tablespoons olive oil

1 onion, chopped

1 carrot, chopped

1 celery stick, chopped

200 g/7 oz Savoy cabbage, cut into strips

200 g/7 oz white cabbage, cut into strips

4 country-style bread slices

4 tablespoons Parmesan cheese, freshly grated

salt and pepper

ESCAROLE SOUP

Bring the stock to the boil. Meanwhile, parboil the escarole in boiling water for 5 minutes. Drain, squeezing out as much liquid as possible, and chop coarsely. Melt the butter in a saucepan, add the escarole and cook over a high heat for about 10 minutes, then add the stock. Beat the eggs with the Parmesan, season with salt and pepper and whisk into the soup. Lightly toast the bread on both sides under a preheated grill, put one slice in each of four soup bowls and ladle in the soup.

ZUPPA DI CICORIA

Serves 4

1.2 litres/2 pints Meat Stock (see page 208)

675 g/1½ lb escarole

25 g/1 oz butter

2 eggs

25 g/1 oz Parmesan cheese, freshly grated

4 country-style bread slices

salt and pepper

MILK AND ONION SOUP

Melt the butter in a saucepan, add the onions, cover and cook, stirring occasionally, over a very low heat for about 30 minutes until very soft and lightly browned. Meanwhile, bring the milk to just below simmering point in another saucepan. Add the milk to the onions, season with salt, increase the heat to medium and cook for a further 30 minutes, making sure that the soup does not boil over. Ladle into a soup tureen and serve with plenty of Parmesan and croûtons.

ZUPPA DI CIPOLLE AL LATTE

Serves 4

25 g/1 oz butter

400 g/14 oz onions, very thinly sliced

1 litre/1¾ pints milk

salt

To serve

Parmesan cheese, freshly grated

croûtons

ONION SOUP AU GRATIN

ZUPPA DI CIPOLLE GRATINATA

Serves 4

50 g/2 oz butter
400 g/14 oz onions, sliced
1.2 litres/2 pints Meat Stock (see page 208)
pinch of plain flour
8 toast slices
80 g/3 oz Emmenthal cheese, freshly grated
salt and pepper

Melt 40 g/1½ oz of the butter in a saucepan, add the onions, cover and cook over a very low heat, stirring occasionally, for about 30 minutes until very soft and lightly browned. Meanwhile, bring the stock to the boil. Sprinkle the onions with the flour, season with salt and pepper, pour in the stock and cook for a further 15 minutes. Meanwhile, preheat the oven to 200°C/400°F/Gas Mark 6. Ladle the soup into four ovenproof soup bowls, place two slices of toast in each and sprinkle with the Emmenthal. Dot with the remaining butter, season with pepper and place on a baking sheet in the oven for a few minutes until the cheese has melted.

MUSSEL SOUP

ZUPPA DI COZZE

Serves 4

20 mussels, scrubbed and beards removed
2 tablespoons olive oil
1 onion, chopped
pinch of saffron threads
2 tomatoes, peeled, seeded and chopped
1.5 litres/2½ pints Fish Stock (see page 208)
4 country-style bread slices
1 garlic clove, halved
1 tablespoon chopped fresh flat-leaf parsley
salt and pepper

Discard any mussels with broken shells or that do not shut immediately when sharply tapped. Put the mussels in a dry frying pan, place over a high heat and cook for about 5 minutes until the shells open. Discard any mussels that remain closed. Remove the mussels from the shells and set aside. Heat the olive oil in a saucepan, add the onion and saffron and cook over a low heat, stirring occasionally, for 5 minutes. Add the tomatoes and stock, season with salt and pepper and cook for 20 minutes. Add the mussels. Toast the bread on both sides under a preheated grill, then rub with the garlic and place a slice in each of four soup bowls. Ladle in the soup and sprinkle with the parsley.

BEAN AND BARLEY SOUP

ZUPPA DI FAGIOLI E ORZO

Serves 4

150 g/5 oz dried red kidney beans, soaked in cold water overnight and drained
2 tablespoons olive oil, plus extra for drizzling
50 g/2 oz pancetta, diced
1 garlic clove, chopped
1 small onion, chopped
150 g/5 oz barley
3 potatoes, diced
2 tablespoons tomato purée
salt and pepper

Put the beans in a saucepan, pour in 1 litre/1¾ pints water, bring to the boil and boil vigorously for 15 minutes, then lower the heat and simmer for 2 hours. Heat the oil in another pan, add the pancetta, garlic and onion and cook over a low heat, stirring occasionally, for 5 minutes. Add the barley and 1 litre/1¾ pints water, bring to the boil, then simmer for 2 hours. Add the beans, with their cooking liquid, the potatoes and tomato purée and season with salt and pepper to taste. Cook for 1 hour, then ladle into a soup tureen, drizzle with oil and serve.

OATMEAL SOUP

Put the potatoes, onion and pancetta into a saucepan, add 1.5 litres/2½ pints water and the oil, bring to the boil and cook for 15 minutes until the potatoes are tender. Season with salt to taste, stir in the rolled oats and cook for 10 minutes; this soup should be fairly thick. Ladle into a soup tureen and serve with Parmesan and croûtons.

ZUPPA DI FIOCCHI D'AVENA

Serves 4

4 potatoes, diced

1 onion, thinly sliced

1 pancetta slice, diced

1 tablespoon olive oil

50 g/2 oz rolled oats

salt

To serve

Parmesan cheese, freshly grated

croûtons

CHEESE AND LEEK SOUP

Bring the stock to the boil. Meanwhile, heat the butter and olive oil in another pan, add the leeks and cook over a low heat, stirring occasionally, for 5 minutes. Sprinkle with the nutmeg, season with salt and pepper, pour in the stock and cook for about 10 minutes. Preheat the oven to 180°C/350°F/Gas Mark 4. Place the bread in each of four ovenproof soup bowls, top with the fontina and sprinkle with the brandy and Emmenthal, then ladle in the soup. Place on a baking sheet in the oven for about 10 minutes, then leave to stand for a few minutes before serving.

ZUPPA DI FORMAGGI E PORRI

Serves 4

1.5 litres/2½ pints Meat Stock (see page 208)

50 g/2 oz butter

1 tablespoon olive oil

3 leeks, sliced

pinch of freshly grated nutmeg

4 country-style bread slices

100 g/3½ oz fontina cheese, sliced

100 g/3½ oz Emmenthal cheese, freshly grated

50 ml/2 fl oz brandy

salt and pepper

BEAN AND MUSHROOM SOUP

Put the beans in a saucepan, add 1.5 litres/2½ pints water, one of the garlic cloves and 1 tablespoon of the oil and bring to the boil, then lower the heat and simmer for 2 hours. Heat the remaining oil in a frying pan, add the onion and cook over a low heat, stirring occasionally, for 10 minutes until lightly browned. Add the porcini, increase the heat to high and cook for a few minutes more, then season with salt and pepper and tip the contents of the pan into the saucepan with the beans. Cook for a few more minutes, then add the parsley and taste and adjust the seasoning. Gently rub the bread with the remaining garlic, spread with a little butter, toast lightly and serve with the soup.

ZUPPA DI FUNGHI E FAGIOLI

Serves 4

300 g/11 oz dried cannellini beans,
soaked in cold water overnight and drained

2 garlic cloves

3 tablespoons olive oil

1 onion

500 g/1 lb 2 oz porcini, thinly sliced

1 tablespoon chopped fresh flat–leaf parsley

8 country-style bread slices

butter, for spreading

salt and pepper

ZUPPA DI GRANCHI

Serves 4

1 onion

1 fresh thyme sprig

1 clove

1 kg/2¼ lb live crabs

2 tomatoes, peeled, seeded and chopped

100 ml/3½ fl oz dry white wine

1 egg yolk

½ tablespoon cornflour

pinch of saffron threads

salt and pepper

thick bread slices, toasted, to serve

CRAB SOUP

Cook the onion in boiling water for about 20 minutes until soft, then drain. Bring 1.2 litres/2 pints lightly salted water to the boil, add the thyme and clove and plunge in the crabs. Cover and cook for 5 minutes, then drain, reserving the cooking liquid. Stand each crab on one edge, then prise the shell apart with your thumbs. Break off the legs and claws, crack them open and pick out the meat. Pull off and discard the gills from the sides of the body, split open the body and prise out the meat. Chop the crab meat and the boiled onion and combine them with the tomatoes. Add the mixture to the reserved cooking liquid, pour in the wine and cook over a medium heat for about 15 minutes. Beat the egg yolk with the cornflour in a bowl, then stir into the soup. Season with salt and pepper and stir in the saffron just before ladling into a soup tureen. Serve the soup very hot with toast.

ZUPPA DI LATTUGHE GRATINATA

Serves 4

65 g/2½ oz butter, plus extra for greasing

4 lettuces, shredded

1 tablespoon plain flour

1 litre/1¾ pints Meat Stock (see page 208)

4 home-made bread slices, toasted

100 g/3½ oz Emmenthal cheese, freshly grated

1 tablespoon chopped fresh flat-leaf parsley

salt and pepper

LETTUCE SOUP AU GRATIN

Melt the butter in a small saucepan, add the lettuces and cook over a low heat, stirring occasionally, for 30 minutes. Season with salt and pepper and stir in the flour. Gradually stir in the stock and simmer for 40 minutes over a low heat. Preheat the oven to 180°C/350°F/Gas Mark 4. Grease an ovenproof soup tureen or dish with butter. Place the toast in the prepared dish, sprinkle with the Emmenthal and ladle in the soup. Cook in the oven for 10 minutes. Sprinkle with the parsley and serve.

ZUPPA DI PANE

Serves 4

250 g/9 oz dried cannellini beans,
soaked in cold water overnight and drained

4 tablespoons olive oil, plus extra for drizzling

$^1/_2$ onion, chopped

2 garlic cloves, chopped

1 carrot, chopped

1 celery stick, chopped

1 fresh flat-leaf parsley sprig, chopped

50 g/2 oz prosciutto

$^1/_2$ Savoy cabbage, shredded

1 bunch of Swiss chard, chopped

2 potatoes, coarsely chopped

2 tablespoons tomato purée

400 g/14 oz day-old bread, thinly sliced

salt and pepper

THICK BREAD SOUP

Put the beans in a saucepan, add cold water to cover and bring to the boil, then lower the heat and simmer for about 2 hours until tender. Heat the oil in another pan, add the onion, garlic, carrot, celery, parsley and prosciutto and cook over a low heat, stirring occasionally, for 10 minutes until lightly browned. Add the cabbage, Swiss chard and potatoes and season with salt and pepper to taste. Stir the tomato purée with 300 ml/$^1/_2$ pint of the bean cooking liquid in a bowl, then stir into the pan of vegetables and prosciutto. Cover and cook over a medium heat for 15–20 minutes until all the vegetables are tender. Meanwhile, drain the beans, pass them through a food mill, then stir them into the vegetable mixture and simmer for a further 10 minutes. Place the bread in a soup tureen, ladle in the soup and leave to stand in a warm place for about 20 minutes so that most of the liquid soaks into the bread. Drizzle with olive oil before serving.

ZUPPA DI PANE E LENTICCHIE

Serves 4

200 g/7 oz lentils, soaked in cold water
for 2 hours and drained

2 garlic cloves, chopped

1 leek, white part only, thinly sliced

1 fresh thyme sprig, chopped

1.5 litres/2$^1/_2$ pints Meat Stock (see page 208)

2 eggs

4 day-old bread slices

3 tablespoons olive oil, plus extra for drizzling

salt and pepper

BREAD AND LENTIL SOUP

Put the lentils, garlic, leek and thyme into a saucepan, pour in the stock and bring to the boil, then lower the heat and simmer for 2 hours. If necessary, add a little hot water during cooking. Beat the eggs with a pinch of salt in a shallow dish and dip in the bread. Heat the oil in a frying pan, add the egg-coated bread and fry until golden on both sides. Drain on kitchen paper and place a slice in each of four soup bowls. Ladle in the lentils, season with salt and pepper and drizzle with oil.

ZUPPA DI PATATE

Serves 4

2 tablespoons olive oil

4 pancetta slices, chopped

6 potatoes, sliced

1 onion, sliced

2 small carrots, grated

salt and pepper

fresh flat-leaf parsley, chopped, to garnish

POTATO SOUP

Heat the oil in a saucepan, add the pancetta and cook, stirring occasionally, for 5 minutes. Add the potatoes, onion and carrots and cook, stirring frequently, for 10 minutes until golden brown. Season with salt and pepper. Pour in 1.5 litres/2$^1/_2$ pints water and bring to the boil. Lower the heat and simmer for about 1 hour until thickened. Serve garnished with parsley.

POTATO AND CLAM SOUP

Discard any clams with broken shells or that do not shut immediately when sharply tapped. Place the clams in a large frying pan, add the wine and cook over a high heat for about 5 minutes until the shells open. Drain the clams, reserving the cooking liquid, and discard any that remain closed. Remove the clams from their shells and strain the cooking liquid through a fine strainer. Heat the oil in a saucepan, add the celery, onion and carrot and cook over a low heat, stirring occasionally, for 10 minutes until lightly browned. Add the tomatoes, potatoes, reserved cooking liquid and 1.2 litres/2 pints water. Bring to the boil and add the rosemary and chervil, then lower the heat and simmer for about 1 hour. Add the clams and season with salt and pepper to taste. Remove and discard the rosemary sprig. Put a slice of bread on the base of each of four soup bowls and ladle in the soup.

ZUPPA DI PATATE E VONGOLE

Serves 4

1.5 kg/3¼ lb clams, scrubbed

100 ml/3½ fl oz dry white wine

3 tablespoons olive oil

1 celery stick, chopped

1 onion, chopped

1 carrot, chopped

4 tomatoes, peeled, seeded and chopped

2 potatoes, diced

1 fresh rosemary sprig

1 tablespoon fresh chervil leaves

4 country-style bread slices

salt and pepper

LEEK AND LENTIL SOUP

Put the pancetta into a saucepan and cook over a low heat until tender, add the lentils and cook for a further 10 minutes. Transfer half the mixture to a food processor and process to a purée. Heat the oil in a frying pan, add the leek and cook over a low heat for about 10 minutes until lightly browned. Remove the leek from the pan and add the slices of bread. Cook until golden brown on both sides. Put the slices of bread and the leek into four soup plates and ladle in the purée and the whole lentils. Season with a pinch of white pepper and serve.

ZUPPA DI PORRI E LENTICCHIE

Serves 4

3 slices pancetta, cut into strips

500 g/1 lb 2 oz cooked or canned lentils, drained

2 tablespoons olive oil

1 leek, white part only, thinly sliced

8 milk bread slices

white pepper

RADICCHIO SOUP

Melt the butter in a saucepan, add the leeks and cook over a low heat, stirring occasionally, for 5 minutes until soft- ened. Add the radicchio, stir in the flour and season with salt and pepper to taste. Pour in the stock, bring to the boil, then lower the heat and simmer for 1 hour. Preheat the oven to 200°C/400°F/Gas Mark 6. Place the slices of bread on the base of an ovenproof soup tureen or dish, sprinkle with the Parmesan and ladle in the soup. Cook in the oven for about 10 minutes.

ZUPPA DI RADICCHIO

Serves 4

50 g/2 oz butter

2 leeks, white parts only, thinly sliced

4 heads radicchio, shredded

50 g/2 oz plain flour

1 litre/1¾ pints Meat Stock (see page 208)

4 home-made bread slices, toasted

4 tablespoons Parmesan cheese, freshly grated

salt and pepper

FROG SOUP

ZUPPA DI RANE

Serves 4

24 frogs

3 tablespoons olive oil

1 onion, sliced

1 carrot, sliced

1 celery stick, chopped

1 garlic clove

3 tomatoes, peeled and chopped

1.5 litres/2¹/₂ pints Meat Stock (see page 208)

1 tablespoon chopped fresh flat-leaf parsley

salt and pepper

4 country-style bread slices, toasted, to serve

Remove the frogs' legs and set aside. Heat the oil in a saucepan, add the onion, carrot, celery and garlic and cook over a low heat, stirring occasionally, for 10 minutes until lightly browned. Add the frogs and mix well, then add the tomatoes and stock and season with salt and pepper. Bring to the boil, then lower the heat and simmer until the frogs have almost disintegrated. Transfer to a food processor and process to a purée. Return the purée to the saucepan, add the frogs' legs and cook for a further 15 minutes. Ladle into a soup tureen, sprinkle with the parsley and serve with toast.

PUMPKIN SOUP

ZUPPA DI ZUCCA

Serves 4

1 kg/2¹/₄ lb pumpkin, peeled, seeded and chopped

1.5 litres/2¹/₂ pints Meat Stock (see page 208)

40 g/1¹/₂ oz butter

2 onions, chopped

2 potatoes, diced

1 garlic clove, chopped

3 day-old bread slices

150 g/5 oz Gruyère cheese, freshly grated

200 ml /7 fl oz double cream

salt and pepper

Steam the pumpkin for about 20 minutes. Bring the stock to the boil. Melt the butter in another pan, add the onions and cook over a low heat, stirring occasionally, for 5 minutes until softened. Add the potatoes, pumpkin and garlic, season with salt and pepper to taste, pour in the hot stock and simmer for about 30 minutes. Lightly toast the bread, then dice it. Mix together the Gruyère, cream, bread and a pinch of pepper in a bowl. Divide the mixture between four individual soup bowls and ladle in the soup.

COURGETTE SOUP

ZUPPA DI ZUCCHINE

Serves 4

6 courgettes, cut into thin batons

3 onions, thinly sliced

500 g/1 lb 2 oz tomatoes, peeled, seeded and chopped

3 tablespoons olive oil

1 litre/1³/₄ pints Meat Stock (see page 208)

1 egg

40 g/1¹/₂ oz Parmesan cheese, freshly grated

4 country-style bread slices, lightly toasted

salt

Put the courgettes, onions, tomatoes and olive oil into a saucepan and cook over a medium heat, stirring occasionally, for 20 minutes. Pour in the stock, season with salt and bring to the boil. Lower the heat and simmer for about 20 minutes until the courgettes are falling apart. Beat the egg with the Parmesan and a pinch of salt. Remove the pan from the heat and stir in the egg mixture. Put a slice of toast in each of four soup bowls and ladle in the soup.

GNOCCHI

Potato gnocchi take pride of place as an all-Italian classic. When making them it is better to steam the potatoes rather than boil them, so that the gnocchi are lighter and, at the same time, tastier and firmer. In either case, the potatoes must always be mashed with a potato masher while they are still hot. This makes the dough easier to knead, and smoother. Gnocchi should be cooked in lightly salted water to prevent them disintegrating. They should be added to the boiling water a few at a time and lifted out gradually with a slotted spoon as they rise to the surface. To cook ricotta, pumpkin, Parmesan or other types of gnocchi, follow the methods shown in the various recipes. Semolina or ricotta gnocchi are particularly suitable for serving at the start of a formal luncheon.

DRY FIRST COURSES

PARISIAN GNOCCHI

Preheat the oven to 200°C/400°F/Gas Mark 6 and grease an ovenproof dish with butter. Heat the milk with a pinch of salt in a fairly deep saucepan and add the butter. When it has melted, tip in all the flour at once, stirring constantly. Lower the heat and stir constantly for about 10 minutes until the mixture comes away from the sides of the saucepan. Remove the pan from the heat, leave to cool slightly, then stir in the eggs, one at a time. Season with salt and pepper. Bring a large pan of lightly salted water to the boil. Using a piping bag with a 1.5-cm/²/₃-inch nozzle drop small pieces of the mixture into the boiling water. The gnocchi rise to the surface when they are ready. Remove with a slotted spoon and spread out in the prepared dish. Spoon the béchamel sauce over them, sprinkle with the Parmesan and bake for about 20 minutes until golden and bubbling.

GNOCCHI ALLA PARIGINA

Serves 4–6

100 g/3¹/₂ oz butter, plus extra for greasing

1 litre/1³/₄ pints milk

275 g/10 oz plain flour

6 eggs

1 quantity Béchamel Sauce (see page 50)

80 g/3 oz Parmesan cheese, freshly grated

salt and pepper

ROMAN GNOCCHI

GNOCCHI ALLA ROMANA

Serves 4–6

150 g/5 oz butter, plus extra for greasing

1 litre/1³/₄ pints milk

250 g/9 oz semolina

2 egg yolks

150 g/5 oz pecorino cheese, freshly grated

salt

Preheat the oven to 200°C/400°F/Gas Mark 6. Grease an ovenproof dish with butter. Pour the milk into a saucepan, add a pinch of salt and bring to the boil. Sprinkle in the semolina, stirring constantly, and cook, stirring, for 10 minutes. Leave to cool slightly, then stir in the egg yolks, one at a time, followed by 40 g/1¹/₂ oz of the pecorino and 50 g/2 oz of the butter. Pour the semolina on to a work surface and spread out to a depth of about 1 cm/¹/₂ inch with a damp knife. Stamp out rounds with a 4-cm/1¹/₂-inch biscuit cutter and place a layer of rounds in the prepared dish. Sprinkle with some of the remaining pecorino and dot with a little of the remaining butter. Continue making layers in this way until all the ingredients are used up. Bake for 15 minutes until golden brown.

BREAD GNOCCHI

GNOCCHI DI PANE

Serves 4

250 g/9 oz day-old bread

500 ml/18 fl oz milk

2 eggs

200 g/7 oz plain flour

pinch of freshly grated nutmeg

50 g/2 oz butter

1 garlic clove

2 fresh sage leaves

50 g/2 oz Parmesan cheese, freshly grated

salt and pepper

Tear the bread into small pieces. Pour the milk into a saucepan and bring to just below boiling point, add a pinch of salt and remove from the heat. Add the bread, leave to soften, then beat with a wooden spoon to a smooth mixture. Beat in the eggs and stir in the flour a little at a time. Stir in the nutmeg and season with salt and pepper. The mixture should have the consistency of a thick purée. Cover and leave to stand in a cool place for about 2 hours. Bring a large pan of water to the boil and add a pinch of salt. Drop in tablespoonfuls of the mixture, a few at a time, and cook for about 5 minutes, then remove with a slotted spoon and keep warm while you cook the remaining gnocchi. Meanwhile, melt the butter in a small saucepan, add the garlic and sage and cook for a few minutes. Place the gnocchi on a warm serving dish, discard the garlic clove and pour the sage butter over them. Sprinkle with Parmesan and serve.

BREAD AND SPINACH GNOCCHI

Tear the bread into pieces, place in a large bowl, add the milk and leave until it has been completely absorbed. Meanwhile, cook the spinach, in just the water clinging to the leaves after washing, for about 5 minutes until tender. Drain, squeezing out as much liquid as possible, and chop. Melt 20 g/³/₄ oz of the butter in a frying pan, add the spinach and 40 g/1¹/₂ oz of the Parmesan and cook, stirring frequently, for 5 minutes. Remove the pan from the heat and stir into the bowl of bread, then stir in the egg and flour. Make long rolls with the mixture, cut them into pieces the same length, dust lightly with flour and shake off any excess. Bring a large pan of lightly salted water to the boil, add the gnocchi, and when they rise to the surface remove with a slotted spoon. Meanwhile, melt the remaining butter. Drain the gnocchi well, arrange on a warm serving dish and pour the melted butter over them. Sprinkle with the remaining Parmesan, mix gently and serve.

GNOCCHI DI PANE E SPINACI

Serves 4

350 g/12 oz day-old bread

200 ml/7 fl oz milk

675 g/1¹/₂ lb spinach

100 g/3¹/₂ oz butter

80 g/3 oz Parmesan cheese, freshly grated

1 egg

100 g/3¹/₂ oz plain flour, plus extra for dusting

salt

PARMESAN GNOCCHI

Grease a broad, shallow ovenproof dish with butter. Melt 100 g/3¹/₂ oz of the butter in a double boiler. Pour the milk into a saucepan, add the melted butter, then tip in all the flour at once, stirring constantly. Beat in the eggs, one at a time. Before adding the next egg, make sure that the previous one has been thoroughly incorporated. Add half the Parmesan and the nutmeg and season with salt and pepper. Place the saucepan over a medium heat and bring to the boil, whisking constantly. Simmer, whisking constantly, for 10 minutes, then pour the mixture on to a work surface and spread out evenly to a depth of 1 cm/¹/₂ inch using a damp knife. Leave to cool. Preheat the oven to 200°C/400°F/Gas Mark 6. Stamp out rounds of the mixture with a biscuit cutter, place the trimmings on the base of the prepared dish and cover with concentric circles of rounds to form a sort of dome. Sprinkle with the remaining Parmesan, dot with the remaining butter and bake for about 30 minutes until light golden brown. Leave to stand for 5 minutes before serving.

GNOCCHI DI PARMIGIANO

Serves 4

150 g/5 oz butter, plus extra for greasing

1 litre/1³/₄ pints milk

250 g/9 oz plain flour

4 eggs

100 g/3¹/₂ oz Parmesan cheese, freshly grated

pinch of freshly grated nutmeg

salt and pepper

GNOCCHI DI PATATE (RICETTA BASE)

Serves 4

1 kg/2¹/₄ lb potatoes

200 g/7 oz plain flour, plus extra for dusting

1 egg, lightly beaten

salt

choice of sauce, to serve

POTATO GNOCCHI (BASIC RECIPE)

Steam the potatoes for 25 minutes or until tender, then mash with a potato masher while they are still hot. Stir in the flour, egg and a pinch of salt and knead to a soft, elastic dough. Be careful with the ratio of potato to flour: if there is too much flour, the gnocchi will be hard; if there is too much potato, they tend to disintegrate while cooking. Shape the dough into long rolls just over 1.5 cm/²/₃ inch in diameter and cut into 2-cm/³/₄-inch lengths. Press them gently against the underside of a grater and arrange on a tea towel dusted with flour. Bring a large pan of lightly salted water to the boil, add the gnocchi, a few at a time, and remove with a slotted spoon as they rise to the surface. Drain, put on a warm serving dish and pour your chosen sauce over them.

GNOCCHI DI PATATE ALLA BAVA

Serves 4

1 quantity Potato Gnocchi (see above)

80 g/3 oz butter

120 g/4 oz fontina cheese, diced

salt

Parmesan cheese, freshly grated, to serve

GNOCCHI ALLA BAVA

Cook the gnocchi, a few at a time, in lightly salted, boiling water. As they rise to the surface, remove with a slotted spoon, drain well and place on a warm serving dish. Dot with the butter, sprinkle with the fontina, mix gently and serve immediately with Parmesan.

GNOCCHI DI PATATE ALLE NOCI

Serves 4

800 g/1³/₄ lb potatoes

120 g/4 oz Parmesan cheese, freshly grated

12 shelled walnuts, finely chopped

2 eggs, lightly beaten

1 tablespoon semolina

40 g/1¹/₂ oz butter, melted

salt and pepper

WALNUT GNOCCHI

Steam the potatoes for 25 minutes until tender, then mash with a potato masher while still hot and knead with 80 g/3 oz of the Parmesan, and the walnuts and eggs. Season with salt to taste, then add the semolina. The dough should be well mixed and the right consistency. If necessary, add more semolina. Shape into long rolls, cut into shorter lengths and press them gently against the underside of a grater. Bring a large pan of lightly salted water to the boil, add the gnocchi, a few at a time, and remove with a slotted spoon as they rise to the surface. Place on a warm serving dish, pour the melted butter over them, sprinkle with the remaining Parmesan and season with pepper.

GNOCCHI DI PATATE ALLE ORTICHE

Serves 4

1 kg/2¼ lb potatoes

200 g/7 oz stinging nettles, finely chopped

200 g/7 oz plain flour

1 egg, lightly beaten

80 g/3 oz butter

1 garlic clove

4 fresh sage leaves

50 g/2 oz Parmesan cheese, freshly grated

salt

POTATO AND NETTLE GNOCCHI

Steam or boil the potatoes for 25 minutes until tender, then mash with a potato masher while still hot. Stir in the nettles, followed by the flour. Beat in the egg, season with salt and knead. Divide the dough into several pieces and shape each into a roll about 1.5cm/²⁄₃ inch in diameter. Cut into 2-cm/³⁄₄-inch lengths and press them gently against the underside of a grater. Bring a large pan of lightly salted water to the boil, add the gnocchi, a few at a time, and remove with a slotted spoon as they rise to the surface. Meanwhile, melt the butter in a small frying pan, add the garlic and sage leaves and cook for a few minutes until the garlic is lightly browned. Remove and discard the garlic. Place the gnocchi on a warm serving dish, pour the sage butter over them, sprinkle with the Parmesan and mix gently.

GNOCCHI DI PATATE CON GLI SCAMPI

Serves 4

1 kg/2¼ lb potatoes

200 g/7 oz plain flour

1 egg, lightly beaten

50 g/2 oz Parmesan cheese, freshly grated

salt

For the sauce

4 tablespoons olive oil

400 g/14 oz langoustines or Dublin Bay prawns, peeled and chopped

1 tablespoon chopped fresh flat-leaf parsley

4 tablespoons dry white wine

100 ml/3½ fl oz double cream

200 g/7 oz tomatoes, peeled and diced

salt and pepper

POTATO GNOCCHI WITH LANGOUSTINES

Cook the potatoes in lightly salted, boiling water for 25 minutes until tender, then mash with a potato masher while still hot. Add the flour, egg, Parmesan and a pinch of salt and knead to a soft, elastic dough. Divide into several pieces and shape into long rolls about 1.5 cm/²⁄₃ inch in diameter. Cut into 2-cm/³⁄₄-inch lengths and press them gently against the underside of a grater. To make the sauce, heat the oil in a frying pan, add the langoustines or prawns and parsley and cook for 2 minutes. Sprinkle with the wine and cook until it has evaporated, then stir in the cream and tomatoes. Cook for 5 minutes, then remove from the heat. Meanwhile, bring a large pan of lightly salted water to the boil. Add the gnocchi, a few at a time, and remove with a slotted spoon as they rise to the surface. Place the gnocchi on a warm serving dish and pour the langoustine sauce over them.

POTATO GNOCCHI FILLED WITH FONDUE

Put the fontina for the fondue in a heatproof bowl, add milk to cover and set aside to soak overnight. The next day, cook the potatoes in lightly salted, boiling water, then drain and mash while still hot. Beat in the flour, egg and a pinch of salt and leave to stand. Meanwhile, prepare the fondue. Add the butter and egg yolks to the fontina and mix well. Set the bowl over a pan of barely simmering water and cook, stirring constantly, to a smooth, thick cream. Season with salt to taste and leave to cool. Halve the potato dough, roll out one piece and arrange small heaps of fondue on top as if making ravioli. Roll out the second piece of dough and cover the first, pressing the edges down well, then cut out with a pastry wheel. Bring a large pan of lightly salted water to the boil, add the gnocchi, a few at a time, and remove with a slotted spoon as they rise to the surface. Meanwhile, melt the butter in a small frying pan, add the sage leaves and cook for a few minutes. Place the gnocchi on a warm serving dish and pour the sage butter over them. Serve with Parmesan.

GNOCCHI DI PATATE
CON RIPIENO DI FONDUTA

Serves 4

1 kg/2¹/₄ lb potatoes

200 g/7 oz plain flour, plus extra for dusting

1 egg, lightly beaten

50 g/2 oz butter

8 fresh sage leaves

salt

Parmesan cheese, freshly grated

For the fondue

400 g/14 oz fontina cheese, thinly sliced

300–425 ml/¹/₂–³/₄ pint milk

4 egg yolks

25 g/1 oz butter

salt

TRIESTIAN POTATO GNOCCHI WITH PRUNES

This regional recipe is traditionally made with fresh plums, blanched for 5–7 minutes, then split, stoned, stuffed with half a sugar cube and put back into shape again. However, when plums are out of season, prunes are often used. Split the prunes and remove the stones, if this has not already been done, and fill the cavity with a pinch of sugar. Cook the potatoes in lightly salted, boiling water for 25 minutes until tender, then mash while still hot. Spoon into a mound on a work surface, add the flour, egg and a pinch of salt and knead to a smooth dough. Make 12 egg-sized gnocchi and press a prune into each one. Bring a large pan of lightly salted water to the boil, add the gnocchi, a few at a time, and remove with a slotted spoon as they rise to the surface. Meanwhile, melt the butter in a small frying pan, add the breadcrumbs, cinnamon and a sprinkling of sugar and cook, stirring frequently, until golden. Place the gnocchi on a warm serving dish and garnish with the breadcrumbs.

GNOCCHI DI PATATE
CON SUSINE ALLA TRIESTINA

Serves 4

12 ready-to-eat prunes

20 g/³/₄ oz sugar, plus extra for sprinkling

1 kg/2¹/₄ lb potatoes

200 g/7 oz plain flour

1 egg

40 g/1¹/₂ oz butter

4 tablespoons breadcrumbs

pinch of ground cinnamon

salt

POTATO AND SPINACH GNOCCHI

Serves 4

675 g/1¹/₂ lb spinach

800 g/1³/₄ lb potatoes

200 g/7 oz plain flour, plus extra for dusting

2 egg yolks, lightly beaten

50 g/2 oz butter, melted

50 g/2 oz Parmesan cheese, freshly grated

salt

Cook the spinach, in just the water clinging to the leaves after washing, for 5 minutes, then drain, squeezing out as much liquid as possible, and chop. Cook the potatoes in lightly salted, boiling water for 25 minutes until tender, then mash while still hot. Mix together the potato, spinach and flour. Season with salt, beat in the egg yolks and knead the dough for a few minutes. Shape the dough into several long rolls, about 1.5cm/²/₃ inch in diameter. Cut into 2-cm/³/₄ inch lengths and press them gently against the underside of a grater. Dust lightly with flour. Bring a large pan of lightly salted water to the boil, add the gnocchi, a few at a time, and remove with a slotted spoon as they rise to the surface. Drain well and arrange on a warm serving dish. Pour the butter over them and sprinkle with the Parmesan. You could use the cooking juices from a roast instead.

RICOTTA AND SPINACH GNOCCHI

Serves 4

1 kg/2¹/₄ lb spinach

350 g/12 oz ricotta cheese

4 tablespoons Parmesan cheese, freshly grated

2 egg yolks, lightly beaten

plain flour, for dusting

50 g/2 oz butter, melted

salt and pepper

Cook the spinach, in just the water clinging to the leaves after washing, for 5 minutes, then drain, squeezing out as much liquid as possible, chop finely and put in a bowl. Add the ricotta, half the Parmesan and the egg yolks and season with salt and pepper. Shape the mixture into balls and dust lightly with flour. Bring a large pan of lightly salted water to the boil, add the gnocchi, a few at a time, and remove with a slotted spoon as they rise to the surface. Place the gnocchi on a warm serving dish, pour the melted butter over them and sprinkle with the remaining Parmesan. You could also serve them with a light Béchamel Sauce (see page 50).

RICE GNOCCHI

Serves 4

400 g/14 oz long-grain rice

4 eggs, lightly beaten

120–175 g/4–6 oz breadcrumbs

1 litre/1³/₄ pints Meat Stock (see page 208)

50 g/2 oz butter, melted

50 g/2 oz Gruyère cheese, freshly grated

50 g/2 oz Parmesan cheese, freshly grated

salt and pepper

Bring a large pan of salted water to the boil, add the rice and cook for 15–18 minutes until tender. Drain well and place in a bowl. Stir in the eggs and enough breadcrumbs to make a thick mixture and season with salt and pepper. Bring the stock to the boil. Shape the rice mixture into small gnocchi and add to the stock, a few at a time, and cook for a few minutes. Remove with a slotted spoon, drain well and arrange on a warm serving dish. Pour the butter over them and sprinkle with the cheeses.

GNOCCHI DI SEMOLINO AL PROSCIUTTO

Serves 4

25 g/1 oz butter, plus extra for greasing

1 litre/1³/₄ pints milk

250 g/9 oz semolina

2 egg yolks, lightly beaten

80 g/3 oz Parmesan cheese, freshly grated

100 g/3¹/₂ oz cooked ham, chopped

salt

SEMOLINA AND HAM GNOCCHI

Preheat the oven to 200°C/400°F/Gas Mark 6. Grease an ovenproof dish with butter. Bring the milk to the boil and add a pinch of salt. Sprinkle in the semolina, stirring constantly, and simmer, stirring, for 10 minutes. Remove the pan from the heat, leave to cool slightly, then stir in the egg yolks, 50 g/2 oz of the Parmesan and the ham. Shape the mixture into slightly squashed gnocchi, arrange in the prepared dish, sprinkle with the remaining Parmesan and dot with the butter. Bake for 30 minutes until golden brown.

GNOCCHI DI ZUCCA E AMARETTI

Serves 4

1 kg/2¹/₄ lb pumpkin, peeled, seeded and cut into chunks

4 eggs, lightly beaten

100 g/3¹/₂ oz amaretti, crushed

200 g/7 oz plain flour

50 g/2 oz butter

8 fresh sage leaves

50 g/2 oz Parmesan cheese, freshly grated

salt and pepper

PUMPKIN AND AMARETTI GNOCCHI

Preheat the oven to 200°C/400°F/Gas Mark 6. Place the pumpkin in an ovenproof dish and bake for about 45 minutes until softened. Mash the pumpkin with a potato masher while still hot. Stir in the eggs, amaretti and flour and season with salt and pepper. Knead well and leave to rest for 30 minutes. Melt the butter in a frying pan, add the sage leaves and cook for a few minutes. Bring a large saucepan of lightly salted water to the boil, add teaspoonfuls of the pumpkin mixture, a few at a time, and remove with a slotted spoon as they rise to the surface. Place on a warm serving dish, pour the sage butter over them and sprinkle with the Parmesan.

GNOCCHI INTEGRALI

Serves 4

200 ml/7 fl oz milk

50 g/2 oz wholemeal flour, plus extra for dusting

150 g/5 oz oat flakes

50 g/2 oz barley flakes

150 g/5 oz Parmesan cheese, freshly grated

1 tablespoon chopped fresh flat-leaf parsley

1 egg, lightly beaten

50 g/2 oz butter, melted

salt

WHOLEMEAL GNOCCHI

Heat the milk in a small pan to just below simmering point, then remove from the heat. Mix together the flour, oat and barley flakes, 100 g/3¹/₂ oz of the Parmesan, the parsley, egg and warm milk. This should produce a soft but thick dough. If necessary, add a few more oat or barley flakes and leave to rest for 30 minutes. Shape into several long rolls about 1.5cm/²/₃ inch in diameter and cut into 2-cm/³/₄-inch lengths. Place on a tea towel and sprinkle with flour. Bring a large pan of lightly salted water to the boil, add the gnocchi and cook for about 15 minutes. Drain, pour on the butter and sprinkle with the remaining Parmesan.

FRESH PASTA

Nowadays, in Italy fresh pasta is usually called egg pasta. It was once known as home-made pasta and was mostly prepared at holiday times. In those days, cappelletti, tortellini, lasagne, timbales, ravioli, pappardelle, tagliatelle, quadretti and agnolotti were invariably made by hand, but today it is more usual to use a pasta machine and other such kitchen appliances that halve the preparation time – or even to buy ready-made egg pasta and egg pasta products. For more information, see page 202.

QUANTITY

For four people, the recommended amounts are 200 g/7 oz flour, 2 eggs and a pinch of salt, which yield 275 g/10 oz fresh pasta, equivalent to about 65 g/2¹/₂ oz per person.

COOKING

Fresh pasta cooks more quickly than dried pasta. When boiling filled pasta, remember that the filing adds extra flavour, so reduce the quantity of salt in the water.

OIL

When boiling sheets of pasta for lasagne, add 1 tablespoon olive oil to the cooking water to prevent them from sticking.

SAUCE AND CHEESE

Fresh pasta is more absorbent than dried pasta, but otherwise the same recommendations apply: the grated cheese should be sprinkled on the pasta before the sauce and serving dish should be warm.

QUANTITIES
AND COOKING TIMES

FRESH PASTA DOUGH (BASIC RECIPE)

PASTA ALL'UOVO (RICETTA BASE)

Serves 4

200 g/7 oz plain flour, preferably Italian type 00,
plus extra for dusting

2 eggs, lightly beaten

salt

Sift the flour and a pinch of salt into a mound on a work surface. Make a well in the centre and add the eggs. Using your fingers, gradually incorporate the flour, then knead for about 10 minutes. If the mixture is too soft, add a little extra flour; if it is too firm, add a little water. Shape the dough into a ball and leave to rest for 15 minutes. Roll out on a lightly floured surface or use a pasta machine to make a thin sheet, and cut out tagliatelle, lasagne, etc.

GREEN PASTA DOUGH (BASIC RECIPE)

PASTA VERDE (RICETTA BASE)

Serves 4

200 g/7 oz plain flour, preferably Italian type 00,
plus extra for dusting

2 eggs, lightly beaten

100 g/3 ½ oz spinach, cooked,
well drained and chopped

salt

Sift the flour and a pinch of salt into a mound on a work surface. Make a well in the centre and add the eggs and spinach. Using your fingers, gradually incorporate the flour, then knead for a few minutes. If the spinach is very damp, add more flour, a little at a time. Shape the dough into a ball and leave to rest for 15 minutes, then roll out on a lightly floured surface or use a pasta machine to make a fairly thick sheet. This pasta may be used for lasagne, tagliatelle, tortellini and ravioli. A dish of green tagliatelle mixed with ordinary tagliatelle is called paglia e fieno, that is, straw and hay. The most suitable seasonings are classic sauces: ragù (meat sauce, see page 52) or butter and cheese.

AGNOLOTTI PIEDMONTESE

AGNOLOTTI ALLA PIEMONTESE

Serves 6

300 g/10½ oz plain flour,
preferably Italian type 00, plus extra for dusting

3 eggs, lightly beaten

salt

For the filling

250 g/9 oz spinach

400 g/14 oz braised beef, minced

2 egg yolks, lightly beaten • 1 egg, lightly beaten

50 g/2 oz Parmesan cheese, freshly grated

150 g/5 oz cooked ham, chopped

salt and pepper

Make the pasta dough (see Fresh Pasta Dough, above) with the quantities specified. Blanch the spinach in boiling water, drain, chop and mix with the beef in a bowl. Stir in the egg yolks, whole egg, Parmesan and ham and season with salt and pepper. If the mixture is a little dry, soften with a few tablespoons of gravy from the braised beef. Roll out the pasta dough into strips. Put mounds of filling at regular intervals along one strip, place another strip on top and press down well around the filling. Cut square agnolotti with a pasta or pastry wheel. Cook in salted, boiling water for about 10 minutes. Drain and dress with gravy from the braised beef or melted butter and grated Parmesan.

BIGOLI WITH ANCHOVIES

Sift the flour with a pinch of salt into a mound on a work surface and make a well in the centre. Add the eggs and enough water to make an elastic dough. Make the bigoli by pressing the dough through the bigolaro, a little at a time. Heat the oil in a pan, add the onions and parsley and cook over a low heat, stirring occasionally, for 5 minutes until the onions are softened. Add the anchovies and cook, mashing with a wooden spoon until they disintegrate. Cook the bigoli in salted, boiling water for 2–3 minutes until al dente. Drain and toss with the onion mixture.

BIGOLI ALLE ACCIUGHE

To make bigoli (thick spaghetti),
you need a small tool called bigolaro which
may be found in specialist kitchenware stores.

Serves 4–6

400 g/14 oz plain flour, preferably Italian type 00

3 eggs, lightly beaten • 4 tablespoons olive oil

2 onions, chopped

1 tablespoon chopped fresh flat-leaf parsley

3 canned anchovy fillets, drained • salt

CANNELLONI WITH BÉCHAMEL SAUCE

Preheat the oven to 200°C/400°F/Gas Mark 6. Grease an ovenproof dish with butter. Cook the spinach, in just the water clinging to the leaves after washing, for five minutes. Drain well and pass through a vegetable mill, then mix together with the veal, ham, Parmesan and egg and season to taste. Roll out the pasta dough into a thin sheet and cut into large rectangles. Cook the rectangles, a few at a time, in a large pan of salted, boiling water for 6–7 minutes. Drain on a damp tea towel. Put some of the spinach mixture and a little béchamel sauce on each rectangle and roll up from one long side. Arrange the cannelloni in a single layer in the prepared dish, pour the remaining béchamel sauce over them and dot with the butter. Bake for 20 minutes, then leave to rest for 5 minutes before serving.

CANNELLONI ALLA BESCIAMELLA

Serves 4

25 g/1 oz butter, plus extra for greasing

300 g/11 oz spinach

200 g/7 oz roast veal, chopped

1 slice cooked ham, chopped

2 tablespoons Parmesan cheese, freshly grated

1 egg, lightly beaten

1 quantity Fresh Pasta Dough (see opposite)

1 quantity Béchamel Sauce (see page 50)

salt and pepper

CHEESE AND PROSCIUTTO CRÊPES

Whisk together the eggs, flour, milk and a pinch of salt to make a smooth batter. Leave to rest for 30 minutes. Brush a 15-cm/6-inch crêpe pan with a little of the melted butter and heat the pan. Pour in 1 tablespoon batter, tilt the pan so that the batter covers the base and cook until the underside is set and golden. Turn over and cook the other side, then slide out of the pan. Continue making crêpes until the batter is used up, bearing in mind that about two crêpes per serving is usual. Preheat the oven to 200°C/400°F/Gas Mark 6. Grease an ovenproof dish with butter. Lay a slice of prosciutto on each crêpe and top with a slice of Gruyère or sottilette. Roll up the crêpes like cannelloni and arrange in layers in the prepared dish. Stir the grated Gruyère and the nutmeg into the béchamel sauce and season with salt and pepper. Pour over the crêpes and bake for 20 minutes. Leave to stand for 5 minutes before serving.

CRESPELLE DI FORMAGGIO E PROSCIUTTO

Serves 4

2 eggs, lightly beaten

100 g/3½ oz plain flour

250 ml/8 fl oz milk

1 teaspoon butter, melted, plus extra for greasing

100 g/3½ oz prosciutto slices

150 g/5 oz Gruyère cheese, or Italian sottilette

80 g/3 oz Gruyère cheese, freshly grated

pinch of freshly grated nutmeg

1 quantity Béchamel Sauce (see page 50)

salt and pepper

FETTUCCINE AL BURRO BRUNO

Serves 4

275 g/10 oz fettuccine

50 g/2 oz butter

4–5 tablespoons pan juices

50 g/2 oz Parmesan cheese, freshly grated

salt

FETTUCCINE IN BROWN BUTTER

Cook the fettuccine in a large pan of salted, boiling water for 2–3 minutes until al dente. Meanwhile, melt the butter in a frying pan over a low heat and stir in the pan juices, which should be fairly concentrated. Drain the pasta, add to the frying pan, toss well and transfer to a warm serving dish. Sprinkle with the Parmesan and serve.

FETTUCCINE IN SALSA BIANCA

Serves 4

1 quantity Fresh Pasta Dough (see page 268)

50 g/2 oz butter

80 g/3 oz Parmesan cheese, freshly grated

4 tablespoons double cream

salt and pepper

FETTUCCINE IN WHITE SAUCE

Roll out the pasta dough into a sheet, fold over and cut into fettuccine. Melt the butter in a small saucepan over a low heat and add half the Parmesan and a little pepper. Cook the fettuccine in a large pan of salted, boiling water for 2–3 minutes until al dente. Drain, return to the pan and toss with the cream and remaining Parmesan. Transfer to a warm serving dish, add the Parmesan and melted butter mixture, season with pepper and serve.

LASAGNE ALLA BOLOGNESE

Serves 4

3 tablespoons olive oil

1 carrot, chopped

1 onion, chopped

300 g/11 oz minced meat

100 ml/3$^{1}/_{2}$ fl oz dry white wine

250 g/9 oz passata

25 g/1 oz butter, plus extra for greasing

1 quantity Fresh Pasta Dough (see page 268)

1 quantity Béchamel Sauce (see page 50)

65 g/2$^{1}/_{2}$ oz Parmesan cheese, freshly grated

salt and pepper

LASAGNE BOLOGNESE

Heat the olive oil in a saucepan, add the carrot and onion and cook over a low heat, stirring occasionally, for 5 minutes. Add the meat and cook until browned, then pour in the wine and cook until it has evaporated. Season with salt, add the passata and simmer for 30 minutes, then season with pepper. Preheat the oven to 200°C/400°F/Gas Mark 6. Grease an ovenproof dish with butter. Roll out the pasta dough into a sheet. Cut into 10-cm/4-inch squares and cook, a few at a time, in plenty of lightly salted, boiling water for a few minutes. Drain and place on a damp tea towel. Arrange a layer of lasagne on the base of the prepared dish, spoon some of the meat sauce, then some of the béchamel sauce on top, sprinkle with some of the Parmesan and dot with some of the butter. Repeat the alternating layers until all the ingredients have been used, ending with a layer of béchamel sauce. Bake for 30 minutes.

LASAGNE NAPOLETANA

LASAGNE ALLA NAPOLETANA
Serves 6

300 g/11 oz plain flour, preferably Italian type 00, plus extra for dusting
3 eggs, lightly beaten
salt

For the filling
5 tablespoons olive oil
1 onion, chopped
1 carrot, chopped
1 celery stick, chopped
1/2 garlic clove, chopped
1 litre/1 3/4 pints passata
5 eggs
300 g/11 oz minced beef
50 g/2 oz Parmesan cheese, freshly grated
40 g/1 1/2 oz butter, plus extra for greasing
150 g/5 oz mozzarella cheese, sliced
salt and pepper

For the filling, heat 3 tablespoons of the oil in a saucepan, add the onion, carrot, celery and garlic and cook over a low heat, stirring occasionally, for 5 minutes, then add the passata. Season with salt and pepper and simmer for about 1 hour. Meanwhile, boil four of the eggs for 12 minutes, then refresh in cold water, shell and slice. Mix together the minced beef, Parmesan and remaining egg in a bowl and season with salt. Shape the mixture into small balls. Heat 25 g/1 oz of the butter and the remaining oil in a frying pan, add the meatballs and cook until browned all over, then add them to the tomato sauce. Make the pasta (see Fresh Pasta Dough, page 268) with the quantities specified and roll out into two thin sheets. Cut into 10-cm/4-inch squares and cook, a few at a time, in plenty of lightly salted, boiling water for a few minutes. Drain and place on a damp tea towel. Preheat the oven to 160°C/325°F/Gas Mark 3. Grease a large ovenproof dish with butter, arrange a layer of lasagne on the base and cover with the tomato sauce with meatballs, then the mozzarella and a few slices of eggs, hard-boiled. Repeat the layers until all the ingredients are used, ending with a layer of tomato sauce. Dot the top with the remaining butter, cover the dish with foil or baking parchment and bake for about 1 hour. Leave to stand for 10 minutes before serving.

AUBERGINE AND RICOTTA LASAGNE

LASAGNE CON MELANZANE E RICOTTA
Serves 4

1 large aubergine, sliced
butter, for greasing
300 g/11 oz lasagne sheets, or made with
300g/11 oz plain flour, preferably Italian type 00, plus extra for dusting
(see Lasagne Napoletana, above)
50 g/2 oz pine nuts, chopped
150 g/5 oz ricotta cheese, crumbled
120 ml/4 fl oz tomato purée
12 fresh basil leaves
olive oil, for drizzling • 4 tablespoons Parmesan cheese, freshly grated • salt

Place the aubergine slices in a colander, sprinkle with salt and leave to drain for 2 hours. Rinse, pat dry and cook under a preheated grill until tender. Preheat the oven to 180°C/350°F/Gas Mark 4. Grease an ovenproof dish with butter. Cook the lasagne in a large pan of salted, boiling water for 6–7 minuteds until al dente, then drain and place on a damp tea towel. Arrange a layer of lasagne on the base of the prepared dish, place half the aubergine slices on top and sprinkle with half the pine nuts, half the ricotta, 4 tablespoons of the tomato purée and six of the basil leaves. Drizzle with olive oil and repeat the layers. Sprinkle with the Parmesan and bake for about 40 minutes.

RADICCHIO LASAGNE

Make the pasta (see Fresh Pasta Dough, page 268) with the quantities specified. Heat the cream in a pan over a low heat, stir in the radicchio, add the butter and cook until the radicchio is soft. Stir in the béchamel sauce and season with salt and pepper to taste. Preheat the oven to 150°C/300°F/Gas Mark 2. Grease an ovenproof dish with butter. Cook the lasagne, a few at a time, in a large pan of salted, boiling water, for 6–7 minutes until al dente, drain and place on a damp tea towel to cool. Place a layer of lasagne on the base of the prepared dish and top with a layer of radicchio sauce. Continue making alternate layers until all the ingredients are used, ending with a layer of radicchio sauce. Bake for 30 minutes, then serve.

LASAGNE DI RADICCHIO

Serves 6

300 g/11 oz plain flour, preferably Italian type 00, plus extra for dusting (see Lasagne Napoletana, above) • 3 eggs, lightly beaten

salt

For the sauce

3 tablespoons double cream

300 g/11 oz radicchio, cut into strips

25 g/1 oz butter, plus extra for greasing

1 quantity Béchamel Sauce (see page 50)

salt and pepper

MACCHERONI ALLA CHITARRA

Make the pasta (see Fresh Pasta Dough, page 268) with the quantities specified and then roll out into a sheet 3 mm/¹/₈ inch thick on a lightly floured surface. Place on the chitarra and roll over it with a rolling pin so that the wires cut the pasta into long square-section ribbons. Heat the olive oil in a frying pan, add the tomatoes and cook, stirring occasionally, for 10 minutes. Season with salt and chilli powder. Cook the maccheroni in a large pan of salted, boiling water for 2–3 minutes until al dente, drain, toss with the tomato sauce and serve immediately.

MACCHERONI ALLA CHITARRA

A speciality of Abruzzo, this ribbon pasta is made with a chitarra, a special utensil that consists of steel wires on a wooden frame.

Serves 6

400 g/14 oz plain flour, preferably Italian type 00, plus extra for dusting

4 eggs, lightly beaten

salt

For the sauce

6 tablespoons olive oil

500 g/1 lb 2 oz plum tomatoes, peeled and diced

pinch of chilli powder

salt

MACCHERONI ALLA CHITARRA WITH CHICKEN LIVERS

Heat the butter and oil in a frying pan, add the onion and cook over a low heat, stirring occasionally, for 5 minutes. Add the chicken livers and cook, stirring occasionally until browned. Add the stock and cook until it has evaporated, then season with salt. Cook the maccheroni in a large pan of salted, boiling water for 2–3 minutes until al dente, drain and toss with the sauce. Sprinkle with the Parmesan and serve.

MACCHERONI ALLA CHITARRA
CON FEGATINI

Serves 6

40 g/1¹/₂ oz butter

3 tablespoons olive oil • 1 onion, chopped

350 g/12 oz chicken livers, trimmed and chopped

4 tablespoons Meat Stock (see page 208)

1 quantity Maccheroni (see above)

3 tablespoons Parmesan cheese, freshly grated

salt

MALTAGLIATI WITH PUMPKIN

MALTAGLIATI CON LA ZUCCA

Serves 6

3 tablespoons olive oil

100 g/3¹/₂ oz butter

500 g/1 lb 2 oz pumpkin, peeled, seeded and diced

400 g/14 oz fresh maltagliati

pinch of freshly grated nutmeg

50 g/2 oz Parmesan cheese, freshly grated

salt and pepper

Heat the oil and 80 g/3 oz of the butter in a saucepan, add the pumpkin and cook over a low heat, stirring occasionally, for 5 minutes. Add a little water, season with salt and simmer, stirring frequently, until the pumpkin is tender. Meanwhile, cook the pasta in a large pan of salted, boiling water for 2–3 minutes until just al dente. Drain, stir into the pumpkin and add the remaining butter, the nutmeg and a little pepper. Mix well, sprinkle with the Parmesan and serve.

ORECCHIETTE (BASIC RECIPE)

ORECCHIETTE (RICETTA BASE)

Serves 4

200 g/7 oz plain flour, preferably Italian type 00

100 g/3¹/₂ oz semolina

salt

Mix together the flour, semolina and a pinch of salt and heap into a mound on the work surface. Make a well in the centre, add a little warm water and mix to a firm, elastic dough. Knead well, then shape into long rolls 2.5 cm/1 inch in diameter. Cut into sections and drag them, one at a time, slowly over the work surface using the tip of a knife to form small shells. Put each shell upside down on the tip of your thumb and press it down on the work surface to accentuate its curvature.

ORECCHIETTE WITH BROCCOLI

ORECCHIETTE CON BROCCOLI

Serves 4

800 g/1³/₄ lb broccoli, cut into florets

2 tablespoons olive oil

1 garlic clove, chopped

1 fresh chilli, seeded and chopped

300 g/11 oz Orecchiette (see above)

salt

Parmesan or pecorino cheese, freshly grated, to serve

Cook the broccoli in salted, boiling water for 5 minutes, then drain. Heat the olive oil in a saucepan, add the garlic and chilli and cook for 3 minutes, then add the broccoli and cook over a low heat, stirring occasionally, for 5 minutes until tender. Meanwhile, cook the orecchiette in a large pan of salted, boiling water for 10 minutes until al dente, then drain and toss with the broccoli. Serve with Parmesan or peconino. Alternatively, the broccoli may be cooked with the orecchiette. In this case, drain everything, then drizzle with olive oil and sprinkle with grated pecorino.

ORECCHIETTE WITH TURNIP TOPS

ORECCHIETTE CON CIME DI RAPA

Serves 4

360 g/12¹/₂ oz Orecchiette (see above)

400 g/14 oz turnip tops

olive oil, for drizzling

salt and pepper

Cook the orecchiette in a large pan of salted, boiling water for 10 minutes until al dente, then add the turnip tops and cook for a further 5 minutes until tender. Drain, transfer to a warm serving dish, drizzle with plenty of olive oil and season with pepper. Alternatively, heat 4 tablespoons olive oil with 2 garlic cloves, add the drained orecchiette mixture, cook for a few minutes, then discard the garlic and serve immediately.

ORECCHIETTE WITH TOMATO AND RICOTTA

ORECCHIETTE CON POMODORO E RICOTTA

Serves 4

4 tablespoons olive oil
250 g/9 oz canned tomatoes
6 fresh basil leaves
360 g/12¹/₂ oz Orecchiette (see page 274)
50 g/2 oz firm ricotta cheese, freshly grated
salt

Heat the oil in a small saucepan, add the tomatoes and a pinch of salt and simmer for about 30 minutes. Mash the tomatoes with a fork, add the basil, turn off the heat and cover. Cook the orecchiette in a large pan of salted, boiling water for 10 minutes until al dente, drain well and transfer to a warm serving dish. Pour the tomato sauce over the pasta and sprinkle with the ricotta.

GENOESE PANSOTTI

PANSOTTI ALLA GENOVESE

Serves 6

400 g/14 oz plain flour, preferably Italian type 00, plus extra for dusting
1 tablespoon dry white wine
25 g/1 oz butter, diced
50 g/2 oz Parmesan cheese, freshly grated
salt

For the filling
1 kg/2¹/₄ lb borage, escarole, Swiss chard or turnip tops
¹/₂ garlic clove
200 g/7 oz ricotta cheese
2 eggs, lightly beaten
4–6 tablespoons Parmesan cheese, freshly grated

For the sauce
1 bread slice, crusts removed
2 tablespoons milk
200 g/7 oz shelled walnuts
¹/₂ garlic clove
150 ml/5 fl oz olive oil

Make the pasta dough (see Fresh Pasta Dough, page 268) with the flour, 5 tablespoons water, the wine and a pinch of salt. Cook the greens in salted, boiling water for 5 minutes or until tender. Drain, reserve some of the water and chop the greens with the garlic, then mix with the ricotta, eggs and enough Parmesan to thicken the mixture. Roll out the pasta dough into a thin sheet and place mounds of the filling at regular intervals on top. Cut the dough into squares around each mound, then fold them in half. To make the sauce, tear the bread into pieces, place in a bowl, add the milk and leave to soak. Blanch the walnuts in boiling water and peel off the skins. Squeeze out the bread. Pound the walnuts, garlic and bread in a mortar and gradually whisk in the oil to make a runny sauce. If necessary, add 1–2 tablespoons of the cooking water from the greens. Cook the pansotti in a large pan of salted, boiling water until al dente, then drain and place in a warm serving dish. Add the walnut sauce, the butter and Parmesan, mix well and serve.

VALTELLINA PIZZOCCHERI

Sift together both flours and a pinch of salt into a mound on the work surface and make a well in the centre. Add the egg, 1 tablespoon warm water and milk and gradually incorporate the flour with your fingers, adding more warm water if necessary. Knead until smooth. Roll in a damp tea towel and leave to stand for 30 minutes. Meanwhile, put the cabbage and potato into a saucepan, add water to cover and season with salt and pepper. Bring to the boil, then lower the heat and simmer for 20 minutes until the cabbage is tender and the potato is almost disintegrating. Divide the butter between three small saucepans and cook the onion, garlic and sage in the separate pans until soft and golden brown. Roll out the pasta dough into a fairly thick sheet on a lightly floured surface and cut into 1-cm/1/2-inch wide ribbons about 20 cm/8 inches long. Add to the pan of vegetables, cook for 5 minutes, then drain and transfer to a large dish. Pour the hot butters over the mixture and toss lightly. Arrange a layer of vegetables and pizzoccheri on the base of a soup tureen, place a layer of cheese slices on top and sprinkle with the Parmesan. Continue making alternating layers until all the ingredients are used. Serve hot.

PIZZOCCHERI DELLA VALTELLINA

Serves 6

150 g/5 oz buckwheat flour

80 g/3 oz plain flour, preferably Italian type 00, plus extra for dusting

1 egg, lightly beaten

2 tablespoons milk

400 g/14 oz Savoy cabbage, shredded

1 potato, chopped

100 g/3 1/2 oz butter

1 onion, thinly sliced

1 garlic clove, thinly sliced

4 fresh sage leaves, shredded

150 g/5 oz low-fat cheese, sliced

80 g/3 oz Parmesan cheese, freshly grated

salt and pepper

RAVIOLI NAPOLETANA

Make the pasta dough (see Fresh Pasta Dough, page 268) with the quantities specified, cover with a damp tea towel and leave to stand for 30 minutes. Meanwhile, beat the ricotta in a bowl with a wooden spoon, then stir in the egg, parsley, Parmesan, ham and mozzarella. Roll out the pasta dough into a fairly thick sheet and place mounds of the filling at regular intervals on half the sheet. Fold over the dough and cut out ravioli, pressing the edges firmly to seal. Cook the ravioli in a large pan of salted, boiling water for 15–20 minutes. Drain, toss with the tomato sauce, transfer to a warm serving dish and serve with Parmesan.

RAVIOLI ALLA NAPOLETANA

Serves 6

300 g/11 oz plain flour, preferably Italian type 00, plus extra for dusting

3 eggs, lightly beaten

salt

For the filling

100 g/3 1/2 oz ricotta cheese

1 egg, lightly beaten

1 tablespoon chopped fresh flat-leaf parsley

100 g/3 1/2 oz Parmesan cheese, freshly grated, plus extra to serve

100 g/3 1/2 oz cooked ham, finely chopped

100 g/3 1/2 oz mozzarella cheese, diced

1 quantity Tomato Sauce (see page 57)

VEGETABLE AND CHEESE FILLED RAVIOLI

For the filling, cook the spinach, in just the water clinging to the leaves after washing, for 5 minutes, then drain well and chop. Beat the ricotta in a bowl with a wooden spoon and stir in the spinach. Stir in the eggs and Parmesan and season with salt and pepper to taste, stirring until very smooth. Make the pasta dough (see Fresh Pasta Dough, page 268) with the flour, eggs and a pinch of salt. Roll out into a sheet, place mounds of the filling at regular intervals on half the sheet, fold over and cut out ravioli (a little larger than normal). Press the edges to seal. Cook in a large pan of salted, boiling water for about 10 minutes, then drain and place in a warm serving dish. Meanwhile melt the butter in a small pan and cook the sage leaves until golden. Sprinkle the ravioli with the ricotta and Parmesan, pour the sage butter over them and serve.

RAVIOLI DI MAGRO

Serves 6

300 g/11 oz plain flour, preferably Italian type 00, plus extra for dusting

3 eggs • 50 g/2 oz butter

8 fresh sage leaves

120 g/4 oz ricotta cheese, crumbled

50 g/2 oz Parmesan cheese, freshly grated

salt

For the filling

1.5 kg/3¼ lb spinach

500 g/1 lb 2 oz ricotta cheese • 2 eggs, lightly beaten

2 tablespoons Parmesan cheese, freshly grated

salt and pepper

STRACCI WITH LOBSTER

Melt the butter in a pan, add the onion and cook over a low heat, stirring occasionally, for 5 minutes until softened. Parboil the celery for a few minutes, then drain. Heat 3 tablespoons of the oil in a pan, add the garlic and parsley and cook for a few minutes. Add the onion, courgette, aubergine, celery and fennel, season and cook, stirring frequently, for about 10 minutes until tender. Meanwhile, plunge the lobsters into a pan of salted water, cover and cook for 8 minutes, drain and extract the meat. Heat the remaining oil in a pan, add the lobster meat and tomatoes and cook for 5 minutes. Cook the stracci in a pan of salted, boiling water for 2–3 minutes until al dente, drain and add to the vegetables. Mix well, add the lobster mixture and transfer to a warm serving dish.

'STRACCI' AGLI ASTICI

Serves 6

25 g/1 oz butter • 1 onion, chopped

1 celery stick, cut into 3-cm/1¼-inch batons

5 tablespoons olive oil • 1 garlic clove

2 fresh flat-leaf parsley sprigs

1 courgette, cut into 3-cm/1¼-inch batons

½ aubergine, cut into 3-cm/1¼-inch batons

½ cooked fennel bulb, cut into 3-cm/1¼-inch batons

2 live lobsters

3 plum tomatoes, peeled and diced

350 g/12 oz stracci pasta (fresh pasta squares)

salt and pepper

TAGLIATELLE WITH MUSHROOMS

Place the mushrooms in a bowl, add warm water to cover and leave to soak for 1 hour. Drain, squeeze out the liquid and chop finely with the onion. Heat the oil in a saucepan, add the mushrooms and onion and cook over a low heat, stirring occasionally, for 5 minutes. Stir in 120 ml/4 fl oz water and season lightly with salt. Add the white wine and cook until it has evaporated, then stir in the tomato purée. Simmer over a medium heat for 30 minutes. Cook the tagliatelle in a large pan of salted, boiling water for 2–3 minutes until al dente. Sprinkle with the Parmesan and toss with the mushroom sauce.

TAGLIATELLE AI FUNGHI

Serves 4

25 g/1 oz dried mushrooms

1 small onion

2 tablespoons olive oil

5 tablespoons dry white wine

3 tablespoons concentrated tomato purée

275 g/10 oz fresh tagliatelle

40 g/1½ oz Parmesan cheese, freshly grated

salt

TAGLIATELLE WITH AUBERGINE

TAGLIATELLE ALLE MELANZANE

Serves 4

6 tablespoons olive oil

2 aubergines, thinly sliced

1 garlic clove

250 g/9 oz tomatoes, peeled and chopped

10 fresh basil leaves

275 g/10 oz fresh tagliatelle

100 g/3¹/₂ oz firm ricotta cheese, freshly grated

salt and pepper

Heat 4 tablespoons of the olive oil in a frying pan, add the aubergine slices and cook over a medium heat for 8–10 minutes until golden brown all over. Heat the remaining oil in a saucepan, add the garlic and the tomatoes and cook over a low heat for 10 minutes, then remove and discard the garlic. Remove the pan from the heat and season with salt and pepper, then chop one of the basil leaves and stir in. Cook the tagliatelle in a large pan of salted, boiling water until al dente, then drain and place in a warm serving dish. Cover with the ricotta, then spoon the tomato sauce over it. Top with the aubergine slices and sprinkle with the remaining basil.

CUTTLEFISH INK TAGLIATELLE

TAGLIATELLE AL NERO DI SEPPIA

Serves 4

200 g/7 oz plain flour, preferably Italian type 00, plus extra for dusting

2 eggs, lightly beaten

1 or 2 cuttlefish ink sacs

150 g/5 oz canned tuna in oil, drained and flaked

1 tablespoon capers, rinsed

3 tablespoons olive oil

salt

Sift the flour with a pinch of salt into a mound on the work surface and make a well in the centre. Add the eggs and cuttlefish ink and gradually incorporate the flour with your fingers. Knead the dough until soft and smooth, then roll out into a sheet, on a lightly floured surface, fold over several times and cut into 5-mm/¹/₄-inch wide tagliatelle. Mix together the tuna, capers and olive oil in a bowl. Cook the tagliatelle in a large pan of salted, boiling water until al dente, then drain and toss with the tuna sauce. Transfer to a warm serving dish.

TAGLIATELLE WITH SALMON

TAGLIATELLE AL SALMONE

Serves 4

50 g/2 oz butter

100 g/3¹/₂ oz smoked salmon, chopped

juice of ¹/₂ lemon, strained

100 ml/3¹/₂ fl oz double cream

5 tablespoons whisky

275 g/10 oz fresh tagliatelle

salt and pepper

Melt the butter in a saucepan, add the salmon, stir and sprinkle with the lemon juice. Cook for a few minutes, then add the cream and whisky and season with salt and pepper. Cook over a low heat for 5 minutes. Cook the tagliatelle in a large pan of salted, boiling water until al dente, drain, add to the sauce and cook for a few minutes. Toss gently and transfer to a warm serving dish.

TAGLIATELLE WITH ARTICHOKES

Break off the artichoke stalks and remove the tough outer leaves and the chokes. Rub all over with lemon juice to prevent discoloration. Cook in lightly salted, boiling water for 7 minutes, then drain and slice thinly. Heat the oil in a frying pan, add the garlic and cook for a few minutes until browned. Remove and discard the garlic and add the artichokes, basil, parsley and tomatoes to the pan. Season with salt and cook over a low heat for 10 minutes. Cook the tagliatelle in a large pan of salted, boiling water until al dente, then drain and add to the frying pan. If necessary, add a few tablespoonfuls of the pasta cooking water to thin the sauce. Drizzle with olive oil and sprinkle with the Parmesan. Remove and discard the parsley, transfer to a warm serving dish and serve.

TAGLIATELLE CON CARCIOFI

Serves 4

4 globe artichokes

juice of 1 lemon, strained

4 tablespoons olive oil, plus extra for drizzling

1 garlic clove

6 fresh basil leaves

1 fresh flat-leaf parsley sprig

5 canned tomatoes, drained and chopped

275 g/10 oz fresh tagliatelle

4 tablespoons Parmesan cheese, freshly grated

salt

TAGLIATELLE WITH SPINACH

Preheat the oven to 200°C/400°F/Gas Mark 6 and grease an ovenproof dish with butter. Cook the spinach, in just the water clinging to the leaves after washing, for 5 minutes, then drain and chop. Heat half the butter in a saucepan, add the onion and cook over a low heat, stirring occasionally, for 5 minutes until softened. Add the spinach and cook for a few minutes more. Season with salt and pepper and sprinkle with half the Parmesan. Cook the tagliatelle in a large pan of salted, boiling water for 2–3 minutes until al dente, then drain, return to the pan and toss with the remaining butter. Make layers of tagliatelle, most of the remaining Parmesan and the spinach in the prepared dish, ending with a layer of spinach. Pour the cream on top, sprinkle with the rest of the Parmesan and bake for 10 minutes until golden and bubbling.

TAGLIATELLE CON SPINACI

Serves 4

65 g/2¹/₂ oz butter, plus extra for greasing

675 g/1¹/₂ lb spinach

1 onion, finely chopped

120 g/4 oz Parmesan cheese, freshly grated

275 g/10 oz fresh tagliatelle

200 ml/7 fl oz double cream

salt and pepper

TAGLIATELLE WITH CREAM, PEAS AND HAM

Heat the butter and oil in a saucepan, add the onion and cook over a low heat, stirring occasionally, for 5 minutes until softened. Add the peas and cook, stirring occasionally, for 20 minutes, then stir in the cream. Cook for 5 minutes, then add the ham. Cook the tagliatelle in a large pan of salted, boiling water until al dente, then drain and toss with the Parmesan and hot sauce. Transfer to a warm serving dish.

TAGLIATELLE PANNA,
PISELLI E PROSCIUTTO

Serves 4

25 g/1 oz butter • 2 tablespoons olive oil

1 onion, very thinly sliced

200 g/7 oz shelled peas

100 ml/3¹/₂ fl oz double cream

2 cooked ham slices, diced

275 g/10 oz fresh tagliatelle

50 g/2 oz Parmesan cheese, freshly grated • salt

TAGLIATELLINE WITH ONIONS

TAGLIATELLINE ALLE CIPOLLE

Serves 4

40 g/1¹/₂ oz butter • 4 tablespoons olive oil

400 g/14 oz white onions, thinly sliced

275 g/10 oz fresh tagliatelline

50 g/2 oz Parmesan cheese, freshly grated

salt and pepper

Heat the butter and oil in a flameproof casserole. Add the onions and cook over a low heat, stirring occasionally, for 5–10 minutes until translucent, then season with salt. Meanwhile, cook the tagliatelline in a large pan of salted, boiling water until al dente, then drain and tip into the casserole. Season lightly with pepper and toss. Remove from the heat and sprinkle with the Parmesan.

TAGLIOLINI WITH LANGOUSTINES

TAGLIOLINI AGLI SCAMPI

Serves 4

400 g/14 oz langoustines or Dublin Bay prawns

1 onion

1 carrot

1 celery stick

3 tablespoons olive oil

1 tablespoon chopped fresh flat-leaf parsley

1 teaspoon concentrated tomato purée

275 g/10 oz fresh tagliolini

salt

Peel the langoustines or prawns, reserving the shells. Put the shells in a pan with the onion, carrot and celery, add water to cover and a pinch of salt. Bring to the boil, lower the heat and simmer for 15 minutes, then strain into a bowl. Reserve some of the stock. Heat the oil in a frying pan, add the langoustines or prawns and cook for 3 minutes, then sprinkle with the parsley. Stir the tomato purée with a little of the shellfish stock in a bowl and add to the pan. Cook the tagliolini in a large pan of salted, boiling water until al dente, then drain, toss with the sauce and transfer to a warm serving dish.

TAGLIOLINI WITH BUTTER AND TRUFFLE

TAGLIOLINI AL BURRO E TARTUFO

Serves 4

80 g/3 oz butter

pinch of freshly grated nutmeg

275 g/10 oz fresh tagliolini

80 g/3 oz Parmesan cheese, freshly grated

1 small white truffle

salt and pepper

Melt the butter in a small saucepan and season with the nutmeg and a pinch each of salt and pepper. Cook the tagliolini in a large pan of salted, boiling water until al dente, then drain and tip into a warm serving dish. Pour the melted butter over the pasta, sprinkle with the Parmesan and then shave the truffle over the top.

TAGLIOLINI WITH SCALLOPS AND LETTUCE

TAGLIOLINI ALLE CAPPESANTE E LATTUGA

Serves 4

2 garlic cloves • 3 tablespoons olive oil

200 g/7 oz shelled scallops with coral

100 ml/3¹/₂ fl oz white wine

150 g/5 oz lettuce, shredded

25 g/1 oz butter pinch of chilli powder

1 tablespoon chopped fresh flat-leaf parsley

275 g/10 oz fresh tagliolini • salt

Heat the oil in a pan, add the garlic and cook for 30 seconds. Remove and discard the garlic and add the scallops to the pan. Sprinkle in the wine, cook until it has evaporated, then season with salt. Add the lettuce and butter and stir well. Stir in the chilli powder and parsley. Cook the tagliolini in a large pan of salted, boiling water until al dente, then drain and add to the sauce. Toss gently and transfer to a warm serving dish.

PUMPKIN TORTELLI

Preheat the oven to 180°C/350°F/Gas Mark 4. Put the pumpkin in a roasting tin, drizzle with the oil, cover with foil and bake for about 1 hour. Pass the pumpkin through a food mill into a bowl, add the Parmesan and eggs and season with salt and pepper. Stir in enough breadcrumbs to make a fairly firm mixture. Roll out the pasta dough into a sheet and stamp out 7.5-cm/3-inch rounds with a pastry cutter. Spoon a little of the pumpkin filling into the centre of each round, fold in half and crimp the edges. Cook the tortelli in a large pan of salted, boiling water for 10 minutes. Meanwhile, melt the butter in a frying pan, add the sage and cook for a few minutes. Drain the tortelli, place in a warm serving dish and sprinkle with the sage butter and extra Parmesan.

TORTELLI DI ZUCCA

Serves 4

500 g/1 lb 2 oz pumpkin, peeled, seeded and chopped

2 tablespoons olive oil

200 g/7 oz Parmesan cheese,

freshly grated, plus extra to serve

2 eggs, lightly beaten

80–120 g/3–4 oz breadcrumbs

200 g/7 oz Fresh Pasta Dough (see page 268)

50 g/2 oz butter

8 fresh sage leaves

salt and pepper

CURRIED TORTELLINI

Melt half the butter in a saucepan, add the peas and ham and cook over a low heat, stirring occasionally, for 10 minutes. Stir in the curry powder and cook for a further 10 minutes. Cook the tortellini in a large pan of salted, boiling water until al dente. Drain and toss with the remaining butter, the Parmesan and cream,and then with the curry sauce. Transfer to a warm serving dish.

TORTELLINI AL CURRY

Serves 4

50 g/2 oz butter

200 g/7 oz shelled peas

50 g/2 oz cooked ham, diced

2 teaspoons curry powder

400 g/14 oz fresh tortellini

50 g/2 oz Parmesan cheese, freshly grated

200 ml/7 fl oz double cream

salt

TORTELLINI BOLOGNESE

Melt the butter in a small saucepan, add the veal and cook over a high heat, stirring frequently, until browned. Transfer to a bowl, leave to cool, then stir in the Parmesan, prosciutto, mortadella and egg. Roll out the pasta dough into a thin sheet, put small mounds of the filling at regular intervals on the sheet and cut it into squares. Fold the squares corner to corner into triangles, then wrap each triangle around your index finger, press the points together and gently push the rest of the dough backwards to make the classic tortellini shape. Make 20 tortellini per person. Serve with tomato sauce.

TORTELLINI ALLA BOLOGNESE

Serves 4

25 g/1 oz butter

50 g/2 oz minced veal

2 tablespoons Parmesan cheese, freshly grated

80 g/3 oz prosciutto, diced

40 g/1¹/₂ oz mortadella, diced

1 egg, lightly beaten

1 quantity Fresh Pasta Dough (see page 268)

Tomato Sauce (see page 57), to serve.

MUSHROOM TORTELLONI

Prepare the pasta dough and leave to rest covered with a damp tea towel for 30 minutes. Heat the oil in a saucepan, add the onion and porcini and cook over a low heat, stirring occasionally, for 5 minutes. Season with salt and cook for a further 15 minutes. Transfer the mixture to a food processor, add the ricotta, Parmesan and parsley and process to a purée. Season with salt and pepper to taste. Roll out the pasta dough to make a thin sheet and cut out 5-cm/2-inch squares. Put a little ricotta mixture into the centre of each square. Fold the squares corner to corner into triangles, then wrap each triangle around your index finger, press the points together and gently push the rest of the dough backwards to make the classic tortellini shape. Melt the butter in a large frying pan, add the sage leaves and cook for a few minutes. Cook the tortelloni in a large pan of salted, boiling water until al dente. Drain, add to the frying pan and stir over a high heat. Transfer to a warm serving dish, sprinkle with Parmesan and serve.

TORTELLONI DI FUNGHI

Serves 4

1 quantity Fresh Pasta Dough (see page 268)

4 tablespoons olive oil

1 small onion, chopped

300 g/11 oz porcini, thinly sliced

250 g/9 oz ricotta cheese, crumbled

50 g/2 oz Parmesan cheese,

freshly grated, plus extra to serve

1 fresh flat-leaf parsley sprig, chopped

40 g/1¹/₂ oz butter

10 fresh sage leaves

salt and pepper

PESTO TORTELLONI WITH SQUID

Make the pasta dough (see Fresh Pasta Dough, page 268) with the flour, eggs and a pinch of salt. For the pesto, put the basil, parsley, pine nuts, walnuts and olive oil into a food processor and process until combined, then scrape into a bowl. Season with salt and stir in the ricotta. Roll out the pasta dough into a sheet and make pesto-filled tortelloni (for method of making tortelloni, see above). For the sauce, heat 3 tablespoons of the oil in a frying pan, add the squid and garlic and cook, stirring frequently, for a few minutes until the squid are light golden brown. Season with salt and pepper to taste, sprinkle with the wine and cook until it has evaporated. Remove the squid from the pan, leaving the cooking juices in the pan.and slice into fairly thin rounds. Cook the pasta in a large pan of salted, boiling water until al dente, drain and tip into the frying pan. Remove and discard the garlic, add the remaining oil, the tomatoes and squid rounds and mix well. Sprinkle with the parsley and basil and mix again. Transfer to a warm serving dish.

TORTELLONI DI PESTO CON CALAMARETTI

Serves 4

300 g/11 oz plain flour, preferably Italian type 00,

plus extra for dusting

3 eggs, lightly beaten • salt

For the pesto

100 g/3¹/₂ oz fresh basil leaves

40 g/1¹/₂ oz fresh flat-leaf parsley

20 g/³/₄ oz pine nuts

10 g/¹/₄ oz walnuts

120 ml/4 fl oz olive oil

200 g/7 oz ricotta cheese • salt

For the sauce

4 tablespoons olive oil

200 g/7 oz small squid, cleaned

1 garlic clove

5 tablespoons dry white wine

2 tomatoes, peeled and diced

1 tablespoon chopped fresh flat-leaf parsley

6 fresh basil leaves, torn

salt and pepper

DRIED PASTA

Pasta is a truly Italian passion that never fades or becomes jaded. It is a wholly Italian speciality made, by law, exclusively from durum wheat flour. In Italy it can be sold only in sealed boxes showing the net weight, producer, type and name (bucatini, fusilli, farfalle, rigatoni, etc.). For more information about the different types and shapes of pasta, see page 202.

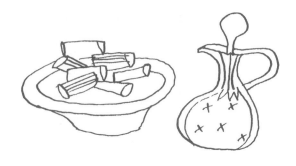

QUANTITY

On average 65–100 g/
2½–3½ oz per person.

SAUCEPAN

This should be large and
also deeper than it is
wide. It is best to choose
an aluminium or steel pan
(special pans with remov-
able metal colanders
inside are available).

WATER AND SALT

The right proportion is
1 litre/1¾ pints water and
10 g/¼ oz salt for every
100 g/3½ oz pasta.

WATER

Add the pasta only when
the water has come to a
rolling boil and, in the case
of spaghetti, fan out the
strands. Stir immediately.
As soon as the water
begins to boil again, put
the lid on. When the water
reaches a rolling boil once
more, remove the lid. Stir
occasionally so that the
pasta does not stick.

TIMING

Follow the packet instructions but check the pasta at
least twice to make sure
that it does not overcook.

COLD WATER

When the pasta is al dente,
some people pour in about
150 ml/¼ pint cold water
to stop it from overcook-
ing. This is useful if, for
some unexpected reason,
the pasta is not drained
immediately. Otherwise it
is unnecessary.

SAUCE AND CHEESE

Grated cheese, if required,
should always be sprinkled
on the pasta before the
sauce and it should always
be freshly grated. Do
not overdo the quantity.
Those who wish may add
more at the table from the
cheese dish. It is worth
pointing out that metal
spoons may rust on con-
tact with fatty particles, so
you should use serve the
cheese with a spoon made
from another material.

BAVETTE WITH CLAMS AND COURGETTES

Serves 4

800 g/1³/₄ lb clams, scrubbed
3 tablespoons olive oil
1 shallot
1 garlic clove
¹/₂ fresh chilli, seeded and chopped
300 g/11 oz courgettes, cut into strips
1 tablespoon chopped fresh flat-leaf parsley
100 ml/3¹/₂ fl oz dry white wine
3 tomatoes, peeled and diced
350 g/12 oz bavette
salt

Discard any clams with broken shells or that do not shut immediately when sharply tapped. Put the clams in a dry frying pan and cook over a high heat for about 5 minutes until they open. Discard any that remain closed. Remove the clams from their shells and set aside. Heat the oil in a saucepan, add the shallot, garlic and chilli and cook over a low heat, stirring occasionally, for 5 minutes until soft. Remove and discard the garlic, add the clams, courgettes and parsley and cook for 5 minutes. Sprinkle in the wine and cook until it has evaporated. Add the tomatoes, season with salt and cook for 20–30 minutes until thickened. Cook the bavette in a large pan of salted, boiling water until al dente, then drain, add to the courgette and clam mixture and toss.

BUCATINI WITH GREEN TOMATOES

Serves 4

2 tablespoons olive oil
100 g/3¹/₂ oz pancetta, diced
¹/₂ garlic clove, chopped
1 fresh flat-leaf parsley sprig, chopped
4 green tomatoes, seeded and chopped
80 g/3 oz canned tuna in oil, drained and flaked
350 g/12 oz bucatini • salt

Heat the oil in a pan, add the pancetta, garlic and parsley and cook over a medium heat for 5 minutes until lightly browned. Add the tomatoes and tuna, season with salt if necessary and cook over a low heat for 40 minutes. Cook the bucatini in a large pan of salted, boiling water until al dente, then drain and tip into the pan of sauce. Mix well and serve.

BUCATINI WITH MUSHROOM SAUCE

Serves 4

25 g/1 oz dried mushrooms
200 g/7 oz fresh porcini
4 tablespoons olive oil
1¹/₂ garlic cloves
50 g/2 oz ricotta cheese
1 tablespoon concentrated tomato purée
350 g/12 oz bucatini
salt and pepper

Place the dried mushrooms in a bowl, add warm water to cover and set aside to soak for 20 minutes, then drain and squeeze out. Chop half the fresh porcini and thinly slice the rest. Heat 3 tablespoons of the oil with the whole garlic clove in a pan, add the drained mushrooms and chopped porcini and cook for about 10 minutes until the mushrooms have given up their liquid. Remove and discard the garlic. Add 150 ml/¹/₄ pint water and cook for 20 minutes. Transfer the mixture to a food processor and process to a purée, then stir into the ricotta. Put the sliced porcini into a pan with the remaining oil, the remaining garlic and the tomato purée. Mix well, add 2 tablespoons water and cook for 15 minutes. Season with salt and pepper. Meanwhile, cook the bucatini in a large pan of salted, boiling water until al dente. Drain, place in a warm serving dish and spoon the ricotta mixture and fried mushrooms on top.

BUCATINI WITH PEPPER SAUCE

Heat the oil in a saucepan, add the onion and garlic and cook over a low heat, stirring occasionally, for 10 minutes until lightly browned. Add the peppers, mix well and cook for a further 10 minutes until tender. Transfer to a food processor and process to a purée. Return to the pan, stir in the cream and season with salt and pepper to taste. Keep warm over a very low heat. Cook the bucatini in a large pan of salted, boiling water until al dente, then drain and tip into the sauce. Cook for 1 minute, stir in the marjoram and serve.

BUCATINI CON SALSA AI PEPERONI

Serves 4

2 tablespoons olive oil

1 baby onion, chopped

$^1/_2$ garlic clove, chopped

3 red or yellow peppers, halved, seeded and sliced

100 ml/3$^1/_2$ fl oz double cream

350 g/12 oz bucatini

2 teaspoons chopped fresh marjoram

salt and pepper

FARFALLE WITH SMOKED PANCETTA

Heat the oil in a pan, add the pancetta and chilli and cook over a medium heat for 5 minutes until lightly browned. Add the tomatoes, season with salt and cook over a low heat for 25 minutes. Stir in the cream and cook over a very low heat for 5 minutes until thickened. Meanwhile, cook the farfalle in a large pan of salted, boiling water until al dente, then drain, tip into the sauce and cook, stirring constantly, for 30 seconds. Sprinkle with the Parmesan and serve.

FARFALLE ALLA PANCETTA AFFUMICATA

Serves 4

1 tablespoon olive oil

100 g/3$^1/_2$ oz smoked pancetta, diced

1 fresh chilli, seeded and chopped

250 g/9 oz tomatoes, peeled and chopped

200 ml/7 fl oz double cream

350 g/12 oz farfalle

25 g/1 oz Parmesan cheese, freshly grated

salt

FUSILLI WITH MUSHROOMS

Heat the oil in a saucepan, add the onion and mushrooms and cook over a low heat, stirring occasionally, for 10 minutes. Season with salt and pepper and add the tomatoes with their can juices. Simmer for 45 minutes, then remove the pan from the heat and add the parsley. Meanwhile, cook the fusilli in a large pan of salted, boiling water until al dente, drain and tip on to a warm serving dish. Sprinkle with the Parmesan, add the butter and toss. Spoon the mushroom sauce on top and serve.

FUSILLI AI FUNGHI

Serves 4

3 tablespoons olive oil

1 onion, chopped

800 g/1$^3/_4$ lb chanterelle mushrooms

or honey fungus, chopped

250 g/9 oz canned tomatoes

1 tablespoon chopped fresh flat-leaf parsley

350 g/12 oz fusilli

25 g/1 oz Parmesan cheese, freshly grated

25 g/1 oz butter

salt and pepper

FUSILLI IN CUTTLEFISH INK

Serves 4

675 g/1¹/₂ lb prepared cuttlefish, ink sacs reserved

2 tablespoons olive oil

1 onion, very thinly sliced

200 ml/7 fl oz dry white wine

2 tablespoons tomato purée

350 g/12 oz fusilli

1 tablespoon chopped fresh flat-leaf parsley

salt and pepper

Cut the cuttlefish into strips. Heat the oil in a saucepan, add the onion and cook over a low heat, stirring occasionally, until softened. Add the cuttlefish and cook over a medium heat, stirring occasionally, until lightly browned. Add the wine and cook until it has evaporated. Stir in the tomato purée, season with salt and pepper, lower the heat, cover and cook for 1 hour. Cook the fusilli in a large pan of salted, boiling water until al dente. Pour the cuttlefish ink into the sauce and stir in the parsley. Drain the pasta, tip it into the sauce, mix well and transfer to a warm serving dish.

FUSILLI SALAD

Serves 4

4 tomatoes, peeled, seeded and diced

16 fresh basil leaves

1 garlic clove

olive oil, for drizzling

350 g/12 oz fusilli

80 g/3 oz canned tuna in oil, drained and flaked

12 black olives, stoned and halved

120 g/4 oz mozzarella cheese, diced

salt

Put the tomatoes, basil and garlic in a serving bowl, drizzle with oil and season with salt. Cook the pasta in a large pan of salted, boiling water until al dente, then drain. Remove and discard the garlic, then tip the fusilli into the bowl. Add the tuna, olives and mozzarella, toss and serve.

LINGUINE WITH GENOESE PESTO

Serves 4

350 g/12 oz linguine

2 potatoes, cut into thin batons

50 g/2 oz French beans

For the pesto

25 fresh basil leaves

2 garlic cloves, chopped

5 tablespoons olive oil

25 g/1 oz pecorino cheese, freshly grated

25 g/1 oz Parmesan cheese, freshly grated

salt

To make the pesto, put the basil, garlic, a pinch of salt and the olive oil in a food processor and process briefly at medium speed. Add both cheeses and process again until blended. Cook the linguine, potatoes and beans together in a large pan of salted, boiling water until al dente, then drain. Toss with the pesto and serve.

MACCHERONI AI FUNGHI PORCINI

Serves 4

25 g/1 oz butter

3 tablespoons olive oil

1 garlic clove

250 g/9 oz porcini, sliced

150 g/5 oz canned chopped tomatoes, drained

1 tablespoon chopped fresh flat-leaf parsley

350 g/12 oz macaroni

salt and pepper

MACARONI WITH MUSHROOMS

Heat the butter and oil in a pan, add the garlic clove and porcini and cook, stirring occasionally, for 5 minutes. Add the tomatoes, season with salt and pepper to taste, cover and cook over a low heat for about 20 minutes. Remove and discard the garlic and stir in the parsley. Cook the macaroni in a large pan of salted, boiling water until al dente, then drain, toss with the porcini sauce and serve. This sauce can also be made without tomatoes, in which case use 40 g/1½ oz butter.

MACCHERONI CON LE SEPPIOLINE

Serves 4

600 g/1 lb 5 oz cleaned cuttlefish

250 g/9 oz canned chopped tomatoes

1 onion, finely chopped

2 garlic cloves

1 large potato, sliced

200 g/7 oz shelled petits pois

2 tablespoons chopped fresh flat-leaf parsley

4 tablespoons olive oil

350 g/12 oz macaroni

salt and pepper

MACARONI WITH CUTTLEFISH

Put the cuttlefish, tomatoes with their can juices, onion, garlic, potato, petits pois, parsley and oil in a large saucepan and cook over a medium heat, stirring frequently, for 10 minutes. Lower the heat, cover and cook for a further 30 minutes. Season with salt and pepper to taste. Cook the macaroni in a large pan of salted, boiling water until al dente, then drain and tip into the sauce. Mix well, transfer to a serving dish and serve.

MACCHERONI GRATINATI

Serves 4

25 g/1 oz butter, plus extra for greasing

1 quantity Béchamel Sauce (see page 50)

50 g/2 oz Parmesan cheese, freshly grated

2 egg yolks

350 g/12 oz macaroni

salt

MACARONI AU GRATIN

Preheat the oven to 240°C/475°F/Gas Mark 9. Grease an ovenproof dish with butter. Mix together the béchamel sauce, Parmesan, butter and egg yolks. Cook the macaroni in a large pan of salted, boiling water until just al dente, then drain and tip into a bowl. Gently stir in half the béchamel sauce mixture and put in the prepared dish, then spoon the remaining béchamel sauce mixture on top. Bake for 15–20 minutes until golden brown.

PASTA WITH SARDINES

Place the sultanas in a bowl, add hot water to cover and set aside to soak. Cook the fennel in lightly salted, boiling water for 15–20 minutes, then drain, reserving the cooking liquid, and chop. Heat the oil in a saucepan, add the onion and cook over a low heat, stirring occasionally, for 5 minutes. Drain the anchovies, add the filleted fish to the pan and mash with a wooden spoon. Drain the sultanas, squeezing out the excess liquid, and add to the pan with the fennel and pine nuts. Sprinkle with the saffron, cover and cook over a low heat for 15 minutes. Open the sardines out like the pages of a book, leaving them attached along their backs. Rinse well, pat dry and dust with flour, shaking off any excess. Heat the vegetable oil in a deep-fryer or large pan to 180–190°C/350–375°F or until a cube of day-old bread browns in 30 seconds. Add the sardines and deep-fry until golden brown, then remove and drain on kitchen paper. Season with a little salt. Preheat the oven to 200°C/400°F/Gas Mark 6 and brush an ovenproof dish with oil. Cook the zite in a large pan of salted, boiling water mixed with the reserved fennel cooking water until al dente, then drain, return to the pan and stir in half the sauce. Spoon a layer of pasta on to the base of the prepared dish and place a layer of sardines on top. Add a layer of the sauce and continue making layers until all the ingredients are used, ending with a layer of sauce. Bake for 10 minutes.

PASTA CON LE SARDE

Serves 4

25 g/1 oz sultanas

4 salted anchovy fillets, heads removed, cleaned and filleted (see page 596), soaked in cold water for 10 minutes and drained

200 g/7 oz wild fennel

2 tablespoons olive oil, plus extra for brushing

1 onion, chopped

25 g/1 oz pine nuts

$^{1}/_{2}$ sachet saffron powder

350 g/12 oz fresh sardines, scaled and cleaned

plain flour, for dusting

vegetable oil, for deep-frying

300 g/11 oz zite (long tubes of dried pasta)

salt

PENNE WITH LETTUCE

Preheat the oven to 180°C/350°F/Gas Mark 6 and grease an ovenproof dish with butter. Place the lettuce in a bowl, add the oil and season with salt and pepper. Cook the penne in a large pan of salted, boiling water until al dente, then drain and tip into the prepared dish. Cover with the lettuce, sprinkle with the Gruyère and dot with the butter. Bake for about 20 minutes.

PENNE ALLA LATTUGA

Serves 4

25 g/1 oz butter, plus extra for greasing

800 g/1$^{3}/_{4}$ lb lettuce, shredded

3 tablespoons olive oil

350 g/12 oz penne

100 g/3 $^{1}/_{2}$ oz Gruyère cheese, freshly grated

salt and pepper

PENNE ARRABBIATA

Heat the oil in a frying pan, add the garlic cloves and chilli and cook until the garlic browns, then remove the cloves from the pan. Add the tomatoes to the pan, season with salt and cook for about 15 minutes. Cook the penne in a large pan of salted, boiling water until al dente, then drain and tip into the frying pan. Toss over a high heat for a few minutes, then transfer to a warm serving dish, sprinkle with the parsley.

PENNE ALL'ARRABBIATA

Serves 4

6 tablespoons oil

2 garlic cloves

^{1}/$_2$ fresh chilli, seeded and chopped

500 g/1 lb 2 oz canned chopped tomatoes, drained

350 g/12 oz penne lisce

1 tablespoon chopped fresh flat-leaf parsley

salt

PENNE WITH BLACK OLIVES

Put the olives and cream in a saucepan and cook over a low heat for about 15 minutes. Cook the penne in a large pan of salted, boiling water until al dente, then drain. Spoon half the olive sauce on to the base of a warm serving dish and top with the pasta. Sprinkle with the Parmesan, then spoon the remaining sauce on top. Mix well and serve.

PENNE ALLE OLIVE NERE

Serves 4

150 g/5 oz black olives, stoned and finely chopped

175 ml/6 fl oz double cream

350 g/12 oz penne lisce

25 g/1 oz Parmesan cheese, freshly grated

salt

PENNE WITH TURNIP TOPS

Cook the turnip tops in salted, boiling water for 10 minutes, then drain and chop. Put the anchovy fillets and the oil in a food processor and process to a purée. Cook the penne in a large pan of salted, boiling water until al dente, then drain and tip into a fairly deep warm serving dish. Add the turnip tops, drizzle with oil, season with pepper and stir. Pour in the anchovy purée, mix again and serve.

PENNE CON CIME DI RAPA

Serves 4

500 g/1 lb 2 oz turnip tops

4 anchovy fillets

3 tablespoons olive oil, plus extra for drizzling

320 g/11^1/$_2$ oz penne

salt and pepper

PENNE WITH SAFFRON

Bring the stock to the boil. Heat the butter and oil in another large saucepan, add the onion and cook over a low heat, stirring occasionally, for 5 minutes until softened. Add the penne and stir until it is shiny and coated with fat. Add a ladleful of hot stock and stir until it has been absorbed. Continue adding stock, a ladleful at a time, as if making risotto, until the pasta is completely cooked. Stir the saffron into the last ladleful of stock before adding it to the pan. Mix well until the dish is an even yellow colour. Remove the pan from the heat, sprinkle with the Parmesan, mix well and stir in a knob of butter if you like. Transfer to a warm serving dish and serve. Saffron threads may be used instead of saffron powder.

PENNE GIALLE

Serves 4

1 quantity Meat Stock (see page 208)

40 g/1^1/$_2$ oz butter, plus extra for serving (optional)

1 tablespoon olive oil

1 onion, thinly sliced

320 g/11^1/$_2$ oz penne lisce

1 sachet saffron powder

40 g/1^1/$_2$ oz Parmesan cheese, freshly grated

CURRIED PENNE SALAD

PENNE IN INSALATA AL CURRY

Serves 4

2 tablespoons olive oil
1 onion, thinly sliced
2 tablespoons curry powder
1 tablespoon plain flour
200 ml/7 fl oz Meat Stock (see page 208)
350 g/12 oz penne
100 ml/3¹/₂ fl oz double cream
1 small cucumber, peeled and finely diced
salt

Heat the oil in a pan, add 1 tablespoon water, a pinch of salt and the onion and cook for 5–6 minutes until softened and translucent. Stir in the curry powder and cook for a few seconds, then stir in the flour and cook for a few seconds more. Gradually stir in the stock, bring to the boil, stirring constantly, then lower the heat and simmer, stirring frequently, for 15 minutes. Remove the pan from the heat and leave to cool. Cook the penne in a large pan of salted, boiling water until al dente, then drain, tip into a serving dish and mix with the cream. Leave to cool, but do not chill in the refrigerator. To serve, spoon the curry sauce over the pasta and sprinkle with the cucumber.

FRIED PENNE

PENNE IN TEGAME

Serves 4

50 g/2 oz butter
1 onion, thinly sliced
350 g/12 oz penne
40 g/1¹/₂ oz Parmesan cheese, freshly grated
salt and pepper

Melt the butter in a pan, add the onion, then add the penne. Mix well to coat the pasta with butter, then pour in enough boiling water to cover. Add salt and cook until the pasta is al dente, adding more boiling water if necessary. Season with pepper, transfer to a warm serving dish and sprinkle with the Parmesan.

PENNE RIGATE WITH ARTICHOKES

PENNE RIGATE AI CARCIOFI

Serves 4

juice of ¹/₂ lemon, strained
4 globe artichokes
4 tablespoons olive oil
1 garlic clove, chopped
1 tablespoon chopped fresh flat-leaf parsley
350 g/12 oz penne rigate
salt and pepper

Half-fill a bowl with water and stir in the lemon juice. Working on one artichoke at a time, break off the stem, remove the coarse, outer leaves and choke, if necessary. Cut into quarters, then slice thinly and drop into the acidulated water to prevent discoloration. Heat the oil in a pan, add the garlic and parsley and cook over a low heat for 2 minutes. Drain the artichokes, add to the pan and mix well. Cover and cook over a low heat for a few minutes, then add 2–3 tablespoons water, season with salt and re-cover the pan so that the artichokes cook in their own steam. Meanwhile, cook the penne in a large pan of salted, boiling water until al dente, then drain and tip into a serving dish. Pour the artichoke sauce, which should not be too runny, over the pasta, season with pepper and serve.

PENNE RIGATE IN VODKA

PENNE RIGATE ALLA VODKA

Serves 4

50 g/2 oz butter

1 thick slice cooked ham, diced

2 tablespoons tomato purée

1 tablespoon chopped fresh flat-leaf parsley

5 tablespoons double cream

3 tablespoons vodka

350 g/12 oz penne rigate

salt and pepper

Melt the butter in a pan, add the ham, tomato purée and parsley, season with salt and pepper and cook, stirring occasionally, for about 10 minutes. Stir in the cream and vodka and cook until the vodka has evaporated. Cook the penne in a large pan of salted, boiling water until al dente, then drain and tip into a warm serving dish. Pour the sauce over the pasta.

RIGATONI WITH MEATBALLS

RIGATONI CON POLPETTINE

Serves 4

300 g/11 oz minced meat

1 fresh flat-leaf parsley sprig, chopped

$^1/_2$ garlic clove, chopped

1 egg, lightly beaten

plain flour, for dusting

3 tablespoons olive oil

1 onion, thinly sliced

1 celery stick, chopped

1 carrot, chopped

1 small fresh rosemary sprig, chopped

400 ml/14 fl oz passata

350 g/12 oz rigatoni

25 g/1 oz Parmesan cheese, freshly grated

salt and pepper

Mix together the minced meat, parsley and garlic in a bowl, then stir in the egg and season with salt and pepper. Shape the mixture into small meatballs, dust with flour and set aside. Heat the oil in a pan, add the onion, celery, carrot and rosemary and cook over a low heat, stirring occasionally, for 5 minutes, then add the meatballs and increase the heat to medium. Cook until the meatballs are lightly browned all over, then add the passata and season with salt. Lower the heat, cover and simmer, stirring occasionally, for about 40 minutes. Cook the rigatoni in a large pan of salted, boiling water until al dente, then drain and tip into the pan with the meatballs. Mix well and heat through for 2 minutes. Transfer to a warm serving dish and sprinkle with the Parmesan.

BAKED WHOLEWHEAT RIGATONI

RIGATONI INTEGRALI AL FORNO

Serves 4

butter, for greasing

1 quantity Béchamel Sauce (see page 50)

200 g/7 oz caciotta or other semi-hard mild cheese, diced

350 g/12 oz wholewheat rigatoni

40 g/1$^1/_2$ oz Parmesan cheese, freshly grated

salt

Preheat the oven to 180°C/350°F/Gas Mark 4. Grease an ovenproof dish with butter. Mix together the béchamel sauce and diced cheese. Cook the rigatoni in a large pan of salted, boiling water until al dente, then drain and tip into the prepared dish. Spoon the béchamel mixture over the pasta, sprinkle with the Parmesan and bake for about 20 minutes. Leave to stand for 5 minutes before serving.

RIGATONI WITH CREAM, PESTO AND TOMATOES

Pour the cream into a saucepan, add the tomatoes and cook over a low heat for 10 minutes. Remove the pan from the heat and stir in the pesto. Meanwhile, cook the rigatoni in a large pan of salted, boiling water until al dente, then drain and tip into a warm serving dish. Sprinkle the pasta with the Parmesan and spoon the sauce over it.

RIGATONI PANNA, PESTO E POMODORO

Serves 4

200 ml/7 fl oz double cream

300 g/11 oz fresh tomatoes, thinly sliced, or canned chopped tomatoes, drained

2 tablespoons Pesto (see page 68)

350 g/12 oz rigatoni

40 g/1¹/₂ oz Parmesan cheese, freshly grated

salt

SPAGHETTI WITH GARLIC AND CHILLI OIL

Heat the oil in a small saucepan, add the garlic and chilli and cook over a low heat for a few minutes until the garlic is golden brown. Season lightly with salt, remove the pan from the heat and add the parsley. Cook the spaghetti in a large pan of salted, boiling water until al dente, then drain, toss with the garlic and chilli oil, and serve.

SPAGHETTI AGLIO, OLIO E PEPERONCINO

Serves 4

5 tablespoons olive oil

2 garlic cloves, thinly sliced

¹/₂ fresh chilli, seeded and chopped

1 fresh flat-leaf parsley sprig, chopped

350 g/12 oz spaghetti

salt

SPAGHETTI WITH BROCCOLI

Parboil the broccoli in salted water for 10 minutes. Heat the oil and butter in a frying pan, add the onion and cook over a low heat, stirring occasionally, for 5 minutes until softened. Drain the broccoli, add to the frying pan and mix well. Stir in the cream and simmer gently for 10 minutes. Transfer the mixture to a food processor and process to a purée. Season with salt and pepper to taste. Meanwhile, cook the spaghetti in a large pan of salted, boiling water until al dente, then drain, toss with the broccoli and cream mixture, sprinkle with the Parmesan and serve.

SPAGHETTI AI BROCCOLETTI

Serves 4

500 g/1 lb 2 oz frozen broccoli

3 tablespoons olive oil

25 g/1 oz butter

1 onion, chopped

4 tablespoons double cream

350 g/12 oz spaghetti

25 g/1 oz Parmesan cheese, freshly grated

salt and pepper

SPAGHETTI WITH CAPERS

Heat the oil in a pan, add the anchovy and garlic and cook over a low heat, stirring frequently, until the anchovy has disintegrated and the garlic has turned golden brown. Remove the pan from the heat, discard the garlic and add the capers. Meanwhile, cook the spaghetti in a large pan of salted, boiling water until al dente, then drain, toss with the sauce and serve.

SPAGHETTI AI CAPPERI

Serves 4

1 salted anchovy, head removed, cleaned and filleted(see page 596), soaked in cold water for 10 minutesand drained

4 tablespoons olive oil • 2 garlic cloves

2 tablespoons capers, rinsed

350 g/12 oz spaghetti

salt

SPAGHETTI CARBONARA

SPAGHETTI ALLA CARBONARA

Serves 4

25 g/1 oz butter

100 g/3 ¹/₂ oz pancetta, diced

1 garlic clove

350 g/12 oz spaghetti

2 eggs, beaten

40 g/1¹/₂ oz Parmesan cheese, freshly grated

40 g/1¹/₂ oz pecorino cheese, freshly grated

salt and pepper

Melt the butter in a pan, add the pancetta and garlic and cook until the garlic turns brown. Remove and discard the garlic. Meanwhile, cook the spaghetti in a large pan of salted, boiling water until al dente, then drain and add to the pancetta. Remove the pan from the heat, pour in the eggs, add half the Parmesan and half the pecorino and season with pepper. Mix well so that the egg coats the pasta. Add the remaining cheese, mix again and serve.

SPAGHETTI AMATRICIANA

SPAGHETTI ALL'AMATRICIANA

Serves 4

olive oil, for brushing

100 g/3¹/₂ oz pancetta, diced

1 onion, thinly sliced

500 g/1 lb 2 oz tomatoes, peeled, seeded and diced

1 fresh chilli, seeded and chopped

350 g/12 oz spaghetti

salt and pepper

Brush a flameproof casserole with oil, add the pancetta and cook over a low heat until the fat runs. Add the onion and cook, stirring occasionally, for 10 minutes until lightly browned. Add the tomatoes and chilli, season with salt and pepper, cover and cook for about 40 minutes, adding a little warm water if necessary. Cook the spaghetti in a large pan of salted, boiling water until al dente, then drain and toss with the sauce in a warm serving dish.

SPAGHETTI WITH RAW TOMATO

SPAGHETTI AL POMODORO CRUDO

Serves 4

500 g/1 lb 2 oz ripe vine tomatoes, peeled, seeded and chopped

4 tablespoons olive oil

10 fresh basil leaves, chopped

2 garlic cloves

350 g/12 oz spaghetti

salt and pepper

Put the tomatoes into a salad bowl, add the oil, basil and garlic and season with salt and pepper. Mix well, cover and set aside in a cool place for 30 minutes to allow the flavours to mingle, then remove and discard the garlic. Cook the spaghetti in a large pan of salted, boiling water until al dente, then drain and toss with the raw tomato sauce and serve.

SPAGHETTI AL ROSMARINO

Serves 4

2 tablespoons olive oil

2 tablespoons fresh rosemary needles,
finely chopped

1 garlic clove, finely chopped

1/2 fresh chilli, seeded and finely chopped

250 g/9 oz canned chopped tomatoes

1 tablespoon plain flour

1 tablespoon milk

350 g/12 oz spaghetti

40 g/1 1/2 oz Parmesan cheese, freshly grated

salt

SPAGHETTI WITH ROSEMARY

Heat the oil in a saucepan, add the rosemary, garlic and chilli and cook for about 2 minutes. Stir in the tomatoes with their can juices and bring to the boil, then lower the heat, cover and simmer for 30 minutes. Stir the flour with 1–2 tablespoons warm water. Season the rosemary sauce with salt, stir in the flour mixture and milk and cook for a further 5 minutes. Cook the spaghetti in a large pan of salted, boiling water until al dente, then drain and transfer to a warm serving dish. Sprinkle with the Parmesan and pour on the sauce.

SPAGHETTI CON ACCIUGHE

Serves 4

150 g/5 oz salted anchovies, heads removed,
cleaned and filleted (see page 596),
soaked in cold water for 10 minutes and drained

1 fresh flat-leaf parsley sprig

1/2 garlic clove

2 tablespoons olive oil

350 g/12 oz spaghetti

salt and pepper

SPAGHETTI WITH ANCHOVIES

Chop the anchovies very finely with the parsley and garlic, then put the mixture in a salad bowl and stir in the olive oil. Cook the spaghetti in a large pan of salted, boiling water until al dente, then drain and tip into the salad bowl. Toss well and season with pepper.

SPAGHETTI CON IL TONNO

Serves 4

3 tablespoons olive oil

1 garlic clove

65 g/2 1/2 oz canned tuna in oil, drained and flaked

3 tablespoons tomato purée

1 tablespoon finely chopped fresh flat-leaf parsley

350 g/12 oz spaghetti

salt and pepper

SPAGHETTI WITH TUNA

Heat the oil in a pan, add the garlic, cook until it has browned, then remove it from the pan. Add the tuna and mix well. Stir the tomato purée with 1–2 tablespoons warm water in a bowl, then stir into the pan and cook over a low heat for 15 minutes. Remove the pan from the heat, stir in the parsley and season with salt and pepper. Meanwhile, cook the spaghetti in a large pan of salted, boiling water until al dente, then drain, toss with the sauce and serve.

SPAGHETTI WITH BREADCRUMBS

Heat 2 tablespoons of the oil in a pan, add the anchovies and cook, mashing with a wooden spoon until they have almost disintegrated, then season with pepper and add the capers and olives. Mix together the breadcrumbs, garlic and a pinch of salt in a bowl. Heat the remaining oil in a small frying pan, add the breadcrumb mixture and cook, stirring frequently, until golden. Cook the spaghetti in a large pan of salted, boiling water until al dente, then drain and return to the pan. Add the anchovy sauce and stir. Transfer to a warm serving dish and sprinkle with the fried breadcrumbs.

SPAGHETTI CON LA MOLLICA

Serves 4

2 salted anchovies, heads removed, cleaned and filleted (see page 596), soaked in cold water for 10 minutes and drained

5 tablespoons olive oil

1 tablespoon capers, rinsed

8 black olives, stoned and halved

80 g/3 oz breadcrumbs

1/2 garlic clove chopped

350 g/12 oz spaghetti

salt and pepper

SPAGHETTI WITH COURGETTES

Heat the oil in a pan, add the garlic clove, whole onion, sage leaves and celery stick and cook over a low heat for 5 minutes. Add the tomatoes and bring to the boil over a medium heat, then add the courgettes. Season with salt and pepper, cover and cook for 15 minutes, then remove the onion, garlic, celery and sage. Meanwhile, cook the spaghetti in a large pan of salted water until al dente, then drain and return to the pan. Toss with the sauce, mozzarella and Parmesan and serve.

SPAGHETTI CON LE ZUCCHINE

Serves 4

3 tablespoons olive oil

1 garlic clove

1 small onion

2 fresh sage leaves

1 celery stick

3 plum tomatoes, peeled, seeded and chopped

350 g/12 oz courgettes, thinly sliced

350 g/12 oz spaghetti

150 g/5 oz mozzarella cheese, diced

25 g/1 oz Parmesan cheese, freshly grated

salt and pepper

SPAGHETTINI WITH BOTTARGA

Crumble half the bottarga and slice the remainder very thinly. Heat the oil in a small saucepan, add the bottarga and cook over a low heat. Meanwhile, cook the spaghettini in a large pan of salted, boiling water until al dente, then drain and tip into the pan of sauce and mix well. Transfer to a warm serving dish.

SPAGHETTINI ALLA BOTTARGA

Serves 4

100 g/3 1/2 oz bottarga

2 tablespoons olive oil

350 g/12 oz spaghettini

salt

303

TORTIGLIONI WITH MUSHROOM AND AUBERGINE

TORTIGLIONI CON FUNGHI E MELANZANE

Serves 4

2 tablespoons olive oil
1 onion, thinly sliced
1 garlic clove
200 g/7 oz mushrooms, chopped
1 aubergine, diced
100 ml/3¹/₂ fl oz double cream
350 g/12 oz tortiglioni
40 g/1¹/₂ oz Parmesan cheese, freshly grated
salt and pepper

Heat the oil in a pan, add the onion and garlic and cook over a low heat until the garlic has browned. Remove and discard the garlic, add the mushrooms and aubergine to the pan and cook, stirring frequently, until light golden brown. Stir in the cream, season with salt and pepper, cover and cook over a low heat for a further 10 minutes. Meanwhile, cook the tortiglioni in a large pan of salted, boiling water until al dente, then drain, tip into the pan of sauce and cook for 1 minute. Transfer to a warm serving dish and sprinkle with the Parmesan.

VERMICELLI WITH CLAMS

VERMICELLI CON LE VONGOLE

Serves 4

1 kg/2¹/₄ lb clams, scrubbed
150 ml/¹/₄ pint olive oil
2 garlic cloves
350 g/12 oz vermicelli
1 tablespoon fresh flat-leaf parsley
salt and pepper

Discard any clams with broken shells or that do not shut immediately when sharply tapped. Heat the oil in a saucepan, add the garlic and clams and cook for about 5 minutes until the shells open. Remove the pan from the heat and lift out the clams with a slotted spoon. Discard any that remain closed. Remove the clams from their shells. Strain the cooking liquid into a frying pan and add the clams. Meanwhile, cook the vermicelli in a large pan of salted, boiling water until al dente, then drain and tip into the frying pan. Cook for 2 minutes, tossing frequently, then season with salt and pepper to taste and sprinkle with the parsley. Tip on to a warm serving dish.

POLENTA

There are two common types of polenta: fine-grained, pale straw-coloured Veneto polenta and large-grained, bright golden-yellow Lombard or Piedmontese polenta. The former is almost always served all'onda (literally 'with wave', meaning with a consistency similar to mashed potato), while the latter is almost always firm. Both, however, are stirred and stirred again in a copper pot with a softwood stick, traditionally over the flames of an open fire. At least, once upon a time it was like that. Today, polenta has caught up with the times and modern kitchen appliances. In fact it can even 'cook itself' in an electric, copper polenta pot or be purchased ready-made at some Italian delicatessens. There is also a third kind of polenta flour, buckwheat flour, which is used to make polenta taragna.

TO SERVE 6

About 500 g/1 lb 2 oz polenta flour and 1.75 litres/ 3 pints water; the proportions vary according to how firm the polenta must be for the recipe.

WATER

Bring salted water to the boil and keep another pan of water boiling in case it is needed.

POLENTA FLOUR

Sprinkle it into the pan while stirring constantly.

ADDITIONS

As soon as the polenta thickens, soften it with a drop of the reserved hot water. This is the secret to cooking polenta successfully, as polenta thickens with heat and softens with water.

COOKING TIME

This ranges from 45 minutes to 1 hour; the longer the cooking time, the more easily the polenta is digested.

SAUCES

Simple cold milk, fresh or melted butter, tomato sauce and cheese such as Gorgonzola or fontina. Polenta can also be served with stews and braised meat, or baked with cheese, butter and ragù (meat sauce).

STORAGE

Polenta flour must be kept dry, otherwise it goes mouldy. Cooked polenta should be stored wrapped in a tea towel in the bottom of the refrigerator.

QUANTITIES AND COOKING METHOD

POLENTA

GNOCCHI DI POLENTA

Serves 4

350 g/12 oz coarse polenta flour

50 g/2 oz butter, plus extra for greasing

40 g/1½ oz Parmesan cheese, freshly grated

salt and pepper

POLENTA GNOCCHI

Make a fairly soft polenta (see page 305). When it is ready, pour it on to a work surface or tray, spread out to a layer 1 cm/½ inch thick and leave to cool and set. When it is cold, stamp out rounds using a wet glass or a biscuit cutter. Preheat the oven to 180°C/350°F/Gas Mark 4. Grease a wide baking sheet with butter and arrange the polenta rounds on it in concentric circles. Top with another layer of polenta rounds, omitting the outer circle, and continue in the same way until a pyramid is formed. Sprinkle with the Parmesan, season with pepper and dot with the butter. Bake for about 20 minutes until golden brown.

MINESTRA DI POLENTA

Serves 4

80 g/3 oz butter

1 onion, chopped

1 litre/1¾ pints milk

250 g/9 oz coarse polenta flour

100 ml/3½ fl oz double cream

40 g/1½ oz Parmesan cheese, freshly grated

salt and pepper

POLENTA SOUP

Melt 40g/1½ oz of the butter in a saucepan, add the onion and cook over a low heat, stirring occasionally, for 10 minutes until lightly browned. Meanwhile, bring the milk to just below simmering point in another pan, then remove from the heat. Stir the polenta flour into the onion and cook, stirring constantly, for 2–3 minutes. Gradually stir in the warm milk and 500 ml/18 fl oz warm water. Season with salt and pepper to taste and cook for 1 hour. Stir in the cream, the remaining butter and the Parmesan and serve.

POLENTA AL GORGONZOLA

Serves 4

350 g/12 oz coarse polenta flour

150 g/5 oz butter, cut into 4 pieces

150 g/5 oz Gorgonzola cheese, sliced

salt

Parmesan cheese, freshly grated, to serve

POLENTA WITH GORGONZOLA

Make a fairly stiff polenta with 1.2 litres/2 pints salted water (see page 305). Preheat the oven to 180°C/350°F/Gas Mark 4. Pour the polenta into soup plates or individual ovenproof dishes while it is still hot. Put a piece of butter in the middle of each, pushing it down slightly into the polenta, and lay a small slice of Gorgonzola on top. Bake until the butter and Gorgonzola have completely melted. Serve with Parmesan.

POLENTA WITH LANGOUSTINES AND RADICCHIO

Make a soft polenta (see page 305). Meanwhile, place the radicchio strips in a large salad bowl. Heat the oil and garlic in a pan and cook for a few minutes until the garlic browns, then remove it from the pan. Add the langoustines or prawns and cook for a few minutes over a high heat. Season with salt and pepper and stir in the lemon juice. Tip into the salad bowl and mix well. When the polenta is ready, pour it over the langoustines or prawns and radicchio, leave to stand for a few minutes, then serve.

POLENTA CON GLI SCAMPI E LA CICORIA

Serves 4

350 g/12 oz coarse polenta flour

2 heads radicchio, cut into strips

2 tablespoons olive oil

1 garlic clove

300 g/11 oz langoustines

or Dublin Bay prawns, peeled

juice of $1/2$ lemon, strained

salt and pepper

POLENTA WITH COD

Heat the oil in a saucepan, add the onion and cook over a low heat, stirring occasionally, for 10 minutes until lightly browned. Add the anchovies, garlic and walnuts, cook for a few minutes, then add the tomatoes, rosemary and parsley and cook for a further 10 minutes. Add the cod and potatoes, season with salt and pepper and cook for about 1 hour or until the potatoes have almost disintegrated and the sauce has thickened. Meanwhile, make the polenta (see page 305). Turn it out on to a warm serving dish, place the cod and sauce in the middle and serve.

POLENTA CON IL MERLUZZO

Serves 4

4 salted anchovies, heads removed, cleaned and

    filleted (see page 596), soaked in cold water for

10 minutes and drained

3 tablespoons olive oil

1 onion, chopped

1 garlic clove, chopped

8 walnuts, chopped

3 tomatoes, peeled, seeded and chopped

pinch of chopped fresh rosemary

1 fresh flat-leaf parsley sprig, chopped

800 g/1$3/4$ lb cod fillet, skinned and diced

2 potatoes, diced

300 g/11 oz coarse polenta flour

salt and pepper

POLENTA WITH MEAT SAUCE

Heat the oil and butter in a saucepan, add the onion, carrot and celery and cook over a low heat, stirring occasionally, for 10 minutes until browned. Add the meat, season with salt and pepper and cook for a few minutes more. Mix the tomato sauce with 1–2 tablespoons warm water in a bowl, add to the pan and cook over a low heat for about 1 hour, adding more water if necessary. Meanwhile, prepare the polenta (see page 305). When it is ready, pour it into a non-stick ring mould, rinsed out with cold water, leave to stand for 2–3 minutes, then turn it out on to a warm serving dish. Pour the hot meat sauce into the middle and serve with Parmesan.

POLENTA CON IL RAGÙ

Serves 4

2 tablespoons olive oil

25 g/1 oz butter

1 onion, chopped

1 carrot, chopped

1 celery stick, chopped

200 g/7 oz minced beef

3 tablespoons Tomato Sauce (see page 57)

350 g/12 oz coarse polenta flour

salt and pepper

Parmesan cheese, freshly grated, to serve

POLENTA WITH FONDUE

POLENTA CON LA FONDUTA

Serves 4

350 g/12 oz coarse polenta flour

40 g/1¹/₂ oz butter

1 quantity Piedmontese Fondue (see page 995)

1 black truffle, thinly sliced

salt

Make a fairly firm polenta (see page 305). When it is ready, beat in the butter. Rinse a non-stick ring mould with cold water, pour in the polenta and smooth the surface. Turn out on to a serving dish. Pour the fondue into the middle of the ring so that it flows over the sides. Sprinkle with the slices of truffle and serve.

POLENTA WITH RICOTTA

POLENTA CON LA RICOTTA

Serves 4

350 g/12 oz coarse polenta flour

300 g/11 oz ricotta cheese

3 tablespoons olive oil

1 onion, chopped

50 g/2 oz pancetta, diced

300 g/11 oz tomatoes, peeled and diced

25 g/1 oz butter, plus extra for greasing

50 g/2 oz Parmesan cheese, freshly grated

salt and pepper

Prepare the polenta (see page 305), pour it on to a work surface or tray and leave to cool and set, then cut it into slices. Beat the ricotta in a bowl until smooth. Heat the oil in a small saucepan, add the onion and pancetta and cook over a low heat, stirring occasionally, for 5 minutes. Add the tomatoes, season with salt and pepper and simmer for 30 minutes. Preheat the oven to 180°C/350°F/Gas Mark 4. Grease an ovenproof dish with butter. Arrange the polenta, ricotta, Parmesan and tomato sauce in layers in the prepared dish, finishing with a layer of polenta. Dot with the butter and bake for 20–25 minutes.

POLENTA WITH SAUSAGE

POLENTA CON LA SALCICCIA

Serves 4

200 g/7 oz Italian sausages, cut into short lengths

2 tablespoons olive oil

1 onion, chopped

1 carrot, chopped

1 celery stick, chopped

500 ml/18 fl oz passata

350 g/12 oz coarse polenta flour

salt and pepper

Prick the sausages, place in a dry frying pan and cook over a medium heat for 5–6 minutes until the fat runs, then remove with a slotted spoon. Heat the oil in a saucepan, add the onion, carrot and celery and cook for 2 minutes. Pour in the passata, season with salt and pepper to taste and cook for 20 minutes. Add the sausages and continue cooking for a further 10 minutes. Meanwhile, make the polenta (see page 305). When it is ready, turn it out on to a warm serving dish, spoon the sausage and tomato sauce all around and serve.

POLENTA WITH EGGS

Make the polenta (see page 305). Preheat the oven to 180°C/350°F/Gas Mark 4. A few minutes before the polenta is ready, beat in the butter. Make shirred eggs (see page 359). Pour the polenta on to a warm serving dish and lay the shirred eggs on top.

POLENTA CON LE UOVA

Serves 4

350 g/12 oz coarse polenta flour
40 g/1¹/₂ oz butter, plus extra for the eggs
8 eggs
salt

VALLE D'AOSTA POLENTA PASTICCIATA

Prepare a fairly stiff polenta (see page 305). Pour it on to a work surface or tray and leave to cool and set, then cut into slices. Preheat the oven to 180°C/350°F/Gas Mark 4 and grease an ovenproof dish with butter. Arrange a layer of polenta in the prepared dish, place the slices of fontina on top, sprinkle with the Parmesan and dot with the butter. Continue making alternate layers, ending with a layer of polenta dotted with the butter. Season with pepper and bake for about 20 minutes.

POLENTA PASTICCIATA ALLA VALDOSTANA

Serves 4

300 g/11 oz coarse polenta flour
80 g/3 oz butter, plus extra for greasing
300 g/11 oz fontina cheese, thinly sliced
80 g/3 oz Parmesan cheese, freshly grated
salt and pepper

POLENTA PASTICCIATA WITH MUSHROOMS

Place the mushrooms in a bowl, add warm water to cover and set aside to soak for 20 minutes. Make a fairly stiff polenta (see page 305). When it is ready, pour it on to a work surface or tray and leave to cool and set. Meanwhile, melt 25 g/1 oz of the butter in a pan, add the garlic and cook until it turns golden brown, then discard it. Drain the mushrooms, squeezing out as much liquid as possible, and add to the pan. Season with salt and pepper and cook for 10 minutes. Stir the mushrooms and their cooking juices into the béchamel sauce with half the Parmesan. Preheat the oven to 180°C/350°F/Gas Mark 4 and grease an ovenproof dish with butter. Cut the cold polenta into slices and arrange in alternating layers with the mushroom mixture in the prepared dish, ending with a layer of polenta. Dot with the remaining butter, sprinkle with the remaining Parmesan and bake for about 1 hour.

POLENTA PASTICCIATA CON I FUNGHI

Serves 4

100 g/3¹/₂ oz dried mushrooms
350 g/12 oz coarse polenta flour
50 g/2 oz butter, plus extra for greasing
1 garlic clove
1 quantity Béchamel Sauce (see page 50)
50 g/2 oz Parmesan cheese, freshly grated
salt and pepper

POLENTA PASTICCIATA WITH ANCHOVIES

POLENTA PASTICCIATA
CON LE ACCIUGHE

Serves 4

300 g/11 oz coarse polenta flour

500 ml/18 fl oz dry white wine

100 g/3½ oz salted anchovies, heads removed, cleaned and filleted (see page 596), soaked in cold water for 10 minutes and drained

80 g/3 oz butter, plus extra for greasing

1 garlic clove

200 ml/7 fl oz double cream

25 g/1 oz Parmesan cheese, freshly grated

salt and pepper

Prepare a fairly stiff polenta (see page 305) using 500ml/18 fl oz salted water and the wine. When it is ready, pour it on to a work surface or tray and leave to cool and set, then cut into slices. Preheat the oven to 180°C/350°F/Gas Mark 4 and grease an ovenproof dish with butter. Melt 50 g/2 oz of the butter in a saucepan, add the garlic and cook for 1 minute. Lower the heat, add the anchovies and cook, mashing with a wooden spoon until they have almost completely disintegrated. Remove the garlic, pour in the cream, season with pepper and cook for a few minutes more. Make alternate layers of polenta and anchovy sauce in the prepared dish, ending with a layer of polenta. Sprinkle with the Parmesan, dot with the remaining butter and bake until golden brown.

POLENTA TARAGNA

POLENTA TARAGNA

Serves 4

300 g/11 oz buckwheat flour

100 g/3½ oz coarse polenta flour

150 g/5 oz butter, cut into pieces

200 g/7 oz soft cheese, thinly sliced

salt

Pour 1.5 litres/2½ pints water into a saucepan and add salt. Bring to the boil and sprinkle in both types of flour together, stirring constantly. Cook, stirring constantly, for 30 minutes, then gradually beat in the butter. When the polenta has absorbed all the butter, add the cheese. Continue to stir for a few minutes more, then serve while hot. Fried sausages may be added if you like.

RICE

Luckily, there is a lot of rice – some 450 million tonnes ar[e] harvested every year throughout the world. Rice belongs t[o] the family Gramineae and contains protein, fats, carbohy[-] drates, sodium, potassium, calcium, phosphorus, iron an[d] other nutritional essentials; and 100 g/3¹/₂ oz provide[s] 350 calories. It is a highly recommended food because i[t] cannot be adulterated and is easy to digest. Furthermore[,] it goes well with meat, pulses, vegetables, fruit and milk.

TYPES OF RICE AND COOKING METHODS

QUANTITIES
Allow 50 g/2 oz per serving in broth, 100 g/3¹/₂ oz for risotto and 70 g/2³/₄ oz as a side dish. The quantity also depends on the other ingredients with which it is served.

ORDINARY
These include Originario and Balilla for soups and desserts; 12–13 minutes cooking time.

SEMI-FINE
These include Maratelli and Ardizzone for antipasti, timbales and croquettes; 13–15 minutes cooking time.

FINE
These include Rizzotto and Vialone for risottos, salads and pilafs; 16 minutes cooking time.

SUPERFINE
These include Arborio, Sesia and Carnaroli for risotto[s] and side dishes; abou[t] 18 minutes cooking time.

EASY COOK
This is a factory-produced parboiled rice that does no[t] overcook and can be store[d] in the refrigerator for three days after cooking.

FOREIGN
Basmati, an Indian rice whic[h] goes well with prawns an[d] crab meat; Jasmine an[d] Thai, which are excellen[t] boiled with red beans o[r] cooked in coconut milk a[s] a side dish; Patna an[d] Carolina rice with a slightly nutty taste, which is stronge[r] when wholegrain; Tilda rices, which are excellent steame[d;] Giant Canadian Wild, a lon[g] black thin rice 'discovered' by Native Americans and currently very fashionable.

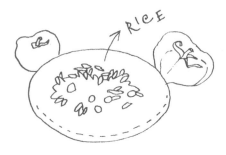

BAKED RICE (BASIC RECIPE)

Cook the rice in a saucepan with plenty of salted, boiling water for no longer than 7–8 minutes. Drain well until the rice is dry. Melt some butter in an ovenproof dish and add the rice. Bake in a preheated oven, 110°C/225°F/Gas Mark ¼, for about 45 minutes. Baked rice may be served with various delicately flavoured or fiery hot sauces, or meat, liver or mushroom ragù. It may also be served with several types of vegetables seasoned in a variety of ways.

COTTURA AL FORNO (RICETTA BASE)
Quantities of rice and water will vary according to requirements (see opposite)

CREOLE RICE (BASIC RECIPE)

Allow 1 litre/1¾ pints water, about 50 g/2 oz butter and a pinch of salt per 500 g/1 lb 2 oz rice. Bring the salted water to the boil in a saucepan, add the butter and when it has melted add the rice. Cook for just under 20 minutes until the rice has absorbed all the liquid. Drain, fluff up the grains with a fork and dot with a little butter. Alternatively, it may be served with light or medium meat, mushroom, liver or vegetable ragù.

COTTURA ALLA CREOLA (RICETTA BASE)
Quantities of rice and water will vary according to requirements (see opposite)

RICE COOKED IN MILK (BASIC RECIPE)

This dish may be sweet or savoury. In both cases, allow 500 ml/18 fl oz milk per 100 g/3 ½ oz rice. Bear in mind that rice absorbs less milk if it is first par-boiled in lightly salted water for 2–3 minutes. When used as a garnish, for making croquettes or as a pudding, use the following proportions: put 150 g/5 oz rice in 1 litre/1¾ pints milk and add 25 g/1 oz butter and a pinch of salt. Cook on the hob for the first 10 minutes, then continue in a medium oven, 180°C/350°F/Gas Mark 4, for about 20 minutes, without stirring. When the rice is tender, beat 2 eggs with a pinch of salt and stir in. Even without eggs, this dish has a delicious, delicate taste. To make dessert rice, proceed in the same way, but add 80 g/3 oz caster sugar and a dash of vanilla essence at the end.

COTTURA AL LATTE (RICETTA BASE)
Quantities of rice and water will vary according to requirements (see opposite)

COTTURA ALL'INDIANA (RICETTA BASE)
Quantities of rice and water will vary according to requirements (see page 312)

INDIAN RICE (BASIC RECIPE)

Cook the rice in plenty of salted, boiling water. When it is tender, drain and refresh under cold running water. Drain again, spread out on a baking sheet or in a roasting tin and put in a warm oven for 10–15 minutes, separating the grains occasionally with a fork. All curries call for rice cooked in this way.

COTTURA PER RISO BOLLITO
(RICETTA BASE)
Quantities of rice and water will vary according to requirements (see page 312)

BOILED RICE (BASIC RECIPE)

This is the simplest way of cooking rice. Pour the rice slowly into salted, boiling water and cook over a high heat for 15–18 minutes according to type. It may be seasoned with melted butter or simply with olive oil and cheese. The same method is used for rice salads. In this case the rice should be a superfine variety, and is drained when tender and rinsed under cold running water before dressing.

COTTURA PER RISO INTEGRALE
(RICETTA BASE)
Quantities of rice and water will vary according to requirements (see page 312)

WHOLEGRAIN RICE (BASIC RECIPE)

Dark wholegrain rice takes a long time to cook. Allow 500 ml/18 fl oz water per 200 g/7 oz rice. Put the required quantity of rice and cold water in a saucepan with a little salt, bring to the boil and cook for about 30 minutes. When it is tender, the rice should be dry and the water should be completely absorbed. Season according to taste.

COTTURA PER RISO PILAF
(RICETTA BASE)
Quantities of rice and water will vary according to requirements (see page 312)

PILAF RICE (BASIC RECIPE)

Preheat the oven to 180°C/350°F/Gas Mark 4. Pilaf means rice in Turkish, so obviously this is Turkish-style rice. Melt the butter in a fairly shallow, ovenproof pan, add the chopped onion and cook over a low heat for 5 minutes until softened. Add the rice and a pinch of salt and stir until the rice is thoroughly coated in the butter. Pour boiling water or stock to cover, 1 litre/1³/₄ pints per 500 g/1 lb 2 oz rice, bring back to the boil, then cover the pan and place in the oven. Bake without uncovering or stirring for 18–20 minutes. Before serving, stir in a knob of butter. Pilaf is usually served with shellfish, prawns, langoustines, chicken in egg sauce, mushrooms, etc.

SICILIAN CROQUETTES

Cook the rice in plenty of salted, boiling water for 15–18 minutes until tender. Drain, tip into a bowl and stir in half the butter and the Parmesan, then spread the rice out on the work surface and leave to cool. Melt the remaining butter in a saucepan, add the beef and cook, stirring frequently, until browned all over. Sprinkle with the wine and cook until it has evaporated. Stir in the tomato purée, cover and cook over a low heat for 15 minutes, then season with salt and remove from the heat. Shape the cooled rice into croquettes as large as small oranges – hence the name arancini – and hollow out the centres. Fill with a little meat sauce and a cube of mozzarella and seal with more rice. Beat the eggs with a pinch of salt in a shallow dish and spread out the flour in another shallow dish. Dip the croquettes in the beaten eggs, then in the flour and shake off any excess. Heat the oil in a deep-fryer or saucepan to 180–190°C/350–375°F or untila cube of day-old bread browns in 30 seconds. Deep-fry the croquettes in the hot oil until golden brown all over. Drain on kitchen paper and serve.

ARANCINI ALLA SICILIANA

Serves 4

300 g/11 oz long-grain rice

50 g/2 oz butter

2 tablespoons Parmesan cheese, freshly grated

100 g/3½ oz minced lean beef

100 ml/3½ fl oz dry white wine

2 tablespoons tomato purée

100 g/3½ oz mozzarella cheese, diced

2 eggs

50 g/2 oz plain flour

vegetable oil, for deep-frying

salt

RICE WITH CURRY SAUCE AND PRAWNS

Preheat the oven to 220°C/425°F/Gas Mark 7 and grease a ring mould with butter. Bring the stock to the boil. Melt the butter in a roasting tin, add the onion and cook over a low heat, stirring occasionally, for 5 minutes until softened. Add the rice and stir until it is thoroughly coated in the butter. Add the stock, cover the tin with foil and place in the oven for about 17 minutes. Meanwhile, cook the prawns in salted, boiling water for 2 minutes, then drain. Take the rice out of the oven, spoon into the prepared mould and tap the mould on the work surface to get rid of any air pockets. Gently turn out on to a warm serving dish and garnish with the prawns. Spoon the curry sauce over the rice and serve.

RISO AL CURRY CON GAMBERI

Serves 4

40 g/1½ oz butter, plus extra for greasing

750 ml/1¼ pints Fish or Chicken Stock (see pages 208–209)

1 onion, sliced

350 g/12 oz long-grain rice

350 g/12 oz large raw prawns, peeled

1 quantity Curry Sauce (see page 54)

salt

CANTONESE RICE

Melt half the butter in a pan, add the rice and stir until it is thoroughly coated in the butter. Add the stock and season with salt and pepper. Cover and simmer for 15 minutes without stirring. Melt the remaining butter in another pan, add the onions and cook over a low heat, stirring occasionally, for 5 minutes. Add the chicken, season with salt and cook, stirring occasionally, for a further 15 minutes. Just before the rice is ready, stir the almonds into it. Spoon the rice and almonds on to a warm serving dish and top with the chicken mixture. Serve with soy sauce.

RISO ALLA CANTONESE

Serves 4

130 g/4¹/₂ oz butter

300 g/11 oz long-grain rice

1 litre/1³/₄ pints Chicken Stock (see page 209)

2 onions, chopped

2 skinless, boneless chicken breasts, diced

25 g/1 oz blanched almonds, coarsely chopped

salt and pepper

soy sauce, to serve

RICE WITH MINT

Mix together the mint, leek, lemon juice and olive oil in a bowl and season with salt and pepper. Cook the rice in plenty of salted, boiling water until tender. Drain well and season with the fresh mint sauce. Be aware that the taste of mint does not go well with wine.

RISO ALLA MENTA

serves 4

8 fresh mint leaves, chopped

1 leek, white part only finely chopped

juice of 1 lemon, strained

120 ml/¹/₄ pint olive oil

350 g/12 oz long-grain rice

salt and pepper

RICE WITH CARROTS AND WALNUTS

Preheat the oven to 180°C/350°F/Gas Mark 4. Rinse the rice under cold running water, then put in a saucepan with 750 ml/1¹/₄ pints water. Add a pinch of salt, bring to the boil and cook over a low heat for 15 minutes. Stir in the carrots, cover and cook for a further 15 minutes until all the water has been absorbed and the rice is tender. Meanwhile, spread out the walnuts on a baking sheet and toast in the oven for a few minutes until golden. When cool enough to handle, chop the nuts. When the rice is tender, stir in the walnuts and corn oil and heat through for a few minutes, then transfer to a warm serving dish.

RISO ALLE CAROTE E NOCI

Serves 4

350 g/12 oz wholegrain rice

200 g/7 oz carrots, sliced

50 g/2 oz shelled walnuts

2 tablespoons corn oil

salt

INDONESIAN RICE

RISO ALL'INDONESIANA

Serves 4

1 chicken, weighing about 500 g/1 lb 2 oz

150 g/5 oz shelled peas

3 tablespoons olive oil

275 g/10 oz long-grain rice

1 litre/1¾ pints Chicken Stock (see page 209)

150 g/5 oz cooked ham, diced

1¼ teaspoons curry powder

salt and pepper

Remove and discard the chicken skin and cut the meat off the bones into fairly neat pieces. Place the chicken meat in a saucepan, add 1.5 litres/2½ pints water and bring to the boil, then lower the heat and simmer for 40 minutes. Add the peas and season lightly with salt and pepper. Heat the oil in another saucepan, add the rice and cook, stirring constantly, until it has changed colour. Stir in a ladleful of stock, and the ham and curry powder. Gradually add more stock as each ladleful is absorbed. Add the chicken and peas to the rice and cook until the rice is tender. Season with salt and pepper to taste and serve in individual bowls or soup plates.

RICE WITH RAW EGG

RISO ALL'UOVO CRUDO

Serves 4

350 g/12 oz long-grain rice • 4 egg yolks

100 g/3½ oz fontina cheese, thinly sliced

25 g/1 oz butter

40 g/1½ oz Parmesan cheese, freshly grated, plus extra to serve • salt

Cook the rice in plenty of salted, boiling water for 15–18 minutes until tender. Meanwhile, beat the egg yolks in a large bowl and add a pinch of salt and the fontina. Drain the rice, spoon it into the bowl and mix quickly so that the egg coats the rice like a cream. Stir in the butter and Parmesan, transfer to a warm serving dish and serve with extra Parmesan.

CURRIED RICE AND LENTILS

RISO CON LENTICCHIE AL CURRY

Serves 4

150 g/5 oz lentils

350 g/12 oz long-grain rice

2 teaspoons curry powder

40 g/1½ oz butter

salt

Put the lentils in a saucepan, add water to cover, bring to the boil and simmer for 30 minutes. Drain, reserving 500 ml/18 fl oz of the cooking liquid. Put the rice in a saucepan, add the reserved cooking liquid, the curry powder, butter and a pinch of salt. Bring to the boil and simmer for 15–20 minutes until the rice is tender and all the liquid has been absorbed. Stir in the lentils and transfer to a warm serving dish.

RICE WITH SPINACH

RISO CON SPINACI

Serves 4

600 g/1 lb 5 oz spinach

40 g/1½ oz butter

350 g/12 oz long-grain rice

40 g/1½ oz Parmesan cheese, freshly grated

salt

Cook the spinach in 500 ml/18 fl oz lightly salted, boiling water for 5 minutes, then drain, reserving the cooking liquid. Squeeze out as much liquid as possible and chop. Melt half the butter in a frying pan, add the spinach and cook over a low heat for 5 minutes. Cook the rice in the reserved cooking liquid for 15–18 minutes until tender, then drain, tip into a warm serving dish and stir in the remaining butter. Top the rice with the spinach and sprinkle with the Parmesan.

SEASONED BOILED RICE

RISO IN CAGNONE

Serves 4

350 g/12 oz long-grain rice
25 g/1 oz butter
8 fresh sage leaves
40 g/1½ oz Parmesan cheese, freshly grated
salt

Cook the rice in plenty of salted, boiling water for 15–18 minutes until tender, then drain. Meanwhile, melt the butter in a small saucepan, add the sage leaves and cook for a few minutes until lightly browned. While the rice is still very hot, pour the sage butter over it, sprinkle with the Parmesan and serve.

MOULDED RICE WITH HAM AND PEAS

RISO IN FORMA
CON PROSCIUTTO E PISELLI

Serves 4

50 g/2 oz butter, plus extra for greasing
½ onion, chopped
250 g/9 oz frozen peas
150 ml/¼ pint Meat Stock (see page 208)
100 g/3½ oz fontina cheese, diced
100 g/3½ oz mozzarella cheese, diced
100 g/3½ oz Emmenthal cheese, diced
200 ml/7 fl oz milk
300 g/11 oz long-grain rice
200 g/7 oz cooked ham, sliced
salt

Preheat the oven to 200°C/400°F/Gas Mark 6. Grease a ring mould with butter. Melt the butter in a small saucepan, add the onion and cook over a low heat, stirring occasionally, for 10 minutes until golden brown. Add the peas, a pinch of salt and the stock, bring to the boil and simmer, uncovered, for 8 minutes or until the peas are tender. Place the cheeses in a bowl, add the milk and set aside. Cook the rice in plenty of salted, boiling water for 15–18 minutes until tender, then drain and tip into a bowl. Drain the cheeses and stir them into the rice. Line the prepared mould with slices of ham, spoon in the rice and press down well. Bake for 5 minutes, then turn out on to a warm serving dish and spoon the peas into the centre.

BAKED RICE WITH PARSLEY

RISO IN FORNO AL PREZZEMOLO

Serves 4

350 g/12 oz long-grain rice
4 tablespoons olive oil
1 shallot, chopped
2 fresh flat-leaf parsley sprigs, chopped
salt and pepper
Parmesan cheese, freshly grated, to serve

Preheat the oven to 180°C/350°F/Gas Mark 4. Cook the rice in plenty of salted, boiling water for 7–8 minutes, then drain until very dry. Tip it into to an ovenproof dish, stir in half the oil, cover with foil and put in the oven for about 20 minutes. Meanwhile, heat the remaining oil in a frying pan, add the shallot and parsley and cook over a low heat, stirring occasionally for 5 minutes until softened. Season with salt and pepper and stir into the rice. Serve with Parmesan.

MINI RICE CROQUETTES WITH MOZZARELLA

Cook the rice in plenty of salted, boiling water for 7–8 minutes, then drain and tip into a large bowl. Add the mozzarella, ham and egg yolks, mix well, then stir in the Parmesan. Shape the mixture into oval croquettes the size of walnuts. Place the flour in a shallow dish, beat the egg with salt and pepper in another shallow dish and place the breadcrumbs in a third shallow dish. Dip the croquettes first in the flour, then in the beaten egg and finally in the breadcrumbs. Heat the oil in a deep-fryer or saucepan to 180–190°C/350–375°F or until a cube of day-old bread browns in 30 seconds. Add the croquettes, in batches, and cook until golden brown. Remove with a slotted spoon and drain on kitchen paper. Serve while still very hot.

MINI SUPPLÌ DI RISO
CON MOZZARELLA

Serves 4

250 g/9 oz long-grain rice

200 g/7 oz mozzarella cheese, diced

100 g/3¹/₂ oz cooked ham, finely diced

2 egg yolks

80 g/3 oz Parmesan cheese, freshly grated

50 g/2 oz plain flour

1 egg

50 g/2 oz breadcrumbs

vegetable oil, for deep-frying

salt and pepper

PAELLA

Preheat the oven to 220°C/425°F/Gas Mark 7. Discard any shellfish with broken shells or that do not shut immediately when sharply tapped. Cut the fish into chunks. Heat 4 tablespoons of the oil in a flameproof casserole, add the fish and cook over a medium heat, stirring occasionally, for 5 minutes, then add the peppers and shellfish, lower the heat, cover and cook until the shells open. Discard any shellfish that remain closed. Meanwhile, heat the remaining oil in a saucepan, add the onion and cook over a low heat, stirring occasionally, for 5 minutes until softened, then stir in the rice. When the rice has changed colour, pour in the stock, stir in the garlic and cook for 12 minutes. Pour the rice into the casserole, mix well, increase the heat and cook for a few minutes more. Drizzle with oil and season with salt and pepper. Transfer the casserole to the oven and bake for 5 minutes. Serve straight from the casserole. There are numerous versions of this classic Spanish dish. Some recipes include artichoke wedges, chicken, pork, turkey, smoked bacon or saffron, depending on the region.

PAELLA

Serves 4

350 g/12 oz shellfish, such as clams and mussels, scrubbed and beards removed

600 g/1 lb 5 oz mixed fish, such as sea bass, hake and red mullet, filleted

7 tablespoons olive oil, plus extra for drizzling

1 red pepper, halved seeded and cut into strips

1 yellow pepper, halved seeded and cut into strips

1 onion, sliced

300 g/11 oz long-grain rice

600 ml/1 pint Chicken or Vegetable Stock (see page 209)

2 garlic cloves, crushed

salt and pepper

RICE SALADS

RISO IN INSALATA AI GAMBERETTI

RICE AND PRAWN SALAD

Serves 4

350 g/12 oz long-grain rice

3 tablespoons olive oil

juice of 1 lemon, strained

200 g/7 oz cooked, peeled prawns

3 tablespoons chopped fresh flat-leaf parsley

8 fresh basil leaves, torn

butter, for greasing

salt and pepper

Cook the rice in plenty of salted, boiling water for about 18 minutes until tender, then drain, rinse under cold running water and drain again. Tip into a bowl. Whisk together the olive oil and lemon juice in a jug and season with salt and pepper. Add the prawns, parsley and basil to the rice, pour the dressing on top and toss gently. Grease a dome-shaped mould with butter and spoon in the rice mixture, pressing it down well. Turn out on to a serving dish and store in a cool place, but not the refrigerator, until ready to serve.

Serves 4

300 g/11 oz long-grain rice

50 g/2 oz French beans

1 courgette • 2 eggs, hard-boiled

1 celery stick, finely chopped

2 tomatoes, peeled, seeded and diced

1 red pepper, halved, seeded and finely chopped

4 radishes, thinly sliced • 3 tablespoons olive oil

1 tablespoon white wine vinegar

2 teaspoons curry powder

1 teaspoon Dijon mustard

salt

CURRIED RICE SALAD

Cook the rice in plenty of salted, boiling water for about 18 minutes until tender, then drain, rinse under cold running water and drain again. Tip into a salad bowl. Meanwhile, cook the French beans and courgette in salted, boiling water for 8–10 minutes until tender, then drain and chop. Shell the eggs, cut in half and scoop out the yolks with a teaspoon. Finely chop the egg whites. Gently stir the beans, courgette, celery, tomatoes, pepper, radishes and egg white into the rice. Whisk together the olive oil and vinegar in a bowl, crumble in the egg yolks, stir in the curry powder and mustard and season with salt. Pour the dressing over the rice, toss gently and serve immediately.

Serves 4

300 g/11 oz long-grain rice

4 tablespoons olive oil • 1 apple

150 g/5 oz Emmenthal cheese, diced

2 celery hearts including leaves, chopped

50 g/2 oz shelled walnuts, chopped

salt and pepper

RICE SALAD WITH CHEESE

Cook the rice in plenty of salted, boiling water for about 18 minutes until tender, then drain, rinse under cold running water and drain again. Tip into a salad bowl and stir in 3 tablespoons of the olive oil. Core and dice the apple and add to the rice with the Emmenthal, celery and walnuts. Stir in the remaining olive oil and season with salt and pepper to taste. Store in a cool place, but not the refrigerator, until ready to serve.

Serves 4

500 g/1 lb 2 oz clams, scrubbed

500 g/1 lb 2 oz mussels, scrubbed and beards removed

300 g/11 oz baby octopuses

250 g/9 oz long-grain rice

2 eggs, hard-boiled

3 tablespoons olive oil

1–2 teaspoons lemon juice, strained

salt

SEAFOOD RICE SALAD

Discard any clams and mussels with broken shells or that do not shut immediately when sharply tapped. Put the shellfish in two separate frying pans and cook on high heat for 5 minutes until they have opened. Remove from the heat and discard any that remain closed. Remove the clams and mussels from their shells and set aside. Cook the baby octopuses in salted, boiling water for about 10 minutes, remove from the heat and leave to cool, then cut in half. Cook the rice in plenty of salted, boiling water for about 18 minutes until tender, then drain, rinse under cold running water and drain again. Tip into a salad bowl and add the clams, mussels and octopuses. Shell the eggs, cut in half and scoop out the yolks. Crumble the yolks into a bowl and gradually whisk in the olive oil a drop at a time. When the dressing has the desired consistency (you may not need all the oil), whisk in lemon juice to taste and season with salt. Sprinkle the dressing over the rice salad and store in a cool place, but not the refrigerator, until ready to serve.

RICE AND BEETROOT SALAD

Cook the rice in plenty of salted, boiling water for about 18 minutes until tender, then drain, rinse under cold running water and drain again. Tip into a salad bowl and add the cheese and capers. Shell and chop two of the eggs and add to the rice. Whisk together the oil, vinegar and mustard in a jug, season with salt and pepper and pour over the salad. Toss well and sprinkle the beetroot and parsley on top. Shell and slice the remaining egg and arrange over the salad.

RISO IN INSALATA CON BARBABIETOLE
Serves 4

300 g/11 oz long-grain rice

100 g/3½ oz Emmenthal cheese, diced

16 capers, rinsed • 3 eggs, hard-boiled

6 tablespoons olive oil

2 tablespoons white wine vinegar

1 teaspoon Dijon mustard

1 cooked beetroot, peeled and diced

1 fresh flat-leaf parsley sprig, finely chopped

salt and pepper

RICE SALAD WITH PICKLED PEPPERS

Cook the rice in plenty of salted, boiling water for about 18 minutes until tender, then drain, rinse under cold running water and drain again. Tip into a bowl and stir in 2 tablespoons of the olive oil. Stir in the peppers and cornichons or gherkins, then mix in the remaining oil and season with salt and pepper to taste. Spoon the rice into a round mould and press down well, then turn out on to a serving dish and cover completely with Parmesan shavings.

RISO IN INSALATA
CON PEPERONI SOTTACETO
Serves 4

300 g/11 oz long-grain rice

3 tablespoons olive oil

1 jar (about 180 g/6¼ oz) pickled peppers,

drained and cut into strips

1 jar (about 180 g/6¼ oz) cornichons or gherkins,

drained and chopped

40 g/1½ oz Parmesan cheese, shaved

salt and pepper

RICE AND CRAB MEAT SALAD

Cook the rice in plenty of salted, boiling water for about 18 minutes until tender, then drain, rinse under cold running water and drain again. Tip into a salad bowl and stir in 1 tablespoon of the oil and a pinch of pepper. Heat 2 tablespoons of the remaining oil in a saucepan, add the leeks and cook, stirring occasionally, for 5 minutes until soft. Add the peas, season with salt and cook over a medium heat for 10 minutes until tender. Beat the eggs with a pinch of salt. Heat the remaining oil in a frying pan, pour in the eggs, tilt the pan to spread them evenly over the base and cook until the underside is set. Flip the omelette over and cook until the second side is set. Slide out of the pan and cut into strips. Pick over the crab meat and remove any pieces of cartilage or shell, then stir the meat into the rice with the leeks and peas and strips of omelette. Taste and adjust the seasoning if necessary. Store in a cool place, but not the refrigerator, until ready to serve.

RISO IN INSALATA
CON POLPA DI GRANCHIO
Serves 4

300 g/11 oz long-grain rice

4 tablespoons olive oil

2 leeks, trimmed and sliced

200 g/7 oz shelled peas

2 eggs

300 g/11 oz crab meat, drained if canned

salt and pepper

LOW–FAT RICE SALAD

Cook the rice in plenty of salted, boiling water for about 18 minutes until tender, then drain and tip into a wide salad bowl while still warm. Arrange the tuna on top, followed by the sweetcorn, then the salmon, then the prawns. Finally, sprinkle the capers on top. Drizzle with olive oil and season with salt and white pepper to taste. Mix thoroughly but gently so that the flavours blend.

RISO IN INSALATA DI MAGRO

Serves 4

250 g/9 oz long-grain rice

150 g/5 oz canned tuna in oil, drained and flaked

150 g/5 oz canned sweetcorn, drained

150 g/5 oz smoked salmon, diced

200 g/7 oz cooked peeled prawns

1 tablespoon capers, rinsed

olive oil, for drizzling

salt and white pepper

SMOKED FISH AND RICE SALAD

Bring the fish stock to the boil in a saucepan. Add the rice and cook for about 18 minutes until tender, then drain and leave to cool. Put the radishes, horseradish, salmon and swordfish into a salad bowl. Whisk together the olive oil, walnut oil, lemon juice and lime juice in a bowl and season with salt and pepper. Pour the dressing over the rice salad, toss and sprinkle with the dill. Store in a cool place, but not the refrigerator, until ready to serve.

RISO IN INSALATA DI PESCE AFFUMICATO

Serves 4

500 ml/18 fl oz Concentrated Fish Stock
 (see page 210)

300 g/11 oz long-grain rice

4 radishes, sliced

1-cm/^{1}/$_2$-inch piece of fresh

horseradish root, chopped

1 smoked salmon slice, cut into strips

1 smoked swordfish slice, cut into strips

2 tablespoons olive oil

1 tablespoon walnut oil

juice of 1 lemon, strained

juice of 1 lime, strained

1 tablespoon chopped fresh dill

salt and pepper

SUMMER RICE SALAD

Cook the rice in plenty of salted, boiling water until tender, then drain, rinse under cold running water and drain again. Meanwhile, put the tuna, cheese, tomatoes and capers into a salad bowl. Add the rice and mix well so that it soaks up the flavours. Whisk together the olive oil and lemon juice in a bowl, then pour the dressing over the salad and toss. Finally, mix in the onions and artichokes.

RISO IN INSALATA ESTIVO

Serves 4

300 g/11 oz easy cook rice

250 g/9 oz canned tuna in oil, drained and flaked

200 g/7 oz Gruyère cheese, diced

4 tomatoes, seeded and diced

2 tablespoons capers, rinsed

3 tablespoons olive oil

juice of 1 lemon, strained

8 pickled pearl onions

8 baby artichokes in oil

salt

RISOTTOS

Rice is the most popular grain in the world but the way of cooking risotto is quintessentially Italian. Its texture varies in relation to regional tastes but the method of its preparation always remains the same. Despite variations in many recipes, the general rule is that, after 'toasting' the rice in a pan with a little oil or butter over a low heat, you need to add hot stock, spoonful by spoonful. It is essential that you choose the right type of rice, such as Arborio or Carnaroli, as these will release starch and create a perfect, creamy mixture.

GARLIC

SEAFOOD RISOTTO

RISOTTO AI FRUTTI DI MARE

Serves 4

4 tablespoons olive oil
1 onion, chopped
1 garlic clove
600 g/1 lb 5 oz cleaned mixed seafood,
such as small octopus, cuttlefish and small squid
about 1.2 litres/2 pints Fish Stock (see page 208)
175 ml/6 fl oz dry white wine
2 tablespoons tomato purée
300 g/11 oz risotto rice
200 g/7 oz shelled mussels
1 tablespoon chopped fresh flat-leaf parsley
salt and pepper

Heat the oil in a saucepan, add the onion and garlic and cook over a low heat, stirring occasionally, for 10 minutes until lightly browned. Remove and discard the garlic, add the seafood to the pan and cook for a few minutes more. Meanwhile, bring the stock to the boil in another pan. Sprinkle the wine over the seafood and cook until it has evaporated, then season with salt and pepper to taste. Pour in 3 tablespoons water, add the tomato purée and cook for a further 10 minutes. Add the rice and cook, stirring constantly, until it has absorbed all the liquid. Add a ladleful of the hot stock and cook, stirring, until it has been absorbed. Continue adding the stock, a ladleful at a time, and stirring until each addition has been absorbed. This will take 18–20 minutes. When the rice is almost tender, add the mussels and mix gently. Sprinkle with the parsley and serve.

BLUEBERRY RISOTTO

Bring the stock to the boil. Meanwhile, melt the butter in another saucepan, add the onion and cook over a low heat, stirring occasionally, for 5 minutes until softened. Add the rice and cook, stirring constantly, until the grains are coated in butter. Sprinkle in the wine and cook until it has evaporated. Set aside 2 tablespoons of the blueberries and add the remainder to the pan. Add a ladleful of the hot stock and cook, stirring, until it has been absorbed. Continue adding the stock, a ladleful at a time, and stirring until each addition has been absorbed. This will take 18–20 minutes. When the rice is tender, stir in the cream and transfer to a warm serving dish. Garnish with the reserved blueberries and serve with Parmesan.

RISOTTO AI MIRTILLI

Serves 4

about 1.5 litres/2^{1}/$_{2}$ pints
Vegetable Stock (see page 209)

40 g/1^{1}/$_{2}$ oz butter

1 onion, finely chopped

350 g/12 oz risotto rice

175 ml/6 fl oz white wine

200 g/7 oz blueberries

100 ml/3^{1}/$_{2}$ fl oz single cream

Parmesan cheese, freshly grated, to serve

JERUSALEM ARTICHOKE RISOTTO

Bring the stock to the boil. Meanwhile, melt the butter in another saucepan, add the onion and cook over a low heat, stirring occasionally, for 5 minutes until softened. Add the artichokes and cook, stirring occasionally, for a further 5 minutes. Add a ladleful of the stock and simmer for 20 minutes, then mash with a fork. Stir in the rice. Add a ladleful of the hot stock and cook, stirring, until it has been absorbed. Continue adding the stock, a ladleful at a time, and stirring until each addition has been absorbed. This will take 18–20 minutes. When the rice is tender, season with salt to taste and stir in the cream. Serve with Parmesan.

RISOTTO AI TOPINAMBUR

Serves 4

about 1.5 litres/2^{1}/$_{2}$ pints Vegetable
Stock (see page 209)

40 g/1^{1}/$_{2}$ oz butter

1 onion, chopped

6 Jerusalem artichokes, sliced

350 g/12 oz risotto rice

1 tablespoon single cream

salt

Parmesan cheese, freshly grated, to serve

BAROLO AND MUSHROOM RISOTTO

Place the mushrooms in a bowl, add hot water to cover and leave to soak for 20 minutes, then drain and squeeze out. Melt the butter with the oil in another saucepan, add the garlic, onion, rosemary, sage and basil and cook over a low heat, stirring occasionally, for 5 minutes. Add the tomatoes and cook for a further 15 minutes. Add the mushrooms, season with salt and pepper to taste, then cover and simmer for 15 minutes. Meanwhile, bring the stock to the boil. Stir the parsley and rice into the pan of vegetables and cook, stirring constantly, until the grains are coated in fat. Sprinkle in the wine and cook until it has evaporated. Add a ladleful of the hot stock and cook, stirring, until it has been absorbed. Continue adding the stock, a ladleful at a time, and stirring until each addition has been absorbed. This will take 18–20 minutes. When the rice is tender, sprinkle with the Parmesan and serve.

RISOTTO AL BAROLO CON FUNGHI

Serves 4

100 g/3^{1}/$_{2}$ oz dried mushrooms

40 g/1^{1}/$_{2}$ oz butter • 2 tablespoons olive oil

1 garlic clove, finely chopped

1 onion, finely chopped • 1 fresh rosemary sprig, finely chopped • 1 fresh sage sprig, finely chopped

1 fresh basil sprig, finely chopped

4 tomatoes, peeled and chopped

about 1.5 litres/2^{1}/$_{2}$ pints Vegetable
Stock (see page 209)

1 fresh flat-leaf parsley sprig, finely chopped

350 g/12 oz risotto rice • 200 ml/7 fl oz Barolo

40 g/1^{1}/$_{2}$ oz Parmesan cheese, freshly grated

salt and pepper

CAVIAR RISOTTO

RISOTTO AL CAVIALE

Serves 4

80 g/3 oz butter

1 onion, chopped

350 g/12 oz risotto rice

350 ml/12 fl oz dry white wine

250 ml/8 fl oz double cream

3 tablespoons caviar

salt and pepper

Melt the butter in a saucepan, add the onion and cook over a low heat, stirring occasionally, for 5 minutes. Stir in the rice, then pour in the wine and bring just to the boil over a low heat. Gradually, stir in the cream and cook, stirring, until the rice is tender, adding a little boiling water if necessary. Season with salt and pepper, remove the pan from the heat and add the caviar. Stir vigorously until the risotto is an even colour, then serve.

MILANESE RISOTTO

RISOTTO ALLA MILANESE

Serves 4

about 1.5 litres/2¹/₂ pints Meat Stock (see page 208)

20 g/³/₄ oz beef bone marrow

80 g/3 oz butter

1 small onion, chopped

350 g/12 oz risotto rice

¹/₂ teaspoon saffron threads

80 g/3 oz Parmesan cheese, freshly grated

salt

Bring the stock to the boil. Heat the beef marrow with 50 g/2 oz of the butter in another saucepan. Add the onion and cook over a low heat, stirring occasionally, for 5 minutes. Stir in the rice and cook, stirring, until the grains are coated in butter. Add a ladleful of the hot stock and cook, stirring, until it has been absorbed. Continue adding the stock, a ladleful at a time, and stirring until each addition has been absorbed. This will take 18–20 minutes. Before adding the final ladleful of stock, stir the saffron into it. When the rice is tender, season with salt to taste, then remove the pan from the heat, stir in the remaining butter and the Parmesan and serve.

SALMON AND WINE RISOTTO

RISOTTO ALLA SALSA DI SALMONE E SPUMANTE

Serves 4

about 1.5 litres/2¹/₂ pints Vegetable Stock (see page 209)

40 g/1¹/₂ oz butter

350 g/12 oz risotto rice

350 ml/12 fl oz sparkling white wine

80 g/3 oz smoked salmon

Bring the stock to the boil. Melt half the butter in another saucepan, stir in the rice and cook, stirring, until the grains are coated in butter. Pour in the wine and cook until it has evaporated. Add a ladleful of the hot stock and cook, stirring, until it has been absorbed. Continue adding the stock, a ladleful at a time, and stirring until each addition has been absorbed. This will take 18–20 minutes. Meanwhile, finely chop half the salmon and coarsely chop the other half. Cream the remaining butter in a bowl and beat in the finely chopped salmon. About 2 minutes before the rice has finished cooking, stir in the butter mixture and coarsely chopped salmon.

CARROT RISOTTO

Serves 4

about 1.5 litres/2^1/$_2$ pints Vegetable
Stock (see page 209)
4 young carrots, chopped
175 ml/6 fl oz dry white wine
50 g/2 oz butter
1 small onion, chopped
350 g/12 oz risotto rice
50 g/2 oz Emmenthal cheese, shaved
2 tablespoons single cream
salt and pepper

Bring the stock to the boil. Meanwhile, put the carrots and wine in a food processor and process to a purée. Melt the butter in another saucepan, add the onion and cook over a low heat, stirring occasionally, for 5 minutes. Add the carrot purée to the pan, increase the heat to medium and cook for a few seconds, then stir in the rice. Add a ladleful of the hot stock and cook, stirring, until it has been absorbed. Continue adding the stock, a ladleful at a time, and stirring until each addition has been absorbed. This will take 18–20 minutes. About 5 minutes before the rice is tender, season with salt and pepper to taste and stir in the Emmenthal and cream. Remove the pan from the heat, cover and leave to stand for 2 minutes before serving.

STRAWBERRY RISOTTO

Serves 4

about 1.5 litres/2^1/$_2$ pints Vegetable
Stock (see page 209)
100 g/3^1/$_2$ oz butter
1 onion, chopped
350 g/12 oz risotto rice
350 ml/12 fl oz dry white wine
300 g/11 oz strawberries, hulled
250 ml/8 fl oz single cream
salt and pepper

Bring the stock to the boil. Melt half the butter in another saucepan, add the onion and cook over a low heat, stirring occasionally, for 5 minutes. Add the rice and cook, stirring, until the grains are coated in butter. Pour in the wine and cook until it has evaporated. Add a ladleful of the hot stock and cook, stirring, until it has been absorbed. Continue adding the stock, a ladleful at a time, and stirring until each addition has been absorbed. This will take 18–20 minutes. Meanwhile, set a few whole strawberries aside, mash the remainder and add to the risotto about halfway through the cooking time. When the rice is almost tender, stir in the cream and season with salt and pepper. Serve garnished with the reserved strawberries.

AUBERGINE RISOTTO

Place the aubergine slices in a colander, sprinkle with salt and leave to drain in the sink for 30 minutes, then rinse well, pat dry with kitchen paper and chop. Bring the stock to the boil. Meanwhile, heat the olive oil in another saucepan, add the garlic and cook for a few minutes until browned, then remove and discard. Add the aubergines, stir in the tomato and oregano, increase the heat to high and cook for a few minutes. Stir in the rice. Add a ladleful of the hot stock and cook, stirring, until it has been absorbed. Continue adding the stock, a ladleful at a time, and stirring until each addition has been absorbed. This will take 18–20 minutes. About 5 minutes before the end of the cooking time, season with salt and pepper to taste and stir in the mozzarella. When the rice is tender, transfer to a warm serving dish.

RISOTTO ALLE MELANZANE

Serves 4

2 aubergines, sliced

about 1.5 litres/2¹/₂ pints Vegetable Stock (see page 209)

2 tablespoons olive oil

1 garlic clove

1 ripe tomato, peeled, seeded and diced

pinch of dried oregano

350 g/12 oz risotto rice

200 g/7 oz mozzarella cheese, diced

salt and pepper

NETTLE RISOTTO

Bring the stock to the boil. Meanwhile, melt the butter with the oil in another saucepan, add the nettles and cook over a low heat, stirring occasionally, for a few minutes. Stir in the rice and cook, stirring, until the grains are coated in fat. Add the wine and cook until it has evaporated. Add a ladleful of the hot stock and cook, stirring, until it has been absorbed. Continue adding the stock, a ladleful at a time, and stirring until each addition has been absorbed. This will take 18–20 minutes. When the rice is almost tender, stir in the cream. When the rice is tender, remove the pan from the heat, stir in the Parmesan, cover and leave to stand for 2 minutes before serving.

RISOTTO ALLE ORTICHE

Serves 4

about 1.5 litres/2¹/₂ pints Vegetable Stock (see page 209)

25 g/1 oz butter

3 tablespoons olive oil

300 g/11 oz fresh young nettles, coarsely chopped

350 g/12 oz risotto rice

5 tablespoons dry white wine

200 ml/7 fl oz single cream

40 g/1¹/₂ oz Parmesan cheese, freshly grated

RADICCHIO RISOTTO

Bring the stock to the boil. Meanwhile, melt half the butter in another saucepan, add the onion and cook over a low heat, stirring occasionally, for 5 minutes. Stir in the radicchio, then stir in the rice and cook, stirring, until the grains are coated in butter. Pour in the wine and cook until it has evaporated. Add a ladleful of the hot stock and cook, stirring, until it has been absorbed. Continue adding the stock, a ladleful at a time, and stirring until each addition has been absorbed. This will take 18–20 minutes. When the rice is tender, season with salt to taste, stir in the remaining butter and the Parmesan and serve.

RISOTTO AL RADICCHIO TREVIGIANO

Serves 4

about 1.5 litres/2¹/₂ pints Vegetable Stock (see page 209)

80 g/3 oz butter

1 onion, chopped

200 g/7 oz radicchio, cut into strips

350 g/12 oz risotto rice

5 tablespoons white wine

2 tablespoons Parmesan cheese, freshly grated

salt

PRAWN RISOTTO

Bring 1 litre/1³/₄ pints salted water to the boil, add the prawns and cook for 2–3 minutes. Remove with a slotted spoon and peel and devein when cool enough to handle, reserving the shells. Crush the shells in a mortar with a pestle. Stick the onion with the cloves and add to the prawn cooking liquid with the celery and carrot, then bring to the boil and simmer for 30 minutes. Remove and discard the cloves, transfer the contents of the pan to a food processor, add the crushed shells and process to a purée. Melt 50 g/ 2 oz of the butter in a saucepan, stir in the rice and cook, stirring, until the grains are coated in butter. Add a ladleful of the purée and cook, stirring, until it has been absorbed. Continue adding the purée, a ladleful at a time, and stirring until each addition has been absorbed. This will take 18–20 minutes. Meanwhile, melt the remaining butter in a frying pan. Add the prawns and cook, stirring occasionally, for 4–5 minutes. When the rice is tender, transfer to a warm serving dish, arrange the prawns around it and serve.

RISOTTO CON I GAMBERI

Serves 4

300 g/11 oz large raw prawns
1 onion
2 cloves
1 celery heart
1 carrot
80 g/3 oz butter
350 g/12 oz risotto rice
salt

APPLE RISOTTO

Bring a pan of water to the boil, add the lemon rind and apples and parboil for 4–5 minutes. Drain well, discarding the lemon rind, and pat dry with kitchen paper. Melt 25 g/1 oz of the butter in a frying pan over a high heat, add the apples and cook, stirring frequently, for 5 minutes. Meanwhile, bring the stock to the boil. Heat the olive oil in another saucepan, stir in the rice and cook, stirring, until the grains are coated in oil. Sprinkle in the wine and cook until it has evaporated. Add a ladleful of the hot stock and cook, stirring, until it has been absorbed. Continue adding the stock, a ladleful at a time, and stirring until each addition has been absorbed. This will take 18–20 minutes. After about 6 minutes of the cooking time, add the apples. When the rice is almost tender, stir in the Parmesan, Worcestershire sauce and remaining butter and season with salt and pepper to taste.

RISOTTO CON LE MELE

Serves 4

thinly pared strip of lemon rind
2 apples, peeled and diced
40 g/1¹/₂ oz butter
about 1.5 litres/2¹/₂ pints Vegetable
Stock (see page 209)
2 tablespoons olive oil
350 g/12 oz risotto rice
5 tablespoons dry white wine
2 tablespoons, Parmesan cheese, freshly grated
1 tablespoon Worcestershire sauce
salt and pepper

RISOTTO CON PANNA E RUCOLA

Serves 4

about 1.5 litres/2¹/₂ pints Vegetable
Stock (see page 209)
40 g/1¹/₂ oz butter • 1 onion, finely chopped
350 g/12 oz risotto rice
5 tablespoons dry white wine
1¹/₂ tablespoons Parmesan cheese, freshly grated
plus extra to serve
175 ml/6 fl oz single cream
small bunch of rocket, chopped
salt and pepper

CREAM AND ROCKET RISOTTO

Bring the stock to the boil. Meanwhile, melt the butter in another saucepan, add the onion and cook over a low heat, stirring occasionally, for 5 minutes. Stir in the rice and cook, stirring, until the grains are coated in butter. Sprinkle in the wine and cook until it has evaporated. Add a ladleful of the hot stock and cook, stirring, until it has been absorbed. Continue adding the stock, a ladleful at a time, and stirring until each addition has been absorbed. This will take 18–20 minutes. Just before the rice is tender, stir in the Parmesan and cream, sprinkle with the rocket and season with salt and pepper to taste. Transfer to a warm serving dish and serve with extra Parmesan.

RISOTTO CON PEPERONI

Serves 4

about 1.5 litres/2¹/₂ pints Vegetable
Stock (see page 209)
4 tablespoons olive oil • 1 onion, finely chopped
3 tomatoes, peeled, seeded and diced
3 red peppers, halved, seeded and cut into strips
1 fresh rosemary sprig, finely chopped
350 g/12 oz risotto rice
4 tablespoons Parmesan cheese, freshly grated

PEPPER RISOTTO

Bring the stock to the boil. Meanwhile, heat the oil in another saucepan, add the onion and cook over a low heat, stirring occasionally, for 5 minutes. Add the tomatoes, peppers and rosemary and cook, stirring occasionally for a further 5 minutes. Stir in the rice and cook, stirring, until the grains are coated in oil. Add a ladleful of the hot stock and cook, stirring, until it has been absorbed. Continue adding the stock, a ladleful at a time, and stirring until each addition has been absorbed. This will take 18–20 minutes. When the rice is tender, stir in the Parmesan and serve.

RISOTTO CON PUNTE DI ASPARAGI

Serves 4

500 g/1 lb 2 oz asparagus, spears trimmed
about 1.5 litres/2¹/₂ pints Vegetable
Stock (see page 209)
65 g/2¹/₂ oz butter
3 tablespoons olive oil
¹/₂ onion, chopped
350 g/12 oz risotto rice
salt
Parmesan cheese, freshly grated, to serve

ASPARAGUS RISOTTO

Cook the asparagus in a pan of salted, boiling water for 10–12 minutes until tender, then drain and cut off and reserve the tips. Chop the stems and set aside. Bring the stock to the boil. Meanwhile, melt 15 g/¹/₂ oz of the butter in a frying pan, add the asparagus tips and cook over a low heat, stirring occasionally, for 5 minutes, then remove from the heat and set aside. Melt 25 g/1 oz of the remaining butter with the oil in a saucepan, add the onion and cook over a low heat, stirring occasionally, for 5 minutes. Stir in the rice and cook, stirring, until the grains are coated in fat, then add the chopped asparagus stems. Add a ladleful of the hot stock and cook, stirring, until it has been absorbed. Continue adding the stock, a ladleful at a time, and stirring until it has been absorbed. This will take 18–20 minutes. When the rice is tender, stir in the remaining butter and the asparagus tips. Serve with Parmesan.

RISOTTO WITH SAUSAGES

Bring the stock to the boil. Meanwhile, melt 25 g/1 oz of the butter in another saucepan, add the onion and crumbled sausages and cook over a low heat, stirring occasionally, for 5 minutes. Stir in the rice and cook, stirring, until the grains are coated in butter. Pour in the wine and cook until it has evaporated. Add a ladleful of the hot stock and cook, stirring, until it has been absorbed. Continue adding the stock, a ladleful at a time, and stirring until each addition has been absorbed. This will take 18–20 minutes. When the rice is tender, remove the pan from the heat, stir in the Parmesan and remaining butter, transfer to a warm serving dish and serve.

RISOTTO CON SALSICCIA

Serves 4

about 1.5 litres/2¹/₂ pints Meat Stock
(see page 208)
40 g/1¹/₂ oz butter
1 onion, chopped
250 g/9 oz Italian sausages, skinned and crumbled
350 g/12 oz risotto rice
175 ml/6 fl oz red wine
4 tablespoons Parmesan cheese, freshly grated

PUMPKIN AND ARTICHOKE RISOTTO

Melt half the butter in a saucepan, add the pumpkin and cook, stirring occasionally, for 5 minutes. Season with salt, stir in 5 tablespoons water and simmer for 20 minutes. Meanwhile, break off the artichoke stems and discard the outer coarse leaves and the chokes, then cut into thin wedges. Add to the pan and cook for a further 15 minutes. Meanwhile, bring the stock to the boil in another pan. Mash the pumpkin with a fork, then stir in the rice and season with salt and pepper. Add a ladleful of the hot stock and cook, stirring, until it has been absorbed. Continue adding the stock, a ladleful at a time, and stirring until each addition has been absorbed. This will take 18–20 minutes. When the rice is tender, stir in the remaining butter and serve with Parmesan.

RISOTTO CON ZUCCA E CARCIOFI

Serves 4

40 g/1¹/₂ oz butter
200 g/7 oz pumpkin flesh, chopped
3 globe artichokes
about 1.5 litres/2¹/₂ pints Vegetable
Stock (see page 209)
350 g/12 oz risotto rice
salt and pepper
Parmesan cheese, freshly grated, to serve

FOUR-CHEESE RISOTTO

Bring the stock to the boil. Meanwhile, melt 25 g/1 oz of the butter in another saucepan, add the onion and cook, stirring occasionally, for 5 minutes. Stir in the rice and cook, stirring, until the grains are coated in butter. Add a ladleful of the hot stock and cook, stirring, until it has been absorbed. Continue adding the stock, a ladleful at a time, and stirring until each addition has been absorbed. This will take 18–20 minutes. About 5 minutes before the rice is cooked, stir in the cheeses. When the rice is tender and the cheeses have melted, remove the pan from the heat, stir in the remaining butter and serve.

RISOTTO MANTECATO
AI QUATTRO FORMAGGI

Serves 4

about 1.5 litres/2¹/₂ pints Vegetable
Stock (see page 209)
40 g/1¹/₂ oz butter
1 onion, thinly sliced
350 g/12 oz risotto rice
50 g/2 oz fontina cheese, diced
50 g/2 oz Emmenthal cheese, diced
50 g/2 oz Gorgonzola cheese, diced
50 g/2 oz Parmesan cheese, freshly grated

BLACK RISOTTO WITH CUTTLEFISH

Cut the cuttlefish into strips. Bring the stock to the boil. Meanwhile, heat the oil in another saucepan, add the onion and garlic and cook over a low heat, stirring occasionally, for 5 minutes. Add the cuttlefish, season with salt and pepper to taste and cook for a few minutes. Pour in the wine and 150 ml/¼ pint water and simmer over a low heat for about 20 minutes. Stir in the rice and cook for a few minutes, then add the hot stock and the cuttlefish ink and cook for a further 20 minutes until the rice and cuttlefish are tender and the liquid has been absorbed. Stir in the butter and serve.

RISOTTO NERO CON LE SEPPIE

Serves 4

1kg/2¼ lb cuttlefish, cleaned and ink sacs reserved

1 litre/1¾ pints Fish Stock (see page 208)

3 tablespoons olive oil

1 small onion, chopped • ½ garlic clove, chopped

175 ml/6 fl oz dry white wine

350 g/12 oz risotto rice

25 g/1 oz butter

salt and pepper

CREAM AND LEEK RISOTTO

Melt the butter in a saucepan, add the leeks and cook, stirring occasionally, for 5 minutes. Add 1 tablespoon water and simmer for 20 minutes, adding more water if necessary. Meanwhile bring the stock to the boil in another pan. Stir the rice into the leeks. Add a ladleful of the hot stock and cook, stirring, until it has been absorbed. Continue adding the stock, a ladleful at a time, and stirring until each addition has been absorbed. This will take 18–20 minutes. When the rice is tender, stir in the cream and season with salt and pepper to taste. Serve with Parmesan.

RISOTTO PANNA E PORRI

Serves 4

25 g/1 oz butter

4 small leeks, white parts only, thinly sliced

about 1.5 litres/2½ pints Vegetable

Stock (see page 209)

350 g/12 oz risotto rice

175 ml/6 fl oz single cream

salt and pepper

Parmesan cheese, freshly grated, to serve

GREEN RISOTTO

Melt 25 g/1 oz of the butter with the oil in a saucepan, add the spinach, carrot, onion, celery and celery leaves and cook over a medium heat for 5 minutes, then lower the heat and cook for a further 10 minutes. Meanwhile, bring the stock to the boil in another pan. Season the vegetables with salt to taste and stir in the rice. Add a ladleful of the hot stock and cook, stirring, until it has been absorbed. Continue adding the stock, a ladleful at a time, and stirring until each addition has been absorbed. This will take 18–20 minutes. When the rice is tender, stir in the remaining butter and serve with Parmesan.

RISOTTO VERDE

Serves 4

40 g/1½ oz butter • 3 tablespoons olive oil

150 g/5 oz spinach, chopped • 1 carrot, chopped

1 onion, chopped

1 celery stick including leaves, chopped

about 1.5 litres/2½ pints Vegetable

Stock (see page 209)

350 g/12 oz risotto rice • salt

Parmesan cheese, freshly grated, to serve

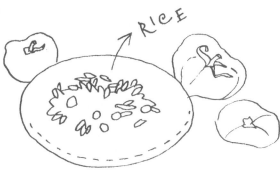

TIMBALES

According to the dictionary a timbale is a puff pastry case filled with cooked ingredients, such as chicken giblets, mushrooms or pasta. Other definitions state that timbale is the name of a cone-shaped mould whose height is equal to its diameter (about 20 cm/8 inches), made of tin-plated iron or stainless steel and at one time called a dariola in Italian. A timbale is usually a cylindrical baked pie. It may be filled with rice or pasta, together with meat, chicken giblets, meatballs, mushrooms or truffles. The timbale is, in any case, a demanding dish – as dishes with fillings often are – which immediately gives the impression of being a rich one. Timbales are, in fact, very rich since they were born from the imagination of chefs who were expected to excel on special occasions, such as princely weddings and royal dinners, and summit meetings as we would say today, and who invented the timbale in order to surprise, intrigue and tempt. On those occasions their golden brown casing made of various types of pastry (puff, shortcrust, pâte brisée, etc.) concealed sophisticated sauces, aromatic spices, delicate meats, rare mushrooms and precious truffles. Even today, timbales mark the most important moment of a formal luncheon.

A FEW RULES

FILLING
Do not overdo the quantity.

BECHAMEL SAUCE
It should be runny and well cooked, otherwise it sticks the pastry together and makes it soggy.

RAGÙ (MEAT SAUCE)
It should be neither too thick nor too thin.

SPICES
Give priority to only one, such as nutmeg or saffron, and do not overdo it.

CHEESE
Cheese should always be freshly grated.

PORTIONS
Timbales should be cut using a special slicer with one sharpened edge or, if you do not have one, with a knife with a broad blade. To serve the slices lay them on a plate using the same utensil.

PHEASANT PIE

PASTICCIO DI FAGIANO

Serves 6

50 g/2 oz butter, plus extra for greasing

200 g/7 oz chicken livers, thawed if frozen and trimmed

2 garlic cloves

2 bay leaves

$^1/_2$ pheasant, skinned, boned and chopped

150 g/5 oz lean pork, finely chopped

3 tablespoons Marsala

2 tablespoons brandy

100 ml/3$^1/_2$ fl oz double cream

350 g/12 oz puff pastry dough, thawed if frozen

plain flour, for dusting

1 egg yolk, lightly beaten

salt and pepper

Preheat the oven to 180°C/350°F/Gas Mark 4. Grease six individual moulds with butter. Melt half the butter in a frying pan, add the chicken livers, garlic and bay leaves and cook, stirring frequently, for 5 minutes. Add the pheasant meat and pork, season with salt and pepper and cook over a medium heat, stirring occasionally, for 15 minutes. Pour in the Marsala and brandy and cook until they have evaporated. Remove and discard the garlic and bay leaves and transfer the mixture to a food processor. Melt the remaining butter. Process the mixture and, with the motor running, gradually add the melted butter and the cream. Roll out the pastry on a lightly floured surface into a thin sheet and use to line the prepared moulds. Fill with the meat mixture, cover with rounds of pastry and crimp the edges to seal. Make a hole in the centre of each pie and prick lines of little holes radiating out from the centre with a fork. Brush the surface with the egg yolk and bake for about 15 minutes. Remove from the oven and leave to stand for 5 minutes before turning out and serving.

PUMPKIN PIE

PASTICCIO DI PASTA DI ZUCCA

Serves 4

50 g/2 oz dried mushrooms

25 g/1 oz butter, plus extra for greasing

$^1/_2$ shallot, chopped

$^1/_2$ carrot, chopped

250 ml/8 fl oz Béchamel Sauce (see page 50)

200 g/7 oz cooked pumpkin

300 g/11 oz plain flour, plus extra for dusting

1 egg, lightly beaten

salt and pepper

Put the mushrooms in a bowl, add hot water to cover and leave to soak for 20 minutes, then drain, squeeze out and chop. Melt the butter in a frying pan, add the shallot and carrot and cook over a low heat until softened, then add the mushrooms. Cover and cook for 15 minutes until tender, then stir into the béchamel sauce. Preheat the oven to 200°C/400°F/Gas Mark 6. Grease an ovenproof dish with butter. Meanwhile, process the pumpkin with a pinch of salt in a food processor. Transfer to a bowl and combine with the flour, then stir in the egg to bind into a dough. Knead quickly and roll out on a lightly floured surface into a fairly thin sheet. Cut out 10–12 rectangles. Bring a pan of salted water to the boil, add the pumpkin rectangles and cook for a few minutes, then drain. Arrange the rectangles in alternate layers with the mushroom sauce and bake for a few minutes.

PENNE AND MUSHROOM PIE

Preheat the oven to 180°C/350°F/Gas Mark 4. Grease an ovenproof timbale mould with butter. Melt 25 g/1 oz of the butter with the oil in a pan. Add the garlic and cook over a low heat for 2–3 minutes until golden brown, then remove and discard. Add the porcini to the pan and sprinkle with a ladleful of stock. Cover and cook over a medium heat for about 10 minutes until soft, sprinkling with a little more stock if necessary. Beat the egg in a bowl with 1 teaspoon of the stock. Season the mushrooms with salt and pepper to taste, stir in the cream and cook for a few minutes more. Remove the pan from the heat and stir in the parsley and egg yolk mixture, making sure that the porcini are evenly coated with the sauce. Cook the pennette in a large pan of salted, boiling water until al dente, then drain. Arrange half the pennette in a layer on the base of the prepared mould, sprinkle with half the Parmesan and dot with half the remaining butter. Place half the porcini on top, spoon on the remaining pasta, sprinkle with the remaining Parmesan and dot with the remaining butter. Top with the remaining porcini. Roll out the pasta frolla on a lightly floured surface to make a round 5 mm/¼ inch thick. Cover the mushrooms with the pasta frolla, trimming to fit. Bake for 15 minutes or until light golden brown.

PASTICCIO DI PENNE AI FUNGHI

Serves 6

50 g/2 oz butter, plus extra for greasing

1 tablespoon olive oil

1 garlic clove

800 g/1¾ lb porcini, thinly sliced

175–200 ml/6–7 fl oz Vegetable Stock (see page 209)

1 egg

5 tablespoons double cream

1 tablespoon chopped fresh flat-leaf parsley

300 g/11 oz pennette lisce

4 tablespoons Parmesan cheese, freshly grated

1 quantity Shortcrust Pastry, made with half quantity sugar (see page 1008)

plain flour, for dusting

salt and pepper

TAGLIATELLE PIE

Preheat the oven to 180°C/350°F/Gas Mark 4. Grease an ovenproof dish with butter. Roll out the dough on a lightly floured surface to a sheet 3 mm/⅛ inch thick and use to line the prepared dish. Cook the spinach, in just the water clinging to its leaves after washing, for 5 minutes then drain, squeezing out as much liquid as possible, and chop. Melt the butter in a frying pan, add the spinach and cook over a low heat for 5 minutes. Add the milk and season with salt. Stir in the cream and season with pepper. Cook the tagliatelle in a large pan of salted, boiling water until al dente, drain, tip into a bowl and mix with the spinach and ham. Spoon the mixture into the dough-lined dish. Beat the eggs with the Parmesan and a small pinch of salt in a bowl, then pour on to the hot tagliatelle. Bake for 30–40 minutes or until the surface is well browned.

PASTICCIO DI TAGLIATELLE

Serves 6

80 g/3 oz butter, plus extra for greasing

300 g/11 oz Pizza Dough (see page 193)

plain flour, for dusting

200 g/7 oz spinach

5 tablespoons milk

3 tablespoons double cream

350 g/12 oz tagliatelle

150 g/5 oz cooked ham, diced

3 eggs

50 g/2 oz Parmesan cheese, freshly grated

salt and pepper

SARTÙ

Serves 6

100 g/3¹/₂ oz butter, plus extra for greasing

80 g/3 oz breadcrumbs

20 g/³/₄ oz dried mushrooms

1 thick bread slice, crusts removed

175 ml/6 fl oz milk

100 g/3¹/₂ oz minced beef

plain flour, for coating

3 tablespoons olive oil

100 g/3¹/₂ oz chicken livers, thawed if frozen, trimmed and chopped

50 g/2 oz Italian sausage, peeled and crumbled

65 g/2¹/₂ oz mozzarella cheese, diced

750 ml/1¹/₄ pints Meat Stock (see page 208)

¹/₂ onion, chopped

50 ml/2 fl oz passata

300 g/11 oz risotto rice

2 eggs, lightly beaten

salt and pepper

SARTÙ

Preheat the oven to 180°C/350°F/Gas Mark 4. Grease an ovenproof dish with butter and sprinkle with the breadcrumbs, turning to coat. Tip out any excess. Put the mushrooms in a bowl, add hot water to cover and leave to soak for 20 minutes, then drain, squeeze and chop coarsely. Tear the bread into pieces, place in a bowl, add the milk and a pinch of salt and leave to soak for 10 minutes, then squeeze out. Combine the minced beef and soaked bread, then roll the mixture into hazelnut-size balls and coat with flour. Heat 25 g/1 oz of the butter with the oil in a frying pan, add the meatballs and cook until golden brown all over. Remove with a slotted spoon, drain on kitchen paper and set aside. Heat 25 g/1 oz of the remaining butter in another pan, add the mushrooms and a pinch of salt, cover and cook over a low heat for 20 minutes. Melt 25 g/1 oz of the remaining butter in another frying pan. Add the chicken livers and cook over a medium heat, stirring frequently, for about 5 minutes until lightly browned. Remove from the heat and season with salt. Heat the sausage and mozzarella in a small saucepan until the cheese has melted. Bring the stock to the boil. Meanwhile, melt the remaining butter in another pan, add the onion and cook over a low heat, stirring occasionally, for 5 minutes, then add the passata and stir in the rice. Add a ladleful of the hot stock and cook, stirring, until it has been absorbed. Continue adding the stock, a ladleful at a time, and stirring until each addition has been absorbed. This will take 18–20 minutes. Cover the base and sides of the prepared dish with a layer of risotto. Mix together all the filling ingredients and spoon them into the dish, pour the eggs over the filling and cover with the remaining risotto. Bake for about 45 minutes. Remove from the oven, leave to stand for 10 minutes, then turn out on to a serving dish and serve.

TIMBALLO DI FUSILLI

Serves 6

50 g/2 oz butter, plus extra for greasing

4 leeks, white parts only, thinly sliced

175 ml/6 fl oz dry white wine

5 tablespoons milk

350 g/12 oz fusilli

80 g/3 oz Parmesan cheese, freshly grated

2 eggs

6 fresh sage leaves

salt and pepper

FUSILLI TIMBALE

Preheat the oven to 180°C/350°F/Gas Mark 4. Grease an ovenproof dish with butter. Melt half the butter in a saucepan, add the leeks, pour in water to a depth of 1.5 cm/²/₃ inch and cook over a low heat for 10 minutes until softened. Add the wine, increase the heat to medium and cook until it has evaporated. Pour in the milk and cook until it has evaporated, then season with salt and pepper to taste. Cook the fusilli in a large pan of salted, boiling water until al dente, then drain. Cover the base of the prepared dish with a thick layer of fusilli, spoon a little of the leek mixture on top, sprinkle with some of the Parmesan and dot with some of the remaining butter. Repeat these layers until all the ingredients are used, ending with a layer of fusilli. Beat the eggs with a pinch of salt and a pinch of pepper, pour them over the fusilli and dot with butter. Garnish with the sage and bake for 40 minutes. Remove the timbale from the oven and leave to stand for 10 minutes before serving.

TIMBALLO DI MACCHERONI
ALLA NAPOLETANA

Serves 6

25 g/1 oz dried mushrooms

50 g/2 oz butter, plus extra for greasing

1 garlic clove, chopped

¹/₂ onion, chopped

250 g/9 oz chicken giblets, trimmed and chopped

100 g/3¹/₂ oz Italian sausages, peeled and crumbled

400 g/14 oz ripe tomatoes, peeled, seeded and diced

85 g/3 oz breadcrumbs

350 g/12 oz macaroni

150 g/5 oz mozzarella cheese, diced

50 g/2 oz Parmesan cheese, freshly grated

salt

MACARONI NAPOLETANA TIMBALE

Preheat the oven to 180°C/350°F/Gas Mark 4. Put the mushrooms in a bowl, add hot water to cover and leave to soak for 20 minutes, then drain and squeeze out. Melt the butter in a saucepan, add the garlic and onion and cook over a low heat, stirring occasionally, for 10 minutes until lightly browned. Add the chicken giblets, sausages and mushrooms, season with salt, stir well and cook for a few minutes. Add the tomatoes, cover and cook over a medium heat for 30 minutes. Meanwhile, grease a high-sided cake tin with butter, sprinkle with the breadcrumbs and turn to coat. Tip out and reserve the excess. Cook the macaroni in a large pan of salted, boiling water until al dente, then drain and tip into a bowl. Add the meat sauce and leave to cool. When cold, stir in the mozzarella and Parmesan and spoon into the prepared tin. Smooth the surface and sprinkle with the reserved breadcrumbs. Bake for about 40 minutes until golden brown. Remove from the oven and leave to stand for 5 minutes, then turn out on to a serving dish and serve.

RICE TIMBALE

Preheat the oven to 180°C/350°F/Gas Mark 4. Cook the rice in a large pan of lightly salted, boiling water for 15–18 minutes until tender, then drain and stir in 25 g/1 oz of the butter, the egg yolks and 4 tablespoons of the Parmesan. Spread out on a large plate or baking sheet and leave to cool. Meanwhile, put the mushrooms in a bowl, add hot water to cover and leave to soak for 20 minutes, then drain, squeeze out and chop. Melt 25 g/1 oz of the remaining butter with the oil, add the garlic and cook for 2–3 minutes, then remove and discard. Add the mushrooms to the pan and cook for 5 minutes. Melt 40 g/1½ oz of the remaining butter in another pan, add the chicken giblets and livers, sweetbreads and sausage. Season with a pinch of salt and a pinch of pepper, stir well and cook for about 5 minutes. Grease an ovenproof dish with plenty of butter and sprinkle with the breadcrumbs, turning to coat. Tip out and reserve the excess. Spoon half the rice mixture on to the base of the dish, cover with the mushrooms and top with the liver and sweetbread mixture. Cover with the remaining rice, dot with the remaining butter and sprinkle with the remaining Parmesan and reserved breadcrumbs. Bake for about 15 minutes.

TIMBALLO DI RISO

Serves 6

350 g/12 oz long-grain rice

120 g/4 oz butter, plus extra for greasing

2 egg yolks, lightly beaten

6 tablespoons Parmesan cheese, freshly grated

25 g/1 oz dried mushrooms

2 tablespoons olive oil

1 garlic clove

250 g/9 oz chicken giblets and livers,

thawed if frozen, trimmed and chopped

200 g/7 oz sweetbreads, chopped

65 g/2 ½ oz Italian sausage, peeled and crumbled

80 g/3 oz breadcrumbs

salt and pepper

CHEESE PIE

Preheat the oven to 180°C/350°F/Gas Mark 4. Lightly grease an ovenproof dish with butter. Roll out the dough on a lightly floured surface to a sheet 3 mm/⅛ inch thick and use to line the prepared dish. Crumble the ricotta into a bowl and add the robiola, Gorgonzola and a pinch of pepper. Cook the tagliatelle in a large pan of salted, boiling water until al dente, then drain and tip on to the cheeses. Toss the pasta with two forks until it is completely covered with cheese and tip into the dough-lined dish. Beat the eggs with the Parmesan, a pinch of salt and a pinch of pepper in a bowl and pour the mixture over the tagliatelle. Bake for 15–20 minutes.

TORTA AI FORMAGGI

Serves 6

butter, for greasing

200 g/7 oz Pizza Dough (see page 193)

plain flour, for dusting

150 g/5 oz ricotta cheese

150 g/5 oz robiola cheese, diced

100 g/3½ oz mild Gorgonzola cheese, diced

250 g/9 oz tagliatelle

2 eggs

4 tablespoons Parmesan cheese, freshly grated

salt and pepper

VINCISGRASSI

VINCISGRASSI

Serves 6–8

butter, for greasing

For the Pasta dough

350 g/12 oz plain flour, preferably Italian type 00, plus extra for dusting

200 g/7 oz semolina

3 tablespoons Vin Santo or Marsala

3 eggs, lightly beaten

salt

For the filling

25 g/1 oz dried mushrooms

100 g/3¹/₂ oz sweetbread

50 g/2 oz butter

2 tablespoons olive oil

¹/₂ onion, chopped

1 black truffle, diced

2 tablespoons Chicken Stock (see page 209)

1 skinless, boneless chicken breast, cut into strips

200 g/7 oz chicken giblets, trimmed and chopped

5 tablespoons dry Marsala

80 g/3 oz Parmesan cheese, freshly grated

1 quantity Béchamel Sauce (see page 50)

salt and pepper

Preheat the oven to 180°C/350°F/Gas Mark 4. Grease an oven-proof dish with butter. For the filling, put the mushrooms in a bowl, add hot water to cover and set aside to soak for 20 minutes, then drain, squeeze dry and chop. Blanch the sweetbread in boiling water for a few minutes, drain and leave to cool, then dice. Melt half the butter in a frying pan, add the sweetbread and cook, stirring occasionally, for a few minutes. Heat the remaining butter with the oil in a saucepan, add the onion and cook over a low heat, stirring occasionally, for 5 minutes, then stir in the mushrooms, truffle and stock. Add the chicken strips and cook over a high heat until browned, then add the giblets and cook for a few minutes more. Pour in the Marsala, lower the heat and cook until half the wine has evaporated. Pour in just enough hot water to cover, season with salt and pepper, cover and cook over a low heat for about 30 minutes. Add the sweetbread. Make the pasta dough (see Fresh Pasta Dough, page 268) using the ingredients specified, then roll out into a sheet and cut into strips about 10 cm/4 inches wide and 50 cm/20 inches long. Bring a large pan of salted water to the boil, add the pasta strips and boil for a few minutes until half-cooked, then remove and refresh in a bowl of cold water. Drain the pasta and spread out on a damp tea towel. Arrange pasta strips in the base of the prepared dish so that they cross to cover the base, allowing the excess to overhang the sides. Cut the remaining strips into rectangles. Fill the dish with alternate layers of filling and pasta, sprinkled with Parmesan and tablespoonfuls of béchamel sauce, ending with a layer of béchamel sauce. Fold over the overhanging ends of the pasta strips to make a pie. Place the dish in a roasting tin, add hot water to come about halfway up the sides and bake for 30 minutes.

RAVIOLINI VOL-AU-VENT

VOL–AU–VENT CON RAVIOLINI

Serves 6

50 g/2 oz butter

100 g/3¹/₂ oz shelled peas

500 g/1 lb 2 oz small ravioli

40 g/1¹/₂ oz Parmesan cheese, freshly grated

1 large, ready-made vol-au-vent case, about 15–20 cm/6–8 inches

1 quantity Béchamel Sauce (see page 50)

salt

Preheat the oven to 150°C/300°F/Gas Mark 2. Line a baking sheet with baking parchment. Melt 25 g/1 oz of the butter in a saucepan, add the peas and 2 tablespoons warm water and cook for about 10 minutes until tender. Season with salt, drain and set aside. Cook the ravioli in a large pan of salted, boiling water until al dente, then drain, tip into a bowl and gently toss with the remaining butter, 25 g/1 oz of the Parmesan and the peas. Fill the vol-au-vent case with the ravioli and spoon in the béchamel sauce. Sprinkle with the remaining Parmesan, place on the baking sheet and heat through in the oven.

SEAFOOD VOL-AU-VENT

Pour 2 litres/3¹/₂ pints water into a large saucepan, add the wine, bay leaf, garlic, clove, parsley, celery, onion and carrot and bring to the boil. Lower the heat and simmer for 15 minutes, then season with salt and pepper and add the hake or cod. Cover and simmer for 20 minutes, then remove from the heat and leave to cool in the stock. Preheat the oven to 150°C/300°F/Gas Mark 2. Tear the bread into pieces, place in a bowl, add the milk and leave to soak for 10 minutes, then squeeze out. Melt the butter in a frying pan, add the prawns and cook for 2 minutes. Sprinkle in the sherry and cook until it has evaporated. Season with salt and pepper, remove the pan from the heat and keep warm. Place the vol-au-vent case on a baking sheet in the oven to warm through. Drain the fish, reserving the stock, flake coarsely and pass through a food mill into a bowl. Add the soaked bread and the egg, season with salt and pepper and mix well. Shape the mixture into balls and dust lightly with flour, shaking off any excess. Strain the fish stock into a clean pan and bring to the boil. Add the fish balls and remove with a slotted spoon as they float to the surface. Drain, dry on kitchen paper and arrange in the vol-au-vent case. Top with the prawns and spoon in the béchamel sauce. Serve immediately.

VOL-AU-VENT DI MARE
Serves 6
350 ml/12 fl oz dry white wine
1 bay leaf
1 garlic clove
1 clove
1 fresh flat-leaf parsley sprig
1 celery stick
1 onion, sliced
1 carrot, sliced
675 g/1¹/₂ lb hake or cod fillet
50 g/2 oz bread, crusts removed
175 ml/6 fl oz milk
25 g/1 oz butter
300 g/11 oz small raw prawns, peeled
3 tablespoons sherry
1 large vol-au-vent case,
about 15–20 cm/6–8 inches
200 ml/7 fl oz Béchamel Sauce (see page 50)
1 egg, lightly beaten
plain flour, for dusting
salt and pepper

EGG

EGG CUP

TURNER

SALT

PEPPER

ALUMINUM FRY PAN

① ②

N-11

350

EGGS →

FRITTATA →

EGGS

Hardly a day goes by in any kitchen without at least one egg being needed – on its own for breakfast or as a snack, as the basis of a sauce such as a wonderful mayonnaise, to thicken a cream, as 'glue' for all fried dishes that need coating in breadcrumbs, or to complete and enrich a salad. Eggs are required for desserts, flans, home-made pasta and even cocktails. They are also the main constituent of a famous tonic. Their nutritional value (156 calories per 50 g/2 oz egg) is more or less equivalent to 200 ml/7 fl oz milk or 100 g/3½ oz meat. However, their proteins are higher quality and more easily assimilated by the human digestive system than those of any other food. Altogether, this small, white or brown, 6-cm/2½-inch tall object, weighing 50–65 g/2–2½ oz, is also a concentrated source of vitamins and minerals. Yet the Italians are among the peoples in the world who consume them the least: only 200 eggs per year per person, compared to 280 for the French, 300 for the Spanish and 400 for the Israelis. On the other hand, Italy exports eggs in large numbers: the most recent figures quote about 70 million eggs in shells and more than 3,000 tonnes of egg-containing products (pasta, desserts, etc.), plus 8,000 tonnes of egg whites for use in the pharmaceutical industry. Soft-boiled or poached eggs, i.e. ones that are briefly cooked, are digested in an hour and a half; whereas fried and hard-boiled eggs take three hours.

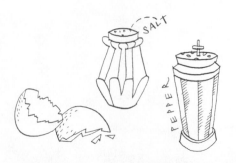

USEFUL TIPS

→ When buying eggs, always check the 'use by' date on the box.

→ The box should also show the size of the eggs, such as medium or large. Differences in size do not affect quality, but do justify the differences in price.

→ Eggs should always be stored in the refrigerator to retain their flavour and keep them fit for consumption. They are best stored in their box with their pointed ends downwards. It is not advisable to store eggs near strong-smelling food as their shells are porous and tend to absorb odours easily.

→ Once shelled, whites will keep in the refrigerator for 2–3 days and yolks for 1–2 days.

→ Remove eggs from the refrigerator 30 minutes before use. This helps to prevent mayonnaise from curdling, egg whites will whisk to a greater volume, and shells are less likely to crack during boiling.

→ Break eggs on to a plate to check their freshness: the yolk should be a bright colour and firm, while the white should be thick, viscous and adhere to the yolk. There is no significance in the precise colour of the yolk, which may range from pale yellow to almost orange – the shade depends on what the hen has eaten. On the other hand the colour of the shell, usually white or brown and sometimes speckled, depends on the breed of bird.

FRITTATA

In Italian cuisine, the frittata family is quite varied and includes omelettes and crêpes. The classic frittata does not include any ingredient other than eggs, salt and, if liked, pepper, along with the oil needed to cook it. Ingredients for other frittata include vegetables or pulses or any other ingredient which may be 'held together' by one or more eggs and fried in a frying pan. It is advisable to use an ordinary non-stick frying pan, which ensures perfect results. Separate sections are devoted to omelettes and crêpes. Both – besides being delicious dishes – may also be served as desserts.

POACHED

Bring a pan of salted water to the boil with 2 tablespoons white wine vinegar – don't use red wine vinegar as it discolours the egg white. Break the eggs into a small bowl, one at a time, and make sure that they are fresh. Plunge each egg into the boiling water and poach for 3–4 minutes. Remove with a slotted spoon and trim the white neatly. If you are poaching several eggs in the same saucepan, make sure that they do not touch.

UOVA AFFOGATE AI CARCIOFI

Serves 4

4 artichoke hearts

1 tablespoon olive oil

200 g/7 oz smoked pancetta, chopped

2 tablespoons white wine vinegar

4 eggs

salt and pepper

For the sauce

40 g/1¹/₂ oz butter

1 teaspoon Dijon mustard

1 teaspoon plain flour

2 tablespoons white wine vinegar

salt and pepper

POACHED EGGS WITH ARTICHOKE HEARTS

To make the sauce, melt the butter in a saucepan, stir in the mustard and flour and cook for a few seconds. Gradually stir in 250ml/ 8 fl oz water, alternating with the vinegar, and season with salt and pepper to taste. Cook, stirring constantly, for 5 minutes. Blanch the artichoke hearts in boiling water for a few minutes, then drain and slice into eight rounds. Arrange in a ring on a warm serving dish. Heat the oil in a frying pan, add the pancetta and cook, stirring occasionally, for 5 minutes until tender. Drain and sprinkle in the middle of the dish. Bring a pan of salted water to the boil, add the vinegar and poach the eggs for 3–4 minutes. Remove with a slotted spoon, place on top of the pancetta and spoon the sauce over them.

POACHED EGGS WITH CHEESE

UOVA AFFOGATE AL FORMAGGIO

Serves 4

4 bread slices, crusts removed
40 g/1½ oz butter, softened
2 tablespoons white wine vinegar
4 eggs
50 g/2 oz Emmenthal cheese, freshly grated
salt

Preheat the oven to 180°C/350°F/Gas Mark 4. Spread the bread with the butter and place on an ovenproof dish. Bring a pan of salted water to the boil, add the vinegar and poach the eggs for 3 minutes. Remove with a slotted spoon, place on the bread, sprinkle with the Emmenthal and bake until the cheese has melted.

POACHED EGGS WITH ASPARAGUS CROQUETTES

UOVA AFFOGATE CON CROCCHETTE DI ASPARAGI

Serves 4

300 g/11 oz asparagus tips
1 quantity thick Béchamel Sauce made with only 200 ml/14 fl oz milk (see page 50)
4 tablespoons Parmesan cheese, freshly grated
6 eggs
plain flour, for dusting
80 g/3 oz breadcrumbs
50 g/2 oz butter
2 tablespoons white wine vinegar
salt

Cook the asparagus tips in salted, boiling water for about 10 minutes, then drain and pass through a food mill. Stir them into the béchamel sauce with the Parmesan and leave to cool slightly. Separate one egg and stir the yolk into the béchamel, then leave to stand in a cool place for about 1 hour. Divide the béchamel mixture into four and shape into four croquettes with a hollow in the centre of each. Dust lightly with flour. Beat one of the remaining eggs in a shallow dish and spread out the breadcrumbs in another shallow dish. Dip each croquette into the beaten egg and then into the breadcrumbs. Melt 40 g/1½ oz of the butter in a frying pan, add the croquettes and cook over a medium heat until golden brown all over. Meanwhile, bring a pan of salted water to the boil, add the vinegar and poach the remaining eggs for 3–4 minutes. Remove with a slotted spoon and place a poached egg in the middle of each croquette. Dot with the remaining butter, transfer to a warm serving dish and serve.

POACHED EGGS
WITH MIXED VEGETABLES

Heat the oil in a frying pan, add the onion and aubergines and cook over a low heat, stirring occasionally, for 5 minutes. Add the tomatoes and courgettes and cook over a low heat for about 30 minutes. Meanwhile, bring a pan of salted water to the boil, add the vinegar and poach the eggs for 3–4 minutes. Remove with a slotted spoon, pat dry with a tea towel and arrange on a warm serving dish. Surround with the hot vegetables and serve.

UOVA AFFOGATE CON VERDURE MISTE

Serves 4

3 tablespoons olive oil

1 onion, chopped

3 aubergines, diced

3 tomatoes, peeled, seeded and diced

3 courgettes, sliced

2 tablespoons white wine vinegar

4 eggs

salt

POACHED EGGS IN GELATINE

Dissolve the gelatine in 500ml/18 fl oz water according to the packet instructions and leave to cool, but do not chill. Bring a pan of salted water to the boil, add the vinegar and poach the eggs for 3–4 minutes. Remove with a slotted spoon and leave to cool. Put each egg in the middle of a slice of ham and roll up. Arrange them on a slightly concave serving dish and garnish with the anchovy fillets, capers and cornichons or gherkins. Spoon the gelatine over the eggs so that it covers the surface and chill in the refrigerator for 3 hours until set.

UOVA AFFOGATE IN GELATINA

Serves 4

500 ml/18 fl oz prepared gelatine

2 tablespoons white wine vinegar

4 eggs

4 cooked ham slices

4 canned anchovy fillets in oil, drained

1 tablespoon capers, drained and rinsed

4 cornichons or gherkins, thinly sliced

salt

SOFT BOILED

Soft-boiled eggs may be cooked in three different ways:
→ *Immerse the eggs in a pan of boiling water. Lower the heat to a simmer and cook for 3–4 minutes.* → *Immerse the eggs in a pan of boiling water and boil for 1 minute. Remove the pan from the heat and leave the eggs to stand in the hot water for 3–4 minutes.* → *Immerse the eggs in a pan of cold water and bring to the boil over a medium heat. Turn off the heat as soon as the water comes to the boil. The cooking time varies according to taste, as some people prefer the white quite firm and others like it more runny. In either case, it is important for the egg yolk to be runny.*

EGGS WITH ASPARAGUS

UOVA ALLA COQUE CON ASPARAGI

Serves 4

800 g/1³/₄ lb asparagus, spears trimmed

4 eggs

salt

lightly salted butter, melted, to serve

Cook the asparagus in salted, boiling water for 20 minutes, then drain. Soft-boil the eggs, place in egg cups and serve with the hot asparagus and individual bowls of melted butter. To eat, dip the asparagus tip into the butter and then into the soft-boiled egg.

EGGS WITH KETCHUP

UOVA ALLA COQUE CON KETCHUP

Serves 4

4 eggs

4 teaspoons tomato ketchup

sesame-seed bread sticks

salt

Soft-boil the eggs according to taste. Place them in egg cups, cut off the tops and season with a teaspoonful of ketchup and a pinch of salt. Mix, using a teaspoon or the bread sticks. The sesame seed flavour of the bread sticks goes well with egg yolk.

SHIRRED

Break the eggs on to a plate to make sure they are fresh. Melt a knob of butter in an ovenproof dish or stainless steel pan over a medium heat and slide in the eggs, one at a time. Season with salt and pepper to taste. Bake in a medium oven (160°C/325°F/Gas Mark 3) for 5–6 minutes without stirring. In this way, the whites set perfectly and the yolks remain soft and runny. Shirred eggs can also be cooked on the hob, but are more successful using the method described above.

EGGS WITH MUSHROOMS

Preheat the oven to 160°C/325°F/Gas Mark 3. Remove the mushroom stems (they may be retained and used for a sauce) and thinly slice the caps. Melt 50 g/2 oz of the butter in a frying pan, add the mushrooms and cook, stirring occasionally, for about 10 minutes until lightly browned, then season with salt and pepper to taste. Grease four individual ovenproof dishes with the remaining butter, divide the mushrooms among them and break an egg on top of each. Season the egg whites with a little salt and bake for about 10 minutes until the egg whites have set. Serve immediately in the same dishes.

UOVA AL PIATTO AI FUNGHI
Serves 4
250 g/9 oz button mushrooms
80 g/3 oz butter
4 eggs
salt and pepper

EGGS WITH PARSLEY

Mix together the parsley and 50 g/2 oz of the butter and season lightly with salt. Melt the remaining butter in a frying pan without letting it brown, break in the eggs and season lightly with salt. Cook for a few minutes until the whites have set but the yolks are still soft. Dot with the parsley butter, remove the pan from the heat and serve immediately on the bread.

UOVA AL PIATTO AL PREZZEMOLO
Serves 4
2 fresh flat-leaf parsley sprigs, chopped
100 g/3¹/₂ oz butter
8 eggs
8 thick bread slices
salt

EGGS WITH TRUFFLE

UOVA AL PIATTO AL TARTUFO

Serves 4

50 g/2 oz butter

8 eggs

50 g/2 oz black truffle

salt and pepper

Melt the butter in a frying pan. When frothy, but not brown, break in the eggs and mix together. Season with salt and pepper and cook over a medium heat for 5–6 minutes. Transfer to a warm serving dish, shave the black truffle over the top and serve immediately.

EGGS WITH ASPARAGUS

UOVA AL PIATTO CON ASPARAGI

Serves 4

800 g/1³/₄ lb asparagus, spears trimmed

4 tablespoons Parmesan cheese, freshly grated

80 g/3 oz butter

4 eggs

salt

Tie the asparagus together in a bunch. Fill a tall, narrow saucepan or asparagus pan with water, bring to the boil and add the bunch of asparagus so that the tips are above the waterline. Steam for about 20 minutes until tender, then drain and arrange on a warm serving dish, half on one side and half on the other with their tips touching. Sprinkle with the Parmesan, then melt 40 g/1¹/₂ oz of the butter and spoon it over the asparagus. Melt the remaining butter in a pan, break in the eggs, one at a time, season with salt and cook until the whites have set. Lift out with a fish slice and place on the asparagus on top of the tips.

EGGS WITH FENNEL AND MOZZARELLA

UOVA AL PIATTO CON FINOCCHI E MOZZARELLA

Serves 4

800 g/1³/₄ lb fennel bulbs

50 g/2 oz butter, plus extra for greasing

200 g/7 oz mozzarella cheese, thinly sliced

4 eggs

4 tablespoons Parmesan cheese, freshly grated

salt and pepper

Cook the fennel in salted, boiling water for about 15 minutes until tender, then drain and chop. Meanwhile, preheat the oven to 160°C/325°F/Gas Mark 3. Grease an ovenproof dish with butter. Melt the butter in a frying pan, add the fennel, season with salt and pepper and cook over a medium heat until light golden brown. Spoon the fennel into the prepared dish, cover with slices of mozzarella and break the eggs on top. Sprinkle with the Parmesan and bake until the cheeses have melted.

EGGS WITH AUBERGINES

Preheat the oven to 160°C/325°F/Gas Mark 3. Grease an ovenproof dish with butter. Dust the aubergines with flour. Heat the oil with the butter in a frying pan, add the aubergines and cook over a medium heat until golden brown. Drain on kitchen paper and season with salt and pepper. Arrange the aubergines in the prepared dish, dot with the tomato purée and break the eggs on top. Bake until the egg whites have set.

UOVA AL PIATTO CON MELANZANE

Serves 4

25 g/1 oz butter, plus extra for greasing

2 aubergines, sliced

plain flour, for dusting

100 ml/3½ fl oz olive oil

3 tablespoons tomato purée

4 eggs

salt and pepper

EGGS WITH POLENTA

Preheat the oven to 160°C/325°F/Gas Mark 3. Grease an ovenproof dish with butter. Melt 40 g/1½ oz of the butter in a frying pan, add the polenta slices and cook over a medium heat until golden brown on both sides. Drain on kitchen paper and arrange in the prepared dish. Break an egg on top of each slice, season with salt and dot with the remaining butter. Bake until the egg whites have set and serve immediately.

UOVA AL PIATTO CON POLENTA

Serves 4

50 g/2 oz butter

4 thick slices ready-made

or home-cooked set polenta (see page 305)

4 eggs

salt

EGGS WITH TOMATOES

Preheat oven to 180°C/350°F/Gas Mark 4. Brush an ovenproof dish with olive oil. Cut the tops off the tomatoes and scoop out the seeds and some of the flesh. Sprinkle the insides with a little salt and place upside down on kitchen paper for 10 minutes to drain. Season the insides of the tomatoes with oregano and pepper and divide the olive oil among them. Place the tomatoes in the prepared dish and bake for 20 minutes. Remove the dish from the oven, break an egg into each tomato, return the dish to the oven and bake for a further 5 minutes. Garnish with parsley and serve.

UOVA AL PIATTO CON POMODORI

Serves 4

2 teaspoons olive oil, plus extra for brushing

4 large tomatoes

pinch of dried oregano

4 eggs

1 fresh flat-leaf parsley sprig, chopped

salt and pepper

EGGS WITH SAUSAGE

Preheat the oven to 180°C/350°F/Gas Mark 4. Grease four individual ovenproof dishes with butter. Heat a frying pan, add the sausages and cook over a medium heat without added oil or fat until well browned. Sprinkle in the wine and cook until it has evaporated. Divide the sausages among the prepared dishes and break an egg on top of each. Season lightly with salt and bake until the egg whites have set. Serve immediately.

UOVA AL PIATTO CON SALSICCIA

Serves 4

butter, for greasing

300 g/11 oz Italian sausages, coarsely chopped

100 ml/3½ fl oz dry white wine

4 eggs

salt

EGGS ON MILK SOAKED BREAD

Preheat oven to 180°C/350°F/Gas Mark 4. Grease an ovenproof dish with butter and place the bread in it in a single layer. Bring the milk to just below boiling point, then pour it over the bread and leave to soak. Heat the oil in a frying pan, add the onion and cook over a low heat, stirring occasionally, for 10 minutes. Set aside and keep warm. Break an egg on top of each piece of bread, season with salt and bake until the egg whites have set and the bread is light golden brown. Sprinkle the onion on top and serve.

UOVA AL PIATTO
SUI CROSTONI AL LATTE

Serves 4

butter, for greasing

4 slices day-old bread, crusts removed

500 ml/18 fl oz milk

3 tablespoons olive oil

1 onion, chopped

4 eggs

salt

FRIED

Break eggs on to a plate one at a time and season with salt. Heat a knob of butter and a teaspoon of oil in a frying pan and slide in the eggs. Gather the whites around the yolks immediately, using a slotted spoon, so that the eggs remain neat and separated. When done, the whites should be a light golden brown and the yolks soft. Lift out the eggs with a fish slice, drain on kitchen paper and arrange on a warm serving dish.

INDIVIDUAL

UOVA FRITTE AL BURRO D'ACCIUGA

Serves 4

100 g/3½ oz butter

4 bread slices, crusts removed

1 tablespoon anchovy paste

4 eggs

salt

4 canned anchovy fillets in oil, drained, to garnish

EGGS WITH ANCHOVY BUTTER

Melt 40 g/1½ oz of the butter in a frying pan, add the bread and fry until golden brown on both sides. Remove from the pan and drain on kitchen paper. Beat 25 g/1 oz of the remaining butter with the anchovy paste in a bowl and spread the mixture on one side of each fried bread slice. Fry the eggs in the remaining butter and sprinkle a little salt on the whites. Lift out with a fish slice and place one on each slice of fried bread. Garnish with the anchovy fillets and serve while hot.

UOVA FRITTE AL CIVET

Serves 4

4 tablespoons olive oil

400 g/14 oz onions, thinly sliced

1 teaspoon sugar

2 tablespoons balsamic vinegar

1 tablespoon sherry vinegar

5 tablespoons red wine

8 eggs

salt and pepper

toast, to serve

EGGS IN RED WINE

Heat the oil in a frying pan, add the onions and stir-fry over a high heat until lightly browned. Add 2 tablespoons water and the sugar, lower the heat and cook for 20–30 minutes until the onions are very soft and caramelized. Sprinkle in the vinegars and cook until they have evaporated. Pour in the wine and cook until about half has evaporated. Season with salt and pepper, then break the eggs into the pan, one at a time, and cook for a few minutes over a medium heat. Transfer the eggs and their sauce to a warm serving dish and serve with toast.

EGGS WITH VINEGAR

Melt 50 g/2 oz of the butter in a frying pan and break in one egg at a time. Season lightly with salt and fry for a few minutes. Transfer to a warm serving dish. Melt the remaining butter in the same pan. When it starts to brown, sprinkle in the vinegar, add the sage and parsley and cook for a few minutes, then pour the sauce over the eggs.

UOVA FRITTE ALL'ACETO

Serves 4

100 g/3¹/₂ oz butter

8 eggs

4 tablespoons white wine vinegar

4 fresh sage leaves, chopped

1 fresh flat-leaf parsley sprig, chopped

salt

AMERICAN-STYLE EGGS

Heat the oil and butter in a frying pan, add the pancetta and cook for 5 minutes until tender, then remove and drain on kitchen paper. Break the eggs into the pan, one at a time, and season with salt and pepper. Using a wooden spoon, flip the egg whites over the yolks to cover. When the whites are set, remove the eggs from the pan using a fish slice and arrange on a warm serving dish. Surround with pancetta and serve with grilled tomatoes.

UOVA FRITTE ALL'AMERICANA

Serves 4

2 tablespoons olive oil

25 g/1 oz butter

100 g/3¹/₂ oz smoked pancetta, cut into strips

4 eggs

salt and pepper

grilled tomatoes, to serve

EGGS ROSSINI

Melt the pâté in a small saucepan with 50 g/2 oz of the butter. Melt the remaining butter in a frying pan, break in the eggs, one at a time, and cook until the whites start to set. Pour the pâté butter on top and cook for a further 2 minutes, then serve.

UOVA FRITTE ALLA ROSSINI

For 4

150 g/5 oz pâté de foie gras

100 g/3¹/₂ oz butter

8 eggs

EGGS WITH BRUSSELS SPROUTS

Bring a large pan of salted water to the boil, add the Brussels sprouts and simmer for 15 minutes, then drain well. Melt 25 g/1 oz of the butter in a frying pan, add the ham and onion and cook over a low heat, stirring occasionally, for 5 minutes. Sprinkle in the flour and cook, stirring, for 1 minute, then stir in 150 ml/¹/₄ pint warm water and simmer for a further 10 minutes. Stir in the cream, season with salt and pepper and heat through. Meanwhile, melt the remaining butter in another frying pan, break in the eggs, one at a time, and fry for a few minutes over a medium heat. Season with salt to taste. Arrange the Brussels sprouts on a warm serving dish, cover with the hot ham sauce, top with the eggs and serve.

*UOVA FRITTE CON CAVOLINI
DI BRUXELLES*

Serves 4

500 g/1 lb 2 oz Brussels sprouts

100 g/3¹/₂ oz butter

1 thick ham slice, diced

1 onion, finely chopped

1 tablespoon plain flour

200 ml/7 fl oz double cream

6 eggs

salt and pepper

EN COCOTTE

Eggs en cocotte can be cooked in a double boiler, on the hob or in the oven. Arrange a layer of chicken livers, ham or similar ingredients in a lightly buttered ramekin and break an egg on top. Add salt and pepper to taste and a knob of butter. Cooking in a double boiler with barely simmering water takes 6–8 minutes. The white must set softly and the yolk remain runny.

UOVA IN COCOTTE AI PORRI

Serves 4

600 g/1 lb 5 oz leeks, trimmed

50g/2 oz butter, plus extra for greasing

pinch of freshly grated nutmeg

4 eggs

salt and pepper

EGGS EN COCOTTE WITH LEEKS

Halve the leeks lengthways, then slice very thinly. Melt the butter in a small frying pan, add the leeks and cook over a low heat, stirring occasionally, for 5 minutes until softened. Season with salt and pepper to taste and sprinkle with the nutmeg. Stir well and add 3 tablespoons warm water, then cover and cook over a low heat for about 20 minutes. Meanwhile, preheat the oven to 180°C/350°F/Gas Mark 4 and grease four ramekins with butter. Divide the leeks among the ramekins, break an egg into each dish and bake for 4 minutes. Turn off the heat, cover the ramekins with a sheet of foil and return to the oven for 2 minutes. Remove the foil, season lightly with pepper and serve.

UOVA IN COCOTTE ALLA PESCATORA

Serves 4

25 g/1 oz butter, plus extra for greasing

80 g/3 oz canned sardines in oil, drained

4 eggs

1 fresh flat-leaf parsley sprig, chopped

salt and pepper

FISHERMAN'S EGGS EN COCOTTE

Preheat the oven to 180°C/350°F/Gas Mark 4 if you wish to bake the eggs. Grease four ramekins with butter. Remove the bones from the sardines and chop the flesh. Divide the flesh among the ramekins, break an egg into each dish, season with salt and pepper to taste and dot with the butter. Place the ramekins in a roasting tin, add boiling water to come about halfway up the sides and bake for 8–10 minutes or until the egg whites are lightly set. Alternatively, place the roasting tin over a low heat for 8–10 minutes. Sprinkle with the parsley and serve.

EGGS EN COCOTTE WITH BACON FAT

UOVA IN COCOTTE AL LARDO

Serves 4

4 small slices bacon fat

4 tablespoons double cream

4 eggs

2 tablespoons Parmesan cheese, freshly grated

Preheat the oven to 180°C/350°F/Gas Mark 4 if you wish to bake the eggs. Parboil the bacon fat in boiling water for about 1 minute, then drain. Put 1 tablespoon cream and a slice of bacon fat in each of four ramekins, break an egg into each and sprinkle with the Parmesan. Place the ramekins in a roasting tin, add boiling water to come about halfway up the sides and bake for 6–8 minutes or until the egg whites are lightly set. Alternatively, place the roasting tin over a low heat for 6–8 minutes. The combination of bacon fat and cream – a strong savoury taste and a milder flavour – gives the eggs a very delicate flavour.

EGGS EN COCOTTE WITH BOLOGNESE MEAT SAUCE

UOVA IN COCOTTE AL RAGÙ

Serves 4

butter, for greasing

1 quantity Bolognese Meat Sauce (see page 52)

8 eggs

salt

Preheat the oven to 180°C/350°F/Gas Mark 4 if you wish to bake the eggs. Grease four ramekins with butter and pour a layer of meat sauce into each. Break the eggs on top, season lightly with salt and cover with another layer of meat sauce. Place the ramekins in a roasting tin, add boiling water to come about halfway up the sides and bake for 8–10 minutes. Alternatively, place the roasting tin over a low heat for 8–10 minutes. Serve hot.

FRAGRANT EGGS EN COCOTTE

UOVA IN COCOTTE AROMATICHE

Serves 4

butter, plus extra for greasing

8 fresh basil leaves, chopped

pinch of dried oregano

4 plum tomatoes, thinly sliced

4 eggs

salt and pepper

Preheat the oven to 180°C/350°F/Gas Mark 4 if you wish to bake the eggs. Grease four ramekins with plenty of butter, sprinkle with half the basil and the oregano, add a few slices of tomato and break an egg into each. Season lightly with salt and pepper and dot with butter, then top with the remaining tomato slices and basil. Place the ramekins in a roasting tin, add boiling water to come about halfway up the sides and bake for 6–8 minutes or until the egg whites are lightly set. Alternatively, place the roasting tin over a low heat for 6–8 minutes.

MEDIUM BOILED

Immerse the eggs in a pan of boiling water, bring back to the boil and cook for 5 minutes. Remove from the pan and refresh under cold running water to prevent any further cooking and to make shelling them without damaging the white easier. Handle them very gently. Medium-boiled eggs are very tasty sprinkled with sauce or with vegetables seasoned in various ways.

BOILED EGGS WITH SPINACH

Cook the spinach, in just the water clinging to the leaves after washing, for 5 minutes, then drain, squeeze out as much liquid as possible and chop finely. Melt the butter in a frying pan, add the spinach and cook over a low heat, stirring occasionally, for 5 minutes. Stir in the cream and season with salt and pepper. Meanwhile, cook the eggs in boiling water for 4–5 minutes, then remove from the pan, refresh under cold water and shell. Place the spinach on a warm serving dish, top with the eggs and serve.

UOVA MOLLETTE AGLI SPINACI

Serves 4

675 g/1¹/₂ lb spinach

50 g/2 oz butter

2 tablespoons double cream

4 eggs

salt and pepper

369

BOILED EGGS WITH MUSHROOMS

UOVA MOLLETTE AI FUNGHI

Serves 4

4 large porcini

olive oil, for brushing

80 g/3 oz butter

1 tablespoon chopped fresh flat-leaf parsley

1 teaspoon lemon juice, strained

4 eggs

salt and pepper

Preheat the grill to medium. Remove the mushroom stems, season the caps with salt and pepper, brush with oil and grill for about 15 minutes. Cream the butter in a bowl and beat in the parsley, lemon juice and salt to taste. Cook the eggs in boiling water for 4–5 minutes, then remove from the pan, refresh under cold water and shell. Place an egg in the hollow of each mushroom cap and add a little parsley butter. Arrange on a warm serving dish and serve immediately.

BOILED EGGS WITH HERBED MUSTARD

UOVA MOLLETTE ALLA SENAPE AROMATICA

Serves 4

50 g/2 oz butter

1 shallot, finely chopped

1 tablespoon plain flour

8 eggs

1 tablespoon herbed mustard or flavoured mustard of choice

1 tablespoon finely chopped fresh chives

salt and pepper

Melt the butter in a pan, add the shallot and cook over a low heat, stirring occasionally, for 8–10 minutes until lightly browned. Sprinkle in the flour and cook, stirring constantly, for 1 minute, then stir in 150 ml/¼ pint warm water, season with salt and pepper and simmer gently for about 20 minutes. Meanwhile, cook the eggs in boiling water for 5 minutes, then remove from the pan, refresh under cold water and shell. Stir the mustard into the sauce and spoon on to a warm serving dish. Place the eggs on top, sprinkle with the chives and serve immediately.

BOILED EGGS WITH TOMATO

UOVA MOLLETTE AL POMODORO

Serves 4

200 ml/7 fl oz passata

1 onion, chopped

1 celery stick, chopped

1 carrot, chopped

1 tablespoon chopped fresh flat-leaf parsley

8 eggs

salt

Heat the tomato sauce in a pan, add the onion, celery, carrot and parsley, season with salt and simmer over a low heat for 20 minutes. Cook the eggs in boiling water for 4–5 minutes, then remove from the pan, refresh under cold water and shell. Spoon half the sauce on to the base of a warm serving dish, place the eggs on top and spoon the remaining sauce over them.

BOILED EGGS WITH BROCCOLI

Cook the broccoli in a pan of salted, boiling water for 10 minutes, then drain. Heat the oil in a frying pan, add the garlic clove and cook until golden brown. Remove and discard the garlic, add the broccoli to the pan and cook over a low heat for a few minutes. Meanwhile, cook the eggs in boiling water for 4–5 minutes, then remove from the pan, refresh under cold water and shell. Arrange the eggs on a warm serving dish, spoon the broccoli around them and serve.

UOVA MOLLETTE CON I BROCCOLI

Serves 4

800 g/1³/₄ lb broccoli, cut into florets

3 tablespoons olive oil

1 garlic clove

4 eggs

salt

BOILED EGGS WITH ARTICHOKE HEARTS

Cook the artichoke hearts in salted, boiling water until just tender, then drain and arrange on a warm serving dish. Melt the butter in a frying pan, add the shallot, thyme and a pinch of pepper and cook over a low heat, stirring occasionally, for 5 minutes Pour in the wine and cook until it has almost completely evaporated. Sprinkle with the flour, stir in 200ml/ 7 fl oz warm water and simmer for 5 minutes. Cook the eggs in boiling water for 4–5 minutes, then remove from the pan, refresh under cold water and shell. Place the eggs on the artichoke hearts and pour the sauce over them. Garnish with the ham and serve.

UOVA MOLLETTE CON I CARCIOFI

Serves 4

4 artichoke hearts

25 g/1 oz butter

1 shallot, chopped

1 fresh thyme sprig, chopped

200 ml/7 fl oz dry white wine

pinch of plain flour

4 eggs

salt and pepper

2 cooked ham slices, cut into strips, to garnish

HARD
BOILED

Add salt to the water to prevent the shells from breaking and bring to the boil. Immerse the eggs and cook over a high heat for about 8 minutes. If the recipe calls for very hard-boiled eggs, cook them for 10 minutes. Refresh the eggs under cold running water to make shelling easier.

ASPIC DI UOVA SODE

Serves 4–6

4 eggs, hard-boiled

150 g/5 oz roast chicken breast, skinned and cut into strips

80 g/3 oz pickled ox tongue, cut into strips

150 g/5 oz cooked ham, trimmed of fat and diced

1 quantity Mayonnaise made with lemon juice (see page 65)

2 gelatine leaves

salt and pepper

radishes, thinly sliced or cut into flowers, to garnish

HARD—BOILED EGGS IN ASPIC

Shell the eggs and cut three of them into equally thick round slices. Chop the remaining egg, place in a bowl with the chicken, tongue and ham and gently stir in the mayonnaise. Prepare the gelatine according to the packet instructions and leave to cool but do not chill in the refrigerator. Pour a little cooled gelatine on to the base of a mould, brush the sides with a generous amount and chill in the refrigerator until set. Arrange some slices of hard-boiled egg on the base, pour a thin layer of gelatine on top and return to the refrigerator until set. Make a layer of the meat mixture in the mould and place a few slices of egg on top. Cover with another layer of gelatine and return to the refrigerator until set. Continue making alternating layers of the meat mixture, egg slices and gelatine until all the ingredients are used, ending with a layer of gelatine. Chill in the refrigerator for 3 hours. To serve, immerse the mould in hot water for a few seconds, then turn out on to a serving dish and garnish with the radishes.

HARD–BOILED EGGS IN CURRY SAUCE

UOVA SODE AL CURRY

Serves 4

butter, for greasing

1 teaspoon curry powder

1 quantity Béchamel Sauce (see page 50)

6 eggs

1 tablespoon Parmesan cheese, freshly grated

salt

Preheat the oven to 180°C/350°F/Gas Mark 4. Grease an ovenproof dish with butter. Stir the curry powder and a pinch of salt into the béchamel sauce. Hard-boil the eggs in salted water, shell and halve lengthways. Scoop out the yolks into a bowl and mash with 2 tablespoons of the curry sauce. Spoon the mixture into the egg whites, arrange them in the prepared dish, spoon the remaining curry sauce over them and sprinkle with the Parmesan. Bake until golden and bubbling.

HARD–BOILED EGGS NAPOLETANA

UOVA SODE ALLA NAPOLETANA

Serves 4

8 eggs

4 tomatoes, peeled, seeded and diced

25 g/1 oz green and black olives, stoned and chopped

4 canned anchovy fillets in oil, drained and finely chopped

4–6 tablespoons Mayonnaise (see page 65)

salt

lettuce leaves, to serve

Hard-boil the eggs in salted water, refresh in cold water and shell. Halve lengthways and scoop out the yolks into a bowl. Mash with a fork and add 1 tablespoon of the tomatoes, and the olives, anchovy fillets and enough mayonnaise to combine. Fill the egg whites with the mixture, doming it up well. Make a bed of lettuce leaves on a serving dish, place the stuffed eggs on top and surround with the remaining tomatoes.

HARD–BOILED EGGS WITH WALNUTS

UOVA SODE ALLE NOCI

Serves 4

4 eggs

10 shelled walnuts

1 tablespoon anchovy paste

40 g/1 1/2 oz butter, softened

juice of 1/2 lemon, strained

salt and pepper

1 tablespoon chopped fresh flat-leaf parsley, to garnish

Hard-boil the eggs in salted water, refresh in cold water, then shell. Halve lengthways, scoop out the yolks into a bowl and mash with a fork. Finely chop two of the walnuts. Add the chopped walnuts, anchovy paste, butter and lemon juice to the egg yolks and mix well. Season with salt and pepper to taste. Fill the egg whites with the mixture and put a shelled walnut in the centre of each. Arrange on a serving dish and garnish with the parsley.

HARD—BOILED EGGS WITH HATS

Hard-boil the eggs in salted water, refresh in cold water and shell. Whisk together the oil and vinegar in a bowl, and season with salt and pepper. Add the salad leaves and toss then arrange on a serving dish. Cut the bottom off each egg so that it stands upright and place the eggs on top of the salad. Cut the top third off the tomatoes, scoop out the seeds and place the thirds on top of the eggs like hats. Slice the remaining parts of the tomatoes and use to garnish the dish. Serve with caper mayonnaise.

UOVA SODE COL CAPELLO

Serves 4

8 eggs

6 tablespoons olive oil

2 tablespoons white wine vinegar

1 bunch of escarole or frisée, cut into strips

1 bunch of rocket, cut into strips

4 tomatoes

salt and pepper

caper mayonnaise, to serve

HARD—BOILED EGGS WITH PRAWNS

Hard-boil the eggs in salted water, refresh under cold running water and shell. Halve lengthways and scoop out the yolks into a bowl. Mash with a fork, add the butter and anchovy paste and mix well. Fill the egg whites with the mixture and sprinkle with the parsley. Arrange the prawns on top.

UOVA SODE CON I GAMBERETTI

Serves 4

4 eggs

25 g/1 oz butter, softened

1 teaspoon anchovy paste

1 fresh flat-leaf parsley sprig, finely chopped

8 cooked, peeled prawns • salt

HARD—BOILED EGGS WITH SMOKED SALMON

Hard-boil the eggs in salted water, refresh in cold water and shell. Halve lengthways, scoop out the yolks into a blender, add the salmon and cream and season with salt and pepper. Process to a thick purée and use to fill the egg whites, doming the mixture on top. Fan out the lettuce leaves on a serving dish, and arrange two half-eggs on each leaf.

UOVA SODE CON IL SALMONE

Serves 4

4 eggs

150 g/5 oz smoked salmon, chopped

3 tablespoons double cream

4 lettuce leaves

salt and pepper

HARD—BOILED EGGS WITH OYSTERS

Hard-boil the eggs in salted water, refresh in cold water and shell. Halve lengthways, scoop out the yolks into a bowl and mash with a fork. Stir in the olive oil and lemon juice to make a smooth sauce and season with salt and pepper. Melt the butter in a frying pan, add the oysters and parsley and cook over a low heat for a few minutes, then spoon into the egg whites. Lightly toast the bread on both sides and spread with a little butter while still hot. Put a small slice of lemon on each slice and top with the oyster-filled eggs. Spoon the egg yolk sauce over them.

UOVA SODE CON LE OSTRICHE

Serves 4

4 eggs

2–3 tablespoons olive oil

2–3 tablespoons lemon juice, strained

25 g/1 oz butter, plus extra for spreading

8 oysters, shucked

1 fresh flat-leaf parsley sprig, chopped

8 bread slices, crusts removed

1 lemon, peeled and thinly sliced

salt and pepper

UOVA SODE IN GELATINA

Serves 4

6 eggs

1 litre/1³/₄ pints gelatine

6–7 cooked ham slices

50 g/2 oz capers, drained and rinsed

12 black olives

salt and pepper

HARD—BOILED EGGS AND HAM IN ASPIC

Hard-boil the eggs in salted water, refresh under cold water and shell. Halve the eggs crossways. Dissolve the gelatine in 1 litre/ 1³/₄ pints water according to the packet instructions, leave to cool slightly, then pour a thin layer on to the base of a serving dish and chill in the refrigerator until set. Using a biscuit cutter or the rim of a glass, cut out 24 rounds of ham a little larger than the maximum diameter of the eggs. Place 12 ham rounds on the layer of set gelatine. Cut the tip off each half—egg so that it stands upright and place one on each ham round. Garnish each egg yolk with capers, a pinch of pepper and an olive and cover with another ham round. Pour the remaining gelatine over the eggs and chill in the refrigerator until set. Remove from the refrigerator 15 minutes before serving.

UOVA SODE RIPIENE E FRITTE

Serves 4

5 eggs

120 g/4 oz ricotta cheese

40 g/1¹/₂ oz Parmesan cheese, freshly grated

2–3 tablespoons double cream

1 tablespoon chopped fresh flat-leaf parsley

80 g/3 oz breadcrumbs

plain flour, for dusting

25 g/1 oz butter

salt and pepper

FRIED STUFFED HARD—BOILED EGGS

Hard-boil four of the eggs in salted water, refresh under cold running water and shell. Halve lengthways, scoop out the yolks into a bowl and mash with a fork. Add the ricotta, Parmesan, 2 tablespoons of the cream and the parsley, season with salt and pepper and mix well. If the mixture is too soft, add 1 tablespoon of the breadcrumbs; if it is too firm, add the remaining cream. Fill the egg whites with the mixture and dust lightly with flour. Beat the remaining egg in a shallow dish and place the breadcrumbs in another shallow dish. Dip the filled eggs first in beaten egg, then in breadcrumbs. Melt the butter in a frying pan, add the filled eggs and cook until lightly browned. Drain on kitchen paper, arrange on a serving dish and serve immediately.

SCRAMBLED

Melt about 100 g/3¹/₂ oz butter in a frying pan for every 6 eggs. Lightly beat the eggs with a pinch of salt and pour into the pan. Stir over a medium heat until creamy, then stir in 25 g/1 oz butter and transfer to to a serving dish. Take care not to overcook the eggs. To be sure that scrambled eggs will be soft, set aside 1 tablespoon beaten egg and add it once the pan has been removed from the heat.

SCRAMBLED EGGS WITH ARTICHOKES

Break off the artichoke stalks, remove the tough, outer leaves and chokes and slice thinly. Melt the butter in a frying pan, add the artichokes and season lightly with salt and pepper. Add 4 tablespoons water, cover and cook for 15 minutes, adding a little more water if necessary. Break the eggs, one at a time, on to a small plate and slide into the pan. Scramble the eggs by stirring them with the artichokes, and remove from the heat as soon as the mixture starts to set. Serve hot.

UOVA STRAPAZZATE AI CARCIOFI

Serves 4

3 artichokes

50 g/2 oz butter

4 eggs

salt and pepper

ABRUZZO
SCRAMBLED EGGS

UOVA STRAPAZZATE ALL'ABRUZZESE

Serves 4

3 tablespoons olive oil

1 onion, finely chopped

1 garlic clove, finely chopped

4 tomatoes, peeled, seeded and diced

1 fresh basil sprig, finely chopped

1 fresh marjoram sprig, finely chopped

1 fresh red chilli, seeded and finely chopped

8 eggs, lightly beaten

100 g/3½ oz stoned black olives

salt and pepper

Heat the oil in a frying pan, add the onion and garlic and cook over a low heat, stirring occasionally, for 5 minutes. Add the tomatoes, herbs and chilli and cook, stirring occasionally, for 10 minutes. Pour in the eggs and mix with a fork to scramble When the mixture is soft, add the olives and season lightly with salt and pepper. Turn off the heat, cover and leave to stand for a few minutes before serving.

SCRAMBLED EGGS
WITH FONTINA

UOVA STRAPAZZATE ALLA FONTINA

Serves 4

5 eggs

80 g/3 oz butter

80 g/3 oz fontina cheese, freshly grated

salt and pepper

Break one egg into a small bowl, beat lightly with a fork and set aside. Break the remaining eggs into another bowl and beat lightly with a fork. Melt 65 g/2½ oz of the butter in a frying pan over a medium heat, pour in the larger bowl of eggs and scramble. Sprinkle in the cheese, season with salt and pepper and continue scrambling. Add the remaining butter, small pieces at a time. When the mixture is soft and creamy, remove the pan from the heat and immediately stir in the reserved beaten egg. Mix well and serve immediately.

SCRAMBLED EGGS
WITH TRUFFLE

UOVA STRAPAZZATE AL TARTUFO

Serves 4

4 bread slices, crusts removed

8 eggs

40 g/1½ oz butter, softened, plus extra for spreading

50 g/2 oz truffle paste

2 tablespoons double cream

salt and pepper

Lightly toast the bread on both sides. Lightly beat the eggs with a pinch of salt and pepper. Cream the butter with the truffle paste in another bowl, then melt in a frying pan over a low heat. Pour in the eggs and as soon as the mixture starts to thicken, add the cream, mix well and remove the pan from the heat. Thinly spread the toast with butter and arrange on a warm serving dish. Spoon the truffled eggs on top and serve immediately.

SCRAMBLED EGGS WITH SPINACH

Cook the spinach, in just the water clinging to the leaves after washing, for 5 minutes, then drain well, squeezing out as much liquid as possible, and chop. Place in a clean pan over a low heat for 1–2 minutes to drive off excess water, then remove from the heat and add the parsley, basil and shallot. Lightly beat the eggs in a bowl with 1 tablespoon water and season with salt and pepper. Stir in the spinach mixture. Heat the oil in a non-stick frying pan, pour in the egg mixture and cook over a medium heat, stirring constantly. When the mixture is green and soft, remove the pan from the heat, leave to stand for 2 minutes, then transfer to a warm serving dish and serve immediately.

UOVA STRAPAZZATE AL VERDE
Serves 4
400 g/14 oz spinach
1 fresh flat-leaf parsley sprig, chopped
6 fresh basil leaves, chopped
1 shallot, chopped
6 eggs
2 tablespoons olive oil
salt and pepper

SCRAMBLED EGGS WITH BEANS

Heat the oil in a frying pan, add the onion and beans and cook over a low heat, stirring occasionally, for 10 minutes. Add the eggs, season with salt and pepper and stir with a fork to scramble. As soon as the eggs become creamy, remove the pan from the heat and serve immediately.

UOVA STRAPAZZATE CON I FAGIOLI
Serves 4
2 tablespoons olive oil
1 onion, cut into thin rings
300 g/11 oz canned borlotti beans,
drained and rinsed
4 eggs, lightly beaten
salt and pepper

SCRAMBLED EGGS WITH CHICKEN LIVERS

Melt half the butter in a frying pan over a high heat, add the chicken livers and cook, stirring frequently, for 5 minutes. Season with salt and pepper and stir in the tomato purée. Add the liver mixture to the eggs. Melt the remaining butter in a clean frying pan, pour in the egg mixture and stir with a fork to scramble until creamy. Remove the pan from the heat and serve immediately.

UOVA STRAPAZZATE CON I FEGATINI
Serves 4
50 g/2 oz butter
200 g/7 oz chicken livers, thawed if frozen,
trimmed and coarsely chopped
1 tablespoon tomato purée
4 eggs, lightly beaten
salt and pepper

SCRAMBLED EGGS WITH SAUSAGE

Put the sausages, garlic and half the butter in a frying pan and cook over a low heat, stirring frequently, until browned, then remove the pan from the heart. Discard the garlic. Lightly beat the eggs with a pinch of salt. Melt the remaining butter in another frying pan and pour in the eggs. Remove the crumbled sausages with a slotted spoon, draining well, and add to the eggs. Stir with a fork until creamy, then remove from the heat and serve immediately.

UOVA STRAPAZZATE CON LA SALSICCIA
Serves 4
200 g/7 oz Italian sausages, skinned and crumbled
1 garlic clove
25 g/1 oz butter
5 eggs
salt

SCRAMBLED EGGS
IN THEIR NESTS

Cook the potatoes in salted, boiling water for 20–30 minutes until tender. Drain, peel and mash in a bowl, then add 25 g/1 oz of the butter, 2–3 tablespoons of the cream, one egg and the Parmesan. Mix well and season with salt. Preheat the oven to 180°C/350°F/Gas Mark 4. Grease a baking sheet with butter. Make four spirals with the potato mixture on the baking sheet and surround each with another higher ring of the mixture. Bake for 20 minutes until golden. Meanwhile, lightly beat the remaining eggs with salt and pepper. Melt the remaining butter in a frying pan, pour in eggs and cook over a low heat for 2 minutes. Stir in the remaining cream and cook, stirring, until thick. Spoon the eggs into the potato 'nests' and serve.

UOVA STRAPAZZATE NEL NIDO

Serves 4

500 g/1 lb 2 oz potatoes

80 g/3 oz butter, plus extra for greasing

50 ml/2 fl oz double cream

6 eggs

50 g/2 oz Parmesan cheese, freshly grated

salt and pepper

THE FRITTATA FAMILY

Italian omelettes – frittate – are economical and quick and are among the tastiest dishes that can be made with eggs. They are also very versatile, as the basic recipe may be enriched and flavoured with a wide range of other ingredients, including herbs, vegetables, fish, cheeses, salami, ham and fruit. As regards quantities, in general allow two eggs per person if the frittata is served as a main course and one if it is an antipasto. As a general rule, 10 g/¹/₄ oz butter or 1¹/₂ teaspoons olive oil is required to cook every two eggs.

COOKING

A FRYING PAN IS ESSENTIAL

No other pan produces the same result. The choice of material, on the other hand, may vary – classic black cast iron, non-stick which does not need butter or oil, or a double pan which may be closed and turned over to brown both sides perfectly. The perfect frittata should be dry and golden brown on the outside, while still slightly soft inside.

THE METHOD IS AS FOLLOWS

Lightly beat the eggs in a bowl, season with salt (pepper is optional) and immediately pour into a frying pan with butter or oil at just the right temperature. Lower the heat and, after 1–2 minutes when the egg starts to set, shake the pan slightly to loosen the frittata and then turn it over. The easiest way to do this is to cover the pan with a flat plate and, holding it tightly, invert the pan then slide the frittata back into the pan and cook it on the other side. Keep the pan over the heat for the necessary time: 2–3 minutes if there are more than four eggs. Although the degree of cooking depends on individual taste, very dry frittata are not recommended.

SAVOURY CRÊPES

Basically, crêpes are only fried eggs, but so many versions exist that you could offer filled crêpes for months without repeating yourself. They may also be used to make timbales, gratins and cannelloni, according to how they are arranged or folded. They may be served as a first course or main course, or as a one-course meal. What is important is that they are thin.

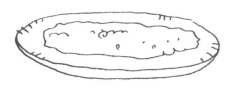

SMOKED SALMON CRÊPES

Prepare the crêpes and while still warm spread lightly with the butter and place 1–2 slices of smoked salmon on top of each. Fold each crêpe into four, arrange on a warm serving dish and sprinkle with the lemon juice. Serve immediately.

CRÊPES AL SALMONE AFFUMICATO
Serves 4
12 crêpes (see page 155)
40 g/1½ oz butter, softened
150 g/5 oz smoked salmon, thinly sliced
juice of 1 lemon, strained

PICKLED SALMON CRÊPES

Put the slices of raw salmon in a soup plate, pour in the lemon juice, sprinkle with the peppercorns and leave to marinate for 1 hour. Prepare the crêpes and leave to cool. Place two slices of salmon on each crêpe, fold into four and arrange on a serving dish.

CRÊPES AL SALMONE MARINATO
Serves 4
8 thin slices raw salmon
juice of 2 lemons, strained
1 tablespoon green peppercorns
12 crêpes (see page 155)

CHEESE AND WALNUT CRÊPES

CRÊPES CON FORMAGGIO E NOCI

Serves 4

12 crêpes (see page 155)

butter, for greasing

150 g/5 oz mild Gorgonzola cheese, crumbled

100 g/3½ oz mascarpone cheese

12 shelled walnuts, chopped

4 tablespoons double cream

Prepare the crêpes and leave to cool. Preheat the oven to 180°C/350°F/Gas Mark 4. Grease an ovenproof dish with butter. Mix together the Gorgonzola and mascarpone in a bowl and add the walnuts. Spread the mixture over the crêpes, fold into four and arrange in the prepared dish. Sprinkle with the cream and bake until the cream is absorbed.

CARDOON CRÊPES

CRÊPES CON I CARDI

Serves 4

500 g/1 lb 2 oz cardoons, trimmed

40 g/1½ oz butter, plus extra for greasing

12 crêpes (see page 155)

¾ quantity Béchamel Sauce (see page 50)

salt

Cook the cardoons in salted, boiling water for 1 hour, then drain well and chop. Melt 25 g/1 oz of the butter in a frying pan, add the cardoons and cook over a low heat, stirring occasionally, for 5 minutes. Prepare the crêpes and leave to cool. Preheat the oven to 180°C/350°F/Gas Mark 4. Grease an ovenproof dish with butter. Spread a little béchamel sauce on each crêpe and arrange a little chopped cardoon on top, then cover with more béchamel sauce and roll up. Place the crêpes in the prepared dish, dot with the remaining butter and bake for 15 minutes. Remove from the oven and leave to stand for about 10 minutes, then serve.

RICOTTA AND SPINACH CRÊPES

CRÊPES CON RICOTTA E SPINACI

Serves 4

12 crêpes (see page 155)

40 g/1½ oz butter, plus extra for greasing

500 g/1 lb 2 oz spinach

1 tablespoon olive oil

200 g/7 oz ricotta cheese

1 egg yolk

2 tablespoons Parmesan cheese, freshly grated

Prepare the crêpes and leave to cool. Preheat the oven to 180°C/350°F/Gas Mark 4. Grease an ovenproof dish with butter. Cook the spinach, in just the water clinging to the leaves after washing, for 5 minutes, then drain, squeeze out as much liquid as possible and chop. Melt 25 g/1 oz of the butter with the oil in a frying pan, add the spinach and cook over a low heat, stirring frequently, for 5 minutes. Transfer to a bowl and mix with the ricotta and egg yolk. Spread the mixture on the crêpes, fold in half and arrange in the prepared dish. Sprinkle with the Parmesan and dot with the remaining butter. Bake for 15 minutes, then remove from the oven and leave to stand for a few minutes before serving.

FRITTATA

Serves 4

40 g/1½ oz butter

4 tablespoons olive oil

2 yellow peppers, halved, seeded and diced

3 tomatoes, peeled, seeded and diced

6 eggs, lightly beaten

salt and pepper

PEPPER FRITTATA

Heat half the butter and the oil in a frying pan, add the peppers and cook, stirring, for 2 minutes. Add the tomatoes, season with salt and pepper, cover and cook over a low heat for 15–20 minutes. Add the eggs. Melt the remaining butter in another frying pan and pour the entire mixture into it. Cook the frittata on both sides and serve.

FRITTATA AL FORMAGGIO

Serves 4

8 eggs

80 g/3 oz fontina cheese, diced

1 small cooked ham slice, diced

1 tablespoon Parmesan cheese, freshly grated

olive oil, for brushing

salt

CHEESE FRITTATA

Lightly beat the eggs with a pinch of salt and stir in the fontina, ham and Parmesan. Heat a frying pan and brush lightly with oil. Pour in the egg mixture and cook over a low heat until browned on both sides. When the frittata is ready, it should be soft and the cheese in the middle should form strings. Transfer to a warm serving dish.

BORAGE FRITTATA

Tear the bread into pieces, place in a bowl, add water to cover and leave to soak, then squeeze out. Heat 3 tablespoons of the oil in a saucepan, add the borage, cover and cook over a low heat until wilted. Lightly beat the eggs with the Parmesan, soaked bread, marjoram and garlic, then stir in the borage and season with salt and pepper. Heat the remaining oil in a frying pan, pour in the mixture and smooth the surface by pressing lightly with a spatula. Cook over a low heat on both sides. This frittata should be very thick and quite soft inside.

FRITTATA ALLA BORRAGINE

Serves 4

50 g/2 oz bread slices, crusts removed

5 tablespoons olive oil

600 g/1 lb 5 oz borage, finely chopped

4 eggs

2 tablespoons Parmesan cheese, freshly grated

6 fresh marjoram leaves, chopped

1/2 garlic clove, finely chopped

salt and pepper

HAM FRITTATA

Lightly beat the eggs and stir in the ham, parsley, Parmesan and cream. Season lightly with salt and pepper. Melt the butter in a frying pan, pour in the mixture and cook until golden brown on both sides. Serve hot.

FRITTATA AL PROSCIUTTO COTTO

Serves 4

6 eggs

120 g/4 oz cooked ham, chopped

1 fresh flat-leaf parsley sprig, chopped

1 tablespoon Parmesan cheese, freshly grated

2 tablespoons double cream

25 g/1 oz butter

salt and pepper

HAM AND SAGE FRITTATA

Lightly beat the eggs, stir in the ham, sage, Parmesan and cream and season with salt and pepper. Melt the butter in a frying pan, pour in the mixture and cook until light golden brown on both sides. The frittata should be dry outside and soft inside.

FRITTATA AL PROSCIUTTO COTTO E SALVIA

Serves 4

6 eggs

120 g/4 oz cooked ham, chopped

6 fresh sage leaves, chopped

1 tablespoon Parmesan cheese, freshly grated

2 tablespoons double cream

25 g/1 oz butter

salt and pepper

CELERY AND SAUSAGE FRITTATA

Lightly beat the eggs, stir in the sausage and celery and season lightly with salt and pepper. Heat the olive oil in a frying pan, pour in the mixture and cook until browned on both sides. This frittata is good eaten both hot or cold.

FRITTATA AL SEDANO E SALSICCIA

Serves 4

6 eggs

150 g/5 oz Italian sausage, skinned and crumbled

1 celery heart, chopped

2 tablespoons olive oil

salt and pepper

TUNA FRITTATA

FRITTATA AL TONNO

Serves 4

25 g/1 oz butter

1 spring onion, thinly sliced

100 g/3¹/₂ oz canned tuna in oil, drained and flaked

6 eggs

1 tablespoon chopped fresh flat-leaf parsley

salt

Melt the butter in a frying pan over a very low heat, add the spring onion and cook, stirring frequently, for 5 minutes until translucent. Stir in the tuna. Lightly beat the eggs, stir in the parsley and a pinch of salt and pour the mixture over the tuna. Cook until the frittata is browned on both sides. Serve warm.

ONION AND THYME FRITTATA

FRITTATA CON CIPOLLE E TIMO

Serves 4

2 tablespoons olive oil

25 g/1 oz butter

300 g/11 oz onions, thinly sliced

2 fresh thyme sprigs, leaves only

6 eggs • salt

Heat the oil and butter in a frying pan, add the onions and cook over a low heat, stirring occasionally, for 5 minutes. Stir in the thyme and cook for a few minutes more. Meanwhile, lightly beat the eggs with a pinch of salt, then pour into the pan. Cook until lightly browned on both sides.

BREAD FRITTATA

FRITTATA CON IL PANE

Serves 4

2 day-old bread slices, crusts removed

200 ml/7 fl oz milk

6 eggs

2 tablespoons Parmesan cheese, freshly grated

1 tablespoon chopped fresh flat-leaf parsley

2 tablespoons olive oil

25 g/1 oz butter

salt and pepper

Tear the bread into pieces, place in a bowl, add the milk and leave to soak for 10 minutes, then squeeze out. Lightly beat the eggs, stir in the bread, Parmesan and parsley and season with salt and pepper. Mix until the bread softens and is incorporated. Heat the oil and butter in a frying pan, pour in the mixture and cook until browned on both sides. This frittata has a simple but delicate taste.

OLIVE FRITTATA

FRITTATA CON LE OLIVE

Serves 4

20 g/³/₄ oz butter

1 shallot, thinly sliced

50 g/2 oz pancetta, cut into strips

5 eggs

2 tablespoons Parmesan cheese, freshly grated

25 g/1 oz green olives, stoned and chopped

25 g/1 oz black olives, stoned and chopped

2 tablespoons olive oil

salt and pepper

Melt the butter in a frying pan, add the shallot and cook over a low heat, stirring occasionally, for 5 minutes until soft. Stir in the pancetta and cook for a few minutes more, then remove the pan from the heat and leave to cool slightly. Lightly beat the eggs with the Parmesan and season with salt and pepper. Stir in the olives and the shallot and pancetta mixture. Heat the oil in a frying pan, pour in the mixture and cook until browned on both sides, but do not let the frittata dry out too much. Serve immediately.

COURGETTE FRITTATA

Heat the oil and half the butter in a pan, add the courgettes and cook, stirring occasionally, for 10 minutes. Season with salt and pepper and remove from the heat. Lightly beat the eggs with a pinch of salt and stir in the courgettes. Melt the remaining butter in a frying pan, pour in the mixture and cook until lightly browned on both sides. This frittata may be served hot or cold.

FRITTATA CON LE ZUCCHINE

Serves 4

2 tablespoons olive oil

50 g/2 oz butter

300 g/11 oz courgettes, thinly sliced

6 eggs

salt and pepper

POTATO AND CINNAMON FRITTATA

Cook the potatoes in salted, boiling water for 20 minutes or until tender, then drain, tip into a large bowl and mash. Add the milk, 40 g/1½ oz of the butter and a pinch of salt and beat to a purée with a wooden spoon. Stir in the egg yolks, one at a time. Whisk two egg whites in a separate grease-free bowl until stiff, then fold into the potato mixture. Add a pinch of cinnamon, season with salt to taste and mix very gently to avoid knocking out the air. Melt the remaining butter with the oil in a frying pan, pour in the potato mixture and cook over a medium heat until browned on both sides.

FRITTATA CON PATATE E CANNELLA

Serves 4

2 potatoes

100 ml/3½ fl oz milk

65 g/2½ oz butter

4 eggs, separated

pinch of ground cinnamon

2 tablespoons olive oil

salt

MEAT FRITTATA

Melt half the butter in a small saucepan, add the meat and a pinch of salt and cook over a medium heat, stirring frequently, until browned. Lightly beat the eggs, season with salt and pepper and stir in the meat and parsley. If the mixture seems too dry, stir in a little milk. Melt the remaining butter with the oil in a frying pan, pour in the mixture and cook until golden brown on both sides. Serve hot or cold. It is also possible to use leftover cooked meat, but in this case sautéing is unnecessary.

FRITTATA DI CARNE

Serves 4

50 g/2 oz butter

150 g/5 oz minced meat

4 eggs

1 fresh flat-leaf parsley sprig, chopped

2–3 tablespoons milk (optional)

1 tablespoon olive oil

salt and pepper

FRITTATA RIPIENA

Serves 4

4 eggs

65 g/2½ oz butter

200 g/7 oz mushrooms, cut into thin strips

50 g/2 oz cooked ham, diced

50 g/2 oz tongue, diced

50 g/2 oz Gruyère cheese, diced

salt and pepper

FILLED FRITTATA

Preheat the oven to 180°C/350°F/Gas Mark 4. Lightly beat the eggs with salt and pepper. Melt 25 g/1 oz of the butter in a large frying pan, pour in the eggs and fry a very thin frittata on both sides. Melt 25 g/1 oz of the remaining butter in a small saucepan, add the mushrooms and cook, stirring occasionally, for about 10 minutes. Add the ham, tongue and cheese to the mushrooms and remove from the heat. Melt the remaining butter. Arrange the mushroom filling on one half of the frittata, brush the other half with melted butter and fold over. Place the frittata on an ovenproof plate and put in the oven for a few minutes until the cheese has melted. Serve immediately while hot.

TORTA DI FRITTATE

Serves 6

200 g/7 oz aubergines, sliced

200 g/7 oz red or yellow peppers

6 eggs

1 fresh flat-leaf parsley sprig, chopped

1 tablespoon Parmesan cheese, freshly grated

25 g/1 oz butter

100 g/3½ oz fontina cheese, sliced

olive oil

salt and pepper

FRITTATA CAKE

Preheat the oven to 200°C/400°F/Gas Mark 6, and preheat the grill. Grill the aubergines until soft and golden brown. Roast the peppers in the oven until blackened and charred, then transfer to a plastic bag and seal the top. Increase the oven temperature to 240°C/475°F/Gas Mark 9. When cool enough to handle, peel and seed the peppers and cut the flesh into strips. Beat two eggs in one bowl and two eggs in another bowl, season both with salt and pepper and divide the parsley between them. Beat the remaining eggs in a third bowl, season with salt and pepper and stir in the Parmesan. Heat the oil and butter in a frying pan, pour in one bowl of the egg and parsley mixture and cook until set on one side, but still quite soft on the other. Slide the frittata out of the pan and cook two more in the same way, with the remaining egg and parsley mixture and the egg and Parmesan mixture. Line a cake tin with baking parchment and place one of the parsley frittatas, soft side up, in it. Cover with the aubergine and half the fontina. Place the Parmesan frittata on top of them, soft side up, and cover with the strips of pepper and the remaining fontina. Finally, place the second parsley frittata on top, soft side down. Bake for 10 minutes. Serve hot or cold.

OMELETTES

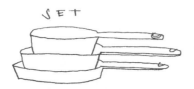

PEPPER OMELETTE

OMELETTE AI PEPERONI

Serves 4

40 g/1¹/₂ oz butter

2 tablespoons olive oil

1 onion, chopped

2 small green peppers, halved, seeded and cut into thick strips

3 tomatoes, peeled, seeded and diced

50 g/2 oz cooked ham, diced

4 eggs • salt and pepper

Melt the butter with the oil in a frying pan, add the onion and cook over a low heat, stirring occasionally, for 10 minutes until lightly browned. Add the peppers and cook for 5 minutes, then add the tomatoes and ham. Cook over a medium heat for about 30 minutes. Lightly beat the eggs with salt and pepper, pour the mixture over the vegetables and increase the heat so that the omelette cooks quickly. This omelette should be soft and puffy; do not turn or fold, but slide whole on to a warm serving dish.

CRAB MEAT OMELETTE

OMELETTE ALLA POLPA DI GRANCHIO

Serves 4

50 g/2 oz butter

50 g/2 oz crab meat, drained if canned, and finely chopped

2 tablespoons double cream

6 eggs

salt and pepper

Melt half the butter in a small saucepan, add the crab meat and cook, stirring occasionally, for 5 minutes. Season with salt and plenty of pepper, add the cream and cook over a low heat for 15 minutes without letting the butter turn brown. Lightly beat the eggs with a pinch of salt, a pinch of pepper and 1 tablespoon cold water. Melt the remaining butter in a frying pan, pour in the eggs and cook until set on the underside and soft on top. Spoon the crab meat on to one half of the omelette, fold over and serve.

PROVENÇAL OMELETTE

OMELETTE ALLA PROVENZALE

Serves 4

2 tablespoons olive oil

2 tomatoes, peeled, seeded and diced

1 garlic clove, finely chopped

100 g/3¹/₂ oz Italian sausages, skinned and crumbled

4 eggs

25 g/1 oz butter

1 fresh flat-leaf parsley sprig, chopped

salt and pepper

Heat the oil in a frying pan, add the tomatoes and garlic and cook, stirring occasionally, until the tomatoes are softened. Meanwhile, pour 1 tablespoon water into another pan, add the sausages and cook over a low heat for 15 minutes, then add to the pan of tomatoes. Lightly beat the eggs with 1 tablespoon water and season lightly with salt and pepper. Melt the butter in a frying pan, pour in the eggs and cook until set on the underside and soft on top. Place the sausage mixture on one half of the omelette, sprinkle with the parsley and fold over. Slide on to a warm serving dish.

OMELETTE WITH SNAILS

Prepare the snails (see page 730). Heat the oil in a pan over a medium heat, add the garlic and cook for a few minutes until browned, then remove and discard. Stir in the parsley, add the snails and season with salt and pepper. Stir gently and sprinkle with the vinegar. Lightly beat the eggs with 1 tablespoon water and a pinch of salt and pepper. Melt the butter in a frying pan, pour in the eggs and cook until set on the underside and soft on top. Spoon the snails, together with their hot cooking juices, on to one half of the omelette, fold over and slide on to a warm serving dish.

OMELETTE ALLE LUMACHE

Serves 4

12 fresh, canned or frozen snails

1 tablespoon olive oil

1 garlic clove

1 tablespoon finely chopped fresh flat-leaf parsley

1 tablespoon white wine vinegar

6 eggs

25 g/1 oz butter

salt and pepper

COURGETTE OMELETTE

Put the courgettes into a non-stick frying pan and place over a high heat for a few minutes so that they dry a little. Sprinkle with salt and pepper and set aside in warm place. Lightly beat the eggs with salt and pepper and stir in the parsley. Heat the oil and butter in a frying pan, pour in the eggs and cook until set on the underside and soft on top. Spoon the courgettes on to one half of the omelette, fold over and leave on the heat for 1 minute. Slide the omelette on to a warm serving dish.

OMELETTE ALLE ZUCCHINE

Serves 4

3 courgettes, cut into thin batons

6 eggs

1 fresh flat-leaf parsley sprig, finely chopped

1 tablespoon olive oil

25 g/1 oz butter

salt and pepper

RADICCHIO OMELETTE

Melt half the butter in a saucepan, add the radicchio and cook over a low heat until softened. Season with salt and pepper to taste, add the cream and flour and cook over a low heat for about 20 minutes. Remove the pan from the heat and set aside in a warm place. Lightly beat the eggs with 1 tablespoon water, salt and pepper. Melt the remaining butter in a frying pan, pour in the eggs and cook until set on the underside and soft on top. Spoon the radicchio on to one half of the omelette and fold over. Slide on to a warm serving dish.

OMELETTE AL RADICCHIO

Serves 4

50 g/2 oz butter

2 radicchio, cut into thin strips

100 ml/3^1/$_2$ fl oz double cream

pinch of plain flour

4 eggs

salt and pepper

AROMATIC OMELETTE

Lightly beat the eggs with salt, pepper and 1 tablespoon water. Mix the herbs together and stir into the eggs. Heat the butter and oil in a frying pan over a medium heat, pour in the egg mixture and cook until set on the underside and soft on top. Slide the omelette on to a warm serving dish. Serve.

OMELETTE AROMATICA

Serves 4

6 eggs • 1 fresh flat-leaf parsley sprig, chopped

6 fresh basil leaves, chopped • 2 fresh mint leaves, chopped • 1 tablespoon chopped fresh chives

25 g/1 oz butter • 1 tablespoon olive oil

salt and pepper

CURRIED MUSHROOM OMELETTE

Melt half the butter in a frying pan, add the onion and cook over a low heat, stirring occasionally, for 5 minutes. Add the mushrooms and cook for a few minutes, then season with salt and pepper to taste and add the flour, curry powder and cream. Mix well and cook over a medium heat for about 30 minutes. Lightly beat the eggs with 1 tablespoon water, a pinch of salt and a pinch of pepper. Melt the remaining butter in a frying pan, pour in the eggs and cook until set on the underside and soft on top. Sprinkle the mushrooms on one half of the omelette, fold over and slide on to a warm serving dish. If you like, this omelette may be served with Curry Sauce (see page 54) or very runny Béchamel Sauce (see page 50).

OMELETTE CON FUNGHI AL CURRY

Serves 4

50 g/2 oz butter

1 onion, thinly sliced

150 g/5 oz button mushrooms, sliced

pinch of plain flour

pinch of curry powder

100 ml/3¹/₂ fl oz double cream

6 eggs

salt and pepper

FOUR CHEESE OMELETTE

Preheat the oven to 160°C/325°F/Gas Mark 3. This is a variation on the classic omelette since milk and different types of cheese are added. Lightly beat the eggs with a little salt and add the Parmesan, milk, salt and pepper. Melt the butter in a small frying pan, pour in the eggs and cook until set on the underside and soft on top. Sprinkle the diced cheeses on one half of the omelette and fold over. Gently slide on to an ovenproof serving dish. Turn off the oven and cook until the cheeses have melted.

OMELETTE VARIANTE
AI QUATTRO FORMAGGI

Serves 4

6 eggs

3 tablespoons Parmesan cheese, freshly grated

100 ml/3¹/₂ fl oz milk

25 g/1 oz butter

25 g/1 oz Emmenthal cheese, finely diced

40 g/1¹/₂ oz mozzarella cheese, finely diced

25 g/1 oz fontina cheese, finely diced

salt and pepper

RICOTTA OMELETTE

Mix together the flour and 1 tablespoon water in a bowl. Add the eggs and beat lightly, then season lightly with salt and pepper. Melt the butter in a frying pan, pour in a ladleful of the mixture and cook until set on the underside and soft on top. Continue making omelettes in the same way until the egg mixture is used. Mix together the ricotta and ham in a bowl, season with salt and, if necessary, dilute with one or more tablespoons warm water. Sprinkle a little of the Parmesan over each omelette, spoon on the ricotta mixture and fold. Arrange on a warm serving dish and serve with tomato sauce.

OMELETTE VARIANTE ALLA RICOTTA

Serves 4

2 tablespoons plain flour

4 eggs

25 g/1 oz butter

200 g/7 oz ricotta cheese

50 g/2 oz cooked ham, chopped

25 g/1 oz Parmesan cheese, freshly grated

salt and pepper

Tomato Sauce (see page 57), to serve

LEMON

OIL BOTTLE

FINE IMITATION OF CUT GLASS

MMM...

VEGETABLES →

VEGETABLES

Italy was once called the garden of Europe. Perhaps this description included the idea of the vegetable garden, given the abundance of salad vegetables, greens, potatoes, peppers, artichokes, mushrooms, tubers, roots, cereals and all the other components that make up the enormous and prolific Italian vegetable family. At one time vegetables were considered a side dish and pulses a poor food – or even food for the poor. Today things are very different. Recently, raw and cooked vegetables have also become first courses, and pulses have been promoted with honour to the highest ranks owing to their high nutritional value. We were once used to eating asparagus and peas in the spring, and cabbages and turnips in the winter. Today, with greenhouse cultivation and international trade, we can find every kind of vegetable all year round. Of course, the taste is not what it was: out-of-season vegetables are often either tasteless or so strongly flavoured that they almost seem chemically synthesized. Nevertheless, whether they are fresh, frozen, canned or bottled, there is no lack of vegetables and they can be prepared in hundreds of ways. Vegetables form an essential part of the healthy diet and nutritionists recommend that we should eat at least five portions a day. While vegetables in general are available fresh and may be eaten either raw or cooked, pulses may be fresh or dried and must always be cooked. Specific cooking times and advice regarding the various recipes are given in the introductions to individual vegetables.

OIL   VINEGAR

STEAMING

This is the best way to cook all vegetables as they absorb less water, retain more taste and, above all, lose fewer nutrients.

BOILING

To retain the bright colour of vegetables when cooking in boiling salted water, do not cover the pan. When boiling some vegetables, it is advisable to add a 'blanching mixture', consisting of 1 tablespoon plain flour, 1 tablespoon olive oil and the juice of 1 lemon. This prevents vegetables such as artichokes, cardoons and scorzonera from turning black and helps retain the bright green colour of French beans, peas, etc.

PARBOILING

This means boiling vegetables for a few minutes before cooking them by the method described in the recipe or before adding them to another dish.

MARINATING

This means leaving ingredients in an aromatic liquid to soak up its flavour. Put 100 ml/3^1/$_2$ fl oz oil, 600 ml/1 pint water, a bouquet garni, consisting of parsley, thyme, a bay leaf and a celery stalk, 1 teaspoon black peppercorns and 1 teaspoon coriander in a saucepan and bring to the boil. Lower the heat and simmer for 20 minutes, then pour the hot or warm marinade (according to the instructions in the recipe) into a bowl, immerse the raw, grilled or fried vegetables (asparagus tips, artichoke hearts, courgettes or aubergines) and leave to marinate for at least 20 minutes or more according to the recipe. Remember to leave vegetables to marinate in a cool place, but not in the refrigerator unless otherwise specified.

FRYING

This is a method of cooking some vegetables – which may be dredged with flour or coated in breadcrumbs or batter – in hot oil. To make a batter, sift 65 g/2^1/$_2$ oz plain flour into a bowl, break an egg into the middle and add 1 tablespoon olive oil and a pinch of salt. Mix thoroughly with a wooden spoon to prevent lumps from forming, then stir in 100 ml/3^1/$_2$ fl oz milk. Cover and leave to stand for at least 30 minutes, then fold in a stiffly whisked egg white. Dip only a few pieces of vegetable in the batter at a time, then fry in hot oil.

ASPARAGUS

Asparagus is elegant, expensive and delicate. Its short season runs from April to June, but it has its best fragrance, firmness and flavour in May. Thanks to imports, however, it can now be found almost all year round. The most widely available types are white, green and violet and there are different varieties for each colour. Choice is a matter of personal taste. Asparagus must be bought fresh. The tips should be straight and green, the stems should be shiny, plump and smooth without blemishes and the bunches should be compact. Asparagus has few calories, but has diuretic properties and is rich in vitamins A and C. Its particularly delicate taste goes well with eggs, prawns, chicken, rabbit and veal. Cream of asparagus soup makes a delicious and sophisticated start to any formal meal. So, too, does a savoury pie containing asparagus among its ingredients. Lastly, on the subject of etiquette, although modern manners allow us to use our fingers to dip asparagus stems in egg yolk or sauces, at least among family and friends, it is more correct to use a fork.

QUANTITIES AND COOKING TIMES

QUANTITIES

Allow 250–300 g/9–11 oz per serving.

BOILING

Cut off the toughest part of the stems and peel the rest if necessary. Rinse and cut the stems to more or less the same length, then tie together in bunches. Place the bunches upright in salted, boiling water with the tips protruding above the waterline and cook for 15–20 minutes.

STEAMING

This is the best cooking method. Bring about 5 cm/ 2 inches salted water to the boil, add the asparagus and steam for about 10 minutes. Just 3 minutes is long enough for blanching.

ASPARAGUS AU GRATIN

Cook the asparagus in salted, boiling water for 15 minutes, then drain and pat dry. Meanwhile, preheat the oven to 180°C/350°F/Gas Mark 4. Grease an ovenproof dish with butter. Arrange half the asparagus spears with the tips pointing inwards in the prepared dish and dot with half the butter. Sprinkle with the Parmesan, cover with the Emmenthal and pour the béchamel sauce over the cheeses while it is still hot. Place the remaining asparagus on top and dot with the remaining butter. Bake for 15 minutes.

ASPARAGI AL GRATIN

Serves 4

1 kg/2¼ lb asparagus, spears trimmed

50 g/2 oz butter, plus extra for greasing

40 g/1½ oz Parmesan cheese, freshly grated

65 g/2½ oz Emmenthal cheese, thinly sliced

300 ml/½ pint Béchamel Sauce (see page 50)

salt

ASPARAGUS BELLA ELENA

Cook the asparagus in salted, boiling water for 15 minutes. Meanwhile, tear the bread into pieces, place in a bowl, pour in the milk and leave to soak. Drain the asparagus, cut off the tips and set aside. Place the stems in a food processor and process to a purée, then scrape into a bowl. Squeeze out the bread and stir it into the purée with the Parmesan. Separate one of the eggs and stir the yolk, together with two whole eggs, into the purée. Season with salt and pepper and stir in the asparagus tips. If the mixture is too runny, add some of the breadcrumbs or more Parmesan. Shape the mixture into balls. Spread out the flour in a shallow dish, beat the remaining egg in another shallow dish and spread out the breadcrumbs in a third. Dip the asparagus balls first in the flour, then in the beaten egg and, finally, in the breadcrumbs. Heat the oil in a pan, add the asparagus balls, in batches if necessary, and fry until golden brown all over. Remove with a fish slice and drain on kitchen paper. Serve immediately.

ASPARAGI ALLA BELLA ELENA

Serves 4

1 kg/2¼ lb asparagus, spears trimmed

50 g/2 oz bread, crusts removed

100 ml/3½ fl oz milk

40 g/1½ oz Parmesan cheese, freshly grated

4 eggs

120 g/4 oz dried breadcrumbs

4 tablespoons plain flour

vegetable oil, for deep-frying

salt and pepper

ASPARAGUS WITH PANCETTA

Cook the asparagus in salted, boiling water for 15 minutes. Meanwhile, preheat the oven to 180°C/350°F/Gas Mark 4. Grease an ovenproof dish with butter. Drain the asparagus and place it in the prepared dish. Stir the Parmesan and egg yolks into the pan of béchamel sauce and season with salt and pepper. Set over a medium heat, stir in the wine and cook until it has evaporated. Remove the pan from the heat and stir in the nutmeg. Place the pancetta slices on top of the asparagus and spoon the sauce over them. Dot with the butter and bake for 15 minutes until golden and bubbling.

ASPARAGI ALLA PANCETTA

Serves 4

1 kg/2¼ lb asparagus, spears trimmed

25 g/1 oz butter, plus extra for greasing

40 g/1½ oz Parmesan cheese, freshly grated

2 egg yolks

300 ml/½ pint Béchamel Sauce (see page 50)

100 ml/3½ fl oz dry white wine

pinch of freshly grated nutmeg

200 g/7 oz pancetta, sliced

salt and pepper

PARMESAN ASPARAGUS

ASPARAGI ALLA PARMIGIANA

Serves 4

1 kg/2¼ lb asparagus, spears trimmed
80 g/3 oz Parmesan cheese, freshly grated
25 g/1 oz butter
salt

Cook the asparagus in salted, boiling water for 15 minutes. Drain and pat dry gently. Arrange on a warm serving dish with the tips pointing inwards. Sprinkle with the Parmesan. Melt the butter, season with a little salt and pour on to the asparagus. Serve immediately.

ASPARAGUS WITH ORANGE

ASPARAGI ALL'ARANCIA

Serves 4

1 kg/2¼ lb asparagus, spears trimmed
1 quantity Mayonnaise (see page 65)
1 teaspoon Dijon mustard
juice of ½ orange, strained
salt

Cook the asparagus in salted, boiling water for 15 minutes. Drain and arrange on a serving dish. Mix together the mayonnaise, mustard and orange juice in a bowl. Spoon a few tablespoons of the dressing on to the asparagus tips and serve the remainder separately in a sauce boat. A few thin slices of orange rind may be added to the sauce if you like.

VALLE D'AOSTA ASPARAGUS

ASPARAGI ALLA VALDOSTANA

Serves 4

butter, for greasing
1 kg/2¼ lb asparagus, spears trimmed
2 cooked ham slices, cut into strips
120 g/4 oz fontina cheese, sliced
2 eggs
2 tablespoons Parmesan cheese, freshly grated
salt and pepper

Preheat the oven to 180°C/350°F/Gas Mark 4. Grease an ovenproof dish with butter. Cook the asparagus in salted, boiling water for 10 minutes. Drain and place in the prepared dish and top with the ham and fontina. Beat the eggs with the Parmesan, season with salt and pepper and pour over the asparagus. Bake for 15–20 minutes until the Parmesan has melted and the eggs have set.

ASPARAGUS MIMOSA

ASPARAGI MIMOSA

Serves 4

1 kg/2¼ lb asparagus, spears trimmed
4 eggs, hard-boiled
1 fresh flat-leaf parsley sprig
1 tablespoon olive oil
salt

Cook the asparagus in salted, boiling water for 15 minutes. Drain and arrange on a serving dish. Shell the eggs and chop with the parsley, place in a bowl and stir in the oil. Sprinkle the egg mixture over the asparagus and serve.

ASPARAGUS MOUSSE

MOUSSE DI ASPARAGI

Serves 4

500 g/1 lb 2 oz asparagus, spears trimmed

3 eggs

2 tablespoons olive oil

250 g/9 oz cream cheese

juice of ¹/₂ lemon, strained

1 egg white

salt and pepper

Cook the asparagus in salted, boiling water for 10 minutes. Drain, set aside the most attractive tips for the garnish and process the remainder to a purée in a blender. Scrape the purée into a saucepan and heat gently to dry slightly. Meanwhile, hard-boil the eggs, refresh under cold water and shell. Halve the eggs, scoop out the yolks and crumble them into a bowl. Season with salt and pepper and stir in the olive oil. Beat in the cheese, then stir in the asparagus purée and lemon juice. Stiffly whisk the raw egg white in a grease-free bowl and gently fold it into the asparagus mixture. Season with salt and pepper to taste. Spoon the mixture into individual dishes and garnish with the reserved asparagus tips. Serve the mousse cold.

ASPARAGUS ROLLS

ROTOLINI DI ASPARAGI

Serves 4

1 kg/2¹/₄ lb asparagus, spears trimmed

50 g/2 oz butter, plus extra for greasing

100 g/3¹/₂ oz prosciutto, sliced

65 g/2¹/₂ oz Parmesan cheese, freshly grated

salt

Cook the asparagus in salted, boiling water for 15 minutes. Meanwhile, preheat the oven to 180°C/350°F/Gas Mark 4. Grease an ovenproof dish with butter. Drain the asparagus and gently pat dry. Spread out the prosciutto on the work surface, lay two large or three small asparagus spears on each slice, roll up and fasten each roulade with a cocktail stick. Place the rolls in the prepared dish, sprinkle with the Parmesan, dot with the butter and bake for 10 minutes. Serve immediately.

BEETROOT

Raging and bloodthirsty are two strong adjectives that have been used to describe beetroots because of their brilliant red colouring, which derives from a pigment in their leaves and roots. Quite the opposite is true – their flesh is soft and sweet. In fact, the sugar beet belongs to the same family. As well as the widely available red beetroot, there are also cream-coloured and lighter-pink beets, all rich in potassium, calcium, sodium and phosphorus, among other nutrients. It has been suggested that eating them regularly helps to prevent cancer. In Italy, beetroots are usually sold ready cooked, but they are also available raw. When choosing them, make sure they are firm and without blemishes or traces of mould. They may be eaten raw – peeled, grated and dressed with oil and lemon juice or sprinkled on salads. When boiled, they go well with soured cream, mayonnaise and mustard. When included in Russian salad, they must be added at the last minute, otherwise they dye the other vegetables red. Lastly, do not worry if the flesh has concentric paler circles, as this is characteristic of a variety that came on the market a few years ago. On the other hand, pay attention to the juice, but only because it stains.

QUANTITIES
AND COOKING TIMES

QUANTITIES
Allow about 150 g/5 oz per serving.

BAKING
Wrap each beetroot separately in foil and bake in a preheated oven, 200°C/ 400°F/Gas Mark 6, for about 2 hours.

STEAMING
Arrange whole or halved beetroots in a steamer and steam until tender. Test by piercing with the prongs of a fork.

BARBABIETOLE ALLA BESCIAMELLA

Serves 4

25g/1 oz butter, melted, plus extra for greasing

600 g/1 lb 5 oz cooked beetroot, peeled
and cut into 5-mm/¼-inch thick slices

300 ml/½ pint Béchamel Sauce (see page 50)

salt

BEETROOT WITH BÉCHAMEL SAUCE

Preheat the oven to 180°C/350°F/Gas Mark 4. Grease an ovenproof dish with butter. Arrange the beetroot slices in the prepared dish and drizzle with the melted butter. Season with salt, spoon the béchamel sauce over the beetroot and bake until hot and bubbling. Serve immediately.

BARBABIETOLE ALLE ACCIUGHE

Serves 4

4 salted anchovies, heads removed,
cleaned and filleted (see page 596),
soaked in cold water for 10 minutes and drained

600 g/1 lb 5 oz cooked beetroot, peeled and diced

1 fresh flat-leaf parsley sprig, chopped

½ garlic clove, chopped

4 tablespoons olive oil

1 tablespoon red wine vinegar

BEETROOT WITH ANCHOVIES

Chop the anchovy fillets. Put the beetroot in a salad bowl and sprinkle with the parsley and garlic. Heat the oil and vinegar in a saucepan, add the anchovies and cook, mashing with a wooden spoon until they have almost disintegrated. Spoon the mixture over the beetroot, mix well and leave to stand for 15 minutes before serving.

BARBABIETOLE ALLE CIPOLLE

Serves 4

25 g/1 oz butter

1 onion, chopped

600 g/1 lb 5 oz cooked beetroot, peeled
and cut into thin batons

salt

BEETROOT WITH ONIONS

Heat the butter in a saucepan, add the onion and cook over a low heat, stirring occasionally, for 5 minutes until softened. Add the beetroot, mix well and season with salt. Cook for a few minutes more, then remove the pan from the heat and serve.

BUCK'S HORN PLANTAIN

This almost uniquely Italian vegetable consists of small sprigs of short, fairly thin green shoots, held together by a root which should be trimmed off before cooking. It is not a common vegetable in other countries and is difficult to obtain outside Italy. It is boiled after being washed several times in cold water. Barba di frate – 'friar's beard' – has a mouth-puckeringly sharp taste, rather like samphire, when served sprinkled with olive oil, salt and lemon juice, which makes it an excellent side dish for boiled meat.

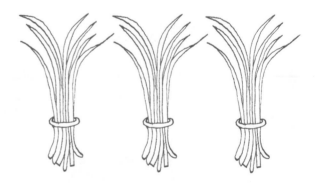

QUANTITIES AND COOKING TIMES

QUANTITIES
Allow about 150 g/5 oz per serving.

BOILING
Cook in salted, boiling water for 10 minutes.

BUCK'S HORN PLANTAIN WITH PANCETTA

Cook the buck's horn plantain or samphire in lightly salted, boiling water for 10 minutes (don't add salt if using samphire). Drain and pat dry with kitchen paper. Heat the butter in a frying pan, add the onion, pancetta and parsley and cook over a low heat, stirring occasionally, for 10 minutes until very lightly browned. Add the buck's horn plantain or samphire, increase the heat to medium and cook for 15 minutes, gradually adding the cream. Season with salt and pepper to taste and serve immediately.

BARBA DI FRATE ALLA PANCETTA

Serves 4

2 bunches of buck's horn plantain or samphire

50 g/2 oz butter

1 onion, finely chopped

100 g/3$^{1}/_{2}$ oz pancetta, finely chopped

1 fresh flat-leaf parsley sprig, chopped

4–5 tablespoons double cream

salt and pepper

TASTY BUCK'S HORN PLANTAIN

Cook the buck's horn plantain or samphire in lightly salted, boiling water for 10 minutes (don't add salt if using samphire), then drain. Meanwhile, chop the anchovy fillets. Heat the oil in a pan, add the garlic and cook over a low heat for a few minutes until golden brown. Remove and discard the garlic and add the anchovies and buck's horn plantain or samphire to the pan. Season with salt and pepper to taste and cook for about 15 minutes more.

BARBA DI FRATE SAPORITA

Serves 4

2 bunches of buck's horn plantain or samphire

4 salted anchovies, heads removed, cleaned and filleted (see page 596), soaked in cold water for 10 minutes and drained

4 tablespoons olive oil

1 garlic clove

salt and pepper

SWISS CHARD

Beetroot tops and true Swiss chard are both widely used in Italy. The former offer a tasty alternative to spinach and are prepared in the same way. Swiss chard, on the other hand, has a sweeter taste and is larger. It is rich in calcium, provides plenty of dietary fibre and has a fair amount of vitamin A. When buying Swiss chard look for brightly coloured, almost shiny green leaves, and fleshy white stalks that snap rather than bend.

QUANTITIES AND COOKING TIMES

QUANTITIES

Allow about 150 g/5 oz per serving.

BOILING

Cook 1 kg/2¹/₄ lb Swiss chard in a large pan of lightly salted, boiling water for 10–15 minutes. If the stalks are very thick, separate them from the leaves, chop into 5–6-cm/2–2¹/₂-inch pieces, remove the fibrous parts and boil for 15–20 minutes. The stalks are usually then sautéed in butter and sprinkled with grated Parmesan. The boiled leaves are served dressed with olive oil, lemon and salt.

SWISS CHARD WITH PARMESAN

Separate the chard leaves from the stalks using kitchen scissors or a sharp knife. (Set the leaves aside to make soup.) Cut the stalks into 5-cm/2-inch pieces and cook in lightly salted, boiling water for 10–15 minutes until tender, then drain well. Heat the milk to just below simmering point, then remove the pan from the heat. Melt the butter in a pan, add the chard stalks and cook over a high heat, stirring frequently, for a few minutes. Pour in the hot milk, lower the heat to medium and simmer for 5–10 minutes. Sprinkle with the Parmesan, season with salt and pepper, and transfer to a warm serving dish.

BIETOLE AL PARMIGIANO

Serves 4

1 kg/2¼ lb Swiss chard

100 ml/3½ fl oz milk

40 g/1½ oz butter

100 g/3½ oz Parmesan cheese, freshly grated

salt and pepper

SWISS CHARD WITH ANCHOVIES

Separate the chard leaves from the stalks using kitchen scissors or a sharp knife. (Set the leaves aside to make soup.) Cut the stalks into 5-cm/2-inch pieces and cook in lightly salted, boiling water for 10–15 minutes until tender, then drain well. Meanwhile, chop the anchovies. Heat the olive oil in a frying pan, add the garlic and anchovies and cook over a low heat, mashing with a wooden spoon until the anchovies have almost disintegrated. Add the chard stalks, increase the heat to high and cook, stirring frequently, for a few minutes. Lower the heat to medium, season with salt and pepper and drizzle with olive oil. Mix well and cook for a further 10 minutes. Remove the pan from the heat, sprinkle with the Parmesan and serve.

BIETOLE CON LE ACCIUGHE

Serves 4

1 kg/2¼ lb Swiss chard

4 salted anchovies, heads removed, cleaned and filleted (see page 596), soaked in cold water for 10 minutes and drained

2 tablespoons olive oil, plus extra for drizzling

1 garlic clove, chopped

40 g/1½ oz Parmesan cheese, freshly grated

salt and pepper

SWISS CHARD AU GRATIN

Preheat the oven to 180°C/350°F/Gas Mark 4. Grease an ovenproof dish with butter. Separate the chard leaves from the stalks using kitchen scissors or a sharp knife. (Set the leaves aside to make soup.) Cook the stalks in lightly salted, boiling water for 10–15 minutes until tender, then drain well and cut into small pieces. Make alternate layers of Swiss chard stalks, béchamel sauce and Parmesan, ending with a layer of Parmesan. Bake for about 15 minutes.

BIETOLE GRATINATE

Serves 4

butter, for greasing

1 kg/2¼ lb Swiss chard

1 quantity Béchamel Sauce (see page 50)

80 g/3 oz Parmesan cheese, freshly grated

salt

BROCCOLI

There are two different types of broccoli: calabrese with a single, compact, dense head similar to a cauliflower but coloured; and sprouting broccoli with lots of small florets, commonly known in Italy as broccoletti. Both are rich in calcium, iron and vitamin C. Fresh broccoli should have bright green leaves and compact firm florets. Prepare it by removing the toughest leaves, cutting the stalks into 6-cm/2¹/₂-inch long pieces and removing the most fibrous parts. Cut the florets in half lengthways.

QUANTITIES AND COOKING TIMES

QUANTITIES

Allow about 250 g/9 oz per serving.

BOILING

Cook in salted, boiling water for 8–10 minutes.

BROCCOLI WITH BOTTARGA

BROCCOLETTI ALLA BOTTARGA

Serves 4

1 kg/2¹/₄ lb sprouting broccoli, cut into florets

100 g/3¹/₂ oz bottarga (dried grey mullet or tuna roe)

juice of 1 lemon, strained

1 garlic clove, chopped

1 fresh flat-leaf parsley sprig, chopped

8 fresh basil leaves, torn

3 tomatoes peeled, seeded and chopped

olive oil, for drizzling

salt and pepper

thin lemon slices, to garnish

Cook the broccoli in salted, boiling water for 15 minutes, then drain and leave to cool slightly. Pound the bottarga in a mortar with the lemon juice, then gradually pound in the garlic, parsley, basil and tomatoes. Season with salt and pepper and, when the sauce is fairly thick, drizzle with olive oil. Mix well and pour into a sauce boat. Place the broccoli on a warm serving dish, garnish with the lemon slices and serve with the sauce.

BROCCOLI WITH ANCHOVIES

Serves 4

1 kg/2¼ lb sprouting broccoli, cut into florets

80 g/3 oz salted anchovies, heads removed, cleaned

and filleted (see page 596), soaked

in cold water for 10 minutes and drained

3 tablespoons olive oil • 2 garlic cloves

¹/₂ fresh chilli, seeded and chopped • salt

Cook the broccoli in salted, boiling water for 15 minutes. Meanwhile, chop the anchovy fillets. Heat the olive oil in a pan, add the garlic and chilli and cook for 1 minute. Add the anchovies and cook, mashing with a wooden spoon until they have almost completely disintegrated. Remove and discard the garlic. Drain the broccoli, add to the pan, mix well and cook over a low heat, stirring occasionally, for about 15 minutes. Serve immediately.

SPICY BROCCOLI WITH YOGURT

Serves 4

1 kg/2¼ lb sprouting broccoli, cut into florets

1 fresh flat-leaf parsley sprig, chopped

1 garlic clove, chopped

1 fresh chilli, seeded and chopped

100 ml/3¹/₂ fl oz low-fat natural yogurt

pinch of mustard powder • salt

Parboil the broccoli in salted, boiling water for a few minutes until just tender, then drain well and place in a large salad bowl. Mix together the parsley, garlic, chilli and yogurt in a bowl, stir in the mustard and season with salt to taste. Pour the sauce over the broccoli and serve warm.

BRAISED BROCCOLI

Serves 4

2 tablespoons olive oil

2 garlic cloves, chopped

1 kg/2¼ lb sprouting broccoli, cut into florets

salt and pepper

Heat the olive oil in a saucepan, add the garlic and broccoli and cook over a low heat, stirring occasionally, for 5 minutes. Season with salt and pepper, add 150 ml/¹/₄ pint water, cover and simmer gently for about 15 minutes until tender. Remove the lid, increase the heat to medium and reduce any excess cooking liquid before serving.

FABULOUS BROCCOLI

Serves 4

1 kg/2¼ lb calabrese broccoli, cut into florets

2 tablespoons olive oil

2 garlic cloves,

2 leeks, trimmed and sliced

1 tablespoon plain flour

100 ml/3¹/₂ fl oz double cream

200 ml/7 fl oz dry white wine

25 g/1 oz butter, plus extra for greasing

6 tablespoons Parmesan cheese, freshly grated

salt and pepper

Parboil the broccoli in salted, boiling water for a few minutes, then drain and leave to cool slightly. Meanwhile, heat the olive oil in a large saucepan, add the garlic and leeks and cook over a low heat, stirring occasionally, until softened. Remove and discard the garlic. Stir in the flour and cook, stirring constantly, for 2 minutes until lightly browned. Stir in the cream, season with salt and pepper and mix well. Add the broccoli, pour in the wine and simmer for about 10 minutes. Meanwhile, preheat the oven to 200°C/400°F/Gas Mark 6. Grease an ovenproof dish with butter. Remove the pan from the heat and transfer the mixture to the prepared dish. Sprinkle with the Parmesan, dot with the butter and bake until golden and bubbling.

GLOBE ARTICHOKES

Globe artichokes may be tapered with thorns or round without thorns. The former are Ligurian and have shiny, firm leaves, and the latter, which are cultivated in central southern Italy, are ball-shaped and known as mammole in Lazio. The artichoke season runs from September to May. Artichokes are rich in iron, phosphorus and calcium, and their considerable fibre content makes them useful for the digestive system. They have another beneficial effect on the digestion because they contain cynarine, a substance which stimulates bile production. Fresh artichokes can be recognized by the compactness and firmness of their leaves, which should break with a sharp crack when folded. They should be prepared by shortening the stem to 4–5 cm/1'/2–2 inches and removing the fibrous part. Discard the toughest and darkest leaves until the lightest and most tender are revealed. Remove the tips by cutting the artichoke a little above its maximum circumference, and scoop out the choke from inside using a teaspoon. As you prepare the artickokes, open out the central leaves and put them in a bowl of water mixed with lemon juice to prevent them going black.

QUANTITIES

If they are served whole and alone, allow 2 per person.

COOKING

Cook in salted, boiling water for 30 minutes if whole and 15 minutes if cut into wedges.

QUANTITIES
AND COOKING TIMES

ARTICHOKES IN GARLIC AND OLIVE OIL

CARCIOFI AGLIO E OLIO

Serves 4

8 globe artichokes, trimmed
1–2 garlic cloves
olive oil (see method)
salt and pepper

Place the artichokes in a fairly tall saucepan. Add the garlic and pour in a mixture of two parts olive oil and one part water until the artichokes are two-thirds covered. Season with salt and pepper to taste, cover and cook over a low heat for about 30 minutes.

ARTICHOKES WITH CHEESE

CARCIOFI AL FORMAGGIO

Serves 4

25 g/1 oz butter, plus extra for greasing
8 globe artichokes, trimmed
250 ml/8 fl oz milk
3 tablespoons rice flour
pinch of saffron threads
pinch of curry powder
150 g/5 oz Emmenthal cheese, freshly grated
1 egg, separated
1 fresh thyme sprig, leaves only
salt

Preheat the oven to 180°C/350°F/Gas Mark 4. Grease an ovenproof dish with butter. Parboil the artichokes for about 10 minutes, then drain well. Meanwhile, heat the milk to just below boiling point, then remove from the heat. Melt the butter in another saucepan, stir in the flour and cook over a low heat, stirring constantly, for 2–3 minutes until lightly browned. Gradually stir in the hot milk, then season with salt and add the saffron and curry powder. Remove the pan from the heat and stir in the Emmenthal, egg yolk and thyme. Stiffly whisk the egg white in a grease-free bowl and fold into the sauce. Fill the artichokes with the sauce and arrange in the prepared dish. Bake for 30 minutes, then remove them from the oven and leave to stand for about 5 minutes before serving.

JEWISH ARTICHOKES

CARCIOFI ALLA GIUDIA

Serves 4

8 Roman artichokes
olive oil (see method)
salt

Young, whole, round (if possible), thornless artichokes are required for this dish. Break off the stems, discard the tough outer leaves and cut the tips off the others with a small sharp knife while holding the artichokes horizontally on a chopping board. They will be wide at the base and rounded at the top. Fill a wide, high-sided, cast-iron frying pan with enough olive oil to half-cover the artichokes and heat gently. Open out the leaves slightly and place the artichokes upright in the oil. Cook over a medium heat for 10–12 minutes, then increase the heat and turn the artichokes upside down. Cook for a further 10 minutes until they have turned golden brown and are crisp at the tips. Remove with a fish slice, taking care not to break them. Serve immediately, sprinkled with a pinch of salt.

Serves 4

juice of ¹/₂ lemon, strained

8 globe artichokes, trimmed

120 g/4 oz butter

150 ml/¹/₄ pint dry white wine

1 shallot, finely chopped

200 g/7 oz chicken livers, thawed if frozen, trimmed

50 ml/2 fl oz brandy

50 ml/2 fl oz Madeira

100 ml/3¹/₂ fl oz double cream

salt and pepper

fresh chervil sprigs, to garnish

ARTICHOKES WITH CHICKEN LIVER MOUSSE

Half-fill a bowl with water and add the lemon juice. Open out the central leaves of the artichokes slightly and place in the acidulated water. Drain and parboil in salted, boiling water for 10–15 minutes, then drain and leave upside down on a tea towel to dry. Preheat the oven to 180°C/350°F/Gas Mark 4. Place the artichokes upright in an ovenproof dish, dot with 15 g/¹/₂ oz of the butter and sprinkle with the wine. Season with salt and pepper, cover with foil and bake for 30 minutes. Meanwhile, melt 25 g/1 oz of the remaining butter in a frying pan, add the shallot and cook over a low heat, stirring occasionally, for 10 minutes until lightly browned. Add the chicken livers, increase the heat to high and cook, stirring frequently, for a few minutes until lightly browned all over. Remove the shallot and livers from the pan and set aside. Pour the brandy into the pan and cook, scraping up the residue from the base, until it has evaporated. Pour in the Madeira and season with salt and pepper. Put the chicken liver mixture in a food processor and process to a purée, then pass through a sieve into a bowl. Stand the bowl in a pan full of ice and beat in the remaining butter and the juices from the frying pan. Finally, beat in the cream. Fill the artichokes with the mousse using a tablespoon or icing bag. Arrange the artichokes on a serving dish and garnish with the chervil.

Serves 4

juice of ¹/₂ lemon, strained

8 globe artichokes, trimmed and cut into wedges

3–4 tablespoons olive oil

2 garlic cloves

1 tablespoon capers, drained and rinsed

100 g/3 ¹/₂ oz green olives, stoned and chopped

1 tablespoon fresh flat-leaaf parsley, chopped

1 lemon, cut into wedges

salt and pepper

ARTICHOKES NAPOLETANA

Half-fill a bowl with water, stir in the lemon juice, add the artichokes and leave to soak for 10 minutes, then drain and pat dry. Heat the olive oil in a pan, add the garlic and cook for a few minutes until golden brown, then remove and discard. Add the artichoke wedges to the pan and cook over a high heat for 5 minutes, then add the capers and olives. Season with salt and pepper to taste and add 150 ml/¹/₄ pint warm water. Mix well, cover and simmer for about 30 minutes until tender. Remove the lid and boil off any excess liquid. Transfer the artichokes to a warm serving dish, sprinkle with the parsley and garnish with the lemon wedges.

PROVENÇAL ARTICHOKES

Half-fill a bowl with water, stir in the lemon juice, add the artichokes and leave to soak for 10 minutes. Heat the olive oil in a frying pan, add the spring onions and pancetta and cook over a low heat, stirring occasionally, for about 8 minutes until lightly browned. Drain the artichokes, add to the pan, increase the heat to high and cook for 5 minutes. Add the basil and thyme, sprinkle in the wine and cook until it has evaporated. Lower the heat, pour in the stock, cover and simmer for 15 minutes. Add the tomatoes, re-cover the pan and cook for a further 5 minutes. Remove the lid, season with salt and pepper and boil off the excess liquid before serving.

CARCIOFI ALLA PROVENZALE

Serves 4

juice of ¹/₂ lemon, strained
4 violet globe artichokes, trimmed and cut into wedges
3 tablespoons olive oil
3 spring onions, chopped
65 g/2¹/₂ oz pancetta, diced
1 fresh basil sprig, chopped
1 fresh thyme sprig, chopped
100 ml/3¹/₂ fl oz dry white wine
5 tablespoons Vegetable Stock (see page 209)
3 tomatoes, peeled and sliced
salt and pepper

ROMAN ARTICHOKES

Half-fill a bowl with water and stir in the lemon juice. Trim the artichokes, reserving the stems, and place in the acidulated water. Remove the tough strings from the stems and chop them with the garlic and parsley, then season with salt and pepper. Drain the artichokes well and fill with the mixture. Place in a saucepan or flameproof casserole, pour in 350 ml/12 fl oz water, drizzle with olive oil, cover and cook over a medium-low heat for 1 hour. Serve warm, garnished with the mint leaves.

CARCIOFI ALLA ROMANA

Serves 4

juice of ¹/₂ lemon, strained
8 globe artichokes
2 garlic cloves
1 fresh flat-leaf parsley sprig
olive oil, for drizzling
salt and pepper
fresh mint leaves, to garnish

SARDINIAN ARTICHOKES

Half-fill a bowl with water, stir in the lemon juice, add the artichokes and leave to soak. Heat the olive oil in a saucepan, add the onion and garlic and cook over a low heat, stirring occasionally, for 10 minutes until lightly browned. Drain the artichokes and add to the pan with the potatoes, season with salt, pour in the stock and simmer for 30 minutes. Sprinkle with the parsley and serve.

CARCIOFI ALLA SARDA

Serves 4

juice of ¹/₂ lemon, strained
4 globe artichokes, trimmed and sliced
3 tablespoons olive oil
1 onion, chopped
1 garlic clove, chopped
500 g/1 lb 2 oz potatoes, diced
150 ml/¹/₄ pint Vegetable Stock (see page 209)
1 fresh flat-leaf parsley sprig, chopped
salt

CARCIOFI AL PECORINO

Serves 4

juice of ¹/₂ lemon, strained

8 globe artichokes, trimmed and cut into wedges

3 tablespoons olive oil

2 garlic cloves

1 fresh flat-leaf parsley sprig, chopped

100 g/3¹/₂ oz pecorino cheese, shaved

65 g/2¹/₂ oz breadcrumbs

salt

ARTICHOKES WITH PECORINO

Half-fill a bowl with water, stir in the lemon juice, add the artichokes and leave to soak for 10 minutes. Heat the olive oil in a saucepan, add the garlic and cook over a low heat for 2 minutes, then remove and discard. Drain the artichokes and add to the pan, season with salt, cover and cook over a low heat for 30 minutes. If necessary, add a little hot water. Arrange the artichokes on a warm serving dish and sprinkle with the parsley, pecorino and breadcrumbs. Mix well and serve.

CARCIOFI AL TONNO

Serves 4

3 tablespoons olive oil, plus extra for brushing

4 large globe artichokes, trimmed

juice of 1 lemon, strained

2 eggs

2 tablespoons single cream

1 fresh flat-leaf parsley sprig, chopped

25 g/1 oz Parmesan cheese, freshly grated

250 g/9 oz canned tuna in oil, drained and flaked

salt

ARTICHOKES WITH TUNA

Preheat the oven to 180 °C/350°F/Gas Mark 4. Brush an ovenproof dish with olive oil. Sprinkle the artichokes with the lemon juice to prevent discoloration and cook in salted boiling water for 10–15 minutes. Drain, open out the central leaves slightly and place in the prepared dish. Season with salt, drizzle with the olive oil, cover with foil and bake for 10 minutes. Meanwhile, beat the eggs with the cream in a bowl and add the parsley, Parmesan and tuna. Fill the artichokes with the tuna mixture. Cover with foil return to the oven and bake for a further 30 minutes.

CARCIOFI FRITTI

Serves 4

juice of 3 lemons, strained

6 globe artichokes

pinch of dried oregano

1 garlic clove, chopped

vegetable oil, for deep-frying

5 tablespoons plain flour

1 egg

salt and pepper

To garnish

lemon slices

fresh flat-leaf parsley sprigs

FRIED ARTICHOKES

Bring a large saucepan of water to the boil and add a pinch of salt and the juice of one of the lemons. Trim the artichokes, reserving the stems. Cut the heads into wedges and chop the stems, then add to the pan of boiling water and simmer for 4–5 minutes. Drain and tip into a bowl. Season with salt and pepper, sprinkle with the oregano and garlic and pour in the remaining lemon juice. Mix well, cover and leave to marinate for 2 hours. Heat the oil in a pan. Place the flour in a shallow dish and beat the egg with a pinch of salt and pepper in another shallow dish. Drain the artichokes, then dip them first in the flour and then in the egg. Fry them, in batches, until golden brown and crisp. Remove with a fish slice and drain on kitchen paper. Arrange on a warm serving dish and garnish with lemon slices and sprigs of parsley.

ARTICHOKES IN HOLLANDAISE SAUCE

Bring a large saucepan of water to the boil, add a pinch of salt and the lemon juice, then add the artichokes and cook for about 20 minutes. Drain, leave to cool slightly, then cut into wedges. Place on a serving dish and pour the hollandaise sauce over them. Garnish with a few sprigs of parsley and serve.

CARCIOFI IN SALSA OLANDESE

Serves 4

juice of 1 lemon, strained

8 globe artichokes, trimmed

1 quantity Hollandaise Sauce (see page 59)

salt

fresh flat-leaf parsley sprigs, to garnish

ARTICHOKES STUFFED WITH SAUSAGE

Preheat the oven to 180°C/350°F/Gas Mark 4. Half-fill a bowl with water and stir in the lemon juice. Trim the artichokes, reserving the stems, open out the leaves slightly and place in the acidulated water. Remove the tough stringy parts from the stems and chop. Heat the olive oil in a frying pan, add the pancetta, garlic, parsley, onion and artichoke stems and cook over a low heat, stirring occasionally, for 5 minutes. Add the sausages, season with salt and pepper and cook over a very low heat for 5 minutes. Drain the artichokes, place upright in an ovenproof dish and stuff with the sausage mixture. Drizzle with olive oil and pour in the wine. Cover with foil and bake for about 1 hour, basting occasionally.

CARCIOFI RIPIENI ALLA SALSICCIA

Serves 4

juice of 2 lemons, strained

8 globe artichokes

3 tablespoons olive oil, plus extra for drizzling

100 g/3¹/₂ oz pancetta, diced

2 garlic cloves, chopped

1 fresh flat-leaf parsley sprig, chopped

1 onion, chopped

100 g/3¹/₂ oz Italian sausages, skinned and crumbled

200 ml/7 fl oz dry white wine

salt and pepper

ARTICHOKES STUFFED WITH PEPPERS

Bring a pan of water to the boil, add half the lemon juice and a pinch of salt, then add the artichokes and cook for 30 minutes. Drain and leave to cool. Mix together the peppers and parsley in a bowl and drizzle with olive oil. Stuff the artichokes with the pepper mixture, arrange on a dish, sprinkle with the remaining lemon juice and season with salt and pepper. Garnish with mushrooms in oil if you like.

CARCIOFI RIPIENI CON PEPERONI

Serves 4

juice of 2 lemons, strained

8 globe artichokes, trimmed

2 yellow peppers, halved seeded and chopped

1 fresh flat-leaf parsley sprig, chopped

olive oil, for drizzling

salt and pepper

mushrooms in oil, to garnish (optional)

ARTICHOKE CLAFOUTIS

CLAFOUTIS DI CARCIOFI

Serves 4

butter, for greasing

juice of ¹/₂ lemon, strained

6 globe artichokes, trimmed • 80 g/3 oz plain flour

3 eggs • 400 ml/14 fl oz milk

1 fresh flat-leaf parsley sprig, chopped

salt and pepper

Preheat the oven to 180°C/350°F/Gas Mark 4. Grease an ovenproof dish with butter. Half-fill a bowl with water, stir in the lemon juice, add the artichokes and leave to soak for 10 minutes. Sift the flour into a bowl, stir in the eggs, one at a time, and gradually whisk in the milk. Season with salt and pepper and stir in the parsley. Drain the artichokes, pat dry and place in the prepared dish. Pour the batter over them and bake for 30 minutes.

ARTICHOKE MOULDS

SFORMATINI DI CARCIOFI

Serves 4

juice of 1 lemon, strained

5 globe artichokes, trimmed and thinly sliced

25 g/1 oz butter, plus extra for greasing

¹/₂ onion, chopped

3 tablespoons Parmesan cheese, freshly grated

200 g/7 oz double cream

pinch of freshly grated nutmeg

3 eggs, lightly beaten

salt and pepper

Half-fill a bowl with water, stir in the lemon juice, add the artichokes and leave to soak for 15 minutes. Preheat the oven to 180°C/350°F/Gas Mark 4. Grease four moulds with butter. Melt the butter in a frying pan, add the onion and cook over a low heat, stirring occasionally, for 5 minutes. Drain the artichokes, add to the pan, season with salt and pepper and mix well. Cover and cook for 15 minutes. Add the Parmesan, cream and nutmeg to the eggs and season with salt, then add the artichokes. Pour into the prepared moulds and place them in a roasting tin. Add hot water to come about halfway up the sides and bake for about 30 minutes until set. Turn out and serve.

SAVOURY ARTICHOKE AND POTATO PIE

TORTA RUSTICA DI CARCIOFI E PATATE

Serves 4

butter, for greasing • juice of ¹/₂ lemon, strained

4–5 globe artichokes, trimmed and cut into thin wedges

500 g/1 lb 2 oz potatoes, thinly sliced

4 tablespoons pecorino cheese, freshly grated

1 fresh thyme sprig, leaves only

5 tablespoons olive oil • salt and pepper

Preheat the oven to 180°C/350°F/Gas Mark 4. Grease an ovenproof dish with butter. Half-fill a bowl with water, stir in the lemon juice, add the artichokes and leave to soak for 10 minutes. Place the potato slices in the prepared dish, then drain the artichokes and place them on top of the potatoes. Sprinkle with the pecorino and thyme, season with salt and pepper and drizzle with the olive oil. Bake for 1 hour. Serve warm.

ARTICHOKE PIE

TORTINO AI CARCIOFI

Serves 4

40 g/1¹/₂ oz butter, plus extra for greasing

5 globe artichokes, trimmed and cut into wedges

50 ml/2 fl oz milk

6 eggs

salt

Preheat the oven to 200°C/400°F/Gas Mark 6. Grease an ovenproof dish with butter. Melt the butter in a frying pan, add the artichokes and cook over a medium heat for a few minutes. Meanwhile, heat the milk in a saucepan. Season the artichokes with salt, pour in the warm milk and simmer for 10 minutes, then transfer the mixture to the prepared dish. Beat the eggs with a pinch of salt and pour them over the artichokes. Bake for about 30 minutes until the eggs have set.

CARDOONS

A member of the globe artichoke family, cardoons are tiresome to clean and take a long time to cook. Even in Italy, they are not as popular as they deserve to be, as is confirmed by the patient gourmets who wait every year for the return of winter, the only season when these delicate vegetables can be found. They are an extremely rare treat outside southern Europe. Cardoons are not so much appreciated for their nutritional value (they are rich in cellulose) as for their delicate, unexpected flavour, which is reminiscent of globe artichokes. Good-quality cardoons have white stems with pale green tints. If they are not fresh, they have a slightly reddish colour. To prepare them, remove the tough, outer stalks until you reach the tender inner ones. Remove the tips, cut the stalks into 5–7.5-cm/2–3-inch long pieces and place in water acidulated with lemon juice to prevent them from turning black. The woody covering of the heart should also be removed before chopping. One of the most mouth-watering dishes that includes raw cardoons in its ingredients is the tasty Piedmontese bagna cauda (see page 424).

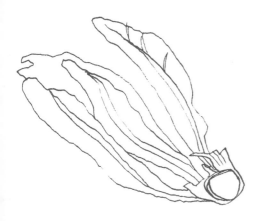

QUANTITIES
Allow about 150 g/5 oz per serving.

BOILING
Almost all recipes involve pre-cooking cardoons in salted, boiling water for over 2 hours.

QUANTITIES AND COOKING TIMES

CARDOONS WITH CHEESE

CARDI AI FORMAGGI

Serves 4

juice of 1 lemon, strained

1 tablespoon olive oil

1 teaspoon plain flour

1 kg/2¼ lb cardoons

25 g/1 oz butter, melted, plus extra for greasing

50 g/2 oz Parmesan cheese, freshly grated

65 g/2½ oz fontina cheese, shaved

65 g/2½ oz Emmenthal cheese, thinly sliced

100 ml/3½ fl oz milk

200 ml/7 fl oz double cream

salt

Pour plenty of water into a saucepan and add the lemon juice, olive oil, flour and a pinch of salt. Trim the cardoons, cut the inner stalks into 5-cm/2-inch lengths and remove all strings, immediately dropping the stalk pieces into the pan. Bring to the boil, then lower the heat and simmer for about 45 minutes. Meanwhile, preheat the oven to 180°C/350°F/Gas Mark 4. Grease an ovenproof dish with butter. Drain the cardoons well, tip into the prepared dish, pour the melted butter on top and sprinkle with the Parmesan and fontina. Cover with a layer of the Emmenthal. Mix together the milk and cream in a jug and carefully pour the mixture over the top. Bake for about 30 minutes and serve.

CARDOONS WITH BAGNA CAUDA

CARDI ALLA BAGNA CAUDA

Serves 4

juice of 1 lemon, strained

1 kg/2¼ lb cardoons

150 g/5 oz butter, plus extra for greasing

2 garlic cloves

10 canned anchovy fillets in oil, drained

40 g/1½ oz Parmesan cheese, freshly grated

salt

Pour 2 litres/3½ pints water into a large saucepan and add the lemon juice and a pinch of salt. Trim the cardoons, cut the inner stalks into 7.5-cm/3-inch lengths and remove all strings, immediately dropping the stalk pieces into the pan. Bring to the boil, lower the heat and simmer for 30 minutes. Meanwhile, preheat the oven to 180°C/350°F/Gas Mark 4. Grease an ovenproof dish with butter. Drain the cardoons well, then tip into the prepared dish. Melt the butter in a small saucepan, add the garlic and cook for a few minutes until lightly browned, then remove and discard. Add the anchovies to the pan and cook, mashing with a fork until smooth. Pour the anchovy-flavoured butter over the cardoons and sprinkle with the Parmesan. Bake for 30 minutes and serve.

DELICATE CARDOONS

CARDI DELICATI

Serves 4

juice of 1 lemon, strained

1 kg/2¼ lb cardoons

25 g/1 oz butter, plus extra for greasing

100 ml/3½ fl oz milk

100 ml/3½ fl oz double cream

40 g/1½ oz Parmesan cheese, freshly grated

salt

Pour plenty of water into a saucepan and add the lemon juice and a pinch of salt. Trim the cardoons, cut the inner stalks into 5-cm/2-inch lengths and remove all strings, immediately dropping the stalk pieces into the pan. Bring to the boil, lower the heat and simmer for about 45 minutes. Meanwhile, grease a flameproof dish with butter. Drain the cardoons well and tip into the prepared dish. Dot the surface with butter, pour in the milk and cook over a low heat for about 30 minutes. Add the cream and cook for about 10 minutes until thickened. Remove from the heat, transfer to a warm serving dish, sprinkle with the Parmesan and serve.

FRIED CARDOONS

Pour plenty of water into a saucepan and add the lemon juice and a pinch of salt. Trim the cardoons, cut the inner stalks into 5-cm/2-inch lengths and remove all strings, immediately dropping the stalk pieces into the pan. Bring to the boil, then lower the heat and simmer for about 1 hour. Drain well and spread out on a tea towel to cool. Meanwhile, sift the flour into a bowl, break the egg in to the middle of the flour and add the olive oil and a pinch of salt. Mix thoroughly with a wooden spoon, then stir in 100 ml/3½ fl oz water. Cover and leave to stand for at least 30 minutes. Stiffly whisk the egg white in a grease-free bowl and fold it into the batter. Heat the oil for deep-frying. Dip the cardoons, a few at a time, into the batter and fry in the hot oil. Remove with a fish slice, drain on kitchen paper and serve as soon as all the cardoons are cooked.

CARDI FRITTI

Serves 4

juice of 1 lemon, strained

1 kg/2¼ lb cardoons

65 g/2½ oz plain flour

1 egg

1 tablespoon olive oil

1 egg white

vegetable oil, for deep-frying

salt

CARDOON SALAD

Pour plenty of water into a saucepan and add the lemon juice and a pinch of salt. Trim the cardoon, cut the inner stalk into 5-cm/2-inch lengths and remove all strings, immediately dropping the stalk pieces into the pan. Bring to the boil, then lower the heat and simmer for about 45 minutes. Meanwhile, hard-boil the eggs, refresh in cold water, shell and chop finely. Drain the cardoon well, dry on a tea towel and put in a salad bowl. Sprinkle with the chopped eggs and the parsley. Heat the olive oil in a small saucepan, add the breadcrumbs and cook, stirring constantly, for a few minutes until golden brown and crisp. Spoon the breadcrumbs over the cardoon mixture, leave to stand for a few minutes, then serve.

CARDI IN INSALATA

Serves 4

juice of 1 lemon, strained

1 cardoon

4 eggs

1 fresh flat-leaf parsley sprig, chopped

3 tablespoons olive oil

1 tablespoon breadcrumbs

salt

SAVARIN DI CARDI AI FUNGHI

Serves 4

juice of 1 lemon, strained

400 g/14 oz cardoons

50 g/2 oz butter, plus extra for greasing

2–3 tablespoons breadcrumbs

1 quantity Béchamel Sauce (see page 50)

40 g/1½ oz Parmesan cheese, freshly grated

1 egg, lightly beaten

1 small shallot, chopped

100 g/3½ oz mushrooms, chopped

4 fresh mint leaves, chopped

1 fresh flat-leaf parsley sprig, chopped

salt and pepper

CARDOON MOULDS WITH MUSHROOMS

Pour plenty of water into a saucepan and add the lemon juice and a pinch of salt. Trim the cardoons, cut the inner stalks into 5-cm/2-inch lengths and remove all strings, immediately dropping the stalk pieces into the pan. Bring to the boil, then lower the heat and simmer for about 45 minutes, then drain well. Meanwhile, preheat the oven to 180°C/350°F/Gas Mark 4. Grease four savarin moulds with butter, sprinkle with the breadcrumbs, turning to coat, and tip out any excess. Melt 20 g/¾ oz of the butter in a frying pan, add the cardoons and cook over a low heat, stirring occasionally, for 5 minutes. Tip into a food processor and process to a purée. Stir the cardoon purée, béchamel sauce and Parmesan into the beaten egg. Spoon the mixture into the prepared moulds. Place on a baking sheet and bake for about 30 minutes. Meanwhile, melt the remaining butter in a frying pan, add the shallot and cook over a low heat, stirring occasionally, for 5 minutes. Add the mushrooms, mint and parsley, season with salt and pepper and cook for about 10 minutes until all the liquid has evaporated and the mushrooms are very tender. Remove the moulds from the oven and turn out in a circle on a warm serving dish. Spoon the hot mushroom sauce over them and serve.

CARROTS

Carrots grow throughout Italy and are harvested in every season of the year. They are eaten in all sorts of ways, both cooked and raw. They are rich in carotene, which the human metabolism transforms into vitamin A, and in sugars, phosphorus, calcium, sodium, potassium, magnesium and other nutrients. They are good for the skin and essential for good eyesight in poor light conditions. When fresh they have a bright orange colour and fragrant flesh. To prevent them from discoloration, carrots should be washed before they are peeled. It is best not to buy ready-prepared carrots since pro-vitamin A oxidizes quickly. One of the simplest and most refreshing raw carrot recipes is a salad consisting of thinly sliced, shaved or grated carrots dressed with olive oil, lemon juice and salt. One of the tastiest side dishes is glazed carrots, which makes even the simplest roast seem more spectacular. It is worth bearing in mind that, according to Angelo Paracucchi, one of the most famous Italian chefs of the last 20 years, carrots only cook in butter – and we agree with him.

QUANTITIES

Allow 2 per person.

BOILING

Wash and scrape young carrots under cold running water, then cook in salted, boiling water for just a few minutes. Peel older carrots with a knife and remove the woody part in the centre. Whole carrots cook in about 40 minutes but if cut into thin strips, they cook in 15 minutes. In both cases, slightly salt the water and add a pinch of sugar which brings out their flavour.

QUANTITIES
AND COOKING TIMES

CARROTS WITH ROQUEFORT

CAROTE AL ROQUEFORT

Serves 4

80 g/3 oz Roquefort cheese, diced

150 ml/¼ pint milk

1 fresh flat-leaf parsley sprig, chopped

600 g/1 lb 5 oz carrots, cut into thin batons

Put the Roquefort into a saucepan and melt over a low heat. Add the milk and stir to make a smooth, runny sauce. Remove the pan from the heat. Do not let the mixture boil. Stir in the parsley, pour the sauce over the carrots and serve.

CARROTS WITH ROSEMARY

CAROTE AL ROSMARINO

Serves 4

750 g/1 lb 10 oz carrots, cut into thin batons

300 ml/½ pint Vegetable Stock (see page 209)

olive oil, for drizzling

1 teaspoon chopped fresh rosemary

salt and pepper

Put the carrots and stock into a saucepan, bring to the boil over a medium heat, then cover and simmer for about 15 minutes. Remove the lid and season with salt and pepper to taste. If the mixture is too runny, continue cooking until it has reduced to the desired consistency. Drizzle with olive oil, sprinkle with the rosemary and cook for a few minutes more. Transfer to a warm serving dish.

SURPRISE RAW CARROTS

CAROTE CRUDE AL RAFANO

Serves 4

½ horseradish root

juice of 1 lemon, strained

1 tablespoon white wine vinegar

1 teaspoon Dijon mustard

pinch of sugar

2 tablespoons olive oil

400 g/14 oz carrots, cut into thin batons

salt and pepper

Scrape the horseradish root under cold running water, chop finely and place in a bowl. Stir in the lemon juice, vinegar, mustard, sugar and olive oil and season with salt and pepper. Beat the mixture until thoroughly combined and creamy. Put the carrots in a salad bowl, spoon the horseradish sauce over them and mix well. Leave to stand for 10 minutes, then serve.

GLAZED CARROTS WITH LEMON

CAROTE GLASSATE AL LIMONE

Serves 4

800 g/1¾ lb carrots, fairly thickly sliced

40 g/1½ oz butter

2 baby onions, chopped

strained juice and grated rind of ½ lemon

1 teaspoon sesame seeds

1 fresh flat-leaf parsley sprig, chopped

olive oil, for drizzling

salt and pepper

Put the carrots in a bowl, add water to cover and a pinch of salt and leave to soak for 15 minutes, then drain. Melt the butter in a saucepan, add the onions and cook over a low heat, stirring occasionally, for 5 minutes. Add the lemon juice and rind and cook for a few minutes more, then add the carrots, season with salt and pepper and cook for a further 10 minutes. Meanwhile, dry-fry the sesame seeds in a heavy-based frying pan for a few seconds until they give off their aroma. Remove the pan of carrots from the heat, transfer to a warm serving dish and sprinkle with the parsley and sesame seeds. Drizzle with olive oil and serve.

CAROTE IN SALSA FRANCESE

Serves 4

2 tablespoons olive oil, plus extra for brushing
600 g/1 lb 5 oz baby carrots
1 egg
1 tablespoon Dijon mustard
1 tablespoon white wine vinegar
salt

CARROTS IN FRENCH SAUCE

Brush a flameproof dish with olive oil. Steam the carrots for about 15 minutes, then drain and pat dry with a tea towel. Cut them into thin batons and place in the prepared dish. Beat the egg with the oil, mustard, vinegar and a pinch of salt in a bowl, then pour the mixture over the carrots and cook over a low heat, stirring constantly, for 10 minutes.

CAROTE MARINATE

Serves 4

500 g/1 lb 2 oz small carrots
2 garlic cloves
1 fresh flat-leaf parsley sprig, chopped
pinch of dried oregano
6 tablespoons olive oil
2 tablespoons white wine vinegar
1 small chilli, seeded and chopped
salt

MARINATED CARROTS

Cook the carrots in salted, boiling water for about 15 minutes until just tender, then drain and dry thoroughly with a tea towel. Cut into thin batons and place in a salad bowl. Rub the garlic around the sides of another bowl, add the parsley, oregano, olive oil, vinegar and chilli, season with salt and mix well. Pour the dressing over the carrots, mix well and leave to marinate in a cool place for 24 hours before serving.

CAROTINE NOVELLE ALLA PANNA

Serves 4

800 g/1³/₄ lb baby carrots
25 g/1 oz butter
150 ml/¹/₄ pint double cream
pinch of freshly grated nutmeg
1 fresh flat-leaf parsley sprig, chopped
4 fresh chives, chopped
salt and pepper

BABY CARROTS IN CREAM

Cook the carrots in salted, boiling water for about 10 minutes, then drain and leave to cool. When cold, cut into thin batons. Melt the butter in a pan over a low heat, pour in the cream, add the nutmeg and season with salt and pepper. Bring to the boil, add the carrots and cook for a few minutes, then add the parsley and chives. Mix well and cook for a further 2 minutes. Serve while hot.

SURPRISE CARROT CROQUETTES

Cook the carrots in salted, boiling water for 15 minutes, then drain and chop. Melt the butter in a saucepan, add the carrots and cook over a low heat, stirring occasionally, for 15 minutes. Remove the pan from the heat and pass the carrots through a sieve into a bowl. Stir in one of the eggs, and the Parmesan and nutmeg, season to taste with salt and pepper and add as many breadcrumbs as needed to obtain a fairly firm mixture. Shape the mixture into small croquettes, make a well in the centre of each and fill with a cube of Emmenthal, then reshape. Spread out the flour in a shallow dish, beat the remaining egg with a pinch of salt in another shallow dish and spread out the remaining breadcrumbs in the third. Heat the oil for deep-frying. Dip the croquettes first in the flour, then in the egg and, finally, in the breadcrumbs. Cook in the hot oil until golden brown on all sides. Arrange the croquettes in a pyramid on a warm serving dish and serve while hot.

CROCCHETTE A SORPRESA

Serves 4

1 kg/2¹/₄ lb carrots

40 g/1¹/₂ oz butter

2 eggs

5 tablespoons Parmesan cheese, freshly grated

pinch of freshly grated nutmeg

120–150 g/4–5 oz breadcrumbs

65 g/2¹/₂ oz Emmenthal cheese, diced

4 tablespoons plain flour

vegetable oil, for deep-frying

salt and pepper

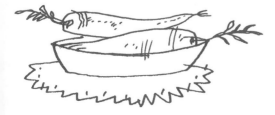

CHESTNUTS

Chestnuts are included in this chapter because, when they are not used for desserts, they make an excellent savoury side dish. It is important to distinguish between the cultivated variety and wild chestnuts. The former has a paler skin with longitudinal streaks and contains a higher percentage of fat. Both types require quite long cooking times. All chestnuts go well with pork, turkey and goose.

QUANTITIES AND COOKING TIMES

QUANTITIES
Allow about 100 g/3½ oz unpeeled chestnuts per serving.

BOILING
Cut a slit in the flat side of each nut and boil for 45 minutes.

ROASTING
Cut a slit in the flat side of each nut and roast in a preheated oven, 180°C/350°F/Gas Mark 4, for 30 minutes.

ROAST CHESTNUTS

CASTAGNE ARROSTITE

Serves 4

600 g/1 lb 5 oz chestnuts

Preheat the oven to 180°C/350°F/Gas Mark 4. Cut a slit in each chestnut with a small sharp knife. Spread out on a baking sheet and roast for 30 minutes. Alternatively, if you have a chestnut roasting pan, put the chestnuts in it and cook over a high heat. Chestnuts are ready when the shells are begin to char. Remove the shells and inner skins and use either whole or mashed chestnuts to stuff roast chicken or turkey. They may also be mashed with melted butter, a bay leaf and a pinch of salt and pepper and served as a side dish.

ROAST CHESTNUTS WITH BRUSSELS SPROUTS

Cut a slit in each chestnut with a small knife, place in a saucepan and add water to cover. Bring to the boil and cook for 20 minutes. Melt half the butter in a saucepan, add the shallot and cook over a low heat, stirring occasionally, for 5 minutes. Add the Brussels sprouts, lemon juice and 120 ml/4 fl oz water. Season with salt and pepper and add the nutmeg. Cover and simmer for about 10 minutes. Meanwhile, preheat the oven to 200°C/400°F/Gas Mark 6. Grease an ovenproof dish with butter. Drain the chestnuts, refresh under cold running water, peel off the shells and inner skins and place in the prepared dish. Add the Brussels sprouts with a little of their cooking liquid. Sprinkle the fontina on top and dot with the remaining butter. Bake for 30 minutes.

CASTAGNE CON CAVOLINI AL FORNO

Serves 4

500 g/1 lb 2 oz chestnuts

50 g/2 oz butter, plus extra for greasing

1 shallot, chopped

500 g/1 lb 2 oz Brussels sprouts, trimmed

juice of 1 lemon, strained

pinch of freshly grated nutmeg

100 g/3^1/$_2$ oz fontina cheese, freshly grated

salt and pepper

BRAISED CHESTNUTS

Preheat the oven to 220°C/425°F/Gas Mark 7. Melt the butter in a small, flameproof casserole, add the chestnuts and cook for 1 minute, then pour in the stock. Add the bay leaf, thyme and celery. Cover and cook in the oven for 45 minutes, gently shaking the casserole occasionally. Do not stir as this can break up the nuts. Season with salt and pepper and serve as a side dish with guinea fowl, duck, goose or roast meat.

MARRONI BRASATI

Serves 4

20 g/^{3}/$_4$ oz butter

600 g/1 lb 5 oz cultivated chestnuts, peeled

1.5 litres/2^1/$_2$ pints Meat Stock (see page 208)

1 bay leaf

1 fresh thyme sprig

1 celery stalk

salt and pepper

CHESTNUT PURÉE

Put the chestnuts in a saucepan, add water to cover, bring to the boil and cook for 45 minutes. Drain and pass through a food mill into a clean pan. Set the pan over a low heat and stir in the cream, followed by the butter, and season with salt and pepper, still stirring constantly. Remove the pan from the heat and serve the hot purée as a side dish with meat, game or wild boar.

PURÉ DI MARRONI

Serves 4

500 g/1 lb 2 oz cultivated chestnuts, peeled

5 tablespoons double cream

25g/1 oz butter

salt and pepper

DANDELION

Catalogna (Italian dandelion) is cultivated in southern Italy and is only ever eaten cooked. It does not have great nutritional properties, but thanks to the bitter substances it contains it acts as a diuretic, and is thought to help purify the system, protect the liver and act as a tonic. The large heads have fairly long leaves. Remove the toughest ones, leaving the hearts intact. Cut off the tops of the remaining leaves and cut into strips. Catalogna has a light but pleasant, slightly bitter taste and is served hot dressed with salt, oil and vinegar or lemon juice. The hearts of the smaller varieties, known as puntarelle, are served raw with pinzimonio (olive oil, salt and pepper). Their leaves are cut into strips and left to soak in cold water where they curl up attractively. They are eaten in salads dressed with oil, vinegar and chopped anchovy. You can substitute other types of dandelion. Pick them while they are young from an unpolluted source well away from the roadside.

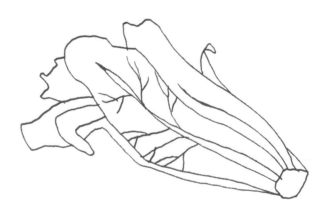

QUANTITIES AND COOKING TIMES

QUANTITIES
Allow about 200 g/7 oz per serving.

BOILING
Cook in salted, boiling water for 15–20 minutes. If the recipe specifies parboiling, a few minutes is sufficient.

DANDELION WITH GARLIC AND OLIVE OIL

Cook the dandelion strips in salted, boiling water for 15 minutes, then drain and squeeze out as much liquid as possible. Heat the oil in a frying pan, add the garlic and cook over a low heat, stirring frequently, until golden brown, then remove and discard. Add the dandelion strips to the pan, increase the heat and cook, stirring occasionally, for about 15 minutes. Season to taste with chilli powder, if you like, or pepper.

CATALOGNA ALL'AGLIO E OLIO

Serves 4

1 kg/2¼ lb Italian dandelion, leaves cut into strips

olive oil

4 garlic cloves

pinch of chilli powder (optional)

salt and pepper

DANDELION WITH PARMESAN

Cook the dandelion strips in salted, boiling water for 15 minutes, then drain, squeeze out as much liquid as possible, chop coarsely and place on a warm serving dish. Melt the butter in a small saucepan and, when it turns slightly golden in colour, pour it over the dandelions. Sprinkle with the Parmesan and serve.

CATALOGNA AL PARMIGIANO

Serves 4

750 g/1 lb 10 oz Italian dandelion, leaves cut into strips

65 g/2½ oz butter

4 tablespoons Parmesan cheese, freshly grated

salt

DANDELION TIP SALAD

Chop the anchovy fillets. Put the dandelion tips in a salad bowl. Mix together the garlic, anchovies, lemon juice and olive oil in another bowl and season lightly with salt. Pour the dressing over the salad, leave to stand for 15 minutes, then serve.

PUNTE DI CATALOGNA IN INSALATA

Serves 4

3 salted anchovies, heads removed,

cleaned and filleted (see page 596),

soaked in cold water for 10 minutes and drained

500 g/1 lb 2 oz Italian dandelion tips

½ garlic clove, chopped

juice of 1 lemon, strained

6 tablespoons olive oil

salt

CAULIFLOWER

In Fano, in the region called Marche in eastern central Italy, they produce some of the very best cauliflowers. There are both all-year-round varieties and ones that are in season only from October to May. For several years now, cross-breeding techniques have produced a 'ball' cauliflower, consisting of white florets, each one shorter than the next, encircled by leaves, which transforms the vegetable into a sort of bouquet. Cauliflower is an attractive vegetable, has a delicate flavour and contains calcium, potassium and magnesium salts, but it's not always easy to digest. When buying cauliflower, make sure it is firm, with white compact florets and whole leaves. To prepare, remove the toughest, outer leaves, cut the stem at the base and either split the florets away from the stem one at a time or leave the cauliflower whole, according to the recipe. To reduce its slightly unpleasant smell during cooking, soak a slice of bread, without crusts, in vinegar and add it to the pan. Boiled cauliflower may be served hot or cold dressed with oil, vinegar or lemon juice, salt and pepper. It may also be sautéed in a frying pan with oil and garlic.

QUANTITIES AND COOKING TIMES

QUANTITIES
Allow about 200 g/7 oz per serving.

BOILING
To cook whole, place upright in a saucepan and add sufficient cold water to come about three-quarters of the way up the sides. Add a pinch of salt, bring to the boil and simmer for 30–40 minutes. If divided into florets, cook for 15–20 minutes.

CAULIFLOWER WITH GORGONZOLA

Put the cauliflower in a saucepan, add cold water, the flour and a pinch of salt and bring to the boil, then simmer for 15 minutes until just tender. Drain and place on a warm serving dish. Meanwhile, put the Gorgonzola, milk, butter and brandy in a blender, add salt and pepper to taste and process until smooth and combined. Spoon the mixture over the cauliflower, sprinkle with the cumin and serve immediately.

CAVOLFIORE AL GORGONZOLA

Serves 4

1-kg/2¼-lb cauliflower, cut into florets

1 teaspoon plain flour

250 g/9 oz strong Gorgonzola cheese, diced

100 ml/3½ fl oz milk

25 g/1 oz butter, softened

2 tablespoons brandy

1 tablespoon cumin seeds

salt and pepper

CAULIFLOWER WITH HAM

Put the cauliflower in a saucepan, add cold water and a pinch of salt and bring to the boil, then simmer for 20 minutes until tender. Drain thoroughly and tip into a bowl. Preheat the oven to 180°C/350°F/Gas Mark 4. Grease an ovenproof dish with butter. Meanwhile, hard-boil the eggs, refresh in cold water, then shell and halve lengthways. Scoop out the yolks and mash in a bowl with a fork. Chop the whites, then add the yolks and whites to the cauliflower. Melt half the butter in a small saucepan, add the breadcrumbs and cook, stirring frequently, until crisp and golden. Spoon the breadcrumbs over the cauliflower, add the ham and Parmesan, season with salt and pepper to taste and mix gently. Spoon the mixture into the prepared dish, dot with the remaining butter and bake for 20 minutes.

CAVOLFIORE AL PROSCIUTTO

Serves 4

1-kg/2¼-lb cauliflower, cut into florets

25 g/1 oz butter, plus extra for greasing

2 eggs

2 tablespoons breadcrumbs

150 g/5 oz cooked ham, diced

4 tablespoons Parmesan cheese, freshly grated

salt and pepper

TWO–COLOUR CAULIFLOWER WITH PEPPER

Parboil the cauliflowers in separate pans of salted water for 5–8 minutes. Drain well and arrange in alternate coloured layers on a serving dish. Mix together the lemon juice, lemon rind, olive oil, red pepper, chilli powder, oregano and garlic in a bowl and season with salt and pepper to taste. Pour the dressing over the cauliflower and leave in a cool place for 1 hour to allow the flavours to mingle, then mix and serve.

CAVOLFIORE BICOLORE AL PEPERONE

Serves 4

1 small white cauliflower, cut into florets

1 small green cauliflower, cut into florets

juice of 1 lemon, strained

2 teaspoons finely grated lemon rind

6 tablespoons olive oil

1 red pepper preserved in brine,

drained and finely chopped

pinch of chilli powder • pinch of dried oregano

1 garlic clove, chopped

salt and pepper

CAULIFLOWER CROQUETTES

Put the cauliflower in a saucepan, add cold water and a pinch of salt and bring to the boil, then simmer for 10 minutes until just tender. Drain thoroughly. Melt the butter in a frying pan, add the cauliflower and cook over a medium heat, stirring occasionally, for 5 minutes. Remove the pan from the heat and leave to cool slightly, then pass through a food mill into a bowl. Add one of the eggs, and the Parmesan, parsley and nutmeg, mix well and season with salt and pepper. Stir in as many breadcrumbs as required to obtain a fairly firm consistency. Shape the mixture into croquettes. Beat the remaining egg with a pinch of salt in a shallow dish. Spread out the flour in another shallow dish and spread out the remaining breadcrumbs in a third. Heat the oil in a large pan. Dip the croquettes first in the flour, then in beaten egg and, finally, in breadcrumbs. Fry in the hot oil, then remove with a fish slice or fish slice and drain on kitchen paper. Place on a warm serving dish.

CROCCHETTE DI CAVOLFIORE

Serves 4

1 cauliflower, cut into florets

25 g/1 oz butter

2 eggs

40 g/1½ oz Parmesan cheese, freshly grated

1 fresh flat-leaf parsley sprig, chopped

pinch of freshly grated nutmeg

80–100 g/3–3½ oz breadcrumbs

3–4 tablespoons plain flour

vegetable oil, for deep-frying

salt and pepper

FRENCH–STYLE CAULIFLOWER

Parboil the cauliflower in salted water for a few minutes, then drain thoroughly. Beat the egg with the flour and milk in a bowl and add enough water to make a slightly runny batter. Heat plenty of oil in a pan over a high heat. Dip the florets in the batter and cook in the hot oil, a few at a time, until golden brown. Remove with a fish slice, drain on kitchen paper and place on a warm serving dish. Heat the tomato sauce in a small frying pan and add the basil. Pour the sauce into a sauce boat and serve separately with the cauliflower.

CAVOLFIORE FRITTO ALLA FRANCESE

Serves 4

1-kg/2¼-lb cauliflower, cut into florets

1 egg

100 g/3½ oz plain flour

200 ml/7 fl oz milk

vegetable oil, for deep-frying

1 quantity Tomato Sauce (see page 57)

4 fresh basil leaves, torn

salt

CAULIFLOWER SALAD

Put the cauliflower in a saucepan, add cold water and a pinch of salt and bring to the boil, then simmer for 15 minutes until just tender. Drain well, tip into a salad bowl and leave to cool. Hard-boil the eggs, refresh briefly in cold water, then shell and chop while warm. Chop the anchovy fillets. Add the anchovies, eggs, capers and olives to the salad bowl and mix gently. Mix the vinaigrette with the parsley, pour it over the salad and leave to stand for 10 minutes.

CAVOLFIORE IN INSALATA

Serves 4

1 small cauliflower • 2 eggs

4 salted anchovies, heads removed, cleaned and filleted (see page 596), soaked in cold water for 10 minutes and drained

1 tablespoon capers, drained and rinsed

10 black olives, stoned and quartered

1 quantity Vinaigrette (see page 76)

1 fresh flat-leaf parsley sprig, chopped

salt

CAVOLFIORE IN SALSA D'UOVA

Serves 4

1-kg/2¹/₄-lb cauliflower, cut into florets

50 g/2 oz butter

1¹/₂ garlic cloves, finely chopped

3 eggs

1 tablespoon plain flour

1 tablespoon white wine vinegar

salt and pepper

CAULIFLOWER
IN EGG SAUCE

Put the cauliflower in a saucepan, add cold water and a pinch of salt and bring to the boil, then simmer for 15–20 minutes until tender. Drain well, pile into a heap on a serving dish and keep warm. Melt the butter in a small pan, add the garlic and cook, stirring occasionally, for a few minutes. Meanwhile, beat the eggs with the flour in a bowl, season with salt, pepper and whisk in the vinegar. Add the mixture to the garlic and mix well, then immediately remove the pan from the heat. Continue stirring until the sauce is thick and creamy, then pour in a continuous thin stream over the cauliflower and serve.

CAVOLFIORE IN SALSA VERDE

Serves 4

800-g/1³/₄-lb cauliflower, cut into florets

1 egg

2 salted anchovies, heads removed, cleaned and filleted (see page 596), soaked in cold water for 10 minutes and drained

1 fresh flat-leaf parsley sprig

1 tablespoon capers, drained and rinsed

3 cornichons or small gherkins, drained

150 ml/¹/₄ pint olive oil

2 tablespoons white wine vinegar

salt

CAULIFLOWER
IN GREEN SAUCE

Put the cauliflower in a saucepan, add cold water and a pinch of salt and bring to the boil, then simmer for 20 minutes until tender. Meanwhile, hard-boil the egg, refresh in cold water, shell and chop coarsely. Chop the anchovy fillets. Drain the cauliflower well, pile into a heap on a serving dish and keep warm. Put the egg, parsley, anchovies, capers and cornichons or gherkins in a food processor and process to a purée. Transfer to a bowl and stir in the olive oil and vinegar until thickened and creamy. Pour the sauce over the cauliflower in a continuous thin stream and serve.

CAVOLFIORE SPEZIATO

Serves 4

1 small cauliflower

2 carrots, cut into thin strips

1 garlic clove, finely chopped

juice of 1 lemon, strained

1 tablespoon dry white wine

3 tablespoons olive oil

¹/₂ teaspoon cumin seeds

pinch of paprika

salt

SPICED CAULIFLOWER

Cut only the most tender florets from the cauliflower and put into a salad bowl. Add the carrots and garlic. Mix together the lemon juice, wine, olive oil, cumin seeds, paprika and a pinch of salt in a jug. Pour the dressing over the florets and mix well.

CABBAGE

The cabbage family is a large one and includes the Savoy cabbage, spring greens, summer and winter cabbages, Chinese cabbages, green and red cabbages, broccoli, cauliflower and Brussels sprouts. All, apart from the Chinese varieties, love the cold weather which even improves their flavour. Because they are so numerous, cabbages can be found all year round, although they are at their best in autumn and winter. The most popular varieties in Italy are the green and Savoy cabbages, both rich in vitamin A, iron and calcium. Green and Savoy cabbages should be firm, compact and without any signs of yellowing. To prepare them, remove the outer, coarse leaves and any damaged ones, cut out the core, split them in half or into segments and wash. They may then be steamed, boiled or braised. Savoy cabbage cut into strips and preserved in brine is called sauerkraut, but as it takes a long time to prepare, it is generally bought ready made.

QUANTITIES

Allow about 150 g/5 oz per serving.

BOILING

Immerse green and Savoy cabbages in salted, boiling water and remove as soon as the water comes back to the boil.

FOR ROULADES

Blanch whole leaves in boiling water, refresh in iced water and spread out on a tea towel.

QUANTITIES AND COOKING TIMES

CABBAGE WITH PAPRIKA

CAVOLO ALLA PAPRICA
Serves 4
40 g/1¹/₂ oz butter
3 onions, chopped
800-g/1³/₄-lb white cabbage, shredded
1 apple, peeled, cored and thinly sliced
300 ml/¹/₂ pint single cream
pinch of sugar
large pinch of paprika
salt
fresh marjoram leaves, to garnish

Melt the butter in a pan, add the onions and cook over a low heat, stirring occasionally, for 5 minutes until softened. Add the cabbage, increase the heat to high and cook for a few minutes. Lower the heat, pour in 150 ml/¹/₄ pint water, cover and cook for 20 minutes. Add the apple to the pan, mix well and cook for a few minutes more, then remove the pan from the heat. Put the cream into a bowl and season with salt, sugar and paprika. Transfer the cabbage mixture to a warm serving dish and spoon the cream mixture over it. Garnish with the marjoram leaves.

BAKED SAVOY CABBAGE

CAVOLO VERZA AL FORNO
Serves 6
1-kg/2¹/₄-lb Savoy cabbage, cored and cut into strips
3 tablespoons olive oil, plus extra for brushing
250 g/9 oz Italian sausages, skinned and crumbled
2 tablespoons tomato purée
300 g/11 oz mozzarella cheese, sliced
200 ml/7 fl oz double cream
40 g/1¹/₂ oz Parmesan cheese, freshly grated
salt and pepper

Bring a large pan of water to the boil, plunge in the cabbage and cook for 5 minutes, then drain and refresh in iced water. Drain well again and spread out on a tea towel. Preheat the oven to 180°C/350°F/Gas Mark 4. Brush an ovenproof dish with olive oil. Put the sausages in a saucepan with the olive oil and heat gently. Stir in the tomato purée and 5 tablespoons water. Season with salt and pepper to taste and cook over a medium heat for 10 minutes. Make a layer of cabbage in the prepared dish, season with salt and pepper, cover with a layer of mozzarella, add a layer of sausage, top with another layer of cabbage and season with salt and pepper. Continue making layers, seasoning each layer of cabbage with salt and pepper, until all the ingredients are used, ending with a layer of cabbage. Pour the cream over the top, sprinkle with the Parmesan and bake for about 40 minutes.

CAPUCHIN SAVOY CABBAGE

CAVOLO VERZA ALLA CAPPUCINA
Serves 4
¹/₂ Savoy cabbage, cored and cut into strips
2 salted anchovies, heads removed, cleaned and filleted (see page 596), soaked in cold water for 10 minutes and drained
2 tablespoons olive oil
2 garlic cloves
1 tablespoon fresh flat-leaaf parsley, chopped
salt and pepper

Parboil the cabbage in salted, boiling water for 5 minutes, then drain well. Chop the anchovy fillets. Heat the oil in a pan, add the garlic and cook for a few minutes until browned, then remove and discard. Add the anchovies to the pan and cook, mashing with a wooden spoon until they have almost completely disintegrated. Add the cabbage and parsley, season with salt and pepper, cover and cook, stirring occasionally, for about 50 minutes.

PAN–COOKED SAVOY CABBAGE

Melt half the butter in a large frying pan and make a layer of half the potato slices on the base, then top with the cabbage and sprinkle with the Parmesan. Beat the eggs with the milk and a pinch of salt and pour into the pan. Make a layer of the remaining potato slices on top, season with salt and pepper and dot with the remaining butter. Cover the pan with a tight-fitting lid and cook over a low heat for 1 hour.

CAVOLO VERZA IN PADELLA

Serves 4

50 g/2 oz butter

3 potatoes, thinly sliced

$^1/_2$ Savoy cabbage, cored and cut into thin strips

1 tablespoon Parmesan cheese, freshly grated

2 eggs

100 ml/3$^1/_2$ fl oz milk

salt and pepper

SAUERKRAUT WITH MUSHROOMS AND POTATOES

Melt the butter in saucepan, add the onion and cook over a low heat, stirring occasionally, for 10 minutes until lightly browned. Add the sauerkraut and mushrooms, increase the heat to high and cook, stirring frequently, for about 8 minutes. Add the potatoes, season with salt, lower the heat, cover and cook for 45 minutes, adding a little water if necessary.

CRAUTI CON FUNGHI E PATATE

Serves 4

25 g/1 oz butter

1 onion, chopped

200 g/7 oz sauerkraut, drained and rinsed

200 g/7 oz mushroom caps, sliced

300 g/11 oz potatoes, thinly sliced

salt

BRAISED SAUERKRAUT

Heat the butter and olive oil in a large saucepan, add the onion and pancetta and cook over a low heat, stirring occasionally, for 5 minutes. Sprinkle in the wine and vinegar and cook until reduced by half. Add the cabbage, thyme and juniper berries, mix well and pour in enough hot stock to cover. Cook over a very low heat, stirring occasionally and adding more hot stock if necessary, for about 2 hours. Season with salt and pepper to taste and serve hot with pork, cotechino (large spiced pork sausage) or zampone (stuffed pig's trotter).

CRAUTI IN UMIDO

Serves 6

25 g/1 oz butter

4 tablespoons olive oil

1 onion, chopped

150 g/5 oz pancetta, chopped

100 ml/3$^1/_2$ fl oz dry white wine

2 tablespoons white wine vinegar

1.5-kg/3$^1/_4$-lb white cabbage, cored and cut into strips

1 fresh thyme sprig, leaves only

6 juniper berries

about 300 ml/$^1/_2$ pint hot Meat Stock (see page 208)

salt and pepper

RICOTTA AND
SAVOY CABBAGE ROLLS

INVOLTINI DI CAVOLO ALLA RICOTTA

Serves 4

8 Savoy cabbage leaves

300 g/11 oz Swiss chard, stalks removed

200 g/7 oz ricotta cheese

4 tablespoons Parmesan cheese, freshly grated

2 eggs, lightly beaten

1 quantity Tomato Sauce (see page 57)

salt and pepper

Blanch the cabbage leaves in salted, boiling water for 5 minutes, then drain and refresh in iced water. Drain again and spread out on a tea towel. Cook the Swiss chard in salted, boiling water for 10–15 minutes, then drain, squeezing out as much liquid as possible. Chop finely, put in a bowl and stir in the ricotta, Parmesan and eggs. Season with salt and pepper, mix well and divide the mixture among the cabbage leaves. Roll up each leaf and tie with kitchen string. Place the cabbage rolls in a wide pan or flameproof casserole, pour in the tomato sauce, cover and simmer for about 20 minutes.

BRUSSELS SPROUTS

The best Brussels sprouts are about the size of walnuts. They come into season in midwinter and make an easy, quick and convenient side dish, as there is very little waste. Like cabbages, to which family they belong, they contain protein, iron and vitamin A, but they are easier to digest as they are not so rich in calcium and vitamin C. When fresh, they should be compact and firm, without any blemished leaves. Brussels sprouts that have opened a little are almost tasteless. Prepare them by washing them in plenty of water, trimming the stems and cutting a cross in their bases. They are good sautéed in the juices of a pork roast, as a side dish with zampone (stuffed pig's trotter) or simply fried in butter.

QUANTITIES AND COOKING TIMES

QUANTITIES
Allow about 6 per person.

BOILING
Plunge them into plenty of salted, boiling water and cook, uncovered, for about 15 minutes.

STEAMING
Place in a steamer, sprinkle with salt, cover and cook for 15 minutes.

SILVER

Serves 4

800 g/1¾ lb Brussels sprouts, trimmed

25 g/1 oz butter

pinch of freshly grated nutmeg

6 tablespoons Parmesan cheese, freshly grated

salt and pepper

PARMESAN BRUSSELS SPROUTS

Cook the Brussels sprouts in salted, boiling water for 15 minutes, then drain. Melt the butter in a pan and, when golden brown, add the sprouts and cook over a low heat for a few minutes. Season with salt and pepper to taste and add the nutmeg. Transfer to a warm serving dish, sprinkle with the Parmesan and serve.

BRUSSELS SPROUTS WITH ALMONDS

CAVOLINI DI BRUXELLES CON LE MANDORLE

Serves 4

675 g/1½ lb Brussels sprouts, trimmed

50 g/2 oz butter

25 g/1 oz blanched almonds

1 garlic clove

thinly pared rind of 1 lemon, chopped

1½ teaspoons breadcrumbs

salt and pepper

Cook the Brussels sprouts in salted, boiling water for 5 minutes, then drain thoroughly, place on a serving dish and keep warm. Heat half the butter in a frying pan, add the almonds and the garlic and stir-fry for a few minutes. Add the lemon rind, season with salt and pepper and remove from the heat. Remove and discard the garlic. Melt the remaining butter in a small saucepan and stir-fry the breadcrumbs until golden, then stir into the almond mixture, spoon over the Brussels sprouts and serve.

BRUSSELS SPROUTS AU GRATIN

CAVOLINI DI BRUXELLES GRATINATI

Serves 4

50 g/2 oz butter, plus extra for greasing

675g/1½ lb Brussels sprouts, trimmed

2 tablespoons olive oil

100 g/3½ oz pancetta, diced

100 g/3½ oz Gruyère cheese, freshly grated

1 quantity Béchamel Sauce (see page 50)

salt and pepper

Preheat the oven to 180°C/350°F/Gas Mark 4. Grease an ovenproof dish with butter. Cook the Brussels sprouts in salted, boiling water for about 10 minutes, then drain, set aside and keep warm. Heat the butter and olive oil in a pan, add the pancetta and cook, stirring occasionally, until lightly browned. Add the Brussels sprouts and 1 tablespoon hot water and cook, stirring occasionally, for about 5 minutes. Stir half the Gruyère into the béchamel sauce and season with salt and pepper. Place the Brussels sprouts in the prepared dish and sprinkle with half the remaining Gruyère. Spoon the béchamel sauce on top and sprinkle with the remaining Gruyère. Bake for about 20 minutes.

VELOUTÉ BRUSSELS SPROUTS

CAVOLINI DI BRUXELLES VELLUTATI

Serves 4

8 black peppercorns

1 lemon, sliced

100 ml/3½ fl oz dry white wine

700 g/1½ lb Brussels sprouts, trimmed

2–3 fresh chives, chopped

1 quantity Velouté Sauce (see page 61)

4 tablespoons Parmesan cheese, freshly grated

salt

Bring a large pan of water to the boil and add the peppercorns, lemon slices, wine and a pinch of salt. Place the Brussels sprouts in a steamer on top, cover and cook for 15 minutes until tender. Transfer the sprouts to a serving dish and keep warm. Stir the chives into the velouté sauce. Sprinkle the Parmesan over the Brussels sprouts, spoon the velouté sauce over them and serve.

CHICKPEAS

Chickpeas come third on the list of the world's most popular pulses. Because of their mouth-watering flavour, they form the main ingredient in a number of rustic dishes, including a traditional soup with rosemary. As dried chickpeas need to be soaked and boiled for an extremely long time, canned ones have become popular. If dried chickpeas are used, either in soups or salads, they must be boiled first in any case and the best way to cook them is in an earthenware pot. Nutritionally, they are rich in protein, calcium, phosphorus and potassium. Chickpea flour is the essential basic ingredient of Ligurian panissa, a kind of polenta, where it is mixed with oil, baby onions, salt and pepper. This may be served hot or cold, but is tastiest when fried and cut into squares or strips.

QUANTITIES
Allow about 50 g/2 oz per serving.

BOILING
Soak in cold water for 24 hours, then drain and cook for 3–4 hours in plenty of boiling water over a medium heat.

QUANTITIES
AND COOKING TIMES

CHICKPEAS WITH ANCHOVIES

Put the chickpeas in a large saucepan, add cold water to cover, bring to the boil and cook over a medium heat for 3–4 hours until tender. Meanwhile, chop the anchovy fillets. Heat the olive oil in a small saucepan, add the anchovies and cook, mashing with a wooden spoon for about 10 minutes until they have almost completely disintegrated. Add the parsley, season with pepper and mix well. Drain the chickpeas, tip into a warm serving dish, add the hot sauce and season with salt to taste.

CECI ALLE ACCIUGHE
Serves 4
200 g/7 oz dried chickpeas,
soaked in cold water for 24 hours and drained
80 g/3 oz salted anchovies, heads removed,
cleaned and filleted (see page 596),
soaked in cold water for 10 minutes and drained
100 ml/3¹/₂ fl oz olive oil
1 fresh flat-leaf parsley sprig, chopped
salt and pepper

CECI CON IL TONNO

Serves 4

200 g/7 oz dried chickpeas

pinch of bicarbonate of soda

150 g/5 oz canned tuna in oil, drained and flaked

6 tablespoons olive oil

2 tablespoons white wine vinegar

salt and pepper

CHICKPEAS WITH TUNA

Put the chickpeas in a bowl, add warm water to cover and the bicarbonate of soda and leave to soak for 24 hours. Rinse, drain and tip into a saucepan. Add water to cover, bring to the boil, then lower the heat and simmer gently for 4–5 hours. Drain and refresh under cold running water. Drain well again, tip into a salad bowl and add the tuna. Whisk together the olive oil and vinegar in a jug, season with salt and pepper and pour the dressing over the salad. Serve immediately.

CECINA O FARINATA

Serves 6

300 g/11 oz chickpea flour

100 ml/3^1/$_2$ fl oz olive oil, plus extra for brushing

salt and pepper

LIGURIAN PANCAKES

Pour 1.5 litres/2^1/$_2$ pints cold water into a large bowl. Gradually add the flour, whisking constantly to prevent lumps from forming. Add the olive oil and 1 teaspoon salt and mix well. Leave to stand for 30 minutes. Preheat the oven to 220°C/425°F/Gas Mark 7. Brush an ovenproof dish with oil. Pour the chickpea mixture into the prepared dish and bake until the top is crisp and golden. Sprinkle with pepper, cut into wedges and serve either hot or warm.

PANISSA

Serves 4

300 g/11 oz chickpea flour

6 tablespoons olive oil

salt

LIGURIAN POLENTA

Pour 1 litre/ 1^3/$_4$ pints water into a large saucepan and heat until warm, then remove the pan from the heat. Pour in the flour, stirring constantly to prevent lumps from forming. Return the pan to the heat and cook, stirring constantly, for about 1^1/$_4$ hours. Rinse several dishes with iced water, ladle the mixture into them and leave to cool and set. When set, cut into thin strips. Heat the olive oil in a heavy-based frying pan, add the strips, in batches if necessary, and fry until golden brown. Remove with a fish slice, drain on kitchen paper, sprinkle with salt and serve hot.

CUCUMBERS

Raw cucumbers have a pleasant aroma, but are not very easy to digest. To reduce this problem, cut them into slices, sprinkle with salt and leave to drain. Any bitter flavour can be eliminated by cutting off the ends and gently rubbing the cut surfaces. This produces a light foam that can then be rinsed off under running water. There are very few recipes for cooked cucumbers. Cucumbers may be green or yellowish, but in both cases they must be firm and compact to the touch. The biggest ones should be cut in half lengthways and the seeds removed with a teaspoon. Small gherkin cucumbers are picked when unripe and pickled in vinegar. They are particularly tasty and mouth-watering.

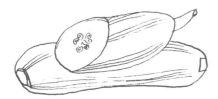

CUCUMBERS IN MAYONNAISE

Put the cucumber slices in a colander, sprinkle with salt and leave to drain for 30 minutes. Rinse, drain, pat dry and put in a salad bowl. Mix with the mayonnaise and sprinkle with the parsley.

CETRIOLI ALLA MAIONESE

Serves 4

3 cucumbers, peeled and thinly sliced

6 tablespoons Mayonnaise (see page 65)

1 fresh flat-leaf parsley sprig, chopped

salt

CUCUMBERS WITH CREAM

CETRIOLI ALLA PANNA

Serves 4

5 cucumbers, peeled

40 g/1½ oz butter

3 tablespoons double cream

salt

Remove the cucumber seeds with a teaspoon, and scoop out balls of the flesh using a melon baller. Blanch the balls in salted, boiling water for a few minutes, then drain. Melt the butter in a pan, add the balls and cook over a low heat for a few minutes, then stir, season with salt to taste and cook gently for 15 minutes. Pour in the cream and cook until it has been absorbed. Transfer to a warm serving dish.

PARISIAN CUCUMBERS

CETRIOLI ALLA PARIGINA

Serves 4

3 cucumbers, peeled and thinly sliced

1 fresh flat-leaf parsley sprig, chopped

1 fresh chervil, sprig, chopped

1 garlic clove, finely chopped

juice of 1 lemon, strained

1 teaspoon Dijon mustard

120 ml/4 fl oz olive oil

salt and pepper

Put the cucumber slices in a colander, sprinkle with salt and leave to drain for 30 minutes. Rinse, drain, pat dry and put in a salad bowl. Add the parsley, chervil and garlic. Mix together the lemon juice, mustard and olive oil in a bowl, season with salt and pepper and pour the dressing over the cucumbers. Toss well and serve.

CUCUMBERS WITH OLIVES

CETRIOLI ALLE OLIVE

Serves 4

2 cucumbers, peeled and thinly sliced

1 tablespoon chopped fresh dill

1 tablespoon lemon juice, strained

1 tablespoon olive oil

20 black olives, stoned and quartered

salt

Put the cucumber slices in a colander, sprinkle with salt and leave to drain for 30 minutes. Rinse, drain, pat dry and put in a salad bowl. Sprinkle with the dill and drizzle with the lemon juice and olive oil. Add the olives, season with salt if necessary and toss. Leave to stand for a few minutes, then serve.

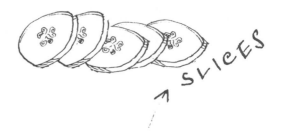

SLICES

CHICORY FAMILY

The chicory family includes various types of radicchio, curly endive, also known as frisée, and escarole, also known as Batavian or broad-leaf endive. They are all very versatile vegetables which – eaten both raw in various salads and cooked – add a distinctive flavour to several recipes. Loose-leaf endives are prepared by gathering the leaves in bunches so that the stems are aligned at the point where the leaves start, then cutting all of them at the same height. The leaves are then cut into strips. Chicories with firm heads must be cleaned by removing the most damaged and toughest leaves. Other chicories, if eaten raw, are cut into large slices of the right size for salads. If they are cooked, the heads should be cut in half or in four. The toughest leaves may be used in minestrones. The pleasantly bitter taste of chicory aids digestion. The chicory family includes several vegetables that are not commonly found outside Italy.

QUANTITIES
Allow about 185 g/6¹/₂ oz per serving.

BOILING
Cook in salted, boiling water for 20–30 minutes.

QUANTITIES
AND COOKING TIMES

CHICORY WITH BÉCHAMEL SAUCE

CICORIA ALLA BESCIAMELLA

Serves 4

1 kg/2¹/₄ lb white chicory heads

25 g/1 oz butter, plus extra for greasing

100 g/3¹/₂ oz cooked ham, coarsely chopped

300 m¹/₂ pint Béchamel Sauce (see page 50)

salt

Cook the chicory in salted, boiling water for 15 minutes. Drain squeeze out the excess liquid and chop coarsely. Preheat the oven to 180°C/350°F/Gas Mark 4. Grease an ovenproof dish with butter. Heat the butter in a frying pan, add the chicory and cook over a low heat, stirring occasionally, for about 10 minutes. Place the chicory in the prepared dish, sprinkle the ham over the top and spoon on the béchamel sauce to cover. Bake for 10 minutes.

CHICORY WITH CHILLI

CICORIA AL PEPERONCINO

Serves 4

1 kg/2¹/₄ lb white chicory heads

3 tablespoons olive oil

3 garlic cloves

1 fresh red chilli, seeded and chopped

salt and pepper

Cook the chicory in salted, boiling water for 15 minutes, then drain and squeeze out the excess liquid. Heat the olive oil in a frying pan, add the garlic and chilli and cook until the garlic is browned. Remove and discard the garlic, add the chicory to the pan, season with salt and pepper and cook for a further 10 minutes.

CHICORY PURÉE

PURÉ DI CICORIA

Serves 4

2 kg/4¹/₂ lb white chicory heads

50 g/2 oz butter, plus extra for greasing

100 ml/3¹/₂ fl oz double cream

pinch of sugar

pinch of freshly grated nutmeg

100 g/3¹/₂ oz Gruyère cheese, freshly grated

salt and pepper

Cook the chicory in salted, boiling water for 15 minutes. Preheat the oven to 180°C/350°F/Gas Mark 4. Grease an ovenproof dish with butter. Drain the chicory and squeeze out the excess liquid, then put into a blender. Add the cream and sugar and process to a purée. Add the nutmeg, season with salt and pepper to taste and process briefly again to mix. Spoon the purée into the prepared dish, dot with butter, sprinkle with the Gruyère and bake until golden brown.

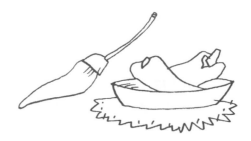

TURNIP TOPS

Turnip tops are the leaves and florets of turnips, sometimes also called broccoletti in Italian (as, somewhat confusingly, are the florets of sprouting broccoli). They are available in autumn and winter and are only eaten cooked. They are exceptionally rich in vitamin C and also contain calcium and phosphorus. To prepare, remove the leaves one at a time, discarding the damaged or very coarse ones and the thickest stalks. The flowery tops are left whole. Boiled turnip tops are served hot, warm or cold, dressed with oil, lemon juice or vinegar and salt. They are very tasty sautéed with oil and garlic.

QUANTITIES

Allow about 50 g/2 oz per serving.

BOILING

Immerse in salted, boiling water and press down with a ladle so that they stay under the surface. Once the water comes back to the boil, lower the heat and simmer for 15 minutes.

QUANTITIES
AND COOKING TIMES

455

TURNIP TOPS BAKED IN A PARCEL

CIME DI RAPA AL CARTOCCIO

Serves 4

olive oil, for brushing and drizzling
1 kg/2¼ lb turnip tops
½ garlic clove, sliced
juice of ½ lemon, strained
salt and pepper

Preheat the oven to 200°C/400°F/Gas Mark 6. Cut four sheets of foil and brush generously with olive oil. Divide the turnip tops among them and put a small slice of garlic in the middle of each. Sprinkle with the lemon juice, drizzle with oil, season with salt and pepper and fold the foil over to enclose. Place on a baking sheet and bake for about 40 minutes. Remove from the oven, leave to stand for a few minutes, then place on a warm serving dish.

PARMESAN TURNIP TOPS

CIME DI RAPA ALLA PARMIGIANA

Serves 4

1 kg/2¼ lb turnip tops
50 g/2 oz butter
40 g/1½ oz Parmesan cheese, freshly grated
salt and pepper

Cook the turnip tops in salted, boiling water for 10 minutes, then drain. Melt the butter in a pan, add the turnip tops and cook over a high heat, stirring frequently with a fork, for 10 minutes. Season with salt and pepper to taste, transfer to a warm serving dish and sprinkle with the Parmesan.

TURNIP TOPS WITH HAM

CIME DI RAPA AL PROSCIUTTO

Serves 4

1 kg/2¼ lb turnip tops
2 tablespoons olive oil
2 garlic cloves
½ fresh chilli, seeded and chopped
100 g/3½ oz cooked ham, cut into strips
25 g/1 oz breadcrumbs
salt

Cook the turnip tops in salted, boiling water for 10 minutes, then drain well, place on a serving dish and keep warm. Heat the olive oil in a pan, add the garlic and cook until lightly browned, then remove and discard. Add the chilli, ham and breadcrumbs to the pan and cook, stirring occasionally, for a few minutes. Spoon the ham mixture over the turnip tops and serve.

SPICY TURNIP TOPS

CIME DI RAPA PICCANTINE

Serves 4

1 kg/2¼ lb turnip tops
100 g/3½ oz salted anchovies, heads removed, cleaned and filleted (see page 596), soaked in cold water for 10 minutes and drained
soaked in water and drained
2 tablespoons olive oil
1 garlic clove
40 g/1½ oz capers, drained, rinsed and chopped
salt

Cook the turnip tops in salted, boiling water for 5 minutes, then drain well. Meanwhile, chop the anchovy fillets. Heat the oil in a pan, add the garlic and cook until lightly browned, then remove and discard it. Add the anchovies and cook over a low heat, mashing with a wooden spoon until they have almost completely disintegrated. Add the turnip tops, mix well and cook over a medium heat for about 20 minutes. Stir in the capers, then remove from the heat and serve.

ONIONS

Onions are invaluable for flavouring broths, meat, vegetable dishes and marinades. To prevent them from making your eyes water excessively when peeling them, hold them under running water while you do so. There are different kinds and colours – round, flat and onion-shaped, and white, red and golden brown. Purple ones have the strongest taste, white ones are the most delicate and red Tropea onions are the sweetest. Baby onions, often sold ready cleaned in bags, are delicate. To make the flavour of onions less intense, blanch them briefly in boiling water.

QUANTITIES AND COOKING TIMES

QUANTITIES
Allow a minimum of 120 g/ 4 oz (1 medium onion) per serving.

BOILING
Cook standard onions for 30 minutes in boiling water and baby onions for 10 minutes.

FRIED ONION RINGS

To make the batter, sift the flour and a pinch of salt into a bowl, make a well in the centre, break the egg into the well and add the olive oil and a pinch of pepper. Mix well until the batter is smooth and even. Leave to rest for 1 hour. Meanwhile, put the onion rings in a dish, add cold water to cover and set aside for about 30 minutes. Drain and pat dry with kitchen paper. Heat the oil for deep-frying in a large pan. Dip the onion rings in the batter and fry, in batches, in the hot oil until golden brown. Remove with a fish slice, drain on kitchen paper and sprinkle with salt and pepper. Serve immediately.

ANELLI FRITTI

Serves 4

2 large onions, cut into thick rings

vegetable oil, for deep-frying

salt and white pepper

For the batter

3 tablespoons plain flour

1 egg

3 tablespoons olive oil

salt and pepper

BABY ONION OMELETTE

Heat the olive oil in a frying pan, add the garlic and cook for a few minutes until browned, then remove and discard it. Add the onions to the pan and cook over a low heat, stirring occasionally, for 5 minutes. Beat the eggs with the Parmesan in a bowl and season with salt and pepper. Pour the mixture into the pan and cook, stirring occasionally with a fork, until the eggs are lightly set. Transfer to a warm serving dish and serve with home-made bread.

CIPOLLATA

Serves 4

4 tablespoons olive oil

1 garlic clove

600 g/1 lb 5 oz baby onions, thinly sliced

6 eggs

40 g/1^1/$_2$ oz Parmesan cheese, freshly grated

1 fresh flat-leaf parsley sprig, chopped

salt and pepper

home-made bread, to serve

GROSSETO ONIONS

Cook the onions in salted, boiling water for 15 minutes. Drain and leave to cool. Scoop out the flesh from the centres using a small sharp knife, leaving hollow 'shells'. Chop the scooped-out flesh and mix with the veal, sausage, Parmesan, olive oil, egg and nutmeg, then season with salt and pepper. Fill the onion shells with the mixture. Place the onions in a large pan in a single layer and pour in the stock. Cover and simmer for about 30 minutes until the sauce thickens. Place on a warm serving dish.

CIPOLLE ALLA GROSSETANA

Serves 4

4 large onions

150 g/5 oz minced lean veal

1 small Italian sausage, skinned and crumbled

2 tablespoons Parmesan cheese, freshly grated

2 tablespoons olive oil

1 egg, lightly beaten

pinch of freshly grated nutmeg

100 ml/3^1/$_2$ fl oz Meat Stock (see page 208)

salt and pepper

STUFFED ONIONS

Tear the bread into pieces, place in a bowl, add the milk and leave to soak. Preheat the oven to 180°C/350°F/Gas Mark 4. Grease an ovenproof dish with butter. Parboil the onions in salted, boiling water for a few minutes, then drain well and leave to cool slightly. Carefully cut them in half without breaking them up. Scoop out the flesh from the centres, leaving the 'shells' intact. Chop the scooped-out flesh and mix it with the meat in a bowl. Squeeze out the bread, add it to the bowl with the parsley, grated Gruyère and egg, season with salt and pepper and mix well. Fill the onion shells with this mixture, top each with a slice of Gruyère and dot with the butter. Arrange the onions in a single layer in the prepared dish, pour in 150 ml/¼ pint water and bake for about 30 minutes or until golden brown.

CIPOLLE RIPIENE

Serves 4

1 bread slice, crusts removed

4 tablespoons milk

40 g/1½ oz butter, plus extra for greasing

4 large onions

150 g/5 oz minced meat, cooked

1 fresh flat-leaf parsley sprig, chopped

1 tablespoon Gruyère cheese, freshly grated

1 egg, lightly beaten

8 small Gruyère cheese slices

salt and pepper

BABY ONIONS WITH SAGE

Heat the oil in a pan, add the pancetta and cook, stirring occasionally, for 5 minutes. Add the onions and sage, season with salt and cook over a high heat until lightly browned all over. Lower the heat, add 5 tablespoons water, cover and cook for about 30 minutes.

CIPOLLINE ALLA SALVIA

Serves 4

1 tablespoon olive oil

50 g/2 oz pancetta, chopped

500 g/1 lb 2 oz baby onions

5 fresh sage leaves

salt

THE SULTAN'S ONIONS

Blanch the onions in salted, boiling water for a few minutes, then drain well and put in a clean pan. Season with salt and pepper, sprinkle with the thyme, then pour in the wine and cook over a high heat until it has evaporated. Meanwhile, heat the stock in another pan. Lower the heat under the pan of onions, pour in the hot stock, cover and cook for 30 minutes. Meanwhile, put the sultanas in a bowl, add lukewarm water to cover and leave to soak. When the onions are tender, drain the sultanas and squeeze out the excess liquid, then stir them into the pan and cook for 5 minutes. Transfer to a warm serving dish.

CIPOLLINE DEL SULTANO

Serves 4

500 g/1 lb 2 oz baby onions

1 fresh thyme sprig, chopped

5 tablespoons dry white wine

175 ml/6 fl oz Vegetable Stock (see page 209)

20 g/¾ oz sultanas

salt and pepper

GLAZED BABY ONIONS

CIPOLLINE GLASSATE

Serves 4

80 g/3 oz butter

500 g/1 lb 2 oz baby onions

1 1/2 teaspoons sugar

salt

Melt the butter in a pan, add the onions and a pinch of salt and cook over a low heat, stirring with a wooden spoon, until the onions have absorbed some of the butter. Sprinkle with the sugar and add just enough warm water to cover. Cover and cook over a low heat until the liquid has completely evaporated and the onions are lightly caramelized. Transfer to a warm serving dish. This delicious dish is an ideal accompaniment to roast meat.

BRAISED BABY ONIONS

CIPOLLINE STUFATE

Serves 4

800 g/1 3/4 lb baby onions

80 g/3 oz butter

1 tablespoon plain flour

100 ml/3 1/2 fl oz Vegetable Stock (see page 209)

salt and pepper

Parboil the onions in salted, boiling water for about 10 minutes, then drain. Melt half the butter in a pan, add the onions, season with salt and pepper and cook, stirring halfway through cooking, for 20 minutes until golden brown all over. Mix the remaining butter with the flour to a paste and add to the pan with the stock. Increase the heat and cook for a further 10 minutes or until the cooking juices thicken. Place the onions on a warm serving dish and spoon the juices over them.

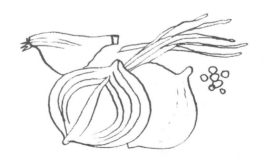

BEANS

There are at least 400 different types of bean. Among the most common in Italy are speckled, red borlotti beans, which are delicious in minestrones and with pasta, thin-skinned cannellini or toscanelli beans, which are tasty in salads and stews, black-eyed beans, which are dark with a small black 'eye' and are excellent boiled or stewed, and large, white kidney beans. Fresh beans are harvested from June to October; dried beans keep for up to three years but are best eaten within 12 months of harvesting. In both cases, their nutritional value is very high and they are rich in protein, potassium, sodium, iron, magnesium and phosphorus.

QUANTITIES

Allow 65–80 g/2½–3 oz dried beans per serving, 80–100 g/3–3½ oz fresh beans per serving.

FRESH

The pods should be undamaged and without blemishes. They must be cooked as soon as they are shelled, for 40 minutes –1½ hours depending on the variety.

DRIED

The beans should not be broken or damaged. Before cooking, soak in cold water to cover for at least 12 hours and remove and discard any that float to the surface. They take 2–3 hours to cook, depending on the variety.

BOILING

Put the beans in a pan of cold water with celery, garlic and sage. Bring to the boil, then cover and simmer. To prevent their skins becoming tough do not interrupt the cooking, and add more hot water when necessary. Some beans, including borlotti, black-eyed and all colours of kidney beans, contain a naturally occurring toxin. This can be destroyed by pre-boiling the beans vigorously for 15 minutes. Drain and then cook in the usual way in fresh water.

QUANTITIES AND COOKING TIMES

THREE PULSE SALAD

FAGIOLI AI TRE LEGUMI

Serves 4

250 g/9 oz canned white beans, drained and rinsed

130 g/4¹/₂ oz canned lentils, drained and rinsed

130 g/4¹/₂ oz canned chickpeas, drained and rinsed

7 tablespoons olive oil

2 tablespoons white wine vinegar

1 tablespoon lemon juice, strained

1 bunch of fresh chives, chopped

salt and white pepper

This is a tasty mixed salad of beans, lentils and chickpeas which is traditionally prepared with freshly cooked pulses boiled in separate pans. However, to speed things up, canned pulses may be used. Tip the beans, lentils and chickpeas into a large salad bowl and drizzle with the olive oil. Mix together the vinegar and lemon juice, season with salt and pepper and add to the salad. Sprinkle with the chives and toss lightly. Transfer to a serving dish and serve immediately.

BEANS PIZZAIOLA

FAGIOLI ALLA PIZZAIOLA

Serves 4

1 kg/2¹/₄ lb fresh beans, shelled

2 celery stalks

3 fresh sage leaves

1 garlic clove

25 g/1 oz butter

4 tablespoons passata

4 fresh basil leaves, torn

1 fresh flat-leaf parsley sprig, chopped

salt and pepper

Put the beans in a saucepan, pour in enough water to cover them by at least 5 cm/2 inches and add one of the celery stalks, the sage and garlic. Bring to the boil, then lower the heat and simmer for 1 hour or until tender. Drain, remove and discard the sage and garlic, place the beans in a serving dish and keep warm. Meanwhile, thinly slice the remaining celery. Melt the butter in a saucepan, add the passata, celery and basil and cook until slightly reduced. Pour the sauce over the beans, season with salt and pepper and mix well. Sprinkle with the parsley and serve.

BEANS UCCELLETTO

FAGIOLI ALL'UCCELLETTO

Serves 4

300 g/11 oz dried beans, soaked in cold water for 12 hours and drained

3 tablespoons olive oil

2 garlic cloves

4–5 fresh sage leaves

400 g/14 oz canned tomatoes

salt and pepper

Place the beans in a saucepan, add water to cover, bring to the boil, then lower the heat and simmer for 2 hours until tender. Meanwhile, heat the oil in a frying pan, add the garlic and sage and cook for a few minutes. Remove and discard the garlic when it turns golden brown. Drain the beans, add to the pan and cook over a medium heat for about 10 minutes. Add the tomatoes, season with salt and pepper and cook, stirring frequently for a further 15 minutes until the sauce starts to thicken. Remove the pan from the heat, and transfer the beans to a warm serving dish.

BEANS WITH SAUSAGES

FAGIOLI CON SALSICCIA

Serves 4

200 g/7 oz dried beans,
soaked in cold water for 12 hours and drained

1 celery stalk

2 garlic cloves

2 fresh sage leaves

2 tablespoons olive oil

8 small Italian sausages

100 ml/3¹/₂ fl oz dry white wine

salt and pepper

Place the beans in a saucepan, pour in water to cover and add the celery, one of the garlic cloves and one of the sage leaves. Cover, bring to the boil, then lower the heat and simmer for 2–3 hours, adding more hot water if necessary. Drain well and keep warm. Heat the oil in a frying pan. Crush the remaining garlic clove, add to the pan with the remaining sage leaf and cook for a few minutes. Prick the sausages with a fork, add to the pan and cook until lightly browned all over. Sprinkle in the wine and cook until it has evaporated. Drain the beans and add to the pan, then cover and cook over a medium heat for 30 minutes. Remove the lid and cook until the excess liquid has boiled off. Season with salt and pepper, mix well and transfer to a warm serving dish.

EXOTIC BEANS

FAGIOLI ESOTICI

Serves 4

¹/₂ avocado, peeled, stoned and sliced

juice of ¹/₂ lemon, strained

25 g/1 oz butter

150 g/5 oz cooked ham, diced

¹/₂ pineapple, peeled, cored and diced

600 g/1 lb 5 oz canned beans, drained and rinsed

2 teaspoons mild or medium mustard

salt

Sprinkle the avocado with the lemon juice to prevent it going brown. Melt the butter in a pan, add the ham, pineapple and beans and mix gently. Season lightly with salt and cook over a medium heat for a few minutes. Mix the mustard with 1–2 tablespoons of the cooking juices in a small bowl and stir into the pan. Add the avocado, cook for a few minutes more and serve.

SUMMER CANNELLINI BEANS

CANNELLINI ESTIVI

Serves 4

3 tablespoons olive oil

1 garlic clove

1 aubergine, diced

1 yellow pepper, halved, seeded and diced

2 fresh tomatoes, peeled, seeded and chopped

350 g/12 oz canned cannellini beans,
drained and rinsed

grated rind of ¹/₂ lemon

4 fresh basil leaves, chopped

1 fresh flat-leaf parsley sprig, chopped

salt and pepper

Heat the oil in a pan, add the garlic and cook until browned, then remove and discard. Add the aubergine and pepper to the pan and cook over a high heat for a few minutes, then add the tomatoes and beans, cover and cook for 5 minutes. Season with salt and pepper and cook, uncovered, for a further 5 minutes. Remove the pan from the heat, transfer the beans to a warm serving dish and sprinkle with the lemon rind, basil and parsley. Mix well and serve.

MIXED BEAN SALAD

Cook the beans and shallot in salted, boiling water for 1–1¹/₂ hours until tender. Cook the French beans in a separate pan of salted, boiling water for 10–15 minutes. Drain all the beans and mix together in a salad bowl with the garlic, olive oil and a pinch of salt. Crumble in the chilli and mix again. Don't dress this mixed bean salad more than 10 minutes before serving.

FAGIOLI MISTI IN INSALATA

Serves 4

450 g/1 lb mixed fresh beans

such as borlotti and cannellini, shelled

1 shallot, chopped

50 g/2 oz French beans, trimmed

¹/₂ garlic clove, chopped

4 tablespoons olive oil

1 dried red chilli

salt

BEAN PURÉE

Put the beans, celery, garlic and sage in a saucepan, add cold water to cover, cover the pan, bring to the boil and simmer for 2–3 hours, adding more hot water if necessary. Drain, discard the herbs and vegetables and pass through a food mill into a clean pan. Season lightly with salt, add the butter and heat gently, stirring constantly. Gradually stir in the stock until the mixture has the desired consistency; you may not need all the stock. Mix well, remove the pan from the heat and season with pepper. This purée is an excellent side dish for roast pork.

FAGIOLI IN PURÉ

Serves 4

250 g/9 oz dried beans,

soaked in cold water for 12 hours and drained

1 celery stalk

1 garlic clove

1 fresh sage sprig

40 g/1¹/₂ oz butter

250 ml/8 fl oz Vegetable Stock (see page 209)

salt and white pepper

GREEN BEANS

Green beans, whether runner, French, wax or any other variety, are best if they have been harvested when young before any strings form. Their colour ranges from yellow to pale or dark green and most varieties are long and thin, but there are also some flat types, and even a miniature one known as fagiolini dall'occhio. As for nutritional value, green beans contain some vitamins A and C, calcium and potassium. When buying, reject any that look withered or are floppy when touched, and choose firm, brightly coloured ones. Green beans cannot be eaten raw and should always be boiled or at least parboiled. Some people prefer to trim the ends and remove any strings before cooking and others prefer to do it afterwards. The latter practice is less widespread, but does mean that the beans absorb less water. The various types of green beans are mostly interchangeable.

QUANTITIES AND COOKING TIMES

QUANTITIES

Allow about 150 g/5 oz per serving as a side dish.

COOKING

Always cook in an uncovered pan to prevent the beans going yellow. The proportions are 1 litre/1³/₄ pints water, 200 g/7 oz beans and 10 g/¹/₄ oz salt. For al dente beans, simmer for 10 minutes; for very teder beans, simmer for 15–20 minutes. Do not overcook or they will become mushy.

FRENCH BEANS IN EGG CREAM

Cook the beans in salted, boiling water for 15 minutes, then drain and chop. Melt the butter in a pan over a low heat, add the onions and cook, stirring occasionally, for 5 minutes. Add the beans, mix well and cook for a few minutes more. Meanwhile, beat the eggs in a bowl, stir in the Parmesan and season with salt and pepper. Pour the egg mixture into the pan, stirring constantly, then remove from the heat. The beans should be pleasantly creamy. This is an elegant side dish.

FAGIOLINI ALLA CREMA D'UOVA

Serves 4

600 g/1 lb 5 oz French beans, trimmed

40 g/1½ oz butter

2 small mild onions, chopped

2 eggs

25 g/1 oz Parmesan cheese, freshly grated

salt and pepper

POLISH BEANS

Cook the beans in salted, boiling water for 15 minutes, then drain and tip into a salad bowl. Add the cannellini beans, spring onion and anchovies, season lightly with salt and pepper and add the frankfurters. Shell and chop the eggs, place in a bowl, mix with the paprika and season with salt and pepper. Sprinkle with the vinegar and drizzle generously with olive oil. Dress the beans with this sauce.

FAGIOLINI ALLA POLACCA

Serves 4

400 g/14 oz French beans, trimmed

250 g/9 oz canned cannellini beans, drained and rinsed

1 spring onion, finely chopped

3 canned anchovy fillets, drained and chopped

4 frankfurters, parboiled, skinned and sliced

2 eggs, hard-boiled • pinch of paprika

1 tablespoon white wine vinegar

olive oil, for drizzling

salt and pepper

GREEN BEANS WITH PARMESAN

Preheat the oven to 180°C/350°F/Gas Mark 4. Grease an ovenproof dish with butter. Cook the beans in salted, boiling water for 15 minutes, then drain and place in the prepared dish. Beat the eggs with the milk and Parmesan and season with salt and pepper. Pour the egg mixture over the beans and bake until just set. Serve immediately.

FAGIOLINI AL PARMIGIANO

Serves 4

butter, for greasing

800 g/1¾ lb French or runner beans, trimmed

3 eggs • 5 tablespoons milk

100 g/3½ oz Parmesan cheese, freshly grated

salt and pepper

FRENCH BEANS WITH TOMATO

Cook the beans in salted, boiling water for 10 minutes. Meanwhile, heat the oil in another pan, add the onion and garlic and cook over a low heat, stirring occasionally, for 5 minutes. Drain the beans, add to the pan and mix well. Stir in the tomatoes, season with salt and pepper, then remove and discard the garlic. Simmer over a low heat for about 10 minutes, then stir in the olives and basil and cook for a further 5 minutes. Serve warm.

FAGIOLINI AL POMODORO

Serves 4

600 g/1 lb 5 oz French beans, trimmed

2 tablespoons olive oil

1 onion, chopped • 1 garlic clove

5 tomatoes, peeled, seeded and chopped

6 green olives, stoned and quartered

6 fresh basil leaves, chopped

salt and pepper

469

FROSTED GREEN BEANS WITH SESAME

FAGIOLINI GLASSATI AL SESAMO

Serves 4

600 g/1 lb 5 oz French or runner beans, trimmed

25 g/1 oz butter

2 spring onions, thinly sliced

strained juice and grated rind of ¹/₂ lemon

1 tablespoon sesame seeds

olive oil, for drizzling

salt and pepper

Cook the beans in salted, boiling water for 10 minutes, then drain and set aside. Melt the butter in a pan, add the spring onions and cook over a low heat, stirring occasionally, for about 5 minutes until softened. Stir in the lemon juice and rind, add the beans, season with salt and pepper and simmer for a further 10 minutes. Meanwhile, dry-fry the sesame seeds, stirring frequently, for about 1 minute until they give off their aroma, then remove from the heat. Transfer the bean mixture to a warm serving dish, sprinkle with the sesame seeds and drizzle with olive oil. Mix well and serve.

RUNNER BEANS AU GRATIN

FAGIOLINI GRATINATI

Serves 4

600 g/1 lb 5 oz runner beans, trimmed

2 tablespoons olive oil

1 garlic clove

2 leeks, trimmed and sliced

1 tablespoon plain flour

100 ml/3¹/₂ fl oz milk

200 ml/7 fl oz dry white wine

25 g/1 oz butter, plus extra for greasing

4 tablespoons Parmesan cheese, freshly grated

salt and pepper

Cook the beans in salted, boiling water for about 10 minutes, then drain and leave to cool slightly. Heat the oil in a large saucepan, add the garlic and leeks and cook over a low heat, stirring occasionally, for 5 minutes. Remove and discard the garlic and stir in the flour. Gradually stir in the milk and season with salt and pepper. Add the beans, pour in the wine, cover and simmer for about 10 minutes. Meanwhile, preheat the oven to 180°C/350°F/Gas Mark 4. Grease an ovenproof dish with butter. Remove the pan from the heat and tip the mixture into the prepared dish. Sprinkle with the Parmesan, dot with the butter and bake for 15 minutes or until golden and bubbling. Remove from the oven and leave to stand for 10 minutes before serving.

FRENCH BEANS IN BÉCHAMEL SAUCE AU GRATIN

FAGIOLINI GRATINATI ALLA BESCIAMELLA

Serves 4

50 g/2 oz butter, plus extra for greasing

2 tablespoons olive oil

1 onion, chopped

400 g/14 oz French beans, trimmed and halved

200 g/7 oz button or chestnut mushrooms, thinly sliced

1 quantity Béchamel Sauce (see page 50)

100 g/3¹/₂ oz cooked ham, diced

1 egg

1 egg yolk

salt and pepper

Divide the butter and olive oil between two small saucepans and heat. Add half the onion to each pan and cook over a low heat, stirring occasionally, for 5 minutes until softened. Add the beans to one pan and the mushrooms to the other and cook over a low heat, stirring occasionally, for 15 minutes. Meanwhile, preheat the oven to 180°C/350°F/Gas Mark 4. Grease a mould with butter. Season the bean and mushroom mixtures with salt and pepper, then stir both into the béchamel sauce with the ham, whole egg and egg yolk. Spoon the mixture into the prepared mould and bake for about 40 minutes. Turn out on to a serving dish.

FRENCH BEAN SALAD

FAGIOLINI IN INSALATA

Serves 4

600 g/1 lb 5 oz green
and yellow French beans, trimmed
1 onion, thinly sliced
1 garlic clove, thinly sliced
1 teaspoon mustard seeds
juice of $^1\!/_2$ lemon, strained
1 fresh flat-leaf parsley sprig, chopped
olive oil, for drizzling
salt and pepper

Cook the beans in salted, boiling water for 15 minutes, then drain and tip into a salad bowl. Add the onion, garlic, mustard seeds, lemon juice and parsley, drizzle with olive oil and season with salt and pepper. Toss and set aside in a cool place for 30 minutes for the flavours to mingle before serving.

BEANS IN GARLIC SAUCE

FAGIOLINI IN SALSA D'AGLIO

Serves 4

1 thick bread slice, crusts removed
100 ml/3$^1\!/_2$ fl oz white wine vinegar
300 g/11 oz yellow French beans
300 g/11 oz green French beans
2 garlic cloves
120 ml/4 fl oz olive oil
salt and pepper

Tear the bread into pieces, place in a bowl, add the vinegar and set aside to soak. Cook the beans in salted, boiling water for about 10 minutes, then drain and place on a serving dish. Crush the garlic in a mortar with a pestle, then gradually stir in the olive oil until thick and smooth. Squeeze out the bread, stir it into the sauce and season with salt and pepper. Spoon the sauce over the warm beans and serve.

FRENCH BEANS IN EGG SAUCE

FAGIOLINI IN SALSA D'UOVA

Serves 4

600 g/1 lb 5 oz French beans
50 g/2 oz butter
1 fresh flat-leaf parsley sprig, chopped
2 egg yolks
juice of 1 lemon, strained
salt

Cook the beans in salted, boiling water for 15 minutes, then drain. Melt the butter in a pan, add the beans and cook over a medium heat, stirring occasionally, for 10 minutes. Stir in the parsley and lower the heat. Beat the egg yolks with the lemon juice, pour the mixture over the beans and stir over a very low heat until slightly thickened. Serve immediately.

BROAD BEANS

The very distinctive flavour of broad beans is more notice-able when they are fresh, small and so young that you need only shell them without peeling off their skins, which are still tender and sweet at this stage. They are delicious eaten raw in the spring with Roman pecorino cheese. Larger, older beans, on the other hand, must be peeled and cooked. These are perfect in minestrones, barley soups or puréed. Deciding whether it is best to remove the skin depends a lot on the recipe. Mostly, however, it is recommended to do so, as the resulting dish will be lighter and tastier. Dried beans, whether with or without skins, should be soaked in cold water for a long period – as much as a whole day. In Calabria, broad beans are used to make an ancient, traditional dish called macco. It is a thick soup seasoned with oil and freshly ground pepper. As for their nutritional value, both dried and fresh broad beans are rich in phosphorus, calcium and potassium.

FRESH

Allow 100 g/3¹/₂ oz shelled broad beans per serving as a side dish. Note that 3 kg/6¹/₂ lb unshelled broad beans correspond to about 600 g/1 lb 5 oz shelled ones.

DRIED

Allow about 80 g/3 oz per serving as a side dish.

BOILING

Cook fresh broad beans in salted, boiling water for 20–30 minutes. Cook dried beans without salt for 2–3 hours.

QUANTITIES AND COOKING TIMES

PIEDMONTESE BROAD BEANS

FAVE ALLA PIEMONTESE

Serves 4

2 kg/4½ lb fresh broad beans, shelled

200 ml/7 fl oz double cream

50 g/2 oz fontina cheese, sliced

salt

Cook the beans in salted, boiling water for 10 minutes, then drain and tip into a frying pan. Stir in the cream and simmer gently for about 10 minutes until thickened. Stir in the fontina and cook until it is just starting to melt.

BROAD BEANS WITH HAM

FAVE AL PROSCIUTTO

Serves 4

2 kg/4½ lb fresh broad beans, shelled

40 g/1½ oz butter

100 g/3½ oz cooked ham, diced

1 onion, chopped

1 carrot, chopped

200 ml/7 fl oz Meat Stock (see page 208)

1 fresh flat-leaf parsley sprig, chopped

salt and pepper

Put the beans in a saucepan, add cold water to cover, bring to the boil and cook for 10 minutes. Meanwhile, melt half the butter in another pan, add the ham, onion and carrot and cook, stirring occasionally, for 5 minutes. Drain the beans and add to the ham mixture, then pour in the stock and season with salt and pepper. Simmer until the sauce is very thick, then stir in the remaining butter, transfer to a warm serving dish and sprinkle with the parsley.

FRESH BROAD BEAN PURÉE

PURÉ DI FAVE FRESCHE

Serves 4

3 kg/6½ lb fresh broad beans, shelled

2 small potatoes, diced

100 ml/3½ fl oz Vegetable Stock (see page 209)

olive oil, for drizzling

salt and pepper

Soak the beans in cold water for 30 minutes, then drain, peel and put into a saucepan. Add enough cold water just to cover and bring to the boil over a low heat. As soon as the water begins to boil, remove the pan from the heat, drain the beans, return to the pan and mash. Season with salt, add the potatoes and stock and cook until soft and creamy. Remove the pan from the heat, drizzle generously with olive oil, then taste and adjust the seasoning if necessary. Serve hot or cold.

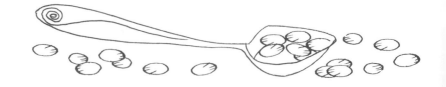

FENNEL

Fennel bulbs are attractive, tasty and aid digestion. They are also the leanest vegetable. Florence fennel bulbs contain no fat and have just 9 calories per 100 g/3¹/₂ oz. On the other hand, they are rich in minerals, including calcium, phosphorus, sodium and potassium. Their delicate aroma is reminiscent of aniseed. When buying fennel, bear in mind that the division into male (round) and female (elongated) bulbs has no scientific basis, but it is worth knowing that the former are better for eating raw – on their own or with other types of salad – while the latter are better cooked. To prepare fennel, rinse very thoroughly under cold running water, remove the outer leaves, which may be very hard, and trim the base. Leave the bulbs whole, or cut them in half or into quarters according to the recipe. Cut surfaces turn brown on exposure to air so fennel should be cooked immediately or dropped into a bowl of acidulated water. Sweet fennel is a highly aromatic herb and is used in roasts as it brings out their fragrance and flavour. Fennel seeds, from both sweet and Florence fennel, are aromatic spices. Fennel also has a noble relative: dill. This light herb has an aroma very like that of fennel and is a favourite with professional and experienced cooks alike. However, it should always be used sparingly.

QUANTITIES AND COOKING TIMES

QUANTITIES
Allow 1 raw Florence fennel bulb per serving and 1¹/₂ bulbs if cooked.

BOILING
Whole fennel bulbs take about 45 minutes to cook. If halved, they take 30 minutes or less.

DEVIL'S FENNEL

Chop the anchovy fillets. Heat the oil in a pan, add the anchovies and cook, mashing with a wooden spoon until they have almost completely disintegrated, then add the fennel. Mix together the mustard and vinegar, season with salt and pepper and sprinkle the mixture over the fennel. Cover and cook over a very low heat, stirring frequently and adding a little water if necessary, until tender. Remove the fennel with a fish slice and place on a warm serving dish. Stir the lemon juice into the cooking juices and cook, stirring, until thickened. Pour the sauce in a continuous stream over the fennel and serve.

FINOCCHI ALLA DIAVOLA

Serves 4

4 salted anchovies, heads removed,
cleaned and filleted (see page 596),
soaked in cold water for 10 minutes
rinsed and drained
100 ml/3¹/₂ fl oz olive oil
4 fennel bulbs, trimmed and cut into wedges
1 teaspoon Dijon mustard
1 tablespoon white wine vinegar
juice of 1 lemon, strained
salt and pepper

FENNEL WITH MOZZARELLA

Cook the fennel in salted, boiling water for about 45 minutes until tender. Drain, pat dry and leave to cool slightly, then cut into thin wedges while still warm Preheat the oven to 160°C/325°F/Gas Mark 3. Melt the butter in a flameproof dish, add the fennel and cook, stirring constantly, until lightly browned. Remove from the heat, cover with the mozzarella slices and sprinkle with the parsley. Beat together the eggs, cream and Parmesan in a bowl, season with salt and pepper and pour the mixture over the fennel. Bake until the eggs are just set. Serve immediately.

FINOCCHI ALLA MOZZARELLA

Serves 4

1 kg/2¹/₄ lb fennel bulbs, trimmed
25 g/1 oz butter
200 g/7 oz mozzarella cheese, sliced
1 fresh flat-leaf parsley sprig, chopped
4 eggs
200 ml/7 fl oz double cream
40 g/1¹/₂ oz Parmesan cheese, freshly grated
salt and pepper

FENNEL WITH WHITE WINE

Put the fennel in a saucepan with the garlic and olive oil and sprinkle with the white wine. Cover and cook for 20 minutes or until the fennel is very tender. Remove the pan from the heat, season with salt and pepper and sprinkle with the parsley.

FINOCCHI AL VINO BIANCO

Serves 4

1 kg/2¹/₄ lb fennel bulbs,
trimmed and cut into wedges
1 garlic clove, chopped • 2 tablespoons olive oil
200 ml/7 fl oz dry white wine
1 fresh flat-leaf parsley sprig, chopped
salt and pepper

FENNEL WITH WALNUTS AND ORANGES

Place the fennel slices in a salad bowl, drizzle with olive oil and season with salt and pepper. Peel the oranges and cut off all traces of pith, then slice and add to the fennel. Add the walnuts, mix and serve.

FINOCCHI CON NOCI E ARANCE

Serves 4

4 tender, round fennel bulbs, trimmed and thinly sliced
olive oil, for drizzling
2 oranges • 6 shelled walnuts, chopped
salt and pepper

FRIED FENNEL

Serves 4

4 fennel bulbs, trimmed

1 egg

40 g/1¹/₂ oz Parmesan cheese, freshly grated

50 g/2 oz butter

salt

Cook the fennel in salted, boiling water for about 45 minutes until tender. Thinly slice crossways and pat dry on kitchen paper. Beat the egg with a pinch of salt in a shallow dish and spread out the Parmesan in another shallow dish. Melt the butter in a non-stick pan. Dip the fennel slices first in the beaten egg and then in the Parmesan. Add to the pan and cook until golden brown on both sides. Serve hot.

FENNEL EN CROÛTE

Serves 8

300 g/11 oz plain flour, plus extra for dusting

100 g/3¹/₂ oz butter, softened

1 kg/2¹/₄ lb fennel bulbs, trimmed

4 salted anchovies, heads removed, cleaned and filleted (see page 596), soaked in cold water for 10 minutes rinsed and drained

100 g/3¹/₂ oz Gruyère cheese, freshly grated

1 egg, separated

salt and pepper

Sift the flour and a pinch of salt into a mound on the work surface, make a well in the centre and add 50 g/2 oz of the butter. Knead to incorporate the flour, adding cold water, 1 tablespoon at a time, to make a smooth dough. Shape the dough into a ball, wrap in cling film and chill in the refrigerator. Meanwhile, melt the remaining butter in a pan, add the fennel and cook over a low heat until softened. Season with salt and remove from the heat. Chop the anchovy fillets and put them, with the Gruyère, egg yolk and fennel in a food processor and process to a purée. Season with salt and pepper to taste. Preheat the oven to 200°C/400°F/Gas Mark 6. Remove the dough from the refrigerator and roll out thinly on a lightly floured surface. Stamp out an even number of rounds using a biscuit cutter or the rim of a glass. Put 1 tablespoon of fennel purée in the centres of half the rounds, place another round on top and crimp the edges to seal. Brush with the lightly beaten egg white, place on a baking sheet and bake for 15 minutes. Serve hot.

FENNEL PIE

Serves 6

7 small fennel bulbs, trimmed

3 eggs

50 g/2 oz butter, plus extra for greasing

5 wholemeal bread slices, crusts removed

6 tablespoons milk

200 g/7 oz taleggio cheese, sliced

4 tablespoons Parmesan cheese, freshly grated

salt

Cook the fennel in salted, boiling water for 45 minutes. Meanwhile hard-boil the eggs, refresh under cold water, then shell and slice thinly. Drain the fennel, pat dry with kitchen paper and cut into crossways slices. Preheat the oven to 180°C/350°F/Gas Mark 4. Grease an ovenproof dish with butter. Sprinkle the slices of bread with milk and make a layer in the base of the prepared dish. Place a layer of fennel on top, followed by a layer of hard-boiled egg and then a layer of taleggio. Continue making layers until all the ingredients are used, then sprinkle with the Parmesan and dot with the butter. Bake until golden, remove from the oven and serve warm.

MUSHROOMS

Honey fungus, chanterelles, pholiotte, porcini, also known as ceps or boletus mushrooms, oyster, morels and Caesar's mushrooms are just some of the best-known and most popular wild mushrooms. For some types you have to wait for the right season, while others are available all year round. Do not pick wild mushrooms unless you are absolutely sure that you can identify the species; and check whether there are restrictions on the quantity you can take. Instead, buy from a reliable supplier to be certain they are safe to eat. From the nutritional point of view, mushrooms contain 90 per cent water and are mainly rich in minerals and phosphorus. They are low in fat and calories and are often included in weight-loss diets. Their main characteristic is their fragrance, which is the product of 38 different substances that remain even after drying. As fresh mushrooms are highly perishable, they should be eaten within a day or two of purchase. When choosing, select the smallest, as these are the most tender; and those with large caps in comparison with their stems. They should be firm to the touch with no trace of an unpleasant smell or any blemishes. They should not look dry or swollen with water or conceal insects. To clean them, wipe gently with a damp cloth, pass them quickly under cold running water and dry them immediately. When cooking, don't cover the pan until all the liquid they give off has evaporated. The time this takes varies according to type but some mushrooms need at least 30 minutes to cook completely. Porcini have a wonderful aroma and are ideal for all methods of preparation. Pholiotte mushrooms are delicious sliced and sautéed with garlic and parsley (trifolati). The highly prized Caesar's mushrooms are wonderful in salads or baked. Chanterelles are excellent in risottos and sauces. Honey fungus is good stewed. Cultivated mushrooms present no problems. Chestnut mushrooms are always available, inexpensive and more or less equivalent to wild mushrooms from a nutritional point of view. There are different types; the white ones stay fresh longer than the brown ones. Lastly, dried mushrooms have more properties and fragrance than fresh ones. Before cooking they should be soaked in warm water. Although some professionals recommend straining the soaking water and adding it to risottos this is not advisable as the liquid may contain invisible traces of soil or dirt which could ruin the final result.

QUANTITIES

Allow about 150–200 g/ 5–7 oz or 2 medium-sized caps per serving.

TRIFOLATI

This is a method of cooking in a frying pan with olive oil, garlic and fresh flat-leaf parsley. The cooking time depends on the kind of mushroom: porcini and chestnut mushrooms, for example, cook in 10 minutes (see page 486).

MUSHROOMS WITH CREAM

Slice the mushrooms and sprinkle with the lemon juice. Melt the butter in a frying pan, add the garlic and cook over a low heat for a few minutes. Add the mushrooms, season with salt and pepper to taste and stir. Cover and cook until tender. Meanwhile, heat the stock in a small saucepan. Remove and discard the garlic from the frying pan and, using a fish slice, transfer the mushrooms to a dish. Sift the flour into the frying pan and cook, stirring constantly, for 2 minutes, then stir in the warm stock. Stir in the cream, mushrooms and egg yolks. Cook for 5 minutes, stirring gently but constantly. Remove the pan from the heat as soon as the sauce thickens, and serve.

FUNGHI ALLA CREMA

Serves 4

80g/3 oz mushrooms

juice of 1 lemon, strained

2 tablespoons butter

1 garlic clove

150 ml/¹/₄ pint Vegetable Stock (see page 209)

1 tablespoon plain flour

150 ml/¹/₄ pint double cream

2 egg yolks

salt and pepper

MUSHROOMS WITH TOMATO

FUNGHI AL POMODORO

Serves 4

2 tablespoons olive oil

1 shallot, finely chopped

1 garlic clove, finely chopped

2 fresh flat-leaf parsley sprigs, finely chopped

600 g/1 lb 5 oz button

or chestnut mushrooms, thinly sliced

100 ml/3½ fl oz dry white wine

350 g/12 oz tomatoes, peeled and chopped

1 tablespoon chopped fresh marjoram

salt and pepper

Heat the oil in a pan, add the shallot, garlic and half the parsley and cook over a low heat, stirring occasionally, for 5 minutes. Add the mushrooms, increase the heat to high and cook for a few minutes. Pour in the wine and cook until it has evaporated. Lower the heat, add the tomatoes and season with salt and pepper, then cover and cook, stirring frequently, for about 10 minutes. Remove the lid, increase the heat slightly and cook until the excess liquid boils off. Stir in the remaining parsley. Transfer to a warm serving dish, sprinkle with the marjoram and serve immediately.

MUSHROOMS WITH PUMPKIN

FUNGHI CON LA ZUCCA

Serves 4

25 g/1 oz butter

2 tablespoons olive oil

1 onion, thinly sliced

300 g/11 oz pumpkin flesh, diced

600 g/1 lb 5 oz mixed mushrooms,

cut into thick slices if large

150 ml/¼ pint Vegetable Stock (see page 209)

3 tablespoons fresh flat-leaf parsley, chopped,

1 tablespoon chopped fresh marjoram

salt and pepper

Heat the butter with the oil in a pan, add the onion and cook over a low heat, stirring occasionally, for 5 minutes. Add the pumpkin and mushrooms, increase the heat to high and cook for a few minutes. Meanwhile, heat the stock in a small saucepan. Season the mushroom mixture with salt and pepper, lower the heat, pour in the hot stock and cook until tender. Stir in the parsley and marjoram, and transfer to a warm serving dish.

MELTING BAKED PORCINI

FUNGHI CROGIOLATI AL FORNO

Serves 4

100 ml/3½ fl oz olive oil, plus extra for brushing

800 g/1¾ lb porcini

1 fresh flat-leaf parsley sprig, chopped

1 garlic clove, chopped

soft part of 2 bread rolls, crumbled

salt and pepper

Preheat the oven to 180°C/350°F/Gas Mark 4. Brush an ovenproof dish with oil. Separate the porcini caps and stems and clean, wash and dry both. Pour 5 tablespoons of the olive oil into a bowl and season with salt and pepper. Add the porcini caps and leave to marinate. Mix together the parsley, garlic, breadcrumbs and remaining oil in another bowl. Take the porcini caps out of the marinade, place on a rack and put in the oven briefly to dry. Chop the porcini stems, place in the prepared dish, place the caps, gill side up, on top and sprinkle with the breadcrumb mixture. Drizzle with a little of the marinade. Bake for 10 minutes.

MUSHROOMS AU GRATIN

Melt 25 g/1 oz of the butter in a pan, add the shallot and cook over a low heat, stirring occasionally, for 5 minutes. Add the mushrooms, increase the heat to high and cook for a few minutes. Add the ham and parsley, season with salt and pepper, lower the heat to medium and cook, stirring occasionally, for about 10 minutes. Meanwhile, preheat the oven to 180°C/350°F/Gas Mark 4. Grease an ovenproof dish with butter. Remove the pan from the heat and transfer the mixture to the prepared dish. Stir the egg yolk, Parmesan and nutmeg into the béchamel sauce and spoon it over the mushrooms. Sprinkle with the breadcrumbs, dot with the remaining butter and bake for about 20 minutes. Remove the dish from the oven, leave to cool slightly, then serve.

FUNGHI GRATINATI

Serves 4

40 g/1$^1/_2$ oz butter, plus extra for greasing

1 shallot, chopped

600 g/1 lb 5 oz mushrooms, cut into thick slices if large

80 g/3 oz cooked ham, diced

1 fresh flat-leaf parsley sprig, chopped

1 egg yolk

2 tablespoons Parmesan cheese, freshly grated

pinch of freshly grated nutmeg

1 quantity Béchamel Sauce (see page 50)

1 tablespoon breadcrumbs

salt and pepper

WARM MUSHROOM SALAD

Heat the olive oil in a pan, add the mushrooms, garlic and speck and cook over a high heat for 2–3 minutes. Lower the heat, remove and discard the garlic and season with salt and pepper. Remove the pan from the heat and leave to cool slightly. Divide the lamb's lettuce among four plates and add the vinaigrette. Place the mushrooms and speck in the middle of each plate and serve immediately.

FUNGHI IN INSALATA TIEPIDA

Serves 4

2 tablespoons olive oil

400 g/14 oz button or chestnut mushrooms, sliced

1 garlic clove

50 g/2 oz speck (Austrian smoked ham), cut into strips

200 g/7 oz lamb's lettuce

1 quantity Vinaigrette, made with balsamic vinegar (see page 76)

salt and pepper

MUSHROOMS WITH AÏOLI

Slice the mushrooms thinly and sprinkle with the lemon juice. Blanch in boiling water for a few minutes, then drain. Heat the oil in a pan, add the mushrooms, herbs and fennel seeds and cook, stirring frequently, for 5 minutes. Lower the heat and cook the mushrooms slowly in their own juices until tender. Season with salt and pepper, remove from the heat and place in a warm serving dish. Serve with the aïoli.

FUNGHI IN SALSA AÏOLI

Serves 4

675 g/1$^1/_2$ lb mushrooms

juice of 1 lemon, strained

2 tablespoons olive oil

1 fresh tarragon sprig, chopped

4 fresh chives, chopped

1 fresh thyme sprig, chopped

1 fresh chervil sprig, chopped

1 teaspoon fennel seeds

1 quantity Aïoli, made with 10 garlic cloves (see page 64)

salt and pepper

PORCINI WITH TARRAGON

FUNGHI PORCINI AL DRAGONCELLO

Serves 4

8 porcini
50 g/2 oz butter
1 fresh tarragon sprig, chopped,
or 1 teaspoon dried tarragon
juice of 1 lemon, strained
salt and pepper

Preheat the oven to 160°C/325°F/Gas Mark 3. Line a roasting tin with foil. Separate the porcini caps and stems and set the stems aside for another dish. Place the caps in the roasting tin and place in the oven until they have dried out. If the caps are very big, make a cut in their tops with a knife. Melt the butter in a pan, add the mushrooms and tarragon, season with salt and pepper and cook over a low heat for 20 minutes. Sprinkle with the lemon juice and cook until it has evaporated, then serve.

PORCINI WITH PROSCIUTTO

FUNGHI PORCINI AL PROSCIUTTO

Serves 4

800 g/1¾ lb small porcini • 2 tablespoons olive oil
130 g/4½ oz prosciutto, diced
100 ml/3½ fl oz dry white wine
1 garlic clove, chopped
1 fresh marjoram sprig, finely chopped
salt and pepper

Separate the porcini caps and stems and chop the stems. Heat the oil in a pan, add the porcini stems and prosciutto and cook over a medium heat for 5 minutes. Add the wine and cook until it has evaporated. Add the garlic and marjoram and cook for a few minutes, then add the porcini caps. Lower the heat, cover and cook, shaking the pan occasionally, for 30 minutes. Season with salt and pepper and serve.

FRIED PORCINI

FUNGHI PORCINI FRITTI

Serves 4

vegetable oil, for deep-frying
plain flour, for dusting
600 g/1 lb 5 oz porcini, chopped
1 egg, lightly beaten
salt

Heat the oil in a large pan. Meanwhile, put the flour in a plastic bag, add the porcini, in batches, and shake to coat, then remove the porcini and dip them in the beaten egg. Deep-fry, in batches, in the hot oil until golden brown. Remove with a fish slice, drain on kitchen paper and transfer to a warm serving dish. Sprinkle with salt and serve immediately.

STUFFED MUSHROOMS

FUNGHI RIPIENI

Serves 4

2 tablespoons olive oil, plus extra
for brushing and drizzling
8 large chestnut mushrooms
3 bread slices, crusts removed
5 tablespoons milk
1 garlic clove
1 egg, lightly beaten
2 tablespoons Parmesan cheese, freshly grated
1 fresh flat-leaf parsley sprig, chopped
salt and pepper

Brush a flameproof casserole with oil. Separate the mushroom caps and stems. Place the caps, gill side up, in the prepared casserole and chop the stems. Tear the bread into pieces, place in a bowl, pour in the milk and leave to soak. Heat the olive oil in a pan, add the garlic and cook for a few minutes, then add the mushroom stems and cook for 5 minutes more. Season with salt and pepper, remove the pan from the heat and discard the garlic. Squeeze out the bread, mix with the mushroom stems, egg, Parmesan and parsley and season with salt and pepper. Fill the mushroom caps with the mixture, drizzle with olive oil, cover and cook over a medium heat for 15–20 minutes.

MUSHROOM TRIFOLATI

FUNGHI TRIFOLATI

Serves 4

3 tablespoons olive oil

50 g/2 oz butter

1 garlic clove

900 g/2 lb porcini

1 fresh flat-leaf parsley sprig, chopped

salt and pepper

Heat the olive oil, half the butter and the garlic in a pan until the garlic is browned, then remove and discard it. Add the porcini to the pan and cook over a high heat for about 30 minutes until all the liquid they release has evaporated, then lower the heat. Beat the parsley into the remaining butter in a bowl, then add to the pan and season with salt and pepper to taste. Serve immediately or set aside and reheat gently before serving.

MUSHROOM CAPS MONTANARA

TESTE DI FUNGHI ALLA MONTANARA

Serves 4

4 large porcini

olive oil, for brushing

350 ml/12 fl oz milk

1 garlic clove

1 teaspoon chopped fresh marjoram

100 g/3 ½ oz polenta flour

50 g/2 oz fontina cheese, cut into thin strips

salt and pepper

Preheat the grill. Separate the porcini caps and stems, brush the caps with olive oil and cook under the grill for a few minutes, then set aside. Reserve the stems for another recipe. Pour the milk into a saucepan, add the garlic and cook over a low heat until just below simmering point. Remove and discard the garlic and stir in the marjoram. Prepare polenta (see page 305) with the flour, substituting the hot, flavoured milk for water. When the polenta is very soft and smooth, season with salt and pepper, remove from the heat and stir in the fontina. Fill the porcini caps with the polenta mixture and arrange on a warm serving dish and serve.

MUSHROOM AND POTATO PIE

TORTINO DI FUNGHI E PATATE

Serves 4

40 g/1½ oz butter

500 g/1 lb 2 oz potatoes, very thinly sliced

500 g/1 lb 2 oz porcini, sliced

100 g/3½ oz Parmesan cheese, freshly grated

3 tablespoons fresh flat-leaaf parsley, chopped

salt

Preheat the oven to 180°C/350°F/Gas Mark 4. Melt the butter in an ovenproof dish and make alternating layers of potato and porcini slices, sprinkling each layer with Parmesan, parsley and a little salt. Add 5 tablespoons water, cover and bake for 1 hour. Remove from the oven, leave to stand for 5 minutes and serve.

BEANSPROUTS

Soya beans are pulses and therefore belong to the same family as chickpeas, beans and lentils. Outside Italy, soya consumption in the form of flour, sauce, oil and tofu is quite common. However, in Italy soya is best known for its sprouts . There are different varieties of soya beans, including yellow, which are very widespread in the United States, green, which have a more delicate flavour, and red, which are generally considered the best. In Britain, mung beansprouts are also widely available and popular. Beansprouts are best bought fresh. They should be white, without any blemishes, and firm enough to snap rather than bend. When they are sold in bags always check the 'use by' date on the packaging. Beansprouts are best eaten on the day of purchase and should not really be stored in the refrigerator unless this is unavoidable. Even then, the maximum period for storing them is 24–48 hours. If you have to put them in the refrigerator, take them out of their packaging, place them in a glass dish and cover. Beansprouts have no waste and simply require rinsing in cold water. They are tasty eaten raw, mixed in salads and are also delicious stir-fried or added to risottos. As for their nutritional value, they contain protein, vitamins A, B and C, potassium salts, magnesium, calcium and phosphorus. Beansprouts are thought to help lower blood cholesterol levels, while the lecithin they contain is considered to have a restorative effect on the central nervous system.

QUANTITIES

According to the recipe.

BOILING

Cook in boiling water for 2 minutes.

**QUANTITIES
AND COOKING TIMES**

GERMOGLI DI SOIA AI GAMBERETTI

Serves 4

1 skinless, boneless chicken breast

400 g/14 oz cooked, peeled prawns

1 celery stalk, sliced

400 g/14 oz beansprouts

1 tablespoon sesame seeds

1 spring onion, green part only, chopped

5 tablespoons dark soy sauce

2 teaspoons sesame oil

salt

BEANSPROUTS WITH PRAWNS

Poach the chicken in lightly salted, simmering water for about 25 minutes until cooked through. Drain and thinly slice. Arrange the chicken slices, prawns, celery and beansprouts on a fairly shallow serving dish and sprinkle with the sesame seeds and spring onion. Mix together the soy sauce and sesame oil in a bowl and season lightly with salt if necessary. Pour the dressing over the salad and serve immediately.

GERMOGLI DI SOIA AL PARMIGIANO

Serves 4

65 g/2$^{1}/_{2}$ oz butter

800 g/1$^{3}/_{4}$ lb beansprouts

40 g/1$^{1}/_{2}$ oz Parmesan cheese, freshly grated

salt

BEANSPROUTS WITH PARMESAN

Melt the butter in a frying pan, add the beansprouts, season with salt and cook over a low heat, stirring frequently, for about 10 minutes. Sprinkle in the Parmesan, cook until the cheese melts, then remove the pan from the heat. Transfer to a warm serving dish and serve immediately.

GERMOGLI DI SOIA PICCANTI

Serves 4

400 g/14 oz beansprouts

3 salted anchovies, heads removed, cleaned and filleted (see page 596), soaked in cold water for 10 minutes and drained

1 tablespoon capers, drained, rinsed and chopped

3 tablespoons olive oil

juice of 1 lemon, strained

10 green olives, stoned and quartered

1 tablespoon fresh flat-leaaf parsley, chopped

salt and pepper

SPICY BEANSPROUTS

Parboil the beansprouts for 2 minutes, then drain well and place in a salad bowl. Chop the anchovy fillets and mix them together with the capers, olive oil and lemon juice in a bowl, season with salt and pepper and spoon the mixture over the beansprouts. Add the olives, sprinkle with the parsley and serve.

ENDIVE

Endive belong to the chicory family. There are two types – curly endive, also called frisée, with curly leaves, and escarole, also called Batavian or broad-leaf endive, with longer flatter leaves. The base of the head, which gives endive their characteristic bitter flavour, may be trimmed according to taste. When cooking, the head may be left whole, or cut in half or even in quarters. Cooked or raw, endive make an excellent side dish for any kind of roast or fried meat.

QUANTITIES AND COOKING TIMES

QUANTITIES
Allow half a head per serving as a raw side dish. When cooking follow the quantity specified in the recipe.

BOILING
Immerse in salted, boiling water for about 10 minutes. Alternatively endive may be blanched, then sautéed in a frying pan with other flavourings.

CURLY ENDIVES IN BATTER

To make the batter, mix together the flour, a pinch of salt, the egg yolk and the olive oil in a bowl and add 150–175ml/5–6 fl oz water to obtain a smooth, runny mixture. Leave to stand for 30 minutes. Whisk the egg white in a grease-free bowl and fold it into the batter. Heat the vegetable oil in a large pan. Dip the endive leaves in the batter, one at a time, and fry in the oil until light golden brown. Remove with a fish slice and drain on kitchen paper. Place the leaves on a warm serving dish, and sprinkle with salt.

INDIVIA FRITTA IN PASTELLA

Serves 4

vegetable oil, for deep-frying

500 g/1 lb 2 oz curly endive, trimmed

For the batter

65 g/2¹/₂ oz plain flour

1 egg, separated

1 tablespoon olive oil

salt

INDIVIA RIPIENA DI OLIVE E CAPPERI

Serves 4

1½ garlic cloves

2 heads of escarole, trimmed

3 tablespoons olive oil, plus extra for brushing

50 g/2 oz breadcrumbs

80 g/3 oz stoned green olives, sliced

25 g/1 oz capers, drained and rinsed

1 fresh flat-leaf parsley sprig, chopped

salt and pepper

ESCAROLE STUFFED WITH OLIVES AND CAPERS

Chop the whole garlic clove. Place the escarole heads, with some of the water from washing still clinging to their leaves, in a frying pan with 2 tablespoons of the olive oil and the chopped garlic. Season with salt and pepper. Cover and cook over a low heat for about 15 minutes. Meanwhile, preheat the oven to 180°C/350°F/Gas Mark 4. Brush an ovenproof dish with oil. Heat the remaining olive oil in a saucepan, add the breadcrumbs and remaining garlic and cook, stirring frequently, until the breadcrumbs are golden. Remove and discard the garlic and stir in the olives, capers and parsley. Gently open out the escarole leaves, stuff the heads with almost all the breadcrumb mixture and press back into their original shapes. Place in the prepared dish and sprinkle with the remaining breadcrumbs. Bake for about 20 minutes.

PURÉ DI INDIVIA

Serves 4

1 kg/2¼ lb curly endive, trimmed

80 g/3 oz butter

pinch of sugar (optional)

25 g/1 oz plain flour

500 ml/18 fl oz milk

salt and pepper

CURLY ENDIVE PURÉE

Cook the endive in salted, boiling water for about 10 minutes until tender, then drain well and chop. Melt half the butter in a pan, add the endive and cook, stirring occasionally, until they are extremely soft – almost mashed – adding a little water if necessary. Season with salt and pepper, taste and, if the flavour is too bitter, add a pinch of sugar. Meanwhile, make a Béchamel Sauce (see page 50) using the remaining butter, the flour and milk. As soon as the sauce is ready, remove the pan from the heat, stir in the endive and serve.

CHICORY

Chicory has a characteristic elongated white head with hints of yellow. The leaves have a delicate, quite bitter taste. To reduce the bitterness, plunge into hot water for a few minutes. To prepare chicory, remove coarse or withered leaves and cut out the core with a small, sharp knife. Rinse the heads whole without opening the leaves. Chicory may be eaten raw in salads (sliced, then cut into strips), boiled and served with a variety of sauces, braised or baked.

QUANTITIES
Allow 1 medium-sized head per serving as a salad.

BRAISING
Blanch the chicory, then put it in a pan with butter and olive oil, cover and braise over a low heat until tender.

RAW
Remove the leaves one at a time. Because they are shaped like little boats they may be filled with tuna or salmon mousse.

QUANTITIES
AND COOKING TIMES

CHICORY WITH PRAGUE HAM

Preheat the oven to 180°C/350°F/Gas Mark 4. Grease an ovenproof dish with butter. Wrap each head of chicory in a slice of ham and place in the prepared dish. Season with salt and pepper, spoon in the béchamel sauce and sprinkle with the nutmeg. Add the stock and sprinkle with the Parmesan. Bake for 15 minutes. Remove the dish from the oven, leave to stand for 5 minutes and serve.

INDIVIA BELGA AL PROSCIUTTO DI PRAGA

Serves 4

butter, for greasing

4 heads of chicory, trimmed

4 large Prague ham or other smoked ham slices

250 ml/8 fl oz Béchamel Sauce (see page 50)

pinch of freshly grated nutmeg

150 ml/¹/₄ pint Meat Stock (see page 208)

4 tablespoons Parmesan cheese, freshly grated

salt and pepper

BAKED CHICORY

Preheat the oven to 180°C/350°F/Gas Mark 4. Grease an ovenproof dish with butter. Cut each head of chicory into four and place in the prepared dish. Season with salt and pepper, pour in the milk and stock and bake for 30 minutes or until the liquid has almost completely evaporated.

INDIVIA BELGA IN TEGLIA

Serves 4

butter, for greasing

800 g/1¾ lb chicory, trimmed

200 ml/7 fl oz milk

200 ml/7 fl oz Vegetable Stock (see page 209)

salt and pepper

BAKED CHICORY WITH NUTMEG

Preheat the oven to 180°C/350°F/Gas Mark 4. Grease an ovenproof dish with butter. Place the chicory in a steamer and steam for about 10 minutes. Remove from the heat, cut each head in half and place in the prepared dish. Season with salt and sprinkle with the breadcrumbs and nutmeg. Bake for 15 minutes until golden.

INDIVIA BELGA IN TEGLIA
ALLA NOCE MOSCATA

Serves 4

butter, for greasing

800 g/1¾ lb chicory, trimmed

80 g/3 oz breadcrumbs

generous pinch of freshly grated nutmeg

salt

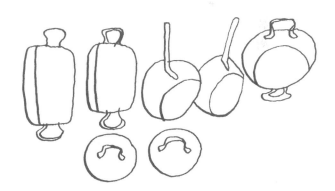

SALADS

Although the following pages are devoted to raw salads, you should not make the mistake of thinking they will cover only lettuce, chicory, radicchio, curly endive and escarole salads. Here, salad means any food – either raw or cooked – which is dressed with oil, vinegar and salt. Therefore you can have rice, crab, lentil, chicken, asparagus and many other types of salad. Dressing a salad is an art that requires a light hand. Tossing it properly is a culinary skill. Salads should be tossed lightly with the hands, as metal spoons can damage and bruise the leaves. Those who do not want to use their hands should choose wooden utensils. The salad bowl should be fairly large and preferably made of glass or porcelain. The classic dressing is salt, vinegar and oil, used in that order, just before serving so that the salad remains crisp. However, there are many other types of dressing and there are also several different types of oil and vinegar, each with a different aroma and flavour. Lemon juice is also widely used and several variations on the theme are possible.

OIL   VINEGAR

Serves 4

1 head of wild dandelion, trimmed

2 Little Gem lettuces, trimmed

1 head of curly endive, trimmed

1 bunch of radishes, thinly sliced

1 spring onion, thinly sliced

150 g/5 oz smoked salmon, cut into strips

juice of 1 lemon, strained

100 ml/3¹/₂ fl oz olive oil • 50 g/2 oz ricotta cheese

1 fresh flat-leaf parsley sprig, chopped

¹/₂ teaspoon chopped fresh dill

salt and pepper

SALMON SALAD WITH 'BEADS'

Place all the salad leaves in a salad bowl and add the radishes, spring onion and smoked salmon. Whisk together the lemon juice and olive oil in a bowl and season with salt and pepper. Pour the dressing over the salad and toss well. Put the ricotta in another bowl and stir in the parsley and dill. Roll into 'beads' with your fingers, sprinkle them over the salad and serve.

MIXED SALAD WITH POMEGRANATE

INSALATA CON MELAGRANA

Serves 4

1 pomegranate
2 carrots, cut into thin batons
1 bunch of lamb's lettuce, trimmed
1 bunch of rocket, trimmed
1 bunch of young spinach, trimmed
100 ml/3¹/₂ fl oz olive oil
1–2 tablespoons balsamic vinegar
juice of ¹/₂ orange, strained
salt

Cut a thin slice from one end of the pomegranate, stand it upright and cut down through the skin at intervals. Holding the pomegranate over a bowl, bend the segments backwards and scrape the seeds into the bowl with your fingers. Remove all traces of pith and membranes. Place the carrots, lamb's lettuce, rocket and spinach in a salad bowl. Whisk together the oil, vinegar and orange juice in another bowl and season with salt to taste. Pour the dressing over the salad and toss. Sprinkle with the pomegranate seeds and serve.

AVOCADO SALAD

INSALATA DI AVOCADO

Serves 4

2 avocados
juice of 1 lemon, strained
2 tangerines
1 Cos lettuce, trimmed
2 tomatoes, sliced
1 spring onion, sliced
2 fresh flat-leaf parsley sprigs, chopped
2 teaspoons Dijon mustard
6 tablespoons olive oil
salt and pepper

Peel, halve and stone the avocados, then cut into slices and sprinkle with the lemon juice. Peel the tangerines, cut away all traces of pith and slice horizontally. Arrange a bed of lettuce leaves on each of four plates. Make a layer with the tomatoes and spring onion, then arrange a ring of avocado slices, top with the tangerine slices and sprinkle with the parsley. Mix together the mustard and olive oil in a bowl, season with salt and pepper, pour the dressing over the salad and serve.

BRESAOLA WITH LAMB'S LETTUCE

INSALATA DI BRESAOLA E SONGINO

Serves 4

150 g/5 oz lamb's lettuce
2 round fennel bulbs, trimmed, halved and thinly sliced
150 g/5 oz bresaola, thinly sliced
1 celery stalk, cut into thin batons
1 egg yolk
3 tablespoons balsamic vinegar
100 ml/3¹/₂ fl oz olive oil
salt and pepper

Arrange a bed of lettuce leaves on each of four plates and top with a fan of fennel. Place the bresaola on top and sprinkle with the celery. Whisk together the egg yolk, vinegar and olive oil in a bowl and season with salt and pepper, then pour into a sauce boat. Serve the salad with the sauce.

WHITE CABBAGE SALAD

INSALATA DI CAVOLO CAPUCCIO

Serves 4

1/2 white cabbage, cored and shredded
2 carrots, cut into thin batons
1 celery stalk, cut into thin batons
1 spring onion, thinly sliced
1 fresh flat-leaf parsley sprig, chopped
120 ml/4 fl oz Mayonnaise (see page 65)
1 teaspoon Worcestershire sauce
salt and pepper

Put the cabbage in a salad bowl and add the carrots and celery. Sprinkle the salad with the spring onion and parsley, season with salt and pepper and toss. Mix together the mayonnaise and Worcestershire sauce in a bowl, add to the salad and toss again.

CUCUMBER SALAD

INSALATA DI CETRIOLI

Serves 4

3 small cucumbers, sliced
2 pears
juice of 1 lemon, strained
200 g/7 oz feta cheese, diced
1 fresh thyme sprig, chopped
4 tablespoons olive oil
1 tablespoon balsamic vinegar
salt and pepper

Blanch the cucumber slices in salted, boiling water for a few minutes, then drain and refresh under cold water. Spread out on a tea towel to dry. Peel and core the pears, then slice thinly and sprinkle with lemon juice. Make a ring of cucumber slices on each of four individual plates. Surround with a ring of pear slices, then another ring of cucumber and, finally, a ring of feta. Sprinkle with the thyme. Whisk together the olive oil and vinegar in a bowl, season with salt and pepper, pour the dressing over the salad and serve.

SWEETCORN AND RADICCHIO SALAD

INSALATA DI MAIS E RADICCHIO

Serves 4

100 g/3 1/2 oz baby spinach leaves, chopped
3 Treviso radicchio, chopped
100 g/3 1/2 oz smoked ham, diced
200 g/7 oz canned sweetcorn, drained
juice of 1 lemon, strained
100 ml/3 1/2 fl oz olive oil
salt

Put the spinach and radicchio in a salad bowl and add the ham and sweetcorn. Put a pinch of salt in a bowl, add the lemon juice and stir to dissolve, then whisk in the olive oil. Pour the dressing over the salad and toss.

CAESAR'S MUSHROOM SALAD WITH MARJORAM

INSALATA DI OVOLI CRUDI ALLA MAGGIORANA

Serves 4

400 g/14 oz Caesar's mushrooms, trimmed
juice of 1/2 lemon, strained
1 small fresh marjoram sprig, chopped
olive oil, for drizzling • salt

Thinly slice the mushrooms, place in a bowl and sprinkle with the lemon juice and marjoram. Season with salt and drizzle with olive oil. Toss and serve.

SPINACH AND SCALLOP SALAD

Holding the shell flat side up, open each scallop by inserting a strong knife between the shells and cutting through the upper muscle. Separate the shells and slide the blade under the scallop to cut the lower muscle. Remove the white flesh and discard the remainder. Heat 1 tablespoon of the olive oil in a small saucepan, add the scallops, then pour in the wine and cook until it has evaporated. Season with salt and pepper and remove from the heat. Place the spinach and tomatoes in a salad bowl. Peel the lemon, remove all traces of pith and dice the flesh, then add to the salad. Mix together the shallot, parsley, vinegar, and remaining olive oil in a bowl and season with salt and pepper. Pour the dressing over the salad and toss. Add the scallops and serve.

INSALATA DI SPINACI E CAPPESANTE

Serves 4

8 scallops

6 tablespoons olive oil

100 ml/3^1/$_2$ fl oz white wine

300 g/11 oz young spinach leaves,

tough stalks removed

8 cherry tomatoes, halved

1 lemon

1 shallot, chopped

1 fresh flat-leaf parsley sprig, chopped

2 tablespoons red wine vinegar

salt and pepper

SPINACH AND MUSHROOM SALAD

Sprinkle the mushrooms with a little of the lemon juice and place in a salad bowl. Add the spinach and pine nuts. Whisk together the olive oil and remaining lemon juice in a bowl and season with salt and pepper. Pour the dressing over the salad, toss and serve.

INSALATA DI SPINACI E FUNGHI

Serves 4

150 g/5 oz mushrooms, thinly sliced

juice of 1 lemon, strained

300 g/11 oz spinach, coarse stalks removed

25 g/1 oz pine nuts

4 tablespoons olive oil

salt and pepper

TURKEY AND BEAN SALAD

Heat 3 tablespoons of the olive oil in a frying pan, add the turkey breast and cook over a medium heat, stirring frequently, until golden brown all over. Season with salt and pepper and remove from the heat. Chop the capers with the parsley, put them in a salad bowl and add the turkey, spring onion and beans. Mix together the mustard, the remaining olive oil and the vinegar in a bowl and season with salt and pepper. Pour the dressing over the salad, toss and serve.

INSALATA DI TACCHINO E FAGIOLI

Serves 4

7 tablespoons olive oil, plus extra for dressing

250 g/9 oz skinless turkey breast fillet, cut into strips

1 tablespoon capers, drained and rinsed

1 fresh flat-leaf parsley sprig

1 spring onion, thinly sliced

350 g/12 oz canned borlotti beans,

drained and rinsed

1^1/$_2$ teaspoons Dijon mustard

1 tablespoon red wine vinegar

salt and pepper

INSALATA DI TREVISANA AI FUNGHI

Serves 4

3 Treviso radicchio, trimmed

300 g/11 oz mushrooms

juice of 1 lemon, strained

200 g/7 oz lamb's lettuce, trimmed

1 bunch of dandelion leaves, trimmed

4 tablespoons olive oil

salt and pepper

TREVISO RADICCHIO SALAD WITH MUSHROOMS

Make a bed of radicchio leaves on each of four plates. Slice the mushrooms, sprinkle with a little of the lemon juice and fan out on top of the radicchio. Add the lamb's lettuce and dandelion leaves. Whisk together the olive oil and 2 tablespoons of the remaining lemon juice in a bowl and season with salt and pepper. Gently pour the dressing over the salad and serve.

INSALATA DI TREVISANA AI GAMBERETTI

Serves 4

3 Treviso radicchio, trimmed

2 avocados

juice of 1 lemon, strained

300 g/11 oz cooked prawns, peeled and deveined

200 g/7 oz canned palm hearts, drained, rinsed and sliced

2 tablespoons olive oil

1 fresh thyme sprig, chopped

1 fresh marjoram sprig, chopped

1 fresh flat-leaf parsley sprig, chopped

salt and pepper

TREVISO RADICCHIO AND PRAWN SALAD

Make a bed of radicchio leaves on each of four plates. Peel, halve, stone and slice the avocados, sprinkle with a little of the lemon juice to prevent discoloration and arrange in rings on top of the radicchio. Top with the prawns and complete with the palm hearts. Whisk together 2 tablespoons of the remaining lemon juice and the olive oil in a bowl, season with salt and pepper and stir in the thyme, marjoram and parsley. Pour the dressing over the salad and serve.

INSALATA GIALLA AL MAIS

Serves 4

1/2 Golden Delicious apple

juice of 1 lemon, strained

50 g/2 oz mature pecorino cheese, diced

2 carrots, cut into thin batons

250 g/9 oz canned sweetcorn, drained

200 g/7 oz beansprouts

5 radishes, thinly sliced

2 tablespoons olive oil

salt and white pepper

YELLOW SALAD WITH SWEETCORN

Peel, core and dice the apple, sprinkle with half the lemon juice and put in a salad bowl. Add the pecorino, carrots, sweetcorn, beansprouts and radishes. Whisk together the olive oil and the remaining lemon juice in a bowl and season with salt and pepper. Pour the dressing over the salad, toss very gently and leave to stand in a cool place for about 30 minutes before serving.

HAWAIIAN SALAD

Put the prawns, sweetcorn and peppers in a salad bowl. Halve the pineapples, lengthways, keeping the leaves attached. Using a small sharp knife, scoop out the insides, leaving about 5 mm/¹/₄ inch around the sides of the 'shells'. Reserve the shells. Discard the core and dice the flesh of one pineapple. Add to the salad and leave to stand in a cool place. Whisk together the lemon juice, olive oil and Tabasco in a bowl and season with salt and pepper. Just before serving, pour the dressing over the salad, toss well and spoon into the pineapple shells. Place on individual plates, garnish with a few watercress leaves and serve.

INSALATA HAWAIANA

Serves 4

200 g/7 oz cooked prawns, peeled and deveined

200 g/7 oz canned sweetcorn, drained

1 red pepper, halved, seeded and diced

¹/₂ green pepper, halved, seeded and diced

2 small pineapples

juice of 1 lemon, strained

4 tablespoons olive oil

dash of Tabasco sauce

salt and pepper

watercress leaves, to garnish

MIXED TUNA SALAD

Put the beans, rocket, radicchio, pepper, celery, fennel and tomatoes in a salad bowl. Add the tuna and olives. Whisk together the olive oil, oregano and a pinch each of salt and pepper in a bowl. Pour the dressing over the salad, toss and serve.

INSALATA MISTA AL TONNO

Serves 4

250 g/9 oz canned cannellini beans, drained and rinsed

1 bunch of rocket, trimmed

1 radicchio, trimmed

1 red pepper, halved seeded and cut into strips

1 celery stalk, cut into thin batons

1 round fennel bulb, trimmed and thinly sliced

2 tomatoes, cut into wedges

250 g/9 oz canned tuna in oil, drained and flaked

50 g/2 oz stoned black olives

4 tablespoons olive oil

pinch of dried oregano

salt and pepper

RICH SALAD

Peel, halve and stone the avocado, then slice thinly and sprinkle with a little of the lemon juice. Put the avocado slices, endive, radicchio, pine nuts and palm hearts in a salad bowl. Whisk together the olive oil, Worcestershire sauce and remaining lemon juice in a bowl and season with salt and pepper. Pour the dressing over the salad, toss and serve.

INSALATA RICCA

Serves 4

1 avocado

juice of 1 lemon, strained

1 head of curly endive, chopped

1 radicchio, cut into strips

40 g/1¹/₂ oz pine nuts

300 g/11 oz canned palm hearts,

drained, rinsed and sliced

4 tablespoons olive oil

1 teaspoon Worcestershire sauce

salt and pepper

INSALATA SICILIANA

Serves 4

1 spring onion, trimmed and soaked in cold water

4 radishes, trimmed and soaked in cold water

2 citrons

2 bunches of rocket, trimmed

2 heads of escarole, trimmed

2 bunches of lamb's lettuce, trimmed

50 g/2 oz beansprouts

juice of 1 lemon, strained

4 tablespoons olive oil

1 fresh flat-leaf parsley sprig, chopped

salt and pepper

SICILIAN SALAD

Drain the spring onion and radishes and slice thinly. Cut off all the peel and pith from the citrons and slice crossways. Put the spring onion, radishes, citrons, rocket, escarole, lamb's lettuce and beansprouts in a salad bowl. Whisk the lemon juice with a pinch of salt and pepper in a bowl, then gradually whisk in the olive oil. Stir in the parsley, pour the dressing over the salad, toss gently and serve immediately.

INSALATINA AI CAPPERI

Serves 4

1 bunch of dandelion leaves, trimmed

1 curly lettuce, such as lollo rosso, trimmed

1 carrot, cut into thin batons

1 round fennel bulb, thinly sliced

4 tablespoons olive oil

2 tablespoons red wine vinegar

2 tablespoons capers, drained and rinsed

6 fresh basil leaves, chopped

salt

CAPER SALAD

Cut the dandelion and lettuce leaves into thin strips and put in a salad bowl. Add the carrot and fennel. Whisk together the olive oil and vinegar in a bowl and season with salt. Add the capers and basil to the salad, pour the dressing over it, toss and serve.

LETTUCE

Lettuce is one of the best-known and most delightful vegetable families. Round lettuces, with soft, light leaves, have a nearly ball-shaped head. Long lettuces, such as Cos, with long crispy leaves, have very large heads. Loose-leaf varieties are early lettuces that grow back after cutting. Their aroma is best appreciated in refreshing salads and, when cooked, they are said to alleviate digestive disorders and induce sleep. Lettuce's reputation for reducing libido, if it is based on the properties of the plant's sap, is undeserved in the light of normal sized portions. Lettuce's true gift is that it is low in calories and at the same time provides plenty of vitamins and minerals. Its juice is said to calm coughing. Cream of lettuce soup is very delicate, and lettuce fried with peas, makes a delicious side dish. Adding lettuce to soups, cutting it into strips or puréeing it enhances their flavour.

QUANTITIES
A medium head is suffi-cient for 2–3 servings of raw salad.

BOILING
Cook for 20 minutes in salted, boiling water.

QUANTITIES
AND COOKING TIMES

LETTUCE HEARTS WITH HERBS

CUORI DI LATTUGA ALLE ERBE

Serves 4

4 lettuce hearts

1 tablespoon Dijon mustard

2 tablespoons balsamic vinegar

5–6 tablespoons olive oil

1 fresh tarragon sprig, chopped

4 fresh chives, chopped

1 fresh chervil sprig, chopped

salt and pepper

Cut each lettuce heart into four and place in a salad bowl. Mix together the mustard and vinegar in a bowl and season with salt and pepper. Gradually whisk in the olive oil. Sprinkle the lettuce with the herbs and pour the dressing over the salad. Toss and leave to stand for 10 minutes before serving.

BRAISED LETTUCE WITH PANCETTA COPPATA

LATTUGA BRASATA CON PANCETTA

Serves 4

4 heads of lettuce, trimmed

200 g/7 oz pancetta coppata

(unsmoked pancetta stuffed with shoulder ham)

40 g/1¹/₂ oz butter

1 shallot, sliced

1 carrot, chopped

150 ml/¹/₄ pint Meat Stock (see page 208)

salt

Parboil the lettuce in salted, boiling water for a few minutes, then drain, pat dry with kitchen paper and chop finely. Cut 12 slices of pancetta coppata and place a mound of lettuce on each slice, then roll up and secure each with a cocktail stick. Chop the remaining pancetta coppata. Melt half the butter in a pan, add the shallot, carrot and chopped pancetta coppata. Add the filled rolls and cook, turning occasionally, until lightly browned all over, then pour in the stock and simmer for 10 minutes. Add the remaining butter and a pinch of salt, stir and cook over a high heat for a few minutes. Transfer the filled rolls to a warm serving dish and spoon the cooking juices over them.

STUFFED LETTUCE

LATTUGA RIPIENA

Serves 4

1 thick bread slice, crusts removed

100 ml/3¹/₂ fl oz milk

100 g/3¹/₂ oz minced meat

100 g/3¹/₂ oz sausage meat

1 tablespoon Parmesan cheese, freshly grated

1 egg, lightly beaten

4 round lettuces

50 g/2 oz lardons

3 tablespoons olive oil

40 g/1¹/₂ oz butter

salt and pepper

Tear the bread into pieces, place in a bowl, add the milk and leave to soak for 10 minutes, then squeeze out. Mix together the meat, sausage meat, bread and Parmesan in a bowl and season with salt and pepper. Add the egg and mix until combined. Remove and discard the outer leaves and part of the centres of the lettuces, wash the lettuces and blanch in salted, boiling water for 3 minutes. Drain, gently open out the leaves and stuff with the meat mixture. Reshape and tie the tops with kitchen string. Spread out the lardons in a flameproof casserole and place the lettuces on top. Pour in the olive oil and dot the lettuces with the butter. Add 100 ml/3¹/₂ fl oz water, cover and cook over a medium heat for about 30 minutes.

LENTILS

Lentils are small but rich in nutrients. They contain a remarkable amount of calcium, phosphorus and iron. There are several different types. In Italy the most famous, owing to their particularly delicate flavour, are Umbrian lentils, which are cultivated on the Castelluccio plateau in the province of Norcia. They are small, dull green in colour and keep their shape when cooked. Orange lentils, which cook more quickly than other kinds, are known in Italy as Egyptian lentils. Like all dried pulses, lentils may be soaked in cold water for a few hours before cooking, but not for too long or they begin to sprout. Discard any that float to the surface during soaking. Lentils lend themselves to a variety of dishes, including soups and side dishes. They can be served warm – dressed with salt, vinegar, oil and basil leaves – as a starter for a summer lunch or at any other time of year.

QUANTITIES AND COOKING TIMES

OIL

QUANTITIES
Allow 65–80 g/2^{1}/$_{2}$–3 oz per serving.

BOILING
Soak, drain and rinse the lentils. Put them in a saucepan, add water to cover, a celery stalk, carrot and small onion and bring to the boil. Lower the heat and simmer for about 1^{1}/$_{2}$ hours, adding hot water if necessary to prevent them drying out. Season with salt once they are cooked.

LENTICCHIE CON SALSICCIA

Serves 4

250 g/9 oz lentils, soaked in cold water
for 3 hours and drained
1 celery stalk • 1 carrot
1 small onion
8 small Italian sausages
2 tablespoons olive oil
6 fresh sage leaves
1 garlic clove

LENTILS WITH SAUSAGES

Put the lentils into a saucepan, add water to cover, and the celery, carrot and onion and bring to the boil. Lower the heat and simmer for about 1^{1}/$_{2}$ hours. Put the sausages in a pan with 2 tablespoons water, prick with a fork and cook for 10 minutes until browned. Meanwhile, heat the olive oil in another pan, add the sage and garlic and cook over a low heat until the garlic is golden brown. Remove and discard the garlic. Drain the lentils and add to the flavoured oil with the sausages. Mix well and serve.

LENTICCHIE IN UMIDO

Serves 4

250 g/9 oz lentils, soaked in cold water
for 3 hours and drained

2 tablespoons olive oil

25 g/1 oz butter

1 fresh sage leaf, chopped

25 g/1 oz pancetta, chopped

1 carrot, chopped

1 celery stalk, chopped

1 onion, chopped

500 ml/18 fl oz passata

salt and pepper

LENTILS IN TOMATO SAUCE

Put the lentils into a saucepan, add water to cover and bring to the boil. Lower the heat and simmer for about 1¹/₂ hours. Heat the olive oil and butter in a pan, add the sage, pancetta, carrot, celery and onion and cook over a low heat, stirring occasionally, for 5 minutes. Add the passata, season with salt and pepper to taste and simmer for 15 minutes. Drain the lentils and tip into the pan of vegetables, mix well and simmer for 10 minutes. Transfer to a warm serving dish.

LENTICCHIE STUFATE AL BACON

Serves 4

300 g/11 oz lentils, soaked in cold water

1 carrot

1 celery stalk

100 g/3¹/₂ oz bacon in a single slice

1 garlic clove

1 onion

salt

LENTILS WITH BACON

Put the lentils into a saucepan, add water to cover, and the carrot and celery and bring to the boil. Add the bacon, garlic and onion, lower the heat, cover and simmer for about 1¹/₂ hours. Remove and discard the vegetables. Remove the bacon, cut it into strips and return to the pan. Season with salt to taste. This side dish may also be served as a fairly thick soup.

PURÉ DI LENTICCHIE

Serves 4

300 g/11 oz lentils, soaked in cold water
for 3 hours and drained

1 celery stalk

1 carrot

200 ml/7 fl oz double cream

25g/1 oz butter

salt and white pepper

LENTIL PURÉE

Put the lentils into a saucepan, add water to cover, and the celery and carrot and bring to the boil. Lower the heat and simmer for about 1¹/₂ hours. Drain and pass through a food mill into a clean pan, then season with salt. Set the pan over a low heat, stir in the cream and cook until the purée has the desired consistency. Remove the pan from the heat, stir in the butter and season with pepper to taste.

AUBERGINES

The round Violetta di Firenze, Violetta Lunga di Napoli, the long Violetta di Rimini, Lunga Nera di Chioggia and Black Beauty are just some of the many varieties of aubergine whose names are inspired by the deep, brilliant colour of the skin of this vegetable, originally from India. Lesser known, but equally good, is the white aubergine. When preparing aubergines it is not always necessary to sprinkle them with salt and leave to drain for 30 minutes. Modern varieties do not usually contain bitter juices. However, salting makes their flavour more delicate and helps to reduce the amount of oil they will absorb. In case of doubt, follow the instructions given in the recipe.

QUANTITIES

Allow about 200 g/7 oz per serving, according to the recipe.

BOILING

Aubergines are not boiled, but they are sliced, then blanched in water and vinegar before being preserved in oil.

SWEATING

Cook in a frying pan over a low heat with garlic, oil, salt and diced tomatoes. This takes about 20 minutes.

**QUANTITIES
AND COOKING TIMES**

AUBERGINE CAVIAR

Slice off and discard the ends of the aubergines, then cook in salted, boiling water until very tender. Tip into a colander and leave to drain so that they lose as much water as possible, but do not allow them to cool completely. Peel the aubergines, place the flesh in a bowl and mash with a potato masher. Alternatively, pass the flesh through a food mill into a bowl. Stir in the lemon juice and olive oil and season with salt and pepper. Mix well and leave to cool. Garnish with tomato slices and serve with buttered toast. Aubergine caviar keeps in an airtight container in the refrigerator for several days.

CAVIALE DI MELANZANE

Serves 4

3 aubergines

juice of 1 lemon, strained

6 tablespoons olive oil

salt and pepper

sliced tomatoes, to garnish

buttered toast, to serve

AUBERGINE FRICASSÉE

FRICASSEA DI MELANZANE

Serves 4

5 aubergines, thickly sliced

25 g/1 oz butter

3 tablespoons olive oil

1 onion, chopped

500 g/1 lb 2 oz ripe plum tomatoes, peeled, seeded and chopped

1 fresh flat-leaf parsley sprig, chopped

1 garlic clove, chopped

2 eggs

juice of 1 lemon, strained

salt and pepper

Place the aubergine slices in a colander, sprinkle with salt and leave to drain for 30 minutes. Meanwhile, melt the butter with the oil in a saucepan, add the onion and cook over a low heat, stirring occasionally, for 5 minutes. Rinse the aubergines, pat dry and add to the pan, then add the tomatoes, parsley and garlic and season with salt and pepper. Mix well and cook over a medium heat for about 15 minutes or until the aubergines are tender. Remove the pan from the heat. Beat the eggs with the lemon juice and pour over the aubergine mixture. Stir rapidly so that the egg does not scramble but coats the mixture like a cream. Transfer the fricassée to a warm serving dish and serve immediately.

AUBERGINES WITH CREAM

MELANZANE ALLA PANNA

Serves 4

3 aubergines, cut into 5-mm/¹/₄-inch thick slices

50 g/2 oz butter

1 shallot, chopped

1 fresh flat-leaf parsley sprig, chopped

4 gherkins, drained and chopped

25 g/1 oz pine nuts, chopped

5 tablespoons white wine vinegar

5 tablespoons double cream

salt and pepper

Blanch the aubergines in salted, boiling water for a few minutes, then drain and leave to cool slightly. Melt half the butter in a pan, add the shallot and cook over a low heat, stirring occasionally, for 5 minutes. Add the parsley, gherkins and pine nuts, stir well, sprinkle in the vinegar and cook until it has evaporated. Pour in the cream, season with salt and pepper and cook over a very low heat for 15 minutes. Meanwhile, melt the remaining butter in a frying pan, add the aubergines and cook over a medium heat until golden brown on both sides. Tip the contents of the frying pan into the cream sauce and cook for a further 10 minutes. Transfer to a warm serving dish.

AUBERGINES WITH ANCHOVIES

MELANZANE ALLE ACCIUGHE

Serves 4

120 ml/4 fl oz olive oil

3 aubergines, cut into 5-mm/¹/₄-inch thick slices

1 garlic clove

4 salted anchovies, heads removed, cleaned and filleted (see page 596), soaked in cold water for 10 minutes and drained

1 fresh flat-leaf parsley sprig, chopped

1 tablespoon white wine vinegar

Heat half the oil in a frying pan, add the aubergines, in batches if necessary, and cook over a medium heat until golden brown all over. Remove with a fish slice, drain on kitchen paper and place on a warm serving dish. Heat the remaining oil in a small saucepan, add the garlic and cook for a few minutes until browned, then remove and discard. Add the anchovies to the saucepan and cook, mashing with a fork until they have almost disintegrated. Stir in the parsley and vinegar, cook for a few minutes more, then pour over the aubergines and serve.

GRILLED AUBERGINES

MELANZANE ARROSTO

Serves 4

3 aubergines, thickly sliced

3 garlic cloves, thinly sliced

18 fresh basil leaves

olive oil, for drizzling

salt and pepper

Place the aubergine slices in a colander, sprinkle with salt and leave to drain for about 30 minutes. Preheat the grill. Rinse the aubergine slices and pat dry with kitchen paper, then grill on both sides for a few minutes. Remove from the heat and leave to cool. Arrange the aubergine slices in layers on a serving dish, sprinkling each layer with garlic, basil leaves, salt and pepper and drizzling with plenty of olive oil. Set aside in a cool place for at least 1 hour to allow the flavours to mingle before serving.

GRANDMOTHER'S AUBERGINES

MELANZANE DELLA NONNA

Serves 4

4 aubergines, halved

2 tablespoons olive oil

2 onions, thinly sliced

2 garlic cloves

5 tomatoes, peeled, seeded and diced

1 fresh flat-leaf parsley sprig, chopped

1 tablespoon capers, drained, rinsed and chopped

1 tablespoon black olives, stoned and sliced

1 tablespoon white wine vinegar

1 teaspoon sugar

salt and pepper

Scoop out and discard the central, seed-filled part of the aubergines and dice the remaining flesh. Place in a colander, sprinkle with salt and set aside for 30 minutes to drain, then rinse and pat dry with kitchen paper. Heat the oil in a frying pan, add the onions and garlic and cook for 1–2 minutes over a low heat until the garlic is light golden brown, then remove and discard it. Add the aubergines to the pan, mix well, then stir in the tomatoes and season with salt and pepper. Cook, stirring frequently, for 15 minutes. Add the parsley, capers, olives, vinegar and sugar and cook for a few minutes more. Taste for the combination of sweet and sour. If the mixture is too sweet, add a little more vinegar; if it is too sour, add a pinch of sugar. After a few minutes, remove the pan from the heat, and transfer the aubergines to a warm serving dish.

AUBERGINES STUFFED WITH MOZZARELLA

MELANZANE FARCITE ALLA MOZZARELLA

Serves 4

2 tablespoons olive oil, plus extra for drizzling

4 small aubergines, halved lengthways

200 g/7 oz mozzarella cheese, diced

2 salted anchovies, heads removed, cleaned and filleted (see page 596), soaked in cold water for 10 minutes and drained

120 ml/4 fl oz passata

salt and pepper

fresh basil sprigs, to garnish (optional)

Preheat the oven to 200°C/400°F/Gas Mark 6. Brush an ovenproof dish with oil. Scoop out the aubergine flesh with a small sharp knife leaving the 'shells' intact. Dice the flesh, place in a bowl and add the mozzarella and anchovies. Mix well, season with salt and pepper and stir in the olive oil. Spoon the mixture into the aubergine shells and top each with 1 tablespoon of the tomato sauce. Place in the prepared dish and bake for about 30 minutes. Transfer to a warm serving dish. This dish may be garnished with fresh basil sprigs if you like.

AUBERGINES AU GRATIN

Place the aubergine slices in a colander, sprinkle with salt and leave to drain for about 30 minutes. Preheat the grill to high. Rinse the aubergines, pat dry and brush with a little oil. Grill until golden on both sides. Heat the oil in a saucepan, add the garlic and onions and cook over a low heat, stirring occasionally, for 5 minutes. Add the parsley and tomatoes, season with salt and pepper, mix well and simmer for about 15 minutes until thickened. Meanwhile, preheat the oven to 200°C/400°F/Gas Mark 6. Brush an ovenproof dish with oil. Make a layer of aubergine slices in the prepared dish, season with salt and pepper and spoon in a layer of the tomato sauce. Continue making alternating layers of aubergine slices and tomato sauce until all the ingredients are used. Mix together the Emmenthal and breadcrumbs and sprinkle over the top. Dot with the butter and bake for about 20 minutes until golden brown.

MELANZANE GRATINATE

Serves 4

600 g/1 lb 5 oz aubergines,
cut into 5-mm/¹/₄-inch thick slices
2 tablespoons olive oil, plus extra for brushing
2 garlic cloves, chopped
2 onions, chopped
1 fresh flat-leaf parsley sprig, chopped
500 g/1 lb 2 oz canned chopped tomatoes
80 g/3 oz Emmenthal cheese, diced
50 g/2 oz breadcrumbs
25 g/1 oz butter
salt and pepper

SURPRISE AUBERGINES IN BREADCRUMBS

Place the aubergine slices in a colander, sprinkle with salt and leave to drain for about 30 minutes. Meanwhile, mix together the prosciutto, scamorza or provolone, parsley and Parmesan in a bowl and season with salt and pepper. Preheat the grill to high. Rinse the aubergines, pat dry carefully and brush with a little oil. Grill until golden brown on both sides. Sandwich the slices together in pairs filled with the prosciutto and cheese mixture. Beat the eggs with a pinch of salt in a shallow dish and spread out the breadcrumbs in another shallow dish. Heat the oil in a large frying pan. Dip each aubergine sandwich first in the beaten eggs, then in the breadcrumbs. Fry in the hot oil until evenly browned all over. Remove with a fish slice and drain on kitchen paper. Arrange on a warm serving dish.

MELANZANE IMPANATE A SORPRESA

Serves 4

600 g/1 lb 5 oz round aubergines,
cut into 5-mm/¹/₄-inch thick slices
100 g/3¹/₂ oz prosciutto, diced
120 g/4 oz smoked scamorza,
provolone or other stretched curd cheese, diced
1 fresh flat-leaf parsley sprig, chopped
2 tablespoons Parmesan cheese, freshly grated
olive oil, for brushing and frying
2 eggs
80 g/3 oz breadcrumbs
salt and pepper

FESTIVE AUBERGINES

MELANZANE IN FESTA

Serves 4

olive oil, for brushing and drizzling

4 small round aubergines

4 large ripe tomatoes, seeded and thinly sliced

250 g/9 oz mozzarella cheese, thinly sliced

2 garlic cloves, finely chopped

1 fresh flat-leaf parsley sprig, finely chopped

4 fresh basil leaves, finely chopped

salt and pepper

Preheat the oven to 180°C/350°F/Gas Mark 4. Brush an ovenproof dish with oil. Cut off the aubergine stalks, then slice lengthways without cutting all the way through, leaving the slices joined at the base. Place the aubergines in the prepared dish. Carefully place alternate slices of tomato and mozzarella between each aubergine slice and the next. Mix together the garlic, parsley and basil in a bowl and sprinkle over the aubergines. Season with salt and pepper to taste and drizzle with olive oil. Cover the dish with foil and bake for 45 minutes. Remove the foil and continue to bake for a further 15–20 minutes. Carefully transfer the aubergines to a warm serving dish and spoon the cooking juices over them.

ROAST AUBERGINES WITH RICOTTA

MELANZANE IN FORNO ALLA RICOTTA

Serves 4

50 g/2 oz dried mushrooms

olive oil, for brushing and drizzling

4 small aubergines, halved lengthways

2 garlic cloves, chopped

1 fresh flat-leaf parsley sprig, chopped

150 g/5 oz ricotta cheese

4 tablespoons Parmesan cheese, freshly grated

1 egg, lightly beaten

pinch of dried oregano

2 salted anchovies, heads removed, cleaned and filleted (see page 596), soaked in cold water for 10 minutes and drained

salt and pepper

Put the mushrooms in a bowl, add hot water to cover and leave to soak for about 30 minutes. Preheat the oven to 180°C/350°F/Gas Mark 4. Brush an ovenproof dish with oil. Scoop out the flesh from the aubergines into a bowl without piercing the 'shells'. Cook the shells in salted, boiling water for 8–9 minutes, then remove with a fish slice and place upside down on kitchen paper to drain. Add half the aubergine flesh to the same water, cook for a few minutes, then drain, squeeze out and mix with the garlic and parsley. Mix together the ricotta, Parmesan, egg and oregano in a bowl and season with salt and pepper, then stir in the aubergine and garlic mixture. Drain and squeeze out the mushrooms. Chop the mushrooms and anchovies together and stir into the mixture. Spoon the mixture into the aubergine shells, place in the prepared dish and drizzle with olive oil. Bake for 40–50 minutes, basting occasionally with the cooking juices. Serve hot.

MARINATED AUBERGINES

Place the aubergine slices in a colander, sprinkle with salt and leave to drain for about 30 minutes. Heat a heavy-based, non-stick frying pan. Rinse the aubergines, pat dry and brush with some of the oil. Add the aubergine slices to the frying pan, in batches if necessary, and cook over a high heat until golden brown on both sides. Mix together the chilli, garlic, capers and mint in a bowl and season with salt and pepper. Make a layer of aubergine slices in a salad bowl, sprinkle with a tablespoon of the chilli dressing and continue making layers until all the ingredients are used. Pour in the remaining olive oil and leave to marinate in a cool place for at least 6 hours. This dish may be served as a first course in summer.

MELANZANE MARINATE

Serves 4

600 g/1 lb 5 oz aubergines,
cut into 5-mm/^{1}/$_4$-inch thick slices
175 ml/6 fl oz olive oil
1 fresh chilli, seeded and chopped
3 garlic cloves, finely chopped
1 tablespoon capers, drained, rinsed and chopped
10 fresh mint leaves, chopped
salt and pepper

PARMESAN AUBERGINES

Place the aubergine slices in a colander, sprinkle with salt and leave to drain for about 1 hour. Meanwhile, put the tomatoes, 4–5 basil leaves and a pinch of salt and pepper in a saucepan and cook over a high heat, stirring frequently, for 20 minutes. Remove from the heat and pass through a food mill into a bowl. Preheat the oven to 180°C/350°F/Gas Mark 4. Rinse the aubergine slices and pat dry. Heat the oil in a frying pan, add the aubergine slices, in batches if necessary, and fry until golden brown on both sides. Remove with a fish slice and drain on kitchen paper. Spoon a little of the tomato sauce into an ovenproof dish and arrange a layer of slightly overlapping aubergine slices on top. Sprinkle with a little of the Parmesan, cover with a few slices of the mozzarella and sprinkle a few basil leaves and 3–4 tablespoons of the beaten eggs on top. Continue making layers until all the ingredients are used, ending with a layer of sliced aubergine sprinkled with tomato sauce. Dot with the butter and bake for 30 minutes. This dish is also good served cold.

PARMIGIANA DI MELANZANE

For 6

4–5 aubergines,
cut lengthways into 5-mm/^{1}/$_4$-inch thick slices
500 g/1 lb 2 oz tomatoes, peeled,
seeded and diced
^{1}/$_2$ bunch of fresh basil
6 tablespoons olive oil
50 g/2 oz Parmesan cheese, freshly grated
100 g/3^1/$_2$ oz mozzarella cheese, sliced
2 eggs, lightly beaten
25 g/1 oz butter
salt and pepper

AUBERGINE TERRINE

Preheat the grill and the oven to 180°C/350°F/Gas Mark 4. Brush an ovenproof dish with oil. Place the peppers on a baking sheet, drizzle with oil and roast, turning frequently, until charred and blackened all over. Remove from the oven, place in a plastic bag and seal the top. Do not switch off the oven. Meanwhile, brush the aubergine slices with oil and grill until golden brown on both sides. When the peppers are cool enough to handle, peel and seed, and chop the flesh. Make a layer of aubergine slices in the prepared dish. Grate 50 g/2 oz of the Emmenthal and slice the remainder. Stir the grated Emmenthal, chopped peppers and a little basil into the eggs and season with salt and pepper. Arrange a layer of Emmenthal slices on top of the aubergines and spoon in some of the egg mixture. Continue making alternate layers until all the ingredients are used, ending with the egg mixture. Place the dish in a roasting tin, add boiling water to come about halfway up the sides and bake for 1 hour. Meanwhile, put the tomatoes, oil and garlic in a small saucepan, season with salt and pepper and cook over a medium heat, stirring frequently, for 20 minutes. Remove and discard the garlic and pass the mixture through a sieve into a bowl. Remove the terrine from the oven, turn out on to a warm serving dish and serve with the tomato sauce.

TERRINA DI MELANZANE

Serves 4

2 tablespoons olive oil,

plus extra for drizzling and brushing

2 yellow peppers

1 red pepper

3 aubergines, cut into 5-mm/¼-inch thick slices

150 g/5 oz Emmenthal cheese

1 fresh basil sprig, chopped

3 eggs, lightly beaten

3 ripe tomatoes, peeled and chopped

1 garlic clove

salt and pepper

COLD AUBERGINE TOWER

Place the aubergine slices in a colander, sprinkle with salt and leave to drain for about 30 minutes. Preheat the grill. Rinse the aubergine slices, pat dry, brush with oil and grill until golden brown on both sides. Lightly toast the bread on both sides and place in a deep serving dish. Arrange a layer of aubergine slices on top and season with salt and pepper. Top with a layer of mozzarella, sprinkle with spring onion and basil leaves, season with salt and pepper, then make a layer of tomato slices and season with salt and pepper. Continue making layers until all the ingredients are used. Drizzle with olive oil and garnish with a few more basil leaves. Leave to stand for 15 minutes, then serve.

TORRE FREDDA DI MELANZANE

Serves 4

600 g/1 lb 5 oz aubergines,

cut into 5-mm/¼-inch thick slices

olive oil, for brushing and drizzling

4 country-style bread slices, crusts removed

350 g/12 oz mozzarella cheese, thinly sliced

1 spring onion, thinly sliced

10 fresh basil leaves, plus extra to garnish

4 ripe tomatoes, peeled, seeded and thinly sliced

salt and pepper

POTATOES

It is almost impossible to find another vegetable as versatile as the potato. It is suitable for both the simplest and most sophisticated dishes. It can even be said that virtually everyone likes potatoes. They boast a fair amount of sodium, potassium, magnesium, calcium and iron, and new potatoes are rich in vitamins B1, B2 and C. They are less fattening than you might think, as long as they are cooked without excessive oil or other fats. Yellow-fleshed, waxy potatoes are excellent boiled, as they keep their shape well. White-fleshed, floury potatoes are ideal for purées, gnocchi, soups and moulds. Steaming is recommended for both types, as they retain more flavour and lose fewer nutrients. New potatoes don't need to be peeled; simply rub them with a tea towel. To make potato balls, use a melon baller to scoop out the flesh from large potatoes. Dress potato salad 1 hour before serving; wine may be substituted for vinegar in the dressing, but ask your guests first whether they might like this unusual taste. Lastly, it should be remembered that potatoes must not be kept in the refrigerator, but in a cool, dark place.

QUANTITIES AND COOKING TIMES

QUANTITIES
Allow about 200 g/7 oz per serving.

BOILING
Immerse whole, unpeeled potatoes in a pan of lightly salted, cold water and bring to the boil. Lower the heat and simmer for about 45 minutes, then drain and peel. Do not leave them standing in the water as they will lose their flavour.

STEAMING
Peel the potatoes, halve or cut into pieces and place in a steamer over boiling water. Cook for 20–30 minutes.

FRYING
Peel the potatoes, cut to the required shape and keep them immersed in cold water until ready to cook to prevent them turning black. Drain and pat dry before cooking.

POTATO AND CAULIFLOWER RING

Steam the potatoes for 20–25 minutes, then tip into a bowl and mash with a potato masher. Preheat the oven to 190°C/375°F/Gas Mark 5. Grease a ring mould with butter. Heat half the butter in a pan, add the shallot and cook over a low heat, stirring occasionally, for 5 minutes, then add the potato, ricotta and fromage frais. Mix well, then remove from the heat and beat in the egg yolks, one at a time. Add the Parmesan and season with salt and pepper. Stiffly whisk the egg whites in a grease-free bowl and fold into the potato mixture. Spoon the mixture into the prepared mould and bake for about 30 minutes. Meanwhile, cook the cauliflower in salted, boiling water for about 15 minutes until just tender, then drain. Heat the remaining butter and the oil in a frying pan, add the cauliflower florets and cook over a low heat, stirring occasionally, for about 5 minutes. Season with salt and pepper. Turn out the potato ring on to a warm serving dish and spoon the cauliflower into the middle.

ANELLO DI PATATE E CAVOLFIORE

Serves 6

1 kg/2¼ lb floury potatoes, diced

50 g/2 oz butter, plus extra for greasing

1 shallot, chopped

200 g/7 oz ricotta cheese, crumbled

200 ml/7 fl oz fromage frais

3 eggs, separated

25 g/1 oz Parmesan cheese, freshly grated

1 small cauliflower, cut into florets

2 tablespoons olive oil

salt and pepper

POTATO BRIOCHES

Cook the whole, unpeeled potatoes in plenty of salted water for about 45 minutes until tender, then drain and peel. Place in a bowl and mash with a potato masher. Preheat the oven to 200°C/400°F/Gas Mark 6. Grease a baking sheet with butter. Heat the milk to just below simmering point, then remove from the heat. Add the butter, Emmenthal and hot milk to the potatoes and mix well, then stir in one of the eggs. Separate the other egg. Stiffly whisk the egg white in a grease-free bowl, fold into the mixture and season with salt. Spoon small, round mounds of the mixture on to the baking sheet and top each with a smaller mound. Lightly beat the remaining egg yolk and brush the mounds with it. Bake until golden brown.

BRIOCHE DI PATATE

Serves 4

675 g/1½ lb potatoes

40 g/1½ oz butter, softened, plus extra for greasing

250 ml/8 fl oz milk

80 g/3 oz Emmenthal cheese, freshly grated

2 eggs

salt

Serves 4

800 g/1³/₄ lb floury potatoes

3 eggs

50 g/2 oz Parmesan cheese, freshly grated

100 g/3¹/₂ oz fontina cheese, cut into sticks

50-g/2-oz cooked ham slice, cut into sticks

80 g/3 oz breadcrumbs

vegetable oil, for deep-frying

salt and pepper

fresh basil leaves, to garnish

POTATO CROQUETTES WITH FONTINA

Cook the whole unpeeled potatoes in plenty of salted water for about 45 minutes until tender, then drain, peel and tip into a bowl. Mash with a potato masher. Separate one of the eggs and stir the yolk and one whole egg into the potato with the Parmesan. Mix well and season with salt and pepper. Shape the mixture into croquettes and push a stick of fontina and a stick of ham into each. Beat the remaining egg with a pinch of salt in a shallow dish and spread out the breadcrumbs in another shallow dish. Heat the oil for deep-frying in a large pan. Dip the croquettes in the beaten egg, then in the breadcrumbs and fry in the hot oil until golden brown. Remove with a fish slice, drain on kitchen paper and pile into a pyramid on a warm serving dish. Garnish with basil leaves.

Serves 4

675 g/1¹/₂ lb potatoes

50 g/2 oz butter

1 carrot, chopped

1 celery stalk, chopped

1 shallot, chopped

5 tablespoons dry white wine

¹/₂ teaspoon plain flour

1 fresh flat-leaf parsley sprig, chopped

4 fresh basil leaves, chopped

salt and pepper

DELICE OF POTATO WITH VEGETABLE SAUCE

Cook the whole, unpeeled potatoes in plenty of salted water for 30–40 minutes. Meanwhile, melt 40 g/1¹/₂ oz of the butter in a pan, add the carrot, celery and shallot and cook over a high heat, stirring frequently, until browned. Add the wine and cook until it has evaporated. Season with salt and pepper, lower the heat and cook, stirring frequently, until the mixture is creamy. Mix the remaining butter with the flour to a paste, stir into the mixture and simmer for a few minutes. Remove from the heat and stir in the parsley and basil. Drain, peel and thinly slice the potatoes. Arrange the slices like sun rays on a warm serving dish and spoon the sauce over them.

SPICY POTATO SALAD

Cook the whole, unpeeled potatoes in plenty of salted water for about 45 minutes until tender, then drain, peel and slice thinly. Place the slices in a salad bowl and leave to cool. Hard-boil the egg, refresh under cold water, shell and halve lengthways. Scoop out the yolk and press through a sieve into a bowl. Chop and add them with the parsley, capers, pickled onions, gherkins and pickled pepper to the egg yolk and mix well. Whisk together the vinegar, olive oil and mustard in another bowl, season with salt and pepper and pour the dressing into the anchovy mixture. Stir well and, if necessary, add a little more olive oil. Pour the anchovy sauce over the potatoes and toss gently.

INSALATA PICCANTE DI PATATE

Serves 4

700 g/1¹/₂ lb waxy potatoes

1 egg

2 salted anchovies, heads removed, cleaned and filleted (see page 596), soaked in cold water for 10 minutes and drained

1 fresh flat-leaf parsley sprig, chopped

1 tablespoon capers, drained and rinsed

4 pickled pearl onions, drained

4 gherkins, drained and chopped

1 pickled pepper, drained and finely chopped

3 tablespoons white wine vinegar

3 tablespoons olive oil

¹/₂ teaspoon Dijon mustard

salt and pepper

HAM AND POTATO ROLLS

Cook the whole, unpeeled potatoes in plenty of salted water for about 45 minutes until tender, then drain, peel and put into a bowl. Mash with a potato masher. Add the fontina, breadcrumbs and egg, season with salt and pepper and mix well. Preheat the oven to 200°C/400°F/Gas Mark 6. Grease an ovenproof dish with butter. Parboil the leek in salted, boiling water for 5 minutes, then drain, leave to cool and cut into eight strips. Spread out the slices of ham and divide the potato mixture among them. Roll up and tie with the strips of leek. Place the rolls in the prepared dish and bake for 10 minutes.

INVOLTINI DI PATATE AL PROSCIUTTO

Serves 4

675 g/1¹/₂ lb potatoes

150 g/5 oz fontina cheese, freshly grated

3 tablespoons breadcrumbs

1 egg, lightly beaten

butter, for greasing

1 leek, white part only

8 cooked ham slices

salt and pepper

POTATO NESTS WITH EGGS

Preheat the oven to 200°C/400°F/Gas Mark 6. Cook the potatoes in salted water for about 10 minutes. Drain, cut off the tops and scoop out the flesh with a teaspoon, leaving the 'shells' intact. Place the potato shells in an ovenproof dish and break an egg into each one. Top each with a slice of butter and a little anchovy paste, season with salt and pepper and bake for 10 minutes.

NIDI DI PATATE CON LE UOVA

Serves 4

4 potatoes

4 eggs

25 g/1 oz butter, cut into 4 slices

1 teaspoon anchovy paste

salt and pepper

POTATOES BAKED IN FOIL WITH YOGURT

Serves 4

8 potatoes

65 g/2¹/₂ oz butter, diced

4 tablespoons low-fat natural yogurt

150 ml/¹/₄ pint double cream

6 fresh chives, chopped

2 fresh flat-leaf parsley sprigs, chopped

juice of 1 lemon, strained

salt and pepper

Preheat the oven to 220°C/425°F/Gas Mark 7. Cut a lengthways slit in the top of each potato with a small sharp knife. Divide the butter among the openings and season with salt and pepper. Wrap each potato in a sheet of foil, place on a baking sheet and bake for about 40 minutes. Meanwhile, mix together the yogurt, cream, chives and parsley in a bowl, stir in the lemon juice and season with salt to taste. Place the potatoes on a warm serving dish and slightly open the foil, top with 1–2 tablespoons of the sauce and serve the remaining sauce separately.

FONTINA POTATO BAKE

Serves 6 – 8

1.5 kg/3¹/₄ lb potatoes

1 garlic clove

butter, for greasing

200 g/7 oz fontina cheese, cubed

100 g/3¹/₂ oz Gruyère cheese, cubed

100 g/3¹/₂ oz cooked ham, cut into strips

250 ml/8 fl oz double cream

salt and pepper

Parboil the unpeeled potatoes in plenty of water for about 20 minutes, then drain, peel and slice thinly. Preheat the oven to 200°C/400°F/Gas Mark 6. Rub the garlic around the inside of an ovenproof dish several times, then grease well with butter. Make a layer of potato slices in the prepared dish, then a layer of the cheeses, followed by a layer of ham. Continue making layers until all the ingredients are used, ending with a layer of potato slices. Pour the cream over the potato slices, season with salt and pepper and bake for 30 minutes. Leave to stand for 5 minutes before serving.

BAKED POTATOES WITH SALMON

Serves 4

8 potatoes

1 smoked salmon slice, coarsely chopped

200 ml/7 fl oz double cream

juice of ¹/₂ lemon, strained

1 bunch of fresh chives, chopped

50 g/2 oz salmon roe

salt and pepper

Preheat the oven to 200°C/400°F/Gas Mark 6. Halve the potatoes lengthways and scoop about one-third of the flesh from the centre. Reassemble in pairs, wrap each par in a sheet of foil, place on a baking sheet and bake for about 40 minutes. Meanwhile, put the smoked salmon, cream and lemon juice in a blender, season with salt and pepper and process until smooth and combined. Remove the potatoes from the oven, fill with the salmon cream and reassemble. Arrange on a warm serving dish, sprinkle with the chives and salmon roe and serve. The contrast between the hot potato and cold salmon cream is delightful. This dish may also be served as a first course.

POTATOES IN BÉCHAMEL SAUCE

Cook the whole, unpeeled potatoes in plenty of salted water for about 45 minutes, then drain, peel and slice. Preheat the oven to 200°C/400°F/Gas Mark 6. Grease an ovenproof dish with butter, arrange the potato slices, slightly overlapping, in it and season with salt and pepper. Stir the cream into the béchamel sauce and pour the mixture over the potatoes to cover. Sprinkle with the Parmesan and melted butter. Bake until golden brown and bubbling, then serve. This dish may also be served as a first course.

PATATE ALLA BESCIAMELLA

Serves 6

1 kg/2¼ lb potatoes

25 g/1 oz butter, melted, plus extra for greasing

100 ml/3½ fl oz single cream

1 quantity Béchamel Sauce (see page 50)

50 g/2 oz Parmesan cheese, freshly grated

salt and pepper

NORMANDY POTATOES

Melt the butter in a flameproof dish or casserole, add the onion, leeks and pancetta and cook over a low heat, stirring occasionally, for 5 minutes. Add the potatoes and pour in the stock to cover. Season with salt and pepper, increase the heat to high and cook for about 30 minutes. When the liquid has evaporated, pour in the cream, lower the heat and cook until thickened. Remove from the heat and serve.

PATATE ALLA NORMANNA

Serves 4

50 g/2 oz butter

1 onion, thinly sliced

2 leeks, trimmed and sliced

100 g/3½ oz pancetta, sliced

675 g/1½ lb potatoes, thinly sliced

500 ml/18 fl oz Meat Stock (see page 208)

400 ml/14 fl oz double cream

salt and pepper

POTATOES WITH SCAMORZA

Cook the whole, unpeeled potatoes in plenty of salted water for about 45 minutes until tender, then drain, peel and cut into 5-mm/¼-inch slices. Grease an ovenproof dish with butter and make alternating layers of potato and cheese slices. Preheat the oven to 180°C/350°F/Gas Mark 4. Melt the butter in a saucepan, stir in the flour and cook, stirring, for a few minutes, then gradually stir in the milk. Cook for 20 minutes, stirring constantly. Add the shallots and curry powder, season with salt and pepper, mix well and simmer for a few minutes. Pour the sauce over the potatoes and bake for 15 minutes.

PATATE ALLA SCAMORZA

Serves 4

675 g/1½ lb potatoes

25 g/1 oz butter, plus extra for greasing

200 g/7 oz scamorza

or provolone cheese, thinly sliced

25 g/1 oz plain flour

500 ml/18 fl oz milk

2 shallots, chopped

1 teaspoon curry powder

salt and pepper

DUCHESSE POTATOES

Serves 4

800 g/1³/₄ lb potatoes

150 g/5 oz butter, plus extra for greasing

4 egg yolks

salt

Cook the whole, unpeeled potatoes in plenty of salted water for about 45 minutes, until tender. Preheat the oven to 200°C/400°F/Gas Mark 6. Grease a baking sheet with butter. Drain and peel the potatoes, then put into a bowl and mash with a potato masher. Transfer to a clean saucepan and place on a low heat. Stir in the butter until it is fully incorporated, then remove from the heat, season with salt and stir in three of the egg yolks. Spoon the mixture into a piping bag fitted with a star nozzle and pipe 'potato meringues' on the prepared baking sheet. Brush with the remaining egg yolk and bake for a few minutes until golden brown.

POTATOES IN WHITE BUTTER SAUCE

PATATE IN SALSA BIANCA

Serves 4

675 g/1¹/₂ lb potatoes

2 small shallots, chopped

100 ml/3¹/₂ fl oz dry white wine

150 g/5 oz butter, softened

3 tablespoons fresh flat-leaaf parsley, chopped

4 fresh chives, finely chopped

salt and pepper

Cook the whole, unpeeled potatoes in plenty of salted water for about 40 minutes until tender, then drain, peel and slice thinly. Put the slices in a serving bowl and keep warm. Put the shallots in a small saucepan, add the wine and 1 tablespoon water and bring to the boil over a medium heat. Lower the heat and simmer until the liquid has reduced by half, then remove from the heat, season with salt and pepper and leave to cool slightly. Whisk in the butter, return to the heat and whisk until smooth and creamy. Remove from the heat, stir in the parsley and chives and pour the sauce over the hot potatoes.

POTATOES AND ONIONS BAKED IN AN EARTHENWARE DISH

PATATE IN TERRACOTTA CON CIPOLLE

Serves 4

olive oil, for brushing and drizzling

400 g/14 oz potatoes, thinly sliced

300 g/11 oz onions, thinly sliced

200 g/7 oz carrots, thinly sliced

6 fresh basil leaves, torn

50 g/2 oz Emmenthal cheese, freshly grated

salt and pepper

Preheat the oven to 180°C/350°F/Gas Mark 4. Brush an earthenware dish with oil. Arrange slightly overlapping slices of the potatoes, carrots and onions in the prepared dish. Sprinkle with the basil, season with salt and pepper and drizzle generously with olive oil. Cover with foil and bake for 40 minutes. Remove the foil, sprinkle the vegetables with the Emmenthal and return to the oven until the cheese melts. Serve hot straight from the dish.

SAUSAGE STUFFED POTATOES

Cook the potatoes in salted water for about 30 minutes until just tender, then drain. Halve lengthways and scoop out the flesh to make barquettes. Preheat the oven to 180°C/350°F/Gas Mark 4. Grease an ovenproof dish with butter. Heat half the butter in a pan with the bay leaf, add the sausage and cook, stirring frequently, until evenly browned. Add the wine and cook until it has evaporated, then season with salt and pepper. Remove and discard the bay leaf and pass the sausage, cooking juices and cooked chicken through a mincer into a bowl. Stir in the parsley and Parmesan. Melt the remaining butter and remove from the heat. Fill the potato barquettes with the meat mixture, place in the prepared dish, sprinkle with the breadcrumbs and melted butter and bake for about 45 minutes.

PATATE RIPIENE ALLA SALSICCIA

Serves 4

8 small potatoes, peeled

50 g/2 oz butter, plus extra for greasing

1 bay leaf

1 Italian sausage, skinned and crumbled

50 ml/2 fl oz dry white wine

100 g/3$^{1}/_{2}$ oz cooked chicken, coarsely chopped

1 fresh flat-leaf parsley sprig, chopped

3 tablespoons Parmesan cheese, freshly grated

4 tablespoons breadcrumbs

salt and pepper

PROVENÇAL SAUTÉED POTATOES

Heat the oil in a saucepan, add the unpeeled garlic and potatoes, season with salt and pepper and cook, stirring frequently, for 20 minutes until golden brown. Meanwhile, mix together the butter and saffron in a bowl until smooth. Remove the potatoes from the pan with a fish slice and drain on kitchen paper. Place them on a serving dish, sprinkle with the parsley and thyme and dot with the saffron butter.

PATATE SALTATE ALLA PROVENZALE

Serves 6

3 tablespoons olive oil

5 garlic cloves

1 kg/2$^{1}/_{4}$ lb new potatoes, diced

50 g/2 oz butter

$^{1}/_{2}$ sachet saffron

1 fresh flat-leaf parsley sprig, chopped

1 fresh thyme sprig, chopped

salt and pepper

STEWED POTATOES WITH TOMATO

Heat the oil in a pan, add the shallot and garlic and cook over a medium heat, stirring occasionally, until golden brown. Add the potatoes and cook over a high heat, stirring frequently, for a few minutes. Add the wine and cook until it has evaporated, then lower the heat and add the tomatoes. Sprinkle with the oregano, season with salt and pepper and add 150 ml/$^{1}/_{4}$ pint water. Cover and cook over a low heat until the potatoes are falling apart. Transfer to a warm serving dish.

PATATE STUFATE AL POMODORO

Serves 4

2 tablespoons olive oil

1 shallot, chopped

1 garlic clove, chopped

600 g/1 lb 5 oz potatoes, diced

5 tablespoons dry white wine

3 tomatoes, peeled, seeded and chopped

pinch of dried oregano

salt and pepper

NEW POTATOES WITH ROSEMARY

PATATINE NOVELLE AL ROSMARINO

Serves 4

25 g/1 oz butter

100 ml/3 ½ fl oz olive oil

1 fresh rosemary sprig

1 garlic clove

675 g/1½ lb new potatoes

salt

Heat the butter and oil in a large pan, add the rosemary, garlic and potatoes, stir and cover. Cook over a low heat until golden brown. Remove and discard the garlic and rosemary, sprinkle with salt and serve.

CREAMY MASHED POTATO

PURÉ DI PATATE CREMOSO

Serves 4

675 g/1½ lb potatoes

50 g/2 oz butter, softened

100 ml/3 ½ fl oz milk

100 g/3½ oz mascarpone cheese

120 ml/4 fl oz single cream

6 fresh chives, chopped

salt and pepper

Steam the potatoes for about 20 minutes, then pass through a potato ricer into a bowl. Gently stir in the butter. Heat the milk to just below simmering point, then remove from the heat. Beat together the mascarpone and cream until smooth in another bowl, then stir in the hot milk and pour the mixture over the potatoes. Mix well, season with salt and pepper to taste and press the mixture through a sieve on to a warm serving dish. Sprinkle with the chives and serve.

PEPPERS

Yellow, red and green peppers ripen from April to October. They are rich in vitamin C, phosphorus, calcium and potassium. Before using them, the stalk, seeds and white membranes should be removed. Green and red peppers are perfect for a peperonata, while yellow peppers are delicious grilled or roasted. Stuffed with meat, rice or other ingredients, peppers may even be served as a main course.

QUANTITIES AND COOKING TIMES

QUANTITIES

Allow about 200 g/7 oz per serving. If stuffed, allow 1 pepper for each person.

ROASTING

Line a roasting tin with foil, lay the peppers on top and cook in a preheated oven, 180°C/350°F/Gas Mark 4, for 1 hour. Remove from the oven, wrap in the foil and leave to cool before peeling.

INSALATA DI PEPERONI E FARRO

Serves 4

2 yellow peppers, seeded and cut into very thin strips

1 red pepper, seeded and cut into very thin strips

1 green pepper, seeded and cut into very thin strips

3 spring onions, sliced

10 black olives, stoned and sliced

$^1/_2$ garlic clove, chopped

200 g/7 oz farro, boiled

juice of $^1/_2$ lemon, strained

120 ml/4 fl oz olive oil

1 tablespoon chopped fresh flat-leaf parsley

salt and ground white pepper

PEPPER AND FARRO SALAD

Put all the peppers, the spring onions, olives, garlic and farro in a salad bowl. Whisk together the lemon juice and olive oil in another bowl and season with a pinch each of salt and white pepper. Pour the dressing over the pepper mixture, sprinkle with the parsley and toss. Place the salad in the refrigerator for 1 hour before serving to allow the flavours to mingle.

PEPPER AND TUNA ROLLS

INVOLTINI DI PEPERONI AL TONNO

Serves 4

1 red pepper

1 yellow pepper

1 green pepper

350 g/12 oz canned tuna in oil, drained and flaked

1 spring onion, chopped

3 tablespoons mushrooms in oil, drained

2 teaspoons capers, rinsed

6 canned anchovy fillets in oil, drained, rinsed and chopped

1 fresh flat-leaf parsley sprig, chopped

1 tablespoon white wine vinegar

olive oil, for drizzling

Preheat the oven to 180°C/350°F/Gas Mark 4. Line a roasting tin with foil. Prick the peppers with a fork, place in the tin and roast for 1 hour. Remove from the oven, wrap in foil and leave to cool. Peel the peppers, cut into quarters, remove the seeds and membranes and pat dry with kitchen paper. Mix together the tuna, spring onion, mushrooms, capers, anchovies and parsley in a bowl and stir in the vinegar. Spread the mixture on the pieces of pepper, roll up tightly and chill in the refrigerator. To serve, place different coloured rolls side by side on a serving dish and drizzle with olive oil.

DELICATE PEPERONATA

PEPERONATA DELICATA

Serves 4

4 mixed peppers

4 tablespoons olive oil

1 garlic clove

1 onion, sliced

4 tomatoes, peeled, seeded and chopped

salt

Preheat the oven to 180°C/350°F/Gas Mark 4. Line a roasting tin with foil. Prick the peppers with a fork, place in the tin and roast for 1 hour. Remove from the oven, wrap in foil and leave to cool. Peel and halve the peppers, remove the seeds and membranes and cut the peppers into large pieces. Heat the oil in a pan with the garlic. Add the peppers and onion and cook over a low heat, stirring occasionally, for 10 minutes. Add the tomatoes, season with salt and cook for 20 minutes until thickened. Remove and discard the garlic before serving.

ROAST PEPPERS

PEPERONI ARROSTO

Serves 4

4 peppers

3 garlic cloves, halved

12 fresh basil leaves

olive oil, for drizzling

salt and pepper

Preheat the oven to 180°C/350°F/Gas Mark 4. Line a roasting tin with foil. Prick the peppers with a fork, place in the tin and roast for 1 hour. Remove from the oven, wrap in foil and leave to cool. Peel and halve the peppers and leave to drain, cut side down, on kitchen paper. Remove the seeds and membranes, cut the peppers into 1.5-cm/²/₃-inch strips and arrange in layers on a fairly deep serving dish, sprinkling each layer with garlic and basil and seasoning with salt and pepper. Drizzle with olive oil and leave to stand in a cool place for 1 hour before serving.

FANCY PEPPERS

Serves 4

3 tablespoons olive oil, plus extra for brushing

4 yellow peppers

6 salted anchovies, heads removed, cleaned and filleted (see page 596), soaked in cold water for 10 minutes and drained

2 garlic cloves, finely chopped

1 fresh flat-leaf parsley sprig, finely chopped

100 g/3¹/₂ oz green olives, stoned and finely chopped

6 fresh basil leaves, finely chopped

250 g/9 oz tomatoes, peeled and diced

250 g/9 oz mozzarella cheese, sliced

salt and pepper

Preheat the oven to 200°C/400°F/Gas Mark 6. Brush an ovenproof dish with oil. Halve the peppers, including the stalks, and remove the seeds and membranes. Place cut side up in the prepared dish and bake for 15–20 minutes. Meanwhile, chop the anchovy fillets. Place them in a bowl, add half the olive oil and mash until smooth. Add the garlic, parsley, olives and basil. Place the tomatoes in another bowl, stir in the remaining olive oil and season with salt and pepper to taste. Remove the peppers from the oven but do not switch it off. Fill each pepper half with the tomatoes, lay a slice of mozzarella on top and add a tablespoon of the anchovy sauce. Return to the oven and bake for 10 minutes.

SWEET–AND–SOUR PEPPERS

PEPERONI IN AGRODOLCE

Serves 4

3 tablespoons olive oil

4 peppers, halved, seeded and thickly sliced

200 ml/7 fl oz white wine vinegar

2 tablespoons sugar

salt

Heat the oil in a pan, add the peppers and cook over a low heat, stirring occasionally, for about 15 minutes. Season with salt, then remove from the pan and set aside. Pour the vinegar into the pan juices, stir in the sugar, increase the heat and cook, stirring, until the vinegar has almost completely evaporated. Return the peppers to the pan and cook for a further 2 minutes, then transfer to a warm serving dish.

SUMMER STUFFED PEPPERS

PEPERONI RIPIENI D'ESTATE

Serves 6

1 aubergine, diced

2 salted anchovies, heads removed, cleaned and filleted (see page 596), soaked in cold water for 10 minutes and drained

2 tablespoons olive oil, plus extra for brushing

150 g/5 oz Gruyère cheese, diced

100 g/3¹/₂ oz olives, stoned and thinly sliced

40 g/1¹/₂ oz fresh flat-leaf parsley, chopped

6 fresh basil leaves, chopped

3 tomatoes, peeled, seeded and chopped

2 potatoes, diced

1 tablespoon capers, drained and rinsed

pinch of dried oregano

6 green peppers • salt and pepper

Place the aubergine cubes in a colander, sprinkle with salt and leave to drain for 30 minutes. Meanwhile, chop the anchovy fillet. Preheat the oven to 180°C/350°F/Gas Mark 4. Brush an ovenproof dish with oil. Place the Gruyère, olives, parsley, basil, tomatoes and potatoes in a large bowl. Rinse the aubergine, pat dry with kitchen paper and add to the bowl with the anchovies, capers and oregano. Season with salt and pepper and mix well. Remove the stalks from the peppers and cut off and reserve the tops. Remove the seeds and membranes using a small sharp knife and a teaspoon. Fill the peppers with the stuffing mixture, pour a teaspoon of olive oil into each, replace the tops and secure with a cocktail stick if necessary. Place the peppers in the prepared dish and bake for 1 hour. Serve hot or cold.

PEAS

Fresh, dried, canned and frozen peas are all rich in potassium, phosphorus, protein and B group vitamins. Good-quality fresh peas can be recognized by their smooth, elastic, bright green pods. They are perfect for numerous recipes, as side dishes and as an ingredient used with pasta and in risottos. Mangetouts are a type of pea with a very thin, edible pod so they do not need shelling. Simply wash them in cold water and gently rub the surface of the pods.

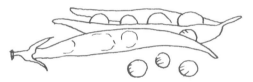

QUANTITIES

Allow about 80 g/3 oz shelled peas per serving. After shelling, 1 kg/2¹/₄ lb pods yields about 500 g/ 1 lb 2 oz peas. After shelling, 1 kg/2¹/₄ lb pods yields about 300 g/11 oz petits pois.

FRYING

Early peas should be treated with great care. Cook over a low heat in butter or oil, but do not allow them to absorb the fat or they will become heavy and indigestible. A high heat makes peas go hard so they should always be cooked over a low heat in a covered frying pan. The steam formed during cooking prevents the peas from absorbing too much fat. If necessary, add a little hot water during cooking.

BOILING

Cook in salted, boiling water for 15–30 minutes, depending on the size and freshness of the peas.

QUANTITIES
AND COOKING TIMES

THREE-COLOUR TERRINE

MATTONELLA TRICOLORE

Serves 6

400 g/14 oz shelled fresh peas

400 g/14 oz carrots, sliced, plus extra to garnish

200 g/7 oz spinach

butter, for greasing

3 eggs, separated

9 tablespoons double cream

25 g/1 oz ricotta cheese

salt and pepper

fresh chervil sprigs, to garnish

Cook the peas and carrots in separate pans of salted, boiling water for 15–30 minutes until tender, then drain. Cook the spinach, in just the water clinging to the leaves after washing, for 5–10 minutes, then drain and squeeze out the excess liquid. Preheat the oven to 190°C/375°F/Gas Mark 5. Grease a terrine or loaf tin with butter. Separately process each vegetable to a purée and put in three different bowls. Add an egg yolk and 3 tablespoons of the cream to each bowl and season with salt and pepper. Add the ricotta to the spinach and carefully mix the ingredients in each bowl. Stiffly whisk the egg whites in a grease-free bowl, then fold one-third into each vegetable purée. Spoon half the pea mixture into the prepared terrine or loaf tin, smooth the surface with a dampened palette knife, spoon in half the carrot mixture and smooth the surface. Spoon all the spinach mixture on top, then the rest of the carrot mixture and the remaining pea mixture, smoothing the surface with a dampened palette knife each time. Cover with foil and bake for 40 minutes. Remove from the oven, leave to cool slightly, then turn out on to a serving dish. Garnish with carrot slices and the chervil sprigs.

PEAS WITH MINT

PISELLI ALLA MENTA

Serves 4

1 kg/2¼ lb fresh peas, shelled

½ teaspoon sugar

10 fresh mint leaves

50 g/2 oz butter

salt and pepper

Cook the peas in salted, boiling water with the sugar and five of the mint leaves for 15–30 minutes until tender. Drain and discard the mint. Melt the butter in a pan, add the peas, stir well and cook over a low heat for 5 minutes. Season with salt and pepper to taste, add the remaining mint leaves and serve.

PEAS WITH PANCETTA

PISELLI ALLA PANCETTA

Serves 4

1 kg/2¼ lb fresh peas, shelled

40 g/1½ oz butter

100 g/3½ oz smoked pancetta, cut into strips

salt

Cook the peas in salted, boiling water for 15–30 minutes until tender, then drain well. Melt the butter in a pan over a very low heat, add the pancetta and cook until golden brown and tender. Add the peas and cook, stirring occasionally, for 5 minutes. Transfer to a warm serving dish.

PEAS WITH PARSLEY

PISELLI AL PREZZEMOLO

Serves 4

4 tablespoons olive oil

1 large onion, thinly sliced

1 kg/2¼ lb fresh peas, shelled

100 ml/3½ fl oz Vegetable Stock (see page 209)

1 fresh flat-leaf parsley sprig, chopped

pinch of sugar

salt and pepper

Heat the oil in a saucepan, add the onion and cook over a low heat, stirring occasionally, for 5 minutes. Stir in the peas, cover and cook for a further 10 minutes. Meanwhile, bring the stock to the boil in another pan. Sprinkle the parsley over the peas and pour in enough boiling stock to cover. Add the sugar, season with salt and pepper to taste and simmer until the stock has been absorbed.

PEAS WITH CARROTS

PISELLI CON CAROTE

Serves 4

50g/2 oz butter

200 g/7 oz baby onions

500 g/1 lb 2 oz baby carrots, sliced

500 g/1 lb 2 oz fresh peas, shelled

1½ teaspoons sugar

2 fresh flat-leaf parsley sprigs, chopped

salt and pepper

Melt half the butter in a pan, add the onions and cook over a medium heat, stirring occasionally, for 5 minutes. Add the carrots and cook, stirring occasionally, for about 10 minutes. Add the peas, sugar and parsley, season with salt and pepper and mix well. Lower the heat, add 5 tablespoons warm water, cover and simmer for about 40 minutes. Remove the lid and boil off any remaining liquid, then stir in the remaining butter and transfer to a warm serving dish.

PEAS WITH LETTUCE

PISELLI CON LATTUGA

Serves 4

40 g/1½ oz butter

2 spring onions, thinly sliced

1 lettuce, cut into strips

1 kg/2¼ lb fresh peas, shelled

salt

Melt the butter in a pan, add the spring onions and cook over a low heat, stirring occasionally, for 5 minutes until softened. Add the lettuce and peas, pour in sufficient boiling water to half-cover the peas, cover and simmer for 20–30 minutes, making sure the mixture does not dry up too much. Season with salt to taste, remove the pan from the heat and serve. This is a delicate and tasty dish.

HOME–COOKED MANGETOUTS

TACCOLE ALLA CASALINGA

Serves 6

1 kg/2¼ lb mangetouts, trimmed

4 tablespoons olive oil

1 small onion, thinly sliced

2 garlic cloves

200 g/7 oz tomatoes, peeled, seeded and diced

salt and pepper

fresh basil leaves, to garnish

Cook the mangetouts in salted, boiling water for 8–10 minutes until just tender, then drain. Heat the oil in a pan, add the onion and cook over a low heat, stirring occasionally, for 5 minutes. Add the garlic and mangetouts, increase the heat to high and cook for 5 minutes. Remove and discard the garlic, add the tomatoes to the pan and season with salt and pepper. Lower the heat to medium, cook for 10–15 minutes, taste and adjust the seasoning if necessary, then transfer to a warm serving dish. Garnish with the basil leaves and serve.

TOMATOES

Tomatoes are so rich in vitamins A, B and C that an adult eating a ripe, 100-g/3¹/₂-oz tomato every day would satisfy their daily requirement for these vitamins. Among the many types available, it is enough to be familiar with the two large families: smooth red tomatoes for salads, mixed grills and frying; and plum tomatoes, which are irreplaceable in sauces. Canned tomatoes include simple peeled tomatoes – which are usually drained before being added to the other ingredients, and whose can-juices may be used to dilute sauces if they become too thick – chopped peeled tomatoes, passata and tomato purée, which may be standard or concentrated. Sliced, seedless green tomatoes coated in breadcrumbs and fried are delicious. So, too, are scooped-out green tomatoes filled with Russian salad.

QUANTITIES AND COOKING TIMES

QUANTITIES

Allow 500 g/1 lb 2 oz fresh tomatoes or a 400-g/14-oz can peeled tomatoes for a sauce. Allow ¹/₂–1 medium tomato per serving as an antipasto, 1 large tomato as a first course and 2 medium tomatoes as a main course.

SALAD

Cut tomatoes into slices rather than wedges as they remain firmer for longer. Season lightly with salt just before serving.

STUFFED

Cut the tomatoes in half, scoop out the seeds and sprinkle the insides with salt. Place upside down on kitchen paper for 10 minutes to drain, then fill.

TOMATO JELLY RING

Put the onion, tomatoes, vinegar, tomato purée and garlic in a large frying pan and cook over a low heat, stirring occasionally, for 10–15 minutes until softened. Transfer to a food processor and process to a purée, then scrape into a bowl. Prepare the gelatine according to the packet instructions, stir into the purée and season with salt and pepper to taste. Rinse a ring mould in extremely cold water, shake and then pour in the mixture. Chill in the refrigerator for at least 2 hours until set. To serve, dip the base of the mould in boiling water for a few seconds, then invert on to a serving dish. Spoon the tuna into the centre and surround the ring with lettuce.

ANELLO DI GELATINA AL POMODORO

Serves 4–6

1 onion, chopped

500 g/1 lb 2 oz plum tomatoes, peeled, seeded and diced

1 tablespoon white wine vinegar

1 teaspoon tomato purée

1 garlic clove

1 sachet gelatine

250 g/9 oz canned tuna in oil, drained and flaked

loose-leaf lettuce, such as lollo rosso

salt and pepper

TOMATO AND MOZZARELLA PARCELS

Preheat the oven to 200°C/400°F/Gas Mark 6. Grease an ovenproof dish with butter. Cut an opening around each tomato stalk with a small sharp knife and remove the seeds with a teaspoon without piercing the skins. Put the mozzarella, basil and parsley in a bowl and drizzle with olive oil. Mix well and spoon the mixture into the tomatoes. Season with salt and pepper. Lightly beat the egg white and yolk in separate bowls. Roll out the pastry on a lightly floured surface and cut into eight squares. Wrap each tomato in a slice of pancetta and place in the middle of each square. Brush the edges with the egg white and enclose the tomatoes in the pastry by pinching together the corners, then brush the parcels with the egg yolk. Place the parcels in the prepared dish and bake for about 20 minutes.

FAGOTTINI DI POMODORI E MOZZARELLA

Serves 4

butter, for greasing

8 cherry tomatoes

200 g/7 oz mozzarella cheese, finely diced

4 fresh basil leaves, chopped

1 fresh flat-leaf parsley sprig, chopped

olive oil, for drizzling

1 egg, separated

300 g/11 oz puff pastry dough, thawed if frozen

plain flour, for dusting

8 pancetta slices

salt and pepper

TOMATO AND GRUYÈRE MOULD

Preheat the oven to 180°C/350°F/Gas Mark 4. Brush a mould with oil. Heat the oil in a small saucepan, add the shallots and cook over a low heat, stirring occasionally, for 5 minutes. Add the passata and cook for a few minutes more, then remove the pan from the heat. Beat the eggs with the cream in a bowl, then stir into the tomato sauce with the herbs and season with salt. Pour the tomato mixture into the mould, place in a roasting tin and add boiling water to come about halfway up the sides. Bake for about 1 hour. Remove from the oven and switch the oven off. Leave the mould to cool for a few minutes, then turn out on to an ovenproof serving dish. Sprinkle with the Gruyère and place in the warm oven until the cheese has melted. Serve immediately.

FLAN DI POMODORI ALLA GROVIERA

Serves 4

3 tablespoons olive oil, plus extra for brushing

2 shallots, finely chopped

500 ml/18 fl oz passata

4 eggs

1 tablespoon double cream

6 fresh basil leaves, chopped

1 fresh flat-leaf parsley sprig, chopped

4 fresh chives, chopped

80 g/3 oz Gruyère cheese, freshly grated

salt

RED TOMATO FRITTATA

FRITTATA ROSSA DI POMODORI

Serves 4

3 tablespoons olive oil

1 shallot, chopped

1/2 garlic clove, chopped

300 g/11 oz plum tomatoes, peeled, seeded and chopped

6 eggs

4 fresh basil leaves, chopped

salt and pepper

Heat the oil in a frying pan, add the shallot and garlic and cook over a low heat, stirring occasionally, for 5 minutes. Add the tomatoes, increase the heat to medium and cook for 5 minutes. Lower the heat and simmer for 15 minutes. Beat the eggs with salt, pepper and the basil leaves in a bowl. Pour the eggs over the tomatoes and cook until evenly set. Do not turn the frittata over. Slide it out of the pan and serve.

TOMATO FRITTERS

FRITTELLINE ROSA DI POMODORO

Serves 4

130 g/4 1/2 oz plain flour

1 egg, lightly beaten

1/2 teaspoon melted butter

4 ripe but firm tomatoes

6 fresh basil leaves, chopped

vegetable oil, for deep-frying

salt and pepper

Sift the flour with a pinch of salt into a bowl and add the egg, melted butter and enough water to make a smooth batter. Leave to stand for about 1 hour. Meanwhile, slice the tomatoes, remove the seeds and sprinkle with pepper and the basil on both sides. Heat the oil for deep-frying in a large pan. Dip the tomato slices in the batter and fry in the hot oil until golden brown. Remove with a fish slice and drain on kitchen paper. Sprinkle with salt and serve.

BAKED TOMATOES

POMODORI AL FORNO

Serves 4

8 tomatoes, halved

1 thick bread slice, crusts removed

4 tablespoons milk

olive oil, for brushing

200 g/7 oz cooked meat, coarsely chopped

3 frankfurters, skinned and coarsely chopped

40 g/1 1/2 oz Parmesan cheese, freshly grated

1 egg

1 egg white

1 fresh flat-leaf parsley sprig, coarsely chopped

1 fresh basil sprig, coarsely chopped

1 garlic clove, coarsely chopped

salt and pepper

Scoop out the tomato seeds and some of the flesh, sprinkle with salt and turn upside down on kitchen paper to drain for 1 hour. Tear the bread into pieces, place in a bowl, add the milk and leave to soak for 10 minutes. Preheat the oven to 180°C/350°F/Gas Mark 4. Brush an ovenproof dish with oil. Put the meat, frankfurters, Parmesan, the bread and milk mixture, the whole egg, the egg white, and the parsley, basil and garlic in a food processor and process until combined. Season with salt and pepper to taste, process briefly again to mix and use to stuff the tomato halves. Place them in the prepared dish and bake for 20 minutes or until golden brown.

TOMATOES AU GRATIN

Scoop out the tomato seeds and some of the flesh, sprinkle with salt and turn upside down on kitchen paper to drain for 1 hour. Preheat the oven to 160°C/325°F/Gas Mark 3. Brush an ovenproof dish with oil. Heat 1 tablespoon of the olive oil in a small saucepan, add 50 g/2 oz of the breadcrumbs and cook, stirring frequently, until golden brown. Remove from the heat and set aside. Heat the remaining oil in another small pan, add the onion and cook over a low heat, stirring occasionally, for 5 minutes. Add the anchovies and parsley, mix well and remove from the heat. Stir in the capers and fried breadcrumbs. Fill the tomato halves with the mixture and place in the prepared dish. Sprinkle with the remaining breadcrumbs, drizzle with olive oil and bake for 40 minutes until golden brown.

POMODORI AL GRATIN

Serves 4

4 tomatoes, halved

3 tablespoons olive oil,

plus extra for brushing and drizzling

100 g/3$\frac{1}{2}$ oz breadcrumbs

1 onion, chopped

3 canned anchovy fillets in oil,

drained and chopped

1 fresh flat-leaf parsley sprig, chopped

1 tablespoon capers, drained, rinsed and chopped

salt

TOMATOES WITH CUCUMBER MOUSSE

Cut off the tops of the tomatoes and reserve. Scoop out the tomato seeds and some of the flesh, sprinkle with salt and turn upside down on kitchen paper to drain for 1 hour. Meanwhile, put the cucumbers, ricotta, mint and milk in a food processor and process to a purée, then scrape into a bowl. Stiffly whisk the egg whites in a grease-free bowl, then fold into the mixture. Fill the tomatoes with the mixture, sprinkle with the chives, replace the tomato tops and chill in the refrigerator for 2–3 hours. Remove the tomatoes from the refrigerator 15 minutes before serving.

POMODORI ALLA MOUSSE DI CETRIOLI

Serves 4

4 tomatoes

2 small cucumbers, peeled and coarsely chopped

200 g/7 oz ricotta cheese

4 fresh mint leaves

2 tablespoons milk

2 egg whites

4 fresh chives, finely chopped

salt

TOMATOES WITH AUBERGINES

Cut off the tops of the tomatoes and reserve. Scoop out the tomato seeds and some of the flesh, sprinkle with salt and turn upside down on kitchen paper to drain for 1 hour. Heat the oil in a pan, add the aubergine and garlic and cook over a high heat, stirring frequently, until the aubergine is lightly browned all over. Add the spring onion, capers and basil and season with salt and pepper. Pour in the vinegar and cook until it has evaporated. Remove from the heat and leave to cool. Fill the tomatoes with the aubergine mixture, replace the tops and serve.

POMODORI ALLE MELANZANE

Serves 4

4 tomatoes

2 tablespoons olive oil

1 aubergine, peeled and diced

1 garlic clove, chopped

1 spring onion, finely chopped

1 tablespoon capers, drained, rinsed and chopped

1 fresh basil sprig, chopped

3 tablespoons white wine vinegar

salt and pepper

TOMATOES WITH COURGETTES

POMODORI ALLE ZUCCHINE

Serves 4

olive oil, for brushing and drizzling

8 tomatoes

2 courgettes, trimmed

1 fresh flat-leaf parsley sprig, chopped

1 garlic clove, chopped

200 g/7 oz mozzarella cheese, sliced

¹/₂ teaspoon dried oregano

salt and pepper

Preheat the oven to 180°C/350°F/Gas Mark 4. Brush an oven-proof dish with oil. Thinly slice the tomatoes without cutting all the way through, leaving them joined at the base. Halve the courgettes lengthways, then slice into thin strips. Slip the strips of courgette between the slices of tomato. Place the tomatoes in the prepared dish, sprinkle with the parsley and garlic, season with salt and pepper and drizzle with olive oil. Bake for 30 minutes. Remove the dish from the oven but do not switch the oven off. Carefully slip slices of mozzarella between the slices of tomato and courgette, sprinkle with the oregano and return to the oven for 10 minutes until the mozzarella starts to form strings. Transfer to a warm serving dish and serve immediately.

TOMATOES WITH ROBIOLA

POMODORI CON ROBIOLA

Serves 4

4 round tomatoes, halved

100 g/3¹/₂ oz robiola cheese, diced

50 g/2 oz mild Gorgonzola cheese, crumbled

25 g/1 oz butter, softened

4 plum tomatoes, peeled and chopped

pinch of paprika

4 fresh chives, chopped

2 tablespoons vodka

salt and pepper

Scoop out the seeds and some of the flesh from the halved tomatoes, sprinkle with salt and turn upside down on kitchen paper to drain for 1 hour. Put the robiola, Gorgonzola and butter in a bowl, season with salt and pepper and beat until smooth and combined. Add the plum tomatoes, paprika and chives, mix well and sprinkle with the vodka. Fill the tomato halves with the mixture, arrange on a serving dish and keep in a cool place until ready to serve. Serve as a tasty summer first course.

TOMATOES WITH BACON AU GRATIN

POMODORI GRATINATI AL BACON

Serves 4

4 tomatoes, halved

3 tablespoons olive oil, plus extra for brushing and drizzling

150 g/5 oz mushrooms, finely chopped

1 onion, finely chopped

150 g/5 oz bacon, finely chopped

1 fresh thyme sprig, chopped

1 fresh flat-leaf parsley sprig, chopped

1 fresh marjoram sprig, chopped

1 egg, lightly beaten

50 g/2 oz breadcrumbs

salt and pepper

Scoop out the tomato seeds and flesh without damaging the 'shells'. Sprinkle the insides with salt and place upside down on kitchen paper to drain for 1 hour. Preheat the oven to 180°C/350°F/Gas Mark 4. Brush an ovenproof dish with oil. Heat the oil in a frying pan, add the mushrooms, onion and bacon and cook over a high heat, stirring frequently, for about 10 minutes. Add the thyme, parsley and marjoram, season with salt and pepper, mix well and remove the pan from the heat. Stir in the egg and spoon the mixture into the tomato shells. Sprinkle with the breadcrumbs, place in the prepared dish and drizzle with olive oil. Bake for 45 minutes.

TOMATOES STUFFED WITH PECORINO

Cut off the tops of the tomatoes. Scoop out the tomato seeds and some of the flesh, sprinkle with salt and turn upside down on kitchen paper to drain for 30 minutes. Preheat the oven to 200°C/400°F/Gas Mark 6. Brush an ovenproof dish with oil. Put both the cheeses in a bowl and stir in the olive oil. Add the oregano, a pinch of pepper and salt to taste if necessary. Spoon the mixture into the tomato 'shells', place in the prepared dish and bake for about 20 minutes. Serve warm.

POMODORI RIPIENI AL PECORINO

Serves 4

8 tomatoes

3 tablespoons olive oil, plus extra for brushing

200 g/7 oz mild pecorino cheese, crumbled

100 g/3¹/₂ oz mature pecorino cheese, freshly grated

large pinch of dried oregano

salt and pepper

TOMATOES STUFFED WITH RUSSIAN SALAD

Scoop out the tomato seeds and some of the flesh, sprinkle with salt and turn upside down on kitchen paper to drain for at least 30 minutes. Meanwhile, hard-boil the eggs, refresh under cold water, shell and cut each one into four wedges. Pat the tomato 'shells' dry and spoon in the Russian salad, doming it up in the centre. Top each filled tomato shell with a wedge of hard-boiled egg. Place in the refrigerator until 15 minutes before you are ready to serve. Arrange the tomatoes on a serving dish and garnish with lettuce leaves. Do not choose overripe tomatoes – delicately flavoured, green-red tomatoes are ideal for this dish.

POMODORI RIPIENI D'INSALATA RUSSA

Serves 4

4 round tomatoes, halved

2 eggs

1 quantity Russian Salad (see page 116)

salt

lettuce leaves, to garnish

TOMATOES STUFFED WITH RICE

Preheat the oven to 180°C/350°F/Gas Mark 4. Brush an ovenproof dish with oil. Cut off the tops of the tomatoes and reserve. Scoop out the tomato seeds and flesh, reserving the flesh and 'shells'. Pass the tomato flesh through a food mill into a bowl. Parboil the rice for 5 minutes in plenty of salted water, then drain and stir into the tomato flesh. Add the parsley, basil, oregano and olive oil, season with salt and pepper and mix well. Spoon the mixture into the tomato shells, replace the tops and place in the prepared dish. Drizzle with olive oil and bake for about 30 minutes. Serve hot or cold.

POMODORI RIPIENI DI RISO

Serves 6

4 tablespoons olive oil,
plus extra for brushing and drizzling

6 large tomatoes

6 tablespoons long-grain rice

1 fresh flat-leaf parsley sprig, chopped

6 fresh basil leaves chopped

pinch of dried oregano

salt and pepper

VERDURE
VEGETABLES

TOMATOES STUFFED WITH TUNA

Cut off the tops of the tomatoes and scoop out the tomato seeds and flesh, reserving the flesh. Sprinkle the 'shells' with salt and turn upside down on kitchen paper to drain for 1 hour. Place the tomato flesh in a strainer and leave to drain. Chop the anchovy fillets and put them with the tuna, capers, yogurt, parsley, chives and lemon juice in a blender. Process, then add the tomato flesh, season with salt and pepper and process again until thoroughly combined. Spoon the mixture into the tomato shells, garnish with basil leaves and keep in the refrigerator until ready to serve.

POMODORI RIPIENI DI TONNO

Serves 4

4 tomatoes

4 salted anchovies, heads removed, cleaned and filleted (see page 596), soaked in cold water for 10 minutes and drained

200 g/7 oz canned tuna in oil, drained

1 tablespoon capers, drained and rinsed

120 ml/4 fl oz low-fat natural yogurt

1 tablespoon fresh flat-leaaf parsley, chopped

5–6 fresh chives, coarsely chopped

juice of 1 lemon, strained

salt and pepper

fresh basil leaves, to garnish

RUSTIC TOMATO PIE

Preheat the oven to 180°C/350°F/Gas Mark 4. Grease a rectangular mould with butter. Heat the oil in a pan, add the spring onions and cook over a low heat, stirring occasionally, for 5 minutes. Lightly season with salt and remove from the heat. Cover the base of the prepared mould with half the bread and spoon the spring onions on top. Place the tomato slices on top, sprinkle with the oregano and cover with remaining the bread. Beat the egg with the milk in a bowl and season with salt and pepper. Pour the mixture over the bread, cover with the pecorino and bake for 30 minutes or until the cheese has melted and turned golden brown. Leave to cool slightly, then turn out on to a serving dish.

TORTINO RUSTICO DI POMODORI

Serves 6

butter, for greasing

3 tablespoons olive oil

3 spring onions, finely chopped

12 thin wholemeal bread slices, crusts removed

500 g/1 lb 2 oz tomatoes, sliced

pinch of dried oregano

1 egg

150 ml/¼ pint milk

50 g/2 oz pecorino cheese, very thinly sliced

salt and pepper

LEEKS

Leeks belong to the same family as garlic and onion, but have a much more delicate flavour. Generally, only the white part of the leek is eaten, so the whole outer leaf and all the green part should be removed. Leeks are mainly used to add flavour to other vegetables. They are also pleasant cut into very thin slices and used raw in mixed salads, or baked or boiled and smothered with melted butter and cheese.

QUANTITIES AND COOKING TIMES

QUANTITIES

1 kg/2¼ lb leeks is sufficient for a side dish for 4; the same amount is enough for a main course if the leeks are combined with other ingredients such as cheese and béchamel sauce.

BOILING

As leeks are very delicate, 15 minutes simmering is enough.

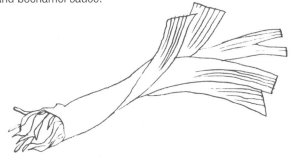

PORRI AL POMODORO

Serves 4

1 shallot, chopped

3 tablespoons olive oil

4 tomatoes, peeled and chopped

1 garlic clove, chopped

1 fresh thyme sprig, chopped

175 ml/6 fl oz dry white wine

1 kg/2¼ lb leeks, white part only, sliced

salt and pepper

LEEKS WITH TOMATO

Cook the shallot in a saucepan with the oil and 100 ml/3½ fl oz water over a medium heat for about 5 minutes until soft. Add the tomatoes, garlic and thyme, season with salt and pepper and cook over a high heat for a few minutes. Sprinkle in the wine and cook until it has evaporated, then lower the heat and simmer for 15 minutes. Parboil the leeks in salted water for 5 minutes, then drain well, add to the tomato mixture, cover and simmer for 15 minutes. Remove the lid, boil off any remaining liquid and transfer to a warm serving dish.

LEEKS WITH HAM

PORRI AL PROSCIUTTO

Serves 4

1 kg/2¹/₄ lb leeks, white parts only
100 g/3¹/₂ oz cooked ham, sliced
100 g/3¹/₂ oz butter
50 g/2 oz plain flour
500 ml/18 fl oz milk
100 g/3¹/₂ oz Gruyère cheese, freshly grated
2 tablespoons Parmesan cheese, freshly grated
salt and pepper

Parboil the leeks in salted water for 5 minutes, then drain well. Preheat the oven to 180°C/350°F/Gas Mark 4. Trim the fat from the ham and place the fat in an ovenproof dish with 25 g/1 oz of the butter. Melt over a medium heat, then add the leeks in two layers and cook, basting frequently, until lightly browned. Season with salt and pepper. Meanwhile, make a Béchamel Sauce (see page 50), using 25 g/1 oz of the remaining butter, the flour and milk. Stir the Gruyère into the sauce. Remove the dish of leeks from the heat, lay the slices of ham on top and spoon the béchamel sauce over them. Dot with the remaining butter, sprinkle with the Parmesan and bake for about 10 minutes.

LEEKS AU GRATIN

PORRI GRATINATI

Serves 4

1 kg/2¹/₄ lb leeks, white parts only
65 g/2¹/₂ oz butter, plus extra for greasing
25 g/1 oz plain flour
350 ml/12 fl oz milk
2 egg yolks
50 g/2 oz Emmenthal cheese, freshly grated
pinch of freshly grated nutmeg
50 g/2 oz Parmesan cheese, freshly grated
4 tablespoons breadcrumbs
salt and pepper

Cook the leeks in salted, boiling water for about 15 minutes, then drain well, spread out on a tea towel and leave to dry. Preheat the oven to 180°C/350°F/Gas Mark 4. Grease an ovenproof dish with butter. Melt 40 g/1¹/₂ oz of the butter in a pan, add the leeks and cook over a low heat, turning occasionally, for a few minutes, then transfer to the prepared dish. Make a Béchamel Sauce (see page 50) with the remaining butter, the flour and milk. Remove the pan of sauce from the heat, beat in the egg yolks, Emmenthal and nutmeg and season with salt and pepper. Pour the sauce over the leeks, sprinkle with the Parmesan and breadcrumbs, dot with the remaining butter and bake for about 20 minutes until golden brown and bubbling.

LEEKS IN HOLLANDAISE SAUCE

PORRI IN SALSA OLANDESE

Serves 4

1 kg/2¹/₄ lb leeks, white parts only
120 g/4 oz butter
3 egg yolks
juice of ¹/₂ lemon, strained
salt and pepper

Cook the leeks in salted, boiling water for about 15 minutes, then drain well, spread out on a tea towel and leave to dry. Meanwhile, prepare a Hollandaise Sauce (see page 59) with the butter, egg yolks and lemon juice and season with salt and pepper. Arrange the leeks on a serving dish, spoon the sauce over them.

RADICCHIO

Radicchio is the generic name of a few types of chicory, a prolific extended family of vegetables. The best-known varieties are the long, red Treviso radicchio, the red Verona radicchio, the variegated red and white Castelfranco Veneto radicchio and the red Chioggia radicchio. Their distinctive features depend on the method of cultivation. Some types are grown in the open and others are grown under glass, which gives them their typically red, white or variegated leaves. The best-known kinds are also the tastiest and most frequently used. As well as being used in classic salads, almost all types of radicchio can be baked or grilled. However, they are no less tasty when used in risottos or for pasta.

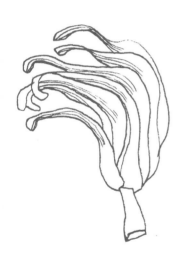

RADICCHIO AND WALNUT ROLLS

Preheat the oven to 180°C/350°F/Gas Mark 4. Grease an oven-proof dish with butter. Blanch the radicchio leaves in boiling water for 2 minutes, then remove and drain on kitchen paper. Mix together the ricotta, walnuts, egg yolk and Parmesan in a bowl and season with salt and pepper. Divide the mixture among the radicchio leaves, roll up and place in the prepared dish. Bake for about 15 minutes.

INVOLTINI DI RADICCHIO ALLE NOCI

Serves 4

butter, for greasing

10 Castelfranco radicchio leaves

100 g/3^1/$_2$ oz ricotta cheese

10 shelled walnuts, chopped

1 egg yolk

2 tablespoons Parmesan cheese, freshly grated

salt and pepper

BAKED RADICCHIO

RADICCHIO AL FORNO

Serves 4

4 tablespoons olive oil

675 g/1 1/2 lb Treviso radicchio, trimmed

juice of 1/2 lemon, strained

salt and pepper

Preheat the oven to 180°C/350°F/Gas Mark 4. Pour half the oil into an ovenproof dish, add the radicchio, sprinkle with the remaining oil and season with salt and pepper. Cover with foil and bake for about 20 minutes. Remove from the oven, transfer to a warm serving dish and sprinkle with the lemon juice.

RADICCHIO WITH PARMESAN

RADICCHIO AL PARMIGIANO

Serves 4

25 g/1 oz butter, plus extra for greasing

8–10 Castelfranco radicchio hearts

2 tablespoons Parmesan cheese, freshly grated

40 g/1 1/2 oz Parmesan cheese, shaved

salt and pepper

Preheat the oven to 180°C/350°F/Gas Mark 4. Grease an ovenproof dish with butter. Blanch the radicchio in boiling water for a few minutes, then remove from the pan and drain on a tea towel. Place the radicchio in the prepared dish, season with salt and pepper and sprinkle with the grated Parmesan and Parmesan shavings. Dot with the butter and bake for 10–15 minutes.

RADICCHIO MIMOSA

RADICCHIO MIMOSA

Serves 4

4 Castelfranco radicchio, cut into strips

5 tablespoons olive oil

2 tablespoons white wine vinegar

4 hard-boiled egg yolks

salt and white pepper

Place the radicchio strips in a salad bowl. Whisk together the olive oil and vinegar in a bowl and season with salt and pepper. Pour the dressing over the radicchio. Press the egg yolks through a sieve over the salad, toss and serve.

TREVISO RADICCHIO SALAD WITH ORANGE

RADICCHIO ROSSO ALL'ARANCIA

Serves 4

juice of 2 oranges, strained

3–4 tablespoons olive oil

1 teaspoon lemon juice (optional)

4 Treviso radicchio, cut into thin wedges

salt and pepper

Whisk together the orange juice and oil in a bowl and season with salt and pepper to taste. Add a few drops of lemon juice to sharpen the taste if the orange juice is too sweet. Place the radicchio in a bowl and pour the orange dressing over it in a continuous stream, then toss gently and serve. The unusual sweet and sour combination of this salad makes it a suitable side dish for boiled fish or mixed boiled meats.

FRIED RADICCHIO

To make the batter, sift the flour with a pinch of salt into a bowl, break the egg into the middle and add the olive oil. Mix thoroughly with a wooden spoon to prevent lumps from forming, then stir in the beer. Cover and leave to stand for at least 30 minutes. Stiffly whisk the egg white in a grease-free bowl, then fold into the batter. Remove the largest outer leaves individually from the radicchio and cut the hearts into thin wedges. Heat the oil for deep-frying in a large pan. Immerse each leaf in the batter and fry in the hot oil, turning frequently so that it browns evenly. Repeat with the radicchio wedges. Drain on kitchen paper, sprinkle with salt and serve immediately.

RADICCHIO ROSSO FRITTO

Serves 4

2–3 Treviso radicchio, trimmed

vegetable oil, for deep-frying

salt

For the batter

65 g/2¹/₂ oz plain flour

1 egg

1 tablespoon olive oil

100 ml/3¹/₂ fl oz beer

1 egg white

salt

RADICCHIO EN CROÛTE

Preheat the oven to 180°C/350°F/Gas Mark 4, and preheat the grill. Grease a baking sheet with butter. Brush the radicchio heads with oil and grill until they wilt slightly, then season with salt and pepper. Roll out the pastry on a lightly floured surface and cut into rectangles (one for each head of radicchio). Lay one head of radicchio on each rectangle and fold over the pastry to enclose it completely. Beat the egg yolk with 1 teaspoon water in a bowl and brush the parcels with it. Place the parcel on the prepared baking sheet and bake for 15–20 minutes until golden brown.

RADICCHIO ROSSO IN CROSTA

Serves 4

butter, for greasing

4–6 Treviso radicchio, trimmed

olive oil, for brushing

250–500 g/9 oz–1 lb 2 oz puff pastry dough,

thawed if frozen

plain flour, for dusting

1 egg yolk

salt and pepper

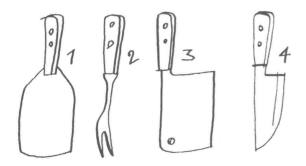

TURNIPS

To enjoy their pleasant flavour at its best, choose small, heavy, very firm and slightly violet-coloured turnips, otherwise they may turn out to be bitter. Turnip stock is fresh and pleasant. When boiled and dressed with oil, vinegar and salt, turnips make a perfect side dish for pork. To prepare, remove the leaves and cut a slice off the top.

QUANTITIES AND COOKING TIMES

QUANTITIES

Allow 2 small turnips per serving as a side dish, otherwise the quantity is specified in the recipe.

BOILING

Immerse turnips whole, if small, or sliced, if large, in salted, boiling water and cook for 20–40 minutes, depending on their size.

TURNIPS WITH BACON

Scoop out a hole in the middle of each turnip with a small sharp knife. Push 15 g/½ oz of the butter into each hole, season with salt and pepper and place in a deep saucepan. Pour 5 tablespoons water into the pan, cover and bring to the boil, then lower the heat and cook until the turnips are tender, adding more boiling water if necessary. Put the bacon in a frying pan and cook over a low heat until the fat runs, then remove and drain on kitchen paper. Make a Béchamel Sauce (see page 50) with the remaining butter, the flour and milk and season with salt and pepper. Stir in the bacon. Remove the turnips from the saucepan, cut into slices, place on a warm serving dish and cover with the sauce.

RAPE AL BACON

Serves 4

8 small turnips, trimmed
165 g/5½ oz butter
80 g/3 oz bacon, cut into strips
40 g/1½ oz plain flour
400 ml/14 fl oz milk
salt and pepper

TURNIPS IN CREAM

Preheat the oven to 180°C/350°F/Gas Mark 4. Line a roasting tin with foil. Pour the cream into a saucepan and bring to the boil, then add the turnip slices and cook for 2 minutes. Remove the turnip slices with a fish slice, drain and arrange in overlapping concentric circles in the roasting tin. Sprinkle with the Parmesan and chives, season with salt and pepper and bake until lightly browned. Transfer to a warm serving dish.

RAPE ALLA PANNA

Serves 4

250 ml/8 fl oz double cream
10 turnips, trimmed and thinly sliced
25 g/1 oz Parmesan cheese, freshly grated
6 fresh chives, chopped
salt and white pepper

STUFFED TURNIPS

Cook the turnips in salted, boiling water until tender, then drain. Meanwhile, heat the oil in a small frying pan, add the chicken and cook over a medium heat, stirring frequently, until golden brown all over, then season with salt and remove from the heat. Preheat the oven to 180°C/350°F/Gas Mark 4. Grease an ovenproof dish with butter. Chop the speck together with the sage. Scoop out the centres of the turnips to make 'bowls' and reserve the flesh. Fill each bowl with chicken and speck and dot the tops with the butter. Place in the prepared dish and bake for about 40 minutes. Put the scooped-out turnip flesh in a double boiler or in a heatproof bowl set over a pan of barely simmering water. Add the egg yolks and cream, season with salt and pepper and cook, stirring constantly, until the sauce has thickened. Serve the stuffed turnips with the sauce.

RAPE FARCITE

Serves 6

12 medium turnips, trimmed
2 tablespoons olive oil
1 small skinless, boneless chicken breast, chopped
40 g/1½ oz butter, plus extra for greasing
5 speck (Austrian smoked ham) slices
5 fresh sage leaves
3 egg yolks
2 tablespoons double cream
salt and white pepper

ROAST TURNIPS WITH POTATOES

RAPE IN TEGLIA CON PATATE

Serves 4

4 tablespoons olive oil

1 onion, thinly sliced

400 g/14 oz turnips, trimmed and sliced

350 g/12 oz potatoes, sliced

150 ml/¼ pint Vegetable Stock (see page 209)

200 g/7 oz mozzarella cheese, diced

pinch of dried oregano

salt and pepper

Preheat the oven to 200°C/400°F/Gas Mark 6. Heat the oil in a roasting tin, add the onion and cook over a low heat, stirring occasionally, for 5 minutes. Add the turnips and potatoes, season with salt and pepper, mix well and pour in the stock. Roast for 30 minutes until the liquid has been completely absorbed. Sprinkle the mozzarella and oregano over the vegetables, return the tin to the oven and cook for a further 10 minutes.

ROAST TURNIPS WITH LEEKS AND PUMPKIN

RAPE IN TEGLIA CON PORRI E ZUCCA

Serves 4

200 g/7 oz pumpkin flesh, sliced

1 teaspoon fresh thyme leaves

3 tablespoons olive oil, plus extra for drizzling

200 g/7 oz leeks, white parts only, sliced

300 g/11 oz turnips, trimmed and sliced

2 tablespoons sesame seeds

salt

Preheat the oven to 200°C/400°F/Gas Mark 6. Place the pumpkin slices on a sheet of foil, season with salt and sprinkle with the thyme leaves. Fold over the foil to enclose the pumpkin completely, place on a baking sheet and bake for 30 minutes. Heat the oil in a large pan, add the leeks and turnips and cook over a medium heat, stirring occasionally, until tender. Add the pumpkin and cook for a few minutes more. Sprinkle with the sesame seeds and drizzle with olive oil, then serve.

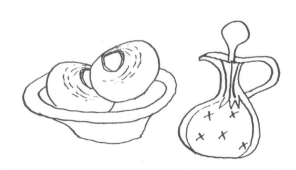

RADISHES

The most common types of radish are red or white, round or elongated. They are eaten raw after they have been trimmed and any blemishes scraped away with a small knife. They may be sliced and added to salads or left whole as a garnish. When served as a dish in their own right, they are simply seasoned with a little salt or served together with thin slices of lightly buttered white or wholemeal bread.

RAVANELLI CON FORMAGGIO

Serves 4

250 g/9 oz crescenza or other stracchino cheese

1 bunch of radishes, trimmed

white pepper

toast slices, to serve

RADISHES WITH CHEESE

Beat the cheese in a bowl with a wooden spoon until smooth and creamy. Cut the radishes into slices and then into thin batons. Add to the cheese with a pinch of pepper, stir and serve with slices of toast.

RAVANELLI GLASSATI

Serves 4

600 g/1 lb 5 oz radishes, trimmed

80 g/3 oz butter

2 tablespoons sugar

salt

GLAZED RADISHES

Halve the radishes, place in a saucepan, add water to cover, and the butter, sugar and a pinch of salt. Bring to the boil, then lower the heat, cover and simmer very gently until the liquid is thick and syrupy. Mix well so that the radishes are evenly coated with syrup. This unusual side dish goes well with roast pork or veal.

RADISH SALAD WITH OLIVES

RAVANELLI IN INSALATA CON LE OLIVE

Serves 4

6 red radishes, trimmed

juice of 1 lemon, strained

100 g/3½ oz lamb's lettuce

10 stoned black olives

olive oil, for drizzling

salt

Cut the radishes into very thin horizontal slices, put in a salad bowl and sprinkle with the lemon juice. Add the lamb's lettuce and olives, drizzle with olive oil and season with salt to taste. Mix gently and leave to stand for 10 minutes before serving.

RADISH SALAD WITH YOGURT

RAVANELLI IN INSALATA CON LO YOGURT

Serves 4

2 large white radishes, thinly sliced

1 green apple

4 tablespoons natural yogurt

salt and white pepper

Put the radishes in a salad bowl, sprinkle with a pinch of salt, stir and leave to stand for 10 minutes. Peel and core the apple and cut into wedges. Using a very sharp knife, cut the wedges into wafer-thin slices and add to the radishes. Mix together the yogurt and a pinch of pepper in a bowl, add to the salad, toss and serve.

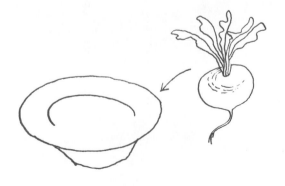

SCORZONERA

Scorzonera is a winter root vegetable with butter-coloured flesh covered with a dark-brown skin. It is also known as black salsify and has a similar flavour. However, true salsify, also known as oyster plant, is lighter in colour and slightly more difficult to peel. All these recipes can be used for both scorzonera and salsify. To prepare, cut off both ends, scrape off the skin and cut the flesh into short pieces or leave whole, depending on the recipe. If there is a woody core in the middle, remove it. As the pieces are prepared, immerse them in cold water mixed with a little vinegar or lemon juice to prevent discoloration. Scorzonera and salsify may also be grated and served dressed with olive oil and lemon juice.

QUANTITIES

Allow about 150 g/5 oz per serving.

BOILING

Cook in lightly salted, boiling water with a little vinegar or lemon juice for about 30 minutes.

QUANTITIES
AND COOKING TIMES

SCORZONERA WITH HORSERADISH

SCORZONERA AL CREN

Serves 4

juice of 1 lemon, strained

600 g/1 lb 5 oz scorzonera

1 tablespoon plain flour

200 ml/7 fl oz double cream

2 tablespoons white wine vinegar

2 tablespoons finely grated horseradish

salt and pepper

Half-fill a bowl with water and add half the lemon juice. Peel and chop the scorzonera, then immerse in the acidulated water. Fill a large pan with water, add the flour, a pinch of salt, the scorzonera and the remaining lemon juice and bring to the boil. Lower the heat and simmer for about 30 minutes. Drain and leave to cool. Meanwhile, stiffly whip cream, season with salt and pepper and gently stir in the vinegar and horseradish. Place the scorzonera on a serving dish and spoon the horseradish cream over it.

SCORZONERA WITH ANCHOVIES

SCORZONERA ALLE ACCIUGHE

Serves 4

juice of 1 lemon, strained

675 g/1½ lb scorzonera, trimmed and peeled

120 g/4 oz salted anchovies, heads removed, cleaned and filleted (see page 596), soaked in cold water for 10 minutes and drained

2 tablespoons olive oil

1 tablespoon capers, drained, rinsed and chopped

1 tablespoon white wine vinegar

1 fresh flat-leaf parsley sprig, chopped

salt

Fill a large pan with water, add the lemon juice, a pinch of salt and the scorzonera and bring to the boil. Lower the heat and simmer for 30 minutes. Meanwhile, Chop the anchovy fillets. Heat the oil in a frying pan, add the anchovies and cook over a low heat, mashing with a wooden spoon until they have almost disintegrated. Add the capers and vinegar and cook until the vinegar has evaporated, then remove the pan from the heat. Drain then chop the scorzonera, and place it on a warm serving dish. Spoon the anchovy sauce over it, sprinkle with the parsley and serve.

SCORZONERA FRICASSÉE

SCORZONERA IN FRICASSEA

Serves 4

juice of 2 lemons, strained

675g/1½ lb scorzonera, trimmed and peeled

25 g/1 oz butter

2 egg yolks

1 fresh flat-leaf parsley sprig, chopped

salt

Fill a large pan with water, add half the lemon juice, a pinch of salt and the scorzonera and bring to the boil. Lower the heat and simmer for 30 minutes, then drain and slice. Melt the butter in a pan, add the scorzonera and cook over a low heat, stirring occasionally, for 5 minutes. Meanwhile, beat the egg yolks with the remaining lemon juice and a pinch of salt in a bowl. Remove the pan from the heat, stir in the egg yolks, return to the heat and cook, stirring constantly until the eggs are lightly cooked. Remove from the heat, sprinkle with the parsley and serve.

CELERY

Green celery is cooked to flavour broths, stews, sauces and boiled meat. White celery is added raw to salads or eaten with pinzimonio (olive oil with pepper and salt). To prepare celery, remove and discard the coarsest sticks and strings. Celery is delicious served raw with creamy cheeses such as Gorgonzola. Recipes for celery may also be used for celeriac. The best months to eat this vegetable are from November to April.

QUANTITIES
Allow 1 celery heart per serving.

BOILING
Halve the sticks lengthways, immerse in salted, boiling water and cook for about 20 minutes.

QUANTITIES
AND COOKING TIMES

CELERIAC CARPACCIO WITH ANCHOVIES

Put the celeriac in a bowl. Mix together the lemon juice and 4 tablespoons of the oil, then pour the mixture over the celeriac and leave to marinate for 30 minutes. Mix together the remaining oil and the vinegar in a bowl, season with salt and pepper and add the anchovies and capers. Arrange a bed of rocket on each of four plates, place slices of celeriac on top, drizzle the dressing over them and sprinkle with the Parmesan.

CARPACCIO DI SEDANO ALLE ACCIUGHE

Serves 4

2 small celeriacs, peeled and thinly sliced

juice of 1 lemon, strained

150 ml/^{1}/$_4$ pint olive oil

2 tablespoons white wine vinegar

3 canned anchovies in oil, drained and chopped

1 tablespoon capers, drained, rinsed and chopped

1 bunch of rocket, chopped

50 g/2 oz Parmesan cheese, shaved

salt and pepper

CELERY WITH GORGONZOLA

Halve the celery stalks lengthways and arrange on a serving dish. Beat the Gorgonzola in a bowl until smooth and season with a few drops of vinegar, salt and pepper. Fill the celery stalks with the mixture.

SEDANO AL GORGONZOLA

Serves 4

2 heads of white celery, trimmed

80 g/3 oz Gorgonzola cheese, crumbled

white wine vinegar, to taste

salt and pepper

CELERY IN BÉCHAMEL SAUCE

SEDANO ALLA BESCIAMELLA

Serves 4

25 g/1 oz butter, plus extra for greasing

3 heads of white celery, trimmed

1 quantity Béchamel Sauce (see page 50)

40 g/1¹/₂ oz Parmesan cheese, freshly grated

salt

Preheat the oven to 200°C/400°F/Gas Mark 6. Grease an oven-proof dish with butter. Halve the celery stalks lengthways and cook in salted, boiling water for 10 minutes, then drain and place in the prepared dish. Spoon the béchamel sauce over them, dot with the butter and sprinkle with the Parmesan. Bake for about 15 minutes until golden and bubbling.

GREEK-STYLE CELERY

SEDANO ALLA GRECA

Serves 4

2 tablespoons sultanas

2 tablespoons olive oil

1 head of white celery, trimmed and sliced

3 small onions, chopped

3 courgettes, sliced

200 ml/7 fl oz dry white wine

2 teaspoons tomato purée

juice of 1 lemon, strained, plus extra to serve

6 fresh basil leaves

salt and pepper

Put the sultanas in a bowl, cover with warm water and leave to soak for 10 minutes, then drain and squeeze out the excess liquid. Heat the oil in a pan, add the celery and cook over a high heat, stirring frequently, for 5 minutes. Add the onions and courgettes, mix well and pour in the wine. Cook until it has evaporated, lower the heat and add the sultanas. Mix together the tomato purée and 1 tablespoon water in a small bowl, add to the pan and simmer for about 20 minutes. Stir in the lemon juice, season with salt and pepper and cook for a few minutes more. Transfer the mixture to a salad bowl, add the basil and leave to cool, then chill in the refrigerator for 3–4 hours. Serve cold with a little extra lemon juice.

MOLISE CELERY

SEDANO ALLA MOLISANA

Serves 4

2 tablespoons olive oil, plus extra for brushing

1 head of green celery, trimmed and sliced

8 spring onions, thinly sliced

100 g/3¹/₂ oz stoned black olives

3 tablespoons breadcrumbs

salt and pepper

Preheat the oven to 200°C/400°F/Gas Mark 6. Brush an oven-proof dish with oil. Cook the celery in salted, boiling water for 10 minutes, then drain, tip into a bowl and leave to cool slightly. Meanwhile, heat the oil and 1 tablespoon water in a pan, add the spring onions and cook over a low heat for 5 minutes until softened, then season with salt and pepper. Place the celery in the prepared dish, top with the spring onions and olives, sprinkle with the breadcrumbs and bake for 15 minutes.

CELERY AND WALNUT SALAD

SEDANO ALLE NOCI

Serves 4

120 g/4 oz white celery, trimmed • 1 green apple, peeled, cored and diced • juice of 1 lemon, strained 120 g/4 oz low-fat tomino or other semi-hard cheese, diced • 1 tablespoon fresh flat-leaf parsley, chopped • 50 g/2 oz shelled walnuts, chopped 5 tablespoons olive oil • salt and pepper

Halve the celery stalks lengthways and cut into thin strips. Place the celery and apple in a salad bowl and stir in half the lemon juice. Add the cheese, parsley and half the walnuts. Whisk together the olive oil and remaining lemon juice in a jug and season with salt and pepper. Stir in the remaining walnuts and pour the dressing over the salad.

SEDANO AL POMODORO

Serves 4

3 tablespoons olive oil

3 heads of white celery, trimmed and sliced

3 tablespoons Tomato Sauce (see page 57)

pinch of sugar

salt and pepper

CELERY IN TOMATO SAUCE

Heat the oil in a saucepan, add the celery and cook over a medium heat, stirring occasionally, for 5 minutes. Add the tomato sauce and sugar, season with salt and pepper and mix well. Lower the heat and simmer for 15 minutes, then transfer to a warm serving dish.

SEDANO FRITTO

Serves 4

1 large celeriac, peeled

1 egg

80 g/3 oz breadcrumbs

3 tablespoons olive oil

25 g/1 oz butter

salt

FRIED CELERIAC

Cook the celeriac in salted, boiling water for 10 minutes, then drain and leave to cool slightly. Meanwhile, beat the egg with a pinch of salt in a shallow dish and spread out the breadcrumbs in another shallow dish. Cut the celeriac into 5-mm/$^1/_4$-inch slices and dip them first in the beaten egg and then in the breadcrumbs. Heat the oil and butter in a frying pan, add the celeriac and fry until light golden brown all over. Remove with a fish slice and drain on kitchen paper, then sprinkle with a little salt and serve.

SEDANO GRATINATO

Serves 4

4 celeriacs, peeled and thinly sliced

40 g/1$^1/_2$ oz butter, plus extra for greasing

2 tablespoons olive oil

1 baby onion, thinly sliced

500 g/1 lb 2 oz canned tomatoes

40 g/1$^1/_2$ oz Parmesan cheese, freshly grated

1 quantity Béchamel Sauce (see page 50)

salt and pepper

CELERIAC AU GRATIN

Sprinkle the celeriac slices with salt. Melt half the butter in a large pan, add the celeriac and cook over a medium heat, stirring occasionally, for 5 minutes. Add 100 ml/3$^1/_2$ fl oz water, cover and cook, stirring occasionally, until tender. Meanwhile, heat the oil in a small saucepan, add the onion and cook over a low heat, stirring occasionally, for 5 minutes until softened. Add the tomatoes, season with salt and pepper, cover and simmer for about 30 minutes. Preheat the oven to 200°C/400°F/Gas Mark 6. Grease an ovenproof dish with butter. Stir 1 tablespoon of the Parmesan into the béchamel sauce. Drain the celeriac and arrange a layer of the slices in the prepared dish. Spoon some of the tomato sauce on top, sprinkle with some of the remaining Parmesan and top with a layer of béchamel sauce. Continue making layers until all the ingredients are used, ending with a layer of béchamel sauce. Bake for about 20 minutes.

SPINACH

Since several varieties are cultivated, spinach is available all year round. The leaves should be firm, fleshy and green with no signs of yellowing. To check for freshness, look at the stalks, which should be firm without any signs of floppiness (although, clearly, they should be removed before using). Spinach should be eaten on the day of purchase but if you must store it, keep it in the salad drawer of the refrigerator for no more than 24 hours. Similarly, leftover cooked spinach should not be kept, as the nitrites absorbed from chemical fertilizers are oxidized into nitrates. Spinach is very rich in vitamin A, calcium, phosphorus and iron. However, there is less iron than is commonly believed and most of it cannot be absorbed by the human digestive system. Raw spinach is very tasty, but in this case choose baby spinach with small, tender leaves. Cream of spinach soup and spinach croquettes are delicious, puréed spinach is flavoursome and spinach moulds look impressive.

QUANTITIES

Spinach shrinks considerably during cooking, so allow about 250 g/9 oz raw leaves per serving.

BOILING

Cook spinach, in just the water clinging to its leaves after washing, in a covered pan for 5–8 minutes. Drain well and press out as much liquid as possible with the back of a spoon.

**QUANTITIES
AND COOKING TIMES**

567

Serves 6

50 g/2 oz sultanas

1 kg/2¼ lb spinach

40 g/1½ oz butter

150 g/5 oz plain flour, plus extra for dusting

500 ml/18 fl oz milk

pinch of freshly grated nutmeg

120 g/4 oz fontina cheese, thinly sliced

4 tablespoons Parmesan cheese, freshly grated

3 egg yolks

olive oil, for brushing

1 egg

80 g/3 oz breadcrumbs

vegetable oil, for deep-frying

salt and pepper

SPINACH CROQUETTES

Put the sultanas in a bowl, add warm water to cover and leave to soak. Cook the spinach, in just the water clinging to the leaves after washing, for about 5 minutes until tender. Drain well, squeeze out the excess liquid and chop finely. Melt the butter in a saucepan, stir in the flour, then gradually stir in the milk. Bring just to the boil, stirring constantly, then season with salt and pepper and add the nutmeg. Remove the pan from the heat, add the fontina and Parmesan and stir until smooth and creamy. Stir in the egg yolks, one at a time. Drain the sultanas, squeeze out and add to the mixture with the chopped spinach. Brush a marble slab or large tray with olive oil, pour the spinach mixture on to it and smooth the surface with a dampened palette knife. Leave to cool. Spread out a little flour in a shallow dish, beat the egg in another shallow dish and spread out the breadcrumbs in a third. Cut the cooled spinach mixture into squares and dip first in the flour, then in the beaten egg and, finally, in the breadcrumbs. Heat the oil for deep-frying in a large pan, add the spinach croquettes and cook until golden brown. Remove with a fish slice, drain on kitchen paper and serve hot.

SPINACI ALLA CREMA

Serves 4

1 kg/2¼ lb spinach

200 ml/7 fl oz double cream

1 teaspoon plain flour, sifted

40 g/1½ oz butter

pinch of freshly grated nutmeg

40 g/1½ oz Parmesan cheese, freshly grated

salt and pepper

SPINACH IN CREAM

Cook the spinach, in just the water clinging to the leaves after washing, for about 5 minutes until tender. Drain well and squeeze out the excess liquid. Mix together the cream and flour in a bowl. Melt the butter in a pan, add the spinach and cook over a low heat, stirring frequently, for a few minutes. Stir in the nutmeg, season with salt and pepper, cover and simmer gently for about 10 minutes. Stir in the cream and simmer gently for a further 20 minutes. Sprinkle with the Parmesan and serve.

SPINACI ALLA GENOVESE

Serves 4

50 g/2 oz sultanas

4 salted anchovies, heads removed, cleaned and fillleted (see page 596), soaked in cold water for 10 minutes and drained

1 kg/2 ¼ lb spinach

4 tablespoons olive oil

1 tablespoon fresh flat-leaaf parsley, chopped

50 g/2 oz pine nuts • salt and pepper

GENOESE SPINACH

Put the sultanas in a bowl, add warm water to cover and leave to soak. Chop the anchovy fillets. Cook the spinach, in just the water clinging to the leaves after washing, for about 5 minutes until tender. Drain well and squeeze out the excess liquid. Heat the oil in a pan, add the anchovies, spinach and parsley and mix well, then add the pine nuts. Drain and squeeze out the sultanas, then add to the pan. Season with salt and pepper to taste and cook for about 10 minutes.

SPINACH AND MUSHROOM SALAD

SPINACI IN INSALATA CON CHAMPIGNON

Serves 4

juice of 1 lemon, strained

150 g/5 oz button mushrooms

1 lettuce, trimmed

300 g/11 oz baby spinach leaves, coarse stalks removed

4 tablespoons olive oil

1 tablespoon Dijon mustard

salt

Half-fill a bowl with water and add half the lemon juice. Thinly slice the mushrooms and add to the acidulated water. Tear the lettuce leaves into pieces and put them in a salad bowl with the spinach leaves. Drain the mushrooms and add to the bowl. Whisk together a generous pinch of salt, the olive oil, mustard and the remaining lemon juice in a bowl. Pour the dressing over the salad, toss gently and serve.

SPINACH IN WHITE BUTTER SAUCE

SPINACI IN SALSA BIANCA

Serves 4

1 lemon, sliced

1 kg/2¼ lb spinach

2 small shallots, chopped

100 ml/3½ fl oz dry white wine

150 g/5 oz butter, softened

½ teaspoon fresh thyme leaves

25 g/1 oz Parmesan cheese, freshly grated

salt and pepper

Bring a pan of salted water to the boil, add the lemon and spinach and cook for about 5 minutes until the spinach is tender. Remove and discard the lemon, drain the spinach and squeeze out the excess liquid. Place in a serving dish and keep warm. Put the shallots, wine and 100 ml/3½ fl oz water in a small saucepan and bring to the boil over a medium heat. Lower the heat and simmer until the liquid has reduced by half. Remove the pan from the heat, season with salt and pepper and leave to cool slightly. Stir in the softened butter and return to the heat, whisking constantly until thickened, then add the thyme. Sprinkle the spinach with the Parmesan, and spoon the sauce over it.

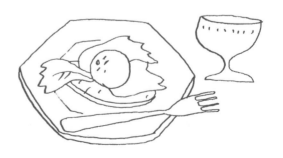

TRUFFLES

*Two Italian regions are famous for their white truffles –
Piedmont, with Alba in the Langhe (the acknowledged capital
of this prized underground fungus) and other areas of the
Monferrato district (the area around Alessandria and the Po
hills) and Marche, whose most famous truffle-growing centres
are Acqualagna, Sant'Angelo in Vado and Visso in the
province of Pesaro, and Amandola, Comunanza and
Montemonaco in the province of Ascoli Piceno. The most
famous region for the esteemed black truffle is Umbria, with
Norcia, Spoleto, Cascia and Scheggino. Truffles mature from
October to April, but the best and most fragrant are those
gathered in the autumn months. Both white and black truffles
are stored in the same way: wrapped in two layers of damp
paper, with two or three dry sheets on the outside, and kept in
the least cold part of the refrigerator for no more than a
week. To clean them, brush gently, then wipe with a damp
cloth. Black truffles are cooked, but white ones are eaten
raw. White truffles go with egg tagliolini, fondues, raw
meat, agnolotti and risottos. Black truffles go with fried eggs,
crostini and frittata.*

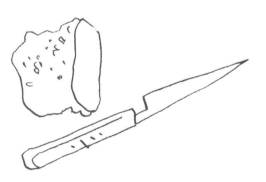

QUANTITIES
Allow about 20 g/³/₄ oz per
serving.

CLASSIC TRUFFLE FRITTATA

FRITTATA CLASSICA DI TARTUFI

Serves 4

5 eggs

100 g/3¹/₂ oz black truffles, chopped

100 ml/3¹/₂ fl oz double cream

juice of ¹/₂–1 lemon, strained

2 tablespoons olive oil

salt

Lightly beat the eggs in a shallow dish and add the truffles, cream, a pinch of salt and lemon juice to taste. Heat the olive oil in a frying pan, pour in the mixture and cook over a medium heat, stirring occasionally with a wooden spoon, turning once. Cook the frittata until just set, but still soft, and the truffles are lightly cooked.

ROAST TRUFFLES WITH POTATOES

TARTUFI AL FORNO CON PATATE

Serves 4

675 g/1¹/₂ lb potatoes, thinly sliced

500 ml/18 fl oz milk

25 g/1 oz butter, plus extra for greasing

1 shallot, chopped

250 ml/8 fl oz double cream

80 g/3 oz black truffles, very thinly sliced

25 g/1 oz Parmesan cheese, freshly grated

salt and pepper

Put the potatoes into a saucepan, pour in the milk and 500 ml/ 18 fl oz water, add a pinch of salt and cook for 30–45 minutes until just tender, then drain. Preheat the oven to 180°C/350°F/Gas Mark 4. Grease an ovenproof dish with butter. Melt the butter in a pan, add the shallot and cook over a low heat, stirring occasionally, for 5 minutes. Add the potatoes and cream, season with salt and pepper and cook for a few minutes more. Remove the potatoes with a fish slice and set aside. Reduce the cooking juices over a low heat. Arrange slightly overlapping slices of potato and truffle in the prepared dish, spoon the thickened cooking juices over them, sprinkle with the Parmesan and bake until golden brown. Serve hot.

PARMESAN TRUFFLES

TARTUFI ALLA PARMIGIANA

Serves 4

40 g/1¹/₂ oz butter

2 black truffles, thinly sliced

40 g/1¹/₂ oz Parmesan cheese, freshly grated

Preheat the oven to 220°C/425°F/Gas Mark 7. Melt 25 g/1 oz of the butter in an ovenproof dish. Remove from the heat and place a layer of the truffle slices in the dish. Sprinkle with the Parmesan and continue making layers until all the ingredients are used. Dot with the remaining butter and bake for a few minutes.

JERUSALEM ARTICHOKES

The Italian name for this vegetable – topinambur – may derive from the name of the Brazilian Topinamba tribe, while the English name is probably a corruption of the Italian for sunflower – girasole – to which family the Jerusalem artichoke belongs. Its shape is similar to that of a knobbly potato and its flavour is quite like that of the globe artichoke. There are both white- and violet-skinned varieties, but the former have the better flavour. When buying Jerusalem artichokes choose those with the smoothest surface. They contain very few calories and so are ideal for anyone trying to lose weight. To prepare them, peel them with a small knife, cut them into slices and immerse in cold water to prevent them turning black. Jerusalem artichokes are tasty raw in salads (grated, sliced or cut in strips), and steamed, trifolati (sliced and fried with garlic and parsley) or boiled.

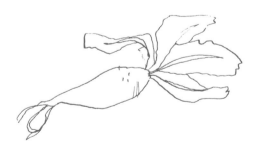

QUANTITIES
Allow 150–200 g/5–7 oz per serving.

BOILING
Immerse in lightly salted, boiling water and cook for 15–30 minutes or more, according to size.

**QUANTITIES
AND COOKING TIMES**

INSALATA DI TOPINAMBUR CON CARCIOFI

Serves 4

400 g/14 oz Jerusalem artichokes, peeled and thinly sliced

4 globe artichoke hearts

juice of 1 lemon, strained

1 carrot, cut into thin batons

4 tablespoons olive oil

salt and pepper

JERUSALEM ARTICHOKE SALAD

Put the Jerusalem artichokes into a salad bowl. Thinly slice the artichoke hearts, sprinkle with a little of the lemon juice and add to the bowl. Add the carrot. Beat together the oil and 2 tablespoons of the remaining lemon juice in a bowl and season with salt and pepper. Pour the dressing over the salad in a continuous trickle, mix gently and serve.

PURÉ DI TOPINAMBUR E PATATE

Serves 6

400 g/14 oz Jerusalem artichokes

800 g/1³/₄ lb potatoes

100 g/3¹/₂ oz butter

200 ml/7 fl oz milk

salt

JERUSALEM ARTICHOKE AND POTATO PURÉE

Boil or steam the Jerusalem artichokes and potatoes in separate pans. Drain, if necessary, peel and pass both through a potato ricer into a clean saucepan. Set the pan over a low heat and stir in the butter. Meanwhile, heat the milk in another pan. When the butter has been completely absorbed, gradually pour in the warm milk, stirring constantly. When the purée is soft and creamy, season with salt, mix well and remove the pan from the heat. Serve hot with roast meat.

TOPINAMBUR ALLA PANNA

Serves 4

25 g/1 oz butter

675g/1¹/₂ lb Jerusalem artichokes, peeled and thinly sliced

250 ml/8 fl oz double cream

1 fresh flat-leaf parsley sprig, chopped

salt

JERUSALEM ARTICHOKES IN CREAM

Melt the butter in a pan, add the artichokes, pour in the cream and cook over a low heat for 5 minutes, then season with salt, cover and cook for 10–15 minutes until tender. If necessary, remove the lid and increase the heat slightly towards the end of cooking in order to thicken the sauce. Remove the pan from the heat, sprinkle in the parsley and stir, then transfer the artichokes and cream to a warm serving dish.

PUMPKIN

Two varieties of pumpkin are very popular in Italy. A green, wrinkled pumpkin is grown in the Po delta. It is very common in Chioggia and Venice, where it is baked, sprinkled with sugar and eaten in slices. The other kind, with a smooth yellow rind, can reach exceptional weights and sizes. The thick rind of both encloses plenty of flesh in varying shades of orange, with seeds hidden in a central cavity. Pumpkins are rich in vitamin A, potassium, calcium and phosphorus. They also have diuretic and refreshing properties. Owing to their weight and size, they are usually sold in slices. However, it is worth bearing in mind that about 30 per cent of a pumpkin consists of rind and seeds. Pumpkin gnocchi, tortelli, moulds, soups and risottos are delicious. There is also an Indian sweet-and-sour chutney, made with pumpkin, tomatoes, onions, garlic, sultanas, white and brown sugar, salt, pepper and ginger. It is sold in jars and served with boiled meats.

QUANTITIES

Allow about 150 g/5 oz flesh per person.

BAKING

Cut the flesh into 1-cm/ ¹/₂-inch slices and bake in a preheated oven, 200°C/400°F/Gas Mark 6, for 15 minutes, then in-crease the temperature to 220°C/425°F/Gas Mark 7 and bake for a further 5 minutes.

STEAMING

Chop the flesh, place in a steamer and cook for 20–30 minutes.

QUANTITIES
AND COOKING TIMES

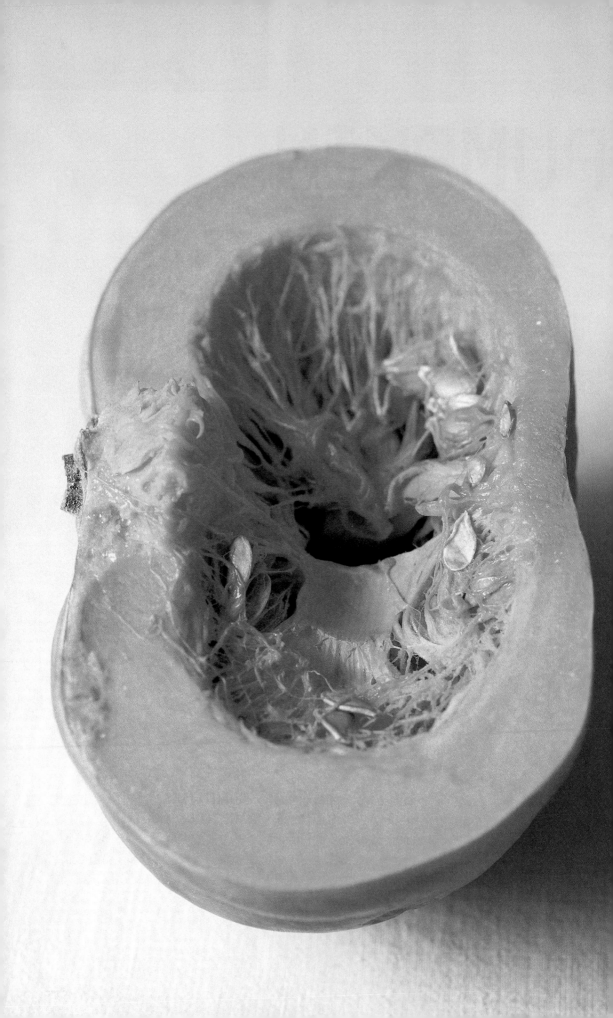

MOZZARELLA PUMPKIN SANDWICH

Preheat the oven to 200°C/400°F/Gas Mark 6. Grease an ovenproof dish with butter. Place the pumpkin slices on a large sheet of foil, season with salt and sprinkle with thyme. Fold over the foil to enclose the pumpkin and seal the edges. Place on a baking sheet and bake for 30 minutes. Take the pumpkin out of the oven but do not switch the oven off. Sandwich a slice of mozzarella between two slices of pumpkin and place in the prepared dish. Repeat with the remaining mozzarella and pumpkin slices. Sprinkle with the Parmesan, dot with the butter and bake for about 10 minutes.

SANDWICH DI ZUCCA ALLA MOZZARELLA

Serves 4

25 g/1 oz butter, plus extra for greasing

600 g/1 lb 5 oz pumpkin flesh,

cut into 1.5-cm/^{2}/$_3$-inch slices

1 fresh thyme sprig, chopped

300 g/11 oz mozzarella cheese, thinly sliced

40 g/1^1/$_2$ oz Parmesan cheese, freshly grated

salt

BAKED PUMPKIN WITH POTATOES

Preheat the oven to 180°C/350°F/Gas Mark 4. Brush an ovenproof dish with oil. Make alternate layers of potatoes, onion and pumpkin in the prepared dish. Sprinkle the tomato over the top, drizzle with olive oil and season with salt and pepper. Bake for 1 hour. Leave to stand for 5 minutes before serving.

ZUCCA AL FORNO CON PATATE

Serves 4

olive oil, for brushing and drizzling

4 waxy potatoes, cut into 5-mm/^{1}/$_4$-inch slices

1 onion, cut into rings

400 g/14 oz pumpkin flesh,

cut into 1-cm/^{1}/$_2$-inch slices

4 ripe tomatoes,

peeled and diced

salt and pepper

PARMESAN PUMPKIN

Heat 2 tablespoons of the oil in a saucepan, add the shallots and cook over a low heat, stirring occasionally, for 5 minutes. Add the tomatoes, season with salt and pepper and cook, stirring occasionally, for 15 minutes. Preheat the oven to 200°C/400°F/Gas Mark 6. Brush an ovenproof dish with oil. Dust the pumpkin slices with flour. Heat the remaining oil in a frying pan, add the pumpkin slices and cook until lightly browned on both sides. Remove with a fish slice and drain on kitchen paper. Make a layer of pumpkin slices in the prepared dish, sprinkle with a little thyme, spoon some of the tomato sauce on top, add some mozzarella slices and sprinkle with a little Parmesan. Continue making alternating layers until all the ingredients are used. Bake until golden brown and bubbling.

ZUCCA ALLA PARMIGIANA

Serves 6

5 tablespoons olive oil, plus extra for brushing

2 shallots, chopped

400 g/14 oz tomatoes, peeled and diced

600 g/1 lb 5 oz pumpkin flesh, sliced

plain flour, for dusting

2 fresh thyme sprigs, chopped

400 g/14 oz mozzarella cheese, thinly sliced

80 g/3 oz Parmesan cheese, freshly grated

salt and pepper

ZUCCA AL ROSMARINO

Serves 4

2 tablespoons olive oil

2 garlic cloves

675 g/1¹/₂ lb pumpkin flesh, thinly sliced

175 ml/6 fl oz dry white wine

1¹/₂ teaspoons finely chopped fresh rosemary

salt and pepper

PUMPKIN WITH ROSEMARY

Heat the oil in a pan, add the garlic and pumpkin and cook over a medium heat, stirring occasionally, until the garlic starts to go brown, then remove and discard it. Pour in the wine and cook until it has evaporated, then lower the heat and simmer until tender. Season with salt and pepper to taste and sprinkle with the rosemary. Cook for a few minutes more, then serve.

COURGETTES

Courgettes are refreshing and delicate and can be bought all year round. As well as classic courgettes in varying shades of dark green, there is also a slightly prickly variety. As the vegetable is so easy to digest, it is recommended as a baby food. When choosing courgettes, bear in mind that elongated ones should be no more than 25–30 cm/10–12 inches long, while round ones should be no more than 12 cm/4¹/₂ inches in diameter. If they grow too big, bitter seeds form inside. Choose courgettes with smooth, bright green skins that are firm to the touch. Before cooking, rinse them under running water and cut off both ends. Courgettes are tasty both raw and cooked. They may be simply boiled, sautéed in a frying pan with oil, garlic and parsley or added to rice soups and frittata. Courgette flowers are also edible. They should be picked as soon as they start to open.

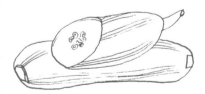

QUANTITIES
Allow about 175 g/6 oz per serving.
BOILING
Cook in boiling water for 15–20 minutes. Be careful not to overcook them.

STEAMING
Small, whole courgettes cook in 15 minutes.
FLOWERS
Gently open the calyx, remove the pistil and rinse quickly under cold water. Stuff and fry in batter or add to frittata or risottos.

QUANTITIES
AND COOKING TIMES

STUFFED COURGETTE BARQUETTES

BARCHETTE DI ZUCCHINE RIPIENE

Serves 4

100 g/3¹/₂ oz cooked ham, chopped
2 tablespoons fresh flat-leaaf parsley, chopped
1 garlic clove, chopped • 50 g/2 oz pancetta, chopped
100 g/3¹/₂ oz minced lean beef
2 tablespoons Parmesan cheese, freshly grated
1 egg, lightly beaten
4 large courgettes, halved lengthways
50 g/2 oz butter • 2 tablespoons olive oil
1 onion, chopped
2 tablespoons bottled Italian tomato sauce
salt and pepper

Mix together the ham, parsley, garlic, half the pancetta, the beef, Parmesan and egg in a bowl and season with salt and pepper. Scoop out the flesh from the courgettes with a small sharp knife, taking care not to pierce the 'shells'. Fill the shells with the meat mixture. Heat the butter and oil in a pan, add the onion and remaining pancetta and cook over a low heat, stirring occasionally, for 5 minutes. Add the courgettes and cook for a few minutes more. Mix the passata with 175 ml/6 fl oz warm water in a bowl and add to the pan. Season with salt, cover and simmer over a low heat for 20–30 minutes until the courgettes are tender and the filling is cooked through. Transfer the courgettes to a warm serving dish and spoon the cooking juices over them.

COURGETTE AND POTATO CHARLOTTE

CHARLOTTE DI ZUCCHINE E PATATE

Serves 4

600 g/1 lb 5 oz potatoes
40 g/1¹/₂ oz butter, plus extra for greasing
50 g/2 oz Parmesan cheese, freshly grated
500 g/1 lb 2 oz courgettes
1 leek, white part only, sliced
100 ml/3¹/₂ fl oz double cream
salt and pepper

Cook the potatoes in salted, boiling water for about 25 minutes until tender. Drain, peel, place in a bowl and mash with a potato masher. Stir in 15 g/¹/₂ oz of the butter and the Parmesan and leave to cool slightly. Cut the largest two courgettes into thin strips and parboil the strips in salted water for a few minutes, then drain and spread out on a tea towel. Preheat the oven to 180°C/350°F/Gas Mark 4. Grease an ovenproof mould with butter. Dice the remaining courgettes. Melt the remaining butter in a pan, add the diced courgettes and leek and cook over a medium heat, stirring occasionally, for 5 minutes. Season with salt and pepper, lower the heat, pour in the cream and cook until it has been absorbed. Remove the pan from the heat and stir the courgette mixture into the mashed potato. Line the prepared mould with the courgette strips and pour in the potato mixture. Smooth the surface and bake for about 30 minutes. Leave to cool slightly before turning out.

FRIED COURGETTE FLOWERS

FIORI DI ZUCCHINE FRITTI

Serves 4

100 g/3¹/₂ oz plain flour
2 tablespoons olive oil
5 tablespoons dry white wine
1 egg, separated
vegetable oil, for deep-frying
12 courgette flowers, trimmed
salt and pepper

Mix together the flour, oil, wine and egg yolk in a bowl and season with salt and pepper. Add 150–200 ml/5–7 fl oz warm water to make a fairly runny, smooth batter. Leave to stand for 1 hour. Whisk the egg white in a grease-free bowl and fold gently into the batter. Heat the oil for deep-frying in a large pan. Dip the flowers in the batter, shake off the excess and fry in the hot oil until golden. Remove with a fish slice and drain on kitchen paper. Sprinkle with salt and serve immediately.

STUFFED COURGETTE FLOWERS

FIORI DI ZUCCHINE RIPIENI

Serves 4

200 g/7 oz robiola cheese, diced

200 g/7 oz Gorgonzola cheese, crumbled

3 gherkins, drained and chopped

1 egg yolk

12 courgette flowers, trimmed

salt

Put the cheeses in a bowl and beat with a wooden spoon until smooth. Season with salt and stir in the gherkins and egg yolk. Mix carefully. Fill the courgette flowers with the cheese mixture, arrange on a serving dish in the shape of a star and serve.

FRIED STUFFED COURGETTE FLOWERS

FIORI DI ZUCCHINE RIPIENI E FRITTI

Serves 4

12 courgette flowers, trimmed

150 g/5 oz mozzarella cheese, cut into sticks

6 canned anchovy fillets in oil, drained and halved

vegetable oil, for deep-frying

For the batter

100 g/3½ oz plain flour

1 egg, separated

5 tablespoons dry white wine

2 tablespoons olive oil

salt

To make the batter, mix together the flour, a pinch of salt, the egg yolk, wine and oil and add 150–200 ml/ 5–7 fl oz warm water to make a fairly runny mixture. Leave to stand for 30 minutes. Whisk the egg white in a grease-free bowl and fold it into the batter. Fill each courgette flower with a stick of mozzarella and half an anchovy fillet and seal with a cocktail stick. Heat the oil for deep-frying in a large pan. Dip the flowers, in the batter and fry in the hot oil until golden brown, then remove with a fish slice and drain on kitchen paper.

BABY COURGETTE SALAD

INSALATA DI ZUCCHINE NOVELLE

Serves 4

6 baby courgettes, thinly sliced

50 g/2 oz Parmesan cheese, shaved

pinch of dried oregano

3 tablespoons olive oil

2 tomatoes, peeled and sliced

salt and pepper

Put the courgettes in a salad bowl, add the Parmesan, oregano and olive oil and season with salt and pepper. Mix well and set aside in a cool place for at least 30 minutes to allow the flavours to mingle. Add the tomatoes just before serving.

SWEET—AND—SOUR COURGETTES

Preheat the oven to 180°C/350°F/Gas Mark 4. Put the sultanas in a bowl, add hot water to cover and set aside to soak. Chop the anchovy fillets. Spread out the pine nuts on a baking sheet and toast lightly in the oven for 5 minutes. Heat the oil in a frying pan, add the courgettes and garlic and cook over a high heat, stirring frequently, for 5 minutes. Drain the sultanas and squeeze out the excess liquid. Lower the heat, add the sultanas, pine nuts, vinegar and sugar to the pan and season with salt. Mix well and cook for a few minutes, then add the anchovies. Cook for 5–10 minutes more, then serve warm.

ZUCCHINE AGRODOLCI

Serves 4

25 g/1 oz sultanas

2 salted anchovies, heads removed, clean and fileted (see page 596) soaked in cold water for 10 minutes and drained

20 g/³/₄ oz pine nuts

2 tablespoons olive oil

6 courgettes, sliced

1 garlic clove, chopped

100 ml/3¹/₂ fl oz white wine vinegar

¹/₂ tablespoon sugar

salt

COURGETTES WITH LEMON

Steam the courgettes for about 15 minutes. Leave to cool slightly, then place on a serving dish. Sprinkle the herbs on top. Drizzle with olive oil, season with salt and pepper to taste and sprinkle with the lemon juice. Toss, set aside in a cool place for the flavours to mingle, then serve.

ZUCCHINE AL LIMONE

Serves 4

600 g/1 lb 5 oz courgettes, cut into thick strips

1 fresh tarragon sprig, chopped

1 fresh flat-leaf parsley sprig, chopped

4 fresh basil leaves, chopped

4 fresh borage leaves, chopped

olive oil, for drizzling

juice of 1 lemon, strained

salt and pepper

ROAST COURGETTES

Preheat the oven to 220°C/425°F/Gas Mark 7. Place the courgettes in a roasting tin, add the olive oil, toss to coat and roast for 20–25 minutes, turning occasionally. Make a layer of some of the courgette slices on a serving dish, sprinkle with some of the garlic, parsley and basil, season with salt and pepper and drizzle with olive oil. Continue making layers until all the ingredients are used. Set aside in a cool place for about 1 hour for the flavours to mingle before serving.

ZUCCHINE ARROSTO

Serves 4

8 courgettes, thickly sliced lengthways

2 tablespoons olive oil, plus extra for drizzling

3 garlic cloves, thinly sliced

2 tablespoons fresh flat-leaaf parsley, chopped

6 fresh basil leaves, chopped

salt and pepper

SURPRISE COURGETTES

ZUCCHINE A SORPRESA

Serves 8

6 courgettes, sliced lengthways

50 g/2 oz plain flour

2 eggs

80 g/3 oz breadcrumbs

$\frac{1}{2}$ teaspoon dried oregano

200 g/7 oz provolone cheese, sliced

vegetable oil, for deep-frying

salt

Sprinkle the courgette slices with salt and leave to stand for about 1 hour, then pat dry with kitchen paper. Meanwhile, spread out the flour in a shallow dish, beat the eggs with a pinch of salt in another shallow dish and spread out the breadcrumbs in a third. Sprinkle a slice of courgette with a little oregano, place a slice of provolone on top and cover with another slice of courgette. Press the 'sandwich' down well, dip first in the flour, then in the beaten eggs and, finally, in the breadcrumbs. Continue making sandwiches until all the ingredients are used. Heat the oil in a frying pan, add the courgette sandwiches, in batches, and cook until golden brown all over. Remove with a fish slice, drain on kitchen paper and serve.

COURGETTES CAPRICCIOSE

ZUCCHINE CAPRICCIOSE

Serves 4

3 tablespoons olive oil, plus extra for brushing

6 courgettes, halved lengthways

4 salted anchovies, soaked in water and drained

1 garlic clove, chopped

1 fresh flat-leaf parsley sprig, chopped

1 fresh basil sprig, chopped

100 g/3$\frac{1}{2}$ oz green olives, stoned

2 tomatoes, peeled, seeded and chopped

150 g/5 oz mozzarella cheese, diced

salt and pepper

Preheat the oven to 200°C/400°F/Gas Mark 6. Brush an ovenproof dish with olive oil. Scoop out the flesh from the courgettes with a small sharp knife, taking care not to pierce the 'shells'. Chop the flesh and set aside. Place the courgette shells, skin side up, in the prepared dish and bake for 10 minutes. Remove from the oven and set aside. Reduce the oven temperature to 180°C/350°F/Gas Mark 4. Meanwhile, place the anchovies skin side up, press along the backbones with your thumb, then turn them over and remove the bones. Chop the flesh, place in a bowl, add 2 table-spoons of the oil and beat with a wooden spoon until smooth. Mix together the garlic, parsley, basil, courgette flesh and olives in another bowl, then stir in the tomatoes. Pour in the remaining oil, add the anchovy mixture and season with salt and pepper. Mix well and spoon the mixture into the courgette shells. Top with the mozzarella and bake for 20 minutes.

COURGETTES CAPRICCIOSE WITH SALMON AND LEEKS

Cook the courgettes in salted, boiling water for about 15 minutes until just tender. Drain, halve lengthways and scoop out the flesh. Preheat the oven to 180°C/350°F/Gas Mark 4. Grease an ovenproof dish with butter. Melt the butter in a frying pan, add the leeks and cook over a low heat, stirring occasionally, for 5 minutes. Stir in the smoked salmon and remove the pan from the heat. Spoon the mixture into the courgette 'shells' and place in the prepared dish. Season with salt, spoon the cream over the filled shells and bake for 10 minutes.

ZUCCHINE CAPRICCIOSE
AL SALMONE E PORRI
Serves 4
4 medium courgettes
25 g/1 oz butter, plus extra for greasing
2 leeks, white part only, chopped
80 g/3 oz smoked salmon, chopped
120 ml/4 fl oz double cream
salt

COURGETTE SALAD WITH THYME

Put the courgettes and chicory into a salad bowl. Mix together the parsley and thyme and sprinkle them over the vegetables. Whisk together the vinegar and olive oil in a jug, season with salt and pepper, pour the dressing over the salad and serve.

ZUCCHINE CON INSALATA BELGA AL TIMO
Serves 4
6 baby courgettes, thinly sliced
2 heads of chicory, cut into 1-cm/¹/₂-inch strips
1 fresh flat-leaf parsley sprig, chopped
3 fresh thyme sprigs, chopped
1 tablespoon white wine vinegar
2¹/₂ tablespoons olive oil • salt and pepper

COURGETTES IN EGG SAUCE

Heat the butter and oil in a pan, add the courgettes and cook over a high heat, stirring frequently, for 8–10 minutes until golden brown. Meanwhile, heat the stock in another pan. Pour the hot stock over the courgettes, lower the heat, season with salt and pepper and cook until the liquid has reduced. Beat the egg yolks with the lemon juice and parsley, pour the mixture over the courgettes, mix well and cook until thickened.

ZUCCHINE IN CREMA D'UOVA
Serves 4
40 g/1¹/₂ oz butter
2 tablespoons olive oil
675 g/1¹/₂ lb baby courgettes, sliced
150 ml/¹/₄ pint Vegetable Stock (see page 209)
2 egg yolks
juice of 1 lemon, strained
1 fresh flat-leaf parsley sprig, chopped
salt and pepper

SHIP

LEMON

YELLOW

FISH →

CRUSTACEANS →

SHELLFISH →

FISH

The term fish is often used to refer to all seafood, although it may then be sub-divided into finned fish, crustaceans, such as crabs, and shellfish, such as mussels. In this chapter, the sub-divisions are sea fish, freshwater fish, crustaceans and shellfish, which are called molluscs and include octopus, squid and cuttlefish. Generally, a wide variety of most types is available throughout the year. However, with the exception of trout, freshwater fish are not so commonly available commercially outside Italy. Finally, this chapter also includes a section on fish soups, which are often more like substantial stews, and a collection of recipes for preparing and cooking snails and frogs, ingredients that do not readily fit into any other category. Although many types of sea fish are becoming increasingly expensive, you do not have to limit your choice to the rarest and most valued. In fact, some of the most common fish are extremely tasty. For example, the fish known as 'blue-scale fish' in Italy, such as sardines and mackerel, are the perfect choice for a number of truly delicious, yet economical recipes. For some years now, nutritionists have been encouraging the inclusion of fish in the diet in preference to many other foods. They are an excellent source of easily digestible protein, and sea fish also contain iodine, as well as other minerals. The flesh of oily fish contains essential fatty acids and fat soluble vitamins that are vital for good health. White fish, such as cod and skate, are very low in fat and even oily fish, such as salmon and herring, contain less fat than meat or poultry. Fish are so highly regarded that we are advised to eat white fish at least twice a week and oily fish once a week, although there are some provisos for pregnant and nursing mothers and the very young about eating certain species. When choosing between white and oily fish, bear in mind that the nutritional value of the former is slightly lower than that of beef, while the nutritional value of the latter is very high indeed. As for the difference between sea fish and freshwater fish, sea fish are more nutritious, although sometimes less digestible. Molluscs and crustaceans are rich in calcium, magnesium, sodium chloride, iodine and, above all, iron. Other seafood is also rich in minerals. In fact, it can be said that all seafood is good for you provided that it is fresh, properly stored, and prepared correctly.

CRUSTACEANS

In spite of their tough-sounding name, under their shells crustaceans are extremely delicate. The flavour, aroma and quality of their flesh is almost beyond comparison. Langoustines, lobsters, crayfish, prawns and crabs all have delicious flesh which needs handling with care – simple short cooking and natural dressings, such as extra virgin olive oil or hot or cold sauces made with top-quality ingredients. Otherwise, your considerable investment will be wasted. Crustaceans are expensive, especially the most highly prized varieties, such as lobster. Canned produce, such as crab meat, is also excellent and may be used in a number of recipes.

SHELLFISH

This group includes mussels, clams, scallops, squid, cuttlefish and many others. Shellfish must be absolutely fresh. While cooking them kills any bacteria, it does not eliminate any toxins that may already have been created if the shellfish have been stored for too long; this may even cause poisoning. This is not intended to be alarmist, but simply to warn you that shellfish require caution. If you are not absolutely sure of their freshness or that they have been stored perfectly in the case of frozen packs, do not buy them. Always buy from a reliable supplier and never gather them from the sea shore yourself. It is advisable to cook shellfish on the day of purchase. Serve them with light sauces, which do not smother their delicate flavour.

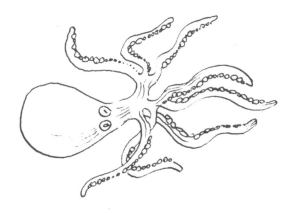

FISH

The quality of fish depends on its freshness. When buying, there are a number of pointers to look for. These include a delicate pleasant smell without any hints of ammonia or strong 'fishiness', a generally healthy appearance, a firm body, close-fitting shiny scales, a naturally coloured taut skin, lively non-red eyes, damp, pink or red gills, no trace of blood along the bones and no inadvertent damage to the abdomen.

QUANTITIES

Some fish produce a high proportion of waste, which makes it quite hard to judge the right quantity for each guest. The amount of waste also affects how much value there is for your money. The table below shows the amount of edible flesh that remains after gutting some types of fish.

YIELD PER 1 KG/2¼ LB FISH	KIND OF FISH	WASTE	YIELD
	Sea bass	50%	500 g/1 lb 2 oz
	Hake	30%	675 g/1½ lb
	Sea bream	45%	650 g/1 lb 7 oz
	Turbot	65%	350 g/12 oz
	Salmon	50%	500 g/1 lb 2 oz
	Sole	55%	450 g/1 lb
	Red mullet	65%	350 g/12 oz

PER SERVING

Allow an average of 150 g/5 oz per serving for fillets, 200 g/7 oz per serving for steaks or slices and 250–300 g/9–11 oz per serving (according to the type) for whole fish.

VARIATIONS

If you feel the fish suggested in a recipe is rather too expensive, try replacing it with a more economical but similar one. For example, less expensive flat fish, such as brill, can be cooked like sole, farmed sea bream may also be used to replace grey mullet or wild sea bass in some cases, and cod (from a sustainable source) can be used in recipes for salmon.

WASTE

The heads (gills removed) and bones of white fish are very good for making fish stock. Do not use those of oily fish.

Although the cooking times given in the recipes are as precise as possible, several things may cause them to vary. These include the size and thickness of the fish, the material the pan or dish is made from and the fuel used for cooking (gas, electricity, charcoal, etc.). In addition, how well done the fish should be is a matter of taste. Remember, however, overcooked seafood loses some of its best qualities. For example, shellfish rapidly become rubbery in texture and fish fillets fall apart or become spongy. You can choose from a variety of cooking methods depending on the type of fish, its size and the way it is to be presented. Whole fish are generally better poached or baked, fillets and steaks are good grilled or fried like small fish. To scale fish, use a scaling knife or small round-bladed knife. Hold the fish by the tail and scrape off the scales from tail to head, then rinse well. Small fish, such as sardines, are best scaled under cold, running water.

POACHING

Most fish may be poached in court-bouillon and served with oil and lemon juice, or mayonnaise flavoured in various ways.

COURT–BOUILLON

This is an aromatic stock. To prepare it, simmer about 2 litres/3½ pints water with a small, sliced onion, ½ sliced carrot, a celery stick, 100 ml/3½ fl oz white wine vinegar or white wine, a few peppercorns and salt for 45 minutes. Strain through a sieve, discard the vegetables and leave the court-bouillon to cool completly. To poach a fish, immerse it in cold or gently simmering court-bouillon and cook for about 10 minutes per 500 g/1 lb 2 oz.

FISH STOCK

This is a 'by-product' of poaching a fish and is excellent for preparing sauces, risottos and rice soups. If you wish to use the stock for such dishes, do not add vinegar, lemon juice or wine to the court-bouillon.

→ Allow 10–12 minutes per 500 g/1 lb 2 oz of fish.

→ Immerse the fish in cold or gently simmering court-bouillon. In both cases, continue cooking at a very gentle simmer.

→ Both court-bouillon and fish stock should be left to cool before being reused.

CONCENTRATED
FISH STOCK

Also known as fish fumet, this is made using the heads and bones of white fish (see page 210).

LARGE WHOLE FISH

These should be immersed in cold court-bouillon.

FISH PORTIONS AND
SMALL WHOLE FISH

Slices, steaks and fillets, and small fish should be immersed in gently simmering court-bouillon. Remember that they cook very quickly.

FRESHWATER FISH

These require a more highly flavoured court-bouillon, so add larger quantities of vegetables.

→ Leave the fish to cool in their cooking liquid, then drain gently to avoid breaking up the flesh.

STEAMING

You will need a combined steamer or a perforated container that can be fitted on an ordinary saucepan. Steaming enhances the flavour of a number of fish, including red mullet, sea bass and most fillets.

BARBECUING

Fish with firm flesh, such as tuna, large fish, such as sea bream, and smaller pieces of fish are excellent when barbecued. You can add all sorts of herbs and spices and splash with red or white wine, fish stock, etc. to bring out their aroma. Use a hinged wire rack to make turning the fish easier.

BAKING

All large or medium fish may be baked. They may be flavoured with herbs, seasoned butter, stock, wine, or even stuffed in the case of large fish. Small fish, fillets, steaks, etc. are also excellent baked in foil parcels. This avoids the problem of lingering smells and has the advantage of concentrating the flavour of the flesh and the added herbs and spices. It is a quick method and results in tender flesh.

GRILLING

Do not scale fish before grilling as the scales help to protect the delicate flesh from the intense heat.

→ Always dry fish before placing on a grill rack, even if it has been marinated first.

→ Be careful not to overcook. For example: sardines, 1 minute each side; small sea bass, 10 minutes each side; giltheaded sea bream, 15 minutes each side.

→ Cook large fish under a low heat and brush frequently with oil.

SHALLOW—FRYING

This method is suitable for whole flat fish, such as sole, as well as for fillets and sliced fish. Briefly cook in a frying pan with a little melted butter over a medium-high heat until golden brown on both sides, then lower the heat and cook until the flesh is tender and flakes easily. As a general rule, almost all fish can be lightly sprinkled with salt and flour before cooking. The cooking time varies from 2–3 minutes each side.

DEEP—FRYING

Small whole fish and larger fish cut into small pieces are ideal for deep-frying, as are white fish such as cod, giltheaded bream and sole. Always dry fish completely first, then coat first with flour, shaking off the excess, and then with a few fine breadcrumbs. Heat plenty of oil in a large pan or deep-fat fryer to 180–190°C/350–375°F or until a cube of day-old bread browns in 30 seconds. This is a quick cooking method, so do not leave the fish in the pan too long. After frying, lift out with a slotted spoon and drain on kitchen paper. Season with salt only after cooking. In Italy, groundnut oil and olive oil (not necessarily extra virgin) are the favourite oils to use. Olive oil would probably be a rather extravagant choice in Britain and, in any case, it does have a low smoke point which makes it more liable to catch fire. One final piece of advice: never reuse the oil, whatever the type, after deep-frying.

MOST SUITABLE SIDE DISHES

Not only do rice, potatoes and other steamed vegetables go well with fish, but so do fresh vegetables in butter.

→ Carrots and French beans go well with sole and cod fillets.

→ Celeriac purée is good served with cod.

→ Courgettes, either sliced or cut into thin batons and steamed or sautéed with a little oil and butter, make a delicious side dish, especially with sole.

→ Cucumbers, when peeled and diced, complement mild-flavoured fish.

→ Leeks, carrots and baby turnips are an ideal combination with baked or steamed giltheaded sea bream.

→ Mayonnaise is delicious with all poached fish, especially if it is flavoured with capers, finely chopped gherkins, thin tomato sauce (which turns it light pink) or chopped black or green olives.

→ Mixed diced vegetables are perfect with tuna.

→ Rice cooked with a pinch of curry powder in the water is colourful and flavoursome. A similar result may be achieved by dissolving a sachet of saffron in the water.

→ Spinach, Swiss chard, lettuce and sorrel have an affinity with almost all fish.

→ Tomatoes, aubergines and peperonata all go well with baked fish.

RECOMMENDED HERBS, SPICES AND FLAVOURINGS

→ Basil, sage and oregano may be added sparingly to sauces, the cooking water of poached fish and the juices of braised fish.

→ Celery may be used together with thyme and bay leaves in a bouquet garni in court-bouillon.

→ Coriander seeds are useful in marinades and court-bouillon.

→ Dill has a fennel-like flavour and goes well with marinated herrings and raw fish carpaccio.

→ Fennel seeds give a lovely flavour to grilled sea bass and other varieties of fish.

→ Garlic is an essential ingredient in fish soup, cod Provençal and with baked fish.

→ Onions, either raw and cut into rings or pickled pearl onions go with almost all steamed fish.

→ Tarragon is used to flavour marinades or grilled fish, especially salmon.

→ Thyme sprinkled generously on baked fish fillets, together with a pinch of salt, brings out their flavour.

➜ In pans and fish kettles: to prevent or reduce the smell, rub the sides of the pan with a little cooking salt and boil 100 ml/ 3¹/₂ fl oz vinegar in it. Keep a pan specially for cooking fish.

➜ On hands: when handling fish, rub your hands frequently with lemon juice or very salty water.

➜ In the kitchen: put a sugar cube in the middle of a plate and ignite it. This should limit the intensity of fishy smells.

➜ Baking in foil: this method is better than ordinary baking because it does not leave unpleasant odours.

To keep cooked fish warm for a short while, cover the dish with foil. Otherwise remember these rules.

➜ If the fish is baked, turn off the heat shortly before the end of the cooking time, cover with foil to prevent the fish from drying out and leave in the oven.

➜ If the fish is boiled, pan-fried or steamed, put it on a serving dish (covered or uncovered) and set over a pan of freshly boiled water with the heat turned off.

ANCHOVIES

SEA FISH

Anchovies belong to a group of oily fish that the Italians call 'blue-scaled'. In recent years, Italian people have come to appreciate their strong mouth-watering flavour and low price more than they did in the past. Anchovies can be prepared in a variety of ways. Whole ones can be salted and fillets are salted and canned in oil. To fillet a whole salted anchovy, cut off its head and tail, and press along the backbones with your thumb. Turn it over and remove the bones which should come away easily. Anchovies are often used in the kitchen to replace sardines. Fresh ones do not travel well and are not widely available outside the Mediterranean. Slightly larger sprats or considerably larger sardines can be substituted in the following recipes. To clean anchovies, snap the backbones of the anchovies just behind the heads with your fingers, then pull off the heads. Most of the innards will come with them. Slit open the bellies and remove any remaining innards, cut off the tails, then rinse and dry the fish.

COMMON SQUARE PAN

FRIED ANCHOVIES

ACCIUGHE FRITTE

Serves 4

675 g/1¹/₂ lb anchovies, cleaned

300 ml/¹/₂ pint milk • plain flour, for dusting

vegetable oil, for deep-frying • salt

For the garnish

1 lemon, cut into wedges

6 small fresh flat-leaf parsley sprigs

Put the anchovies in a dish, add the milk and leave to soak for 30 minutes. Spread out the flour in a shallow dish. Heat the oil in a large pan. Drain the anchovies, dip in the flour to coat and deep fry in the hot oil until golden brown (see page 593). Remove with a slotted spoon, drain on kitchen paper and season with salt. Transfer to a warm serving dish and garnish with the lemon wedges and parsley sprigs.

ANCHOVIES AU GRATIN

ACCIUGHE GRATINATE

Serves 4

4–5 tablespoons olive oil, plus extra for brushing

800 g/1³/₄ lb anchovies, cleaned

50 ml/2 fl oz white wine vinegar

¹/₂ teaspoon dried oregano

1 garlic clove, chopped

salt and pepper

Preheat the oven to 200°C/400°F/Gas Mark 6. Brush an ovenproof dish with oil. Place the anchovies skin side up and press along the backbones with your thumb, then turn over and remove the bones, leaving the fish joined along their backs. Place the anchovies in the prepared dish. Mix together the vinegar, olive oil, oregano and garlic in a bowl and season with salt and pepper. Pour the mixture over the anchovies and bake for 15 minutes. Arrange on a serving dish and serve hot or cold.

ANCHOVIES WITH TRUFFLES

ACCIUGHE TARTUFATE

Serves 4

600 g/1 lb 5 oz salted anchovies, heads and tails removed, cleaned and filleted (see page 596), rinsed and drained

1 white truffle, thinly sliced

olive oil

Pat the anchovy fillets dry. Arrange a layer of anchovies in a glass jar, cover with a layer of truffle and drizzle with olive oil. Continue making alternate layers until all the ingredients are used, filling the jar with plenty of olive oil. Leave in a cool place for a few days for the flavours to mingle.

MIXED FISH FRY

FRITTO MISTO DI PESCI AZZURRI

Serves 4

plain flour, for dusting

1 kg/2¼ lb mixed small oily fish, such as anchovies, sardines and sprats, cleaned

vegetable oil, for deep-frying

4 fresh sage leaves, plus extra to garnish

salt and white pepper

1 lemon, cut into wedges, to garnish

Spread out the flour in a shallow dish. Dip the fish in the flour to coat and shake off any excess. Heat the oil in a large pan with the sage leaves. Remove the sage and fry the larger fish in the hot oil until golden brown, then fry the smaller ones. As the fish are ready, remove with a slotted spoon and drain on kitchen paper (see page 593). Keep warm while you cook the remaining batches, then arrange on a warm serving dish, garnish with lemon wedges and sage leaves and season with salt and pepper.

LAYERED ANCHOVIES AND POTATOES

TEGLIA D'ACCIUGHE E PATATE

Serves 4

olive oil, for brushing and drizzling

600 g/1 lb 5 oz anchovies, heads and tails removed, cleaned and filleted (see page 596), rinsed and drained

1 fresh flat-leaf parsley sprig, chopped

1 garlic clove, chopped

10 fresh mint leaves, chopped

juice of 2 lemons, strained

600 g/1 lb 5 oz potatoes, peeled and thinly sliced

50 g/2 oz breadcrumbs

200 ml/7 fl oz dry white wine

salt and pepper

Preheat the oven to 180°C/350°F/Gas Mark 4. Brush an ovenproof dish with oil. Remove the bones from the anchovies, but leave the fish joined along their backs. Mix together the parsley, garlic and half the mint in a bowl. Make a layer of anchovies in theprepared dish, sprinkle with some of the herb mixture, season with salt and pepper, pour in some of the lemon juice and drizzle with olive oil. Cover with a layer of potatoes, sprinkle with more of the herb mixture and season with salt and pepper. Continue making alternate layers until all the ingredients are used. Mix together the remaining mint and the breadcrumbs in a bowl. Pour the wine over the final layer of potatoes and sprinkle with the breadcrumb mixture. Bake for 1 hour.

SHAD

Like salmon, shad are sea fish that swim upstream to spawn. In Italy, they are found in Lake Como, Lake Garda and Lake Maggiore, but in Britain they are usually taken from estuaries. They may be 25–30 cm/10–12 inches long. Their flesh is not among the most highly prized, perhaps because they are extremely bony, but it is tasty, and when fried, soused or grilled, shad are absolutely delicious.

SHAD WITH SAGE

Place the fish in a dish, add the milk and leave to soak for 10 minutes. Drain, pat dry with kitchen paper and dust lightly with flour. Heat the olive oil and butter in a frying pan, add the sage leaves and cook until lightly browned. Add the shad and cook for 7 minutes on each side. Season with salt, remove from the pan with a slotted spoon, drain on kitchen paper and serve.

AGONI ALLA SALVIA

Serves 4

800 g/1³/₄ lb shad, scaled and cleaned

300 ml/¹/₂ pint milk

plain flour, for dusting

4 tablespoons olive oil

40 g/1¹/₂ oz butter

6 fresh sage leaves

salt

SHAD WITH TOMATO SAUCE

Serves 4

800 g/1³/₄ lb shad, scaled and cleaned

4 tablespoons olive oil

1 carrot, finely chopped

1 onion, finely chopped

1 garlic clove, finely chopped

1 celery stick, finely chopped

1 fresh flat-leaf parsley sprig, finely chopped

6 plum tomatoes, peeled, seeded and chopped

1 tablespoon capers, drained and rinsed

salt

Cut each fish into three pieces. Heat the oil in a saucepan, add the carrot, onion, garlic, celery and parsley and cook over a low heat, stirring occasionally, for 10 minutes until lightly browned. Add the tomatoes, cover and simmer for about 10 minutes until slightly thickened. Add the fish and capers, season with salt and cook for about 20 minutes until the flesh flakes easily. This recipe may be used with most kinds of fish.

FRIED SHAD

Serves 4

800 g/1³/₄ lb shad, scaled and cleaned

300 ml/¹/₂ pint milk

plain flour, for dusting

7 tablespoons olive oil

1 lemon, sliced

salt

Place the fish in a dish, add the milk and leave to soak for 10 minutes. Drain, pat dry with kitchen paper and dust lightly with flour. Heat the olive oil in a frying pan, add the fish and cook for a few minutes on each side until golden brown. Remove with a slotted spoon, drain on kitchen paper, season with salt, place on a warm serving dish and surround with the slices of lemon.

SOUSED SHAD

Serves 4

800 g/1³/₄ lb shad, scaled and cleaned

plain flour, for dusting

120 ml/4 fl oz olive oil

1 onion, thinly sliced

1 celery stick, chopped

1 garlic clove, thinly sliced

4 fresh sage leaves

1 bay leaf

1 rosemary sprig

6 peppercorns

300 ml/¹/₂ pint red wine vinegar

salt

Dust the fish with flour, shaking off any excess. Heat 7 tablespoons of the oil in a frying pan, add the fish, a few at a time, and cook for a few minutes on each side until golden brown. Remove with a slotted spoon, drain on kitchen paper, season with salt and place in a dish. Put the onion, celery, garlic, sage leaves, bay leaf, rosemary, peppercorns, vinegar, the remaining olive oil and a pinch of salt in a pan. Bring to the boil, then lower the heat and cook until the mixture comes back to the boil. Remove from the heat and pour the mixture over the fish. Leave in a cool place for 24 hours before serving.

HERRINGS

Herrings live in the waters of the North Atlantic and the Arctic. The most highly prized variety is the Norwegian herring and, of these, the younger ones are the best. Fresh herrings are not available in Italy but preserved herrings are imported. The most common preserved herring is the salted smoked golden kipper. To prepare kippers, remove the skins and heads, slit open the backs and remove the bones without disturbing the delicious roe. Soak the fillets in a mixture of water and vinegar for 4 hours to remove the salt, then drain and sprinkle with garlic, oregano and chilli or with chopped onion and chopped parsley. If you prefer a more delicate taste, soak the kipper fillets in milk and then dress with oil and mixed herbs. Another kind of herring that is easily found in Italy is the pickled herring. The flavour is quite strong so if you are adding it to green salads or potato salads, be careful with the quantities.

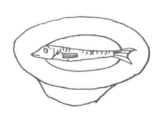

KIPPERS WITH GRAPEFRUIT

Mix together the grapefruit juice, lemon juice, olive oil and mustard in a bowl and season with salt and pepper. Place the fennel slices on a serving dish, top with the kippers, pour the grapefruit sauce over them and sprinkle with the dill. Put in the refrigerator to marinate for 15 minutes before serving.

ARINGHE AL POMPELMO

Serves 4

juice of 1 grapefruit, strained

juice of ¹/₂ lemon, strained

4 tablespoons olive oil • ¹/₂ teaspoon herb mustard

1 round fennel bulb, thinly sliced

8 kippers, skinned and filleted

1 teaspoon chopped fresh dill

salt and pepper

HERRING AND CAULIFLOWER SALAD

Cook the cauliflower in a pan of salted, boiling water for 5 minutes. Drain and refresh under cold running water. Roll up the herring fillet halves and secure with a cocktail stick. Mix together the cream, mustard, vinegar, olive oil and baby onion in a bowl and season with salt and pepper. Place the lettuce and red onion in a large salad bowl and top with the cauliflower and herring rolls. Pour the dressing over the salad and keep in a cool place until ready to serve.

INSALATA D'ARINGHE CON CAVOLFIORI

Serves 4

1 cauliflower, cut into florets

1 jar (about 120 g/4 oz) herring fillets in oil,

drained and halved lengthways

175 ml/6 fl oz double cream

1 tablespoon Dijon mustard

1 tablespoon red wine vinegar

3 tablespoons olive oil • 1 baby onion, chopped

1 loose-leaf lettuce heart, such as lollo rosso, chopped

1 red onion, thinly sliced • salt and pepper

SALT COD

AND STOCKFISH

In Italy, there are two, or rather three, names for the same fish – merluzzo (cod) when it is fresh (see page 627), baccalà (salt cod) when it is cut into small pieces and preserved in salt, and stocafisso (stockfish) when it is dried and sold whole. Salt cod has white flesh and a black skin. It must be left, skin side uppermost, under cold, running water for 18–24 hours to remove all the salt it has absorbed. Alternatively, soak it in cold water for 24 hours, changing the water frequently. To cook, place it in a pan, add cold water to cover and bring just to the boil over a medium heat, then lower the heat, cover and simmer for 10 minutes; do not cook it any longer or the flesh becomes tough. Stockfish is completely rigid. To soften, beat, then soak for 2 days and cook thoroughly for up to 3 hours.

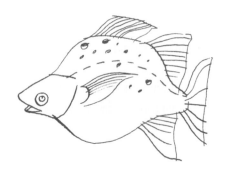

SALT COD AU GRATIN

Preheat the oven to 180°C/350°F/Gas Mark 4. Cut the salt cod into fairly large pieces and remove the skin and bones. Heat 4 tablespoons of the olive oil in a roasting tin, add the onion and garlic and cook over a low heat, stirring occasionally, for 5 minutes. Add the salt cod and cook until golden brown on both sides, then pour in the milk and season with salt and pepper. Cover the tin with foil, transfer to the oven and bake for about 2 hours or until the milk is completely absorbed. Preheat the grill. Put the anchovy fillets and the remaining olive oil in a small saucepan and cook over a low heat, mashing with a wooden spoon until the anchovies have almost completely disintegrated. Spoon the anchovy sauce over the salt cod, sprinkle with the parsley and mix gently. Sprinkle with the Parmesan and grill until golden brown.

BACCALÀ AL GRATIN

Serves 4

800 g/1¾ lb salt cod, soaked and drained

7 tablespoons olive oil

1 onion, chopped

2 garlic cloves

1 litre/1¾ pints milk

4 canned anchovy fillets in oil, drained

1 fresh flat-leaf parsley sprig, chopped

50 g/2 oz Parmesan cheese, freshly grated

salt and pepper

SALT COD LIVORNO–STYLE

Place the tomatoes in a food processor and process to a purée. Cut the salt cod into fairly large pieces, pat dry and dust lightly with flour. Heat the oil in a large pan, add the salt cod and cook until lightly browned on both sides. Add the tomatoes, season with salt and pepper and cook over a medium heat for a few minutes. Sprinkle with the parsley and garlic and simmer for a further 5 minutes. Serve hot or warm.

BACCALÀ ALLA LIVORNESE

Serves 4

500 g/1 lb 2 oz canned tomatoes

675 g/1½ lb salt cod, soaked and drained

plain flour, for dusting

100 ml/3½ fl oz olive oil

1 fresh flat-leaf parsley sprig, chopped

1 garlic clove, chopped

salt and pepper

SALT COD WITH OLIVES AND CAPERS

Cut the salt cod into fairly large pieces. Chop the anchovy fillets. Heat the olive oil in a pan, add the anchovies and cook over a low heat, mashing with a wooden spoon. Add the onion and cook, stirring occasionally, for 5 minutes. Add the salt cod and cook for 5 minutes on each side. Pour in the wine and add the capers and olives. Season with salt if necessary, then simmer, stirring occasionally, for 10–15 minutes and serve.

BACCALÀ CON OLIVE E CAPPERI

Serves 4

800 g/1¾ lb salt cod, soaked and drained

2 salted anchovies, heads removed,

cleaned and filleted (see page 596),

soaked in cold water for 10 minutes and drained

2 tablespoons olive oil

1 onion, chopped

175 ml/6 fl oz dry white wine

1 tablespoon capers, drained and rinsed

100 g/3½ oz black olives, stoned and chopped

salt

BACCALÀ CON PATATE E PEPERONI

Serves 4

800 g/1³/₄ lb salt cod, soaked and drained

120 ml/4 fl oz olive oil

1 onion, sliced

1 green pepper, halved, seeded and cut into strips

1 red pepper, halved, seeded and cut into strips

4 tomatoes, peeled and sliced

300 g/11 oz potatoes, sliced

pinch of cayenne pepper

5 black peppercorns

1 fresh thyme sprig, chopped

1 fresh flat-leaf parsley sprig

1 bay leaf

175 ml/6 fl oz dry white wine

100 g/3¹/₂ oz black olives

SALT COD WITH POTATOES AND PEPPERS

Cut the salt cod into large pieces. Heat half the olive oil in a large pan, add the salt cod and cook until lightly browned on both sides. Heat the remaining olive oil in another pan, add the onion and peppers and cook, stirring occasionally, for 5 minutes, then add the tomatoes and potatoes and cook for a further 10 minutes. Make alternate layers of salt cod and vegetables in a flameproof casserole. Sprinkle with the cayenne, peppercorns and thyme, add the parsley sprig and bay leaf, pour in the wine and simmer for 50 minutes. Remove and discard the bay leaf and parsley, add the olives and cook for a further 10 minutes.

BACCALÀ FRITTO

Serves 4

800 g/1³/₄ lb salt cod, soaked and drained

vegetable oil, for frying

1 quantity Batter for Frying (see page 1017)

salt

FRIED SALT COD

Cut the salt cod into fairly large pieces and pat dry. Heat plenty of oil in a wide frying pan. Dip the pieces of fish in the batter to coat, then fry, in batches, for 5 minutes on each side. Drain on kitchen paper, season lightly with salt and serve.

STOCCAFISSO ALLA MEDITERRANEA

Serves 4

800 g/1³/₄ lb stockfish, soaked and drained

80 g/3 oz salted anchovies, heads removed, cleaned and filleted (see page 596), soaked in cold water for 10 minutes and drained

100 ml/3¹/₂ fl oz olive oil

1 onion, chopped

1 garlic clove, chopped

1 fresh flat-leaf parsley sprig, chopped

250 g/9 oz tomatoes, peeled and chopped

1 tablespoon capers, drained and rinsed

salt and pepper

MEDITERRANEAN STOCKFISH

Cut the stockfish into fairly large pieces. Chop the anchovy fillets. Heat the olive oil in a pan, add the onion, garlic and parsley and cook over a low heat, stirring occasionally, for 5 minutes. Add the stockfish and cook for 5 minutes on each side. Add the tomatoes, season with salt and pepper and cook for 10 minutes. Add the anchovies, mash them well with a wooden spoon and cook for 5 minutes more. Add the capers, heat through for 1 minute and serve.

VENETO–STYLE CREAMED STOCKFISH

Place the stockfish in a saucepan, add water to cover and bring to the boil, then lower the heat and simmer for 25–35 minutes. Remove the pan from the heat and leave the fish to cool in the liquid. When cold, drain the fish, remove the skin and bones and cut into small pieces. Heat 4 tablespoons of the oil in a pan, add the onion and cook over a low heat, stirring occasionally, for 5 minutes. Meanwhile, bring the milk to simmering point in another saucepan. Add the stockfish to the onion, then gradually add the hot milk and remaining olive oil stirring, vigorously. Simmer for 1 hour until white, frothy and creamy. Season with salt and pepper to taste and serve with polenta.

STOCCAFISSO MANTECATO ALLA VENETA

Serves 4

600 g/1 lb 5 oz stockfish, soaked and drained

150 ml/¹/₄ pint olive oil

¹/₂ onion, chopped

100 g/3¹/₂ fl oz milk

salt and pepper

polenta, to serve

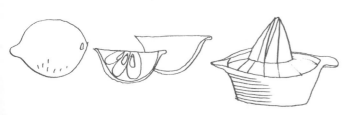

WHITEBAIT

In Ligurian cuisine, whitebait refers to anchovy and sardine fry. They are very small, fragile and white, are available in February and March and are appreciated for their delicate flavour. Wash them carefully to get rid of any sand or other impurities. They cook very quickly – a few minutes in boiling water – and are usually eaten dressed with oil and lemon juice. Whitebait are also used in frittata and other simple recipes.

WHITEBAIT IN EGG CREAM

BIANCHETTI ALLA CREMA D'UOVA

Serves 4

4 eggs
5 tablespoons olive oil
1 onion, finely chopped
400 g/14 oz whitebait, washed and drained
juice of 1 lemon, strained
salt and pepper

Lightly beat the eggs with 1 tablespoon hot water and salt and pepper in a bowl. Heat the olive oil in a pan, add the onion and cook over a low heat, stirring occasionally, for 5 minutes. Add the whitebait and pour in the egg. Cook, stirring to keep the mixture runny and slightly creamy as it heats. Sprinkle with the lemon juice, mix and serve.

WHITEBAIT WITH OLIVE OIL AND LEMON

BIANCHETTI ALL'OLIO E LIMONE

Serves 4

300 g/11 oz whitebait, washed and drained
150 ml/¼ pint olive oil
juice of 1 lemon, strained
1 teaspoon Dijon mustard
salt

Cook the whitebait in salted, boiling water for 2–3 minutes. Drain and leave to cool. Whisk together the olive oil, lemon juice and mustard in a bowl, pour the mixture over the fish and serve.

SEA BASS

Sea bass are fairly widespread in the Mediterranean and this large family of fish is found all over the world. Most types are about 40 cm/16 inches long and weigh about 1 kg/2¹/₄ lb, but there are even bigger ones. They are highly prized for their white, lean and delicate flesh. Farmed sea bass are also excellent. The Australian Mulloway is similar in texture to sea bass and a good alternative.

SEA BASS BAKED IN A PARCEL

Preheat the oven to 200°C/400°F/Gas Mark 6. Cut out a sheet of baking parchment and brush with olive oil. Place the rosemary sprig and one of the garlic cloves in the cavity of the sea bass, season with salt and pepper and place the fish on the baking parchment. Slice the remaining garlic. Sprinkle the fish with the parsley and cover with the lemon slices, onion rings, spring onions and garlic slices. Spoon the wine over the fish, fold over the baking parchment to enclose it completely, and seal the edges. Place on a baking sheet and bake for 15 minutes. Serve with olive oil, lemon slices and salt.

BRANZINO AL CARTOCCIO

Serves 4

olive oil, for brushing and serving

1 fresh rosemary sprig • 2 garlic cloves

1-kg/2¹/₄-lb sea bass, spines trimmed, scaled and cleaned

1 fresh flat-leaf parsley sprig, chopped

1 lemon, sliced, plus extra for serving

1 onion, sliced into rings

2 spring onions, sliced

5 tablespoons dry white wine

salt and pepper

SEA BASS WITH FENNEL

BRANZINO AL FINOCCHIO

Serves 4

Preheat the oven to 180°C/350°F/Gas Mark 4. Sprinkle the dried fennel inside the cavity of the fish. Make several diagonal slashes on each side of the fish, brush it with olive oil and place on a baking sheet. Bake, turning and brushing with more olive oil occasionally, for about 20 minutes. Season with salt and pepper. Make a bed of fresh fennel slices on a serving dish and place the sea bass on top. Gently warm the brandy in a ladle, then pour it over the fish and ignite. Serve when the flames have died down.

large pinch of dried fennel

1-kg/2¼-lb sea bass, spines trimmed, scaled and cleaned

olive oil, for brushing

50 ml/2 fl oz brandy

salt and pepper

fresh fennel slices, to serve

JELLIED SEA BASS

BRANZINO IN GELATINA

Serves 4

Put the sea bass in a fish kettle or large pan, pour in the court-bouillon, bring just to the boil, then lower the heat and poach gently for about 20 minutes. Remove from the heat and leave to cool in the cooking liquid. Prepare the gelatine according to the packet instructions and stir in the sherry or wine. Cook the carrot in salted, boiling water for 15–20 minutes until tender, then drain. Drain the sea bass and pat dry with kitchen paper. When the gelatine begins to cool, pour a thin layer on to a serving dish and place the fish on top. Garnish with the carrot, egg slices and mayonnaise. Cover carefully with the remaining gelatine, then chill in the refrigerator until set.

1-kg/2¼-lb sea bass, spines trimmed, scaled and cleaned

1 quantity Court-bouillon (see page 591)

500 ml/18 fl oz dissolved gelatine

1 tablespoon sherry or white wine

1 carrot, sliced

1 egg, hard-boiled, shelled and sliced

1 quantity Mayonnaise (see page 65)

BAKED MARINATED SEA BASS

BRANZINO MARINATO AL FORNO

Serves 4

Pour the olive oil into a dish and add the onion, bay leaf, thyme and parsley. Place the fish in the dish, turning to coat, and leave to marinate, turning occasionally, for about 1 hour. Preheat the oven to 200°C/400°F/Gas Mark 6. Remove and discard the herbs. Transfer the fish to an ovenproof dish or roasting tin, season with salt and pepper and brush with some of the marinade. Bake, basting occasionally with the marinade, for about 20 minutes. Serve with boiled or, better still, steamed potatoes.

5 tablespoons olive oil

1 onion, thinly sliced

1 bay leaf

1 fresh thyme sprig

1 fresh flat-leaf parsley sprig

1-kg/2¼-lb sea bass, spines trimmed, scaled and cleaned

salt and pepper

boiled or steamed potatoes, to serve

GREY MULLET

Grey mullet are very widespread along Italian coasts and their white flesh has a very pleasant taste, although it is not highly prized. They can reach 50–60 cm/20–24 inches in length and weigh as much as 6 kg/13 $^1/_4$ lb, on average, they weigh 675-900g/1 $^1/_2$–2lb. Grey mullet are usually roasted or barbecued whole, but are also good poached. Bottarga is made from their pressed cured roe. It looks like a firm, light-brown sausage and crumbles when cut. It makes a tasty antipasto and is used to season spaghetti (see Spaghettini whit Bottarga, page 303). Grey mullet is known as diamond-scale mullet or sea mullet in Australia and New Zealand.

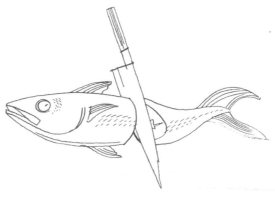

GREY MULLET IN VINEGAR

CEFALO ALL'ACETO

Serves 4

3 tablespoons olive oil

1 garlic clove

4 grey mullet, scaled and cleaned

175 ml/6 fl oz white wine vinegar

25 g/1 oz butter

$^1/_2$ teaspoon cornflour

salt and pepper

Heat the olive oil in a pan, add the garlic clove and cook until it turns brown, then remove and discard it. Add the fish and cook until browned on both sides, then add the vinegar and cook until it has evaporated. Season with salt and pepper and cook over a medium heat for 15 minutes. Mix together the butter and cornflour to a paste, add to the pan and stir into the cooking juices to thicken. Cook for a few minutes more and serve.

GREY MULLET WITH PARSLEY

Heat the olive oil in a pan, add the garlic and cook until it turns brown, then remove and discard it. Add the fish, season with salt and pepper to taste and cook over a medium heat for about 15 minutes. Sprinkle with the parsley, transfer to a warm serving dish, spoon the cooking juices over the fish and garnish with the lemon wedges.

CEFALO AL PREZZEMOLO

Serves 4

3 tablespoons olive oil

1 garlic clove

4 grey mullet, scaled and cleaned

1 fresh flat-leaf parsley sprig, chopped

salt and pepper

1 lemon, cut into wedges, to garnish

GREY MULLET AND DILL PARCELS

Preheat the oven to 200°C/400°F/Gas Mark 6. Cut four squares of foil, each large enough to hold a fish, and brush with oil. Season the cavities of the fish with salt and pepper and place a dill sprig in each. Put one fish on each foil square and divide the onion and garlic among them. Place a few lemon slices on top of each fish and sprinkle with the wine and brandy. Fold over the foil to enclose the fish completely, place on a baking sheet and bake for about 10 minutes. Remove from the oven, transfer to a warm serving dish and open the foil parcels just before serving.

CEFALO IN CARTOCCIO ALL'ANETO

Serves 4

olive oil, for brushing

4 grey mullet, scaled and cleaned

4 fresh dill sprigs

1 onion, chopped

1 garlic clove, chopped

1 lemon, sliced

175 ml/6 fl oz dry white wine

4 teaspoons brandy

salt and pepper

STUFFED GREY MULLET IN OLIVE SAUCE

Place a slice of pancetta and a sage leaf in the cavity of each fish and season lightly with salt and pepper. Heat the olive oil in a pan, add the parsley and remaining sage leaves and cook for a few minutes, then remove the pan from the heat and leave to cool. Place the fish in the pan, return to the heat, cover and cook for 5–6 minutes on each side. Add the wine and cook for about 10 minutes until it has evaporated. Gently stir in the olives, cook for 2 minutes and serve.

CEFALO RIPIENO IN SALSA D'OLIVE

Serves 4

4 pancetta slices

8 fresh sage leaves, chopped

4 grey mullet, scaled and cleaned

5 tablespoons olive oil

1 fresh flat-leaf parsley sprig, chopped

5 tablespoons dry white wine

20 mixed green and black olives, stoned and chopped

salt and pepper

no

GROUPER

Grouper are among the most highly prized sea fish because their white flesh is tasty and tender. They are best cooked simply; for example, by poaching (their stock is excellent) or baking. Another way to enjoy them and bring out their flavour is to braise them, when they are excellent on spaghetti. Many grouper are more than 80 cm/31 inches long and some members of the family can reach as much as 150 cm/5 feet in length and 50 kg/110 lb in weight. Large grouper are usually sold as steaks, while smaller grouper, sufficient for two to four servings, are available whole. If you have difficulty finding grouper, you can substitute sea bass or sea trout. In Australia, members of the grouper family are called rock cods.

BAKED GROUPER

CERNIA AL FORNO

Serves 4

3 tablespoons olive oil, plus extra for brushing
1-kg/2¼-lb grouper, fins trimmed and cleaned
175 ml/6 fl oz white wine
juice of ½ lemon, strained
2 tablespoons capers, drained and rinsed
1 fresh red chilli, seeded and chopped
salt and pepper

Preheat the oven to 180°C/350°F/Gas Mark 4. Brush an ovenproof dish with olive oil. Season the fish inside and out with salt and pepper and place in the dish. Brush with the oil and pour in the wine and lemon juice. Bake for 15 minutes, then add the capers and chilli. Continue to cook, basting occasionally, for a further 30 minutes until cooked through. Transfer to a warm dish, spoon the sauce over the fish and serve.

CERNIA ALL'AVOCADO

GROUPER WITH AVOCADO

CERNIA ALL'AVOCADO

Serves 4

1 shallot, sliced

1 carrot, sliced

1 celery stick, chopped

1 garlic clove

1 fresh flat-leaf parsley sprig

1 fresh thyme sprig

juice of 1 lemon, strained

4 black peppercorns

1-kg/2¼-lb grouper, fins trimmed and cleaned

salt

For the sauce

2 avocados

3 tablespoons olive oil

3–4 tablespoons lemon juice, strained

½ onion, chopped

salt and pepper

For the garnish

lemon slices

fresh flat-leaf parsley leaves

Pour 2 litres/3½ pints water into a large pan, add the shallot, carrot, celery, garlic, parsley, thyme, lemon juice, peppercorns and a pinch of salt and bring to the boil. Lower the heat, cover simmer for about 30 minutes. Remove from the heat and leave to cool. Add the fish to the cooled stock and bring just to the boil, then lower the heat and simmer for 30 minutes. Transfer the fish to a dish, leave to cool, then chill in the refrigerator for at least 3 hours. Prepare the sauce just before serving. Halve and stone the avocados and scoop out the flesh into a food processor. Add the olive oil, lemon juice and onion, season with salt and pepper and process to a purée. The sauce should have the consistency of mayonnaise, so if it is too thick, thin it with more lemon juice. Place the fish on a serving dish, spread with a little avocado sauce, leaving the head and tail uncovered, and garnish with lemon slices and parsley leaves. Serve with the remaining sauce.

GROUPER WITH OLIVES

CERNIA ALLE OLIVE

Serves 4

4 grouper steaks

plain flour, for dusting

2 tablespoons olive oil

1 onion, finely chopped

400 g/14 oz plum tomatoes, peeled, seeded and diced

150 g/5 oz green or black olives, stoned

salt and pepper

Lightly dust the fish with flour. Heat the oil in a pan, add the onion and cook over a lowheat, stirring occasionally, for 5 minutes. Stir in the tomatoes and simmer for 10 minutes. Add the fish, 2 tablespoons hot water and the olives and season with salt and pepper to taste. Cover and simmer gently for about 30 minutes. Remove the lid and, if the cooking juices are too runny, increase the heat to medium and cook for a few more minutes until thickened. Transfer the fish and sauce to a warm serving dish.

MONKFISH

In Italy, monkfish are known as coda di rospo − toad's tail − because only their long fleshy tails are sold, although in Veneto the large, ugly heads, which are sold separately, are used for delicious stocks and jellies. The alternative English name for monkfish is angler fish. In Australia and New Zealand, a similar species is called either monkfish or stargazer. Monkfish tails are almost always sold skinned, making them very easy to prepare. However, you may still need to remove the transparent, greyish membrane that covers the flesh. Otherwise, all you need do is rinse quickly and pat dry. The flavoursome, pink flesh turns white when cooked, and although it has compact fibres it is very tender. In addition, it is nearly completely boneless so there is very little waste. During cooking the volume of monkfish decreases considerably so this must be taken into account when calculating quantities. Monkfish are ideal for a number of fabulous dishes.

MONKFISH WITH LEMON

Preheat the oven to 220°C/425°F/Gas Mark 7. Remove and discard the membrane from the monkfish and snap the backbone in a few places. Make small slits in the flesh and insert the garlic slivers. Season with salt and place in an ovenproof dish. Halve one of the lemons and squeeze the juice from one of the halves. Peel the remaining lemon and lemon half, removing all traces of pith, and slice thinly. Cover the fish with the lemon slices. Pour in half the olive oil and put the dish in the oven. When quite a lot of liquid has formed on the base of the dish, carefully pour it off. Add the remaining olive oil and the lemon juice. Lower the oven temperature to 180°C/350°F/Gas Mark 4 and bake for about 40 minutes. Transfer to a warm serving dish.

CODA DI ROSPO AL LIMONE

Serves 4

1 kg/2¼ lb monkfish

1 garlic clove, very thinly sliced

2 lemons

175 ml/6 fl oz olive oil

salt

MONKFISH IN RED WINE

CODA DI ROSPO AL VINO ROSSO
Serves 4
50 g/2 oz butter
1 shallot, chopped
1 carrot, chopped
2 tablespoons brandy
350 ml/12 fl oz red wine
4 fresh sage leaves
1 fresh thyme sprig, leaves only
1 tablespoon red wine vinegar
1 kg/2¼ lb monkfish fillets, cut into chunks
1 tablespoon plain flour
2 tablespoons olive oil
100 g/3½ oz baby onions, chopped
100 g/3½ oz mushrooms
salt and pepper

CODA DI ROSPO AL VINO ROSSO

Serves 4

50 g/2 oz butter

1 shallot, chopped

1 carrot, chopped

2 tablespoons brandy

350 ml/12 fl oz red wine

4 fresh sage leaves

1 fresh thyme sprig, leaves only

1 tablespoon red wine vinegar

1 kg/2¼ lb monkfish fillets, cut into chunks

1 tablespoon plain flour

2 tablespoons olive oil

100 g/3½ oz baby onions, chopped

100 g/3½ oz mushrooms

salt and pepper

Melt half the butter in a pan, add the shallot and carrot and cook over a low heat, stirring occasionally, for 10 minutes until lightly browned. Add the brandy and cook until it has evaporated. Add the red wine, sage, thyme and vinegar and season with salt and pepper. Cover and simmer very gently for about 20 minutes. Strain the sauce, return it to the pan and reheat thoroughly. Add the fish and cook for 10 minutes. Remove the fish from the pan with a slotted spoon and keep warm. Increase the heat under the sauce to high and cook until reduced. Meanwhile, mix together the remaining butter and the flour to a paste, then stir it into the sauce to thicken. Cook, stirring constantly, for 10 minutes. Heat the olive oil in another pan, add the onions and cook, stirring frequently, until softened. Add the mushrooms and stir in the sauce, then add the fish and cook over a low heat for 5 minutes. Transfer to a warm serving dish.

MONKFISH WITH CAULIFLOWER AND SPRING ONIONS

CODA DI ROSPO CON CAVOLFIORE E CIPOLLE

Serves 4

1 bunch of spring onions

1 cauliflower, cut into florets

100 g/3½ oz butter

juice of ½ lemon, strained

1 kg/2¼ lb monkfish fillets, thickly sliced

350 ml/12 fl oz dry white wine

3 tablespoons double cream

1 tablespoon fresh flat-leaf parsley, chopped

salt and pepper

Chop the white and green parts of the spring onions separately. Blanch the cauliflower in salted, boiling water for 5 minutes, then drain and refresh under cold, running water. Melt half the butter in a pan, add the white parts of the spring onions and cook over a low heat, stirring occasionally, until softened. Add the cauliflower, lemon juice and the green parts of the spring onions and cook over a low heat for 10 minutes. Melt the remaining butter in another pan, add the fish and cook for 3 minutes on each side. Pour in the wine, cover and cook over a medium heat for about 15 minutes. Gently stir in the cream, season with salt and pepper and cook for a few minutes more until thickened. Transfer the fish to a warm serving dish, surround with the cauliflower and spring onions and sprinkle with the cooking juices and parsley.

MONKFISH WITH ANCHOVY SAUCE

Preheat the oven to 200°C/400°F/Gas Mark 6. Grease an ovenproof dish with butter and place the fish in it. Thinly pare the lemon rind and sprinkle it over the fish with the shallot and parsley. Add 2 tablespoons of the olive oil and the wine, season with salt and pepper and bake for 30 minutes. Chop the anchovy fillets. Place the flesh in a bowl and mash. Squeeze the juice from half the lemon and strain. Hard-boil the eggs, refresh under cold water and shell, then halve lengthways and scoop out the yolks. Add the egg yolks and lemon juice to the anchovies, mix well and gradually stir in the remaining olive oil to make a fairly thick sauce. Transfer the slices of monkfish to a warm serving dish and spoon the sauce over them. Serve with steamed potatoes.

CODA DI ROSPO CON SALSA D'ACCIUGHE

Serves 4

butter, for greasing

4 monkfish slices

1 lemon

1 shallot, finely chopped

1 fresh flat-leaf parsley sprig, chopped

7 tablespoons olive oil

5 tablespoons white wine

4 salted anchovies, heads removed,

cleaned and filleted (see page 596),

soaked in cold water for 10 minutes and drained

2 eggs

salt and pepper

steamed potato wedges, to serve

MONKFISH AND PRAWN ROULADES

Preheat the oven to 180°C/350°F/Gas Mark 4. Slice the monkfish fillets, make incisions in the flesh and insert the prawns. Heat half the olive oil in a small, nonstick frying pan, add the aubergine slices and cook over a medium heat until light golden brown on both sides, then remove from the pan. Place the monkfish slices on the aubergine slices, roll up and tie with kitchen string. Place the rolls in a roasting tin and bake for 25 minutes. Remove the tin from the oven and prick the roulades all over with a fork. Leave to stand for 5 minutes, then transfer to a plate and keep warm. Set the roasting tin over a low heat and stir in the flour, then stir in the wine, lemon juice and Worcestershire sauce. Gradually stir in the stock and cook, stirring constantly, until thickened. Heat the remaining olive oil in a small saucepan, add the shallots and garlic and cook over a low heat, stirring occasionally, for 5 minutes. Add the olives, rocket and stock mixture, season with salt and pepper and cook for a further 5 minutes. Cut the roulades into thick slices, place on a warm serving dish and spoon the hot sauce over them.

INVOLTINI DI CODA DI ROSPO CON GAMBERETTI

Serves 6

1.2 kg /2¹/₂ lb monkfish fillets

200 g/7 oz cooked prawns, peeled and deveined

2 tablespoons olive oil

3 long aubergines, thinly sliced lengthways

25 g/1 oz plain flour

5 tablespoons dry white wine

juice of 1 lemon, strained

dash of Worcestershire sauce

150 ml/¹/₄ pint Concentrated Fish Stock (see page 210)

4 shallots, chopped

1 garlic clove, chopped

50 g/2 oz black olives, stoned and chopped

¹/₂ bunch of rocket, chopped

salt and pepper

MONKFISH STEW
WITH TURMERIC RICE

Lightly dust the monkfish with flour. Heat the olive oil and 25 g/1 oz of the butter in a pan, add the onions and cook over a low heat, stirring occasionally, for 5 minutes. Add the fish and cook, stirring, for 2 minutes, then add the wine and cook until it has evaporated. Add the orange and lemon rind, ginger and Tabasco, season with salt and pepper and cook for a further 10 minutes, then add the tomato and parsley. Meanwhile, put the rice in a pan, add cold water to cover, a pinch of salt and enough turmeric to turn the water bright yellow. Bring to the boil, cover and simmer for 15 minutes. Drain the rice, spread it out well on a warm serving dish, dot with the remaining butter and serve with the hot fish stew.

SPEZZATINO DI CODA DI ROSPO
CON RISO ALLA CURCUMA

Serves 6

900 g/2 lb monkfish fillets, cut into chunks
plain flour, for dusting
2 tablespoons olive oil
40 g/1½ oz butter
2 onions, finely chopped
175 ml/6 fl oz dry white wine
rind of 1 orange, cut into thin strips
rind of 1 lemon, cut into thin strips
2.5-cm/1-inch piece of fresh root ginger, cut into strips
dash of Tabasco sauce
1 tomato, peeled, seeded and diced
1 fresh flat-leaf parsley sprig, chopped
200 g/7 oz long-grain rice
½–1½ teaspoons ground turmeric
salt and pepper

SEA BREAM

GARLIC

Sea bream is a large family of fish found in many parts of the world. Red and black sea bream are among the most commonly available outside Italy, although other types, including dentex and giltheaded sea bream, are also sold. Red sea bream is an excellent all-round member of the family that can be substituted for others if they are not available; sea bass is also a good substitute. The black bream and yellow fin bream are close relatives commonly found in Australian and New Zealand waters. The three most popular varieties in Italy are dentex, giltedheaded sea bream and white sea bream. A Mediterranean member of the sea bream family, dentex can be large – up to 1 metre/3'/4 feet long and up to 12 kg/26'/2 lb in weight. This is why they are often sold as fillets. Giltheaded sea bream, sometimes known by their French name daurade, are mainly caught in the European waters of the eastern Atlantic coast and the Mediterranean. They are among the most highly prized sea fish because of their delicate flavour. They vary from 30–60 cm/12–24 inches long and their weight may, exceptionally, reach as much as 10 kg/22 lb. White sea bream are similar to giltheaded sea bream, but much larger. They have darker, richer flesh and can be recognised by the large black ring around the base of the tail. Their tasty flesh is particularly suitable for adding flavour to fish soups. White sea bream easily exceed 1.5 kg/3'/4 lb in weight, but the best fish for cooking whole weigh about 1 kg/2'/4 lb. The cooking methods and recipes are virtually the same as those for grouper (see page 612).

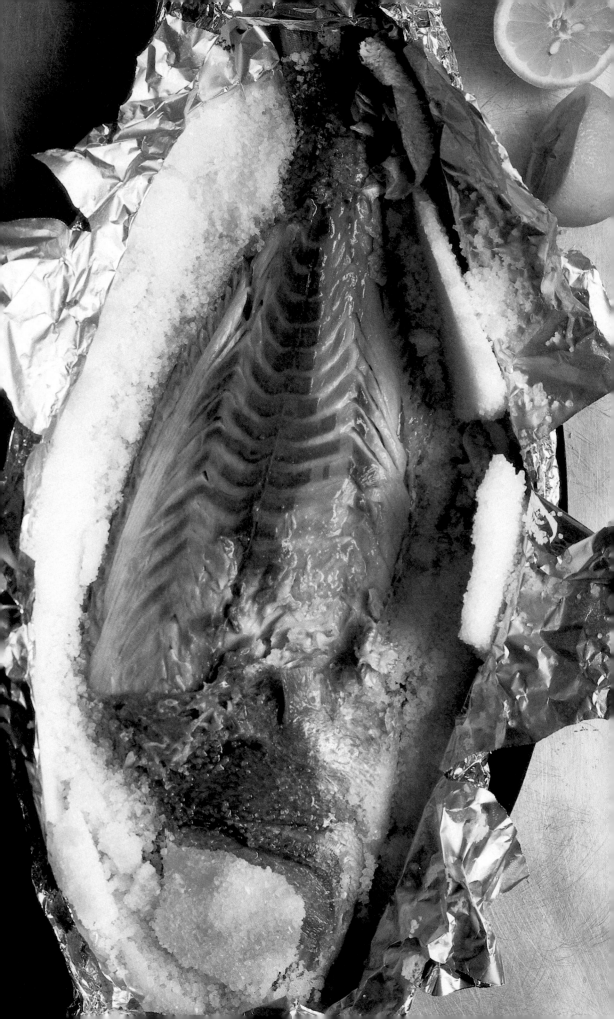

DENTICE AL SALE

Serves 6

1.5-kg/3¼-lb dentex, scaled and cleaned
1.8 kg/4 lb coarse sea salt
olive oil, for drizzling
juice of 1 lemon, strained
salt and pepper

SEA BREAM BAKED
IN A SALT CRUST

Preheat the oven to 200°C/400°F/Gas Mark 6. Season the cavity of the fish with salt and pepper. Line a roasting tin with a sheet of foil, sprinkle 400 g/14 oz of the sea salt on the base and place the fish on top. Cover it completely with the remaining salt and bake for about 45 minutes (allow 15 minutes per 500 g/1 lb 2 oz). Remove the tin from the oven, break the salt crust and lift out the fish. Remove and discard the skin, place the fish on a warm serving dish and drizzle with olive oil and the lemon juice.

DENTICE BRASATO

Serves 4

½ onion, chopped
1 carrot, chopped
1 celery stick, chopped
1-kg/2¼-lb dentex, scaled and cleaned
olive oil, for drizzling
350 ml/12 fl oz white wine
salt and pepper

BRAISED SEA BREAM

Preheat the oven to 180°C/350°F/Gas Mark 4. Mix together the onion, carrot and celery and spread out the mixture in a roasting tin. Place the fish, whole or sliced, on top and season with salt and pepper to taste. Drizzle with olive oil, pour in the wine and add enough water almost to cover the fish. Bring to the boil over a medium heat, then transfer to the oven. Cook, basting frequently, for about 30 minutes (allow about 15 minutes per 500 g/1 lb 2 oz).

DENTICE IN GELATINA

Serves 4

1-kg/2¼-lb dentex, scaled and cleaned
1 quantity Court-bouillon (see page 591)
500 ml/18 fl oz dissolved gelatine
1 tablespoon sherry or dry white wine
1 carrot, sliced
1 egg, hard-boiled, shelled and sliced
1 quantity Mayonnaise (see page 65)

JELLIED SEA BREAM

Put the dentex in a fish kettle or large pan, pour in the court-bouillon, bring just to the boil, then lower the heat and poach gently for about 20 minutes. Remove from the heat and leave to cool in the cooking liquid. Prepare the gelatine according to the packet instructions and stir in the sherry or wine. Cook the carrot in salted, boiling water for 15–20 minutes until tender, then drain. Drain the fish and pat dry with kitchen paper. When the gelatine begins to cool, pour a thin layer on to a serving dish and place the fish on top. Garnish with the carrot, egg slices and mayonnaise. Cover carefully with the remaining gelatine, then chill in the refrigerator until set.

GRILLED SEA BREAM

Mix together the olive oil, lemon juice and parsley in a dish, season with salt and pepper, and add the fish, turning to coat, and leave in a cool place to marinate for 3 hours. Preheat the grill. Drain the fish, reserving the marinade, and sprinkle with the breadcrumbs, pressing them on with your fingers. Cook the fish under the grill, turning and brushing with the reserved marinade two or three times, for about 15 minutes until the flesh flakes easily.

ORATA AI FERRI

Serves 4

4 tablespoons olive oil

juice of 1 lemon, strained

1 fresh flat-leaf parsley sprig, chopped

4 x 250–300-g/9–11-oz giltheaded sea bream, scaled and cleaned

175–225 g/6–8 oz fine breadcrumbs

salt and pepper

SEA BREAM WITH FENNEL BULBS

Preheat the oven to 180°C/350°F/Gas Mark 4. Cook the fennel in salted, boiling water for 10 minutes, then drain. Put the thyme sprig in the cavity of the fish and season the cavity with salt and pepper. Place the fish in an ovenproof dish, add the garlic, drizzle with olive oil and season with salt and pepper. Arrange the fennel all round the fish and bake, turning halfway through cooking, for about 30 minutes. Drizzle the fish with the lemon juice and serve.

ORATA AI FINOCCHI

Serves 4

4 fennel bulbs, trimmed and halved

1 fresh thyme sprig

1-kg/2¼-lb giltheaded sea bream, scaled and cleaned

1 garlic clove

olive oil, for drizzling

juice of 2 lemons, strained

salt and pepper

BAKED SEA BREAM

Preheat the oven to 200°C/400°F/Gas Mark 6. Spread out the onions in an ovenproof dish and place the fish on top. Place the tomatoes around the fish and cover it with the lemon slices. Season with salt and pepper, pour in the olive oil and wine and add the bay leaf. Bake for about 20 minutes. Sprinkle with the parsley and thyme before serving.

ORATA AL FORNO

Serves 4

2 onions, thinly sliced

1-kg/2¼-lb giltheaded sea bream, scaled and cleaned

3 tomatoes, cut into wedges and seeded

2 lemons, thinly sliced

1 tablespoon olive oil

200 ml/7 fl oz dry white wine

1 bay leaf • 1 fresh thyme sprig, chopped

1 fresh flat-leaf parsley sprig, chopped

salt and pepper

SEA BREAM WITH OLIVES

ORATA ALLE OLIVE

Serves 4

25 g/1 oz butter

2 tablespoons olive oil • 2 shallots, chopped

2 tomatoes, peeled, seeded and chopped

1 yellow pepper, halved, seeded and cut into strips

1 fresh thyme sprig, chopped

1 fresh chervil sprig, chopped

350 ml/12 fl oz dry white wine

80 g/3 oz stoned green olives

80 g/3 oz stoned black olives

1-kg/2¹/₄-lb giltheaded sea bream, scaled and cleaned

salt and pepper

Preheat the oven to 180°C/350°F/Gas Mark 4. Heat the butter and oil in a pan, add the shallots and cook over a low heat, stirring occasionally, for 5 minutes. Add the tomatoes, yellow pepper and herbs, season with salt and pepper and cook for a few minutes more. Pour in the wine and add the green and black olives. Season the cavity of the fish with salt and pepper, place it in an ovenproof dish and spoon the olive sauce over it. Bake for about 30 minutes.

SEA BREAM WITH COURGETTES

SARAGO ALLE ZUCCHINE

Serves 4

1 shallot • 1 carrot

1 bouquet garni

pinch of curry powder

375 ml/13 fl oz dry white wine

4 courgettes

2 egg yolks

1 teaspoon Dijon mustard

200 ml/7 fl oz olive oil, plus extra for brushing

120 ml/4 fl oz fl oz natural yogurt

1-kg/2¹/₄-lb white sea bream, scaled and cleaned

1 fresh chervil sprig, chopped

salt and pepper

Put the shallot, carrot, bouquet garni and curry powder in a saucepan, pour in 500 ml/18 fl oz water and the wine and season with salt and pepper. Bring to the boil, then lower the heat and simmer for 30 minutes. Meanwhile, steam the courgettes for about 15 minutes, then cut into fairly thick slices. Preheat the oven to 180°C/350°F/Gas Mark 4. Mix together the egg yolks, mustard and a pinch of salt in a bowl, then gradually whisk in the olive oil and stir in the yogurt. Brush a sheet of foil with olive oil, place the fish on top and place on a baking sheet. Bake for 30 minutes, sprinkling with the curry stock as the skin dries. Remove the fish from the oven and leave to cool slightly. Transfer to a warm serving dish, surround with the courgettes and sprinkle with the chervil. Serve with the yogurt sauce.

AROMATIC SEA BREAM

SARAGO AROMATICO

Serves 4

2 garlic cloves

1 tablespoon fresh rosemary needles

1 fresh flat-leaf parsley sprig

1 small fresh thyme sprig

1-kg/2¹/₄-lb white sea bream, scaled and cleaned

40 g/1¹/₂ oz breadcrumbs • 6 tablespoons olive oil

juice of 1 lemon, strained

salt and pepper

Preheat the oven to 180°C/350°F/Gas Mark 4. Chop one of the garlic cloves, the rosemary needles, parsley and thyme together with a pinch of salt. Fill the cavity of the fish with the herbs and place the fish in an ovenproof dish. Season with salt and pepper and sprinkle with the breadcrumbs. Mix together the olive oil, lemon juice, 2 tablespoons water and the remaining garlic clove in a bowl and pour the mixture over the fish. Bake for 20 minutes.

ROAST SEA BREAM

Preheat the oven to 180°C/350°F/Gas Mark 4. Make small incisions in the thickest parts of the fish and insert the strips of bacon fat and strips of anchovy. Brush a sheet of foil with oil, place the fish on top and fold the foil over to enclose it completely. Place on a baking sheet and bake for 30 minutes. Remove the baking sheet from the oven, unwrap the fish and pour the cooking juices into a small frying pan. Wrap the fish again and keep warm. Add the wine to the pan and cook over a high heat until reduced by at least one-third. Remove the pan from the heat and gradually stir in the butter. Place the fish on a warm serving dish and serve with the sauce.

SARAGO ARROSTO

Serves 4

1.5-kg/3¼-lb white sea bream, scaled and cleaned

25 g/1 oz bacon fat, cut into strips

50 g/2 oz canned anchovy fillets in oil,

drained and cut into strips

olive oil, for brushing

350 ml/12 fl oz white wine

80 g/3 oz butter, cut into pieces

SEA BREAM WITH MUSHROOMS

Pour the wine and 750 ml/1¼ pints water into a saucepan, add the onion, lemon juice, herbs and peppercorns and season with salt. Bring to the boil, then lower the heat and simmer for 15 minutes. Add the fish and cook for 20 minutes, then drain and strain the stock. Preheat the oven to 180°C/350°F/Gas Mark 4. Skin the fish, remove and discard the bones and cut the flesh into chunks. Place the fish in an ovenproof dish and surround it with the mushrooms. Mix the cornflour with 2 tablespoons of the cold stock in a bowl. Bring 500 ml/18 fl oz of the stock to the boil, pour in the cornflour mixture and cook, stirring constantly, until thickened. Season with salt and pepper to taste and stir in the cream. Pour the sauce over the fish and mushrooms and bake for about 10 minutes.

SARAGO CON FUNGHI

Serves 4

350 ml/12 fl oz white wine

1 onion, sliced

juice of 1 lemon, strained

1 fresh thyme sprig

6 fresh basil leaves

1 fresh chervil sprig

5 black peppercorns

800-g/1¾-lb white sea bream, scaled and cleaned

250 g/9 oz mushrooms

2 teaspoons cornflour

1 tablespoon double cream

salt and pepper

FISH TARTARE
WITH KIWI FRUIT

Mix together the lemon juice, lime juice, olive oil and peppercorns in a dish and season with salt. Using a very sharp knife, cut the sea bream and sardines into thin slices. Add them to dish with the smoked salmon and mix gently. Leave to marinate in a cool place, but not in the refrigerator, for 1 hour. Drain the fish and pat dry with kitchen paper. Put each type of fish in the middle of a separate plate and garnish each with the kiwi slices in the shape of a flower.

TARTARA DI PESCI AI KIWI

Serves 4

juice of 5 lemons, strained

juice of 2 limes, strained

4 tablespoons olive oil

4 black peppercorns, lightly crushed

800-g/1¾-lb giltheaded sea bream, filleted

3 sardines, filleted

2 smoked salmon slices, cut into strips

salt

4 kiwi fruits, peeled and sliced, to garnish

625

Serves 4

juice of 3 lemons, strained

6 tablespoons olive oil

1 garlic clove, finely chopped

1 fresh mint sprig, finely chopped

1 fresh thyme sprig, finely chopped

pinch of dried oregano

1 fresh flat-leaf parsley sprig, finely chopped

4 dentex fillets

salt and pepper

MARINATED SEA BREAM

Mix together the lemon juice, 2 tablespoons of the olive oil, the garlic, mint, thyme, oregano and parsley in a dish. Add the fish, turning to coat, and leave to marinate in a cool place for 3 hours. Drain the fish, reserving the marinade. Heat the remaining oil in a frying pan, add the fish and cook on both sides over a high heat for a few minutes, then sprinkle with 2 tablespoons of the reserved marinade and turn the fish. Cook for a few minutes more until the flesh flakes easily, season with salt and pepper and carefully transfer to a warm serving dish with a slotted spoon.

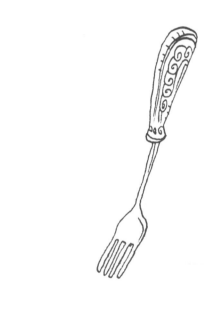

COD

Cod is a tasty, white fish from the North Atlantic. In Italy it is also popular dried, and dried and salted (see Salt Cod – Stockfish page 602). Cod can reach considerable sizes – up to 1.5 metres/5 feet – and are usually sold as steaks or fillets. It was once an inexpensive fish, but over-fishing has caused prices to rise. The Australian flathead is a good alternative for all cod recipes.

COD WITH LEEKS

Melt the butter in a saucepan, add the leeks and cook over a medium heat, stirring occasionally, for 5 minutes. Lower the heat, cover and cook very gently for 15 minutes, then season with salt and pepper. Meanwhile, spread out the flour in a shallow dish, lightly beat the egg in another shallow dish and spread out the breadcrumbs in a third. Heat the oil in a large pan. Dip the cod first in the flour, then in the egg and, finally, in the breadcrumbs. Fry in the hot oil, turning occasionally, for about 10 minutes until golden brown and cooked through (see page 593). Remove with a slotted spoon, drain on kitchen paper and season with salt. Arrange on a warm serving dish and surround with the leeks.

MERLUZZO AI PORRI

Serves 4

50 g/2 oz butter

4 leeks, white parts only, sliced

50 g/2 oz plain flour

1 egg

50 g/2 oz breadcrumbs

vegetable oil, for deep-frying

4 x 150-g/5-oz cod fillets

salt and pepper

COD IN CURRY SAUCE

Put the cod in a pan, add water to cover and a pinch of salt and bring just to the boil, then lower the heat and simmer gently for 15 minutes. Remove with a slotted spoon, drain well and keep warm. Heat the olive oil in a pan, add the onion and cook over a low heat, stirring occasionally, for 5 minutes. Add 150 ml/¼ pint of the stock, sprinkle with the curry powder and saffron and simmer for 2 minutes. Beat the egg yolk with the remaining stock, pour into the pan and cook until the sauce has thickened. Season with salt and pepper and pour the sauce over the cod.

MERLUZZO AL CURRY

Serves 4

800 g/1¾ lb cod fillets

1 tablespoon olive oil

1 onion, thinly sliced

175 ml/6 fl oz Fish Stock (see page 208)

1 teaspoon curry powder

pinch of saffron powder

1 egg yolk

salt and pepper

BAKED COD WITH VEGETABLES

MERLUZZO AL FORNO CON VERDURE

Serves 4

4 cod fillets

juice of 1 lemon, strained

80 g/3 oz pancetta, sliced

50 g/2 oz butter

4 tomatoes, peeled and chopped

1 leek, white part only, thinly sliced

2 carrots, sliced

1 onion, thinly sliced

200 ml/7 fl oz milk

salt and pepper

Preheat the oven to 200°C/400°F/Gas Mark 6. Sprinkle the cod with the lemon juice, season with salt and wrap in the pancetta slices. Melt the butter in a flameproof casserole, add the tomatoes, leek, carrots and onion and cook, stirring constantly, for about 10 minutes, then season with salt and pepper. Add the fish, cover and bake for about 25 minutes. Lower the oven temperature to 180°C/350°F/Gas Mark 4. Pour the milk into the casserole, return to the oven and bake for a further 15 minutes. Transfer the fish to a serving dish, ladle the hot cooking juices over it and serve.

PROVENÇAL COD

MERLUZZO ALLA PROVENZALE

Serves 4

800 g/1³/₄ lb cod fillets

100 ml/3¹/₂ fl oz white wine vinegar

1 fresh thyme sprig

2 potatoes, unpeeled

olive oil, for drizzling

50 ml/2 fl oz milk

2 shallots, chopped

25 g/1 oz butter

juice of ¹/₂ lemon, strained

1 fresh flat-leaf parsley sprig, chopped

salt and pepper

toasted croûtons, to serve

Put the fish into a pan, pour in water to cover and add a pinch of salt, the vinegar and thyme. Bring just to the boil, then lower the heat and simmer gently for about 10 minutes. Remove the pan from the heat and leave the fish to cool in its own stock. Meanwhile, cook the potatoes in lightly salted, boiling water for about 30 minutes until tender, then drain, peel and mash. Drain the fish and flake the flesh, removing any remaining pin bones. Place the fish in a large, heatproof bowl or the top of a double boiler. Season with pepper, drizzle with olive oil, add the milk, potatoes, shallots and butter and mix gently. Set over a pan of barely simmering water and heat through. Sprinkle with the lemon juice and parsley and serve with toasted croûtons.

SICILIAN COD

MERLUZZO ALLA SICILIANA

Serves 4

3 tablespoons olive oil, plus extra for brushing

100 g/3¹/₂ oz salted anchovies, heads removed, cleaned and filleted (see page 596), soaked in cold water for 10 minutes and drained

1-kg/2¹/₄-lb cod, cleaned and boned

1 fresh rosemary sprig, plus extra chopped

2 fresh basil leaves, plus extra chopped

50 g/2 oz breadcrumbs

salt and pepper

100 g/3¹/₂ oz stoned black olives, to garnish

Preheat the oven to 200°C/400°F/Gas Mark 6. Brush an ovenproof dish with oil. Chop the anchovy fillets. Heat 2 tablespoons of the olive oil in a saucepan, add the anchovies and cook, mashing with a wooden spoon until they have almost completely disintegrated. Spoon a little of the anchovy mixture inside the cavity of the cod and add the rosemary sprig, basil leaves and remaining olive oil. Close the cavity. Spoon the remaining anchovy mixture into the prepared dish, add the fish, sprinkle with chopped rosemary and basil and the breadcrumbs, season with salt and pepper to taste and bake for 30 minutes. Serve surrounded by the olives.

COD STEW WITH OLIVES AND CAPERS

Lightly dust the courgettes with flour, shaking off the excess. Heat half the olive oil in a frying pan, add the courgette slices, in batches, and cook until they are golden brown on both sides. Remove with a slotted spoon and drain on kitchen paper, then sprinkle with salt and keep warm. Heat the remaining olive oil in a pan, add the onion and celery and cook over a low heat, stirring occasionally, for 5 minutes. Add the passata, capers and olives and simmer for about 10 minutes. Increase the heat to high, add the cod and cook for a few more minutes. Season with salt and pepper, add the courgettes, lower the heat, cover and simmer for 30 minutes.

SPEZZATINO DI MERLUZZO
CON OLIVE E CAPPERI

Serves 4

4 courgettes, thinly sliced

plain flour, for dusting

6 tablespoons olive oil

1 onion, chopped

1 celery stick, chopped

200 ml/7 fl oz passata

1 tablespoon capers, drained, rinsed and chopped

100 g/3½ oz green olives, stoned and chopped

600 g/1 lb 5 oz cod fillets, coarsely chopped

salt and pepper

COD AND WALNUT TERRINE

Preheat the oven to 140°C/275°F/Gas Mark 1. Line a terrine or loaf tin with baking parchment. Season the cod with salt and place a layer of the fillets in the terrine or loaf tin. Mix together the parsley, chervil and breadcrumbs in a bowl. Sprinkle a little of the breadcrumb mixture into the terrine or loaf tin, then some walnuts, some capers, a few leaves of rocket and a few thyme leaves. Continue making alternate layers until all the ingredients are used, ending with a layer of cod. Drizzle generously with olive oil, cover with foil and place in a roasting tin. Pour in boiling water to come about halfway up the sides and bake for 40 minutes. Remove the terrine or loaf tin from the oven and set aside, still covered, to cool, then turn out on to a serving dish. To make the sauce, whisk together the vinegar and olive oil in a bowl, stir in the capers and garlic and season with salt and pepper. Serve the cod terrine with the sauce.

TERRINA DI MERLUZZO CON LE NOCI

Serves 4

600 g/1 lb 5 oz cod fillets

1 fresh flat-leaf parsley sprig, chopped

1 fresh chervil sprig, chopped

100 g/3½ oz breadcrumbs

50 g/2 oz shelled walnuts, chopped

2 tablespoons salted capers, rinsed

1 bunch of rocket

1 fresh thyme sprig

olive oil, for drizzling

salt

For the sauce

1 tablespoon balsamic vinegar

4–5 tablespoons olive oil

1 tablespoon capers, drained and rinsed

½ garlic clove, chopped

salt and pepper

HAKE

Hake is a similar fish to cod, but, unlike cod, is found in the Mediterranean Sea. It can grow up to 1 metre/3¹/₄ feet long and is mostly sold in portions. The delicate, easily digestible flesh is excellent poached and seasoned with oil and lemon juice or served with mayonnaise. Hake are easy to bone and may also be bought frozen. The southern hake from New Zealand can be cooked in exactly the same way as its European relative.

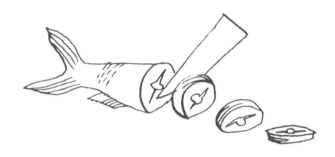

HAKE WITH POTATOES

NASELLO CON PATATE

Serves 4

olive oil, for brushing and drizzling

4 potatoes, thinly sliced

800 g/1³/₄ lb hake fillets

1 fresh thyme sprig

1 fresh rosemary sprig

salt and white pepper

Preheat the oven to 200°C/400°F/Gas Mark 6. Brush an oven-proof dish with olive oil and arrange half the potatoes in a layer on the base. Place the fish on top, add the thyme and rosemary and season with salt and pepper. Cover with the remaining potato slices and drizzle with olive oil. Bake for 30 minutes.

HAKE IN GREEN SAUCE

NASELLO IN SALSA VERDE

Serves 4

2 tablespoons olive oil, plus extra for brushing

4 hake steaks

1 fresh flat-leaf parsley sprig, chopped

1 celery stick, chopped plus a few leaves

juice of 1 lemon, strained

salt and pepper

Preheat the oven to 200°C/400°F/Gas Mark 6. Brush an oven-proof dish with oil, place the fish in it and bake for about 10 minutes. Meanwhile, heat the olive oil in a saucepan, add the onion and cook over a low heat, stirring occasionally, for 5 minutes until softened. Season with salt and pepper, remove from the heat and keep warm. Stir in the parsley, celery leaves and lemon juice. Serve the hake with this green sauce.

HAKE IN SHALLOT SAUCE

NASELLO INSAPORITO AGLI SCALOGNI

Serves 4

juice of 2 lemons, strained

2 tablespoons olive oil

600 g/1 lb 5 oz hake fillets, cut into chunks

25 g/1 oz butter

2 shallots, finely chopped

100 ml/3½ fl oz dry white wine

salt and pepper

Preheat the grill. Mix together the lemon juice and olive oil. Season the fish with salt and pepper and sprinkle with the lemon and olive oil mixture. Grill for 8 minutes, then transfer to a serving dish and keep warm. Melt the butter in a pan, add the shallots and cook over a low heat, stirring occasionally, for 5 minutes. Increase the heat to medium, add the wine and cook for a further 5 minutes. Season with salt and pepper to taste, spoon the sauce over the fish and serve.

FRIED HAKE

NASELLO IN TEGAME

Serves 4

4 tablespoons olive oil

2 shallots, thinly sliced

1 leek, white part only, thinly sliced

1 celery stick, chopped

2 carrots, chopped

1 garlic clove, chopped

1 fresh flat-leaf parsley sprig, chopped

1 fresh thyme sprig, chopped

100 ml/3½ fl oz dry white wine

200 g/7 oz tomatoes, peeled, seeded and chopped

1 teaspoon tomato purée

1 tablespoon capers, drained and rinsed

10 stoned black olives

2 gherkins, drained and sliced

1 teaspoon Dijon mustard

1 kg/2¼ lb hake steaks

salt and pepper

Heat half the olive oil in a pan over a medium heat, add the shallots, leek, celery, carrots, garlic and herbs and cook, stirring frequently, for about 10 minutes. Pour in the wine and cook until it has evaporated, then add the tomatoes and season with salt and pepper. Mix the tomato purée with 1 tablespoon hot water in a small bowl and stir into the pan. Cook over a medium heat, stirring occasionally, for about 20 minutes. Stir in the capers, olives, gherkins and mustard and cook for a further 5 minutes. Meanwhile, heat the remaining olive oil in a nonstick frying pan, add the fish and cook over a medium heat until lightly browned on both sides. Season with salt and pepper, transfer to the pan of vegetables and cook for 10 minutes, then serve.

HUSS

Known as sea veal in some parts of Italy and popularly called rock salmon in Britain, this fish is actually dogfish and a member of the shark family. It is always sold in fillets and there is no waste. Although huss is nutritious, low in fat and easy to digest, it is not very highly prized. It is good stewed, but also lends itself to the cooking methods used for tuna and swordfish.

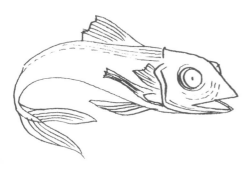

HUSS WITH VEGETABLES

Heat the olive oil in a saucepan or flameproof casserole. Add the onions, then the aubergine, carrots and courgettes and, finally, the tomatoes and cook for 10 minutes. Place the fish fillets on top of the vegetables, season with salt and pepper and cook for 20 minutes. Arrange the fish and vegetables on a warm serving dish and garnish with basil leaves.

PALOMBO ALLE VERDURE

Serves 4

3 tablespoons olive oil

2 onions, thinly sliced

1 aubergine, diced

3 carrots, diced

3 courgettes, diced

4 tomatoes, diced

4 huss fillets

salt and pepper

fresh basil leaves, to garnish

633

HUSS WITH CELERY

PALOMBO AL SEDANO

Serves 4

3 tablespoons olive oil

4 huss fillets

4 tomatoes, peeled, seeded and coarsely chopped

1 celery stick, chopped

pinch of chilli powder

4 fresh basil leaves, chopped

50 g/2 oz stoned black olives

salt and pepper

Heat the olive oil in a pan, add the fish and cook until lightly browned on both sides. Add the tomatoes, celery, chilli powder and basil, season with salt and pepper and mix gently. Cover and cook for about 30 minutes. Add the olives, cook for a few minutes more and serve.

HUSS WITH POTATOES AU GRATIN

PALOMBO CON PATATE AL GRATIN

Serves 4

50 g/2 oz butter, plus extra for greasing

4 potatoes, thinly sliced

800 g/1³/₄ lb huss fillets

1 quantity Béchamel Sauce (see page 50)

40 g/1¹/₂ oz Parmesan cheese, freshly grated

salt and pepper

Preheat the oven to 180°C/350°F/Gas Mark 4. Grease an oven-proof dish with butter and arrange half the potatoes on the base. Melt the butter in a frying pan, add the fish and cook, turning once, until golden brown on both sides. Using a slotted spoon, place the huss fillets on top of the layer of potatoes, season lightly with salt and pepper and cover with the remaining potatoes. Pour the béchamel sauce over the top, sprinkle with the Parmesan and bake for about 30 minutes.

HUSS WITH GREEN TOMATOES

PALOMBO CON POMODORI VERDI

Serves 4

4 huss fillets

3–4 green tomatoes, peeled, seeded and diced

1 onion, thinly sliced

1 tablespoon chopped fresh oregano

olive oil, for drizzling

50 g/2 oz breadcrumbs

salt and pepper

Preheat the oven to 180°C/350°F/Gas Mark 4. Place the fish in an ovenproof dish, season with salt and pepper, top with the tomatoes, onion and oregano and drizzle with olive oil. Sprinkle the breadcrumbs on top, cover with foil and bake for 30 minutes.

SWORDFISH

Swordfish are a feature of Sicilian cuisine. Their firm, tasty flesh, which is sold as steaks, is highly valued in Europe (though less so in Australia) and is ideal for a wide range of recipes, many of which are also suitable for fresh tuna. Swordfish live in temperate seas and can grow up to 4 metres/13 feet long.

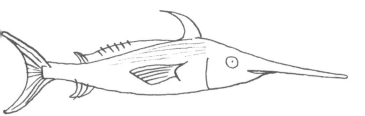

FABULOUS SMOKED SWORDFISH

To make the sauce, put the fennel, mascarpone, olive oil and egg yolk in a food processor and process to a smooth, thick purée. Add 1 tablespoon warm water, the white wine vinegar and the balsamic vinegar, season with salt and pepper and process briefly again. Arrange the radicchio leaves on a serving dish in the shape of a garland. Put the slices of fish in the middle and the celery strips all around. Spoon a little vinegar sauce on top and serve.

PESCE SPADA AFFUMICATO IN FANTASIA

Serves 6

2 Treviso radicchio

12 smoked swords

150 g/5 oz celery, cut into thin strips

For the sauce

200 g/7 oz fennel bulbs, boiled, drained and chopped

150 g/5 oz mascarpone cheese

50 ml/2 fl oz olive oil

1 egg yolk

1 teaspoon white wine vinegar

1 tablespoon balsamic vinegar

salt and pepper

BAKED SWORDFISH

Preheat the oven to 180°C/350°F/Gas Mark 4. Mix together the onion, garlic and parsley in a bowl. Place half the mixture in an ovenproof dish and place the fish on top. Season with salt and pepper and cover with the remaining chopped mixture. Pour in the olive oil and white wine. Bake, basting frequently, for 30 minutes.

PESCE SPADA AL FORNO

Serves 4

1 onion, chopped • 1 garlic clove, chopped

3 tablespoons chopped fresh flat-leaf parsley

4 swordfish steaks

175 ml/6 fl oz olive oil

175 ml/6 fl oz white wine

salt and pepper

Serves 4

250 g/9 oz mussels, scrubbed and beards removed

250 g/9 oz clams, scrubbed

150 ml/¼ pint olive oil, plus extra for drizzling

1 garlic clove

150 g/5 oz raw prawns, peeled and deveined

2 tomatoes, coarsely chopped

1 yellow pepper, halved, seeded and cut into large slices

6 fresh basil leaves, chopped

1 fresh chilli, seeded and chopped

4 swordfish steaks

1 fresh flat-leaf parsley sprig, chopped

salt and pepper

SWORDFISH PARCELS

Preheat the oven to 200°C/400°F/Gas Mark 6. Cut four large squares of foil. Discard any mussels or clams that do not shut immediately when sharply tapped, then place the shellfish in a pan with 3 tablespoons of the olive oil and the garlic. Cook over a high heat for about 5 minutes until the shells open. Discard any that remain closed. Drain the shellfish, reserving the cooking liquid. Heat 2 tablespoons of the remaining olive oil in another pan, add the prawns and cook for a few minutes. Add the mussels and clams, still in their shells, the tomatoes, yellow pepper, basil, chilli and reserved cooking liquid and simmer for 5 minutes. Heat the remaining oil in a frying pan, add the swordfish and cook for 5 minutes on each side. Place a swordfish steak on each square of foil, season with salt and pepper and spoon the seafood mixture on top. Sprinkle with the parsley and drizzle with olive oil. Fold the foil over and seal the edges, transfer the parcels to a baking sheet and bake for about 10 minutes. Place the parcels on a warm serving dish, opening them slightly.

Serves 4

4 swordfish steaks

1 small bay leaf

1 garlic clove

1 fresh chervil sprig, chopped

6 fresh basil leaves, chopped

2 tablespoons olive oil, plus extra for drizzling

120 ml/4 fl oz dry white wine

1 onion, chopped

1 celery stick, chopped

1 carrot, chopped

300 g/11 oz canned chopped tomatoes

15 g/½ oz capers, drained and rinsed

50 g/2 oz black olives, stoned

40 g/1½ oz Parmesan cheese, shaved

salt and pepper

BRAISED SWORDFISH

Place the fish in a flameproof casserole with the bay leaf and garlic, sprinkle with the chervil and basil, drizzle generously with olive oil and season with salt and pepper. Cook over a medium heat, turning the fish occasionally, for 30 minutes. Meanwhile, preheat the oven to180°C/350°F/Gas Mark 4. Transfer the casserole to the oven and cook, sprinkling in the wine during cooking, for just under 15 minutes. Meanwhile, heat the olive oil in a pan, add the onion, celery and carrot and cook over a low heat, stirring occasionally, for 5 minutes. Add the tomatoes, capers and olives and simmer for about 10 minutes, adding a little water if necessary. Pour the sauce over the fish, sprinkle with the Parmesan and return to the oven for about 15 minutes. Leave to stand for a few minutes before serving.

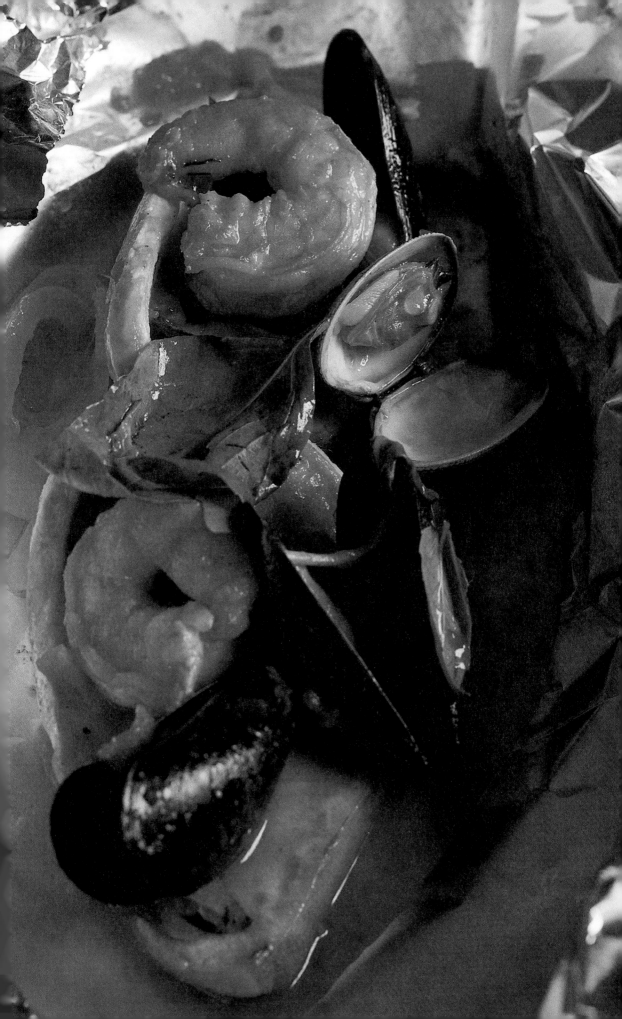

PESCE SPADA MARINATO

Serves 4

300 g/11 oz swordfish, very thinly sliced

olive oil, for drizzling

juice of 2 lemons, strained

100 g/3¹/₂ oz rocket, chopped

100 g/3¹/₂ oz escarole, chopped

leaves from 2 fresh chervil sprigs

salt and pepper

1 lemon, sliced, to garnish

MARINATED SWORDFISH

Place the swordfish on a plate, drizzle with olive oil and the lemon juice and season with salt and pepper. Cover and chill in the refrigerator for about 2 hours. Mix together the rocket, escarole and chervil in a bowl. Drain the slices of fish, reserving the marinade, and place in a ring on a serving dish, then put the salad leaves in the centre. Spoon the marinade over the dish and garnish with the lemon slices.

TRANCE DI PESCE SPADA
ALL'ACETO BALSAMICO

Serves 4

4 swordfish steaks

100 ml/3¹/₂ fl oz milk

plain flour, for dusting

200 g/7 oz butter

¹/₂ teaspoon ground cinnamon

1 clove

100 ml/3¹/₂ fl oz cider vinegar

2 tablespoons balsamic vinegar

salt and pepper

SWORDFISH STEAKS
IN BALSAMIC VINEGAR

Put the fish in a dish, add the milk and set aside for 10 minutes. Drain and dust with flour. Melt half the butter in a frying pan, add the fish and cook over a medium heat until golden brown on both sides. Season with salt and pepper, remove with a slotted spoon and drain on kitchen paper. Transfer to a serving dish and keep warm. Melt the remaining butter over a low heat, add the cinnamon, clove, cider vinegar and balsamic vinegar and simmer for about 10 minutes or until the sauce is fairly thick. Pour it over the fish and serve.

ROASTING

SKATE

Skates and rays are virtually interchangeable. They are kite-shaped, cartilaginous, flat fish with long thin tails. The flesh from the wings is lean with a very subtle flavour. Though it is not highly prized in Italy it is more popular elsewhere.

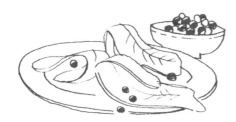

SKATE WITH CAPERS

Cut the skate wings into fairly large pieces. Heat the olive oil in a pan, add the onion, garlic and parsley and cook over a low heat, stirring occasionally, for about 10 minutes until the onion is lightly browned. Add the tomatoes and capers, season with salt and pepper to taste and cook, stirring occasionally, for 10 minutes. Place the skate in the pan, add 2–3 tablespoons warm water, if necessary, and cook for about 30 minutes.

RAZZA AI CAPPERI

Serves 4

1 kg/2¼ lb skate wings
4 tablespoons olive oil
1 onion, chopped
1 garlic clove
1 fresh flat-leaf parsley sprig, chopped
800 g/1¾ lb tomatoes, peeled and chopped
1 tablespoon capers, drained and rinsed
salt and pepper

SKATE NIÇOISE

Pour 1 litre/1¾ pints water into a pan and add one of the onions, the carrot, celery, wine, vinegar and thyme and season with salt. Bring just to the boil, then lower the heat and simmer for 15 minutes. Add the fish and cook over a low heat for 5 minutes. Remove the skate, drain and carefully remove the skin. (This may not be necessary, as skate wings are usually sold already skinned.) Place on a serving dish and keep warm. Chop the remaining onion. Heat the olive oil in a pan, add the onion, shallot and parsley and cook over a low heat, stirring occasionally, for 5 minutes. Spoon the mixture over the skate and serve.

RAZZA ALLA NIZZARDA

Serves 4

2 onions
1 carrot, sliced
1 celery stick
100 ml/3½ fl oz dry white wine
100 ml/3½ fl oz white wine vinegar
1 fresh thyme sprig
800 g/1¾ lb skate wings
2 tablespoons olive oil
1 shallot, chopped
1 fresh flat-leaf parsley sprig, chopped
salt

TURBOT
AND BRILL

The Italian name for this fish – rombo, meaning rhombus – derives from its shape, which is similar to that of sole and John Dory, with which it shares recipes. Both brill and turbot are called rombo and, perhaps surprisingly, the former is preferred in Italy. Brill grow to 25–75 cm/10–30 inches long and live in the Mediterranean and along the European Atlantic coast. They are highly prized for their firm, white, tasty flesh, which is easy to digest. They do not need skinning as they have no scales. It is best to have them filleted by a professional to avoid damaging them. When poaching turbot or brill, it is advisable to leave them whole and cook them in a light court-bouillon, possibly even made with milk.

TURBOT FILLETS WITH VEGETABLES

FILETTO DI ROMBO CON VERDURE

Serves 6

1 white onion, thinly sliced
1 carrot, thinly sliced
2 celery sticks, cut into thin strips
200 g/7 oz mushrooms, thinly sliced
175 ml/6 fl oz dry white wine
4 turbot or brill fillets
3 tablespoons double cream
salt and pepper

Place the onion, carrot, celery and mushrooms in a large saucepan, pour in the wine and 250 ml/8 fl oz water, cover and simmer for about 15 minutes or until the liquid has reduced. Add the fish fillets, cover and cook for 3–4 minutes. Remove the pan from the heat, transfer the fish to a serving dish and keep warm. Stir the cream into the vegetables, season with salt and pepper and heat gently for a few minutes. Spoon the vegetable sauce over the fish and serve.

TURBOT FILLETS
WITH A POTATO TOPPING

Preheat the oven to 200°C/400°F/Gas Mark 6. Grease an ovenproof dish with butter. Cook the potatoes in lightly salted, boiling water for 10–15 minutes until just tender, then drain and refresh under cold, running water. Put the fish in the prepared dish and cover with slightly overlapping slices of potato, like fish scales. Brush with the bea-ten egg, season with salt and pepper and bake for 15–20 minutes. Meanwhile, pour the wine and stock into a saucepan, add the shallots and cook over a medium heat until the liquid has reduced and the mixture is quite thick. Remove from the heat, leave to cool slightly, then pour into a food processor, add the basil and process to a purée. Transfer to a bowl and keep warm. Cream the butter in a bowl, then beat in the shallot mixture. Remove the fish from the oven, garnish with the chives and tomatoes and serve with the sauce.

FILETTO DI ROMBO VESTITO DI PATATE

Serves 6

80 g/3 oz butter, plus extra for greasing

3 potatoes, thinly sliced

6 turbot or brill fillets

1 egg, lightly beaten

5 tablespoons dry white wine

175 ml/6 fl oz Vegetable Stock (see page 209)

6 shallots, chopped

4 fresh basil leaves

salt and pepper

For the garnish

¹/₂ bunch of fresh chives, chopped

3 tomatoes, peeled and diced

BAKED TURBOT
WITH LENTIL SAUCE

Put the lentils and one of the bay leaves in a pan, add water to cover and bring to the boil, then lower the heat and simmer for 30–45 minutes until tender. Drain well and discard the bay leaf. Preheat the oven to 180°C/350°F/Gas Mark 4. Heat 2 tablespoons of the olive oil in a saucepan, add one-quarter of the shallots, the bacon and a bay leaf and cook over a low heat, stirring frequently, for 5 minutes. Add the lentils, 50 ml/2 fl oz of the wine and 5 tablespoons of the stock and simmer for about 5 minutes. Remove from the heat, transfer half the mixture to a food processor and process to a purée, then scrape into a clean pan. Heat the remaining olive oil, stock, wine, bay leaf and chopped shallot in a roasting tin. Lightly season the fish fillets with salt, add to the tin and cook for 5 minutes, then transfer to the oven and bake for a further 15 minutes. Remove the tin from the oven, transfer the fish to a serving dish and keep warm. Strain the cooking juices into a bowl and stir in the curry powder. Add the mixture to the lentil purée, heat gently and gradually whisk in the butter. Sprinkle the marjoram over the fish and serve with the lentil mixture and sauce.

ROMBO AL FORNO
CON SUGO DI LENTICCHIE

Serves 6

250 g/9 oz lentils

3 bay leaves

175 ml/6 fl oz olive oil

2 shallots, chopped

50 g/2 oz bacon, diced

175 ml/6 fl oz dry white wine

250 ml/8 fl oz Concentrated Fish Stock (see page 210)

2-kg/4¹/₂-lb turbot or brill, filleted

pinch of curry powder

40 g/1¹/₂ oz butter, cut into small pieces

1 fresh marjoram sprig, chopped

salt

ROMBO ALL'ARANCIA

Serves 4

2 oranges

1 tablespoon olive oil

4 turbot or brill fillets

2 tablespoons sugar

salt

orange slices, to garnish

TURBOT IN ORANGE SAUCE

Thinly pare the rind of one of the oranges, discarding all traces of pith, and chop very finely. Squeeze the juice from both oranges and strain into a measuring jug. Heat the olive oil in a pan and add the fish. Season lightly with salt, add half the orange juice and cook over a medium heat, turning the fish occasionally, for 15 minutes. Pour 2 tablespoons water into a saucepan, add the orange rind and sugar, heat for 2–3 minutes and stir in the remaining orange juice. Pour the sauce over the fish and cook for a further 10 minutes. Transfer to a warm serving dish and garnish with orange slices.

ROMBO ALLO SPUMANTE

Serves 4

65 g/2^1/$_2$ oz butter

1 shallot, chopped

100 g/3^1/$_2$ oz mushrooms, finely chopped

4 x 150-g/5-oz turbot or brill fillets

200 ml/7 fl oz dry sparkling wine

2 tablespoons double cream

1 teaspoon cornflour

salt and pepper

TURBOT IN SPARKLING WINE

Heat half the butter in a frying pan, add the shallot and cook over a low heat, stirring occasionally, for 5 minutes. Stir in the mushrooms and cook until lightly browned. Melt the remaining butter in another frying pan, add the fish and cook until lightly browned on both sides. Remove from the pan with a slotted spoon and add to the other pan. Add half the wine and cook for 5 minutes, then season with salt and pepper. Using a slotted spoon, transfer the fish to a serving dish and keep warm. Stir the cream into the mushroom mixture over a low heat. Mix the cornflour to a paste with 1 tablespoon warm water, then stir into the pan. Increase the heat to medium and cook for a few minutes more until thickened. Add the remaining wine and cook, stirring constantly, until piping hot. Spoon the sauce over the fish and serve.

TURBOT WITH SAFFRON IN CLAM SAUCE

ROMBO ALLO ZAFFERANO
CON SUGO DI VONGOLE

Serves 6

Discard any clams that do not shut immediately when sharply tapped. Heat half the olive oil and half the wine in a frying pan, add the garlic and clams and cook over a high heat for about 5 minutes until the clams open. Discard any that remain closed. Drain the clams, reserving the cooking liquid, leave to cool, then remove from their shells. Strain the cooking liquid into a bowl. Heat the remaining olive oil in a saucepan, add the shallot and cook over a low heat, stirring occasionally, for 5 minutes. Add the potatoes, pour in the remaining wine and cook until it has evaporated. Add the stock and about half the reserved cooking liquid and simmer until the potatoes are tender. Meanwhile, preheat the oven to 180°C/350°F/Gas Mark 4. Brush an ovenproof dish with oil. Ladle half the potato mixture into a food processor and process to a purée, then return the purée to the pan. Add the clams and tomato and season with salt and pepper to taste. Season the fish fillets with salt and pepper, place them in the prepared dish and bake for 20 minutes. Beat together the butter, saffron and chilli powder in a bowl until thoroughly combined. Spoon the saffron butter over the fish, sprinkle with the parsley and serve with the potato and clam mixture.

500 g/1 lb 2 oz clams, scrubbed

4 tablespoons olive oil, plus extra for brushing

250 ml/8 fl oz dry white wine

1 garlic clove

1 shallot, chopped

3 potatoes, diced

150 ml/¼ pint Concentrated Fish Stock (see page 210)

1 tomato, peeled, seeded and diced

2-kg /4½-lb turbot or brill, filleted

80 g/3 oz butter, softened

10 saffron threads

pinch of chilli powder

1 tablespoon fresh flat-leaf parsley, chopped

salt and pepper

TURBOT WITH OLIVE SAUCE

ROMBO CON SALSA DI OLIVE

Serves 6

Preheat the oven to 200°C/400°F/Gas Mark 6. Grease an ovenproof dish with butter. Chop the anchovy fillets. Heat the butter in a frying pan, add the pine nuts and cook, stirring frequently, for a few minutes until golden brown. Remove from the pan and drain on kitchen paper. Put the anchovy, olives, parsley, shallots and stock in a food processor and process to a purée, then scrape into a bowl and whisk in enough olive oil to make a smooth sauce. Place the fish in the prepared dish, season with salt and pepper, pour the sauce over it and bake for 20 minutes. Transfer to a warm serving dish and sprinkle with the pine nuts. Boiled or steamed potatoes make an excellent side dish.

25 g/1 oz butter, plus extra for greasing

1 salted anchovy, head removed, cleaned and filleted (see page 596), soaked in cold water for 10 minutes and drained

25 g/1 oz pine nuts

300 g/11 oz black olives, stoned

½ bunch of fresh flat-leaf parsley, chopped

2 shallots, chopped

1–2 tablespoons Concentrated Fish Stock (see page 210)

150 ml/¼ pint olive oil

1.2-kg/2½-lb turbot or brill, filleted

salt and pepper

SALMON

Salmon are among the most highly prized fish. Although they live in the ocean, they swim upstream against the current to reproduce in the rivers in which they were born. Salmon grow up to 1.5 metres/5 feet in length and weigh as much as 36 kg/ 79 lb, but they normally range from 1.5–9 kg/3¹⁄₄–19³⁄₄ lb. Italy imports quite a lot of salmon, usually smoked, but occasionally frozen. However, salmon can also be found fresh, in fillets, steaks or whole in some places. An oily fish, salmon has pink, firm flesh with a delicious flavour.

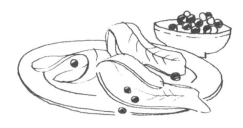

SALMON AND BACON BITES

BOCCONCINI DI SALMONE CON BACON

Serves 4

butter, for greasing

2 fresh sage sprigs

675 g/1¹⁄₂ lb salmon fillets, cut into cubes

150 g/5 oz bacon rashers, halved

salt and pepper

Preheat the oven to 200°C/400°F/Gas Mark 6. Grease an oven-proof dish with butter. Pull the sage leaves off the stems and cut them in half. Season the salmon cubes with salt and pepper and wrap each cube in a small slice of bacon with half a sage leaf. Secure with cocktail sticks and place in the prepared dish. Bake, turning occasionally, for 10–15 minutes.

SALMON AND CHICORY PARCELS

FAGOTTINI DI SALMONE CON INDIVIA

Serves 4

5 tablespoons olive oil

5 tablespoons dry white wine

4 salmon steaks

1 head of chicory, cut into strips

1 garlic clove, chopped

400 g/14 oz puff pastry dough, thawed if frozen

plain flour, for dusting

1 egg yolk, lightly beaten

salt and pepper

Mix together 3 tablespoons of the olive oil and the wine in a dish, season with salt and pepper and add the salmon, turning to coat. Leave to marinate for 2 hours. Preheat the oven to 200°C/400°F/Gas Mark 6. Heat the remaining olive oil in a pan, add the chicory and garlic and cook, stirring occasionally, for 5 minutes. Divide the pastry into four and roll each piece out on a lightly floured surface. Drain the salmon and place a steak on each piece of pastry. Divide the chicory among them, then fold the pastry over and press the edges to seal. Prick with a fork, place on a baking sheet and brush with the egg yolk. Bake for about 30 minutes.

SALMON FISHCAKES

SVIZZERE DI SALMONE

Serves 4

100 g/3¹/₂ oz bread, crusts removed

200 ml/7 fl oz milk

1 lemon

400 g/14 oz salmon fillet, chopped

65 g/2¹/₂ oz butter, softened

80 g/3 oz breadcrumbs

25 g/1 oz Clarified Butter (see page 88)

salt and white pepper

Tear the bread into pieces, place in a bowl, add milk to cover and leave to soak for 10 minutes, then drain and squeeze out. Grate the rind of half the lemon and peel the other half, removing all traces of pith from both halves, and slice thinly. Mix together the salmon, soaked bread and butter in a bowl and season with salt and pepper. Divide the mixture into four, shape into balls, then flatten gently with your hand. Pour the remaining milk into a shallow dish and mix together the breadcrumbs and lemon rind in another shallow dish. Melt the clarified butter in a frying pan. Dip the fishcakes first in the milk, then in the breadcrumb mixture and fry for 4 minutes on each side. Remove with a slotted spoon and drain on kitchen paper. Place on a warm serving dish and garnish with the lemon slices.

SALMON TARTARE

TARTARA DI SALMONE

Serves 4

3 lemons

5 tablespoons olive oil • dash of Tabasco sauce

600 g/1 lb 5 oz salmon fillets, diced

2 yellow peppers, halved, seeded and cut into squares

50 g/2 oz capers, drained and rinsed

8 green olives, stoned and chopped • 4 egg yolks

salt and pepper

1 tablespoon fresh flat-leaf parsley, chopped, to garnish

Peel one of the lemons, removing all traces of white pith, and chop the flesh. Squeeze the juice from the remaining lemons. Mix together the olive oil, lemon juice and Tabasco in a bowl and season with salt and pepper. Mix together the salmon, yellow peppers, capers, olives and chopped lemon in a dish, add the lemon dressing, mix well and leave to marinate for 20 minutes. Divide the mixture among four dishes and place an egg yolk in the middle of each. Garnish with the parsley.

SMOKED SALMON TERRINE

TERRINA DI SALMONE AFFUMICATO

Serves 6

200 g/7 oz smoked salmon, coarsely chopped

200 g/7 oz smoked trout, coarsely chopped

100 ml/3¹/₂ fl oz double cream

1 jar (40–50 g/1¹/₂–2 oz) lumpfish roe

Put the salmon in a food processor, process to a purée and scrape into a bowl. Clean the food processor, add the trout, process to a purée and scrape into another bowl. Whisk the cream and stir half into each purée. Line a rectangular cake tin with plenty of cling film, allowing it to overlap the sides. Spoon the salmon mixture evenly over the base of the tin, sprinkle with the lumpfish roe and cover with the trout mixture. Fold over the overhanging cling film and chill in the refrigerator for about 6 hours. Turn out on to a serving dish.

JOHN DORY

John Dory are highly-prized, thin-bodied fish with excellent flesh and no pin bones. They are easy to cut into four fillets and are suitable for many sole, turbot and brill recipes. John Dory are tasty grilled whole. A 1.5-kg/3¹/₄-lb fish is sufficient for four servings. The leatherjacket, which lives in Australian and New Zealand waters, closely resembles the John Dory.

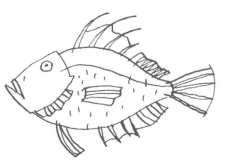

JOHN DORY FILLETS IN SAUCE

Put the fish fillets in a pan, pour in 1 litre/1³/₄ pints water, add the onion, carrot, parsley and vinegar and season with salt and pepper. Bring just to the boil, then lower the heat and poach for 10 minutes. Mix together the ketchup and brandy in a bowl and stir into the mayonnaise. Drain the fish, transfer to a warm serving dish and serve with the sauce.

FILETTI DI SAN PIETRO IN SALSA

Serves 4

800 g/1³/₄ lb John Dory fillets

1 onion

1 carrot, sliced

1 fresh flat-leaf parsley sprig

1 tablespoon white wine vinegar

1 tablespoon brandy

4 tablespoons tomato ketchup

1 quantity Mayonnaise (see page 65)

salt and pepper

JOHN DORY FILLETS IN BÉCHAMEL SAUCE

FILETTI DI SAN PIETRO
IN SALSA BESCIAMELLA

Serves 4

1 tablespoon olive oil

25 g/1 oz butter

1 shallot, chopped

1 celery stick, chopped • 1 carrot, chopped

4 John Dory fillets

5 tablespoons dry white wine

25 g/1 oz dried mushrooms,
soaked in warm water for 30 minutes and drained

1 egg yolk

250 ml/8 fl oz Béchamel Sauce (see page 50)

1 fresh flat-leaf parsley sprig, chopped

salt and pepper

Heat the olive oil and butter in a flameproof casserole, add the shallot, celery and carrot and cook over a low heat, stirring occasionally, for 5 minutes. Add the fish to the pan and cook until lightly browned on both sides. Pour in the wine, season with salt, add the mushrooms and cook for 15 minutes. Meanwhile, preheat the oven to 180°C/350°F/Gas Mark 4. Beat the egg yolk into the béchamel sauce, stir in the parsley and season with pepper. Pour the sauce over the fish, transfer to the oven and bake for about 15 minutes.

BAKED JOHN DORY ROULADES

INVOLTINI DI SAN PIETRO AL FORNO

Serves 4

1 tablespoon olive oil, plus extra for brushing

2 salted anchovies, heads removed,
cleaned and filleted (see page 596),
soaked in cold water for 10 minutes and drained

2 tablespoons breadcrumbs

1 fresh flat-leaf parsley sprig, chopped

1 garlic clove, chopped • 50 g/2 oz pine nuts

50 g/2 oz Parmesan cheese, freshly grated

600 g/1 lb 5 oz John Dory fillets

1 fresh thyme sprig, chopped

1 fresh rosemary sprig, chopped

juice of 1 lemon, strained • salt and pepper

Preheat the oven to 180°C/350°F/Gas Mark 4. Brush an oven-proof dish with oil. Chop the anchovy fillets. Heat the olive oil in a pan, add the anchovies and cook, mashing with a wooden spoon until they have almost disintegrated. Add the breadcrumbs, parsley, garlic, pine nuts and Parmesan, season with salt and pepper and mix well, adding a drop of olive oil if the mixture seems too dry. Season the fillets with salt and pepper, divide the anchovy mixture among them and roll up. Secure with cocktail sticks and place in the prepared dish, then sprinkle with the thyme, rosemary and lemon juice and bake for about 15 minutes.

JOHN DORY WITH MANGETOUTS

SAN PIETRO CON TACCOLE

Serves 4

100 g/3½ oz butter

500 g/1 lb 2 oz mangetouts, trimmed

1.5-kg/3¼-lb John Dory, filleted

plain flour, for dusting

salt and pepper

fresh fennel fronds, to garnish

Melt half the butter in a pan, add the mangetouts and cook over a low heat, stirring occasionally, for about 5 minutes, then season with salt and pepper to taste. Add 150 ml/¼ pint water, cover and simmer for 30 minutes. Lightly dust the fish with flour, shaking off the excess. Melt the remaining butter in a frying pan, add the fish and cook over a medium heat until golden brown all over and cooked through. Drain the mangetouts and transfer them and the fish fillets to a warm serving dish and garnish with fennel fronds.

SARDINES

Sardines and pilchards are inexpensive, tasty and nutritious, which explains why these fish – common in Italian seas – are so popular. Pilchards are simply adult sardines and in Britain they are now being rebranded as Cornish sardines to lose their association with the canned product. They must be scaled and cleaned before cooking and, in some cases, you will need to cut off their heads and remove the bones. To do this, open them out, place skin side up and press along the backbones with your thumb. Turn them over, cut through the ends of their bones and remove. Rinse well and pat dry with kitchen paper.

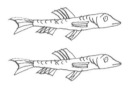

SARDINE ROLLS

Preheat the oven to 180°C/350°F/Gas Mark 4. Brush an oven-proof dish with oil. Season the sardines with salt and pepper, wrap each in a slice of pancetta and secure with a cocktail stick. Place the rolls in the prepared dish, add the bay leaves and thyme and pour in the lemon juice and olive oil. Bake for about 15 minutes.

INVOLTINI DI SARDINE

Serves 4

1–2 tablespoons olive oil, plus extra for brushing

800 g/1³/₄ lb sardines, scaled, cleaned and boned

120 g/4 oz smoked pancetta, thinly sliced

2 bay leaves

1 fresh thyme sprig

juice of 1 lemon, strained

salt and pepper

GRILLED SARDINES

Preheat the grill. Brush the sardines with olive oil. Place them, still opened out, on the grill rack and grill for 4–5 minutes. Mix together the olive oil, lemon juice, chilli, garlic and Worcestershire sauce in a bowl and season with salt and pepper. Serve the sardines with the sauce.

SARDINE ALLA GRIGLIA

Serves 4

800 g/1³/₄ lb sardines, scaled, cleaned and boned

5 tablespoons olive oil, plus extra for brushing

juice of 1 lemon, strained

¹/₂ red chilli , seeded and chopped

¹/₂ garlic clove, chopped

1 teaspoon Worcestershire sauce

salt and pepper

SARDINES MARINARA

SARDINE ALLA MARINARA

Serves 4

olive oil, for brushing and drizzling

800 g/1¾ lb sardines, scaled, cleaned and boned

3 fresh rosemary sprigs, chopped

1 garlic clove, chopped

pinch of dried oregano

1 tablespoon white wine vinegar

salt

Lightly brush a heavy-based pan with olive oil. Make two layers of the sardines in the pan with the rosemary and garlic between them. Sprinkle with the oregano, season with salt and drizzle generously with olive oil. Cook over a medium-low heat for 15 minutes. Sprinkle with the vinegar and cook until the flesh flakes easily. Serve the sardines cold.

SARDINES WITH SHALLOTS

SARDINE ALLO SCALOGNO

Serves 4

plain flour, for dusting

1 egg

175 ml/6 fl oz olive oil

800 g/1¾ lb sardines, scaled, cleaned and boned

4 shallots, finely chopped

1 fresh flat-leaf parsley sprig, finely chopped

5 tablespoons white wine vinegar

salt and pepper

Spread out the flour in a shallow dish and lightly beat the egg in another shallow dish. Heat the oil in a large frying pan. Dip the sardines first in the flour, then in the egg and fry for 5 minutes or longer, depending on their size. Mix together the shallots, parsley and vinegar in a bowl and season with salt and pepper. Remove the sardines with a slotted spoon and drain on kitchen paper. Place them on a warm serving dish and serve with the shallot sauce.

SARDINES IN BREADCRUMBS

SARDINE IMPANATE

Serves 4

50 g/2 oz plain flour

1 egg

80 g/3 oz breadcrumbs

vegetable oil, for deep-frying

800 g/1¾ lb sardines, scaled, cleaned and boned

salt

lemon wedges, to serve

Spread out the flour in a shallow dish, lightly beat the egg with a pinch of salt in another shallow dish and spread out the breadcrumbs in a third. Heat the oil for deep-frying. Dip the sardines first in the flour, then in the egg and, finally, in the breadcrumbs. Fry in the hot oil for about 7 minutes, turning once (see page 593). Remove from the pan and drain on kitchen paper. Serve with lemon wedges.

SARDINES BELLAVISTA

SARDINE IN BELLAVISTA

Serves 4

25 g/2 oz butter

2 tablespoons olive oil, plus extra for brushing

1 onion, chopped

250 g/9 oz porcini, chopped

1 fresh flat-leaf parsley sprig, chopped

2 tablespoons tomato purée

600 g/1 lb 5 oz sardines, boned, scaled and cleaned

2 yellow peppers

10 canned anchovy fillets in oil, drained

– salt and pepper

Heat the butter and oil in a pan, add the onion and cook over a low heat, stirring occasionally, for 5 minutes. Add the porcini and cook, stirring occasionally, until all the liquid they give off has evaporated. Season with salt and pepper, stir in the parsley and tomato purée and cook until thickened. Meanwhile, preheat the oven to 180°C/350°F/Gas Mark 4 and preheat the grill. Brush an ovenproof dish with oil. Place the sardines, still opened out, in the prepared dish, spoon the porcini sauce over them and bake for 20 minutes. Meanwhile, grill the peppers, peel, seed and cut into strips. Transfer the sardines to a warm serving dish and surround with a ring of alternating anchovy fillets and pepper strips.

STUFFED SARDINES

SARDINE RIPIENE

Serves 4

½ bunch of fresh flat-leaf parsley

1 fresh bergamot sprig

1 garlic clove

3 eggs

2 tablespoons breadcrumbs

1 tablespoon Parmesan cheese, freshly grated

800 g/1¾ lb sardines, scaled, cleaned and boned

plain flour, for dusting

5 tablespoons olive oil

salt and pepper

Chop the parsley, bergamot and garlic together, place in a bowl, add the eggs and mix well. Add the breadcrumbs and Parmesan, season with salt and pepper and mix again. Spread the mixture on the inside of the opened-out sardines, fold them back over, dust lightly with flour and shake off any excess. Heat the oil in a frying pan, add the sardines and cook for 5–6 minutes, turning once. Remove with a slotted spoon, drain on kitchen paper, season with salt and serve.

SUCCULENT SARDINES

SARDINE SAPORITE

Serves 4

800 g/1¾ lb sardines, scaled, cleaned and boned

plain flour, for dusting

3 tablespoons olive oil

1 garlic clove

1 fresh rosemary sprig

1 bay leaf

175 ml/6 fl oz white wine

salt and pepper

Preheat the oven to 180°C/350°F/Gas Mark 4. Dust the sardines with flour. Heat the olive oil in a pan with the garlic, rosemary and bay leaf, add the sardines and cook for a few minutes until lightly browned on both sides. Season with salt and pepper and transfer the fish to an ovenproof dish. Remove and discard the herbs and garlic and pour the wine into the pan. Mix well and cook over a high heat until reduced by half. Pour the sauce over the sardines and bake for about 20 minutes.

SCORPION FISH

There are several types of scorpion fish, which are also known by their French name rascasse. Brown scorpion fish, which are actually grey, have a much better flavour than the much more common red variety. All are proverbially ugly and have thickset bodies and strong spines on their backs that can cause injury. However, their firm, white flesh is tasty and can be prepared in a number of ways, although traditionally it is mainly used in soups and stews. Brown scorpion fish are fairly small – 20–30 cm/8–12 inches long – and a lot is wasted because of their big heads. Red scorpion fish are about 50 cm/20 inches long.

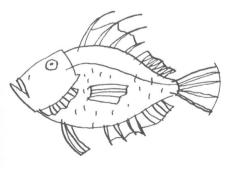

CAPPON MAGRO

Serves 12

6–8 wholewheat crackers

2 garlic cloves

2–3 tablespoons white wine vinegar

175 ml/6 fl oz olive oil, plus extra for drizzling

1.5 kg/3¼ lb scorpion fish, spines trimmed, cleaned

1 large live spiny lobster

juice of 1 lemon, strained

200 g/7 oz salted anchovies, heads removed, cleaned and filleted (see page 596), soaked in cold water for 10 minutes and drained

3 egg yolks

50 g/2 oz capers, drained and rinsed

200 g/7 oz green olives, stoned

1 fresh flat-leaf parsley sprig, coarsely chopped

50 g/2 oz pine nuts

2 bread rolls, crusts removed

12 oysters

150 g/5 oz tuna mosciame (salted and dried tuna fillet)

500 g/1 lb 2 oz French beans, cooked (see page 468)

400 g/14 oz potatoes, cooked (see page 518) and sliced

300 g/11 oz scorzonera, cooked (see page 561) and sliced

5 globe artichokes, cut into wedges and cooked (see page 415)

4 carrots, sliced and cooked (see page 427)

1 cauliflower, cut into florets and cooked (see page 436)

1 beetroot, cooked (see page 405) and sliced

1 celery heart, cooked (see page 563) and sliced

120 g/4 oz small mushrooms in oil, drained

10 large cooked prawns, peeled and deveined

6 eggs, hard-boiled, shelled and sliced

salt and pepper

GENOESE SALAD

Rub the crackers with one of the garlic cloves, place in a bowl and add water to cover and 1 tablespoon of the vinegar, then drain and place on the base of a large serving dish. Drizzle with olive oil, season with salt and pepper and set aside. Poach the scorpion fish in gently simmering water for 20–30 minutes until the flesh flakes easily. Drain, then remove and discard the skin and bones. Cut the flesh into chunks, place in a dish, drizzle with olive oil and about half the lemon juice, season with salt and leave to cool completely. Plunge the lobster into a pan of boiling water, cover and cook for 10–15 minutes, depending on the size. Drain and remove the meat (see page 689), place in a dish, drizzle with olive oil and the remaining lemon juice, season with salt and leave to cool completely. Meanwhile, chop the anchovy fillets. Put the anchovies, egg yolks, capers, half the olives, the parsley, pine nuts, the remaining garlic and the rolls in a food processor and process to a purée. Scrape into a bowl and stir in the olive oil and remaining vinegar. Open the oysters (see page 716). Place a layer of mosciame on top of the crackers, spoon a little anchovy sauce on top and make alternating layers of the cooked vegetables, most of the anchovy sauce, fish and lobster, piling them up in a pyramid, until all the ingredients are used. Thread the remaining olives, the mushrooms and prawns alternately on to four or five long wooden skewers and insert them into the top of the pyramid. Garnish with the egg slices, the oysters, any remaining prawns and any other leftover ingredients. Sprinkle with the remaining sauce and keep in a cool place until just before serving.

SCORPION FISH WITH MUSHROOMS

Preheat the oven to 180°C/350°F/Gas Mark 4. Grease an oven-proof dish with butter. Spread out the mushrooms in the dish, season the fish with salt and pepper and place it on top of them. Dot with the butter, top with the lemon slices and pour in the wine. Bake, basting frequently, for 20–30 minutes.

SCORFANO AI FUNGHI

Serves 4

50 g/2 oz butter, plus extra for greasing

150 g/5 oz mushrooms, thinly sliced

800 g/1³/₄ lb scorpion fish,

spines trimmed, cleaned

3 lemon slices

175 ml/6 fl oz dry white wine

salt and pepper

SCORPION FISH WITH THYME

Preheat the oven to 180°C/350°F/Gas Mark 4. Season the cavities of the fish with salt and pepper and fill with some of the thyme. Sprinkle the remainder of the thyme in an ovenproof dish, add the fish and season with salt and pepper. Mix together the olive oil and lemon juice and pour the mixture over the fish. Bake, basting frequently, for 20–30 minutes. Meanwhile, chop the anchovy fillets. Pass the anchovies through a sieve into a bowl and combine with the butter. Serve the fish with the anchovy butter.

SCORFANO AL TIMO

Serves 4

4 scorpion fish, spines trimmed, cleaned

¹/₂ bunch of fresh thyme, chopped

4 tablespoons olive oil

juice of 1 lemon, strained

100 g/3¹/₂ oz salted anchovies, heads removed,

cleaned and filleted (see page 596),

soaked in cold water for 10 minutes and drained

100 g/3¹/₂ oz butter, softened

salt and pepper

SCORPION FISH IN WHITE WINE AND SAFFRON

Put the fish in a flameproof casserole with the olive oil and sprinkle the tomatoes on top of them. Season with salt and pepper, add the garlic and saffron and pour in the wine. Bring to the boil, cover and simmer over a medium heat for 15–20 minutes. Remove from the heat and leave the fish to cool in the cooking liquid. Serve cold with the white wine sauce.

SCORFANO AL VINO BIANCO E ZAFFERANO

Serves 4

2 x 300-g/11-oz scorpion fish,

spines trimmed, cleaned

3 tablespoons olive oil

400 g/14 oz tomatoes, peeled, seeded and diced

1 garlic clove

pinch of saffron threads

500 ml/18 fl oz dry white wine

salt and pepper

MACKEREL

Like sardines and pilchards, mackerel belong to what is known in Italy as the 'blue-scale' fish family. They vary in length from 25–45 cm/10–18 inches. They are plentiful in the Mediterranean (as are the blue mackeral in Australian and New Zealand waters) and their greyish flesh is not very highly prized. However, it is firm and tasty with a distinctive flavour. Mackerel are excellent barbecued or cooked in oil. If they are freshly caught and weigh more than 500 g/1 lb 2 oz, it is best to store them in the refrigerator for a day before cooking.

MACKEREL WITH FRENCH BEANS

SGOMBRI AI FAGIOLINI

Serves 4

5 tablespoons olive oil
1 onion, sliced
1 carrot, chopped
1 fresh flat-leaf parsley sprig, chopped
1 fresh thyme sprig, chopped
150 g/5 oz French beans, trimmed
1 tomato, peeled seeded and chopped
2 tablespoons capers, drained and rinsed
4 mackerel, cleaned
plain flour, for dusting
salt and pepper

Heat 2 tablespoons of the olive oil in a pan, add the onion, carrot, parsley and thyme and cook over a low heat, stirring occasionally, for 5 minutes. Add the beans and cook, stirring frequently, for 15 minutes. Add the tomato and capers, season with salt and pepper and cook for a further 5 minutes. Dust the mackerel with flour, shaking off the excess. Heat the remaining olive oil in a frying pan, add the mackerel and cook until golden brown and the flesh flakes easily with a fork. Remove with a slotted spoon, add to the pan of vegetables and cook for a further 5 minutes. Taste and adjust the seasoning if necessary, then serve.

MACKEREL WITH SAGE BUTTER

SGOMBRI AL BURRO

Serves 4

4 mackerel, cleaned
plain flour, for dusting
25 g/1 oz butter
1 quantity Sage Butter (see page 87)
juice of ½ lemon, strained
salt

Make several diagonal slashes on each side of the mackerel, then dust lightly with flour, shaking off the excess. Melt the butter in a frying pan, add the fish and cook over a medium heat for about 5 minutes on each side. Season with salt and transfer to a warm serving dish. Put a little of the sage butter on each fish and sprinkle with the lemon juice.

SGOMBRI ALLA GRECA

Serves 4

2 tablespoons olive oil, plus extra
for brushing and drizzling
2 small onions, chopped
4 mackerel, cleaned
2 fresh sage leaves
1 tablespoon fresh flat-leaf parsley, chopped
1 fresh thyme sprig • juice of 1 lemon, strained
100 g/3¹/₂ oz black olives, stoned
salt and pepper

GREEK MACKEREL

Preheat the oven to 180°C/350°F/Gas Mark 4. Brush an oven-proof dish with oil. Heat the oil in a small frying pan, add the onions and cook over a low heat, stirring occasionally, for 5 minutes. Place the mackerel in the prepared dish, sprinkle the onions on top, drizzle with olive oil and add the sage, parsley and thyme. Sprinkle with the lemon juice, season with salt and pepper, add the olives and cover the dish with foil. Bake for 30 minutes.

SGOMBRI AL RIBES

Serves 4

350 g/12 oz currants
4 mackerel, cleaned
25 g/1 oz butter
1 onion, chopped
1 garlic clove
175 ml/6 fl oz dry white wine
1 teaspoon sugar
salt and pepper

MACKEREL WITH CURRANTS

Preheat the oven to 180°C/350°F/Gas Mark 4. Place the currants in a bowl, add warm water to cover and leave to soak. Make several diagonal slashes in each side of the fish and place in an ovenproof dish. Melt the butter in a pan, add the onion and garlic and cook over a low heat, stirring occasionally, for about 10 minutes. Drain the currants, reserving the soaking liquid. Set about 80 g/3 oz aside and squeeze the remainder over the bowl of soaking liquid, then discard. Pour the wine and soaking liquid into the pan, add the sugar and season with salt and pepper. Heat through and pour the mixture over the fish. Bake for about 10 minutes. Add the reserved currants and cook the fish for a further 10 minutes. Serve with the sauce.

TERRINA DI SGOMBRI AL VINO BIANCO

Serves 4

1 carrot, sliced
1 onion, sliced
¹/₂ lemon, sliced
1 fresh flat-leaf parsley sprig, chopped
1 fresh thyme sprig, chopped
375 ml/13 fl oz white wine
100 ml/3¹/₂ fl oz white wine vinegar
6 black peppercorns
4 mackerel, cleaned
salt

MACKEREL AND WHITE WINE TERRINE

Put the carrot, onion, lemon, parsley, thyme, wine, vinegar, peppercorns and a pinch of salt in a pan and bring to the boil. Simmer for a few minutes, then remove from the heat and leave to stand for 1 hour. Make several diagonal slashes in both sides of the mackerel. Bring the wine mixture back to the boil, lower the heat, add the fish and simmer for 5 minutes. Remove the slices of lemon with tongs and place in a bowl. Remove the mackerel with a slotted spoon and place on top. Boil the cooking juices over a high heat for 5 minutes until reduced, then remove and discard the herbs. Pour the mixture into a food processor and process to a purée. Pour the sauce over the fish, leave to cool and then chill in the refrigerator for about 1 hour.

SOLE

Italian sole are about 20 cm/8 inches long, whereas sole found in northern seas can reach 40–45 cm/16–18 inches. Sole have firm flesh with a delicate flavour and are easy to digest. They are flat fish that live on the seabed. Their bodies are surrounded by a 'frill', which should be cut off. Their upper sides have a characteristic dark skin, which should be removed by making a cut near the tail and tearing it off with one sharp tug. The skin on their undersides is pale and covered with extremely small scales. You can either scale the undersides or remove the skin in the same way as before. If sole are prepared whole, their spines must be snapped in several places so they remain flat during cooking. If you need fillets, on the other hand, it is best to have them cut by the fishmonger.

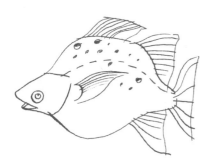

ALMOND–COATED SOLE FILLETS

Lightly dust the fish with flour. Beat the eggs with a little salt and pepper in a shallow dish. Place the almonds in another shallow dish. Melt the butter in a frying pan. Dip the sole fillets first in the egg and then in the almonds to coat. Add to the pan and cook for a few minutes on each side. Transfer to a warm serving dish and garnish with parsley sprigs.

FILETTI DI SOGLIOLE ALLE MANDORLE

Serves 4

8 sole fillets, skinned

plain flour, for dusting

2 eggs

120 g/4 oz almonds, coarsely chopped

80 g/3 oz butter

salt and pepper

fresh flat-leaf parsley sprigs, to garnish

SOLE SALAD

Put the fillets in a dish, pour the lemon juice over them and cover with cling film. Chill in the refrigerator for 2 hours. Put the peppers, carrot, cucumber and tomatoes in a salad bowl. Whisk together the olive oil, rosemary and vinegar in a bowl, season with salt and pepper and pour the dressing over the salad. Drain the fish and dice, then add to the salad and toss. Season lightly with salt and serve.

FILETTI DI SOGLIOLE IN INSALATA
Serves 4
8 large sole fillets, skinned
juice of 2 lemons, strained
2 green peppers, halved, seeded and diced
1 yellow pepper, halved, seeded and diced
1 carrot, thinly sliced
1 cucumber, thinly sliced
2 tomatoes, peeled, seeded and diced
4–5 tablespoons olive oil
1 tablespoon fresh rosemary needles, chopped
1 tablespoon white wine vinegar
salt and pepper

SOLE AND PRAWN ROULADES

Melt 25 g/1 oz of the butter in a pan, add the prawns and cook, stirring occasionally, for 2 minutes. Season with salt and pepper and remove from the pan with a slotted spoon. Leave to cool slightly, then place one of the prawns on each sole fillet, roll up and secure with a cocktail stick. Melt the remaining butter in a pan, add the roulades and cook for about 10 minutes, until light golden brown all over. Season lightly with salt, add the wine and cook until it has evaporated. Mix together the chives, cream and lemon juice in a bowl. Place the roulades on a warm serving dish and spoon the sauce over them.

INVOLTINI DI SOGLIOLE CON I GAMBERI
Serves 4
80 g/3 oz butter
8 raw Mediterranean
or tiger prawns, peeled and deveined
8 sole fillets, skinned
4 tablespoons dry white wine
1/2 bunch of fresh chives, chopped
100 ml/3 1/2 fl oz double cream
juice of 1/2 lemon, strained
salt and pepper

SOLE WITH MUSHROOMS

Heat 2 tablespoons of the olive oil in a frying pan, add the porcini and cook over a medium-low heat, stirring occasionally. Meanwhile, place the fish in a saucepan, pour in the wine and brandy, add the garlic and rosemary and season with salt and pepper to taste. Bring just to the boil, then lower the heat and simmer for 15 minutes. Transfer the fish to the frying pan and keep warm. Strain the cooking juices into a clean pan, bring to the boil over a high heat and cook until reduced. Lower the heat, add the egg yolks, the remaining olive oil and the lemon juice and mix quickly. As soon as the egg sets, remove the pan from the heat. Place the fish on a warm serving dish, garnish with the porcini and spoon the sauce over them.

SOGLIOLE AI FUNGHI
Serves 4
6 tablespoons olive oil
200 g/7 oz porcini, thinly sliced
8 sole fillets, skinned
100 ml/3 1/2 fl oz dry white wine
50 ml/2 fl oz brandy
1 garlic clove
1 fresh rosemary sprig
2 egg yolks
juice of 1/2 lemon, strained
salt and pepper

GRILLED SOLE

SOGLIOLE ALLA GRIGLIA

Serves 4

4 sole, cleaned, trimmed and skinned

olive oil, for brushing

salt and pepper

lemon wedges, to serve

Preheat the grill. Season the fish with salt and pepper and brush with olive oil. Place the fish on the grill rack and cook under the grill, brushing frequently with olive oil, for 7–8 minutes on each side. Transfer to a warm serving dish and serve with lemon wedges.

SOLE IN CIDER

SOGLIOLE AL SIDRO

Serves 4

25 g/1 oz butter

1 onion, thinly sliced

1 garlic clove

80 g/3 oz smoked pancetta, cubed

1 tablespoon plain flour

350 ml/12 fl oz cider

1 bay leaf

8 sole fillets, skinned

1 egg yolk, lightly beaten

3 tablespoons double cream

salt and pepper

fried bread, to serve

Melt the butter in a pan, add the onion, garlic and pancetta and cook over a low heat, stirring occasionally, for 5 minutes. Sprinkle with the flour and cook, stirring, for a few minutes more. Pour in the cider, season with salt and pepper, add the bay leaf, increase the heat to medium and cook for 15 minutes until reduced. Lower the heat, place the sole fillets in the pan and simmer gently for 7–8 minutes. Transfer the sole to a warm serving dish. Remove and discard the garlic and bay leaf. Stir the egg yolk and cream into the pan juices, heat through for a few minutes, then pour the sauce over the fish. Serve with thick slices of bread fried in butter.

SOLE WITH THYME

SOGLIOLE AL TIMO

Serves 4

4 sole, cleaned, trimmed and skinned

120–150 ml/4–5 fl oz olive oil, plus extra for drizzling

juice of ½ lemon, strained

3 tablespoons fresh thyme leaves

salt and white pepper

This is a very easy recipe. Place the fish in a pan, add water to cover and a pinch of salt and bring just to the boil, then lower the heat and poach until tender. Drain and place on a serving dish. Drizzle with olive oil and sprinkle with the lemon juice. Put the thyme leaves, a pinch of salt and a pinch of pepper in a bowl and gradually stir in the olive oil. Spoon the thyme sauce over the fish and keep in a cool place until ready to serve.

SOLE IN MELTED BUTTER

Put the sole in a dish, add the milk and leave to soak for at least 15 minutes, then drain, pat dry with kitchen paper and dust lightly with flour. Melt 50 g/2 oz of the butter in a frying pan, add the fish and cook over a medium-low heat for about 5 minutes on each side until golden brown and tender. Season with salt and transfer to a serving dish. Melt the remaining butter in a double boiler or in a heatproof bowl set over a pan of barely simmering water and continue to heat until it starts to froth, then pour it over the sole. Serve immediately.

SOGLIOLE CON BURRO FUSO
Serves 4
4 sole, cleaned, trimmed and skinned
300 ml/½ pint milk
plain flour, for dusting
150 g/5 oz butter
salt

SOLE IN PIQUANT SAUCE

Chop the anchovy fillets. Lightly dust the sole with flour. Melt half the butter in a frying pan, add the sole and cook until browned on both sides. Sprinkle with the lemon juice, transfer to a serving dish and keep warm. Melt the remaining butter in a small saucepan, add the anchovies and capers and cook over a medium heat, then pour the sauce over the fish. Sprinkle with the parsley and serve.

SOGLIOLE IN SALSA PICCANTE
Serves 4
2 salted anchovies, heads removed, cleaned and filleted (see page 596), soaked in cold water for 10 minutes and drained
4 sole, cleaned, trimmed and skinned
plain flour, for dusting
80 g/3 oz butter
juice of 2 lemons, strained
2 tablespoons capers, drained and rinsed
2 tablespoons chopped fresh flat-leaf parsley

STURGEON

Sturgeon are sea fish that swim up rivers to spawn in early spring. The common sturgeon can reach 3 metres/10 feet in length. Their roe is used to make caviar and their swim bladders to make gelatine. Their white, firm and tasty flesh is highly prized and is excellent poached, grilled or fried. Sturgeon may be bought as fresh or frozen steaks, dried, smoked or canned. They are not widely available outside Italy and are very expensive. Over-fishing and the destruction of their habitat has severely reduced their numbers. However, white sturgeon have been farmed in Italy for several years. You could substitute a firm white-fleshed fish, such as halibut, for sturgeon in these recipes.

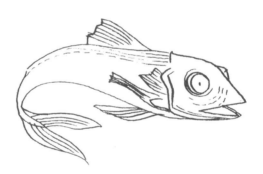

STURGEON IN SWEET-AND-SOUR SAUCE

SCALOPPE DI STORIONE AGRODOLCI

Serves 4

200 ml/7 fl oz milk
600 g/1 lb 5 oz sturgeon fillet, thinly sliced
plain flour, for dusting
25 g/1 oz butter
2 tablespoons olive oil
salt and pepper

For the sauce
80 g/3 oz butter
1 teaspoon sugar
2.5-cm/1-inch cinnamon stick
1 clove
200 ml/7 fl oz balsamic vinegar
salt

Pour the milk into a dish, season the fish with salt and pepper and add to the milk. Drain and dust with flour. Heat the butter and olive oil in a frying pan, add the fish and cook for 4 minutes on each side until evenly browned. Remove with a slotted spoon, drain on kitchen paper, place on a plate, cover and keep warm. To make the sauce, melt the butter over a very low heat, add the sugar, cinnamon, clove and a pinch of salt and mix well. Pour in the vinegar and cook, stirring frequently, until thickened. Remove and discard the cinnamon and clove. Pour the sauce on to a warm serving dish, place the fish on top and serve.

STURGEON IN ANCHOVY SAUCE

Pour 1 litre/1³/₄ pints water into a saucepan and add the wine, bay leaf and a little salt. Bring to the boil, add the fish and cook for 10 minutes. Drain, reserving about 1 tablespoon of the cooking liquid, place on a serving dish, cover and keep warm. Meanwhile, heat the olive oil in a small saucepan, add the anchovies and cook over a medium heat, mashing with a fork until they have almost disintegrated. Stir in 1–2 teaspoons of the reserved cooking liquid, add the vinegar and mix well. Remove the pan from the heat and stir in the capers. Spoon the sauce over the fish and serve.

SCALOPPE DI STORIONE ALLE ACCIUGHE

Serves 4

200 ml/7 fl oz dry white wine

1 bay leaf

4 thin sturgeon fillet slices

salt

For the sauce

3–4 tablespoons olive oil

6 canned anchovy fillets in oil, drained and chopped

1 tablespoon balsamic vinegar

1 tablespoon capers, drained and rinsed

STURGEON IN BALSAMIC VINEGAR

Mix together the onion, celery and two-thirds of the garlic in a bowl. Place half the mixture in a dish, place the fish on top and sprinkle with the remaining chopped mixture. Season with salt and pepper and sprinkle with the vinegar and wine. Leave to marinate for about 2 hours. Chop the anchovy fillets. Heat the olive oil in a frying pan, add the anchovies and cook, mashing with a wooden spoon until they have almost disintegrated. Stir in the remaining garlic and the parsley, add the fish and cook until golden brown on both sides.

STORIONE ALL'ACETO BALSAMICO

Serves 4

1 onion, chopped

1 celery stick, chopped

1¹/₂ garlic cloves, chopped

4 sturgeon steaks

1 tablespoon balsamic vinegar

4 tablespoons dry white wine

4 salted anchovies, heads removed,

cleaned and filleted (see page 596),

soaked in cold water for 10 minutes and drained

3 tablespoons olive oil

1 fresh flat-leaf parsley sprig, chopped

salt and pepper

GRILLED STURGEON

Put the olive oil, wine, lemon juice, thyme, a rosemary sprig and the parsley in a dish, season with salt and pepper and add the fish, turning to coat. Leave to marinate for 1 hour. Preheat the grill. Drain the fish, reserving the marinade, and make small incisions in the flesh. Insert pieces of garlic and rosemary needles from the remaining sprig into the cuts. Cook under the grill, occasionally brushing with the marinade, for 25 minutes.

STORIONE ALLA GRIGLIA

Serves 4

175 ml/6 fl oz olive oil

5 tablespoons dry white wine

juice of 1 lemon, strained

1 fresh thyme sprig

2 fresh rosemary sprigs

1 fresh flat-leaf parsley sprig

4 sturgeon steaks

1 garlic clove, sliced

salt and pepper

STURGEON WITH ARTICHOKES

STORIONE CON CARCIOFI

Serves 4

4 globe artichokes

6 tablespoons olive oil

2 garlic cloves

1 small fresh bergamot sprig

4 sturgeon steaks

4 tomatoes, halved and seeded

salt and pepper

Cut off the artichoke stems, remove the coarse outer leaves and trim the remainder. Scoop out and discard the chokes, then place the artichokes upright in a small saucepan. Pour in enough water to half-cover them and add half the olive oil, one of the garlic cloves, the bergamot, a pinch of salt and a pinch of pepper. Cover and cook over a medium-low heat for about 40 minutes until the liquid is almost completely absorbed. Preheat the oven to 180°C/350°F/Gas Mark 4. Heat the remaining olive oil in a frying pan and cook the fish for 3–4 minutes on each side. Chop the remaining garlic and sprinkle it over the tomatoes. Place on a baking sheet and bake for 5–6 minutes. Halve the artichokes and arrange in a ring on a warm serving dish, then place the fish in the centre, overlapping the steaks slightly, and put the tomato halves between the artichokes.

STURGEON WITH RED PEPPER SAUCE

STORIONE CON SALSA AI PEPERONI

Serves 4

3 tablespoons olive oil, plus extra for brushing

1 onion, chopped

800 g/1³/₄ lb red peppers, halved, seeded and sliced

800-g/1³/₄-lb sturgeon fillet

1 fresh chervil sprig, chopped

1 fresh tarragon sprig, chopped

1 garlic clove, chopped

1 bay leaf

5 tablespoons dry white wine

salt and pepper

Preheat the oven to 180°C/350°F/Gas Mark 4. Brush an ovenproof dish with oil. Heat the olive oil in a pan, add the onion and cook over a low heat, stirring occasionally, for 5 minutes. Add the peppers, increase the heat to medium, season with salt and pepper, cover and cook for about 30 minutes, adding 2–3 tablespoons hot water during cooking. Meanwhile, put the fish in the prepared dish, brush with olive oil and add the chervil, tarragon, garlic and bay leaf. Season with salt and pepper and bake for about 30 minutes, adding the wine during cooking. When the peppers are tender, transfer them to a food processor and process to a purée. If the sauce seems too runny, reduce it over a high heat. If it seems too thick, add a little warm water. Pour the sauce over the base of a warm serving dish and place the fish on top.

TUNA

Tuna-fishing in the Mediterranean is highly profitable as the fish are greatly appreciated and demand is high. Tuna easily reach 2.5 metres/8¹/₄ feet in length, but much bigger ones, up to 4.5 metres/14³/₄ feet long and weighing upwards of 600 kg/1,322 lb, have also been caught. Canned tuna often appears on Italian tables, but fresh tuna is seen rather less frequently, as it is quite expensive. Tuna steaks can be cooked like meat – stewed, braised or roasted.

TUNA IN VINEGAR

Heat the olive oil in a large, shallow pan, add the garlic and cook for a few minutes, then add the tuna and 2 tablespoons water. Season with salt and pepper to taste and sprinkle with the parsley. Cover and cook over a low heat for about 20 minutes. Add the vinegar and cook until it has evaporated, then serve.

TONNO ALL'ACETO

Serves 4

3 tablespoons olive oil

1 garlic clove, sliced

4 tuna steaks

1 fresh flat-leaf parsley sprig, chopped

2 tablespoons white wine vinegar

salt and pepper

TUNA WITH CELERY

TONNO AL SEDANO

Serves 4

2 tablespoons olive oil

25 g/1 oz butter

900 g/2 lb tuna steaks, cut into cubes

4 tomatoes, peeled, seeded and diced

4 fresh basil leaves, chopped

1 head of celery, chopped

pinch of chilli powder

50 g/2 oz black olives, stoned

salt and pepper

Heat the olive oil and butter in a pan, add the tuna and cook, stirring frequently, until lightly browned all over. Add the tomatoes, basil, celery and chilli powder and season with salt and pepper. Cover and cook over a medium heat for 30 minutes. Stir in the olives, heat through briefly and serve.

TUNA AND BEAN SALAD

TONNO IN INSALATA CON FAGIOLINI

Serves 4

1 kg/2¼ lb fresh white beans, shelled

400-g/14-oz tuna steak

olive oil, for brushing and drizzling

1 garlic clove, halved

10 fresh basil leaves, chopped

40 g/1½ oz pine nuts

4 leeks, white parts only, thinly sliced

1 tomato, seeded and sliced

1 head of escarole

salt and pepper

Cook the beans in a pan of boiling water for 40–60 minutes until tender, then drain. Preheat the grill. Brush the tuna generously with olive oil, place on the hot grill rack and cook, brushing with more oil occasionally, for 10 minutes on each side. Cut the cooked fish into cubes. Rub the garlic around the inside of a salad bowl and put the basil and pine nuts in the bowl. Season with salt and pepper, drizzle with olive oil and mix well. Add the beans, leeks, tomato, escarole and fish and serve while the tuna is still warm.

SLOW-COOKED TUNA

TONNO STUFATO

Serves 4

2 tablespoons olive oil

4 tuna steaks, halved

1 shallot, chopped

200 g/7 oz carrots, chopped

200 g/7 oz turnips, chopped

200 g/7 oz French beans, halved

1 fresh thyme sprig

1 fresh rosemary sprig

100 ml/3½ fl oz white wine

salt and pepper

Heat the olive oil in a large shallow pan, add the tuna and cook over a high heat until browned on both sides. Remove the tuna from the pan, skim off any excess fat, then add the shallot and cook, stirring occasionally, for about 5 minutes. Add the carrots, turnips, beans, thyme and rosemary, season with salt and pepper and cook over a medium heat, stirring occasionally, for about 10 minutes. Place the tuna on top of the vegetables, add the wine and 150 ml/¼ pint warm water, lower the heat, cover and simmer for about 30 minutes. Remove and discard the herbs and transfer the tuna and vegetables to a warm serving dish.

RED MULLET

Red mullet are highly prized fish with an unmistakable colour, especially the Mullus surmuletus, which is strangely sometimes called golden mullet. It is also the larger type of mullet and can exceed 300 g/11 oz. Its firm flesh is very tasty, but unfortunately very bony. Small, very fragile red mullet are best simply fried, but golden mullet can be cooked in a variety of ways – they are very good roasted or baked in a parcel, for example. In Australia, red mullet is often called goatfish. Mullet are also an important ingredient in fish soups. During cooking, they should be touched as little as possible and only very gently, since their tender flesh breaks up easily.

RED MULLET WITH FENNEL

Preheat the oven to 180°C/350°F/Gas Mark 4. Sprinkle the fennel over the base of an ovenproof dish. Season the cavities of the fish with salt and pepper, place them on top of the fennel and pour in the lemon juice, wine and 4 tablespoons of the olive oil. Bake, basting occasionally, for about 30 minutes. Meanwhile, mix together the shallot, chilli, mustard, egg yolk and a pinch of salt in a bowl, then gradually whisk in the remaining olive oil. Serve the red mullet straight from the dish with the sauce handed separately.

TRIGLIE AL FINOCCHIO

Serves 4

2 fresh fennel sprigs, chopped

1 kg/2¼ lb red mullet, scaled and cleaned

juice of 2 lemons, strained

175 ml/6 fl oz dry white wine

200 ml/7 fl oz olive oil

1 shallot, chopped

1 dried chilli, crushed

1 tablespoon herb mustard

1 hard-boiled egg yolk, mashed

salt and pepper

TRIGLIE ALLA LIVORNESE

Serves 4

4 tablespoons olive oil

1 fresh flat-leaf parsley sprig,
chopped, plus extra for for sprinkling

$^1/_2$ garlic clove, chopped

200 ml/7 fl oz passata

1 kg/2$^1/_4$ lb red mullet, scaled and cleaned

salt and pepper

RED MULLET
LIVORNO–STYLE

Heat the olive oil in a large frying pan, add the parsley and garlic and cook over a low heat, stirring frequently, for a few minutes. Add the passata, season with salt and pepper and simmer for 5 minutes. Place the fish in the sauce and simmer gently, shaking the pan occasionally, for 20 minutes. Do not turn the fish over, to avoid breaking them. Sprinkle with parsley and serve.

TRIGLIE ALLE ERBE AROMATICHE

Serves 4

3 tablespoons olive oil

1 kg/2$^1/_4$ lb red mullet, filleted

juice of 1 lemon, strained

2 tablespoons double cream

1 fresh flat-leaf parsley sprig, chopped

1 fresh thyme sprig, chopped

1 fresh chervil sprig, chopped

salt and pepper

RED MULLET
WITH HERBS

Heat the olive oil in a frying pan, add the fish, skin side down, and cook for 3–4 minutes, then carefully turn them over and cook for 1 minute more. Remove from the pan with a slotted spoon and keep warm. Skim off the olive oil from the pan juices, stir in the lemon juice and bring to simmering point. Stir in the cream and cook until thickened. Season with salt and pepper and stir in the herbs. Place the fish on a warm serving dish, spoon the hot sauce over them.

TRIGLIE CON FAGIOLI

Serves 4

200 g/7 oz dried cannellini beans,
soaked overnight in cold water and drained

1 onion

2 fresh sage leaves

1 fresh tarragon sprig

1 fresh chervil sprig

1 kg/2$^1/_4$ lb red mullet, scaled and cleaned

plain flour, for dusting

6 tablespoons olive oil

1 tablespoon white wine vinegar

1 shallot, finely chopped

salt and pepper

RED MULLET
WITH BEANS

Put the beans in a saucepan, add water to cover, and the onion, sage, tarragon and chervil and bring to the boil, then lower the heat and simmer for 1–2 hours until tender. Drain the beans and discard the onion and herbs. Lightly dust the fish with flour. Heat half the olive oil in a frying pan, add the fish and cook for about 4 minutes on each side. Beat together the remaining olive oil and the vinegar in a bowl, stir in the shallot and season with salt and pepper. Pour the dressing over the beans and mix gently. Arrange the fish on a warm serving dish and surround with the beans.

EEL

In Italy eels are found in Lake Bolsena and the Comacchio marshes, where they are famously bred and processed. But eel travel enormous distances during migration and can be found all the world over. They look like snakes and are often still slithering when they reach the fishmonger as they are very lively. Young, thin eel fry are called cieche in Italian, meaning blind. When they mature, after four or five years, some are eaten fresh, and others are salted or – and this is the speciality of Comacchio – smoked. The females, called capitoni in central southern Italy and bisati in Veneto, are larger than the males. They sometimes reach 1 metre/3'/4 feet in length and are highly prized. Eels must be skinned for some recipes and it's best to ask the fishmonger to prepare them for you. Otherwise, use a small, sharp, pointed knife and make a T-shaped cut under the head. Take hold of the two flaps and pull the skin inside out. As eels are slippery, it is advisable to hold them firmly with a tea towel.

FRESHWATER FISH

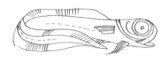

BRETON EEL

Pour the wine and 500 ml/18 fl oz water into a saucepan, add the carrot, onion and thyme, season with salt and pepper and bring to the boil. Lower the heat and simmer for 15 minutes. Add the eels and simmer for 10 minutes, then remove from the heat and leave to cool in the cooking liquid. Heat the olive oil in a pan, add the mushrooms, pancetta and garlic and cook over a low heat, stirring frequently, for about 10 minutes until browned. Stir in the tomato purée and 150 ml/¼ pint of the eel cooking liquid and season with salt and pepper. Simmer for 20 minutes. Arrange the slices of eel on a warm serving dish and spoon the hot sauce over them.

ANGUILLE ALLA BRETONE

Serves 4

175 ml/6 fl oz dry white wine

1 carrot

1 onion

1 fresh thyme sprig

800 g/1¾ lb eels, skinned, cleaned and sliced and cut into 4-cm/1½-inch slices

2 tablespoons olive oil

200 g/7 oz mushrooms, sliced

100 g/3½ oz smoked pancetta, diced

½ garlic clove, chopped

1 tablespoon tomato purée

salt and pepper

671

ROAST EEL

ANGUILLE ARROSTO

Serves 4

1-kg/2¼-lb eels, skinned and cleaned

4 bay leaves

salt

Preheat the oven to 180°C/350°F/Gas Mark 4. Make a cut in the back of the eel, coil it into a casserole, add the bay leaves and sprinkle with salt. Cook in the oven for at least 40 minutes, where it will roast in its own fat. Transfer to a warm serving dish.

EEL WITH SAVOY CABBAGE

ANGUILLE CON LE VERZE

Serves 4

1 small Savoy cabbage, cored and quartered

25 g/1 oz butter

2 tablespoons olive oil

4 shallots, chopped

2 carrots, sliced

100 g/3½ oz smoked pancetta, cubed

5 tablespoons dry white wine

5 tablespoons white wine vinegar

1 bay leaf

800 g/1¾ lb eels, skinned, cleaned and sliced

salt and pepper

Parboil the cabbage in salted, boiling water for 10 minutes, then drain. Heat the butter and olive oil in a saucepan, add the shallots, carrots and pancetta and cook over a low heat, stirring occasionally, for 10 minutes. Add the wine, vinegar and bay leaf and season with salt and pepper. Add the cabbage to the pan, cover and cook for 30 minutes. Add the eels to the pan, re-cover and cook, shaking the pan occasionally, for 20 minutes. Remove and discard the bay leaf and transfer the mixture to a warm serving dish.

EEL IN GREEN SAUCE

ANGUILLE IN SALSA VERDE

Serves 4

25–40 g/1–1½ oz butter

900 g/2 lb eels, skinned, cleaned and sliced

1 fresh flat-leaf parsley sprig, chopped

1 fresh red sorrel sprig, chopped

1 fresh chervil sprig, chopped

1 tablespoon fresh rosemary needles, chopped

1 onion, chopped

175 ml/6 fl oz dry white wine

1 egg yolk, lightly beaten

pinch of potato flour

juice of 1 lemon, strained

salt and pepper

Melt 25 g/1 oz of the butter in a pan, add the eels and cook over a medium heat, turning occasionally, for 15 minutes. Season with salt and pepper, remove from the pan and set aside. Add the parsley, sorrel, chervil, rosemary and onion to the pan and cook over a low heat, stirring occasionally, for 5 minutes, adding the remaining butter if necessary. Pour in the wine, return the eels to the pan and cook for a further 5 minutes. Stir in the egg yolk, potato flour and lemon juice and cook until the sauce has thickened.

BRAISED EEL

Heat the olive oil in a pan, add the onion, garlic and parsley and cook over a low heat, stirring occasionally, for 5 minutes. Add the tomatoes, season with salt and pepper and simmer, stirring occasionally, for 10 minutes. Add the eels and cook for a few minutes more, then pour in the wine. Simmer over a very low heat for 30 minutes until the eels are tender, adding a little water if necessary. Sprinkle with parsley and serve.

ANGUILLE IN UMIDO

Serves 4

3 tablespoons olive oil

1 onion, chopped

1 garlic clove

1 fresh flat-leaf parsley sprig, chopped,

plus extra for sprinkling

400 g/14 oz tomatoes, peeled, seeded and chopped

900 g/2 lb eels, skinned, cleaned and thickly sliced

175 ml/6 fl oz red or white wine

salt and pepper

EEL KEBABS

Mix together the olive oil, vinegar, lemon juice and one of the bay leaves in a dish, season with salt and pepper and add the eels, turning to coat. Leave in a cool place to marinate for 1¹/₂ hours. Preheat the oven to 180°C/350°F/Gas Mark 4. Drain the eels, reserving the marinade, and thread on to skewers, alternating with the remaining bay leaves and the bread cubes. Put the kebabs into a roasting tin, sprinkle with the marinade and cook in the oven, turning and brushing with olive oil occasionally, for about 20 minutes.

SPIEDINI D'ANGUILLA

Serves 4

150 ml/¹/₄ pint olive oil, plus extra for brushing

50 ml/2 fl oz red wine vinegar

juice of 1 lemon, strained

17 bay leaves

800 g/1³/₄ lb eels, skinned, cleaned and sliced,

(cut into 3-cm/1¹/₄-inch slices)

1 white loaf, crusts removed, cut into cubes

salt and pepper

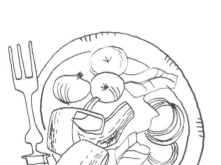

CARP

Carp live in still waters or sluggish rivers with muddy beds. Their flesh is highly prized, but, unfortunately, they have a lot of bones. They easily reach 50–60 cm/20–24 inches in length and a weight of 2–3 kg/4¹⁄₂–6¹⁄₂ lb. When preparing carp, it is important to leave them under cold, running water or soak them in water acidulated with a little vinegar for several hours, so that their flesh loses any slight muddy taste it may have retained.

CARP WITH MAÎTRE D'HÔTEL BUTTER

CARPA ALLA MAÎTRE D'HÔTEL

Serves 4

50 g/2 oz butter, softened

juice of 1 lemon, strained

1 tablespoon fresh flat-leaf parsley, chopped

4 carp, cleaned and soaked

olive oil, for brushing

salt

Beat the butter with 3 tablespoons of the lemon juice, the parsley and a pinch of salt in a bowl until thoroughly combined. Shape the mixture into cubes and chill in the refrigerator until required. Preheat the grill. Brush the fish with olive oil and some of the remaining lemon juice and cook under the grill until the flesh flakes easily. Serve garnished with the butter cubes.

CARP WITH OLIVES

Preheat the oven to 180°C/350°F/Gas Mark 4. Brush an ovenproof dish with olive oil. Mix together the garlic and parsley in a bowl, season with salt and pepper and stuff the cavities of the carp with the mixture. Place the carp in the prepared dish, pour 1 tablespoon of the vinegar over each fish and sprinkle with the olives. Bake for about 40 minutes. Transfer the carp to a warm serving dish and spoon the cooking juices over them.

CARPA ALLE OLIVE

Serves 4

olive oil, for brushing

2 garlic cloves, chopped

1 fresh flat-leaf parsley sprig, chopped

4 carp, cleaned and soaked

4 tablespoons white wine vinegar

12 green olives, stoned and chopped

salt and pepper

ORIENTAL CARP

Put the raisins in a bowl, add water to cover and leave to soak for 30 minutes, then drain and squeeze out. Meanwhile, sprinkle the carp with cooking salt and leave to stand for 30 minutes, then rinse and cut into fairly large slices. Arrange a layer of onions and almonds on the base of a saucepan, sprinkle with the raisins and place the fish on top. Pour in just enough water to cover, add the sugar cubes and season with salt and pepper. Cover and cook over a low heat for 1 hour. Gently lift out the slices of fish and place on a serving dish. Strain the cooking juices into a bowl, pressing down with the back of a spoon. Spoon the contents of the sieve over the slotted spoons and spoon the liquid around them. Leave to cool.

CARPA ALL'ORIENTALE

Serves 4

15 g/¹/₂ oz raisins

1-kg/2¹/₄-lb carp, cleaned and soaked

cooking salt, for sprinkling

400 g/14 oz onions, chopped

12 almonds, chopped

2 sugar cubes

salt and pepper

CARP IN WINE

Heat the olive oil and half the butter in a pan, add the carrots, onions and celery and cook over a low heat, stirring occasionally, for 15 minutes. Add the carp, season with salt and pepper to taste and pour in the wine and 5 tablespoons water. Bring to the boil, then cover and simmer gently for 45 minutes. Transfer the fish to a serving dish. Pass the vegetables through a food mill and return them to the pan with the cooking juices. Cook until thickened and stir in the remaining butter. Serve the carp with the sauce.

CARPA AL VINO

Serves 4

2 tablespoons olive oil

50 g/2 oz butter

2 carrots, finely chopped

2 onions, finely chopped

1 celery stick, finely chopped

1-kg/2¹/₄-lb carp, cleaned and soaked

500 ml/18 fl oz red wine

salt and pepper

CHAR

Char, sometimes spelt charr, are caught in almost all Italian lakes, where they were introduced from northern Europe at the beginning of the twentieth century. They are, on average, 15–40 cm/6-16 inches long and weigh 500 g–3 kg/ 1 lb 2 oz–6¹/₂ lb, although smaller fish are available. They have firm, white flesh and may be cooked in the same way as trout, to which they are related. The flesh takes on a pink tinge if they have been feeding on crustaceans. They are rarely available commercially in Britain, so it's worth cultivating a friendship with a keen fisherman, who may also be able to supply the similar grayling.

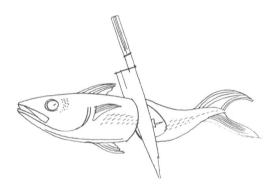

CHAR WITH HERBS

LAVARELLI ALLE ERBE

Serves 4

4 x 200-g/7-oz char, cleaned
1 small fresh bergamot sprig, chopped
1 small fresh marjoram sprig, chopped
1 small fresh rosemary sprig, chopped
1 tablespoon capers, drained and rinsed
5 tablespoons olive oil
juice of ¹/₄ lemon, strained
plain flour, for dusting
5 tablespoons dry white wine
salt and pepper

Open out the fish like a book, place them skin side up and press along the backbones with your thumb. Turn them over and use a knife to prise the backbones away from the flesh, then remove them. Put the bergamot, marjoram, rosemary and capers in a bowl and mix. Add 1 tablespoon of the olive oil and the lemon juice and season with salt and pepper. Sprinkle this mixture on to the insides of the open fish, then close and press firmly together with the palm of your hand. Lightly dust the fish with flour. Heat the remaining olive oil in a frying pan, add the fish and cook until browned on both sides. Add the wine and cook until it has evaporated and the fish flakes easily. Lightly season with salt, remove from the heat and serve.

FRIED CHAR

Put the fish in a dish, add the milk and leave to soak for 15 minutes. Drain, pat dry and dust with flour. Heat the oil in a frying pan, add the fish and cook over a medium heat for about 8 minutes on each side until browned. Remove the fish with a slotted spoon, drain on kitchen paper and season with salt. Char fried in a little butter are more delicate.

LAVARELLI FRITTI

Serves 4

4 x 200-g/7-oz char, cleaned

300 ml/½ pint milk

plain flour, for dusting

6 tablespoons olive oil

salt

POACHED CHAR WITH HORSERADISH SAUCE

Put the fish in a fish kettle or large pan, add the court-bouillon and bring just to the boil, then lower the heat and simmer gently for about 20 minutes until the flesh flakes easily. Remove from the heat and leave the fish to cool in the stock. Mix together the mayonnaise, horseradish, mustard, a pinch of salt and 1 tablespoon of the cooled stock. Drain the fish, remove the bones and transfer carefully to a serving dish. Spoon the horseradish sauce over the fish and serve.

LAVARELLI LESSATI
CON SALSA AL RAFANO

Serves 4

1-kg/2¼-lb char, cleaned

1 quantity Court-bouillon (see page 591)

1 quantity Mayonnaise,

made with 1 egg (see page 65)

2 tablespoons grated horseradish

½ teaspoon English mustard

salt

CHAR AND POTATO PIE

Preheat the oven to 180°C/350°F/Gas Mark 4. Brush a roasting tin with oil. Cut several diagonal slashes on each side of each fish. Make layers of the potatoes in the roasting tin, drizzle with olive oil, sprinkle with the garlic and season with salt and pepper. Place the fish on top, sprinkle with the herbs and drizzle with olive oil. Bake for about 30 minutes and transfer to a warm serving dish.

TORTINO DI LAVARELLI CON PATATE

Serves 4

olive oil, for brushing and drizzling

4 x 200-g/7-oz char, cleaned

3–4 potatoes, thinly sliced

1 garlic clove, chopped

1 fresh thyme sprig, chopped

1 fresh marjoram sprig, chopped

salt and pepper

PIKE

Pike are caught in fresh water in central northern Italy and are appreciated for their firm, white but fairly bony flesh. Female pike may grow to 1 metre/3¹/₄ feet long. It is best to leave large pike in the refrigerator for 24 hours. Pike roe should be discarded because it is often poisonous.

PIKE IN BEURRE BLANC

LUCCIO AL BURRO BIANCO

Serves 4

1-kg/2¹/₄-lb pike, cleaned
1 small onion slice
1 fresh flat-leaf parsley sprig
1 garlic clove
40 g/1¹/₂ oz butter, melted
salt and pepper

For the beurre blanc
3 shallots, finely chopped
1 tablespoon white wine vinegar
1 tablespoon dry white wine
200 g/7 oz butter, softened and cut into small pieces
juice of ¹/₂ lemon, strained
salt and white pepper

Preheat the oven to 180°C/350°F/Gas Mark 4. Season the cavity of the pike with salt and pepper and place the onion, parsley and garlic inside it, then season the fish with salt and pepper. Brush the melted butter over the fish, place in an ovenproof dish and bake for 30 minutes, brushing every 5 minutes with the remaining melted butter. Meanwhile, make the beurre blanc. Put the shallots in a saucepan with the vinegar and wine and cook over a medium-high heat until reduced. Remove the pan from the heat and whisk in the butter, a little at a time. Return the pan to the heat for a few seconds after each addition. Stir in the lemon juice and season with salt and pepper to taste. Serve the pike with the beurre blanc handed separately.

OLD-FASHIONED PIKE

Heat the olive oil in a frying pan. Season the fish fillets with salt and pepper on both sides, add to the pan and cook over a high heat until golden brown on both sides. Transfer the fish to a plate and keep warm. Pour the wine into the pan, add the onion and garlic and cook, stirring occasionally, until the liquid has reduced by half. Add the butter, a little at a time, and mix well. Finally, stir in 3 tablespoons warm water and the lemon juice. Keep warm over a very low heat. Put the pancetta in another pan and heat until the fat runs, then remove with a slotted spoon. Place the fish in the butter sauce, add the pancetta and simmer gently for 10–15 minutes. Garnish the pike fillets with parsley and serve.

LUCCIO ALL'ANTICA

Serves 4

2 tablespoons olive oil

1-kg/2¼-lb pike, cleaned and filleted

5 tablespoons dry white wine

1 onion, thinly sliced

½ garlic clove, chopped

50 g/2 oz butter, softened and cut into pieces

juice of ½ lemon, strained

100 g/3½ oz smoked pancetta, cubed

salt and pepper

chopped fresh flat-leaf parsley, to garnish

PIKE BLANQUETTE

Lightly dust the fish pieces with flour. Melt the butter in a pan and when it has turned light golden brown, add the fish and cook until evenly browned on both sides. Add the mushrooms, season with salt and pepper to taste and cook over a low heat for about 20 minutes. Meanwhile, beat together the egg yolks and cream in a small bowl and season lightly with salt. Remove the pan from the heat and pour the egg mixture over the fish. Return to a very low heat and heat through gently. Transfer the fish pieces to a warm serving dish and spoon the sauce over them.

LUCCIO IN BLANQUETTE

Serves 4

1-kg/2¼-lb pike, cleaned and cut into chunks

plain flour, for dusting

50 g/2 oz butter

200 g/7 oz mushrooms, thinly sliced

2 egg yolks

200 ml/7 fl oz double cream

salt and pepper

PERCH

Perch are highly prized freshwater fish. They live along the banks of lakes and slow-flowing rivers in central and northern regions of Italy and Sicily and are found in many other parts of Europe and North America. On average they are 20–35 cm/8–14 inches long, but may grow as long as 60 cm/24 inches. They have firm, white flesh with a delicate flavour and are easy to cut into fillets. They share a number of recipes with trout, and are delicious fried in oil or sautéed in butter.

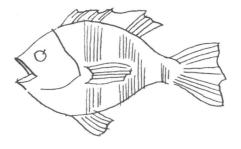

PERCH BAKED IN CREAMY HERB SAUCE

PESCE PERSICO IN TEGLIA ALLA CREMA VERDE

Serves 4

8 perch fillets

50 g/2 oz butter

3 fresh chervil sprigs, chopped

8 fresh basil leaves, chopped

200 ml/7 fl oz dry white wine

200 ml/7 fl oz single cream

50 g/2 oz breadcrumbs

salt and pepper

Preheat the oven to 180°C/350°F/Gas Mark 4. Place the perch fillets in an ovenproof dish, dot with the butter, sprinkle with the chervil and basil and season with salt and pepper. Pour in the wine and cream and sprinkle the breadcrumbs over the top. Bake for 10–15 minutes, then serve straight from the dish.

MILANESE PERCH

Mix together the lemon juice and olive oil in a dish, add the fish, turning to coat, and leave to marinate for 1 hour. Spread out the flour in a shallow dish, beat the egg with a pinch of salt in another shallow dish and spread out the breadcrumbs in a third. Drain the fish, dust lightly with flour, shake off the excess, and dip in the egg and then in the breadcrumbs. Melt the butter in a frying pan over a medium heat, add the fish and fry for 3–4 minutes on each side until light golden brown all over. Remove the fish with a slotted spoon and drain on kitchen paper. Transfer to a warm serving dish and sprinkle with salt.

PESCE PERSICO ALLA MILANESE

Serves 4

juice of 1 lemon, strained

4 tablespoons olive oil

600 g/1 lb 5 oz perch fillets

50 g/2 oz plain flour

1 egg

80 g/3 oz breadcrumbs

50 g/2 oz butter

salt

PERCH WITH SAGE

Lightly dust the fish fillets with flour and shake off any excess. Melt the butter with the sage in a frying pan, add the fish and cook over a medium heat for 3–4 minutes on each side until light golden brown all over. Season with salt and pepper and serve.

PESCE PERSICO ALLA SALVIA

Serves 4

600 g/1 lb 5 oz perch fillets

plain flour, for dusting

50 g/2 oz butter

8 fresh sage leaves

salt and pepper

PERCH WITH ANCHOVIES

Dice the anchovy fillets. Lightly dust the perch fillets with flour, shaking off any excess. Heat 2 tablespoons of the olive oil in a frying pan, add the fish and cook on both sides until lightly browned. Mix together the anchovies, garlic, parsley, lemon juice, cayenne, the remaining olive oil and the wine in a bowl and pour the mixture over the perch. Season with salt and cook over a low heat for about 15 minutes.

PESCE PERSICO ALLE ACCIUGHE

Serves 4

3 salted anchovies, heads removed, cleaned and filleted (see page 596), soaked in cold water for 10 minutes and drained

600 g/1 lb 5 oz perch fillets

plain flour, for dusting

3 tablespoons olive oil

1 garlic clove, chopped

1 fresh flat-leaf parsley sprig, chopped

juice of $1/2$ lemon, strained

pinch of cayenne pepper

5 tablespoons dry white wine

salt

681

TENCH

*A member of the carp family, tench is a bony freshwater fish.
Its flesh is pleasant-tasting, provided it comes from rivers that
are not too muddy. If you are in doubt, soak in a bowl of
water acidulated with a little vinegar for 15 minutes. Tench
should be cleaned and washed, but not scaled. Small tench are
excellent fried.*

TINCA ALLE ERBE

Serves 4

4 x 250-g/9-oz tench, cleaned

3 tablespoons olive oil

2 shallots, chopped

1 carrot, chopped

1 celery stick, chopped

1 fresh flat-leaf parsley sprig, chopped

4 fresh basil leaves, chopped

1 fresh thyme sprig, chopped

1 fresh marjoram sprig, chopped

5 tablespoons dry white wine

50 g/2 oz green olives, stoned

juice of 1 lemon, strained

salt and pepper

TENCH WITH HERBS

Remove as many bones as possible from the fish. Heat the olive oil in a frying pan, add the fish and cook until lightly browned on both sides, then remove from the pan. Add the shallots, carrot, celery and herbs to the pan and cook over a low heat for about 10 minutes, then return the fish to the pan, add the wine and season with salt and pepper. Simmer gently for about 30 minutes, adding a little water if the mixture is drying out. Just before the end of the cooking time, add the olives. Transfer the fish to a serving dish and keep warm. Tip the contents of the pan into a food processor, add the lemon juice and process to a purée. Reheat the mixture briefly, then pour the sauce over the fish and serve.

SOUSED TENCH WITH HERBS

Dust the fish with flour and shake off any excess. Heat 4 tablespoons of the olive oil in a frying pan, add the tench and cook for 10 minutes, then transfer to a serving dish. Heat the remaining olive oil in another pan, add the onion, carrot, garlic, parsley, sage and rosemary and cook over a low heat, stirring occasionally, for 10 minutes. Season with salt and pepper, add the vinegar and bring to the boil. Pour the mixture over the fish and leave to marinate for 6–7 hours in a cool place, but not in the refrigerator.

TINCA IN CARPIONE ALLE ERBE

Serves 4

4 x 250-g/9-oz tench, cleaned

plain flour, for dusting

150 ml/¼ pint olive oil

1 large onion, chopped

1 carrot, chopped

½ garlic clove, chopped

1 fresh flat-leaf parsley sprig, chopped

4 fresh sage leaves, chopped

1 fresh rosemary sprig, chopped

5 tablespoons white wine vinegar

salt and pepper

TENCH IN A SALT CRUST

Preheat the oven to 240°C/475°F/ Gas Mark 9. Fill the cavity of the fish with the mixed herbs. Line a roasting tin with foil and cover with a 2-cm/¾-inch thick layer of the coarse salt. Place the tench on top and cover with the remaining coarse salt. Bake for about 35 minutes, then remove from the oven and leave to stand for 10 minutes. Meanwhile, mix together the garlic, parsley, olive oil and lemon juice in a bowl and season with salt and pepper. To serve, break the salt crust and carefully extract the fish. Remove and discard the skin, cut the fish in half and slice into fillets. Serve with the sauce.

TINCA IN CROSTA DI SALE

Serves 4

1-kg/2¼-lb tench, cleaned

1 bunch of mixed fresh herbs, chopped

3–4 kg/6½–9 lb coarse sea salt

1 garlic clove, chopped

1 fresh flat-leaf parsley sprig, chopped

100 ml/3½ fl oz olive oil

juice of 1 lemon, strained

salt and pepper

STUFFED TENCH

Preheat the oven to 180°C/350°F/Gas Mark 4. Grease an ovenproof dish with butter. Mix together 4 tablespoons of the breadcrumbs, the Parmesan, garlic, parsley and olive oil in a bowl and season with salt and plenty of pepper. Fill the cavities of the fish with the mixture. Place the bay leaves in the prepared dish, put the tench on top and sprinkle with the remaining breadcrumbs. Bake, basting occasionally, for 1 hour. When the fish are ready, plenty of tasty sauce should have formed which goes well with polenta or mashed potato.

TINCA RIPIENA

Serves 4

butter, for greasing

50 g/2 oz breadcrumbs

4 tablespoons Parmesan cheese, freshly grated

2 garlic cloves, chopped

2 tablespoons chopped fresh flat-leaf parsley

1 tablespoon olive oil

4 x 250-g/9-oz tench, cleaned

3 bay leaves

salt and pepper

TROUT

There are various types of trout. The most commonly caught in Italian lakes and rivers are brown trouts. These average 20–40 cm/8–16 inches in length and 600 g–3 kg/1 lb 5 oz–6¹/₂ lb in weight. Rainbow trout, originally imported from the United States, are farmed. Trout are easy to digest and highly prized, especially sea trout, which are readily identified by their pink flesh. Trout are available both fresh and frozen (the latter are usually farmed).

SEA TROUT ROLL

ROTOLO DI TROTA SALMONATA

Serves 4

4 sea trout fillets

2 gelatine leaves

200 ml/7 fl oz double cream

2 teaspoons grated horseradish

juice of 1 lemon, strained

1 jar (about 40 g/1¹/₂ oz) sea trout roe

salt and white pepper

rocket, to garnish

Remove any remaining pin bones from the fish and place the fillets in a shallow dish. Set the dish over a pan of boiling water and steam for 10 minutes. Put the gelatine in a bowl, add water to cover and leave to soak for 5 minutes. Pour the cream into a double boiler or heatproof bowl and heat over barely simmering water. Squeeze out the gelatine and stir it into the cream. Flake the fish into a bowl, add the cream mixture, horseradish and lemon juice, season with salt and pepper and mix. Transfer the mixture to a food processor and process until smooth and combined. Scrape out the mixture and shape it into a roll, then wrap tightly in foil and chill in the refrigerator for about 4 hours until set. Thinly slice the roll, place on a serving dish and surround with the roe and garnish with rocket.

SMOKED TROUT WITH MELON

Halve the melon, scoop out and discard the seeds and cut the flesh into thin strips. Thinly slice four of the onions and chop the fifth. Pour the yogurt into a salad bowl, add the chopped onion, cream and vinegar and season with salt and pepper. Mix well and add the sliced onions. Put a trout fillet on each of four plates, add some melon strips, sprinkle with the sauce and garnish with cucumber slices.

TROTA AFFUMICATA AL MELONE

Serves 4

1 small melon

5 baby white onions

250 ml/8 fl oz natural yogurt

2 tablespoons double cream

1 tablespoon white wine vinegar

4 smoked trout fillets

salt and pepper

$^1/_2$ cucumber, sliced, to garnish

SEA TROUT WITH JUNIPER BERRIES

Put the bay leaf, carrot, thyme and parsley in a pan, pour in 500 ml/18 fl oz water and bring to the boil. Place the fish in a steamer over the pan, cover and steam for 10 minutes. Remove the fish from the heat, pat dry and place in a serving dish. Bring the liquid in the pan back to the boil and continue to boil over a high heat until reduced, then add the wine, vinegar and juniper and season with salt. Bring back to the boil, then pour the mixture over the fish and leave to cool to room temperature.

TROTA AL GINEPRO

Serves 4

1 bay leaf

1 carrot, sliced

1 fresh thyme sprig, chopped

1 fresh flat-leaf parsley sprig, chopped

8 sea trout fillets

175 ml/6 fl oz dry white wine

175 ml/6 fl oz white wine vinegar

4 juniper berries

salt

PROVENÇAL TROUT

Parboil the potatoes in 500 ml/18 fl oz water and the wine for 10 minutes. Drain and season with salt and pepper. Heat 4 tablespoons of the olive oil in a frying pan, add the potatoes and cook, turning occasionally, until tender. Put the tomatoes and red pepper in separate saucepans and heat gently without any additional oil or fat, then divide the butter between them. Heat the remaining olive oil in a frying pan, add the trout and cook for 10 minutes on each side. Lift the fish out of the pan with a slotted spoon and remove and discard their skins. Spoon the tomatoes on to a warm serving dish, place the trout in the middle of them and surround with the potatoes, olives and red pepper.

TROTA ALLA PROVENZALE

Serves 4

3 potatoes, sliced

350 ml/12 fl oz dry white wine

6 tablespoons olive oil

4 tomatoes, peeled and chopped

1 red pepper, halved, seeded and cut into strips

50 g/2 oz butter

4 small trout, cleaned

100 g/3$^1/_2$ oz black olives, stoned

salt and pepper

TROUT WITH MUSHROOMS AND MUSSELS

TROTA CON FUNGHI E COZZE

Serves 4

25 g/1 oz butter, plus extra for greasing

25 g/1 oz dried mushrooms

4 small trout, cleaned

1 tablespoon chopped fresh thyme

olive oil, for brushing

½ onion, chopped

1 carrot, chopped

1 celery stick, chopped

350 ml/12 fl oz dry white wine

12 mussels, cooked and shelled (see page 713)

salt and pepper

Preheat the oven to 180°C/350°F/Gas Mark 4. Grease an oven-proof dish with butter. Put the mushrooms in a bowl, add warm water to cover and leave to soak. Season the cavities of the trout with salt and pepper and sprinkle with the thyme. Brush the fish with olive oil, place in the prepared dish and add the onion, carrot and celery. Dot with the butter, cover with foil and bake for 10 minutes. Drain and squeeze out the mushrooms. Remove the foil from the dish, add the wine and mushrooms and bake for a further 10 minutes. Add the mussels and bake for a few more minutes to heat through, then serve.

SMOKED SEA TROUT AND VEGETABLE CASSEROLE

TROTA CON VERDURE

Serves 6

50 g/2 oz butter, plus extra for greasing

2 eggs, separated

200 g/7 oz smoked sea trout fillet, flaked

1 quantity Béchamel Sauce (see page 50)

500 g/1 lb 2 oz spinach

500 g/1 lb 2 oz red sorrel

4 tablespoons double cream

2 tablespoons chopped almonds

salt and pepper

Preheat the oven to 220°C/425°F/Gas Mark 7. Grease six ramekins or individual moulds with butter. Lightly beat the egg yolks and stiffly whisk the whites in a separate, grease-free bowl. Stir the yolks and fish into the cold béchamel sauce, fold in the egg whites and season with salt and pepper. Pour the mixture into the prepared dishes and place them in a roasting tin. Add boiling water to come about halfway up the sides and bake for 25 minutes. Meanwhile, melt the butter in a pan, add the spinach and sorrel and cook over a low heat, stirring frequently, until wilted. Season with salt and pepper, stir in 1 tablespoon of the cream and spoon the mixture over the base of an ovenproof dish. Remove the roasting tin from the oven and lower the temperature to 180°C/350°F/Gas Mark 4. Turn out the ramekins or moulds on top of the spinach mixture, spoon the remaining cream over them and sprinkle with the almonds. Bake for about 15 minutes.

SEA TROUT ROE WITH POTATOES

UOVA DI TROTA E PATATE

Serves 4

4 potatoes, unpeeled

50 g/2 oz butter, softened

1 tablespoon chopped fresh chervil

2 tablespoons double cream

1 jar (about 40 g/1½ oz) sea trout roe

salt • lemon slices, to garnish

Preheat the oven to 180°C/350°F/Gas Mark 4. Wrap each potato in a sheet of foil and bake for about 50 minutes. Unwrap the potatoes and peel them, then cut in half and arrange on a warm serving dish. Cream the butter, beat in the chervil, cream and a pinch of salt and spread the mixture over the potatoes. Divide the roe among and garnish with slices of lemon.

CRUSTACEANS

The crustacean family is quite large especially when you consider how many different species of shrimp and prawn there are. However, all crustaceans have relatively elongated bodies covered at the front by a carapace – a shell of varying hardness which protects part of the head and the part of the upper body where the viscera are. They also have eyes, feelers and five pairs of legs. The pair of legs nearest the mouth are often modified into heavy claws or pincers used to grip food and for defence. The end of the body, popularly called the tail, is actually the abdomen. It is the choice part from the culinary point of view and is protected by a segmented shell. The true tail, which opens out like a fan, is technically called the telson. All crustaceans have compact flesh with a mild yet distinctive flavour and a pleasant hint of sweetness. Ideally, they should still be alive when purchased. Traditionally, they are thrown into boiling water where the shell protects the flesh from the fierce heat and keeps it soft and delicate. A more humane alternative is to place crabs and lobsters in the freezer for a couple of hours to induce hypothermia before boiling them. The shell also protects the flesh during frying and grilling. Remember that the most delicate flesh is in the legs and claws. Spiny and European lobsters are both top-ranking crustaceans but no one will ever settle the elegant culinary question of which is the most highly prized. More common crustaceans are also good and tasty.

LOBSTER

Spiny and European lobsters find equal favour with gourmets, although the flesh of the latter is milder and more delicate. Both should be boiled for 15 minutes per 1 kg/2¹/₄ lb. Increase the time by 5 minutes for every additional 200 g/7 oz. Small spiny lobsters – 300 g/11 oz – should be boiled for 5 minutes and 800-g/1³/₄-lb spiny lobsters should be boiled for 10 minutes. The best spiny lobsters are medium-size females. Given that about 70 per cent is waste, you need a 1-kg/2¹/₄-lb spiny lobster for two servings. Live lobsters should be immersed in a large saucepan of boiling water, tightly covered and cooked for 1 minute. To prevent them from jumping out, it is advisable to tie their tails to a wooden stick. To extract the meat, place the lobster on a board, cut it in half lengthways, open it up and remove the meat from each half of the tail. Remove the dark intestinal tract with the point of a knife and discard. Break off the claws in the case of European lobsters, crack open and remove the meat. The soft green tomalley (liver) and the coral (roe) are considered delicacies. If you're going to use the shells to serve the lobster, remove and discard the stomach sac.

CREOLE SPINY LOBSTER

Bring a large saucepan of water to the boil with the onions, celery, carrots, herbs, juniper, garlic, peppercorns and a pinch of salt and simmer for 20 minutes. Bring back to a rolling boil, immerse the lobsters, cover tightly and cook for 10 minutes. Remove the pan from the heat and leave the lobsters to cool in the cooking liquid. Drain the lobsters, reserving the cooking liquid, cut open and remove the meat (see above), reserving the coral. Bring the cooking liquid to the boil and boil until reduced to about 500 ml/18 fl oz, then strain into a bowl. For the dressing melt half the butter in a pan, add the onion and cook over a low heat, stirring frequently, for 10 minutes until lightly browned. Pour in the brandy and cook over a low heat until the liquid is reduced by half, then strain. Melt the remaining butter in another saucepan, stir in the flour and curry powder, then gradually stir in the lobster stock. Cook, stirring until thickened and smooth, then add the coral and reduced brandy. Serve the lobsters with the dressing.

ARAGOSTA ALLA CREOLA

Serves 4

2 onions, halved

1 celery stick, halved • 2 carrots, halved

1 bay leaf

¹/₂ bunch of fresh flat-leaf parsley

8 juniper berries • 1 garlic clove

6 black peppercorns

2 x 800-g/1³/₄-lb live spiny lobsters

salt

For the dressing

50 g/2 oz butter

1 onion, chopped

100 ml/3¹/₂ fl oz brandy

25 g/1 oz plain flour

pinch of curry powder

SPICY LOBSTER

ARAGOSTA ALLE SPEZIE

Serves 4

4 spiny lobster tails, thawed if frozen

80 g/3 oz butter

$^1/_2$ teaspoon ground ginger • $^1/_2$ teaspoon curry powder

1 teaspoon ground coriander

juice of 1 lemon, strained

salt and pepper

lemon slices, to garnish

Preheat the grill. Make a deep cut in the hard outer covering on the undersides of the lobster tails. Melt the butter in a saucepan, remove from the heat as soon as it has melted, stir in the ginger, curry powder, coriander and lemon juice and season with salt and pepper. Arrange the lobster tails with the back shells uppermost in a roasting tin and grill for about 3 minutes, then turn over, pour the spiced butter into the cuts in the undersides and grill for a further 3–4 minutes. Season with pepper and garnish with lemon slices.

LOBSTER IN TARRAGON SAUCE

ARAGOSTA IN SALSA DI DRAGONCELLO

Serves 4

2 x 800-g/1$^3/_4$-lb spiny lobsters, boiled

100 g/3$^1/_2$ oz butter

1 onion, finely chopped

1 celery stick, finely chopped

1 carrot, finely chopped

50 ml/2 fl oz brandy

1 teaspoon herb mustard

1 fresh tarragon sprig, finely chopped

175 ml/6 fl oz dry white wine

juice of $^1/_2$ lemon, strained

salt and pepper

Cut open the lobsters and remove the meat (see page 689), reserving the tomalley and coral . Melt 50 g/2 oz of the butter in a pan, add the onion, celery and carrot and cook over a low heat, stirring occasionally, for 5 minutes. Add the lobster meat and cook until lightly browned, then season. Add half the brandy and cook until it has evaporated, then add the mustard and tarragon. Pour in the wine, cover and simmer for 10 minutes. Remove the pan from the heat, transfer the lobsters to a plate and keep warm. Strain the cooking liquid into a clean pan. Chop the tomalley and coral and add to the pan with the remaining butter, remaining brandy and the lemon juice. Cook over a medium heat until slightly reduced, then season. Serve the lobsters covered with the sauce.

ARMORICAN LOBSTER

ASTICI ALL'ARMORICANA

Serves 4

1.5 kg/3$^1/_4$ lb live European lobsters

2 onions, finely chopped

$^1/_2$ garlic clove, finely chopped

50 g/2 oz butter

2 tablespoons olive oil

5 tablespoons brandy

1 tablespoon fresh flat-leaf parsley, chopped

300 g/11 oz canned chopped tomatoes

250 ml/8 fl oz dry white wine

salt and pepper

To garnish

cucumber slices

lemon slices

Bring a large saucepan of water to a rolling boil, add the lobsters, cover tightly and cook for 2 minutes. Drain, open the lobsters and remove the meat (see page 689), then cut it into fairly large pieces. Cook the onions and garlic in salted, boiling water until soft, then drain, reserving the cooking liquid, place in a food processor and process to a purée. Heat the butter and olive oil in a saucepan, add the lobster meat and cook until lightly browned all over. Transfer to another pan, add half the brandy and ignite. Scrape the onion back into the saucepan of reserved cooking liquid, stir in the parsley and tomatoes and heat gently. When the sauce is hot pour it over the lobsters and stir well. Add the wine, season with salt and pepper and cook over a medium heat for about 20 minutes. Pour in the remaining brandy, lower the heat, cover and cook for a further 5 minutes. Remove the pan from the heat, transfer the mixture to a warm serving dish and garnish with slices of cucumber and lemon.

Serves 6

1 carrot

1 onion

1 lemon

175 m/6 fl oz white wine

1 tablespoon white wine vinegar

5 live European lobsters

40 large raw Mediterranean prawns, peeled and deveined

6 fresh basil leaves, chopped

5 vine tomatoes, chopped

1 celery stick, chopped

175 ml/6 fl oz olive oil

juice of ¹/₂ lemon, strained

salt and pepper

25 g/1 oz olives, to garnish

LOBSTER AND PRAWN SALAD

Put the carrot, onion, lemon, wine and vinegar in a large saucepan, bring to the boil, then lower the heat and simmer for 15 minutes. Bring back to a rolling boil, add the lobsters, cover tightly and cook for 7 minutes, then add the prawns and cook for 3 minutes more. Drain, open the lobsters and extract the flesh (see page 689), then cut it into large pieces. Put the basil, tomatoes and celery in a bowl and add the lobster meat and prawns. Whisk together the olive oil and lemon juice in a bowl and season with salt and pepper. Pour the dressing over the salad, toss gently and serve on individual plates garnished with the olives

Serves 4

1 quantity Court-bouillon (see page 591)

1-kg/2¹/₄-lb live spiny lobster

300 ml/¹/₂ pint dissolved gelatine

1 white loaf of bread, sliced and crusts removed

40 g/1¹/₂ oz butter

1 bunch of rocket

Mayonnaise (see page 65), to serve

MAGNIFICENT MEDALLIONS OF LOBSTER

Bring the court-bouillon to a rolling boil in a large saucepan, add the lobster, cover tightly and cook for 15 minutes. Remove the pan from the heat and leave the lobster to cool in its cooking liquid. Drain, cut open and extract the meat (see page 689), then slice into medallions. Prepare the gelatine according to the packet instructions. Place the lobster medallions on a plate, brush with several coatings of gelatine and chill in the refrigerator until set. Stamp out the same number of rounds of bread as there are lobster medallions. Melt the butter in a frying pan, add the bread rounds and fry until golden brown on both sides. Remove with a slotted spoon and drain on kitchen paper. Place on a serving dish, top with the lobster medallions, surround with rocket leaves and serve with mayonnaise handed separately.

MY KNIFE

PRAWNS

There are many different species, colours and sizes of prawns and shrimp. Three types, in particular, feature in Italian cooking. Mediterranean prawns are 23 cm/9 inches long, greyish brown in colour with stripes and tinges of purple. Their flesh, which turns pink on cooking, has a very delicate flavour. Pink and red prawns from the Mediterranean Sea grow to about 21 cm/8¹/₂ inches while those from the Atlantic reach as much as 33 cm/13 inches in length. These vary in colour from red to pink, may be variegated and have a delicate but distinctive flavour. Shrimp, at 10 cm/4 inches long, may be pink or grey and have a hint of sweetness. It is usually better to peel prawns and shrimp after cooking rather than before to protect their delicate flesh. Finally, the freshwater crayfish should also be mentioned. Once these could be found without difficulty in Italian rivers but today they are nearly all imported from Asia.

ASPARAGUS AND PRAWNS

Bring a pan of salted water to the boil, add the vinegar and blanch the prawns for 2 minutes, then drain. Tie the asparagus into a bunch and cook it, standing upright, in salted, boiling water for 15–20 minutes, then drain and leave to cool. Put the carrot and celery on a serving dish and top with the prawns and asparagus. Drizzle with olive oil, season with salt and pepper and sprinkle with the lemon juice. Mix gently and serve immediately.

ASPARAGI E GAMBERI

Serves 4

2 tablespoons white wine vinegar

20 raw Mediterranean prawns, peeled and deveined

800 g/1³/₄ lb asparagus, spears trimmed

1 carrot, thinly sliced

1 celery heart, thinly sliced

olive oil, for drizzling

juice of ¹/₂ lemon, strained

salt and pepper

FRIED PRAWNS IN PINK SAUCE

CODE DI GAMBERI FRITTE IN SALSA ROSA

Serves 4

4 tablespoons tomato purée

3 tablespoons double cream

juice of ½ lemon, strained

350 ml/12 fl oz dry white wine

1 teaspoon grated fresh root ginger

1 garlic clove

16 raw Mediterranean prawns, peeled and deveined

2 egg whites

vegetable oil, for deep-frying

plain flour, for dusting

salt and pepper

Mix together the tomato purée, cream and lemon juice in a bowl, season with salt and pepper and set aside. Pour the wine into a dish and add a pinch of salt and the ginger and garlic. Add the prawns, mix well and leave to marinate for about 1 hour. Stiffly whisk the egg whites in a grease-free bowl. Drain the prawns and immerse them in the egg white. Heat the oil for deep frying in a large pan. Spread out the flour in a shallow dish. Holding each prawn by the tip of its tail, dip it in the flour, then put it in to the hot oil and cook until golden brown. Remove with a slotted spoon and drain on kitchen paper. Season with salt and serve with the pink sauce handed separately.

PRAWNS WITH SALMON MOUSSE

GAMBERI DI SPUMA DI SALMONE

Serves 4

275 g/10 oz raw prawns, peeled and deveined

500 ml/18 fl oz dissolved gelatine

3 salmon steaks

100 ml/3½ fl oz double cream

2 tablespoons brandy

salt and pepper

Cook the prawns in salted, boiling water for 4 minutes, then drain. Prepare the gelatine according to the packet instructions. Coat the base of a mould with some of the gelatine and chill in the refrigerator until set. Meanwhile, cook the salmon in a nonstick pan, turning occasionally, for 5 minutes. Remove from the pan with a slotted spoon, flake the flesh, removing any bones, and put it in a food processor with the cream and brandy. Process to a smooth purée and season with salt and pepper to taste. Set aside a few prawns for the garnish and arrange the remainder on the base of the mould. Spoon the salmon mousse into the mould, cover with a thin layer of gelatine and chill in the refrigerator for 2 hours. To serve, turn out the mould on to a serving dish and garnish with the reserved prawns.

PRAWN SALAD WITH BEANS

GAMBERI IN INSALATA CON FAGIOLI

Serves 4

1 lemon slice

500 g/1 lb 2 oz raw prawns, peeled and deveined

200 g/7 oz cooked (see page 460) or canned cannellini beans, drained and rinsed

2 tablespoons white wine vinegar

5 tablespoons olive oil

1 fresh flat-leaf parsley sprig, chopped

salt and pepper

Bring 1 litre/1¾ pints salted water to the boil in a saucepan with the slice of lemon. Add the prawns and cook for 5–6 minutes. Drain well, tip into a bowl and leave to cool. When the prawns are cold, add the beans. Whisk together the vinegar and olive oil in a bowl and season with salt and pepper. Pour the dressing over the salad, mix gently, sprinkle with the parsley and serve.

GAMBERI IN SALSA DOLCEFORTE

Serves 6

24 raw Mediterranean prawns, peeled and deveined

5 tablespoons olive oil

2 carrots, finely chopped

2 celery sticks, finely chopped

1/2 onion, finely chopped

1 leek, finely chopped

50 ml/2 fl oz brandy

175 ml/6 fl oz dry white wine

200 ml/7 fl oz Concentrated Fish Stock (see page 210)

1 fresh thyme sprig

1 bay leaf

2 ripe tomatoes, peeled, seeded and chopped

2 lemons

1 tablespoon sugar

plain flour, for dusting

1/2 teaspoon ground cinnamon

50 g/2 oz sultanas

1 tablespoon pine nuts

salt and pepper

PRAWNS IN STRONG SWEET SAUCE

Pull off the heads and peel the prawns, reserving the heads and shells. Heat 3 tablespoons of the oil in a pan, add the prawn heads and shells, carrots, celery, onion and leek and cook over a low heat, stirring occasionally, for 5 minutes. Add the brandy and cook until it has evaporated, then pour in the wine and bring to the boil. Add the fish stock, thyme, bay leaf and tomatoes and simmer, stirring occasionally, until thickened. Strain the stock into a clean pan and return to the heat. Simmer until reduced to about 5 tablespoons. Remove from the heat and reserve. Thinly pare the lemons, avoiding all traces of white pith, and cut the rind into very thin batons. Blanch the rind in three separate changes of boiling water, then drain and place in a small saucepan with the sugar and 2 tablespoons of water. Bring to the boil, stirring until the sugar has dissolved, then boil without stirring until the lemon rind is coated in syrup, then remove from the heat. Meanwhile, squeeze the lemons and strain the juice. Lightly dust the prawns with flour. Heat the remaining oil in a frying pan, add the prawns, season with salt and pepper and cook, stirring frequently, until lightly browned. Sprinkle in the cinnamon, add the reserved stock, lemon juice, lemon rind, sultanas and pine nuts and mix well. Season with salt according to taste and serve.

ZUCCHINE AI GAMBERETTI

Serves 4

8 courgettes

1 quantity Mayonnaise (see page 65)

1 onion, finely chopped

dash of Tabasco sauce

1 tablespoon tomato ketchup

200 g/7 oz cooked, peeled prawns

salt

COURGETTES WITH PRAWNS

Cook the courgettes in salted, boiling water for about 8 minutes, then drain and leave to cool slightly. Mix together the mayonnaise, onion, Tabasco and ketchup in a bowl. Halve the courgettes lengthways and scoop out the flesh without piercing the 'shells'. Fill the shells with the mayonnaise mixture and the prawns. Serve immediately while warm.

SPIDER CRAB

Spider or spiny crabs are large crabs which are found in the Adriatic, among many other places, and in Venice they know just how to cook them. Their flavour is delicate and the most prized part is the central body and claws. The roe – known as coral – is delicious. Simply season it with olive oil and lemon juice. Live spider crabs are plunged into boiling water and cooked for about 30 minutes if large or 20 minutes if small. They should be left to cool in the cooking liquid before you open them and extract the flesh. To do this, break off the legs and claws and cut open the body shell in a circle with a knife or scissors. Remove and discard the gills and scoop out the meat, reserving the coral. Crack the claws with a nutcracker or the handle of a heavy knife, but take care not to shatter the cartilage which could then penetrate the flesh. The extracted flesh is usually served in the crab shell, in which case you should also remove the mouth and stomach sac.

SPIDER CRAB IN OLIVE OIL AND LEMON

Bring a large pan of salted water to a rolling boil. Add the spider crabs, cover and cook for just under 10 minutes. Leave in the water to cool a little. Cut open the shells and extract the meat (see above), and coral, if any. Thoroughly wash and dry the insides of the shells and line with one or two lettuce leaves. Fill with crab meat. Mix together the olive oil and lemon juice in a bowl, add the parsley and garlic if using and season with salt and pepper. Drizzle the dressing over the crabs. If there is any coral, mix it with a little olive oil and use as a garnish.

GRANCEOLA ALL'OLIO E LIMONE
Serves 4
4 live spider crabs
4–8 lettuce leaves
4 tablespoons olive oil
juice of 1 lemon, strained
fresh flat-leaf parsley, chopped (optional)
1 garlic clove (optional)
salt and pepper

SPIDER CRAB WITH MAYONNAISE

Bring a large saucepan of water to a rolling boil with a pinch of salt and pepper, the thyme and marjoram. Add the spider crabs, cover tightly and cook for 10 minutes. Remove the pan from the heat, leave the crabs in the water to cool slightly and then drain. Cut open the shells and extract the meat (see page 697). Thoroughly wash and dry the insides of the shells and line with one or two lettuce leaves. Gently stir the crab meat into the mayonnaise, then spoon the mixture into the shells and garnish with the prawns. Keep in a cool place, but not the refrigerator, until ready to serve.

GRANCEOLA CON MAIONESE

Serves 4

1 fresh thyme sprig

1 fresh marjoram sprig

4 live spider crabs

4–8 lettuce leaves

1 quantity Mayonnaise (see page 65)

salt and pepper

100 g/3¹/₂ oz cooked, peeled prawns, to garnish

SPIDER CRAB MIMOSA

Bring the court-bouillon to a rolling boil in a large saucepan, add the spider crabs, cover tightly and cook for about 10 minutes. Remove from the heat and leave to cool slightly in the cooking liquid. Open the shells and extract the meat (see page 697). Chop the white meat and mix it with the brown meat in a bowl. Press the egg yolks through a fine sieve and add two-thirds to the crab meat, season with salt and pepper and gently stir in the olive oil and lemon juice. Thoroughly wash and dry the crab shells, then spoon the crab meat mixture into them. Sprinkle the remaining egg yolk and the parsley on top and serve.

GRANCEOLA MIMOSA

Serves 4

1 quantity Court-bouillon (see page 591)

4 live spider crabs

3 hard-boiled egg yolks

4 tablespoons olive oil

juice of 1 lemon, strained

1 tablespoon fresh flat-leaf parsley, chopped

salt and white pepper

CRAB

There are two well-known and highly popular types of crab in Italy – the green crab (called moleca in Venice), which lives in lagoons and has soft tasty flesh, and the shore crab (known as the granchio di sabbia in Italian), which lives in shallow waters near rivers. The brown, common or edible crab, as well as the spider crab (see pages 697–99), also make excellent eating. Australia and New Zealand also have a wide variety of native crab species that are particularly delicious. Canned crab meat from northern seas is widely available. It is very tasty dressed with oil and lemon juice or mixed with tomato sauce and served with spaghetti. To remove the meat from a cooked crab, place it on its back and break off the claws and legs, then break off the tail flap. Insert a heavy-bladed knife between the body shell and the back shell, twist and then prise apart with your thumbs. Remove and discard the 'dead man's fingers' (gills). Using a spoon, scoop the brown meat out into a bowl. Halve the body with a sharp knife and carefully scoop out the remaining white meat from the shell. Crack the claws and legs and carefully pick out the meat. Finally, press on the back shell just behind the eyes, then remove and discard the mouth and stomach sac. Scoop out the remaining brown meat.

CHERRY TOMATOES STUFFED WITH CRAB

CILIEGINE RIPIENE DI GRANCHIO

Serves 4

12 red cherry tomatoes

250 g/9 oz canned crab meat, drained

4 tablespoons Mayonnaise (see page 65)

salt and pepper

12 black olives, stoned, to garnish

Cut off the tops of the cherry tomatoes, scoop out a little of the flesh without piercing the 'shells' and season the insides with salt. Place upside down on kitchen paper for 1 hour to drain. Pick over the crab meat and remove any cartilage. Mix together the crab meat and mayonnaise in a bowl and season with salt and pepper. Fill the cherry tomatoes with the mixture and garnish each with an olive.

CRAB WITH AVOCADO

GRANCHIO CON AVOCADO

Serves 4

2 avocados

juice of 1 lemon, strained

25 g/1 oz butter

120 g/4 oz canned crab meat, drained

100 g/3½ oz double cream

2 tablespoons bottled prawn cocktail sauce

dash of Tabasco sauce

salt and pepper

Peel, stone and slice the avocados, then sprinkle with the lemon juice. Melt the butter in a frying pan, add the avocado slices and cook over a low heat for 10 minutes. Season with salt and pepper and arrange on a serving dish. Pick over the crab meat and remove any cartilage, then add to the frying pan. Stir in the cream, prawn cocktail sauce and Tabasco. Heat gently for a few minutes until thickened, then pour the mixture over the slices of avocado.

CRAB SALAD

GRANCHIO IN INSALATA

Serves 4

1 quantity Court-bouillon (see page 591)

1 live crab

1 Treviso radicchio, cut into strips

300 g/11 oz canned palm hearts, drained, rinsed and sliced

olive oil, for drizzling

white wine vinegar, for drizzling

2 gherkins, drained and coarsely chopped

1 quantity Sauce Aurore (see page 61)

salt and white pepper

Bring the court-bouillon to a rolling boil in a large saucepan, add the crab, cover tightly and cook for 20 minutes, then drain. Open the crab (see page 700), carefully extract all the meat and chop the white meat. Season the crab meat, radicchio and palm hearts separately with a drizzle of olive oil, a drizzle of vinegar, a pinch of salt and a pinch of pepper. Line a large salad bowl with a bed of radicchio, arrange the crab meat and palm hearts on top and sprinkle with the gherkins. Drizzle the sauce aurore in decorative spirals on top.

CRAB ROLLS

INVOLTINI DI GRANCHIO RIPIENI

Serves 4

1 quantity Court-bouillon (see page 591)

1 live crab

8 large aubergine slices

olive oil, for brushing

50 g/2 oz butter

1 shallot, finely chopped

100 ml/3½ fl oz dry white wine

salt

Preheat the grill. Bring the court-bouillon to a rolling boil in a large saucepan, add the crab, cover tightly and cook for 20 minutes. Meanwhile, brush the aubergine slices with oil and grill on both sides until golden brown. Remove from the grill and leave to cool. Drain and open the crab (see page 700), carefully extract all the meat and chop the white meat. Melt the butter in a pan, add the shallot and cook over a low heat, stirring occasionally, for 5 minutes. Stir in the chopped crab meat, add the wine and cook until it has evaporated. Season lightly with salt. Divide the mixture among the aubergine slices, roll up and secure with cocktail sticks. Brush a pan with olive oil, add the rolls and set over a medium heat until warmed through. Transfer to a warm serving dish.

LANGOUSTINES

Italians differentiate between scampi, which are shorter than 20 cm/8 inches long, and what are called scamponi, which are longer. In Britain, their equivalents are langoustines, Dublin Bay prawns or Norwegian lobster, although the deep-fried breaded tails are sometimes called scampi. (Similar species to langoustines are widely available in Australia and New Zealand.) Dublin Bay prawns have a thicker carapace than langoustines, but are otherwise very similar. Both should be eaten extremely fresh because their flesh deteriorates very quickly. The only edible part is the flesh in the tail, which has a delicate delicious flavour that some prefer to lobster. Both whole langoustines and just the tails, are cooked, then the tails are shelled and deveined – i.e. the black intestine is removed. The cooking time varies according to size. When added to boiling water, allow 5 minutes from when the water returns to the boil. If added to cold water, allow 3 minutes after it comes to the boil.

LANGOUSTINES WITH TOMATOES

Melt the butter in a pan, add the onion and cook over a low heat, stirring occasionally, for 5 minutes, then add the tomatoes. Mix the tomato purée with 2 tablespoons warm water, stir into the pan and simmer for about 10 minutes. Transfer the mixture to a food processor and process to a purée, then return to the pan. Add salt and pepper to taste. Add the langoustines or prawns and cook, stirring constantly, for 2–3 minutes. Stir in the cream and cook until the sauce has thickened. Arrange the langoustines or prawns on a warm serving dish and spoon the sauce over them.

SCAMPI AI POMODORI

Serves 4

50 g/2 oz butter

1 onion, finely chopped

300 g/11 oz tomatoes, peeled, seeded and cubed

1 tablespoon tomato purée

20 langoustines or Dublin Bay prawns, peeled

100 ml/3¹/₂ fl oz double cream

salt and pepper

LANGOUSTINES WITH CURRY SAUCE

Bring a large saucepan of water to the boil with the herbs, and the carrot and onion if using. Add the langoustines or prawns, bring back to the boil and cook for 5 minutes, then drain, peel and devein. Melt the butter in a pan, add the shallots and cook over a low heat, stirring occasionally, for 5 minutes. Stir in the curry powder, then pour in the wine and cook until it has reduced by half. Stir in the cream and season with salt and pepper. Arrange the langoustines or prawns on a warm serving dish, sprinkle with the lemon juice and spoon the sauce over them.

SCAMPI ALLA SALSA DI CURRY

Serves 4

$^1/_2$ bunch of fresh parsley

$^1/_2$ bunch of fresh thyme

1 carrot (optional)

1 onion (optional)

20 langoustines or Dublin Bay prawns

40 g/1$^1/_2$ oz butter

2 shallots, finely chopped

1 teaspoon curry powder

100 ml/3$^1/_2$ fl oz dry white wine

100 ml/3$^1/_2$ fl oz double cream

juice of 1 lemon, strained

salt and pepper

LANGOUSTINES WITH SAGE

Put the langoustines or prawns in a bowl, season with salt and pepper, pour in the lemon juice and leave to marinate for about 1 hour. Preheat the grill. Drain the langoustines or prawns, reserving the marinade, wrap each in a slice of pancetta together with a sage leaf and secure with a cocktail stick. Brush lightly with olive oil, arrange on the grill rack and cook under the grill, turning twice and occasionally drizzling with the reserved marinade, for 10–12 minutes.

SCAMPI ALLA SALVIA

Serves 4

20 langoustines or Dublin Bay prawns, peeled

juice of 2 lemons, strained

20 smoked pancetta slices

20 small fresh sage leaves

olive oil, for brushing

salt and pepper

GRILLED LANGOUSTINES

Put the langoustines or prawns in a large bowl, sprinkle with the herbs, add the lemon juice and olive oil and season with salt and pepper. Leave to marinate for about 45 minutes. Preheat the grill. Spread out a sheet of foil in a grill pan and brush with olive oil. Drain the langoustines or prawns, reserving the marinade, place them on the foil and cook under the grill, turning twice and occasionally drizzling with a little reserved marinade, for about 12 minutes.

SCAMPI GRIGLIATI

Serves 4

20 langoustines or Dublin Bay prawns, peeled

1 fresh flat-leaf parsley sprig, finely chopped

1 fresh chervil sprig, finely chopped

1 fresh marjoram sprig, finely chopped

juice of 1 lemon, strained

4 tablespoons olive oil, plus extra for brushing

salt and pepper

SHELLFISH

Warty venus clams, smooth venus clams, mussels, razor clams, carpet shell clams, queen scallops, whelks, great scallops – and we could go on. Scientifically, molluscs are classified into eight classes with eight thousand different species. However, only three classes are commonly used in the kitchen. These are cephalopods, which do not have external shells, such as octopus and cuttlefish, gastropods, which have a single shell, such as whelks, murex and other marine snails, and bivalves with two shells, such as clams, scallops and mussels. While the freshness of fish can easily be judged by looking at the liveliness of the eyes, the shininess of the scales and the texture of the flesh, molluscs require more attention and not everyone knows what to look for. Here are the main rules to follow when buying them. The shells should be shiny and completely closed. The more open they are, the longer they have been out of the sea. They should have a mild, pleasant smell – if they have a strong smell, their freshness is at the extreme limit. Shellfish require careful cleaning under plenty of running water. If they are not going to be eaten immediately, they should be cooked anyway and stored in their cooking juices for not longer than 24 hours in the refrigerator.

SQUID

The most delicious squid are small, tender ones that are cooked whole. The larger ones are not quite so tender and should be cut into rings. In Australia, squid can also be called inkfish and are sometimes referred to by their Italian name, calamari. To prepare squid, rinse well and pull the head and body apart. Cut off the tentacles, then squeeze out and discard the beak. Discard the rest of the head. Remove and discard the quill and ink sac from the body and remove any remaining membrane (most of the innards will have come out with the head). Rinse the body sac well and peel off the skin. Some of the ink may be added to risottos and spaghetti sauces to give them an unusual black colour and a stronger flavour of the sea.

MARCHE–STYLE SQUID

Chop the anchovy fillets. Heat the olive oil in a pan with the garlic and parsley. Add the squid and anchovies and season lightly with salt and pepper. Cook over a low heat for 10 minutes, then stir in the wine and 2–3 tablespoons water. Simmer gently for about 20 minutes until tender.

CALAMARI ALLA MARCHIGIANA

Serves 4

2 salted anchovies, heads removed, cleaned and
filleted (see page 596), soaked in cold water
for 10 minutes and drained

5 tablespoons olive oil

1 garlic clove

1 fresh flat-leaf parsley sprig, chopped

800 g/1³/₄ lb small squid, cleaned

5 tablespoons white wine

salt and pepper

FRIED SQUID

CALAMARI FRITTI

Serves 4

800 g/1³/₄ lb small squid, cleaned

plain flour, for dusting

6 tablespoons olive oil

salt

Dust the squid with flour. Heat the olive oil in a frying pan, add the squid and cook until golden brown all over. Remove with a slotted spoon and drain on kitchen paper, then season lightly with salt. Squid cooked this way are often served with fried langoustines or other delicate fried seafood.

SQUID STUFFED WITH PRAWNS

CALAMARI RIPIENI AI GAMBERETTI

Serves 4

1 potato, unpeeled

4 large squid, cleaned

300 g/11 oz cooked prawns, peeled and chopped

2 egg yolks, lightly beaten

4 tablespoons olive oil

1 garlic clove

4 tablespoons double cream

250 ml/8 fl oz passata

1 fresh flat-leaf parsley sprig, chopped

salt and pepper

Cook the potato in salted, boiling water for 20–30 minutes until tender, then drain, peel and mash with a potato masher. Cook the squid tentacles in salted, boiling water for 3 minutes, then drain and chop. Mix together the mashed potato, tentacles, prawns and egg yolks in a bowl and season with salt and pepper to taste. Spoon the mixture into the body sacs of the squid, being careful not to overfill them, and secure with cocktail sticks. Heat the olive oil in a large frying pan, add the garlic and cook for a few minutes until browned, then remove and discard it. Add the squid to the pan and cook over a low heat for about 30 minutes. Stir the cream into the passata, sprinkle with the parsley and pour the mixture over the squid. Heat through briefly, then serve.

GRILLED STUFFED SQUID

CALAMARI RIPIENI ALLA GRIGLIA

Serves 4

4 squid, cleaned

1 fresh flat-leaf parsley sprig, plus extra to garnish

¹/₂ garlic clove

50 g/2 oz breadcrumbs

olive oil, for drizzling and brushing

salt and pepper

lemon wedges, to garnish

Preheat the grill to hot. Chop the squid tentacles with the parsley and garlic. Put the mixture in a bowl, add the breadcrumbs, drizzle with olive oil and season with salt and pepper. Spoon the mixture into the body sacs of the squid and secure with cocktail sticks. Brush the outside of the squid with olive oil seasoned with salt and pepper, place on the grill rack and grill, turning frequently, until golden brown and tender. Serve hot with lemon wedges and sprigs of parsley.

SCALLOPS

The scallop has a very flat lower shell and a distinctly convex upper shell. It is off-white and often has shades of pink and hazelnut. Scallops are among the most highly prized shellfish and are sold both alive and shelled. They consist of three parts – a firm white muscle, a yellow or orange coral and a brown bearded part, called the skirt, which is not eaten. The best ones are 10–15 cm/4–6 inches in diameter. Scallop dishes are often served in the shells, so even if you're buying prepared scallops, it's worth asking the fishmonger for the upper half-shell. To open a scallop, hold it flat side up, insert the blade of a knife between the shells and cut the muscle attached to the top shell. Carefully remove the top shell, then slide the knife underneath the scallop to sever the lower muscle. Remove and discard the skirt and black stomach sac. The simplest way of enjoying scallops is to poach them. Soak the muscle and coral in cold water for 15 minutes to get rid of any residual sand. Then poach in salted, simmering water for 10 minutes, leave to cool and slice or leave whole. They may be served with mayonnaise or with oil and lemon juice, or mixed with a lettuce and watercress salad.

CAPPESANTE AL FORNO

Serves 4

12 scallops, shelled (above)

4 tablespoons olive oil, plus extra for drizzling

1 garlic clove

juice of 1 lemon, strained

6 fresh basil leaves, chopped

salt and white pepper

BAKED SCALLOPS

Scrub the curved half-shells and put in a low oven to keep warm. Heat the oil and garlic in a frying pan, add the scallops and cook for 4 minutes. Stir, season with salt, remove the pan from the heat and put the scallops in the half-shells. Sprinkle each with $^1/_2$ teaspoon of the cooking juices, a drizzle of olive oil and a pinch of pepper. Sprinkle with the lemon juice and basil and serve.

CAPPESANTE IN INSALATA

Serves 4

7 tablespoons olive oil

8 scallops, shelled (see page 710)

200 g/7 oz lettuce, shredded

1 bunch of rocket

3 tomatoes, peeled, seeded and diced

2 tablespoons white wine vinegar

salt and pepper

SCALLOP SALAD

Heat 2 tablespoons of the olive oil in a pan, add the scallops and cook for about 2 minutes on each side. Put the lettuce, rocket and tomatoes in a salad bowl. Whisk together the vinegar, a pinch of salt and the remaining olive oil in a bowl, season with pepper and pour the dressing over the salad. Add the scallops and toss.

CAPPESANTE IN SALSA DI ZAFFERANO

Serves 4

12 scallops, shelled (see page 710)

1 carrot, diced

1 spring onion, thinly sliced

175 ml/6 fl oz dry white wine

50 g/2 oz butter, cut into pieces

1 tablespoon double cream

pinch of saffron threads

salt

SCALLOPS IN SAFFRON SAUCE

Scrub the curved half-shells and dry with kitchen paper. Put the carrot, spring onion, wine, a pinch of salt and 4 tablespoons water in a pan, bring to the boil and simmer for 10 minutes. Add the scallops and cook for a further 4 minutes. Remove the scallops with a slotted spoon, halve them, place in the half-shells and keep warm. Boil the cooking juices until reduced, then stir in the butter, cream and saffron. Pour the hot sauce over the scallops and serve.

MUSSELS

These molluscs have several different names in Italian – cozze, muscoli, peoci and mitili. Nowadays, most commercially available mussels are farmed, which guarantees a high level of cleanliness. However, they should still be thoroughly scrubbed under cold, running water, but not left to soak in water. Pull off the beards with the help of a short, sharp knife and knock off any barnacles from the shells with the knife handle. Discard any mussels with broken shells or those that do not shut immediately when sharply tapped. To open them, place in a frying pan over a high heat for a few minutes. Discard any that remain closed. Their tender tasty flesh is very easy to digest and their cooking juices are a delicious addition to soups, sauces and risottos.

CREAMY MUSSELS

Put the mussels in a pan with the olive oil, garlic and lemon juice, cover and cook over a high heat, shaking the pan occasionally, for about 5 minutes until the shells open. Drain, reserving the cooking liquid. Discard any mussels that remain shut and the empty half-shells. Place the mussels in their half-shells on a serving dish. Mix the mayonnaise with 1–2 tablespoons of the reserved cooking liquid and spoon the mixture over the mussels. Season with a little pepper and garnish with the basil and diced tomato.

COZZE ALLA CREMA
Serves 4
1.5 kg/3¼ mussels,
scrubbed and beards removed
3 tablespoons olive oil
1 garlic clove
juice of ½ lemon, strained
1 quantity Mayonnaise (see page 65)
pepper

For the garnish
8 fresh basil leaves
1 tomato, diced

MUSSELS

COZZE ALLA MARINARA

Serves 4

1.5 kg/3¹/₄ lb mussels, scrubbed
and beards removed

3 tablespoons finely chopped fresh flat-leaf parsley

pepper

MUSSELS MARINARA

Put the mussels in a pan over a high heat with plenty of pepper but no water and cook for about 5 minutes until they open. Discard any that remain closed. Drain, reserving the cooking juices and place in a deep serving dish. Strain the cooking juices thorough a muslin-lined sieve into a bowl. Stir in the parsley, pour the mixture over the mussels and serve.

COZZE CON PEPERONI VERDI

Serves 4

1 kg/2¹/₄ lb mussels, scrubbed and beards removed

3 tablespoons olive oil

2 garlic cloves

2–3 green peppers, halved, seeded and sliced

2 fresh thyme sprigs, chopped

salt

MUSSELS WITH GREEN PEPPERS

Put the mussels in a frying pan with 1 tablespoon of the olive oil and one of the garlic cloves and cook over a high heat for about 5 minutes until they open. Discard any that remain closed. Remove the mussels from their shells and set aside. Chop the remaining garlic. Heat the remaining olive oil in a frying pan, add the green peppers and remaining garlic and cook over a medium heat, stirring frequently, for 10 minutes. Season with salt, add the mussels and cook, stirring gently, for a few minutes. Transfer to a warm serving dish and sprinkle with the thyme.

COZZE GRATINATE

Serves 4

1 kg/2¹/₄ lb mussels, scrubbed and beards removed

3 tablespoons chopped fresh flat-leaf parsley

2 garlic cloves, chopped

large pinch of dried oregano

olive oil, for drizzling

80 g/3 oz breadcrumbs

salt and pepper

1 lemon, cut into wedges, to garnish

MUSSELS AU GRATIN

Preheat the oven to 200°C/400°F/Gas Mark 6. Put the mussels in a frying pan and place over a high heat for about 5 minutes until they open. As they open, remove from the frying pan and place the half-shells containing the mussels in a roasting tin. Discard any that remain closed and the empty half-shells. Sprinkle the mussels with the parsley, garlic and oregano, season with salt, drizzle generously with olive oil and sprinkle with the breadcrumbs. Bake for 5 minutes, then transfer to a warm serving dish, season with pepper and garnish with the lemon wedges.

IMPEPATA DI COZZE

Serves 4

2 kg/4¹/₂ lb mussels, scrubbed and beards removed

3 tablespoons chopped fresh flat-leaf parsley

pepper

PEPPERED MUSSELS

Put the mussels in a frying pan with plenty of pepper and cook over a high heat for about 5 minutes until they open. Discard any that remain closed. Sprinkle with the parsley, remove the pan from the heat and serve.

OYSTERS

Oysters are the favourite antipasto of the most demanding gourmets worldwide, but which type is the best, flat ones or bowl-shaped ones? Flat oysters have smooth, flattened, often rounded shells and come in two varieties: belons with white flesh and marennes with green flesh. The belon is the queen of oysters owing to its plumpness and length, 13–15 cm/5–6 inches. Bowl-shaped oysters are longer and deeper. Oysters must reach the kitchen alive. This means that, before they are opened, the shells must be tightly closed and, once opened with a special knife, they must draw away from the slightest touch. To open an oyster, hold it flat side up in the hollow of one hand – it's safest to wrap your hand in a tea towel first to help avoid injury if the knife slips. Insert a strong knife, preferably an oyster knife, into the hinge of the shell and prise the two shells apart. Sever the muscle that holds the oyster to the top shell and lift the shell off, then sever the lower muscle. Pour the liquid out of the bottom half-shell into a bowl and strain. Leave the oysters in their half-shells on a bed of ice for 30 minutes to release their liquor, that is what makes their flavour unforgettable. Provide your guests with suitable metal forks to remove the oysters from the half-shells, bearing in mind that silver forks will turn black. According to connoisseurs, oysters should be eaten raw and without any dressing or, at most, with a small dash of lemon juice. Some accept combining them with slices of lightly buttered rye bread. Nevertheless, oysters may also be fried, marinated or prepared American-style. How many oysters per person? Experts vary in recommending between six and nine. We consider six to be the right number when they are served with a simple sauce or dressing. In seafood restaurants, oysters are usually served by the dozen.

GREEK OYSTERS

Open the oysters (see opposite), discard the top shells and arrange the half-shells on a tray. Mix together the lemon juice and olive oil in a sauce boat, season with salt and pepper and stir in the parsley. Make a bed of crushed ice on a serving dish and place the oysters on top. Serve with the sauce handed separately.

OSTRICHE ALLA GRECA

Serves 4

24 live oysters

juice of 2 lemons, strained

100 ml/3¹/₂ fl oz olive oil

1 small fresh flat-leaf parsley sprig, chopped

crushed ice

salt and pepper

AMERICAN OYSTERS

Preheat the oven to 240°C/475°F/Gas Mark 9. Open the oysters (see opposite), discard the top shells and season with a pinch of salt, a few drops of lemon juice and a pinch of cayenne. Crumble the bread over them and drizzle with the melted butter. Bake for 5 minutes and serve.

OSTRICHE ALL'AMERICANA

Serves 4

24 live oysters

dash of lemon juice

pinch of cayenne pepper

2–3 day-old bread slices, crusts removed

40 g/1¹/₂ oz butter, melted

salt

HOT OYSTERS IN BEURRE BLANC

Preheat the oven to 110°C/225°F/Gas Mark ¹/₄. Put the shallots, half the wine and the vinegar in a pan, season with salt and pepper and set over a medium heat until reduced by two-thirds. Add the cream and bring to the boil. Stir in the butter, a little at a time. Remove the pan from the heat, season with salt and pepper to taste and stir in the onion. Return the pan to the heat and keep warm, stirring occasionally, but do not allow the sauce to boil. Open the oysters (see opposite), discard the top shells, tip the liquor into a saucepan and remove the oysters from the half-shells. Add the remaining wine to the liquor, season with salt and pepper, bring to the boil and simmer until reduced by two-thirds. Wash the empty half-shells thoroughly, dry and arrange on a bed of sea salt on an ovenproof dish. Place the shells in the oven for 10 minutes. Dip the oysters in the warm liquor and wine mixture and place in the hot-half shells. Strain the liquor and wine mixture into the butter sauce, pour it over the oysters and serve.

OSTRICHE CALDE AL BURRO BIANCO

Serves 4

2 shallots, chopped

3 tablespoons dry white wine

1 tablespoon white wine vinegar

1 tablespoon double cream

150 g/5 oz butter, chilled and cut into pieces

1 onion, chopped

24 live oysters

coarse sea salt

salt and pepper

CURRIED OYSTERS

OSTRICHE CALDE AL CURRY

Serves 4

16 live oysters

400 g/14 oz spinach

6 tablespoons double cream

100 g/3½ oz butter

1 teaspoon curry powder

2 egg yolks

salt and pepper

Open the oysters (see page 716), discard the top shells, tip the liquor into a bowl and remove the oysters from the half-shells. Steam the spinach for about 5 minutes, then drain, pressing out as much liquid as possible, and pass through a food mill. Heat the spinach purée in a pan with 4 tablespoons of the cream and a pinch of salt. Divide the spinach among the half-shells. Strain the oyster liquor into a small saucepan and heat gently, then add the oysters and simmer for 5 minutes. Drain the oysters and place them on top of the spinach mixture. Mix together the butter and curry powder and set aside. Whisk the egg yolks and remaining cream in a double boiler or heat-proof bowl set over a pan of barely simmering water until light and fluffy. Stir in the curry butter, cook for a few minutes more and season with salt and pepper to taste. Spoon the sauce over the oysters and serve.

OYSTERS IN SALTED SABAYON SAUCE

OSTRICHE CON LO ZABAIONE SALATO

Serves 4

16 live oysters

200 g/7 oz courgettes, sliced

50 g/2 oz butter, cut into pieces

4 egg yolks

1 shallot, finely chopped

100 ml/3½ fl oz sparkling dry white wine

coarse sea salt

salt and pepper

Preheat the oven to 220°C/425°F/Gas Mark 7. Open the oysters (see page 716), remove from the half-shells and place in a dish. Discard the top shells and wash the bottom shells well under cold running water. Cook the courgettes in salted, boiling water for 5 minutes, then drain, tip into a food processor and process to a purée. Gently heat the purée with a knob of the butter and a pinch of salt in a small saucepan. Beat the egg yolks with the shallot in a double boiler or heat-proof bowl, then whisk in the wine. Set the double boiler over a medium heat or place the bowl over a pan of barely simmering water and heat, whisking constantly, for about 10 minutes until thickened. Do not allow the mixture to boil. Remove the sauce from the heat and stir in the remaining butter, a pinch of salt and a pinch of pepper. Make a bed of coarse salt on a baking sheet and arrange the half-shells on top. Place a tablespoon of the courgette purée in each shell, top with an oyster and cover with a tablespoon of the sauce. Bake for 4–5 minutes and serve.

OCTOPUS

Octopuses are cephalopods with a highly prized but tough flesh. They require careful preparation to tenderize. Immediately after they are caught, they should be beaten thoroughly, then cooked slowly in a covered pan. Young male octopuses are the tastiest and most tender. To clean an octopus, remove the eyes, beak and only bone, then turn the body sac inside out and empty it. All the rest is edible. Italians also cook very small octopuses. There are two types — musky octopuses, which have a characteristic aroma, and curled octopuses, which are tougher in texture and lack the musky scent. Their Italian name, moscardini, is Ligurian and this is also how they are known in many other Italian regions, but in Naples they are called polpetelli and in Veneto polpetti. They are very small with lean, tender, tasty flesh that is easy to digest. They must be washed well and, if they are really very small, they can be left whole. Otherwise, remove the beak and eyes. Musky octopuses are excellent simply poached and dressed with olive oil and lemon juice. They are often prepared in the same ways as cuttlefish and young squid, which may be substituted for them in the recipes here. Similarly, you could use very small, baby octopuses of another variety.

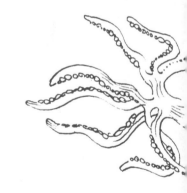

OCTOPUS AND POTATO SALAD

Put the octopus in a large pan and add water to cover and a pinch of salt. Bring to the boil, then lower the heat, cover and simmer for 30 minutes or until tender. Remove from the heat and leave to cool in the cooking liquid, then drain, skin and cut into pieces. Meanwhile, cook the potatoes in salted, boiling water for about 30 minutes until tender, then drain, peel and dice them. Put them in a salad bowl and sprinkle with the wine. Add the octopus, season with salt and pepper to taste, sprinkle with the rosemary and drizzle with olive oil.

INSALATA DI POLPI E PATATE

Serves 4

1-kg/2¹/₄-lb octopus, cleaned

4 potatoes, unpeeled

1 tablespoon dry white wine

pinch of fresh rosemary needles

olive oil, for drizzling

salt and pepper

LIGURIAN MUSKY OCTOPUS

Cut the octopuses into pieces unless they are very small. Bring a pan of lightly salted water to the boil, add one of the onions, 2–3 tablespoons of the vinegar and the octopuses and simmer for 10–15 minutes. Drain and set aside. Thinly slice the remaining onions. Heat the olive oil in a pan, add the onions, garlic, sage and bay leaf and cook over a low heat, stirring occasionally, for about 10 minutes. Pour in the remaining vinegar, remove and discard the garlic and simmer gently for about 30 minutes. Season with salt and pepper to taste. Pack the octopuses in layers in a jar and pour in the warm vinegar to cover. Close the jar tightly and keep in a cool place. Musky octopuses prepared in this way keep for quite a long time.

MOSCARDINI ALLA LIGURE

Serves 4

1.5 kg/3^1/$_4$ lb musky octopuses, cleaned

3 onions

1 litre/1^3/$_4$ pints white wine vinegar

4 tablespoons olive oil

1 garlic clove

1 fresh sage sprig

1 bay leaf

salt and pepper

MUSKY OCTOPUS NAPOLETANA

Cook the octopuses in salted, boiling water for 10 minutes or more, depending on their size. Drain, cut into pieces and place in a dish. Mix together the olive oil, parsley, garlic and lemon juice in a jug, season with salt and pepper and pour the dressing over the octopuses. Leave in a cool place for 1 hour for the flavours to mingle before serving.

MOSCARDINI ALLA NAPOLETANA

Serves 4

1 kg/2^1/$_4$ lb musky octopuses, cleaned

6 tablespoons olive oil

2 tablespoons chopped fresh flat-leaf parsley

1 garlic clove, chopped

juice of 1 lemon, strained

salt and pepper

BRAISED MUSKY OCTOPUS

Heat the olive oil in a pan with the garlic and chilli, add the octopuses and cook, stirring occasionally, until golden brown all over, then remove from the pan. Add the tomatoes to the pan and cook for 5 minutes over a low heat. Season with salt and pepper and cook for a further 10 minutes. Return the octopuses to the pan, sprinkle with the parsley, heat through and serve.

MOSCARDINI IN UMIDO

Serves 4

3 tablespoons olive oil

1 garlic clove, chopped

^{1}/$_2$ fresh red chilli, seeded and chopped

1 kg/2^1/$_4$ lb musky octopuses, cleaned

3 tomatoes, peeled, seeded and chopped

2 tablespoons chopped fresh flat-leaf parsley

salt and pepper

POLPI AFFOGATI

Serves 4

900 g/2 lb small octopuses, cleaned

150 ml/¹/₄ pint olive oil

400 g/14 oz tomatoes, peeled, seeded and sliced

3 tablespoons chopped fresh flat-leaf parsley

1 garlic clove, chopped

salt

POACHED OCTOPUS

Put the octopuses in a flameproof casserole, preferably earthenware, with the olive oil, tomatoes, parsley and garlic. Do not add salt or water. Cover tightly and cook over a low heat for 30 minutes. Do not remove the lid during cooking. Season with salt and serve in their sauce, which should be plentiful.

POLPI AL VINO ROSSO

Serves 4

3 tablespoons olive oil

1 onion, chopped

1 garlic clove

1 fresh sage leaf

1 fresh rosemary sprig

1-kg/2¹/₄-lb octopus, cleaned and cut into pieces

5 tablespoons red wine

2 bay leaves

salt and pepper

OCTOPUS IN RED WINE

Heat the olive oil in a saucepan, add the onion, garlic, sage and rosemary and cook over a low heat, stirring occasionally, for 5 minutes. Add the octopus and cook for a few minutes more, then pour in the wine, add the bay leaves and season with salt and pepper to taste. Simmer over a very low heat for 1¹/₂ hours. Serve hot or cold.

POLPI DEL MARINAIO

Serves 4

1-kg/2¹/₄-lb octopus, cleaned

1 garlic clove, crushed

1 onion, thinly sliced

olive oil, for drizzling

1 tomato, peeled, seeded and chopped

5 tablespoons white wine

salt and pepper

MARINER'S OCTOPUS

Put the octopus into a flameproof casserole, preferably earthenware, add the garlic and onion, season with salt and pepper and drizzle with olive oil. Cover and cook over a low heat for 1 hour. Add the tomato and wine and cook for 1 hour more until the octopus is tender. Remove the octopus from the casserole and cut into pieces. Serve with the cooking juices, which should be fairly thick; if they are too thick, add a little lukewarm water.

CUTTLEFISH

Cuttlefish are cephalopods with long tentacles and a character-istic oval bone, called a quill or cuttlebone. The most highly prized cuttlefish are young – 10–12 cm/4–4½ inches long – with tender, easy-to-digest flesh that cooks quickly. Adult cuttlefish are tougher and require longer cooking times. Preparation is simple. Cut off the tentacles just in front of the eyes and discard the beak in their centre. Separate and skin the tentacles and pull off the skin from the body. Cut along the back and remove the cuttlebone, then remove the ink sac. Remove and discard the innards and the head. Cut the body in half, unless you're going to stuff it, and wash well. Cuttlefish ink may be used to add flavour and colour to spaghetti sauces or risottos.

WARM CUTTLEFISH SALAD WITH GREEN ASPARAGUS

Halve the pieces of asparagus lengthways, then parboil in salted water for about 5 minutes. Drain and refresh under cold, running water. Heat the olive oil in a frying pan, add the cuttlefish and cook, stirring frequently, until lightly browned. Season with salt and pepper, add the parsley, garlic, coriander and asparagus and mix well. Remove the pan from the heat, transfer to a serving dish and serve warm.

INSALATA TIEPIDA DI SEPPIE CON ASPARAGI VERDI

Serves 6

300 g/11 oz green asparagus, spears cut into 5-cm/2-inch lengths

3 tablespoons olive oil

500 g/1 lb 2 oz medium cuttlefish, cleaned and cut into thin strips

1 tablespoon fresh flat-leaf parsley, chopped

1 garlic clove, chopped

1 teaspoon coriander seeds • salt and pepper

CUTTLEFISH WITH SPINACH

Cook the spinach, in just the water clinging to the leaves after washing, for about 5 minutes, then drain, squeeze out as much liquid as possible and chop. Heat the olive oil in a pan, add the onion and garlic and cook, stirring occasionally, until the garlic turns brown, then remove and discard it. Add the cuttlefish and mix well, then season and pour in the wine. Cook until it has evaporated, then cover and simmer over a low heat for about 10 minutes. Add the spinach and passata and simmer for about 30 minutes. Meanwhile, preheat the oven to 160°C/325°F/Gas Mark 3. Spread the pine nuts on a baking sheet and toast in the oven, stirring occasionally, until golden brown. Stir into the cuttlefish for the last few minutes of the cooking time.

SEPPIE AGLI SPINACI

Serves 4

250 g/9 oz spinach

2 tablespoons olive oil

1 onion, thinly sliced

1 garlic clove

800 g/1¾ lb small cuttlefish, cleaned and halved

175 ml/6 fl oz dry white wine

250 ml/8 fl oz passata

20 g/¾ oz pine nuts

salt and pepper

CUTTLEFISH WITH PEAS

SEPPIE AI PISELLI

Serves 4

4 tablespoons olive oil1 garlic clove

800 g/1³/₄ lb cuttlefish, cleaned and cut into strips

675g/1¹/₂ lb shelled peas

or canned peas, drained and rinsed

175 ml/6 fl oz dry white wine

salt and pepper

Heat the oil and garlic in a saucepan until the garlic tuns brown, then remove and discard it. Add the cuttlefish to the pan, season with salt and pepper, stir well and cook for a few minutes. Add the wine and cook until it has evaporated. Pour in just enough water to almost cover the cuttlefish and bring to the boil. Lower the heat, cover and simmer for about 1 hour. Add the peas and cook for about 30 minutes until tender.

CUTTLEFISH WITH ARTICHOKES

SEPPIE CON I CARCIOFI

Serves 4

4 tablespoons olive oil • 1 garlic clove

800 g/1³/₄ lb cuttlefish, cleaned and cut into strips

175 ml/6 fl oz dry white wine

6 globe artichokes, trimmed, chokes removed

and cut into wedges

salt and pepper

Heat the oil and garlic in a pan until the garlic turns brown, then remove and discard it. Add the cuttlefish to the pan, season, mix well and cook for a few minutes. Add the wine and cook until it has almost completely evaporated. Pour in just enough water to almost cover the cuttlefish and bring to the boil. Lower the heat, cover and simmer for 30–40 minutes. Add the artichokes and simmer for a further 15 minutes until tender. Season with salt and pepper to taste.

STUFFED CUTTLEFISH

SEPPIE FARCITE

Serves 4

300 g/11 oz baby squid,

cleaned (see page 707) and chopped

1 tablespoon capers, drained, rinsed and chopped

1 tablespoon pine nuts

1 small fresh flat-leaf parsley sprig, chopped

2 eggs, lightly beaten

2–3 bread rolls, crusts removed

4 large cuttlefish, cleaned

3–4 tablespoons olive oil • salt and pepper

Preheat the oven to 180°C/350°F/Gas Mark 4. Mix together the squid, capers, pine nuts, parsley and eggs in a bowl, crumble in the rolls, mix well and season with salt and pepper. Stuff the cuttlefish with the mixture. Place the cuttlefish in a single layer in an ovenproof dish, drizzle with the olive oil and season with salt and a little pepper. Bake for about 30 minutes.

CUTTLEFISH AU GRATIN

SEPPIE GRATINATE

Serves 6

6 tablespoons olive oil, plus extra for drizzling

2 garlic cloves, chopped

1 kg/2¹/₄ lb cuttlefish, cleaned and cut into strips

1 tablespoon capers, drained and rinsed

50 g/2 oz green olives, stoned and chopped

1 fresh flat-leaf parsley sprig, chopped

50 g/2 oz breadcrumbs • salt and pepper

Heat the olive oil in a flameproof casserole, add the garlic and cuttlefish and cook over a high heat until golden brown. Season with salt and pepper, add the capers and olives, lower the heat, cover and simmer gently for about 45 minutes. Preheat the oven to 180°C/350°F/Gas Mark 4. Mix together the parsley and breadcrumbs and sprinkle the mixture over the cuttlefish. Drizzle with olive oil and bake for about 10 minutes.

FISH SOUPS

We have fishermen to thank for fish soups, which were originally created to avoid wasting unsold fish from the day's catch. They simply put everything into a large pot, cooked it and then ate it. To begin with, the poorest and least prized fish were the ones used, but this simple dish gradually developed and improved over the years. Today we have both simple soups and sophisticated stews that often include fine fish, crustaceans and shellfish. Around Italy's 7,000 km/4,350 miles of coastline, there are as many kinds of fish soup as there are region bordering the sea – and they all have different names, such as brodetto, cacciucco, buridda and ciuppin.

→ For 6 servings, allow 2.5–3 kg/5$\frac{1}{2}$–6$\frac{1}{2}$ lb fish, consisting of five or six different varieties. There are also soups made with only one type of fish. Scorpion fish adds more flavour than almost any other.

→ As a general rule, there should be at least three different types of fish in the soup: one stock-making fish, such as scorpion fish, one sauce-making fish, such as red mullet, and a sliced fish, such as huss.

→ Large fish should be cut into chunks and small ones should be left whole.

→ Add firm-fleshed fish first, then the delicate ones.

→ Cook on a high heat for about 20 minutes, then serve immediately. Do not overcook the fish.

→ Add only small quantities of tomato. Pepper, on the other hand, may be used generously. If you like, lightly toasted slices of homemade bread may be gently rubbed with a clove of garlic and served separately. Alternatively, place them in the base of soup plates and ladle the soup over them.

QUANTITIES AND COOKING TIMES

725

MARCHE–STYLE FISH SOUP

BRODETTO MARCHIGIANO

Serves 8–10

300 g/11 oz mussels, scrubbed
and beards removed

300 g/11 oz clams, scrubbed

4–5 tablespoons olive oil

1 onion, finely chopped

300 g/11 oz large cuttlefish, cleaned

1 green pepper, halved, seeded and sliced

5 just-ripe tomatoes, peeled, seeded and chopped

1 fresh chilli, seeded and finely chopped

100 ml/3¹/₂ fl oz white wine vinegar

2.5 kg/5¹/₂ lb mixed fish, such as scorpion fish,
monkfish fillet, mackerel and red mullet, cleaned
and cut into chunks if necessary

300 g/11 oz mantis shrimp,
slipper lobsters or langoustines

300 g/11 oz small cuttlefish, cleaned

salt and pepper

There are as many recipes for brodetto as there are regions along the Adriatic coast. This version is traditionally made at San Benedetto di Tronto in Marche. Discard any mussels and clams with broken shells or those that do not shut immediately when sharply tapped. Place them in two separate frying pans over a high heat until they open. Discard any that remain closed. Remove some of the mussels and clams from their shells and leave the rest in situ. Heat the olive oil in a large flameproof casserole, add the onion and cook over a low heat, stirring occasionally, for 5 minutes. Add the large cuttlefish and cook for 10 minutes, then add the green pepper, season with salt and pepper and mix well. Cook over a low heat for a further 10 minutes. Add the tomatoes, chilli and vinegar and cook until the vinegar has evaporated. Gradually add the fish and shellfish in layers, beginning with the least delicate and finishing with the mussels, and the mantis shrimp, slipper lobsters or langoustines. Cover and simmer gently for about 20 minutes.

LIVORNO–STYLE FISH SOUP

CACCIUCCO

Serves 8

175 ml/6 fl oz olive oil

1 onion, chopped

1 fresh flat-leaf parsley sprig, chopped

2 garlic cloves, chopped

1 small fresh chilli, seeded and chopped

500 ml/18 fl oz red or white wine

300 g/11 oz tomatoes, peeled, seeded and chopped

2.5 kg/5¹/₂ lb mixed fish (see method), cleaned
and cut into chunks if necessary

fish stock (see page 208), optional

500 g/1 lb 2 oz mussels, scrubbed
and beards removed

salt and pepper

toast rubbed with garlic, to serve

For this typical Tyrrhenian-coast fish soup, you need a few slices of monkfish, a conger or freshwater eel, a few squid or cuttlefish and some mussels. Heat the olive oil in a flameproof casserole, preferably earthenware, add the onion, parsley, garlic and chilli, season with salt and pepper and cook over a low heat, stirring occasionally, for about 10 minutes until the onion is golden brown. Add the wine and cook for 10 minutes more, then add the tomatoes and simmer for a further 10 minutes. Add the firmer fish, pour in a little warm water or fish stock, and cook on a high heat for 10 minutes. Gradually add the more delicate fish, finishing with the mussels. (Discard any with broken shells or that do not shut immediately when sharply tapped, and any that remain closed after cooking.) The total cooking time for the fish is about 30 minutes. Serve with slices of toast rubbed with garlic.

FISHERMAN'S SOUP

Serves 4

1 onion

1 clove

5 carrots

1 celery stick, chopped

400 g/14 oz sea bass, cleaned

500 g/1 lb 2 oz monkfish fillet

400 g/14 oz gurnard, cleaned

1 bunch of fresh mixed herbs

4 potatoes

4 leeks

4 courgettes

1 kg/2¼ lb mussels, scrubbed and beards removed

salt and pepper

1 quantity Vinaigrette (see page 76), to serve

Stud the onion with the clove and slice one of the carrots. Put the onion, sliced carrot, celery, any fish trimmings and the herbs in a large pan, season with salt and pepper and add 2.5 litres/4¼ pints water. Bring just to the boil, then lower the heat, cover and simmer for 30 minutes to make a court-bouillon. Meanwhile, put the potatoes in cold salted water and bring to the boil. Add the remaining carrots and other vegetables and cook for about 20 minutes, then drain and slice. Discard any mussels with broken shells or that do not shut immediately when sharply tapped. Place the mussels in a frying pan over a high heat until the shells open. Discard any that remain closed. Put the fish in a large pan and strain the court-bouillon over them. Bring to the boil and cook over a medium heat for about 30 minutes. Transfer the fish to the middle of a warm serving dish and place the mussels on one side and the vegetables on the other. Serve the soup with a vinaigrette.

PIRATE'S FISH SOUP

Serves 6

1 red pepper, halved, seeded and sliced

1 green pepper, halved, seeded and sliced

2 dried chillies, seeded and crumbled

4 garlic cloves, chopped

1 bunch of fresh mixed herbs, such as marjoram, thyme, basil, sage and chives

200 ml/7 fl oz olive oil

200 ml/7 fl oz red wine

300 g/11 oz octopuses, cleaned

300 g/11 oz cuttlefish, cleaned and halved if large

300 g/11 oz musky or curled octopuses, cleaned

100 ml/3½ fl oz white rum

500 g/1 lb 2 oz mussels, scrubbed and beards removed

300 g/11 oz clams, scrubbed

pinch of freshly grated nutmeg (optional)

salt and pepper

Put the peppers, chillies, garlic, herbs, olive oil and wine in a flameproof casserole and cook over a medium heat for 10 minutes. Add the octopuses and cuttlefish and simmer for 20 minutes. Add the musky or curled octopuses and rum and cook for a further 10 minutes. Discard any mussels and clams with broken shells or that do not shut immediately when sharply tapped. Add the mussels and clams to the casserole, stir well, cover and cook for 5–10 minutes until the shells have opened. Discard any that remain shut. Season with salt and pepper to taste, sprinkle with nutmeg if using, and serve.

MIXED FISH SOUP WITH ORANGE

Put the leek, carrots, wine and any fish trimmings in a large saucepan, season with salt and add 2 litres/3½ pints water. Bring to the boil, then lower the heat and simmer for 30 minutes. Strain and reserve 1.5 litres/2½ pints. Heat the olive oil in a flameproof casserole, add the onion and cook over a low heat, stirring occasionally, for 5 minutes. Add half the reserved stock and simmer for 20 minutes or until the onion has almost disintegrated. Put the hake, grey mullet, scorpion fish, sole, cod, squid and cuttlefish into a large pan, pour in the remaining reserved stock, season with salt and poach for 30 minutes. Discard any clams with broken shells or that do not shut immediately when sharply tapped. Add the onion mixture, orange juice, langoustines or prawns, clams, tomato and basil, season with salt and pepper, cover and cook for about 3 minutes until the clam shells have opened. Discard any that remain closed. Serve the soup with croûtons.

ZUPPA DI PESCE MISTO ALL'ARANCIA

Serves 6

1 leek
2 carrots
5 tablespoons dry white wine
1 hake, cleaned and cut into chunks
1 grey mullet, cleaned and cut into chunks
1 scorpion fish, cleaned and cut into chunks
1 sole, cleaned and cut into chunks
2 tablespoons olive oil
1 onion, finely chopped
500 g/1 lb 2 oz cod fillet, cut into chunks
3 squid, cleaned
3 cuttlefish, cleaned and halved if large
400 g/14 oz clams, scrubbed
175 ml/6 fl oz freshly squeezed orange juice, strained
10 langoustines or Dublin Bay prawns
1 tomato, peeled, seeded and cubed
8 fresh basil leaves, chopped
salt and pepper
croûtons, to serve

MIXED SHELLFISH SOUP

Discard any mussels, cockles and clams with broken shells or that do not shut immediately when sharply tapped. Pour the wine into a large pan, add the parsley and celery leaves, onions, lemon rind, scallops and all the other shellfish. Cover and cook over a medium-high heat until the shells open. Discard any that remain closed. Season generously with pepper, but taste before adding any salt, as shellfish are already quite salty. Garnish with lemon slices and serve.

ZUPPA DI PESCE MISTO DI CONCHIGLIE

Serves 4

12 mussels, scrubbed and beards removed
12 scallops, shelled
12 cockles, scrubbed
12 carpet shell clams, scrubbed
12 warty venus clams, scrubbed
150 ml/¼ pint dry white wine
1 fresh flat-leaf parsley sprig, coarsely chopped
leaves of 1 celery stick, coarsely chopped
2 onions, thinly sliced
grated rind of ½ lemon
salt and pepper
1 lemon, sliced, to garnish

SNAILS

The most highly prized snails – the ones used for the famous Bourguignonne recipe – are the so-called vineyard snails, widespread in Piedmont and Lombardy. The others are almost all farmed. Cleaned, ready-to-cook, frozen or canned snails are available. If you obtain fresh – that is, live – snails, the task of rendering them edible is long, complicated and requires a ruthlessness that not everyone possesses. However, in order to be comprehensive, an outline of how to prepare live snails is given below.

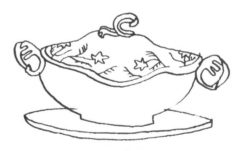

→ Cover the snails with coarse salt and leave in a fairly large, covered ventilated box for 24 hours.

→ Wash them several times in water, vinegar and salt until there are no traces of sliminess left in the water.

→ Dip them several times in cornmeal and rinse again under cold, running water.

→ Parboil by immersing in boiling water for 5 minutes.

→ Carefully extract the snails from the shells and remove and discard the black end part.

→ Place in a court-bouillon made with carrot, onion, thyme, bay leaf and parsley and simmer for 4 hours.

→ Drain and prepare according to the chosen recipe.

→ Allow 6 per serving as an antipasto and 12 as a main course.

BOURGUIGNONNE SNAILS

Preheat the oven to 190°C/375°F/Gas Mark 5. Mix together the butter, parsley, garlic and shallots in a bowl, season with salt and pepper and beat until smooth. Put a little of the mixture in the base of each shell, then place the snails on top and spread with a little more of the butter mixture. Place the shells in an ovenproof dish and bake for about 10 minutes.

LUMACHE ALLA BOURGUIGNONNE

Serves 4

350 g/12 oz butter, softened

1 fresh flat-leaf parsley sprig, finely chopped

2 garlic cloves, finely chopped

2 shallots, finely chopped

48 prepared snails, with shells

salt and pepper

LIGURIAN SNAILS

Place the mushrooms in a bowl, add lukewarm water to cover and leave to soak for 2 hours. Heat the olive oil in a pan, add the onion, garlic and parsley and cook over a low heat, stirring occasionally, for 5 minutes. Drain the mushrooms, squeeze out and chop. Stir the mushrooms, rosemary and oregano into the pan and cook for 5 minutes. Add the snails and cook for a few minutes more, then add the wine and cook until it has evaporated. Pour in the passata, season with salt and pepper to taste, cover and simmer over a low heat for 45 minutes, adding a little water if the mixture seems to be drying out.

LUMACHE ALLA LIGURE

Serves 4

10 g/¼ oz dried mushrooms

3 tablespoons olive oil

1 onion, chopped

1 garlic clove, chopped

1 fresh flat-leaf parsley sprig, chopped

1 teaspoon chopped fresh rosemary

½ teaspoon dried oregano

48 prepared snails

5 tablespoons dry white wine

400 ml/14 fl oz passata

salt and pepper

LOMBARD SNAILS

Chop the anchovy. Heat the olive oil with the garlic in a pan until the garlic turns brown, then remove and discard it. Add the anchovies, butter, parsley and onion and cook over a low heat, mashing the anchovies until they have almost disintegrated. Stir in the flour, then add the snails and cook for a few minutes. Pour in the wine, season with salt and pepper to taste, cover and simmer for about 1 hour. Serve hot.

LUMACHE ALLA LOMBARDA

Serves 4

50 g/2 oz salted anchovies, heads removed, cleaned and filleted (see page 596), soaked in cold water for 10 minutes and drained

3 tablespoons olive oil

1 garlic clove

50 g/2 oz butter

1 fresh flat-leaf parsley sprig, chopped

¼ onion, chopped

1 tablespoon plain flour

48 prepared snails

175 ml/6 fl oz dry white wine

salt and pepper

FROGS

Frog flesh is lean and white, with a delicate flavour that is highly appreciated by connoisseurs. They are mainly found in Piedmont and Lombardy. Frogs are sold cleaned and skinned. Generally, only the legs are cooked, but frog aficionados usually eat them whole, bones and all. A standard portion is a dozen frogs' legs per person.

GENOESE FROGS' LEGS

RANE ALLA GENOVESE

Serves 4

1 onion, chopped

1 fresh flat-leaf parsley sprig, chopped

pinch of dried oregano

1 bay leaf

175 ml/6 fl oz white wine vinegar

1 kg/2¹/₄ lb frogs' legs

plain flour, for dusting

5 tablespoons olive oil

salt and pepper

Mix together the onion, parsley, oregano, bay leaf and vinegar in a bowl, season with salt and pepper, add the frogs' legs and leave to marinate for 30 minutes. Drain the frogs' legs and coat with flour. Heat the olive oil in a frying pan, add the frogs' legs and cook, turning occasionally, until golden brown all over. Sprinkle with salt and serve.

FROGS' LEGS IN WHITE WINE

RANE AL VINO BIANCO

Serves 4

250 ml/8 fl oz white wine

1 onion, sliced

1 fresh flat-leaf parsley sprig, chopped

1 kg/2¹/₄ lb frogs' legs

25 g/1 oz butter

1 teaspoon plain flour

1 egg yolk

juice of 1 lemon, strained

salt and pepper

Put the wine, onion and parsley in a saucepan, season with salt and pepper and bring to the boil. Add the frogs' legs and cook over a medium heat for 10 minutes. Remove the frogs' legs and boil the cooking liquid until it has reduced by two-thirds. Melt the butter in a small pan, stir in the flour and then stir the mixture into the reduced cooking liquid. Pass through a food mill into another pan, return to the heat and bring to the boil. Add the frogs' legs and cook for a further 5 minutes. Meanwhile, beat together the egg yolk and lemon juice in a bowl. Move the pan to the edge of the hob and stir in the egg yolk mixture.

FRIED FROGS' LEGS IN TOMATO SAUCE

Heat 2 tablespoons of the olive oil in a pan, add the tomatoes and a pinch of salt and cook over a medium heat, stirring frequently, for 10 minutes. Melt the butter in another pan, add the garlic and cook over a low heat, stirring frequently, for a few minutes, then add to the tomatoes. Stir in the lemon juice. Heat the remaining olive oil in a frying pan. Dust the frogs' legs with flour, then dip them in the cream and cook in the hot oil until golden brown all over. Transfer to a warm serving dish and spoon the tomato sauce over them.

RANE FRITTE IN SALSA

Serves 4

7 tablespoons olive oil

500 g/1 lb 2 oz tomatoes, peeled, seeded and chopped

25 g/1 oz butter

1 garlic clove, chopped

1 tablespoon lemon juice

1 kg/2¼ lb frogs' legs

plain flour, for dusting

200 ml/7 fl oz double cream

salt

FROGS' LEGS IN BREADCRUMBS

Spread out the flour in a shallow dish, lightly beat the eggs with a pinch of salt in another shallow dish and spread out the breadcrumbs in a third. Sprinkle the frogs' legs with salt and pepper. Dip the frogs' legs first in the flour, then in the eggs and, finally, in the breadcrumbs. Heat the olive oil and butter in a frying pan and cook the frogs' legs, in batches, until golden brown. Remove from the pan, drain on kitchen paper and season with salt. Sprinkle with the parsley and surround with the lemon.

RANE IMPANATE

Serves 4

50 g/2 oz plain flour

2 eggs

50 g/2 oz breadcrumbs

1 kg/2¼ lb frogs' legs

3 tablespoons olive oil

40 g/1½ oz butter

½ bunch of fresh flat-leaf parsley, chopped

1 lemon, peeled and sliced

salt and pepper

FROGS IN BATTER

Soak the frogs in cold water for 3 hours. Mix together the vinegar, parsley and a generous pinch of pepper in a bowl. Drain the frogs and add them to the bowl so that they are immersed. Mix together the flour, egg, egg yolk and a pinch of salt in another bowl and stir in the wine and olive oil to make a smooth batter. Heat the oil for deep-frying in a large pan. Drain the frogs, dip them in the batter and fry in the hot oil. Remove with a slotted spoon, drain on kitchen paper and season lightly with salt. Serve with the lemon wedges.

RANE IN PASTELLA

Serves 4

1 kg/2¼ lb frogs

500 ml/18 fl oz white wine vinegar

1 fresh flat-leaf parsley sprig, chopped

100 g/3½ oz plain flour

1 egg

1 egg yolk

5 tablespoons white wine

1 tablespoon olive oil

vegetable oil, for deep-frying

salt and pepper

1 lemon, cut into wedges, to serve

MEAT →

OFFAL →

MEAT

Meat? Yes, but always high-quality meat. Since the 1950s, consumption of this superb, protein-rich food has increased in Italy. Today's meat is finer, leaner, more tender and tastier than ever. This has happened in response to the demands of consumers and their determination to obtain the high-quality they expect. The nutritional value of contemporary meat means that, it is even included in some slimming diets. But you need to be choosy. It is certainly possible to identify the quality of meat at a glance, but it is also important to know how to pick the best cut for each recipe. This is also important for the family budget because it does not automatically follow that the most highly prized and expensive cuts are also the most nutritious and tasty. Equally, it would be absurd to ask for fillet steak every time. Less expensive cuts for stewing or braising, for example, certainly do not lack flavour.

CLASSIFICATION

In Italy meat is categorized in various ways. It is divided into:

ANIMALI DA MACELLO ('BUTCHERED' ANIMALS)

Beef, kid, lamb, mutton, pork, veal and also horse.

ANIMALI DA CORTILE (FARMYARD ANIMALS)

Chicken, duck, goose, guinea fowl, pigeon, turkey and rabbit.

SELVAGGINA E CACCIAGIONE (GAME)

Chamois (an Alpine, deer-like animal), hare, pheasant, quail, and wild boar. Meat can also divided into: red (beef, horse and mutton); white (kid, lamb, veal and poultry); and black (game). Finally, there are two more categories to remember:

MEAT DERIVATIVES

Meat extract and stock cubes.

SAUSAGES AND CURED MEATS

Whole or minced meat is often mixed with fat, flavoured with herbs and seasoned before being used to fill natural or artificial skins. Most sausages and cured meats are made from pork and are divided into cooked (cotechino, ham, etc.) and raw (salami, sausages, etc.).

N.B. For this edition, rabbit is included within Game (see pages 947 to 985) but recipes for all other 'farmyard animals', such as chicken and duck appear in Poultry (see pages 875 to 945).

Time is increasingly precious and today's lifestyles, however relaxed, all attach great importance to health, Therefore, the proper storage of food has become even more vital. As there is usually little time to go shopping and to cook, refrigerators and freezers have become essential. It is always best to wrap meat in foil or cling film or to put it in food bags or glass dishes before placing it in the refrigerator or freezer. This wrapping should, be tight and the meat should be perfectly sealed to avoid contact with the air and protect its flavour and nutritional content. To prevent cross-contamination in the refrigerator, it is essential to store raw meat where the juices cannot drip on to cooked meat or other ingredients. This is usually at the bottom. Many modern refrigerators are multi-temperature. This means that the internal space is divided into various 'compartments' that provide different levels of cold depending on the type of food to be stored. This ranges from 7–8°C/45–46°F for mature cheeses, salamis and cold pork meats, and 5°C/41°F for soft cheeses, yogurt and sauces, to 0°C/32°F for meat, fish and delicate foods. Storing food in this way ensures that it stays fresh for three or four times longer than in traditional refrigerators. This has been made possible by no-frost technology – the best storage temperature is reached through a system of internal air-circulation. This has the additional advantage of preventing the refrigerator from icing up, making defrosting unnecessary.

OFFAL

Offal is delicious and exists in a range of forms which may be prepared in many different ways. In Italy, the most valued offal are brains, bone marrow and sweetbreads, followed by liver, kidney, heart and tripe. Also in this category, but with a stronger flavour more suitable for robust dishes, is tongue, calf's head and trotters.

LAMB

As tender as a lamb, as they say in Italian to describe something soft. The tenderness of this meat derives from the fact that the animal is not yet one-year-old and has fed only on its mother's milk. Baby lamb, or abbacchio as it is called in Lazio, is even younger – just five or six weeks old. However milk-fed lamb is less common outside Italy and, as a rule, most meat available comes from grazing animals of between four months and a year, the younger ones being known as spring lamb. The meat from sheep over a year old is known as hogget or hogget lamb and if it comes from animals over two years old it is mutton. Lamb is a pale, tender, fairly fatty meat. It should be eaten fresh and preferably between October and June.

COOKING

→ As lamb tends to shrink during cooking, be generous with the weight when buying and always allow an extra portion.

→ The most common preparation methods are roasting or stewing after marinating in white wine with a drop of vinegar, inserting garlic into incisions in the meat and seasoning with herbs, such as rosemary, thyme, sage and mint.

→ Barbecued chops are very tasty and roast leg of lamb en croûte with herbs is an impressive dish for special occasions.

ROASTING

The best cuts for roasting are first of all the leg, especially if it includes half the lamb with the kidney right up to the first rib. Then comes the saddle, then the shoulder. The shoulder is tender and tasty, but rather fatty and difficult to carve neatly. Oven roast-

TOMATO

ing is perfect but pot-roasting also produces excellent results.

BRAISING, STEWING, BLANQUETTES AND CURRIES

The front part of the lamb is particularly suitable for stewing or braising with vegetables and early seasonal produce, such as petits pois, artichokes and baby onions. It is also ideal for curries, blanquettes (the meat must remain white), and cooking in an egg sauce (mixed with butter and cream) or with lemon juice.

CHOPS

Small lamb chops cut from the loin are particularly tender. They need cooking very quickly – just 2–3 minutes on each side. They are also delicious dipped in egg, then in breadcrumbs, and fried in butter, especially clarified butter.

ITALIAN CUTS
AND COOKING
TECHNIQUES

1. COLLO
   Stewing and braising
2. SPALLA
   Roasting and stewing
3. CARRÉ
   Ideal for grilling

4. PETTO
   Suitable for stews
5. SELLA
   Excellent for roasting
6. COSCIOTTO
   The best part for roasting

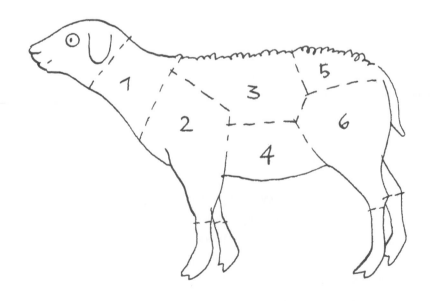

1. **SCRAG END OF NECK**
Stewing and braising
2. **MIDDLE NECK**
Stewing and casseroles
3. **SHOULDER**
Roasting, barbecues, kebabs, casseroles
3b. **FORE SHANK**
Braising
4. **BEST END OF NECK**
(Also known as rack of lamb.) Roasting, and cut into chops for grilling and stewing
5. **LOIN**
Roasting, including whole saddle, and cut into chops for grilling or frying, into fillet or into noisettes

6. **CHUMP**
Roasting, and cut into chops for grilling or frying
7. **LEG**
Roasting, and cut into leg chops for grilling
7b. **HIND SHANK**
Braising
8. **BREAST**
Boned and rolled for roasting or braising

BRITISH CUTS AND COOKING TECHNIQUES

If you are in doubt over which cut to choose or cannot find one that is listed here, ask a reputable butcher for advice.

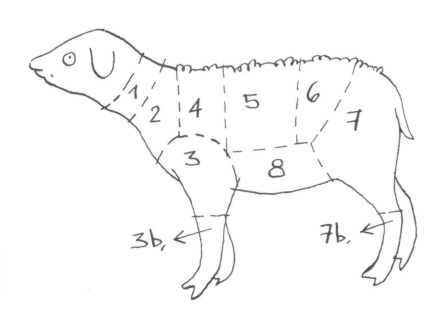

ROMAN SPRING LAMB

ABBACCHIO ALLA ROMANA
Serves 4
1-kg/2¼-lb leg of lamb
plain flour, for dusting
3 tablespoons olive oil
3 fresh rosemary sprigs
4 fresh sage leaves, chopped
1 garlic clove, crushed
175 ml/6 fl oz white wine
5 tablespoons white wine vinegar
4 potatoes, sliced
salt and pepper

Chop the leg into pieces or ask the butcher to do this for you. Preheat the oven to 180°C/350°F/Gas Mark 4. Dust the pieces of lamb with flour. Heat the oil in a wide roasting tin, add the lamb and cook over a high heat, turning frequently, for about 10 minutes until browned all over. Season with salt and pepper, add the rosemary sprigs and sprinkle with the sage and garlic. Turn the pieces over several times so that they soak up the flavour. Mix together the wine and vinegar, add to the roasting tin and cook until the liquid has almost completely evaporated. Add 150 ml/¼ pint boiling water and the potatoes, cover and roast for 30 minutes or until tender. If the gravy seems to be drying out, add a little hot water mixed with white wine vinegar. Transfer the lamb to a warm serving dish and serve while still hot. For an even tastier alternative, omit the potatoes, and when the lamb is nearly ready transfer 2–3 tablespoons of the gravy to a small pan, add three boned and chopped salted anchovies (see page 596) and cook over a low heat, mashing the anchovies with a wooden spoon until they have almost disintegrated. Mix well, pour the sauce over the meat and roast for a few minutes more before serving.

LAMB WITH MUSHROOMS

AGNELLO AI FUNGHI
Serves 4
1-kg/2¼-lb shoulder of lamb, boned and rolled
4 tablespoons olive oil, plus extra for brushing
500 g/1 lb 2 oz porcini
250 ml/8 fl oz double cream
25 g/1 oz butter
2 garlic cloves
1 fresh parsley sprig, chopped
salt and pepper

Preheat the oven to 200°C/400°F/Gas Mark 6. Season the meat with salt and pepper and brush it all over with lightly salted olive oil. Place in a roasting tin with the oil and roast for 1 hour. Meanwhile, separate the stems and caps of the porcini, then slice the caps and chop 100g/3½ oz of the stems. Remove the lamb from the tin, cover with foil and keep warm. Pour 175 ml/6 fl oz warm water and the cream into a pan, add the chopped porcini stems and simmer for 15 minutes. Meanwhile, melt the butter in a frying pan, add the porcini caps and cook over a high heat until lightly browned. Add the garlic, season with salt and pepper, lower the heat to medium and cook for a further 15 minutes. Remove and discard the garlic and add the parsley. Carve the lamb into thin slices, place on a warm serving dish, pour the hot sauce over them and serve surrounded by the porcini caps.

ARABIAN LAMB

AGNELLO ALL'ARABA

Serves 4

4 tablespoons olive oil

3 onions, thinly sliced

1-kg/2¼-lb saddle of lamb,
boned and cut into 5-cm/2-inch cubes

2 tablespoons clear honey

1 sachet saffron

pinch of ground cumin

pinch of ground ginger

250 ml/8 fl oz hot Meat Stock
(see page 208) or water

80 g/3 oz green olives, stoned

80 g/3 oz almonds

1 bunch of fresh coriander, finely chopped

salt and pepper

Preheat the oven to 200°C/400°F/Gas Mark 6. Heat the oil in a roasting tin, add the onions and cook over a low heat, stirring occasionally, for 5 minutes, then remove from the tin. Add the lamb and cook, stirring frequently, for 5 minutes until browned all over. Return the onions to the tin. Mix together the honey, saffron, cumin, ginger and stock or water in a jug and season with salt and pepper. Pour the mixture over the meat, cover the roasting tin with foil and roast for 1 hour or until tender. Meanwhile, blanch the olives in boiling water for 5 minutes, then drain. Dry-fry the almonds in a heavy-based frying pan, stirring frequently, for a few minutes. About 10 minutes before the end of the roasting time, add the olives and almonds to the roasting tin, mix well and return to the oven to finish cooking. Transfer to a warm serving dish, sprinkle with the coriander and serve. As a side dish, we suggest fresh broad beans boiled in water for 15 minutes, then tossed with butter.

LEG OF LAMB À LA PÉRIGOURDINE

COSCIOTTO ALLA PERIGORDINA

Serves 6

3 tablespoons olive oil

20 g/¾ oz butter

2-kg/4½-lb leg of lamb, skinned

2 tablespoons brandy

6 garlic cloves

1 onion, chopped

1 leek, trimmed and chopped

1 fresh thyme sprig, chopped

1 fresh flat-leaf parsley sprig, chopped

1 celery stick, chopped

1 clove

1 bottle (750 ml/1¼ pints) dry white wine

salt and pepper

Preheat the oven to 150°C/300°F/Gas Mark 2. Heat the oil and butter in a roasting tin, add the lamb and cook over a medium heat, turning frequently, until browned all over. Add the brandy, heat for a few seconds, then ignite and cover the tin with a large saucepan lid or baking sheet to extinguish the flames. Put the garlic around the lamb, add the onion, leek, thyme, parsley, celery and clove, season with salt and pepper and pour in the wine. Cover tightly and roast for 5 hours. Carefully transfer the lamb to a warm serving dish. Remove and discard the garlic from the roasting tin and pour the gravy into a sauce boat. This dish goes well with courgette purée or mashed potato.

ROAST LEG OF LAMB

Preheat the oven to 200°C/400°F/Gas Mark 6. Grease a roasting tin with the butter. Lard the lamb with the pancetta and, using a small, pointed knife, make small incisions all over it. Insert the sage and some of the rosemary into the incisions. Brush the lamb all over with oil, place in the prepared roasting tin and season with salt and pepper. Sprinkle the garlic and remaining rosemary on top, pour in the vinegar and wine and roast for 1½ hours. Turn the lamb halfway through the cooking time and baste occasionally with the cooking juices. Serve with baby spinach salad.

COSCIOTTO ARROSTO

Serves 6

80 g/3 oz butter

2-kg/4½-lb leg of lamb

80 g/3 oz pancetta, cut into strips

6 fresh sage leaves, cut into strips

1 tablespoon rosemary needles

olive oil, for brushing

4 garlic cloves, chopped

5 tablespoons white wine vinegar

5 tablespoons white wine

salt and pepper

baby spinach salad, to serve

ROAST LEG OF LAMB IN A HERB CRUST

Preheat the oven to 240°C/475°F/Gas Mark 9. Mix together the thyme, oregano, parsley and rosemary in a bowl, add the oil and breadcrumbs, season with salt and pepper and mix well. Place the lamb in a large roasting tin, spread the herb mixture over it and roast for 15 minutes. Lower the oven temperature to 180°C/350°F/Gas Mark 4, add 150 ml/¼ pint warm water to the roasting tin and roast for a further 15 minutes. Remove the lamb from the roasting tin, cover with foil and leave to stand for 10 minutes. Carve the meat and place on a warm serving dish. For a side dish, halve and seed some tomatoes, fill with breadcrumbs and chopped oregano, drizzle with olive oil, season with salt and pepper and bake for 15 minutes.

COSCIOTTO IN CROSTA D'ERBE

Serves 6

1 tablespoon chopped fresh thyme

1 tablespoon chopped fresh oregano

1 tablespoon fresh flat-leaf parsley, chopped

1 tablespoon chopped fresh rosemary needles

4 tablespoons olive oil

2 tablespoons breadcrumbs

2-kg/4½-lb leg of lamb

salt and pepper

LAMB CUTLETS WITH ANCHOVY BUTTER

Preheat the grill. Brush the cutlets on both sides with olive oil and grill for 4–6 minutes on each side, depending on how well done you like your lamb. Season with salt, transfer to a serving warm dish and dot with the anchovy butter.

COSTOLETTE AL BURRO D'ACCIUGA

Serves 4

8 lamb cutlets

olive oil

1 quantity Anchovy Butter (see page 85)

salt

LAMB CUTLETS COOKED IN VINEGAR

Mix together the vinegar, half the oil, the onion, parsley and cloves in a dish and season with salt and pepper. Add the lamb cutlets and leave to marinate for 1 hour. Heat the remaining oil in a frying pan, drain the lamb cutlets, add to the pan and cook for 2 minutes on each side until golden brown. Transfer to a warm serving dish.

COSTOLETTE ALL'ACETO

Serves 4

175 ml/6 fl oz white wine vinegar

6 tablespoons olive oil

1 onion, sliced

1 fresh flat-leaf parsley sprig, chopped

2 cloves

8–12 lamb cutlets

salt and pepper

LAMB CUTLETS WITH MINT

Mix together the lemon juice, 3 tablespoons of the oil and the mint in a dish, add the lamb cutlets and leave to marinate, turning occasionally, for 1–2 hours. Heat the butter and the remaining oil in a frying pan. Drain the lamb cutlets, add to the pan and cook for 2 minutes on each side. Season with salt and pepper and serve with peas or courgettes.

COSTOLETTE ALLA MENTA

Serves 4

juice of 1 lemon, strained

plenty of olive oil, for brushing

1 fresh mint sprig, chopped

8 lamb cutlets

20 g/³⁄₄ oz butter

salt and pepper

peas or courgettes cooked in butter, to serve

LAMB CUTLETS SCOTTADITO

Brush the lamb cutlets with oil and season with salt and pepper. Cover and leave to stand in a cool place for 15 minutes. Meanwhile, preheat the grill to high. Drain the lamb cutlets carefully to get rid of any excess seasoning, then grill for about 1 minute on each side. Alternatively, brush a non-stick frying pan with a little oil and cook the lamb cutlets over a high heat for 1 minute on each side, seasoning with salt and pepper on turning them. Before removing the cutlets from the heat, sprinkle with lemon juice, if you wish. Transfer to a warm serving dish.

COSTOLETTE A SCOTTADITO

Serves 4

8–12 lamb cutlets

5 tablespoons olive oil

salt and pepper

juice of 1 lemon, strained (optional)

LAMB FRICASSÉE WITH ONIONS

FRICASSEA CON CIPOLLINE

Serves 4

800-g/1³/₄-lb leg of lamb
40 g/1¹/₂ oz butter
3 tablespoons olive oil
400 g/14 oz baby onions
500 ml/18 fl oz dry white wine
2 egg yolks
juice of 1 lemon, strained
salt and pepper

Ask your butcher to cut the leg into fairly small pieces. Heat the butter and oil in a saucepan, add the pieces of lamb and cook, turning frequently, until golden brown all over. Remove the lamb from the pan and keep warm. Add the onions to the pan and cook over a medium heat, stirring frequently, for about 10 minutes until golden brown. Return the pieces of lamb to the pan, season with salt and pepper and pour in the wine. Cover and cook over a medium heat for 40 minutes. Beat the egg yolks with the lemon juice in a bowl. Move the pan to the edge of the hob and pour in the egg yolk mixture. Stir quickly so that the mixture thickens and coats the pieces of lamb without drying out. Transfer to a warm serving dish.

LAMB MEATBALLS WITH AUBERGINE

POLPETTE ALLE MELANZANE

Serves 4

2 aubergines
500 g/1 lb 2 oz lean minced lamb
pinch of dried oregano
2 egg yolks
1 fresh flat-leaf parsley sprig, chopped
4 tablespoons olive oil
salt and pepper

Preheat the oven to 180°C/350°F/Gas Mark 4. Wrap the aubergines in foil, place on a baking sheet and bake for about 30 minutes. Unwrap the aubergines and leave to cool slightly, then cut them in half and scoop out the flesh with a teaspoon. Mix together the lamb, aubergine flesh, oregano, egg yolks and parsley in a bowl and season with salt and pepper. Shape the mixture into small meatballs. Heat the oil in a frying pan, add the meatballs and cook over a medium heat, stirring frequently, until golden brown all over. Transfer to a warm serving dish.

SHOULDER OF LAMB IN A PARCEL

SPALLA AL CARTOCCIO

Serves 6

olive oil, for brushing
1-kg/2¹/₄-lb boneless shoulder of lamb, trimmed of fat
1 fresh flat-leaf parsley sprig, chopped
1 fresh chervil sprig, chopped
1 fresh oregano sprig, chopped
1 bay leaf
175 ml/6 fl oz dry white wine
juice of ¹/₂ lemon, strained
salt and pepper

Preheat the oven to 200°C/400°F/Gas Mark 6. Brush a large sheet of baking parchment generously with olive oil. Season the top and underside of the lamb with salt and pepper and place it in the middle of the baking parchment. Sprinkle with the herbs and add the bay leaf. Pour the wine and lemon juice on top and wrap carefully so that the liquid does not leak out. Place on a baking sheet and roast for 1 hour or until cooked through and tender. Open the parcel slightly to let the steam escape, then serve.

SPALLA ALLA FORNAIA

Serves 6

25 g/1 oz butter, plus extra for greasing

1 kg/2¼ lb potatoes, thinly sliced

1 tablespoon chopped fresh thyme

500 g/1 lb 2 oz onions, thinly sliced

2 garlic cloves, thinly sliced

1-kg/2¼-lb boneless shoulder of lamb

500 ml/18 fl oz Meat or Vegetable Stock
(see pages 208 and 209)

salt and pepper

SHOULDER OF LAMB À LA BOULANGÈRE

Preheat the oven to 200°C/400°F/Gas Mark 6. Grease an ovenproof dish with butter. Make a layer of potatoes on the base of the dish, season with salt and pepper, sprinkle with a little of the thyme and cover with a layer of onions and garlic. Continue making layers until all these ingredients have been used. Make a few incisions in the lamb with a small sharp knife, place it on top of the vegetables and season with salt and pepper. Pour the stock into the dish, dot the lamb with the butter and roast, basting the potatoes occasionally, for 30 minutes. Remove the dish from the oven and cover with a sheet of foil, then return it to the oven and roast for a further 30–45 minutes. Leave the meat to stand, without uncovering it, for about 10 minutes before serving.

SPALLA AL MIRTO

Serves 4

1.2-kg/2½-lb shoulder of lamb

3 garlic cloves

2 tablespoons olive oil, plus extra for brushing

5 tablespoons dry white wine

50 ml/2 fl oz mirto (myrtle liqueur) or gin

salt and pepper

SHOULDER OF LAMB WITH MIRTO

Preheat the oven to 200°C/400°F/Gas Mark 6. Rub the lamb with the garlic clove, then cut the cloves in half and dip them in salt. Make six fairly deep incisions in the meat with a small knife and insert half a garlic clove in each. Brush the meat with olive oil and season with salt and pepper. Then place the lamb in a roasting tin, add the oil, half the wine and half the mirto or gin and roast for 30 minutes. Turn the shoulder over and spoon the remaining wine and mirto or gin over it, baste well, return to the oven and roast for a further 30 minutes.

SPEZZATINO ALLE CAROTE

Serves 6

4 tablespoons olive oil
50 g/2 oz butter
500 g/1 lb 2 oz carrots, cut into thin batons
1 shallot, finely chopped
1 kg/2¼ lb boneless shoulder of lamb, cut into cubes
1 onion, chopped
1 garlic clove, chopped
pinch of dried oregano
10 celery leaves, chopped
salt and pepper

CHOPPED LAMB AND CARROTS

Heat half the oil and half the butter in a pan, add the carrots and shallot and cook over a low heat, stirring occasionally, for 20 minutes. Meanwhile, heat the remaining oil and butter in another pan, add the lamb and cook over a high heat, stirring frequently, until browned all over. Season with salt and pepper to taste and continue cooking, stirring constantly, for a few minutes more. Add the onion, garlic, oregano and celery leaves, lower the heat to medium and cook for 10 minutes. When the carrots are almost tender, transfer them to the pan with the lamb and cook for a further 5 minutes.

KID

In Italy, the best breeds of goat are the Girgentana, the Alpine, the Apulian and the Sardinian. A suckling kid of 6–12 kg/13¼–26½ lb in weight is ideal for cooking. The nutritional value of kid is similar to that of lamb, but the beautiful pale pink meat is not as tasty and so requires more seasoning. Consequently, most recipes include herbs and wine. When roasting, allow 1 hour per 1 kg/2¼ lb. As kid may be difficult to obtain outside Italy, it is worth noting that many recipes can be used for either lamb or kid, and the best parts of both are the leg, shoulder and loin.

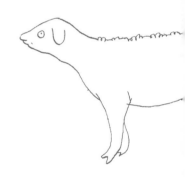

LEG OF KID WITH TRUFFLE CREAM

Put the rosemary, sage and garlic in a large pan (not aluminium) with the oil, half the brandy and a pinch each of salt and pepper. Add the meat and leave to marinate overnight. The next day, put the pan over a medium heat, add the pieces of butter and cook, turning occasionally, for 1 hour. Pour in the remaining brandy, ignite it and leave until the flames die down. Take the kid out of the pan and cut the meat off the bone. Strain the cooking juices and reserve 175 ml/6 fl oz. Mix the reserved juices with the truffle paste and cream. Return the meat to the pan, add the sauce and simmer over a low heat for about 10 minutes. Transfer to a warm serving dish.

COSCIOTTO ALLA CREMA TARTUFATA

Serves 4

1 tablespoon fresh rosemary needles, chopped

3 fresh sage leaves, chopped

2 garlic cloves, chopped

2 tablespoons olive oil

175 ml/6 fl oz brandy

1-kg/2¼-lb leg of kid

25 g/1 oz butter, cut into pieces

1 tablespoon truffle paste

250 ml/8 fl oz double cream

salt and pepper

PIEDMONTESE LEG OF KID

COSCIOTTO ALLA PIEMONTESE

Serves 4

1-kg/2¼-lb leg of kid

100 g/3½ oz pancetta, cut into strips

3 tablespoons olive oil

1 onion, chopped

1 garlic clove, chopped

1 carrot, sliced

1 celery stick, sliced

1 fresh rosemary sprig

500 ml/18 fl oz dry white wine

3 tablespoons tomato purée

salt and pepper

Lard the kid with the pancetta. Heat the oil in a pan, add the meat and cook over a high heat, turning frequently, until browned all over. Season with salt and pepper, add the onion, garlic, carrot, celery and rosemary and cook for a few minutes. Add the wine, tomato purée and 5 tablespoons water and simmer for 1 hour. Remove and discard the rosemary, transfer the vegetables to a food processor and process to a purée. Cut the meat from the bone, place on a warm serving dish and spoon the vegetable purée on top.

EASTER LEG OF KID

COSCIOTTO PASQUALE

Serves 4

1-kg/2¼-lb leg of kid

1 fresh rosemary sprig, chopped

4 fresh sage leaves, chopped

1 garlic clove, chopped

5 tablespoons olive oil

800 g/1¾ lb new potatoes, diced

500 g/1 lb 2 oz carrots, cut into thin batons

400 g/14 oz baby onions

1 fresh flat-leaf parsley sprig, chopped

salt and pepper

Preheat the oven to 180°C/350°F/Gas Mark 4. Place the leg in a roasting tin, season with salt and pepper and sprinkle with the rosemary, sage and garlic. Pour the oil over the kid and roast, basting occasionally, for about 1 hour. Meanwhile, parboil the potatoes, carrots and onions in separate pans for about 10 minutes, then drain and transfer to the roasting tin with the meat. When the meat is tender, cut it off the bone and place on a warm serving dish. Surround with the vegetables and sprinkle with the parsley.

KID CUTLETS WITH CREAM

COSTOLETTE ALLA PANNA

Serves 4

20 g/¾ oz butter

1 tablespoon olive oil

12 kid cutlets

250 ml/8 fl oz double cream

juice of 1 lemon, strained

2 fresh flat-leaf parsley sprigs, finely chopped

salt and pepper

lemon slices, to garnish

Heat the butter and oil in a frying pan, add the cutlets and cook over a high heat for 2 minutes on each side. Season with salt and pepper, lower the heat, add the cream and simmer for 15 minutes. Pour in the lemon juice and simmer for a further 5 minutes. Sprinkle the cutlets with parsley, place on a warm serving dish and garnish with slices of lemon.

PORK, BACON
HAM

It is well known that no part of the pig is ever thrown away – everything can be successfully transformed into tasty and nutritious foods which delight the taste buds and add flavour to many dishes. In Italy, as in many other countries, so-called lean pork is the favourite choice. It comes from selected breeds that produce meat that is much lower in fat than the breeds of the past. Only some cuts are sold as fresh meat, while the others are used to make salamis, preserved meats, sausages and a variety of other preparations. Good quality fresh pork can be recognized by its fine grain, pink colour and slight marbling of white fat.

COOKING

Pork requires rather long cooking times – about 25 minutes per 500 g/1 lb 2 oz.

ROASTING

Loin should be roasted in a preheated low to medium oven so that the heat can penetrate to the centre before a crust forms on the outside.

CAUL

Also known as caul fat, this is a lattice-like membrane that encloses the pig's stomach. It is used to wrap and contain other ingredients. In Italy, it can be bought from delicatessens and is used after being soaked in warm water for 3 minutes to soften.

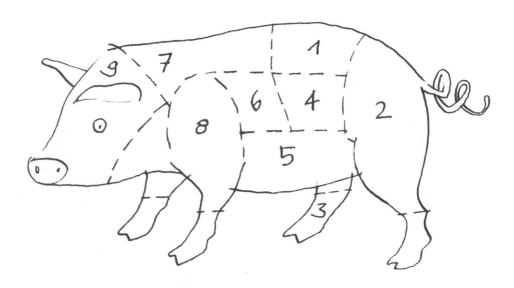

ITALIAN CUTS AND COOKING TECHNIQUES

1. LONZA
   Ideal for roasting
2. COSCIOTTO
   The part used to make ham
3. PIEDINI
   Boiling and frying
4. PUNTINE COSTINE
   Stewing and braising
5. PANCETTA, GUANCIALE
   For forcemeats or for larding and wrapping dry meats

6. FILETTO, LOMBO
   Recommended for roasting and grilling
7. CARRÉ
   Extremely tasty chops
8. SPALLA
   For roasting and stewing
9. TESTA
   Boiling

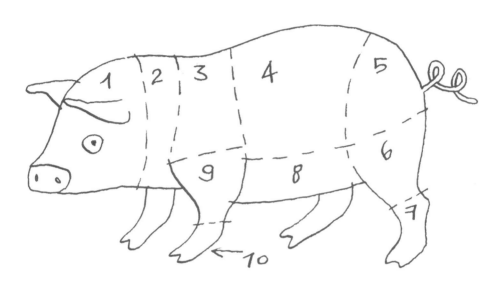

1. HEAD
Brawn and pet food

2. SPARE RIB
Cut into spare-rib chops for grilling or frying, sliced for stir-fries

3. BLADE
Roasting and braising

4. LOIN
Roasting, cut into fillets for roasting, frying and medallions and into chops for grilling

5. CHUMP AND LEG (FILLET END)
Roasting, cut into chops for grilling and braising

6. LEG (KNUCKLE END)
Roasting

7. HOCK
Braising

8. BELLY (FLANK)
Stuffing and roasting, minced for terrines, adds flavour to casseroles, spare ribs

9. HAND
Braising

10. TROTTER
Braising

BRITISH CUTS AND COOKING TECHNIQUES

If you are in doubt over which cut to choose or cannot find one that is listed here, ask a reputable butcher for advice.

ROAST LOIN OF PORK

ARISTA AL FORNO

Serves 6

25 g/1 oz butter

3 tablespoons olive oil • 1 fresh rosemary sprig

1-kg/2¼-lb hind loin of pork, chined

175 ml/6 fl oz dry white wine

4–5 tablespoons hot milk

salt and pepper

boiled Tuscan or cannellini beans, to serve

Preheat the oven to 180°C/350°F/Gas Mark 4. Heat the butter, oil and rosemary in an oval roasting tin, add the pork and cook, turning frequently, for 5–10 minutes until browned all over. Add the wine and cook until it has evaporated, then season with salt and pepper. Transfer to the oven and roast, turning occasionally and basting with hot milk, for 1 hour or until cooked through. Remove the pork from the oven and leave to stand for 10 minutes, then carve, serve with a side dish of boiled Tuscan or cannellini beans seasoned with extra-virgin olive oil, salt and pepper.

ROAST PORK WITH ORANGE

ARROSTO ALL'ARANCIA

Serves 6

40 g/1½ oz butter

350 ml/12 fl oz orange juice, strained

1 teaspoon grated orange rind • 1 garlic clove

pinch of chilli powder • pinch of dried oregano

1-kg/2¼-lb loin of pork, boned • salt and pepper

Preheat the oven to 180°C/350°F/Gas Mark 4. Melt the butter in a pan, add the orange juice, grated rind, garlic, chilli powder and oregano, season with salt and pepper and mix well. Rub the meat with salt and pepper and place in a roasting tin. Pour in the mixture and roast, basting frequently, for about 1½ hours. Carve and serve with the cooking juices.

ROAST PORK IN GRAPE JUICE

ARROSTO ALL'UVA

Serves 6

1-kg/2¼-lb fillet

6 tablespoons olive oil

250 ml/8 fl oz grape juice

salt and pepper

Tie the meat neatly with kitchen string and brush with some of the olive oil. Put the remaining oil in a deep pan, add the pork and cook over a high heat, turning frequently, until browned all over. Add the grape juice, lower the heat, cover and simmer for about 1½ hours until the pork is tender and the sauce has thickened. Season with salt and pepper to taste. Lift out the meat, untie it and carve into slices. Place on a warm serving dish and spoon the sauce over them.

BRAISED PORK WITH ROSEMARY

ARROSTO CON IL ROSMARINO

Serves 6

needles from 1–2 rosemary sprigs

1-kg/2¼-lb loin of pork , boned

25 g/1 oz butter

6 tablespoons olive oil

1 garlic clove, crushed • ½ onion, chopped

175 ml/6 fl oz dry white wine

1 tablespoon white wine vinegar

1 teaspoon Dijon mustard

salt and pepper

Push half the rosemary needles into the meat and tie neatly with kitchen string. Heat the butter and 4 tablespoons of the olive oil in a pan, add the pork and cook, turning frequently, until golden brown all over. Add the garlic, onion and remaining rosemary, then pour in the wine and cook until evaporated. Season, cover and simmer for about 1½ hours. Remove the pork from the pan and leave to stand for 10 minutes, then untie, carve into fairly thick slices and place on a warm serving dish. Meanwhile, stir the vinegar, the remaining oil, the mustard and a pinch of pepper into the cooking juices. Pour into a sauce boat and serve with the meat.

ROAST PORK WITH APPLES

ARROSTO CON LE MELE

Serves 6

1-kg/2¼-lb loin of pork, boned
2 tablespoons olive oil
350 ml/12 fl oz red wine
175 ml/6 fl oz Vegetable Stock (see page 209)
4 cloves
½ tablespoon mustard powder
2 tablespoons sugar
10 black peppercorns, crushed
2 green apples, peeled, cored and cubed
salt and pepper

Preheat the oven to 200°C/400°F/Gas Mark 6. Lightly season the meat with salt and pepper, roll and tie with kitchen string. Heat the oil in a pan, add the meat and cook, turning frequently, until browned all over. Meanwhile, pour the wine and stock into another pan, add the cloves, mustard powder, sugar and peppercorns, season with salt and bring to the boil. Transfer the pork to an ovenproof dish, season with salt and pepper and surround with the apples. Pour the hot wine mixture over it, cover with foil and roast for 20 minutes, then lower the oven temperature to 180°C/350°F/Gas Mark 4 and roast, basting frequently, for a further 45 minutes. Remove and discard the foil, return the pork to the oven and roast for 15 minutes more until tender. Lift the meat out of the dish and leave to stand. Strain the sauce into a pan, pressing down the apples with a spoon. Cook over a high heat until thickened and caramelized, then season with salt and pepper to taste. Untie the meat and carve into slices. Place on a warm serving dish and spoon the hot sauce over.

ROAST PORK WITH LEMON

ARROSTO CON LIMONE CARAMELLATO

Serves 6

1-kg/2¼-lb loin of pork, boned
2 tablespoons fresh rosemary needles, chopped
175 ml/6 fl oz dry white wine
50 g/2 oz sugar
5 tablespoons lemon juice, strained
1 tablespoon brandy
1 lemon, sliced
salt and pepper

Make a few incisions in the meat, along the grain, using a small knife. Insert a pinch of rosemary needles in each incision until half have been used. Place the pork in a deep bowl, pour in the wine and sprinkle with the remaining rosemary. Leave to marinate in a cool place, turning occasionally, for 2 hours. Preheat the oven to 230°C/450°F/Gas Mark 8. Drain the pork, reserving the marinade, and tie neatly with kitchen string. Put the meat in a roasting tin and roast for 15 minutes, then lower the temperature to 180°C/350°F/Gas Mark 4 and roast for a further 30 minutes. Pour the reserved marinade over the pork, season with salt and pepper, return to the oven and roast for about 1 hour more. Meanwhile, dissolve the sugar in the lemon juice and brandy in a bowl. Remove the roasting tin from the oven and skim off the fat with a tablespoon. Pour the lemon mixture over the pork, return to the oven and roast, basting every 10 minutes, until the sauce has thickened and the meat is dark and shiny. Remove the pork and leave to stand for a few minutes, then untie and carve it into slices. Place on a warm serving dish, surround with the lemon slice and spoon the cooking juices over the meat.

PAN-FRIED PORK FILLET

BISTECCHE DI FILETTO

Serves 4

4 fillet slices, 1 cm/½ inch thick

plain flour, for dusting

25 g/1 oz butter

175 ml/6 fl oz dry white wine

1 flat-leaf parsley sprig, chopped

salt

Lightly dust the pork with flour and shake off any excess. Melt the butter in a pan, add the meat and cook over a high heat for 2 minutes on each side. Turn the slices several times, then pour in the wine, cover and cook for 5 minutes. Remove the lid, season with salt and, if necessary, cook for a little longer until the pan juices have thickened. Transfer the meat to a warm serving dish, spoon the cooking juices over it and sprinkle with the parsley. Mashed or roast potatoes seasoned with rosemary go well as a side dish.

CASSOEULA

BOTTAGGIO ALLA MILANESE

Serves 8

5 tablespoons olive oil

50 g/2 oz butter

1 onion, chopped

160 g/5½ oz pork rind

1 pig's trotter, chopped

1 quantity Meat Stock (see page 208)

1 kg/2¼ lb spare ribs

3 carrots, cut into thin batons

1 celery stick, chopped

1 Savoy cabbage

4 small mild salamis or Italian sausages

salt and pepper

Heat the oil and butter in a large pan, add the onion and cook over a low heat, stirring occasionally, for 10 minutes. Add the pork rind and trotter and cook, turning occasionally, until browned all over. Season with salt and pepper to taste, pour in enough stock to cover and cook until the liquid has reduced by half. Add the ribs and cook for about 10 minutes, then add the carrots and celery. Cover and simmer gently for 30 minutes. Meanwhile, briefly blanch the cabbage leaves in boiling water, then refresh under cold water. Add the cabbage to the pan, re-cover and simmer for a further 20 minutes, adding more stock if necessary. Prick the salamis or sausages with a fork, add to the pan, re-cover and simmer for 20 minutes more. When the mixture is ready it will have a slightly glutinous consistency owing to the pork rind and trotter.

PORK CHOPS WITH BLUEBERRIES

BRACIOLE AI MIRTILLI

Serves 4

4 spare-rib chops

plain flour, for dusting

25 g/1 oz butter

3 tablespoons olive oil

175 ml/6 fl oz red wine

300 g/11 oz blueberries

100 g/3½ oz clear honey

salt

Preheat the oven to 200°C/400°F/Gas Mark 6. Dust the chops with flour. Heat the butter and oil in a small flameproof casserole, add the chops and cook, turning occasionally, until browned all over. Pour in the wine and cook until it has partly evaporated, then season with salt. Pass the blueberries through a food mill and mix with the honey in a bowl. Spread this mixture over the chops, then cover the casserole, transfer to the oven and cook for 15 minutes. Leave to stand for 10 minutes, then serve.

CURRIED PORK CHOPS

BRACIOLE AL CURRY

Serves 4

25 g/1 oz butter • 2 tablespoons olive oil

4 spare-rib chops • 50 ml/2 fl oz brandy

1 teaspoon curry powder

1 tablespoon double cream

2 tablespoons warm Vegetable Stock (see page 209)

Heat the butter and oil in a pan, add the chops and cook, turning occasionally, until browned all over. Add the brandy and cook until it has evaporated. Mix together the curry powder, cream and stock in a bowl and add to the pan. Cover and simmer for 15–20 minutes. Transfer to a warm serving dish.

PORK CHOPS IN GORGONZOLA

BRACIOLE AL GORGONZOLA

Serves 4

25 g/1 oz butter

4 spare-rib chops

5 tablespoons dry white wine

100 g/3¹/₂ oz mild Gorgonzola cheese

salt

Melt the butter in a frying pan, add the chops and cook over a high heat for 6 minutes on each side. Transfer to a warm serving dish. Leave the frying pan to cool, then pour in the wine and heat gently until half has evaporated, then crumble in the cheese and cook over a low heat until melted. Season to taste with salt and pour the sauce over the meat.

PORK CHOPS IN CREAM

BRACIOLE ALLA PANNA

Serves 4

4 spare-rib chops

25 g/1 oz butter

1 tablespoon olive oil

175 ml/6 fl oz port

250 ml/8 fl oz double cream

1 teaspoon plain flour

salt and pepper

Lightly pound the chops. Heat the butter and oil in a frying pan, add the chops and cook, turning occasionally, for 6 minutes on each side. Season, then remove from the pan, drain and keep warm. Pour the port into the pan and cook over a low heat, scraping up any sediment from the base of the pan, until the liquid has reduced by half. Mix together the cream and flour in a bowl, stir into the pan and season lightly with salt and pepper. Simmer for 5 minutes, then pour the sauce over the chops and serve.

PORK SHOULDER WITH PRUNES

CARRÉ ALLE PRUGNE

Serves 6

1-kg/2¹/₄-lb shoulder of pork, main bone removed and ribs uncovered

150 g/5 oz prunes, stoned

50 g/2 oz butter

2 tablespoons olive oil

1 shallot, chopped

2 tablespoons brandy

salt and pepper

Preheat the oven to 200°C/400°F/Gas Mark 6. Open out the meat like a book and arrange a row of prunes along the join. Chop the remaining prunes. Roll the pork and tie with kitchen string passed between the ribs, then season. Heat half the butter and the oil in a roasting tin, then remove from the heat, add the pork and roast, basting occasionally, for about 1¹/₄ hours. Melt the remaining butter in a pan, add the shallot and cook over a low heat for 5 minutes. Add the prunes and cook for a further 5 minutes. Pour in the brandy and ignite. Remove the meat from the roasting tin and leave to stand. Skim off the fat from the cooking juices and strain the juices into the prune sauce. Untie the meat and carve it into slices. Serve with the prune sauce.

PORK SHOULDER WITH CARDOONS

Push the cloves into the meat. Mix together the rosemary, sage and a pinch of salt in a bowl and gently rub the mixture over the pork, then tie the meat neatly with kitchen string. Place half the onion in a saucepan with the peppercorns, half the butter and half the oil and heat gently. Place the pork on top and cook until browned on both sides. Pour in the wine and cook until it has reduced by half. Season with salt and simmer over a low heat. Heat the remaining butter and oil in another pan, add the pancetta, garlic and the remaining onion and cook over a low heat, stirring occasionally, for 5 minutes. Add the tomatoes and 150 ml/$\frac{1}{4}$ pint hot water and cook until the liquid has almost completely evaporated. Cook the cardoons in a pan of salted, boiling water for about 30 minutes until tender but still quite firm to the bite. Drain and add to the sauce. Remove the meat from the pan, untie and carve it into slices. Place on a warm serving dish, spoon the cooking juices over them and serve with the cardoons.

CARRÉ CON I CARDI

Serves 4

3 cloves
800-g/1$\frac{3}{4}$-lb shoulder of pork, boned
pinch of dried rosemary
pinch of dried sage
1 onion, chopped
6 black peppercorns
40 g/1$\frac{1}{2}$ oz butter
2 tablespoons olive oil
175 ml/6 fl oz red wine
50 g/2 oz pancetta, chopped
1 garlic clove, chopped
200 g/7 oz canned tomatoes
1.5 kg/3$\frac{3}{4}$ cardoons, trimmed
and chopped (see page 423)
salt

SPARE RIBS WITH POLENTA

Melt the butter in a pan, add the onion and garlic clove and cook over a low heat, stirring occasionally, for 10 minutes until golden brown. Remove and discard the garlic. Add the ribs to the pan, pour in the wine and cook until it has evaporated. Add the tomatoes, chilli and basil and season with salt and pepper. Simmer over a low heat for 1 hour or until the meat starts to fall off the bones. If necessary, add a little warm water and wine to prevent the mixture from drying out during cooking. Serve the spare ribs with soft polenta.

COSTINE CON POLENTA

Serves 4

50 g/2 oz butter
1 onion, chopped
1 garlic clove
800 g/1$\frac{3}{4}$ lb spare ribs
175 ml/6 fl oz red wine
400 g/14 oz canned tomatoes
1 fresh chilli, seeded and chopped
6 fresh basil leaves, chopped
salt and pepper
Polenta (see page 305), to serve

PORK CHOPS IN BUTTER AND SAGE

Trim the bones and flatten the chops slightly with a meat mallet. Melt the butter in a pan, add the sage and cook until light golden brown. Add the meat and cook for 5 minutes on each side until tender and cooked through. Season lightly with salt and pepper.

COSTOLETTE AL BURRO E SALVIA

Serves 4

4 loin chops
40 g/1$\frac{1}{2}$ oz butter
6 fresh sage leaves
salt and pepper

PORK CHOPS WITH TUSCAN CABBAGE

COSTOLETTE AL CAVOLO NERO

Serves 4

400 g/14 oz Tuscan cabbage, shredded

4 tablespoons olive oil

2 garlic cloves

4 loin chops

175 ml/6 fl oz red wine

1 fresh flat-leaf parsley sprig, chopped

salt and pepper

Cook the cabbage in salted, boiling water for about 30 minutes, then drain. Meanwhile, heat the oil in a frying pan, add the garlic and cook until golden brown, then remove and discard it. Add the chops to the pan, pour in the wine and season with salt and pepper. Simmer over a low heat until the wine has evaporated. Remove the chops from the pan and keep warm. Add the cabbage and parsley to the pan and cook over a low heat for 10 minutes. Return the chops to the pan and heat through for a few minutes before serving.

PORK CHOPS WITH YELLOW PEPPERS

COSTOLETTE CON PEPERONI

Serves 4

25 g/1 oz butter

1 tablespoon olive oil

4 loin chops

4 yellow peppers, halved, seeded and cut into strips

1 garlic clove, crushed (optional)

salt

Heat the butter and oil in a frying pan, add the chops, season with salt and cook until golden brown on both sides. Add the peppers, lower the heat and cook gently for about 15 minutes, adding the garlic, if using, about halfway through the cooking time.

CROÛTES WITH PORK FILLET AND PÂTÉ DE FOIE GRAS

CROSTONI DI FILETTO AL FOIE GRAS

Serves 4

80 g/3 oz butter

4 fillet slices

4 white bread slices, crusts removed

5 tablespoons Marsala

100 g/3½ oz pâté de foie gras

salt and pepper

Heat half the butter in a frying pan, add the meat and cook for 3 minutes on each side. Season with salt and pepper, remove from the pan and keep warm. Melt the remaining butter in another frying pan, add the slices of bread and cook until golden brown on both sides. Remove with a fish slice, drain on kitchen paper and place on a warm serving dish. Place a slice of pork on each slice of bread. Pour the Marsala into the pan where the meat was cooked and heat gently, scraping up the sediment from the base with a wooden spoon. Cook until slightly reduced. Lightly spread each slice of meat with the pâté de foie gras and spoon the hot sauce on top.

PORK EN CROÛTE

Heat the butter and oil in a pan, add the onion and cook over a low heat, stirring occasionally, for 10 minutes. Stir in the mushrooms and cook for a few minutes, then add 1 tablespoon of the lemon juice, the lemon rind, parsley and crumbled rolls and mix well. Season generously with salt and pepper. Remove the pan from the heat and leave to cool. Preheat the oven to 200°C/400°F/Gas Mark 6. Trim any fat from the meat and make a deep, lengthways cut in each piece without cutting through completely. Open out each piece of meat like a book and flatten with a meat mallet. Season with salt and pepper and sprinkle with the remaining lemon juice. Spread half the mushroom mixture on each piece of meat, then place one piece on top of the other and press down well so that they form a single block. Roll out the pastry on a lightly floured surface into a rectangle 5 cm/2 inches longer than the meat and three times the width. Place the meat in the middle of the pastry, brush the side edges with a little water and fold in towards the middle, then repeat for the two ends. Press down well to seal the parcel. Decorate with any pastry trimmings and brush with the beaten egg. Place the parcel on a baking sheet and bake for 30 minutes. Lower the oven temperature to180°C/350°F/Gas Mark 4 and bake for a further 45 minutes. If the pastry begins to brown too much, cover with foil to prevent it from burning. Remove the parcel from the oven and leave to stand for 10 minutes, then slice and reassemble on a serving dish.

FILETTO FARCITO IN CROSTA

Serves 4

25 g/1 oz butter

1 tablespoon olive oil

1 onion, chopped

225 g/8 oz mushrooms

juice and grated rind of ¹/₂ lemon

1 fresh flat-leaf parsley sprig, chopped

2 rolls, crusts removed, crumbled

800-g/1³/₄-lb fillet, halved

375 g/13 oz puff pastry dough, thawed if frozen

plain flour, for dusting

1 egg, lightly beaten

salt and pepper

PORK ROULADES WITH APRICOTS

If you're not using ready-to-eat apricots, put them in a bowl, add lukewarm water to cover and leave to soak. Heat the oil and butter in a pan, add the slices of pork and cook until golden brown on both sides. Remove from the pan and set aside. Squeeze out the apricots, if necessary, and chop them. Add the apricots and pancetta to the pan and cook, stirring occasionally, until the pancetta is lightly browned, then season with salt. Divide the apricot mixture equally among the slices of pork, roll up and tie with kitchen string. Put the roulades in the pan, add the brandy and cook until it has evaporated, then serve.

INVOLTINI ALLE ALBICOCCHE

Serves 4

100 g/3¹/₂ oz dried apricots

2 tablespoons olive oil

25 g/1 oz butter

8 loin of pork slices

100 g/3¹/₂ oz pancetta, cut into strips

50 ml/2 fl oz brandy

salt

LOMBO TONNATO

Serves 4

800-g/1³/₄-lb loin of pork, boned

250 ml/8 fl oz dry white wine

2 carrots, cut into thin batons

1 celery stick, chopped

1 onion

1 tablespoon black peppercorns

1 tablespoon olive oil

salt

1 lemon, sliced, to garnish

For the sauce

3 hard-boiled egg yolks

1 tablespoon Dijon mustard

1 tablespoon white wine vinegar

175 ml/6 fl oz olive oil

2 tablespoons capers, drained, rinsed and chopped

4 canned anchovy fillets in oil, drained and chopped

200 g/7 oz canned tuna in oil, drained and flaked

salt

LOIN OF PORK WITH TUNA SAUCE

Tie the pork neatly with kitchen string and place in a snug-fitting pan. Pour in the wine and add water to cover. Add the carrots, celery, onion, a pinch of salt, the peppercorns and olive oil, bring to the boil, then lower the heat, cover and simmer gently for 1 hour. Remove the pan from the heat and leave the meat to cool in the cooking liquid. Drain the pork, reserving the vegetables, place on a plate, cover with cling film and put a weight (such as a couple of cans of tomatoes) on top. Chill in the refrigerator. Meanwhile, make the sauce. Mash the egg yolks in a bowl, then beat in the mustard, a generous pinch of salt and the vinegar until smooth. Gradually beat in the olive oil, adding it in a thin, continuous stream. Stir in the capers, anchovies and tuna. Put the reserved vegetables in a food processor and process to a purée. Stir the purée into the sauce. Uncover the meat and carve it into thin slices. Place the slices, overlapping slightly, in concentric rings on a serving dish. Spoon the sauce over them to cover completely. Garnish with slices of lemon and serve.

LONZA AL GINEPRO

Serves 4

800-g/1³/₄-lb loin of pork, boned

1 shallot, chopped

1 onion, chopped

10–15 juniper berries, lightly crushed

2 bay leaves

5 tablespoons white wine

5 tablespoons oil

100 g/3¹/₂ oz pancetta, sliced

salt and pepper

LOIN OF PORK WITH JUNIPER

Make small incisions in the meat and insert pieces of shallot. Put the onion, juniper berries, bay leaves, wine and half the oil in a dish and season with salt and pepper. Add the pork, turning to coat, and leave to marinate for 2 hours. Preheat the oven to 180°C/350°F/Gas Mark 4. Drain the pork, reserving the marinade, wrap it in the slices of pancetta and tie with kitchen string. Put the pork in a roasting tin with the remaining oil and roast, basting occasionally with the reserved marinade, for about 1 hour or until tender and cooked through. Remove the meat from the roasting tin, untie and carve into thin slices. Place them on a warm serving dish and spoon the cooking juices over them.

BACON AND POTATO PIE

Preheat the oven to 200°C/400°F/Gas Mark 6. Mix together the bacon and onion in a large bowl, add the potatoes, sprinkle with the flour and mix well. Beat the eggs with a little salt and pepper in another bowl, stir in the milk, pour into the bacon mixture and stir until fully combined. Melt the butter in a roasting tin and when it has turned golden brown, pour in the mixture, then smooth the surface and mark with the prongs of a fork. Bake for about 45 minutes. Slice the pie and serve hot.

PASTICCIO DI BACON E PATATE

Serves 4

8 bacon rashers, coarsely chopped

$1/2$ onion, coarsely chopped

300 g/11 oz potatoes, cut into thin batons

1 tablespoon plain flour

2 eggs

5 tablespoons milk

40 g/1$1/2$ oz butter

salt and pepper

BAKED HAM

Preheat the oven to 240°C/475°F/Gas Mark 9. Using a sharp knife, score the skin of the ham in a diamond pattern. Mix together a generous pinch of sea salt and pepper in a small bowl and rub the mixture into the ham, particularly along the score marks, so that it penetrates well. Put the ham on a rack over a roasting tin and pour the wine and 350 ml/12 fl oz water into the tin beneath. Bake for 15 minutes, then lower the oven temperature to 150°C/300°F/Gas Mark 2 and bake for 3 hours, turning the ham halfway through the cooking time. Do not baste as the skin should be crisp when done. Meanwhile, put the butter, 175 ml/6 fl oz water, the sugar, vinegar and table salt and pepper in a pan and bring to the boil. Add the cabbage, cover, lower the heat and simmer for 15 minutes. Add the redcurrant jelly and apples, re-cover and cook for a further 40 minutes. If necessary, remove the lid during the end of the cooking period so that any excess liquid boils off. When the ham is cooked, switch off the oven, open the door and leave it in the oven for 20 minutes. Carve the ham into slices, place on a warm serving dish and surround with the cabbage. Stir 150 ml/$1/4$ pint warm water into the cooking juices and serve in a sauce boat with the ham.

PROSCIUTTO AL FORNO

Serves 10

3-kg/6$1/2$-lb raw cured ham

250 ml/8 fl oz dry white wine

50 g/2 oz butter

25 g/1 oz sugar

2 tablespoons red wine vinegar

1 red cabbage, shredded

4 tablespoons redcurrant jelly

2 apples, peeled, cored and chopped

sea salt

table salt and pepper

SMOKED HAM WITH MARSALA

PROSCIUTTO AL MARSALA

Serves 10

3-kg/6¹/₂-lb Prague ham or other smoked ham

500 ml/18 fl oz dry Marsala

6 tablespoons olive oil

80 g/3 oz butter

1 onion, diced

2 carrots, diced

2 celery sticks, diced

1 fresh flat-leaf parsley sprig, chopped

salt and pepper

For the sauce

200 ml/7 fl oz hot Meat Stock
(see page 208) or hot water

1 teaspoon cornflour

100 ml/3¹/₂ fl oz dry Marsala

25 g/1 oz butter

Cut off the skin and part of the fat from the ham and place the ham in a snug-fitting pan. Add the Marsala and leave to marinate for 6 hours. Preheat the oven to 180°C/350°F/Gas Mark 4. Drain the ham, reserving the marinade, and tie neatly with kitchen string. Heat the oil and butter in a large roasting tin, add the ham and cook, turning carefully, until lightly browned all over. Add the vegetables, parsley and salt and pepper. Transfer to the oven and roast, basting frequently with the cooking juices and the reserved marinade, for 2 hours. Remove the ham from the roasting tin and keep warm. To make the sauce, pass the vegetable and the ham juices through a food mill into a pan, add any remaining marinade and the stock or water and bring to the boil. Boil until slightly reduced. Mix the cornflour to a paste with 2 tablespoons cold water in a bowl, stir the mixture into the sauce and cook, stirring constantly, until thickened, then remove from the heat. Whisk in the Marsala and butter. Untie the ham and carve into fairly thick slices. Place on a warm serving dish and serve covered with the sauce.

HAM IN WHITE WINE

PROSCIUTTO AL VINO BIANCO

Serves 4

butter, for greasing

8 thick cooked ham slices

350 ml/12 fl oz dry white wine

300 g/11 oz mushrooms, sliced

1 small shallot, chopped

175 ml/6 fl oz double cream

1 tablespoon white port

salt

Preheat the oven to 150°C/300°F/Gas Mark 2. Grease a fairly large, ovenproof dish with butter and place the ham on the base. Pour in half the wine, cover with foil and bake for 3 hours, making sure that the liquid does not come to the boil. Put the mushrooms, shallot and remaining wine in a pan, bring to the boil, then stir in the cream and simmer gently. Add the ham cooking juices and cook until reduced to the required consistency. Stir in the port and season with salt to taste. Place the ham on a warm serving dish and cover with the sauce.

SPARE RIBS IN WHITE WINE

PUNTINE AL VINO BIANCO

Serves 4

2 tablespoons olive oil

40 g/1¹/₂ oz butter

4 fresh sage leaves

12 spare ribs

175 ml/6 fl oz dry white wine

salt and pepper

Heat the oil, butter and sage leaves in a fairly large pan until the leaves are light golden brown. Add the spare ribs and cook over a high heat for a few minutes, turning constantly, until evenly browned. Lower the heat and cook for 20 minutes. Season with salt and pepper and cook, occasionally sprinkling the ribs with the wine, for 40 minutes (do not pour in all the wine at once). Transfer to a warm serving dish.

Serves 6

12 spare ribs

3 tablespoons olive oil

1 spring onion, sliced

$^1/_2$ fresh pineapple, peeled, cored and chopped

1 yellow pepper, halved, seeded and cut into squares

1 green pepper, halved, seeded and cut into squares

1 red pepper, halved, seeded and cut into squares

2 tablespoons sugar

salt and pepper

SWEET–AND–SOUR SPARE RIBS

Preheat the oven to 200°C/400°F/Gas Mark 6. Season the spare ribs with salt and pepper, put in a roasting tin and roast for 20 minutes, turning them halfway through the cooking time. Meanwhile, preheat the grill. Place the roasting tin under the grill and cook for a further 10 minutes. Heat the oil in a pan, add the spring onion and cook over a low heat, stirring occasionally, for 5 minutes. Add the pineapple and peppers and cook over a low heat for about 10 minutes, adding a little water if necessary. Sprinkle with the sugar, season with salt and pepper, mix well and simmer for a further 10 minutes. Add the ribs and cook for a few minutes more, then serve.

SPEZZATINO CON LE PRUGNE

Serves 6

300 g/11 oz prunes

500 ml/18 fl oz port or Marsala

500 g/1 lb 2 oz fillet, diced

plain flour, for dusting

50 g/2 oz butter

1 shallot, finely chopped

2 tablespoons double cream

salt and pepper

CHOPPED PORK WITH PRUNES

Place the prunes in a bowl, add the port or Marsala and leave to soak overnight. Preheat the oven to 180°C/350°F/Gas Mark 4. Drain the prunes, reserving the port or Marsala, and stone them, then place them in a an ovenproof dish and dry in the oven for 6 minutes. Season the pork with salt and pepper and dust lightly with flour. Melt the butter in a frying pan, add the pork and cook, stirring frequently, for 5 minutes. Remove the meat from the pan and keep warm. Add the shallot to the pan and cook over a low heat, stirring occasionally, for 10 minutes until lightly browned. Pour in the reserved port or Marsala and cook until it has evaporated. Whisk in the cream. Place the meat on a warm serving dish, spoon the sauce over it and surround with the prunes.

SPEZZATINO CON SALSICCIA AFFUMICATA

Serves 4

1 Savoy cabbage, trimmed and separated into leaves

200 g/7 oz carrots, sliced

400 g/14 oz boneless blade of pork, cut into large cubes

400 g/14 oz boneless shoulder of pork, cut into large cubes

2 Italian smoked sausages

salt and pepper

PORK STEW WITH SMOKED SAUSAGES

Blanch the cabbage leaves in salted, boiling water for 5 minutes, then drain and place in a large pan. Add the carrots and all the pork and season with salt and pepper. Cover and cook over a low heat for 1$^1/_4$ hours. Prick the sausages with a fork, add to the pan and cook for 10 minutes. Mix well and transfer to a warm serving dish.

SWEET–AND–SOUR PORK STEW

Mix together the brandy and soy sauce in a dish, add the pork and leave to marinate for about 2 hours. Meanwhile, prepare the sauce. Heat half the butter and half the oil in a frying pan, add all the vegetables and stir-fry for a few minutes. Add 5 tablespoons water and the vinegar, sprinkle with the sugar and ketchup and season with salt and pepper. Simmer for about 20 minutes. Meanwhile, drain the pork. Heat the remaining butter and the remaining oil in pan, add the pork and cook over a medium heat, stirring frequently, until browned all over. Pour the sauce on top of the pork, stir well and simmer for 30 minutes. Serve the stew with boiled rice.

SPEZZATINO IN AGRODOLCE

Serves 4

50 ml/2 fl oz brandy

4 tablespoons dark soy sauce

600 g/1 lb 5 oz boneless shoulder of pork,

cut into cubes

50 g/2 oz butter

4 tablespoons olive oil

3 green peppers, halved, seeded and finely chopped

3 red peppers, halved, seeded and finely chopped

1 onion, finely chopped

4 gherkins, drained and finely chopped

1 tablespoon red wine vinegar

25 g/1 oz sugar • 1 tablespoon tomato ketchup

salt and pepper

boiled rice, to serve

PORK STEW WITH PEAS

Tip the tomatoes with their can juices into a food processor and process to a purée. Heat the butter and oil in a pan, add the onion and garlic and cook over a low heat, stirring occasionally, for 5 minutes. Add the pork and cook, stirring frequently, until lightly browned all over, then season with salt and pepper. Add the wine and cook until it has evaporated, then add the puréed tomatoes and the peas. Simmer gently for about 1 hour. Transfer the stew to a warm serving dish.

SPEZZATINO CON PISELLI

Serves 4

200 g/7 oz canned tomatoes

40 g/1½ oz butter

2 tablespoons olive oil

1 onion, chopped

1 garlic clove, chopped

600 g/1 lb 5 oz boneless shoulder of pork,

cut into cubes

175 ml/6 fl oz red wine

1 kg/2 ¼ lb fresh peas, shelled

salt and pepper

SPICY PORK STEW

Melt the butter in a pan, add the pork and cook over a high heat, stirring frequently, until browned all over. Pour in half the wine, add the cumin and garlic and season with salt and plenty of pepper. Mix well and bring to the boil, then cover, lower the heat and simmer for 30 minutes until tender. Add the remaining wine and the lemon, increase the heat to medium and cook, stirring constantly, until thickened. Stir in the coriander and serve.

SPEZZATINO SPEZIATO

Serves 6

50 g/2 oz butter

1 kg/2¼ lb boneless shoulder of pork, cut into cubes

350 ml/12 fl oz dry white wine

1 teaspoon ground cumin

1 garlic clove, chopped

5 lemon slices, chopped

2 tablespoons ground coriander

salt and pepper

PORK KEBABS
WITH PRUNES

SPIEDINI ALLE PRUGNE

Serves 4

500 g/1 lb 2 oz boneless loin of pork,
cut into 24 cubes

24 ready-to-eat prunes

plain flour, for dusting

25 g/1 oz butter

50 ml/2 fl oz dry Marsala

50 ml/2 fl oz dry white wine

salt and pepper

Thread three cubes of pork alternately with three prunes on to eight skewers, then dust the kebabs with flour. Melt the butter in a frying pan, add the kebabs and cook, turning frequently, until browned all over. Season with salt and pepper, pour in the Marsala and cook until it has evaporated. Pour in the wine, lower the heat, cover and simmer gently, basting occasionally, for about 15 minutes.

PORK HOCK
WITH VEGETABLES

STINCO CON VERDURE

Serves 4

2 pork hocks

4 carrots, thickly sliced

2 large onions, thinly sliced

4 potatoes, quartered

1 small Savoy cabbage, shredded

salt and pepper

Put the hocks in a wide pan, add water to cover and bring to the boil. Lower the heat, cover and simmer for about 1$\frac{1}{2}$ hours. Season with salt and pepper, add the carrots, onions and potatoes and simmer for a further 15 minutes. Add the cabbage and cook until the all vegetables are tender, but still slightly firm to the bite.

PORK TENERELLE

TENERELLE

Serves 4

20 g/^{3}/$_4$ oz dried mushrooms

4 tablespoons olive oil

100 g/3^1/$_2$ oz smoked pancetta, diced

1 onion, finely chopped

1 celery stick, finely chopped

1 carrot, finely chopped

600 g/1 lb 5 oz boneless loin of pork, minced

150 ml/^{1}/$_4$ pint hot Meat Stock (see page 208)

1 garlic clove

5 tablespoons dry white wine

2 tablespoons passata

fresh flat-leaf parsley, chopped

salt and pepper

Put the mushrooms in a bowl, add hot water to cover and leave to soak for 20 minutes, then drain and squeeze out. Meanwhile, heat 2 tablespoons of the oil in a pan, add the pancetta and cook over a medium heat, stirring frequently, for 5 minutes. Add the onion, celery and carrot, mix well and add the pork, then season with salt and pepper. Cook, stirring frequently, until the meat is evenly browned, occasionally adding a little hot stock, if necessary. Remove from the heat. Heat the remaining oil and the garlic in another pan, then add the mushrooms, wine and passata and season with salt and pepper. Simmer gently until reduced by half, then sprinkle with the parsley. Meanwhile, shape the pork mixture into small meatballs and flatten them slightly. Add the meatballs to the mushroom sauce and simmer for a few minutes, then transfer to a warm serving dish.

BEEF

Beef is tasty and nutritious. Its tenderness depends on the age of the animal it comes from, the type of fodder on which it was raised and the length of time it has been hung to mature. For several years, some Italian breeders have issued certificates of origin – a sort of beef identity card which makes the meat traceable and shows its quality. The aim is to provide the consumer with greater guarantees. Certification is voluntary as, currently, no law obliges breeders to give such information. Today, Italian meat stands up handsomely against the famed excellent meat in the rest of the world. Since 1993–4, the European Community has granted funds so that high-quality beef produced by member states, which is strictly checked and certified, can be exported. Only beef which has obtained EC approval bears the European Quality Beef mark (EQB).

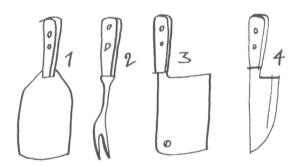

COOKING

→ It is important to prevent raw meat from losing its juices during preparation. It is therefore best to put it on a plate, rather than on a wooden board.

→ For the same reason, it is best to salt meat after browning. Avoid 'pricking' with a fork during cooking: use a slotted wooden or metal spatula to turn.

→ Meat loses only a small part of its nutritional value in cooking. The only exception is when simmering it in salted water. In this case it 'releases' its soluble components (mainly minerals) into the water thus forming a good stock.

→ If water or stock is to be added during cooking, it must be hot. Wine should be poured down the side of the pot to prevent sudden changes in temperature. When butter is stirred into ground (minced) meat to make stuffing, it should be melted first.

ROASTING

The best technique is spit-roasting: the fierce heat causes a light protective layer to form around the meat which helps retain the juice.

→ Pot roasts can be cooked in the oven or on the ring. They must in any case be cooked briefly on the ring in order to brown and sear the meat to retain the juice. After this, salt is added and the casserole is placed in a preheated oven. To prevent meat from drying out, baste occasionally with its cooking juices.

→ Medium and large pieces cook better if they are compact: that is why we always suggest tying them neatly in our recipes with a few twists of thin but tough kitchen string which will not leave unsightly marks on the meat.

STEAKS

In general these are large slices of well-hung meat (loin, fillet, sirloin, T-bone, shoulder or rump) weighing from 120–150 g/4–5 oz, which require quick cooking over a high heat with oil or butter.

BOILING

Topside, flank, brisket, neck and clod are the ideal cuts. They are cooked in plenty of salted water and flavoured with vegetables, such as celery, carrot and onion.

→ If you want to make good stock, immerse the meat in slightly salted cold water and gradually bring it to the boil.

→ If you want good boiled meat, immerse the meat in boiling water so that the protein and muscle fibres

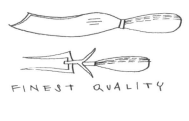

FINEST QUALITY

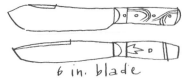

6 in. blade

seal, keeping the meat tender and moist.

→ Since it takes a long time to prepare stock, make more than necessary and pour what is left over into an ice tray. That way you can have excellent tasting stock cubes on hand in the freezer.

BRAISING AND STEWING

The most suitable parts for braising are topside, chuck, blade, neck and clod. After browning and moistening with water or wine, the meat is cooked on a low heat for a long time in a pot with a heavy lid.

→ A few vegetables and herbs or spices are normally also added to the pot, such as onions, carrots, celery and cloves.

→ Stewing and 'in umido' are similar techniques to braising, except the latter usually involves adding tomatoes and contains a very small quantity of liquid.

FRICASSÉE

This is a chopped white meat stew. Cream mixed with egg and lemon juice is added, or egg and lemon juice are added shortly before cooking is complete.

FRYING

For frying there is nothing better than olive oil, which – when light and very hot – adds flavour to any type of food. Here are a few things to bear in mind:

→ there are two main types of frying: pan-frying and deep-frying

→ in pan-frying, the oil comes up to about half the thickness of the food which is turned with a slotted spatula so that it browns and cooks evenly and completely

→ in deep-frying, the food is immersed in plenty of oil which covers it completely

→ while frying, the oil must never smoke

→ to judge the temperature, put a cube of day-old bread in the pan: if the oil is medium hot, it browns in 40 seconds; if it is very hot, it turns golden in 30 seconds; if it is extremely hot, it turns golden in 25 seconds

→ non-stick pans may be used for foods with long frying times so that the amount of oil needed can be reduced

→ fried food must be salted after cooking or very lightly salted at the start, otherwise there is a risk (for example with Milanese veal chops) that breadcrumbs may come away or crispy crusts will not form

→ it is best not to reuse oil after frying

→ dredging with flour: meat is usually dusted with flour and any excess flour is shaken off

→ browning: first of all dust with flour, then dip in lightly salted beaten egg

→ breadcrumbs: first dust with flour, then dip in beaten egg, then in breadcrumbs

→ batter: batter is made of flour and various liquids; it solidifies on contact with hot oil and forms a crust or puffs up.

STRACOTTO STEW

in this type of stew, the meat is larded, lightly browned all over, then moistened with wine, stock or water. The liquid is then kept at a gentle simmer for 3-4 hours. When cooked, the stew will be thickened and rich.

ITALIAN CUTS
AND COOKING
TECHNIQUES

1. FIOCCO
   Boiling
2. BRIONE
   Stewing and boiling
3. FUSELLO
   Fairly lean. Stewing, boiling,
   roulades and cutlets
4. COLLO
   Boiling and stewing
5. REALE
   Boiling and braising
6. BIANCOSTATO
   DI REALE
   Boiling
7. CAPPELLO DEL PRETE
   Its Italian name means
   priest's hat and derives from
   its slightly triangular shape.
   It is soft and gelatinous.
   Braising, stewing and boiling
8. GERETTO
   Boiling, braising and stewing
9. FESONE DI SPALLA
   Steaks, boiling, roulades,
   cutlets and escalopes

10. COSTE DELLA CROCE
    Boiling
11. BIANCOSTATO
    DI CROCE
    Soups
12. PUNTA DI PETTO
    Boiling and stewing
13. PANCIA
    O BAMBORINO
    Soups, stews and meatballs
14. BIANCOSTATO
    DI PANCIA
    Stocks and boiling
15. COSTATA
16. CONTROFILETTO
    (LOMBATA)
    Steaks and Florentine steaks
17. FILETTO
    The most tender and tastiest
    cut. Roasting and grilling
18. SCALFO
    Stewing
19. SCAMONE
    A tender tasty cut. Large
    roasts

20. NOCE
    Very tender. Escalopes, slices,
    steaks and roasting
21. SPINACINO
    Stuffed roasts
22. PESCE O PICCIONE
    Boiling
23. GIRELLO
    O MAGATELLO
    Steaks, escalopes, roasting,
    stewing and boiling, and
    also raw for carpaccio
24. ROSA
    Steaks and slices
25. CULACCIO
    O SCAMONE
    Roasting, boiling, braising
    and grilling
26. CODONE
    Stewing and boiling

BRITISH CUTS
AND COOKING
TECHNIQUES

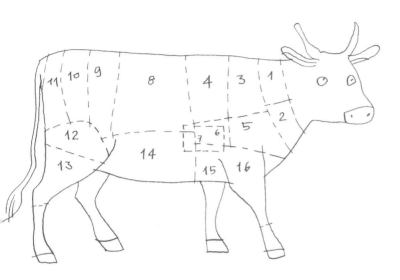

1. **NECK**
   Stewing
2. **CLOD**
   Stewing
3. **CHUCK AND BLADE**
   Braising and stewing
4. **FORE RIB**
   Roasting
5. **THICK RIB**
   Roasting
6. **THIN RIB**
   Roasting
7. **ROLLED RIBS**
   Roasting
8. **SIRLOIN**
   Roasting and cut into steaks and fillet
9. **RUMP**
   Roasting and cut into steaks

10. **SILVERSIDE**
    Pot-roasting, braising
11. **TOPSIDE**
    Braising, pot-roasting
12. **THICK FLANK**
    Pot-roasting and braising, and slow-frying in slices
13. **LEG**
    Stewing, casseroles
14. **FLANK**
    Stewing, and minced for pies
15. **BRISKET**
    Boiling, braising, pot roasting and salt beef
16. **SHIN**
    Stewing, casseroles

If you are in doubt over which cut to choose or cannot find one that is listed here, ask a reputable butcher for advice.

POT—ROAST BEEF WITH BRANDY AND GRAPEFRUIT

ARROSTO AL BRANDY E POMPELMO

Serves 6

800-g/1¾-lb beef topside
40 g/1½ oz butter
3 tablespoons olive oil
175 ml/6 fl oz dry white wine
50 ml/2 fl oz brandy
juice of 1 ruby grapefruit, strained
2 yellow grapefruits, peeled and segmented
salt and pepper

Tie the meat neatly with kitchen string. Heat the butter and olive oil in a flameproof casserole, add the meat and cook, turning frequently, until browned on all sides. Mix together the wine and brandy in a jug and pour the mixture over the meat. Cook until the liquid has evaporated, then season with salt and pepper. Lower the heat and cook for 1¼ hours, gradually adding the grapefruit juice. Transfer 3—4 tablespoons of the cooking juices to a pan, add the grapefruit segments and heat gently. Untie the meat, carve into slices, place on a warm serving dish and surround with the grapefruit segments and gravy.

POT—ROAST BEEF IN CREAM

ARROSTO ALLA PANNA

Serves 6

40 g/1½ oz butter
2 tablespoons olive oil
1 onion, thinly sliced
800-g/1¾-lb topside or silverside
3 tablespoons white wine vinegar
200 ml/7 fl oz double cream
salt and pepper

Heat the butter and olive oil in an oval, flameproof casserole, add the onion and cook, stirring occasionally, for 10 minutes until golden brown. Tie the meat neatly with kitchen string, add to the casserole, increase the heat to high and cook, turning frequently, until browned all over. Season with salt and pepper, add the vinegar, lower the heat, cover and simmer gently for about 2 hours, occasionally adding a little hot water if it seems to be drying out. When the meat is cooked through and tender, remove it from the casserole and leave it to stand for 10 minutes in a warm place. Stir the cream into the cooking juices and heat until thickened. Untie the beef, carve into slices, place on a warm serving dish and spoon the sauce over them.

POT—ROAST BEEF WITH ANCHOVIES AND TOMATO

ARROSTO ALLE ACCIUGHE E POMODORO

Serves 6

4 salted anchovies, heads removed, cleaned and filleted (see page 596), soaked in cold water for 10 minutes and drained
2 tablespoons olive oil
40 g/1½ oz butter • 1 onion, chopped
150 g/5 oz Italian sausages, skinned and crumbled
800-g/1¾-lb topside or silverside
plain flour, for dusting
5 tablespoons dry white wine
4 tomatoes, peeled and diced
salt and pepper

Chop the anchovy fillets. Heat the oil and butter in a pan, add the onion and cook over a low heat, stirring occasionally, for 5 minutes. Add the anchovies and cook, mashing with a wooden spoon until they have almost disintegrated, then add the sausages. Tie the meat neatly with kitchen string, dust lightly with flour, and add to the pan. Increase the heat to high and cook, turning frequently, until browned on all sides, then season with salt and pepper. Pour in the wine and cook until it has evaporated. Add the tomatoes, cover, and simmer gently for about 2 hours. Remove the meat from the pan and leave it to stand for 10 minutes. Untie the meat, carve into slices and serve with the cooking juices.

ROAST BEEF WITH CARROTS

Preheat the oven to 120°C/250°F/Gas Mark ¹/₂. Cover the base of a roasting tin with two-thirds of the pancetta. Heat the oil in a saucepan, add the carrots, garlic and thyme and cook over a medium-high heat, stirring frequently, until lightly browned. Season with salt and sprinkle with the nutmeg, then transfer to a dish and keep warm. Tie the meat neatly with kitchen string, add to the pan and cook, turning frequently, until browned on both sides. Season with salt, add the brandy and cook until it has evaporated. Transfer the beef to the roasting tin, spoon the carrot mixture and celery leaves around it and sprinkle the remaining pancetta on top. Cover and roast for 2 hours until the carrots have caramelized. Remove the meat from the roasting tin, discard the string, carve into slices and season with pepper. Transfer to a warm serving dish together with the vegetables.

ARROSTO ALLE CAROTE

Serves 6

150 g/5 oz pancetta, chopped

3 tablespoons olive oil

1 kg/2¹/₄ lb carrots, sliced

1 garlic clove, chopped

1 fresh thyme sprig, chopped

pinch of freshly grated nutmeg

800-g/1³/₄-lb topside

2 tablespoons brandy

4–5 celery leaves

salt and pepper

POT—ROAST MARINATED BEEF

Mix together all the marinade ingredients in a dish, add the meat, turning to coat, and leave to marinate for 6 hours. Drain the meat, reserving the marinade. Heat the oil and half the butter in a flame-proof casserole, add the beef and cook, turning frequently, until browned all over. Season with salt and cook over a low heat for 1¹/₂ hours or until cooked through and tender. Remove the meat from the casserole and leave to stand. Meanwhile, mix together the remaining butter and the flour and stir the paste into the cooking juices. Cook, stirring until slightly thickened, then strain in a little of the reserved marinade. Carve the beef and serve with the sauce.

ARROSTO MARINATO

Serves 6

900-g/2-lb topside

2 tablespoons olive oil

50 g/2 oz butter • 15 g/¹/₂ oz plain flour

salt

For the marinade

200 ml/7 fl oz olive oil

1 onion, sliced • ¹/₂ bunch of mixed fresh herbs, including flat-leaf parsley • 6 black peppercorns

STEAK WITH MUSHROOMS

Melt half the butter in a pan, add the shallot and cook over a low heat, stirring occasionally, for 5 minutes. Add the mushrooms, mix well, then add the wine and cook until it has evaporated. Mix the tomato purée with 3 tablespoons warm water, add the mixture to the pan and season lightly with salt. Cover and cook until the sauce is reduced by half. Heat the oil in a frying pan, add the slices of bread and cook until brown on both sides. Remove with a fish slice and drain on kitchen paper. Melt the remaining butter in another frying pan, add the steaks and cook for 2–3 minutes on each side. Season lightly with salt, place a steak on each slice of bread, spoon the mushroom sauce over them and sprinkle with the parsley.

BISTECCHE AI FUNGHI

Serves 4

50 g/2 oz butter

1 shallot, finely chopped

250 g/9 oz mushrooms, sliced

5 tablespoons dry white wine

1 tablespoon tomato purée

3 tablespoons olive oil

4 thick bread slices, crusts removed

4 fillet steaks

1 fresh flat-leaf parsley sprig, chopped

salt

STEAK IN BALSAMIC VINEGAR

BISTECCHE ALL'ACETO BALSAMICO

Serves 4

25 g/1 oz butter
2 tablespoons olive oil
4 entrecôte steaks
1 shallot, chopped
2 teaspoons balsamic vinegar
fresh flat-leaf parsley sprig, chopped
salt

Heat 20 g/³⁄₄ oz of the butter and the oil in a frying pan. Add the steaks and cook over a high heat for 2–4 minutes on each side, depending on how well done you like your steak. Season with salt, transfer to a serving dish and keep warm. Add the shallot to the pan and cook over a low heat, stirring occasionally, for 5 minutes. Add the remaining butter and reduce a little, then stir in the vinegar. Remove the pan from the heat and pour the sauce over the steaks, sprinkle with the parsley and serve.

STEAK PIZZAIOLA

BISTECCHE ALLA PIZZAIOLA

Serves 4

2 tablespoons olive oil
25 g/1 oz butter
2 garlic cloves
4 rump steaks
600 g/1 lb 5 oz ripe tomatoes, peeled and diced
pinch of dried oregano
salt and pepper

Heat the oil and butter in a frying pan, add the garlic and cook until it turns brown, then remove and discard it. Add the steaks to the pan and cook on a high heat for 1 minute on each side. Season with salt and pepper, transfer to a plate and keep warm. Add the tomatoes and oregano to the pan and simmer for 10 minutes until thickened and pulpy. Return the steaks to the pan and cook until done to your liking.

STEAK WITH MUSTARD

BISTECCHE ALLA SENAPE

Serves 4

3 tablespoons olive oil
25 g/1 oz butter
4 rump steaks
1 tablespoon brandy
200 ml/7 fl oz double cream
4 tablespoons Dijon mustard
salt

Heat the oil and butter in a frying pan, add the steaks and cook over a high heat for 2–4 minutes on each side, depending on how well done you like your steak. Season with salt on both sides, transfer to a serving dish and keep warm. Pour the brandy into the pan and cook, scraping up the sediment on the base, until the liquid has evaporated. Stir in the cream, season with salt if necessary and cook until thickened. Stir in the mustard, pour the sauce over the steaks and serve.

BEEF PATTIES
WITH CREAM AND MUSHROOMS

Put the mushrooms in a bowl, add warm water to cover and leave to soak for 1 hour, then drain, squeeze out and chop. Melt 40 g/ 1½ oz of the butter in a pan, add the mushrooms and cook over a low heat, stirring occasionally, for 20–30 minutes. Meanwhile, tear the bread into pieces, place in a bowl, add milk to cover and leave to soak. When the mushrooms are cooked, remove with a fish slice, pass through a food mill and return to the pan. Stir in the cream and cook until thickened. Drain and squeeze out the bread and mix with the meat in a bowl. Shape the mixture into rounds, flatten gently and dust with flour. Melt the remaining butter in a frying pan, add the beef patties and cook, turning once, for 7–8 minutes. Season with salt, transfer the patties to a warm serving dish and pour the sauce over them.

BISTECCHE TRITATE
CON PANNA E FUNGHI

Serves 4

50 g/2 oz dried mushrooms

65 g/2½ oz butter

1–2 bread slices, crusts removed

150–175 ml/5–6 fl oz milk

200 ml/7 fl oz double cream

500 g/1 lb 2 oz lean minced beef

plain flour, for dusting

salt

PIEDMONTESE BOILED MEAT

Bring 5 litres/8¾ pints salted water to the boil in a large pan together with the celery, onion and carrot. Add the beef, lower the heat to medium and simmer for 1 hour. Add the veal, boiling fowl and calf's tongue and simmer for a further 2 hours. Cook the calf's head separately (see page 870). Meanwhile, prick the cotechino skin with a needle, immerse it in a pan of cold water, bring to the boil and simmer for about 2 hours. Remove the pan from the heat, leave the cotechino to stand in the cooking liquid for 10 minutes, then lift it out and drain well. Put the various meats together on a large warm serving dish and serve with boiled potatoes and green sauce.

BOLLITO ALLA PIEMONTESE

Serves 8

1 celery stick

1 onion • 1 carrot

1-kg/2¼-lb beef fillet

1-kg/2¼-lb boneless breast of veal

½ boiling fowl • 1 small calf's tongue

1 kg/2¼ lb calf's head

1 small cotechino sausage

salt

boiled potatoes and Green Sauce

(see page 74), to serve

MILANESE MIXED BOILED MEAT

Half-fill a large saucepan with water, add the onion, celery and carrots and bring to the boil. Add the beef and veal and simmer for about 2 hours. If using the cotechino, prick the skin with a needle, place it another pan of water, bring to the boil and simmer for about 2 hours. Place the calf's head in another pan with just enough water to cover, bring to the boil and simmer for 1½ hours. Drain and slice the beef, veal and calf's head and place on a warm serving dish. Surround with slices of cotechino and serve with green sauce and Cremona mustard. Strain the beef and veal stock and serve with the meats.

BOLLITO MISTO ALLA MILANESE

Serves 6

1 onion • 1 celery stick

2 carrots

800-g/1¾-lb topside

500-g/1 lb 2-oz boneless breast of veal

500-g/1 lb 2-oz calf's head

1 cotechino sausage (optional)

Green Sauce (see page 74),

and Cremona mustard to serve

BRASATO

Serves 6

1-kg/2¼-lb topside of beef or
another fairly lean cut

50 g/2 oz butter

3 tablespoons olive oil

1 onion, finely chopped

2 carrots, finely chopped

1 celery stick, finely chopped

175 ml/6 fl oz red wine

1 ripe tomato, peeled and chopped

4 canned tomatoes, chopped

1 tablespoon tomato purée

1 quantity Meat Stock (see page 208)

salt and pepper

BRAISED BEEF

Tie the meat neatly with kitchen string. Melt the butter with the oil in a large saucepan, add the onion, carrots and celery and cook over a low heat, stirring occasionally, for 10 minutes. Add the meat and cook, turning frequently, until lightly browned. Season with salt and pepper, add the wine and cook until it has evaporated, then add the fresh and canned tomatoes. Mix the tomato purée with 5 tablespoons warm water in a bowl, add to the pan and cook for a few minutes more. Add enough stock to half-cover the meat, bring to the boil, lower the heat, cover and simmer for about 1½ hours, adding more hot stock as necessary. Remove the meat from the pan, untie and carve into slices. Place the slices on a warm serving dish and strain the cooking juices over them. Hot braised beef may be served with grilled sliced polenta or soft polenta.

BRASATO AL BAROLO

Serves 6

1-kg/2¼-lb topside or another fairly lean cut

3 tablespoons olive oil

40 g/1½ oz butter

25 g/1 oz prosciutto fat, chopped

pinch of cocoa powder

1 teaspoon rum (optional)

salt

For the marinade

1 bottle (750 ml/1¼ pints) Barolo

2 carrots, sliced

2 onions, sliced

1 celery stalk, chopped

4 fresh sage leaves

1 small fresh rosemary sprig

1 bay leaf

10 black peppercorns

salt

BRAISED BEEF WITH BAROLO

Tie the meat neatly with kitchen string, place in a dish and pour in the wine for the marinade. Add the carrots, onions, celery, sage, rosemary, bay leaf, peppercorns and a pinch of salt and leave to marinate for 6–7 hours. Drain the meat, reserving the marinade, and pat dry with kitchen paper. Heat the oil, butter and prosciutto fat in a saucepan, add the meat and cook over a high heat, turning frequently, until browned all over. Season with salt, pour in the reserved marinade, lower the heat, cover and simmer for 1½ hours until tender. Remove the meat from the pan, untie and carve. Arrange the slices, slightly overlapping, on a warm serving dish. Discard the herbs from the cooking liquid and pass it through a food mill, then stir in the cocoa and rum if using. Pour the sauce over the meat and serve.

BEEF STROGANOFF

BUE ALLA STROGONOFF

Serves 6

120 g/4 oz butter

4 onions, thinly sliced

120 g/4 oz mushrooms, sliced

juice of 1 lemon, strained

20 g/³/₄ oz plain flour

250 ml/8 fl oz double cream

1 teaspoon sugar

1 tablespoon strong mustard

1 tablespoon olive oil

800 g/1³/₄ lb thinly sliced sirloin
or rump steak, cut into thin strips

salt and pepper

Melt 100 g/3¹/₂ oz of the butter in a pan, add the onions and cook over a low heat, stirring occasionally, for 10 minutes until golden brown. Add the mushrooms and lemon juice, cover and simmer gently, shaking the pan occasionally, for 10 minutes. Melt the remaining butter in a frying pan, stir in the flour and cook, stirring for 2 minutes. Stir in the cream and sugar and cook, stirring frequently, for 7–8 minutes. Season with salt and pepper, remove from the heat and stir in the mustard. Cut the strips of steak into squares. Heat the oil in a frying pan over a high heat. Add the steak and cook, stirring frequently, for a few minutes until browned and tender. Stir the steak into the mushroom and onion mixture and spoon the sauce on top, then transfer to a warm serving dish.

BRAISED BEEF WITH ONIONS

BRASATO ALLE CIPOLLE

Serves 6

1-kg/2¹/₄-lb topside
or another fairly lean cut

25 g/1 oz pancetta, cut into thin strips

1 kg/2¹/₄ lb onions, thickly sliced

salt and pepper

Lard the beef with the pancetta and tie neatly with kitchen string. Put the onions in a large pan, place the meat on top, cover and cook over a very low heat for 1 hour. Turn the meat over, season well with salt and pepper, re-cover and cook, stirring occasionally, for 1 hour more or until tender. Remove the meat from the pan, untie and carve into fairly thin slices. Place the slices, slightly overlapping, on a warm serving dish and spoon the onion sauce over them. If you prefer a more even consistency, pass the sauce through a food mill first. This dish is excellent served with soft polenta.

CARPACCIO

CARPACCIO

Serves 4

400 g/14 oz sirloin steak, cut into wafer-thin slices

1 quantity Mayonnaise (see page 65)

1 tablespoon Worcestershire sauce

1 tablespoon lemon juice

3 tablespoons milk

salt and white pepper

Spread out the slices of steak on a serving dish. Mix together the mayonnaise, Worcestershire sauce, lemon juice and milk in a bowl, season with salt and pepper and spoon the mixture over the meat. This is the original version of carpaccio invented by Arrigo Cipriani and served in his world-famous Venetian restaurant, but there are several variations. For example, a little mustard may be added to the mayonnaise. The steak may be drizzled with olive oil and lemon juice, seasoned with salt and pepper and then covered with Parmesan shavings and truffle shavings, or even thinly sliced raw mushrooms dressed with oil, pepper and lemon juice. A more exotic version can be made by dressing the meat with olive oil, lemon juice, salt and pepper and covering with sliced palm hearts and Parmesan shavings.

FLORENTINE T-BONE STEAK

COSTATA ALLA FIORENTINA

Serves 4

2 x 600-g/1 lb 5-oz T-bone steaks

olive oil, for drizzling

salt and pepper

Those who wish to serve authentic Florentine T-bone steaks should follow the rules of the Articles of Association of the Florentine T-bone Steak Academy, founded in 1991 by representatives of the Florentine Butchers' Association. For over 200 years, a Florentine steak has been defined as a T-bone steak cut from a chianina calf and hung for 5–6 days. The steak must be cut from the loin through the fillet and sirloin with the T-bone in the middle. The meat must be 2–3 cm/³⁄₄–1¹⁄₄ inches thick and weigh 600–800 g/1 lb 5 oz–1³⁄₄ lb. It must be cooked for 5 minutes on each side without seasoning over hot charcoal, preferably oak charcoal, about 20 cm/8 inches above the embers. The steak must be turned once only with a spatula and seasoned only when cooked. The meat should be brown on the outside and slightly rare inside. To serve, lightly drizzle a warm serving dish with olive oil and arrange the seasoned steaks on it.

SALTED T-BONE STEAK IN SAUCE

COSTATA DI BUE AL SALE CON SALSA

Serves 6

2.5-kg/5¹⁄₂-lb T-bone steak

80 g/3 oz butter

salt and pepper

For the sauce

40 g/1¹⁄₂ oz butter

2 tablespoons olive oil

6 shallots, chopped

5 tablespoons dry white wine

2 egg yolks

1 tablespoon fresh flat-leaf parsley, chopped

1 tablespoon white wine vinegar

salt and pepper

Preheat the oven to 200°C/400°F/Gas Mark 6. Spread the steak with about half the butter and season well with salt and pepper. Generously grease a frying pan with the remaining butter, set over a medium-high heat, add the steak and cook for 2 minutes on each side. Transfer the pan to the oven and cook for 15–20 minutes until tender. (If the pan has a wooden handle, cover it with foil first.) Place the steak on a warm serving dish, tent with foil and leave to stand for 10 minutes before carving. Meanwhile, prepare the sauce. Heat the butter and oil in a pan, add the shallots and cook over a low heat, stirring occasionally, for 5 minutes. Add the wine and cook until it has evaporated, then season with salt and pepper. Remove the pan from the heat and stir in the egg yolks, one at a time. Add the parsley and sprinkle with the vinegar. Return to the heat for a few minutes but do not allow the sauce to boil. Slice the steak fairly thickly and serve with the sauce.

BEEF WELLINGTON

Preheat the oven to 220°C/425°F/Gas Mark 7. Brush an oval ovenproof dish with oil. Wrap the beef in the pancetta slices and tie with kitchen string, then place in the prepared dish. Cover and cook in the oven for 10 minutes, then remove from the oven and leave to cool slightly. Lower the oven temperature to 200°C/400°F/Gas Mark 6. Meanwhile, roll out the pastry on a lightly floured surface. Untie the beef and remove the pancetta. Carefully spread the pâté over the whole fillet, then place the meat on the pastry and wrap the pastry around to enclose it, crimping the edges to seal. Beat the egg yolk with the milk in a bowl and brush the mixture over the parcel. Make two small holes in the dough to allow steam to escape during cooking. Place the parcel on a baking sheet and bake for 20 minutes until golden brown. Leave to stand for 5 minutes, then slice and transfer to a warm serving dish.

FILETTO IN CROSTA AL PÂTÉ

Serves 6

olive oil, for brushing

1-kg/2¼-lb beef fillet

100 g/3½ oz pancetta, sliced

250 g/9 oz puff pastry dough, thawed if frozen

plain flour, for dusting

100 g/3½ oz truffle pâté

1 egg yolk

1 tablespoon milk

FONDUE BOURGUIGNONNE

Dice the meat and place in a serving dish. Place the sauces in small bowls. Place a fondue set on the table, add the oil and a little salt to the pan and keep it hot with a lighted burner. Each guest pierces a piece of meat with a fondue fork and cooks it according to taste in the hot oil. They then dip it in one of the sauces. Provide a selection of sauces with different characteristics and flavours, some hot and some not, such as mayonnaise, curry sauce, tartar sauce, aïoli, hot cream sauce, mustard, etc. (see Sauces, pages 45 to 89).

FONDUE BOURGUIGNONNE

Serves 4

800 g/1¾ lb tender lean beef

various sauces (see method)

500 ml/18 fl oz olive oil

salt

GOULASH

Heat the butter and oil in a large saucepan, add the onions and cook over a low heat, stirring occasionally, for 5 minutes. Add the meat and stir well. Mix the paprika with 150 ml/¼ pint hot water, pour the mixture into the pan and cook for a few minutes, then add the tomatoes. Cook over a very low heat until the meat starts to brown, then add 150 ml/¼ pint hot water. Cover and simmer gently for about 1 hour. Season with salt to taste, add the potatoes and simmer for a further 45 minutes.

GULASCH

Serves 4

40 g/1½ oz butter

4 tablespoons olive oil

4 onions, thinly sliced

600 g/1 lb 5 oz lean beef, cut into coarse cubes

1 tablespoon hot paprika

500 g/1 lb 2 oz ripe tomatoes,

peeled and chopped or canned chopped tomatoes

500 g/1 lb 2 oz potatoes, diced

salt

HAMBURGERS AMERICAN-STYLE

HAMBURGER ALL'AMERICANA
Serves 4
400 g/14 oz lean minced beef
1 small onion, finely chopped
1 egg, lightly beaten
olive oil, for drizzling
4 soft round rolls
4 small lettuce leaves
8 tomato slices
tomato ketchup, to taste
salt and pepper

Preheat the grill. Mix the meat and onion together in a large bowl, then stir in the egg and season with salt and pepper. Divide the mixture into four, shape into balls and gently flatten into patties. Drizzle with a little oil. Cook the hamburgers under the grill for 3 minutes on each side, turning them with a fish slice. Alternatively, cook in a heavy-based frying pan over a high heat for 3 minutes on each side. Halve the rolls and place a hamburger on the bottom half of each. Add a lettuce leaf, two tomato slices and a little ketchup to each and replace the tops of the rolls.

HAMBURGERS WITH HAM

HAMBURGER CON PROSCIUTTO
Serves 4
400 g/14 oz lean beef, chopped
50 g/2 oz smoked cooked ham, chopped
4 egg yolks, lightly beaten
1 fresh flat-leaf parsley sprig, chopped
2 tablespoons olive oil
salt and pepper

Mix the beef and ham together in a bowl, stir in the egg yolks and parsley and season with a little pepper. Divide the mixture into four, shape into balls and gently flatten into patties. Heat the oil in a frying pan, add the hamburgers and cook on a medium-high heat for 3 minutes on each side until browned on the outside but rare on the inside. Season with salt and serve.

BEEF AND SPINACH ROULADES

INVOLTINI AGLI SPINACI
Serves 4
400 g/14 oz spinach
50 g/2 oz butter
8 thin lean beef slices
8 thin Gruyère cheese slices
3 carrots, chopped
1 tablespoon olive oil
5 tablespoons dry white wine
2 shallots, chopped
1 tomato, peeled and diced
salt and pepper

Cook the spinach, in just the water clinging to the leaves after washing, for about 5 minutes until wilted, then drain and squeeze out as much liquid as possible. Melt half the butter in a frying pan, add the spinach and cook over a low heat, stirring occasionally, for 5 minutes. Spread out the slices of beef and pound until thin and even. Place a slice of cheese on each and divide two-thirds of the carrots and two-thirds of the spinach among them. Roll up and tie with kitchen string. Heat the oil and the remaining butter in a frying pan, add the roulades and cook, turning frequently, until lightly browned all over. Add the wine and cook until it has evaporated, then add the shallots and tomato and season with salt and pepper. Cover and cook over a low heat for 20 minutes. Add the remaining carrot and cook for 5 minutes, then add the remaining spinach and cook for a further 5 minutes. Remove the string from the roulades and serve in their sauce.

BEEF AND BRESAOLA ROULADES

Pound the meat until it is thin and even and place two slices of bresaola on each piece. Roll up, tie with kitchen string and dust with flour. Melt the butter in a frying pan, add the roulades and cook, turning frequently, until browned all over. Add the wine and cook until it has evaporated, then add the stock, cover and simmer over a low heat for 15 minutes. Add the cream and juniper berries and cook until thickened. Season with salt if necessary. Remove the string from the roulades, place on a warm serving dish and spoon the sauce over them.

INVOLTINI CON BRESAOLA

Serves 4

400 g/14 oz lean beef, cut into 4 slices

8 bresaola slices

plain flour, for dusting

40 g/1¹/₂ oz butter

175 ml/6 fl oz dry white wine

150 ml/¹/₄ pint Meat Stock (see page 208)

4 tablespoons double cream

8 juniper berries

salt

TASTY ROULADES

Mix together the salami, basil, garlic and butter in a bowl. Spread the mixture on the slices of meat, season with salt and pepper, roll up and tie with kitchen string. Heat the oil in a frying pan, add the rosemary, onion and roulades and cook, turning the roulades frequently, until browned all over. Lower the heat, cover and cook for 15 minutes. Remove the string before serving.

INVOLTINI GUSTOSI

Serves 4

100 g/3¹/₂ oz salami, chopped

6 fresh basil leaves, chopped

¹/₂ garlic clove, chopped

25 g/1 oz butter, softened

8 lean beef slices

3 tablespoons olive oil

1 fresh rosemary sprig

¹/₂ onion, chopped

salt and pepper

SIMPLE POACHED BEEF

The most suitable cuts of beef for poaching are chuck and blade or brisket. You can also add breast of veal. Although this is a simple, home-cooked dish, it needs a fairly large piece of lean meat. To make sure that the meat is tasty, always add it to hot water in which vegetables have been simmering for about 20 minutes. Season with salt and simmer on a low heat for about 2 hours. Remove the meat from the pan, leave to stand for 10 minutes, then carve and place on a warm serving dish. Serve with Green Sauce (see page 74) and boiled potatoes if you like. Strain the stock and serve boiling hot in bowls or use for risotto or Stracciatella (see page 238).

LESSO CASALINGO

Serves 6

1 kg/2¹/₄ lb beef or 500 g/1 lb 2 oz beef and 500 g/1 lb 2 oz veal

1 onion

1 celery stick

1 carrot

salt

793

SIMPLE POACHED BEEF SALAD

Leave the beef to cool, then chop. Put it in a salad bowl, sprinkle with the spring onion and parsley and add the capers and gherkins. Whisk together the olive oil, vinegar, mustard and a pinch of salt in a bowl. Add the dressing to the salad, toss and set aside for 1 hour to let the flavours mingle. Shell the eggs and halve or slice. Garnish the salad with the eggs and put a green peppercorn in the middle of each yolk. You can also use leftover beef cooked according to the recipe on page 793 for this salad.

LESSO IN INSALATA

Serves 4

500-g/1 lb 2-oz Simple Poached Beef (see page 793)

1 spring onion, finely chopped

1 fresh flat-leaf parsley sprig, chopped

2 tablespoons capers, drained and rinsed

5 gherkins, drained and sliced

100 ml/3¹/₂ fl oz olive oil

3 tablespoons red wine vinegar

1 tablespoon Dijon mustard • salt

2 eggs, hard-boiled, and green peppercorns,

to garnish

SIMPLE POACHED BEEF WITH ROSEMARY

Heat the oil in a pan, add the meat and cook for a few minutes. Chop the garlic and rosemary together, place in a bowl, stir in the vinegar and pour the mixture over the meat. Cover and simmer for 5–10 minutes. Season with salt to taste. Transfer to a warm serving dish and serve with a side dish of boiled potatoes or beetroot.

LESSO INSAPORITO AL ROSMARINO

Serves 4

2 tablespoons olive oil

4 slices leftover Simple Poached Beef (see page 793)

1 garlic clove

1 fresh rosemary sprig

5 tablespoons white wine vinegar

salt

boiled potatoes or boiled beetroot, to serve

STEAK WITH SAGE

Lightly dust the steaks with flour. Melt the butter in a frying pan, add the steaks and cook until golden brown on both sides. Add the sage and cook for a few more minutes. Season with salt and serve. Boiled potatoes sautéed with a few tablespoons of oil and a little pepper make a good accompaniment.

LOMBATE ALLA SALVIA

Serves 4

4 sirloin steaks

plain flour, for dusting

25 g/1 oz butter • 4 fresh sage leaves

salt

STEAK IN WHITE WINE

Melt the butter in a frying pan, add the steaks and cook until lightly browned on both sides. Transfer to a plate and keep warm. Add the onions and carrots to the pan and cook over a low heat, stirring occasionally, for 5 minutes. Return the steaks to the pan, add the wine and cook until it has evaporated, then add the passata and season with salt and pepper. Cover and cook over a low heat for 15 minutes. Switch off the heat and leave to stand for a few minutes without uncovering. Serve with white turnips in butter.

LOMBATE AL VINO BIANCO

Serves 4

40 g/1¹/₂ oz butter

4 sirloin steaks • 2 onions, thinly sliced

2 carrots, cut into thin strips

175 ml/6 fl oz dry white wine

2 tablespoons passata

salt and pepper

white turnips in butter, to serve

795

MEATBALLS IN BRANDY

POLPETTE AL BRANDY

Serves 4

400 g/14 oz lean minced beef

50 g/2 oz cooked ham, chopped

2 egg yolks

50 g/2 oz Parmesan cheese, freshly grated

1 fresh flat-leaf parsley sprig, chopped

3–4 tablespoons Béchamel Sauce (see page 50)

plain flour, for dusting

50 g/2 oz butter

1 tablespoon olive oil

1 small onion, chopped

1 tablespoon brandy

salt and pepper

Mix together the beef, ham, egg yolks, Parmesan, parsley and béchamel sauce in a bowl and season with salt and pepper. Shape the mixture into balls and dust with flour. Heat the butter and oil in a pan. Add the onion and cook over a low heat, stirring occasionally, for 5 minutes. Increase the heat to high, add the meatballs and cook for 1 minute on each side, then lower the heat and cook gently for about 15 minutes. Transfer the meatballs to a serving dish and keep warm. Stir 2–3 tablespoons warm water and the brandy into the pan and cook until thickened. Remove the pan from the heat, stir the sauce, pour it over the meatballs and serve immediately.

MEATBALLS WITH ANCHOVIES

POLPETTE ALLE ACCIUGHE

Serves 4

2 rolls, crusts removed

150 ml/¼ pint milk

1 fresh flat-leaf parsley sprig, finely chopped

1 garlic clove, finely chopped

2 canned anchovy fillets in oil, drained and finely chopped

400 g/14 oz lean minced beef • 1 egg yolk

2 tablespoons Parmesan cheese, freshly grated

50 g/2 oz fine breadcrumbs

olive oil, for brushing • salt and pepper

spinach in butter, to serve

Tear the rolls into pieces, place in a bowl, add the milk and leave to soak for 10 minutes, then drain and squeeze out. Mix together the parsley, garlic, anchovy fillets and beef in a bowl. Stir in the egg yolk, soaked rolls and Parmesan and season with salt and pepper. Shape the mixture into 8–10 meatballs and flatten slightly. Spread out the breadcrumbs in a shallow dish and roll the meatballs in them to coat. Brush the base of a frying pan with a little oil, add the meatballs and cook over a high heat for 1 minute on each side. Lower the heat, cover and cook gently for about 10 minutes. Serve with spinach in butter.

MEATBALLS WITH POTATO

POLPETTE ALLE PATATE

Serves 4

2 potatoes, boiled and drained

300 g/11 oz lean beef, finely chopped

2 mortadella slices, finely chopped

1 egg, lightly beaten

1 tablespoon Parmesan cheese, freshly grated

1 fresh flat-leaf parsley sprig, chopped

50 g/2 oz breadcrumbs

2 tablespoons olive oil

salt and pepper

Mash the potatoes in a bowl while they are still hot and mix in the beef, mortadella and egg. Stir in the Parmesan and parsley and season with salt and pepper. Shape the mixture into eight balls. Spread out the breadcrumbs in a shallow dish and roll the meatballs in them to coat. Heat the oil in a frying pan, add the meatballs and cook, turning frequently, until golden brown all over and cooked through. Remove with a fish slice and drain on kitchen paper.

MEATBALLS IN LEMON

POLPETTE AL LIMONE

Serves 4

400 g/14 oz lean minced beef

50 g/2 oz Parmesan cheese, freshly grated

4 tablespoons Béchamel Sauce (see page 50)

dash of Worcestershire sauce

40 g/1½ oz butter

4 tablespoons double cream

juice of ½ lemon, strained

1 teaspoon breadcrumbs

salt

Mix together the minced beef, Parmesan, béchamel sauce and Worcestershire sauce in a bowl and season with salt. Shape the mixture into eight meatballs, then flatten them slightly. Melt the butter in a pan and when it starts to go golden brown, add the meatballs. Cook over a medium heat, turning frequently for about 15 minutes. Transfer to a serving dish and keep warm. Pour the cream into a pan, add the lemon juice and breadcrumbs and cook, stirring frequently, until slightly thickened. Pour the sauce over the meatballs and serve.

MEATBALLS WITH SPINACH

POLPETTE CON SPINACI

Serves 4

250 g/9 oz spinach

250 g/9 oz lean minced beef

120 ml/4 fl oz Béchamel Sauce (see page 50)

25 g/1 oz Parmesan cheese, freshly grated

1 egg, lightly beaten

plain flour, for dusting

25 g/1 oz butter

2 tablespoons olive oil

salt

Cook the spinach, in just the water clinging to the leaves after washing, for about 5 minutes until wilted, then drain, squeeze out as much liquid as possible and chop. Mix together the spinach, beef, béchamel sauce, Parmesan and egg in a bowl and season with salt. Shape the mixture into eight balls and dust with flour. Heat the butter and oil in a frying pan, add the meatballs and cook, turning frequently, until browned all over and cooked through. Remove with a fish slice, drain on kitchen paper and serve.

MEATBALLS WITH A TASTY ONION GARNISH

POLPETTE SAPORITE

Serves 4

65 g/2½ oz butter

1 large onion, sliced

400 g/14 oz lean minced beef

2 egg yolks

salt and pepper

Melt half the butter in a pan, add the onion and cook over a low heat, stirring occasionally, for 10 minutes, then season with salt. Mix together half the onion, the beef and egg yolks in a bowl and season with salt and pepper. Shape the mixture into eight meatballs. Melt the remaining butter in a frying pan, add the meatballs and cook over a high heat, turning frequently, until browned all over and cooked through. Transfer to a dish, spoon the cooking juices over them and garnish with the remaining onion.

ROAST BEEF

Preheat the oven to 200°C/400°F/Gas Mark 6. Sprinkle the butter and 1 tablespoon of the oil over the base of a roasting tin. Tie the beef neatly with kitchen string, brush with the remaining oil, place in the roasting tin and cook over a high heat, turning frequently, until browned all over. Season with salt and pepper. Cover, transfer to the oven and roast for 30 minutes or longer, depending on how well done you like your beef. Test by piercing the meat with a skewer. If the juices are red, it is rare, if they are pink, it is medium and if no juices run, it is well done. Remove from the roasting tin and leave to stand for 5 minutes before removing the string and carving. Place the roasting tin over a low heat and stir in 150 ml/¼ pint hot water, scraping up the sediment on the base. If the gravy is too runny, stir in a knob of butter dipped in flour. Cook, stirring until thickened. Pour the gravy into a sauce boat and serve with the meat.

ROAST–BEEF

Serves 6

40 g/1½ oz butter, cut into pieces,
plus extra for the gravy (optional)
2 tablespoons oil
1-kg/2¼-lb fillet of beef
plain flour, for the gravy (optional)
salt and pepper

ROAST BEEF WITH CHESTNUTS

Preheat the oven to 200°C/400°F/Gas Mark 6. Tie the meat neatly with kitchen string. Heat the butter and oil in a roasting tin, add the meat and cook, turning frequently, until browned all over. Season with salt and pepper, add the celery, onion, carrot and rosemary to the tin and cook, stirring occasionally, for a further 10 minutes. Add the wine and cook until it has evaporated. Cover with foils, transfer to the oven and roast for 30–40 minutes, depending on how well done you like your beef. After 30 minutes the beef will be rare and after 40 minutes it will be medium. Meanwhile, cook the chestnuts in boiling water until tender, then drain and press through a sieve into a bowl. Remove the meat from the roasting tin, leave to stand for about 10 minutes, then remove the string and carve. Place the roasting tin over a low heat, stir in the cream and the chestnut purée and cook, stirring frequently, until slightly thickened. Pour into a sauce boat and serve with the meat.

ROAST–BEEF CON LE CASTAGNE

Serves 4

1-kg/2¼-lb fillet of beef
25 g/1 oz butter
1 tablespoon olive oil
1 celery stick, chopped
1 onion, chopped
1 carrot, chopped
1 fresh rosemary sprig, chopped
5 tablespoons dry white wine
100 g/3½ oz dried white chestnuts,
soaked in warm water for 6 hours and drained
3 tablespoons double cream
salt and pepper

RAPID ROAST WITH ROCKET

Preheat the oven to 240°C/475°F/Gas Mark 9. Place the beef in an ovenproof dish and cover completely with the rocket. Drizzle with olive oil and season with salt and pepper. Roast for about 1 minute. An alternative version of this simple but tasty recipe uses radicchio instead of rocket, but it has a slightly more bitter flavour.

'SCOTTATA' ALLA RUCOLA

Serves 6

600 g/1 lb 5 oz beef fillet, thinly sliced
100 g/3½ oz rocket, coarsely chopped
olive oil, for drizzling
salt and pepper

BEEF STEW

SPEZZATINO DI MANZO

Serves 4

2 tablespoons olive oil

25 g/1 oz butter

¹/₂ onion, chopped

1 celery stick, chopped

1 carrot, chopped

600 g/1 lb 5 oz lean stewing steak, cut into cubes

5 tablespoons dry white wine

2 tomatoes, peeled and diced or

2–3 canned tomatoes

salt and pepper

Heat the oil and butter in a pan, add the onion, celery and carrot and cook over a low heat, stirring occasionally, for 10 minutes. Add the meat and cook, stirring constantly, until browned all over. Pour in the wine and cook until it has evaporated, then season with salt and pepper to taste. Put the tomatoes into a food processor and process to a purée, then add to the pan with 150 ml/¹/₄ pint warm water. Cover and simmer over a low heat, stirring occasionally, for about 1 hour.

BEEF STEW WITH COFFEE

SPEZZATINO AL CAFFÉ

Serves 4

2 tablespoons olive oil

600 g/1 lb 5 oz lean stewing steak, cut into cubes

2 onions, thinly sliced

1 garlic clove, chopped

2 green peppers, halved, seeded and thickly sliced

25 g/1 oz plain flour

5 tablespoons dry white wine

5 tablespoons brewed coffee

salt and pepper

This is a Brazilian recipe. Heat the oil in a pan, add the meat and cook, stirring frequently, until browned all over. Remove the meat with a fish slice and keep warm. Add the onions, garlic and peppers to the pan and cook over a low heat, stirring occasionally, for 10 minutes. Sprinkle in the flour and cook, stirring constantly, for 2–3 minutes. Gradually stir in the wine and coffee and bring to the boil, stirring constantly. Return the meat to the pan, season with salt and pepper to taste, cover and cook for 1 hour or until the meat is tender.

BEEF STEW WITH WINE AND ONIONS

SPEZZATINO AL VINO E CIPOLLE

Serves 4

65 g/2¹/₂ oz butter

800 g/1³/₄ lb onions, finely chopped

150 g/5 oz pancetta, diced

600 g/1 lb 5 oz lean stewing steak, cubed

25 g/1 oz plain flour

375 ml/13 fl oz dry white wine

375 ml/13 fl oz red wine

salt and pepper

Melt the butter in a pan, add the onions and pancetta and cook over a low heat, stirring occasionally, for 10 minutes. Stir in the meat, sprinkle with the flour and cook, stirring constantly, for 2 minutes. Gradually stir in the white and red wines and cook over a low heat until the liquid is almost completely absorbed. Season with salt and pepper to taste and serve.

FLORENTINE
BEEF STEW

Cut a few strips from one of the carrots and chop the remainder. Lard the beef with the carrot strips and pancetta and rub with salt and pepper. Tie neatly with kitchen string. Put the celery, onion and chopped carrots into a saucepan and add the meat and oil. Cook over a high heat, turning the meat frequently, until browned all over. Pour in the wine and cook until it has evaporated. Add the tomatoes, lower the heat, cover and simmer gently for about 2 hours. Remove the meat from the pan, cut off the string, carve and place the slices on a warm serving dish. Pass the cooking juices and vegetables through a food mill and pour them over the meat.

STRACOTTO ALLA FIORENTINA
Serves 6
3 carrots
1-kg/2^1/$_4$-lb lean beef, such as topside
40 g/1^1/$_2$ oz pancetta, cut into strips
1 celery stick, chopped
^{1}/$_2$ onion, chopped
4 tablespoons olive oil
175 ml/6 fl oz red wine
500 g/1 lb 2 oz tomatoes, peeled, seeded and chopped
salt and pepper

BEEF STEW
WITH WHITE WINE

Using a larding needle, lard the beef with the strips of pancetta. Put the pork fat, half the onions and three of the carrots in a deep saucepan, or better still, earthenware casserole and season with salt and pepper. Place the meat on the bed of vegetables and put the remaining onions and carrots on top. Pour in the wine, cover and simmer for 2 hours or until most of the liquid has been absorbed. Serve with mashed potatoes.

STRACOTTO AL VINO BIANCO
Serves 6
1-kg/2^1/$_4$-lb lean beef, such as topside
100 g/3^1/$_2$ oz pancetta, cut into strips
100 g/3^1/$_2$ oz pork fat, chopped
500 g/1 lb 2 oz onions, thinly sliced
1 kg/2^1/$_4$ lb carrots, sliced
500 ml/18 fl oz dry white wine
salt and pepper
Creamy Mashed Potato (see page 526), to serve

BEEFBURGERS

Tear the bread into pieces, place in a bowl, add the milk and leave to soak for 10 minutes, then drain and squeeze out. Mix together the beef, soaked bread and parsley in a bowl. Shape the mixture into meatballs, flatten slightly and dust lightly with flour. Heat the oil and butter in a frying pan, add the patties and cook for 6–8 minutes until done to your liking. Season with salt and serve.

SVIZZERE
Serves 4
1 bread slice, crusts removed
150 ml/^{1}/$_4$ pint milk
450 g/1 lb lean minced beef
1 tablespoon fresh flat-leaf parsley, chopped
plain flour, for dusting
2 tablespoons olive oil
25 g/1 oz butter
salt

STEAK TARTARE

TARTARA DI MANZO

Serves 4

450 g/1 lb lean minced steak

4 egg yolks

1 onion, thinly sliced

1 tablespoon capers, drained and rinsed

2 tablespoons fresh flat-leaf parsley, chopped,

2 canned anchovy fillets in oil, drained and chopped

mild or medium French mustard (optional)

olive oil and lemon wedges, to serve

Divide the steak among four dishes, shaping each portion into a mound. Make a shallow well in the centre of each mound and pour in a raw egg yolk. Surround the meat each mound with onion, capers, parsley and anchovies. Serve with olive oil and lemon wedges. Each guest may season the meat to taste and can mix in the surrounding ingredients using a fork. If you like, a little mustard may be used to spice up the dish.

TOURNEDOS ROSSINI

TOURNEDOS ALLA ROSSINI

Serves 6

6 x 3-cm/1^1/$_4$-inch thick tournedos, trimmed

40 g/1^1/$_2$ oz butter

100 ml/3^1/$_2$ fl oz Madeira or dry Marsala

6 tablespoons double cream

50 g/2 oz truffle pâté

salt

For the garnish (optional)

6 black truffle slices

6 white truffle slices

Tournedos are steaks cut from the heart of the fillet. They are usually 3–5 cm/1^1/$_4$–2 inches thick and weigh 100–150 g/3^1/$_2$–5 oz. Tie the tournedos neatly with kitchen string so that they keep their rounded shape while cooking. Melt the butter in a frying pan and, when it turns hazel, add the steaks. Cook over a high heat for 1 minute on each side, turning with a fish slice. Lower the heat and cook for 7–8 minutes for rare or 10 minutes for medium. Pour in the Madeira or Marsala, tilt the frying pan and ignite. When the flames die down transfer the tournedos to a warm serving dish and remove the string. Stir the cream into the cooking juices, add the truffle pâté and a pinch of salt and mix well. Cook over a medium heat until the sauce has thickened. Pour the sauce over the tournedos and serve. Garnish each steak with a slice each of black and white truffle, if you like.

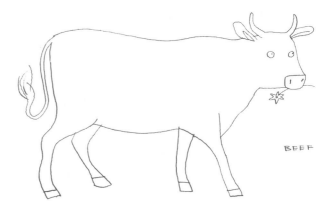

BEEF

MUTTON

Mutton is a highly prized, flavoursome, deep-red meat. It comes from sheep over two years old. Strictly, lambs slaughtered between one and two years old are called hogget lambs but they can be used in mutton recipes and quite often shops make no distinction between hogget and mutton. The best sheep farms in Italy are found in Piedmont, Lazio and Puglia. In the rest of Europe, there are excellent farms in Great Britain and Ireland, where mutton is used to prepare dishes such as tasty mutton chops and the famous Irish stew. New Zealand is the world's largest lamb producer, closely followed by Australia. France, on the other hand, is famous for its pré-salé mutton, reared in pastures near the sea, which makes the meat particularly tasty. Mutton is currently enjoying a revival and is often featured in fashionable restaurants.

COOKING

Mutton and hogget have a fairly strong flavour, so it is worth marinating them for several hours in wine with a little vinegar, vegetables and herbs (celery, carrot, onion, parsley, thyme and bay leaf), salt and black peppercorns. Don't leave to marinate in the refrigerator, simply choose a cool place.

→ When choosing the oil or fat to add, remember that mutton is a fatty meat, so avoid making it heavier with excessive quantities of oil and butter.

→ To appreciate the flavour of mutton fully, it should be served rare and very hot.

→ Among the most traditional and fragrant herbs used with mutton are rosemary, mint and fennel, but myrtle and thyme also go well.

ROASTING

It is best to choose the leg for roasting, as this is the most suitable cut and the result is predictable.

→ If it is to be cooked rare, allow 18–20 minutes per 1 kg/2¼ lb meat. If you prefer it medium or well done, simply increase the time (but not by too much), according to taste. Italians generally prefer mutton well done.

BRAISING AND STEWING

These methods of cooking take about 1½ hours, and in the case of large pieces of meat, even 2 hours.

→ The meat should be cut into pieces and cooked with vegetables such as carrots, celery and onion. Other vegetables that go well with mutton are Savoy cabbage and aubergines as they help to reduce the amount of fat.

CHOPS

The best and tastiest are the double chops cut from the loin. They are excellent brushed well with oil, seasoned with pepper and grilled.

LEG OF MUTTON IN VODKA

Bring the stock to the boil in a large pan, add the mutton and simmer for about 40 minutes. Meanwhile, place the prunes in a bowl, add warm water to cover and leave to soak for at least 30 minutes, then drain. Melt the butter in a pan and, when it starts to sizzle, stir in the passata, then add the onion, garlic, celery and bay leaf. Cook, stirring occasionally, for about 5 minutes, then pour in the vodka, season with salt and paprika and cook, stirring constantly, for a few minutes more. Add the hot stock, a little at a time, stirring constantly, then add the mutton, rice and prunes. Continue to cook, stirring constantly, for about 20 minutes. Remove and discard the bay leaf, transfer the mutton mixture to a warm, fairly deep serving dish and serve with slices of buttered toast.

COSCIOTTO ALLA VODKA

Serves 4

1 litre/1³/₄ pints Meat Stock (see page 208)

800-g/1³/₄-lb leg of mutton, cut into pieces

12 prunes, stoned

100 g/3¹/₂ oz butter

2 tablespoons passata

1 onion, chopped

1 garlic clove, chopped

1 celery heart, sliced

1 bay leaf

50 ml/2 fl oz vodka

large pinch of paprika

100 g/3¹/₂ oz risotto rice

salt

buttered toast, to serve

LEG OF MUTTON WITH TURNIPS

Tie the meat neatly with kitchen string, then cook in a heavy-based pan without adding any fat, turning occasionally, until browned all over. Sprinkle with the flour, turn the meat several times and add the onions, garlic, rosemary, thyme and celery. Pour in 150 ml/¹/₄ pint of the stock or water, lower the heat and simmer. Meanwhile, melt the butter in a frying pan, add the turnips and cook over a medium heat, stirring frequently, until browned all over. Drain, add to the meat and season with salt and pepper. Cover and cook for 1¹/₂ hours, adding more hot stock or water as required. Remove the meat from the pan, untie and carve into slices. Place on a warm serving dish and surround with the turnips.

COSCIOTTO CON LE RAPE

Serves 6

1-kg/2¹/₄-lb leg of mutton, boned

2 tablespoons plain flour

2 onions, thinly sliced

1 garlic clove

1 fresh rosemary sprig

1 fresh thyme sprig

1 celery stick

500 ml/18 fl oz hot Meat Stock

(see page 208) or water

25 g/1 oz butter

1 kg/2¹/₄ lb turnips, quartered

salt and pepper

ENGLISH MUTTON CHOPS

These famous mutton chops are usually cut fairly thick, the way the English are said to like them. Preheat the grill to high. Meanwhile, melt the butter. Brush the chops with the butter and grill for 5 or 6 minutes on each side, brushing occasionally with more melted butter. Season with salt and pepper and serve.

COSTOLETTE ALL'INGLESE

Serves 4

40 g/1¹/₂ oz butter

4 mutton chops

salt and pepper

IRISH STEW

Boned shoulder or breast of mutton is ideal for this dish. Arrange alternate layers of meat, potatoes and onions in a flameproof casserole, sprinkling each layer with salt, pepper, thyme and parsley. Add the bay leaf and pour in just enough water to cover. Bring to the boil over a high heat, cover, lower the heat and simmer for 1¼ hours until tender. In Ireland — famous for its tasty mutton — this stew is considered a national dish. It can also be made with beef.

SPEZZATINO ALL'IRLANDESE

Serves 4

800 g/1¾ lb boneless mutton, sliced or cut into cubes

800 g/1¾ lb potatoes, thinly sliced

3 onions, thinly sliced

1 tablespoon chopped fresh thyme

2 tablespoons fresh flat-leaf parsley, chopped

1 small bay leaf

salt and pepper

MUTTON STEWED IN CITRUS JUICE

Heat the oil and butter in a pan, add the onion and cook over a low heat, stirring occasionally, for about 10 minutes. Add the mutton and cook, stirring constantly, until browned all over. Add the potatoes and 150 ml/¼ pint warm water. Cook for 20 minutes, then season with salt and pepper and cook for a further 20 minutes. Add the pecorino, cook for 10 minutes more, then pour in the lemon and orange juice and cook until they have evaporated.

SPEZZATINO AL SUCCO DI AGRUMI

Serves 4

2 tablespoons olive oil

25 g/1 oz butter

1 onion, thinly sliced

600 g/1 lb 5 oz boneless shoulder

of mutton, coarsely chopped

500 g/1 lb 2 oz new potatoes

80 g/3 oz pecorino cheese, diced

juice of 1 lemon, strained

juice of 2 oranges, strained

salt and pepper

MUTTON AND BEAN STEW

Melt the butter in a pan, add the meat and cook, stirring frequently, until browned all over. Add the carrots, onions, garlic, thyme and rosemary and season with salt and pepper. Cook, stirring occasionally, for a further 10 minutes, then pour in 150 ml/¼ pint water, cover and simmer over a medium heat for 30 minutes. Add the beans, re-cover the pan and simmer for a further 45 minutes. Remove and discard the garlic and rosemary before serving.

SPEZZATINO CON FAGIOLI

Serves 4

25 g/1 oz butter

600 g/1 lb 5 oz boneless shoulder of mutton,

cut into cubes

2 carrots, thinly sliced

2 onions, thinly sliced

2 garlic cloves

1 fresh thyme sprig, chopped

1 fresh rosemary sprig

600 g/1 lb 5 oz cooked fresh beans

or canned beans, such as broad beans

salt and pepper

MUTTON AND POTATO STEW

SPEZZATINO CON PATATE

Serves 4

2 tablespoons olive oil

600 g/1 lb 5 oz boneless mutton, cut into cubes

2 onions, thinly sliced

2 garlic cloves, chopped

4 tomatoes, peeled and diced

500 g/1 lb 2 oz potatoes, quartered

1 fresh flat-leaf parsley sprig, chopped

salt and pepper

Heat the oil in a saucepan, add the mutton and cook, stirring frequently, for a few minutes until browned. Add the onions and garlic, season with salt and pepper and cook, stirring occasionally, for 10 minutes. Stir in the tomatoes. Put the potatoes in another pan, add boiling water to cover and cook over a medium heat for 25–30 minutes until tender. Drain, season lightly with salt and sprinkle with the parsley. Bring the mutton cooking juices to the boil and cook over a high heat for a few minutes until reduced, then place the meat on a warm serving dish and surround with the potatoes. Spoon the cooking juices over the meat and potatoes.

CHOPPED MUTTON WITH PRUNES

SPEZZATINO CON PRUGNE

Serves 4

200 g/7 oz prunes, stoned

300 ml/¹/₂ pint dry white wine

600 g/1 lb 5 oz boneless breast of mutton,
cut into cubes

1 onion, thinly sliced

1 garlic clove

50 g/2 oz butter

2 tablespoons passata

salt and pepper

Place the prunes in a bowl, pour in the wine and set aside. Put the meat in a pan, add cold water to cover and bring to simmering point. Add the onion and garlic, cover and simmer over a medium heat for about 1 hour, then season with salt and pepper and drain well, reserving the cooking liquid. Melt the butter in another pan, add the passata and meat and cook over a high heat, stirring frequently, for a few minutes, then lower the heat, drain the prunes and add them to the pan. Simmer for about 20 minutes. If the meat seems to be drying out, add some of the reserved cooking liquid. Transfer to a warm serving dish.

MARINATED MUTTON KEBABS

SPIEDINI MARINATI

Serves 4

5 tablespoons olive oil

1 garlic clove

1 fresh thyme sprig

6 black peppercorns

500 g/1 lb 2 oz boneless leg of mutton,
cut into cubes

salt

Mix together the oil, garlic, thyme and peppercorns in a dish, season with salt and add the meat. Stir well and leave to marinate for 1 hour. Drain the mutton and divide it among four metal skewers. The skewers can be cooked on a barbecue, under the grill or in a griddle pan – all at a very high heat. Cook, turning frequently, for 3 minutes until almost crisp on the outside, but tender in the middle.

VEAL

Veal is synonymous with tender meat. This is because it comes from animals that are butchered when they are very young – 5–7 months or younger – are not very heavy – 130–150 kg/300–350 lb – and are fed exclusively on a milk formula. This also explains the delicate pale-pink colour of the meat. Grass-fed veal is also available and veal is a meat that is gradually gaining popularity, though it can be difficult to obtain and prohibitively expensive in some countries, e.g. Australia. Chief among veal's benefits are that it is easy to digest and cooks rapidly. As it is dry and rather lean, larding with strips of pancetta or bacon, or pancetta or bacon fat, is an ideal way of cooking it. Some cuts, such as breast, may be prepared with 'pockets' that are then stuffed with other minced meats mixed with eggs, grated cheese and spices. Cooking methods used for beef may also be used for veal.

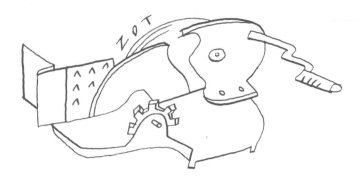

ITALIAN CUTS
AND COOKING
TECHNIQUES

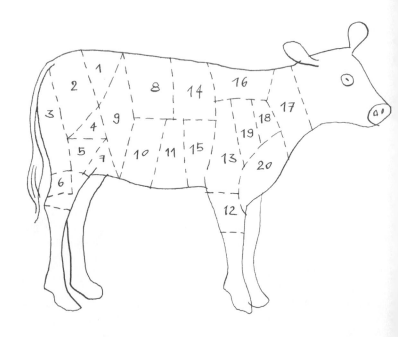

1. CODONE
   O CODONCINO
   Roasting
2. SOTTOFESA
   Roasting, grilling and
   sliced and roulades
3. GIRELLO
   Roasting, and sliced and
   escalopes
4. FESA FRANCESE
   Grilling, and sliced, roulades,
   stuffed rolls and escalopes
5. NOCE
   Roasting, and chops,
   sliced and escalopes
6. PESCE
   O PICCIONE
   Boiling and stewing

7. SPINACINO
   Meat loaves and stuffed
   rolls and pockets
8. NODINI
   Grilling
9. SCAMONE
   Roasting
10. PANCETTA
    Stuffed pockets
11. PUNTA DI PETTO
    Boiling and stewing
12. GERETTO
    Boiling, and chops with
    marrowbone
13. FESA
    DI SPALLA
    Ideal sliced and for stuffed
    rolls

14. COSTOLETTE
    Grilling, and chops and
    escalopes
15. FIOCCO
    Stewing and braising
16. REALE
    Roasting, boiling, stewing
    and braising
17. COLLO
    Boiling and stewing
18. FUSELLO
    Roasting, braising, boiling
    and sliced
19. CAPPELLO
    DEL PRETE
    Boiling, stewing and braisin
20. BRIONE
    Boiling, stewing and braising

BRITISH CUTS AND COOKING TECHNIQUES

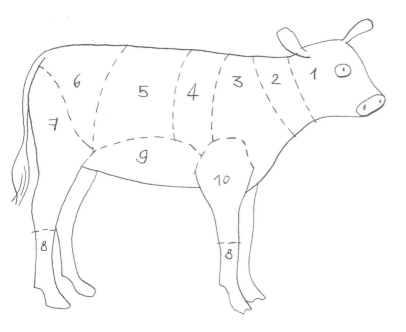

1. **HEAD**
   Stewing
2. **SCRAG END**
   Casseroles and stocks, and chopped or minced for pies
3. **MIDDLE NECK**
   Casseroles and stocks, and chopped or minced for pies
4. **BEST END**
   Roasting, and cut into cutlets for grilling and frying
5. **LOIN**
   Roasting, and cut into chops and medallions for grilling and frying
6. **RUMP**
   Roasting, and cut into steaks for grilling and frying
7. **LEG, SILVERSIDE, TOPSIDE**
   Roasting, pot-roasting, and cut into escalopes and fillets for grilling and frying
8. **KNUCKLE, SHIN**
   Stewing, and chopped for pies
9. **BREAST**
   Roasting, braising, and stewing, and minced
10. **SHOULDER**
    Roasting

ROASTING

If you are in doubt over which cut to choose or cannot find one that is listed here, ask a reputable butcher for advice.

813

MILK POT-ROAST

ARROSTO AL LATTE

Serves 6

800-g/1³/₄-lb boneless breast of veal

plain flour, for dusting

3 tablespoons olive oil

40 g/1¹/₂ oz butter

about 1 litre/1³/₄ pints milk

salt and pepper

Tie the veal neatly with kitchen string and dust lightly with flour. Heat the oil and butter in an oval saucepan, add the meat and cook, turning frequently, until browned all over. Meanwhile, heat 175 ml/6 fl oz of the milk until it is lukewarm. Season the veal with salt and pepper, pour in the warm milk, bring to just below simmering point and add as much of the remaining milk as required to cover the meat completely. Simmer over a medium heat for about 1 hour. Remove the veal from the pan, leave to stand for 10 minutes, then untie and slice. Place on a warm serving dish and spoon the cooking juices over the meat.

VEAL BRAISED IN MILK WITH PROSCIUTTO

ARROSTO AL LATTE E PROSCIUTTO

Serves 6

40 g/1¹/₂ oz butter

2 tablespoons plain flour

2 prosciutto slices, cut into thin strips

800-g/1³/₄-lb boneless breast of veal

900 ml/1¹/₂ pints milk

salt

Melt the butter in a pan, stir in the flour, then add the prosciutto and cook, stirring constantly, until browned. Tie the veal neatly with kitchen string, add to the pan and cook over a high heat, turning frequently, until browned all over. Season with salt to taste, pour in 175 ml/6 fl oz of the milk and cook until it has been absorbed. Repeat this three times without covering the pan. Finally, add the remaining milk and cook until it has been absorbed. Remove the veal from the pan, untie, carve into slices and serve with the cooking juices.

POT-ROAST VEAL WITH WALNUTS

ARROSTO ALLE NOCI

Serves 6

50 g/2 oz butter

4 tablespoons olive oil

800-g/1³/₄-lb boneless breast of veal

50 g/2 oz shelled walnuts, chopped

juice of 1 lemon, strained

175 ml/6 fl oz double cream

175 ml/6 fl oz Meat Stock (see page 208)

salt and pepper

Melt the butter and oil in a pan, add the veal and cook, turning frequently, for 15 minutes until browned all over. Add the walnuts, lemon juice, cream and stock and season with salt and pepper. Cover and simmer for 45 minutes, making sure that the meat does not stick to the base of the pan. If necessary, add a little more hot stock. Remove the veal and leave to stand. Tip the cooking juices into a food processor and process to a purée. Carve the veal, place the slices on a warm serving dish and spoon the purée over them.

BRAISED VEAL WITH OLIVES

Make small incisions in the veal with a small, sharp knife, insert the olive halves and tie neatly with kitchen string. Heat the oil and butter in a pan, add the onion, carrot, rosemary and celery and cook over a low heat, stirring occasionally, for 10 minutes. Add the meat and cook, turning frequently, until browned all over. Pour in the wine and cook until it has evaporated, then season with salt and pepper. Simmer gently over a low heat, turning occasionally and adding a little warm water if necessary, for about 1 hour. Remove the veal from the pan and leave to stand for 10 minutes. Untie, carve into slices and place on a warm serving dish. Pass the cooking juices through a food mill into a bowl. If they are too thick, thin with a little hot stock; if they are too runny, add a paste of equal quantities of butter and plain flour. Spoon the juices over the meat and serve.

ARROSTO ALLE OLIVE

Serves 6

800-g/1³/₄-lb topside

200 g/7 oz green olives, stoned and halved

2 tablespoons olive oil

50 g/2 oz butter

1 onion, chopped

1 carrot, chopped

1 fresh rosemary sprig, chopped

1 celery stick, chopped

175 ml/6 fl oz dry white wine

salt and pepper

BRAISED VEAL WITH LEMON

Beat together the olive oil and lemon juice in a dish, season with salt and pepper and add the veal, turning to coat. Leave to marinate, turning occasionally, for 3 hours. Transfer the veal and the marinade to a saucepan, add 150 ml/¹/₄ pint water and bring to the boil. Lower the heat and simmer for about 1 hour until tender. Remove the veal from the pan, carve into slices and place on a warm serving dish. Boil the cooking juices until slightly reduced, then pour into a sauce boat and serve with the veal.

ARROSTO AL LIMONE

Serves 4

6 tablespoons olive oil

juice of 1 lemon, strained

800-g/1³/₄-lb topside

salt and pepper

POT–ROAST VEAL WITH KIDNEY

Make several cuts in the veal and insert a few grains of sea salt, then tie the meat neatly with kitchen string. Melt the butter in a pan, add the veal and cook, turning frequently, until browned all over. Pour in the cream, cover and simmer gently for 1 hour. Remove the veal from the pan and leave to stand. Add the kidney slices to the pan, cover and cook for 15 minutes. Untie the veal, carve into slices and place on a warm serving dish. Spoon the kidney and sauce on top.

ARROSTO CON ROGNONE

Serves 6

800-g/1³/₄-lb boneless breast of veal

40 g/1¹/₂ oz butter

175 ml/6 fl oz double cream

1 veal kidney, peeled, cored and sliced

sea salt

BRAISED VEAL TOPSIDE

ARROSTO DI GIRELLO

Serves 6

800-g/1³/₄-lb topside
50 g/2 oz butter
25 g/1 oz pancetta, sliced
1 onion, thinly sliced
3 carrots, thinly sliced
1 bunch of fresh herbs, chopped
175 ml/6 fl oz dry white wine
salt and pepper

Tie the veal neatly with kitchen string. Melt the butter in a saucepan, add the veal and cook, turning frequently, for about 10 minutes until browned all over. Season with salt and pepper and remove the veal from the pan. Place the pancetta on the base of the pan, return the veal to the pan, cover with the onion and carrots and add the herbs. Pour in 175 ml/6 fl oz warm water and the wine, cover and simmer over a low heat for about 1½ hours. Remove the veal and leave to stand for about 10 minutes. Pour the cooking juices into a food processor and process to a purée. Untie the veal, carve into slices and place on a warm serving dish. Spoon the cooking juices over the veal.

SIMPLE ROAST VEAL

ARROSTO SEMPLICE

Serves 6

800-g/1³/₄-lb topside
3 tablespoons olive oil
40 g/1½ oz butter, plus extra for greasing
salt and pepper
150 ml/¼ pint warm meat stock (see page 208) or water (optional)

Preheat the oven to 120°C/250°F/Gas Mark ½. Tie the veal neatly with kitchen string. Heat the oil and butter in a flameproof casserole, add the veal and cook, turning frequently, until brown all over. Season with salt and pepper, cover with greased greaseproof paper, transfer to the oven and roast, turning occasionally, for 1 hour. If the meat becomes too dry during cooking, add the warm stock or water. Remove the veal from the casserole, leave to stand for 10 minutes, then untie and carve into slices. Spoon the cooking juices over a warm serving dish and place the slices of meat in a row on top.

BRAISED VEAL WITH TRUFFLE

ARROSTO TARTUFATO

Serves 6

1-kg/2¼-lb loin of veal, boned
100 g/3½ oz pancetta, diced
1 black truffle, sliced
5 tablespoons olive oil
25 g/1 oz butter
salt and pepper

Make small incisions in the veal using a sharp knife. Season the incisions with salt and pepper and insert a piece of pancetta and a small slice of truffle into each. Tie the meat neatly with kitchen string. Heat the oil and butter in a pan, add the veal and cook, turning frequently, until browned all over. Lower the heat, cover and cook gently for about 1 hour, adding a little warm water if necessary. Remove the meat and leave to stand for 10 minutes. Untie and carve into slices. Place the slices on a warm serving dish and spoon the cooking juices over them.

VEAL CUTLETS WITH ARTICHOKES

Half-fill a bowl with water and stir in the lemon juice. Cut off the tough outer leaves from the artichokes, remove and discard the chokes, cut into quarters and drop into the acidulated water. Bring a pan of lightly salted water to the boil, drain the artichokes, add to the pan and parboil for 5 minutes, then drain. Mix together the ham and 15 g/^{1}/$_2$ oz of the butter in a bowl and spread the mixture over the artichoke quarters. Pound the veal cutlets with a meat mallet and season with salt and pepper. Place an artichoke quarter on each, roll up and tie with kitchen string. Heat the oil and the remaining butter in a frying pan, add the onion and cook over a low heat, stirring occasionally, for 5 minutes. Add the roulades and cook, turning frequently, until golden brown all over. Add 150 ml/^{1}/$_4$ pint hot water and simmer for about 10 minutes until tender and cooked through, then serve.

BRACIOLINE CON CARCIOFI

Serves 6

juice of 1 lemon, strained

2 tender globe artichokes

50 g/2 oz cooked ham, chopped

50 g/2 oz butter

8 best end veal cutlets, boned

1 tablespoon olive oil

1 small onion, chopped

salt and pepper

BRAISED VEAL

Lard the veal with the strips of pancetta and tie neatly with kitchen string. Heat the oil in a saucepan, add the prosciutto fat, onions and carrots and cook over a medium heat, stirring occasionally, for 10 minutes until browned. Add the meat, season with salt and pepper and cook, turning frequently, for about 10 minutes until browned all over. Pour in half the wine, increase the heat and cook until it has evaporated. Cook for a further 10 minutes, then pour in the remaining wine and cook until it has evaporated. Pour in the hot stock, lower the heat to medium, cover and simmer for 1^1/$_2$ hours. Remove the veal from the pan, untie and carve into slices. Pass the cooking juices through a food mill. Place the slices of veal on a warm serving dish and spoon the cooking juices over them.

BRASATO

Serves 6

1-kg/2^1/$_4$-lb topside

40 g/1^1/$_2$ oz pancetta, cut into strips

2 tablespoons olive oil

50 g/2 oz prosciutto fat

2 onions, thinly sliced

2 carrots, thinly sliced

350 ml/12 fl oz dry white wine

1 litre/1^3/$_4$ pints hot Meat Stock (see page 208)

salt and pepper

SUMMER VEAL

Bring a saucepan of water to the boil with the celery, carrot and onion. Tie the veal neatly with kitchen string, add to the pan and simmer for 2 hours. Remove the pan from the heat and leave the meat to cool in its stock. Drain the veal, untie and carve very thinly. Arrange the slices on a serving dish and sprinkle with the capers. Whisk together the oil and lemon juice in a bowl, season with salt and pour the dressing over the meat. Leave to marinate for 30 minutes, then serve.

CARNE ESTIVA

Serves 6

1 celery stick

1 carrot • 1 onion

1-kg/2^1/$_4$-lb topside

100 g/3^1/$_2$ oz capers, drained and rinsed

100 ml/3^1/$_2$ fl oz olive oil

juice of 4 lemons, strained

salt

CIMA ALLA GENOVESE

Serves 6

1-kg/2¹/₄-lb boneless breast of veal
1 onion
1 carrot
2 bay leaves
salt

For the stuffing
50 g/2 oz bread slices, crusts removed
200 g/7 oz minced veal
100 g/3¹/₂ oz sweetbreads
or brains, blanched and diced
40 g/1¹/₂ oz pork fat, chopped, or lardons
200 g/7 oz Swiss chard, boiled, drained
and coarsely chopped
pinch of freshly grated nutmeg
2 tablespoons chopped fresh marjoram
2 eggs, lightly beaten
2 tablespoons Parmesan cheese, freshly grated
salt and pepper

GENOESE STUFFED BREAST OF VEAL

First prepare the stuffing. Tear the bread into pieces, place in a bowl, add water to cover and leave to soak for 10 minutes, then drain and squeeze out. Put the minced veal in a bowl and add the sweetbreads or brains and pork fat or lardons, Swiss chard and soaked bread. Mix well, stir in the nutmeg and marjoram and season with salt and pepper. Bind the mixture with the beaten eggs and Parmesan. Make a horizontal cut in the breast of veal along one of the long sides to create a 'pocket'. Fill the pocket with the stuffing, sew up the opening and tie neatly with kitchen string. Bring a large pan of lightly salted water to the boil with the onion, carrot and bay leaves. Add the stuffed breast and simmer gently for about 2 hours. Drain the meat and put on a plate. Cover and place a weight on top. Leave to cool, then untie and carve into slices. Arrange on a serving dish.

CODINO ARROSTO

Serves 4

850-g/1 lb 14-oz rump
1 tablespoon meat seasoning
25 g/1 oz butter
4 tablespoons olive oil
1 fresh flat-leaf parsley sprig, finely chopped
1 fresh rosemary sprig, finely chopped
4 fresh sage leaves, finely chopped
2 spring onions, white parts only, chopped
1 carrot, thinly sliced
175 ml/6 fl oz dry white wine
salt and pepper

POT—ROAST CODINO OF VEAL

Preheat the oven to 200°C/400°F/Gas Mark 6. Gently rub the veal with the meat seasoning and tie neatly with kitchen string. Heat the butter and oil in a flameproof casserole, add the veal and cook, turning frequently, until browned all over. Add the parsley, rosemary and sage to the casserole and mix well, then add the spring onions and carrot. Cook until lightly browned, then pour in the wine and cook until it has evaporated. Season with salt and pepper, pour in 5 tablespoons hot water, transfer to the oven and cook for about 1¹/₂ hours, adding a few tablespoons of warm water to prevent drying out if necessary. Remove the meat from the casserole and leave to stand for 10 minutes. Meanwhile, put the cooking juices in a food processor and process until smooth. Untie the veal, carve it into slices, place on a warm serving dish and spoon the sauce over them.

CARNI – FRATTAGLIE
MEAT – OFFAL

MILANESE VEAL CHOPS

Only chops should be used, but nowadays this dish is often made with slices of thickly cut rump. Pound the meat to an even thickness with a meat mallet. Beat the egg with a pinch of salt in a shallow dish. Spread out the breadcrumbs in another shallow dish. Melt the clarified butter in a frying pan. Dip each chop first in the beaten egg and then in the breadcrumbs, pressing them on with your fingers. Fry the chops over a low heat for about 10 minutes on each side until golden brown. Remove with a fish slice and drain on kitchen paper, then transfer to a warm serving dish. The chops go well with any vegetables served with butter, or with fresh salads.

COSTOLETTE ALLA MILANESE
Serves 4
4 veal chops, boned
1 egg
80 g/3 oz fine breadcrumbs
50 g/2 oz Clarified Butter (see page 88)
salt

VALLE D'AOSTA VEAL CHOPS

Cut through the centre of each chop horizontally, leaving the meat attached to the bone, and open out like a book. Put a slice of fontina and a few truffle shavings between the two halves, then the bring the halves together again, pressing along the edges. Secure with two cocktail sticks and season with salt and pepper. Beat the eggs with a pinch of salt in a shallow dish. Spread out the breadcrumbs in another shallow dish. Dust the chops with flour, then dip them first in the beaten egg and then in the breadcrumbs. Heat the butter and oil in a frying pan, add the chops and cook for about 10 minutes on each side until browned. Drain, remove the cocktail sticks and serve.

COSTOLETTE ALLA VALDOSTANA
Serves 4
4 x 150-g/5-oz veal chops
4 slices fontina cheese
1 white truffle, shaved
2 eggs
80 g/3 oz breadcrumbs
plain flour, for dusting
40 g/1½ oz butter
2 tablespoons olive oil
salt and pepper

VILLEROY VEAL CUTLETS

Beat the egg with a pinch of salt in a shallow dish. Spread out the breadcrumbs in another shallow dish. Lightly dust the cutlets with flour. Heat half the clarified butter in a frying pan, add the cutlets and cook until lightly browned on both sides. Season with salt and pepper. Stir the egg yolks and nutmeg into the béchamel sauce. Immerse the cutlets in the béchamel sauce, then remove and drain off the excess. Dust with flour, dip in the beaten egg and then dip in the breadcrumbs to coat. Heat the remaining clarified butter in a frying pan, add the cutlets and cook until browned on both sides. Remove with a fish slice, drain on kitchen paper and serve.

COSTOLETTE ALLA VILLEROY
Serves 4
1 egg
80 g/3 oz breadcrumbs
4 veal cutlets
plain flour, for dusting
100 g/3½ oz Clarified Butter (see page 88)
2 egg yolks
pinch of freshly grated nutmeg
1 quantity hot Béchamel Sauce (see page 50)
salt and pepper

VEAL IN 'REDUCED STOCK'

Lightly pound the slices of veal with a meat mallet. Beat the eggs with a pinch of salt in a shallow dish. Spread out the breadcrumbs in another shallow dish. Dust the veal slices with flour, dip in the beaten eggs, then dip in the breadcrumbs and shake off any excess. Heat the clarified butter in a pan, add the veal and cook until lightly browned on both sides. Pour in the warm stock, cover and cook over a low heat until the stock has reduced completely. Increase the heat, pour in the vinegar and cook until it has evaporated. Transfer the veal to a warm serving dish.

COTOLETTE AL 'CONSUMATO DI BRODO'

Serves 4

500 g/1 lb 2 oz veal slices

2 eggs

80 g/3 oz breadcrumbs

plain flour, for dusting

40 g/1½ oz Clarified Butter (see page 88)

200 ml/7 fl oz warm Meat Stock (see page 208)

1 tablespoon white wine vinegar

salt

VEAL BOLOGNESE

Beat the egg with a pinch of salt and a pinch of pepper in a shallow dish. Spread out the breadcrumbs in another shallow dish. Pound the veal until even with a meat mallet, dip in the beaten egg and then in the breadcrumbs. Melt the butter in a frying pan, add the veal and cook until golden brown on both sides. Put a slice of prosciutto, grana padano shavings and 2–3 slices of truffle on each slice. Pour in the stock, cover and cook until the prosciutto and cheese are translucent. Just before serving, coat the veal slices with the clarified butter. For a lighter version of this classic recipe, proceed as above but without dipping the meat in breadcrumbs.

COTOLETTE ALLA BOLOGNESE

Serves 4

1 egg

80 g/3 oz breadcrumbs

4 veal slices

80 g/3 oz butter

4 prosciutto slices

100 g/3½ oz grana padano cheese, shaved

1 small black truffle, sliced

200 ml/7 fl oz Meat Stock (see page 208)

25 g/1 oz Clarified Butter (see page 88)

salt and pepper

VEAL STEAKS IN VINEGAR

Pound the veal steaks with a meat mallet until even. Whisk together the oil and vinegar in a dish and season with salt and pepper. Add the meat, leave to marinate for 1 hour, then drain. Melt the butter in a frying pan, add the steaks and cook over a medium heat for 5 minutes on each side. Season with salt to taste and transfer to a warm serving dish. These steaks have a wonderful aroma and an unusual flavour.

FETTINE ALL'ACETO

Serves 4

400 g/14 oz veal steaks

100 ml/3½ fl oz olive oil

200 ml/7 fl oz white wine vinegar

40 g/1½ oz butter

salt and pepper

VEAL STEAKS WITH EGG AND LEMON

FETTINE ALL'UOVO E LIMONE

Serves 4

500 g/1 lb 2 oz veal steaks
plain flour, for dusting
40 g/1½ oz butter
2 egg yolks
juice of 1 lemon, strained
1 fresh flat-leaf parsley sprig, chopped
salt

Dust the steaks with flour. Melt the butter in a frying pan, add the steaks and cook for 5 minutes. Season with salt, remove from the pan and keep warm. Beat together the egg yolks and lemon juice in a bowl. Pour 2 tablespoons water into the pan and heat, scraping up the sediment from the base. Add the egg yolk mixture and mix quickly. Spoon the egg sauce over the meat and sprinkle with the parsley.

VEAL KNOTS

FETTINE ANNODATE

Serves 4

2 tablespoons olive oil
25 g/1 oz butter
1 fresh rosemary sprig, chopped
4 fresh sage leaves, chopped
1 garlic clove, chopped
1 onion, chopped
500 g/1 lb 2 oz thin veal slices, cut into strips
plain flour, for dusting
5 tablespoons dry Marsala
1 fresh flat-leaf parsley sprig, chopped
salt and pepper

Heat the oil and butter in a frying pan, add the rosemary, sage, garlic and onion and cook over a low heat, stirring occasionally, for 5 minutes. Tie a knot in each strip of meat and dust with flour. Add to the pan and cook, turning occasionally, until browned all over. Season with salt and pepper, cover and cook for 20 minutes. Uncover the pan and increase the heat to reduce the cooking juices, then add the Marsala and cook until it has evaporated. Sprinkle with the parsley and serve.

VEAL STEAKS IN OLIVE SAUCE

FETTINE IN SALSA D'OLIVE

Serves 4

40 g/1½ oz butter
3 tablespoons olive oil
500 g/1 lb 2 oz veal steaks
plain flour, for dusting
5 tablespoons dry white wine
12 stoned green olives
1 slice bottled red pepper in oil, drained and chopped
salt and pepper

Heat the butter and oil in a frying pan. Dust the steaks with flour, add to the pan and cook until browned all over. Season with salt and pepper, remove from the pan and keep warm. Pour the wine into the pan and cook until it has evaporated. Add 3 tablespoons water and cook, scraping the sediment from the base of the pan with a wooden spoon, then add the olives and pepper. Return the meat to the pan and cook over a high heat for a few minutes.

VEAL RIBBONS

Put the veal strips, olive oil and herbs in a pan, season with salt and pepper and cook over a low heat, occasionally adding a little hot water, until browned. Cook the onions in salted, boiling water for 10 minutes, then drain and add to the meat. Cook, gradually adding the Marsala, until the meat is tender and cooked through. Stir in the butter and serve.

'FETTUCCINE' DI CARNE

Serves 4

500 g/1 lb 2 oz veal steaks, cut into strips

3 tablespoons olive oil

1 tablespoon fesh flat-leaf parsley, chopped

4 fresh sage leaves, chopped

1 tablespoons chopped fresh thyme

10 baby onions

100 ml/3¹/₂ fl oz Marsala

25 g/1 oz butter

salt and pepper

FILLET OF VEAL IN CONZA

Cut the fillet into extremely thin slices and place in a layer in a bowl. Cover with a layer of rosemary needles, sage, basil, onion slices and strips of lemon rind. Drizzle with olive oil and lemon juice and season with salt and pepper. Continue making alternate layers until all the ingredients are used, ending with a layer of herbs, onion and lemon rind. Drizzle with a little more oil, cover the bowl with cling film and chill in the refrigerator for 24 hours.

FILETTO IN CONZA

Serves 6

500 g/1 lb 2 oz veal fillet

1 fresh rosemary sprig

8 fresh sage leaves, chopped

8 fresh basil leaves, chopped

1 onion, thinly sliced

thinly pared rind of 1 lemon, cut into strips

120–150 ml/4–5 fl oz olive oil

juice of 2 lemons, strained

salt and pepper

MEAT MOULD

Preheat the oven to 180°C/350°F/Gas Mark 4. Grease a soufflé dish or individual ramekins with butter and sprinkle with the breadcrumbs, tipping out the excess. Melt the butter in a frying pan, add the veal and cook, stirring occasionally, until browned. Transfer the veal to a bowl and add the ham. Season the béchamel sauce with salt and pepper and stir in the egg yolk, veal mixture and enough Parmesan, to achieve the desired consistency. Pour the mixture into the prepared dish or ramekins, sprinkle with a pinch of breadcrumbs and bake for about 40 minutes until golden brown.

FLAN DI CARNE

Serves 4

25 g/1 oz butter, plus extra for greasing

40 g/1¹/₂ oz breadcrumbs

250 g/9 oz minced veal

50 g/2 oz cooked ham, chopped

1 quantity Béchamel Sauce (see page 50)

1 egg yolk

2–3 tablespoon Parmesan cheese, freshly grated

salt and pepper

VEAL BUNDLES WITH TRUFFLES

INVOLTINI AI TARTUFI

Serves 4

450 g/1 lb veal steaks

1 white truffle, thinly shaved

25 g/1 oz Parmesan cheese, thinly shaved

2 eggs

80 g/3 oz breadcrumbs • 40 g/1½ oz butter

salt

Pound the steaks with a meat mallet until thin and even, season with salt and sprinkle with a few shavings of truffle and Parmesan. Fold in half and press down well all around the edges. Beat the eggs with a pinch of salt in a shallow dish. Spread out the breadcrumbs in another shallow dish. Dip each steak bundle into the beaten eggs and then into the breadcrumbs. Melt the butter in a frying pan, add the steak bundles and cook, turning frequently, for 10 minutes.

VEAL ROULADES WITH VEGETABLES

INVOLTINI ALLE VERDURE

Serves 4

450 g/1 lb veal slices • 2 carrots, cut into batons

1 celery stick, cut into batons

40 g/1½ oz butter • 3 tablespoons olive oil

5 tablespoons dry white wine

4 tablespoons passata

salt and pepper

Pound the slices of veal with a meat mallet. Divide the carrots and celery among the slices of meat, then roll up and tie with kitchen string. Heat the butter and oil in a frying pan, add the roulades and cook, turning frequently, until browned all over. Pour in the wine and cook until it has evaporated, then season with salt and pepper. Add the passata, cover and simmer gently for 30 minutes.

SIMPLE POACHED VEAL

LESSO SEMPLICE

Serves 4

1 carrot • 1 celery stick

1 onion • 1-kg/2¼-lb boned breast of veal

salt

Pour 4 litres/7 pints water into a saucepan, add a pinch of salt, the carrot, celery and onion and bring to the boil. Add the veal, lower the heat, cover and simmer gently for about 2 hours. Drain the meat and serve while still hot with mustard or a choice of sauces.

VEAL ROULADES IN ASPIC

MESSICANI IN GELATINA

Serves 6

1 bread slice, crusts removed

150 g/5 oz minced beef

50 g/2 oz prosciutto, chopped

50 g/2 oz Parmesan cheese, freshly grated

1 egg

1 egg yolk

500 g/1 lb 2 oz veal steaks

4 tablespoons olive oil

25 g/1 oz butter

4–5 fresh sage leaves

175 ml/6 fl oz dry white wine

1 litre/1¾ pints dissolved gelatine

salt and pepper

Tear the bread into pieces, place in a bowl, add water to cover and leave to soak for 10 minutes, then drain and squeeze out. Mix together the beef, soaked bread, prosciutto and Parmesan in a bowl. Stir in the egg and egg yolk and season. Pound the veal steaks with a meat mallet until thin and divide the filling among them. Roll up and tie with kitchen string. Heat the oil and butter in a pan, add the sage and roulades and cook, turning frequently, until browned. Pour in all but 1 tablespoon of the wine and cook until it has evaporated. Pour in 150 ml/¼ pint water and cook for 15 minutes. Add 2–3 tablespoons water, increase the heat and cook for 1 minute. Remove the pan from the heat and place the roulades on a serving dish. Prepare the gelatine according to the instructions, add the remaining wine and pour it over the roulades until completely covered. Chill in the refrigerator for a few hours until set.

VEAL NOISETTES IN BUTTER, SAGE AND ROSEMARY

Pound the noisettes lightly with a meat mallet and place in a pan with the butter. Sprinkle with the rosemary and sage and cook over a medium heat for 4 minutes on each side. Season with salt and pepper, pour in the wine and cook until it has evaporated. Add the stock, lower the heat, cover and simmer for 30 minutes, adding more stock if necessary.

NODINI AL BURRO, SALVIA E ROSMARINO
Serves 4
4 veal noisettes
80 g/3 oz butter, cut into pieces
2 fresh rosemary sprigs, chopped
8 fresh sage leaves, chopped
5 tablespoons white wine
300 ml/½ pint Meat Stock (see page 208)
salt and pepper

VEAL NOISETTES À LA FINANCIÈRE

Melt half the butter in a frying pan, add the mushrooms and cook over a low heat, stirring occasionally, for 20 minutes. Add the peas, sweetbreads and bone marrow, pour in the Marsala and cook until it has evaporated. Season with salt and pepper and cook for a few minutes more. Melt the remaining butter in a another frying pan. Dust the veal noisettes with flour, add to the pan and cook for 4 minutes on each side. Pour in the stock, cover and simmer until tender. Place the veal noisettes on a warm serving dish and spoon the sauce over them.

NODINI ALLA FINANZIERA
Serves 4
100 g/3½ oz butter
100 g/3½ oz mushrooms, sliced
2 tablespoons frozen peas
150 g/5 oz sweetbreads and
bone marrow, chopped
5 tablespoons dry Marsala
4 veal noisettes
plain flour, for dusting
300 ml/½ pint Meat Stock (see page 208)
salt and pepper

MILANESE OSSO BUCO

Melt the butter in a saucepan, add the onion and cook over a low heat, stirring occasionally, for 5 minutes. Dust the veal with flour, add to the pan and cook over a high heat, turning frequently, until browned all over. Season with salt and pepper and cook for a few minutes more, then pour in the wine and cook until it has evaporated. Add the stock, celery and carrot, lower the heat, cover and simmer for 30 minutes, adding more stock if necessary. Mix the tomato purée with 1 tablespoon hot water in a bowl and stir into the pan. Prepare the gremolata by mixing together the lemon rind and parsley in a bowl, add the mixture to the veal, turn carefully and cook for a further 5 minutes.

OSSIBUCHI ALLA MILANESE
Serves 4
80 g/3 oz butter • ½ onion, chopped
4 osso buco (5-cm/2-inch thick rounds of veal knuckle)
plain flour, for dusting
5 tablespoons dry white wine
175 ml/6 fl oz Meat Stock (see page 208)
1 celery stick, chopped
1 carrot, chopped
2 tablespoons tomato purée
salt and pepper

For the gremolata
thinly pared rind of ½ lemon, finely chopped
1 fresh flat-leaf parsley sprig, finely chopped

VEAL OSSO BUCO WITH PEAS

Lightly dust the veal with flour. Melt the butter in a frying pan, add the onion, carrot and veal and cook over a high heat, stirring and turning frequently, until the veal is browned all over. Pour in the wine and cook until it has evaporated. Put the tomatoes in a food processor, process to a purée and add to the pan with the peas and 150 ml/¼ pint water. Season with salt and pepper, lower the heat, cover and simmer for about 1 hour.

OSSIBUCHI CON PISELLI

Serves 4

4 osso buco (5-cm/2-inch thick rounds of veal knuckle)

plain flour, for dusting

80 g/3 oz butter

1 onion, finely chopped • 1 carrot, finely chopped

175 ml/6 fl oz dry white wine

150 g/5 oz canned tomatoes

500 g/1 lb 2 oz fresh peas, shelled

salt and pepper

MEAT PIE

Pound the veal with a meat mallet until thin and even. Place one slice on the base of a deep heatproof dish (it should be just the right size to fit). Sprinkle with a little Parmesan and a pinch of salt and lay a slice of mortadella and a slice of ham on top. Spoon a little of the beaten eggs over the meat. Continue to make layers until all the ingredients are used, ending with beaten eggs. Stand the dish in saucepan and add water to come about halfway up the sides. Bring just to the boil, then lower the heat and simmer for 2 hours. Turn the pie out on to a dish — it should slide out easily. Put a weight on top and leave for about 1 hour. Drain off the jelly-like liquid which forms and use to garnish. Chill in the refrigerator, then serve cut into slices. This pie can even be served the next day.

PASTICCIO DI CARNE

Serves 6–8

4 thick lean veal slices

2 tablespoons Parmesan cheese, freshly grated

4 thick mortadella slices

4 cooked ham slices

4 eggs, lightly beaten

salt

ROAST BREAST OF VEAL

Ask your butcher to pound the breast of veal into a fairly broad slice. Preheat the oven to 180°C/350°F/Gas Mark 4. Grease a roasting tin with butter. Season the veal with salt and pepper, place the slices of prosciutto on top and sprinkle with the rosemary and sage. Roll up the meat and tie with kitchen string. Place the veal in the roasting tin, dot with the butter, drizzle with the oil and roast, basting and turning the meat occasionally, for about 1½ hours. Leave to stand for about 10 minutes before untying and carving into slices.

PETTO AL FORNO

Serves 6

50 g/2 oz butter, plus extra for greasing

800-g/1¾-lb boneless breast of veal

2 thick prosciutto slices

1 fresh rosemary sprig, chopped

4 fresh sage leaves, chopped

2 tablespoons olive oil

salt and pepper

BREAST OF VEAL
WITH MAYONNAISE

PETTO ALLA MAIONESE

Serves 4

500-g/1 lb 2-oz boneless breast of veal

25 g/1 oz butter

6 tablespoons Mayonnaise (see page 65)

3 gherkins, drained and chopped

10 black olives, stoned and quartered

salt and pepper

Season the veal on both sides with salt and pepper. Melt the butter in a frying pan, add the veal and cook, turning frequently, until cooked through and golden brown all over. Remove from the pan and leave to cool. Mix together the mayonnaise, gherkins and olives in a bowl and spread the mixture over the meat. Roll up and wrap securely in foil. Chill in the refrigerator for 3 hours before slicing and serving.

BREAST OF VEAL
WITH HERBS

PETTO ALLE ERBE

Serves 6

3 eggs

4 tablespoons Parmesan cheese, freshly grated

1-kg/2¼-lb boneless breast of veal

300 g/11 oz Swiss chard

1 fresh flat-leaf parsley sprig, chopped

1 fresh basil sprig, chopped

3 cooked ham slices

1 garlic clove, chopped (optional)

2 tablespoons olive oil

40 g/1½ oz butter

500 ml/18 fl oz Meat Stock (see page 208)

salt and pepper

Beat the eggs in a bowl, add the Parmesan, season with salt and make a small frittata (see page 382). Spread out the meat and place the frittata on top. Blanch the Swiss chard in salted, boiling water for a few minutes, then drain and chop. Mix together the Swiss chard, parsley, basil, ham, and garlic if using. Sprinkle the mixture over the frittata and season with salt and pepper. Roll up the meat and tie with kitchen string. Heat the oil and butter in a frying pan, add the veal and cook, turning frequently, until golden brown all over, then season with salt. Pour in the stock, cover and simmer over a low heat, turning and basting occasionally, for 1½ hours. Remove the veal from the pan and leave to stand for 10 minutes, then untie, slice and serve.

BREAST OF VEAL
WITH SAUSAGES

PETTO ALLE SALSICCE

Serves 6

6 small Italian sausages

4 tablespoons diced day-old bread

1 onion, chopped

300 ml/½ pint Meat Stock (see page 208)

1-kg/2¼-lb boneless breast of veal

4 tablespoons olive oil, plus extra for brushing

50 g/2 oz butter

Cook the sausages without additional oil or fat in a frying pan until browned and cooked through, then skin and crumble into a bowl. Add the bread and onion and mix well. If the mixture is too dry, stir in a little of the stock. Make a horizontal cut in the breast of veal along one of the long sides to create a 'pocket'. Spoon the mixture into the pocket and sew up the opening. Brush the veal with oil and put it into in a pan with the oil and butter. Cook over a medium heat, turning occasionally, until browned all over. Cover and cook on a low heat, turning the meat occasionally and gradually adding the stock as necessary, for 1½ hours. Carve into slices and spoon the cooking juices over them.

BRAISED BREAST OF VEAL

Open out the veal well and make several small incisions in the surface. Slip rosemary needles, a slice of garlic and a piece of pancetta dipped in pepper and a little salt into each incision. Roll up the meat and tie with kitchen string. Heat the butter and oil in a pan, add the veal and cook, turning frequently, until browned all over. Cover and cook over a low heat, gradually adding the Marsala, for 1 hour or until cooked through and tender. Remove the meat from the pan and leave to stand. Add 1–2 tablespoons hot water to dilute the cooking juices, if necessary. Untie the veal, carve into slices, place on a warm serving dish and spoon the cooking juices over them. You could serve this with a side dish of spinach in butter.

PETTO ARROSTO

Serves 6

1-kg/2¹/₂-lb boneless breast of veal

1 fresh rosemary sprig

1 garlic clove, sliced

50 g/2 oz pancetta, chopped

25 g/1 oz butter

3 tablespoons olive oil

175 ml/6 fl oz dry Marsala

salt and pepper

VEAL ESCALOPES IN LEMON

Pound the escalopes lightly with a meat mallet and dust with a little flour. Melt 65 g/2¹/₂ oz of the butter in a frying pan, add the escalopes and cook over a high heat for 5 minutes, turning several times, then season with salt. Mix the lemon juice with 4 tablespoons water, pour the mixture into the pan and cook until slightly reduced. Sprinkle with the parsley, scatter with the remaining butter, then remove from the heat when the butter has melted. Serve the veal escalopes in the sauce.

PICCATA AL LIMONE

Serves 4

500 g/1 lb 2 oz veal escalopes

plain flour for dusting

80 g/3 oz butter

juice of 1 lemon, strained

1 fresh flat-leaf parsley sprig, chopped

salt

VEAL ESCALOPES WITH MARSALA

Dust the veal escalopes with flour. Melt the butter in a large frying pan, and when it turns hazel add the veal and cook over a high heat for about 5 minutes on each side. Lower the heat, season with salt to taste and cook for a few more minutes more, then remove from the pan and keep warm. Pour in the Marsala and cook over a low heat, scraping up the sediment from the base of the pan with a wooden spoon. Place the escalopes on a warm serving dish and spoon the sauce over them.

PICCATA AL MARSALA

Serves 4

500 g/1 lb 2 oz veal escalopes

plain flour, for dusting

80 g/3 oz butter

250 ml/8 fl oz dry Marsala

salt

VEAL MEATLOAF

Mix together the veal, ham, eggs and nutmeg in a bowl and season with salt and pepper. Shape the mixture into an ovoid and dust with flour. Heat the butter and oil in a pan, add the onion, carrot and celery and cook over a low heat, stirring occasionally, for 10 minutes. Add the meatloaf and cook, turning carefully, until browned all over. Mix the tomato purée with 2 tablespoons warm water and stir into the pan. Cover and simmer gently for about 1 hour. Remove the meatloaf from the pan, cut into fairly thick slices, place them on a warm serving dish and spoon the cooking juices over them.

POLPETTONE CASALINGO

Serves 4

500 g/1 lb 2 oz minced rump

100 g/3 ¹/₂ oz cooked ham, chopped

2 eggs, lightly beaten

pinch of freshly grated nutmeg

plain flour, for dusting

50 g/2 oz butter

2 tablespoons olive oil

1 onion, chopped

1 carrot, chopped

1 celery stick, chopped

2 teaspoons tomato purée

salt and pepper

ROMAN SALTIMBOCCA

This is the only main course in Italian cuisine whose recipe has been officially approved and laid down. This is the recipe that the panel of cooks agreed upon in Venice in 1962. Saltimbocca, incidentally, means jump into the mouth. Place a half-slice of prosciutto on each escalope, put a sage leaf on top and fasten with a cocktail stick. Melt the butter in a frying pan and cook the veal over a high heat on both sides until golden brown. Season with salt, pour in the wine and cook until it has evaporated, then remove the cocktail sticks and serve.

SALTIMBOCCA ALLA ROMANA

Serves 4

100 g/3¹/₂ oz prosciutto slices, halved

500 g/1 lb 2 oz veal escalopes

8–10 fresh sage leaves

50 g/2 oz butter

100 ml/3¹/₂ fl oz dry white wine

salt

VEAL ESCALOPES WITH MUSHROOMS

Heat half the oil and 20 g/³/₄ oz of the butter in a frying pan, add the mushrooms and garlic and cook over a low heat, stirring occasionally, for 20 minutes. Remove the pan from the heat, discard the garlic, season the mushrooms with salt and sprinkle with the parsley. Dust the veal escalopes with flour. Heat the remaining oil and remaining butter in another pan, add the veal and cook over a high heat for 10 minutes on each side until golden brown. Season with salt and pepper, remove from the pan and keep warm. Stir 2–3 tablespoons hot water into the cooking juices and add to the mushrooms. Place the veal escalopes on a warm serving dish and pour the mushroom mixture over them.

SCALOPPINE AI FUNGHI

Serves 4

120 ml/4 fl oz olive oil

50 g/2 oz butter

300 g/11 oz mushrooms, sliced

1 garlic clove

1 fresh flat-leaf parsley sprig, chopped

4 veal escalopes

plain flour, for dusting

salt and pepper

VEAL ESCALOPES PIZZAIOLA

Dust the veal escalopes with flour. Heat the oil and butter in a frying pan, add the onion and garlic and cook over a low heat, stirring occasionally, for 5 minutes. Add the veal, increase the heat to high and cook for 5 minutes on each side. Add the tomatoes and cook for a few minutes more. Remove and discard the garlic, add the capers and the olives and season lightly with salt and pepper. Simmer for a further 5 minutes, then transfer the veal escalopes to a warm serving dish and spoon the cooking juices over them.

SCALOPPINE ALLA PIZZAIOLA

Serves 4

4 veal escalopes

plain flour, for dusting

3 tablespoons olive oil

40 g/1¹/₂ oz butter

¹/₂ onion, chopped

1 garlic clove

4 ripe tomatoes, peeled and chopped

2 tablespoons capers, drained and rinsed

10 green olives, stoned

salt and pepper

VEAL ESCALOPES WITH MUSTARD

Dust the veal escalopes with flour. Heat the butter and oil in a large frying pan, add the veal escalopes and cook over a medium heat for 8–10 minutes until golden brown on both sides. Season with salt, remove from the pan and keep warm. Stir 1–2 tablespoons hot water into the cooking juices, add the mustard and mix well to dissolve. Chop the parsley, thyme and chives together, add to the pan and cook for a few minutes. Pour the sauce over the veal escalopes and serve.

SCALOPPINE ALLA SENAPE

Serves 4

4 veal escalopes

plain flour, for dusting

40 g/1¹/₂ oz butter

2 tablespoons olive oil

1 tablespoon Dijon mustard

1 fresh parsley sprig

1 fresh thyme sprig

4 fresh chives

salt

VEAL ESCALOPES WITH MILK

Lightly pound the veal escalopes with a meat mallet and dust with flour. Beat the egg with a little salt and pepper in a shallow dish. Spread out the breadcrumbs in another shallow dish. Dip the veal escalopes first in the beaten egg, then in the breadcrumbs and shake off the excess. Melt the butter in a frying pan, add the veal and cook for 3 minutes on each side. Pour in the milk, cover the pan and simmer for about 20 minutes until the veal is tender. Arrange the veal escalopes on a warm serving dish. Stir the capers into the hot cooking juices and pour the mixture over the meat.

SCALOPPINE AL LATTE

Serves 4

4 veal escalopes

plain flour, for dusting

1 egg

50 g/2 oz breadcrumbs

25 g/1 oz butter

500 ml/18 fl oz milk

1 tablespoon capers, drained

rinsed and chopped

salt and pepper

VEAL ESCALOPES WITH HERBS

SCALOPPINE ALLE ERBE

Serves 4

50 g/2 oz butter

1 tablespoon olive oil

¼ onion, in one piece

4 veal escalopes

1 fresh rosemary sprig, chopped

1 fresh sage sprig, chopped

1 fresh thyme sprig, chopped

5 tablespoons dry white wine

salt and pepper

Heat the butter and oil in a frying pan, add the onion and cook over a low heat for 10 minutes, stirring occasionally to make sure the onion stays intact, then remove from the pan. Add the veal escalopes to the pan and cook over a high heat for 2 minutes on each side, then lower the heat and season with salt and pepper. Add the rosemary, sage and thyme and cook for a few minutes. Pour in the wine and cook over a medium heat for about 10 minutes until the veal is tender. Remove the veal escalopes from the pan. Add 1–2 tablespoons hot water to the pan and cook, scraping up the sediment from the base with a wooden spoon, then pour the sauce over the meat and serve.

VEAL ESCALOPES WITH GRAPEFRUIT

SCALOPPINE AL POMPELMO

Serves 4

40 g/1½ oz butter

1 fresh thyme sprig

4 veal escalopes

plain flour, for dusting

5 tablespoons dry white wine

juice of ½ grapefruit, strained

salt and pepper

grapefruit slices, to garnish

Heat the butter in a frying pan and add the thyme. Lightly dust the veal escalopes with flour, add to the pan and cook over a high heat until golden brown on both sides. Mix together the wine and grapefruit juice and pour the mixture into the pan. Cover and simmer over a low heat for 15 minutes until the liquid has thickened. Season with salt and pepper. Transfer the veal escalopes to a warm serving dish and spoon the cooking juices over them discarding the thyme. Garnish with slices of grapefruit.

VEAL FRITTERS

SGONFIOTTI DI CARNE

Serves 4

2 onions, chopped

1 garlic clove, chopped

1 chilli, seeded and chopped

250 g/9 oz minced veal

50 g/2 oz butter

2 eggs, hard-boiled and chopped

8 green olives, stoned and chopped

50 g/2 oz sultanas

pinch of dried oregano

250 g/9 oz puff pastry dough, thawed if frozen

plain flour, for dusting

1 egg, lightly beaten

vegetable oil, for deep-frying

salt and pepper

Mix together the onions, garlic, chilli and veal in a bowl. Melt the butter in a frying pan, add the veal mixture and cook, stirring constantly, until evenly browned. Remove from the heat and leave to cool. Stir in the eggs, olives, sultanas and oregano and season with salt and pepper. Roll out the pastry on a lightly floured surface and stamp out 10-cm/4-inch rounds. Put a little filling on each round, brush the edges with the beaten egg, fold in half and crimp to seal. Heat the oil in a large pan, add the fritters and cook until golden brown. Remove with a fish slice, drain and serve.

SIX-AROMA VEAL STEW

Season the veal with salt and pepper and place in a bowl with the garlic, parsley and basil. Add the lemon and orange juice, lime rind and cumin seeds and mix well. Leave the veal to marinate, stirring occasionally, for 2 hours. Heat the oil and butter in a saucepan. Drain the veal, reserving the marinade, add to the pan and cook, stirring frequently, for about 5 minutes. Strain the reserved marinade into the pan, cover and simmer for 45 minutes, adding a little warm water if necessary.

SPEZZATINO AI SEI PROFUMI

Serves 4

800 g/1³/₄ lb boneless shoulder
of veal, cut into cubes
1 garlic clove, chopped
1 fresh flat-leaf parsley sprig, chopped
1 fresh basil sprig, chopped
juice of 1 lemon, strained
juice of 1 orange, strained
grated rind of 1 lime
1 tablespoon cumin seeds
3 tablespoons olive oil
40 g/1¹/₂ oz butter
salt and pepper

CURRIED VEAL

Heat the oil and butter in a saucepan, add the onions and cook over a low heat, stirring occasionally, for 5 minutes. Lightly dust the veal with flour, add to the pan, increase the heat to high and cook, stirring frequently, for 5 minutes or until browned all over. Season with salt and pepper. Stir the curry powder into 2–3 tablespoons warm water in a bowl and pour the mixture over the meat. Mix well, cover and simmer over a medium heat for 1 hour. Add the thyme and parsley, then transfer to a warm serving dish. This curry is delicious served with a pilaf or plain boiled rice.

SPEZZATINO AL CURRY

Serves 4

2 tablespoons olive oil
25 g/1 oz butter
2 onions, chopped
600 g/1 lb 5 oz boneless shoulder
of veal, cut into cubes
plain flour, for dusting
2 tablespoons curry powder
leaves of 1 fresh thyme sprig
1 fresh flat-leaf parsley sprig, chopped
salt and pepper

VEAL AND VEGETABLE STEW

Heat the oil and butter in a pan, add the onion and celery and cook over a low heat, stirring occasionally, for 5 minutes. Dust the veal with flour, add to the pan and cook over a high heat, stirring frequently, until browned all over. Season with salt and pepper and cook for a further 5 minutes, then add the carrots and passata. Lower the heat, cover and simmer for about 45 minutes, occasionally adding 2–3 tablespoons warm water if the stew starts to dry out. Add the courgettes, re-cover the pan and cook for a further 15 minutes.

SPEZZATINO CON VERDURE

Serves 4

2 tablespoons olive oil
25 g/1 oz butter
1 onion, finely chopped
1 celery stick, finely chopped
600 g/1 lb 5 oz boned shoulder of veal, cut into cubes
plain flour, for dusting
3 carrots, cut into thin batons
100 ml/3¹/₂ fl oz passata
3 courgettes, cut into thin batons
salt and pepper

BREAST OF VEAL WITH ARTICHOKE HEARTS

SPINACINO AI CARCIOFI

Serves 8

1.2-kg/2¹/₂-lb boned breast of veal

300 g/11 oz minced meat,

50 g/2 oz Parmesan cheese, freshly grated

1 egg, lightly beaten

3 very tender artichoke hearts

4 tablespoons olive oil

juice of ¹/₂ lemon, strained

25 g/1 oz butter

salt

Using a sharp knife, cut a deep 'pocket' in the veal. Mix together the minced meat, Parmesan and egg in a bowl and season with salt. Place 2-3 tablespoons of the minced meat mixture in the veal 'pocket' and gently push it down towards the end. Insert an artichoke heart with the base towards the opening. Stuff the pocket with another 2-3 tablespoons of the minced meat mixture, pushing it down well, then insert another artichoke heart. Add another 2-3 tablespoons of the minced meat mixture, then the remaining artichoke heart and, finally, add the remaining minced meat mixture. Sew up the opening with trussing thread. Mix 1 tablespoon of the oil with the lemon juice in a small bowl and brush the mixture all over the veal. Heat the butter and the remaining oil in a large pan or flameproof casserole, add the veal, cover and cook over a low heat for about 1 hour. After the first 30 minutes, start turning the veal occasionally. About 5 minutes before the end of the cooking time, remove the lid, increase the heat and cook the veal, turning frequently, until browned all over. Remove the pan from the heat and leave the veal to stand for 10 minutes before carving into slices. Arrange the slices on a serving dish and spoon some of the cooking juices over them.

SHIN OF VEAL IN CIDER

STINCO AL SIDRO

Serves 6

150 g/5 oz butter

4 shallots, thinly sliced

1 veal shin

1 tablespoon Calvados

750 ml/1¹/₄ pints dry cider

300 g/11 oz baby onions

4 red apples, cored and chopped

250 ml/8 fl oz double cream

1 egg yolk

salt and pepper

Melt 50 g/2 oz of the butter in a pan, add the shallots and cook over a low heat, stirring occasionally, for 10 minutes. Increase the heat to high, add the veal shin and cook, turning frequently, for 10 minutes until browned all over. Season with salt and pepper, add the Calvados and cook until it has evaporated. Pour in the cider, add a little more salt, lower the heat, cover and simmer for about 1¹/₂ hours. Meanwhile, melt 50 g/2 oz of the remaining butter in another pan, add the onions and cook over a low heat, stirring occasionally, for 15 minutes. Melt the remaining butter in another pan, add the apples and cook over a low heat, stirring occasionally, until just tender. Remove the meat from the pan and keep warm. Stir the cream into the cooking juices, then stir in the egg yolk and heat gently without allowing the sauce to boil. Carve the veal, place the slices on a warm serving dish, pour the sauce over them and surround with the apples and onions.

ROAST SHIN OF VEAL

STINCO ARROSTO

Serves 6

3 tablespoons olive oil

40 g/1½ oz butter

1 fresh myrtle sprig or 6 juniper berries

1 fresh rosemary sprig

2 shallots, finely chopped

1 veal shin

175 ml/6 fl oz red wine

salt and pepper

Preheat the oven to 190°C/375°F/Gas Mark 5. Put the oil, butter, myrtle or juniper berries, rosemary and shallots in a roasting tin and cook over a low heat, stirring occasionally, for 10 minutes. Add the veal and cook, turning frequently, until golden brown on all sides. Season with salt and pepper, transfer to the oven and roast for about 1 hour. Pour in the wine, return the tin to the oven and roast, basting occasionally, for 1 hour more. If necessary, add a ladleful of hot water. Remove the veal and carve it, then place the slices on a warm serving dish and spoon the cooking juices over them.

HOT VEAL IN TUNA SAUCE

VITELLO TONNATO CALDO

Serves 6

40 g/1½ oz butter • 3 tablespoons olive oil

800-g/1¾-lb topside

175 ml/6 fl oz dry white wine

1 carrot • 1 celery stick

2 salted anchovies, heads removed, cleaned and filleted (see page 596), soaked in cold water for 10 minutes, drained and rinsed

100 g/3½ oz canned tuna in oil, drained and flaked

4 gherkins, drained and chopped

juice of 1 lemon, strained

salt and pepper

Heat the butter and oil in a saucepan, add the veal and cook, turning frequently, until browned all over. Season with salt and pepper and cook for a further 5 minutes, then pour in the wine and cook until it has evaporated. Add the carrot and celery and pour in 175 ml/6 fl oz water. Cover and simmer over a low heat, turning the meat occasionally, for 1½ hours. Meanwhile, chop the anchovy fillets. Mix together the anchovies, tuna, gherkins and lemon juice in a bowl. When the meat is tender, remove it from the pan. Remove the carrot and celery, pour the tuna mixture into the pan and mix with the cooking juices. Carve the meat into fairly thin slices, place them on a warm serving dish and spoon the hot tuna sauce over them.

COLD VEAL IN TUNA SAUCE

VITELLO TONNATO FREDDO

Serves 6

800-g/1¾-lb topside

1 carrot • 1 onion • 1 celery stick

1 tablespoon white wine vinegar

1 tablespoon olive oil • salt

For the sauce

200 g/7 oz canned tuna in oil, drained

3 canned anchovy fillets in oil, drained

2 tablespoons capers, drained and rinsed

2 hard-boiled egg yolks

3 tablespoons olive oil

juice of 1 lemon, strained

Tie the veal neatly with kitchen string. Bring a pan of salted water to the boil and add the veal, carrot, onion, celery, vinegar and olive oil. Cover and simmer over a low heat for 2 hours until the meat is tender. Remove the pan from the heat and leave the veal to cool in the stock. For the sauce, put the tuna, anchovy fillets, capers and egg yolks through a mincer or process in a food processor. Stir in the olive oil, 2–3 tablespoons of the stock and the lemon juice. Untie the meat, carve into slices and place on a serving dish. Spoon the sauce over the slices and leave for a few hours for the flavours to mingle before serving

SAUSAGES

Italian sausages include cotechino, cappello del prete, zampone and salame da sugo – or salamina, as this particular variety are more affectionately called by the inhabitants of Ferrara, who love it. Although the family of Italian sausages for cooking is not as big as the family of sausages eaten raw, the distinctiveness of their ingredients, their specific flavour and their aroma make them true delicacies which, particularly in the winter, provide comfort against the rigours of the climate and help create a cheerful mood. They are of very different shapes and sizes and include a wide variety of ingredients. For example, meat from the pig's snout predominates in cotechino. In boned trotters, there is a mixture of a number of coarsely minced meats seasoned with spices. Lean meat predominates in sausages sold by length or in links, and the mixture must be fairly even. Prized cuts predominate in the salama da sugo – a sausage that seems to have no equivalent anywhere else in the world – such as fillet, lean meat and tongue. And every region of Italy, from Lombardy and Tuscany to Veneto, Emilia Romagna and Campania, boasts its special sausages. Lastly, the gastronomic symbol that marks the arrival of the new year in Italy is the zampone from Modena, which has rightly become part of Italian culinary tradition.

CAPPELLO DEL PRETE EN CROÛTE

Prick the sausage, wrap it in foil and boil for 1½ hours. Meanwhile, cook the beetroot tops in salted, boiling water for about 15 minutes until tender. Drain and squeeze out as much liquid as possible, then mix with the butter, garlic and Parmesan. Drain the cappello del prete and skin. Preheat the oven to 200°C/400°F/Gas Mark 6. Roll out the pastry on a lightly floured surface to a triangle large enough to enclose the cappello del prete. Sprinkle half the beetroot tops on the pastry, place the cappello del prete on top and cover with the remaining beetroot tops. Lift the pastry corners up and over to the middle to enclose. Place on a baking sheet, brush with egg yolk and bake for 40 minutes until golden brown.

CAPPELLO DEL PRETE IN CROSTA
Serves 4

1 cappello del prete sausage
('priest's-hat' pork sausage)
500 g/1 lb 2 oz beetroot tops
25 g/1 oz butter
1 garlic clove, finely chopped
2 tablespoons Parmesan cheese, freshly grated
300 g/11 oz puff pastry dough, thawed if frozen
plain flour, for dusting
1 egg yolk, lightly beaten
salt

COTECHINO

COTECHINO

Serves 4

600-g/1 lb 5-oz cotechino sausage

Prick the cotechino all over and wrap in foil so that it does not burst. Place in a large pan, add water to cover, bring just to the boil, then lower the heat and simmer gently for about 2 hours. Leave in the water for 10 minutes before draining and slicing. It is worth noting that most cotechini sold outside Italy are pre-cooked, so this preliminary step is not required for cotechino recipes. You may, however, need to heat the cotechino before adding it to other ingredients or before serving.

WRAPPED COTECHINO

COTECHINO ARROTOLATO

Serves 6

250 g/9 oz spinach

50 g/2 oz butter

1 garlic clove, crushed

50 g/2 oz Parmesan cheese, freshly grated

675-g/1¹/₂-lb veal rump steak

600-g/1 lb 5-oz cooked cotechino, skinned

3 tablespoons olive oil

1 fresh rosemary sprig, chopped

6 fresh sage leaves, chopped

175 ml/6 fl oz dry white wine

salt and pepper

Preheat the oven to 190°C/375°F/Gas Mark 5. Cook the spinach, in just the water clinging to the leaves after washing, for about 5 minutes, then drain, squeeze out as much liquid as possible and chop. Mix the spinach with half the butter and the garlic and season with salt and pepper. Put the spinach on the veal, sprinkle with the Parmesan and put the cotechino in the centre. Roll up and tie with kitchen string. Heat the oil and the remaining butter in a flameproof casserole, add the rosemary and sage and cook for a few minutes, then add the meat and cook, turning frequently, until browned all over. Pour in the wine and cook until it has evaporated, then season with salt and pepper. Transfer to the oven and roast for about 1 hour. Remove from the oven, leave to stand for 10 minutes, untie and carve into slices.

COTECHINO WITH LENTILS

COTECHINO CON LENTICCHIE

Serves 4

400 g/14 oz lentils

1 onion, halved

2 celery sticks

2 tablespoons olive oil

20 g/³/₄ oz butter

600-g/1 lb 5-oz cooked cotechino, skinned, sliced and heated through

salt and pepper

Put the lentils, one onion-half and one of the celery sticks in a large pan, add cold water to cover and bring to the boil, then lower the heat and simmer for 45–50 minutes until the lentils are tender. Meanwhile, chop the remaining onion-half and celery. Heat the oil and butter in a pan, add the chopped onion and celery and cook over a low heat, stirring occasionally, for 5 minutes. Drain the lentils, discard the onion and celery and add to the pan. Cook over a low heat, stirring constantly. Season with salt and pepper to taste, transfer to a warm serving dish and arrange the cotechino on top.

COTECHINO WITH MUSHROOM SAUCE

COTECHINO CON SALSA DI FUNGHI

Serves 6

2 tablespoons olive oil

1 shallot, chopped

600 g/1 lb 5 oz mushrooms, thinly sliced

200 ml/7 fl oz double cream

12 white bread slices

melted butter, for brushing

5 tablespoons milk

600-g/1 lb 5-oz cooked cotechino, skinned, sliced and heated through

salt and pepper

Preheat the oven to 200°C/400°F/Gas Mark 6. Heat the oil in a pan, add the shallot and cook over a low heat, stirring occasionally, for 5 minutes. Add the mushrooms and cream, season with salt and pepper and cook for 10–20 minutes until tender. Meanwhile, stamp out 12 rounds from the slices of bread, brush with melted butter, place on a baking sheet and cook in the oven until golden brown. Bring the milk to simmering point in a small saucepan. Transfer the mushroom mixture to a food processor, add the hot milk and process until smooth. Put a slice of cotechino on each round of bread and pour the mushroom sauce over the rounds.

COTECHINO IN A JACKET

COTECHINO VESTITO

Serves 4

50 g/2 oz dried mushrooms

300-g/11-oz lean veal

400-g/14-oz cooked cotechino, skinned

20 g/³/₄ oz butter

¹/₄ onion, finely chopped

1 celery stick, finely chopped

1 carrot, finely chopped

50 g/2 oz pancetta, finely chopped

Put the mushrooms in a bowl, add warm water to cover and leave to soak for 15–30 minutes, then drain and squeeze out. Pound the veal with a meat mallet until thin and even, place the cotechino on top and roll up, then tie with kitchen string. Melt the butter in a pan, add the onion, celery, carrot and pancetta and cook over a low heat, stirring occasionally, for about 5 minutes. Add the meat, increase the heat to medium and cook, turning frequently, until browned all over. Pour in enough water to half-cover, add the mushrooms and simmer for about 1 hour. Remove the meat from the pan, untie, carve and serve with the cooking juices.

TEN–HERB SAUSAGES

SALSICCE ALLE DIECI ERBE

Serves 4

8 Italian sausages

fresh rosemary needles, chopped

fresh sage leaves, chopped

fresh basil leaves, chopped

fresh thyme leaves, chopped

fresh flat-leaf parsley, chopped

fresh marjoram leaves, chopped

fresh mint leaves, chopped

fresh tarragon leaves, chopped

celery stick(s), chopped

shallot(s), chopped

100 ml/3¹/₂ fl oz dry white wine

The quantities of the various herbs, celery and shallot to use depend on individual taste, but it is best to go easy with the stronger ones, such as rosemary. Prick the sausages, put them in a pan with 2 tablespoons water and cook, turning occasionally, for about 10 minutes until golden brown. Add the herbs, celery and shallot(s) and cook for a few minutes more. Pour in the wine and cook until it has evaporated, then serve.

SAUSAGES IN TOMATO

SALSICCE AL POMODORO

Serves 4

8 Italian sausages
100 ml/3¹/₂ fl oz dry white wine
250 ml/8 fl oz passata
salt and pepper

Prick the sausages with a fork, put them in a pan, add 2 table-spoons water and cook over a low heat, turning occasionally, for 10 minutes until golden brown. Pour in the wine and cook until it has evaporated. Add the passata and season with salt and pepper to taste. Cover and simmer for a further 15 minutes, then serve the sausages in the sauce.

SAUSAGES WITH CARROTS

SALSICCE CON CAROTE

Serves 4

40 g/1¹/₂ oz butter
8 carrots, cut into thin batons
500 g/1 lb 2 oz Italian sausages, cut into pieces
salt and pepper

Melt 25 g/1 oz of the butter in a pan, add the carrots and cook over a low heat, stirring occasionally, for 10 minutes. Put the sausages in a pan, add 2–3 tablespoons water and cook, stirring frequently, for about 10 minutes until browned. Add the carrots and remaining butter, season with salt and pepper to taste, cook for a few minutes and serve.

SAUSAGES WITH LEEKS AU GRATIN

SALSICCE CON PORRI AL GRATIN

Serves 4

3 leeks, trimmed and thinly sliced
1 quantity Meat Stock (see page 208)
butter, for greasing
8 small Italian sausages
150 ml/¹/₄ pint double cream

Put the leeks in a small saucepan and pour in stock to cover. Bring to the boil, then lower the heat and simmer for about 15 minutes until tender. Drain and leave to cool. Preheat the oven to 200°C/400°F/Gas Mark 6. Grease an ovenproof dish with butter. Prick the sausages and cook in a pan, turning frequently, until browned all over. Put the leeks in the prepared dish and place the sausages on top. Spoon the cream over them and bake until hot and bubbling.

SAUSAGES WITH POTATO TART

SALSICCE CON TORTA DI PATATE

Serves 4

6 potatoes, unpeeled
300 g/11 oz Italian sausages
3 tablespoons olive oil
2 onions, thinly sliced
salt and pepper

Cook the potatoes in a pan of lightly salted, boiling water for 25–30 minutes until tender. Drain, peel and mash with a fork. Prick the sausages, put them in a pan, add 2 tablespoons water and cook, turning frequently, for about 10 minutes until browned all over. Heat the oil in another pan, add the onions and cook over a low heat, stirring occasionally, for about 5 minutes. Add the mashed potato, season with salt and pepper and stir well. Using a spatula, shape the mixture into a 2.5-cm/1-inch thick round. Cook over a high heat until brown and crisp on the underside, then turn over and brown the second side. Turn out the potato tart on to a warm serving dish and surround with the hot sausages.

SAUSAGES AND TURNIPS

Put the sausages, rosemary and garlic in a pan and cook, turning frequently, until browned all over. Remove the sausages from the pan, add the turnips and cook, stirring and turning frequently, for 5 minutes. Season lightly with salt and pepper, cover the pan and cook for about 30 minutes. If the turnips seem a little watery towards the end of the cooking time, remove the lid and reduce the liquid. Add the sausages and cook for a few minutes more. Place on a warm serving dish.

SALSICCE E RAPE
Serves 4
400 g/14 oz Italian sausages, cut into pieces
1 fresh rosemary sprig
1 garlic clove, chopped
600 g/1 lb 5 oz turnips, sliced
salt and pepper

FRIED SAUSAGES

Prick the sausages, place them in a heavy-based pan and cook over a medium-high heat, turning frequently, until browned all over. Pour in the wine and cook until it has evaporated. These sausages are good served with a side dish of Savoy cabbage cut into strips and seasoned with oil flavoured with a clove of garlic.

SALSICCE IN TEGAME
Serves 4
8 Italian sausages
100 ml/3¹/₂ fl oz dry white wine

FRANKFURTERS WITH SAVOY CABBAGE

Heat the oil in a pan, add the cabbage, season with salt and pepper and cook over a medium heat, stirring frequently, for 5 minutes. Lower the heat, cover and cook for 1 hour. Drizzle the cabbage with vinegar and stir, then remove from the pan and place on a warm serving dish. Meanwhile, cook the frankfurters in simmering water for 10 minutes, then drain. Place on the bed of Savoy cabbage and serve.

WÜRSTEL CON VERZA
Serves 4
5 tablespoons olive oil
1 Savoy cabbage, shredded
white wine vinegar, for drizzling
8 frankfurter sausages
salt and pepper

ZAMPONE

Prick the skin of the zampone with a large needle. Wrap in muslin, place in a pan, add water to cover and bring to the boil. Lower the heat, cover and simmer gently for 3 hours. (The cooking time increases by about 30 minutes for each additional 500g/1 lb 2 oz). Leave to stand in the water for 10 minutes, then drain and slice. Zampone goes well with mashed potatoes or stewed lentils.

ZAMPONE
Serves 4–6
1-kg/2¹/₄-lb zampone (stuffed pig's trotter), soaked overnight in cold water and drained

OFFAL

Pâté de foie gras is one of the gastronomic symbols of France, home of culinary elegance. Its sophisticated flavour has raised the prestige of liver to its highest level. It is, in fact, one of the most highly prized members of the vast offal family, which also includes heart, lights, kidney ('red offal'), brains, sweetbreads, bone marrow ('white offal'), tripe and tongue, as well as the head, trotters and tail. Kidney is the basic ingredient of some very tasty recipes. Heart and liver have a lot of recipes in common. Lights and pluck, one of the least popular and most inexpensive kinds of offal are, nevertheless, an essential ingredient for some authentic soups. Brains, sweetbreads and bone marrow are delicious and delicate. Fresh, pickled or smoked tongue is used in a variety of tasty and fairly popular recipes. Calf's head is also part of the offal family. Trotters, which involve laborious preparation, are the key ingredient of the famous tasty nervetti. Offal may not suit every cook's sensibilities, but it forms an essential part of Italian meat cookery and can provide many of the richest and most delicious flavours of this cuisine.

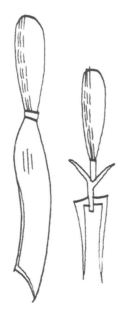

SWEETBREADS

Sweetbreads – almost always from calves, although lamb sweetbreads may also be available – are delicate and have a high nutritional value. The classic way to bring out their flavour is to fry them in butter. They are also delicious coated in breadcrumbs and fried. They are highly recommended for thickening and softening stuffing and giving it a hint of sophistication.

QUANTITIES
AND COOKING TIMES

→ Allow about 120 g/4 oz per serving.

→ Soak the sweetbreads in plenty of cold water, changing it at least three or four times.

→ Parboil for about 5–6 minutes in lightly salted, boiling water, drain and leave to cool.

→ Carefully remove all membrane, paying care not to damage the delicate texture.

ANIMELLE AL CRESCIONE

Serves 6

2 carrots

1 fresh flat-leaf parsley sprig

1 fresh thyme sprig

800 g/1³/₄ lb sweetbreads, soaked and drained

65 g/2¹/₂ oz butter

1 onion, finely chopped

1 tablespoon plain flour

100 ml/3¹/₂ fl oz Madeira

350 ml/12 fl oz white wine

1 tablespoon double cream

1 bunch of watercress

salt and pepper

SWEETBREADS WITH WATERCRESS

Put one of the carrots and the parsley and thyme into a pan, add about 1 litre/1³/₄ pints water, bring to the boil and simmer for 30 minutes. Finely chop the remaining carrot. Remove the stock from the heat and leave to cool slightly, then add the sweetbreads and bring back to the boil. Lower the heat and simmer for 10 minutes, then drain and remove the membrane. Melt the butter in a pan, add the chopped carrot and the onion and cook over a low heat, stirring occasionally, for 5 minutes. Add the sweetbreads and cook for a few minutes, then season with salt and pepper to taste. Stir in the flour, then stir in the Madeira and white wine and cook until evaporated. Add the cream and cook until thickened. Transfer the sweetbreads to a warm serving dish. Add the leaves and thinnest stems of the watercress to the pan and simmer for 10 minutes. Ladle the sauce into a food processor and process to a purée. Pour the sauce over the sweetbreads and serve.

SWEETBREADS AU GRATIN WITH PEAS

Parboil the sweetbreads in lightly salted, boiling water for 5–6 minutes, then drain, leave to cool slightly and remove the membrane. Melt 25 g/1 oz of the butter in a pan, add the carrots and onions and cook over a low heat, stirring occasionally, for 5 minutes. Add the thyme and season with salt and pepper. Add the sweetbreads to the pan, pour in the wine and 150 ml/¼ pint water and cook for 5 minutes. Remove the sweetbreads from the pan, slice thinly and keep warm. Pass the cooking juices and vegetables through a food mill. Melt 50 g/2 oz of the remaining butter in a frying pan, stir in the flour and add the puréed cooking juices. Stir over a low heat for about 10 minutes. Preheat the oven to 180°C/350°F/Gas Mark 4. Grease an ovenproof dish with butter. Meanwhile, cook the peas in a pan with the remaining butter and 2 tablespoons warm water. In another pan mix the sauce made from the puréed cooking juices with the cream and the peas, season with salt and cook over a medium heat until thickened. Place the sweetbreads in the prepared dish, spoon the pea sauce over them and sprinkle with the Parmesan. Bake for about 10 minutes until golden, then serve straight from the dish.

ANIMELLE AL GRATIN CON PISELLI
Serves 6
675 g/1½ lb sweetbreads, soaked and drained
120 g/4 oz butter, plus extra for greasing
2 carrots, chopped
2 small onions, chopped
1 fresh thyme sprig
175 ml/6 fl oz dry white wine
40 g/1½ oz plain flour
250 g/9 oz frozen peas
1 tablespoon double cream
25 g/1 oz Parmesan cheese, freshly grated
salt and pepper

SWEETBREADS WITH CREAM AND MUSHROOMS

Lightly dust the sweetbreads with flour and gently shake off any excess. Melt 50 g/2 oz of the butter in a pan, add the sweetbreads and cook, turning frequently, for about 10 minutes, then season with salt and pepper. Mix together the cream and lemon juice in a bowl, pour the mixture over the sweetbreads, cover and cook over a medium heat until thickened. Meanwhile, heat the remaining butter and the oil in another saucepan, add the mushrooms and cook over a very low heat, stirring occasionally, for 20 minutes. Gently stir the mushrooms into the sweetbreads, season with salt and transfer to a warm serving dish.

ANIMELLE ALLA PANNA E FUNGHI
Serves 4
500 g/1 lb 2 oz sweetbreads,
soaked, drained and thinly sliced
plain flour, for dusting
80 g/3 oz butter
200 ml/7 fl oz double cream
juice of ½ lemon, strained
2 tablespoons olive oil
300 g/11 oz mushrooms, thinly sliced
salt and pepper

SWEETBREADS WITH MADEIRA

ANIMELLE AL MADERA

Serves 4

600 g/1 lb 5 oz sweetbreads, soaked and drained

plain flour, for dusting

40 g/1¹/₂ oz butter

175 ml/6 fl oz dry Madeira

salt and pepper

Parboil the sweetbreads in lightly salted water for 5–6 minutes, then drain and leave to cool slightly. Carefully remove the membrane with a small sharp knife, cut into even pieces and dust lightly with flour. Melt the butter in a pan, add the sweetbreads and cook over a low heat, shaking the pan frequently, until golden brown. Season lightly with salt and pepper and cook for a further 10 minutes. Pour in the Madeira, bring just to the boil and cook, stirring occasionally, until the cooking juices have thickened. Transfer to a warm serving dish.

SWEETBREADS IN WHITE WINE

ANIMELLE AL VINO BIANCO

Serves 4

600 g/1 lb 5 oz sweetbreads, soaked and drained

plain flour, for dusting

40 g/1¹/₂ oz butter

2 tablespoons olive oil

1 garlic clove

175 ml/6 fl oz dry white wine

1 fresh flat-leaf parsley sprig, chopped

salt

Parboil the sweetbreads in lightly salted water for 5–6 minutes, then drain and leave to cool slightly. Carefully remove the membrane and slice thinly. Dust lightly with flour. Heat the butter and oil in a pan, add the garlic and cook until browned, then remove and discard it. Add the sweetbreads and cook until browned on both sides. Pour in the wine, cook until it has evaporated, then lower the heat and cook for a further 10 minutes. Season with salt to taste, sprinkle with the parsley and serve.

SWEETBREADS WITH GLOBE ARTICHOKES

ANIMELLE CON I CARCIOFI

Serves 4

juice of ¹/₂ lemon, strained

4 globe artichokes

50 g/2 oz butter

1 tablespoon olive oil

500 g/1 lb 2 oz sweetbreads, soaked and drained

100 g/3¹/₂ oz prosciutto, cut into strips

175 ml/6 fl oz dry white wine

salt and pepper

Half-fill a bowl with water and stir in the lemon juice. Break off the artichoke stems and remove the tough outer leaves and chokes. As each one is ready, place it in the acidulated water to prevent discoloration. Drain the artichokes, cut into wedges, then slice thinly. Heat 40 g/1¹/₂ oz of the butter and the olive oil in a pan, then add the artichokes and 5 tablespoons water and cook over a low heat for about 30 minutes. Parboil the sweetbreads in lightly salted water for 5–6 minutes, then drain and leave to cool slightly. Carefully remove the membrane, then chop. Heat the remaining butter and the prosciutto in a frying pan, add the sweetbreads, season lightly with salt and pepper and cook for 10 minutes. Add the cooked artichokes, sprinkle with the wine and cook until the liquid has evaporated. Transfer to a warm serving dish.

SWEETBREADS WITH JERUSALEM ARTICHOKES

Parboil the sweetbreads in lightly salted water for 5–6 minutes, then drain and leave to cool slightly. Carefully remove the membrane, then slice thinly. Melt the butter in a frying pan, add the onion and cook over a low heat, stirring occasionally, for about 10 minutes. Sprinkle with the Marsala and flour, season with salt and pepper and cook until the liquid has evaporated. Add the sweetbreads and cook for 10 minutes, adding the stock a ladleful at a time as it is absorbed. (You will not need it all.) Preheat the oven to 180°C/350°F/Gas Mark 4. Generously grease an ovenproof dish with butter. Parboil the Jerusalem artichokes for 10 minutes, then drain and slice. Arrange them on the base of the prepared dish, sprinkle with the Parmesan, place the sweetbreads on top and spoon the cooking juices over them. Sprinkle with 5 tablespoons of the remaining stock and bake for 10 minutes. Serve straight from same dish.

ANIMELLE CON I TOPINAMBUR

Serves 4

500 g/1 lb 2 oz sweetbreads, soaked and drained

50 g/2 oz butter, plus extra for greasing

1 small onion, very finely chopped

100 ml/3¹/₂ fl oz Marsala

1 tablespoon plain flour

1 quantity Vegetable Stock (see page 209)

400 g/14 oz Jerusalem artichokes

2 tablespoons Parmesan cheese, freshly grated

salt and pepper

SWEETBREADS IN BREADCRUMBS

Parboil the sweetbreads in lightly salted water for 5–6 minutes, then drain and leave to cool slightly. Carefully remove the membrane, then slice thinly and dust with flour, shaking off any excess. Beat the egg with a pinch of salt in a shallow dish and spread out the breadcrumbs in another shallow dish. Dip the sweetbreads first in the beaten egg, then in the bread-crumbs. Melt the clarified butter in a frying pan, add the sweetbreads and cook for 5–6 minutes until golden brown. Season with salt to taste, remove from the pan with a fish slice and drain on kitchen paper. Serve on a bed of Milanese risotto.

ANIMELLE IMPANATE

Serves 4

600 g/1 lb 5 oz sweetbreads, soaked and drained

plain flour, for dusting

1 egg

80 g/3 oz breadcrumbs

50 g/2 oz Clarified Butter (see page 88)

salt

Milanese Risotto (see page 330), to serve

BRAINS

Brains are delicate and have a high nutritional value. They should only be eaten when extremely fresh. They are mostly used in quick, simple dishes, for example cooked in butter or covered in breadcrumbs and fried, or to soften and thicken meat and vegetable stuffings. Their flavour goes very well with the fragrance of truffles. In almost all recipes brains may be used interchangeably with sweetbreads. Outside Italy lamb's and sheep's brains are the most popular. Calf's and ox brains are also sometimes available, however there are still concerns about BSE. In some countries, brains can also be purchased frozen. Ox and calf's brains weigh 300–400 g/11–14 oz, lamb's brains weigh about 120 g/ 4 oz and sheep's brains about 150 g/5 oz.

QUANTITIES AND COOKING TIMES

→ In general, allow about 150 g/5 oz per serving.

→ Soak brains in warm water for 30 minutes. Remove the membrane and any traces of blood very gently with a small sharp knife.

→ Soak in cold water, which should be changed several times until the brains become white.

→ For recipes where the brains need pre-cooking, bring plenty of water to the boil with 1 tablespoon vinegar and the juice of half a lemon. Immerse ox brains and simmer for a few minutes. Calves' brains need a little less time. Drain and refresh under cold, running water.

→ To boil brains, first of all prepare a thick Vegetable Stock (see page 209), strain and leave to cool slightly. Immerse the brains in the stock, bring to the boil and cook over a very low heat for about 10 minutes.

BRAINS WITH TOMATO SAUCE

Soak the brains in cold water for 10 minutes. Meanwhile, prepare the sauce. Mix together the tomatoes, onion, garlic and basil in a bowl and blend for 2 minutes with a hand-held food processor. Stir in a dash of Tabasco, season with salt and pepper and set aside in a cool place. Drain the brains and cut into medium-sized cubes with a small sharp knife. Beat the egg with a pinch of salt in a shallow dish. Mix together the cornflour and lemon rind in another shallow dish and spread out the breadcrumbs in a third. Dip the brains first in the egg, then in the cornflour mixture and, finally, in the breadcrumbs. Heat the oil and butter in a frying pan, add the brains and cook over a medium heat, turning once, for 4–5 minutes until golden brown. Season with salt, transfer to a warm serving dish and serve with the tomato sauce.

BOCCONCINI DI CERVELLA

Serves 4

600 g/1 lb 5 oz lamb's brains, cleaned

1 egg • 3 tablespoons cornflour

1 teaspoon grated lemon rind

2 tablespoons olive oil

50 g/2 oz breadcrumbs • 25 g/1 oz butter

salt

For the sauce

4 cherry tomatoes, peeled, seeded and chopped

1 onion, thinly sliced • 1 garlic clove

5–6 fresh basil leaves

dash of Tabasco sauce • salt and pepper

BRAINS WITH CAPERS

Preheat the oven to 180°C/350°F/Gas Mark 4. Brush an oven-proof dish with olive oil. Put the brains in a saucepan, add water to cover, bring to the boil and cook for 1 minute. Drain, refresh under cold, running water and drain again. Cut in half and place in the prepared dish. Season with salt and pepper and sprinkle with the capers and olives. Sprinkle with the breadcrumbs and drizzle the oil over them. Bake for about 20 minutes until golden brown and transfer to a warm serving dish.

CERVELLA AI CAPPERI

Serves 4

4 tablespoons olive oil, plus extra for brushing

600 g/1 lb 5 oz brains, cleaned

1 tablespoon capers, drained and rinsed

10 black olives, stoned and sliced

25 g/1 oz fine breadcrumbs

salt and pepper

BRAINS WITH BUTTER AND SAGE

Melt the butter in a frying pan, add the sage and cook over a low heat, stirring occasionally, for about 5 minutes. Add the brains and cook for about 10 minutes until golden brown on both sides. Season with salt and pepper to taste and arrange on a warm serving dish.

CERVELLA AL BURRO E SALVIA

Serves 4

40 g/1½ oz butter

8 fresh sage leaves

600 g/1 lb 5 oz brains, cleaned and thinly sliced

salt and white pepper

BRAINS AU GRATIN

Preheat the oven to 180°C/350°F/Gas Mark 4. Grease an ovenproof dish with butter and sprinkle with sea salt. Briefly blanch the brains in boiling water, then drain and slice. Place the brains in the prepared dish. Mix together the breadcrumbs and parsley and sprinkle the mixture over the brains. Dot with the butter and season with pepper. Bake for 15 minutes, then serve straight from the dish.

CERVELLA AL GRATIN

Serves 4

40 g/1½ oz butter, plus extra for greasing

600 g/1 lb 5 oz brains, cleaned

4 tablespoons coarse breadcrumbs

1 fresh flat-leaf parsley sprig, chopped

sea salt and white pepper

MILANESE-STYLE BRAINS

CERVELLA ALLA MILANESE

Serves 4

600 g/1 lb 5 oz brains, cleaned and sliced

plain flour, for dusting

2 eggs

80 g/3 oz breadcrumbs

100 g/3¹/₂ oz Clarified Butter (see page 88)

salt and pepper

lemon wedges, to garnish

Lightly dust the brains with flour. Beat the eggs with a pinch of salt in a shallow dish and spread out the breadcrumbs in another shallow dish. Dip the brains first in the eggs and then in the breadcrumbs to coat. Melt the clarified butter in a frying pan over a low heat, add the brains and cook until browned on both sides. Season with salt and pepper to taste. Remove with a fish slice and drain on kitchen paper. Place on a warm serving dish and garnish with wedges of lemon.

BRAINS AND BONE MARROW IN CURRY SAUCE

CERVELLA CON FILONI AL CURRY

Serves 4

300 g/11 oz lamb's brains, cleaned

200 g/7 oz calf's brains, cleaned

200 g/7 oz bone marrow

1 onion, halved

1 carrot

1 celery stick

50 g/2 oz butter, plus extra for greasing

3 tablespoons plain flour

1 tablespoon curry powder

salt

Put the brains and bone marrow in a saucepan, add cold water to cover, one of the onion halves, the carrot and celery and season with salt. Bring to the boil, lower the heat and simmer for 20 minutes. Finely chop the remaining onion half. Melt the butter over a low heat, add the chopped onion and cook for about 5 minutes. Sprinkle with the flour and stir in. Pour a ladleful of the offal cooking juices into a bowl, stir in the curry powder and pour the mixture into the pan with sauce. Cook over a low heat, stirring frequently, for about 30 minutes. Preheat the oven to 180°C/350°F/Gas Mark 4. Lightly grease an ovenproof dish. Drain and chop the meat, place in the prepared dish and pour the curry sauce over it. Bake for 10–15 minutes, then remove from the oven and leave to stand for 5 minutes. Serve straight from the dish.

BRAINS IN ANCHOVY SAUCE

CERVELLA IN SALSA DI ACCIUGHE

Serves 4

600 g/1 lb 5 oz brains, cleaned • ¹/₂ onion

1 carrot • 1 celery stick

1 fresh flat-leaf parsley sprig • salt

For the sauce

2 salted anchovies, heads removed, cleaned and filleted (see page 596), soaked in cold water for 10 minutes and drained • 50 g/2 oz butter

1 tablespoon capers, drained and rinsed

1 tablespoon fresh flat-leaf parsley, chopped

2 tablespoons white wine vinegar

salt and pepper

Put the brains in a saucepan, add cold water to cover, the onion, carrot, celery and parsley and season with salt. Bring to the boil, then lower the heat and simmer for 10–15 minutes. Drain, slice and place the brains on a warm serving dish. Set aside and keep warm. Make the sauce. Chop the anchovy fillets. Melt the butter in a frying pan over a low heat, add the parsley, capers and anchovies and mix well. Sprinkle with the vinegar and cook until it has evaporated, then season with salt and pepper to taste. Cook for a further 5 minutes, then remove the pan from the heat, pour the sauce over the brains and serve.

BRAIN ROULADES WITH TRUFFLE

Blanch the brains briefly in boiling water, then drain and slice. Melt 25 g/1 oz of the butter in a frying pan, add the prosciutto, porcini and truffle and cook over a low heat, stirring occasionally, for about 5 minutes. Season with salt and pepper and pour the mixture into the béchamel sauce. Cut the caul into eight or more squares and place two or more slices of brains and 1 tablespoon of the sauce mixture in the middle of each. Roll up and secure with cocktail sticks. Beat the egg with a pinch of salt in a shallow dish and spread out the breadcrumbs in another shallow dish. Dip the roulades first in the egg and then in the breadcrumbs. Melt the remaining butter in a frying pan, add the roulades and cook, turning frequently, until browned all over. Remove with a fish slice and drain on kitchen paper. Place on a warm serving dish and garnish with lemon slices.

INVOLTINI DI CERVELLA AL TARTUFO

Serves 4

600 g/1 lb 5 oz brains, cleaned

80 g/3 oz butter

100 g/3¹/₂ oz prosciutto, diced

1 porcini, diced

1 small black truffle, diced

1 quantity Béchamel Sauce (see page 50)

1 pig's caul, soaked in warm water

for 3 minutes and drained

1 egg

80 g/3 oz fairly coarse breadcrumbs

salt and pepper

lemon slices, to garnish

SMALL BRAIN MOULDS WITH HERBS

Heat the oil and butter in a pan, add the onion and cook over a low heat, stirring occasionally, for 5 minutes. Stir in the herbs, add 150 ml/¹/₄ pint water and simmer for 15 minutes. Add the brains, sprinkle with the lemon juice and season with salt and pepper. Simmer, uncovered, over a low heat the until liquid has reduced Meanwhile, preheat the oven to 180°C/350°F/Gas Mark 4. Grease four ramekins with butter. Remove the brains from the pan and chop. Beat the eggs with a pinch of salt, then stir them into the herb sauce. Divide the brains and sauce among the ramekins, place on a baking sheet and bake for about 30 minutes or until a cocktail stick inserted into the moulds comes out dry. Remove the moulds from the oven, turn out in a ring on a warm serving dish and garnish with a few leaves of radicchio.

SFORMATINI ALLE ERBE

Serves 4

2 tablespoons olive oil

25 g/1 oz butter, plus extra for greasing

1 onion, chopped

1 tablespoon chopped fresh chives

1 tablespoon chopped fresh tarragon

1 tablespoon fresh flat-leaf parsley, chopped

600 g/1 lb 5 oz brains, cleaned

juice of ¹/₂ lemon, strained

5 eggs

salt and pepper

radicchio leaves, to garnish

OXTAIL

Oxtail is a very tasty, inexpensive cut of meat with lots of bone. It is particularly recommended for braising and stewing, and is an excellent ingredient in mixed boiled meat dishes. Calf's codino (literally: small tail) is something completely different. It is recommended for roasting and is a true cut of meat. It is called codino because it is the rump of the animal. Where fresh oxtail is difficult to obtain, frozen may be available.

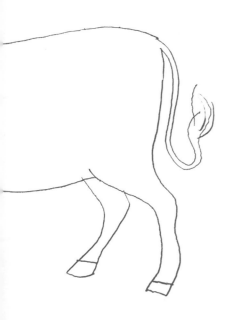

**QUANTITIES
AND COOKING TIMES**

→ Allow about 1 kg/2¹/₄ lb oxtail for four servings.

→ Ask the butcher to cut the tail into fairly large pieces, then leave to soak in cold water for a few hours.

→ To separate the meat from the bone more easily, it is useful to parboil the pieces for a few minutes in lightly salted water before following the recipe.

OXTAIL WITH PANCETTA

Soak the oxtail in three changes of cold water for a total of 2 hours, then drain and pat dry with kitchen paper. Heat the oil and butter in a pan, add the pancetta and cook, stirring occasionally, for 5 minutes. Add the oxtail and cook, turning frequently, until browned all over. Add the wine and cook until it has evaporated. Add the onion, carrots, celery and garlic and season with salt and pepper to taste. Stir and cook for a few minutes more, then add enough hot water to cover. Cover with a lid and simmer over a medium heat for about 3 hours until the meat comes away from the bones and the cooking juices have thickened.

CODA DI MANZO ALLA PANCETTA

Serves 4

1 kg/2¼ lb oxtail, cut into pieces

2 tablespoons olive oil

25 g/1 oz butter

65 g/2½ oz pancetta, chopped

175 ml/6 fl oz dry white wine

1 onion, finely chopped

2 carrots, finely chopped

1 celery stick, finely chopped

1 garlic clove, finely chopped

salt and pepper

OXTAIL VACCINARA

Bring a large pan of salted water to the boil, add the oxtail, carrot, one of the onions and the bouquet garni and simmer for 1 hour. Chop the remaining onion. Heat the oil and pork fat in another pan, add the chopped onion and the garlic and cook until the garlic turns brown, then remove and discard it. Drain the oxtail, add it to the pan and cook, turning frequently, for a few minutes until browned all over. Pour in the wine and cook until it has evaporated. Season with salt and pepper, add the passata, cover and simmer over a medium heat for 1½ hours, adding a little stock if necessary. Stir in the celery and simmer gently for a further 10–15 minutes until tender.

CODA DI MANZO ALLA VACCINARA

Serves 4

1 kg/2¼ lb oxtail, cut into pieces

1 carrot

2 onions

1 bouquet garni

4 tablespoons olive oil

50 g/2 oz pork fat, pounded

1 garlic clove, lightly crushed

175 ml/6 fl oz dry white wine

750 ml/1¼ pints passata

4 celery hearts, cut into batons

150–300 ml/¼–½ pint Meat Stock

(see page 208) (optional)

salt and pepper

ROASTING

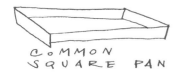

COMMON SQUARE PAN

PLUCK
AND LIGHTS

Lights refers only to the lungs, but the Italian expression coratella d'agnello and the somewhat archaic English term 'pluck' also include the heart, liver and other lamb offal. It is rarely, if ever, sold as pluck nowadays, outside Italy. This is a very tasty form of offal and suitable for a number of recipes.

QUANTITIES AND COOKING TIMES

→ Allow 150 g/5 oz per serving.

→ The individual parts are normally used in this order: first the lungs, then the heart and other offal, and finally the liver, which cooks most rapidly.

TOMATO

CORATELLA D'AGNELLO ALLA ROMANA

Serves 4

50 g/2 oz butter

6 tablespoons olive oil

4 globe artichokes, cut into wedges

500 g/1 lb 2 oz lights or pluck, chopped

salt and pepper

ROMAN LAMB'S LIGHTS

Heat half the butter and half the oil in a pan, add the artichokes and 2 tablespoons hot water and simmer for about 15 minutes until tender. Meanwhile, heat the remaining butter and oil in another pan, add the meat (in the order described above if using pluck) and cook until lightly browned all over and cooked through. Season with salt and pepper, add the meat to the artichokes and mix well. Cook for a few minutes more, then serve.

LIGHTS IN MARSALA

Lightly dust the meat with flour. Melt the clarified butter in a frying pan, add the meat (in the order described opposite if using pluck) and cook over a high heat until browned all over. Season with salt and pepper and remove the meat from the pan. Mix together the flour and Marsala in a bowl, stir into the cooking juices and cook until reduced by half. Stir in the Worcestershire sauce and pour the mixture over the meat.

CORATELLA D'AGNELLO AL MARSALA

Serves 4

600 g/1 lb 5 oz lights or pluck, sliced

1 tablespoon plain flour, plus extra for dusting

65 g/2¹/₂ oz Clarified Butter (see page 88)

175 ml/6 fl oz dry Marsala

dash of Worcestershire sauce

salt and pepper

GREENGROCER'S LIGHTS

Chop the lights. If using pluck, chop the lungs, heart, spleen and other offal and slice the liver. Mix together the onion, carrot, garlic and parsley in a bowl. Heat the oil in a frying pan, add the vegetable mixture and cook over a low heat, stirring occasionally, for 5 minutes. Add the lights and cook for a few minutes, then, if using pluck, add all the other offal, except the liver, and cook for 3 minutes. Add the liver and cook for a further 2 minutes. Season with salt and pepper to taste, stir in the lemon juice and serve.

CORATELLA D'AGNELLO DELL'ORTOLANO

Serves 4

600 g/1 lb 5 oz lights or pluck

1 onion, finely chopped

1 carrot, finely chopped

1 garlic clove, finely chopped

1 fresh flat-leaf parsley sprig, chopped

3 tablespoons olive oil

juice of ¹/₂ lemon, strained

salt and pepper

FRIED LIGHTS

Dice the lights. If using pluck, dice the heart, spleen and other offal and slice the liver. Heat the oil and garlic in a frying pan and cook until the garlic turns brown, then remove and discard it. Add the celery and carrots and cook for a few minutes. Add the lights, mix gently and cook for a few minutes, then add all the other offal except the liver and cook over a medium heat for 3 minutes. Finally, add the liver, mix well and cook for a further 3–4 minutes. Season with salt and pepper to taste, stir in the vinegar and cook until it has evaporated. Sprinkle with the thyme and serve.

CORATELLA D'AGNELLO IN TEGAME

Serves 4

600 g/1 lb 5 oz lights or pluck

3 tablespoons olive oil

1 garlic clove

1 celery stick, chopped

2 carrots, chopped

50 ml/2 fl oz cider vinegar

2 fresh thyme sprigs, chopped

salt and pepper

HEART

Ox or calf's heart may be considered an excellent and economical alternative to other meat, as its nutritional value is equal to that of lean veal. However, owing to its tougher muscle fibres, it is more difficult to digest. A calf's heart weighs 800 g–1 kg/1³/₄–2¹/₄ lb. An ox heart may even reach 2 kg/4¹/₂ lb. When choosing, make sure the meat is elastic and the colour bright. Heart is prepared by slicing, then removing any lumps together with the larger nodes with arteries and veins.

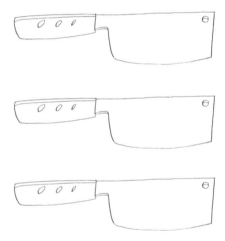

**QUANTITIES
AND COOKING TIMES**

→ Allow about 150–200 g/ 5–7 oz per serving.

→ Grill 1-cm/¹/₂-inch thick slices for 2 minutes on each side.

→ Allow no longer than 10 minutes in a frying pan, turning halfway through the cooking time.

HEART KEBABS

Put the heart in a bowl. Mix together the oil, lemon juice, wine, oregano and a pinch of pepper, pour the mixture over the meat and leave to marinate for 3 hours. Preheat the grill. Drain the meat, reserving the marinade, and thread on to skewers, alternating with the pepper and onion slices. Brush with the reserved marinade and grill under a medium-high heat, turning frequently, for 4 minutes. Season with salt and pepper and serve.

CUBETTI DI CUORE ALLO SPIEDO

Serves 4

800 g/1³/₄ lb heart, cut into cubes

2 tablespoons olive oil • juice of 1 lemon, strained

175 ml/6 fl oz dry white wine

generous pinch of dried oregano

2 red peppers, halved, seeded and cut into thick slices

1 onion, sliced • salt and pepper

HEART WITH HERBS

Reserve 2 tablespoons of the olive oil and mix the remainder with the lemon juice in a dish. Add the heart and leave to marinate for 1 hour. Drain the heart and lard with the strips of pancetta. Heat the reserved oil and the butter in a frying pan, add the onion and garlic and cook over a low heat, stirring occasionally, for 5 minutes. Lightly dust the heart with flour, add to the pan and cook for 2 minutes. Pour in the wine and cook until it has evaporated. Season with salt and pepper to taste and add the herbs. Add the stock or water, cover and simmer for 25 minutes. Slice the heart and serve in its gravy.

CUORE AGLI AROMI

Serves 4

175 ml/6 fl oz olive oil

juice of 1 lemon, strained

800 g/1³/₄ lb heart, halved and cleaned

50 g/2 oz pancetta, cut into strips • 25 g/1 oz butter

1 onion, chopped • 1 garlic clove, crushed

plain flour, for dusting

175 ml/6 fl oz dry white wine

1 fresh flat-leaf parsley sprig, chopped

4 fresh sage leaves, chopped

4 fresh basil leaves, chopped

150 ml/¹/₄ pint hot Meat Stock (see page 208) or water

salt and pepper

GRILLED HEART

Preheat the grill. Melt the butter with a little salt in a double boiler and brush on both sides of the slices of heart, then dip the slices in the breadcrumbs. Place the bacon on the grill rack and put a slice of heart on each. Grill for 2 minutes on each side. Transfer to a warm serving dish and serve with mashed potatoes.

CUORE ALLA GRIGLIA

Serves 4

50 g/2 oz butter

800 g/1³/₄ lb heart, cut into 1-cm/¹/₂-inch slices

80 g/3 oz fine breadcrumbs

100 g/3¹/₂ oz bacon rashers, halved

salt

mashed potatoes, to serve

HEART WITH ANCHOVIES

Heat the butter and olive oil in a frying pan, add the heart and cook, turning frequently, for 5 minutes. Add the anchovies and cook until they have disintegrated. Sprinkle with the parsley and serve.

CUORE ALLE ACCIUGHE

Serves 4

25 g/1 oz butter

2 tablespoons olive oil • 800 g/1³/₄ lb heart, sliced

5 canned anchovy fillets in oil, drained and chopped

1 tablespoon fresh flat-leaf parsley, chopped

LIVER

Calf's liver is delicate and flavoursome, whereas ox liver is less tender. Both contain quite a bit of fat. The most valuable liver from the dietary point of view is pig's liver, followed by lamb's, ox, calf's and chicken's. Pâtés, terrines and numerous pies owe their distinctive flavour to liver.

QUANTITIES AND COOKING TIMES

→ Allow about 150 g/5 oz per person.

→ Liver should be eaten extremely fresh and, like all offal, it needs careful rinsing in cold water.

→ Fresh liver is a brownish-red colour. When it is not fresh it has tints of purple and a limp consistency.

→ Remove the membrane and any sinewy parts. Liver should be cooked for a few minutes over a high heat and turned frequently.

→ Pig's liver takes longer to cook and is nearly always prepared by cutting it into small pieces and wrapping it in white caul fat.

→ Salt should be added after cooking, otherwise liver becomes tough.

FEGATELLI NELLA RETE

Serves 4

1 pig's caul

12–24 bay leaves

600 g/1 lb 5 oz pig's liver, cut into large cubes

50 g/2 oz lard or 4 tablespoons olive oil

salt and pepper

PIG'S LIVER IN A NET

Soak the caul in warm water for 3 minutes, then drain and cut into large squares. Place a bay leaf in the middle of each square with a cube of liver on top. Wrap the caul into a parcel and secure with a cocktail stick. Melt the lard or heat the oil in a frying pan, add the parcels and cook, turning frequently, for a few minutes. Season with salt and pepper and stir. Transfer to a warm serving dish.

LIVER WITH SHALLOTS

Dust the liver with flour. Heat 25 g/1 oz of the butter and the oil in a frying pan, add the liver and cook for 2 minutes on each side. Season with salt and pepper. Transfer the liver to a serving dish and keep warm. Add the shallots to the pan and cook over a low heat, stirring occasionally, for about 10 minutes. Pour in the wine and cook until reduced by half. Add the remaining butter and remove the pan from the heat. Pour the sauce over the liver and serve.

FEGATO AGLI SCALOGNI

Serves 4

600 g/1 lb 5 oz liver, sliced

plain flour for dusting

40 g/1¹/₂ oz butter

2 tablespoons olive oil

4 shallots, sliced

175 ml/6 fl oz dry white wine

salt and pepper

LIVER WITH BUTTER AND SAGE

Beat the eggs with a pinch of salt in a shallow dish, add the liver and leave for a few minutes. Melt the butter over a low heat with the garlic and sage in a frying pan until they turn brown, then remove and discard. Drain the liver, add to the pan, increase the heat to medium and cook for 2 minutes on each side, then lower the heat cook for a few minutes more, turning frequently, until cooked through. Season with salt and pepper to taste and serve.

FEGATO AL BURRO E SALVIA

Serves 4

2 eggs

600 g/1 lb 5 oz liver, sliced

50 g/2 oz butter

1 garlic clove

5–6 fresh sage leaves

salt and pepper

VENETO–STYLE LIVER

Heat the oil in a frying pan, add the onions and cook over a low heat, stirring occasionally, for about 10 minutes until lightly browned. Add the wine, increase the heat to high and cook until it has evaporated. Stir in the parsley and add the liver. Cook, turning frequently, for 4–5 minutes. Season with salt and pepper to taste and transfer to a warm serving dish.

FEGATO ALLA VENETA

Serves 4

4–5 tablespoons olive oil

250 g/9 oz onions, thinly sliced

175 ml/6 fl oz dry white wine

1 tablespoon fresh flat-leaf parsley, chopped

500 g/1 lb 2 oz liver, sliced

salt and pepper

LIVER WITH LEMON

Lightly dust the liver with flour and shake off the excess. Heat the butter and oil in a frying pan over a low heat, add the liver, increase the heat to high and cook, turning frequently, for a few minutes until cooked through. Season lightly with salt and pepper and cook for a few minutes more. Transfer the liver to a serving dish and keep warm. Stir the lemon juice into the pan and heat. Stir in the parsley, then pour the sauce over the liver and serve.

FEGATO AL LIMONE

Serves 4

600 g/1 lb 5 oz liver, sliced

plain flour, for dusting

25 g/1 oz butter

2 tablespoons olive oil

juice of 1 lemon, strained

1 tablespoon fresh flat-leaf parsley, chopped

salt and pepper

LIVER UCCELLETTO

FEGATO ALL'UCCELLETTO

Serves 4

80 g/3 oz prosciutto, sliced
500 g/1 lb 2 oz liver, thinly sliced
8 fresh sage leaves • 50 g/2 oz pancetta, diced
8 bread slices, crusts removed, cubed
2 tablespoons olive oil
25 g/1 oz butter • salt and pepper

Put a small slice of prosciutto on each slice of liver and roll up. Thread the roulades on to long wooden or metal skewers, alternating with the sage leaves, pancetta and slices of bread. Heat the oil and butter in a frying pan, add the kebabs and cook over a high heat, turning frequently, for 5 minutes. Season lightly with salt and pepper and serve immediately.

LIVER IN MERLOT

FEGATO AL MERLOT

Serves 4

600 g/1 lb 5 oz liver, thinly sliced
plain flour, for dusting
50 g/2 oz butter
175 ml/6 fl oz Merlot wine
salt and pepper

Lightly dust the liver with flour and shake off any excess. Melt the butter in a frying pan over a low heat, add the liver and cook for 2 minutes on each side. Add 1 tablespoon hot water and the wine, increase the heat to high and cook for 5 minutes or until the wine has evaporated. Season and transfer to a warm serving dish. This liver is traditionally served with fried polenta.

LIVER WITH GLOBE ARTICHOKES

FEGATO CON CARCIOFI

Serves 4

juice of 1 lemon, strained
4 globe artichokes stems,
outer leaves and chokes removed
7 tablespoons olive oil
600 g/1 lb 5 oz liver, sliced
salt and pepper

Half-fill a bowl with water and stir in half the lemon juice. Cut the artichokes in half and add to the acidulated water as soon as each one is prepared to prevent discoloration. Drain and slice thinly. Heat 4 tablespoons of the oil in a saucepan, add the artichokes and cook over a low heat for 20 minutes. Add 1 tablespoon hot water if necessary and season lightly with salt. Heat the remaining oil in a frying pan, add the liver and cook for 2 minutes on each side, then sprinkle with the remaining lemon juice. Season with salt and pepper, stir well, then transfer to the pan of artichokes. Spoon the mixture on to a warm serving dish.

SWEET–AND–SOUR LIVER

FEGATO IN AGRODOLCE

Serves 4

50 g/2 oz sultanas, soaked in warm water
25 g/1 oz butter
2 tablespoons olive oil
600 g/1 lb 5 oz pig's liver, sliced
1 tablespoon plain flour
1 tablespoon white wine vinegar
salt and pepper

Heat the butter and oil in a frying pan, add the liver and cook, turning frequently, for a few minutes until tender. Season lightly with salt and pepper, then transfer to a serving dish and keep warm. Drain and squeeze out the sultanas, dust with the flour and sprinkle into the pan. Season lightly with salt and cook for 3 minutes, then stir well. Add the vinegar and 1 tablespoon cold water, season with pepper, increase the heat to high and cook until the liquid has evaporated. Simmer for a further 3 minutes, then pour the sauce over the liver and serve.

TONGUE

The most delicate tongue, as it is the smallest and most tender, is calf's tongue. Ox tongue is larger and heavier, and needs longer cooking which decreases its nutritional value. It also has a more powerful flavour. Tongue is delicious boiled, braised or pickled.

QUANTITIES AND COOKING TIMES

→ Allow about 1 kg/2¼ lb for 4 servings.

→ Both calf's and ox tongue are available whole or already cleaned.

→ Before cooking, soak the tongue in cold water for several hours, changing the water a number of times.

→ A calf's tongue weighs about 500 g/1 lb 2 oz and cooks in 1–1½ hours. An ox tongue may weigh up to 2 kg/4½ lb and cooks in 3–3½ hours. A pig's tongue weighs 300–400 g/11–14 oz and cooks in about 35 minutes.

→ To boil tongue, immerse it in cold, salted water with an onion, celery stick, carrot and a few cloves. When cooked, drain and skin. Tongue should always be served with spicy sauces.

→ When the cooking liquid is to be used later as stock, parboil the tongue for 15 minutes, skin it and then return it to the pan and continue to cook it as normal.

→ Tongue should be sliced diagonally into very thin slices.

→ Preparing smoked tongue requires a lot of skill, so it is best to buy it ready smoked from a butcher or a delicatessen. It is delicious sliced and served with liver pâté and aspic.

BOILED SMOKED TONGUE

Fill a large saucepan with cold water, add the tongue, carrot, celery, onion and a pinch of salt and bring to the boil. Lower the heat and simmer for about 3 hours, depending on the thickness of the tongue. Drain the tongue, skin and slice. Serve with a selection of spicy sauces (see pages 64 to 76) or with mashed potatoes flavoured with 2 tablespoons Parmesan cheese, freshly grated.

LINGUA AFFUMICATA E LESSATA

Serves 4

½ smoked tongue, soaked overnight in cold water and drained

1 carrot

1 celery stick

1 onion

salt

TONGUE WITH GREEN OLIVES

LINGUA ALLE OLIVE VERDI

Serves 4

1 tongue, soaked overnight in cold water and drained

25 g/1 oz butter

1 tablespoon olive oil

1 onion, finely chopped

1 carrot, finely chopped

1 celery stick, finely chopped

20 stoned green olives

salt and pepper

Cook the tongue in salted, boiling water for 20 minutes, then drain and skin without allowing it to cool. Heat the butter and oil in a frying pan, add the onion, carrot and celery and cook over a low heat, stirring occasionally, for 5 minutes. Meanwhile, coarsely chop 10 of the olives. Stir the chopped olives into the pan, add the tongue, pour in 150 ml/¼ pint warm water and simmer until the tongue is tender. Season with salt and pepper to taste, stir in the remaining olives, mix and cook for a further 3–4 minutes. Slice the tongue, place on a warm serving dish and spoon the sauce over it.

BRAISED TONGUE

LINGUA BRASATA

Serves 4

1 tongue, soaked overnight in cold water and drained

40 g/1½ oz butter

3 tablespoons olive oil

2 onions, thinly sliced

3 carrots, sliced

175 ml/6 fl oz dry white wine

250 g/9 oz canned tomatoes

salt and pepper

Parboil the tongue in salted, boiling water for 20 minutes, then drain and skin. Meanwhile, heat the butter and oil in a pan, add the onions and carrots and cook over a low heat, stirring occasionally, for 5 minutes. Add the tongue, cover and cook for 30 minutes. Pour in the wine and cook until it has evaporated, then season with salt and pepper to taste and cook for a further 2 minutes. Mash the tomatoes with their can juices in a bowl, add to the pan, cover and simmer for about 1½ hours until the tongue is tender. Remove the tongue from the pan. Ladle the cooking juices into a food processor and process to a purée. Reheat the purée for a few minutes. Slice the tongue, place on a warm serving dish and spoon the hot purée over it.

TONGUE IN TARTARE SAUCE

LINGUA IN SALSA TARTARA

Serves 4

600 g/1 lb 5 oz tongue

175 ml/6 fl oz white wine vinegar

1 garlic clove • salt and pepper

1 quantity Tartare Sauce (see page 73)

Prepare and boil the tongue as described on page 865. Drain, skin and cut into strips. Mix together the vinegar and garlic in a dish, season with salt and pepper, add the tongue and leave to marinate for 4–5 hours. Just before serving, drain the tongue strips, place on a serving dish and spoon the tartare sauce over them.

SPICY TONGUE

LINGUA PICCANTE

Serves 4

3–4 tablespoons Dijon mustard

8 boiled tongue slices

80 g/3 oz breadcrumbs

40 g/1½ oz Clarified Butter (see page 88)

salt and pepper

Mix the mustard with a pinch of pepper in a bowl and spread the mixture on both sides of the tongue slices. Cover with the breadcrumbs, pressing them in place with the palms of your hands. Melt the clarified butter in a frying pan, add the slices of tongue and cook until golden brown on both sides. Season lightly with salt and pepper, remove with a fish slice and drain on kitchen paper.

KIDNEYS

Kidneys are highly regarded as ingredients in sophisticated European cuisine. They have a high nutritional value and contain some fat. It is advisable to buy lamb's or calf's kidneys as they have a more delicate and pleasant taste than ox or pig's kidneys, which are much tougher and have a decidedly stronger flavour.

→ Allow about 150 g/5 oz per serving.

→ Kidneys should be eaten extremely fresh and must not be kept in the refrigerator for more than 24 hours.

→ If kidneys are not bought already cleaned, halve them vertically, wash carefully under cold, running water, skin with a small sharp knife and remove the inner white spongy core.

→ To reduce the strong flavour of ox kidneys, slice them and leave to soak in cold water with a little added lemon juice or vinegar.

→ To prevent kidneys from becoming tough during cooking, which in any case should take only a few minutes, chop or cut them into fairly thick slices.

→ Many chefs suggest precooking before use. This consists of quickly sautéing sliced kidneys in a pan lightly brushed with oil, then leaving them to drain in a sieve for about 30 minutes.

→ Kidneys may be grilled, fried in butter and flambéed in brandy, or trifolato (sliced and fried with garlic and parsley).

QUANTITIES
AND COOKING TIMES

KIDNEYS WITH MUSTARD

ROGNONE ALLA SENAPE

Serves 4

50 g/2 oz butter
1 tablespoon olive oil
2 kidneys, cleaned and cored
175 ml/6 fl oz double cream
2 tablespoons Dijon mustard
salt and pepper

Heat the butter with the oil in a frying pan, add the kidneys and cook over a high heat for 4 minutes. Season with salt and pepper, remove from the pan and keep warm. Mix together the cream and mustard, stir into the cooking juices and cook until heated through. Thinly slice the kidneys, place on a warm serving dish and pour the sauce over them.

KIDNEYS IN MADEIRA

ROGNONE AL MADERA

Serves 4

50 g/2 oz butter
1 1/2 teaspoons olive oil
2 kidneys, cleaned, cored and sliced
2 tablespoons plain flour
2 tablespoons Madeira
salt and pepper

Melt 40 g/1 1/2 oz of the butter with the oil in a frying pan, add the kidneys and cook over a high heat for 4 minutes. Season with salt and pepper, remove from the pan, place on a warm serving dish and keep warm. Mix together the remaining butter and the flour to make a paste – beurre manié. Stir 1 tablespoon hot water into the cooking juices, pour in the Madeira and heat gently. Gradually stir in the beurre manié (see page 88), small pieces at a time. As soon as the sauce has thickened, pour it over the kidneys.

KIDNEYS IN BORDEAUX

ROGNONE AL VINO DI BORDEAUX

Serves 6

3 kidneys, cleaned, cored and sliced
2 shallots, chopped
1 1/2 teaspoons plain flour
175 ml/6 fl oz red Bordeaux wine
175 ml/6 fl oz Meat Stock (see page 208)
50 g/2 oz bone marrow, chopped
50 g/2 oz smoked pancetta, diced
50 g/2 oz mushrooms, thinly sliced
salt and pepper

Heat a non-stick frying pan, add the kidneys and cook for a few minutes. Remove from the pan and keep warm. Add the shallots to the frying pan and cook for about 5 minutes until soft. Sprinkle with the flour and mix well. Pour in the wine and stock and cook until the liquid has reduced. Season with salt and pepper, add the marrow and melt over a low heat. Whisk the sauce gently. Cook the pancetta in another non-stick pan for about 5 minutes, then add the mushrooms and cook for a further 5 minutes. Stir the mushroom mixture into the pan of shallots, add the kidneys, heat through for a few minutes and serve.

KIDNEYS WITH RAW SPRING ONIONS

ROGNONE CON CIPOLLINE CRUDE

Serves 4

2 kidneys, cleaned, cored and thinly sliced diagonally

2 tablespoons olive oil

1 shallot, finely chopped

250 ml/8 fl oz double cream

4 spring onions, thinly sliced

salt and pepper

Season the kidneys with salt and pepper. Heat the oil in a frying pan, add the kidneys and stir gently with a wooden spoon, then add the shallot. When the kidneys are pink in colour, add the cream and bring to the boil over a low heat, stirring constantly. Remove the pan from the heat, add the spring onions and serve.

KIDNEYS, SAUSAGE AND MUSHROOMS

ROGNONE CON SALSICCIA E FUNGHI

Serves 4

20 g/³⁄₄ oz dried mushrooms,

400 g/14 oz Italian sausages, chopped

5 tablespoons dry white wine

2 tablespoons olive oil

1 garlic clove

20 g/³⁄₄ oz butter

2 kidneys, cleaned, cored and sliced

4 canned tomatoes,

5 tablespoons Meat Stock (see page 208)

salt and pepper

mashed potato, to serve

Put the mushrooms in a bowl, add warm water to cover and leave to soak for 2 hours. Cook the sausages in a pan with the wine for about 10 minutes until tender. Heat the oil in a frying pan, add the garlic and cook over a high heat until browned, then remove and discard it. Add the butter and when it has melted, add the kidneys and cook for 1 minute. Add the tomatoes, mash carefully and stir. Drain the mushrooms, reserving 1 tablespoon of the soaking liquid, and squeeze out. Add the mushrooms, reserved soaking liquid and stock to the pan and simmer for 5 minutes. Drain the sausages, add to the pan and cook for 15 minutes. Season with salt and pepper to taste and serve with mashed potatoes.

CALF'S HEAD

Although tasty, calf's head is not to everyone's taste. More than anything else, the thought of it is rejected both by those who have to cook it and those who are not 'brave enough' to eat it and therefore do not know what it tastes like. Nevertheless, calf's head is still an important ingredient in the Italian traditional dish of mixed boiled meats, albeit less frequently than in the past. It should not be used to make stock. Calf's head is normally bought from the butcher already boned and rolled. If bought whole, the following preparation, which takes some time, is necessary – singe, wash, soak in cold water for a few hours and parboil. A calf's head generally weighs around 5 kg/11 lb.

FORK

QUANTITIES AND COOKING TIMES

→ Allow about 150 g/5 oz per serving.

→ A calf's head should be cooked on its own and not with other meat. It takes about 1¹/₂ hours if whole and 1¹/₄ hours if boned. Add a pinch of salt to the water, and an onion, celery stick and carrot or herbs, according to taste.

→ To keep the meat white, it is advisable to add a little lemon juice and 1–2 tablespoons plain flour to the cooking water, and then stir quickly to prevent lumps from forming.

→ To check to see if the calf's head is cooked, prick with a fork. It is ready when it is no longer gelatinous.

→ Once drained, the calf's head should be left to cool, then chopped into small pieces. Discard the cooking liquid.

→ Calf's head may be eaten both hot and cold, together with spicy sauces – green sauce (see page 74) is particularly recommended.

BOILED CALF'S HEAD

Wash the calf's head, singe and leave to soak in cold water for a few hours. Pour 2 litres/3½ pints water into a large saucepan and bring to the boil. Stir the flour into a little water in a bowl and pour the mixture into the pan and stir well. Add the onion, carrot, celery, lemon juice, thyme, bay leaf, peppercorns and a generous pinch of salt. Simmer gently for 15 minutes, making sure the liquid does not boil over. Drain the calf's head, add to the pan, cover and simmer for about 2 hours. Check to see whether it is ready by pricking it with a fork. It should be tender but not jelly-like. Drain well, carve into thin slices and serve with two or three fairly spicy sauces.

TESTINA DI VITELLO BOLLITA

Serves 4

600 g/1 lb 5 oz boned calf's head

2 tablespoons plain flour

1 onion

1 carrot

1 celery stick, chopped

juice of 1 lemon, strained

1 fresh thyme sprig

1 bay leaf

6 black peppercorns

salt and pepper

FRIED CALF'S HEAD

Bring a large saucepan of salted water to the boil with the onion, carrot and celery. Add the calf's head and simmer for 1½ hours. Drain, place a weight on top and leave to cool, then carve into slices. Beat 4 tablespoons of the oil with the lemon juice and a pinch each of salt and pepper in a dish, add the slices of calf's head and leave to marinate for 1 hour. Beat the eggs in a shallow dish and spread out the breadcrumbs in another shallow dish. Drain the meat and dust lightly with flour. Dip in the beaten eggs and then in the breadcrumbs. Heat the remaining oil in a frying pan, add the meat and cook over a medium heat, turning occasionally, until golden brown on both sides. Remove with a fish slice, drain on kitchen paper and serve.

TESTINA DI VITELLO FRITTA

Serves 4

1 onion

1 carrot

1 celery stick

600 g/1 lb 5 oz boned calf's head

120 ml/4 fl oz olive oil

juice of 1 lemon, strained

2 eggs

80 g/3 oz breadcrumbs

plain flour, for dusting

salt and pepper

CALF'S HEAD SALAD

Boil the calf's head as described above. Drain, leave to cool, then cut into strips. Line a salad bowl with lettuce leaves. Place the strips of calf's head in another bowl with the tuna, anchovy fillets and celery. Drizzle with olive oil, season with salt and pepper, transfer to the salad bowl and serve.

TESTINA DI VITELLO IN INSALATA

Serves 4

400 g/14 oz boned calf's head

1 lettuce

150 g/5 oz canned tuna, drained and flaked

10 canned anchovy fillets in oil, drained and chopped

1 celery heart, sliced

olive oil, for drizzling

salt and pepper

TRIPE

Tripe was always considered an excellent 'working-class' dish, but it is also enjoyed by those with sophisticated palates, although it has gone out of favour outside Italy and may be difficult to obtain. Italians serve tripe as a first course but it may be served as a main course, especially in the winter. Tripe may be ox or calf's, the latter being more tender and quicker to cook. It is divided into various types including plain and honeycomb, which is considered the best by connoisseurs.

QUANTITIES AND COOKING TIMES

→ Allow about 150 g/5 oz per serving.

→ Rinse several times in cold water and then cut into thin strips.

→ If tripe is to be cooked the day after purchase, store it covered with water in the refrigerator.

→ Tripe does not have a particularly strong flavour, so choose a rich sauce and add vegetables and herbs when cooking.

→ The longer tripe cooks, the more flavour it has.

TRIPPA AI FUNGHI

Serves 4

15 g/¹/₂ oz dried mushrooms

80 g/3 oz butter

2 tablespoons olive oil

1 onion, chopped

1 carrot, chopped

1 celery stick, chopped

675 g/1¹/₂ lb tripe, soaked, drained and cut into strips

500 g/1 lb 2 oz tomatoes, peeled, seeded and diced

1 quantity Meat Stock (see page 208)

40 g/1¹/₂ oz Parmesan cheese, freshly grated

salt and pepper

TRIPE WITH MUSHROOMS

Place the mushrooms in a bowl, add warm water to cover and set aside to soak for 15–30 minutes, then drain and squeeze out. Heat half the butter and the oil in a pan, add the onion, carrot and celery and cook over a medium heat, stirring occasionally, for 5 minutes. Add the mushrooms and cook for 5 minutes, then add the tripe and season with salt and pepper. Add the tomatoes and pour in just enough stock to cover. Bring to the boil, lower the heat, cover and simmer for 3 hours. Remove the pan from the heat, stir in the remaining butter and sprinkle with the Parmesan.

MILANESE TRIPE

Heat 25 g/1 oz of the butter and the oil in a pan, add the pancetta and cook over a low heat, stirring occasionally, for 5 minutes. Add the onion and cook, stirring occasionally, for a further 5 minutes, then add the tripe. Cook for about 15 minutes, then add the carrot, celery, tomatoes and eight of the sage leaves and season with salt and plenty of pepper. Cook for 10 minutes, then pour in the hot stock a little at a time. Bring to the boil and simmer for 3 hours or until the tripe is tender. Meanwhile, cook the beans separately in a large pan of boiling water with the remaining sage leaves and the garlic for about 3 hours until tender. Drain the beans, discarding the sage and garlic, and add to the tripe. Sprinkle with the Parmesan and serve.

TRIPPA ALLA MILANESE

Serves 6

80 g/3 oz butter

2 tablespoons olive oil

150 g/5 oz pancetta, chopped

1 onion, chopped

1 kg/2¼ lb tripe, soaked, drained and cut into strips

1 carrot, chopped

1 celery stick, chopped

500 g/1 lb 2 oz tomatoes, peeled, seeded and diced

20 fresh sage leaves

1 litre/1¾ pints hot Meat Stock (see page 208)

100 g/3½ oz dried white beans,
soaked overnight and drained

1 garlic clove

50 g/2 oz Parmesan cheese, freshly grated

salt and pepper

TRIPE WITH HERBS

Put the tripe in a large pan, add water to cover, the bouquet garni and one onion stuck with the cloves, and season with salt and pepper. Bring to the boil, then lower the heat and simmer for 1 hour. Meanwhile, thinly slice the remaining onions. Heat the olive oil in a pan, add the sliced onions, tomatoes and garlic and season with salt and pepper. Simmer gently, uncovered, for 15 minutes. Drain the tripe, cut into strips and stir it into the pan. Add the wine and simmer over a low heat for 1 hour. Season with salt and pepper to taste, cover and simmer for a further 30 minutes. Remove the pan from the heat, sprinkle with the parsley and serve.

TRIPPA AROMATICA

Serves 6

1 kg/2¼ lb tripe, soaked and drained

1 bouquet garni

3 onions

2 cloves

4 tablespoons olive oil

1 kg/2¼ lb tomatoes, peeled, seeded and diced

3 garlic cloves, unpeeled

175 ml/6 fl oz dry white wine

2 tablespoons fresh flat-leaf parsley, chopped

salt and pepper

SIMPLE TRIPE

Melt the butter in a pan, add the onion and cook over a low heat, stirring occasionally, for 5 minutes. Add the tripe, cover and cook, occasionally adding a ladleful of the stock, for 3 hours or until tender. Season with salt and pepper, sprinkle with the Parmesan and serve.

TRIPPA IN BIANCO

Serves 4

100 g/3½ oz butter

1 onion, chopped

675 g/1½ lb tripe, soaked, drained and cut into strips

1 quantity hot Meat Stock (see page 208)

100 g/3½ oz Parmesan cheese, freshly grated

salt and pepper

POULTRY →

POULTRY

The term poultry covers all domesticated birds bred and reared for eating. Even though some Italian breeders specify the birds are 'free-range', chickens, turkeys and geese are no longer free to scratch about in barnyards at will. Despite their often cramped conditions, Italian poultry farms are considered to offer birds a quality of life above the European average and the same is said for the flavour of the meat. That said, there is an increasing movement in some countries to raise free-range and organic birds, a trend that is widely supported by consumers. However, such poultry tends to be more expensive and although many people claim that the birds are healthier and taste better than intensively reared ones, little scientific research has been undertaken to support this view. Poultry fit into two groups – white meat, such as chickens and turkeys, and red meat, such as ducks, guinea fowl and pigeon. Chicken is the most popular type of poultry as it is relatively inexpensive and can be prepared in an almost infinite number of ways. Guinea fowl, which have been domesticated since the sixteenth century, have a stronger flavour and firmer meat. Turkeys too have established a place in our eating habits – the breast is much sought after. Ducks and geese are almost exclusively eaten in Italy during the winter and are mainly part of the gastronomic traditions of a few regions, such as Lombardy and Veneto, where there are numerous farms. The same is true of pigeons, which are mainly eaten in Umbria. When buying frozen poultry, make sure the packaging is undamaged and thaw the meat completely before cooking.

DUCK

Ducks may be domesticated or wild, the latter being available in Italy during the hunting season. European domesticated ducks include large, fat autumn birds, with strong-tasting meat, and spring ducks, which are smaller, more tender and with a more delicate flavour. Strictly speaking, a duckling does not become a duck until it is about two months old, at the stage of its second plumage. Most birds on sale are, in fact, ducklings and can weigh as much as 3.2 kg/7 lb oven-ready, although smaller specimens – 1.5–1.6 kg/3'|₄–3'|₂ lb – are also available. Ducklings are more tender than mature birds. Duck meat is tender and nutritious, but as it is very fatty it is not recommended for people on diets or with gastric problems. Ducks may be cooked in several ways – roasted, braised, in a casserole or as the now legendary à l'orange. Breast fillets are also available, as well as products such as the famous duck pâté de foie gras, terrines and pies. It is essential to follow a few rules when cooking a whole bird. Truss it with kitchen string so that it stays in shape while cooking. It must not be overcooked. Allow 30 minutes per 500 g/1 lb 2 oz. Season the cavity with salt and pepper, then season the outside with a large pinch of salt. Pre-cooking is recommended although not essential. Season the cavity with salt and pepper, put the duck in a pan and pour in water to cover it by two-thirds. Add a large onion, bring to the boil and simmer for 20 minutes, then drain, pat dry and follow your chosen recipe.

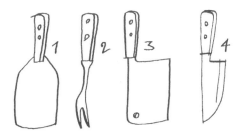

DUCK À L'ORANGE

ANATRA ALL'ARANCIA

Serves 4

40 g/1¹/₂ oz butter

3 fresh sage leaves

1.5-kg/3¹/₄-lb duck

150 g/5 oz lean pancetta, sliced

1 tablespoon olive oil

175 ml/6 fl oz white wine

150–300 ml/¹/₄–¹/₂ pint Chicken Stock

(see page 209)

5 oranges

salt and pepper

Put a pinch of salt, a pinch of pepper, 15 g/¹/₂ oz of the butter and the sage in the cavity of the duck. Wrap it in the pancetta and truss with kitchen string. Heat the oil and remaining butter in a deep pan, add the duck and cook, turning frequently, for 15 minutes until browned all over. Pour in the wine and 150 ml/¹/₄ pint of the stock, cover and simmer, seasoning with salt and basting two or three times, for 1 hour until tender. If it seems to be drying out, add another 150 ml/¹/₄ pint hot stock. Meanwhile, pare the rind of two of the oranges and cut into thin strips. Blanch in boiling water for a few minutes, then drain. Squeeze the juice from two of the remaining oranges and cut the third into segments. Remove the duck from the pan and keep warm. Add the orange juice and strips of rind to the pan and heat gently without allowing the sauce to boil. Untie the duck and carve. Place the meat on a warm serving dish, spoon a little of the sauce on top and garnish with the orange segments. Serve with the remaining sauce.

DUCK COOKED IN BEER

ANATRA ALLA BIRRA

Serves 4

25 g/1 oz butter

1 onion, thinly sliced

1.5-kg/3¹/₄-lb duck

1 litre/1³/₄ pints beer

1 fresh rosemary sprig

1 fresh thyme sprig

2 fresh sage leaves

1 tablespoon sultanas

salt and pepper

Melt the butter in a deep pan, add the onion and cook over a low heat, stirring occasionally, for 5 minutes. Add the duck and cook, turning frequently, for 15 minutes until browned all over. Pour in the beer, bring to the boil, then lower the heat to a simmer. Season with salt and pepper to taste, add the rosemary, thyme and sage and simmer, basting and turning occasionally, for 1 hour until tender. Meanwhile, place the sultanas in a bowl, add lukewarm water to cover and leave to soak for 30 minutes, then drain and squeeze out. Remove the duck from the pan and keep warm. Remove and discard the herbs from the pan and increase the heat to thicken the cooking juices if necessary. Stir in the sultanas and simmer for a few minutes. Cut the duck into pieces, place them on a warm serving dish and spoon the sauce over them.

DUCK IN ALMOND SAUCE

Set the liver aside and cut the bird into pieces. Season with salt and pepper and dust with flour. Heat 2 tablespoons of the oil in a pan over a low heat, add the liver and cook for a few minutes until browned on the outside but still pink in the middle. Remove from the pan and set aside. Add the onion and garlic to the pan and cook over a medium heat, turning frequently, for 8–10 minutes until browned all over. Remove from the pan and set aside with the liver. If necessary, add 1 tablespoon oil to the pan, then add the duck and cook, turning frequently, until browned all over. Add the tomatoes, lower the heat, cover and cook. Meanwhile, chop the almonds together with the liver, onion and garlic. Place in a bowl, stir in the wine and add the mixture to the duck. Add the parsley, season with salt, re-cover the pan and simmer gently for 1 hour more, adding a little warm water if necessary to prevent drying out. Place the pieces of duck in the middle of a warm serving dish, surround with two rings of potatoes mashed with cheese and serve.

ANATRA ALLA SALSA DI MANDORLE

Serves 6

2-kg/4¹/₂-lb duck, with liver

plain flour, for dusting

2–3 tablespoons olive oil

1 onion

1 garlic clove

3 tomatoes, chopped

12 blanched almonds, roasted

5 tablespoons dry white wine

1 fresh flat-leaf parsley sprig, chopped

salt and pepper

potatoes mashed

with Parmesan cheese, freshly grated to serve

DUCK WITH PEACHES

Place the duck in a pan with the sage and bay leaf and pour in water to cover. Season with salt and pepper and cook over a low heat for 1¹/₂ hours. Remove the duck from the pan. Remove and discard the skin, cut the breast fillets off the bones and return to the pan. Simmer over a low heat until the liquid has evaporated completely. Cut the peach halves in half again. Melt the butter in a frying pan, add the peaches and cook over a low heat until lightly browned all over. Sprinkle with the cinnamon and cook for a few minutes more, then add to the duck. Season with salt and pepper to taste. Transfer the duck and peaches to a warm serving dish and serve with thickly sliced toast. This dish is also pleasant cold. The cold dish and peaches go well with white wines that have a peach-like aroma.

ANATRA ALLE PESCHE

Serves 4

1.5-kg/3¹/₄-lb duck

3 fresh sage leaves

1 bay leaf

500 g/1 lb 2 oz white peaches,

peeled, halved and stoned

25 g/1 oz butter

pinch of ground cinnamon

salt and pepper

thick toast slices, to serve

ANATRA AL PEPE VERDE

Serves 6

40 g/1¹/₂ oz butter

1 onion, thinly sliced

1 carrot, sliced

1 celery stick, sliced

1 fresh flat-leaf parsley sprig

1 fresh thyme, sprig

2-kg/4¹/₂-lb duck

1 tablespoon green peppercorns

175 ml/6 fl oz dry white wine

350 ml/12 fl oz Chicken Stock (see page 209)

1 small red pepper, halved seeded and chopped

salt and pepper

DUCK WITH GREEN PEPPERCORNS

Preheat the oven to 220°C/425°F/Gas Mark 7. Heat 25g/1oz of the butter in a roasting tin, add the onion and cook over a low heat, stirring occasionally, for 5 minutes. Add the carrot, celery, parsley and thyme. Rub the skin of the duck with salt and pepper, put three of the peppercorns, the remaining butter and a pinch of salt inside the cavity and truss with kitchen string. Place in the roasting tin with the vegetables. Cover the tin with foil, transfer to the oven and cook for 15 minutes. Remove the duck from the oven and lower the temperature to 190°C/375°F/ Gas Mark 5. Pour the wine over the duck and cook over a medium heat until it has evaporated. Add the stock and bring to the boil, then re-cover the roasting tin and return it to the oven for 45 minutes. If it seems to be drying out, add a little more stock. Do not switch off the oven, but remove the duck from the roasting tin and strain the cooking juices into a bowl. Stir in 5 tablespoons boiling water, pour back into the roasting tin and cook over a medium heat until slightly reduced. Add the red pepper and remaining peppercorns. Return the duck to the roasting tin and roast in the oven for a further 15 minutes. Carve the duck, place on a warm serving dish and spoon the sauce over it.

ANATRA FARCITA AL MIELE

Serves 6

2-kg/4¹/₂-lb duck, with liver

25 g/1 oz butter

3 tablespoons soy sauce

2 onions, chopped

¹/₂ garlic clove

5 tablespoons brandy

2 tablespoons clear honey

1 thick cooked ham slice, chopped

salt

STUFFED DUCK WITH HONEY

Preheat the oven to 180°C/350°F/Gas Mark 4. Rub the inside and outside of the duck with salt. Melt the butter in a frying pan, add the liver and cook over a low heat, turning frequently, for a few minutes, then remove from the pan and chop. Mix together the soy sauce, onions, garlic and brandy in a bowl. Transfer half the mixture to another bowl and stir in the honey. Rub the duck with the honey mixture making sure it penetrates well. Stir 350 ml/12 fl oz boiling water into the leftover mixture. Stir the liver and ham into the remaining soy, onion, garlic and brandy mixture and stuff the duck with it. Truss with kitchen string, place on a rack set over a roasting tin and pour a little water into the tin. Roast for about 1¹/₂ hours, basting occasionally with the diluted honey mixture. Remove the duck from the rack, untie, carve and place on a warm serving dish.

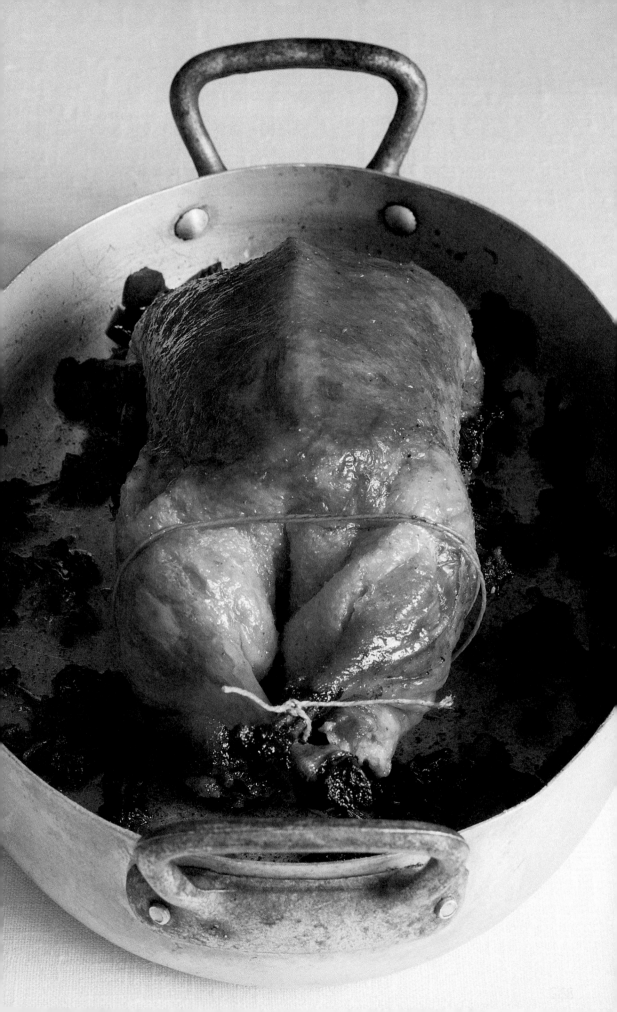

SWEET–AND–SOUR DUCK

ANATRA IN AGRODOLCE

Serves 4

1.5-kg/3¼-lb duck

40 g/1½ oz butter

2 onions, finely chopped

1 fresh sage leaf

350 ml/12 fl oz hot Chicken Stock (see page 209)

1 fresh mint sprig, chopped

2 tablespoons sugar

2 tablespoons white wine vinegar

salt and pepper

Season the cavity of the duck with salt and pepper and truss with kitchen string. Melt the butter in a large saucepan or flameproof casserole, add the onions and cook over a medium heat, stirring occasionally, for 5 minutes. Add the sage, then add the duck and cook, turning frequently, until browned all over. Pour in the hot stock, lower the heat, cover and simmer, turning the duck occasionally, for 1½ hours until tender. Remove the duck from the pan and keep warm. Add 150 ml/¼ pint boiling water to the cooking juices and sprinkle in the mint. Put the sugar and 1 tablespoon cold water in a saucepan, bring to the boil, stirring until the sugar has dissolved, then heat until caramelized and light golden in colour. Pour the caramelized sugar on to the cooking juices, stir in the vinegar and season with salt to taste. Untie the duck and carve. Place on a warm serving dish and serve with the sauce.

DUCK IN HERB SAUCE

ANATRA IN SALSA AROMATICA

Serves 6

2 tablespoons olive oil

1 small onion

2 fresh sage leaves

1 bay leaf

1 fresh rosemary sprig

1 fresh marjoram sprig

2 fresh thyme leaves

2-kg/4½-lb duck

50 g/2 oz butter

5 tablespoons balsamic vinegar

1 fresh chervil sprig

1 fresh tarragon sprig, chopped

6 fresh basil leaves, chopped

3 black peppercorns, lightly crushed

3 egg yolks

2 tablespoons tomato purée

2 tablespoons double cream

salt and pepper

Preheat the oven to 180°C/350°F/Gas Mark 4. Heat the oil in a small saucepan, then remove from the heat and set aside. Put the onion, sage, bay leaf, rosemary, marjoram and thyme in the cavity of the duck and season with salt and pepper. Truss with kitchen string, place in a roasting tin with half the butter and the hot oil, cover with foil and roast, basting and turning occasionally, for about 1½ hours. Meanwhile, pour the vinegar into a saucepan, add the chervil, tarragon, half of the basil and the peppercorns and cook over a low heat until the liquid has reduced. Strain into a bowl and leave to cool slightly, then whisk the mixture into the egg yolks in a double boiler or heatproof bowl. Stir in the tomato purée and cream and season with salt and pepper. Heat over barely simmering water and gradually beat in the remaining butter in small pieces at a time. Carve the duck, place in the middle of a warm serving dish, spoon the herb sauce over it and sprinkle with the basil.

Serves 6

2-kg/4¹/₂-lb duck, with giblets

50 g/2 oz smoked pancetta, diced

1 onion, chopped

1 garlic clove, chopped

4 leeks, white parts only thinly sliced

4 carrots, grated

1 tablespoon breadcrumbs

1 egg white

50 g/2 oz ricotta cheese

pinch of freshly grated nutmeg

800 g/1³/₄ lb turnips, sliced

2 tablespoons double cream

salt and pepper

STUFFED DUCK IN TURNIP SAUCE

Preheat the oven to 180°C/350°F/Gas Mark 4. Chop the giblets. Cook the pancetta in a pan, without any additional oil or fat, over a low heat, stirring frequently, for 5 minutes. Add the onion, garlic and giblets and cook over a high heat for 5 minutes. Put the mixture into a bowl, add the leeks, carrots, breadcrumbs, egg white, ricotta and nutmeg, season with salt and pepper and mix well. Stuff the duck with the mixture, sew up the opening and truss with kitchen string. Prick the skin all over with a fork, place in a roasting tin and roast for 1 hour. Meanwhile, steam the turnips for 30 minutes, then transfer to a food processor and process to a purée. Scrape the turnip purée into a bowl, stir in the cream, season with salt and pepper and keep warm. Remove the duck from the roasting tin, pull off the legs and wings and carve the breast. Place on a warm serving dish and spoon the turnip sauce over it.

Serves 4

4 duck legs, boned

350 ml/12 fl oz red wine

2 garlic cloves

1 leek, sliced

1 bay leaf

2 carrots, thinly sliced

2 onions, thinly sliced

salt and pepper

JUGGED DUCK LEGS

Roll up the duck legs and tie with kitchen string. Mix together 250 ml/8 fl oz of the wine, the garlic, leek and bay leaf in a dish, season with salt, add the legs and leave to marinate, turning occasionally, for 6 hours. Preheat the oven to 200°C/400°F/Gas Mark 6. Drain the legs, reserving the marinade, put in a roasting tin with the carrots and onions and roast for 20 minutes. Meanwhile, strain the marinade into a saucepan, season with salt and pepper and cook over a low heat until the liquid has reduced. Remove the legs from the roasting tin and keep warm. Skim off the fat from the roasting tin and stir the remaining wine into the cooking juices, then pour into the saucepan. Heat gently until the sauce has reduced. Untie the legs and carve into slices. Arrange on a warm serving dish and spoon the sauce over them.

DUCK FILLETS WITH FIGS

FILETTI DI ANATRA AI FICHI

Serves 4

1 small duck, with liver

1 tablespoon olive oil

50 g/2 oz butter, plus extra for greasing

250 ml/8 fl oz red wine

1 tablespoon lemon juice

2.5 kg/5½ lb fresh figs

½ white loaf, sliced and crusts removed

1 lemon

salt and pepper

Preheat the oven to 230°C/450°F/Gas Mark 8. Set the liver aside. Season the cavity of the duck with salt and pepper and truss with kitchen string. Place the duck in a roasting tin, add the oil and 10 g/¼ oz of the butter. Roast the duck for 1 hour, then remove from the oven and lower the temperature to 200°C/400°F/Gas Mark 6. Cut off the wings, breast and legs and break up the carcass with a meat mallet. Stir the red wine into the roasting tin, add the carcass and cook in the oven for 10 minutes, then remove from the oven but do not switch it off. Pass the cooking juices through a food mill into a saucepan and stir in the lemon juice. Chop the liver and add to the sauce. Cut the figs almost in half and open out slightly. Grease another roasting tin with butter, add the figs and put a small piece of the remaining butter in each, then bake until lightly browned. Remove the figs from the oven and season with salt and pepper. Melt the remaining butter in a frying pan, add the slices of bread and cook until golden brown on both sides. Carve the legs into slices and cut the breast into fillets. Place the fried bread and duck in the middle of a warm serving dish arrange the figs around them and spoon the sauce over the duck.

BREAST OF DUCK WITH GRAPEFRUIT

PETTO DI ANATRA AL POMPELMO

Serves 4

2 grapefruit

juice of 1 orange, strained

2 tablespoons sugar

2 black peppercorns, lightly crushed

pinch of ground cinnamon (optional)

2 duck breasts

1 tablespoon olive oil

5 tablespoons white wine vinegar

25 g/1 oz butter

salt and pepper

Preheat the oven to 200°C/400°F/Gas Mark 6. Holding the grapefruit over a bowl to catch the juice, peel and cut off the pith. Dice the flesh, add to the bowl and pour in the orange juice. Stir in the sugar, peppercorns, 1 tablespoon water and the cinnamon, if using. Pour into a pan and cook over a medium heat for 15 minutes. Meanwhile, slash the thickest parts of the duck breasts. Heat the oil in a frying pan, add the duck breasts and cook over a high heat until lightly browned. Transfer to the oven and cook for 10 minutes. (If your frying pan does not have an ovenproof handle, cover it with foil first.) Remove the duck from the pan and keep warm. Stir the vinegar into the pan, add 2 tablespoons of the juice mixture, season with salt and pepper and cook over a low heat until reduced. Season with salt and pepper to taste and stir the butter into the mixture. Slice the duck diagonally, place on a warm serving dish and spoon the sweet-and-sour sauce over it.

CAPON

Capons are young cockerels that have been castrated and fattened, producing birds with a weight range of 2–2.5 kg/4¹/₂–5¹/₂ lb. Despite their production having died out in many countries, capons are so popular in Italy that they are still commercially available there. Sometimes, large roasters outside Italy are described as 'capon-style' but this is not strictly accurate as they do not have the same tenderness or flavour as true capons, but they may be used as a substitute in the following recipes. In Italy, capon is synonymous with Christmas, when these delicious birds are much sought after for their flavoursome meat. They are generally cooked whole and served boiled with mixed pickles and mostarda, a preserve made with mustard, or with boiled rice and béchamel sauce flavoured with curry powder. Skimmed capon stock is excellent for cooking cappelletti and raviolini. Capons may also be roasted.

CAPON ROAST IN A PARCEL

Put the dried mushrooms in a bowl, add warm water to cover and leave to soak for 15–30 minutes, then drain, squeeze out and chop coarsely. Preheat the oven to 180°C/350°F/Gas Mark 4. Mix together the butter and parsley in a bowl and place the mixture in the cavity of the capon. Wrap the capon with the slices of pork fat or bacon and truss with kitchen string. Spread out a large sheet of foil, place the carrots and onions in the middle, sprinkle with the prosciutto and mushrooms and top with the capon. Fold over the sides of the foil and wrap the capon so that it is completely enclosed. Roast the capon for 1¹/₂–2 hours, depending on its size. Remove the capon from the oven, unwrap and untie, then cut into pieces and place on a warm serving dish. Tip the other ingredients in the parcel into a food processor and process to a purée. Scrape the purée into a saucepan, stir in the Marsala and cook over a low heat, stirring constantly, until hot. Season with salt and pepper to taste and serve the sauce with the capon.

CAPPONE AL CARTOCCIO

Serves 8

150 g/5 oz dried mushrooms

25 g/1 oz butter

1 tablespoon chopped fresh flat-leaf parsley

1 capon

100 g/3¹/₂ oz pork fat or streaky bacon, sliced

2 carrots, sliced

2 onions, sliced

1 thick prosciutto slice, chopped

175 ml/6 fl oz Marsala

salt and pepper

CAPON IN CARDOON SAUCE

CAPPONE IN SALSA DI CARDI

Serves 4

½ capon, about 1 kg/2¼ lb, with giblets

800 g/1¾ lb cardoons (see page 423)

2 tablespoons plain flour

1 lemon slice

25 g/1 oz butter

20 g/¾ oz Parmesan cheese, freshly grated

salt

For the stock

1 veal shin

1 green celery stick with leaves

1 carrot

1 onion

2 bay leaves

2 cloves

1 fresh flat-leaf parsley sprig

First, make the stock. Pour 2 litres/3½ pints water into a saucepan, add all the stock ingredients and the capon giblets and season with salt. Bring to the boil, lower the heat and simmer for 1½ hours. Strain the stock into a bowl and set aside. Wrap the capon in piece of muslin, tie with kitchen string, place in a saucepan and add enough stock to cover. Cover the pan and simmer over a low heat for 1½ hours. Meanwhile, trim, peel and chop the cardoons, place in a saucepan, add half the flour, the lemon, 10 g/¼ oz of the butter and a pinch of salt and pour in water to cover. Bring to the boil, then lower the heat and simmer for 30–50 minutes until tender. Drain and pass through a food mill into a double boiler or heatproof bowl. Mix the remaining flour and remaining butter to a paste – beurre manié (see page 88). Heat the cardoon purée over barely simmering water and gradually stir in the beurre manié, a small piece at a time, and the Parmesan, then season with salt. Transfer the capon to a carving board, unwrap, remove the skin and carve the meat into thin slices. Place them on a warm serving dish and spoon the sauce over them.

POACHED CAPON

CAPPONE LESSATO

Serves 8

1 capon

1 onion • 1 carrot

1 celery stick

salt and pepper

Green Sauce (see page 74)

or spicy fruit mostarda, to serve

Season the cavity of the capon with salt and pepper, place in a large saucepan and add plenty of water. Season with salt, add the onion, carrot and celery, bring just to the boil, then lower the heat and simmer gently for 2 hours until tender and cooked through. Remove from the heat and leave to cool slightly in the cooking liquid, then drain. Remove the skin, cut the capon into pieces and place on a serving dish. Serve with green sauce or spicy fruit mostarda.

STUFFED CAPON

CAPPONE RIPIENO

Serves 8

1 thick bread slice, crusts removed

100 g/3½ oz cooked ham, chopped

100 g/3½ oz cooked tongue, chopped

100 g/3½ oz cooked spinach, chopped

1 carrot, chopped

1 fresh flat-leaf parsley sprig, chopped

2 eggs, lightly beaten

1 capon • 3 tablespoons olive oil

25 g/1 oz butter • salt and pepper

new potatoes or mixed salad, to serve

Tear the bread into pieces, place in a bowl, add water to cover and leave to soak for 10 minutes, then drain and squeeze out. Mix together the soaked bread, ham, tongue, spinach, carrot and parsley in a bowl, stir in the beaten eggs and season with salt and pepper. Stuff the capon with the mixture and truss with kitchen string. Heat the oil and butter in a large saucepan, add the capon and cook, basting occasionally with the cooking juices, for 1½–2 hours until tender and cooked through. If necessary, add 1–2 tablespoons warm water to prevent the bird from drying out. Serve the capon with new potatoes or a mixed salad.

TRUFFLED CAPON

Mix together 1 tablespoon of the olive oil, the brandy and Marsala in a bowl, season with salt and pepper, add the truffles and leave to marinate for 1 hour. Preheat the oven to 180°C/350°F/Gas Mark 4. Stir the pork fat or bacon into the truffle mixture and spoon it into the cavity of the capon. Sew up the opening. Put the remaining oil into a casserole, add the capon and roast for about 2 hours.

CAPPONE TARTUFATO

Serves 8

5 tablespoons olive oil

1 tablespoon brandy

1 tablespoon Marsala

250 g/9 oz black truffles, chopped

50 g/2 oz pork fat or streaky bacon, chopped

1 capon

salt and pepper

SIMPLE CAPON GALANTINE

Bring a large pan of salted water to the boil, add the capon so that it is completely immersed and cook for 15 minutes. Remove the capon, leave to cool slightly, then peel off the skin, keeping the pieces as large as possible. Cut the meat off the bones and chop, then mix with the veal and ham in a bowl. Place the capon carcass, carrots and beef bone in a saucepan, add plenty of water and bring to the boil. Shape the chopped meat mixture into a meatloaf, then wrap first in the capon skin and then in muslin, tying both ends. Remove the carcass and beef bone from the stock, immerse the meatloaf and simmer for about 3 hours. Drain, cover and place a weight on top to flatten it evenly. (You can use a chopping board weighted down with several cans of tomatoes, beans, etc.) Leave to cool. Untie and discard the muslin, cut the capon into thin slices, place on a serving dish and garnish with diced gelatine.

GALANTINA SEMPLICE DI CAPPONE

Serves 8

1 capon

300 g/11 oz lean veal, chopped

100 g/3¹/₂ oz cooked ham, chopped

2 carrots

1 beef bone

salt

diced gelatine, to garnish

TOMATO

GUINEA FOWL

Guinea fowl is a great choice for an elegant dinner party. It is much tastier than chicken with a flavour somewhat similar to that of pheasant. To guarantee success, choose a bird between eight and ten months old. If a guinea fowl is more than a year old its meat is rather tough and needs thorough hanging. It should be cooked over a low heat for 40–60 minutes, depending on the size. When roasting guinea fowl, it is advisable to cover the breast with a few slices of pancetta or bacon so that the meat stays tender.

POT-ROAST GUINEA FOWL

ARROSTO DI FARAONA

Serves 6

1 guinea fowl
1 fresh rosemary sprig
2 fresh sage leaves
50 g/2 oz pancetta slices
40 g/1¹/₂ oz butter
3 tablespoons olive oil
175 ml/6 fl oz dry white wine
salt and pepper

Season the cavity of the guinea fowl with salt and pepper and place the rosemary, sage, one of the pancetta slices and 15 g/¹/₂ oz of the butter in the cavity. Cover the breast of the bird with the remaining pancetta and tie with kitchen string. Season with salt and pepper. Heat the remaining butter and the oil in a pan, add the guinea fowl and cook, turning frequently, until browned all over. Add half the wine and cook until it has evaporated, then cover and cook over a low heat for 50 minutes. Remove the pancetta slices, re-cover the pan and cook for a further 10 minutes. Remove the guinea fowl from the pan and keep warm. Stir the remaining wine into the pan and cook until reduced by half. Cut the guinea fowl into pieces, place on a warm serving dish and spoon the cooking juices over it.

GUINEA FOWL WITH ARTICHOKE HEARTS

Preheat the oven to 200°C/400°F/Gas Mark 6. Season the cavity of the guinea fowl with salt and pepper. Heat 3 tablespoons of the oil with one of the garlic cloves in a pan, add the artichoke hearts and cook until tender, then sprinkle with the parsley and season lightly with salt and pepper. Leave to cool, then place in the cavity of the guinea fowl, sew up the opening and truss with kitchen string so that the bird keeps its shape. Place in a roasting tin with the remaining oil, the pancetta, butter, remaining garlic and rosemary. Roast until the upper surface is browned, then turn over to brown the other side. Add the wine, lower the oven temperature to 180°C/350°F/Gas Mark 4 and roast for about 1 hour until tender. Remove the guinea fowl from the roasting tin and untie. Carve the breast into fairly thick slices, pull off the wings and legs and cut the back into four pieces. Place the meat on a warm serving dish and spoon the hot cooking juices over it.

FARAONA AI CARCIOFI

Serves 6

1 guinea fowl, boned

5 tablespoons olive oil

2 garlic cloves

5 globe artichoke hearts

1 fresh parsley sprig, chopped

2 pancetta slices, chopped

25 g/1 oz butter

1 fresh rosemary sprig

5 tablespoons dry white wine

salt and pepper

GUINEA FOWL WITH PINEAPPLE

Set two of the pineapple slices aside and chop the remainder. Heat the butter and oil in a pan, add the guinea fowl and cook, turning frequently, until browned all over. Season with salt and pepper, add the onion, carrot, celery, garlic and chopped pineapple and cook, stirring occasionally, for about 10 minutes. Pour in the stock, cover and simmer over a low heat for 1 hour. Remove the pieces of guinea fowl and keep warm. Stir 2 tablespoons hot water into the pan, scraping up the sediment from the base, then pass the cooking juices through a food mill into a bowl and return to the pan. Stir in the cream and heat gently until slightly thickened. Place the pieces of guinea fowl on a warm serving dish, spoon the sauce over them and garnish with the reserved pineapple slices.

FARAONA ALL'ANANAS

Serves 6

1/2 pineapple, peeled, cored and sliced

25 g/1 oz butter

3 tablespoons olive oil

1 guinea fowl, cut into pieces

1 onion, chopped

1 carrot, chopped

2 celery sticks, chopped

1 garlic clove, chopped

300 ml/1/2 pint Chicken Stock (see page 209)

250 ml/8 fl oz double cream

salt and pepper

GUINEA FOWL WITH SAGE

FARAONA ALLA SALVIA

Serves 6

10 fresh sage leaves
40 g/1½ oz butter
1 guinea fowl
100 g/3½ oz pancetta, sliced
2 tablespoons olive oil
salt and pepper

Preheat the oven to 180°C/350°F/Gas Mark 4. Chop half the sage leaves and mix them with 15g/1 oz of the butter. Season the cavity of the guinea fowl with salt and pepper, place the sage and butter mixture inside the cavity and sew up the opening. Wrap the bird in the pancetta slices and truss with kitchen string. Place the guinea fowl in a roasting tin with the oil, half the remaining butter and the remaining sage leaves. Roast, turning occasionally, for about 1 hour until tender. Remove the guinea fowl from the roasting tin and place the tin over a low heat. Stir 2 tablespoons hot water into the cooking juices, scraping up any sediment from the base of the tin, then stir in the remaining butter and pour into a sauce boat. Slice the breast of the bird, remove the wings and legs, cut the back into four pieces and serve with the sauce.

GUINEA FOWL ORTOLANA

FARAONA ALL'ORTOLANA

Serves 4

50 g/2 oz butter
6 tablespoons olive oil
4 fresh sage leaves
1 celery stick, chopped
1 guinea fowl, cut into pieces
175 ml/6 fl oz white wine
8 baby onions
3 potatoes, diced
300 g/11 oz diced pumpkin
salt and pepper

Heat half the butter and half the oil in a large pan with the sage, celery and a pinch each of salt and pepper, add the guinea fowl and cook, turning frequently and occasionally adding the wine, until browned all over. Heat the remaining butter and oil in another pan, add the onions, potatoes and pumpkin, season with salt and pepper and cook over a low heat, stirring occasionally, for 40 minutes. Preheat the oven to 180°C/350°F/Gas Mark 4. Transfer the vegetables and guinea fowl to a roasting tin and roast for about 30 minutes.

GUINEA FOWL WITH MASCARPONE

FARAONA AL MASCARPONE

Serves 6

150 g/5 oz mascarpone cheese
120 ml/4 fl oz brandy
1 guinea fowl
25 g/1 oz butter
1 fresh rosemary sprig, chopped
salt and pepper

Mix together the mascarpone and half the brandy in a bowl and spoon into the cavity of the guinea fowl. Sew up the opening and truss with kitchen string. Melt the butter in a pan, add the guinea fowl and cook, turning frequently, until browned all over. Season with salt and pepper, sprinkle with the rosemary, lower the heat and cover. Cook, turning occasionally, for 1 hour until tender. Transfer the guinea fowl to a warm serving dish, sprinkle with the remaining brandy and ignite. Carve when the flames have died down.

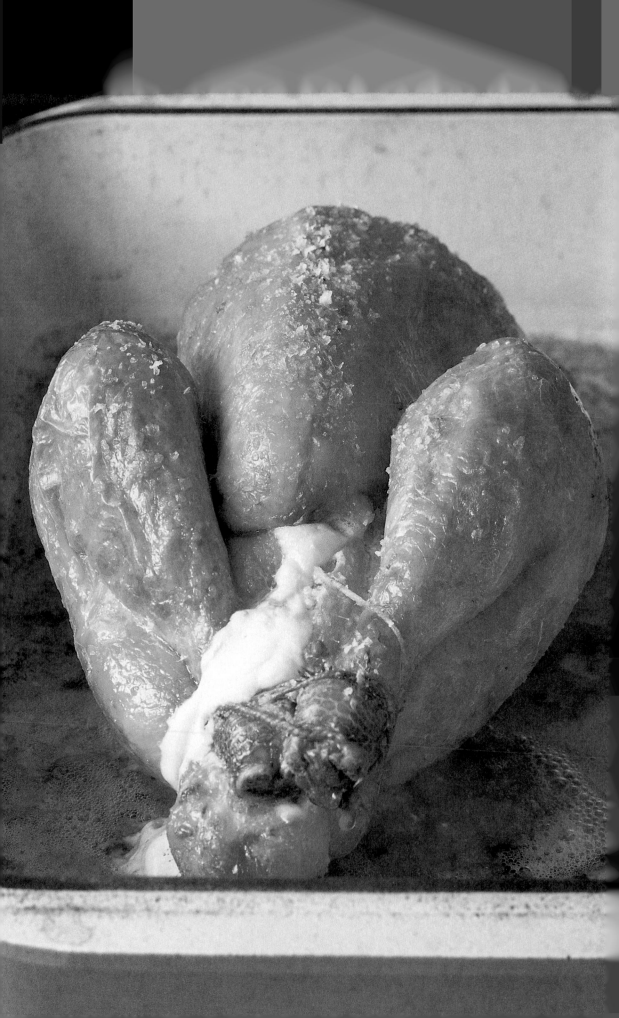

GUINEA FOWL WITH RED WINE

Dust the guinea fowl with flour. Heat the oil and 25 g/1 oz of the butter in a pan, add the pancetta, onions and guinea fowl and cook over a low heat, stirring and turning frequently, for 15 minutes. Season with salt and pepper, add the nutmeg and pour in the wine. Cover and simmer over a low heat for 1 hour. Meanwhile, put the mushrooms in a bowl, add warm water to cover and leave to soak for 30 minutes, then drain and squeeze out. Remove the pieces of guinea fowl from the pan and keep warm. Stir 2 tablespoons hot water into the cooking juices, add the mushrooms, sausage and remaining butter and cook for 20 minutes. Place the guinea fowl on a warm serving dish and spoon the sauce over it.

FARAONA AL VINO ROSSO
Serves 6

1 guinea fowl, cut into pieces
plain flour, for dusting
2 tablespoons olive oil
40 g/1½ oz butter
50 g/2 oz pancetta
2 onions, chopped
pinch of freshly grated nutmeg
1 litre/1¾ pints red wine
20 g/¾ oz dried mushrooms
100 g/3½ oz Italian sausages, chopped
salt and pepper

GUINEA FOWL WITH CREAM AND LEMON

Melt the butter in a pan, add the guinea fowl and cook over a high heat, turning frequently, until browned all over. Season with salt and pepper, lower the heat, cover and cook for about 45 minutes. Stir in the cream, re-cover the pan and cook for a further 15 minutes. Transfer to a warm serving dish and sprinkle with the lemon juice.

FARAONA CON PANNA E LIMONE
Serves 6

50 g/2 oz butter
1 guinea fowl, cut into pieces
5 tablespoons double cream
juice of ½ lemon, strained
salt and pepper

STUFFED GUINEA FOWL WITH MUSHROOMS

Chop the liver, place in a bowl, and add the sausages, mushrooms, onions, garlic, parsley and oregano and mix well. Season with salt and pepper and stir in the brandy. Heat 1 tablespoon of the oil in a frying pan, add the mixture and cook over a medium heat, stirring occasionally, for 5 minutes. Spoon the mixture into the cavity of the guinea fowl and sew up the opening. Cover the breast of the bird with the pancetta slices and truss with kitchen string. Heat the butter and the remaining oil in a pan, add the guinea fowl and cook over a medium heat, turning frequently, until browned all over. Season with salt and pepper, lower the heat and cook for about 1 hour.

FARAONA FARCITA CON I FUNGHI
Serves 6

1 guinea fowl, with liver
150 g/5 oz Italian sausages, chopped
120 g/4 oz mushrooms, chopped
2 onions, chopped
1 garlic clove, chopped
1 fresh flat-leaf parsley sprig, chopped
1 fresh oregano sprig, chopped
50 ml/2 fl oz brandy
3 tablespoons olive oil
50 g/2 oz pancetta slices
25 g/1 oz butter
salt and pepper

GUINEA FOWL STUFFED WITH SULTANAS

FARAONA RIPIENA CON UVETTA

Serves 6

25 g/1 oz sultanas
50 ml/2 fl oz brandy
1 thick bread slice, crusts removed
150 g/5 oz Italian sausages, chopped
1 fresh thyme sprig, chopped
1 small fresh rosemary sprig, chopped
1 fresh flat-leaf parsley sprig, chopped
4 fresh sage leaves, chopped
pinch of freshly grated nutmeg
1 egg, lightly beaten
1 guinea fowl
25 g/1 oz butter
2 tablespoons olive oil
salt and pepper

Put the sultanas in a bowl, add half the brandy, stir in 2 tablespoons water and leave to soak for 10 minutes, then drain. Tear the bread into pieces, place in another bowl, add water to cover and leave to soak for 10 minutes, then drain and squeeze out. Mix together the sausages, soaked bread, half the sultanas and the thyme, rosemary, parsley and sage in a bowl, stir in the nutmeg and egg and season with salt and pepper. Spoon the mixture into the cavity of the guinea fowl, sew up the opening and truss with kitchen string. Heat the butter and oil in a pan, add the guinea fowl and cook over a medium heat, turning frequently, until browned all over. Season with salt and pepper, sprinkle with the remaining brandy, lower the heat and cook for about 30 minutes. Turn the bird over, sprinkle with the remaining sultanas and cook for a further 30 minutes. To serve, thinly carve the stuffed part of bird and pull off the wings and legs.

GUINEA FOWL WITH TRUFFLES BAKED IN A PARCEL

FARAONA TARTUFATA AL CARTOCCIO

Serves 6

200 g/7 oz lean veal, chopped
1 egg, lightly beaten
1 small white truffle, chopped
150 g/5 oz celery, chopped
1 carrot, chopped
1 fresh flat-leaf parsley sprig, chopped
600 ml/1 pint double cream
1 guinea fowl, boned
5 tablespoons olive oil
5 tablespoons white wine
1 fresh rosemary sprig, chopped
1 garlic clove, chopped
salt and pepper
mashed potatoes, to serve

Preheat the oven to 200°C/400°F/Gas Mark 6. Mix together the veal, egg, truffle, celery, carrot and parsley in a large bowl, stir in the cream and season with salt and pepper. Spread out a sheet of baking parchment and place the guinea fowl on top. Stuff with the veal mixture, sew up the opening and fold over the baking parchment to enclose the bird completely. Pour 3 tablespoons of the oil into a roasting tin, add the parcel and roast, occasionally sprinkling the parcel with the wine, for about 1 hour. Remove the parcel from the oven, open out slightly and leave to stand for 15 minutes, then remove the guinea fowl, thinly carve the stuffed part and pull off the wings and legs. Arrange on a serving dish and keep warm. Heat the remaining olive oil in a pan, add the rosemary and garlic and cook over a low heat for a few minutes. Spoon the mixture over the meat and serve with mashed potatoes.

CHICKEN BOILERS

It has long been known that mature birds – between 15 and 16 months old – make good stock. It is probably less well known that young hens, also known as pullets – between seven and eight months old – are excellent in stews and casseroles.

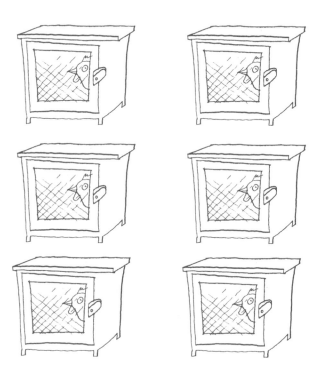

→ As boilers produce fairly fatty stock, remove the skin and underlying fat before immersing the bird in lightly salted water.

→ Cooking takes 1 hour or more, depending on the size of the bird. If the hen is old, it takes at least 2 hours.

→ When the stock is ready, remove the fat by filtering it through a muslin-lined sieve.

COOKING

897

CHICKEN WITH POMEGRANATE

GALLINA ALLA MELAGRANA

Serves 4

2 tablespoons olive oil

40 g/1½ oz butter

1 boiler chicken

2 baby onions

20 g/¾ oz dried mushrooms,

4 pomegranates

250 ml/8 fl oz double cream

4 fresh sage leaves, chopped

salt and pepper

Preheat the oven to 180°C/350°F/Gas Mark 4. Heat half the oil and half the butter in a flameproof casserole, add the chicken and cook, turning frequently, until browned all over. Add one of the onions and sprinkle with hot water. Transfer to the oven and roast for about 1 hour. Meanwhile, place the mushrooms in a bowl, add warm water to cover and leave to soak for 15–30 minutes, then drain and squeeze out. Cut off and discard a slice from one end of a pomegranate, stand it upright and cut downwards through the skin at intervals. Bend back the segments and scrape the seeds into a bowl with your fingers. Repeat with the remaining pomegranates, then crush the seeds with a potato masher and pour the juice over the chicken. Return the casserole to the oven. Reserve the seeds. Chop the remaining onion. Heat the remaining oil and butter in a pan, add the chopped onion and cook over a low heat, stirring occasionally, for 5 minutes. Add the mushrooms and cook, stirring occasionally, for a further 15 minutes, then add to the casserole. When the bird is tender, remove it and the whole onion from the casserole. Transfer the cooking juices to a food processor and process to a purée. Scrape the purée into a saucepan, stir in the cream and sage, season and cook over a low heat until thickened. Cut the bird into pieces and chop the onion. Serve the chicken with the sauce, reserved pomegranate seeds and chopped onion.

RUSTIC CHICKEN

GALLINA CAMPAGNOLA

Serves 6

1 boiler chicken, with giblets

1 onion, thinly sliced

80 g/3 oz cooked ham, chopped

2 tablespoons breadcrumbs

1 fresh flat-leaf parsley sprig, chopped

1 egg yolk

40 g/1½ oz butter

25 g/1 oz pancetta, sliced

12 baby onions

175 ml/6 fl oz dry white wine

3–4 potatoes, diced

salt and pepper

Chop the giblets, place in a frying pan with the onion and ham and cook over a medium heat, stirring frequently, for a few minutes until browned. Remove the pan from the heat and stir in the breadcrumbs, chopped parsley and egg yolk. Season with salt and pepper, return the pan to the heat and cook for a few minutes more. Stuff the chicken with the mixture, sew up the opening and truss with kitchen string. Melt the butter in a flameproof casserole, add the chicken and cook over a high heat, turning frequently, until browned all over. Add the pancetta and baby onions, lower the heat to medium, cover and cook for about 10 minutes. Pour in the wine and cook, uncovered, until it has evaporated, then cover the casserole and simmer for 45 minutes. Add the potatoes and, if necessary, a little hot water to prevent drying out, and cook for a further 30 minutes. Remove the chicken from the casserole, untie and cut into pieces. Serve with the potatoes, baby onions and cooking juices.

GALLINA CON CAROTE E CIPOLLE

Serves 4

1-kg/2¼-lb boiler chicken

25 g/1 oz butter

300 g/11 oz baby onions

500 g/1 lb 2 oz carrots, cut into thin batons

350 ml/12 fl oz dry white wine

salt and pepper

CHICKEN WITH CARROTS AND ONIONS

Season the cavity of the chicken with salt and pepper. Melt the butter in a pan, add the chicken and cook, turning frequently, until browned all over. Add the onions and carrots and cook, stirring frequently, for about 10 minutes until golden brown. Pour in the wine and cook until it has evaporated. Season with salt and pepper to taste, cover and cook over a low heat for about 1 hour.

GALLINA IN SALSA ROSA

Serves 6

500g/1 lb 2 oz canned tomatoes

80 g/3 oz butter

1 boiler chicken, cut into pieces

175 ml/6 fl oz white wine

17⅚ fl oz milk

salt and pepper

boiled or pilaf rice, to serve

CHICKEN IN PINK SAUCE

Pass the tomatoes through a food mill into a bowl. Melt the butter in a large pan, add the chicken pieces and cook, turning frequently, until browned all over. Add the wine, milk and tomatoes, season well with salt and pepper, cover and cook over a medium heat for about 1½ hours. A thick, tasty pink sauce will have formed which, besides tasting exquisite, is also very attractive. Serve the chicken on a warm serving dish, completely covered with the sauce and accompanied with boiled or pilaf rice.

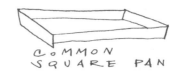

COMMON
SQUARE PAN

GOOSE

Geese are beautiful, white, plump and appealing when alive, but not exactly easy to digest when cooked. By removing the excess fat, however, you can make goose meat much lighter and less of a strain on the digestive system. However, you should bear in mind that the youngest geese have the leanest meat. Generally, in Italy, geese are roasted with plenty of turnips and potatoes to help absorb the fat released during cooking. To make sure the skin is crisp, never baste a goose with its own cooking juices. It is best to place the bird on a rack so that the fat can drip into a roasting tin or tray beneath – pour about 175 ml/6 fl oz water into the tin before roasting. As far as cooking times are concerned, allow 1 hour for the first 1 kg/2'/₄ lb and then 15 minutes for every additional 1 kg/2'/₄ lb. If you are buying a whole goose, choose one aged between eight and nine months and weighing about 3 kg/6'/₂ lb so that it can be roasted perfectly in an ordinary oven. When roasting a goose, parboiling is recommended to decrease its fattiness (see below).

COOKING

→ Season the cavity of the goose with salt, add a large pinch of rosemary needles and sew up the opening.

→ Fill a deep pan one-third full with water, add a large onion and the goose. Bring to the boil, cover and simmer for 30 minutes or more, depending on the size of the bird.

→ Drain the goose, discard the water and follow the recipe.

→ This method should also be used before roasting.

ARROSTO DI OCA CON PEPERONI
IN AGRODOLCE

Serves 8

3-kg/6¹/₂-lb goose

350 g/12 oz dried chestnuts

120 ml/4 fl oz olive oil

1 onion, chopped

1 carrot, chopped

1 celery stick, chopped

1 fresh rosemary sprig, chopped

175 ml/6 fl oz white wine

1 quantity hot Chicken Stock (see page 209)

2 yellow peppers, halved, seeded and cut into strips

2 red peppers, halved, seeded and cut into strips

2 green peppers, halved, seeded and cut into strips

2 tablespoons sugar

175 ml/6 fl oz white wine vinegar

salt and pepper

ROAST GOOSE WITH SWEET–AND–SOUR PEPPERS

Season the cavity of the goose with salt and pepper, fill with the dried chestnuts and truss with kitchen string. Heat half the olive oil in a flameproof casserole, add the goose, onion, carrot, celery and rosemary and cook, turning the bird frequently, for about 20 minutes until well browned. Meanwhile, preheat the oven to 180°C/350°F/Gas Mark 4. Pour the wine and 5 tablespoons of the hot stock into the casserole, then transfer to the oven and roast for 2 hours, adding a ladleful of hot stock every 15 minutes and turning the goose every 30 minutes. Heat the remaining oil in a pan, add all the peppers and cook over a low heat, stirring occasionally, for 20 minutes. Stir in the sugar and vinegar and simmer gently for a further 10 minutes. Remove the goose from the oven and discard the chestnuts. Pass the cooking juices through a food mill. Carve the goose breast into slices, remove the legs and wings and place on a warm serving dish. Surround with the sweet-and-sour peppers and serve with the cooking juices.

COSCE DI OCA IN AGRODOLCE

Serves 4

250 ml/8 fl oz balsamic vinegar

1 shallot

1 carrot

120 g/4 oz sugar

4 goose legs

50 g/2 oz butter

2 tablespoons cornmeal

salt

SWEET–AND–SOUR GOOSE LEGS

Pour the vinegar into a saucepan, add the shallot, carrot, 25 g/1 oz of the sugar and the goose legs, season with salt and simmer until the goose is tender and cooked through. Drain the goose legs and leave to cool, then slice the meat off the bones. Strain the stock into a bowl and leave to cool, then remove and reserve the fat that solidifies on the surface. Melt the butter in a pan, add the goose meat and cook, turning frequently, until browned all over. Sprinkle with half the remaining sugar and a little of the reserved fat from the stock, then sprinkle with the remaining sugar and cook over a low heat until caramelized. Remove the meat, place on a serving dish and keep warm. Stir the cornmeal into the pan and cook, stirring, for a few minutes, then gradually stir in 175 ml/6 fl oz of the stock and heat gently until thickened. Spoon the sauce over the slices of goose and serve.

GERMAN GOOSE WITH APPLES

Preheat the oven to 160°C/325°F/Gas Mark 3. Chop half the apples and slice the remainder. Season the cavity of the goose with salt and stuff with the chopped apples, then sew up the opening and truss with kitchen string. Place on a rack set over a roasting tin or oven tray and pour a little water into the tin or tray. Roast until the goose has browned, then pat the skin dry with kitchen paper. Pour the wine over the goose, add 150 ml/¼ pint warm water, return to the oven and roast for a further 2 hours. Meanwhile, blanch the apple slices in boiling water for 1 minute, then drain. Melt the butter in a frying pan, add the sliced apples and cook over a low heat, stirring frequently, until softened. Place the goose on a warm serving dish, surround with the apples and season with pepper.

OCA ALLA TEDESCA CON LE MELE
Serves 8
1 kg/2¼ lb eating apples, peeled and cored
3-kg/6½-lb goose
175 ml/6 fl oz dry white wine
40 g/1½ oz butter
salt and pepper

BRAISED GOOSE

Preheat the oven to 150°C/300°F/Gas Mark 2. Melt the butter in a flameproof casserole, add the goose and cook, turning frequently, until browned all over. Add the onions and garlic and cook over a low heat, stirring occasionally, for 5 minutes. Pour in the wine, add the tomatoes and herbs and season with salt and pepper. Cover, transfer to the oven and cook for about 3 hours until the meat comes away from the bones. Remove the goose from the casserole, cut the meat off the bones, place on a serving dish and keep warm. Remove and discard the garlic and herbs and heat the cooking juices to reduce if necessary. Pour in the brandy and mix well, season with salt and pepper to taste and serve the goose with the sauce.

OCA BRASATA
Serves 8
50 g/2 oz butter
3-kg/6½-lb goose, cut into pieces
2 onions, thinly sliced
2 garlic cloves
1 bottle (750 ml/1¼ pints) dry white wine
6 large tomatoes, peeled, seeded and chopped
1 fresh rosemary sprig
2 fresh sage leaves
50 ml/2 fl oz brandy
salt and pepper

GOOSE STUFFED WITH POTATOES

OCA RIPIENA DI PATATE

Serves 8

400 g/14 oz potatoes, unpeeled

25 g/1 oz butter

1 onion, chopped

1 fresh parsley sprig, chopped

pinch of chopped fresh rosemary

3-kg/6¹/₂-lb goose

300 ml/¹/₂ pint hot Chicken Stock (see page 209)

salt and pepper

Cook the potatoes in salted, boiling water for 10 minutes, then drain, peel and dice. Preheat the oven to 200°C/400°F/Gas Mark 6. Melt the butter in a pan, add the onion and parsley and cook over a low heat, stirring occasionally, for 5 minutes. Add the potatoes, increase the heat to medium and cook, shaking the pan occasionally, until browned. Season with salt and pepper and stir in the rosemary. Stuff the goose with the vegetable mixture, sew up the opening and truss with kitchen string. Prick the skin all over with a fork. Place the goose, breast side down, on a rack set over a roasting tin or oven tray, cover with a sheet of foil and pour a little water into the tin or tray underneath. Roast for 1 hour, then lower the oven temperature to 180°C/350°F/Gas Mark 4 and roast for 1 hour more. Remove and discard the foil, turn the goose over, return to the oven and roast, basting occasionally with hot stock, for 1 more hour. Skim off the fat from the cooking juices and pour them into a sauce boat. Carve the goose and serve with the cooking juices.

BREAST OF GOOSE IN BALSAMIC VINEGAR

PETTO D'OCA ALL'ACETO BALSAMICO

Serves 4

25 g/1 oz butter

2 tablespoons olive oil

2 garlic cloves

500 g/1 lb 2 oz boneless breast of goose, sliced

6 tablespoons balsamic vinegar

salt and pepper

For the sauce

100 ml/3¹/₂ fl oz olive oil

100 ml/3¹/₂ fl oz balsamic vinegar

2 garlic cloves

¹/₂ fresh chilli, seeded and chopped

salt

First, make the sauce. Whisk together the oil and vinegar in a bowl and add the garlic, chilli and a pinch of salt, then set aside. Heat the butter and olive oil in a pan, add the garlic and cook over a low heat until the cloves have turned brown, then remove and discard them. Add the goose slices to the pan, increase the heat to high and cook, turning frequently, for a few minutes until browned. Season with salt and pepper, sprinkle with the vinegar and cook for 15–20 minutes until reduced. Transfer to a warm serving dish and pour the sauce on top.

STRACOTTO D'OCA

Serves 8

3-kg/6¹/₂-lb goose

50 g/2 oz pancetta, thinly sliced

2 tablespoons olive oil

1 bottle (750 ml/1¹/₄ pints) dry white wine

350 ml/12 fl oz white wine vinegar

1 quantity Chicken Stock (see page 209)

6 black peppercorns, lightly crushed

1 bay leaf

2 onions

pinch of chopped fresh marjoram

pinch of chopped fresh rosemary

For the sauce

2 salted anchovies, heads removed, cleaned and filleted (see page 596), soaked in cold water for 10 minutes and drained

2 lemons

25 g/1 oz butter

GOOSE STEW

Preheat the oven to 190°C/375°F/Gas Mark 5. Wrap the goose in the slices of pancetta, place on a rack set over a roasting tin or oven tray and roast for 1¹/₂ hours. Take the goose out of the oven and remove the pancetta. Place the goose in a snug-fitting pan with the olive oil. Pour in the wine, vinegar and stock to cover. Add the peppercorns, bay leaf, onions, marjoram and rosemary and season with salt. Simmer over a low heat for 1 hour, then remove the goose from the pan and keep warm. To make the sauce, first chop the anchovy fillets. Peel one of the lemons and cut off all traces of white pith. Dice the flesh and add to the goose cooking juices with the anchovies, heat through gently, then remove the pan from the heat and stir in the butter. Slice the remaining lemon. Carve the goose into slices and place on a warm serving dish. Spoon the sauce over it and garnish with the lemon slices.

PIGEON

Reared pigeons should more properly be called squab – young pigeons – and have lean, white, tasty, easily digestible meat. In fact, experts say that only young birds should be cooked as they are sure to have tender, tasty flesh. Otherwise, you risk having tough, unpleasant meat on your plate. Pigeons are excellent roast, grilled or fried with peas. Wild pigeons – better known as wood pigeons – have darker meat with a more gamy flavour. One pigeon is usually enough for two people.

ROAST PIGEONS

ARROSTO DI PICCIONI

Serves 4

2 pigeons, with livers

4 thin pancetta slices

1 tablespoon olive oil

25 g/1 oz butter

salt and pepper

Preheat the oven to 180°C/350°F/Gas Mark 4. Chop the livers and set aside. Wrap each pigeon in two slices of pancetta and truss with kitchen string. Heat the oil and butter in a flameproof casserole, add the pigeons and cook, turning frequently, until browned all over. Season with salt and pepper to taste, transfer to the oven and roast for 40 minutes. Remove the pancetta, return the casserole to the oven and roast for a further 10 minutes. Remove the pigeons from the casserole and keep warm. Stir 1 tablespoon hot water into the cooking juices, add the chopped livers and cook over a medium heat, stirring constantly, for a few minutes. Cut the pigeons in half, place on a warm serving dish and spoon the sauce over them.

GRILLED PIGEONS

PICCIONI ALLA GRIGLIA

Serves 4

5 tablespoons olive oil

1 fresh flat-leaf parsley sprig, chopped

juice of 2 lemons, strained

4 black peppercorns, lightly crushed

2 pigeons, halved • salt

potatoes baked in foil, to serve

Mix together the oil, parsley, lemon juice and peppercorns in a dish, season with salt, add the pigeons and leave to marinate for 4–6 hours. Preheat the grill. Drain the pigeons, reserving the marinade, and place under the grill. Cook for 45 minutes, turning frequently and brushing with the reserved marinade. Serve with potatoes baked in foil.

PIQUANT PIGEONS

PICCIONI ALL'AGRO

Serves 4

2 fresh rosemary sprigs, chopped

2 bay leaves

2 fresh sage leaves

2 pancetta slices

2 pigeons

juice of 2 lemons, strained

salt and pepper

boiled rice, to serve

Put a pinch of salt, a pinch of pepper, half the rosemary, a bay leaf, a sage leaf and a slice of pancetta in the cavity of each pigeon. Place in a pan, season with salt and pour in the lemon juice. Cover and cook over a low heat for 45 minutes. Serve with boiled rice seasoned with a knob of butter.

PIGEONS WITH OLIVES

PICCIONI ALLE OLIVE

Serves 4

50 g/2 oz pancetta slices

2 pigeons

50 g/2 oz butter

1 onion, thinly sliced

1 teaspoon cornflour

175 ml/6 fl oz white wine

250 ml/8 fl oz hot Meat Stock (see page 208)

100 g/3¹/₂ oz stoned black olives

salt and pepper

Preheat the oven to 180°C/350°F/Gas Mark 4. Put a pinch of salt and a slice of pancetta in the cavity of each pigeon. Place the remaining slices of pancetta over the breasts of the birds and truss with kitchen string. Season with salt and pepper. Place the pigeons in a casserole with 25 g/1 oz of the butter and roast until well browned. Melt the remaining butter in a pan, add the onion and cook over a low heat, stirring occasionally, for 5 minutes. Sprinkle in the cornflour, then gradually stir in the wine and cook, stirring constantly, until it has evaporated. Pour in the stock, add the olives and cook until the sauce has thickened. Remove the pigeons from the casserole, untie and cut in half. Place on a warm serving dish and spoon the sauce over them.

STUFFED PIGEONS

PICCIONI FARCITI

Serves 4

1 thick white bread slice, crusts removed

2 pigeons, with livers

50 g/2 oz cooked ham, chopped

50 g/2 oz prosciutto, chopped

1 fresh flat-leaf parsley sprig, chopped

50 g/2 oz butter

1 celery stick, chopped

1 fresh sage leaf

175 ml/6 fl oz Meat Stock (see page 208)

175 ml/6 fl oz dry white wine

salt and pepper

Tear the bread into pieces, place in a bowl, add water to cover and leave to soak for 10 minutes, then drain and squeeze out. Chop the livers, place in a bowl, add the ham, prosciutto, parsley and soaked bread and mix well. Season with salt and pepper and spoon the mixture into the cavities of the pigeons. Melt the butter in a pan, add the celery and sage and cook over a low heat, stirring occasionally, for 5 minutes. Add the pigeons and cook, turning frequently, until browned all over Pour in the stock and wine, cover and simmer over a low heat for 1 hour.

CHICKEN

Chickens may be bought whole or in portions – breast, legs, wings, thighs and livers. Today most chickens in Italy and elsewhere are intensively reared and are sold plucked, gutted, without head, neck and feet and ready for cooking. There is increasing desire for free-range and organic birds and, although expensive, such chicken is growing in popularity. Chicken is tender and therefore cooks very quickly, but it is not always very tasty and the flavour sometimes needs enriching with marinades, sauces and herbs. The quality of chicken may be judged by its skin, which should have a velvety consistency and pale colour with slight sky-blue glints.

JOINTING CHICKEN

→ A cooked or raw chicken may be easily cut along its joints with poultry shears or a short-bladed kitchen knife.

→ Always start from the legs. Cut into the point where they are attached to the body, then cut through the joint. Do the same with the wings. After removing the legs and wings, turn the chicken on its back, cut in along the central bone and remove the two breast fillets. Divide the body in half, first lengthways, then crossways.

COOKING

→ The chickens described here and used in the following recipes weigh about 1 kg/2¼ lb. To test whether the bird is cooked, pierce the thickest part with the point of a sharp knife. If the juices run clear, the chicken is ready, but if there are any traces of pink, it should be cooked for a little longer.

IN THE OVEN

It is best to cook chicken slowly at a moderate temperature, increasing the heat only towards the end of the cooking time, to brown the bird. That way the meat stays tender, especially if the bird is fairly large.

GRILLING

The ideal method is over charcoal, but chicken can also be cooked successfully under a preheated conventional grill. Open the bird out by cutting along its back and pounding to flatten it evenly. Poussins are excellent grilled as they cook in 45 minutes.

ROASTING

Always choose a young bird. To begin with, only season the cavity with salt. Near the end of the cooking time, season the outside too. It cooks in 40–45 minutes.

ON THE SPIT

Some modern ovens come with a spit. Season the cavity of the chicken with salt and occasionally brush the bird with oil or melted butter while it is cooking. It cooks in about 50 minutes.

STEWING

Cut the chicken into pieces. To provide extra flavour, add ingredients such as tomatoes, fresh or dried mushrooms, fragrant herbs, etc. It cooks in about 1 hour.

POACHING

Before immersing the chicken in water, rub the skin with half a lemon to keep the meat white. Always add a carrot, a celery stick and an onion to the pan. When the chicken has finished cooking, drain it well, remove and discard the skin, carve the meat and serve, still warm, with a selection of sauces. It cooks in 1 hour.

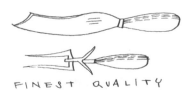

FINEST QUALITY

CHICKEN PIE

Preheat the oven to 180°C/350°F/Gas Mark 4. Line the base and sides of a deep ovenproof pie dish with some of the bacon, place the chicken on top and cover with the slices of egg. Season very lightly with salt, bearing in mind that the bacon will be salty. Make a layer of the onion and parsley, top with a layer of the mushrooms and, finally, cover with the remaining bacon. Roll out the pastry on a lightly floured surface into a sheet large enough to cover the pie dish. Place the pastry on top of the pie and tuck in the sides to seal. Brush with the egg yolk mixture and lightly prick all over the surface with a fork. Transfer to the oven and bake for 1¼ hours. Remove from the oven and leave to stand for about 10 minutes, then serve straight from the dish.

CHICKEN PIE

Serves 4

200 g/7 oz smoked bacon rashers

500 g/1 lb 2 oz boneless chicken, diced

2 eggs, hard-boiled, shelled and sliced

1 onion, chopped

2 tablespoons chopped fresh parsley

150 g/5 oz mushrooms, chopped

200 g/7 oz puff pastry dough, thawed if frozen

plain flour, for dusting

1 egg yolk beaten with 2 tablespoons water

salt

CHICKEN LEGS IN RED WINE

Put the mushrooms in a bowl, add hot water to cover and leave to soak for 15 minutes, then drain and squeeze out. Melt the butter in a pan, add the rosemary and bay leaf, then add the chicken legs and cook, turning frequently, until golden brown all over. Season with salt and pepper and add the mushrooms, then pour in the wine and cook until it has evaporated. Remove the chicken legs from the pan, wrap each in a slice of pancetta, secure with a cocktail stick and return to the pan. Cook, uncovered, over a medium heat for 30 minutes until tender and cooked through. If necessary, thicken the cooking juices by adding a pinch of plain flour stirred into 1 tablespoon water and cooking for a further 5 minutes.

GIAMBONETTI DI POLLO AL VINO ROSSO

Serves 4

25 g/1 oz dried mushrooms

25 g/1 oz butter

1 fresh rosemary sprig

1 bay leaf

4 chicken legs

350 ml/12 fl oz red wine

4 pancetta slices

salt and pepper

AMERICAN CHICKEN SALAD

Put the chicken and celery in a bowl. Mix together the mayonnaise and cream in another bowl, season with salt and pepper and stir gently into the chicken mixture. Transfer to a serving dish and sprinkle the capers and olives on top. Garnish the dish with the wedges of egg.

INSALATA DI POLLO ALL'AMERICANA

Serves 4

300 g/11 oz cooked chicken, skinned and cut into strips

1 bunch of white celery, cut into thin batons

250 ml/8 fl oz Mayonnaise (see page 65)

2 tablespoons double cream

1 tablespoon capers, drained and rinsed

12 black olives

salt and pepper

2 eggs, hard-boiled, shelled and cut into wedges, to garnish

CHICKEN AND CELERIAC SALAD

INSALATA DI POLLO CON SEDANO-RAPA

Serves 4

300 g/11 oz cooked chicken, skinned and cut into strips

1 celeriac, cut into thin batons

1 quantity Mayonnaise (see page 65)

3 tablespoons natural yogurt

1 teaspoon Dijon mustard

Put the chicken and celeriac into a salad bowl. Mix together the mayonnaise, yogurt and mustard in another bowl and season with salt. Gently stir the dressing into the salad and serve.

CHICKEN ROULADES WITH SAGE

INVOLTINI DI POLLO ALLA SALVIA

Serves 4

4 skinless, boneless chicken breast portions

8 fresh sage leaves

100 g/3¹/₂ oz pancetta, thinly sliced

2 tablespoons olive oil

salt and pepper

radicchio salad, to serve

Lightly pound the chicken with a meat mallet. Place two of the sage leaves on each portion and season with salt and pepper. Roll up, wrap in the pancetta slices and secure with cocktail sticks. Heat the oil in a frying pan, add the roulades and cook, turning frequently, until browned all over. Cover and cook over a low heat for about 20 minutes, adding 1 tablespoon hot water if necessary. Serve with a radicchio salad.

CHICKEN, ANCHOVY AND CAPER ROULADES

INVOLTINI DI POLLO ALLE ACCIUGHE E CAPPERI

Serves 4

4 salted anchovies, soaked in water and drained

4 skinless, boneless chicken breast portions

25 g/1 oz capers, drained and rinsed

25 g/1 oz butter

1 tablespoon olive oil

1 onion, thinly sliced

50 ml/2 fl oz dry white wine

salt and pepper

Place the anchovies skin side up and press along the backbones with your thumb, then turn them over and remove the bones. Lightly pound the chicken with a meat mallet. Divide the boned anchovies and capers among the chicken portions, roll up and secure with cocktail sticks. Heat the butter and oil in a frying pan, add the onion and cook over a low heat, stirring occasionally, for 5 minutes. Add the roulades and cook, turning frequently, until browned all over. Season with salt and pepper, increase the heat to high, pour in the wine and cook until it has reduced slightly. Lower the heat, cover and simmer for 20 minutes. Transfer to a warm serving dish.

CHICKEN ROULADES WITH CHIVES

INVOLTINI DI POLLO
ALL'ERBA CIPOLLINA

Serves 4

4 skinless, boneless chicken breast portions

50 g/2 oz butter

2 tablespoons chopped fresh chives

plain flour, for dusting

3 tablespoons olive oil

salt and pepper

peas in butter, to serve

Cut the chicken portions in half horizontally and pound to 5 mm/¼ inch thick with a meat mallet. Cut the butter in half and cut one of the halves into 4 slices. Put a slice of butter, a pinch of salt and a pinch of pepper on each chicken portion and divide the chives among them. Roll up the portions, dust with flour, shake off any excess and secure with cocktail sticks. Heat the olive oil and the remaining butter in a frying pan, add the roulades and cook over a high heat, turning frequently, until browned all over. Lower the heat to medium, cover and cook for 15 minutes. Serve the roulades with peas in butter.

POACHED STUFFED CHICKEN

LESSO RIPIENO

Serves 6

300 g/11 oz minced veal

25 g/1 oz Parmesan cheese, freshly grated

1 tablespoon breadcrumbs

1 fresh flat-leaf parsley sprig, finely chopped

1 fresh rosemary sprig, finely chopped

1 garlic clove, finely chopped

1 egg, lightly beaten

1 chicken

1 carrot • 1 onion

1 celery stick

salt and pepper

Mix together the veal, Parmesan and breadcrumbs in a bowl and add the parsley, rosemary and garlic. Stir in the beaten egg, season with salt and pepper and stuff the chicken with the mixture. Sew up the opening. Place the chicken in a pan, add the carrot, onion, celery and a pinch of salt and pour in water to cover. Bring just to the boil, then lower the heat and simmer for 25 minutes. Prick the chicken with a fork, return to the heat and simmer for a further 20 minutes until tender and cooked through. Remove the chicken from the pan, cut off the wings and legs and carve the central part filled with stuffing. Place on a warm serving dish. The stock may be used to cook cappelletti pasta.

CHICKEN BREASTS IN VINEGAR

PETTI ALL'ACETO

Serves 4

4 skinless, boneless chicken breast portions

80 g/3 oz butter

2 shallots, chopped

350 ml/12 fl oz white wine vinegar

salt and pepper

Lightly pound the chicken portions with a meat mallet. Heat 50 g/2 oz of the butter in a pan, add the chicken and cook over a medium heat, turning occasionally, until browned on both sides. Season with salt and pepper, lower the heat, cover and cook for 20 minutes until tender and cooked through. Meanwhile, heat half the remaining butter in a small frying pan, add the shallots and cook over a low heat, stirring occasionally, for about 8 minutes until lightly golden. Pour in the vinegar and cook until reduced by half. Remove the pan from the heat and stir in the remaining butter. Place the chicken on a warm serving dish, and pour the shallot sauce on top.

CHICKEN BREASTS AND FENNEL AU GRATIN

PETTI CON FINOCCHI AL GRATIN

Serves 4

butter, for greasing

2 fennel bulbs, trimmed

4 skinless, boneless chicken breast portions, diced

1 quantity Béchamel Sauce (see page 50)

salt

Preheat the oven to 180°C/350°F/Gas Mark 4. Grease a roasting tin with butter. If the fennel bulbs are young and tender, blanch in boiling water for 2–3 minutes, then drain. Otherwise cook the bulbs in boiling water for 5 minutes, then drain. Slice the fennel and spread out in the prepared roasting tin, then top with the chicken and season with salt. Spoon the béchamel sauce over the chicken and bake for 30 minutes or until golden brown.

CHICKEN BREASTS STUFFED WITH MASCARPONE

PETTI FARCITI AL MASCARPONE

Serves 4

40 g/1½ oz butter, plus extra for greasing

250 g/9 oz mushrooms

juice of 1 lemon, strained

1 garlic clove

1 tablespoon chopped fresh flat-leaf parsley

4 skinless, boneless chicken breast portions

2 cooked ham slices, halved

100 g/3½ oz mascarpone cheese

1 tomato

salt and pepper

Preheat the oven to 200°C/400°F/Gas Mark 6. Grease a roasting tin with butter. Chop the mushrooms and sprinkle with the lemon juice to prevent discoloration. Melt 25 g/1 oz of the butter in a small frying pan, add the garlic and cook until it turns brown, then remove and discard it. Add the parsley and mushrooms and cook over a high heat, stirring occasionally, for 5 minutes. Season with salt and pepper and cook for a further 2 minutes, then remove the pan from the heat. Slice horizontally through the chicken portions without cutting all the way through. Open out each portion like a book, pound with a meat mallet and season with salt and pepper. Place a piece of ham on one side of each piece of chicken, divide the mascarpone among the portions and top each one with 1 tablespoon of the mushrooms. Fold the portions together again and secure with cocktail sticks. Cut four slices out of the centre of the tomato, put one on each chicken, season with salt and dot with the remaining butter. Place the chicken in the prepared roasting tin, cover with foil and roast for 15 minutes. Meanwhile, preheat the grill. Discard the foil and brown the chicken under the grill.

SOUSED CHICKEN BREASTS

Pound the chicken with a meat mallet until evenly thin. Beat the eggs with a pinch of salt in a dish, add the chicken and leave to stand for 15 minutes. Spread out the breadcrumbs in a shallow dish. Drain the chicken and dip in the breadcrumbs to coat. Heat the butter and 2 tablespoons of the oil in a pan, add the chicken and cook over a medium heat, turning occasionally, for about 10 minutes until golden brown on both sides. Meanwhile, heat the remaining oil in another pan, add the onion, celery and carrot and cook over a low heat, stirring occasionally, for 5 minutes. Season with salt and pepper to taste, add the vinegar and wine and bring to the boil, then immediately remove from the heat and add the sage and garlic. Place the chicken in a dish, pour the hot marinade over it, leave to cool, then chill in the refrigerator for at least 4 hours before serving. This dish can be prepared the day before.

PETTI IN CARPIONE

Serves 4

4 skinless, boneless chicken breast portions

2 eggs

80 g/3 oz breadcrumbs

25 g/1 oz butter

5 tablespoons olive oil

1 onion, thinly sliced

1 celery stick, thinly sliced

1 carrot, thinly sliced

350 ml/12 fl oz white wine vinegar

100 ml/3¹/₂ fl oz dry white wine

4 fresh sage leaves

2 garlic cloves, sliced

salt and pepper

CHICKEN BREASTS IN ALMOND SAUCE

Melt half the butter in a frying pan, add the chicken and cook over a low heat, turning occasionally, until lightly browned on both sides. Add the lemon juice, season with salt and pepper, cover and cook for 20 minutes. Remove the chicken from the pan and add half the remaining butter, the almonds, garlic and onion. Cook, stirring occasionally, until the almonds have browned, then add the remaining butter, pour in the wine and cook until it has evaporated. Return the chicken to the pan and heat through. Transfer the chicken to a warm serving dish, spoon the sauce over it and sprinkle with the parsley.

PETTI IN SALSA DI MANDORLE

Serves 4

40 g/1¹/₂ oz butter

4 skinless, boneless chicken breast portions

juice of ¹/₂ lemon, strained

40 g/1¹/₂ oz almonds, chopped

1 garlic clove, crushed

1 onion, thinly sliced

50 ml/2 fl oz dry white wine

2 tablespoons chopped fresh flat-leaf parsley

salt and pepper

CHICKEN WITH MUSHROOMS

Put the mushrooms in a bowl, add warm water to cover and leave to soak for 15 minutes, then drain and squeeze out. Lightly dust the chicken portions with the flour. Heat the butter and oil in a pan, add the chicken and cook, turning frequently, until browned all over. Add the mushrooms and onions and cook for a few minutes, then pour in the wine and cook until it has evaporated. Add the passata and 3 tablespoons water and season with salt and pepper. Cover and cook over a medium heat for about 1 hour until tender and cooked through. Place the chicken portions with their cooking juices on a warm serving dish and sprinkle with the parsley.

POLLO AI FUNGHI

Serves 4

150 g/5 oz dried mushrooms

1 chicken, cut into 4 portions

2 tablespoons plain flour

25 g/1 oz butter • 3 tablespoons olive oil

2 baby onions, chopped

5 tablespoons dry white wine

2 tablespoons passata

2 tablespoons chopped fresh flat-leaf parsley

salt and pepper

CHICKEN ROASTED IN A PARCEL

POLLO AL CARTOCCIO

Serves 4

1 chicken
4 black peppercorns
4 fresh flat-leaf parsley sprigs
12 baby onions
2 cloves
25 g/1 oz butter, melted
sea salt

Preheat the oven to 200°C/400°F/Gas Mark 6. Sprinkle the cavity of the chicken with sea salt and add the peppercorns, two of the parsley sprigs and two of the onions studded with the cloves. Sew up the opening and fold the wings on to the back. Rub the outside of the bird with sea salt, brush with the melted butter and place in the middle of a fairly large sheet of foil. Surround with the remaining onions and parsley and wrap the foil over the chicken to enclose it completely. Roast for 30 minutes, then lower the oven temperature to 180°C/350°F/Gas Mark 4 and roast for a further 30 minutes until tender and cooked through. Serve in the parcel and open at the table.

CHICKEN CURRY

POLLO AL CURRY

Serves 4

25 g/1 oz butter
1 chicken, cut into pieces
2 tablespoons curry powder
2 onions, chopped
2 apples, peeled, cored and chopped
2 tablespoons double cream
salt and pepper
boiled rice or pilaf, to serve

Melt the butter in a pan, add the chicken and cook, turning frequently, until very lightly browned, then season with salt and pepper. Stir the curry powder into 150 ml/¼ pint hot water and add to the pan. Add the onions and apples, cover and cook over a low heat for 35 minutes, adding a little hot water during cooking if necessary. Pour in the cream and cook for a further 10 minutes. Serve with boiled rice or pilaf.

CHICKEN BABI

POLLO ALLA BABI

Serves 4

1 chicken
5 tablespoons olive oil
1 garlic clove, crushed
1 fresh rosemary sprig
salt and pepper

In Piedmontese dialect, babi means toad. To make the chicken look like a toad, open it along the breast and pound several times with a meat mallet. Gently rub the inside of the bird with salt and pepper. Heat the oil in a heavy-based frying pan, add the chicken and cook over a high heat for about 15 minutes until browned on both sides. Add the garlic and rosemary, lower the heat and cook for a further 30 minutes until tender and cooked through. Drain the chicken carefully and serve.

CHICKEN IN BEER

POLLO ALLA BIRRA

Serves 4

1 chicken

1 carrot, finely chopped • 1 onion, finely chopped

1 leek, trimmed and finely chopped

1 celery stick, finely chopped

1 litre/1¾ pints lager beer • salt and pepper

Season the chicken cavity with salt and pepper and place in a large pan. Add the carrot, onion, leek and celery and pour in the beer, which should almost completely cover the bird. Bring to the boil, then lower the heat and simmer, turning once, for about 1 hour until the beer has almost completely evaporated and the chicken is golden brown, tender and cooked through.

CHICKEN CACCIATORE

POLLO ALLA CACCIATORA

Serves 4

1 chicken, cut into pieces

25 g/1 oz butter

3 tablespoons olive oil

1 onion

6 tomatoes, peeled, seeded and chopped

1 carrot, chopped

1 celery stick, chopped

1 fresh flat-leaf parsley sprig, chopped

salt and pepper

Put the chicken in a flameproof casserole with the butter, oil and onion and cook over a medium heat, stirring and turning frequently, for about 15 minutes until browned. Add the tomatoes, carrot and celery, pour in 150 ml/¼ pint water, cover and simmer for 45 minutes until the chicken is tender and cooked through. Sprinkle in the parsley and season with salt and pepper. This is the simplest way to prepare chicken cacciatore – in some regions more celery and carrots are added, in others white wine is used instead of water or stock, and in still others sliced mushrooms are added.

DEVILLED CHICKEN

POLLO ALLA DIAVOLA

Serves 4

1 chicken

3 tablespoons olive oil

generous pinch of chilli powder

salt

Traditionally, devilled chicken is grilled, but this version is cooked on the hob. Open the chicken out lengthways along the back and pound it well with a meat mallet. Heat the oil in a pan, add the chicken and cook, turning frequently, for 15 minutes until golden brown all over. Season with salt, sprinkle with the chilli powder and cook over a low heat for a further 45 minutes until tender and cooked through.

PHILIPPINES CHICKEN

POLLO ALLA FILIPPINA

Serves 4

2 tablespoons olive oil

1 chicken, cut into pieces

5 tablespoons white wine vinegar

3 tablespoons dark soy sauce

2 garlic cloves, chopped

1 bay leaf

4 black peppercorns

salt

Heat the oil in a pan, add the chicken and cook, stirring and turning frequently, until golden brown all over. Meanwhile, put the vinegar, soy sauce, garlic, bay leaf, peppercorns and a pinch of salt in a saucepan over a low heat. When the chicken is evenly golden brown, pour the mixture over it, cover and simmer, basting occasionally, for 30 minutes until tender and cooked through. Remove the chicken from the pan and transfer to a warm serving dish. Stir 1 tablespoon hot water into the cooking juices, cook until heated through and pour into a sauce boat. Serve the chicken with the sauce.

CHICKEN WITH GARLIC

POLLO ALL'AGLIO

Serves 4

25 g/1 oz butter

2 tablespoons olive oil

1 chicken, cut into pieces

1 garlic bulb, separated into unpeeled cloves

5 tablespoons dry white wine

salt and pepper

Heat the butter and oil in a saucepan, add the chicken and cook, stirring and turning frequently, for about 15 minutes until golden brown all over. Add the garlic cloves and cook until the papery skins have turned golden brown, then season well with salt and pepper. Pour in the wine and cook until it has evaporated, then cover the pan and simmer over a low heat for 30 minutes until tender and cooked through. Remove the lid, increase the heat and cook until the sauce has thickened slightly. Remove the garlic and place the chicken on a warm serving dish.

GREEK CHICKEN

POLLO ALLA GRECA

Serves 4

1 chicken

5 tablespoons olive oil

juice of 1 lemon, strained

1 tablespoon chopped fresh oregano

salt and pepper

Gently rub the outside of the chicken with salt and pepper and put a pinch of each in the cavity. Whisk 4 tablespoons of the oil with the lemon juice and half the oregano in a bowl, season, add the chicken and leave to marinate for at least 2 hours. Preheat the oven to 180°C/350°F/Gas Mark 4. Drain the chicken, reserving the marinade, and place in a roasting tin with the remaining oil. Roast, turning frequently and basting with the reserved marinade, for 1½ hours until tender. Serve sprinkled with the remaining oregano.

CHICKEN WITH CREAM

POLLO ALLA PANNA

Serves 4

1 chicken, cut into pieces • plain flour, for dusting

40 g/1½ oz butter • 275 ml/9 fl oz double cream

juice of ½ lemon, strained

50 g/2 oz cooked ham, chopped

salt and pepper

Season the chicken and dust with flour. Melt the butter in a pan, add the chicken and cook over a low heat, turning occasionally, until lightly browned. Pour in the cream and simmer for about 30 minutes until tender and cooked through. Season to taste, pour in the lemon juice and mix thoroughly. Add the ham and cook for a further 2 minutes, then place on a warm serving dish.

CHICKEN RATATOUILLE

POLLO ALLA RATATOUILLE

Serves 4

50 g/2 oz butter • 6 tablespoons olive oil

2 onions, quartered • 3 courgettes, cut into cubes

2 aubergines, cut into cubes

3 red or yellow peppers,

halved, seeded and thickly sliced

4 tomatoes, peeled, quartered and seeded

1 chicken, cut into pieces • 2 garlic cloves

salt and pepper

Heat half the butter and half the oil in a pan, add the onions, courgettes, aubergines and peppers, season with salt and pepper and cook over a high heat for a few minutes. Lower the heat, add the tomatoes, cover and simmer gently for about 1 hour. Heat the remaining butter and oil in another pan, add the chicken and garlic and cook, stirring and turning frequently, until golden brown all over. Season with salt and pepper and cook for a further 30 minutes until tender and cooked through. Remove and discard the garlic and add the chicken to the vegetables. Mix well and serve.

CHICKEN WITH ONIONS

POLLO ALLE CIPOLLE

Serves 4

25 g/1 oz butter

2 tablespoons olive oil

1 chicken, cut into pieces

1 large onion, thinly sliced

500 g/1 lb 2 oz baby onions

1 fresh thyme sprig

1 bay leaf

1 garlic clove

salt and pepper

Heat the butter and olive oil in a pan, add the chicken, sliced onion and baby onions and cook over a low heat, stirring and turning occasionally, until golden brown all over. Season with salt and pepper, add the thyme, bay leaf and garlic, cover and cook gently for 40 minutes until tender and cooked through. Remove and discard the bay leaf and garlic. Place the chicken and onions on a warm serving dish.

POLLO ALLE CIPOLLE

Serves 4

25 g/1 oz butter

2 tablespoons olive oil

1 chicken, cut into pieces

1 large onion, thinly sliced

500 g/1 lb 2 oz baby onions

1 fresh thyme sprig

1 bay leaf

1 garlic clove

salt and pepper

CHICKEN WITH APPLES

POLLO ALLE MELE

Serves 4

1 chicken

2 red apples, peeled, cored and grated

4 pork fat slices or 4 streaky bacon rashers

salt and pepper

Preheat the oven to 240°C/475°F/Gas Mark 9. Season the cavity of the chicken with salt and pepper and stuff with the grated apples. Sew up the opening, wrap the chicken in the pork fat or bacon and tie with kitchen string. Place in a roasting tin and roast until the pork or bacon fat melts and collects on the base of the tin. Lower the oven temperature to 190°C/375°F/Gas Mark 5 and roast for 1 hour, basting frequently during the last 30 minutes, until tender and cooked through. If the skin seems to go brown too quickly, lower the temperature and cover the tin with a sheet of foil. Remove the chicken from the oven and untie. Cut off the legs and wings and carve the central part filled with stuffing.

CHICKEN WITH OLIVES

POLLO ALLE OLIVE

Serves 4

3 tablespoons olive oil

1 chicken, cut into pieces

175 ml/6 fl oz white wine

6 tomatoes, peeled, seeded and chopped

2 garlic cloves, chopped

1 fresh thyme sprig, chopped

4 fresh sage leaves, chopped

1 fresh marjoram sprig, chopped

50 g/2 oz stoned black olives

juice of ¹/₂ lemon, strained

6 fresh basil leaves

salt and pepper

Heat the oil in a pan, add the chicken and cook, stirring and turning frequently, for 15 minutes until golden brown all over. Season with salt and pepper, then remove from the pan and keep warm. Stir the wine into the pan and cook until it has evaporated. Add the tomatoes, garlic, thyme, sage and marjoram. Return the chicken to the pan and cook, stirring occasionally, for 30 minutes until tender and cooked through. Add the olives, lemon juice and basil and cook for a few minutes more, then serve.

CHICKEN WITH LEMON (1)

POLLO AL LIMONE (1)

Serves 4

1 chicken
1 lemon, halved
25 g/1 oz butter
1 garlic clove
2 tablespoons olive oil
juice of 1 lemon, strained
1 fresh flat-leaf parsley sprig, chopped
salt and pepper

Preheat the oven to 180°C/350°F/Gas Mark 4. Gently rub the chicken cavity with one of the lemon halves, then slice the remaining half. Stuff the cavity with the lemon slices, half the butter and the garlic. Place the chicken in a roasting tin with the olive oil and remaining butter, season with salt and pepper and roast for 35 minutes. Sprinkle the lemon juice over the chicken, return to the oven and roast for a further 40 minutes until tender and cooked through. Cut the back and breast of the chicken into four pieces, pull off the wings and legs and place the meat on a warm serving dish. Sprinkle with the parsley and serve.

CHICKEN WITH LEMON (2)

POLLO AL LIMONE (2)

Serves 4

1 lemon
1 chicken
olive oil, for brushing
salt

Preheat the oven to 180°C/350°F/Gas Mark 4. Put the lemon and a pinch of salt in the cavity of the chicken and sew up the opening. Brush a roasting tin with oil, place the chicken in it, cover with a sheet of foil and roast for 1½ hours until tender and cooked through. Remove the string from the opening and take the lemon out. Cut the chicken into portions and place on a warm serving dish.

CHICKEN ON THE SPIT

POLLO ALLO SPIEDO

Serves 4

1 chicken
3 tablespoons olive oil
salt and pepper
green salad or roast new potatoes
with rosemary, to serve

Fold the wings against the back, season the chicken with salt and pepper inside and out and brush well with the oil. Thread the chicken on to a spit, put in the oven and turn slowly, basting occasionally with the cooking juices, for 35–50 minutes until tender and cooked through. If you are using an infrared oven, it is not necessary to brush the chicken with oil as the bird will cook in its own fat. Remove the chicken from the spit and season with salt and pepper. Serve hot with a green salad or roast new potatoes with rosemary.

CHICKEN WITH SPARKLING WINE

Heat the oil and butter in a large pan, add the chicken and cook, turning frequently, until golden brown all over, then remove from the pan and keep warm. Add the shallots to the pan and cook over a low heat, stirring occasionally, for about 5 minutes, then return the chicken to the pan. Pour in the wine and stock, season with salt and pepper and add the chilli powder, parsley, thyme and rosemary. Cover and simmer for 50 minutes until tender and cooked through. Transfer the chicken to a warm serving dish. Reduce the cooking juices slightly, stir in the cream and simmer for 3 minutes. Strain the sauce over the chicken and serve.

POLLO ALLO SPUMANTE

Serves 4

3 tablespoons olive oil

25 g/1 oz butter

1 chicken, cut into pieces

2 shallots, sliced

350 ml/12 fl oz sparkling dry white wine

350 ml/12 fl oz Chicken Stock (see page 209)

pinch of chilli powder

1 fresh flat-leaf parsley sprig, chopped

1 fresh thyme sprig, chopped

1 fresh rosemary sprig, chopped

100 ml/3¹/₂ fl oz double cream

salt and pepper

CHICKEN WITH TUNA

Preheat the oven to 180°C/350°F/Gas Mark 4. Heat the olive oil in a flameproof casserole, add the chicken and cook, turning frequently, until lightly golden all over. Add the wine and cook until it has evaporated. Season with salt and pepper and add the bay leaf, garlic, onion, carrot and celery. Cover, transfer to the oven and roast for about 1 hour until tender and cooked through. Meanwhile, chop the anchovy fillets. Mix together the mayonnaise, tuna and anchovies, then stir in the capers. Remove the chicken from the casserole and leave to cool. Strain the cooking juices into the mayonnaise mixture. When the chicken is cold, cut it into pieces and place on a serving dish. Spoon the mayonnaise mixture over it and chill in the refrigerator for 2 hours.

POLLO AL TONNO

Serves 4

3 tablespoons olive oil

1 chicken

175 ml/6 fl oz dry white wine

1 bay leaf • 1 garlic clove

1 onion, chopped • 1 carrot, chopped

1 celery stick, chopped

2 salted anchovies, heads removed, cleaned and filleted (see page 596), soaked in cold water for 10 minutes and drained

1 quantity Mayonnaise (see page 65)

250 g/9 oz canned tuna in oil, drained and flaked

1 tablespoon capers, drained and rinsed

salt and pepper

CHICKEN IN WHITE WINE

Preheat the oven to 180°C/350°F/Gas Mark 4. Heat the oil in a roasting tin, add the garlic and rosemary, then add the chicken and cook, turning frequently, until golden brown all over. Season with salt and pepper and pour in the wine so that the chicken is almost covered. Cover the tin with a double layer of foil and roast for 30 minutes. Remove the foil, return the roasting tin to the oven and roast until the wine has evaporated and the chicken is tender and cooked through.

POLLO AL VINO BIANCO

Serves 4

2 tablespoons olive oil

1 garlic clove

1 fresh rosemary sprig

1 chicken, cut into pieces

1 bottle (750 ml/1¹/₄ pints) dry white wine

salt and pepper

CHICKEN IN RED WINE

POLLO AL VINO ROSSO

Serves 4

50 g/2 oz butter

100 g/3¹/₂ oz pancetta, diced

100 g/3¹/₂ oz baby onions

1 garlic clove

100 g/3¹/₂ oz mushrooms

1 fresh thyme sprig

1 tablespoon plain flour

1 chicken, cut into pieces

500 ml/18 fl oz red wine

salt

Melt the butter in a pan, add the pancetta, onions, garlic, mushrooms and thyme and cook over a low heat, stirring occasionally, for 5 minutes, then sprinkle with the flour. Remove and discard the garlic and add the chicken pieces. Cover and cook for 10 minutes, then pour in the wine and season with salt. Cover and simmer over a low heat for about 30 minutes until tender and cooked through.

POT-ROAST CHICKEN

POLLO ARROSTO

Serves 4

1 chicken

4 tablespoons olive oil

1 onion, chopped

1 carrot, chopped

1 celery stick, chopped

1 fresh rosemary sprig

salt and pepper

carrots in butter, to serve

Lightly season the cavity of the chicken and tie with kitchen string. Heat the oil in a pan, add the onion, carrot, celery and rosemary and cook over a low heat, stirring occasionally, for about 10 minutes. Place the chicken on top, increase the heat to high and cook, turning occasionally, for 15 minutes. Season with salt, lower the heat, cover and cook for 40–50 minutes until tender and cooked through. If necessary, add a little hot water to prevent the meat from drying out. Remove the chicken from the pan, untie, carve and serve with carrots in butter.

STUFFED CHICKEN

POLLO ARROSTO RIPIENO

Serves 4

4 bread slices, crusts removed

1 chicken, with giblets

2 chicken livers, thawed if frozen and chopped

100 g/3¹/₂ oz prosciutto, chopped

25 g/1 oz Parmesan cheese, freshly grated

1 egg, lightly beaten

1 fresh rosemary sprig

4 fresh sage leaves

25 g/1 oz butter

3 tablespoons olive oil

salt and pepper

Preheat the oven to 180°C/350°F/Gas Mark 4. Tear the bread into pieces, place in a bowl, add water to cover and leave to soak for 10 minutes, then drain and squeeze out. Season the cavity of the chicken with salt and pepper. Chop the giblets and mix with the chicken livers, prosciutto, soaked bread and Parmesan in a bowl. Season with salt and pepper and stir in the beaten egg. Stuff the chicken with the mixture and sew up the opening. Fold the wings against the back and tuck the rosemary and sage underneath them. Put the chicken in a roasting tin with the butter and olive oil and roast, basting frequently, for about 1 hour until tender and cooked through. Season with salt to taste, cut the chicken into quarters, take out and slice the stuffing. Place the chicken and stuffing on a warm serving dish.

CHICKEN WITH YELLOW PEPPERS

Preheat the grill. Place the peppers on a baking sheet and grill, turning frequently, until the skins are blistered and charred. Remove with tongs, place in a plastic bag and seal the top. When the peppers are cool enough to handle, rub off the skins, then halve, seed and cut into strips. Heat the oil and garlic in a pan until the garlic has turned brown, then remove and discard it. Add the chicken and cook, turning frequently, until browned all over. Season with salt and pepper, pour in the wine and cook until it has evaporated. Stir in the tomatoes and strips of pepper and simmer over a medium heat, stirring occasionally, for about 20 minutes until the chicken is tender and cooked through.

POLLO CON PEPERONI GIALLI

Serves 4

3 large yellow peppers

2 tablespoons olive oil

1 garlic clove, lightly crushed

1 chicken, cut into pieces

175 ml/6 fl oz dry white wine

600 g/1 lb 5 oz tomatoes, peeled, seeded and diced

salt and pepper

CHICKEN WITH GREEN PEPPERS

Heat the butter and 4 tablespoons of the oil in a pan, add the chicken and cook, turning frequently, for 15 minutes until golden brown all over. Season with salt and pepper, cover and cook over a low heat for about 20 minutes. Add the peppers, garlic and the remaining oil if necessary. Simmer over a low heat for about 30 minutes until the chicken is tender and cooked through. If necessary, add 1–2 tablespoons hot water to prevent the pan from drying out.

POLLO CON PEPERONI VERDI

Serves 4

40 g/1$\frac{1}{2}$ oz butter

4–5 tablespoons olive oil

1 chicken, cut into pieces

300 g/11 oz small, thin green peppers

1 garlic clove, chopped

salt and pepper

FRIED MARINATED CHICKEN

Season the chicken with salt and pepper. Mix together 175 ml/6 fl oz of the oil, the lemon juice, garlic, parsley, onion and bay leaf in a dish, add the chicken and leave to marinate for at least 2 hours. Drain the chicken, pat dry with kitchen paper and dust with flour. Beat the egg with a pinch of salt and dip the chicken in the mixture to coat. Heat the remaining oil in a frying pan, add the chicken and cook over a medium heat, turning frequently, for about 10 minutes until golden brown all over and cooked through. Remove the chicken from the pan, drain well on kitchen paper, and garnish with slices of lemon.

POLLO FRITTO MARINATO

Serves 4

1 chicken, cut into pieces

250 ml/8 fl oz olive oil

juice of 1 lemon, strained

1 garlic clove, chopped

1 fresh flat-leaf parsley sprig, chopped

1 onion, thinly sliced

1 bay leaf, crumbled

plain flour, for dusting

1 egg

salt and pepper

lemon slices, to garnish

FRIED CHICKEN IN BREADCRUMBS

POLLO IMPANATO E FRITTO

Serves 4

175 ml/6 fl oz olive oil
juice of 1 lemon, strained
1 chicken, cut into pieces
2 eggs
80 g/3 oz fresh breadcrumbs
50 g/2 oz Clarified Butter (see page 88)
plain flour, for dusting
salt and pepper

Mix together the olive oil and lemon juice in a dish and season with salt and pepper. Add the chicken and leave to marinate for 1 hour. Beat the eggs with a pinch of salt in a shallow dish and spread out the breadcrumbs in another shallow dish. Drain the chicken, dust lightly with flour and dip first in the beaten eggs and then in the breadcrumbs. Melt the clarified butter in a frying pan, add the chicken and cook over a medium-high heat, turning frequently, for 15–20 minutes until crisp on the outside and tender and cooked through on the inside. Remove the chicken from the pan, drain on kitchen paper and serve.

CHICKEN IN A SALT CRUST

POLLO IN CROSTA DI SALE

Serves 4

1 kg/2¼ lb plain flour
1 kg/2¼ lb sea salt
1 egg white
1 chicken
1 fresh rosemary sprig
1 bay leaf
salt and pepper

Preheat the oven to 160°C/325°F/Gas Mark 3. Mix together the flour, sea salt and egg white in a bowl until thoroughly combined. Season the inside of the chicken with salt and pepper and put the rosemary and bay leaf in the cavity. Place the chicken in an ovenproof dish and cover completely with the salt mixture. Cover the dish tightly and bake for 1½ hours. Break the salt crust and cut the chicken into pieces.

CHICKEN IN A BRICK

POLLO IN TERRACOTTA

Serves 4

1 fresh rosemary sprig, chopped
1 fresh thyme sprig, chopped
1 fresh summer savory sprig, chopped
2 teaspoons dried oregano
4 fresh sage leaves, chopped
2 fresh flat-leaf parsley sprigs, chopped
1 chicken
salt and pepper

Preheat the oven to 220°C/425°F/Gas Mark 7. Soak a chicken brick in warm water for 5 minutes, then tip out any excess water but do not dry. Mix together all the herbs in a bowl and put half of them in the base of the chicken brick. Season the chicken with salt and pepper and tie neatly with kitchen string. Place the chicken in the brick and sprinkle with the remaining herbs. Roast for 1¼ hours until tender and cooked through.

SPICY INDIAN MEATBALLS

POLPETTE PICCANTI ALL'INDIANA

Serves 4

2 onions

2 cloves

400 g/14 oz minced chicken

1 garlic clove, finely chopped

1 small fresh red chilli, seeded and chopped

50 g/2 oz butter

juice of 1 lemon, strained

salt

Finely chop one of the onions and stud the other with the cloves. Mix together the chicken, chopped onion, garlic and chilli in a bowl, season with salt and mix well. Shape the mixture into balls. Melt the butter in a pan, add the remaining onion and cook over a medium heat, turning frequently, until browned, then discard. Add the meatballs and cook, stirring frequently, for 10 minutes. Lower the heat and cook for 20 minutes, basting with 1 tablespoon hot water if necessary. Pour the lemon juice over the meatballs, stir and serve.

CHOPPED CHICKEN WITH LEMON BALM

SPEZZATINO ALLA MELISSA

Serves 4

10 fresh lemon balm leaves

2 tablespoons vegetable oil

25 g/1 oz butter

1 chicken, cut into pieces

4 tablespoons sugar

2 tablespoons soy sauce

Put the lemon balm leaves in a heatproof bowl, pour in 5 tablespoons boiling water and leave to infuse for 2 hours. Heat the oil and butter in a pan, add the chicken pieces and cook over a medium heat, turning frequently, for 5 minutes. Meanwhile, put the sugar in a large saucepan, add 1 tablespoon water and cook, stirring until the sugar has dissolved, then boil without stirring until it has caramelized. Strain the lemon balm infusion into the caramelized sugar, stir in the soy sauce and add the chicken. Cook over a low heat for 30 minutes. Mix well and serve.

CHICKEN STEW WITH OLIVES

SPEZZATINO ALLE OLIVE

Serves 4

2 tablespoons olive oil • 25 g/1 oz butter

1 garlic clove • 1 chicken, cut into pieces

4 tomatoes, peeled and coarsely chopped

150 g/5 oz stoned black olives

1 fresh flat-leaf parsley sprig, chopped

4 fresh basil leaves, chopped • salt and pepper

Heat the oil and butter in a pan with the garlic. Add the chicken and cook over a medium-high heat, turning frequently, until browned all over. Season with salt and pepper, add the tomatoes and olives, lower the heat, cover and simmer for about 30 minutes. Transfer the mixture to a warm serving dish and sprinkle with the parsley and basil.

CHOPPED CHICKEN WITH ALMONDS

SPEZZATINO CON LE MANDORLE

Serves 4

4 skinless, boneless chicken breast portions, cut into strips

2 tablespoons vegetable oil

100 g/3¹/₂ oz blanched almonds

2 tablespoons soy sauce • salt

Cut the chicken strips into smaller pieces. Heat the oil in a frying pan, add the chicken and almonds and stir-fry over a high heat for a few minutes until golden brown all over. Pour in the soy sauce, season lightly with salt and stir in 1–2 tablespoons water. Lower the heat to medium, cover and simmer for 20 minutes.

OSTRICH

Ostrich could become the meat of the third millennium, so it is worth trying it straight away. It is already familiar in the United States and ostrich farms have also been established in several European countries as well as further afield, including Australia and New Zealand. Ostrich farms are multiplying in Italy – at the moment there are about 400. Some Italian supermarkets offer a variety of ostrich cuts and several restaurants have dishes devoted to this exotic bird on their menus. From a nutritional point of view its red, lean and tender meat deserves respect mainly because of its iron content and high levels of protein. In addition, its low fat content, compared with other more common red meats, makes it particularly digestible. It has minimal cholesterol and sodium levels too. As regards flavour, it is similar to beef but slightly stronger. Ostrich meat is lean and 100 g/3¹/₂ oz provides 105 kcal. A 100–kg/220–lb ostrich provides about 25–30 kg/55–66 lb of prime meat – fillets, steaks, etc. – and 5 kg/11 lb of other cuts – slices, minced meat, etc. Ostrich sausages and cold cuts, such as ham, salami and dried salted meat are also available. As ostrich is a suitable alternative to beef, and more or less the same preparation and cooking techniques apply, from carpaccio onwards. This has been proved conclusively since 1995 by chef Fabio Beretta at the Conte Rosso restaurant, the first in Milan – maybe in the whole of Italy – to offer this new meat on its menu. The recipes in this section are his.

OSTRICH EGGS

UOVA DI STRUZZO

Ostrich eggs weigh about 1.5 kg/3¹/₄ lb – the shell alone weighs 200 g/7 oz. The shell should be kept intact because of its commercial value. Drill a hole in the bottom with a 2-cm/³/₄-inch conical bit, insert a thin stick and whisk the yolk and white inside the egg. Pour the egg out through the hole and store in a screw-top jar in the refrigerator. Weigh out the required amount.

FILETTO DI STRUZZO ALLA CONTE ROSSO

Serves 4

2 porcini, cut into thin strips

1 teaspoon breadcrumbs

1 garlic clove, chopped

3 fresh basil leaves, chopped

1 teaspoon chopped fresh rosemary needles

720-g/1 lb 9-oz ostrich fillet

plain flour, for dusting

4 tablespoons olive oil

350 ml/12 fl oz double cream

40 g/1$^{1}/_{2}$ oz butter

1 tablespoon Worcestershire sauce

dash of brandy

8 white bread slices, toasted and cut into triangles

salt

CONTE ROSSO OSTRICH FILLET

Mix together the porcini, breadcrumbs, garlic, basil and rosemary in a bowl. Cut the ostrich fillet into quarters, make a slit in each to create a 'pocket' and stuff with the porcini mixture. Secure with cocktail sticks and dust with flour. Heat the olive oil in a pan, add the ostrich fillets and cook for 5 minutes on each side. Pour off the oil, then add the cream, butter, Worcestershire sauce, brandy and a pinch of salt. Cook over a low heat until the sauce is creamy. Place the fillets on a warm serving dish, spoon the sauce over them and arrange the toast triangles around them.

STRACOTTO DI STRUZZO

Serves 4

2 carrots, finely chopped

1 celery stick, finely chopped

1 onion, finely chopped

7 tablespoons olive oil

500 g/1 lb 2 oz ostrich slices, cut into large cubes

plain flour, for dusting

500 ml/18 fl oz white wine

500 ml/18 fl oz Vegetable Stock (see page 209)

200 g/7 oz tomato purée

1 bouquet garni, (1 bay leaf, 2 cloves,

1 fresh sage sprig,1 fresh rosemary sprig,

6 juniper berries, 1 small cinnamon stick

and a pinch of freshly grated nutmeg

in a muslin square)

salt and pepper

OSTRICH STEW

Put the carrots, celery and onion in a deep pan, add 4 tablespoons of the olive oil and cook over a medium heat, stirring occasionally, for 5 minutes. Dust the meat with flour. Heat the remaining oil in another pan, add the meat and cook, stirring and turning frequently, until browned. Transfer the meat to the pan of vegetables, add the wine, stock, tomato purée and bouquet garni and season with salt and pepper. Cover and cook over a medium heat for 40 minutes.

TURKEY

Turkey is the honoured guest at Christmas Day in Britain, Australia and New Zealand. In the United States it is a key ingredient of Thanksgiving. The United States observes this festival every year on the fourth Thursday of November in remembrance of the day in 1621 when the Pilgrim Fathers celebrated their first, successful, harvest after enduring a year of hardship following their arrival in the New World in 1620. The turkey is, in fact, native to America. Christopher Columbus wrote about it in his journals. However, the bird has been farmed for a long time and, through selective breeding, it has developed from a lean wild bird to a fat domesticated one. It is so large today that some turkeys are more than twice the size of their ancestors. They put on weight very quickly – with current breading techniques, males reach 14–15 kg/31–33 lb and females 7–8 kg/15–18 lb in five months. Turkey is often stuffed; classic stuffings include chestnuts, prunes and sausage, celery and carrot, and sausage and breadcrumbs.

COOKING

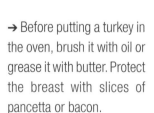

→ Before putting a turkey in the oven, brush it with oil or grease it with butter. Protect the breast with slices of pancetta or bacon.

→ Place the turkey on one side for the first 45 minutes, then on the other, so that the breast does not come into contact with the roasting tin. Finally, place it on its back.

→ Baste frequently while it is cooking. If there are not enough cooking juices, sprinkle with a little hot water.

→ As soon as the skin goes golden brown, cover with foil.

→ Cooking takes about 40 minutes per 1 kg/ 2¼ lb, at a temperature of 220°C/425°F/Gas Mark 7 for the first hour, and 180°C/350°F/Gas Mark 4 after that.

POT–ROAST TURKEY

ARROSTO DI TACCHINELLA

Serves 8

3-kg/6½-lb turkey
2 fresh rosemary sprigs
4 fresh sage leaves
2 prosciutto slices, cut into strips
100 g/3½ oz pancetta, sliced
3 tablespoons olive oil
25 g/1 oz butter
2 tablespoons grappa
salt and pepper

Season the cavity of the turkey with salt and pepper and put one of the rosemary sprigs, the sage and prosciutto in the cavity. Sew up the opening, wrap the turkey breast with pancetta and truss with kitchen string. Put the oil, butter and remaining rosemary in a large shallow pan, add the turkey and cook over a low heat, turning and basting occasionally, for 1¾–2 hours until tender and cooked through. Season lightly with salt once or twice during cooking. About 10 minutes before the end of the cooking time, remove the pancetta to allow the turkey to brown completely. Sprinkle with the grappa and ignite. Serve when the flames have died down.

TURKEY À L'ORANGE

ARROSTO DI TACCHINO ALL'ARANCIA

Serves 4

800-g/1¾-lb turkey breast
25 g/1 oz butter
2 tablespoons olive oil
1 onion, chopped
1 celery stick, chopped
1 carrot, chopped
2 oranges
5 tablespoons dry white wine
pinch of plain flour (optional)
50 ml/2 fl oz double cream
salt and pepper

Tie the turkey breast neatly with kitchen string. Heat the butter and oil in a pan, add the onion, celery and carrot and cook over a low heat, stirring occasionally, for 10 minutes. Add the turkey, increase the heat to medium and cook, turning several times, until browned all over. Meanwhile, peel the oranges and blanch three or four pieces of rind, making sure that they are free of pith, in boiling water for a few minutes, then drain. Squeeze the juice from one of the oranges and strain. Separate the other orange into segments. As soon as the turkey is golden brown, pour in the wine and orange juice, add the blanched orange rind and season with salt and pepper. Lower the heat, cover and simmer for 1 hour until cooked through and tender. Remove the turkey from the pan, carve into slices and place on a warm serving dish. Stir 2 tablespoons hot water into the cooking juices, scraping up any sediment on the base of the pan. If the sauce seems a little thin, stir in a pinch of flour to thicken. Stir in the cream and season with a little pepper. Spoon the sauce over the slices of turkey and garnish with the orange segments.

TURKEY LEG WITH SPINACH

Open out the turkey leg like a book and pound with a meat mallet to flatten slightly. Tear the bread into pieces, place in a bowl, add all but 1 tablespoon of the wine and leave to soak for 10 minutes, then drain and squeeze out. Preheat the oven to 180°C/350°F/Gas Mark 4. Cook the spinach, in just the water clinging to the leaves after washing, for about 5 minutes, then drain, squeeze out and chop. Melt half the butter in a frying pan, add the onion, garlic and soaked bread and stir well, then add the spinach and marjoram and season with salt and pepper. Cook for a few minutes, then remove the pan from the heat. Combine the spinach mixture with the beaten egg in a bowl, then spread it over the turkey and roll up. Tie with kitchen string, put in a roasting tin with the remaining butter and roast for about 50 minutes. Remove the turkey from the roasting tin and leave to stand for 10 minutes. Meanwhile, stir the remaining wine and 1 tablespoon warm water into the cooking juices, scraping up any sediment on the base of the tin, over a low heat. Pour into a sauce boat and serve with the turkey carved into even slices.

COSCIA AGLI SPINACI

Serves 4

900-g/2-lb turkey leg, skinned and boned

1 thick bread slice, crusts removed

175 ml/6 fl oz dry white wine

250 g/9 oz spinach

50 g/2 oz butter

1 onion, chopped

1 garlic clove, chopped

pinch of dried marjoram

1 egg, lightly beaten

salt and pepper

TURKEY LEG WITH HERBS

Finely chop the herbs in quantities according to taste, mix with 50 g/2 oz of the butter and the lemon juice in a bowl and season with salt and pepper. Remove the skin from the turkey leg in one piece. Spread the herb butter over the leg, wrap it up in its skin and tie with kitchen string. Heat the olive oil and the remaining butter in a pan, add the turkey leg and cook, turning frequently, until browned all over. Cover and cook over a low heat, adding a little hot water if necessary to prevent drying out, for 1 hour until tender and cooked through. Carve the meat into slices, place on a warm serving dish and spoon the cooking juices over. Serve with potatoes.

COSCIA ALLE ERBE AROMATICHE

Serves 4

fresh flat-leaf parsley

fresh tarragon

fresh thyme

fresh rosemary

fresh marjoram

fresh basil

fresh mint

fresh sage

80 g/3 oz butter, softened

juice of $^1/_2$ lemon, strained

900-g/2-lb turkey leg

4 tablespoons olive oil

salt and pepper

potatoes, to serve

TURKEY BREAST WITH CHEESE

FESA AL FORMAGGIO

Serves 4

600 g/1 lb 5 oz turkey breast steaks

plain flour, for dusting

25 g/1 oz butter

175 ml/6 fl oz white wine

50 g/2 oz Parmesan cheese, shaved

black truffle, thinly shaved (optional)

salt and pepper

Pound the turkey steaks with a meat mallet and dust with flour. Melt the butter in a pan, add the turkey steaks and cook, turning occasionally, until browned on both sides. Pour in the wine and cook until it has evaporated, then season with salt and pepper. Cook over a low heat for about 10 minutes, then sprinkle each steak with Parmesan, cover and cook until the cheese has melted. Transfer to a warm serving dish. To enrich the dish, sprinkle with a few thin shavings of black truffle.

TURKEY BREAST WITH ALMONDS

FESA ALLE MANDORLE

Serves 4

40 g/1½ oz butter

1 onion, chopped

1 carrot, chopped

1 celery stick, chopped

600 g/1 lb 5 oz turkey breast steaks

5 tablespoons white wine

50 g/2 oz blanched almonds

175 ml/6 fl oz milk

1 tablespoon brandy

salt and pepper

Melt the butter in a pan, add the onion, carrot and celery and cook over a low heat, stirring occasionally, for 5 minutes. Place the turkey steaks on top and cook until browned on both sides, then season with salt and pepper. Increase the heat to medium, pour in the wine and cook until it has evaporated, then cover and cook over a low heat for about 10 minutes. Meanwhile, put the almonds in a pan, add the milk and brandy and simmer for 15 minutes. Transfer to a food processor and process to a purée. Pour the purée over the meat, simmer for a few more minutes and serve.

TURKEY FRICASSÉE WITH PORCINI

FRICASSEA AI PORCINI

Serves 4

40 g/1½ oz butter

3 tablespoons olive oil

600 g/1 lb 5 oz skinless, boneless turkey breast, cut into medium cubes

1 small onion, chopped

2 garlic cloves

175 ml/6 fl oz dry white wine

400 g/14 oz porcini, sliced

1 fresh flat-leaf parsley sprig, chopped

5 tablespoons hot chicken or turkey stock made with a stock cube

2 egg yolks

juice of ½ lemon, strained

salt and pepper

Heat the butter and 2 tablespoons of the olive oil in a pan, add the turkey and cook over a high heat, stirring frequently, until golden brown. Remove with a fish slice and set aside. Lower the heat, add the onion and one of the garlic cloves to the pan and cook, stirring occasionally, for 5 minutes, then remove and discard the garlic. Return the turkey to the pan, add the wine, cover and simmer for 30 minutes. Brush the porcini with the remaining olive oil and stir into the pan. Chop the remaining garlic and add to the pan with the parsley, pour in the hot stock and simmer for about 30 minutes more. Beat the egg yolks with 1 tablespoon water, the lemon juice, a pinch of salt and a pinch of pepper in a bowl. Move the pan to the edge of the hob, pour in the egg mixture and mix quickly so that it does not curdle, but remains soft and creamy and coats the meat lightly. Transfer to a warm serving dish.

TASTY TURKEY ROULADES

Preheat the oven to 200°C/400°F/Gas Mark 6. Place the yellow pepper on a baking sheet and roast until the skin blackens and blisters, then remove from the oven, wrap in foil and set aside for 20 minutes. Meanwhile, chop the anchovy fillets. Tear the roll into pieces, place in a bowl, add water to cover and leave to soak for 10 minutes, then drain and squeeze out. Unwrap the pepper, peel, seed and cut into strips. Place the pepper, anchovies, soaked roll, parsley and a pinch of salt in a food processor and process to a purée. Place a slice of pancetta on each slice of turkey and spread with the purée, then roll up, tie with kitchen string and dust with the flour. Heat the oil and butter in a pan, add the onion and cook over a low heat, stirring occasionally, for 5 minutes. Add the roulades and cook, turning frequently, until browned all over, then season with salt and pepper and cook for a few minutes more. Add the tomatoes and basil leaves and simmer for 10 minutes. Taste and add more salt if necessary. Transfer the roulades to a warm serving dish and spoon the cooking juices over them.

INVOLTINI SAPORITI

Serves 4

1 yellow pepper

4 salted anchovies, heads removed, cleaned and filleted (see page 596), soaked in cold water for 10 minutes and drained

1 bread roll, crust removed

1 fresh flat-leaf parsley sprig, coarsely chopped

100 g/3½ oz pancetta, sliced

600 g/1 lb 5 oz sliced turkey breast

25 g/1 oz plain flour

2 tablespoons olive oil

25 g/1 oz butter

½ onion, chopped

400 g/14 oz canned chopped tomatoes

5 fresh basil leaves

salt and pepper

TURKEY ROLL WITH OLIVES

Spread out the turkey breast and pound well with a meat mallet. Place the ham and olives on top, season with salt and pepper, roll up and tie with kitchen string. Heat the butter and olive oil in a pan, add the sage, rosemary and rolled turkey and cook, turning frequently, for 10 minutes until browned all over. Pour in the wine and cook until it has evaporated. Season with salt and pepper, cover and cook over a low heat for 1 hour. This dish is excellent both hot and cold.

ROTOLO ALLE OLIVE

Serves 4

800-g/1¾-lb turkey breast, boned

80 g/3 oz cooked ham, sliced

50 g/2 oz green olives

25 g/1 oz butter

2 tablespoons olive oil

4 fresh sage leaves

1 fresh rosemary sprig

5 tablespoons dry white wine

salt and pepper

TURKEY STEW WITH MUSTARD

SPEZZATINO ALLA SENAPE
Serves 4

2 tablespoons olive oil
25 g/1 oz butter
1 onion, chopped
1 garlic clove, chopped
600 g/1 lb 5 oz skinless, boneless turkey breast, cut into cubes
175 ml/6 fl oz dry white wine
250 ml/8 fl oz hot Chicken Stock (see page 209)
2 tablespoons Dijon mustard
1 fresh flat-leaf parsley sprig, chopped
salt and pepper

Heat the oil and butter in a frying pan, add the onion and garlic and cook over a low heat, stirring occasionally, for 5 minutes. Increase the heat to medium, add the turkey and cook, stirring frequently, for 10 minutes until golden brown. Season with salt and pepper, pour in the wine and cook until it has evaporated. Pour in 175 ml/6 fl oz of the hot stock, cover and simmer for about 30 minutes. Mix together the remaining stock and the mustard in a bowl and stir into the pan. Sprinkle with the parsley and simmer for a further 15 minutes.

GLAZED TURKEY

TACCHINELLA GLASSATA
Serves 8–10

1.5-kg/3¼-lb turkey
bunch of fresh mixed herbs
thinly pared rind of 1 orange, cut into thin strips
3 tablespoons olive oil
5 tablespoons dry white wine
175 ml/6 fl oz hot Chicken Stock (see page 209)
20 g/¾ oz dried mushrooms
1 carrot, chopped
1 celery stick, chopped
1 onion, chopped
40 g/1½ oz butter
500 g/1 lb 2 oz shelled chestnuts, boiled for about 45 minutes
5 tablespoons dry Marsala
salt and pepper

Preheat the oven to 200°C/400°F/Gas Mark 6. Season the turkey inside and out with salt and pepper and place the herbs and orange rind in the cavity. Put the bird in a fairly large roasting tin, sprinkle with the olive oil and roast until the skin is golden brown. Lower the temperature to 180°C/350°F/Gas Mark 4, sprinkle with the wine, return to the oven and roast, basting occasionally with the hot stock, for a further 1½ hours. Meanwhile, place the mushrooms in a bowl, add hot water to cover and leave to soak for 30 minutes, then drain and squeeze out. Add the carrot, celery and onion to the roasting tin, cover the turkey with a sheet of foil, return to the oven and roast for a further 30 minutes. Melt the butter in a pan, add the chestnuts and mushrooms and cook over a low heat, stirring occasionally, for about 10 minutes. Add the Marsala and 1 tablespoon of the turkey cooking juices, season with salt and pepper and simmer until thickened. Transfer the turkey to a warm serving dish and surround with the glazed chestnuts. Pour the sauce that remains into a sauce boat and serve with the turkey.

CHRISTMAS TURKEY

Preheat the oven to 220°C/425°F/Gas Mark 7. First make the stuffing. Tear the bread into pieces, place in a bowl, add water to cover and leave to soak for 10 minutes, then drain and squeeze out. Chop the turkey giblets, pancetta and sausages together, place in a bowl, add the soaked bread, apples, prunes and chestnuts and mix well. Spoon the mixture into the cavity of the turkey, dip the butter into a pinch each of salt and pepper, add to the cavity and sew up the opening. Cover the turkey breast with the pancetta slices and put in a roasting tin with the butter. Roast for 1 hour, then lower the temperature to 180°C/350°F/Gas Mark 4 and roast, basting occasionally, for about a further 1¼ hours. Remove the pancetta, return the turkey to the oven and roast for 15 minutes more until golden brown, tender and cooked through.

TACCHINO DI NATALE

Serves 8

3-kg/6½-lb turkey, with giblets
100 g/3½ oz pancetta, sliced
50 g/2 oz butter

For the stuffing
1 thick slice bread, crusts removed
40 g/1½ oz pancetta
100 g/3½ oz Italian sausages
2 apples, peeled, cored and sliced
100 g/3½ oz ready-to-eat prunes
250 g/9 oz shelled chestnuts, boiled for about 45 minutes
25 g/1 oz butter
salt and pepper

TURKEY STUFFED WITH CHESTNUTS

Peel off the skins and mash the chestnuts. Preheat the oven to 180°C/350°F/Gas Mark 4. Add the sausages and olives to the chestnuts, season with salt and pepper and mix well. Spoon the mixture into the cavity of the turkey and sew up the opening. Cover the turkey breast with the pancetta slices, tie with kitchen string and season with salt and pepper. Generously brush a roasting tin with oil, put the turkey in it and roast, basting occasionally, for 1½ hours. Remove the pancetta slices, return the turkey to the oven and roast for a further 30 minutes until browned, cooked through and tender. Place the turkey on a warm serving dish and surround with large lettuce leaves as a garnish.

TACCHINO RIPIENO DI CASTAGNE

Serves 6–8

250 g/9 oz shelled chestnuts, boiled for about 45 minutes
300 g/11 oz Italian sausages, skinned and crumbled
150 g/5 oz stoned green olives, chopped
3-kg/6½-lb turkey
100 g/3½ oz pancetta, sliced
olive oil, for brushing
salt and pepper
lettuce leaves, to garnish

TURKEY STUFFED
WITH BRUSSELS SPROUTS

Preheat the oven to 180°C/350°F/Gas Mark 4. Cook the Brussels sprouts in a large pan of salted, boiling water, uncovered, for about 15 minutes, then drain and halve. Put them in a bowl, add the ham, season with salt and pepper and mix well. Spoon the mixture into the cavity of the turkey and sew up the opening. Cover the turkey breast with the pork fat or bacon, tie with kitchen string and season with salt and pepper. Generously brush a roasting tin with oil, put the turkey in it and roast, basting occasionally, for 1½ hours. Remove the slices of pork fat or bacon, return the turkey to the oven and roast for a further 30 minutes until browned, cooked through and tender. Remove the turkey from the roasting tin and leave to stand for about 10 minutes, then place on a warm serving dish.

TACCHINO RIPIENO
DI CAVOLINI DI BRUXELLES

Serves 6–8

300 g/11 oz Brussels sprouts, trimmed

250 g/9 oz cooked ham, chopped

3-kg/6½-lb turkey

100 g/3½ oz pork fat, thinly sliced,

or streaky bacon rashers

olive oil, for brushing

salt and pepper

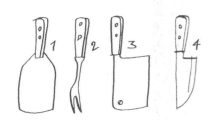

CASTLE

SALT

PHEASANT?

1

PEPPER

2

KNIFE

ONION

GAME →

GAME

This chapter on game has been written in the hope that the reader will, whenever possible, buy farmed animals. Many game species, such as rabbit, deer and 'wild' boar, are reared nowadays in very much the same way as cattle and pigs. This helps to conserve wildlife in its natural habitat. Each individual section of this chapter provides specific details about the particular animal. However, in general, young game is more suitable for roasting, frying and grilling, whereas adult game is better stewed, braised and jugged. Jugged game is one of the most classic, traditional recipes. The flavour of game often goes well with some fruits, such as cherries, grapes, blueberries and apples, which may be added to the pan during cooking or served separately as sauces.

WOODCOCK AND SNIPE

Woodcock and snipe are similar-looking, migratory birds with characteristically long beaks. They are known as beccacce throughout Italy, but in the north they are also called gallinazze, pizzacre or pole and in the south, pizzarde or arcere. They are not farmed and are only found in Italy at certain times of year – in October and November and in February and March. Different countries specify various hunting seasons. Both woodcock and snipe are pleasantly tasty and need hanging for between three and five days. One woodcock or snipe is sufficient for two people.

FEATHERED GAME

CURRIED WOODCOCK

Season the birds with salt and pepper and dust with flour. Melt half the butter in a frying pan, add the birds and cook over a medium heat, turning frequently, for 15 minutes. Melt the remaining butter in another pan, add the onion and cook over a low heat, stirring occasionally, for 5 minutes. Add the curry powder and hot stock and simmer for 20 minutes. Just before serving, transfer the birds to the curry sauce, heat through and add the lemon juice.

BECCACCIA AL CURRY

Serves 4

2 woodcock or snipe, drawn and plucked

plain flour, for dusting

50 g/2 oz butter

1 onion, sliced

2 teaspoons curry powder

300 ml/¹/₂ pint hot Meat Stock (see page 208)

juice of ¹/₂ lemon, strained

salt and pepper

WOODCOCK WITH JUNIPER

BECCACCIA AL GINEPRO

Serves 4

12 juniper berries
100 g/3¹/₂ oz butter
4 fresh thyme sprigs
2 woodcock or snipe, drawn and plucked
175 ml/6 fl oz gin
salt and pepper

Crush the juniper berries in a mortar with a pestle until mashed. Blend one-third of the berries with 40 g/1¹/₂ oz of the butter and shape the mixture into four balls. Put one butter ball and a sprig of thyme in the cavity of each bird. Heat the remaining butter in a pan, add the birds and cook over a high heat, turning frequently, until browned. Season with salt and pepper, sprinkle with the remaining juniper berries, lower the heat to medium and cook until the birds are tender and cooked through. Gently heat the gin in a small pan, pour it over the birds and ignite, then serve.

WOODCOCK WITH TRUFFLE

BECCACCIA AL TARTUFO

Serves 4

2 woodcock or snipe, drawn and plucked
with livers and hearts
80 g/3 oz pancetta slices
25 g/1 oz butter
2 tablespoons olive oil
1 carrot, chopped
1 celery stick, chopped
¹/₂ onion, chopped
1 bay leaf
350 ml/12 fl oz red wine
2 small black truffles, shaved
8 polenta slices
salt and pepper

Chop the livers and hearts and set aside. Tie the beaks of the birds between their legs, season the cavities with a pinch each of salt and pepper and wrap them with the pancetta. Heat the butter and olive oil in a pan, add the carrot, celery, onion and bay leaf and cook over a low heat, stirring occasionally, for 10 minutes. Add the birds to the pan and cook, turning frequently, until browned all over. Season with salt and pepper, pour in 275 ml/9 fl oz of the wine and simmer over a low heat for about 20 minutes. Remove the birds from the pan, cut them in half and keep warm. Add the livers and hearts to the pan and mix well. Pour in the remaining wine, add half the truffle shavings and cook until the sauce is slightly reduced. Place the polenta on a warm serving dish and put the birds on top. Spoon the sauce over them and sprinkle with the remaining truffle.

WOODCOCK WITH GREEN APPLES

BECCACCIA CON MELE VERDI

Serves 4

2 woodcock or snipe, drawn and plucked
olive oil, for brushing
25 g/1 oz butter
4 bread slices
2 green apples, peeled, cored
and cut into 5-mm/¹/₄-inch thick slices
salt and pepper

Preheat the oven to 220°C/425°F/Gas Mark 7. Put the birds in a roasting tin, brush with olive oil and season with salt. Roast for 10 minutes or until golden brown and tender. Melt half the butter in a frying pan, add the slices of bread and cook until golden brown on both sides, then remove from the pan and set aside. Heat the remaining butter, add the apples and cook until lightly browned, then season with pepper. Serve the birds on the slices of fried bread surrounded by the hot apples.

PHEASANT

Pheasants are highly valued birds originating in Asia. The most obvious difference between the male and the female is that the former has coloured feathers. The hen has duller plumage which merges into the vegetation. In Italy, farm-reared pheasants, which need hanging for about a day in the refrigerator, are the most widespread, but this is not usually necessary for pheasants bought commercially outside Italy. If the bird comes from a shoot, it needs to be hung for three days. A large cock pheasant is more or less enough for four people.

PHEASANT WITH FRUIT

Squeeze the juice from 500 g/1 lb 2 oz of the grapes. Truss the pheasant with kitchen string. Melt half the butter in a pan, add the pheasant and cook, turning frequently, until browned all over. Pour the grape juice, orange juice, wine and brandy over the bird, season with salt and pepper, cover and simmer over a low heat for 30 minutes. Meanwhile, blanch the remaining grapes in boiling water for 1 minute, then drain, refresh under cold water and peel. Add the grapes and walnuts to the pheasant and simmer for a further 10 minutes. Transfer the pheasant to a serving dish, remove the string and keep warm. Add the remaining butter to the cooking juices, sprinkle with the flour and stir well. Bring to the boil, add the orange rind and remove from the heat. Surround the pheasant with slices of orange and the peeled grapes and serve with the sauce.

FAGIANO ALLA FRUTTA

Serves 4

750 g/1 lb 10 oz mixed white and black grapes

1 pheasant, drawn and plucked

50 g/2 oz butter

juice of 2 oranges, strained

175 ml/6 fl oz dry white wine

50 ml/2 fl oz brandy

20 shelled walnuts, coarsely chopped

1 tablespoon plain flour

grated rind of $^{1}/_{2}$ orange

salt and pepper

orange slices, to garnish

PHEASANT IN CREAM SAUCE

Season the cavity of the pheasant with salt and pepper, then wrap the breast in the pancetta slices and truss with kitchen string. Heat the olive oil and butter in a pan, add the pheasant and cook, turning frequently, until browned all over, then season lightly with salt. Lower the heat, cover and cook gently for about 30 minutes. Sprinkle the pheasant with the cream and cook, basting frequently, for a further 15 minutes. Finally, add the lemon juice to the sauce and serve.

FAGIANO ALLA PANNA

Serves 4

1 pheasant, drawn and plucked

130 g/4¹/₂ oz pancetta, thinly sliced

2 tablespoons olive oil

25 g/1 oz butter

4 tablespoons double cream

1 tablespoon lemon juice

salt and pepper

PHEASANT WITH OLIVES

Preheat the oven to 180°C/350°F/Gas Mark 4. Season the cavity of the pheasant with salt and pepper and put the rosemary and 25 g/1 oz of the of butter in it. Wrap the bird in the pancetta and truss with kitchen string. Place in a flameproof casserole dish, dot with remaining the butter and roast, basting frequently with the Marsala and cooking juices, for about 1 hour. Remove the dish from the oven, sprinkle the olives over the pheasant and cook over a low heat for a further 40 minutes.

FAGIANO ALLE OLIVE

Serves 4

1 pheasant, drawn and plucked

1 fresh rosemary sprig

80 g/3 oz butter

6 pancetta slices

5 tablespoons dry Marsala

200 g/7 oz stoned black olives

salt and pepper

STUFFED POT—ROAST PHEASANT

If possible, choose a hen pheasant rather than a cock as the meat is more tender. Chop the liver, mix with the pork fat or bacon, parsley, and truffle if using, in a bowl and season with salt and pepper. Spoon the mixture into the cavity of the pheasant and sew up the opening. Cover the breast of the bird with the pancetta slices, tie with kitchen string and season with salt and pepper. Heat the butter in a pan, add the pheasant and cook for 20 minutes. Remove the pancetta to allow the meat to brown and cook for a further 10 minutes. Add the cream and cook for 15 minutes more, then serve.

FAGIANO ARROSTO RIPIENO

Serves 4

1 pheasant, drawn and plucked, with liver

50 g/2 oz smoked pork fat or streaky bacon, chopped

1 fresh flat-leaf parsley sprig, chopped

1 small black truffle, chopped (optional)

50 g/2 oz pancetta, sliced

25 g/1 oz butter

2 tablespoons double cream

salt and pepper

FAGIANO CON I FUNGHI

Serves 4

1 pheasant, drawn and plucked
1 tablespoon olive oil
50 g/2 oz butter
1 onion, chopped
1 shallot, chopped
1 carrot, chopped
100 g/3^1/$_2$ oz cooked ham, diced
1 fresh rosemary sprig
4 fresh sage leaves, chopped
1 bay leaf
1 litre/1^3/$_4$ pints Chicken Stock (see page 209)
200 g/7 oz button mushrooms
200 g/7 oz chanterelle mushrooms
1 garlic clove
200 g/7 oz stoned green olives
salt and pepper

PHEASANT WITH MUSHROOMS

Season the cavity of the pheasant with salt and pepper and truss with kitchen string. Heat the olive oil and half the butter in a pan, add the pheasant and cook, turning frequently, until browned all over, then remove from the pan. Add the onion, shallot, carrot, ham and herbs to the pan, season with salt and pepper and pour in the stock. Cover and simmer over a low heat for about 15 minutes. Return the pheasant to the pan, re-cover and simmer for a further 40 minutes. Melt the remaining butter in another pan, add the mushrooms and garlic and cook, stirring occasionally, for about 10 minutes. Remove the mushrooms from the pan, add the olives and cook gently for 5 minutes. Add the olives and mushrooms to the pheasant and cook for a few minutes more. Transfer the bird and vegetables to a warm serving dish, discarding the rosemary, bay leaf and garlic.

FILETTI DI FAGIANO ALL'ARANCIA

Serves 4

1 pheasant, drawn and plucked boned and carcass reserved
50 g/2 oz butter
5 juniper berries, lightly crushed
175 ml/6 fl oz dry white wine
200 ml/7 fl oz Meat Stock (see page 208)
4 black peppercorns, lightly crushed
juice of 1 orange, strained
salt

PHEASANT WITH ORANGE

Slice the pheasant meat. Melt the butter in a frying pan with the juniper berries, add the slices of pheasant and cook over a medium heat, stirring and turning occasionally, for about 20 minutes. Meanwhile, put the wine, stock, peppercorns and a pinch of salt in another pan, add the carcass and bring to the boil, then cook until the liquid has reduced by half. Strain and skim off the fat if necessary. Bring the pheasant stock to a simmer, add the orange juice and slices of pheasant and simmer for a further 2 minutes. Transfer to a warm serving dish.

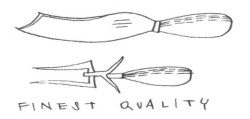

FINEST QUALITY

PARTRIDGE

Red-legged partridges, commonly eaten in Italy, are related to grey partridges, which are more widespread in Britain. They differ in having brightly coloured feet, a white patch on the throat and being slightly larger. In Australia and New Zealand, a different variety, the chukar, is farmed widely. Farmed partridges do not require hanging, but birds from shoots should be hung for 2–4 days. Partridge meat is red and flavoursome and is excellent roasted in the oven or on a spit. Allow one small partridge or half a large one per serving. To cook, allow 20 minutes per 250 g/9 oz.

PARTRIDGE WITH MUSTARD

PERNICE ALLA SENAPE

Serves 4

2 partridges, drawn and plucked with livers

pinch of chilli powder

2 slices pork fat or streaky bacon

3 tablespoons olive oil

50 g/2 oz butter

150 ml/¼ pint Meat Stock

(see page 208), plus extra for the sauce

25 g/1 oz plain flour

½ teaspoon English mustard

3–4 tablespoons double cream

salt

Season the cavities of the partridges with the chilli powder and a pinch of salt and wrap the birds in the pork fat or bacon. Heat the olive oil and 25 g/1 oz of the butter in a pan, add the partridges and cook over a medium-high heat, turning frequently, until browned all over. Pour in the stock and simmer, basting occasionally, for 20–25 minutes. Meanwhile, finely chop the livers. Mix together the flour and remaining butter in a bowl and stir in the mustard. Remove the partridges from the pan, place on a serving dish and keep warm. Add the mustard mixture and the partridge livers to the pan and pour in a little extra stock if necessary. Lower the heat and cook, stirring constantly, until the sauce has the desired consistency. Add the cream and cook over a medium heat for a few minutes. Spoon the sauce over the partridges and serve.

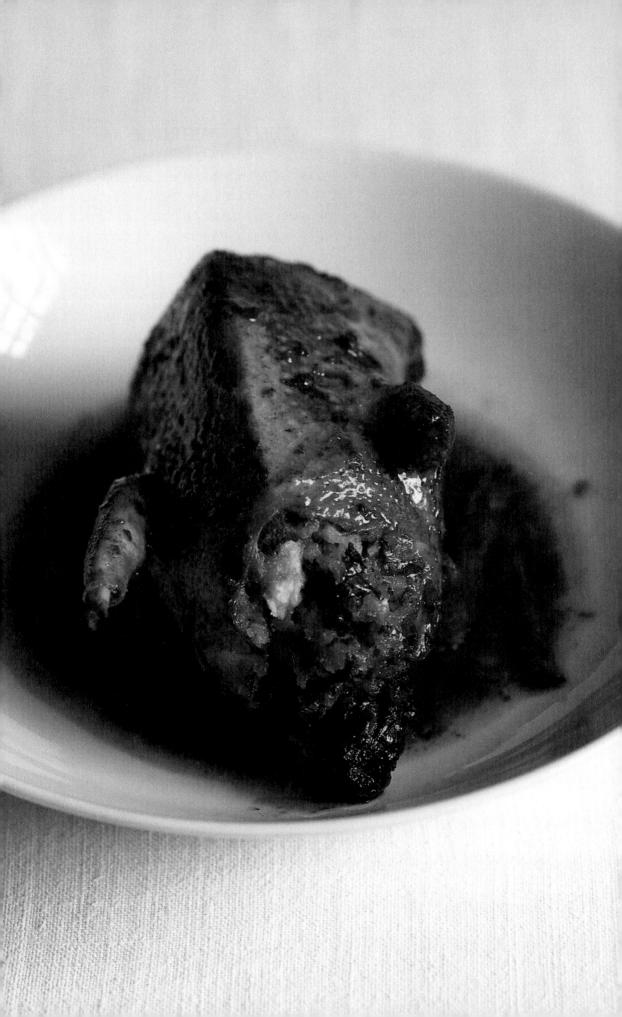

PERNICE FARCITA

Serves 4

25 g/1 oz butter, plus extra for greasing

1 thick bread slice, crusts removed

5 tablespoons milk

500 g/1 lb 2 oz mushrooms

2 partridges, drawn and plucked

with livers and hearts

100 g/3¹/₂ oz smoked pancetta, diced

salt and pepper

STUFFED PARTRIDGE

Preheat the oven to 180°C/350°F/Gas Mark 4. Generously grease an ovenproof dish with butter. Tear the bread into pieces, place in a bowl, add the milk and leave to soak for 10 minutes, then drain and squeeze out. Separate the caps of half the mushroom from their stems and chop the stems with the livers and hearts. Place in a bowl, stir in the soaked bread and season with salt and pepper to taste. Divide the mixture between the cavities of the partridges and sew up the openings. Chop the remaining mushrooms. Place the partridges in the prepared dish, surround them with the chopped mushrooms and pancetta and dot with the butter. Cover and roast for about 20 minutes. Remove the lid, stir in the cooking juices and roast until the partridges are cooked through and tender. Serve straight from the dish.

PERNICE MARINATA

Serves 4

4 partridges, drawn and plucked

4 tablespoons olive oil

1 onion, chopped

1 garlic clove, chopped

1 red pepper, halved, seeded and diced

¹/₂ celeriac, diced

2 bay leaves

4 black peppercorns, lightly crushed

300 ml/¹/₂ pint dry white wine

300 ml/¹/₂ pint white wine vinegar

5 tablespoons Meat Stock (see page 208), optional

salt and pepper

MARINATED PARTRIDGE

Season the partridges inside and out with salt. Heat the olive oil in a frying pan, add the partridges and cook, turning frequently, for 10 minutes until browned all over, then season with pepper. Transfer the birds to a flameproof dish and add the onion, garlic, red pepper, celeriac, bay leaves, peppercorns, wine and vinegar. Cover and cook over a low heat for about 1 hour, adding the stock if necessary to prevent drying out. Leave the partridges to cool slightly, then serve in their vegetable sauce, discarding the bay leaves.

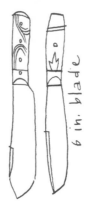

QUAIL

Quail are widespread and naturally live in fields and on grazing land. In Britain, wild quail are a protected species and quail bought in supermarkets or at butchers' shops are farmed, as they also are in Australia and New Zealand. They are sold oven-ready, and have lean, easily digestible flesh. Frozen quail are also available.

QUAIL WITH YOGURT

Mix together the lemon rind, onion, garlic and paprika in a bowl, strain in 2 tablespoons of the lemon juice and season with salt and pepper. Spread some of the mixture on the quail to cover. Place the birds in a frying pan with the olive oil and cook for 10 minutes on each side. Add the remaining lemon mixture, pour in the hot stock, cover and cook for about 15 minutes. Transfer the quail to a warm serving dish. Stir the yogurt into the cooking juices and strain in the remaining lemon juice to taste. Cook until thickened, then serve the quail with the sauce.

QUAGLIE ALLO YOGURT

Serves 4

grated rind and juice of 1 lemon

1 onion, chopped

1 garlic clove, chopped

1 teaspoon paprika

8 quail

2 tablespoons olive oil

200 ml/7 fl oz hot Meat Stock (see page 208)

400 ml/14 fl oz natural yogurt

salt and pepper

QUAIL IN WHITE WINE

Put half a garlic clove, 1 teaspoon of the rosemary needles and a sage leaf in the cavity of each bird and season with salt and pepper. Put the quail in a pan with the olive oil and cook, turning frequently, until browned all over. Season with salt, pour in the wine, cover and simmer over a low heat for 20 minutes.

QUAGLIE AL VINO BIANCO

Serves 4

4 garlic cloves, halved

8 teaspoons fresh rosemary needles

8 fresh sage leaves

8 quail

2 tablespoons olive oil

175 ml/6 fl oz white wine

salt and pepper

QUAIL WITH RISOTTO

QUAGLIE CON RISOTTO

Serves 4

4 quail

80 g/3 oz butter

2 tablespoons olive oil

2 tablespoons plain flour

about 1.5 litres/2¹/₂ pints hot Chicken Stock
(see page 209)

1 fresh thyme sprig

1 bay leaf

175 ml/6 fl oz dry white wine

1 onion, chopped

300 g/11 oz risotto rice

40 g/1¹/₂ oz Parmesan cheese, freshly grated

salt and pepper

Truss the quail with kitchen string and season with salt and pepper. Heat 25 g/1 oz of the butter and the oil in a pan, add the quail and cook over a high heat, turning frequently, for about 10 minutes until golden brown. Sprinkle the quail with half the flour and mix well. Mix together the remaining flour and 150 ml/¹/₄ pint of the stock in a bowl. Add the thyme and bay leaf to the quail, pour in the wine and the flour mixture and cook for a further 10 minutes. Meanwhile, prepare a risotto (see page 328) with the remaining butter, the onion, rice and stock and sprinkle with the Parmesan. Spoon the risotto on to a warm serving dish, flatten slightly and top with the quail and the cooking juices, discarding the herbs.

QUAIL ON THE SPIT

SPIEDO DI QUAGLIE

Serves 4

25 g/1 oz butter, softened

2 teaspoons fresh rosemary needles

1 small onion, finely chopped

8 quail

16 pancetta slices

8 rustic bread slices

olive oil, for brushing

salt and pepper

plain risotto, to serve

Preheat the oven to 180°C/350°F/Gas Mark 4. Mix together the butter, rosemary and onion in a bowl and season with salt and pepper. Divide the herb butter among the quails' cavities, then wrap each bird in two pancetta slices and truss with kitchen string. Thread the quail on to a spit, alternating with the slices of bread, brush with oil and roast for about 25 minutes. Brush occasionally with the cooking juices. Serve with a plain risotto.

GARLIC

CHAMOIS

FURRED GAME

Chamois, a wild mammal found in the Alps, is not widely available in other parts of the world. Even in Italy, chamois have become rare on the table and even rarer in the wild. The chamois meat found in shops is often frozen and is mainly imported. It tends to be less tasty, but more tender and is best jugged – the universal recipe for furred game. Other cooking methods are similar to those shown for venison, which may used as a substitute in this section. Mocetta is a speciality of Valle d'Aosta. It is cured meat made from a chamois leg that has been dried after soaking in a special marinade.

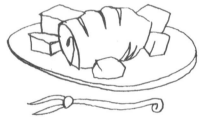

ALSACE CHAMOIS

CAMOSCIO ALSAZIANO

Serves 8

2 kg/4¹/₂ lb chamois or venison, cut into large pieces
175 ml/6 fl oz olive oil
100 g/3¹/₂ oz pancetta, diced
50 g/2 oz butter
50 g/2 oz plain flour
4 tablespoons double cream
salt and pepper

For the marinade
1 bottle (750 ml/1¹/₄ pints) white wine
5 tablespoons white wine vinegar
1 carrot
1 onion
1 garlic clove
2 celery sticks
1 fresh flat-leaf parsley sprig
4 juniper berries
4 black peppercorns
salt

To make the marinade, pour the wine and vinegar into a pan, add the carrot, onion, garlic, celery, parsley, juniper berries, peppercorns and a pinch of salt, bring to the boil and simmer for 15 minutes. Pour the marinade into a bowl, add the meat and leave in a cool place, turning occasionally, for 12 hours. Drain the meat, reserving the marinade, and pat dry with kitchen paper. Heat the olive oil in a pan, add the pancetta and meat and cook over a medium heat, stirring and turning frequently, until browned all over. Season with salt and pepper, lower the heat and cook, basting occasionally with the marinade until half has been used. Strain the remaining marinade into a bowl. Melt the butter in a saucepan, stir in the flour and cook, stirring constantly, until golden brown. Gradually stir in the remaining marinade and continue to cook, stirring constantly, until the sauce begins to thicken. Turn the heat to its lowest setting and simmer for 20 minutes. Just before serving, stir the cream into the sauce, season with salt and heat through. Serve the meat with the sauce.

CHAMOIS IN RED WINE

Pour the wine into a dish, add the cloves, juniper berries, bay leaves, celery, carrot and onion and season with salt and pepper. Add the meat and leave to marinate in a cool place, but not in the refrigerator, for at least 12 hours. Drain the meat, reserving the marinade, put it in a saucepan with the butter and olive oil and cook over a medium heat, turning and stirring frequently, until browned all over. Pour in the reserved marinade, add the apple, lower the heat and simmer gently for about 2 hours. Remove the pan from the heat and, using a slotted spoon, transfer the meat to a warm serving dish. Strain the cooking juices, stir in a little warm water if they are too thick and reheat. Spoon the cooking juices over the meat and serve.

CAMOSCIO AL VINO ROSSO

Serves 6

1 bottle (750 ml/1^1/$_4$ pints) Barolo or Nebbiolo wine

2 cloves

4 juniper berries

2 bay leaves

1 celery stick, sliced

1 carrot, sliced

1 onion, sliced

1 chamois or venison leg, cut into small pieces

25 g/1 oz butter

3 tablespoons olive oil

1 apple, peeled, cored and chopped

salt and pepper

CHAMOIS CHOPS WITH MUSHROOMS AND DRIED FRUIT

Put the porcini in a bowl, add hot water to cover and leave to soak for 30 minutes, then drain and slice thinly. Put the prunes and apricots in another bowl, add the tea and leave to soak for 30 minutes, then drain. Heat the olive oil and half the butter in a frying pan, add the chops and cook for about 10 minutes on each side, then season with salt to taste. Transfer the chops to a serving dish. Put the sugar in the pan and cook over a high heat for a few minutes but do not allow it to caramelize. Stir in the vinegar and cook over a high heat until the liquid has reduced by about half. Add the dried fruit, hot stock and juniper berries, bring to the boil and simmer for 5 minutes. Remove the fruit with a slotted spoon and arrange it around the chops. Stir the remaining butter into the cooking juices, in small pieces at a time, add the porcini, cover and cook, occasionally adding a tablespoonful of hot water if necessary. Season with salt to taste, spoon the sauce over the chops and serve.

COSTOLETTE DI CAMOSCIO AI FUNGHI E FRUTTA SECCA

Serves 4

40 g/1^1/$_2$ oz dried porcini

16 prunes

16 dried apricots

300 ml/^{1}/$_2$ pint freshly brewed tea

2 tablespoons olive oil

50 g/2 oz butter

8 chamois or venison chops

2 tablespoons sugar

100 ml/3^1/$_2$ fl oz red wine vinegar

100 ml/3^1/$_2$ fl oz hot Meat Stock (see page 208)

3 juniper berries

salt

VENISON

Roe deer, which live in the mountains, especially the Alps, as well as on the plains, are the main source of venison in Italy. However, they are increasingly rare in the wild and rightly protected, but their numbers are increasing on farms. Farmed venison has a less gamey flavour and the meat needs hanging for only eight days. Besides roe deer, three other types are also found in Britain - some wild, others in parks and increasing numbers reared on farms. Venison is also imported from New Zealand, where it is sold as Cervena. Australia also farms venison, which it largely exports to South-East Asia and Europe. Venison may be prepared in numerous ways – frozen meat may be used for stews and braising, the saddle of a young deer is ideal for roasting and the haunch and ribs are tasty grilled or fried.

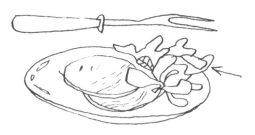

ROAST VENISON

CAPRIOLO ARROSTO

Serves 6

1 leg or haunch of venison
100 g/3¹⁄₂ oz pancetta, cut into thin strips
175 ml/6 fl oz olive oil, plus extra for brushing
500 ml/18 fl oz dry white wine
1 fresh thyme sprig, chopped
1 fresh summer savory sprig, chopped
1 fresh oregano sprig, chopped
salt and pepper

Make small incisions in the meat and insert the strips of pancetta. Mix together the olive oil, wine and herbs in a dish, season with salt and pepper and add the meat. Cover and leave to marinate in a cool place overnight. Preheat the oven to 220°C/425°F/Gas Mark 7. Generously brush a roasting tin with oil. Drain the leg of venison, reserving the marinade, place it in the roasting tin and roast for 10 minutes. Pour the reserved marinade into the tin, lower the temperature to 180°C/350°F/Gas Mark 4 and roast, basting frequently, for about 30 minutes. This will result in slightly rare venison. If you prefer it well done, roast for a further 10 minutes, but do not overcook or it will become tough. Remove the venison from the roasting tin and carve, then place the slices on a warm serving dish and spoon the cooking juices over them.

VENISON STEW

Mix together the wine, half the spices, the celery, carrots, onion, garlic, sage and bay leaves in a dish, season with salt and pepper and add the meat. Leave to marinate, stirring and turning occasionally, for 12 hours. Remove the venison from the marinade and pat dry with kitchen paper. Strain the marinade into a bowl and reserve the liquid and the vegetables separately, but discard the cloves and bay leaves. Heat the olive oil and butter in a pan, add the pancetta and cook, stirring occasionally, until crisp. Add the venison and cook, stirring frequently, until browned all over. Add the remaining spices, season with salt to taste and stir in the reserved vegetables. Cook, stirring occasionally, for 10 minutes, then pour in the reserved marinade and bring to the boil. Lower the heat, cover and simmer for 2 hours. Transfer the meat to a warm serving dish. Remove and discard the cloves and transfer the cooking juices to a blender. Process to a purée, pour into a sauce boat and serve with the venison.

CAPRIOLO IN SALMÌ

Serves 8

1 bottle (750 ml/1¹/₄ pints) red wine
2 pinches of freshly grated nutmeg
2 pinches of ground cinnamon
4 cloves
1 celery stick, chopped
2 carrots, sliced
1 onion, chopped
1 garlic clove, chopped
4 fresh sage leaves
2 bay leaves
2 kg/4¹/₂ lb stewing venison, cut into cubes
3 tablespoons olive oil
50 g/2 oz butter
1 pancetta slice, diced
salt and pepper

ROAST SADDLE OF VENISON WITH CRANBERRIES

Preheat the oven to 180°C/350°F/Gas Mark 4. Gently rub the meat with salt and pepper. Heat the olive oil and half the butter in a large frying pan, add the venison and cook, turning frequently, until browned all over. Transfer to a roasting tin, surround with the vegetables and garlic and roast, basting frequently with the cooking juices and stock, for 1¹/₂ hours. Remove the venison from the roasting tin, carve into thin slices, place on a serving dish and keep warm. Remove and discard the garlic from the cooking juices, pour in the wine and cook over a high heat until reduced. Cut the remaining butter into small pieces, add to the roasting tin and stir until the sauce is thick and velvety, then spoon it over the venison. Stir the sugar into 175 ml/6 fl oz water to dissolve, then pour into a saucepan, bring to the boil and boil for a few minutes. Add the cranberries and simmer over a low heat for 5 minutes. Stir in the cream and cook until thickened. Serve the venison with the warm cranberry sauce.

SELLA DI CAPRIOLO ARROSTO AI MIRTILLI ROSSI

Serves 6–8

1 saddle of venison
4 tablespoons olive oil
50 g/2 oz butter
2 carrots, chopped
1 onion, chopped
1 celery stick, chopped
1 garlic clove
200 ml/7 fl oz hot Meat Stock (see page 208)
100 ml/3¹/₂ fl oz red wine
3 tablespoons sugar
400 g/14 oz cranberries, thawed if frozen
2 tablespoons double cream
salt and pepper

WILD BOAR

Italian wild boar are large and robust, sometimes reaching a weight of 180 kg/397 lb, and live in a few restricted areas of Tuscany and Lazio. Wild boar is also hunted elsewhere, including Australia and New Zealand. Although there are moves to reintroduce boar to the wild in Britain, most wild boar there is, in fact, farmed. The cuts of meat and the most suitable cooking techniques correspond to those of pork. The loin, ribs and legs of young boar are popular for grilling and roasting. The loin is best for roasting and the ribs are recommended for cooking on the barbecue. Other cuts of young boar are best stewed. Adult wild boar are best fried or stewed after marinating. As with all other game, frozen wild boar is tastiest when stewed.

WILD BOAR WITH APPLES

Preheat the oven to 200°C/400°F/Gas Mark 6. Melt half the butter in a flameproof casserole, add the meat and cook, stirring frequently, until browned. Stir in the onion and carrot, sprinkle in the flour and cook, stirring constantly, for 2–3 minutes, then gradually stir in the wine. Add the garlic and bay leaf, season with salt and pepper and bring to the boil. Transfer the casserole to the oven and cook for 1 hour, then stir in the brandy. Meanwhile, melt the remaining butter in a pan, add the apples and cook, stirring occasionally, for 10 minutes until golden. Discard the garlic and bay leaf, serve the meat in the cooking juices and hand the apples separately.

CINGHIALE ALLE MELE

Serves 4

50 g/2 oz butter

1 kg/2¼ lb lean wild boar, diced

1 onion, finely chopped

1 carrot, finely chopped

1 tablespoon plain flour

375 ml/13 fl oz red wine

1 garlic clove

1 bay leaf

50 ml/2 fl oz brandy

3 apples, peeled, cored and sliced

salt and pepper

WILD BOAR WITH OLIVES

Pour the wine and vinegar into a large pan and add the carrot, garlic, onion, thyme, sage, bay leaves, parsley, peppercorns and a generous pinch of salt. Bring to the boil, then lower the heat and simmer for 15 minutes. Remove the pan from the heat, leave to cool and pour into a bowl. Add the meat, cover and leave to marinate in a cool place, stirring occasionally, for up to 2 days. Heat the olive oil and butter in a pan. Drain the meat, reserving the marinade, add to the pan and cook, stirring frequently, until browned all over. Season with salt and pepper, pour in about half the reserved marinade, bring to the boil, then lower the heat and simmer for 1½ hours. Add the olives and simmer for a further 30 minutes. Discard the garlic and herbs and serve with mashed potatoes.

CINGHIALE ALLE OLIVE

Serves 6

1 bottle (750 ml/1¼ pints) white wine

5 tablespoons white wine vinegar

1 carrot

1 garlic clove

1 onion

1 fresh thyme sprig

2 fresh sage leaves

2 bay leaves

1 fresh flat-leaf parsley sprig

6 black peppercorns

1.2 kg/2½ lb lean wild boar, diced

175 ml/6 fl oz olive oil

25 g/1 oz butter

150 g/5 oz stoned green olives

salt and pepper

mashed potatoes, to serve

WILD BOAR IN SAUCE

First make the marinade. Put the carrots, onions, garlic, parsley, thyme, bay leaf, cloves, wine, vinegar and olive oil in a pan, season with salt and pepper and bring to the boil, then lower the heat and simmer for 15 minutes. Remove the pan from the heat and leave to cool, then pour into a dish. Gently rub the leg of boar with salt, place in the cooled marinade, cover and leave to marinate in a cool place for 24 hours. Preheat the oven to 200°C/400°F/Gas Mark 6. Drain the meat, reserving the marinade, and pat dry with kitchen paper. Strain the marinade into a bowl. Place the meat in a roasting tin with the strips of pancetta and cook over a medium heat, turning frequently, until browned all over. Add enough of the reserved marinade to half-cover the meat and transfer to the oven. Roast, turning occasionally, for 1¾ hours, covering the roasting tin with foil halfway through the cooking time. Remove the meat from the roasting tin and keep warm. Add the remaining marinade and cook over a high heat until reduced by half, then purée the mixture with a hand-held blender. Season with pepper, remove from the heat and stir in the butter in small pieces at a time. Serve the wild boar with the sauce.

CINGHIALE IN SALSA

Serves 12

2.5 kg/5½ lb leg of wild boar

150 g/5 oz pancetta, sliced into strips

25 g/1 oz butter

salt and pepper

For the marinade

2 carrots, chopped

2 onions, chopped

1 garlic clove, chopped

1 fresh flat-leaf parsley sprig, chopped

1 fresh thyme sprig, chopped

1 bay leaf

2 cloves

2 litres/3½ pints red wine

175 ml/6 fl oz red wine vinegar

3 tablespoons olive oil

salt and pepper

RABBIT

Rabbit meat is white, lean, tender, tasty and eaten mainly in the winter. Both wild rabbits and farmed rabbits are widely available. The former have more flavoursome, aromatic meat as they are free to feed on the herbs found in the wooded areas where they live. The best rabbits for eating are between three months and a year old and at this age they have short necks and feet. Rabbit meat does not need hanging and may be bought whole or in pieces. Keep to the following few basic rules when cooking rabbit. Before starting to cook, soak the rabbit in a mixture of 1.5 litres/2¹/₂ pints water and 175 ml/6 fl oz white wine vinegar for 30 minutes. The best herbs for flavouring rabbit are rosemary, sage, bay leaf, thyme, fennel and basil. Do not forget to add one or more garlic cloves to the pan. Rabbit meat is a little watery, so heat it in a frying pan for a few minutes until dry. It takes 45–60 minutes to cook, depending on its age.

CONIGLIO AL FORNO

Serves 6

5 tablespoons olive oil

1 fresh rosemary sprig

2 garlic cloves

1 rabbit, cut into pieces

salt and pepper

ROAST RABBIT

Preheat the oven to 180°C/350°F/Gas Mark 4. Heat the olive oil in a flameproof casserole with the rosemary and garlic, add the rabbit and cook, turning frequently, until browned all over. Season with salt and pepper, transfer the casserole to the oven and cook, stirring and turning occasionally, for 1 hour or until tender. Transfer to a warm serving dish.

RABBIT CACCIATORE

Melt the butter in a pan, add the onion and prosciutto and cook over a low heat, stirring occasionally, for 5 minutes. Add the rabbit, increase the heat to medium and cook, turning frequently, until browned all over. Season with salt and pepper to taste, stir in the wine and add the thyme, then cover and cook for 20 minutes. Add the tomatoes, lower the heat and simmer for about 1 hour. If the cooking juices are too runny, thicken them by stirring in a pinch of flour. Transfer the stew to a warm serving dish, discarding the thyme, and serve with a soft polenta.

CONIGLIO ALLA CACCIATORA

Serves 6

25 g/1 oz butter

1 onion, chopped

50 g/2 oz prosciutto, chopped

1 rabbit, cut into pieces

175 ml/6 fl oz dry white wine

1 fresh thyme sprig

500 g/1 lb 2 oz tomatoes, peeled, seeded and coarsely chopped

pinch of plain flour (optional)

salt and pepper

soft Polenta (see page 305), to serve

RABBIT IN VINEGAR

Heat the butter and olive oil in a pan, add the sage, rosemary and garlic, season with pepper and stir-fry for a few minutes. Add the rabbit and cook over a medium heat, turning frequently, until browned all over. Mix the vinegar with 3 tablespoons water and add to the pan. Season with salt to taste, cover and simmer for about 50 minutes. Stir in the olives and capers and simmer for a further 10 minutes, then serve.

CONIGLIO ALL'ACETO

Serves 6

25 g/1 oz butter

3 tablespoons olive oil

1 fresh sage sprig, chopped

1 fresh rosemary sprig, chopped

1 garlic clove, crushed

1 rabbit, cut into pieces

175 ml/6 fl oz white wine vinegar

100 g/3½ oz stoned green olives

50 g/2 oz capers, drained and rinsed

salt and pepper

RABBIT IN OLIVE OIL AND LEMON

Heat the olive oil in a pan, add the rosemary, sage, parsley, garlic and bay leaf and cook over a medium heat, stirring occasionally, for 3 minutes. Add the rabbit and cook, turning frequently, until browned all over. Season with salt and pepper, pour in the wine and cook until it has evaporated. Lower the heat, cover and simmer for 45 minutes. Remove the lid and simmer for a further 15 minutes until tender. Remove and discard the garlic and bay leaf, stir in the lemon juice, increase the heat to high and cook for 5 minutes more.

CONIGLIO ALL'AGRO

Serves 6

5 tablespoons olive oil

1 fresh rosemary sprig, chopped

1 fresh sage leaf, chopped

1 fresh flat-leaf parsley sprig, chopped

1 garlic clove

1 bay leaf

1 rabbit, cut into pieces

175 ml/6 fl oz dry white wine

juice of 2 lemons, strained

salt and pepper

RABBIT WITH BAY LEAVES

Heat the olive oil in a pan, add the rabbit and bay leaves and cook over a medium heat for a few minutes. Lower the heat, cover and cook, turning the meat occasionally, for 1 hour. Season with salt and pepper, cook for 1 minute more and serve.

CONIGLIO ALL'ALLORO

Serves 6

5 tablespoons olive oil

1 rabbit, cut into pieces

6 bay leaves

salt and pepper

RABBIT WITH MUSTARD

Brush the rabbit with some of the olive oil and season generously with salt and pepper. Heat the remaining oil in a pan, add the rabbit and cook over a medium heat, turning frequently, until browned all over. Pour in the wine and lemon juice, season lightly with salt and pepper and add the rosemary, marjoram, parsley, garlic, spring onion and bay leaf. Lower the heat, cover and simmer for about 50 minutes. Mix the mustard with 1 tablespoon hot water, pour into the pan and simmer, uncovered, for a further 10 minutes until the sauce has thickened. Discard the bay leaf and serve with mashed potatoes.

CONIGLIO ALLA SENAPE

Serves 6

1 rabbit, cut into pieces

4 tablespoons olive oil

175 ml/6 fl oz dry white wine

juice of 1 lemon, strained

1 fresh rosemary sprig, chopped

2 fresh marjoram leaves, chopped

1 fresh flat-leaf parsley sprig, chopped

1 garlic clove, crushed

1 spring onion, white part only, sliced

1 bay leaf

2 tablespoons strong mustard

salt and pepper

mashed potatoes, to serve

RABBIT IN MILK

Melt the butter in a pan, add the onion and rosemary and cook over a low heat, stirring occasionally, for 5 minutes. Dust the rabbit with flour, add to the pan, increase the heat to medium and cook, turning frequently, until browned all over. Season with salt and pepper, pour in the milk and bring to the boil, then lower the heat, cover and simmer for about 30 minutes. Add the fennel seeds, re-cover the pan and simmer for a further 30 minutes. Mix the cornflour to a paste with 1 tablespoon water, add to the pan and cook, stirring constantly, until the sauce has thickened. Transfer the meat to a warm serving dish and spoon the sauce over it.

CONIGLIO AL LATTE

Serves 6

50 g/2 oz butter

1 onion, chopped

1 fresh rosemary sprig, chopped

1 rabbit, cut into pieces

plain flour, for dusting

500 ml/18 fl oz milk

1 tablespoon fennel seeds

1 teaspoon cornflour

salt and pepper

RABBIT WITH HONEY AND VEGETABLES

CONIGLIO AL MIELE CON VERDURE

Serves 4

80 g/3 oz butter

1 tablespoon clear honey

1 rabbit, cut into pieces

5 tablespoons white wine vinegar

4 carrots, sliced

4 turnips, sliced

100 g/3¹/₂ oz peas

100 g/3¹/₂ oz French beans

1 fresh tarragon sprig, chopped

salt and pepper

Preheat the oven to 200°C/400°F/Gas Mark 6. Heat the butter and honey in a flameproof casserole, add the rabbit and cook over a medium heat, turning frequently, until browned all over. Season with salt and pepper, remove from the casserole and keep warm. Pour the vinegar into the casserole and cook, scraping up any sediment from the base with a wooden spoon, then simmer over a low heat until the liquid has evaporated. Meanwhile, cook the vegetables in separate pans of salted, boiling water for 5 minutes, then drain. Return the rabbit to the casserole, add the vegetables and tarragon, cover, transfer to the oven and cook for about 45 minutes until tender.

RABBIT IN CIDER

CONIGLIO AL SIDRO

Serves 6

25 g/1 oz butter • 2 tablespoons olive oil

1 rabbit, cut into pieces

1 onion, sliced

100 g/3¹/₂ oz pancetta, diced

1 tablespoon plain flour • 600 ml/1 pint dry cider

175 ml/6 fl oz Meat Stock (see page 208)

100 g/3¹/₂ oz mushrooms, sliced

1 fresh thyme sprig

strip of thinly pared lemon rind

salt and pepper

Heat the butter and oil in a pan, add the rabbit and cook over a medium heat, turning frequently, until browned all over. Remove the rabbit from the pan and keep warm. Add the onion and pancetta to the pan and cook over a low heat, stirring occasionally, for about 10 minutes. Sprinkle with the flour and stir well, then gradually stir in the cider and stock. When all the liquid has been incorporated, bring to the boil, stirring constantly. Return the rabbit to the pan, add the mushrooms, thyme and lemon rind and season with salt and pepper. Cover and cook over a low heat for 1 hour until tender. Remove and discard the thyme and lemon rind, season with salt and pepper to taste and serve.

RABBIT IN RED WINE

CONIGLIO AL VINO ROSSO

Serves 6

1 rabbit, with liver

1 onion • 2 cloves

1 fresh thyme sprig, chopped

1 fresh rosemary sprig, chopped

1 fresh sage sprig, chopped

pinch of ground cinnamon

1 garlic clove

1 carrot, chopped • 1 celery stick, chopped

1 bottle (750 ml/1¹/₄ pints) red wine

40 g/1¹/₂ oz butter • 2 tablespoons olive oil

salt and pepper

Chop the liver and set aside. Cut the rabbit into pieces. Put them in a dish, add the onion stuck with the cloves, the thyme, rosemary, sage, cinnamon, garlic, carrot and celery and pour in the wine. Leave to marinate, turning occasionally, for 12 hours. Drain the meat, reserving the marinade. Heat the butter and olive oil in a pan, add the rabbit and cook over a medium heat, turning frequently, until browned all over. Season with salt and pepper, pour in the reserved marinade, lower the heat, cover and simmer for 30 minutes. Add the liver, re-cover and simmer for a further 30 minutes. Transfer the rabbit to a warm serving dish. Ladle the cooking juices into a blender and process to a purée. Spoon the sauce over the rabbit and serve

BRAISED RABBIT WITH ROSEMARY

CONIGLIO ARROSTO AL ROSMARINO

Serves 6

4 fresh rosemary sprigs
1 rabbit
3 tablespoons olive oil
25 g/1 oz butter
1 garlic clove
salt and pepper
roast potatoes, to serve

Chop the needles of one of the rosemary sprigs and set aside. Brush the rabbit with some of the olive oil and stuff with the whole rosemary sprigs, half the butter and the garlic and season the cavity with a pinch of salt. Place in a pan with the remaining oil and butter, sprinkle with the chopped rosemary and season with salt and pepper to taste. Cover and cook over a low heat, turning occasionally and adding a few tablespoons of hot water if necessary, for 1½ hours. Remove the rabbit from the pan, cut into pieces and place on a warm serving dish. Serve with roast potatoes.

RABBIT WITH PEPERONATA

CONIGLIO CON PEPERONATA

Serves 6

6 tablespoons olive oil
25 g/1 oz butter
1 carrot, chopped
1 fresh sage sprig, chopped
1 fresh rosemary sprig, chopped
1 rabbit, cut into pieces
5 tablespoons white wine vinegar
1 red pepper, halved, seeded and thickly sliced
1 green pepper, halved, seeded and thickly sliced
1 yellow pepper, halved, seeded and thickly sliced
1 onion, thinly sliced
3 tomatoes, peeled, seeded and diced
salt and pepper

Heat half the olive oil and the butter in a pan, add the carrot, sage and rosemary and cook over a low heat, stirring occasionally, for 5 minutes. Add the rabbit, increase the heat to medium and cook, turning frequently, for 10 minutes until browned all over, then season with salt and pepper to taste. Mix the vinegar with 5 tablespoons water, add to the pan, lower the heat, cover and simmer for 1 hour or until the rabbit is tender. Meanwhile, heat the remaining olive oil in a frying pan, add the peppers and onion and cook over a medium heat, stirring occasionally, for about 15 minutes. Add the tomatoes, lower the heat, cover and simmer until all the vegetables are softened and cooked through. Season with salt and pepper, transfer the pepper mixture to the pan of rabbit and cook for a few minutes more, then serve.

FRIED RABBIT

CONIGLIO FRITTO

Serves 6

2 eggs
80 g/3 oz breadcrumbs
1 rabbit, cut into pieces
150 ml/¼ pint olive oil
salt
lemon wedges, to garnish

Beat the eggs with a pinch of salt in a shallow dish and spread out the breadcrumbs in another shallow dish. Dip the pieces of rabbit first into the beaten eggs and then in the breadcrumbs to coat. Heat the oil in a frying pan, add the pieces of rabbit and cook, turning frequently, for about 10 minutes until crisp and golden brown on the outside and tender and cooked through on the inside. Remove from the pan and drain on kitchen paper. Serve immediately, garnished with wedges of lemon.

STEWED RABBIT

Heat the olive oil in a pan, add the rabbit and cook over a medium heat, turning frequently, for 15 minutes until browned all over. Add the garlic, thyme and parsley, mix well and season with salt and pepper. Pour in the wine and cook until it has evaporated. Add the tomatoes, lower the heat, cover and simmer, stirring occasionally, for about 1¼ hours.

CONIGLIO IN UMIDO

Serves 6

3 tablespoons olive oil

1 rabbit, cut into pieces

1 garlic clove, chopped

1 fresh thyme sprig, chopped

1 fresh flat-leaf parsley sprig, chopped

175 ml/6 fl oz dry white wine

2 tomatoes, peeled, seeded and coarsely chopped

salt and pepper

MARINATED RABBIT

Stud the onion with the cloves and place in a dish with the wine, vinegar, celery, carrot and peppercorns. Add the rabbit and leave to marinate, turning occasionally, for at least 6 hours. Drain the meat, reserving the marinade, and pat dry with kitchen paper. Strain the marinade. Heat the butter and olive oil in a pan, add the pieces of rabbit and cook over a medium heat, turning frequently, until browned all over. Season with salt and pepper, add 300 ml/½ pint of the reserved marinade and cook until it has evaporated slightly. Lower the heat, cover and simmer for about 1¼ hours, adding 2–3 tablespoons of the remaining marinade if necessary.

CONIGLIO MARINATO

Serves 6

1 onion • 2 cloves

500 ml/18 fl oz dry white wine

2 tablespoons white wine vinegar

1 celery stick

1 carrot

6 black peppercorns

1 rabbit, cut into pieces

25 g/1 oz butter

3 tablespoons olive oil

salt and pepper

STUFFED RABBIT

Preheat the oven to 200°C/400°F/Gas Mark 6. Tear the bread into pieces, place in a bowl, add water to cover and leave to soak for 10 minutes, then drain and squeeze out. Chop the liver. Mix together the ham and sausages in a bowl. Heat half the butter and the olive oil in a pan, add the liver and onion and cook over a low heat, stirring occasionally, for 5 minutes. Remove the pan from the heat and stir in the soaked bread, then add the mixture to the bowl of ham and sausages, stir in the parsley, thyme and egg and season with salt and pepper. Spoon the mixture into the cavity of the rabbit and sew up the opening. Place the rabbit in a roasting tin, brush with olive oil, dot with the remaining butter and sprinkle with the garlic and carrot. Roast until golden brown, then pour in the wine, cover with foil and roast for a further 1½ hours.

CONIGLIO RIPIENO

Serves 6

1 thick bread slice, crusts removed

1 rabbit, with liver

100 g/3½ oz cooked ham, chopped

200 g/7 oz Italian sausages, skinned and crumbled

50 g/2 oz butter

1 tablespoon olive oil, plus extra for brushing

1 onion, chopped

1 fresh flat-leaf parsley sprig, chopped

1 fresh thyme sprig, chopped

1 egg, lightly beaten

1 garlic clove, finely chopped

1 carrot, chopped

350 ml/12 fl oz dry white wine

salt and pepper

ROTOLO DI CONIGLIO CON IL TONNO

Serves 6

300 g/11 oz boneless rabbit, diced

plain flour, for dusting

pinch of curry powder

2 tablespoons olive oil

185 g/6½ oz canned tuna in oil, drained

1 canned anchovy fillet in oil, drained

120 ml/4 fl oz double cream

3 egg yolks

50 g/2 oz pistachios

5 tablespoons white wine

1 shallot, chopped

25 g/1 oz butter

500 ml/18 fl oz Meat Stock (see page 208)

1 tablespoon white truffle pâté

juice of ½ lemon, strained

200 ml/7 fl oz sunflower oil

2 tablespoons white wine vinegar

80 g/3 oz rocket

salt and pepper

radicchio salad, to serve

RABBIT AND TUNA ROLL

Dredge one-third of the diced rabbit with flour and sprinkle with the curry powder. Heat the olive oil in a frying pan, add the coated meat and cook over a low heat, stirring occasionally, for 30 minutes. Put the remaining rabbit and the tuna and anchovy in a food processor and process. Add the cream and one of the egg yolks, season with salt and pepper and process again. Scrape into a bowl and stir in the pistachios, cooked rabbit, wine, shallot and butter. Knead the mixture and shape into a sausage. Wrap in muslin and tie both ends. Bring the stock to the boil in a large pan, add the muslin-wrapped roll and simmer for 20 minutes. Remove the pan from the heat and leave the roll to cool in the cooking liquid, then drain and chill in the refrigerator for at least 2 hours. Meanwhile, beat the remaining egg yolks with the truffle pâté and lemon juice in a bowl and season with salt. Gradually whisk in the sunflower oil until fully incorporated, then stir in the vinegar. Remove the rabbit roll from the refrigerator, unwrap and slice. Make a bed of rocket on a serving dish, place the slices of rabbit roll on top and spoon the sauce over them. Serve with a radicchio salad.

SPEZZATINO ALLE ACCIUGHE

Serves 6

5 tablespoons olive oil

1 fresh rosemary sprig

2 fresh sage leaves

1 garlic clove, chopped

1 rabbit, cut into pieces

4 salted anchovies, heads removed, cleaned and filleted (see page 596), soaked in cold water for 10 minutes and drained

5 tablespoons white wine vinegar

salt and pepper

RABBIT STEW WITH ANCHOVIES

Heat the olive oil in a large saucepan with the rosemary, sage and garlic. Add the rabbit and cook over a high heat, turning frequently, until browned all over. Season, lower the heat, cover and cook, stirring occasionally, for 1¼ hours until tender. Meanwhile, chop the anchovy fillets. Mix together the anchovies, vinegar and 1 tablespoon water in a bowl. Remove the rabbit from the pan and drain well. Discard the herbs. Pour the vinegar and anchovy mixture into the pan, increase the heat and cook until reduced. Return the meat to the pan, lower the heat and cook for a further 10 minutes. Transfer to a warm serving dish.

RABBIT STEW WITH WALNUTS

Put the garlic, thyme, rosemary and juniper berries in a dish, season with salt and pepper and pour in the wine and vinegar. Add the rabbit and leave to marinate, turning occasionally, for 12 hours. Drain the meat, reserving the marinade, and pat dry with kitchen paper. Melt the butter in a pan, add the rabbit and cook, turning frequently, until browned all over. Add about half the marinade and cook over a high heat for 30 minutes or until the liquid has almost completely evaporated. Chop 50 g/2 oz of the walnuts and stir into the cream, then pour into the pan and cook until thickened. Transfer the rabbit to a warm serving dish. Stir the remaining walnuts into the sauce, spoon it over the rabbit and serve.

SPEZZATINO ALLE NOCI

Serves 6

1 garlic clove, chopped

1 fresh thyme sprig, chopped

1 fresh rosemary sprig, chopped

3 juniper berries, lightly crushed

375 ml/13 fl oz dry white wine

1 tablespoon white wine vinegar

1 rabbit, cut into pieces

25 g/1 oz butter

100 g/3¹/₂ oz shelled walnuts, halved

5 tablespoons double cream

salt and pepper

RABBIT STEW WITH TOMATOES AND BASIL

Heat the olive oil in a pan, add the rabbit and cook, turning frequently, until browned all over. Transfer to a plate, cover and keep warm. Add the tomatoes and onion to the pan and cook, stirring occasionally, for 20 minutes. Return the rabbit to the pan, add the garlic and season with salt and pepper. Cover and cook over a low heat for 1 hour. Sprinkle with the basil and serve.

SPEZZATINO AL POMODORO
E BASILICO

Serves 6

3 tablespoons olive oil

1 rabbit, cut into pieces

1 kg/2¹/₄ lb tomatoes, peeled, seeded and diced

1 onion, thinly sliced

1 garlic clove, crushed

10 fresh basil leaves, chopped

salt and pepper

RABBIT 'TUNA'

Cook the rabbit in a large pan of simmering water with the onion, carrot, celery, bay leaf and a pinch of salt for 1¹/₂ hours. Drain the rabbit, cut the meat off the bones and chop while still warm, then season with salt and pepper. Make a layer of meat in a glass or ceramic dish and sprinkle with some of the sage and garlic. Continue making layers until the dish is three-quarters full. Gently pour the olive oil over the surface, cover and leave to stand in a cool place for a few days.

'TONNO' DI CONIGLIO

Serves 6

1 rabbit

1 onion

1 carrot

1 celery stick

1 bay leaf

6 fresh sage leaves, chopped

2 garlic cloves, finely chopped

175 ml/6 fl oz olive oil

salt and pepper

HARE

Hares are often mistaken for wild rabbits, but differ in that their ears and feet are longer. For the best results when cooking, the age of the animal should be considered as it will affect the choice of recipe. Leverets from two to four months old, weighing about 1.5 kg/3 1/4 lb, can be roasted. One-year old hares, weighing 2.5–3 kg/5 1/2–6 1/2 lb, are best jugged. Older hares, weighing 4–6 kg/8 3/4–18 1/4 lb, are best used in terrines. Young female hares are preferable for their tender meat. Hares should be hung for about two days. They are available in Italy whole or cut into pieces. Outside Italy they are difficult to buy commercially but are usually available from specialist game suppliers.

HARE CACCIATORE

LEPRE ALLA CACCIATORA

Serves 6–8

1 hare, cut into pieces

white wine vinegar, for rinsing

2 fresh thyme sprigs

2 fresh marjoram, sprigs

4 fresh sage leaves

2 bay leaves

1 bottle (750 ml/1 1/4 pints) full-bodied red wine

4 tablespoons olive oil

1 garlic clove

2 tablespoons tomato purée

salt and pepper

Wash the hare in plenty of vinegar, then put the pieces in a bowl with a thyme sprig, a marjoram sprig, two sage leaves and a bay leaf and pour in the wine. Cover and leave to marinate in a cool place, turning occasionally, for at least 12 hours. Drain the meat, reserving the marinade, put in a pan and cook over a high heat, turning frequently, for 10 minutes, then season. Add the olive oil, garlic and remaining herbs and cook, turning frequently, until the pieces of hare are browned all over. Strain the reserved marinade into the pan and bring to the boil, then lower the heat, cover and simmer for about 2 hours. If the meat seems to be drying out during cooking, add a little warm water. Mix the tomato purée with 2 tablespoons water, add to the pan, re-cover and simmer for a further 30 minutes. Transfer to a warm serving dish.

HARE WITH WINE

Stud the onion with the cloves and place in a dish with the wine, carrot, shallot, thyme, bay leaf, sage leaf, juniper berries and vinegar. Set the liver and blood aside. Cut the hare into small pieces, season with pepper, add to the marinade and season with salt. Leave to marinate, turning occasionally, for at least 12 hours. Heat the butter and oil in a pan. Drain the meat, reserving the marinade, add to the pan and cook over a medium heat, turning frequently, until lightly browned all over. Remove and discard the herbs from the marinade, pour it into a blender and process to a purée. Sprinkle the pieces of hare with the flour and mix well, then pour in the puréed marinade. If necessary, add a little warm water so that the liquid covers the meat. Lower the heat and simmer for 2 hours until tender. Meanwhile, finely chop the liver. Stir the blood, liver and cream into the pan and simmer for 3 minutes, then serve.

LEPRE AL VINO

Serves 6–8

1 onion

2 cloves

1 bottle (750 ml/1¼ pints) full-bodied red wine

1 carrot, sliced

1 shallot, sliced

1 fresh thyme sprig

1 bay leaf

1 fresh sage leaf

6 juniper berries

1 tablespoon white wine vinegar

1 hare, with liver and blood

25 g/1 oz butter

2 tablespoons olive oil

1 tablespoon plain flour

5 tablespoons double cream

salt and pepper

HARE WITH JUNIPER BERRIES

Mix together the wine, juniper berries, bay leaf, shallot, garlic, onion, peppercorns and a pinch of salt in a dish. Add the pieces of hare, cover and leave to marinate in a cool place, turning occasionally, for at least 12 hours. Preheat the oven to 180°C/350°F/Gas Mark 4. Generously brush a roasting tin with olive oil. Drain the meat, reserving the marinade, and pat dry with kitchen paper. Wrap the slices of pancetta around the pieces of hare, place in the prepared roasting tin and cook for 45–50 minutes or until the hare is medium rare. If you prefer well-done meat, cook for an extra 15 minutes. Strain the marinade into a saucepan, bring to the boil over a high heat and cook until reduced by half. Remove the roasting tin from the oven and unwrap the pieces of hare. Gently heat the brandy in a small saucepan, pour it over the meat and ignite. When the flames have died down, transfer the hare to a warm serving dish. Strain the reduced marinade into the cooking juices and bring to the boil over a high heat, scraping up any sediment from the base of the roasting tin with a wooden spoon. Remove the tin from the heat, stir in the butter and pour into a sauce boat.Serve the hare with the sauce.

LEPRE CON IL GINEPRO

Serves 6–8

500 ml/18 fl oz dry white wine

10 juniper berries

1 bay leaf, torn into pieces

1 shallot, very finely chopped

1 garlic clove, crushed

1 onion, sliced

4 black peppercorns

1 hare, cut into fairly large pieces

olive oil, for brushing

100 g/3½ oz pancetta, sliced

3 tablespoons brandy

25 g/1 oz butter

salt

SWEET AND STRONG HARE

Heat the olive oil and butter in a pan, add the pancetta and hare and cook over a medium heat, turning and stirring frequently, until the pieces of hare are browned all over. Season with salt and pepper, sprinkle with half the flour, mix well and cook for about 10 minutes. Pour in the wine and stock, add the bay leaf, lower the heat and simmer for about 1½ hours. Meanwhile, put the sultanas in a bowl, add warm water to cover and leave to soak for 15 minutes, then drain and squeeze out. Stir the sultanas and pine nuts into the pan and simmer for a further 30 minutes. Mix together the chocolate, the remaining flour, the vinegar, sugar and a pinch of salt in a bowl, then stir in 3–4 tablespoons water. Pour the mixture into the pan and bring just to the boil. Taste and add more salt if necessary. Serve the hare covered in this ancient chocolate sauce.

LEPRE DOLCE FORTE

Serves 6–8

2 tablespoons olive oil

25 g/1 oz butter

40 g/1½ oz pancetta, diced

1 hare, cut into pieces

2 tablespoons plain flour

175 ml/6 fl oz red wine

175 ml/6 fl oz Meat Stock (see page 208)

1 bay leaf

50 g/2 oz sultanas

25 g/1 oz pine nuts

25 g/1 oz plain chocolate, grated

1 teaspoon white wine vinegar

2 teaspoons sugar

salt and pepper

ROASTING

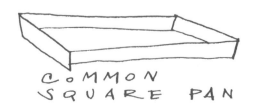

COMMON
SQUARE PAN

WILD GAME DISHES

Today it is unusual to buy game that is not farmed, but some animals are still hunted in the wild to be served at the table, and there may be occasions when you need to cook wild hare, woodcock or venison, for example. Generally, the recipes are not particularly difficult, but they are often quite time consuming and complicated.

ANATRA SELVATICA CON I FICHI

Serves 4

1 wild duck, drawn and plucked, liver reserved

white wine vinegar, for rinsing

2 tablespoons olive oil

1 bottle (750 ml/1¼ pints) red wine

25 ml/1 fl oz brandy

juice of 1 lemon, strained

400 g/14 oz figs

25 g/1 oz butter

salt and pepper

WILD DUCK WITH FIGS

Preheat the oven to 200°C/400°F/Gas Mark 6. Rinse the duck well with plenty of vinegar and season the cavity with salt and pepper. Rinse and trim the liver and place in the cavity, then put the duck in a roasting tin with the olive oil and wine and roast for 1 hour until cooked through and tender. Remove the duck from the roasting tin, cut into slices and keep warm. Finely dice the liver. Reduce the oven temperature to 180°C/350°F/Gas Mark 4. Stir the brandy and lemon juice into the cooking juices and cook over a low heat, scraping up any sediment from the base of the tin with a wooden spoon. Stir in the liver. Meanwhile, cut the figs in half, leaving them attached at the stalks. Place in an ovenproof dish, season with salt and pepper and dot with the butter. Transfer to the oven and cook for about 10 minutes. Place the slices of duck on a warm serving dish, spoon the sauce over them and surround with the figs.

VENISON WITH CREAM

First make the marinade. Stud the onion with the cloves. Pour the wine into a large pan, add the studded onion, carrot, celery, parsley, bay leaf, thyme, nutmeg and juniper berries and season with salt and pepper. Bring to the boil, then lower the heat and simmer for 15 minutes. Remove the pan from the heat and pour the marinade into a dish. Pound the venison with a meat mallet, add to the marinade, cover and leave to marinate in a cool place, stirring occasionally, for 3 days. Preheat the oven to 200°C/400°F/Gas Mark 6. Generously brush a roasting tin with olive oil. Drain the venison, place in the roasting tin, add the carrot, onion and celery, pour in the wine, sprinkle with the breadcrumbs and season lightly with pepper. Roast for 15 minutes, add the cream and season with salt to taste, then return to the oven and roast for a further 15 minutes. Carve the venison into slices and place on a warm serving dish. Add 2 tablespoons hot water to the cooking juices and heat gently, scraping up the sediment from the base of the tin with a wooden spoon. Strain the cooking juices over the slices of venison. Serve with sliced polenta.

CERVO ALLA PANNA

Serves 6

1.5 kg/3¼ lb loin or haunch of venison

olive oil, for brushing

1 carrot, chopped • 1 onion, chopped

1 celery stick, chopped

1 litre/1¾ pints dry white wine

1 tablespoon breadcrumbs

150 ml/¼ pint double cream

salt and pepper

sliced Polenta (see page 305), to serve

For the marinade:

1 onion • 2 cloves

1 litre/1¾ pints dry white wine

1 carrot, thinly sliced • 1 celery stick

1 tablespoon chopped fresh flat-leaf parsley

1 bay leaf • 1 fresh thyme sprig

pinch of freshly grated nutmeg

5 juniper berries

salt and pepper

MUSHROOM AND GAME PIE

Place the venison and partridge in a dish, add the carrot, shallot, celery, sage, bay leaf and juniper berries and season with salt and pepper. Pour in the wine and leave to marinate in a cool place, stirring occasionally, for 12 hours. Drain the meat, reserving the marinade. Heat the butter and olive oil in a pan, add the meat and cook over a medium heat, stirring frequently, until browned all over. Remove the meat from the pan and set aside. Add the onion and ham to the pan and cook over a low heat, stirring occasionally, for 10 minutes, then add the porcini. Cover and simmer gently for 20 minutes. Return the meat to the pan, pour in the reserved marinade, cover and cook over a low heat for 1½ hours. Preheat the oven to 220°C/425°F/Gas Mark 7. Divide the pastry into two pieces and roll out on a lightly floured surface. Line the base of a pie dish with one piece of pastry and spoon in the meat and porcini mixture. Cover with the remaining pastry, prick all over with a fork and brush with the beaten egg. Bake for 20 minutes, then lower the oven temperature to 190°C/375°F/Gas Mark 5 and bake for a further 15 minutes. Serve warm.

TORTA DI FUNGHI E SELVAGGINA

Serves 12

500 g/1 lb 2 oz lean venison, diced

500 g/1 lb 2 oz skinless, boneless partridge, diced

1 carrot, chopped • 1 shallot, chopped

1 celery stick, chopped

1 fresh sage sprig

1 bay leaf

5 juniper berries

500 ml/18 fl oz red wine

25 g/1 oz butter

3 tablespoons olive oil

1 onion, chopped

50 g/2 oz cooked ham, diced

500 g/1 lb 2 oz fresh porcini

250 g/9 oz puff pastry dough, thawed if frozen

plain flour, for dusting

1 egg, lightly beaten

salt and pepper

CHEESE →

CHEESE

Parmesan and grana padano on pasta and risottos, mozzarella on pizzas, fontina in dishes from Valle d'Aosta, mascarpone in Tiramisu, Gorgonzola with polenta, macaroni with four cheeses – we could go on, as hundreds of antipasti, first courses, main dishes, lunches and snacks depend upon on at least 451 different kinds of cheese. That is the number of cheeses produced in Italy. Their quality is overseen by the various national consortia for each type. There are also Italian controlling bodies that assign cheeses the Denominazione di Origine Controllata, and European controlling bodies that assign them the coveted Protected Designation of Origin (PDO). As cheese is simultaneously both a food and a flavouring, it is important to follow some rules about how it is cooked and the quantity used. This is to avoid altering the flavour of the dish and of the cheese itself. Remember that cooking makes cheese taste stronger, so pay attention to the quantity specified in the recipe, the stage at which it is added and the way it is mixed.

ADVICE

→ Grated cheese should always be sprinkled on pasta before the sauce, which then softens and melts it. In the specific case of bucatini amatriciana, professional cooks advise serving the pecorino separately so that guests can help themselves, thus preserving its fragrance.

→ As a general rule with risottos, the cheese or cheeses should not be added during cooking, but at the end after removing the pan from the heat. At most, the cheese may be added 3 minutes before the end of the cooking time for a stronger flavour, in which case, you should continue stirring to prevent it from sticking to the base of the saucepan.

→ In the case of soups and purées, freshly grated cheese should be handed separately at the table.

→ Grated cheese should be brought to the table in a cheese dish with lid, complete with a bone or other non-metallic teaspoon. Metal teaspoons oxidize easily in contact with cheeses.

→ When using savoury cheeses – whether grated, thinly sliced, melted or shaved – together with other ingredients (for example in soufflés, savoury pies, fried mozzarella sandwiches, etc.) season the dish itself only lightly.

Store cheeses on the bottom shelf of the refrigerator in sealed plastic or glass containers. As they are in the least cold part of the refrigerator, they remain softer and, being sealed, do not transfer smells to other dishes and ingredients or absorb them.

→ Put one or two sugar cubes in the containers to absorb any moisture.

→ Place each kind of cheese in its own container or wrap it in foil.

→ Store mozzarella in its original packaging, complete with its original liquid, or transfer it to one of the upper shelves in a bowl full of a mixture of water and milk.

→ It is advisable to take cheeses out of the refrigerator 1 hour before serving and open the containers to allow them to breathe. When cold, they tend to be less flavoursome and more difficult to digest, especially fattier cheeses.

→ Avoid putting grana padano, provolone and pecorino in the refrigerator. Simply store in a cool place instead.

→ Remove cheeses from their wrappings and place on a wooden board or glass plate garnished with lettuce leaves.

→ Adjust quantities according to the number of guests. Offer at least three different types of cheese – soft, semi-hard and hard – ranging from mild to strong in flavour. Alternatively, serve an Italian mild or strong cheese, a French soft cheese and an English hard or medium cheese.

→ It is probably wise to avoid serving very strong-smelling cheeses, which are not to everyone's taste.

→ Provide one or two cheese knives or slicer.

→ For authentic Italian presentation, serve cheese before dessert and fruit, offering them once only.

→ The wines served at the table should come from the same regions as the cheeses.

ETIQUETTE

→ Hard cheeses: Cut one piece at a time with a knife, remove any rind, put on a bite-sized piece of bread or a biscuit and lift to the mouth.

→ Soft cheeses: Use only a fork.

TASTY COMBINATIONS

→ Blue cheeses and soft cheeses may be served with mixed grilled vegetables, or steamed vegetables dressed with olive oil.

→ Mascarpone and other cream cheeses go very well with mostarda (a preserve made with mustard).

→ Caciotta goes with both black and green olives.

→ Caprino loves radishes.

→ Gorgonzola and fontina go perfectly with polenta.

→ Almost all semi-hard and hard cheeses are good with walnuts, pears and grapes.

→ Blue, cream and ricotta-type cheeses mixed with icing sugar turn into delicate creams for decorating biscuits, fruit salads or sour black cherries in syrup.

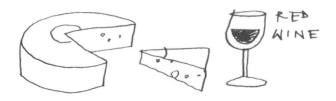

RED WINE

CAPRINO BAVAROIS

Soak the sheets of gelatine in cold water for 10 minutes, then squeeze out. Heat a little water in a double boiler or in a heatproof bowl set over a pan of barely simmering water. Add the gelatine and dissolve, following the packet instructions. Stir into the cream in a bowl. Mash the cheese in another bowl with a fork, drizzle with olive oil and add the vinegar. Beat the mixture with a whisk until light and frothy. Pour in the cream mixture. Whisk the egg whites in a grease-free bowl and fold them into the cheese mixture, a little at a time. Season with salt and pepper to taste. Brush four moulds with olive oil, then divide the mixture among them. Cover and leave in a cool place for a few hours to set. When set, turn out the moulds and arrange the creams in the middle of a serving dish. Cover with the radish slices and a little shredded rocket and place the tomatoes around one side and the celery around the other. Drizzle with olive oil and a little vinegar and season with salt and pepper to taste.

BAVARESE DI CAPRINI

Serves 4

50 g/2 oz gelatine sheets

100 ml/3^1/$_2$ fl oz double cream

120 g/4 oz caprino or other high-fat goats' cheese

olive oil, for drizzling and brushing

1 teaspoon white wine vinegar, plus extra for drizzling

2 egg whites

10 radishes, sliced

1 bunch of rocket, shredded

2 tomatoes, peeled, seeded and sliced

2 celery sticks, chopped

salt and pepper

BUFFALO MILK MOZZARELLA CAPRESE SALAD

Drain the mozzarella and cut into 3-mm/^{1}/$_8$-inch thick slices. Arrange the mozzarella and tomato slices alternately in concentric rings on a serving dish. Sprinkle with the basil leaves, drizzle with olive oil and season with salt. Keep in a cool place until ready to serve.

CAPRESE DI MOZZARELLA DI BUFALA

Serves 4

300 g/11 oz buffalo milk mozzarella cheese

3–4 tomatoes, peeled, seeded and sliced

8 fresh basil leaves

olive oil, for drizzling

salt

SCAMORZA CARPACCIO

Place the cheese in the middle of a serving dish and arrange the cucumber slices around it. Whisk together the oil and lemon juice in a bowl and season with salt and pepper to taste. Pour the dressing over the cheese and garnish with the mint leaves.

CARPACCIO DI SCAMORZA

Serves 4

400 g/14 oz scamorza

or provolone cheese, peeled and thinly sliced

1 cucumber, thinly sliced

3 tablespoons olive oil

juice of ^{1}/$_2$ lemon, strained

salt and pepper

6 fresh mint leaves, to garnish

CHEESE RINGS

CIAMBELLINE DI FORMAGGIO

Serves 4–6

100 g/3¹/₂ oz butter, softened

100 g/3¹/₂ oz Parmesan cheese, freshly grated

100 g/3¹/₂ oz plain flour

1 egg yolk

1 tablespoon milk

salt

Preheat the oven to 150°C/300°F/Gas Mark 2. Line a baking sheet with baking parchment. Beat the butter with the Parmesan, flour and a pinch of salt in a bowl until smooth and combined. Roll into thin cylinders and shape into rings. Lightly beat the egg yolk with the milk and brush the rings with the mixture. Place on the prepared baking sheet and bake for about 12 minutes. Remove the rings from the oven while they are still pale because overcooking makes the cheese taste unpleasantly strong and the rings become hard. These cheese rings go well with pre-dinner drinks.

MASCARPONE AND ANCHOVY CREAM

CREMA DI MASCARPONE E PASTA D'ACCIUGHE

Serves 4

200 g/7 oz mascarpone cheese

50 g/2 oz anchovy paste

lightly toasted croûtons, to serve

Gently beat the mascarpone and anchovy paste in a bowl until smooth and even. Put the cream into individual small bowls and serve with very hot, lightly toasted croûtons.

CREAM OF RICOTTA AND VEGETABLE SOUP

CREMA DI RICOTTA E VERDURE

Serves 4

2 small potatoes, diced

2 lettuces, finely chopped

100 g/3¹/₂ oz red sorrel or spinach, finely chopped

2 leeks, white parts only, finely chopped

200 g/7 oz ricotta cheese

2 tablespoons olive oil

1 fresh flat-leaf parsley sprig, chopped

salt and pepper

Put the potatoes, lettuces, sorrel or spinach and leeks into a pan, pour in 1 litre/1³/₄ pints water, bring to the boil and season with salt and pepper. Lower the heat to medium, cover and simmer for about 30 minutes. Remove the pan from the heat, transfer the mixture to a food processor and process until smooth, then pour back into the pan. Press the ricotta through a sieve, stir into the pan and set over a medium-low heat. When the soup is heated through, pour it into a tureen and add the olive oil. Sprinkle with the parsley and serve.

POPPY-SEED CROQUETTES

Cook the potatoes in salted, boiling water for 20–25 minutes until tender, then drain, peel, place in a bowl and mash with a potato masher. Stir in the Emmenthal, and a pinch each of salt and pepper. Shape the mixture into round croquettes. Beat the eggs in a shallow dish and mix together the breadcrumbs and poppy seeds in another shallow dish. Dip the croquettes first in the beaten eggs and then in the breadcrumb mixture. Heat the oil in a frying pan, add the croquettes and cook until golden brown on both sides. Remove with a fish slice, drain on kitchen paper and serve.

CROCCHETTE AI SEMI DI PAPAVERO

Serves 4

200 g/7 oz potatoes, unpeeled

200 g/7 oz Emmenthal cheese, shaved

1 tablespoon finely chopped mixed fresh herbs,

such as fresh basil, flat-leaf parsley,

thyme and marjoram

2 eggs

65 g/2¹/₂ oz breadcrumbs

2 tablespoons poppy seeds

5 tablespoons olive oil

salt and pepper

TALEGGIO TOASTS

Preheat the oven to 180°C/350°F/Gas Mark 4 and the grill. Place the aubergine and courgette slices on the rack in the grill pan and grill briefly on both sides. Drizzle with a little olive oil, season with salt and pepper and set aside. Grill the slices of bread on both sides, drizzle with oil and season lightly with salt. Divide the vegetables among the toasts, cover with two slices of Taleggio and season lightly with pepper. Place on a baking sheet and bake for a few minutes without allowing the cheese to melt. Serve warm.

CROSTONI AL TALEGGIO

Serves 4

1 aubergine, cut lengthways into 3-mm/¹/₈-inch slices

1 courgette, cut lengthways into 3-mm/¹/₈-inch slices

olive oil, for drizzling

8 bread slices, crusts removed

250 g/9 oz taleggio cheese, sliced

salt and pepper

AUBERGINE AND MOZZARELLA ROUNDS

Put the aubergine slices in a colander, sprinkling each layer with salt, and leave to drain for 30 minutes, then rinse and pat dry. Preheat the oven to 180°C/350°F/Gas Mark 4. Heat the oil in a frying pan, add the aubergine slices, in batches if necessary, and cook until light golden brown on both sides. Remove from the pan with a fish slice and drain on kitchen paper. Place the aubergine slices in a single layer on a baking sheet and top each with a slice of mozzarella. Put 1 teaspoon of the passata on each slice of cheese and bake for a few minutes until the mozzarella has melted. Serve hot or cold.

DISCHETTI DI MELANZANE E MOZZARELLA

Serves 4

2 aubergines, cut into 1-cm/¹/₂-inch thick slices

3 tablespoons olive oil

150 g/5 oz mozzarella cheese, thinly sliced

3 tablespoons passata

salt

993

SPICY BUNDLES

FAGOTTINI PICCANTI

Serves 4

100 g/3¹/₂ oz ricotta cheese

100 g/3¹/₂ oz strong provolone cheese, shaved

pinch of paprika

8 prosciutto slices

¹/₂ melon, seeded

pepper

Mix together the ricotta, provolone and paprika in a bowl. Spread out the prosciutto and place 1 tablespoon of the cheese mixture on each slice, then roll each up and secure with cocktail sticks. Scoop out balls from the melon using a melon baller. Place the roulades on a serving dish and surround with the melon balls. Just before serving, season with pepper.

PUFF PASTRY FLOWERS WITH TOMA

FIORE DI SFOGLIA CON TOMA

Serves 4

butter, for greasing

500 g/1 lb 2 oz puff pastry dough, thawed if frozen

plain flour, for dusting

2 egg yolks

200 g/7 oz toma paglierina cheese

salt

Preheat the oven to 180°C/350°F/Gas Mark 4. Grease a baking sheet with butter. Roll out the pastry on a lightly floured surface and cut out four or five 15-cm/6-inch rounds. Place one dough round on the base of the prepared baking sheet and arrange the others, slightly overlapping, all around it. Beat the egg yolks with 1 tablespoon water and brush the mixture over the pastry rounds. Place the toma on the central round and season lightly with salt. Fold over the other rounds to form a flower shape. Bake for 15 minutes or until the cheese has completely melted. Serve hot.

SAVOYARD FONDUE

FONDUTA ALLA SAVOIARDA

Serves 4

1 garlic clove

600 g/1 lb 5 oz Gruyère or Emmenthal cheese, diced

1 bottle (750 ml/1¹/₄ pints) dry white wine

1 teaspoon potato flour

50 ml/2 fl oz kirsch

salt and pepper

triangles of lightly toasted bread, to serve

Rub the inside of a terracotta dish or ceramic fondue pot with the garlic. Put the cheese in the pot, pour in the wine and leave to stand for 3 hours. Mix together the potato flour and kirsch in a small bowl. Place the fondue pot over a medium heat and melt the cheese, stirring constantly, then gradually add the kirsch mixture, stirring constantly, until thickened and smooth. Season lightly with salt and pepper. Serve immediately in small warm dishes with triangles of lightly toasted bread.

PIEDMONTESE FONDUE

FONDUTA PIEMONTESE

Serves 4

400 g/14 oz fontina cheese, diced

250 ml/8 fl oz milk

25 g/1 oz butter

4 egg yolks

1 white truffle, sliced

salt

triangles of lightly toasted bread, to serve

Put the fontina in a bowl and add the milk to cover. Leave to soften for at least 2 hours. Melt the butter in a double boiler or in a heatproof bowl set over a pan of barely simmering water. Stir in the fontina mixture and egg yolks and cook, stirring constantly, until the cheese has completely melted. Season lightly with salt and cook for a further 5 minutes but do not allow the mixture to boil. Pour into soup plates, sprinkle with slices of white truffle and serve with small triangles of lightly toasted bread.

GRUYÈRE GOURGÈRE

GOURGÈRE ALLA GROVIERA

Serves 6

150 g/5 oz butter, plus extra for greasing

250 g/9 oz Gruyère cheese

250 g/9 oz plain flour, sifted

5 eggs

salt

For the garnish

80 g/3 oz butter

2 aubergines, diced

2 courgettes, diced

3 tomatoes, peeled, seeded and diced

salt and pepper

Preheat the oven to 180°C/350°F/Gas Mark 4. Grease a baking sheet with butter. Grate 200g/7 oz of the Gruyère and dice the remainder. Bring 300 ml/½ pint water to the boil in a saucepan and add the butter and a pinch of salt. When the butter has melted, remove the pan from the heat and tip in the flour all at once, stirring constantly. Return the pan to the heat and cook, stirring constantly, for 10 minutes. Leave to cool slightly, then beat in the eggs, one at a time. Stir the grated cheese into the mixture. Place tablespoons of the mixture in a ring on the prepared baking sheet and sprinkle them with the diced cheese. Bake for about 30 minutes. Meanwhile, prepare the garnish. Melt the butter in a frying pan, add the aubergines and courgettes and cook, stirring constantly, for 5 minutes, then add the tomatoes and cook until all the vegetables are tender and light golden brown. Season with salt and pepper. Transfer the gougère to a warm serving dish and spoon the vegetables into the centre. If you prefer a stronger flavour, substitute mature provolone for the Gruyère.

CHICORY, CHEESE AND WALNUTS

Serves 4

16 walnuts
2 celery sticks, chopped
2 heads of chicory, sliced
200 g/7 oz Emmenthal cheese, diced
olive oil, for drizzling
salt and pepper

Blanch the walnuts in boiling water for a few minutes, then drain, refresh under cold water, peel and chop coarsely. Put the walnuts, celery, chicory and cheese in a salad bowl, drizzle with olive oil and season with salt and pepper. Toss gently and leave in a cool place for a few minutes to allow the flavours to mingle.

BRESAOLA ROLLS WITH RICOTTA

INVOLTINI DI BRESAOLA ALLA RICOTTA

Serves 4

200 g/7 oz ricotta cheese
200 g/7 oz bresaola, thinly sliced
bunch of rocket, chopped
olive oil, for drizzling
salt
lightly toasted bread, to serve

Beat the ricotta in a bowl until smooth, then place a tablespoon of the cheese on each slice of bresaola. Sprinkle with the rocket, drizzle with a little olive oil and season with a pinch of salt. Roll up and put in a cool place. Serve with lightly toasted bread.

MIXED GREENS WITH CAPRINO

MISTO VERDE AL CAPRINO

Serves 4

4 potatoes
200 g/7 oz mangetouts
3 green peppers
olive oil, for drizzling
300 g/11 oz caprino
or other high-fat goats' cheese, sliced
salt and pepper

Preheat the grill. Cook the potatoes in lightly salted, boiling water for 20–25 minutes until tender. Drain, peel and cut into wedges. Cook the mangetouts in lightly salted, boiling water for 8–10 minutes until tender, then drain. Meanwhile, place the green peppers on a baking sheet and grill, turning frequently, until blackened and charred. Transfer to a plastic bag, seal the top and leave to cool, then peel, seed and cut into large slices. Place the potatoes, mangetouts and pepper slices in a salad bowl, drizzle with olive oil, season with salt and add the cheese. Season with pepper, toss gently and serve.

TOASTED MOZZARELLA

Beat the eggs in a shallow dish and mix together the breadcrumbs, thyme and a pinch of salt in another shallow dish. Dust the mozzarella slices with flour, dip in the beaten eggs, then in the breadcrumb mixture. Chill in the refrigerator for 2 hours. Place a baking sheet under the grill and preheat the grill and the baking sheet. Remove the mozzarella slices from the refrigerator and place on the hot baking sheet. Brown under the grill without melting the cheese. Place on a serving dish, drizzle with oil and sprinkle with the chopped parsley, capers and anchovies.

MOZZARELLA ALLA PIASTRA

Serves 4

2 eggs

65 g/2¹/₂ oz breadcrumbs

1 tablespoon fresh thyme leaves

8 mozzarella cheese slices

plain flour, for dusting

olive oil, for drizzling

1 tablespoon chopped fresh flat-leaf parsley

1 tablespoon capers, rinsed

4 canned anchovy fillets, drained and chopped

salt

FRIED MOZZARELLA SANDWICHES

Place the slices of mozzarella on half the bread and top with the remaining bread to make sandwiches. Beat the eggs in a shallow dish with the milk and season with salt. Dust the sandwiches with flour and place in the beaten eggs, pressing down gently with a fish slice until they have absorbed some of the mixture. Heat the olive oil and butter in a frying pan, add the sandwiches and cook for about 2 minutes on each side until crisp and golden brown. Remove with a fish slice and drain on kitchen paper. Serve hot.

MOZZARELLA IN CARROZZA

Serves 4

8 bread slices, halved

150 g/5 oz mozzarella cheese, sliced

2 eggs

175 ml/6 fl oz milk

plain flour, for dusting

100 ml/3¹/₂ fl oz olive oil

25 g/1 oz butter

salt

CHEESE AND HAM PÂTÉ

Beat the ricotta in a bowl until smooth, then stir in the ham, pine nuts, cream and brandy and season with salt and pepper. Line a rectangular mould with cling film and pour in the mixture. Smooth the surface with a palette knife and chill in the refrigerator for 3–4 hours. Turn out on to a serving dish and serve with small, warm, brown bread croûtons.

*PÂTÉ DI FORMAGGIO
E PROSCIUTTO COTTO*

Serves 6

250 g/7 oz ricotta cheese

250 g/9 oz cooked ham, finely chopped

2 tablespoons pine nuts

5 tablespoons double cream

50 ml/2 fl oz brandy

salt and pepper

warm brown bread croûtons, to serve

ROTOLO DI FONTINA E PROSCIUTTO

Serves 4

300 g/11 oz plain flour, plus extra for dusting
3 eggs
100 g/3½ oz cooked ham, sliced
200 g/7 oz fontina cheese, sliced
40 g/1½ oz butter
6 fresh sage leaves
salt and pepper

FONTINA AND HAM ROLL

Sift the flour into a mound on the work surface and make a well in the centre. Break the eggs into the well and add a pinch each of salt and pepper. Knead the mixture for 10 minutes, then gather into a ball, wrap in cling film and leave to rest for 15 minutes. Roll out the dough on a lightly floured surface to a thin sheet. Place the dough on a linen cloth and sprinkle with the ham and fontina. Using the cloth to help you, roll up into a sausage shape and tie the ends with kitchen string. Bring a large pan of salted water to the boil, add the wrapped roll and simmer for 20 minutes. Meanwhile, melt the butter with the sage leaves. Drain the roll and unwrap. Slice, place on a serving dish and spoon the sage butter over the slices.

ROTOLO DI PATATE E FORMAGGIO

Serves 6

1 kg/2¼ lb potatoes,
350 g/12 oz plain flour
2 eggs, lightly beaten
80 g/3 oz fontina cheese, sliced
80 g/3 oz Taleggio cheese, sliced
100 g/3½ oz butter, melted
6 fresh sage leaves
50 g/2 oz Parmesan cheese, freshly grated
salt

POTATO AND CHEESE ROLL

Cook the potatoes in lightly salted, boiling water for 20–25 minutes, then drain, peel, place in a bowl and mash with a potato masher. Stir in the flour and eggs and season with salt. Knead to an elastic dough, then roll out to a 1-cm/½-inch thick round with a rolling pin and place on a tea towel. Place the cheese slices on the potato dough and roll up, using the tea towel to help you. Tie the ends of the roll with kitchen string. Bring a pan of salted water to the boil, add the wrapped roll and simmer for 20 minutes. Meanwhile, melt the butter with the sage leaves. Drain the roll and leave to cool slightly, then unwrap and place on a wooden chopping board. Cut into 1-cm/½-inch thick slices and place on a serving dish. Sprinkle with the Parmesan and sage butter.

CHEESE PIE

Preheat the oven to 180°C/350°F/Gas Mark 4. Line a pie tin with baking parchment and grease lightly with butter. Cut the pastry dough in half. Roll out one piece on a lightly floured surface and place in the prepared tin. Beat the ricotta in a bowl with a wooden spoon, stir in the mozzarella, Emmenthal, beaten eggs and Parmesan and season with salt and pepper to taste. Sprinkle the mixture over the pastry case. Roll out the remaining pastry dough, place it over the pie and press along the edges to seal. Lightly beat the egg yolk and brush it over the pie. Bake for about 35 minutes, then remove the pie from oven and leave to stand for 10 minutes before serving.

TORTA DI FORMAGGIO

Serves 6

butter, for greasing

250 g/9 oz puff pastry dough, thawed if frozen

plain flour, for dusting

250 g/9 oz ricotta cheese

150 g/5 oz mozzarella cheese, diced

150 g/5 oz Emmenthal cheese, diced

2 eggs, lightly beaten

1 tablespoon Parmesan cheese, freshly grated

1 egg yolk

salt and pepper

ROBIOLA TRIANGLES

Preheat the oven to 180°C/350°F/Gas Mark 4. Grease a baking sheet with butter. Cut each slice of bread into two triangles, drizzle each with olive oil and season with a pinch of salt. Mash the robiola in a bowl and stir in the Parmesan, egg and cream until fully mixed. Spread the mixture on the bread triangles, place on the prepared baking sheet and bake for about 10 minutes. Serve hot.

TRIANGOLINI ALLA ROBIOLA

Serves 4

butter, for greasing

8 bread slices, crusts removed

olive oil, for drizzling

200 g/7 oz robiola cheese

1 tablespoon Parmesan cheese, freshly grated

1 egg, lightly beaten

2 tablespoon double cream

salt

DESSERTS →

BAKING →

DESSERTS AND SWEET TREATS

Ready-made and instant puddings and commercial ice creams have not destroyed the sheer pleasure of home-made desserts, prepared by hand from recipes we have dreamed up ourselves or taken from books and magazines. It would, of course, be foolish, when time is often so short, to reject the benefits of ready-made shortcrust and puff pastry dough, which halve the time and effort and are usually of excellent quality. However, the joy of savouring the aroma of a freshly baked tart, decorating a meringue with cream or icing a cake never goes out of fashion. That is why desserts are talked about, invented and reinvented and why old recipes are revised, lightened and still made at home. The following is a survey of the various techniques.

PASTRY AND DOUGH

Flour, eggs, butter, sugar, milk or water and yeast are ingredients that appear time and again in numerous desserts and form the basis of pastries and cakes. The following pages provide recipes for them, and in some cases more than one recipe, as small variations on a theme mean greater choice and variety. The recipes may be divided into ones for pastries (firm) and doughs (soft). Pastries, such as shortcrust, puff and pâte brisée, are baked in tart or cake tins or on baking sheets, and are eaten as they are or used as the base for creams, fillings, etc. Doughs, such as the mixtures for puffs, brioches and savarins, are kneaded with yeast or lightened with whisked egg white and cooked in special moulds. They are eaten as they come or finished with creams, fillings and liqueurs, depending on the recipe.

FLOUR

Flour should be absolutely fresh, extremely fine, white and dry. When adding it to eggs, it is always a good idea to sift it first so that there will be no lumps. When rolling out pastry, dust it and the work surface lightly with flour to prevent it from sticking. The rolling pin may also be dusted with flour.

BUTTER

Like flour, butter must be extremely fresh, top quality and stored correctly. It should usually be removed from the refrigerator some time before use to soften it slightly. Sometimes it is added to flour in small pieces. When the recipe calls for melted butter, it is always best to heat it in a double boiler or a heatproof bowl set over a pan of barely simmering water. Unsalted butter is invariably used in Italian recipes and is, in any case, the best choice for sweet dishes.

SUGAR

Always use the type of sugar specified in the recipe – caster, icing, granulated (simply described as sugar with no further qualification) or brown. You can grind coarse sugar in a food processor to make it finer if necessary. You can buy vanilla sugar, which usually has a very strong aroma, but it is better and more economical to make your own. Put a vanilla pod in a glass jar, fill the jar with sugar, seal and store in a cool place. In this way the sugar takes on a natural, delicate vanilla fragrance.

MILK

Of course milk should be fresh. Although long-life milk can give excellent results, fresh full-fat milk is preferable.

RAISING AGENTS

Fresh and dried yeast should always be activated in lukewarm water or milk before adding it to the other ingredients. Easy-blend dried yeast can be added with the flour. The average amount of fresh yeast needed in summer is 10–12 g/^{1}/$_4$–^{3}/$_8$ oz for every 500 g/1 lb 2 oz flour. In winter, use 15–20 g/^{1}/$_2$–^{3}/$_4$ oz for every 500 g/ 1 lb 2 oz flour. Dried yeast is stronger, so use half these quantities, the equivalent of 2 teaspoons. With easy-blend dried yeast, 1 sachet is the equivalent, but do check the packet instructions. After adding yeast to the mixture, leave to rise in a warm place and, when the dough has doubled in volume, put the dessert straight into the oven. In the case of baking powder, follow the packet instructions and remember that the raising action begins immediately the baking powder becomes wet, so do not leave the mixture to stand unless instructed to do so in the recipe.

OCTAGON

DOUGH AND PASTRY CASES

It is always best to leave dough and pastry covered with a tea towel or wrapped in cling film before use so that the surface does not become hard on contact with the air. To prevent a tart case from puffing up during baking, prick it all over with a fork after placing it in the tin, or cover with a sheet of baking parchment and sprinkle with baking beans. These may be metal or ceramic or simply dried beans, such as kidney beans, kept specifically for the purpose.

Most ovens are fitted with thermostats that regulate the internal temperature and allow dishes to be cooked with accuracy. The table below gives the correspondence between the temperature shown on the thermostat and the general indications given in the recipes.

LOW HEAT
110–140°C/225–275°F/
Gas Mark ¼–1

MEDIUM
140–180°C/275–350°F/
Gas Mark 1–4

HOT
180–200°C/350–400°F/
Gas Mark 4–6

VERY HOT
200–240°C/400–475°F/
Gas Mark 6–9

Bear in mind, however, that dessert cooking times vary depending on the size, the material the tin or dish is made from and the quantity of ingredients. Individual ovens also vary and you should check the manufacturer's instructions if using a fan oven. As a general rule, it is advisable not to put desserts in a very hot oven and a medium temperature is usually preferable for even cooking. If desserts brown quickly on the surface, they are often not equally well cooked inside. To make sure, use the old trick of inserting a wooden cocktail stick – if it comes out clean and dry, the dessert is ready.

BAKING

Puddings, soufflés and custards may be cooked in a bain-marie, or water bath, in the oven and on the hob. This technique keeps the mixture softer. It consists of standing the cake tin or dish in another container half-full of water that is kept constantly at simmering point. If the water starts to boil away too quickly, top up with more boiling water.

BAIN-MARIE

TURNING OUT CAKES

Cakes, including those served hot, should not be turned out immediately after they have been removed from the oven, but left to stand for a few minutes first. If you're not using a springform tin or a loose-based tin, put a plate on top and, holding the plate and tin firmly together, invert and tap the base of the tin so that the cake slides out on to the plate. Then gently lift off the tin. The cake will be upside down, so to serve it, cover with a serving dish and invert again immediately so that the surface is not damaged.

TURNING OUT MOULDS

After removing a mould from the refrigerator it is sometimes necessary to wrap it in a tea towel wrung out in hot water to loosen its edges. To turn out the mould place a plate on top of it and, holding the plate and mould firmly together, invert, then tap the base of the mould. You can usually hear if the pudding slides on to the plate. If this doesn't work, wring out the tea towel in hot water again and repeat. You can also immerse the base of the mould in hot water and then invert on to a serving dish.

DECORATING

Whipped cream, candied fruit, walnuts, hazelnuts, crystallized violets, chopped almonds, silver balls and hundreds and thousands are among the most popular decorations. However, do not over-decorate your desert as you may alter its flavour.

PASTRY AND DOUGH

This section provides basic recipes that are essential when tackling the vast subject of preparing pastry- or dough-based dishes, and they range from shortcrust pastry and pâte brisée to marzipan and Genoese pastry. These recipes are, of course, essential when preparing desserts but the section also contains recipes for biscuit dough and two specialist pastries that are used for savoury dishes – Savoury Choux Paste and Easy Pâte Brisée. Desserts themselves are usually finished with custards, fruit, ricotta or other ingredients. Ready-made pastry dough may also be an invaluable aid – all you have to do is carefully follow the packet's instructions.

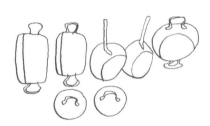

PÂTE BRISÉE

Sift the flour into a mound, make a well in the centre, add the butter and a pinch of salt and rub in with your fingertips. Add just enough iced water to form a springy dough. Wrap in cling film and chill in the refrigerator for about 1 hour. Preheat the oven to 180°C/350°F/Gas Mark 4. Briefly knead the pastry, then roll out on a lightly floured surface to a 3-mm/^{1}/$_8$-inch thick sheet. If making a tart, line a tart tin greased with butter with the pastry and bake for 40 minutes. If you are preparing barquettes or tartlet cases, bake for 15–20 minutes.

PASTA BRISÉE

Serves 6

300 g/11 oz plain flour, plus extra for dusting

150 g/5 oz unsalted butter, cut into pieces

2–3 tablespoons iced water

salt

ALMOND PASTE (1)

Preheat the oven to 180°C/350°F/Gas Mark 4. Grease a baking sheet with butter. Mix together the almonds and sugar in a bowl, crushing them to a coarse paste. Stiffly whisk the egg whites in another, grease-free bowl and fold into the almond mixture, then stir in the flour. Spoon the mixture into a piping bag and squeeze out small balls on to the prepared baking sheet, spacing them well apart. Bake for 15–20 minutes, then remove from the oven and leave to cool.

PASTA DI MANDORLE (1)

Makes 30–35 petits fours

unsalted butter, for greasing

100 g/3^1/$_2$ oz blanched almonds

100 g/3^1/$_2$ oz caster sugar

3 egg whites

25 g/1 oz plain flour, sifted

ALMOND PASTE (2)

PASTA DI MANDORLE (2)

Sufficient to stuff 40 dates or make 20 bonbons

100 g/3¹/₂ oz blanched almonds, finely chopped

100 g/3¹/₂ oz icing sugar

2 egg whites

pink or green food dye (for dates)

1 tablespoon white rum (for dates) or strong coffee

or maraschino liqueur (for bonbons)

40 dates, stoned

1 quantity caramel (see page 1019), optional

caster sugar, for decorating (for bonbons)

Mix together the almonds and sugar in a bowl. Stiffly whisk the egg whites in another, grease-free bowl and fold into the almond mixture. If stuffing dates, stir a drop of your chosen food dye into the rum and then stir the rum into the almond paste until the colour is even. Cut the dates in half and stuff with a little of the mixture. If you like, you can pour caramel over the dates. To make bonbons, add the coffee or liqueur to the almond mixture. Shape into 20 balls, roll in caster sugar and arrange in fluted paper cases.

SHORTCRUST PASTRY (1)

PASTA FROLLA (1)

Serves 6

200 g/7 oz plain flour, plus extra for dusting

100 g/3¹/₂ oz caster sugar

100 g/3¹/₂ oz unsalted butter,

softened and cut into pieces

2 egg yolks

2 teaspoons lemon rind, grated

salt

Sift the flour and sugar together into a mound, make a well in the centre and add the butter, egg yolks, lemon rind and a pinch of salt. Mix thoroughly and knead briefly. Wrap the pastry in cling film and chill in the refrigerator for 1 hour. Roll out the pastry on a lightly floured surface and use to line a pie dish. Trim the edges and follow the recipe instructions for your chosen pie.

SHORTCRUST PASTRY (2)

PASTA FROLLA (2)

Serves 6

200 g/7 oz plain flour, plus extra for dusting

100 g/3¹/₂ oz caster sugar

80 g/3 oz unsalted butter, softened

and cut into pieces, plus extra for greasing

1 egg

1 egg yolk

jam

salt

This recipe is used for extra-light tarts. Sift together the flour and sugar into a mound, make a well in the centre and add the butter, egg, egg yolk and a pinch of salt. Knead together, then wrap the pastry in cling film and chill in the refrigerator for at least 1 hour. Preheat the oven to 180°C/350°F/Gas Mark 4. Grease a tart tin with butter. Take the pastry out of the refrigerator and set a small piece aside, then roll out the remainder on a lightly floured surface to 3 mm/¹/₈ inch thick. To make a jam tart, line the prepared tart tin with the pastry and spread with your chosen jam. Roll out the reserved pastry, cut into thin strips and place in a lattice pattern over the tart, securing at the rim with a little water. Alternatively, use a lattice cutter. Bake for about 20 minutes.

EGGLESS SHORTCRUST PASTRY

PASTA FROLLA SENZA UOVA

Serves 6

150 g/5 oz unsalted butter, softened
100 g/3¹/₂ oz caster sugar
1 teaspoon grated lemon rind
120 g/4 oz plain flour, plus extra for dusting
120 g/4 oz potato flour

Cream together the butter, sugar and lemon rind in a bowl. Sift together the plain and potato flours into a mound, make a well in the centre, add the creamed mixture and knead lightly. Wrap the pastry in cling film and chill in the refrigerator for 1 hour. Roll out the pastry on a lightly floured surface and use according to the recipe. This shortcrust pastry has a more delicate flavour than the version with egg, but contains more butter.

GENOESE PASTRY

PASTA GENOVESE

Serves 6

50 g/2 oz unsalted butter, softened, plus extra for greasing
120 g/4 oz plain flour, plus extra for dusting
5 eggs
150 g/5 oz caster sugar
salt

Preheat the oven to 180°C/350°F/Gas Mark 4. Grease a cake tin with butter and dust lightly with flour. Put the eggs and sugar in the top of a double boiler or in a heatproof bowl set over a pan of barely simmering water. Beat the mixture with a hand-held electric whisk or a balloon whisk until it doubles in volume, then remove from the heat and whisk until the mixture has cooled. Whisk in a pinch of salt, the butter and flour, a little at a time, and continue whisking until smooth. Pour the mixture into the prepared tin and bake for about 40 minutes.

MARGHERITA SPONGE

PASTA MARGHERITA

Serves 6

100 g/3¹/₂ oz unsalted butter, melted, plus extra for greasing
150 g/5 oz plain flour, plus extra for dusting
6 eggs, separated
200 g/7 oz caster sugar
50 g/2 oz potato flour
rind of 1 lemon, grated
salt

Preheat the oven to 180°C/350°F/Gas Mark 4. Grease a cake tin with butter and dust lightly with flour. Beat the egg yolks with the sugar in a large bowl until pale and fluffy. Sift together the plain and potato flour on to a sheet of greaseproof paper, then add to the egg yolk mixture, a little at a time, followed by the melted butter, a pinch of salt and the lemon rind. Stiffly whisk the egg whites in another, grease-free bowl, then gently fold into the mixture. Pour into the prepared tin and bake for 30–35 minutes. This cake may be served sprinkled with icing sugar and sliced and filled with jam or cream.

CHOUX PASTE

Preheat the oven to 200°C/400°F/Gas Mark 6. Grease a baking sheet with butter and dust lightly with flour. Put 250 ml/8 fl oz water, the butter, sugar and a pinch of salt in a saucepan, bring just to the boil and remove the pan from the heat. Tip in the flour, all in one go, and mix with a wooden spoon. Return the pan to the heat and cook, stirring constantly, for 7–8 minutes until the mixture comes away from the side of the pan. Remove the pan from the heat, leave to cool, then beat in the eggs, one at a time, making sure each egg has been fully absorbed before adding the next. Spoon the dough into a piping bag and pipe walnut-size heaps on to the prepared baking sheet, spacing them well apart. Alternatively, use two dessertspoons. Bake for about 20 minutes until the puffs have doubled in size. Transfer the puffs to a wire rack, making a slit in the side of each to allow the steam to escape and leave to cool, then fill with custard, chocolate or whipped cream.

PASTA PER BIGNÈ

Serves 6

100 g/3^1/$_2$ oz unsalted butter, plus extra for greasing

150 g/5 oz plain flour, sifted, plus extra for dusting

15 g/^{1}/$_2$ oz caster sugar

4 eggs

salt

SAVOURY CHOUX PASTE

Preheat the oven to 180°C/350°F/Gas Mark 4. Grease a baking sheet with butter and dust lightly with flour. Pour 250 ml/8 fl oz water into a saucepan, add the butter and a little salt and pepper and bring to the boil. Remove the pan from the heat, tip in the flour, all in one go, then cook, stirring constantly, until the mixture comes away from the sides of the pan. Remove the pan from the heat and leave to cool. Beat the eggs into the mixture, one at a time, making sure each egg has been fully absorbed before adding the next. Stir in the Parmesan. Scoop out a tablespoon of the mixture at a time, shape it into a walnut-size ball and place on the prepared baking sheet. Bake for about 20 minutes until the puffs have doubled in size. Transfer the puffs to a wire rack, making a slit in the side of each to allow the steam to escape and leave to cool. Fill with melted cheese, béchamel sauce or other creamy, savoury mixture. You can substitute 200 g/7 oz diced cooked ham or finely chopped Hungarian salami for the Parmesan. You can also use half Emmenthal and half Parmesan cheese.

PASTA PER BIGNÈ SALATA

Serves 6

100 g/3^1/$_2$ oz unsalted butter, plus extra for greasing

150 g/5 oz plain flour, sifted, plus extra for dusting

4 eggs

200 g/7 oz Parmesan cheese, freshly grated

salt and white pepper

PASTA PER BRIOCHE

Serves 6–8

10 g/¹/₄ oz fresh yeast

250 g/9 oz plain flour, plus extra for dusting

4 eggs

15 g/¹/₂ oz caster sugar

200 g/7 oz unsalted butter, softened and

cut into pieces,

plus extra for greasing

salt

BRIOCHE

Pour a little lukewarm water into a bowl, add the yeast and mash with a fork to a smooth paste. Sift 50 g/2 oz of the flour into a mound, make a well in the centre and add the dissolved yeast. Knead well and shape into a ball. Cut a cross in the surface, cover with a tea towel and leave to rise in a warm place for 2–3 hours. Sift the remaining flour into a mound, make a well in the centre, break one of the eggs into it and add the sugar and a pinch of salt. Mix well, gradually incorporating the butter, then knead in two of the remaining eggs, one at a time. Once the first batch of dough has doubled in size, combine the two mixtures, knead into a large ball, cover with a tea towel and leave to rise in a warm place for 2–3 hours until doubled in size. Grease a brioche mould with butter. Lightly dust your hands with flour and lightly knead the dough again. Cut off one-third of the dough and set aside. Shape the larger piece of dough into a ball, place in the prepared mould and cut a cross in the top. Shape the smaller piece of dough into a pear shape and place, pointed end down, on top of the first piece, then leave to rise in a warm place for a further 30 minutes. Preheat the oven to 200°C/400°F/Gas Mark 6. Lightly beat the remaining egg and brush it over the surface of the dough. Bake for about 50 minutes or until a cocktail stick inserted into the brioche comes out dry. You can use individual fluted moulds to make small brioches. Shape as before, brush with beaten egg and prick with a fork. Bake for 15–20 minutes.

PASTA PER DOLCI LIEVITATA

Serves 4–6

100 ml/3¹/₂ fl oz lukewarm milk

25 g/1 oz caster sugar

³/₄ teaspoon dried yeast

1 egg

40 g/1¹/₂ oz unsalted butter, softened,

plus extra for greasing

225 g/8 oz plain flour

YEAST CAKE

Pour the milk into a bowl and stir in 1 teaspoon of the sugar. Sprinkle the yeast on the surface and leave to stand for 10–15 minutes until frothy, then stir to a smooth paste. Tip the yeast mixture into a mixing bowl and add the remaining sugar, the egg and butter. Sift the flour over the mixture, stirring constantly, then knead to a smooth dough. Cover and leave to rise in a warm place for 1¹/₂ hours. Preheat the oven to 180°C/350°F/Gas Mark 4. Grease two cake tins with butter. Divide the dough in half and roll out, leaving the edges fairly thick. Place in the prepared tins and bake for 30 minutes. Sandwich the cakes together with your chosen filling.

TART CASE

Cream the butter with the sugar and a pinch of salt in a bowl, then stir in the egg and all the flour in one go. Turn out on to the work surface and knead until the flour has been completely absorbed. Divide the dough into four pieces, put one on top of the other and press down. Repeat this process twice more, then wrap in cling film and leave to stand for about 1 hour. Preheat the oven to 180°C/350°F/Gas Mark 4. Grease a tart tin or cake tin with butter. Roll out the dough to a round 5 mm/^{1}/$_4$ inch thick and line the prepared tin with it. Cover the tart case with a sheet of foil or greaseproof paper and fill with baking beans. Bake for about 25 minutes. Remove from the oven and remove the foil or paper and beans. Leave to cool before filling with fresh fruit or a filling of your choice.

PASTA PER FONDO TORTA

Serves 6

130 g/4^1/$_2$ oz unsalted butter, plus extra for greasing

80 g/3 oz caster sugar

1 egg, lightly beaten

250 g/9 oz plain flour

salt

SPONGE CAKE

Preheat the oven to 180°C/350°F/Gas Mark 4. Grease a cake tin with butter and dust lightly with flour. Beat the egg yolks with the sugar in a bowl until pale and fluffy. Stiffly whisk the egg whites in another, grease-free bowl, then gently fold into the egg yolk mixture. Sift in the potato flour and plain flour, adding a little at a time. Spoon the mixture into the prepared tin and smooth the surface. Bake for about 40 minutes. Remove from the oven and leave to cool in the tin, then turn out. Slice horizontally and spread with the filling of your choice before sandwiching together again.

PASTA PER PAN DI SPAGNA

Serves 6

unsalted butter, for greasing

80 g/3 oz plain flour, sifted, plus extra for dusting

6 eggs, separated

150 g/5 oz caster sugar

80 g/3 oz potato flour, sifted

SABLÉ DOUGH

Chop the almonds together with half the sugar. Sift the flour into a mound, make a well in the centre and add the butter, remaining sugar, egg yolks, almond mixture and a pinch of salt. Knead lightly and shape into a ball, then wrap in cling film and leave to rest for 1 hour. Preheat the oven to 180°C/350°F/Gas Mark 4. Roll out the dough into a fairly thick sheet on a lightly floured surface and stamp out rounds or other shapes with a cutter. Place on a dampened baking sheet and bake for 15 minutes. Leave the biscuits on the baking sheet to cool.

PASTA PER SABLÉ

Serves 6

65 g/2^1/$_2$ oz blanched almonds

100 g/3^1/$_2$ oz caster sugar

200 g/7 oz plain flour, plus extra for dusting

120 g/4 oz unsalted butter, softened

3 egg yolks

salt

SPEEDY PUFF PASTRY

PASTA SFOGLIA RAPIDA

Serves 6

100 g/3¹/₂ oz unsalted butter

150 g/5 oz plain flour, plus extra for dusting

salt

Making puff pastry is so time-consuming that it is almost always best to buy it ready-made. However, if you want to make it at least once, it is worth trying this simplified version. Mix together the butter and 25 g/1 oz of the flour using a palette knife. (This helps to prevent the heat of your hands making the mixture too soft. In fact, the secret of successful puff pastry is the right balance of temperature between the different ingredients.) When the butter has absorbed all the flour, shape the dough into a 5-mm/¹/₄-inch thick square on a lightly floured surface. Knead the remaining flour with a little water and a pinch of salt until soft. Shape into a round and place it in the middle of the dough square. Gently lift the four corners of the square and bring them together in the middle covering the round. Using a rolling pin, roll out into a rectangle with the short side towards you. Turn the dough a quarter turn. Lift up the right-hand short side and fold it in towards the middle of the rectangle. Do the same with the left-hand side. Fold the pastry in half again so that it looks like a sort of square book. This is the first 'pastry fold'. Roll out the square into a long rectangle, always rolling in the same direction, and repeat the pastry fold. Do this four times. Between each fold, chill the dough in the refrigerator for 10 minutes. Puff pastry should be baked in an oven preheated to 200–220°C/400–425°F/Gas Mark 6–7 for about 20 minutes for small dishes and slightly longer for petits fours and cakes.

EASY PÂTE BRISÉE

PASTA TIPO BRISÉE

Serves 6

300 g/11 oz plain flour, plus extra for dusting

100 g/3¹/₂ oz unsalted butter, softened and cut into pieces

1 egg

3–4 tablespoons milk

salt

Sift the flour into a mound, make a well in the centre and add the butter, egg and a pinch of salt. Mix together with your fingertips until the mixture resembles breadcrumbs. Add the milk, a little at a time, and knead briefly into a smooth dough. Wrap in cling film and chill in the refrigerator for 1 hour. Remove the dough from the refrigerator, knead lightly, then roll out on a lightly floured surface to a sheet about 1 cm/¹/₂ inch thick. This dough is used for savoury pies.

SWEET
SAUCES AND
DECORATIONS

Sauces and decorations may be used to transform an ordinary ice-cream cake or plain home-made pudding into an elegant dessert. Just pour on melted chocolate, decorate with smooth liqueur-flavoured icing or liven up with colourful fruit sauces and wrap in a cloud of whipped cream. This section reveals the secrets, big and small, of how to present simple dishes with style.

MELTED CHOCOLATE

Pour 275ml/9 fl oz water into a saucepan, add the sugar and heat gently, stirring constantly, until the sugar has dissolved. Bring to the boil, then simmer, without stirring, until the syrup has reduced by half. Add the chocolate and melt over a low heat, stirring constantly with a wooden spatula. Stir in the butter and when it has melted remove the pan from the heat. This chocolate sauce may be served with ice creams or used to decorate or fill cakes and choux puffs.

CIOCCOLATA FUSA

50 g/2 oz caster sugar

150 g/5 oz plain chocolate, broken into pieces

10 g/¹/₄ oz unsalted butter

COLD ICING

This simple icing is used to decorate cakes and petits fours. Put the sugar in a bowl and stir in 2–3 tablespoons water to make a fairly thick mixture. Stir in the liqueur, or the vanilla or orange rind. Stir the mixture with a wooden spatula until smooth and of a spreading consistency. To give the icing a shine after it has been spread on a cake, put the cake in an oven preheated to 180°C/350°F/Gas Mark 4 for a few seconds.

GLASSA A FREDDO

150 g/5 oz icing sugar

2 tablespoons liqueur of your choice

or ¹/₂ teaspoon vanilla essence or orange rind, grated

BUTTER ICING

GLASSA AL BURRO

65 g/2¹/₂ oz unsalted butter
350 g/12 oz icing sugar, sifted
1–2 drops vanilla essence
2 tablespoons double cream

Cream the butter in a bowl with a wooden spoon, then beat in the sugar and vanilla. Add the cream, a little at a time, until the icing has a spreading consistency. To make sure the icing adheres well, spread the surface of the cake or the petits fours with a light film of gelatine first.

COFFEE ICING

GLASSA AL CAFFÈ

300 ml/¹/₂ pint freshly brewed strong coffee
250 g/9 oz icing sugar

Pour the hot coffee into a bowl and sift in the sugar, a little at a time, stirring until the mixture is fairly thick. Leave to cool. Spread the icing evenly over the surface of the cake with a palette knife. Place in an oven preheated to 180°C/350°F/Gas Mark 4 for a few seconds so that it becomes shiny.

CHOCOLATE ICING

GLASSA AL CIOCCOLATO

2 tablespoons icing sugar
150 g/5 oz plain chocolate, broken into pieces

Put the sugar in a saucepan, add 120 ml/4 fl oz water and heat, stirring constantly, for a few minutes until thickened. Meanwhile, melt the chocolate in a heatproof bowl set over a pan of barely simmering water. Add the syrup to the melted chocolate, a drop at a time, stirring constantly. Spread the icing over the cake while it is still hot.

DECORATIVE ICING

GLASSA PER DECORARE

1 egg white
150 g/5 oz vanilla icing sugar (see page 1003)

Whisk the egg white in a grease-free bowl, then gradually sift in the sugar, whisking constantly. Add 2 tablespoons warm water, a drop at a time, and stir gently for 20 minutes with a regular movement from the bottom upwards to avoid knocking out the air. Use a piping bag to decorate the cake.

MERINGUES

MERINGA

Makes 20

unsalted butter, for greasing
plain flour, for dusting
5 egg whites
200 g/7 oz icing sugar, sifted

Preheat the oven to 150°C/300°F/Gas Mark 2. Grease a baking sheet with butter and dust lightly with flour. Stiffly whisk the egg whites in a grease-free bowl, then gently stir in the sugar. Spoon a little of the meringue into a piping bag and squeeze out 1-cm/¹/₂-inch thick rounds on to the prepared baking sheet. Lower the oven temperature to its minimum setting and cook the meringues for 30–40 minutes without allowing them to brown. Meringues should not cook, but simply dry out.

WHIPPED CREAM

Chill a bowl in the freezer for 15–30 minutes, then remove and pour the cream into it. Whip with an electric mixer until thickened. If you want a sweetened cream, add the sugar to the cream before whipping.

PANNA MONTATA

300 ml/¹/₂ pint double cream, chilled

1–2 tablespoons vanilla icing sugar (optional, see page 1003)

BATTER FOR FRYING

Put the flour, wine and grappa into a large bowl, add a pinch of salt and mix well. Stir in the egg yolk to make a fairly thick, but still runny mixture. Leave to stand for 30 minutes. Whisk the egg white in a grease-free bowl, then fold it into the mixture. Quickly dip the ingredients to be fried in the batter and cook in hot oil – 180–190°C/350–375°F or until a cube of day-old bread browns in 30 seconds. Remove with a slotted spoon or fish slice and drain on kitchen paper.

PASTELLA PER FRIGGERE

150 g/5 oz plain flour

5 tablespoons white wine

2 tablespoons grappa

1 egg, separated

salt

HOT CHOCOLATE SAUCE

Melt the chocolate in a heatproof bowl set over a pan of barely simmering water. Stir with a wooden spoon, then add the cream, a little at a time, stirring until the sauce has the required consistency. Remove the bowl from the heat just as the sauce reaches simmering point. This chocolate sauce may be poured on to moulds and mousses, as well as various flavours of ice cream, such as hazelnut, banana or even chocolate ice cream itself.

SALSA AL CIOCCOLATO

250 g/9 oz plain chocolate, broken into pieces

200 ml/7 fl oz double cream

COLD CHOCOLATE SAUCE

Whip the cream until thickened. Melt the chocolate in a heatproof bowl set over a pan of barely simmering water, then remove from the heat and leave to cool slightly. Stir in the custard and leave to cool completely, then fold in the whipped cream. This chocolate sauce may be used to fill sponge cakes.

SALSA AL CIOCCOLATO FREDDA

3 tablespoons double cream

50 g/2 oz plain chocolate, broken into pieces

1 quantity Custard (see page 1039)

ORANGE SAUCE

SALSA ALL'ARANCIA
rind of 1 orange, finely pared
200 g/7 oz orange jelly
200 g/7 oz apricot jam
2 tablespoons orange liqueur

Slice the orange rind into fine strips and blanch in boiling water for 5 minutes, then drain and dry with kitchen paper. Press the orange jelly and apricot jam through a fine sieve into a saucepan and stir in the orange liqueur. Add the orange rind and heat gently, stirring constantly. This sauce may be poured, hot or cold, on to ice creams and creamy desserts.

APRICOT SAUCE

SALSA DI ALBICOCCHE
150 g/5 oz caster sugar
250 g/9 oz apricots, stoned

Put the sugar and 200 ml/7 fl oz water in a saucepan and bring to the boil over a medium heat, stirring until the syrup thickens. Pass the apricots through a food mill, add to the syrup and heat until the sauce is thick enough to coat the back of a tablespoon. Pour the sauce through a muslin-lined sieve into a bowl. This sauce is used for filling or covering desserts and cakes, especially those made with chocolate. It may be used hot or cold.

CHERRY SAUCE

SALSA DI CILIEGE
300 g/11 oz cherries, stoned
120 g/4 oz caster sugar
175 ml/6 fl oz kirsch

Place the cherries and sugar in a small saucepan, pour in 100 ml/3$\frac{1}{2}$ fl oz water, cover and cook over a medium heat until softened. Remove the cherries with a slotted spoon and pass through a food mill into a bowl. Reduce the cooking liquid over a low heat, then remove from the heat and leave to cool. Stir the cooled liquid into the cherry purée, then add the kirsch. Serve this sauce with plain ice cream or panna cotta. It may also be used to fill cakes.

STRAWBERRY SAUCE

SALSA DI FRAGOLE
50 g/2 oz caster sugar
300 g/11 oz strawberries
50 ml/2 fl oz kirsch or maraschino liqueur

Pour 100 ml/3$\frac{1}{2}$ fl oz water into a saucepan, add the sugar and cook over a medium heat, stirring constantly, for 8–10 minutes. Pass the strawberries through a food mill, stir the purée into the syrup and add the liqueur. This sauce may be served with all types of ice cream, particularly pistachio.

HAZELNUT SAUCE

Preheat the oven to 200°C/400°F/Gas Mark 6. Spread out the hazelnuts on a baking sheet and place in the oven for about 10 minutes but do not allow them to brown. Tip the nuts on to a clean tea towel and rub to remove the skins, then crush finely and stir into the custard. Finally, stir in the brandy. This sauce goes particularly well with zabaglione ice cream or plain zabaglione.

SALSA DI NOCCIOLE

100 g/3½ oz hazelnuts, shelled
475 ml/16 fl oz Confectioner's Custard
(see page 1039)
50 ml/2 fl oz brandy

THICK SYRUP

Pour 250ml/8 fl oz water into a saucepan, add the sugar and heat gently, stirring constantly, until the sugar has dissolved. Bring to the boil, then simmer, without stirring, until the syrup has thickened. The quantities of sugar and water vary depending on the consistency required. For example, halve the amount of sugar for a runny syrup. When making syrup, it is best to use a stainless steel or heavy-based double boiler.

SCIROPPO DI ZUCCHERO DENSO

800 g/1¾ lb caster sugar

CARAMEL

Rinse out a small stainless steel saucepan with cold water, add the sugar and pour in 120 ml/4 fl oz warm water. Cook over a very low heat, stirring until the sugar has dissolved completely and turned golden brown and stringy. This may take as long as 30 minutes. Caramel is used for lining pudding moulds and, in particular, when making classic Crème Caramel (see page 1028). It may also be poured over ice cream and is one of the main ingredients of mulled milk.

ZUCCHERO CARAMELLATO

100 g/3½ oz caster sugar

BAVAROIS

All you need is a little practice and your bavarois or Bavarian cream – a delicious dessert for all seasons of the year – is sure to make a great impression. This may be partly thanks to the tall, often fluted or decorated moulds that give the bavarois an elegant shape or to their colour – yellow, green, red or brown from fruit, coffee or chocolate. They may be two-colour – cream and chocolate or strawberry and lemon – or even three-colour – coffee, zabaglione and hazelnut. They are based on egg custard, whipped cream and flavoured sugars. The bavarois is left to cool and set in the refrigerator and then turned out by inverting the mould. The dessert is completed to perfection with fresh fruit, fruit in syrup or a sauce handed separately.

BAVARESE ALL'ARANCIA

Serves 6

3 gelatine leaves

3 oranges

100 g/3¹/₂ oz caster sugar

400 ml/14 fl oz evaporated milk

6–8 candied orange slices

ORANGE BAVAROIS

Fill a small bowl with water, add the gelatine and leave to soak. Grate the rind of two of the oranges and squeeze the juice from all three. Strain the orange juice into a saucepan, add the sugar and orange rind, bring to the boil and cook until reduced by half. Drain the gelatine, squeeze out and stir into the warm orange syrup, one sheet at a time. Whisk the evaporated milk in a bowl until foamy, then whisk in the orange mixture. Arrange the slices of candied orange on the base of a cake tin and pour the mixture on top. Chill in the refrigerator for at least 4 hours until set, then turn out.

VANILLA BAVAROIS

BAVARESE ALLA VANIGLIA

Serves 6

250 ml/8 fl oz milk

1 vanilla pod, slit

1 gelatine leaf

4 egg yolks

150 g/5 oz caster sugar

500 ml/18 fl oz double cream

Bring the milk just to the boil in a small pan, remove from the heat, add the vanilla pod and leave for about 1 hour, then remove the vanilla pod. Fill a small bowl with water, add the gelatine and leave to soak. Beat the egg yolks with the sugar until pale and fluffy, then fold in the flavoured milk a little at a time. Drain the gelatine, squeeze out and stir into the mixture. Pour into a pan and cook over a medium heat, stirring constantly, until thick enough to coat the back of the spoon. Do not allow the mixture to boil. Remove the pan from the heat, pour the resulting custard into a bowl and leave to cool, stirring occasionally to prevent a skin forming on the surface. Stiffly whip the cream, then gently fold into the cooled custard. Rinse out a cake tin with cold water and spoon the mixture into it. Cover and chill in the refrigerator for about 4 hours until set. To serve, dip the base of the cake tin in hot water for a few seconds, then invert on to a serving dish. This bavarois, which is excellent on its own, is also used as the base for fruit, coffee, chocolate and other flavoured Bavarian creams.

PLUM BAVAROIS

BAVARESE ALLE PRUGNE

Serves 6

400 g/14 oz plums, stoned

1 litre/1³/₄ pints red wine

1 quantity Genoese Pastry (see page 1010)

175 ml/6 fl oz brandy

2 gelatine leaves

1 quantity Custard (see page 1039)

400 ml/14 fl oz double cream

Place the plums in a dish, pour in the red wine and leave to soak for about 20 minutes. Line a loose-based cake tin with the Genoese pastry. Drain the plums and place five or six of them in a bowl with the brandy. Arrange some of remaining plums on the base of the lined tin and the remainder upright around the side. Fill a small bowl with water, add the gelatine and leave to soak for 3 minutes, then drain and squeeze out. Stir the gelatine into the custard in a bowl and leave to cool. Stiffly whip the cream and gently fold it into the custard. Pour the mixture into the cake tin, being careful not to disturb the plums. Chill in the refrigerator for at least 2 hours until set. Drain the remaining plums. Transfer the bavarois to a serving dish and decorate with the drained plums.

BAVARESE AL VINO

Serves 6

2 gelatine leaves

5 tablespoons sweet white wine

juice of ½ lemon, strained

4 eggs yolks

150 g/5 oz caster sugar

500 ml/18 fl oz double cream

unsalted butter, for greasing

1 quantity Genoese Pastry (see page 1010)

plain flour, for dusting

For the syrup

5 tablespoons sweet white wine

250 g/9 oz black grapes

100 g/3½ oz caster sugar

WINE BAVAROIS

Fill a small bowl with water, add the gelatine and leave to soak. Gently heat the wine and lemon juice in a saucepan. Beat the egg yolks with the sugar in another saucepan until pale and fluffy. Whisk in the hot wine mixture and heat gently, stirring constantly, until thick enough to coat the back of the spoon. Remove from the heat and leave to cool slightly. Drain the gelatine and squeeze out, then stir into the custard and leave to cool completely. Stiffly whip the cream and gently fold it into the cold custard. Chill in the refrigerator. Preheat the oven to 180°C/350°F/Gas Mark 4. Grease two shallow cake tins with butter. Make the syrup. Heat the wine, 50 g/2 oz of the grapes and the sugar in a pan, stirring until the sugar has dissolved. Drain and reserve the grapes and reserve the syrup. Place the remaining grapes in a food processor and process to a purée. Strain the purée into the hot syrup, mix well and leave to cool slightly. Divide the pastry in half, place in the prepared tins to a depth of 2cm/¾ inch and bake for about 40 minutes. Remove from the oven and leave to cool. Place a pastry round on a serving dish, sprinkle with some of the syrup, spread a layer of bavarois on top, then a layer of the reserved grapes, then another layer of bavarois. Top with the second pastry round and sprinkle with syrup. Spread the remaining bavarois over the whole cake. Keep cool until ready to serve, then decorate with the remaining grapes.

MOULDS
AND PUDDINGS

This group of desserts encompasses a large number of techniques and recipes. To Italians, moulds bring back happy childhood memories and are often served as tempting snacks for children. They are made from milk, eggs and flour – and sometimes potato flour, semolina, rice and bread – and are flavoured with vanilla or other ingredients, depending on what you like best. Moulds are served cold with fruit sauces or biscuits.

PIEDMONT PUDDING

Heat the milk to simmering point in a small saucepan, then remove from the heat. Beat the eggs with 4 heaped tablespoons of the sugar in a bowl until pale and fluffy. Gradually stir in the warm milk, then add the amaretti, chocolate, and rum if using. Mix well. Put the remaining sugar in a small saucepan, add 2 tablespoons water and heat until caramelized. When the sugar has begun to turn brown, remove it from the heat and pour into a warm rectangular mould, tipping and turning so that the caramel coats the base and sides evenly. Leave to cool. Preheat the oven to 180°C/350°F/Gas Mark 4. Pour the chocolate mixture into the mould. Stand the mould in a roasting tin, add boiling water to come halfway up the sides and bake for 1 hour or until a cocktail stick inserted into the centre comes out clean. Alternatively, simmer over a low heat for 1 hour. Remove from the water bath and leave to cool, then turn out.

BONET

Serves 6

500 ml/18 fl oz milk

4 eggs

165 g/5½ oz caster sugar

50 g/2 oz amaretti, crumbled

3 tablespoons dark chocolate, grated

50 ml/2 fl oz rum (optional)

CHOCOLATE MOULD

BUDINO AL CIOCCOLATO

Serves 6

100 g/3¹/₂ oz unsalted butter, softened,
plus extra for greasing
3 eggs, separated
100 g/3¹/₂ oz caster sugar
100 g/3¹/₂ oz plain chocolate, broken into pieces
500 ml/18 fl oz milk
50 g/2 oz plain flour
Zabaglione (see page 1039) or whipped cream,
to serve (optional)

Preheat the oven to 180°C/350°F/Gas Mark 4. Grease a mould with plenty of butter. Cream the butter in a bowl, then beat in the egg yolks, one at a time, followed by the sugar. Melt the chocolate in a heatproof bowl set over a pan of barely simmering water. Meanwhile, bring the milk just to the boil. Gradually add the milk to the chocolate, a little at a time, then pour on to the creamed mixture, mixing well. Pour into a pan, sift in the flour and simmer, stirring constantly, for 5 minutes. Remove from the heat and leave to cool, stirring occasionally. Stiffly whisk the egg whites in a grease-free bowl and fold into the mixture. Pour the chocolate mixture into the prepared mould. Stand the mould in a roasting tin, add boiling water to come halfway up the sides and bake for 30 minutes. Alternatively, set the roasting tin over a low heat, add boiling water and simmer for 30 minutes. Remove the mould from the water bath and leave to cool, then turn out gently on to a serving dish. Serve with zabaglione or whipped cream, if you like.

LIME MOULD

BUDINO AL LIME

Serves 4–6

1 quantity Caramel (see page 1019)
5 eggs
200 g/7 oz caster sugar
100 ml/3¹/₂ fl oz lime juice, strained
lemon rind, thinly pared, to decorate

Prepare the caramel and pour into a mould, tipping and turning so that it covers the base and sides evenly. Beat the eggs with the sugar in a saucepan over a low heat until pale and fluffy. Stir in the lime juice and pour the mixture into the prepared mould. Stand the mould in a roasting tin, add boiling water to come halfway up the sides and simmer for 1 hour or until a cocktail stick inserted into the dessert comes out dry. Remove the mould from the water bath and leave to cool. Turn out on to a serving dish and decorate with lemon rind.

HONEY PUDDING

BUDINO AL MIELE

Serves 4

500 ml/18 fl oz sweet white wine
150 ml/¹/₄ pint clear honey
pinch of ground cinnamon
1 teaspoon lemon rind, grated
6 eggs
130 g/4¹/₂ oz caster sugar

Pour the wine into a saucepan and bring to the boil. Stir in the honey, cinnamon and lemon rind, then remove from the heat and leave to cool. Beat the eggs in a bowl and beat in the wine mixture. Prepare the caramel (see page 1019) with the quantity of sugar specified. Pour into a round mould, tipping and turning so that it coats the base and sides evenly, and leave to cool. Preheat the oven to 180°C/350°F/Gas Mark 4. Pour the egg and wine mixture into the mould, place in a roasting tin and add boiling water to come halfway up the sides. Bake for 30 minutes, then remove from the water bath and leave to cool. Turn out just before serving.

CHESTNUT MOULD

Cook the chestnuts in a pan of boiling water for about 20 minutes, then drain and peel off the skins. Put them in a saucepan, add the milk and vanilla and season with a pinch of salt. Cover and cook over a medium heat for about 35 minutes until tender. Press the chestnuts and their cooking liquid through a sieve into another saucepan. Toast the almonds in the oven or under the grill, then chop. Gently heat the chestnut purée and stir in the sugar and almonds, then remove from the heat and stir in the cream. Pour the mixture into a mould, leave to cool and then chill in the refrigerator for 3 hours. Just before serving, turn out on to a dish and garnish with almonds.

BUDINO DI CASTAGNE

Serves 6

500 g/1 lb 2 oz chestnuts, shelled

500 ml/18 fl oz milk

a few drops of vanilla essence

100 g/3½ oz blanched almonds,

plus extra to garnish

50 g/2 oz caster sugar

150 ml/¼ pint single cream

salt

FRUIT JELLY

Pour the orange and lemon juices into a saucepan, add the sugar and cook over a low heat, stirring constantly, until the sugar has dissolved. Add the jelly, prepared according to the packet instructions, bring just to the boil, then remove from the heat and strain. Place the strawberries in a food processor and process to a purée. Stir the purée into the fruit juice mixture, leave to cool slightly, then pour into a ring mould. Chill in the refrigerator for several hours or overnight until set. Using a melon baller, scoop out balls of melon flesh. Turn out the mould on to a serving dish, fill the centre with the melon balls and serve.

BUDINO DI FRUTTA IN GELATINA

Serves 6

juice of 1 kg/2¼ lb oranges, strained

juice of 2 lemons, strained

185 g/6½ oz caster sugar

1 tablespoon instant jelly

500 g/1 lb 2 oz strawberries

1 small melon, halved and seeded

ALMOND PUDDING

Preheat the oven to 180°C/350°F/Gas Mark 4. Brush a marble slab or metal baking sheet with oil. Grease a mould with butter. Spread out the almonds on another baking sheet and bake for a few minutes, until dry. Melt the sugar in a saucepan, stir in the almonds and cook, stirring constantly, until they are golden brown. Pour the mixture on to the prepared slab or baking sheet and leave to cool, then crush extremely finely. Stiffly whisk the egg whites in a grease-free bowl, then fold in the crushed almond mixture. Pour into the prepared mould, place in a roasting tin, pour in boiling water to come halfway up the sides and bake for 30 minutes or until a cocktail stick inserted in the centre comes out clean. Turn out and serve cold.

BUDINO DI MANDORLE

Serves 4–6

sunflower or olive oil, for brushing

unsalted butter, for greasing

175 g/6 oz blanched almonds

175 g/6 oz caster sugar

8 egg whites

ENGLISH BREAD
AND BUTTER PUDDING

Put the sultanas and raisins in a bowl, add warm water to cover and leave to soak for 1 hour, then drain and squeeze out. Grease a large ovenproof dish with butter. Spread both sides of the slices of bread with the butter and make a layer of half the slices on the base of the prepared dish, cutting them into two or more pieces to fit well. Sprinkle with half the dried fruit and place the remaining bread on top. Beat the eggs with the sugar in a bowl, then stir in the milk, cream and remaining dried fruit, a little at a time. Pour the mixture over the bread and leave to stand for 30 minutes or until the bread has absorbed the liquid. Meanwhile, preheat the oven to 180°C/350°F/Gas Mark 4. Cover the dish with foil and bake for 45 minutes. Remove and discard the foil, return the dish to the oven and bake for a further 15 minutes. Serve warm with apricot sauce.

BUDINO DI PANE ALL'INGLESE

Serves 6

80 g/3 oz sultanas

80 g/3 oz raisins

100 g/3¹/₂ oz unsalted butter, softened,

plus extra for greasing

8–10 white bread slices, crusts removed

4 eggs

130 g/4¹/₂ oz caster sugar

500 ml/18 fl oz milk

200 ml/7 fl oz double cream

Apricot Sauce (see page 1018), to serve

SEMOLINA PUDDING

Put the sultanas in a bowl, add warm water to cover and leave to soak for 15 minutes, then drain and squeeze out. Preheat the oven to 180°C/350°F/Gas Mark 4. Grease a mould with butter and sprinkle with breadcrumbs to coat. Pour the milk into a saucepan, add 120 ml/4 fl oz water and the sugar and bring to the boil. Sprinkle in the semolina, add a pinch of salt and simmer, stirring constantly, for 10 minutes. Remove the pan from the heat and stir in the butter, sultanas, lemon rind and eggs. Pour the mixture into the prepared mould and bake for 40 minutes. This pudding may be made more flavoursome by adding a little candied citron peel.

BUDINO DI SEMOLINO

Serves 6

50 g/2 oz sultanas

25 g/1 oz unsalted butter, plus extra for greasing

breadcrumbs, for sprinkling

750 ml/1¹/₄ pints milk

100 g/3¹/₂ oz caster sugar

150 g/5 oz fine semolina

grated rind of 1 lemon

4 eggs, lightly beaten

salt

SEMOLINA PUDDING
WITH BLACK CHERRIES

Pour the milk into a saucepan, add the sugar, lemon rind and a pinch of salt and bring to the boil. Sprinkle in the semolina, stir quickly and immediately remove from the heat. Stir in the butter and cherries and leave to cool. Meanwhile, preheat the oven to 180°C/350°F/Gas Mark 4. Grease an ovenproof dish with butter. Stir the egg yolks into the cooled semolina mixture, one at a time. Stiffly whisk the egg whites in a grease-free bowl and fold into the mixture. Pour into the prepared dish and bake for 40 minutes.

BUDINO DI SEMOLINO ALLE AMARENE

Serves 4

1 litre/1³/₄ pints milk

100 g/3¹/₂ oz caster sugar

grated rind of 1 lemon

200 g/7 oz semolina

50 g/2 oz unsalted butter, plus extra for greasing

300 g/11 oz black cherries, stoned

3 eggs, separated

salt

CRÈME CARAMEL

CRÈME CARAMEL

Serves 6

500 ml/18 fl oz milk

1 vanilla pod, slit

2 eggs

3 egg yolks

150 g/5 oz caster sugar

Pour the milk into a saucepan, add the vanilla pod and bring to simmering point, then remove from the heat and leave to infuse for 15 minutes. Remove the vanilla pod. Beat the eggs and egg yolks with 120 g/4 oz of the sugar in a bowl until pale and fluffy. Gradually stir in the flavoured milk, then strain the mixture into another bowl. Preheat the oven to 180°C/350°F/Gas Mark 4. Put the remaining sugar and 1 tablespoon water into a non-stick saucepan and heat gently until caramelized. Remove from the heat and pour into individual moulds, tipping and turning so that the base and sides are covered. Pour the custard into the moulds, place them in a roasting tin, add boiling water to come halfway up the sides and bake for 20 minutes. Remove from the water bath and leave to cool, then turn out.

CHOCOLATE DELIGHT

DELIZIA AL CIOCCOLATO

Serves 4–6

unsalted butter, for greasing

25 g/1 oz plain flour, plus extra for dusting

100 g/3¹⁄₂ oz plain chocolate, broken into pieces

5 eggs, separated

200 g/7 oz icing sugar

25 g/1 oz vanilla sugar (see page 1003)

50 g/2 oz unsalted butter, melted

20 g/³⁄₄ oz cornflour

Preheat the oven to 150°C/300°F/Gas Mark 2. Grease a cake tin with butter and lightly dust with flour. Melt the chocolate in a heatproof bowl set over a pan of barely simmering water, then remove from the heat. Beat the egg yolks with half the icing sugar and the vanilla sugar in a bowl. Beat in the melted butter and chocolate, sift in the flour and cornflour and mix well. Stiffly whisk the egg whites in a grease-free bowl, then whisk in the remaining icing sugar. Gently fold into the chocolate mixture and pour into the prepared tin. Bake for about 40 minutes, then remove from the oven and leave to cool. Chill in the refrigerator before turning out and serving.

RICE PUDDING

DELIZIA AL RISO

Serves 4

150 g/5 oz short-grain rice

250 ml/8 fl oz milk

150 g/5 oz caster sugar

150 ml/¹⁄₄ pint double cream

50 g/2 oz candied citron peel, cut into pieces

Cook the rice in a pan of boiling water for 10 minutes, then drain immediately. Bring the milk to simmering point in a pan, add the rice and cook until all the milk has been absorbed. Stir in the sugar, then remove the pan from the heat and leave to cool. Stiffly whip the cream. Fold the citron peel and the whipped cream into the rice. Rinse out a ring mould with water, pour in the rice mixture and place in the freezer until the mixture becomes firm. Turn out and serve.

LATTE BRÛLÉE

Serves 6

1 litre/1³/₄ pints milk

185 g/6¹/₂ oz caster sugar

8 egg yolks

2 egg whites

whipped cream, to serve

MILK BRÛLÉE

Pour the milk into a saucepan, add 100 g/3¹/₂ oz of the sugar and cook over a medium heat, stirring until the sugar has dissolved. Lower the heat and simmer for about 1 hour, then remove from the heat and leave to cool. Heat the remaining sugar in a small saucepan until it melts and turns golden brown, then pour into a mould, tipping and turning so that the base and sides are evenly covered. Return the excess caramelized sugar to the heat and cook until it turns dark brown. Add 150 ml/¹/₄ pint water to prevent the sugar from burning and cook, stirring constantly, until a thick, dark syrup forms. Remove the pan from the heat and leave to cool. Preheat the oven to 180°C/350°F/Gas Mark 4. Beat together the egg yolks and egg whites in a saucepan with a fork, stir in the milk mixture and dark syrup and strain into the caramel-lined mould. Stand in a roasting tin, add boiling water to come halfway up the sides and bake for 20 minutes or until a cocktail stick inserted into the centre comes out clean. Turn out and serve with whipped cream. This dessert has a sophisticated bitter-sweet flavour that finishes off a meal perfectly.

PANNA COTTA

Serves 6

10 g/¹/₄ oz gelatine leaves

100 ml/3¹/₂ fl oz milk

500 ml/18 fl oz double cream

100 g/3¹/₂ oz caster sugar

1 vanilla pod, slit

Hazelnut Sauce (see page 1019), to serve (optional)

PANNA COTTA

Fill a small bowl with water, add the gelatine and leave to soak. Pour the milk into a saucepan and bring to just below simmering point, then remove the pan from the heat. Do not allow it to boil. Drain and squeeze out the gelatine and add to the milk. Pour the cream into another saucepan, add the sugar and vanilla pod and bring to the boil over a low heat, stirring constantly. Immediately remove the pan from the heat, remove the vanilla pod and stir in the milk mixture. Rinse out a rectangular cake tin with ice-cold water, shaking out any excess, and fill with the mixture. Chill in the refrigerator for several hours until set. Turn out on to a serving dish and serve by itself or with hazelnut sauce.

CHARLOTTES

A charlotte is a dessert based on fruit and custard, which may be covered or encircled in sliced bread, sponge fingers or sponge cake softened with fresh fruit juice, liqueur, tea or coffee.

AMARETTI CHARLOTTE

Beat the butter with 100 g/3½ oz of the sugar in a bowl until pale and fluffy. Melt the chocolate with 2 tablespoons water in a heatproof bowl set over a pan of barely simmering water. Beat the egg yolk with the milk in a small bowl, then stir into the melted chocolate. Stir in the butter mixture. Mix the rum with 5 tablespoons water and the remaining sugar in another bowl. Make a layer of amaretti in a dish and sprinkle with some of the rum mixture. Make another layer of amaretti on top and sprinkle with the rum mixture again. Continue making layers in this way until all the amaretti have been used. Line the base and sides of a charlotte mould with some of the softened amaretti. Pour in a little of the chocolate mixture and make alternating layers of amaretti and chocolate mixture, ending with a layer of amaretti. Press down gently, cover and chill in the refrigerator for 4–5 hours. To make the icing, put the chocolate, sugar, butter and 1 tablespoon water in a heatproof bowl set over a pan of barely simmering water and stir until melted and combined, then remove from the heat. Turn out the charlotte and spread with the icing. If you want to make the icing shiny, put the charlotte in a hot oven for a minute.

CHARLOTTE AGLI AMARETTI

Serves 6

120 g/4 oz unsalted butter, softened

120 g/4 oz caster sugar

250 g/9 oz plain chocolate, broken into pieces

1 egg yolk

200 ml/7 fl oz milk

5 tablespoons rum

400 g/14 oz small amaretti

For the icing

65 g/2½ oz plain chocolate, broken into pieces

50 g/2 oz icing sugar

25 g/1 oz unsalted butter

CHARLOTTE AI FRUTTI DI BOSCO

Serves 6

4 gelatine leaves

500 ml/18 fl oz milk

a few drops of vanilla essence

6 egg yolks

150 g/5 oz caster sugar

24 sponge cake slices

100 ml/3½ fl oz double cream

200 g/7 oz raspberries

200 g/7 oz mixed redcurrants and blackcurrants, stripped

100 g/3½ oz blueberries

100 g/3½ oz strawberries

FRUITS OF THE FOREST CHARLOTTE

Fill a small bowl with water, add the gelatine and leave to soak. Pour the milk into a saucepan, add the vanilla and bring to simmering point, then remove from the heat. Beat the egg yolks with the sugar in a saucepan until pale and fluffy, then gradually stir in the hot milk. Drain the gelatine, squeeze out and add to the custard, then cook over a low heat, stirring constantly, until thick enough to coat the back of the spoon. Remove from the heat and leave to cool. Preheat the grill and lightly toast the slices of sponge cake, then line the base and sides of a charlotte mould with them, reserving enough to cover the top. Stiffly whip the cream and stir it into the cooled custard with the fruit. Pour the mixture into the mould and cover with the remaining slices of sponge cake. Cover the mould with foil and chill in the refrigerator for 24 hours.

CHARLOTTE ALLE PRUGNE E ALLE PERE

Serves 6

500 g/1 lb 2 oz pears, peeled, cored and chopped

juice of ½ lemon, strained

150 g/5 oz caster sugar

200 g/7 oz plums, stoned

1 litre/1¾ pints red wine

65 g/2½ oz redcurrant jelly

300 ml/½ pint double cream

unsalted butter, for greasing

24 sponge fingers

PLUM AND PEAR CHARLOTTE

Place the pears and lemon juice in a food processor and process to purée, then scrape into a pan and stir in the sugar. Put the plums and wine into another saucepan, bring to the boil, then lower the heat and simmer for 15 minutes, then drain. Set aside a few plums for decoration and place the remainder in a food processor and process to purée. Add the plum purée to the pear purée and heat gently but do not allow to boil. Add the redcurrant jelly and stir until it has melted completely, then remove from the heat and leave to cool. Stiffly whip the cream and fold it into the fruit mixture. Grease a charlotte mould with butter and line the base and sides with sponge fingers. Reserve enough sponge fingers to cover the top of the mould and crumble the remainder. Make a layer of the fruit mixture in the mould and cover with a layer of crumbled sponge fingers. Continuing making layers, ending with the reserved whole sponge fingers. Chill in the refrigerator for 3 hours, then turn out and decorate with the reserved plums.

BLACKCURRANT CHARLOTTE

CHARLOTTE AL RIBES

Serves 6–8

1 quantity Custard (see page 1039)

2 gelatine leaves

2 tablespoons brandy

200 g/7 oz blackcurrants

40 g/1½ oz Chestnut Jam (see page 1116)

4 egg whites

150 ml/¼ pint double cream

sponge fingers

Leave the custard to cool slightly. Fill a small bowl with water, add the gelatine and leave to soak for 3 minutes, then drain and squeeze out. Stir the gelatine into the custard and leave to cool completely. Stir the brandy, blackcurrants and chestnut jam into the custard. Stiffly whisk the egg whites in a grease-free bowl and fold into the custard. Line a mould with baking parchment, pour the mixture into it and chill in the refrigerator for 6 hours. Stiffly whip the cream. Turn out the charlotte on to a serving dish, spread the whipped cream over it and arrange upright sponge fingers all around it, leaving the top uncovered.

CHARLOTTE DELIGHT

CHARLOTTE DELIZIA

Serves 6

50 g/2 oz unsalted butter

120 g/4 oz plain chocolate, broken into pieces

5 eggs

100 g/3½ oz ricotta cheese

100 g/3½ oz caster sugar

3 tablespoons double cream

1 teaspoon instant coffee powder

150 g/5 oz langues-de-chat

whipped cream, to serve

Put half the butter, the chocolate and 3 tablespoons water into a saucepan and cook over a low heat, stirring constantly, until melted and combined, then remove the pan from the heat. Separate two of the eggs, stir the yolks into the chocolate mixture and leave to cool. Stiffly whisk the two egg whites in a grease-free bowl and fold into the cooled chocolate mixture, then chill in the refrigerator. Separate the remaining eggs and stir the yolks into the ricotta, one at a time. Stir in the sugar, cream and coffee powder. Stiffly whisk the egg whites in a grease-free bowl and fold into the ricotta mixture, then leave in a cool place until ready to use. Grease a shallow round mould with the remaining butter, place a layer of langues-de-chat on the base and top with the chocolate mixture. Make another layer of langues-de-chat and top with the coffee mixture. Cover with a final layer of langues-de-chat. Cover the mould with foil and chill in the refrigerator for 24 hours. To serve, dip the base of the mould in warm water for a few seconds, then turn out. Serve with whipped cream.

BLACK GRAPE CHARLOTTE

Heat the wine in a saucepan, add the grapes and parboil for a few minutes, then drain, reserving the wine. Peel, halve and seed the grapes, then put them in a bowl. Return the wine to the saucepan, add 130 g/4$\frac{1}{2}$ oz of the sugar and heat gently, stirring constantly, until the sugar has dissolved, then remove from the heat and leave to cool slightly. Add half the grapes to the wine mixture and leave to infuse for about 2 hours. Drain the grapes, reserving the wine mixture, and pat dry with kitchen paper. Stiffly whip the cream, fold in the remaining sugar and chill in the refrigerator until required. Dip the sponge fingers, one at a time, into the reserved wine and use some to line the base and sides of a charlotte mould. Spread a layer of whipped cream on the base and arrange a layer of wine-infused grapes on top. Continue making alternating layers until all the ingredients have been used, ending with a layer of sponge fingers. Chill in the refrigerator for 2 hours, then turn out on to a serving dish and decorate with the remaining grapes.

CHARLOTTE DI UVA NERA

Serves 6

350 ml/12 fl oz red wine

1.5 kg/3$\frac{1}{4}$ lb black grapes

150 g/5 oz caster sugar

175 ml/6 fl oz double cream

24 sponge fingers

CUSTARDS AND CREAMS

Custards and creams are an enormous family, a mainstay in dessert preparation, and have a truly wide and versatile range of uses. They are used to fill cakes, tartlets, puff pastry spirals and choux puffs, to enrich traditional cakes such as pandoro and panettone – Christmas cakes from Verona and Milan respectively – and to decorate charlottes, and can be served alone as mouth-watering desserts in their own right. Following a few basic rules and being a little patient when cooking will result in a delicious home-made cream that can even be prepared a few days in advance.

CREMA AI MARRONI

Serves 6

1 kg/2¼ lb chestnuts, shelled

200 g/7 oz caster sugar

50 g/2 oz vanilla sugar (see page 1003)

200 ml/7 fl oz double cream

salt

CHESTNUT CREAM

Blanch the chestnuts in boiling water for 5 minutes, then drain and peel. Bring a pan of lightly salted water to the boil, add the chestnuts and simmer for 30 minutes. Meanwhile, put the caster sugar, vanilla sugar and 250 ml/8 fl oz water into a saucepan and cook over a low heat, stirring until the sugar has dissolved, then simmer for about 10 minutes. Drain the chestnuts, remove the syrup from the heat and add the chestnuts. Return the pan to the heat and boil for 10 minutes, then remove the chestnuts with a slotted spoon and pass through a food mill into a bowl. Stir the syrup into the chestnuts and leave to cool. Stiffly whip the cream and fold it into the cooled chestnut mixture, then divide among individual dishes and keep cool until ready to serve.

BLUEBERRY CREAM

CREMA AI MIRTILLI

Serves 4

1 tablespoon caster sugar

200 g/7 oz blueberries

1 quantity Custard (see page 1039), cooled

Put the sugar and 2 tablespoons water in a saucepan and cook over a low heat, stirring constantly, until the sugar has dissolved. Add the blueberries, reserving a few, increase the heat to medium and cook for 15 minutes, then remove from the heat and leave to cool, then drain. Divide the custard among individual dishes and decorate with the reserved fruit.

APRICOT CREAM

CREMA DI ALBICOCCHE

Serves 6

600 g/1 lb 5 oz apricots, peeled, stoned and chopped

185 g/6½ oz caster sugar

2 gelatine leaves

300 ml/½ pint single cream

1–2 ice cubes, crushed

1 egg white

Put the apricots and 130 g/4½ oz of the sugar in a saucepan and cook over a low heat until tender. Meanwhile, fill a small bowl with water, add the gelatine and leave to soak. Transfer the apricots to a food processor and process to a purée, then scrape into a bowl. Drain and squeeze out the gelatine, stir it into the purée and chill in the refrigerator. Mix together the cream and ice cubes and beat well. Stiffly whisk the egg white with the remaining sugar in a heatproof bowl over a pan of barely simmering water until firm and foamy. Remove from the heat and leave to cool. Mix the three mixtures together and divide among individual dishes.

BANANA CREAM

CREMA DI BANANE

Serves 4

2 bananas

400 g/14 oz curd cheese

50 g/2 oz milk powder

2 tablespoons clear honey

generous pinch of ground cinnamon

Peel and slice the bananas, then place in a bowl with the cheese, milk powder, honey and cinnamon. Mash together thoroughly until evenly combined. Pour into a dish and chill in the refrigerator for at least 1 hour before serving.

MASCARPONE CREAM

CREMA DI MASCARPONE

Serves 6

3 eggs, separated

3 tablespoons caster sugar

300 g/11 oz mascarpone cheese

3 tablespoons rum

biscuits, to serve

Beat the egg yolks with the sugar in a bowl until pale and fluffy. Stiffly whisk the egg whites in a grease-free bowl and fold into the egg yolk mixture, then fold in the mascarpone, a little at a time. Gently mix in the rum, pour into individual dishes and chill in the refrigerator until required. Serve with biscuits.

CUSTARD

Pour the milk into a pan, stir in the vanilla sugar and bring just to the boil, then remove from the heat. Beat the egg yolks with the caster sugar in another pan until pale and fluffy, then gradually pour in the hot milk. Cook over a very low heat, stirring constantly, until the mixture is thick enough to coat the back of the spoon. Do not allow it to boil. Remove from the heat and leave to cool slightly. Custard may be served cold with light biscuits as a simple dessert, or it may be used hot or cold as a sauce or filling for cakes or other desserts.

CREMA INGLESE

Serves 6

500 ml/18 fl oz milk

15 g/¹/₂ oz vanilla sugar (see page 1003)

4 egg yolks

130 g/4¹/₂ oz caster sugar

CONFECTIONER'S CUSTARD

Beat the egg yolks with the sugar in a pan until pale and fluffy. Gradually stir in the flour until evenly mixed. Bring the milk just to boiling point in another pan and add the vanilla or lemon rind, then remove from the heat. Gradually add the hot milk to the egg yolk mixture then cook over a low heat, stirring constantly, for 3–4 minutes until thickened. Pour the custard into a bowl and leave to cool, stirring occasionally to prevent a skin from forming. This custard is used for filling a wide variety of pastries and cakes. The flour makes it thicker but a little less delicate than plain custard.

CREMA PASTICCERA

Serves 4

4 egg yolks

100 g/3¹/₂ oz caster sugar

25 g/1 oz plain flour

500 ml/18 fl oz milk

a few drops of vanilla essence

or 1 teaspoon grated lemon rind

OLD-FASHIONED CREME BRÛLÉE

Pour the milk and cream into a small pan and bring to the boil. Beat the egg yolks with the sugar in another pan until pale and fluffy and pour in the hot milk mixture. Cook over a low heat, stirring constantly, until thick enough to coat the back of the spoon. Pour the custard into a large flameproof dish and chill in the refrigerator for 5–6 hours. Preheat the grill to high. Sprinkle the surface of the custard with sugar. Place the dish on a baking sheet and surround with ice cubes, then cook under the grill for a few minutes to caramelize the sugar. Return to the refrigerator until ready to serve.

CRÈME BRÛLÉE D'ALTRI TEMPI

Serves 6

500 ml/18 fl oz milk

100 ml/3¹/₂ fl oz double cream

4 egg yolks

85 g/3 oz caster sugar

sugar, for sprinkling

ZABAGLIONE

Beat the egg yolks with the sugar in a heatproof bowl until pale and fluffy, then stir in the Marsala or wine, a little at a time. Place the bowl over a pan of barely simmering water and cook over a low heat, stirring constantly, until the mixture starts to rise. Remove from the heat and serve hot or cold in glasses. Alternatively, zabaglione may be used as a sauce on coffee or hazelnut ice cream.

ZABAIONE

Serves 4

4 egg yolks

4 tablespoons caster sugar

120 ml/4 fl oz Marsala, dry white wine

or sparkling wine

SOUFFLÉS

Soufflés are classic dishes and both savoury and sweet soufflés are seen as a test of culinary skill. However, following a few basic rules will help to ensure success. The milk, flour and eggs – the basic ingredients – should be extremely fresh. The whisked egg whites should be folded into the mixture at the last minute and the spatula or spoon used should be turned very gently from the bottom to the top of the mixture to avoid knocking out the air. Other essential instructions are to never open the oven during cooking, as the soufflé will go flat, and to calculate the timing carefully so that the desert may be brought immediately to the table and served as soon as it is ready. The spongy airy structure of these desserts gives them a soft delicate taste.

CHOCOLATE SOUFFLÉ

SOUFFLÉ AL CIOCCOLATO

Serves 6

15 g/¹/₂ oz unsalted butter, plus extra for greasing

vanilla sugar (see page 1003), for dusting

80 g/3 oz plain chocolate, broken into pieces

300 ml/¹/₂ pint milk

35 g/1¹/₄ oz plain flour

50 g/2 oz caster sugar

3 egg yolks

1 egg white

Preheat the oven to 200°C/400°F/Gas Mark 6. Grease a soufflé dish with butter and dust with vanilla sugar. Put the chocolate and 175 ml/6 fl oz of the milk in a heatproof bowl set over a pan of barely simmering water and stir constantly until the chocolate has melted and the mixture is smooth. Put the flour in another saucepan, pour in the remaining milk and mix well. Stir in the sugar and chocolate mixture, bring to the boil and cook, stirring constantly, for 2–3 minutes. Remove from the heat and leave to cool slightly, then stir in the butter, then the egg yolks one at a time. Stiffly whisk the egg white in a grease-free bowl and gently fold it into the mixture. Spoon the mixture into the prepared dish so that it is two-thirds full and bake for about 30 minutes until risen and set. Serve immediately.

VANILLA SOUFFLÉ (BASIC RECIPE)

SOUFFLÉ ALLA VANIGLIA

Serves 6

15 g/¹/₂ oz unsalted butter, plus extra for greasing

50 g/2 oz caster sugar, plus extra for sprinkling

200 ml/7 fl oz milk

1 vanilla pod, slit

35 g/1¹/₄ oz plain flour

3 eggs, separated

1 egg white

salt

Vanilla soufflé is a basic recipe which can be adapted for other flavours. Preheat the oven to 200°C/400°F/Gas Mark 6. Grease a soufflé dish with butter and sprinkle with sugar. Pour 120 ml/4 fl oz of the milk into a small saucepan, add the sugar and a pinch of salt and bring to the boil. Remove the pan from the heat, add the vanilla pod and leave to infuse for 15 minutes, then remove the vanilla pod. Put the flour in a small saucepan, stir in the remaining cold milk and gradually add the hot milk. Bring to the boil and cook, stirring constantly, for 2–3 minutes. Remove from the heat and leave to cool slightly. Stir in the egg yolks, one at a time, then stir in the butter. Stiffly whisk all the egg whites in a grease-free bowl, then gently fold into the mixture. Spoon the mixture into the prepared dish so that it is two-thirds full and bake for 30 minutes. Serve immediately.

RHUBARB SOUFFLÉ

SOUFFLÉ AL RABARBARO

Serves 6

200 g/7 oz rhubarb, cut into thin batons

100 g/3¹/₂ oz icing sugar

unsalted butter, for greasing

40 g/1¹/₂ oz caster sugar, plus extra for sprinkling

4 egg whites

Custard (see page 1039), to serve

Place the rhubarb in a dish, sprinkle the icing sugar over it and leave to soften for 2 hours. Preheat the oven to 160°C/325°F/Gas Mark 3. Grease an ovenproof dish or mould with butter and sprinkle with caster sugar. Stiffly whisk the egg whites in a grease-free bowl. Put the caster sugar and 2 tablespoons water in a small saucepan and bring to the boil, then add the rhubarb and cook for 2 minutes. Pour the rhubarb mixture on to the egg whites and whisk with an electric mixer for 1 minute. Spoon the mixture into the prepared dish or mould and bake for 25 minutes. Serve with immediately with custard.

RUM SOUFFLÉ

SOUFFLÉ AL RUM

Serves 4

unsalted butter, for greasing

25 g/1 oz plain flour

120 g/4 oz caster sugar

200 ml/7 fl oz milk

3 eggs, separated

50 ml/2 fl oz rum

1 egg white

Preheat the oven to 180°C/350°F/Gas Mark 4. Grease a cake tin with butter. Mix together the flour, sugar and milk in a saucepan and bring to just below boiling point, stirring constantly. Remove the pan from the heat as soon as the mixture thickens. Stir in the egg yolks, one at a time, then add the rum and leave to cool. Stiffly whisk the egg whites in a grease-free bowl and fold into the mixture. Spoon the mixture into the prepared cake tin and bake for 35–40 minutes. Serve immediately.

TORRONE SOUFFLÉ

Preheat the oven to 200°C/400°F/Gas Mark 6. Grease a soufflé dish with butter and sprinkle with sugar. Bring 200 ml/7 fl oz of the milk to the boil in a small saucepan, then remove from the heat and add the sugar, a pinch of salt and the vanilla pod. Cover and leave to infuse for 15 minutes, then remove the vanilla pod. Mix together the flour and remaining cold milk in a small saucepan, and bring to the boil over a medium heat, stirring constantly. Stir in the vanilla milk, then as soon as the mixture thickens, remove from the heat and leave to cool slightly. Stir in the egg yolks, one at a time, then stir in the butter and torrone. Stiffly whisk the egg whites in a grease-free bowl and fold into the mixture. Spoon the mixture into the prepared dish and bake for 30 minutes. Serve immediately.

SOUFFLÉ AL TORRONE

Serves 6

25 g/1 oz unsalted butter, plus extra for greasing

50 g/2 oz caster sugar, plus extra for sprinkling

300 ml/½ pint milk

1 vanilla pod, slit

35 g/1¼ oz plain flour

4 egg yolks

40 g/1½ oz torrone (Italian nougat), finely chopped

5 egg whites

salt

ZABAGLIONE SOUFFLÉ

Preheat the oven to 200°C/400°F/Gas Mark 6. Sprinkle the sponge fingers with the Marsala and use to line a soufflé dish. Cook the peaches in a pan with 1 tablespoon water for a few minutes, then drain and sprinkle them into the soufflé dish. Bring 120 ml/4 fl oz of the milk to the boil with the sugar and a pinch of salt. Mix together the flour and remaining milk, pour the mixture into the boiling milk and cook, stirring constantly, for 2–3 minutes. Remove from the heat and leave to cool, then stir into the zabaglione. Stiffly whisk the egg whites in a grease-free bowl, fold gently into the zabaglione mixture and pour the mixture over the peaches. Bake for 30 minutes. Serve immediately.

SOUFFLÉ CON ZABAIONE

Serves 6

100 g/3½ oz sponge fingers

4 tablespoons Marsala

250 g/9 oz peaches, peeled, stoned and diced

175 ml/6 fl oz milk

50 g/2 oz caster sugar

35 g/1¼ oz plain flour

1 quantity Zabaglione (see page 1039)

4 egg whites

salt

BAKING

Cakes, pastries, gâteaux and other confectionery provide an opportunity to cook creatively. At first, the different doughs were shaped by hand, then moulds were created that have ended up characterizing many desserts over time. Just think of the dozens of biscuit shapes, from the shell-shaped madeleines, made famous by Marcel Proust, to the finger-shaped langues-de-chat (literally cats' tongues) not to mention the animals, stars, hearts, diamonds, houses and little figures so often seen in petits fours and biscuits. Consider the numerous lovely cake tins, from babà, charlotte, plum cake and ciambella tins to other fluted or tower-shaped ones, with protrusions and indentations that produce amazing sculptures that are often small masterpieces of design in themselves. Then there is cake decoration — the search for the right combination of colours that turns a plate of assorted sweet pastries into a mosaic of jewels. Petits fours fall into this section, together with family cakes and other cakes from the simplest to the most elaborate. As a general rule, cakes should be brought to the table whole and guests should serve themselves by cutting their own portions with a serving knife. Remember also that soft cakes should be eaten with a special pastry fork, whereas a knife may be required for firmer cakes and tarts. Biscuits that accompany ice cream, for example, should be served directly from the tray or dish. The same goes for sweet pastries, which should be transferred from the tray or dish to the plate without removing the fluted paper cases.

TEA–TIME CAKES

This section includes some of the most popular, classic Italian recipes from ciambella – ring cake – to plum-cake – actually a dried fruit cake – as well as some treats from other corners of the world such as American-style muffins and British-style scones.

A LOVELY CUP OF TEA

CARROT RING CAKE

Preheat the oven to 180°C/350°F/Gas Mark 4. Grease a ring mould with butter. Sift together the flour, sugar, baking powder, ginger, nutmeg and a pinch of salt into a bowl. Add the milk, oil, butter and eggs and mix well. Stir in the raisins and walnuts, followed by the carrots. Pour the mixture into the prepared mould and bake for about 1 hour. Remove from the oven and leave to cool in the mould, then turn out, sprinkle with plenty of icing sugar and serve.

CIAMBELLA ALLE CAROTE

Serves 4–6

25 g/1 oz unsalted butter, melted, plus extra for greasing

150 g/5 oz plain flour

150 g/5 oz soft brown sugar

2 teaspoons baking powder

pinch of ground ginger

pinch of freshly grated nutmeg

2 tablespoons milk

5 tablespoons olive or sunflower oil

2 eggs, lightly beaten

50 g/2 oz raisins

20 g/³⁄₄ oz shelled walnuts, chopped

2 carrots, finely chopped

icing sugar, for sprinkling

salt

EASY RING CAKE

CIAMBELLA FACILE

Serves 4

100 g/3¹/₂ oz unsalted butter, softened, plus extra for greasing

plain flour, for dusting

200 g/7 oz caster sugar

3 eggs, separated

250 g/9 oz potato flour

2 teaspoons baking powder

25 g/1 oz vanilla sugar (see page 1003)

3 tablespoons milk

salt

Preheat the oven to 180°C/350°F/Gas Mark 4. Grease a ring mould with butter and lightly dust with flour. Cream the butter with the caster sugar until pale and fluffy, then beat in a pinch of salt and the egg yolks. Sift together the potato flour, baking powder and vanilla sugar into the butter mixture, mix gently and stir in the milk. Stiffly whisk the egg whites in a grease-free bowl and fold into the mixture. Half-fill the prepared mould with the mixture and bake for about 40 minutes. Leave to cool in the mould before turning out.

MARBLED RING CAKE

CIAMBELLA MARMORIZZATA

Serves 6–8

80 g/3 oz unsalted butter, melted, plus extra for greasing

400 g/14 oz plain flour, plus extra for dusting

2 teaspoons baking powder

80 g/3 oz caster sugar

2 eggs

175 ml/6 fl oz milk

25 g/1 oz cocoa powder

icing sugar, for sprinkling

salt

Preheat the oven to 180°C/350°F/Gas Mark 4. Grease a ring mould with butter and lightly dust with flour. Sift together the flour, baking powder, sugar and a pinch of salt into a bowl, add the eggs, melted butter and milk and mix until smooth and even. Pour one-third of the mixture into another bowl and stir in the cocoa powder. Pour the plain mixture into the prepared mould, then pour the cocoa mixture on top and bake for 35–40 minutes. Remove from the oven and leave to stand for 15 minutes, then turn out. Sprinkle with icing sugar and serve.

VELVETY RING CAKE

CIAMBELLA VELLUTATA

Serves 4

5 tablespoons lukewarm milk

40 g/1¹/₂ oz caster sugar

1 teaspoon dried yeast

200 g/7 oz plain flour

100 g/3¹/₂ oz unsalted butter, softened and cut into pieces, plus extra for greasing

2 eggs

2 tablespoons rum

salt

Pour the milk into a bowl and stir in the sugar until it has dissolved. Sprinkle the yeast over the surface and leave to stand for 10–15 minutes until frothy, then stir into a paste. Sift the flour and a pinch of salt into a mound in a bowl, make a well in the centre and add the yeast mixture. Mix well with a wooden spoon, then knead in the butter. Add the eggs, one at a time, and the rum, kneading after each addition. Cover with a tea towel and leave to rise for 8 hours. Preheat the oven to 180°C/350°F/Gas Mark 4. Grease a ring mould with butter. Spoon the dough evenly into the ring mould and bake for 40 minutes. Remove from the oven and leave to stand for 15 minutes, then turn out.

KUGELHOPF

KUGELHUPF

Serves 6

100 g/3¹/₂ oz muscatel raisins

175 ml/6 fl oz milk

25 g/1 oz fresh yeast

300 g/11 oz plain flour, plus extra for dusting

80 g/3 oz unsalted butter, plus extra for greasing

4 eggs

80 g/3 oz caster sugar, plus extra for sprinkling

grated rind of 1 lemon

5 tablespoons double cream

Put the raisins in a bowl, add warm water to cover and leave to soak for 15 minutes, then drain and squeeze out. Heat 3 tablespoons of the milk until lukewarm, pour into a bowl and add the yeast. Mash with a fork to a smooth paste, then add 3 tablespoons of the flour and leave to rise. Preheat the oven to 180°C/350°F/Gas Mark 4. Grease a kugelhopf mould with butter and lightly dust with flour. Cream the butter in a bowl, then beat in the eggs, sugar and lemon rind. When the yeast mixture has doubled in volume, add it to the butter mixture with the remaining flour, the raisins and cream and mix well. Gently heat the remaining milk and add just enough to make a soft dough. Place the dough in the mould and leave to rise until it reaches about 5 cm/2 inches below the rim of the mould. Bake for 1¹/₄ hours. Serve cold, sprinkled with sugar.

MUFFINS

MUFFINS

Serves 6

50 g/2 oz unsalted butter, softened, plus extra for greasing

40 g/1¹/₂ oz caster sugar

1 egg

5 tablespoons milk

200 g/7 oz plain flour

2 teaspoons baking powder

salt

butter and jam, to serve

Preheat the oven to 180°C/350°F/Gas Mark 4. Grease a six-cup patty tin with butter or line the cups with paper cases. Cream the butter with the sugar in a bowl until pale and fluffy, then beat in the egg and milk. Sift together the flour, baking powder and a pinch of salt into the mixture and mix gently. Turn out and knead for about 15 minutes. Divide the dough among the prepared cups in the patty tin, but do not fill them completely. Bake for 15 minutes until golden brown. Remove the muffins from the oven and serve hot with butter and jam.

FRUIT CAKE

Preheat the oven to 180°C/350°F/Gas Mark 4. Grease a rectangular cake tin with butter. Cream the butter in a bowl, then gradually beat in the sugar, a little at a time, until pale and fluffy. Beat in the eggs and egg yolks, one at a time, followed by the flour and a pinch of salt. Add the rum, raisins, currants, sultanas and chopped peel. Pour the mixture into the prepared cake tin and bake for 30 minutes or until cooked through. Remove from the oven and leave to cool, then turn out.

PLUM−CAKE

Serves 8

250 g/9 oz unsalted butter, softened, plus extra for greasing

250 g/9 oz caster sugar

3 eggs

2 egg yolks

250 g/9 oz plain flour

2 tablespoons rum

100 g/3½ oz muscatel raisins

50 g/2 oz currants

50 g/2 oz sultanas

100 g/3½ oz candied peel, chopped

salt

SCONES

Cream the butter in a bowl and beat in the sugar and eggs. Sift together the flour, baking powder and a pinch of salt and stir into the mixture. Add just enough milk to make a soft dough, then shape into a ball, cover and leave to stand for 1 hour. Preheat the oven to 180°C/350°F/Gas Mark 4. Grease a baking sheet with butter. Roll out the dough to a 2-cm/¾-inch thick sheet on a lightly floured surface. Stamp out rounds with a biscuit cutter or the rim of an upturned glass and cut a cross in the surface of each. Place on the prepared baking sheet and bake for 15 minutes until well risen. Remove and serve immediately while still very hot. Traditionally, scones are served halved and spread with butter and jam.

SCONES

Serves 4

50 g/2 oz unsalted butter, softened, plus extra for greasing

20 g/¾ oz caster sugar

2 eggs, lightly beaten

200 g/7 oz plain flour, plus extra for dusting

2 teaspoons baking powder

2–3 tablespoons milk

salt

4 AFTERNOON

PETITS FOURS AND BISCUITS

Making petits fours, biscuits, pralines and meringues at home requires a little practice, but their flavour and aroma certainly reward the work involved.

CINNAMON BISCUITS

BISCOTTI ALLA CANNELLA

Serves 6

250 g/9 oz plain flour, plus extra for dusting

5 tablespoons olive oil

130 g/4½ oz caster sugar

rind of 1 lemon, grated

unsalted butter, for greasing

ground cinnamon, for dusting

Sift the flour into a mound, make a well in the centre, pour in the oil and add the sugar and lemon rind. Mix until well combined, then leave to stand for about 20 minutes at room temperature. Preheat the oven to 200°C/400°F/Gas Mark 6. Grease a baking sheet with butter and dust lightly with flour. Shape the mixture into balls, flatten slightly and place on the prepared baking sheet. Dust with cinnamon and bake for about 20 minutes. Remove the baking sheet from the oven, leave the biscuits to cool slightly, then transfer to a wire rack to cool completely.

YOGURT BISCUITS

BISCOTTI ALLO YOGURT

Serves 6

unsalted butter, for greasing

175 g/6 oz plain flour, plus extra for dusting

4 eggs

200 g/7 oz caster sugar

120 ml/4 fl oz full-fat natural yogurt

Preheat the oven to 220°C/425°F/Gas Mark 7. Grease a baking sheet with butter and dust lightly with flour. Beat the eggs with the sugar in a bowl until light and fluffy. Beat in the yogurt, then sift in the flour, stirring constantly until evenly combined and smooth. Spoon small heaps of the mixture on to the prepared baking sheet and bake for 15 minutes. Remove from the oven and cool on a wire rack.

UGLY–BUT–GOOD BISCUITS

Stiffly whisk the egg whites in a grease-free bowl, then gradually fold in the hazelnuts, sugar and vanilla. Pour the mixture into a non-stick pan and cook over a low heat, stirring constantly with a wooden spoon, for about 30 minutes. Preheat the oven to 180°C/350°F/Gas Mark 4. Grease a baking sheet with butter and dust lightly with flour. Remove the pan from the heat and place tablespoons of the mixture on the prepared baking sheet, spaced well apart. Bake for about 40 minutes without opening the oven door. Remove from the oven and leave to cool on the baking sheet, then remove with a palette knife.

BISCOTTI BRUTTI MA BUONI

Makes 20

6 egg whites

400 g/14 oz toasted hazelnuts, finely chopped

330 g/11½ oz caster sugar

a few drops of vanilla essence

unsalted butter, for greasing

plain flour, for dusting

ENGLISH BISCUITS

Preheat the oven to 180°C/350°F/Gas Mark 4. Cream the butter with both types of sugar in a bowl, then beat in the egg and vanilla. Mix together the flour, baking powder and a pinch of salt in another bowl, then sift into the creamed mixture, beating constantly with a wooden spoon. If necessary, soften the mixture with a little milk. Stir in the hazelnuts and chocolate. Place about 15 tablespoons of the mixture, spaced well apart, on an ungreased baking sheet and bake for about 7–8 minutes. Remove the baking sheet from the oven and leave to cool slightly, then remove the biscuits with a palette knife and leave to cool on a wire rack. Cook the remaining mixture in the same way.

BISCOTTI INGLESI

Makes 30

100 g/3½ oz unsalted butter

50 g/2 oz soft brown sugar

50 g/2 oz caster sugar

1 egg, lightly beaten

a few drops of vanilla essence

175 g/6 oz plain flour

2 teaspoons baking powder

2 tablespoons milk (optional)

50 g/2 oz shelled hazelnuts, coarsely chopped

50 g/2 oz plain chocolate, coarsely chopped

salt

SABLÉS

Preheat the oven to 200°C/400°F/Gas Mark 6. Grease a baking sheet with butter. Sift the flour into a bowl, add the butter and 50 g/2 oz of the sugar and mix until combined. Shape the mixture into three or four rolls, then cut into slices and flatten to about 1 cm/½ inch thick. Sprinkle with the remaining sugar and place on the prepared baking sheet. Switch off the oven, put the baking sheet inside and leave until the oven has cooled completely, by which the time the biscuits will be ready.

BISCOTTI SABLÉ

Makes 20

80 g/3 oz unsalted butter, softened, plus extra for greasing

120 g/4 oz plain flour

65 g/2½ oz caster sugar

Serves 10–12

500 g/1 lb 2 oz caster sugar

500 g/1 lb 2 oz ground almonds

100 ml/3^1/$_2$ fl oz maraschino liqueur

a few drops of pink food colouring

a few drops of green food colouring

20 shelled walnuts, halved

20 dates, stoned

DATE AND WALNUT BONBONS

Put the sugar in a saucepan, add 4 tablespoons water and bring to a simmer over a low heat. Simmer for 2 minutes, then remove the pan from the heat and stir in the almonds. Colour half the maraschino liqueur with a drop of pink food colouring and half with a drop of green food colouring. Divide the almond mixture in half and knead the pink liqueur into one half and the green into the other until evenly coloured. Shape the mixture into small balls. Sandwich each green ball between two walnut halves and press each pink ball into the centre of a date. Place in fluted paper petits fours cases and arrange in alternate concentric rings.

Serves 6

100 g/3^1/$_2$ oz unsalted butter, softened, plus extra for greasing

65 g/2^1/$_2$ oz caster sugar

65 g/2^1/$_2$ oz plain flour, plus extra for dusting

2–3 egg whites

ROLLED WAFERS

Preheat the oven to 200°C/400°F/Gas Mark 6. Grease a baking sheet with butter. Cream the butter in a bowl until soft and fluffy, then beat in the sugar and flour. Stiffly whisk two of the egg whites in another, grease-free bowl and fold in gently. If the mixture seems too stiff, add another whisked egg white. Roll out the mixture on a lightly floured surface into a thin sheet, then stamp out rounds and place on the prepared baking sheet. Bake for 7–8 minutes until golden brown, then remove from the oven. Lift the biscuits off the baking sheet with a palette knife, roll up and leave to cool on a wire rack.

Serves 6

olive oil, for brushing

130 g/4^1/$_2$ oz caster sugar

150 g/5 oz blanched almonds, chopped

15 g/^{1}/$_2$ oz unsalted butter

^{1}/$_2$ teaspoon lemon juice

fresh bay leaves, to serve

PRALINE

Brush a marble slab or a baking sheet with oil. Melt the sugar with 1^1/$_2$ teaspoons water in a heavy-based saucepan over a medium-low heat. Stir in the almonds, then add the butter and lemon juice. Lower the heat and cook until the mixture is golden brown. Remove the pan from the heat and pour the mixture on to the oiled surface and spread out to 1 cm/^{1}/$_2$ inch thick. Cut into diamond shapes with a knife and leave to cool and set. Break up the praline into diamonds and place each piece on a bay leaf.

MERINGUES WITH WHIPPED CREAM

Makes 24

unsalted butter, for greasing

plain flour, for dusting

3 egg whites

150 g/5 oz icing sugar, plus extra for sprinkling

500 ml/18 fl oz double cream

ground cinamon, grated chocolate,

tamarind or black cherry syrup (optional)

Preheat the oven to 110°C/225°F/Gas Mark $^1/_4$. Grease a baking sheet with a little butter and dust lightly with flour. Stiffly whisk the egg whites in a grease-free bowl, then gradually whisk in the sugar. Spoon the mixture into a piping bag fitted with a round nozzle and pipe half-shell shapes on to the prepared baking sheet. Sprinkle with sugar and place in the oven for 30–35 minutes. Meringues must not cook, but simply dry without browning. Remove from the oven and leave to cool. Whip the cream until thickened and quite stiff. Hollow out part of the flat side of each meringue with a teaspoon and fill with the cream. Leave the cream plain or sprinkle with ground cinnamon, grated chocolate, tamarind syrup or black cherry syrup. Put the meringues together in pairs and serve.

CARAMEL TARTLETS

Makes 10

150 g/5 oz unsalted butter, plus extra for greasing

100 g/3$^1/_2$ oz icing sugar

1 egg, lightly beaten

250 g/9 oz plain flour, plus extra for dusting

For the walnut paste

30 shelled walnuts, chopped

25 g/1 oz icing sugar

1 egg yolk

2 egg whites

For the walnut caramel

200 ml/7 fl oz double cream

250 g/9 oz caster sugar

1 tablespoon clear honey

100 g/3$^1/_2$ oz shelled walnuts

Prepare the pastry the day before serving. Cream the butter and icing sugar together in a bowl, then beat in the egg and stir in the flour. Knead the pastry lightly, then shape into a ball, cover and leave to stand in a cool place until the next day. Preheat the oven to 200°C/400°F/Gas mark 6. Grease 10 cups in one or two tartlet tins with butter. Roll out the pastry on a lightly floured surface to 5 mm/$^1/_4$ inch thick. Stamp out rounds and line in the prepared tartlet tins. Make the walnut paste. Mix together the walnuts, icing sugar and about 1 tablespoon water in a bowl, then stir in the egg yolk. Stiffly whisk the egg whites in another, grease-free bowl, then fold into the walnut paste, a little at a time. Spread the walnut paste in the pastry cases. Bake for 30 minutes. Leave to cool, then remove from the tins. Meanwhile, prepare the walnut caramel. Pour the cream into a small saucepan and heat gently. Put the caster sugar in another saucepan, add the honey and cook, without stirring, until golden brown. Remove the pan from the heat and stir in the hot cream and the walnuts. Pour the caramel over the tartlets and leave to cool, but do not chill.

DESSERT CAKES

The wide range of recipes here includes cakes from a number of countries and of various levels of difficulty, from the famous Viennese Sachertorte and babà to simpler strudels and light sponge cakes. The choice of dessert depends on the other dishes on the menu, although it is usually best to choose something light for the end of an evening meal or lunch. More elaborate gâteaux and substantial cakes may be offered at tea time.

CIAMBELLA

COFFEE BABÀ

Cream the yeast with the milk in a bowl, mashing it to a smooth paste with a fork. Sift the flour and a pinch of salt into a mound, make a well in the centre and add the yeast and eggs. Mix well, then add the butter and sugar and mix again until thoroughly combined and smooth. Cover with a tea towel and leave to rise until almost doubled in volume. Grease a ring mould with butter. Shape the dough into a 'sausage' and place in the ring mould to half-fill, then leave to rise until almost doubled in volume. Preheat the oven to 180°C/350°F/Gas Mark 4, then bake the baba for about 40 minutes. Remove from the oven and leave to cool in the mould. Meanwhile, make the syrup. Pour the coffee and rum into a small saucepan, add the sugar and bring to the boil. Simmer gently until the sugar has dissolved. Turn out the cooled baba on to a serving dish and gradually pour the coffee syrup on top so that it is completely absorbed. Decorate with sweetened whipped cream.

BABÀ AL CAFFÈ

Serves 6

10 g/¼ oz fresh yeast

175 ml/6 fl oz lukewarm milk

200 g/7 oz plain flour

3 eggs

100 g/3½ oz unsalted butter,

cut into pieces, plus extra for greasing

25 g/1 oz caster sugar

salt

sweetened whipped cream, to decorate

For the syrup

175 ml/6 fl oz freshly brewed coffee

5 tablespoons rum

50 g/2 oz caster sugar

CHESTNUT CAKE

CASTAGNACCIO

Serves 8

3 tablespoons sunflower or olive oil, plus extra for brushing and drizzling
400 g/14 oz chestnut flour
250 ml/8 fl oz milk
50 g/2 oz caster sugar
20 g/³/₄ oz pine nuts
needles from 1 fresh rosemary sprig
salt

Preheat the oven to 180°C/350°F/Gas Mark 4. Brush a 2-cm/³/₄-inch deep sandwich tin with oil. Sift the flour into a bowl and gradually whisk in the milk and 350 ml/12 fl oz cold water until thoroughly combined but runny. Stir in the sugar, a pinch of salt and the oil, then spoon into the prepared tin. Sprinkle with the pine nuts and rosemary and drizzle with a little oil. Bake for 40 minutes, then leave to cool before serving.

APRICOT CLAFOUTIS

CLAFOUTIS ALLE ALBICOCCHE

Serves 6

20 g/³/₄ oz unsalted butter, melted, plus extra for greasing
330 g/11¹/₂ oz caster sugar
25 g/1 oz vanilla sugar (see page 1003)
rind of 1 lemon, grated
500 g/1 lb 2 oz apricots, halved and stoned
3 eggs, separated
50 g/2 oz plain flour
150 ml/¹/₄ pint warm milk

Preheat the oven to 200°C/400°F/Gas Mark 6. Grease a cake tin with butter. Pour 250 ml/8 fl oz water into a saucepan, add 250 g/9 oz of the caster sugar, the vanilla sugar and the lemon rind and bring to the boil, stirring until the sugar has dissolved. Boil for 5 minutes, then add the apricots and simmer for a few minutes more. Drain and set aside. Beat the egg yolks with the remaining sugar in a bowl until pale and fluffy, then stir in the melted butter, flour and milk. Stiffly whisk the egg whites in a grease-free bowl and fold into the mixture. Pour into the prepared cake tin, arrange the apricot halves on top and then push them down into the mixture. Bake for 40 minutes and serve warm or cold.

CHERRY CLAFOUTIS

CLAFOUTIS ALLE CILIEGE

Serves 6

unsalted butter, for greasing
100 g/3¹/₂ oz plain flour
2 eggs, lightly beaten
100 g/3¹/₂ oz caster sugar
250 ml/8 fl oz milk
300 g/11 oz black cherries, stoned
vanilla sugar (see page 1003), for sprinkling

Preheat the oven to 200°C/400°F/Gas Mark 6. Grease a cake tin with butter. Sift the flour into a mound in a bowl, make a well in the centre, add the eggs, sugar and milk and mix well until smooth. Pour the mixture into the prepared tin so that it is two-thirds full. Sprinkle the cherries on top and bake for 40 minutes. Sprinkle with vanilla sugar before serving.

PEAR CROWN

CORONA ALLE PERE

Serves 6

6 Williams pears
juice of 1 lemon, strained
250 g/9 oz caster sugar
1 litre/1¾ pints red wine
50 g/2 oz unsalted butter, melted,
plus extra for greasing
3 eggs, separated
3 tablespoons warm milk
120 g/4 oz plain flour
pinch of baking powder

Peel and core the pears, leaving them whole, then sprinkle with the lemon juice to prevent discoloration. Place in a saucepan, sprinkle with 100 g/3½ oz of the sugar and pour in the red wine. Bring to the boil over a low heat and simmer gently for about 10 minutes. Remove the pan from the heat and leave the pears to cool in their syrup. Preheat the oven to 180°C/350°F/Gas Mark 4. Grease a ring mould with butter. Beat the egg yolks with the remaining sugar in a bowl until pale and fluffy. Stir in the milk, sift in the flour and add the melted butter. Mix gently until combined. Stiffly whisk the egg whites in a grease-free bowl, then gently fold into the mixture. Finally, add the baking powder. Pour the mixture into the prepared ring mould and bake for about 30 minutes. Remove from the oven and leave to cool completely. Meanwhile, remove the pears from the syrup with a slotted spoon. Turn out the cake on to a serving dish. Reheat the pear syrup, then sprinkle it on to the cake, a little at a time, so that it is completely absorbed. Place the pears in the middle of the crown and serve warm or cold.

RHUBARB TART

CROSTATA AL RABARBARO

Serves 6

unsalted butter, for greasing
plain flour, for dusting
300 g/11 oz Shortcrust Pastry (see page 1008)
2 eggs
200 g/7 oz caster sugar
400 g/14 oz rhubarb, chopped
vanilla icing sugar (see page 1003),
to decorate (optional)

Preheat the oven to 180°C/350°F/Gas Mark 4. Grease a medium-sized rectangular pie dish with butter, dust with flour and shake out any excess. Roll out the pastry into a very thin sheet on a lightly floured surface, line in the prepared dish and prick the base with a fork. Leave to rest for 10 minutes. Meanwhile, whisk the eggs with the sugar in a bowl until pale and fluffy, then gently stir in the rhubarb. Spoon the mixture evenly over the base of the pie and bake for 45–50 minutes. Remove from the oven, leave to cool and transfer to a serving dish. Sprinkle with vanilla icing sugar if you like.

FIG TART

Cut the figs into quarters, without peeling, and place in a bowl. Sprinkle with the sugar and half the rum and set aside for about 1 hour. Preheat the oven to 180°C/350°F/Gas Mark 4. Grease a tart tin with butter. Roll out two-thirds of the pastry into a round on a lightly floured surface and line in the prepared tart tin. Prick the base with a fork, cover with foil and fill with baking beans. Bake for about 20 minutes, then remove from the oven but do not switch it off. Remove the foil and beans and leave to cool. Drain the figs and arrange them on the base of the tart case. Mix together the jam and remaining rum in a small saucepan and heat gently, stirring frequently, until smooth. Gently pour the mixture over the figs. Shape the remaining pastry into very thin rolls and arrange in a lattice over the tart and as piping around the edge, pressing gently to seal. Bake for about 10 minutes, then remove from the oven and leave to cool.

CROSTATA DI FICHI

Serves 6

400 g/14 oz ripe green figs

50 g/2 oz caster sugar

350 ml/12 fl oz rum

unsalted butter, for greasing

300 g/11 oz Shortcrust Pastry (see page 1008)

plain flour, for dusting

50 g/2 oz plum jam

BLACKBERRY TART

Preheat the oven to 180°C/350°F/Gas Mark 4. Grease a tart tin with butter. Roll out the pastry to a round on a lightly floured surface, line in the prepared tin and prick the base with a fork. Make sure the confectioner's custard has cooled, then pour it into the tart case and bake for 35–40 minutes. Meanwhile, set aside about 350–450 g/12–16 oz of the blackberries for decoration and place the remainder in a food processor. Process to a purée, scrape into a bowl and stir in the raspberry jam, diluting the mixture with a little water, if necessary (the mixture should be thick). Remove the tart from the oven and leave to cool. Spread the purée evenly over the tart, then cover with the reserved blackberries.

CROSTATA DI MORE

Serves 6

unsalted butter, for greasing

300 g/11 oz Shortcrust Pastry (see page 1008)

plain flour, for dusting

1 quantity Confectioner's Custard (see page 1039)

1 kg/2^1/$_4$ lb blackberries

200 g/7 oz raspberry jam

TUTTI FRUTTI TART

CROSTATA TUTTI FRUTTI

Serves 6

25 g/1 oz unsalted butter, plus extra for greasing

300 g/11 oz Pâte Brisée (see page 1007)

plain flour, for dusting

1 vanilla pod, slit

500 ml/18 fl oz milk

4 egg yolks

100 g/3¹/₂ oz caster sugar

15 g/¹/₂ oz plain flour, sifted

250 g/9 oz blackcurrants

100 g/3¹/₂ oz blueberries

250 g/9 oz raspberries

8 apricots, peeled, stoned and sliced

1 kiwi fruit, peeled and sliced

Preheat the oven to 200°C/400°F/Gas Mark 6. Grease a tart tin with butter. Roll out the pastry into a round on a lightly floured surface and line in the prepared tin. Prick the base with a fork, cover with baking parchment and fill with baking beans, then bake for about 30 minutes. Remove from the oven, discard the parchment and beans and leave to cool. Meanwhile, place the vanilla pod in a saucepan with the milk and heat to simmering point. Beat the egg yolks with the sugar in another saucepan until pale and fluffy and add the flour. Remove the vanilla pod and gradually stir the flavoured milk into the egg yolk mixture, then heat gently, stirring constantly, until thickened. Remove the pan from the heat, stir in the butter and leave to cool. Pour the cooled custard into the tart case. Arrange all the fruit in a decorative pattern on top of the tart. Keep in a cool place until ready to serve.

WALNUT AND COFFEE CAKE

DOLCE ALLE NOCI E AL CAFFÈ

Serves 8–10

50 g/2 oz unsalted butter, softened, plus extra for greasing

5 eggs, separated

375 g/13 oz caster sugar

300 g/11 oz shelled walnuts, finely chopped

100 g/3¹/₂ oz plain flour, sifted

120 ml/4 fl oz freshly brewed espresso or strong black coffee

1 tablespoon rum

120 g/4 oz icing sugar

walnut halves and coffee beans, to decorate

Preheat the oven to 200°C/400°F/Gas Mark 6. Grease two shallow square cake tins with butter. Beat four of the egg yolks with 250 g/9 oz of the caster sugar in a bowl until pale and fluffy. Stir in 250 g/9 oz of the walnuts, then stir in the flour, a little at a time. Stiffly whisk the egg whites in a grease-free bowl and gently fold into the mixture. Divide the mixture between the prepared tins and bake for 25 minutes, then remove from the oven and leave to cool. Cream the butter in a bowl, then beat in the remaining egg yolk and caster sugar, half the coffee, the rum and the remaining walnuts. Spread this mixture on one cake, then place the other on top, aligning the sides. Sift the icing sugar into a shallow bowl, stir in the remaining coffee and gradually add water until the mixture is spreadable. Pour the icing over the cake and spread using a warm palette knife. Leave to dry, then decorate with walnut halves and coffee beans.

CHERRY TART

To make the pastry, beat together the sugar, egg, one of the egg yolks, the lemon rind and a pinch of salt in a bowl until pale and fluffy. Beat in the butter, a little at a time, then stir in the flour. Tip out on to a work surface and knead gently, then shape into a ball and leave to rest in a cool place for 30 minutes. Lightly beat the remaining egg yolk. To make the filling, put the milk and vanilla pod in a saucepan and bring just to the boil, then remove from the heat. Beat together the egg yolks with 50 g/2 oz of the sugar and stir in the flour. Remove the vanilla pod from the milk and add the milk to the mixture in a thin continuous trickle, stirring constantly. Pour the mixture into a saucepan and bring to the boil over a low heat, stirring constantly. Remove the pan from the heat and place the butter on top, then spread it gently with a knife blade to prevent a skin from forming. Leave to cool. Put the cherries into a saucepan, sprinkle with the remaining sugar, add the brandy and bring to the boil over a low heat, then simmer for 10 minutes. Meanwhile, preheat the oven to 200°C/400°F/Gas Mark 6. Grease a tart tin with butter. Roll out two-thirds of the pastry on a lightly floured surface and line the prepared tin. Pour in the cooled custard and spread the cherries evenly on top. Roll out the remaining pastry into a round and place over the filling. Crimp the edges well to seal, brush with the beaten egg yolk, score with a fork and pierce with the point of a knife. Bake for 45 minutes, then leave to cool in the tin before serving.

DOLCE DI CILIEGE

Serves 6–8

150 g/5 oz caster sugar

1 egg

2 egg yolks

rind of ¹/₂ lemon, grated

150 g/5 oz unsalted butter, softened and diced, plus extra for greasing

200 g/7 oz plain flour, sifted, plus extra for dusting

salt

For the filling

250 ml/8 fl oz milk

¹/₂ vanilla pod, slit

2 egg yolks

100 g/3¹/₂ oz caster sugar

25 g/1 oz plain flour, sifted

20 g/³/₄ oz unsalted butter

250 g/9 oz black cherries, stoned

2 tablespoons brandy

STRAWBERRY DESSERT

Melt the jelly over a low heat with 3 tablespoons water until syrupy. Sprinkle the sugar and lemon rind over the strawberries and spread evenly in the tart case. Spoon the raspberry syrup over them.

DOLCE DI FRAGOLE

Serves 6

200 g/7 oz raspberry jelly

50 g/2 oz caster sugar

rind of 1 lemon, grated

400 g/14 oz strawberries

1 Tart Case (see page 1013), cooled

DOLCE DI MASCARPONE

Serves 6

50 g/2 oz unsalted butter, softened, plus extra for greasing
500 g/1 lb 2 oz mascarpone cheese
150 g/5 oz caster sugar
a few drops of vanilla essence
25 g/1 oz cornflour
4 eggs
200 ml/7 fl oz double cream
2 teaspoons lemon juice

MASCARPONE DESSERT

Preheat the oven to 150°C/300°F/Gas Mark 2. Grease a round mould with butter. Beat together the butter and mascarpone in a bowl until evenly combined, then beat in the sugar, vanilla and cornflour. Stir in the eggs, one at a time, then add the cream and lemon juice. The resulting mixture should be fairly thick. Pour into the prepared mould and bake for about 30 minutes until golden brown, then increase the oven temperature to 240°C/475°F/Gas Mark 9 and bake for a further 10 minutes. Remove the mould from the oven and leave to cool, then turn out and store in the refrigerator until ready to serve.

MILLEFOGLIE AI TRE CIOCCOLATI

Serves 6

600 g/1 lb 5 oz puff pastry dough, thawed if frozen
plain flour, for dusting
1 egg yolk, lightly beaten
100 g/3½ oz plain chocolate, broken into pieces
150 ml/¼ pint single cream
100 g/3½ oz milk chocolate, broken into pieces
100 g/3½ oz white chocolate, broken into pieces

THREE–CHOCOLATE MILLEFEUILLE

Preheat the oven to 180°C/350°F/Gas Mark 4. Line a baking sheet with baking parchment. Roll out the pastry on a lightly floured surface and cut out four 25-cm/10-inch rounds. Place a round on the prepared baking sheet, brush with the egg yolk and bake for 20 minutes. Transfer to a wire rack to cool and leave the baking sheet to cool. Bake the remaining pastry rounds in the same way, but without brushing with egg yolk. Meanwhile, melt the plain chocolate in a heatproof bowl over a pan of barely simmering water. Stir in 3 tablespoons of the cream, then remove from the heat and whisk until fairly thick. Repeat with the milk chocolate and 3 tablespoons of the cream and, finally, with the white chocolate and remaining cream. Place a plain pastry round on a serving dish and spread with the plain chocolate cream. Top with a second plain round and spread with the white chocolate cream. Place the remaining plain pastry round on top and spread with the milk chocolate cream. Cover with the glazed pastry round, leave to stand for a few minutes, then serve.

MOCHA CAKE

Preheat the oven to 180°C/350°F/Gas Mark 4. Grease a cake tin with butter and lightly dust with flour. To make the cake, beat the egg yolks with the caster sugar and lemon rind in a bowl until the mixture has trebled in volume. Stiffly whisk the egg whites in a grease-free bowl and fold into the mixture. Sift in the flour, stirring gently. Pour the mixture into the prepared tin and bake for 30 minutes. Leave to stand in the tin for a few minutes, then turn out on to a wire rack to cool. To make the syrup, put the caster sugar in a small saucepan, add 4 tablespoons water and bring to the boil, stirring until the sugar has dissolved. Remove the pan from the heat, add the brandy and leave to cool. To make the coffee cream, cream the butter in a bowl until light and smooth, then beat in the egg yolks, one at a time. Beat in the coffee and icing sugar. Set 1 tablespoon of the cream aside. Slice the cake in half horizontally. Sprinkle the lower half with one-third of the syrup and spread with one-third of the cream. Top with the other half of the cake, spoon the remaining syrup over the top and sides and spread all except the reserved tablespoon of cream over the top and sides. Decorate the sides with the almonds and arrange the candied cherries and curls of the reserved coffee cream alternately on top.

MOKA

Serves 6

For the cake
unsalted butter, for greasing
100 g/3½ oz plain flour, plus extra for dusting
4 eggs, separated
100 g/3½ oz caster sugar
grated rind of 1 lemon

For the syrup
50 g/2 oz caster sugar
120 ml/4 fl oz brandy

For the coffee cream
200 g/7 oz unsalted butter, softened
3 egg yolks
50 ml/2 fl oz freshly brewed strong coffee
250 g/9 oz icing sugar

To decorate
50 g/2 oz blanched almonds, roasted
50 g/2 oz candied cherries

ITALIAN BREAD AND BUTTER PUDDING

Preheat the oven to 150°C/300°F/Gas Mark 2. Grease an ovenproof dish with butter. Put the raisins in a bowl, add warm water to cover and leave to soak. Cut the slices of bread in half, spread out on a baking sheet and dry in the oven. Remove from the oven and increase the temperature to 180°C/350°F/Gas Mark 4. Beat the eggs with the sugar in a bowl and stir in the milk. Drain the raisins and squeeze out. Spread the bread with the butter and place a layer on the base of the prepared dish, then sprinkle with the raisins and the egg mixture. Continue making layers, ending with a layer of moistened bread. Bake for about 40 minutes. Serve warm or cold in the same dish.

PAN DOLCE

Serves 4

175 g/6 oz unsalted butter, plus extra for greasing
120 g/4 oz raisins
20 white bread slices, crusts removed
4 eggs
120 g/4 oz caster sugar
1 litre/1¾ pints milk

FRUITS OF THE FOREST CRUMBLE

SBRICIOLATA AI FRUTTI DI BOSCO

Serves 6

200 g/7 oz plain flour

225 g/8 oz soft brown sugar

120 g/4 oz unsalted butter

500 g/1 lb 2 oz mixed berries, such as blackberries, blueberries and raspberries

Sift the flour into a large bowl, stir in half the sugar and add the butter. Cut the butter into the dry ingredients, then rub in with your fingertips. Leave to stand in a cool place, but not in the refrigerator, for about 30 minutes. Preheat the oven to 180°C/350°F/Gas Mark 4. Meanwhile, put all the fruit in a deep ovenproof dish, sprinkle with the remaining sugar and mix well. Spoon the crumble mixture over the fruit to cover and bake for 30 minutes until golden brown. Serve warm.

SPLENDID MARIA–CAKE

SPLENDIDA TORTA MARIA

Serves 6–8

250 g/9 oz blanched almonds

200 g/7 oz caster sugar

250 g/9 oz plain chocolate, broken into pieces

1 egg

4 egg yolks

250 g/9 oz unsalted butter, softened and cut into pieces

6 egg whites

a few drops of vanilla essence

1 teaspoon potato flour

icing sugar, for sprinkling

Preheat the oven to 150°C/300°F/Gas Mark 2. Line a loose-based 25-cm/10-inch round cake tin with baking parchment. Lightly toast the almonds in a heavy-based frying pan over a low heat until golden, then remove from the heat and leave to cool. Chop the almonds with 1 tablespoon of the sugar. Melt the chocolate in a heatproof bowl set over a pan of barely simmering water, then remove from the heat, stir gently and leave to cool. Beat the egg, egg yolks and remaining sugar in a large bowl until pale and fluffy, then stir in the butter, one piece at a time, until thoroughly combined. Stir in the cooled chocolate. Stiffly whisk the egg whites in a grease-free bowl and fold in the almond mixture, vanilla and potato flour, then fold the egg white mixture into the chocolate mixture. Pour into the prepared tin and bake for $1^1/_4$ hours. If necessary, lower the oven temperature for the last 15 minutes of the cooking time. Remove the cake from the oven and leave to cool in the tin. Turn out on to a serving dish and sprinkle with icing sugar.

APRICOT STRUDEL

STRUDEL DI ALBICOCCHE

Serves 4

250 g/9 oz plain flour, plus extra for dusting

1 egg

100 g/3$^1/_2$ oz caster sugar

100 g/3$^1/_2$ oz unsalted butter, melted, plus extra for greasing

1 kg/2$^1/_4$ lb apricots, peeled, stoned and sliced

salt

Sift the flour into a mound, make a well in the centre and add the egg, 50 g/2 oz of the sugar, 80 g/3 oz of the butter, a pinch of salt and 1–2 tablespoons water. Knead to a smooth, elastic dough, then leave to rest for 30 minutes. Preheat the oven to 220°C/425°F/Gas Mark 7. Grease a baking sheet with butter. Roll out the pastry into a very thin rectangle on a lightly floured surface. Place the apricots along one side, sprinkle with the remaining sugar and roll into a sausage shape. Seal the ends and brush the surface with the remaining melted butter. Place the strudel on the prepared baking sheet and bake for about 1 hour.

RICOTTA STRUDEL

Place the raisins in a bowl, add warm water to cover and leave to soak for 15 minutes, then drain and squeeze out. Preheat the oven to 220°C/425°F/Gas Mark 7. Grease a baking sheet with butter. Roll out the pastry into a very thin rectangle on a lightly floured surface. Beat the ricotta in a bowl until smooth, then stir in the raisins, sugar, butter, egg, egg yolk and lemon rind. Spoon the mixture on to one half of the pastry, roll up and seal the ends. Brush with the melted butter, place on the prepared baking sheet and bake for about 1 hour.

STRUDEL DI RICOTTA
Serves 4
25 g/1 oz raisins
50 g/2 oz unsalted butter, plus extra for greasing
250 g/9 oz puff pastry dough, thawed if frozen,
or 1 quantity Speedy Puff Pastry (see page 1014)
plain flour, for dusting
500 g/1 lb 2 oz ricotta cheese
100 g/3½ oz caster sugar
1 egg
1 egg yolk
rind of 1 lemon, grated
1 tablespoon melted butter

SIMPLE STRUDEL

Place the raisins for the filling in a bowl, add warm water to cover and leave to soak for 15 minutes, then drain and squeeze out. Meanwhile, sift the flour into a mound, make a well in the centre and add 20 g/¾ oz of the butter, the egg, 6 tablespoons water and a pinch of salt. Knead to a smooth and elastic dough and leave to rest for 30 minutes. For the filling, beat the butter with the egg yolks and sugar, then stir in the cream, breadcrumbs, raisins, grapes and cinnamon. Whisk the egg whites in a grease-free bowl and fold into the filling mixture. Preheat the oven to 220°C/425°F/Gas Mark 7. Grease a baking sheet with butter. Roll out the pastry into a very thin rectangle on a lightly floured surface and spread the filling on top. Roll up, brush the surface with the remaining butter, place on the prepared baking sheet and bake for about 30 minutes. Brush with milk, return the strudel to the oven and bake for a further 30 minutes. Transfer the strudel to a serving dish and sprinkle with plenty of icing sugar.

STRUDEL SEMPLICE
Serves 4
250 g/9 oz plain flour, plus extra for dusting
45 g/1¾ oz unsalted butter, melted,
plus extra for greasing
1 egg
milk, for brushing
icing sugar, for sprinkling
salt

For the filling
65 g/2½ oz raisins
65 g/2½ oz unsalted butter, softened
4 eggs, separated
100 g/3½ oz caster sugar
250 ml/8 fl oz double cream
50 g/2 oz breadcrumbs
100 g/3½ oz seedless grapes
pinch of ground cinnamon

TARTE TATIN

TARTE TATIN

Serves 6

150 g/5 oz plain flour, plus extra for dusting

65 g/2¹/₂ oz unsalted butter, cut into pieces, plus extra for greasing

65 g/3 oz caster sugar

single cream, to serve

For the filling

5–6 apples

120 g/4 oz caster sugar

Sift the flour into a mound, make a well in the centre and add the butter and 5 tablespoons water. Knead to a smooth dough and leave to rest for 1 hour. Preheat the oven to 240°C/475°F/Gas Mark 9. Generously grease a round ovenproof dish with butter and sprinkle with the sugar. To make the filling, peel, core and thickly slice the apples. Place half the apple slices in the prepared dish and sprinkle with half the sugar. Arrange another layer of apple slices on top and sprinkle with the remaining sugar. Roll out the pastry into a 3-cm/1¹/₄-inch thick round on a lightly floured surface, place it over the apples to cover completely and tuck in around the side. Bake for 30 minutes. Meanwhile, preheat the grill. Turn out the tart on to a flameproof dish and place under the grill for 10 minutes until the sugar has caramelized. Serve the tart warm with cream.

CHOCOLATE CAKE

TORTA AL CIOCCOLATO

Serves 6

50 g/2 oz unsalted butter, plus extra for greasing

100 g/3¹/₂ oz plain chocolate, broken into pieces

3 eggs

150 g/5 oz caster sugar

100 g/3¹/₂ oz plain flour, sifted

salt

whipped cream, to serve

Preheat the oven to 160°C/325°F/Gas Mark 3. Grease a cake tin with butter. Melt the butter and chocolate in a heatproof bowl set over a pan of barely simmering water, whisking occasionally. Beat the eggs with the sugar in another bowl, then stir in the flour and a pinch of salt. Stir the egg mixture into the chocolate mixture and continue to stir for about 10 minutes. Pour the mixture into the prepared cake tin and bake for 20 minutes. Remove the tin from the oven and leave to cool, then turn out. Serve the cake with whipped cream.

CHOCOLATE CAKE WITH JAM

TORTA AL CIOCCOLATO CON MARMELLATA

Serves 6

Chocolate Cake (see above)

200 g/7 oz apricot jam

2 tablespoons pineapple syrup

5 tablespoons rum

Cut the chocolate cake in half horizontally. Stir the jam well. Mix the pineapple syrup with the rum in a bowl and sprinkle generously on both cake halves. Spread one half with jam and top with the other. Leave to stand for 1 hour before serving.

CHOCOLATE AND PEAR TART

Make a pâte brisée (see page 1007) with the flour, 100 g/3½ oz of the butter, 5 tablespoons iced water, a pinch of salt and 1 teaspoon of the sugar and leave to stand for 1 hour. Meanwhile, peel, core and halve the pears, place in a dish and sprinkle with the remaining sugar and the Grand Marnier. Preheat the oven to 180°C/350°F/Gas Mark 4. Roll out the pastry on a lightly floured surface into a round 5 mm/¼ inch thick and line in a tart tin. Cover the base with foil, fill with baking beans and bake for 10 minutes. Remove the tart from the oven, remove the foil and beans and place the pear halves in the tart case. Return the tart to the oven and bake until the crust is golden brown, then remove and leave to cool. Meanwhile, melt the chocolate with 1 tablespoon water in a small saucepan over a low heat, then stir in the remaining butter. Remove the pan from the heat and leave to cool. Whip the cream and fold it into the chocolate mixture. Pour the chocolate topping over the tart, sprinkle with the almonds and serve.

TORTA AL CIOCCOLATO E ALLE PERE

Serves 8

200 g/7 oz plain flour, plus extra for dusting

150 g/5 oz unsalted butter

80 g/3 oz caster sugar

4 pears

4 tablespoons Grand Marnier

130 g/4½ oz plain chocolate, broken into pieces

100 ml/3½ fl oz double cream

25 g/1 oz blanched almonds, chopped

salt

CAKE WITH ORANGE ICING

Preheat the oven to 180°C/350°F/Gas Mark 4. Grease a cake tin with butter. Melt the butter in a heatproof bowl set over a pan of barely simmering water. Whisk together the eggs, caster sugar and half the icing sugar in a large bowl until light and fluffy. Stir in the melted butter. Sift the flour and baking powder into the mixture, mix well and gently stir in half the orange juice. Pour the mixture into the prepared cake tin and bake for 20–25 minutes. Meanwhile, mix together the remaining orange juice and the remaining icing sugar in a bowl. Remove the cake from the oven and leave to cool, then turn out on to a serving dish. Spread the orange icing evenly over the cake and leave to set in a cool place.

TORTA ALLA GLASSA D'ARANCIA

Serves 6

100 g/3½ oz unsalted butter, cut into small pieces, plus extra for greasing

2 eggs

100 g/3½ oz caster sugar

200 g/7 oz icing sugar

100 g/3½ oz plain flour

¾ teaspoon baking powder

juice of 2 oranges, strained

LEMON TART

Preheat the oven to 180°C/350°F/Gas Mark 4. Grease a tart tin with butter. Beat the eggs with the caster sugar in a large bowl, stir in the lemon rind and lemon juice, then stir in the butter. Roll out the pastry into a round on a lightly floured surface and line in the prepared tart tin. Trim the edges, then pour the lemon mixture into the tart case. Bake for 30 minutes, then remove from the oven and transfer to a wire rack to cool. Place a few lemon leaves or decorative paper shapes on the surface of the tart, sprinkle with icing sugar, then carefully remove the leaves or shapes.

TORTA AL LIMONE

Serves 6

150 g/5 oz unsalted butter, softened,
plus extra for greasing

3 eggs

150 g/5 oz caster sugar

rind of 2 lemons, grated

juice of ¹/₂ lemon, strained

300 g/11 oz Shortcrust Pastry (see page 1008)

plain flour, for dusting

icing sugar, sifted, for sprinkling

YOGURT CAKE

Preheat the oven to 180°C/350°F/Gas mark 4. Grease a cake tin with butter. Mix together an equal quantity of sugar and flour and dust the cake tin with the mixture, tipping out any excess. Beat the eggs in a bowl, add the flour, cornmeal, yogurt, sugar, oil and a pinch of salt and stir well. Pour the mixture into the prepared cake tin and bake for about 40 minutes. Do not open the oven door for at least the first 20 minutes. Remove from the oven and leave to cool, then turn out.

TORTA ALLO YOGURT

Serves 6

unsalted butter, for greasing

140 g/5 oz caster sugar, plus extra for dusting

170 g/6 oz self-raising flour, plus extra for dusting

2 eggs

170 g/6 oz cornmeal

120 ml/4 fl oz natural yogurt

5 tablespoons sunflower or olive oil

salt

YOGURT AND RICOTTA CAKE

Preheat the oven to 200°C/400°F/Gas Mark 6. Grease a cake tin with butter. Separate two of the eggs and beat the third in a small bowl. Pour the yogurt into a saucepan, sift the cornflour over it and stir well. Add the sugar and cook over a low heat, stirring constantly, until thickened. Stir in the ricotta, then remove from the heat and leave to cool. Stiffly whisk the egg whites in a grease-free bowl. Stir the egg yolks into the ricotta mixture, then gently fold in the egg whites. Pour the mixture into the prepared cake tin, smooth the surface and brush with the beaten egg. Bake for about 30 minutes, then remove from the oven and leave the cake to cool in the tin.

TORTA ALLO YOGURT E RICOTTA

Serves 6

butter, for greasing

3 eggs

150 ml/¹/₄ pint natural yogurt

100 g/3¹/₂ oz cornflour

100 g/3¹/₂ oz caster sugar

400 g/14 oz mild ricotta cheese, crumbled

ALSACE TART

TORTA ALSAZIANA

Serves 6

250 g/9 oz caster sugar

4 eggs

120 g/4 oz unsalted butter,
cut into pieces, plus extra for greasing

250 g/9 oz plain flour, plus extra for dusting

5 tablespoons milk

2 tablespoons double cream

4 eating apples

juice of 1 lemon, strained

Beat together 100 g/3½ oz of the sugar and one of the eggs in a bowl until light and fluffy, then beat in the butter. Sift the flour into a mound in a bowl, make a well in the centre, pour in the butter mixture and mix with your fingertips, then knead until smooth. Shape into a ball, wrap and leave to rest in the refrigerator for 1 hour. Preheat the oven to 200°C/400°F/Gas Mark 6. Grease a tart tin with butter. Roll out the pastry into a round on a lightly floured surface, place on the base of the prepared tin and set aside in a cool place. Meanwhile, whisk together the remaining eggs and remaining sugar in a saucepan. Combine the milk and cream, pour into the pan and cook over a low heat, stirring constantly, until thickened and smooth, then remove from the heat. Peel the apples, cut into quarters, core and arrange in the cake tin. Sprinkle with the lemon juice, pour the custard on top, allowing it to cover the base of the tart, and bake for 30 minutes. Remove from the oven and leave to stand for 15 minutes, then turn out.

APPLE CAKE

TORTA CON LE MELE

Serves 6

80 g/3 oz unsalted butter, softened,
plus extra for greasing

300 g/11 oz self-raising flour, plus extra for dusting

3 eggs

150 g/5 oz caster sugar

3 apples, peeled, cored and chopped

whipped cream, to serve (optional)

Preheat the oven to 180°C/350°F/Gas Mark 4. Grease a cake tin or mould with butter and dust lightly with flour. Whisk together the eggs and sugar until pale and fluffy, then beat in the butter until thoroughly combined. Sift the flour into the mixture, then add the apples and mix gently. Pour the mixture into the prepared tin or mould and bake for 30–40 minutes. Remove from the oven and leave to cool, then turn out, or serve immediately while hot. Serve with whipped cream, if you like.

ALMOND CAKE

TORTA DI MANDORLE

Serves 6–8

115 g/4 oz unsalted butter, softened,
plus extra for greasing

120 g/4 oz blanched almonds, chopped

4 egg yolks

250 g/9 oz caster sugar

50 g/2 oz plain flour

50 g/2 oz potato flour

2 tablespoons orange liqueur

sifted icing sugar, for dusting

Preheat the oven to 180°C/350°F/Gas Mark 4. Grease a cake tin with butter and sprinkle with 2 tablespoons of the almonds to coat. Whisk together the egg yolks and sugar in a bowl until pale and fluffy. Fold in both flours, the remaining almonds, the orange liqueur and butter until thoroughly mixed. Pour the mixture into the prepared tin and bake for about 40 minutes. Transfer the cake to a wire rack and leave to cool. Dust the surface with plenty of icing sugar.

APPLE AND PEAR TART

TORTA DI MELE E PERE

Serves 6

80 g/3 oz unsalted butter, softened, plus extra for greasing

plain flour, for dusting

120 g/4 oz caster sugar

100 g/3¹/₂ oz blanched almonds, finely chopped

3 apples

3 pears

300 g/11 oz Pâte Brisée (see page 1007)

1 egg yolk, lightly beaten

Preheat the oven to 200°C/400°F/Gas Mark 6. Grease a tart tin with butter and dust lightly with flour. Cream the butter and sugar in a bowl until smooth, then stir in the almonds. Peel, core and dice the apples and pears and stir into the mixture. Roll out two-thirds of the pastry into a round on a lightly floured surface and line in the prepared tin. Spread the fruit mixture over the base of the tart case. Roll out the remaining pastry to a round and place it on top of the tart. Crimp the edges to seal, make a hole in the centre and brush with the egg yolk. Bake for about 45 minutes and serve warm.

HAZELNUT CAKE

TORTA DI NOCCIOLE

Serves 6

100 g/3¹/₂ oz unsalted butter, melted, plus extra for greasing

200 g/7 oz self-raising flour, plus extra for dusting

2 eggs

200 g/7 oz caster sugar

200 g/7 oz toasted hazelnuts, finely chopped

grated rind of 1 lemon

50 ml/2 fl oz milk

Preheat the oven to 180°C/350°F/Gas Mark 4. Grease a shallow cake tin with butter and lightly dust with flour. Sift the flour into a mound, make a well in the centre, add the eggs, sugar, hazelnuts, melted butter, lemon rind and milk and mix well. Pour the mixture into the prepared tin and bake for about 30 minutes. Remove the cake from the oven, leave to stand for 15 minutes, then turn out.

WALNUT CAKE

TORTA DI NOCI

Serves 6

150 g/5 oz unsalted butter, softened, plus extra for greasing

4 eggs, separated

150 g/5 oz caster sugar

200 g/7 oz shelled walnuts, chopped

150 g/5 oz plain flour

2 teaspoons baking powder

grated rind of 1 lemon

pinch of ground cinnamon

1 tablespoon rum (optional)

Custard (see page 1039) or whipped cream, to serve

Preheat the oven to 180°C/350°F/Gas Mark 4. Grease a cake tin with butter. Cream the butter with a wooden spoon, then beat in the egg yolks, one at a time. Stir in the sugar and walnuts, sift in the flour and baking powder and mix well. Add the lemon rind, cinnamon, and rum if using. Stiffly whisk the egg whites in a grease-free bowl and fold into the mixture. Pour into the prepared tin and bake for about 1 hour. Remove the cake from the oven, leave to cool and then turn out. Serve with custard or whipped cream.

WALNUT AND HONEY TART

TORTA DI NOCI E MIELE

Serves 6

unsalted butter, for greasing

plain flour, for dusting

175 g/6 oz caster sugar

150 ml/¼ pint double cream

1 tablespoon clear honey

185 g/6½ oz shelled walnuts, chopped

300 g/11 oz Shortcrust Pastry (see page 1008)

1 egg yolk, lightly beaten

Grease a tart tin with butter and lightly dust with flour. Caramelize the sugar (see page 1019) in a pan over a low heat. When it has turned golden brown, add the cream and stir in the honey and walnuts, then remove from the heat and leave to cool. Preheat the oven to 180°C/350°F/Gas Mark 4. Halve the pastry dough. Roll out one half on a lightly floured surface and line the prepared tin. Spoon the walnut mixture evenly on top. Roll out the remaining pastry and place on top of the tart. Crimp the edges to seal, brush with the egg yolk and bake for 25–30 minutes. Leave to cool before serving.

PEACH PIE

TORTA DI PESCHE

Serves 6

unsalted butter, for greasing

40 g/1½ oz breadcrumbs

1 kg/2¼ lb peaches, peeled, stoned and sliced

150 g/5 oz caster sugar

25 g/1 oz cocoa powder

4 eggs, lightly beaten

200 g/7 oz amaretti, crushed

Preheat the oven to 180°C/350°F/Gas Mark 4. Grease an ovenproof dish with butter and sprinkle with the breadcrumbs, tipping out any excess. Put the peaches in a saucepan with the sugar and cook over a low heat for about 10 minutes. Remove from the heat and mash with a fork. Stir in the cocoa, eggs and amaretti, then pour the mixture into the prepared dish. Bake for about 30 minutes, then remove from the oven, leave to stand for a few minutes and serve.

RICOTTA CAKE

TORTA DI RICOTTA

Serves 6

unsalted butter, for greasing

250 g/9 oz plain flour, plus extra for dusting

4 eggs

100 g/3½ oz soft brown sugar, plus extra for sprinkling

400 g/14 oz ricotta cheese

grated rind of ½ lemon

5 tablespoons sunflower or olive oil

175 ml/6 fl oz milk

1 tablespoon baking powder

Preheat the oven to 180°C/350°F/Gas Mark 4. Grease a tart tin with butter and lightly dust with flour. Whisk together the eggs and sugar in a bowl until pale and fluffy. Stir in the ricotta, lemon rind, oil and milk. Sift in the flour and baking powder, mix well and pour into the prepared tin. Sprinkle with extra sugar and bake for about 40 minutes. Remove from the oven and leave to cool, then turn out.

RICOTTA AND SULTANA TART

TORTA DI RICOTTA E UVETTA

Serves 6

50 g/2 oz sultanas

5 tablespoons Marsala

185 g/6½ oz plain flour, plus extra for dusting

120 g/4 oz unsalted butter, plus extra for greasing

80 g/3 oz caster sugar

2 egg yolks

grated rind of 1 lemon

350 g/12 oz ricotta cheese

25 g/1 oz breadcrumbs

Put the sultanas in a bowl, pour in the Marsala and leave to soak. Sift the flour into a mound, make a well in the centre, add the butter, 50 g/2 oz of the sugar, one of the egg yolks and half the lemon rind and mix well. Shape the dough into a ball, wrap and leave to rest for 1 hour. Preheat the oven to 180°C/350°F/Gas Mark 4. Grease and dust a tart tin. Drain the sultanas and squeeze out. Beat the remaining egg yolk with the remaining sugar in a bowl until pale and fluffy, then add the ricotta, breadcrumbs, sultanas and remaining lemon rind. Halve the pastry and roll out one piece on a lightly floured surface to a 5-mm/¼-inch thick round. Line the tin and sprinkle the ricotta mixture on top. Roll out the remaining pastry, cut into strips and make a lattice on top of the tart. Arrange the remaining pastry strips around the side and press lightly to seal. Bake for 45 minutes, remove from the oven and leave to cool.

RICOTTA AND SOUR CHERRY TART

TORTA DI RICOTTA E VISCIOLE

Serves 6

185 g/6½ oz plain flour, plus extra for dusting

120 g/4 oz unsalted butter, cut into pieces, plus extra for greasing

100 g/3½ oz caster sugar

1 egg yolk

grated rind of ½ lemon

300 g/11 oz sour cherries, stoned

350 g/12 oz ricotta cheese

Sift the flour into a mound, make a well in the centre, add the butter, half the sugar, the egg yolk and the lemon rind and mix well. Shape the dough into a ball, wrap and leave to rest for 1 hour. Put the cherries in a pan with 4 tablespoons water and the remaining sugar and cook over a low heat for 20 minutes. Meanwhile, preheat the oven to 180°C/350°F/Gas Mark 4. Grease and dust a tart tin. Place the ricotta in a bowl. Drain the cherries and stir them into the ricotta. Halve the pastry and roll out one piece on a lightly floured surface to a 5-mm/¼-inch thick round. Line the prepared tin and sprinkle the ricotta mixture on top. Roll out the remaining pastry, cut into strips and make a lattice on top of the tart. Arrange the remaining pastry strips around the side and press lightly to seal. Bake for 45 minutes, then remove from the oven and leave to cool.

PUMPKIN CAKE

TORTA DI ZUCCA

Serves 6–8

100 g/3½ oz unsalted butter, softened, plus extra for greasing

150 g/5 oz cooked pumpkin or canned pumpkin purée

200 g/7 oz caster sugar • 2 eggs

225 g/8 oz self-raising flour

grated rind of 1 lemon • 8 amaretti, crushed

5 tablespoons milk

Preheat the oven to 180°C/350°F/Gas Mark 4. Grease a cake tin with butter. If using cooked pumpkin, pass it through a food mill. Cream the butter and sugar in a bowl, then beat in the eggs until the mixture is light and fluffy. Add the pumpkin purée, flour, lemon rind, amaretti and milk. (The exact quantity of amaretti may need to be adjusted to produce a soft mixture.) Pour the mixture into the prepared tin and bake for 45 minutes. Remove the cake from the oven, leave to cool and then turn out.

SACHERTORTE

Preheat the oven to 180°C/350°F/Gas Mark 4. Grease a spring-form cake tin with butter and lightly dust with flour. Melt the chocolate with 2 tablespoons water in a heatproof bowl set over a pan of barely simmering water. Remove from the heat and leave to cool. Stiffly whisk the egg whites in a grease-free bowl. Cream the butter with the caster sugar in a bowl, then stir in the egg yolks, one at a time. Stir in the chocolate and fold in the egg whites. Sift in the flour and vanilla sugar, stirring gently. Pour the mixture into the prepared tin, smooth the surface with a palette knife and bake for about 1¹/₂ hours. Remove the cake from the oven and leave to cool in the tin, then turn out and slice in half horizontally. Heat the jelly in a small saucepan until melted, then spread it over the lower half of the cake and top with the other half. Spread the chocolate icing over the whole cake with a palette knife, then leave until set.

TORTA TIPO SACHER

Serves 6

100 g/3¹/₂ oz butter, softened,
plus extra for greasing
150 g/5 oz plain flour, plus extra for dusting
80 g/3 oz plain chocolate, broken into pieces
6 eggs, separated
100 g/3¹/₂ oz caster sugar
25 g/1 oz vanilla sugar (see page 1003)
3 tablespoons apricot jelly
1 quantity Chocolate Icing (see page 1016)

VIENNESE APPLE PIE

Sift the flour and a pinch of salt into a mound, make a well in the centre and add the sugar, lemon rind and eggs. Mix with your fingertips to a fine, crumbly mixture, then gradually work in the butter. Shape into a ball and leave to rest in a cool place for 1 hour. Meanwhile, prepare the filling. Place the sultanas in a bowl, add warm water to cover and leave to soak for 15 minutes, then drain and squeeze out. Peel, core and dice the apples, place in a large bowl, add the sponge fingers, sultanas, walnuts, sugar, cinnamon and melted butter and mix well. Preheat the oven to 180°C/350°F/Gas Mark 4. Grease a rectangular pie dish with butter. Roll out two-thirds of the pastry on a lightly floured surface and line the prepared dish. Spoon the filling evenly on top. Roll out the remaining pastry, place on top of the pie and crimp the edges to seal. Brush with the beaten egg yolk and bake for 45 minutes. Leave to cool before serving.

TORTA VIENNESE ALLE MELE

Serves 8

320 g/11¹/₂ oz plain flour, plus extra for dusting
80 g/3 oz caster sugar
grated rind of ¹/₂ lemon
2 eggs
165 g/5¹/₂ oz unsalted butter, softened and cut into
pieces, plus extra for greasing
1 egg yolk, lightly beaten
salt

For the filling
100 g/3¹/₂ oz sultanas
4 apples
4 sponge fingers, crumbled
100 g/3¹/₂ oz shelled walnuts, chopped
65 g/2¹/₂ oz caster sugar
pinch of ground cinnamon
1 tablespoon melted unsalted butter

FRUIT
DESSERTS

This section includes a collection of delicious recipes based on a wide range of fruits presented in a variety of fabulous ways – with liqueur, cream, wine or custard. Fruit can be served hot, cold or iced and is always a popular way to end a meal.

SUMMER PINEAPPLE

Serves 6

1 pineapple

1 orange

1 banana, sliced

250 g/9 oz raspberries

250 g/9 oz strawberries, halved if large

1 pear, peeled, cored and diced or 1 peach, peeled, stoned and diced

4 tablespoons caster sugar

175 ml/6 fl oz champagne or sparkling white wine

100 ml/3½ fl oz brandy

vanilla ice cream, to serve

Cut the pineapple in half horizontally and scoop out the flesh, leaving the 'shells' intact. Core and dice the pineapple flesh and place it in a bowl. Peel the orange, removing all traces of pith, and cut into segments, then dice the flesh. Add the orange, banana, raspberries, strawberries and pear or peach to the bowl and mix well. Sprinkle with the sugar, champagne or wine and brandy. Chill the fruit salad and pineapple shells in the refrigerator for 2–3 hours. To serve, fill the shells with the fruit salad and top with a dome of vanilla ice cream. Make a layer of crushed ice on a serving dish, place the filled pineapple shells on top and serve.

WATERMELON WITH RUM

Cut a slice off the top of the watermelon about a quarter of the way down and reserve. Scoop out the flesh from the large part of the watermelon and discard the seeds. Dice the flesh, place it in a bowl and stir in the sugar, rum and brandy. Spoon the mixture into the watermelon 'shell' and cover with the reserved 'lid'. Chill in the refrigerator for 2–3 hours before serving.

ANGURIA AL RUM

Serves 6

2-kg/4^1/$_2$-lb watermelon

100 g/3^1/$_2$ oz caster sugar

2 tablespoons rum

2 tablespoons brandy

CARAMELIZED ORANGES

Thinly pare the rind from the oranges, avoiding the white pith, and cut it into strips. Put the sugar in a saucepan, add 1 tablespoon water and heat gently, without stirring, until melted and golden brown. Mix the wine with 1 tablespoon water and stir it into the caramel, then stir in the brandy. Add the strips of orange rind and cook over a very low heat for 1^1/$_2$ hours. Blanch the oranges in boiling water for 2–3 minutes, then drain, and cut off any white pith with a small, sharp knife. Place them on a serving dish, sprinkle with the syrup and candied orange rind and decorate with mint leaves.

ARANCE CARAMELLATE

Serves 4

4 oranges

200 g/7 oz caster sugar

5 tablespoons dry white wine

5 tablespoons brandy

fresh mint leaves, to decorate

CHERRIES IN ALCOHOL

Spread out the cherries on a tea towel and leave to dry for 24 hours. Cut off the first half of the stems and pack the cherries into one or two sterilized preserving jars. Add two of the cloves, a cinnamon stick and a heaped tablespoon of sugar to each jar. Fill the jar or jars with vodka or eau-de-vie so that the fruit is completely covered. Seal the jars and store in a cool, dark, dry place for 2 months before using.

CILIEGE SOTTO SPIRITO

900 g/2 lb large firm cherries

2–4 cloves

2 x 5-cm/2-inch cinnamon sticks

65 g/2^1/$_2$ oz caster sugar

1 bottle (750 ml/1^3/$_4$ pints) vodka or eau-de-vie

STRAWBERRY AND RHUBARB COMPOTE

Put the strawberries in a dish, add the orange juice and leave to soak. Blanch the rhubarb in boiling water for 5 minutes, then drain. Mix the vanilla with ^{1}/$_2$ teaspoon water, stir into the syrup and bring to the boil over a low heat. Add the rhubarb and simmer gently for 10 minutes. Pour the mixture over the strawberries and leave to cool, then chill in the refrigerator until ready to serve

COMPOSTA DI FRAGOLE AL RABARBARO

Serves 6

300 g/11 oz strawberries

juice of 1 orange, strained

400 g/14 oz rhubarb, trimmed and cut into short lengths

1 teaspoon vanilla essence

250 ml/8 fl oz Thick Syrup (see page 1019)

SPICED FIGS

FICHI ALLE SPEZIE

Serves 6

¹/₂ teaspoon ground cinnamon
¹/₂ teaspoon ground coriander
2 cloves
¹/₂ teaspoon ground ginger
100 g/3¹/₂ oz caster sugar
rind of 1 orange, thinly pared and cut into strips
12 ripe figs

Put the spices, sugar and orange rind in a saucepan, add 500 ml/18 fl oz water and bring to the boil. Lower the heat and simmer for 10 minutes, then add the figs and simmer for 5 minutes more. Do not allow the syrup to boil. Remove the pan from the heat and leave to cool. Drain the figs, reserving the syrup, and put them in a dish. Bring the syrup back to the boil and cook over a medium heat until reduced by half, then pour it over the figs. Leave to cool completely.

STRAWBERRIES WITH ORANGE

FRAGOLE ALL'ARANCIA

Serves 6

750 g/1 lb 10 oz strawberries
130 g/4¹/₂ oz caster sugar
175 ml/6 fl oz orange juice, strained

Put 250 g/9 oz of the strawberries in a food processor and process to a purée. Add half the sugar and the orange juice and process briefly again until mixed. Pour the mixture into a dish, arrange the remaining whole strawberries on top and sprinkle with the remaining sugar. Cover and chill until ready to serve.

FRESH FRUIT JELLY

FRUTTA FRESCA IN GELATINA

Serves 6

3 gelatine leaves
1 bottle (750 ml/1¹/₄ pints) sweet white wine
100 g/3¹/₂ oz caster sugar
1 apple
1 pear
1 banana
2 kiwi fruit
2 clementines
12 raspberries
2 fresh mint leaves, chopped

Fill a small bowl with water, add the gelatine and leave to soak for 3 minutes, then drain and squeeze out. Pour the wine into a saucepan, add the sugar and gelatine and heat gently until the sugar and gelatine have dissolved. Remove from the heat, leave to cool and then chill in the refrigerator overnight. Peel, core and chop the apple and pear. Peel and chop the banana, kiwi fruit and clementines. Arrange all the fruit in a fairly large dish, alternating the colours to make an attractive design. Chill in the refrigerator for 3–4 hours. Just before serving, pour the wine jelly – which should be slightly runny – into the dish. Sprinkle with the mint and serve.

FRUIT SALAD

MACEDONIA

Serves 6

1 kg/2¹/₄ lb mixed fresh fruit
juice of 1 lemon, strained
50 ml/2 fl oz maraschino liqueur
50 g/2 oz slivered almonds
150 g/5 oz caster sugar
vanilla or lemon ice cream, to serve

There should be equal quantities of each type of fruit. Prepare the fruit, peeling and coring as necessary, and cut it into cubes. Put it into a large dish, sprinkle with the lemon juice, maraschino liqueur, almonds and sugar and stir well. Leave in a cool place for a few hours to soak up the flavour before serving. Serve with ice cream.

EXOTIC FRUIT SALAD

MACEDONIA DI FRUTTA ESOTICA

Serves 8

750 g/1 lb 10 oz pineapple

250 g/9 oz papaya, halved and seeded

2 mangoes

3 kiwi fruit, peeled and diced

2 star fruits, trimmed and sliced

250 g/9 oz lychees, peeled and stoned

4 tablespoons caster sugar

175 ml/6 fl oz sweet white wine

2 tablespoons rum

1 pomegranate

Cut off the leafy top of the pineapple, then cut off the skin, removing the 'eyes' from the flesh with a small, pointed knife. Cut the flesh into slices, core and dice. Cut the papaya halves in half again, then peel and dice the flesh. Cut a thick lengthways slice from a mango, keeping the knife as close to the stone as possible. Turn the mango round and cut a lengthways slice from the other side of the stone. Score the flesh in each thick slice in criss-cross lines, spaced about 1 cm/ 1/2 inch apart. Turn the skin inside out and cut off the flesh. Trim any remaining flesh from the stone. Repeat with the other mango. Put the pineapple, papaya, mangoes, kiwis, star fruits and lychees in a dish and sprinkle with the sugar, wine and rum. Cut off a thin slice from one end of the pomegranate, then stand it upright and cut through the skin at intervals. Bend back the segments and push the seeds into a bowl with your fingers. Remove all traces of pith and membrane, then sprinkle the seeds over the fruit salad. Cover the dish with cling film and chill in the refrigerator for 4 hours. To serve, stir the fruit salad gently and leave to stand at room temperature for 10 minutes.

MELON FRUIT SALAD

MACEDONIA DI MELONI

Serves 6–8

1/2 watermelon

1 white-fleshed melon, halved and seeded

1 yellow-fleshed melon, halved and seeded

juice of 1 orange, strained

175 ml/6 fl oz port

3 tablespoons caster sugar

Cut a slice off the top of the watermelon about one-third of the way down the fruit. Cut decorative notches around the edge of the larger portion with a knife. Scoop out balls of melon flesh with a melon baller, discarding the seeds. Chill the empty 'shell' in the refrigerator. Scoop out balls of flesh from the other two melons and place them, with the watermelon balls, in a bowl. Sprinkle with the orange juice, port and sugar, cover and leave to infuse in the refrigerator for 3 hours. To serve, spoon the mixture into the watermelon shell.

APPLE DUMPLINGS

MELE IN CROSTA

Serves 4

unsalted butter, for greasing

250 g/9 oz puff pastry dough, thawed if frozen

plain flour, for dusting

4 cooking apples

4 tablespoons vanilla sugar (see page 1003)

150 ml/1/4 pint double cream

1–11/2 teaspoons ground cinnamon

1 egg yolk, beaten with 1 tablespoon water

Preheat the oven to 180°C/350°F/Gas Mark 4. Grease an ovenproof dish with butter. Roll out the pastry to 3 mm/1/8 inch thick on a lightly floured surface and cut it into four squares, each large enough to enclose an apple. Peel and core the apples and place one in the middle of each pastry square. Sprinkle with the vanilla sugar and fill each cavity with a quarter of the cream and a pinch of cinnamon. Bring the corners of the pastry squares up to the top of each apple and pinch together, leaving a small opening to allow steam to escape. Brush the dumplings with the egg yolk mixture, place in the prepared dish and bake for 40 minutes.

APPLES IN THEIR NESTS

MELE NEL NIDO

Serves 6

50 g/2 oz unsalted butter, cut into pieces, plus extra for greasing

6 russet apples, peeled and cored

2 eggs, separated

65 g/2¹/₂ oz caster sugar

130 g/4¹/₂ oz plain flour • 2 tablespoons milk

4–6 tablespoons raspberry jam

salt

Preheat the oven to 200°C/400°F/Gas Mark 6. Grease an oven-proof dish with butter. Place the apples in the prepared dish. Beat the egg yolks with the sugar in a bowl until pale and fluffy. Sift in the flour with a pinch of salt, a little at a time, and stir in the milk. Stiffly whisk the egg whites in a grease-free bowl and fold into the mixture. Pour the batter around the apples, but do not cover them completely. Fill the cavities in the apples with raspberry jam and pieces of butter. Bake for about 45 minutes or until golden brown. Remove from the oven and leave to cool slightly, then serve.

SPICED APPLES WITH SULTANAS

MELE SPEZIATE CON UVETTA

Serves 4

80 g/3 oz sultanas

25 g/1 oz unsalted butter, plus extra for greasing

1 teaspoon ground cinnamon

¹/₂ teaspoon ground ginger

pinch of ground cumin • 4 apples

5 tablespoons moscato or other sparkling sweet dessert wine

Put the sultanas in a bowl, add hot water to cover and leave to soak for 15 minutes. Meanwhile, preheat the oven to 160°C/325°F/ Gas Mark 3. Grease an ovenproof dish with butter. Drain the sultanas, squeeze out and sprinkle with the cinnamon, ginger and cumin. Core the apples, fill the cavities with the sultana mixture and place in the prepared dish. Dot the tops of the apples with the butter and sprinkle with the wine. Bake for about 30 minutes, then remove from the oven and leave to cool slightly before serving.

MELON SURPRISE

MELONE SORPRESA

Serves 6

1 melon, halved and seeded

350 g/12 oz raspberries

350 g/12 oz seedless white grapes

3 peaches, peeled, stoned and diced

4 tablespoons caster sugar

5 tablespoons sweet liqueur, such as maraschino

Scoop out balls of the melon flesh using a melon baller and place in a bowl. Reserve the 'shells'. Add the raspberries, grapes and peaches to the melon balls and sprinkle with the sugar and liqueur. Divide the fruit salad between the melon shells and chill in the refrigerator for at least 2 hours before serving.

BLUEBERRIES IN SYRUP

MIRTILLI SCIROPPATI

Serves 4

500 g/1 lb 2 oz blueberries

500 g/1 lb 2 oz caster sugar

5 tablespoons grappa

Put the blueberries in a saucepan, add 5 tablespoons water and heat gently for 10 minutes. Add the sugar and cook, stirring constantly until it has dissolved completely, then simmer, stirring occasionally, for 15 minutes. Remove from the heat and leave to cool slightly. Sprinkle with the grappa and leave to cool completely. Spoon the berries and syrup into one or two sterilized jars and seal the tops. Use for decorating a variety of desserts and for serving with ice cream.

PEARS IN CHOCOLATE

Preheat the oven to 160°C/325°F/Gas Mark 3. Sprinkle half the sugar evenly over the base of an ovenproof dish. Peel, halve and core the pears, place them in the dish and sprinkle with the remaining sugar. Bake for 15 minutes. Meanwhile, melt the chocolate and butter in a heatproof bowl set over a pan of barely simmering water. Add the pear brandy and stir until smooth and velvety. Pour the chocolate sauce over the pears and serve warm.

PERE AL CIOCCOLATO

Serves 4

25 g/1 oz caster sugar

4 pears

100 g/3½ oz plain chocolate, broken into pieces

20 g/¾ oz butter

1–2 tablespoons pear brandy

CINNAMON PEARS

Peel and core the pears, then sprinkle with half the lemon juice to prevent discoloration. Put them in a saucepan, add the wine, 100 g/3½ oz of the sugar and the cinnamon and bring to the boil. Lower the heat and simmer for about 10 minutes, then leave to cool. Remove the pears with a slotted spoon and put one pear in the centre of each of six individual dishes. Slice the remaining pears and arrange the slices around the whole pears like flower petals. Add the remaining lemon juice and remaining sugar to the cooking juices, bring to the boil and simmer over a medium heat until reduced by about half. Strain the liquid through a fine sieve and pour it over the pears. Chill in the refrigerator for at least 2 hours before serving.

PERE ALLA CANNELLA

Serves 6

12 pears

juice of 2 lemons, strained

1 bottle (750 ml/1¼ pints) rosé wine

130 g/4½ oz caster sugar

4-cm/1½-inch cinnamon stick

PEARS WITH LEMON

Peel, quarter and core the pears, then cut each quarter into two or three wedges, depending on the size of the fruit. Place the pear wedges in a fairly large dish, pour in the lemon juice to cover and sprinkle with the sugar. Chill in the refrigerator for 2–3 hours.

PERE AL LIMONE

Serves 6

8 pears

juice of 8 lemons, strained

50 g/2 oz caster sugar

SPICY CANDIED PEARS

Peel the pears and leave whole. Place them upright in a saucepan, pour in water to cover and add the cinnamon, sugar, cloves, butter and orange rind. Bring to the boil, then lower the heat and simmer for 20 minutes. Drain the pears, reserving the syrup. Bring the syrup to the boil and cook until reduced by one-third. Strain into a clean saucepan, stir in the cream and bring to the boil. Remove from the heat, leave to cool slightly and then bring back to the boil. Slice the pears and arrange like the rays of the sun on a serving dish. Spoon the spicy cream over them and sprinkle the surface with a pinch of cinnamon. Serve with biscuits.

PERE PRALINATE ALLE SPEZIE

Serves 4

4 pears

1 teaspoon ground cinnamon, plus extra to sprinkle

20 g/¾ oz caster sugar

2 cloves

20 g/¾ oz unsalted butter

rind of 1 orange, thinly pared

120 ml/4 fl oz double cream

biscuits, to serve

PEACHES WITH CHOCOLATE

Blanch the white peaches in boiling water for a few minutes, then drain and peel carefully without damaging the flesh. Set aside. Place the canned peaches and their syrup in a food processor and process to a purée. Transfer to a bowl and chill in the freezer for 1 hour. Place the chocolate, cream and sugar in a saucepan and heat gently until melted and smooth. Remove the saucepan from the heat and leave to cool, stirring constantly. Remove the peach purée from the freezer when it starts to take on a granular consistency and before it becomes completely frozen and place on a serving dish. Cut the white peaches in half, remove the stones and arrange on top of the purée. Chill in the refrigerator. Pour the cold sauce over the peaches and decorate with the hazelnuts.

PESCHE AL CIOCCOLATO

Serves 4

4 white peaches

400g /14 oz canned peaches in syrup

100 g/3¹/₂ oz dark chocolate

50 ml/2 fl oz double cream

25 g/1 oz icing sugar

100 g/3¹/₂ oz hazelnuts, chopped, to decorate

PEACHES WITH STRAWBERRIES

Blanch the peaches in boiling water for a few minutes, then drain and peel. Halve and stone them, then place on a serving dish. Sprinkle with the sugar and fill the cavities with the strawberries. Dilute the jam with the wine and pour the mixture over the strawberries. Leave in a cool place for a few hours to absorb the flavour before serving.

PESCHE ALLE FRAGOLINE

Serves 4

6 yellow peaches

100 g/3¹/₂ oz caster sugar

300 g/11 oz strawberries

3 tablespoons strawberry jam

2–3 tablespoons sweet white wine

PEACHES IN RED WINE

Blanch the peaches in a saucepan of boiling water for 5 minutes, then drain and peel. Halve and stone them. Pour the wine into a saucepan, add the caster sugar, vanilla sugar, clove and nutmeg and simmer for 10 minutes. Add the peaches and simmer for a further 10 minutes. Remove the peaches with a slotted spoon and place in a dish. Bring the syrup to the boil and cook until reduced and thickened. Pour it over the peaches and leave to infuse for 12 hours.

PESCHE AL VINO ROSSO

Serves 4

800 g/1³/₄ lb white peaches

1 litre/1³/₄ pints red wine

175 g/6 oz caster sugar

25 g/1 oz vanilla sugar (see page 1003)

1 clove

pinch of freshly grated nutmeg

STUFFED PEACHES

PESCHE RIPIENE

Serves 4

25 g/1 oz unsalted butter, plus extra for greasing
5 yellow peaches
50 g/2 oz caster sugar
4 amaretti, crushed
2 egg yolks
25 g/1 oz cocoa powder

Preheat the oven to 160°C/325°F/Gas Mark 3. Grease an ovenproof dish with butter. Peel, halve, stone and chop one of the peaches and place in a bowl. Halve and stone the remaining peaches. Scoop out a little flesh from the cavity of each and add to the bowl. Stir in the sugar, amaretti, egg yolks and cocoa powder. Divide the mixture among the cavities of the peach halves, piling it up into a dome. Dot each dome with the butter, place the peaches in the prepared dish and bake for 1 hour. Serve hot or warm.

PLUMS IN WINE

PRUGNE AL VINO

Serves 6

1 bottle (750 ml/1¼ pints) sweet rosé wine
pinch of ground cinnamon
130 g/4½ oz caster sugar
thinly pared rind of 1 lemon
1 kg/2¼ lb plums, halved and stoned

Mix together the wine, cinnamon and sugar in a saucepan, add the lemon rind and bring to the boil over a low heat. Add the plums, bring back to the boil and cook for 10 minutes. Transfer to a dish and leave to cool, then chill in the refrigerator until ready to serve.

SWEET CRÊPES

Crêpes may be either sweet or savoury and can be filled with béchamel sauce, vegetables, custard, fruit, jam and many other things. In fact, they are equally successfully as an antipasto or a dessert. Crêpes are very easy to make – simply prepare a batter with milk, flour, eggs and sugar and you're ready to cook them. The real secret of success lies in their thinness, and achieving this soon comes with practice. An ordinary frying pan will do when making crêpes, but to guarantee success it's worth buying a crêpe pan. Once you get the hang of it, making crêpes is quick and easy. Crêpes can also be prepared in advance. If you fill them, heat them at the last minute and serve them flambéed at the table – with the aroma of brandy, they are guaranteed to delight your guests.

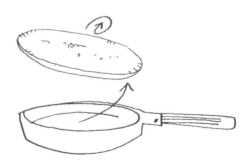

CHOCOLATE CRÊPES

Cook 12 crêpes, stack them, interleaved with greaseproof paper, on a plate and keep warm. Pour the milk into a saucepan, add the chocolate and melt over a low heat, stirring constantly until smooth, then remove the pan from the heat. Gently stir in the butter and spread the filling over the crêpes while still hot. Fold each crêpe into a half-moon shape, arrange, slightly overlapping, on a serving dish and serve with whipped cream.

CRÊPES AL CIOCCOLATO

Serves 6

1 quantity Crêpe Batter (see page 155)

2 tablespoons milk

250 g/9 oz plain chocolate, broken into pieces

25 g/1 oz unsalted butter

stiffly whipped double cream, to serve

JAM CRÊPES

CRÊPES ALLA MARMELLATA

Serves 6

1 quantity Crêpe Batter (see page 155)

2 tablespoons apricot jam

2 teaspoons grated orange rind

2 tablespoons caster sugar

50 ml/2 fl oz brandy

vanilla sugar (see page 1003), for sprinkling

Cook 12 crêpes, stack them, interleaved with greaseproof paper, on a plate and keep warm. Put the apricot jam, orange rind, sugar and 5 tablespoons water in a small saucepan and bring to the boil. Cook, stirring constantly, for a few minutes, then remove from the heat and add the brandy. Spread a little of the jam mixture on each crêpe and fold into four. Place on a serving dish, sprinkle with vanilla sugar and serve warm.

APPLE CRÊPES

CRÊPES ALLE MELE

Serves 6

1 quantity Crêpe Batter (see page 155)

100 g/3$\frac{1}{2}$ oz caster sugar

$\frac{1}{2}$ teaspoon ground cinnamon

juice of 1 lemon, strained

strip of thinly pared lemon rind

500 g/1 lb 2 oz apples, peeled, cored and diced

Cook 12 crêpes, stack them, interleaved with greaseproof paper, on a plate and keep warm. Pour 175 ml/6 fl oz water into a saucepan and add the sugar, cinnamon, lemon juice and strip of lemon rind. Bring to the boil, stirring until the sugar has dissolved, and cook for a few minutes over a high heat until syrupy. Remove and discard the lemon rind, add the apples and cook, stirring frequently, until coated with caramel, then remove from the heat. Fill each crêpe with a little of the apple mixture and roll up loosely, then place on a serving dish. Serve warm.

SUGAR CRÊPES

CRÊPES ALLO ZUCCHERO

Serves 6

25 g/1 oz unsalted butter, cut into pieces

1 quantity Crêpe Batter (see page 155)

sugar, for sprinkling

Melt a piece of the butter in a small frying pan over a low heat. Pour in 1 tablespoon of the batter and tilt the pan so that it covers the base evenly. Cook for a few seconds until the underside is set and golden brown, then flip over with a spatula and cook the second side for a few seconds more. Slide the crêpe out of the pan on to a plate. Cook more crêpes in the same way, adding more butter as required. As the crêpes are cooked, stack them interleaved with greaseproof paper and keep warm. Sprinkle each crêpe with a little sugar, fold into four and place on a serving dish. Serve warm.

CRÊPES SUZETTE

CRÊPES SUZETTE

Serves 6

1 quantity Crêpe Batter (see page 155)

100 g/3$\frac{1}{2}$ oz unsalted butter

100 g/3$\frac{1}{2}$ oz caster sugar

juice of 1 mandarin, strained • 50 ml/2 fl oz curaçao

vanilla sugar (see page 1003), for sprinkling

Cointreau, or another sweet liquer (optional)

Cook 12 crêpes, stack them, interleaved with greaseproof paper, on a plate and keep warm. Cream the butter in a bowl, then beat in the sugar, mandarin juice and curaçao. Spread the crêpes with the mixture, fold into four and sprinkle with vanilla sugar. Place on a serving dish and serve warm. The crêpes may also be flambéed after sprinkling with Cointreau or another sweet liqueur.

PANCAKES

Sift together the flour, sugar and a pinch of salt into a bowl, make a well in the centre, add the egg and beat well. Add the milk, oil and baking powder and mix well, then cover and leave to stand for 2 hours. Stir the batter. Melt a piece of the butter in a small frying pan, pour in a ladleful of batter and tilt the pan so that the batter covers the base evenly. Cook on both sides without letting the pancake brown too much. Continue making pancakes until all the batter is used, adding more butter as required. Serve the pancakes piping hot with a choice of syrups such as maple, apple or other fruits.

PANCAKES

Serves 4

100 g/3¹/₂ oz plain flour

15 g/¹/₂ oz caster sugar

1 egg

175 ml/6 fl oz milk

1 tablespoon sunflower or olive oil

1 teaspoon baking powder

25 g/1 oz unsalted butter, cut into pieces

salt

syrup of choice, to serve

BLUEBERRY PANCAKES

Sift together the flour, sugar, cinnamon and a pinch of salt into a bowl, make a well in the centre, add the eggs and mix well. Add the milk, oil and baking powder and mix well, then cover and leave to stand for at least 2 hours. Stir the batter. Melt a piece of the butter in a small frying pan, pour in a ladleful of batter, and cook on both sides. Continue making pancakes until all the batter is used, adding more butter as required. As the pancakes are ready, place on a serving dish and sprinkle with a little of the blueberries in syrup and some of the icing sugar. Keep warm until ready to serve.

PANCAKES AI MIRTILLI

Serves 6

120 g/4 oz plain flour

25 g/1 oz caster sugar

pinch of ground cinnamon

3 eggs

300 ml/¹/₂ pint milk

1 tablespoon sunflower or olive oil

1 teaspoon baking powder

50 g/2 oz unsalted butter, cut into pieces

175 ml/6 fl oz Blueberries in Syrup
(see page 1084)

3 tablespoons icing sugar

salt

SWEET OMELETTES

Sweet omelettes are made in the classic way, that is, cooked on one side only and usually folded. They are almost always filled with jam or caramelized fruit, often enhanced with a few tablespoonfuls of liqueur. Omelettes may round off a lunch or dinner menu consisting of fairly light dishes. They are also served as nourishing snacks for children. They may be decorated by sprinkling them with sugar and then caramelizing it with a hot skewer in a variety of patterns.

OMELETTE DOLCE (RICETTA BASE)

Serves 4

6 eggs

25 g/1 oz caster sugar

40 g/1½ oz unsalted butter

SWEET OMELETTE (BASIC RECIPE)

Lightly beat the eggs with the sugar and 3 tablespoons water in a bowl. Melt 25 g/1 oz of the butter in a frying pan over a low heat, pour in the egg mixture and tilt the pan to cover the base evenly. Cook until the omelette is set underneath but still soft on top, then fold the left side over to the middle and the right side over on top of it. Slide the omelette on to a warm serving dish and 'glaze' by gently spreading the remaining butter over the surface. Alternatively, sprinkle with sugar and flash under the grill.

APRICOT JAM AND CREAM OMELETTE

Whip the cream, put it in a serving bowl and sprinkle with the almonds. Put the jam and rum in a small saucepan and stir over a medium heat until melted and smooth. Lightly beat the eggs with the sugar and 4 tablespoons water in a bowl. Melt the butter in a frying pan over a low heat, pour in the egg mixture and tilt the pan to cover the base evenly. Cook until the omelette is set underneath but still soft on top. Spoon the jam mixture over it, fold the left side in towards the middle and fold the right side over on top. Slide the omelette on to a warm serving dish. Serve the omelette immediately and hand the cream separately. This omelette can also be filled with canned fruit. In this case, drain and dice the fruit and place it in the middle of the omelette.

OMELETTE ALLA MARMELLATA DI ALBICOCCHE E PANNA

Serves 4

40 g/1½ oz apricot jam

2 tablespoons rum

6 eggs

2 tablespoons caster sugar

25 g/1 oz unsalted butter

200 ml/7 fl oz double cream

2 tablespoons chopped blanched almonds

RASPBERRY OMELETTE

Put the jam and kirsch in a small saucepan and stir over a medium heat until melted and smooth. Lightly beat the eggs with the sugar and 4 tablespoons water in a bowl. Melt the butter in a frying pan over a low heat, pour in the egg mixture and tilt the pan to cover the base evenly. Cook until the omelette is set underneath but still soft on top, then fold the left side over to the middle and the right side over on top of it. Slide the omelette on to a warm serving dish and pour the jam mixture on top. Serve immediately.

OMELETTE DI LAMPONI

Serves 4

50 g/2 oz raspberry jam

2 tablespoons kirsch

6 eggs

20 g/¾ oz caster sugar

25 g/1 oz unsalted butter

OMELETTE WITH DRIED FRUIT AND ALMONDS

Put the raisins, prunes and apricots in a bowl, add warm water to cover and leave to soak. Lightly beat the eggs with the sugar, 4 tablespoons water and orange rind in another bowl. Melt the butter in a frying pan over a low heat, pour in the egg mixture and tilt the pan to cover the base evenly. Cook until the omelette is set underneath but still soft on top. Drain the fruit and squeeze out, then place it in the middle of the omelette. Fold the left side over the fruit and the right side over on top of it. Slide the omelette on to a warm serving dish, sprinkle with sugar almonds, and the rum, ignite and serve.

OMELETTE CON FRUTTA SECCA ALLA FIAMMA

Serves 4

50 g/2 oz raisins

2 prunes, stoned

2 dried apricots, stoned and chopped

6 eggs

2 tablespoons caster sugar, plus extra for sprinkling

rind of 1 orange, grated

25 g/1 oz unsalted butter

2 tablespoons rum

chopped almonds, to serve

FRITTERS

Although they are sometimes a little heavy, these delicacies are almost irresistible. It is a good rule to fry only a few fritters at a time and to drain them on kitchen paper.

AMARETTI FRITTI

Serves 4

130 g/4¹/₂ oz plain flour

1 egg, separated

1 tablespoon brandy

1 tablespoon olive oil, plus extra for frying

200 g/7 oz amaretti

2 tablespoons rum

icing sugar, for dusting

AMARETTI FRITTERS

Prepare a soft batter (see page 1017) with the flour, egg yolk, brandy, olive oil and as much water as required and leave to rest for 1 hour. Stiffly whisk the egg white in a grease-free bowl and fold into the batter. Soak the amaretti in the rum, then dip them in the batter. Heat the oil for frying in a frying pan, add the amaretti and cook until golden brown. Drain on kitchen paper and dust with icing sugar.

CHIACCHIERE

Serves 6

250 g/9 oz plain flour, plus extra for dusting

50 g/2 oz caster sugar

1 egg

1 egg yolk

2 tablespoons olive oil, plus extra for frying

175 ml/6 fl oz white wine

icing sugar, for dusting

SWEET FRITTERS

Sift the flour into a bowl, stir in the sugar and make a well in the centre. Add the egg, egg yolk, olive oil and the wine, mix well and leave to rest for at least 30 minutes. Roll out the dough into a thin sheet on a lightly floured surface and, using a fluted pastry wheel, cut it into strips 10 cm/4 inches long and 3 cm/1¹/₄ inches wide. Tie the strips together as if they were ribbons but do not pull too tightly. Heat the oil for frying in a frying pan, add the fritters and cook until light golden brown. Remove with a slotted spoon and drain on kitchen paper. Dust with icing sugar.

Serves 8

1 pineapple

4 apples

2 bananas

olive oil, for frying

50 g/2 oz icing sugar

For the batter

150 g/5 oz plain flour

1 egg

100 ml/3¹⁄₂ fl oz sweet champagne

2 egg whites

For the sauce

500 g/1 lb 2 oz raspberries

2–3 tablespoons icing sugar

2 tablespoons kirsch

FRUIT AND CHAMPAGNE FRITTERS

To make the batter, sift the flour into a large bowl, make a well in the centre and add the egg and half the champagne. Mix thoroughly with a whisk until smooth and even, then stir in the remaining champagne. Cover the bowl and leave to rest in a cool place for 1 hour. Stiffly whisk the egg whites in a grease-free bowl and gently fold them into the batter and set aside. Meanwhile, prepare the sauce. Mash the raspberries in a bowl and stir in sugar to taste and the kirsch. Press through a sieve into another bowl and keep in a cool place until required. Peel the pineapple and cut out the 'eyes' with a small, pointed knife. Cut the flesh into 1-cm/¹⁄₂-inch slices and stamp out the cores. Peel and core the apples, then cut into 1-cm/¹⁄₂-inch round slices. Peel the bananas and cut into 2-cm/³⁄₄-inch diagonal slices. Heat plenty of oil in a large frying pan. Dip the pieces of fruit in the batter and fry, a few at a time, until golden brown. Remove with a slotted spoon, drain on kitchen paper and keep warm. Dust with the icing sugar and serve with the raspberry sauce.

Serves 4

4 apples

100 ml/3¹⁄₂ fl oz rum

or juice of 1 lemon, strained

1 quantity Fruit and Champagne Fritters batter (see above)

olive oil, for frying

icing sugar, for dusting

APPLE FRITTERS

Peel and core the apples, then cut into fairly thick slices and sprinkle with the rum or lemon juice. Leave to stand for 15 minutes. Dip the apple slices in the batter, making sure they are evenly covered. Heat plenty of oil in a large frying pan, add the apple slices, a few at a time, and fry until light golden brown. Remove with a slotted spoon, drain on kitchen paper and transfer to a warm serving dish. Dust with plenty of icing sugar. Pineapple, peach, pear and other fruit fritters may be prepared in the same way.

DOUGHNUTS

Mix together the yeast and caster sugar in a bowl, add the milk and mash to a smooth paste. Stir in 50 g/2 oz of the flour, knead well and shape into a miniature loaf, then leave to rise in a warm place for 20 minutes or until doubled in size. Sift the remaining flour on to a work surface, place the miniature loaf in the centre and add the butter, egg yolks and a pinch of salt. Knead thoroughly, then leave to rise in warm place for 1 hour. Roll out the dough on a lightly floured surface to about 5 mm/1/4 inch thick and stamp out 5-cm/2-inch rounds with a plain biscuit cutter or the rim of a glass. Put 1 tablespoon of the jam in the middle of half the rounds, brush the edges with a little milk and top with the remaining rounds, pressing down gently to seal. Leave to rise in a warm place for 30 minutes. Heat the oil in a deep pan, add the doughnuts, a few at a time, and cook until golden brown. Remove with a slotted spoon and drain on kitchen paper. Serve dusted with icing sugar. You can also fill the doughnuts with Confectioner's Custard (see page 1039).

KRAPFEN

Makes 20

15 g/1/2 oz fresh yeast

1 tablespoon caster sugar

120 ml/4 fl oz lukewarm milk, plus extra for brushing

200 g/7 oz plain flour, plus extra for dusting

50 g/2 oz unsalted butter, melted

2 egg yolks

275 g/10 oz apricot jam

sunflower or olive oil, for deep-frying

icing sugar, for dusting

salt

FRITTERS

Sift the flour into a bowl, make a well in the centre and add the caster sugar, a pinch of salt, the butter and eggs. Knead lightly with your fingers to form a soft dough. Wrap in cling film, flatten slightly with a rolling pin and leave to rest in the refrigerator for at least 12 hours. Roll out the dough on a lightly floured surface to a sheet about 4 cm/1 1/2 inches thick. Stamp out shapes, such as stars, hearts or animals, with biscuit cutters. Heat the oil in a deep pan. Add the fritters and cook for 5–6 minutes until puffed up and golden brown. Remove with a slotted spoon, drain on kitchen paper and dust with plenty of vanilla icing sugar.

SGONFIOTTI

Serves 6

250 g/9 oz plain flour, plus extra for dusting

100 g/31/2 oz caster sugar

50 g/2 oz unsalted butter, softened

2 eggs, lightly beaten

sunflower or olive oil, for deep-frying

vanilla icing sugar (see page 1003), for dusting

salt

ICE CREAMS AND SORBETS

Home-made ice creams consist of a basic mixture of egg, milk, sugar and cream, combined with chocolate or other flavourings. Sorbets, on the other hand, are fat-free and based on syrup or fruit purée with additional sugar. As well as serving them as desserts, they make great palate cleansers between two savoury courses. Both ice creams and sorbets are easy to make with an ice-cream maker, which allows the consistency of the mixture to be adjusted from firm and creamy to grainy. Ice creams and sorbets are wonderful with spirits such as whisky, vodka, rum and brandy, including fruit brandies. They also go with sweet liqueurs – coffee liqueur goes with creamy ice creams and orange liqueur with chocolate and vanilla ones.

SILVER SPOON

FRUITS OF THE FOREST ICE CREAM

GELATO AI FRUTTI DI BOSCO

Serves 6

400 g/14 oz berries, such as blackberries, loganberries and raspberries

juice of ½ lemon, strained

175 g/6 oz caster sugar

250 ml/8 fl oz double cream

Put the berries into a food processor, add the lemon juice, sugar and cream and process until smooth. Pour the mixture into an ice-cream maker and freeze for about 20 minutes or according to the manufacturer's instructions.

MARRON GLACÉ ICE CREAM

GELATO AI MARRON GLACÉ

Serves 6

250 g/9 oz marrons glacés

150 ml/¼ pint double cream

200 ml/7 fl oz milk

1 egg yolk

100 g/3½ oz caster sugar

liqueur of your choice

Put the marrons glacés, cream and milk in a food processor and process until combined. Beat the egg yolk with the sugar in a bowl until pale and fluffy, then stir in a dash of your choice of the liqueur and the marron glacé mixture. Pour into an ice-cream maker and freeze for about 20 minutes or according to the manufacturer's instructions.

COFFEE ICE CREAM

GELATO AL CAFFÈ

Serves 6

200 ml/7 fl oz milk

1 vanilla pod, halved

2 eggs

150 g/5 oz caster sugar

175 ml/6 fl oz extra strong coffee

200 ml/7 fl oz double cream

Pour the milk into a saucepan. Scrape the pulp from the vanilla pod into the milk and bring to the boil. Remove from the heat and leave to cool. Beat the eggs with the sugar in a bowl until pale and fluffy, then add the coffee, followed by the cream and vanilla milk. Mix well, then pour the mixture into an ice-cream maker and freeze for about 20 minutes or according to the manufacturer's instructions.

CARAMEL ICE CREAM

GELATO AL CARAMELLO

Serves 4

100 g/3½ oz caster sugar

3 egg yolks, lightly beaten

350 ml/12 fl oz double cream

Put the sugar in a pan with 1 tablespoon cold water and set over a low heat until it has melted. Increase the heat to medium, skim and, when it goes golden red in colour, pour in 5 tablespoons hot water and remove from the heat. Cover the pan and return to a very low heat for about 20 minutes until a thick caramel has formed. Gradually whisk the caramel into the egg yolks in a bowl and continue whisking until the mixture is light, frothy and cool. Place the bowl in the freezer for 30 minutes. Stiffly whip the cream and fold it into the mixture. Pour into an ice-cream maker and freeze for about 20 minutes or according to the manufacturer's instructions.

CHOCOLATE ICE CREAM

GELATO AL CIOCCOLATO

Serves 6

750 ml/1¼ pints milk

100 g/3½ oz plain chocolate, broken into pieces

6 egg yolks

120 g/4 oz caster sugar

Bring the milk to the boil in a small saucepan, then remove from the heat. Place the chocolate and a few tablespoons of the milk in a heatproof bowl and melt over a pan of barely simmering water. Pour the chocolate mixture into the hot milk. Beat the egg yolks with the sugar in a small saucepan until pale and fluffy, then gradually whisk in the chocolate mixture. Place the pan over a low heat and cook, stirring constantly, until thickened. Do not allow the mixture to boil. Strain the mixture into a bowl and leave to cool, stirring occasionally. Pour into an ice-cream maker and freeze for about 20 minutes or according to the manufacturer's instructions.

VANILLA ICE CREAM

This is a basic recipe for several types of ice cream. Bring the milk to the boil in a small saucepan, remove from the heat and add the vanilla sugar. Beat the egg yolks with the caster sugar in a saucepan until pale and fluffy. Set the pan over a low heat and gradually beat in the hot milk. Do not allow the mixture to boil but continue beating until it is just thick enough to coat the back of the spoon. Remove from the heat, strain into a bowl and leave to cool, stirring occasionally. Pour into an ice-cream maker and freeze for about 20 minutes or according to the manufacturer's instructions.

GELATO DI CREMA ALLA VANIGLIA

Serves 6

750 ml/1¼ pints milk

25 g/1 oz vanilla sugar (see page 1003)

6 egg yolks

175 g/6 oz caster sugar

STRAWBERRY ICE CREAM

Set some whole strawberries aside for decoration and mash the remainder with a fork. Add the mashed strawberries to the ice cream, put the mixture in an ice-cream maker and freeze for about 20 minutes. Serve in individual dishes and decorate with the reserved whole strawberries. Peach, apricot and banana ice cream may be made in the same way.

GELATO DI FRAGOLE

Serves 6

500 g/1 lb 2 oz strawberries

1 quantity Vanilla Ice Cream (see above)

LEMON ICE CREAM

Beat together the lemon juice and sugar, using an electric mixer, then stir in the apple, milk and lemon syrup. Whip the cream in another bowl and very gently fold it into the mixture. Pour the mixture into an ice-cream maker and freeze for about 20 minutes or according to the manufacturer's instructions.

GELATO DI LIMONE

Serves 6

juice of 3 lemons, strained

150 g/5 oz caster sugar

1 apple, peeled, cored and grated

120 ml/4 fl oz milk • 2 tablespoons lemon syrup

200 ml/7 fl oz double cream

HAZELNUT ICE CREAM

Preheat the oven to 200°C/400°F/Gas Mark 6. Spread out the hazelnuts on a baking sheet and roast for 15–20 minutes. Tip the nuts on to a tea towel and rub off the skins, then chop finely and place in a bowl. Bring the milk to the boil and stir in the vanilla sugar. Mix a few tablespoons of the milk with the chopped hazelnuts, then stir in the remaining milk. Beat the egg yolks with the caster sugar in a saucepan until pale and fluffy, then stir in the hazelnut mixture. Cook over a medium heat, stirring constantly, until the mixture just comes to the boil. Remove from the heat and leave to cool, then pour the mixture into an ice-cream maker and freeze for about 20 minutes or according to the manufacturer's instructions.

GELATO DI NOCCIOLE

Serves 6

100 g/3½ oz hazelnuts

750 ml/1¼ pints milk

25 g/1 oz vanilla sugar (see page 1003)

6 egg yolks

175 g/6 oz caster sugar

YOGURT ICE CREAM

GELATO DI YOGURT

Serves 4

500 ml/18 fl oz natural yogurt

2 tablespoons vanilla icing sugar (see page 1003)

Pour the yogurt into an ice-cream maker and stir in the vanilla sugar. Freeze for about 20 minutes or according to the manufacturer's instructions.

RASPBERRY SEMIFREDDO

SEMIFREDDO AL LAMPONE

Serves 6–8

6 eggs

250 g/9 oz caster sugar

250 g/9 oz raspberries

750 ml/1¼ pints double cream

Whisk the eggs with the sugar in a heatproof bowl set over a pan of barely simmering water until thickened, then remove from the heat and continue whisking the mixture until completely cool. Mash the raspberries in a shallow dish. Stiffly whip the cream and stir in the egg mixture and mashed raspberries. Line a rectangular loaf tin with cling film, pour in the mixture and smooth the surface. Put in the freezer overnight or for at least 4 hours. To serve, turn out and remove the cling film.

CREAM SEMIFREDDO

SEMIFREDDO ALLA PANNA

Serves 6

3 eggs, separated

500 ml/18 fl oz double cream, chilled

150 g/5 oz caster sugar

200 g/7 oz plain chocolate, chopped

Stiffly whisk the egg whites in a grease-free bowl. Stiffly whip the cream in another bowl. Beat the egg yolks with the sugar in a third bowl until pale and fluffy, then fold in the egg whites, followed by the whipped cream. Mix very gently. Line a mould with cling film, sprinkle a layer of chocolate on the base and top with a layer of the cream mixture. Continue making alternate layers until all the ingredients are used. Chill in the freezer overnight. Turn out and remove the cling film.

TORRONE SEMIFREDDO

SEMIFREDDO AL TORRONE

Serves 6

3 eggs, separated

50 g/2 oz caster sugar

300 g/11 oz torrone (Italian nougat), chopped

2 tablespoons brandy

350 ml/12 fl oz double cream

Beat the egg yolks with the sugar until pale and fluffy, then stir in the torrone and brandy. Stiffly whisk the egg whites in a grease-free bowl. Stiffly whip the cream in another bowl. Gently fold the egg whites into the torrone mixture, followed by the cream. Line a mould with cling film, pour in the mixture and place in the freezer overnight. Turn out the semifreddo 30 minutes before serving and remove the cling film.

CREAM AND CHOCOLATE SEMIFREDDO

SEMIFREDDO DI CREMA DI CIOCCOLATO

Serves 6–8

3 eggs

100 g/3¹/₂ oz caster sugar

15 g/¹/₂ oz plain flour

250 ml/8 fl oz milk

25 g/1 oz cocoa powder

250 ml/8 fl oz double cream

1 tablespoon vanilla sugar (see page 1003)

Make confectioner's custard (see page 1039) with the eggs, caster sugar, flour and all but 3 tablespoons of the milk. Pour half the custard into a bowl and set aside. Stir the cocoa powder and remaining milk into the remaining custard and reheat for a few minutes, then pour into another bowl. When cold, chill both custards in the refrigerator. Stiffly whip the cream with the vanilla sugar and fold half into each custard. Line a mould with cling film and pour in the first custard, followed by the second. Put in the freezer overnight. Turn out and remove the cling film.

MARRON GLACÉ SEMIFREDDO

SEMIFREDDO DI MARRON GLACÉ

Serves 6–8

500 ml/18 fl oz double cream

40 g/1¹/₂ oz caster sugar

6 marrons glacés, chopped

5 sponge fingers, crumbled

1 teaspoon bitter cocoa powder

Hot Chocolate Sauce (see page 1017), to serve

(optional)

Stiffly whip the cream with the sugar, then gently stir in the marrons glacés, sponge fingers and cocoa. Line a mould with cling film, pour in the mixture and smooth the surface. Put in the freezer overnight or for at least 4 hours. Turn out, remove the cling film and serve with hot chocolate sauce, if you like.

KIWI SORBET

SORBETTO AL KIWI

Serves 4

200 g/7 oz caster sugar

4 kiwi fruits

juice of 1 lemon, strained

strawberries, to decorate

Pour 500 ml/18 fl oz water into a pan, add the sugar and bring to the boil, stirring until the sugar has dissolved, then boil for about 15 minutes. Peel the kiwi fruits, place in a food processor and process to a purée. Mix together the kiwi purée, syrup and lemon juice in a bowl, then pour the mixture into an ice-cream maker and freeze for about 20 minutes or according to the manufacturer's instructions. Serve decorated with strawberries.

BANANA SORBET

SORBETTO ALLA BANANA

Serves 4

juice of 1 orange, strained
juice of 1 lemon, strained
150 g/5 oz caster sugar
1 kg/2¼ lb bananas

Pour the orange and lemon juice into a saucepan, add the sugar and dissolve it over a low heat, then remove the pan from the heat. Peel and coarsely chop the bananas, then place them in a food processor and process to a purée. Scrape the banana purée into the fruit juice and mix well. Pour the mixture into an ice-cream maker and freeze for about 20 minutes or according to the manufacturer's instructions.

LEMON SORBET

SORBETTO AL LIMONE

Serves 6

3 lemons
200 g/7 oz caster sugar
50 ml/2 fl oz vodka

Thinly pare the rind of one of the lemons and squeeze the juice from all of them. Pour 500 ml/18 fl oz water into a saucepan, add the sugar and lemon rind and bring to the boil, stirring until the sugar has dissolved. Boil for 15 minutes, then remove from the heat. Remove and discard the lemon rind and leave the syrup to cool. Strain the lemon juice into the syrup and add the vodka. Pour into an ice-cream maker and freeze for about 20 minutes or according to the manufacturer's instructions.

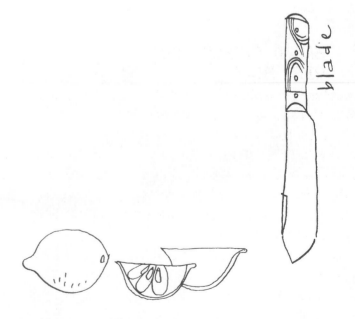

OTHER DESSERTS

Here are some desserts that do not fall neatly into any specific category. This section includes some very contemporary recipes together with other more traditional desserts.

BAKED CITRUS FRUIT WITH MINT

Preheat the oven to 200°C/400°F/Gas Mark 6. Peel the oranges, grapefruit and lemons, removing all traces of pith, then cut each fruit into four, holding it over a bowl to catch the juice. Place the pieces of fruit in an ovenproof dish and reserve the juice. Beat the egg yolks with the sugar and vanilla in a saucepan, then beat in the reserved citrus juice. Cook over a low heat, whisking constantly until thickened. Do not allow the mixture to boil. Remove the pan from the heat, stir in the chopped mint and pour the sauce over the fruit. Bake for 5–10 minutes until golden brown and heated through. Decorate with mint leaves and strips of lemon rind before serving.

GRATIN DI AGRUMI ALLA MENTA

Serves 4

4 oranges

4 grapefruit

4 lemons

3 egg yolks

20 g/³/₄ oz caster sugar

a few drops of vanilla essence

1 tablespoon chopped fresh mint

To decorate

fresh mint leaves

strips of lemon rind

GRATIN FRUITS OF THE FOREST WITH ZABAGLIONE

GRATIN DI FRUTTI DI BOSCO ALLO ZABAIONE

Serves 4

500 g/1 lb 2 oz mixed berries, such as strawberries, blackberries and blueberries

3 egg yolks

50 g/2 oz caster sugar

2 tablespoons Grand Marnier

grated rind of ¹/₂ lemon

Preheat the grill. Cut larger berries in half and place all the fruit in a flameproof dish or in individual ramekins. Beat together the egg yolks, sugar and Grand Marnier in a heatproof bowl. Set the bowl over a pan of barely simmering water and cook, whisking constantly, until the mixture has thickened. Do not allow it to boil. Remove from the heat and stir in the lemon rind. Pour the sauce over the fruit and cook under the grill until golden brown. Serve hot, warm or cold.

CHOCOLATE MARQUISE

MARQUISE AL CIOCCOLATO

Serves 6

250 g/9 oz plain chocolate, broken into pieces

2 tablespoons rum (optional)

200 g/7 oz unsalted butter, softened

5 eggs, separated

50 g/2 oz candied orange peel, chopped

80 g/3 oz icing sugar

Orange Sauce (see page 1018), to serve

Rinse out a mould with iced water and place in the refrigerator until required. Put the chocolate, and rum if using, in a heatproof bowl and melt over a pan of barely simmering water. Remove the bowl from the heat. Beat the butter with a wooden spoon until creamy, then add it to the melted chocolate. Beat well, then beat in the egg yolks, one at a time. Add the candied peel and sugar. Stiffly whisk the egg whites in a grease-free bowl, then gently fold into the chocolate mixture. Pour the mixture into the prepared mould and chill in the refrigerator for 24 hours. Turn out and serve with orange sauce.

PLUM MERINGUE

MERINGATA ALLE PRUGNE

Serves 6–8

300 g/11 oz stoned plums

1 litre/1³/₄ pints red wine

1 quantity Genoese Pastry, baked (see page 1010)

For the meringue

6 egg whites

500 g/1 lb 2 oz caster sugar

juice of ¹/₂ lemon, strained

For the cream

250 ml/8 fl oz milk

3 egg yolks

65 g/2¹/₂ oz caster sugar

185 g/6¹/₂ oz unsalted butter, softened

Preheat the oven to 110°C/225°F/Gas Mark ¹/₄. Line a baking sheet with baking parchment. First, make the meringue. Stiffly whisk the egg whites with the sugar and lemon juice in a grease-free bowl. Spoon or pipe the meringue into thin strips on the prepared baking sheet and bake for 1¹/₂ hours. Remove from the oven. Meanwhile, place the plums in a pan, add the wine and bring to the boil, then lower the heat and simmer for about 20 minutes. Drain the plums, reserving the cooking liquid, and leave to cool, then chop. To prepare the cream, pour the milk into a small pan and bring to just below boiling point, then remove from the heat. Beat the egg yolks and sugar in another small pan until thick and frothy, then gradually add the hot milk. Cook over a low heat, stirring constantly, until thick enough to coat the back of the spoon. Remove from the heat and leave to cool slightly, then stir in the butter. Leave to cool completely, then stir in the plums. Place the Genoese pastry on the base of a serving dish and sprinkle with the reserved cooking liquid. Pour half the cream on top and sprinkle with half the meringue strips. Top with the remaining cream. Crumble the remaining meringue and sprinkle them over the dessert.

GRAPE MERINGUE PIE

Crush half the grapes and strain the juice. Place the Genoese pastry on the base of a serving dish and sprinkle with the grape juice. Stiffly whip the cream and spread half of it over the pastry base. Crumble the meringue. Reserve some of the meringue and a few grapes for decoration and sprinkle the remaining grapes and meringue over the cream. Cover with the remaining cream and decorate with the reserved meringue and grapes.

MERINGATA ALL'UVA

Serves 6

600 g/1 lb 5 oz white grapes

1 quantity Genoese pastry, baked (see page 1010)

400 ml/14 fl oz double cream

1 quantity Meringue (see Plum Meringue, opposite)

MONTEBIANCO

Tie the fennel seeds in a small square of muslin. Bring a pan of lightly salted water to the boil, add the chestnuts and fennel seeds and simmer for about 40 minutes. Drain and peel the chestnuts, then place them in a saucepan, pour in the milk and simmer, mashing with a wooden spoon, for 15 minutes. If necessary, add a little more warm milk. As the mixture is just beginning to thicken, stir in the sugar and remove from the heat. Sprinkle in the rum and cocoa and mix well. Pass the mixture through a food mill on to a serving dish to create a cone of 'chestnut vermicelli'. Decorate with rosettes of whipped cream and crystallized violets.

MONTE BIANCO

Serves 6

pinch of fennel seeds

800 g/1³/₄ lb chestnuts, shelled

175 ml/6 fl oz milk

50 g/2 oz caster sugar • 50 ml/2 fl oz rum

2 tablespoons cocoa powder • salt

To decorate

1 quantity Whipped Cream

crystallized violets

CHOCOLATE PROFITEROLES

Preheat the oven to 190°C/375°F/Gas Mark 5. Grease a baking sheet with butter and dust with flour. Pour the milk and 5 tablespoons water into a small saucepan, add the butter and bring to the boil over a low heat. Remove the pan from the heat, tip in the flour all at once and stir well. Return the saucepan to the heat and cook, stirring constantly until the mixture comes away from the base and sides. Remove from the heat and leave to cool, then beat in the eggs one at a time. Do not add the second egg until the first has been fully absorbed. Spoon the mixture into a piping bag and pipe 16 mounds on to the prepared baking sheet, spaced well apart. Bake for 15 minutes until the mounds are puffed up and golden brown. Transfer to a wire rack to cool. Meanwhile, prepare the topping. Melt the chocolate with 1 tablespoon water in a small saucepan over a low heat. Stir in the butter and sugar and cook until thickened. Remove from the heat and leave to cool. Make a slit in the side of the puffs and fill them with the whipped cream. Arrange the puffs in a pyramid on a serving dish and pour the chocolate topping over them.

PROFITEROLES AL CIOCCOLATO

Serves 4–6

50 g/2 oz unsalted butter, softened,

plus extra for greasing

75 g/2³/₄ oz plain flour, plus extra for dusting

6 tablespoons milk

2 eggs

200 ml/7 fl oz double cream, whipped

For the topping

100 g/3¹/₂ oz plain chocolate, broken into pieces

25 g/1 oz unsalted butter

50 g/2 oz caster sugar

SEMOLINA WITH CHERRIES

SEMOLINO ALLE CILIEGE

Serves 6

unsalted butter, for greasing

250 ml/8 fl oz sweet white wine

120 g/4 oz semolina

2 eggs

120 g/4 oz caster sugar

500 g/1 lb 2 oz cherries, stoned

50 g/2 oz blanched almonds, chopped

1 egg white

Preheat the oven to 200°C/400°F/Gas Mark 6. Grease a mould with butter. Pour the wine and 500 ml/18 fl oz water into a saucepan and bring to the boil. Sprinkle in the semolina and cook, stirring constantly, for 15 minutes. Remove the pan from the heat and leave to cool slightly. Stir in the eggs, one at a time, then stir in the sugar, cherries and almonds. Stiffly whisk the egg white in a grease-free bowl and fold into the semolina mixture. Pour the mixture into the prepared mould and place it in a roasting tin. Add boiling water to come about halfway up the sides and bake for 45 minutes. Remove from the oven and leave to cool to room temperature before turning out.

TIRAMISU

TIRAMI SU

Serves 6

2 egg whites • 4 egg yolks

150 g/5 oz icing sugar

400 g/14 oz mascarpone cheese

200 g/7 oz sponge fingers

175 ml/6 fl oz freshly brewed extra strong coffee, cooled

200 g/7 oz plain chocolate, grated

cocoa powder, for dusting

Stiffly whisk the egg whites in a grease-free bowl. Beat the egg yolks with the sugar in another bowl until pale and fluffy. Gently fold in the mascarpone, then the egg whites. Make a layer of sponge fingers on the base of a deep, rectangular serving dish and brush them evenly with coffee. Cover with a layer of the mascarpone cream and sprinkle with a little grated chocolate. Continue making layers until all the ingredients are used, ending with a layer of mascarpone cream. Dust with cocoa and chill in the refrigerator for about 3 hours.

ZUCCOTTO

ZUCCOTTO

Serves 4–6

150 g/5 oz sponge fingers

150 ml/¼ pint Grand Marnier

350 ml/12 fl oz double cream

65 g/2½ oz cocoa powder

2 tablespoons icing sugar

100 g/3½ oz plain chocolate, chopped

10 blanched almonds, chopped

You will need a hemispherical zuccotto mould for an authentic version of this dessert, but you can adapt the recipe for other shapes. Line the mould with some of the sponge fingers and sprinkle with a little Grand Marnier. Stiffly whip the cream and divide it between two bowls. Sift together the cocoa and sugar into one bowl of cream. Add the chocolate and almonds to the other bowl of cream. Spoon or pour the cocoa cream on to the base of the lined mould, then tap firmly on a work surface to remove any pockets of air. Cover the cocoa cream with a layer of sponge fingers and sprinkle them evenly with Grand Marnier. Spoon or pour the almond cream on top and cover with the remaining sponge fingers. Sprinkle with the remaining Grand Marnier. Chill in the refrigerator for about 4 hours, then turn out on to a serving dish. If you prefer frozen zuccotto, put the mould in the freezer for 3–4 hours.

ITALIAN TRIFLE

ZUPPA INGLESE

Serves 6

1 quantity Confectioner's Custard (see page 1039)

1 tablespoon cochineal

2 tablespoons rum

250 g/9 oz sponge cake, sliced

To decorate

100 ml/3¹/₂ fl oz double cream

mixed crystallized fruit

chocolate chips or fresh berries

Reserve 250 ml/8 fl oz of the confectioner's custard. Mix the cochineal with 1 tablespoon water in a shallow dish. Mix the rum with 1 tablespoon water in another shallow dish. Arrange a layer of sponge cake on the base of a broad glass dish, sprinkle with the cochineal mixture and pour on a layer of confectioner's custard. Make another layer of sponge cake, sprinkle with the rum and pour on another layer of confectioner's custard. Continue making alternating layers, ending with a layer of sponge cake. Chill in the refrigerator for 1 hour. Remove the bowl from the refrigerator and leave to stand for about 10 minutes. Meanwhile, stiffly whip the cream. Spread the reserved confectioner's custard on top of the last layer of sponge cake. Fill a piping bag fitted with a star nozzle with the whipped cream and use to decorate the trifle, then add crystallized fruit and chocolate chips or fresh berries.

JELLIES AND JAMS

Jellies and jams are different kinds of fruit preserve. Raspberries, strawberries, apricots, apples and redcurrants are the best fruits for preparing delicate transparent jellies, while a wider variety of fruits may be used for jam-making. Preparation is based on a few simple rules. The fruit should be ripe, in prime condition, well washed, and peeled and seeded. The quantity of sugar depends on the tartness of the fruit. As a general guide, the sharpest fruits require their own weight in sugar, whereas sweeter ones need less. The fruit should not be cooked for too long as this may destroy the flavour or even leave a slightly burnt taste. It should not, however, be cooked too briefly either, or harmful fermentation may arise. To test for the setting point, remove the pan from the heat and put a teaspoon of jam on a cold saucer. Cool quickly, then push with your finger. If the surface wrinkles, the jam is ready.

GELATINA DI FRAGOLE

strawberries

sugar

(See introduction for advice on quantities)

STRAWBERRY JELLY

Hull the strawberries, place them in a saucepan and cook over a low heat, without adding any liquid and stirring constantly, for 8 minutes. Place a large sieve, or suspend a jelly bag, over a bowl, pour in the strawberries and leave to drain. If you want clear jelly, leave to drip without pressing or squeezing the fruit. When all the juice has collected, weigh it and add the same weight of sugar. Pour the juice into a saucepan and bring to the boil over a medium heat, stirring constantly. When the juice comes to the boil, stop stirring, skim and cook for exactly 3 more minutes. Remove from the heat and leave to cool slightly, then ladle the warm jelly into warm, sterilized glass jars and leave to cool. Seal the jars and store in a cool, dry place.

QUINCE JELLY

Thinly slice the quinces, place them in a saucepan and add water to cover. Cook over a medium heat until almost mushy. Place a large sieve, or suspend a jelly bag, over a bowl, pour in the quinces and leave to drain. If you want clear jelly, leave to drip without pressing or squeezing the fruit. When all the juice has collected, weigh it and add the same weight of sugar. Pour the juice into a saucepan and cook, stirring occasionally, until the jelly comes away from the spoon and falls in large drops. Add lemon juice to taste according to the quantity of jelly. Ladle into warm, sterilized glass jars while still hot, leave to cool and then seal. Store in a cool, dry place.

GELATINA DI MELE COTOGNE

quinces, unpeeled

sugar

freshly squeezed lemon juice, strained

(See introduction for advice on quantities)

REDCURRANT JELLY

Put the redcurrants in a saucepan and add water to cover. Cook over a medium heat, stirring constantly, for about 8 minutes. Place a large sieve, or suspend a jelly bag, over a bowl, pour in the redcurrants and leave to drain. If you want clear jelly, leave to drip without pressing or squeezing the fruit. When all the juice has collected, weigh it and add the same weight of sugar. Pour the mixture into a saucepan and bring to the boil over a low heat, stirring constantly. Do not stop stirring, skim carefully and cook for exactly 3 more minutes. Ladle the jelly into warm, sterilized glass jars and leave to cool. Seal and store in a cool, dry place.

GELATINA DI RIBES

redcurrants

sugar

(See introduction for advice on quantities)

GRAPE JELLY

Crush the grapes and strain the juice. Measure the juice and pour it into a saucepan. Add 300g/11 oz sugar for every 1 litre/1³/₄ pints juice. Bring the juice to the boil, stirring until the sugar has dissolved and skimming if necessary. Boil until reduced by about one-third. Remove from the heat and leave to cool slightly, then ladle into warm, sterilized glass jars. When cool, seal tightly and store in a cool, dry place.

GELATINA D'UVA

white grapes

sugar

(See introduction for advice on quantities)

MARMELLATA D'ALBICOCCHE

900 g/2 lb sugar

2 kg/4¹/₂ lb apricots, halved and stoned

APRICOT JAM

Pour 500 ml/18 fl oz water into a saucepan, add the sugar and bring to the boil over a low heat, stirring constantly, then simmer for about 10 minutes. Add the apricots and cook, stirring and skimming occasionally, for about 2¹/₂ hours until the jam reaches setting point. Ladle into warm, sterilized glass jars while still hot, leave to cool and seal tightly.

MARMELLATA D'ARANCE

2 kg/4¹/₂ lb oranges

sugar

(See introduction for advice on quantities)

ORANGE MARMALADE

Prick the oranges all over with a fork and place them in a large bowl. Add water to cover and leave to soak for 12 hours. Drain, dry and peel the oranges, reserving the rind from three of them. Using a small, sharp knife, remove all traces of white pith from the reserved rind and cut the rind into extremely thin strips. Bring a small pan of water to the boil, add the strips of orange rind and cook for 3–4 minutes, then drain. Weigh the peeled oranges, slice thinly and remove the pips. Put the slices in a saucepan with an equal weight of sugar. Bring to the boil over a medium heat and simmer gently, without adding any water, stirring frequently for about 1 hour or until the sugar starts to form threads. Add the strips of orange rind and cook, stirring constantly, for 2–3 minutes. Ladle the marmalade into warm, sterilized glass jars while still hot. Leave to cool and then seal tightly. Store in a cool, dry place.

MARMELLATA DI CASTAGNE

2 kg/4¹/₂ lb chestnuts, shelled

1 teaspoon sea salt

1 kg/2¹/₄ lb sugar

200 ml/7 fl oz rum

CHESTNUT JAM

Put the chestnuts in a saucepan and add the salt and enough water to cover. Cover and cook over a medium heat for about 45 minutes. Drain, remove the skins and press through a sieve into a clean saucepan. Add the sugar and 250 ml/8 fl oz water and cook over a medium heat, stirring constantly, for about 40 minutes. About 10 minutes before removing the pan from the heat, add the rum and stir carefully. Ladle into warm, sterilized glass jars, leave to cool and seal tightly. This jam should be thick and dry.

CHERRY JAM

Place the cherries in a saucepan, add the sugar and leave to stand in a cool place for 3 hours. Sprinkle the cherries with the lemon juice and cook over a medium heat, stirring occasionally, for about 1 1/2 hours until the jam is of an even consistency. Ladle into warm, sterilized glass jars while still hot and leave to cool, then seal tightly.

MARMELLATA DI CILIEGE

2 kg/4 1/2 lb black cherries, stoned

1 kg/2 1/4 lb sugar

juice of 1 lemon, strained

FIG JAM

Pour 500 ml/18 fl oz water into a saucepan, add the sugar and bring to the boil, stirring until the sugar has dissolved. Add the figs and cinnamon and cook over a medium heat, stirring occasionally until the jam thickens. Ladle into warm, sterilized glass jars while still hot, leave to cool then seal tightly.

MARMELLATA DI FICHI

500 g/1 lb 2 oz sugar

1 kg/2 1/4 lb figs, peeled and chopped

pinch of ground cinnamon

STRAWBERRY JAM

Hull the strawberries and place in a heavy-based saucepan. Add the sugar and bring to the boil over a medium heat, stirring constantly. When the mixture starts to boil, gradually increase the heat and cook, stirring constantly, for 20–25 minutes. Ladle the jam into warm, sterilized glass jars while still hot and leave to cool then seal and store in a cool, dry place.

MARMELLATA DI FRAGOLE

1 kg/2 1/4 lb strawberries

1 kg/2 1/4 lb sugar

BERRY JAM

Place the berries in a saucepan, add the sugar and cook over a medium heat, without any additional liquid and stirring constantly, for 30 minutes. Remove the pan from the heat, leave to cool slightly, then ladle into warm, sterilized glass jars. When cool, seal the jars and store in a cool, dry place.

MARMELLATA DI FRUTTI DI BOSCO

1 kg/2 1/4 lb mixed berries, such as raspberries, strawberries, blackberries, blueberries and redcurrants

500 g/1 lb 2 oz sugar

2 kg/4¹/₂ lb kiwi fruit, peeled and chopped

2 kg/4¹/₂ lb sugar

KIWI JAM

Place the kiwis in a saucepan, add the sugar and cook over a medium heat, stirring constantly, for 30 minutes. Ladle the jam into warm, sterilized glass jars while still hot. When cool, seal the jars and store in a cool, dry place.

MARMELLATA DI MELE

2 kg/4¹/₂ lb apples, peeled and cored

juice of 2 lemons, strained

1 kg/2¹/₄ lb sugar

APPLE JAM

Brush the apples with the lemon juice to stop them from turning brown. Grate the apples into a saucepan, add the sugar and 4 tablespoons water and cook over a low heat, stirring constantly, for 2¹/₂ hours. Ladle the jam into warm, sterilized glass jars, leave to cool, then seal. Store in a cool, dry place. If you use russet apples, peel and thinly slice them, place them in a saucepan, add just enough water to cover and cook over a very low heat. Pass through a food mill, then weigh them and add an equal weight of sugar. Return the mixture to the pan and cook until it reaches setting point.

MARMELLATA DI PERE

2 kg/4¹/₂ lb pears, peeled, cored and chopped

1 kg/2¹/₄ lb sugar

juice of 1 lemon, strained

PEAR JAM

Put the pears, sugar and lemon juice in a saucepan and cook over a low heat, stirring constantly, for 1 hour. Ladle the jam into warm, sterilized glass jars and leave to cool, then seal tightly. Store in a cool, dry place.

MARMELLATA DI PESCHE

2 kg/4¹/₂ lb peaches, peeled, halved and stoned

800 g/1³/₄ lb sugar

PEACH JAM

Slice the peach halves thinly and place in a saucepan. If the peaches are very ripe and juicy, it is not necessary to add water, otherwise add 5 tablespoons water. Cook over a low heat until the peaches start to become mushy, then add the sugar and cook, stirring occasionally, for about 2¹/₂ hours. Ladle the jam into warm, sterilized glass jars and leave to cool, then seal tightly. Store in a cool, dry place.

GREEN TOMATO JAM

Put the tomatoes in a bowl and add the sugar, lemon juice and rind and a pinch of salt. Cover and leave to stand for a few hours. Pour the mixture into a saucepan and cook over a medium heat until it reaches setting point. Ladle into warm, sterilized glass jars while still hot and leave to cool, then seal tightly. Store in a cool, dry place.

MARMELLATA DI POMODORI VERDI

1 kg/2¼ lb green tomatoes, chopped
400 g/14 oz sugar
juice and grated rind of ½ lemon
salt

PLUM JAM

Put the plums in a saucepan, add the sugar and cook, stirring occasionally, for 35 minutes. Remove from the heat and leave the jam to cool, then ladle into warm, sterilized glass jars and seal. Store in a cool, dark place.

MARMELLATA DI PRUGNE

1 kg/2¼ lb plums, halved and stoned
500 g/1 lb 2 oz sugar

RHUBARB JAM

Put the rhubarb in a bowl, add the sugar, cover and leave to stand for 2 hours. Pour the mixture into a saucepan, bring to the boil and cook, stirring constantly, for about 30 minutes. To see if it is done, pour a little of the mixture on to a small plate. If it slides slowly, the jam is almost ready. Stir in the orange rind and cook for a further 5 minutes. Ladle into warm, sterilized glass jars and leave to cool, then seal. Store in a cool, dry place.

MARMELLATA DI RABARBARO

2 kg/4½ lb rhubarb, trimmed and chopped
1 kg/2¼ lb sugar
grated rind of 1 orange

GRAPE JAM

Any type of grapes may be used. Put the grapes in a saucepan and crush. Remove all the seeds but leave the skins. Add the sugar and cook over a low heat, stirring occasionally, until the mixture reaches setting point. Ladle the jam into warm, sterilized glass jars and seal tightly. Store in a cool, dry place.

MARMELLATA D'UVA

2 kg/4½ lb grapes
1 kg/2¼ lb sugar

GARLIC

WINE

1

MENUS BY CELEBRATED CHEFS

→

THE MENUS

Pulling together a menu requires equal amounts of skill and imagination. *The Silver Spoon* rounds off its presentation of over 2,000 recipes with a set of truly exquisite menus supplied by some of the best-known Italian chefs of the past fifty years.

Italian cuisine is revered throughout the world and, for this new English-language edition we have included a number of international chefs who are truly worldwide ambassadors of fine Italian cuisine. Though they may not be working in Italy (and, in fact, some of them were not even born there), each is playing their part in keeping the standard of Italian cuisine at the level of excellence now acknowledged throughout the world.

This section includes signature dishes from some of the most highly respected chefs in the world, be they Italian born or American, living in the centre of Rome or the heart of Sydney. The list below illustrates not only the immense regard in which we hold Italian cuisine, but also its universal appeal.

The Silver Spoon Guest Chefs:

Aimo & Nadia	Italy
Lidia Bastianich	United States
Mario Batali	United States
Nino Bergese	Italy
Gianfranco Bolognesi	Italy
Carlo Brovelli	Italy
Arrigo Cipriani	Italy
Franco Colombani	Italy
Enzo Deprà	Italy
Maria Pia de Razza-Klein	New Zealand
Alfonso e Livia Jaccarino	Italy
Giorgio Locatelli	United Kingdom
Stefano Manfredi	Australia
Gualtiero Marchesi	Italy
Karen Martini	Australia
Gianluigi Morini	Italy
Fulvio Pierangelini	Italy
Stefano de Pieri	Australia
Ruth Rogers and Rose Gray	United Kingdom
Ezio Santin	Italy
Nadia Santini	Italy
Gianfranco Vissani	Italy
Aldo Zilli	United Kingdom

Aimo & Nadia

Il Luogo di Aimo e Nadia
Via Montecuccoli 6
Milan
Italy

This is a perfect husband and wife partnership in the kitchen as well as in real life. Aimo knows the secrets of every type of meat, vegetable or other ingredient, while Nadia transforms Aimo's daily shopping trip into recipes. Having moved to Milan in 1946, Aimo started his long and splendid career as a kitchen help and quickly worked his way up, moving to manage his own restaurant in 1955. He has never forgotten the lessons learned from his mother (an excellent cook in private homes who spent seven years in France) and her recipes, which he has perfected with flair and skill. He is a keen researcher of raw ingredients, which are always strictly Italian and strictly seasonal, enhanced by the extra virgin olive oil that underlines the simplicity of all dishes by Aimo and Nadia. In their elegant Milan restaurant these two Tuscan nomads (they met when very young and have been married for over 40 years) test and test again, approve and change when change is needed. Chefs and custodians of Italian traditions, yet aware of modern ideas, Aimo and Nadia have strong principles – fast cooking, no cream, very little butter, a lot of olive oil as dressing and an abundance of vegetables and aromatic herbs. Typical dishes from their restaurant include cream of cannellini beans with black borlotti beans, fresh anchovies with a ricotta filling, spaghetti with spring onions and red chilli, warm Italian bacon with a purée of spinach, warm ricotta with radicchio, Norcia lamb with fresh ginger and frozen honey mousse.

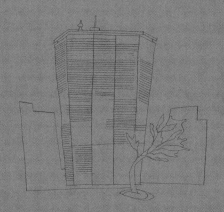

MENUS

ZUPPETTA DI MARE CON LENTICCHIE

SPAGHETTI AL CIPOLLOTTO E PEPERONCINO

CAPPELLO DI VITELLO SANATO ALL'UVA FRAGOLA

CROSTATA DI FARINA DI CASTAGNE FARCITA CON PERE

SEAFOOD STEW WITH LENTILS

ZUPPETTA DI MARE CON LENTICCHIE

Serves 4

3 tablespoons olive oil, plus extra for drizzling
1 celery stick, chopped
1 carrot, chopped
1 onion, chopped
100 g/3½ oz cooked lentils
250 g/9 oz fish and seafood, such as sea bass fillets, prepared squid, peeled prawns, peeled langoustines and scrubbed clams
300 ml/½ pint Fish Stock (see page 208–9)
1 tomato, chopped
1 fresh flat-leaf parsley sprig, chopped
1 fresh basil sprig, chopped
salt and pepper

Heat 1 tablespoon of the olive oil in a frying pan, add 1 tablespoon each of the celery, carrot and onion and cook over a low heat, stirring occasionally, for 5 minutes. Stir in the lentils and cook for a few minutes more. Heat the remaining olive oil in a shallow saucepan, add the remaining celery, carrot and onion and cook over a low heat, stirring occasionally, for 5 minutes. Add the sea bass and the squid, increase the heat to high and cook for 1 minute, then add the prawns, langoustines, clams and lentil mixture. Pour in the stock, season with salt and pepper and cook until the fish is tender. Just before removing the pan from the heat, add the tomato, parsley and basil. Serve with a drizzle of olive oil.

SPAGHETTI WITH SPRING ONIONS AND RED CHILLI

SPAGHETTI AL CIPOLLOTTO E PEPERONCINO

Serves 4

3 tablespoons olive oil, plus extra for drizzling
2 bay leaves
5 fresh thyme leaves
5 fresh oregano leaves
3 garlic cloves, chopped
500 g/1 lb 2 oz spring onions, white part only, cut into thin strips
100 g/3½ oz tomatoes, peeled, seeded and diced
½ tablespoon chopped fresh red chilli
175 ml/6 fl oz Vegetable Stock (see page 209)
300 g/11 oz spaghetti
5 fresh basil leaves, shredded
salt

Heat the oil a shallow saucepan with the bay leaves, thyme and oregano over a low heat, add the garlic and spring onions and cook for 15–20 minutes until the spring onions are reduced in volume to about 60 per cent. Add the tomatoes and chilli to the pan and cook for about 5 minutes, gradually adding the stock. Cook the pasta in a large pan of salted, boiling water for 8–10 minutes until al dente, then drain. Tip it into the sauce and toss over a high heat for 1 minute. Garnish with the basil, drizzle with a little olive oil and serve.

SHOULDER OF VEAL WITH UVA FRAGOLA

Place the grapes in a saucepan, add 150 ml/ ¼ pint of the stock and cook over a medium heat for 15 minutes, then strain the liquid into a bowl. Put the celery, carrot, onion and shallot into a shallow saucepan. Season the veal with salt and pepper and add it to the pan with the pork fat or bacon, bouquet garni, cloves, garlic and olive oil. Cook over a medium-high heat until the meat is browned all over, then lower the heat to medium and cook for 45 minutes, basting with the remaining stock. Pour in the grape juice and cook for a further 45 minutes, adding a little more stock if necessary. Lift the meat out of the pan and remove and discard the cloves, bouquet garni and pork fat or bacon. Strain the cooking juices into a jug and season with salt and pepper. Slice the meat, place it on a warm serving dish and pour the sauce over it. Serve with a purée of potatoes.

CAPPELLO DI VITELLO SANATO ALL'UVA FRAGOLA

Serves 4

200 g/7 oz uva fragola (strawberry-flavoured grapes)

750 ml/1¼ pints Meat Stock (see page 208)

½ celery stick, chopped

½ carrot, chopped

½ onion, chopped

1 shallot, chopped

1-kg/2¼-lb shoulder of veal

40 g/1½ oz pork fat or streaky bacon

1 bouquet garni

2 cloves

1 garlic clove

5 tablespoons olive oil

salt and pepper

puréed potatoes, to serve

CHESTNUT FLOUR PIE WITH PEARS

Sift together both types of flour into a mound and make a well in the centre. Add the egg, 50 g/2 oz of the sugar and the butter. Knead to make a smooth dough, then wrap and leave to rest in the refrigerator for 30 minutes. Chop 50 g/2 oz of the pears, place in a saucepan with the remaining sugar and cook over a medium heat for 30 minutes. Transfer the cooked pears to a food processor and process to a purée. Preheat the oven to 180°C/350°F/Gas Mark 4. Cut off two-thirds of the dough and roll out on a lightly floured surface, then use to line a tart tin. Slice the remaining pears. Pour the confectioner's custard into the pastry case and top with the remaining pears. Spoon the melted chocolate over them. Roll out the remaining pastry and use to cover the pie, sealing and trimming the edges. Bake for 30 minutes.

CROSTATA DI FARINA DI CASTAGNE FARCITA CON PERE

Serves 4

50 g/2 oz plain flour, plus extra for dusting

75 g/2¾ oz chestnut flour

1 egg

65 g/2½ oz caster sugar

75 g/2¾ oz unsalted butter

100 g/3½ oz pears, peeled and cored

6 tablespoons Confectioner's Custard (see page 1039)

50 g/2 oz plain or dark chocolate, melted

Lidia Bastianich

Felidia
243 East 58th Street
New York
United States of America

For Lidia Bastianich, every meal is a celebration. The genesis of this love for food, and the desire to share it, was her early childhood by the Adriatic Sea in the Istrian town of Pula. Her grandparents operated a trattoria, cultivating the produce that they ate and served. She has fond memories of distilling grappa and making wine, harvesting olives for olive oil, and curing meats such as prosciutto and pancetta. With her grandmother she would visit the communal mill to grind wheat for bread and pasta. In 1959 Lidia Bastianich and her family embarked on new lives in the United States of America. She mastered baking and cake decorating as a teenager working part time in a bakery, but soon opened her first restaurant where she refined further dishes. Other restaurant businesses followed. In 1981 her flagship, the award-winning Felidia, was launched, housed in an elegantly appointed brownstone building on the Upper East Side of Manhattan. Felidia clearly established Lidia Bastianich as a leader in the development of Italian cuisine: fine cooking with the freshest of ingredients; pure unaffected flavours; and provincial delicacies with an innovative touch. It is the culinary heritage and regional fare of her native soil, especially Friuli-Venezia-Giulia in northern Italy, that Lidia Bastianich interprets in her restaurants, on television and in print. She is renowned for the warmth and passion she brings to all her culinary endeavours and for encouraging families to cook and dine together. Lidia Bastianich's formative affinity with the yield of the land engendered her profound respect for seasonal ingredients and has delivered ongoing popular and critical acclaim.

MENUS

GAMBERI 'STILE SCAMPI'

ZITE CON SALSICCIA, CIPOLLE E FINOCCCHIO

POLLO E PATATE DI NONNA ERMINIA

CROSTATA DI CIOCCOLATO, NOCCIOLE E ARANCIA

PRAWNS IN THE SCAMPI STYLE

Heat the olive oil in a small frying pan over a medium heat. Add the garlic and cook for about 1 minute until pale golden. Stir in the shallots, season generously with salt and pepper and cook, shaking the pan, for about 2 minutes until the shallots are wilted. Add half the wine, bring to the boil and cook until about half of the liquid has evaporated. Stir in 1 tablespoon of the lemon juice and cook until almost all the liquid has evaporated. Transfer the mixture to a small bowl and leave to cool completely. Add the butter, parsley and tarragon and beat until blended. Spoon the flavoured butter on to a 30-cm/12-inch length of cling film and roll it into a log shape, wrapping it up completely. Chill in the refrigerator. (The flavoured butter can be made several hours or up to a few days in advance.) Preheat the oven to 240°C/475°F/Gas Mark 9. Peel the prawns, leaving the tail and last shell segment intact, and devein them. Place the prawns flat on a work surface and, starting at the thick end, make a horizontal cut along the centre of the prawns extending about three-quarters of the way through. Pat the prawns dry. Using some of the flavoured butter, lightly grease a shallow baking tin, such as a Swiss roll tin, or ovenproof sauté pan into which the prawns will fit comfortably without touching. Place each prawn on the work surface with the underside of the tail facing away from you. With your fingers, roll each half of the slit part of the prawn in towards and underneath the tail, forming a number 6-shape on each side of the prawn and lifting the tail up. Arrange the prawns, tails upwards, in the prepared tin or sauté pan as you work, leaving a space between them. Cut the remaining flavoured butter into 1-cm/½-inch cubes and scatter them among the prawns. Mix the remaining wine and lemon juice and add to the pan. Sprinkle the thyme sprigs over and around the prawns, season with salt and pepper and roast for about 5 minutes until the prawns are firm, crunchy and barely opaque in the centre. Transfer the prawns to a hot serving dish or divide among hot plates. Drain the cooking juices into a small pan. Bring to the boil over a high heat and boil for 1–2 minutes until the sauce is slightly thickened. Spoon or strain the sauce over the prawns and serve.

GAMBERI 'STILE SCAMPI'

Serves 6

2 tablespoons extra virgin olive oil

3 large garlic cloves, crushed

2 tablespoons finely chopped shallots

120 ml/4 fl oz dry white wine

2 tablespoons freshly squeezed lemon juice, strained

120 g/4 oz unsalted butter, at room temperature

2 teaspoons finely chopped fresh flat-leaf parsley

2 teaspoons finely chopped fresh tarragon

36 unpeeled raw tiger prawns (about 1.6 kg/3½ lb)

6–8 fresh thyme sprigs

salt and pepper

ZITE CON SALSICCIA,
CIPOLLE E FINOCCHIO

ZITE WITH SAUSAGE, ONIONS AND FENNEL

Serves 6

1 tablespoon sea salt

450 g/1 lb sweet Italian sausage
(without fennel seeds)

1 large fennel bulb with stem
and fronds (about 450 g/1 lb), trimmed
and halved lengthways

5 tablespoons extra virgin olive oil

2 onions, halved and sliced

$\frac{1}{2}$ teaspoon salt

$\frac{1}{2}$ teaspoon chilli flakes

150 g/5 oz tomato purée

450 g/1 lb zite (long tubes of dried pasta)

fennel fronds

80 g/3 oz pecorino, Parmesan
or grana padano cheese, freshly grated

Bring a large pan of water with the salt to boiling point. Meanwhile, remove the sausage from its casing and break the meat up with your fingers. Slice the fennel halves lengthways into 5-mm/$\frac{1}{4}$-inch thick slices. Separate the slivers of fennel if they are attached at the base and cut into 5-cm/2-inch long batons. Heat the olive oil in a frying pan over a medium-high heat, add the sausage meat and cook, stirring and breaking it up with a wooden spoon, for about 1–1$\frac{1}{2}$ minutes until it is sizzling and beginning to brown. Push the sausage to one side, add the onion slices and cook, stirring constantly, for about 2 minutes until they are sizzling and wilting, then stir them in with the meat. Push the mixture to one side, add the fennel batons and cook for about 1 minute until wilted, then stir into the sausage and onion mixture. Sprinkle in half the salt and push to one side again. Add the chilli flakes and toast for 30 seconds, then stir them in. Move the mixture to the sides of the pan, add the tomato purée and cook, stirring constantly, for 1–2 minutes until it is sizzling and caramelizing, then stir it into the sausage mixture. Ladle 750 ml/1$\frac{1}{4}$ pints of the salted, boiling water into the frying pan, stir well and bring the liquid to the boil. Lower the heat and simmer for about 6 minutes until the fennel is soft but not mushy. Meanwhile, add the pasta to the pan of boiling water, stir and bring back to the boil, then cook for about 8 minutes until almost al dente. Check the sauce which should not become too thick – if necessary, stir in another 250 ml/8 fl oz of the boiling pasta water. When the sauce is done, adjust the seasoning if necessary. When the pasta is al dente, lift it out of the pan with a spider (pasta spoon) or slotted spoon, drain briefly and add to the simmering sauce. Toss the pasta with the sauce, adding more pasta cooking water if the sauce seems too thick. Sprinkle with the fennel fronds and cook, tossing constantly, for 2 minutes until the pasta is perfectly al dente and coated with the sauce. Remove the frying pan from the heat, sprinkle the grated cheese over the pasta and toss to combine. Transfer to warm pasta bowls and serve.

ERMINIA'S CHICKEN AND POTATOES

Trim off excess skin and all visible fat from the chicken and cut the drumsticks from the thighs. If using breast halves, cut into two small pieces. Halve the bacon rashers crossways, roll each strip into a neat, tight cylinder and secure with a cocktail stick, cutting off the end so only a small piece protrudes. Pour the rapeseed oil into a frying pan and set over a high heat. Sprinkle the chicken with ¼ teaspoon salt on all sides. When the oil is very hot, add the chicken pieces skin side down, about 2.5 cm/ 1 inch apart. Cook for several minutes to brown the underside, then turn and cook for 7–10 minutes until golden brown on all sides. If using breast pieces, cook for only about 5 minutes, removing them from the oil as soon as they are golden. Adjust the heat to maintain a steady sizzling and colouring. Remove the crisped chicken pieces with tongs to a bowl. Meanwhile, toss the potatoes with the olive oil and ¼ teaspoon salt in a bowl. When all the chicken has been cooked, pour off the frying oil from the pan. Return the pan to medium heat and, when hot, add all the potatoes, cut side down, in a single layer. Scrape all the olive oil out of the bowl into the frying pan with a spatula; drizzle over a little more oil if the pan seems dry. Cook the potatoes for about 4 minutes to form a crust, then move them around the pan, still cut side down, for about 7 minutes more until brown and crisp. Turn them over and cook for a further 2 minutes. Add the onion wedges and rosemary to the pan and toss with the potatoes. Return the chicken pieces – not breast pieces – to the pan, together with any juices that have accumulated, and add the bacon rolls. Increase the heat slightly and carefully turn and tumble the chicken, potatoes and onion to coat with the pan juices. Spread everything out in the pan with as many potatoes on the base as possible to keep crisping up, and cover. Lower the heat to medium and cook, shaking the pan occasionally, for about 7 minutes, then uncover and tumble the chicken pieces and potatoes again. Cover and cook for a further 7–8 minutes, adding the breast pieces, if using, at this point. Tumble the mixture again, cover and cook for 10 minutes more. Remove the lid, turn the chicken pieces again and cook, un-covered, for about 10 minutes to evaporate the moisture and caramelize the mixture. Taste and adjust the seasoning if neces-sary. Turn the chicken pieces occasionally until they are golden and the potatoes are cooked through. Serve immediately.

POLLO E PATATE DI NONNA ERMINIA

Serves 4–6

1.2 kg/2½ lb chicken legs or portions

120–175 g/4–6 oz bacon rashers

120 ml/4 fl oz rapeseed oil

½ teaspoon salt or more to taste

450 g/1 lb new potatoes, halved

2 tablespoons extra virgin olive oil,

plus extra if necessary

2 medium-small onions, quartered lengthways

2 fresh rosemary sprigs with plenty of needles

1 –2 pickled cherry peppers, seeded

CROSTATA WITH CHOCOLATE, HAZELNUTS AND ORANGE

CROSTATA DI CIOCCOLATO, NOCCIOLE E ARANCIA

Serves 6–8

1 quantity Shortcrust Pastry (1) (see page 1008), chilled
150 g/5 oz plain chocolate, cut into pieces
whipped cream, to serve (optional)

For the filling
40 g/1½ oz hazelnuts, toasted and skins rubbed off
1 orange
130 g/4½ oz sugar
80 g/3 oz butter, softened
2 eggs
1 tablespoon plain flour
80 g/3 oz plain chocolate, chopped in very small pieces
2 tablespoons orange liqueur, such as Cointreau or Grand Marnier

Place a baking stone, if you have one, on the middle rack of the oven and preheat the oven to 180°C/350°F/Gas Mark 4. Roll out the dough and use to line a 23-cm/9-inch fluted, loose-based quiche tin, then chill in the refrigerator. Melt the chocolate in a heatproof bowl set over a pan of barely simmering water, stirring until it is completely smooth. Pour the chocolate into the pastry case and spread it evenly over the base. Put the hazelnuts in a food processor and pulse to chop finely but be careful not to overprocess. Tip the nuts into a bowl. Using a vegetable peeler, pare thin strips of orange rind about 5 cm/2 inches long. Stack up a few strips at a time and slice them lengthways into very thin slivers, then cut the slivers crossways into tiny pieces like glitter or small confetti – you should have about 2 tablespoons. Put the sugar and butter in the food processor and process for about 30 seconds until smooth. With the motor running, add the eggs through the feeder tube and process for about 1 minute until smooth and slightly thickened. Scrape down the sides of the bowl. With the motor running, add the flour through the feeder tube and process until smooth. Scrape down the sides of the bowl again. Add the orange rind, chocolate and hazelnuts and pulse for 1–2 seconds to incorporate. Finally, add the orange liqueur and process for just 1 second. Scrape the filling from the sides and blade of the processor bowl, stir and pour it into the pastry case. Smooth the surface with a spatula. Bake for 35–40 minutes until the filling is puffed, firm in the centre and a cocktail stick inserted in the centre comes out clean. The crust should be nicely browned as well. Transfer the tart to a wire rack to cool and serve slightly warm or at room temperature, with whipped cream if you like.

Mario Batali

Across the West Village and theatre district of Manhattan, in an expanding empire of eateries, Mario Batali is reinventing and redefining Italian culinary traditions. His landmark restaurant is Babbo Ristorante e Enoteca where distinctive, innovative food with vibrant and complex flavours is served. After studying the Golden Age of Spanish theatre at university, Mario Batali briefly enrolled at Le Cordon Bleu in London, England. However, his real culinary adventure began in earnest with an apprenticeship to London's legendary chef, Marco Pierre White. Several years of intense training followed in the small hillside village of Borgo Capanne in Northern Italy. Now, traditional and regionally inspired recipes and techniques steer his contemporary interpretations. Mario Batali's devotion to regional food extends outside Italy to the seasonal markets and artisan-made goods of New York's Greenwich Village. While Italian staples are imported, local farmers provide fresh produce including forgotten or heirloom varietals. Mario Batali proudly makes his own salumi, such as pancetta and coppa. The overarching philosophy that guides him is to ask, 'what are the best ingredients at hand today?' Accordingly, new, original dishes are constantly added to the menu at Babbo and full-bodied flavours abound. From marinated fresh anchovies with watermelon, radishes and lobster oil, to gooseliver ravioli with balsamic vinegar and brown butter, to yogurt cheesecake with lemon cream and blackcurrant jam. In his cookbooks and on television he invites people to revel in spirited Italian cuisine. Combined with flattering reviews and prestigious awards this has made Mario Batali one of the most recognisable chefs in the United States.

Babbo Ristorante e Enoteca
110 Waverly Place
New York
United States of America

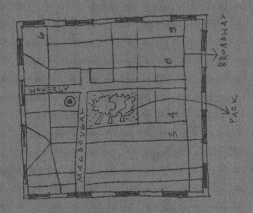

MENUS

SFORMATO DI PISELLI IN VINAIGRETTE DI CAROTA

RAVIOLI DI GUANCIA DI VITELLO CON FEGATINI E TARTUFO NERO

PICCIONE 'AL MATTONE' CON MOSTARDA DI PORCINI

BUDINO DI SEMOLINA CON RABARBARO E SCIROPPO DI MENTUCCIA

SWEET PEA FLAN WITH CARROT VINAIGRETTE

*SFORMATO DI PISELLI
IN VINAIGRETTE DI CAROTA*

Serves 6

cooking spray, for oiling

50 g/2 oz fresh mint leaves

350 g/12 oz fresh or frozen peas

3 eggs

175 ml/6 fl oz double cream

1 teaspoon freshly squeezed lemon juice

300 ml/½ pint carrot juice

1 teaspoon clear honey

1 tablespoon champagne vinegar

120 ml/4 fl oz extra virgin olive oil

350 g/12 oz young pea vines

50 ml/2 fl oz Parsley Oil (see below)

sea salt and pepper

Parmesan cheese shavings, to garnish

For the parsley oil

475 ml/16 fl oz extra virgin olive oil

1 bunch of fresh flat-leaf parsley, chopped

1 teaspoon sea salt

Before preparing the parsley oil, chill the olive oil for 2 hours, then process all the ingredients in a food processor until nearly smooth and uniformly green. These quantities will make about 475 ml/16 fl oz which may be stored in the refrigerator for 24 hours. Preheat the oven to 180°C/350°F/Gas Mark 4. Oil six ramekins with cooking spray. Bring about 2.8 litres/5 pints water to the boil and add 1 tablespoon sea salt. Prepare an ice bath. Blanch the mint leaves and peas in the boiling water for 1 minute, then drain and immerse in the ice bath. Drain again, transfer to a food processor and process to a purée. Pass the mixture through a food mill into a bowl, stir in the eggs, cream and lemon juice and season with salt and pepper. Spoon the pea mixture into the ramekins so that they are about two-thirds full. Place the ramekins in a roasting tin, add boiling water to come about halfway up the sides and cover the tin with foil. Bake for 25–30 minutes until the mixture is just set in the centres. Remove from the oven and leave to cool. Meanwhile, bring 250 ml/8 fl oz of the carrot juice to the boil in a heavy-based saucepan over a high heat. Lower the heat to medium and cook until reduced to 50 ml/2 fl oz. Pour the reduced juice into a bowl and whisk in the honey and vinegar. Gradually whisk in the olive oil and then stir in the remaining carrot juice. Season to taste with salt and pepper. To serve, carefully run a knife around the edge of each cooled flan and turn out on to the centre of each of six chilled plates. Toss the pea vines with the carrot vinaigrette and season with salt and pepper if necessary. Divide the pea vines among the plates, partially covering the flans. Drizzle with any remaining vinaigrette and the parsley oil, garnish with the Parmesan and serve immediately.

BEEF CHEEK RAVIOLI

Preheat the oven to 200°C/400°F/Gas Mark 6. Heat the olive oil in a large, ovenproof frying pan with a lid. Add the onion and celery and cook over a low heat, stirring occasionally, for about 10 minutes until very soft but not browned. Increase the heat to high, add the meat, in batches if necessary, and cook, turning frequently until browned all over. Add the wine and bring the mixture to the boil, stirring and scraping up the sediment from the base of the pan. Stir in the tomatoes and rosemary and bring back to the boil. Cover the pan, transfer to the oven and cook for 1 hour or until the meat is very tender. Remove from the oven and leave to cool, then skim off any excess fat. Transfer the mixture to a food processor and pulse until smooth. Roll out the pasta dough with a pasta machine on its thinnest setting, then cut the dough into 10-cm/4-inch squares. Place 1 tablespoon of the beef filling in the centre of each square, bring two opposite corners together to form a triangle and press the edges firmly together to seal. (You can freeze the ravioli on baking sheets interleaved with greaseproof paper or baking parchment at this point.) Bring about 5.5 litres/9½ pints water to the boil and add 2 tablespoons salt. Meanwhile, heat the butter in a sauté pan over a high heat until it begins to brown, then add the chicken canapés and cook for 1 minute. Add a few tablespoons of the salted, boiling water, then add the truffles and cook for 1 minute more. Cook the ravioli in the salted, boiling water for 2 minutes or until they rise to the surface, then remove with a slotted spoon and add to the sauté pan. Add half the chopped parsley and the pecorino and toss gently for 1 minute over a medium heat. Place three ravioli on each of eight warmed plates, spoon the sauce over them, top with the remaining parsley and sprinkle with extra pecorino.

RAVIOLI DI GUANCIA DI VITELLO CON FEGATINI E TARTUFO NERO

Serves 8

3 tablespoons extra virgin olive oil

1 white onion, cut into 5-mm/¼-inch dice

½ celery stick, cut into 5-mm/¼-inch dice

900 g/2 lb beef cheeks, brisket

or chuck steak, trimmed

and cut into 2.5-cm/1-inch cubes

475 ml/16 fl oz red wine

175 g/6 oz fresh tomatoes, chopped

or drained canned chopped tomatoes

1 teaspoon fresh rosemary, chopped

1 quantity Fresh Pasta Dough (see page 268)

225 g/8 oz unsalted butter

1 quantity Chicken Liver Canapés (see page 123)

2 tablespoons sliced black truffles

1 bunch of fresh flat-leaf parsley, chopped

4 tablespoons pecorino cheese, freshly grated,

plus extra for serving

PICCIONE 'AL MATTONE' CON MOSTARDA DI PORCINI

Serves 4

2 tablespoons clear honey

50 ml/2 fl oz balsamic vinegar

250 ml/8 fl oz extra virgin olive oil

$^1/_2$ bunch of fresh thyme, leaves only

1 large red onion, thinly sliced

4 pigeons, cleaned and breast and backbones removed

salt and pepper

For the roasted beetroot farrotto

2 large red beetroots, trimmed

2 tablespoons extra virgin olive oil

2 tablespoons pomegranate molasses

175 g/6 oz farro

120 ml/4 fl oz Chicken Stock (see page 209)

sea salt and pepper

Parmesan cheese, freshly grated, to serve

For the porcini mustard

$^1/_2$ red onion, finely chopped

250 ml/8 fl oz balsamic vinegar

50 g/2 oz dried porcini

4 tablespoons Dijon mustard

4 tablespoons extra virgin olive oil

4 tablespoons finely chopped, drained bottled or canned black truffles

BARBECUED PIGEON AL MATTONE WITH PORCINI MUSTARD

You will need four house bricks, well wrapped in foil. Mix together the honey, vinegar, olive oil, thyme leaves and onion in a non-metallic dish large enough to hold the pigeons in one layer. Add the pigeons, turning to coat, cover and leave to marinate in the refrigerator, turning occasionally, for at least 4 hours. Meanwhile, make the porcini mustard. Mix together the onion, vinegar, porcini and 250 ml/8 fl oz water in a heavy-based saucepan and bring to the boil, then lower the heat and simmer until the liquid has reduced by half. Pour the mixture into a bowl and leave to cool, then transfer to a food processor, add the mustard and olive oil and process until thoroughly combined. Pass the mixture through a strainer into a bowl and stir in the truffles. This quantity makes 475 ml/16 fl oz which may be stored in an airtight container in the refrigerator for up to 2 weeks. For the roasted beetroot farrotto, preheat the oven to 200°C/400°F/Gas Mark 6 and cut out two squares of foil each large enough to contain a beetroot. Place the beetroots on the foil squares, drizzle with the olive oil and season. Wrap and roast for about 40 minutes until tender. Remove from the oven and leave until cool enough to handle, then peel, halve and cut into half-moon slices about 5 mm/$^1/_4$ inch thick. Place the slices in a bowl, toss gently with the molasses and season, then set aside. Bring about 2.75 litres/4$^3/_4$ pints water to the boil and add 1 tablespoon salt. Set up an ice bath. Cook the farro in the boiling water for about 20 minutes until tender but not quite cooked through, then drain and immerse in the ice bath. Drain again and transfer to a sauté pan. Add the stock and beetroots and toss over a high heat for about 3 minutes until most of the stock has been absorbed and the farro is completely cooked through. Adjust the seasoning and sprinkle with the Parmesan. Preheat the barbecue. Place the bricks on the grill and heat until very hot; use tongs to handle them from here on. Remove the pigeons from the marinade and pat dry with kitchen towels, then place them, breast side down, on the grill. Carefully place a hot brick on top of each and cook for 6 minutes. Remove the bricks, turn the pigeons, replace the bricks and grill for a further 4–6 minutes until medium rare. To serve, divide the farrotto among four warm plates, placing it in the centre of each. Place a pigeon on top of each mound and top each with 1 tablespoon porcini mustard.

SEMOLINA BUDINO WITH RHUBARB AND MINT MARMELLATA

Grease eight ramekins with butter, then sprinkle them with sugar, turning to coat evenly, and tip out the excess. Place the ramekins in a roasting tin large enough to hold them with at least 2.5 cm/1 inch between them. Melt the remaining butter and leave to cool. Put the sliced rhubarb and 120 g/4 oz of the sugar in a saucepan and scrape in the pulp from inside one vanilla pod using the point of a knife. Cook over a medium heat, stirring frequently, for about 15 minutes until the rhubarb is soft. Remove from the heat and leave to cool completely. Meanwhile, preheat the oven to 200°C/400°F/Gas Mark 6. Beat the egg yolks with 175 g/6 oz of the remaining sugar with an electric mixer. Add the vanilla essence and melted butter, then beat in the milk. Mix together the two types of flour in another bowl, then gradually beat them into the egg yolk mixture. Fold in the rhubarb with a rubber spatula. Whisk the egg whites with the salt until foamy, then gradually whisk in 2 tablespoons of the remaining sugar until soft peaks form. Fold the egg whites into the egg yolk mixture. Divide the mixture among the ramekins and add boiling water to the roasting tin to come about one-third of the way up their sides. Cover with foil and bake for 25–30 minutes until the budini begin to puff up. Remove the foil and bake for a further 10–15 minutes until the budini are pale golden in colour and set. Transfer the ramekins to a rack to cool. To make the marmellata, put the rhubarb and sugar in a large saucepan and cook over a low heat, stirring until the sugar has dissolved. Scrape the pulp from the inside of the vanilla pod into the pan, add the mint and cook, stirring, for about 10 minutes until the rhubarb is tender but not mushy. Transfer the mixture to a shallow dish and leave to cool, then discard the mint. Pour the cream into a bowl and scrape the pulp from the remaining vanilla pod into it. Whip with an electric mixer on medium speed until soft peaks form. Gradually add the remaining sugar and whip until the cream holds its shape. Turn out each budino on to individual plates, top with some of the marmellata and serve with a spoonful of the vanilla cream.

BUDINO DI SEMOLINA CON RABARBARO E SCIROPPO DI MENTUCCIA

Serves 8

120 g/4 oz unsalted butter, plus extra for greasing

350 g/12 oz sugar, plus extra for sprinkling

3 rhubarb sticks, cut into 2-cm/³/₄-inch slices

2 vanilla pods, split lengthways

4 eggs, separated

¹/₂ teaspoon vanilla essence

175 ml/6 fl oz milk

4 tablespoons semolina flour

5 tablespoons cake flour

pinch of sea salt

250 ml/8 fl oz double cream

For the rhubarb and mint marmellata

8 rhubarb sticks, finely chopped

350 g/12 oz sugar

1 vanilla pod, split lengthways

3–4 large fresh mint sprigs

Nino Bergese

Nino Bergese was possibly the most authoritative Italian chef of the twentieth century. Even in retirement he still retained the unquestioned authority of a true master and every young chef would have loved to have worked within his great shadow. He was born in 1904 and died in 1977 and his career was meteoric. At the age of 16 he was already assistant chef in the distinguished kitchens of the Piedmont Count Costa Carrù della Trinità, at whose tables Italian and Egyptian royalty and the dukes of Aosta and Genoa were guests. He moved to work for Count Arborio Mella di Sant'Elia, master of ceremonies of the royal house of Savoy. The twenty-second birthday of Prince Umberto di Savoia was celebrated on 15 September 1926 at the royal family's summer residence at Villa Crocetta, between Intra and Pallanza. Bergese prepared his famous torta fiorentina for the heir to the Italian throne who went on to request it for a further three days. Later, there were other great houses and other noble names, then all this was interrupted by war. With the return of peace, Bergese said goodbye to aristocratic homes and made his debut among the winding alleys of Genoa in Vico Indoratori. His tiny, yet chic restaurant La Santa became a landmark in the 1960s for all those intent on discovering culinary delights such as creamed risotto and spaghetti. 'Dishes should be created with the best ingredients and with a clear aim in mind,' explained Nino Bergese to those who, wanting to enter his profession, asked for his advice. His book Mangiare da Re (Eat Like a King) is a collection of 512 of his countless recipes – an expert's pantry from which we have taken three of his most famous dishes.

MENUS

RISO MANTECATO

SELLA DI VITELLO ALLA BERGESE

TORTA FIORENTINA

CREAMED RISOTTO

Heat the oil with 50 g/2 oz of the butter in a deep saucepan, add the onion and cook over a low heat, stirring occasionally, for about 20 minutes until golden brown. Pass the onion through a fine nylon sieve and return it to the saucepan. Add the wine and vegetable stock, bring to the boil, add the rice and cook for 15 minutes over a medium heat. Remove the pan from the heat and stir in the remaining butter and the Parmesan. Serve the risotto in individual dishes, dressed with the meat stock.

RISO MANTECATO

Serves 8

4 tablespoons olive oil

300 g/11 oz butter • 1 large onion, thinly sliced

350 ml/12 fl oz dry white wine

450 ml/³/₄ pint Vegetable Stock (see page 209)

500 g/1 lb 2 oz risotto rice

100 g/3¹/₂ oz Parmesan cheese, freshly grated

175 ml/6 fl oz hot Meat Stock (see page 208)

SADDLE OF VEAL ALLA BERGESE

Melt the butter in a large, flameproof pan, add the veal and cook, turning occasionally, until brown all over. Pour in the vodka and light it. When the flames have died, pour in the cream, bring to the boil and lower the heat. Add the pancetta and season with pepper. Cook, uncovered, over a medium heat for about 40 minutes until tender. Season with salt if necessary and drain well. Using a sharp knife, detach the meat from the bones and place the bones on a warm serving dish. Slice the meat and arrange it in tiers over the bones. Cover and keep warm. Strain the cooking liquid, reheat if necessary and pour into a sauce boat. Serve the veal with the sauce and vegetables, such as finely diced, buttered carrots, potato browned in butter and baby onions in a sweet and sour sauce.

SELLA DI VITELLO ALLA BERGESE

Serves 8

50 g/2 oz butter

2.5-kg/5¹/₂-lb saddle of veal

350 ml/12 fl oz vodka • 500 ml/18 fl oz double cream

80 g/3 oz smoked pancetta, sliced

salt and white pepper

FLORENTINE TART

Preheat the oven to 180°C/350°F/Gas Mark 4. Grease one or two baking sheets and dust with flour. Prepare a shortcrust pastry dough (see page 1008). Roll out four sheets of dough on a floured surface to 5 mm/¹/₄ inch thick and 30 cm/12 inches square. Place on the prepared baking sheets and bake for 15 minutes, then remove from the oven and leave to cool. Meanwhile, make the confectioner's custard (see page 1039) and leave to cool, stirring occasionally. Spread the custard over three of the pastry squares, place them on top of each other and top with the fourth. Place the sugar and cocoa powder in a heatproof bowl set over barely simmering water and cook, stirring constantly, until melted and smooth. Remove from the heat, quickly cover the pastry with the mixture and leave to cool. To make the royal icing, beat the egg white with 2 tablespoons of the icing sugar in a bowl, beating in more sugar if necessary. Use a small piping bag to decorate the tart with a lattice. Finally, place a dot of icing in the centre of each diamond.

TORTA FIORENTINA

Serves 8-10

For the dough

300 g/11 oz unsalted butter, plus extra for greasing

500 g /1 lb 2 oz plain flour, plus extra for dusting

150 g/5 oz caster sugar • 100 g/3¹/₂ oz cocoa powder

For the confectioner's custard

100 g/3¹/₂ oz plain flour • 125 g/4¹/₄ oz unsalted butter

100 g/3¹/₂ oz cocoa powder • 1 litre/1³/₄ pints milk

200 g/7 oz caster sugar

For the fondant

350 g/12 oz caster sugar • 25 g/1 oz cocoa powder

For the royal icing

¹/₂ egg white • 40 g/1¹/₂ oz icing sugar

Gianfranco Bolognesi

La Frasca
Via Matteotti 38
Castrocaro Terme (FO)
Italy

Pellegrino Artusi's book La scienza in cucina o l'arte di mangiar bene (Science in the Kitchen or The Art of Eating Well), which was first published in 1891, is still a bestseller. However, the doctor from Forlimpopoli in the Romagna region was incapable of even cooking tagliatelle. It was simply a fondness for and an enjoyment of good cooking and a powerful cultural urge that led him to write this highly successful collection of recipes with wisdom and shrewdness. Today it remains as an invaluable benchmark and guide. Gianfranco Bolognesi is an exponent and follower of the same philosophy. By adjusting the generous portions of recipes to modern dietary standards, he perpetuates Artusi's style and ideas. Although, like Artusi, he does not cook, unlike the famous master he can boast an expertise in wine that he puts into practice with great discernment when choosing specific wines to accompany the food. At La Frasca, his restaurant in Castrocaro, his chefs prepare typical local recipes to very high standards and, at the same time, develop ideas that have grown out of Bolognesi's research and creativity. Among the many dishes that regularly star on his menus, the rice savarin with goose salami and porcini, sole with rosemary, black truffle and crispy spinach and the Artusi vegetable mould with giblets must be mentioned. Such dishes have won him his much coveted Michelin stars and have been endorsed by diners, meal after meal, since 1971.

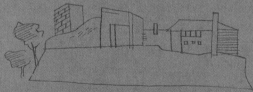

MENUS

TAGLIATELLE ALL'ANTICA CON TARTUFI

PERNICE CON VERZE, SALVIA FRITTA E VERDURE

PANNA COTTA, TORTA DI MANDORLE E ZABAIONE ARTUSIANO

TAGLIATELLE ALL'ANTICA WITH TRUFFLES

Make the pasta dough (see page 268) with the flour and eggs, forming a firm and elastic dough. Roll it out very thinly on a lightly floured surface and cut into 5-mm/¼-inch ribbons. For the sauce, melt the butter in a frying pan, add the prosciutto and cook over a medium heat until softened, taking care that it does not colour. Meanwhile, cook the tagliatelle in plenty of salted, boiling water until al dente, then drain and toss in the frying pan with the prosciutto and butter. Add the Parmesan and mix carefully. Transfer the tagliatelle to a warm serving dish and garnish with the strips of truffle.

TAGLIATELLE ALL'ANTICA CON TARTUFI

Serves 4

For the pasta dough

400 g/14 oz plain flour, plus extra for dusting

4 eggs

For the sauce

100 g/3½ oz butter

100 g/3½ oz prosciutto, diced

50 g/2 oz Parmesan cheese, freshly grated

100 g/3½ oz black truffle,

ideally from Dovadola (Forlì), cut into thin strips

salt

PARTRIDGES WITH SAVOY CABBAGE, FRIED SAGE AND VEGETABLES

Steam or boil the diced vegetables until al dente. Heat 1 tablespoon of the olive oil in a frying pan, add the cabbage, garlic and pancetta and cook over a low heat, stirring occasionally, until crispy. Season to taste with salt and pepper. Separate the breasts and legs of the partridges. Heat 2 tablespoons of the remaining oil in a frying pan, add the partridges and two of the sage leaves and cook, turning occasionally, until tender and golden brown. Remove from the pan and keep warm. Drain off the oil and any fat from the pan, pour in the wine and heat until it has evaporated. Add the game stock and simmer over a low heat for a few minutes, then stir in 25 g/1 oz of the butter. Thinly slice the partridges. Toss the mixed vegetables with the remaining butter and spoon them on to one side of a warm serving dish. Spoon the crispy Savoy cabbage on to the other side, place the partridges on top and sprinkle with the slivers of truffle. Dust the remaining sage leaves with flour. Heat the remaining oil, add the sage leaves and fry until golden brown, then place in the centre of the plate. Spoon the sauce over the partridges and serve. (Make game stock by simmering the discarded parts of the partridges, some vegetables, aromatic herbs and white wine for a few hours, occasionally adding a little Meat Stock [see page 208].)

PERNICE CON VERZE, SALVIA FRITTA E VERDURE

Serves 4

300 g/11 oz mixed diced vegetables, such as carrots, fennel, baby onions and new potatoes

150 ml/¼ pint olive oil

200 g/7 oz Savoy cabbage, shredded

2 garlic cloves, chopped

100 g/3½ oz lean pancetta, diced

4 partridges

18 fresh sage leaves

175 ml/6 fl oz dry white wine

150 ml/¼ pint game stock

100 g/3½ oz butter

50 g/2 oz white truffle, cut into slivers

plain flour, for dusting

salt and pepper

PANNA COTTA, ALMOND TART AND ZABAGLIONE

PANNA COTTA, TORTA DI MANDORLE
E ZABAIONE ARTUSIANO

Serves 4

For the panna cotta
3 eggs
2 egg yolks
120 g/4 oz caster sugar
500 ml/18 fl oz double cream
50 g/2 oz amaretti, lightly crushed

For the caramel
150 g/5 oz caster sugar
150 ml/¼ pint water

For the tart
80 g/3 oz ground almonds
80 g/3 oz plain flour
80 g/3 oz caster sugar
80 g/3 oz unsalted butter
pinch of salt
icing sugar, for dusting

For the zabaglione
2 egg yolks
2 tablespoons caster sugar
175 ml/6 fl oz Marsala

To decorate
red fruits
fresh mint leaves

Preheat the oven to 180°C/350°F/Gas Mark 4. To make the panna cotta, beat together the eggs, egg yolks and sugar until pale and fluffy, then beat in the cream. Strain the mixture into another bowl and stir in the amaretti crumbs. To make the caramel, stir the sugar and water in a saucepan over a low heat until the sugar has dissolved, then cook until hazelnut in colour. Pour the caramel into an ovenproof dish, tilting to coat the inside, then pour in the panna cotta mixture. Place the dish in a roasting tin, add boiling water to come about halfway up the side and bake for about 45 minutes. Remove from the oven, but do not switch it off, and leave to cool. Meanwhile, make the almond tart. Mix all the ingredients, except the icing sugar, to a dough, then shape into a round about 1 cm/½ inch thick. Place on a baking sheet and bake for about 10 minutes. To prepare the zabaglione, beat the egg yolks with the sugar in a heatproof bowl set over a pan of barely simmering water, gradually beating in the Marsala a little at a time. Cut the panna cotta into drop shapes and divide among four dishes, then pour the caramel over the shapes. Place a slice of almond tart, dusted with icing sugar next to the panna cotta and pour the warm zabaglione on the other side. Decorate with red fruits and mint leaves.

Carlo Brovelli

In the 1950s, Il Sole, in Ranco, on the Lombardy side of Lake Maggiore, was a traditional restaurant for day trippers and families. Fish from the lake, fried or cooked in a carpione (sweet and sour sauce), was excellent and finding a free table was no easy task. However, Carlo Brovelli, whose family had been restaurateur-chefs for four generations since 1872, decided that the time had come to change his style of cooking. He had learned all kinds of subtle ways of using local ingredients from his grandmother and uncle and had attended the excellent catering school at Stresa, yet he felt he needed more. As a result, he travelled the world for ten years, 'studying' in the greatest restaurants in Switzerland, France, Germany and Austria, where the excellence of the food is matched by the sophisticated presentation and service. Back in Ranco, assisted by his wife Itala, a wine expert, he revolutionized his old restaurant and, within a few years, had fulfilled his dream: the creation of haute cuisine with fish from his lake, such as red char al Barbaresco, shrimp pastries with foie gras and whitefish with jus, and masterpieces using game, such as mallard, duck and pigeon. His recipes are sophisticated yet never lose touch with local flavours. Carlo Brovelli should also be given credit for having taught a new generation of promising chefs, including his son Davide, who continues the family tradition.

Ristorante Il Sole
Piazza Venezia 5
Ranco (VA)
Italy

MENUS

CAPPESANTE E SEDANO FRITTO

MARGHERITE ALLE UOVA E ASPARAGI

OSSOBUCO DI STORIONE IN GREMOLATA

SPUMONE D'ARANCIA E GRAND MARNIER

SCALLOPS AND FRIED CELERY

CAPPESANTE E SEDANO FRITTO

Serves 4

200 g/7 oz shelled scallops, skirts and corals reserved

250 ml/8 fl oz milk

50 g/2 oz butter

50 ml/2 fl oz dry white wine

1 tablespoon chopped fresh dill

1 tablespoon olive oil

1 celery stick, cut into thin batons

salt and pepper

Rinse the scallops under cold running water for 15 minutes, then place in a bowl, add the milk and leave to soften. Melt the butter in a saucepan, add the scallop skirts and cook for about 4 minutes. Pour in the wine and 250 ml/ 8 fl oz water, season with salt and pepper and bring to the boil. Add the dill, lower the heat and simmer for about 15 minutes, then remove from the heat and strain into a clean pan. Add the scallops and corals and cook for about 5 minutes until tender. Remove the scallops and corals with a slotted spoon, bring the cooking liquid to the boil and cook until slightly reduced. Meanwhile, heat the olive oil in a small pan, add the celery and cook, stirring, for a few minutes. Slice the scallops and arrange them like petals on four warm plates, alternating the white and the coral to create a coloured flower shape. Drizzle with the reduced cooking liquid and garnish with the celery.

RAVIOLI WITH EGGS AND ASPARAGUS

MARGHERITE ALLE UOVA E ASPARAGI

Serves 4

50 g/2 oz butter, melted

1 tablespoon chopped fresh basil

For the pasta dough

250 g/9 oz plain flour, plus extra for dusting

3 egg yolks

1 egg

200 ml/7 fl oz olive oil

salt

For the filling

1 bunch of wild asparagus

5 eggs

50 g/2 oz butter, melted

1 bunch of rocket, finely chopped

salt and pepper

Prepare the pasta dough (see page 268). For the filling, cut off the asparagus tips and steam them until just al dente, then remove from the heat and dice. Beat the eggs with salt and pepper in a bowl. Mix together the butter, eggs, asparagus tips and rocket. Roll out the pasta dough on a lightly floured surface. Spread the filling over one half of the dough. Fold over the other half of the dough and cut out the ravioli with a wheel into a flower shape. Cook in salted boiling water until al dente, then drain, toss gently with the melted butter and the basil.

STURGEON STEAKS IN GREMOLATA

Chop the parsley with the garlic, lemon rind, anchovies and sage. Pour the stock and wine into a saucepan, add the butter and cook over a low heat until slightly reduced. Add the fish and simmer for 10 minutes. Shortly before the end of the cooking time, sprinkle the parsley mixture – gremolata – over the fish, cover and simmer for a further 2 minutes. Transfer the fish steaks to four warm plates and pour the sauce over them. Serve with mixed, boiled vegetables flavoured with vanilla and coriander.

OSSOBUCO DI STORIONE IN GREMOLATA

Serves 4

2 salted anchovies, heads removed,
cleaned and filleted (see page 596),
soaked in cold water for 10 miutes and drained
2 fresh flat-leaf parsley sprigs
1 garlic clove
thinly pared rind of ½ lemon
1 fresh sage sprig
250 ml/8 fl oz Fish Stock (see page 208–9)
5 tablespoons dry white wine
50 g/2 oz butter
4 sturgeon steaks
mixed vegetables, to serve

ORANGE AND GRAND MARNIER MOUSSE

Grate the rind of two of the oranges and thinly pare the rind of the other two, avoiding all traces of bitter white pith. Separate the oranges into segments, removing all traces of pith. Pour the milk into a saucepan, add the grated orange rind and 120 g/4 oz of the sugar, stir well and bring to the boil. Beat the egg yolks in another pan, then pour in the milk in a steady stream, stirring constantly. Cook over a low heat, stirring constantly, until thickened. Strain the mixture into a bowl and leave to cool completely. Stiffly whisk the egg whites in a grease-free bowl, then fold them into the egg yolk mixture, followed by the Grand Marnier. Pour the mousse into a mould or loaf tin and place in the freezer for 6 hours. Cut the remaining orange rind into thin strips. Pour 250 ml/8 fl oz water into a saucepan, add the remaining sugar and the strips of orange rind and bring to the boil, stirring until the sugar has dissolved. Boil the mixture until a thick, translucent syrup forms. Turn out the mousse and cut it into 2-cm/³⁄₄-inch slices. Place the slices on four plates, spoon the syrup and orange rind over them and decorate with the orange segments, arranged like flowers.

SPUMONE D'ARANCIA E GRAND MARNIER

Serves 4

4 oranges
250 ml/8 fl oz milk
200 g/7 oz caster sugar
4 eggs, separated
50 ml/2 fl oz Grand Marnier

Arrigo Cipriani

Harry's Bar
Calle Vallaresso, 1323
Venice
Italy

Giuseppe Cipriani founded his legendary Harry's Bar in Venice in 1931 and was succeeded by his son Arrigo at the end of the 1950s. Nevertheless, he continued to eat at Harry's Bar at least twice a week, simply sitting at a table, perusing the menu, ordering and passing judgement on the dishes just like the other demanding customers. Indeed, Giuseppe Cipriani's school bears fruit: the Bellini, a cocktail made from white peach juice and sparkling white wine, was created in 1948, on the occasion of a great Venetian exhibition devoted to the painter Giovanni Bellini. The Carpaccio Cipriani consists of thin slices of meat covered with a special sauce, which was originally known as universal sauce. However, following the historic Carpaccio exhibition in Venice in 1950, it was renamed in honour of the painter. The colours of the dish – red and yellow – were his favourites. During those years Giuseppe Cipriani created other dishes – still on the menu today – with the aid of Berto Toffolo, his top-ranking chef. These include sole Casanova, langoustines armoricaine, croque monsieur and cream crêpes. Arrigo Cipriani has hired other talented chefs over the years and each one of them has contributed towards the fame of Harry's Bar, not just the original bar in Venice, but also his restaurant in New York, where the ambience and dishes match those which continue to attract swarms of illustrious guests to the Venetian lagoon each year.

MENUS

CARPACCIO CIPRIANI

RISOTTO ALLA PRIMAVERA

SCAMPI AL FORNO

CRESPELLE ALLA CREMA PASTICCIERA

CARPACCIO CIPRIANI

Trim all traces of fat, sinew and gristle from the beef, leaving a small, cylindrical piece, then chill in the refrigerator. When the meat is cold, cut it into extremely thin slices with a very sharp knife. Place the slices of meat on six plates to cover each one entirely. Season lightly with salt and chill in the refrigerator for at least 5 minutes. Stir the Worcestershire sauce and lemon juice into the mayonnaise and add just enough milk so that the sauce is thick enough to coat the back of a tablespoon. Add salt and pepper to taste and add more Worcestershire sauce or lemon juice if necessary. Chill in the refrigerator until required. Remove the meat and sauce from the refrigerator just before serving and drizzle the sauce over the beef.

CARPACCIO CIPRIANI

Serves 6

675-g/1¹/₂-lb lean sirloin

salt

For the Carpaccio sauce

1–2 teaspoons Worcestershire sauce

1 teaspoon lemon juice

200 ml/7 fl oz Mayonnaise (see page 65)

2–3 tablespoons milk

salt and white pepper

SPRING RISOTTO

To prepare the vegetables, heat the olive oil in a large frying pan over a medium heat, add the garlic and cook for about 30 seconds, then remove it from the pan. Add the mushroom caps and cook for 5–6 minutes until softened and the liquid has evaporated. Add the artichokes and cook for 8–10 minutes, then add the onion and cook for a further 2 minutes. Finally, add the courgettes, asparagus, red pepper and leek, increase the heat to high and cook for 10 minutes, stirring frequently. Season to taste with salt and pepper, remove the pan from the heat and set aside. To prepare the risotto, heat the olive oil in a large saucepan, add the onion and cook over a medium heat, stirring occasionally, for 3–5 minutes. Stir in the rice, lower the heat, add about 120 ml/4 fl oz of the stock and bring to the boil, stirring constantly. Gradually add more stock as each addition is absorbed. After about 10 minutes, when the risotto is half-cooked, add the vegetables and continue to cook for a further 10–15 minutes until the rice is tender and creamy. Remove the pan from the heat and stir in the butter and Parmesan. Season with salt and pepper to taste. For a softer risotto stir in a few more tablespoons of stock. Serve with extra grated Parmesan.

RISOTTO ALLA PRIMAVERA

Serves 6

For the spring vegetables

1 tablespoon olive oil

¹/₂ garlic clove, crushed

115 g/4 oz mushroom caps, thinly sliced

3 small artichokes, thinly sliced

1 teaspoon finely chopped onion

2 small courgettes, diced

6 asparagus spears, cut into short lengths

1 large red pepper slice, cut into pieces

1 small leek, white part only, cut into short lengths

salt and pepper

For the risotto

1 tablespoon olive oil

1 small onion, chopped

250 g/9 oz risotto rice

1.5 litres/2¹/₂ pints Chicken Stock (see page 209)

40 g/1¹/₂ oz butter

3 tablespoons freshly grated Parmesan cheese, plus extra for serving

salt and pepper

BAKED LANGOUSTINES

SCAMPI AL FORNO

Serves 6

1 kg/2¹/₄ lb peeled langoustines or
Dublin Bay prawns
plain flour, for dusting
100 ml/3¹/₂ fl oz olive oil
50 g/2 oz butter
1 small fresh flat-leaf parsley sprig,
chopped dash of Worcestershire sauce
juice of ¹/₂ lemon, strained
salt and pepper

Preheat the oven to 240°C/475°F/Gas Mark 9. Season the langoustines or prawns and dust with flour. Heat the oil in a frying pan, add the prawns, a few at a time, and cook for 2–3 minutes until lightly coloured. Remove with a slotted spoon, arrange in a single layer in an ovenproof dish and bake for 3–4 minutes. Drain off the oil from the frying pan, add the butter and parsley and cook for about 30 seconds until the butter starts to darken. Remove from the oven, sprinkle with the Worcestershire sauce and lemon juice and pour the parsley butter on top.

ITALIAN CRÊPES WITH CUSTARD CREAM

CRESPELLE ALLA CREMA PASTICCIERA

Serves 6

375 ml/13 fl oz milk
100 g/3¹/₂ oz caster sugar, plus extra for sprinkling
thinly pared rind of 2 lemons
3 large egg yolks
40 g/1¹/₂ oz plain flour
¹/₂ teaspoon vanilla essence
150 ml/¹/₄ pint Cointreau

For the Italian crêpes
3 eggs
25 g/1 oz plain flour
1 tablespoon olive oil
120 ml/4 fl oz milk
50–65 g/2–2¹/₂ oz unsalted butter
salt

Pour the milk into a heavy-based saucepan, add half the sugar and the lemon rind and bring to the boil. Remove the pan from the heat and remove the lemon rind. Beat the egg yolks with the remaining sugar in a bowl, then beat in the flour. Gradually stir in the milk, then transfer the custard to a pan and cook over a medium heat, stirring constantly, until thickened. Continue cooking for 3–4 minutes, then stir in the vanilla. Remove the pan from the heat and leave to cool, stirring frequently to prevent a skin from forming. When the custard is cold, chill in the refrigerator until required. To make the crêpes, beat the eggs in a bowl with the flour, oil and a pinch of salt. Stir in the milk and strain into a jug. Melt a little of the butter in a crêpe pan or small frying pan (about 15 cm/6 inches in diameter) over a medium heat. Pour in enough batter to cover the base and cook until golden brown on the underside, then flip over and brown the other side. Slide out of the pan. Continue making crêpes, occasionally adding a little more butter to the pan as required. When the crêpes are served, the golden brown side of the crêpe – the one cooked first – should be on the outside, so fill the crêpes on the least cooked side. Sprinkle a tablespoon of the custard on one half, fold the other half over the top and fold again to form a triangle. Place on a baking sheet and store in the refrigerator until ready to cook. Preheat the oven to 240°C/475°F/Gas Mark 9. Sprinkle the crêpes with sugar and bake for 5–10 minutes until heated through and the sugar has melted. Bring the crêpes to the table on the baking sheet, pour the Cointreau over and ignite carefully. Tip and turn the baking sheet until the flames die down. Serve the crêpes in their hot juices.

Franco Colombani

Albergo del Sole
via Monsignor Trabattoni 22
Maleo (LO)
Italy

'There is no nouvelle or traditional cuisine, just good or bad, and the client is the ultimate judge of a restaurateur's capabilities.' This is the pure and simple philosophy of Franco Colombani (1929–96), who spent a lifetime defending this firmly held view. A cultured and jealous guardian of Italian traditional cooking, Colombani was also the founder of Linea Italia in Cucina, an association for top-level restaurant owners committed to promoting local products and to using only produce in season. For over 60 years, his family owned the fifteenth-century Albergo del Sole in Maleo, near Lodi and this was where Colombani started to research traditional Italian recipes in 1958. (He was particularly interested in those of the areas around Cremona and Piacenza.) His mother and sister helped out initially, and then he was joined by his capable wife, Silvana. Today, she and the couple's sons, Francesco and Mario, continue the tradition and run the restaurant. The daily menu has always been restricted to a few dishes, but these are invariably rich in flavour – pesto minestrone, capon alla Stefani (named by a cook for the Gonzagas in the seventeenth century), braised beef with polenta in the Padania style and a fine pound cake with mascarpone cream. Finally, cured salami, one of the restaurant's specialities, should not be overlooked. This was always a feature of the celebrations in December each year.

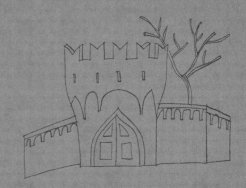

MENUS

INSALATA DI CAPPONE

STRACOTTO

SABBIOSA CON CREMA DI MASCARPONE

CAPON SALAD

INSALATA DI CAPPONE

Serves 4

1 tablespoon sultanas

300 g/11 oz poached capon or chicken

20 g/³/₄ oz candied citron peel, cut into thin strips

4 tablespoons extra virgin olive oil,

plus extra for drizzling • 1¹/₂ teaspoons white

wine vinegar, plus extra for drizzling

dash of balsamic vinegar

salad leaves • salt and pepper

Put the sultanas in a bowl, add warm water to cover, soak for 15 minutes, then drain and squeeze out. Carefully remove the skin and bones from the capon or chicken, then cut the meat into strips 1 cm/¹/₂ inch thick and place them in a salad bowl. Add the sultanas and candied peel, season and drizzle with the olive oil. Add the wine and balsamic vinegars and mix thoroughly. Make a bed of salad leaves on a dish and drizzle with olive oil and white wine vinegar. Spoon the meat mixture on top.

BRAISED BEEF

STRACOTTO

Serves 4

1 kg/2¹/₄ lb topside of beef

2 garlic cloves

50 g/2 oz butter

200 ml/6 fl oz olive oil

500 ml/18 fl oz Barbera or other fruity red wine

2 onions, diced • 80 g/3 oz carrots, diced

50 g/2 oz celery, diced • 3 tablespoons passata

1 litre/1³/₄ pints Meat Stock (see page 208)

3 cloves • pinch of freshly grated nutmeg

pinch of ground cinnamon

salt and pepper

Make two incisions in the meat and insert the garlic, then truss neatly with kitchen string. Heat the butter and oil in a saucepan, add the meat and cook, turning frequently, until browned all over. Pour in the wine and cook, turning the meat occasionally, until the liquid has reduced by half. Add the onions, carrots, celery and passata and season with salt and a little pepper. Pour in the stock, add the spices, lower the heat, cover and simmer for about 2 hours until the meat is tender. Remove the meat from the pan and keep warm. Press the vegetables through a sieve and return to the pan. Reheat the sauce. Meanwhile, slice the beef and place it on a dish, then spoon the sauce over it.

POUND CAKE WITH MASCARPONE CREAM

SABBIOSA CON CREMA DI MASCARPONE

Serves 6

400 g/14 oz unsalted butter, plus extra for greasing

breadcrumbs, for sprinkling

50 ml/2 fl oz brandy

1 sachet dried yeast

400 g/14 oz caster sugar

400 g/14 oz potato flour

4 eggs

For the cream

5 eggs, separated

100 g/3¹/₂ oz caster sugar

500 g/1 lb 2 oz mascarpone cheese

50 ml/2 fl oz rum or brandy

Preheat the oven to 180°C/350°F/Gas Mark 4. Grease a 30-cm/12-inch round cake tin with butter and sprinkle with breadcrumbs. To make the cake, pour the brandy into a small bowl, sprinkle the yeast on top and set aside for 10–15 minutes until frothy, then stir to a smooth paste. Beat the sugar with the butter, then add the potato flour and one egg at a time, beating well until thoroughly incorporated. Add the yeast mixture. Pour the mixture into the tin and bake until the cake has shrunk from the sides and a cocktail stick inserted in the centre comes out clean. Do not open the oven door during baking. Leave the cake to cool. Meanwhile, prepare the cream. Beat the egg yolks with the sugar until pale and fluffy, then beat in the mascarpone a little at a time. Stiffly whisk the egg whites in a grease-free bowl and fold into the egg yolk mixture, followed by the rum or brandy.

Enzo Deprà

Enzo Deprà is the grandson and son of chefs. His Dolada restaurant in Pieve Dalpago in the province of Belluno is the same one that was opened by his grandfather in 1923. As a young man, like many others from the Veneto region, he emigrated to Switzerland, where he attended catering school and worked in his brother's restaurant. It was there that he learned the techniques of classic international cuisine and, also from his brother, (who had gained experience on cruise ships that sailed to the East), the secrets of Indonesian cooking. On his return to Italy in 1965 he was one of the first to take up nouvelle cuisine, a style in which he achieved wide acclaim. His skill led to his appointment as consultant to a large multinational company in the food industry, where he researched raw ingredients extensively. In 1982 he decided that the time had come to re-evaluate the produce from his locality and his restaurant succeeded in transforming traditional dishes into haute cuisine very quickly. He achieved yet another evolution in taste, replacing the sophisticated recipes of an aristocratic cuisine with traditional country dishes which he made lighter and tastier without altering their basic characteristics. His most celebrated creations include his patora soup of barley, corn and beans, exquisite chicken liver pâté with herbs and truffle and fillet of red deer served with small polenta gnocchi.

Dolada
località Plois
Pieve Dalpago (BL)
Italy

MENUS

TERRINA DI FEGATINI ALLE ERBE E TARTUFO

CASUNZJEI DI PATATE E RICOTTA FORTE

INTINGOLO DI CHIOCCIOLE AL SEDANO RAPA E DADOLATA DI POLENTA

DOLCE DI PANE CON SALSA ALLA VANIGLIA

1149

CHICKEN LIVER PÂTÉ WITH HERBS AND TRUFFLE

TERRINA DI FEGATINI
ALLE ERBE E TARTUFO

Serves 4

1 tablespoon Madeira

1 tablespoon port

300 g/11 oz butter

1 shallot, chopped

1 tablespoon white wine

400 g/14 oz chicken livers, thawed if frozen and trimmed

2 eggs • 4 teaspoons truffle juice

pinch of freshly grated nutmeg

1¹/₂ tablespoons chopped truffle

150 g/5 oz unsalted pork fat or streaky bacon, cut into thin strips

2 bay leaves

2 fresh thyme sprigs • 2 fresh marjoram sprigs

salt and pepper

Preheat the oven to 110°C/225°F/Gas Mark ¹/₄ or lower if possible. Pour the Madeira and port into a small saucepan and reduce by half over a low heat, then leave to cool. Melt 10 g/¹/₄ oz of the butter in a shallow saucepan, add the shallot and cook over a low heat for 3–4 minutes, then add the white wine and cook until reduced by half. Remove from the heat and leave to cool. Put the chicken livers, remaining butter, the eggs, truffle juice, Madeira mixture, wine mixture and nutmeg in a food processor, season with salt and pepper and process until smooth. Pass the mixture through a sieve into a bowl and gently stir in the truffle. Line a terrine or loaf tin with the pork fat or bacon and spoon the chicken liver mixture into it. Smooth the surface, place the bay leaves, thyme and marjoram on top and cover with the remaining slices of pork fat or bacon. Cover the terrine or loaf tin tightly with a lid or a double thickness of foil. Place in a roasting tin, add boiling water to come halfway up the sides and bake for 1 hour. Leave to cool completely before serving.

CASUNZJEI PASTA WITH POTATOES AND SEASONED RICOTTA

CASUNZJEI DI PATATE E RICOTTA FORTE

Serves 4

For the pasta

300 g/11 oz plain flour, plus extra for dusting

2 eggs • 2 egg yolks • 1 tablespoon olive oil

For the filling

butter, for greasing

250 g/9 oz potatoes, cut into thin batons

¹/₂ onion, finely chopped

50 g /2 oz mascarpone cheese

50 g /2 oz fresh ricotta cheese

1¹/₂ tablespoons freshly grated Parmesan cheese

1 egg yolk • pinch of freshly grated nutmeg

1 tablespoon olive oil • salt and pepper

For the sauce

4 tablespoons olive oil • ¹/₂ onion, finely chopped

2 potatoes, diced

50 g/2 oz fresh smoked ricotta cheese, very thinly sliced • salt and pepper

To make the filling, grease a frying pan, make a layer of the potatoes and cook over a low heat until browned on both sides. About 5 minutes before the end of cooking, add the onion and cook until softened, then remove the pan from the heat. When cooled, stir in the mascarpone, ricotta, Parmesan, egg yolk, nutmeg and olive oil and season. Make the pasta dough (see page 268) with the ingredients listed and roll out on a floured surface to a thin sheet. Stamp out 7.5-cm/3-inch rounds with a biscuit cutter. Place a little filling in the centre of each, brush the edges with water and fold them in half to form casunzjei, pressing firmly to seal. To prepare the sauce, heat 1 tablespoon of oil in a saucepan, add the onion and cook over a low heat, stirring occasionally, for 5 minutes. Add the potatoes and 300 ml/¹/₂ pint water, increase the heat to medium and simmer for 30 minutes until tender. Pass the potato mixture through a food mill, add the remaining oil and season. Divide the sauce among four plates. Bring a large pan of salted water to the boil, add the casunzjei and cook for 3–4 minutes until al dente, then drain and arrange in a sunray pattern over the sauce. Top with the slices of ricotta.

RAGÙ OF SNAILS WITH CELERIAC

Blanch the snails, shell them and remove and discard the intestines (see page 730). Wash well and cut into small pieces. Heat the olive oil in a shallow saucepan, add the onion and celery and cook over a low heat, stirring occasionally, for 5 minutes. Add the snails and cook for a few minutes, then pour in the wine, increase the heat to medium and cook until evaporated. Add the stock a little at a time and simmer for about 2 hours. Preheat the oven to 180°C/350°F/Gas Mark 4. Season the snails with salt, if necessary, and plenty of pepper, add the celeriac and cook for a further 5 minutes. Sprinkle with the breadcrumbs, mix well and leave to stand for a few minutes. Meanwhile, heat the polenta in the oven, arrange it on a dish and drizzle with oil. Serve with the snail ragù.

INTINGOLO DI CHIOCCIOLE
AL SEDANO RAPA
E DADOLATA DI POLENTA

Serves 4

1 kg/2¼ lb snails

1 onion, finely chopped

2 green celery sticks, finely chopped

3 tablespoons olive oil, plus extra for drizzling

200 ml/6 fl oz aromatic white wine

1 litre/1¾ pints Meat Stock (see page 208)

100 g/3½ oz celeriac, diced

1 tablespoon breadcrumbs

5 slices of polenta, cut into cubes

salt and pepper

BREAD PUDDING WITH VANILLA SAUCE

Tear the bread into pieces and place it in a bowl. Bring the milk to the boil, remove from the heat and stir in the sugar until it has dissolved. Pour the mixture over the bread and leave until the liquid has been absorbed and the mixture has cooled. Place the sultanas in another bowl, add warm water to cover and leave to soak for about 15 minutes, then drain and squeeze out. Dust with flour, gently shaking off any excess. Preheat the oven to 160°C/325°F/Gas Mark 3. Grease individual moulds with butter and dust them with sugar. Pass the soaked bread through a sieve into a bowl and add the sultanas, liqueur, egg and egg yolk, mixing well. Spoon the mixture into the moulds until they are three-quarters full. Dot the surface with the butter and bake for 20 minutes, then increase the oven temperature to 180°C/350°F/Gas Mark 4 and bake for a further 10 minutes. Remove from the oven, to cool, then serve with the vanilla sauce. To prepare the vanilla sauce, bring the milk just to the boil, then remove from the heat. Meanwhile, put the egg yolks and sugar in a heatproof bowl and scrape in the contents of the vanilla pod. Beat vigorously until light and fluffy. Gradually beat in the hot milk. Set the bowl over a pan of barely simmering water and cook, stirring constantly with a wooden spoon until thickened, taking care that the eggs do not curdle. Strain and leave to cool before serving.

DOLCE DI PANE
CON SALSA ALLA VANIGLIA

Serves 8–10

100 g/3½ oz day-old bread, crusts removed

350 ml/12 fl oz skimmed milk

100 g/3½ oz caster sugar, plus extra for dusting

50 g/2 oz sultanas

plain flour, for dusting

15 g/½ oz unsalted butter, plus extra for greasing

50 ml/2 fl oz fior d'agno or citrus liqueur

1 egg

1 egg yolk

Vanilla Sauce, to serve

For the vanilla sauce

500 ml/18 fl oz milk

5 egg yolks

120 g/4 oz caster sugar

1 vanilla pod, halved lengthways

Maria Pia de Razza-Klein

Maria Pia's Trattoria
55 Mulgrave Street
Thorndon, Wellington
New Zealand

Far from her adopted homeland of New Zealand, the town of Morciano di Leuca in Puglia is the setting for the early culinary education of Maria Pia de Razza-Klein. There, near the southeastern-most tip of the Italian Peninsula, she learnt to respect the products that were cultivated on her family's farm and made in their artisanal pasta shop. She produced handmade pasta such as orecchiette, pre-empting the rediscovery of regional cooking in Italy. From these lessons of the land emerged her adherence to a philosophy of holistic connections between food, well-being and the environment. She studied macrobiotics in Florence, and at the Steiner elementary school in Bologna she prepared meals for small, yet demanding, vegetarian children, which she found as satisfying as creating banquets for discerning gourmets. She now heads her local chapter of the world-wide Slow Food Movement. Concurrent with her quest for the integrity of ingredients is her observance of the traditions of authentic Italian cuisine. Working in a restaurant in the Apennines of Emilia Romagna, Maria Pia de Razza-Klein was taught the secrets of Emilian cuisine by the women who were its custodians. She overheard and understood their declaration: 'But who invented tagliatelle? And tortellini? A statue, that's what they should dedicate to that person – a statue.' It is this philosophy of treasuring rustic dishes, along with her expertise in traditional and regional fare, that draws diners to Maria Pia's Trattoria in Wellington, New Zealand. Widely acclaimed for superb, truly homemade food, her restaurant's menu includes the freshly made pasta that began Maria Pia de Razza-Klein's gastronomic journey.

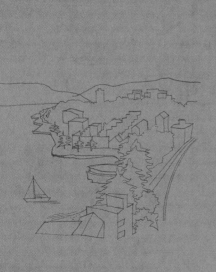

MENUS

INSALATA DI POLIPO SU LETTO DI FINOCCHIETTI E SCAGLIE DI PECORINO STAGIONATO

SPAGHETTI ALLA CHITARRA VERDI E BIANCHI CON SUGHETTO DI COZZE, POMODORINI ED OLIV

AGNELLO AL FORNO CON CONTORNO DI RADICCHIO TREVISANO ALLE MELE COTOGNE E PANCETT

RADICCHIO TREVISANO ALLE MELE COTOGNE E PANCETTA

FIOR DI LATTE ALLO ZAFFERANO CON SALSA ALLE ARANCE ROSSE E VINCOTTO

MARINATED OCTOPUS AND FENNEL SALAD WITH MATURE PECORINO CHEESE

Cut the tentacles from the head of the octopus. Remove and discard the eyes and innards, taking care not to break the ink sac. Remove the long strip of cartilage. Under running water remove the hard scales from the suckers on the tentacles, but do not remove the skin as it is the tastiest part and turns a lovely pink colour when cooked. Beat the tentacles with a meat mallet for a few minutes until soft. Place the octopus in a large pan and add cold water to cover. Bring to the boil and skim off the foam from the surface for the first few minutes of cooking. Add the onion, bay leaves, celery, garlic, cloves and a cork, but do not add salt. Lower the heat and simmer for 1½ hours. Drain the octopus, reserving 250 ml/ 8 fl oz of the cooking liquid. Discard the vegetables and flavourings, cut the octopus into 4–cm/1½-inch long strips and transfer to a bowl. Add the lemon juice, reserved cooking liquid, olive oil and parsley, season, mix well and leave to marinate at room temperature for at least 1 hour before serving. Prepare the fennel by removing the feathery fronds and the base. Slice the bulb thinly and leave to soak in a bowl of very cold water. Just before serving, drain and pat dry. Arrange the fennel slices on the base of individual serving plates. Drain the strips of octopus and arrange them on top. Sprinkle with the pecorino. Add several spoonfuls of the marinade, drizzle with extra virgin olive oil and season with pepper. Serve with good bread such as pane pugliese, grilled and rubbed with garlic.

INSALATA DI POLIPO SU LETTO DI FINOCCHIETTI E SCAGLIE DI PECORINO STAGIONATO

Serves 8

1-kg/2¼-lb octopus (or 1 large or 2 small ones)

1 large onion

2 bay leaves

1 celery stick

2 garlic cloves

2 cloves

juice of 3 lemons, strained

150 ml/¼ pint extra virgin olive oil, plus extra for drizzling

25 g/1 oz fresh flat-leaf parsley, finely chopped

3 large fennel bulbs

100 g/3½ oz mature pecorino cheese, shaved

salt and pepper

grilled garlic-flavoured bread, to serve

In Puglia we are voracious eaters of seafood. We also know how to cook octopus and squid so that it is tender and not tough: we boil it together with a cork from a wine bottle. I learned this trick from my grandmother and my mother and can't tell you why it works but can assure that it does!

1153

FRESH 'GUITAR STRING' SPAGHETTI WITH MUSSELS, CHERRY TOMATOES AND OLIVES

SPAGHETTI ALLA CHITARRA
VERDI E BIANCHI
CON SUGHETTO DI COZZE,
POMODORINI ED OLIVE

Serves 8

For the spinach pasta
200 g/7 oz spinach
200 g/7 oz semolina flour plus extra for dusting
200 g/7 oz spelt flour
2 large eggs
1 egg yolk
1 tablespoon warm water (optional)

For the plain pasta
200 g/7 oz semolina flour
200 g/7 oz spelt flour
4 large eggs

For the sauce
1 kg/2$^{1}/_{4}$ lb New Zealand green lip mussels, scrubbed and beards removed
7 tablespoons extra virgin olive oil
3 garlic cloves, finely chopped
450 g/1 lb canned cherry tomatoes
100 g/3$^{1}/_{2}$ oz stoned black olives
100 g/3$^{1}/_{2}$ oz stoned green olives
1 tablespoon capers, drained
35 g/1$^{1}/_{4}$ oz rock salt
3 tablespoons finely chopped fresh flat-leaf parsley
salt and pepper

In Italy we use a tool called a chitarra to make the fresh spaghetti. It is a box strung with steel wire (it looks like a guitar) on to which the fresh pasta sheets are placed. They are then forced through the wires with a small rolling pin. If you don't have one, you can of course use the spaghetti form on your pasta machine. For this recipe I use our wonderful New Zealand green lip mussels which are so juicy and large. You can also use the black Mediterranean or other varieties.

For the spinach pasta, cook the spinach in a little boiling water until wilted. Drain and squeeze out well, then place in a food processor and process to a purée. Mix the two types of flour in a bowl, make a well in the centre and add the eggs, egg yolk and puréed spinach in the well. Work with your hands to a soft and thoroughly mixed dough, adding the water if necessary. Knead for 15 minutes, cover with a clean tea towel and leave to rest for 20 minutes at room temperature. Halve the dough and roll out each piece on a lightly floured surface (preferably marble or stone) to 5-mm/$^{1}/_{4}$-inch thick sheets. Sprinkle with flour and leave to dry for 30 minutes, turning once and sprinkling with more flour to prevent them from sticking. Make the pasta sheets into spaghetti and leave to rest until ready to cook. Follow the same process to make the plain pasta with the ingredients listed. Meanwhile, make the sauce. Discard any mussels with broken shells or that do not shut when sharply tapped. Pour water into a saucepan to a depth of about 12 cm/4$^{1}/_{2}$ inches, add the mussels and cover with a tight-fitting lid. Bring to the boil and steam, shaking the pan occasionally, for 3–5 minutes until the shells have opened. Discard any mussels that are still closed. Remove the mussels with a slotted spoon, strain the cooking liquid through a fine sieve and reserve. Heat the olive oil in a pan, add the garlic and cook, stirring occasionally, until translucent. Add the tomatoes, olives, capers and reserved cooking liquid, bring to the boil and cook until reduced by half. Season with salt and pepper, then add the mussels and cook for 2–3 minutes. Meanwhile, bring 5 litres/8$^{3}/_{4}$ pints water to the boil, dissolve the rock salt and bring back to the boil. Add both pastas, stir gently with a wooden fork and cook for 3–5 minutes. Drain in a colander and toss with the sauce in a large bowl. Transfer to individual plates and arrange the mussels on the top and around the sides of each plate. Garnish with chopped parsley and season with freshly grated black pepper.

ROAST LAMB WITH RADICCHIO TREVISANO, QUINCE AND PANCETTA

Preheat the oven to 230°C/450°F/Gas Mark 8. Season the lamb with the rosemary and garlic, then roll up and tie with kitchen string. Mix the paprika with 3 tablespoons of the olive oil and rub the mixture all over the lamb with your fingers. Place the lamb in a roasting tin and add the celery, onions, carrot and bay leaves. Pour over the remaining olive oil and roast uncovered for 20 minutes. Add the wine and stock, cover the tin with dampened baking parchment and foil, lower the oven temperature to 180°C/350°F/Gas Mark 4 and roast for 1 hour more until the meat is cooked but still tender and pink inside. Remove the lamb from the roasting tin and leave to rest. Strain the cooking liquid, reserving the vegetables but discarding the bay leaves, and skim off as much fat as possible. Pass the vegetables through a food mill or process in a food processor to reduce to a purée, adding half the strained cooking juices. Mix the other half of the cooking juices with the Vincotto in a saucepan, bring to the boil and cook until reduced by one-quarter. Season with salt and pepper. Slice the meat thickly and cover with the sauce. Serve with the radicchio Trevisano (see below).

AGNELLO AL FORNO CON CONTORNO DI RADICCHIO TREVISANO ALLE MELE COTOGNE E PANCETTA

Serves 8

2 kg/4$^{1}/_{2}$-lb leg of lamb, boned and butterflied

2 tablespoons fresh rosemary, finely chopped

3 garlic cloves, crushed • 1 tablespoon sweet paprika • 120 ml/4 fl oz extra virgin olive oil

3 celery sticks, finely diced

3 onions, each cut into 6 wedges

1 carrot, coarsely chopped • 4 bay leaves,

500 ml/18 fl oz rosé wine

(preferably rosato del salento)

200 ml/7 fl oz Vegetable Stock (see page 209)

50 ml/2 fl oz Vincotto • salt and pepper

Radicchio Trevisano with Quince

and Pancetta (see below), to serve

We Pugliese are not great carnivores but lamb is high on our list of preferred meats. Living in New Zealand, I naturally make great use of our delicious, grass-fed lamb and this recipe is one of my favourites.

RADICCHIO TREVISANO WITH QUINCE AND PANCETTA

Cook the quince in a small saucepan with 350 ml/12 fl oz of water for about 10 minutes until soft. Meanwhile, heat the butter and olive oil in a large frying pan, add the pancetta and cook until crisp. Remove the pancetta from the pan and set aside. Add the onion and Jerusalem artichokes to the pan and cook over a low heat for a few minutes, then add 2–3 tablespoons water and cook until the Jerusalem artichokes are soft. Add the radicchio leaves, the quince with its cooking liquid and the Vincotto and simmer for 10 minutes until most of the liquid has evaporated. Add the pancetta and cook for a further 5 minutes. Season with salt and pepper.

RADICCHIO TREVISANO ALLE MELE COTOGNE E PANCETTA

Serves 8

1 quince, quartered • 25 g/1 oz butter

3 tablespoons extra virgin olive oil

150 g/5 oz pancetta pepata

(pepper coated belly pork), diced

1 red onion, thinly sliced

3 Jerusalem artichokes, thinly sliced

3 heads of radicchio Trevisano,

leaves separated and kept whole

3 tablespoons Vincotto • salt and pepper

Radicchio Trevisano originates from the city of Treviso in the Veneto region. It has long red and white leaves and a slightly bitter taste that I absolutely adore.

FIOR DI LATTE ALLO ZAFFERANO
CON SALSA ALLE ARANCE ROSSE
E VINCOTTO

Serves 6

For the cooked milk puddings

sunflower or olive oil, for brushing

350 ml/12 fl oz milk

250 ml/8 fl oz double cream

60 g/2¹/₄ oz caster sugar

¹/₄ teaspoon saffron threads, soaked
in 2 tablespoons boiling water

5 gelatine leaves

For the sauce

juice of 2 blood oranges, strained

juice of 1 lemon, strained

50 ml/2 fl oz Vincotto

1 teaspoon honey, such as New Zealand Manuka
or other aromatic variety

2 tablespoons Grand Marnier or other orange liqueur

1 blood orange, to decorate

*I find fior di latte – literally 'flower of the milk' – to
be much lighter and more digestible than the
ubiquitous panna cotta. In this version I use saffron
to give it a gorgeous orange colour. The sauce
uses Vincotto, a typical product of my region,
Salento (Puglia), made from the cooked must of
Negramaro and Malvasia grapes, which is
available from Italian speciality shops and
delicatessens.*

COOKED SAFFRON MILK PUDDINGS WITH BLOOD ORANGE AND VINCOTTO SAUCE

Lightly brush six individual moulds with oil. Place the milk, cream and sugar in a saucepan and bring to the boil, stirring until the sugar has dissolved. Remove from the heat and stir in the saffron water. Soak the gelatine leaves in a small bowl of cold water for 5 minutes until softened, then drain and squeeze out. Stir the gelatine into the hot milk mixture and leave to cool to room temperature. Stir briefly, then pour into the prepared moulds and chill in the refrigerator for at least 6 hours. To make the sauce, mix together the orange juice, lemon juice and Vincotto in a small saucepan and bring to the boil. Stir in the honey until it dissolves, then remove from the heat. Stir in the Grand Marnier and leave to cool, then store in the refrigerator until ready to serve. To serve, loosen the edges the milk puddings with a knife and invert on to individual plates. Peel the orange, removing all traces of pith, cut into rounds and then divide each round into six triangular pieces. Spoon a small amount of the sauce on the fior di latte and spoon the remainder around the plates. Decorate with the orange triangles.

Alfonso e Livia Jaccarino

Don Alfonso 1890
c.so Sant'Agata 11
Sant'Agata sui Due Golfi (NA)
Italy

Four generations of Sorrento hoteliers provided Alfonso Jaccarino with sufficient experience and skill to scale the heights of Italian and then European cuisine during the 1980s and 1990s. His talents as a chef are matched, at each stage, by those of his wife Livia, an authority on wine. Both travel a great deal, gathering wisdom in their visits to both vineyards and to fruit, meat and fish markets all over the world. This love of local producers and retailers led to their decision to study local food and wine in greater depth in order to discover how to preserve their characteristics and quality. This is how Le Peracciole farm came into being, a farm unique in the world and covering three hectares (7½ acres) at Punta Campanella, looking out towards the island of Capri. Here, an ideal microclimate gives lettuce, tomatoes, potatoes, onions, aromatic herbs and olives those unique flavours and aromas that, when combined with the freshest of fish or most succulent meat, make the Jaccarino's cooking worthy of their coveted three Michelin stars – dishes such as vermicelli with clams and courgettes, swordfish with celery, lavender and wild spinach, and new potatoes with oysters, chives, prawns and lentils. You also can't forget the desserts, with their delightful flavours and combinations, such as baked aubergine bound with a chocolate sauce.

MENUS

BACINI DI COZZE CON FIORI DI ZUCCA

RAVIOLI DI CACIOTTA AL POMODORINO E BASILICO

SCORFANO AL VINO BIANCO

PASTICCIO DI MELANZANE CON CIOCCOLATO

MUSSEL PURSES WITH COURGETTE FLOWERS

BACINI DI COZZE
CON FIORI DI ZUCCA

Serves 4

600 g/1 lb 5 oz live mussels

courgettes, as required

100 g/3¹/₂ oz breadcrumbs

2 tablespoons chopped fresh flat-leaf parsley

50 ml/2 fl oz olive oil

dry white wine, for drizzling

salt

Preheat the oven to 180°C/350°F/Gas Mark 4. Open the mussels and remove the meat, reserving the shells. Carefully clean the courgette flowers, remove and discard their pistils and steam briefly. Mix together the breadcrumbs, parsley and a pinch of salt in a bowl and add the mussels. Place the mussels, one by one, in each courgette flower. Lay the flowers in the mussel shells, place in an ovenproof dish, drizzle with the olive oil and bake for 4 minutes. Remove the dish from the oven and drizzle the wine over the mussels. Transfer to a platter and serve.

CACIOTTA RAVIOLI WITH TOMATO AND BASIL

RAVIOLI DI CACIOTTA
AL POMODORINO E BASILICO

Serves 4

400 g/14 oz plain flour, plus extra for dusting

100 ml/3¹/₂ fl oz extra virgin olive oil

250 g/9 oz fresh caciotta cheese, diced

1 fresh marjoram sprig, chopped

1 egg, separated

1 garlic clove, finely chopped

500 g/1 lb cherry tomatoes, quartered

150 ml/¹/₄ pint passata

10 fresh basil leaves

salt

Mix the flour with half the oil to a dough and leave to rest in a cool place. Meanwhile, prepare the filling. Mix together the caciotta, marjoram, egg yolk and a pinch of salt. Lightly beat the egg white. Roll out the half the dough on a lightly floured surface and brush with beaten egg white to seal. Spoon the cheese mixture into a piping bag fitted with a 1-cm/¹/₂-inch plain nozzle and pipe small mounds of filling at regular intervals on the dough. Roll out the remaining dough, brush with egg white and place on top of the first sheet. Press around the mounds of filling and cut out the ravioli using a small round cutter. Heat the remaining oil in a frying pan, add the garlic and cook for 1–2 minutes, then add the tomatoes and passata and season with salt if necessary. Add the basil, stir and turn off the heat. Cook the ravioli in a large pan of salted, boiling water for about 2 minutes, then drain well and tip into a serving dish. Pour the sauce over them and serve.

SCORPION FISH IN WHITE WINE

Preheat the oven to 180°C/350°F/Gas Mark 4. Heat 3 table-spoons of the olive oil in a flameproof casserole, add the garlic cloves and cook for 2–3 minutes, then remove and discard them. Add the fish fillets and cook until lightly browned on both sides. Season lightly with salt, add the olives and capers, drizzle with the wine and cook until the liquid has evaporated. Sprinkle with the breadcrumbs, transfer the casserole to the oven and bake for 20–30 minutes until tender. Meanwhile, roast the red pepper until charred and blackened, then remove from the oven. Peel, seed and dice the flesh. Heat the remaining oil in frying pan, add the bread cubes and cook, turning frequently, until golden brown all over. Remove with a slotted spoon and drain on kitchen paper. Transfer the fish fillets to a warm serving dish and sprinkle with the croûtons, red pepper and parsley.

SCORFANO AL VINO BIANCO

Serves 4

4 tablespoons olive oil

2 garlic cloves

600 g/1 lb 5 oz scorpion fish fillets

80 g/3 oz stoned green olives

40 g/1½ oz capers, drained, rinsed and chopped

150 ml/5 fl oz dry white wine

50 g/2 oz fresh breadcrumbs

1 red pepper

4 tomato bread slices, cut into cubes

2 tablespoons chopped fresh flat-leaf parsley

salt

AUBERGINE PIE WITH CHOCOLATE

Thoroughly combine the ricotta, sugar, candied fruit and 50 g/2 oz of the chocolate in a bowl. Steam the aubergine slices until tender. Melt the remaining chocolate in a heatproof bowl set over a pan of barely simmering water, then remove from the heat and stir in the Marsala. Arrange the cubes of sponge cake on a serving dish and cover them with the ricotta mixture, mounding it up in the centre. Place the aubergine slices on top and pour the melted chocolate over them.

PASTICCIO DI MELANZANE
CON CIOCCOLATO

Serves 4

150 g/5 oz ricotta cheese

50 g/2 oz icing sugar

50 g/2 oz candied fruit, diced

250 g/9 oz plain or dark chocolate,

broken into pieces

8 aubergine slices

2 tablespoons Marsala

1 sponge cake, cut into 2.5-cm/1-inch cubes

Giorgio Locatelli

Locanda Locatelli
8 Seymour Street
London
United Kingdom

Giorgio Locatelli is one of the finest Italian chefs in the United Kingdom, one who is celebrated for his use of the freshest and best quality produce. So vital is this to his cooking that he imports many of his ingredients directly from Italy. He was raised on the banks of Lake Maggiore in the village of Corgeno, where his family owned a Michelin-starred restaurant. This ensured he enjoyed an intense appreciation and understanding of Northern Italian cuisine from an early age. Building on this solid foundation he honed his skills working in local restaurants in the north of Italy and in Switzerland. In 1986 he moved to England to join the kitchens of Anton Edelmann at The Savoy in London. Then he moved to Paris, cooking at Restaurant Laurent and La Tour D'Argent. On his subsequent return to London, Giorgio Locatelli became head chef at Olivio, Eccleston Street, and subsequently opened Zafferano in 1995. It was at Zafferano that his culinary talents received critical acclaim. He made his name in London and, at the same time, he earned international repute with a host of accolades including Best Italian Restaurant (Carlton London Restaurant Awards) and, in the best family tradition, his first Michelin star. Further restaurants in London followed but, in 2002, Giorgio Locatelli opened his first independent restaurant: the Michelin-starred Locanda Locatelli in Marylebone, London. The restaurant soon had a coveted Diploma di Cucina Eccellente, which was conferred on it by the Accademia Italiana della Cucina. Despite its prestigious status in the restaurant scene of London, Locanda Locatelli is renowned for its friendly service and relaxed atmosphere. At Locanda Locatelli, Giorgio Locatelli serves the traditional Italian dishes of his youth enhanced by his signature innovative interpretations: embracing the natural flavours of the freshest produce.

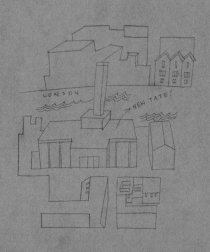

MENUS

CAPPESANTE ALL'ASPRETTO DI ZAFFERANO

RAVIOLI DI FAGIANO

CONIGLIO AL FORNO CON PROSCIUTTO CRUDO E POLENTA

DEGUSTAZIONE DI CIOCCOLATO AMEDEI

PAN—FRIED SCALLOPS WITH SAFFRON VINAIGRETTE

Serves 4

8 large scallops or 12 small ones, shelled and corals reserved

4–5 celery sticks, cut into thin batons

2 tablespoons lemon juice, strained

3 tablespoons extra virgin olive oil

4 tablespoons vinaigrette

salt and pepper

For the vinaigrette

200 ml/7 fl oz white wine vinegar

1 level tablespoon saffron threads

100 ml/3$\frac{1}{2}$ fl oz extra virgin olive oil

freshly ground sea salt

For the purée

$\frac{1}{2}$ celeriac, diced

1 tablespoon olive oil

3 tablespoons double cream

50 g/2 oz butter

salt

Put the vinegar into a pan with the saffron over a low heat and let it reduce by half. Leave it to cool down. When cold, whisk in the oil and season with salt. If the scallops have been stored in the refrigerator, remove them and let them to come to room temperature before cooking. Preheat the oven to 180°C/350°F/Gas Mark 4. To make the purée, put the celeriac in an oven-proof dish with 5 tablespoons water, a pinch of salt and the olive oil, cover, seal completely with foil and bake for about 30 minutes until soft. Transfer the celeriac mixture to a food processor and process, adding the cream as the motor is running, then pass through a fine sieve to produce a smooth purée. (It is important to process the celeriac while it is still hot, as it makes the purée smoother and it will pass more easily through the sieve). Set the purée aside. Put the celery in a bowl with a handful of ice to crisp up. Mix together the lemon juice and half the olive oil. Heat an ovenproof frying pan – two if you have 12 scallops. When it is hot but not smoking, pour in the rest of the oil, then add the scallops (don't season at this stage as the salt will make them leach out their moisture and they will become dry). Cook the scallops for 1 minute (or 1$\frac{1}{2}$ minutes if large), until golden underneath, then turn them over and put into oven for 1 further minute. Season and transfer them to the bowl of saffron vinaigrette. Gently reheat the celeriac purée in a small pan and season if necessary. Remove the pan from the heat and beat in the butter. Spoon the purée on to individual plates and arrange the scallops on top. Drain the celery from the ice, season with the lemon and oil mixture and arrange on top of the scallops. Drizzle the remaining saffron vinaigrette around.

PHEASANT RAVIOLI WITH ROSEMARY JUS

RAVIOLI DI FAGIANO

Serves 6

1 large drawn and plucked pheasant, boned

4 teaspoons vegetable oil

100 g/3½ oz pancetta, finely diced

3 shallots, finely chopped

175 ml/6 fl oz white wine

3 tablespoons Parmesan cheese, freshly grated

1 tablespoon fresh breadcrumbs

1 egg, plus 1 egg, beaten, to brush the pasta

4 tablespoons double cream

½ quantity of Fresh Pasta Dough (see page 268)

50 g/2 oz unsalted butter

1 fresh rosemary sprig

salt and pepper

Preheat the oven to 220°C/425°F/Gas Mark 7. Cut the breasts of the pheasants in half crossways, put them on a work surface, skin side up, and season. Heat an ovenproof sauté pan (large enough to hold all the pheasant) until it smokes, then pour in the vegetable oil and add the pheasant, skin side down. Cook quickly until the skin turns golden, then add the pancetta and shallots, turn the pheasant over and cook for a further 2–3 minutes. Add the wine, cook for 1 minute to allow the alcohol to evaporate, then transfer to the oven for 2-3 minutes until the meat is cooked through, but not overcooked (it will continue to cook as it cools). Leave the mixture to cool then, while it is still warm, put it into a food processor and process to a coarse paste. Transfer the paste to a plate and then spoon a little at a time on to a chopping board. Pass the paste through a sieve or run over it with a spatula or table knife to feel whether any shot has been left in the meat. If so, remove it. Put the mixture into a bowl, add the Parmesan, breadcrumbs and egg and season, if necessary. Gradually stir in the cream and then chill in the refrigerator. When the mixture is cold, scoop out small quantities, roll them into about 32 balls with your hands and place ready to fill the pasta. Make the pasta dough and pass through a pasta machine to make strips. Mark a faint line along the centre of the first pasta strip with the back of a knife. Brush one half with beaten egg, then place little mounds of the pheasant mixture, in pairs, on one side of the strip, leaving a space of about 4 cm/ 1½ inches between each mound. Fold the other half of the pasta strip over the top, carefully matching the top edges and pressing them together. Then with your hand, gently press down over the rest (don't worry if you compress the filling a little), so that the two halves of pasta fit together. Press around each mound of filling, making sure the pasta is quite smooth. Using a fluted cutter about 1 cm/½ inch bigger in circumference than the filling, cut out each raviolo. Discard the trimmings. Press out air trapped inside, by pinching with your thumbs around the outside of each raviolo until there are no air pockets left. (If you pierce the pasta, just pinch it together again.) Make more ravioli in the same way. Bring a large pan of salted water to the boil. Meanwhile, melt the butter with the rosemary in a large sauté pan and cook until the butter begins to foam. Cook the ravioli in the boiling water for 3-4 minutes, then drain with a slotted spoon and transfer to the pan of sauce. Toss gently for 1–2 minutes and serve.

RABBIT WITH PROSCIUTTO AND POLENTA

Preheat the oven to 120°C/250°F/Gas Mark ¹/₂. Wrap each rabbit leg in two slices of prosciutto. Heat half the oil in a large, shallow, flameproof casserole, add the rabbit legs and cook over a medium heat until they start to colour, then add the butter. Turn the legs over and cook for a further 2 minutes. Cover the legs completely with the melted lard, then cover the casserole with foil and cook in the oven for 1 hour until very tender. Meanwhile, cook the polenta. Put it in a large jug so that it can be poured in a steady stream. Bring the milk to the boil in a large saucepan (it should half-fill the pan). Add 1 teaspoon salt and then gradually add the polenta in a continuous stream, stirring constantly with a long-handled whisk until completely blended. When the polenta starts to bubble vigorously, lower the heat to the lowest possible setting and cook, stirring occasionally, for 20 minutes. Cut each radicchio into three pieces and season with salt and pepper. Brush with the remaining oil and cook on a medium-hot griddle pan until wilted. Spoon the polenta on to individual serving plates and put the rabbit legs on top. Add the radicchio on the side and serve immediately.

CONIGLIO AL FORNO

CON PROSCIUTTO CRUDO E POLENTA

Serves 6

6 rabbit legs, boned

12 thin prosciutto slices

2 tablespoons groundnut oil

50 g/2 oz butter

500 g/1 lb 2 oz lard, melted

120 g/4 oz polenta

1.2 litres/2 pints milk

2 heads of radicchio Trevisano

sea salt and pepper

DEGUSTAZIONE DI
CIOCCOLATO AMEDEI

Serves 4

For the dark chocolate mousse
$^{1}/_{2}$ gelatine leaf
5 tablespoons milk
80 g/3 oz Amedei Chuao chocolate
65 g/2$^{1}/_{2}$ oz egg whites • 25 g/1 oz dextrose

For the white chocolate mousse
$^{1}/_{2}$ gelatine leaf
140 g/4$^{3}/_{4}$ oz Amedei white chocolate
150 ml/$^{1}/_{4}$ pint whipping cream
7 tablespoons milk • $^{1}/_{2}$ vanilla pod

For the nougatine
40 g/1$^{1}/_{2}$ oz fondant • 20 g/$^{3}/_{4}$ oz glucose
1$^{1}/_{2}$ tablespoons honey
50 g/2 oz ground roasted pine nuts

For the chocolate crisps
100 g/3$^{1}/_{2}$ oz icing sugar
10 g/$^{1}/_{4}$ oz cocoa powder • 50 g/2 oz plain flour
pinch of ground cinnamon
70 g/2$^{3}/_{4}$ oz unsalted butter, melted
100 g/3$^{1}/_{2}$ oz egg whites
pine nuts, to decorate

For the crème anglaise
100 ml/3$^{1}/_{2}$ fl oz whipping cream
400 ml/14 fl oz milk
thinly pared rind of $^{1}/_{2}$ orange
100 g/3$^{1}/_{2}$ oz caster sugar • 90 g/3$^{1}/_{4}$ oz egg yolks

For the pine nut ice cream
567 ml/19$^{1}/_{4}$ fl oz milk
172 ml/5$^{3}/_{4}$ fl oz double cream • 137 g/4$^{3}/_{4}$ oz dextrose
40 g/1$^{1}/_{2}$ oz skimmed milk powder
50 g/2 oz sucrose
6 g/$^{1}/_{8}$ oz ice cream stabilizer
25 g/1 oz inverted sugar
100 g/3$^{1}/_{2}$ oz pine nuts, roasted and chopped

AMEDEI CHOCOLATE TASTERS

To make the dark chocolate mousse, soak the gelatine for 5 minutes, then squeeze out. Boil the milk, then remove from the heat. Melt the chocolate over a pan of barely simmering water, then add the milk, making sure that the mixture doesn't split. Stir in the gelatine. Stiffly whisk the egg whites with the dextrose, then carefully fold into the chocolate. To make the white chocolate mousse, soak the gelatine for 5 minutes, then squeeze out. Melt the chocolate in a bowl set over a pan of barely simmering water. Whip the cream. Pour the milk into a saucepan and scrape the seeds from the vanilla pod into the pan. Bring to the boil, then add to the chocolate, whisking constantly. Stir in the gelatine. Let the mixture to cool to 35°C/95°F. Gently fold in the whipped cream. To make the nougatine, put the fondant, glucose and honey in a pan and heat the mixture to 163°C/325°F. Remove from the heat and stir in the pine nuts. Put the mixture between two sheets of baking parchment and roll as thinly as possible. Let it cool. Preheat the oven to 165°C/330°F/Gas Mark 3–4. Peel off the parchment, break into pieces, place on a baking sheet, heat for 2 minutes until soft. Remove from the oven, flatten with the rolling pin and cut into 6 x 10-cm/2$^{1}/_{4}$ x 4-inch rectangles, 1 mm/$^{1}/_{24}$ inch thick. Return to the oven for 20 seconds, then take out and roll around a metal cylinder or spoon. To make the chocolate crisps, mix all dry ingredients together. Add the butter, mix well, then add the egg whites and mix again. Chill in the refrigerator for at least 2 hours. Preheat the oven to 180°C/350°F/Gas Mark 4. With a palette knife, shape the mixture into 16 x 3-cm/6$^{1}/_{4}$ x 1$^{1}/_{4}$-inch rectangles, place on a baking sheet, sprinkle with pine nuts and bake for 5 minutes. Remove from the oven and place on a rolling pin to cool. To make the crème anglaise, bring the cream, milk and orange rind to the boil, then let cool for 30 minutes. Beat the egg yolks with the sugar. Remove the orange rind from the milk mixture and reheat to 60°C/140°F, then add the egg yolk mixture. Cook, stirring, until 85°C/185°F, remove from the heat and let cool. For the pine nut ice cream, put the milk, cream, dextrose and milk powder in a pan and heat, whisking, to 40°C/104°F. Add the sucrose, stabilizer and inverted sugar and bring to 85°C/185°F. Remove the pan from the heat and stand it in a bowl of iced water to cool, then chill for 6–12 hours. Add the pine nuts to the mixture, then freeze in an ice cream machine. To serve, fill two nougatine cylinders with dark chocolate mousse and one with white. Place on a plate, next to a bowl of ice cream with a crisp on top of it. Spoon some of the crème anglaise on the side.

Stefano Manfredi

Stefano Manfredi is a leading exponent of modern Italian cooking. Born in the Lombardy region of northern Italy, he settled on Australian shores with his family in 1961. His culinary journey was launched when his first restaurant opened in 1983. It transformed the way the cuisine of Italy was perceived and is the only Italian restaurant to have attained the coveted highest rating from The Sydney Morning Herald Good Food Guide. As one of Australia's leading chefs his success comes from paying tribute to his family's traditional fare in a revitalised contemporary context, in his eateries, cookbooks and food journalism. His latest venture after a distinguished line of restaurant projects is Manta Restaurant: Italian seafood dining located in an historic wharf building with spectacular views across the marina to the city skyline. Simplicity and freshness is the mantra at Manta Restaurant where exquisite dishes of unadulterated flavours are created. Stefano Manfredi believes that 'good cooking involves a lot of work even before one starts to cook'. At Manta Restaurant the selection and preparation of exceptional quality ingredients is fundamental and the menu is changed daily to honour seasonal availability. The fruits of the sea, in peak condition, are selected each morning at the fish market auction. Handpicked oysters are delivered directly from the grower. As each day's fish haul arrives in the kitchen, it is carefully dry-filleted, without using running water, to maintain the integrity of the texture and flavor. Dedicated to this freshest of produce, Stefano Manfredi has received critical and popular acclamation for his sophisticated reinvention of his proud Italian heritage.

Manta Restaurant
The Wharf,
Cowper Wharf Road
Woolloomooloo
Australia

MENUS

CROSTINI CON PEPERONI E CIPOLLE AL AGRODOLCE

TAGLIATELLE CON GAMBERI DI FIUME, BURRO E SESAMO

FAGIANO ARROSTO CON VERZA, CASTAGNE E SALSA AL VINO ROSSO

TORTA SBRISOLONA CON MELA COTOGNA, CREMA DI MASCARPONE E VINCOTTO

STEFANO MANFREDI

STEFANO MANFREDI

CROSTINI WITH PEPPERS AND ONIONS IN AGRODOLCE

CROSTINI CON PEPERONI E CIPOLLE AL AGRODOLCE

Serves 6

2 red peppers, seeded
2 yellow peppers, seeded
2 red onions
extra virgin olive oil, for drizzling and brushing
2 tablespoons balsamic vinegar
6 x 1-cm/½-inch thick bread slices
salt and pepper

Preheat the oven to 180°C/350°F/Gas Mark 4. Cut all the peppers into eight strips and cut both onions into eight wedges. Spread them out in a roasting tin, drizzle with olive oil, season with salt and pepper and toss well to coat. Bake for about 20 minutes until softened. Remove the tin from the oven, add the balsamic vinegar, mix well and leave to cool to room temperature. Preheat the grill. Cut each slice of bread into three or four pieces, brush with olive oil and toast on both sides. Top the crostini with the vegetables and serve.

TAGLIATELLE WITH YABBIES, BUTTER AND SESAME SEEDS

TAGLIATELLE CON GAMBERI DI FIUME, BURRO E SESAMO

Serves 6

For the tagliatelle
600 g/1 lb 5 oz plain flour
6 eggs

For the topping
30 live yabbies or other freshwater crayfish
120 g/4 oz sesame seeds, toasted
120 g/4 oz butter, softened and thinly sliced
100 g/3½ oz grana padano, finely grated
salt and pepper

To make the tagliatelle, sift the flour into a mound on a work surface and make a well in the centre. Crack the eggs directly into the well and gradually bring the mixture together to form a dough. Add a little more flour if the mixture is too wet. Roll the dough through a pasta machine until it is very thin, then cut into 5-mm/¼ inch wide tagliatelle. For the topping, bring a large pan of salted water to the boil, add the yabbies or crayfish and bring to the boil, then immediately remove the seafood from the water, peel off the shells and cut each tail in half lengthways. Cook the tagliatelle in a large pan of salted, boiling water for a few minutes until al dente, then drain and toss with the sesame seeds, butter, yabbies or crayfish, cheese and salt and pepper to taste. Serve immediately.

ROAST PHEASANT WITH SAVOY CABBAGE, CHESTNUTS AND RED WINE

For the red wine sauce, heat the olive oil in a saucepan, add the onion, celery and garlic and cook over a low heat, stirring occasionally, for a few minutes until softened but not coloured. Add the vinegar, increase the heat to medium and cook until the liquid has reduced by three-quarters. Pour in the wine and cook, skimming off any scum that rises to the surface, until the liquid has reduced by half. Strain the mixture through a muslin-lined sieve into a clean pan, return to the heat and cook until reduced to 250 ml/8 fl oz. To prepare the cabbage and chestnuts, heat the olive oil in a saucepan, add the onion and pancetta and cook over a low heat, stirring occasionally, until softened and light golden brown. Add the cabbage, season with salt and cook, stirring constantly, until wilted. Add the chestnuts and simmer gently until the cabbage is tender but still retains a little texture. Season to taste. To prepare the pheasants, preheat the oven to 240°C/475°F/Gas Mark 9. Rub each bird with a little olive oil, sprinkle with salt and place them in a roasting tin. Roast for 15–20 minutes until each pheasant is cooked through. Remove the roasting tin from the oven but do not switch it off. Remove the pheasants from the roasting tin and leave to rest in a warm place for about 10 minutes. Meanwhile, add the red wine reduction to the roasting tin, mix thoroughly with the cooking juices and return the tin to the oven for 5–6 minutes. Strain the sauce through a muslin-lined sieve and keep warm. To serve, cut the breast meat off the bones and remove the legs from each bird. Place half a bird on each of six plates and serve with the cabbage and chestnuts and red wine sauce.

FAGIANO ARROSTO CON VERZA, CASTAGNE E SALSA AL VINO ROSSO

Serves 6

3 x 800-g/1³/₄-lb pheasants, drawn and plucked

extra virgin olive oil, for rubbing

salt

For the red wine sauce

3 tablespoons extra virgin olive oil

1 onion, chopped

1 celery heart, chopped

10 garlic cloves, chopped

250 ml/8 fl oz balsamic vinegar

1.5 litres/2¹/₂ pints red wine

For the cabbage and chestnuts

3 tablespoons extra virgin olive oil

1 onion, finely diced

100g/3¹/₂ oz pancetta, finely diced

¹/₂ Savoy cabbage, cored and shredded

30 chestnuts, cooked and peeled (see page 432)

salt and pepper

TORTA SBRISOLONA CON MELA COTOGNA,
CREMA DI MASCARPONE E VINCOTTO

Makes 20

For the torta sbrisolona
120 g/4 oz plain flour
80 g/3 oz fine polenta flour
100 g/3¹/₂ oz ground almonds
80 g/3 oz caster sugar
1 egg yolk
juice of ¹/₂ lemon
1 teaspoon vanilla essence
grated rind of 1 lemon
65 g/2¹/₂ oz butter
50 g/2 oz duck fat

For the quinces
6 quinces
1 litre/1³/₄ pints dry white wine
300 g/11 oz sugar
2 cinnamon sticks
8 black peppercorns
1–2 tablespoons vincotto

For the mascarpone cream
2 egg whites
75 g/2³/₄ oz caster sugar
300 g/11 oz mascarpone cheese
1 teaspoon vanilla essence

TORTA SBRISOLONA WITH QUINCE, MASCARPONE CREAM AND VINCOTTO

Preheat the oven to 160°C/325°F/Gas Mark 3. Line a baking sheet with baking parchment. To make the torta sbrisolona, mix together the flour, polenta, ground almonds, sugar, egg yolk, lemon juice, vanilla essence and lemon rind in a bowl. Add the butter and duck fat and gradually incorporate into the dry ingredients to form a dough. Roll out the dough to a thickness of 5 mm/¹/₄ inch and stamp out rounds with an 8-cm/3¹/₄-inch biscuit cutter. Place the rounds on the prepared baking sheet and bake for 30 minutes. Remove from the oven and leave to cool. Preheat the oven to 110°C/225°F/Gas Mark ¹/₄. Peel the quinces, cut them into quarters, leaving the cores intact, place in an ovenproof dish and pour in the wine to cover. Sprinkle with the sugar and bake for 6–8 hours until tender. Remove from the oven and leave to cool, then core the fruit and thinly slice each quarter. To make the mascarpone cream, whisk the egg whites in a grease-free bowl until soft peaks form. Gradually whisk in the sugar until stiff peaks form. Fold in the mascarpone and vanilla essence. To serve, place a spoonful of mascarpone cream on each of the sbrisolona and top with the quince slices, then sprinkle with the vincotto.

Gualtiero Marchesi

1977 witnessed the dawn of a new age in Italian food when Gualtiero Marchesi opened his restaurant in Via Bonvesin de la Riva in Milan. A single example of one of his dishes defines his nouvelle-cuisine style of conceptual cooking – 7 pasta penne, 20 g/¼ oz sliced back Norcia truffle and 7 asparagus tips (bevel cut). However, this style of cooking was one with which the public grew weary. After fifteen years, Marchesi reconsidered his menu and at the Albereta, his restaurant at Erbusco in Franciacorta, which opened in 1993, he reinvented the ancient recipe for lasagne. He opened out the pasta sheets instead of layering them, covered them with a light meat sauce and flour-free béchamel, using less stock and cream. Marchesi's fame travelled afar and for a few years he became for some 'the divine Marchesi', the first Italian to be awarded the prestigious three Michelin stars. On 22 October 2002, the International Academy of Gastronomy awarded Gualtiero Marchesi the Grand Prix Mémoire et Gratitude, the most prestigious prize that the Academy gives.

L'Albereta
Via Vittorio Emanuele 23
Erbusco (BS)
Italy

MENUS

INSALATA DI STORIONE CON LE SUE UOVA

RAVIOLO APERTO

FILETTO DI VITELLO ALLA ROSSINI

SFORMATO DI PANETTONE

STURGEON SALAD WITH CAVIAR

INSALATA DI STORIONE CON LE SUE UOVA

Serves 4

4 tablespoons Vinaigrette made with lemon juice (see page 76)

250-g/9-oz sturgeon fillet

100 g/3¹/₂ oz mixed salad leaves

1 onion, finely chopped

40 g/1¹/₂ oz oscietra caviar

fresh chervil sprigs, to garnish

Pour 2 tablespoons of the vinaigrette into a dish. Thinly slice the sturgeon, pound the slices lightly and place in the dish with the dressing. Toss the salad leaves in 1 tablespoon of the remaining vinaigrette and divide them among four plates. Add the onion and caviar to the remaining vinaigrette. Place the slices of fish on the salad leaves, sprinkle with the caviar mixture and garnish with chervil.

OPEN RAVIOLO

RAVIOLO APERTO

Serves 6

For the parsley pasta dough

100 g/3¹/₂ oz plain flour, plus extra for dusting

1 egg

1–2 tablespoons olive oil

For the green pasta dough

100 g/3¹/₂ oz plain flour, plus extra for dusting

80 g/3 oz spinach

1 egg

1–2 tablespoons olive oil

salt

For the filling

6 large parsley leaves

600 g/1 lb 5 oz scallops, shelled

5-cm/2-inch piece of fresh root ginger, grated

120 g/4 oz butter

100 ml/3¹/₂ fl oz dry white wine

salt and white pepper

Make the parsley pasta dough (see page 268) with the flour, egg and oil and roll out on a lightly floured surface to 3 mm/¹/₈ inch thick. Cut out twelve 5-cm/2-inch squares. Place a parsley leaf in the centre of half the squares, cover with the remaining squares and pass them through a pasta machine several times until the pasta is reduced to a thickness of about 1 mm/¹/₂₅ inch. Make the green pasta dough (see page 268) and roll out on a lightly floured surface to 1 mm/¹/₂₅ inch thick. Cut out six 10-cm/4-inch squares. To prepare the filling, cut the scallops in half crossways and season them. Squeeze out the juice from the grated ginger and reserve 1 tablespoon. Melt 20 g/³/₄ oz of the butter in a frying pan, add the scallops and cook them for a few seconds, then pour in the wine and cook for a few minutes. Remove the scallops from the pan. Heat the cooking liquid until it has reduced, add the ginger juice and whisk in the remaining butter to make the sauce. Return the scallops to the pan and cook for a few minutes more. Cook the pasta squares in a large pan of salted, boiling water until al dente. Pour a tablespoon of sauce on to each of six warm plates, place a green pasta square on top, divide the scallops and remaining sauce among them and top with the parsley pasta.

FILLET OF VEAL ALLA ROSSINI

Preheat the oven to 180°C/350°F/Gas Mark 4. Melt 20 g/³/₄ oz of the butter in an ovenproof frying pan. Season the veal with salt, add to the pan and cook until lightly browned on both sides, then transfer to the oven for 7 minutes. Remove the pan from the oven, set the veal aside and keep warm. Set the pan over a low heat, pour in the Madeira and cook, stirring and scraping up the sediment from the base, until the liquid has evaporated. Add the truffle juice and cook until it has reduced, then add the stock and truffle and season with salt. Bring to the boil and whisk in 10 g/¹/₄ oz of the remaining butter. Briefly cook the slices of foie gras in a non-stick pan and place them on the veal. Put the sultanas in a bowl, add warm water to cover and leave to soak for 5 minutes, then drain and squeeze out. Meanwhile, dry-fry the pine nuts until golden brown. Melt the remaining butter in another pan, add the spinach and cook until just wilted, then add the pine nuts and sultanas and season to taste. Arrange a bed of spinach on each of four warm plates, place the fillets on top and pour the sauce around them.

FILETTO DI VITELLO ALLA ROSSINI

Serves 4

50 g/2 oz butter

4 x 150-g/5-oz veal fillets

50 ml/2 fl oz Madeira

3 tablespoons truffle juice

100 g/3¹/₂ fl oz Meat Stock (see page 208)

20 g/³/₄ oz black truffle, chopped

4 x 40-g/1¹/₂-oz foie gras slices

2¹/₂ tablespoons sultanas

3 tablespoons pine nuts

400 g/14 oz spinach

salt and pepper

PANETTONE PUDDING

Cut the orange and lemon rinds into thin batons and place in a small saucepan with the orange juice, candied peel, sultanas, candied orange, Grand Marnier and sugar syrup. Bring to the boil and cook until reduced by half. Meanwhile, soak the gelatine in cold water for 5 minutes, then squeeze out. Remove the saucepan from the heat and, while it is still warm, mix the resulting syrup with half the custard and the gelatine. Blend well and leave to cool, stirring occasionally. Meanwhile, stiffly whisk the egg whites and gently fold them into the mixture, then fold in the caster sugar. Thickly whip the cream in another bowl and fold it into the mixture. Cut the panettone into cubes and add it to the mixture. Divide the mixture among four moulds and chill in the refrigerator for 3–4 hours. To serve, divide the remaining custard among four dishes, carefully turn the puddings out of their moulds and place one in the centre of each dish. To make the custard, pour the milk into a saucepan and bring to the boil, then remove from the heat. Beat the egg yolks with the sugar in another saucepan until pale and fluffy. Pour in the milk in a continuous stream, whisking constantly. Cook the custard over a medium heat, stirring constantly, until thickened. Do not allow it to boil.

SFORMATO DI PANETTONE

Serves 4

thinly pared rind of ¹/₂ orange

thinly pared rind of ¹/₂ lemon

2 tablespoons orange juice

2 tablespoons chopped candied citron peel

2¹/₂ tablespoons sultanas, chopped

20 g/³/₄ oz candied orange, chopped

2 tablespoons Grand Marnier

2 tablespoons Sugar Syrup (see page 1019)

2 gelatine leaves

300 ml/¹/₂ pint Custard (see below)

2 egg whites

2 tablespoons caster sugar

100 ml/3¹/₂ fl oz double cream

80 g/3 oz panettone, crusts removed

For the custard

250 ml/8 fl oz milk

4 egg yolks

120 g/4 oz caster sugar

Karen Martini

Melbourne Wine Room
125 Fitzroy Street
St Kilda, Victoria
Australia

Definitively original, the cooking of Karen Martini is a Mediterranean affair of inventive flavour combinations. The celebrated Australian chef, restaurateur, writer and television presenter draws inspiration from her rich cultural heritage. Bistecca fiorentina, her signature dish, has its roots in Florence but thrives under her care. The aged rib-eye steak is charbroiled over charcoal or wood, encrusted in Sicilian sea salt and served with horseradish. Karen Martini determined when young that her sole aim was to cook. Her gastronomic direction was shaped by family influences, including those of her father's parents who hailed from Tuscany and Nice and had been pastry chefs in Tunisia. Karen Martini spent her youth learning Tuscan and other recipes from her province as well as the Italian-influenced cuisine of North Africa. Together with her grandparents, she prepared the classics that now comprise her style. At 15 years old her training commenced with apprenticeships followed by trade school. She went on to absorb the basics of French cuisine in the kitchens of Melbourne restaurant, Tansy's. Next, travelling in Europe, she consolidated her repertoire of regional Italian dishes. Returning to Australia she held several head-chef positions before becoming founding chef at The Melbourne Wine Room. The popular bustling wine bar with adjoining dining room has won numerous prestigious awards. Complemented by an impressive wine cellar, the menu is celebrated for its combinations of intense flavours and textures that excite without overwhelming the palate. The award-winning wine list, with over 800 listings, embraces outstanding wines from the world's boutique and smaller winemakers.

MENUS

CARPACCIO DI TONNO CON FINOCCHIO BOTTARGA

INSALATA DI GAMBERETTI E FAGIOLI BIANCHI, CONDITA CON OLIO DI TARTUFO

COSTOLETTINE DI AGNELLO CON PATATE E CONDITE CON FETA E ORIGANO

PASTA DI CHOUX CON CREMA PASTICCIERA DI MANDORLE E SALSA CIOCCOLATO E MANDORLE CROCCANTI

YELLOW FIN TUNA CARPACCIO WITH SHAVED FENNEL, LEMON AND BOTTARGA

Cut the tuna into four even-sized slices, place them between sheets of baking parchment and press out gently with the back of the knife to form four even rounds. Set aside. Stiffly whip the cream with the yogurt, then fold in salt and lemon juice to taste. Thinly shave the fennel into ribbons with a mandoline and sprinkle with the reserved fennel fronds. Place the tuna on four plates, season with salt and pepper and sprinkle with the diced shallot, fennel ribbons and lemon triangles. Add a spoonful of the cream mixture to each plate and thinly shave the bottarga over the plates using a sharp knife. Drizzle generously with the oil and place a grissini across each plate of carpaccio.

CARPACCIO DI TONNO CON FINOCCHIO E BOTTARGA

Serves 4

500-g/1 lb 2-oz tuna mid-loin, sashimi grade
120 ml/4 fl oz double cream
1 tablespoon natural yogurt
dash of lemon juice
1 fennel bulb, trimmed with fronds reserved
1 purple shallot, finely diced
1 lemon, peeled, segmented
and cut into little triangles
80 g/3 oz bottarga • 4 grissini
200 ml/7 fl oz extra virgin olive oil
sea salt and pepper

SEARED PRAWNS WITH CANNELLINI BEAN SALAD AND TARTUFO DRESSING

Remove the prawn heads, peel the bodies, but leave the tail shells intact, and devein. Mix together the beans, half the lemon juice and the extra virgin olive oil in a bowl, season with salt and pepper and set aside in a warm place. Heat a large frying pan, add a little oil for frying, then add the prawns and stir-fry quickly without colouring. Season with salt and pepper, add the shallots and garlic to the pan, then stir in the beans. Remove the pan from the heat. Stir in the fennel, celery leaves and chives and transfer the mixture to a dish. To make the dressing, mix together the truffle paste, lemon juice and olive oil and pour it over the prawns and beans. Drizzle any extra dressing over the salad before serving. Finally, shave over the white truffle.

INSALATA DI GAMBERETTI E FAGIOLI BIANCHI, CONDITA CON OLIO DI TARTUFO

Serves 4

12 raw king prawns
300 /11 oz cooked cannellini beans,
drained and cooled to room temperature
100 ml/3¹/₂ fl oz freshly
squeezed lemon juice, strained
150 ml/¹/₄ pint extra virgin olive oil
olive oil, for frying • 3 shallots, finely diced
2 garlic cloves, finely diced
1 fennel heart, thinly shaved, with fronds reserved
fine yellow leaves of 1 celery heart, thinly sliced
¹/₂ bunch of chives, finely chopped
1 small fresh white truffle (optional)
salt and pepper

For the truffle dressing
1 tablespoon truffle paste
5 teaspoons lemon juice
100 ml/3¹/₂ fl oz extra virgin olive oil
4 teaspoons truffle oil
1 tablespoon roasted garlic
filament scraped from 1 large,
broken-up field mushroom

COSTOLETTINE DI AGNELLO CON PATATE E CONDITE CON FETA E ORIGANO

Serves 6

2 racks of lamb, each with about 8 cutlets

6 garlic cloves, crushed with the flat of a knife

½ bunch of fresh oregano

100 ml/3½ fl oz extra virgin olive oil, plus extra for drizzling

juice of 1 lemon, strained

4 teaspoons sherry vinegar

12 potatoes, sliced lengthways

200 g/7 oz curly endive

2 bunches of baby leeks, trimmed

120 ml/4 fl oz Vinaigrette (see page 76)

80 g/3 oz Ligurian olives

200 g/7 oz soft marinated feta cheese

salt and pepper

CHARGRILLED LAMB CUTLETS WITH OREGANO AND HOT FETA DRESSING

Trim the racks of lamb but leave a layer of fat, then score the fat in criss-cross lines. Cut the racks into separate cutlets. Mix together the garlic, half the oregano, the oil, lemon juice and vinegar in a large, non-metallic dish, season with pepper, add the lamb and leave to marinate. Meanwhile, cook the potatoes in salted, boiling water until tender, then drain, drizzle with olive oil and season with salt and pepper. Add the curly endive while the potatoes are still hot, toss gently and set aside in a warm place. Preheat the grill. Cook the leeks in another pan of boiling water for 2–3 minutes, then drain, drizzle with olive oil and season with salt and pepper. Drain the cutlets, season with salt and cook for 4–6 minutes until browned. Pour the vinaigrette into a shallow pan, add the olives, the remaining oregano leaves and the feta. Stir gently over a low heat to warm through. Place the warm potatoes on a serving dish, top with the lamb cutlets, sprinkle with the leeks and spoon the hot dressing over the dish. Season with a little black pepper and serve.

CHOUX PASTRY CREST WITH ALMOND CREAM, PRALINE, CHOCOLATE SAUCE AND GOLD LEAF

PASTA DI CHOUX CON CREMA
PASTICCIERA DI MANDORLE E SALSA
CIOCCOLATO E MANDORLE CROCCANTI

Serves 6

1 quantity Choux Paste (see page 1011)

For the almond cream

500 ml/18 fl oz milk

25 g/1 oz butter

100 g/3¹/₂ oz caster sugar

finely grated rind of ¹/₂ lemon

¹/₂ vanilla pod

4 egg yolks

50 g/2 oz cornflour

1 drop almond essence

For the chocolate sauce

200 g/7 oz dark chocolate, broken into pieces

100 ml/3¹/₂ fl oz double cream

25 g/1 oz cocoa powder

65 g/2¹/₂ oz clear honey

25 g/1 oz butter, cut into small pieces

1 teaspoon vanilla essence

For the praline

olive oil, for brushing

150 g/5 oz sugar

50 g/2 oz almonds, toasted

To serve

150 ml/¹/₄ pint single cream

icing sugar, for sprinkling (optional)

gold leaf filament (optional)

Preheat the oven to 220°C/425°F/Gas Mark 7. Spoon the choux paste into a piping bag fitted with a star nozzle and pipe doughnut-shaped rounds on a baking sheet. Sprinkle the baking sheet with a little water and bake for 5 minutes, then open the oven door and let the steam escape. Lower the oven temperature to 180°C/350°F/Gas Mark 4 and bake for a further 10–15 minutes until dried out. Remove from the oven and leave to cool. To make the almond cream, heat the milk, butter, half the sugar, the lemon rind and vanilla pod in a saucepan. Meanwhile, beat the egg yolks with the remaining sugar in a bowl, then whisk in the cornflour in three batches. Remove the hot milk from the heat and stir it into the egg yolk mixture. Return the mixture to the pan and bring to simmering point, whisking constantly. Lower the heat and simmer gently for 5 minutes. Stir in the almond essence and discard the vanilla pod. Pour the cream into a tray and cover with cling film. To make the chocolate sauce, place the chocolate, cream and honey in a pan over a low heat. Whisk the cocoa powder with 5 tablespoons water and the vanilla essence in a bowl and add to the chocolate mixture. Cook, stirring constantly, until melted and almost simmering. Remove from the heat and stir in the butter in small pieces at a time. Oil a baking sheet for the praline. Put the sugar in a pan, add about 2 tablespoons water and bring to the boil, then cook until the sugar caramelizes and turns golden brown. Stir in the almonds, remove the pan from the heat and pour the mixture on to the prepared baking sheet. Leave to cool and set. Wrap a rolling pin in baking parchment and use to crush the praline, then store in an airtight container until required. To serve, beat 250 ml/8 fl oz of the almond cream with sufficient single cream to give a smooth consistency. Spoon the mixture into a piping bag. Cut off a small 'lid' from each choux pastry and fill with the almond cream. Replace the lids. Place the pastries on a serving plate and pour the chocolate sauce over them and into a pool on the plate. Sprinkle with the praline and icing sugar or garnish with gold leaf filament and serve.

Gianluigi Morini

San Domenico
via Sacchi 1
Imola (BO)
Italy

Gianluigi Morini was born in Imola in 1935 in the very house where, on 7 March 1970, he opened the restaurant that was to become one of the most prestigious in Italy. A man with diverse interests, Morini had finally discovered his true vocation. But this was no passing whim – he sought out Nino Bergese, the legendary chef of kings, as his private tutor. It was not easy to persuade Bergese to leave his retirement in the peace and quiet of his home by the sea, but in the end Morini won him over. Bergese generously taught him the secrets of the trade, introduced him to the great dishes that had been created in the kitchens of the most prestigious Italian dynasties, drew up the menus at the San Domenico, organized service and guided the skills of the young chef Valentino Marcattilii. Today, Marcattilii is one of the most successful and internationally recognized Italian chefs, one who won his first Michelin star at the age of twenty and his second at twenty-two. Marcattilii's style became increasingly sophisticated, its success springing from the reintroduction of aristocratic dishes with a balanced blend of tradition and innovation. Morini meanwhile continued to perfect every detail of his restaurant, even providing a background of classical music each day that had been selected by Piero Buscaroli, a musicologist of world renown.

MENUS

TORTELLINI CON CREMA DI FEGATO D'OCA

QUAGLIE FARCITE CON VERDURE E PISELLI

CIOCCOCOCCO

TORTELLINI WITH GOOSE LIVER CREAM

Cook the goose liver in a non-stick pan with the bay leaves but without any additional fat for a few minutes. Remove the pan from the heat and leave to cool. Discard the bay leaves, put the liver in a food processor with the butter and process until smooth. Pass the mixture through a fine sieve into a bowl. Gently heat the cream in the same pan, add the liver mixture and nutmeg and season with salt and pepper if necessary. Cook the tortellini in a large pan of salted, boiling water until al dente, then drain and transfer to the pan of sauce. Cook, stirring constantly, for 2 minutes. Sprinkle with the Parmesan and serve with slivers of black truffle if you like.

TORTELLINI CON CREMA DI
FEGATO D'OCA

Serves 4

200 g/7 oz goose liver, sliced

3 bay leaves

100 g/3^1/$_2$ oz butter

100 ml/3^1/$_2$ fl oz double cream

pinch of freshly grated nutmeg

400 g/14 oz tortellini bolognesi

50 g/2 oz Parmesan cheese, freshly grated

salt and pepper

thinly shaved black truffle (optional), to serve

QUAIL STUFFED WITH GREEN VEGETABLES AND PEAS

Heat the half the oil and half the butter in a frying pan, add the peas and spinach and cook over a low heat, gradually adding the stock, until tender. Remove from the heat and leave to cool. Put the vegetable mixture in a food processor with the chicken and process until smooth. Mix together the goose liver and eggs, season with salt and pepper if necessary and add the vegetable mixture. Stuff the quail with the mixture and leave to stand for about 3 hours. Preheat the oven to 180°C/350°F/Gas Mark 4. Grease the reserved bones with the remaining oil and butter and place in an ovenproof dish with the quail. Season with salt and pepper, add the garlic and roast until the quail are browned all over and cooked through. (Test by piercing the thickest part with the point of a sharp knife. If the juices run clear, the quail are cooked.) Add the balsamic vinegar and return to the oven for a few minutes. Add the wine and cook until it has evaporated. Remove the quail, strain the cooking juices and season if necessary. Serve on warm plates with grilled or baked aubergines.

QUAGLIE FARCITE
CON VERDURE E PISELLI

Serves 4

2 tablespoons olive oil

25 g/1 oz butter

100 g/3^1/$_2$ oz shelled peas

150 g/5 oz spinach

475 ml/16 fl oz Chicken Stock (see page 209)

100 g/3^1/$_2$ oz skinless, boneless chicken breast, coarsely chopped

150 g/5 oz poached goose liver, cut into cubes

2 eggs

4 quail, boned with bones reserved

4 garlic cloves

5 tablespoons balsamic vinegar

175 ml/6 fl oz dry white wine

salt and pepper

grilled or baked aubergines, to serve

CHOCOCOCONUT

CIOCCOCOCCO

Serves 4

For the chocolate mousse
1 gelatine leaf
3 egg yolks
80 g/3 oz caster sugar
20 g/³/₄ oz cocoa powder
300 ml/¹/₂ pint milk
250 ml/8 fl oz double cream

For the coconut mousse
1 gelatine leaf
3 egg yolks
80 g/3 oz caster sugar
300 ml/¹/₂ pint milk
150 g/5 oz desiccated coconut
250 ml/8 fl oz double cream

For the caramel sauce
100 g/3¹/₂ oz caster sugar
300 ml/¹/₂ pint double cream

To decorate
4 fresh mint sprigs
25 g/1 oz plain or dark chocolate, shaved

To make the chocolate mousse, soak the gelatine in a bowl of cold water for 5 minutes, then squeeze out. Beat the egg yolks with the sugar and the cocoa powder until smooth and thoroughly combined. Bring the milk just to the boil and pour it into the egg mixture, stirring constantly, then add the gelatine and leave to cool, stirring occasionally. Stiffly whip the cream and fold it into the custard. Half-fill four large moulds with the mixture and chill in the refrigerator until set. To make the coconut mousse, soak the gelatine in a bowl of cold water for 5 minutes, then squeeze out. Beat the egg yolks with the sugar until combined. Pour the milk into a saucepan, add the coconut and bring to the boil. Remove the pan from the heat and strain the milk into the egg yolk mixture, stirring constantly, then add the gelatine and leave to cool, stirring occasionally. Reserve the coconut and leave to dry. Stiffly whip the cream and fold it into the cooled custard. Remove the moulds from the refrigerator, spoon in the coconut mixture and chill for several hours. To make the caramel sauce, put the sugar in a saucepan, add 5 tablespoons water and stir over a low heat until the sugar has dissolved, then continue cooking until the mixture turns a golden colour. Add the cream, bring to the boil, stirring constantly, and simmer for a few minutes. Remove the pan from the heat, strain the sauce and leave to cool. Pour the caramel sauce into four dishes. Turn out the chocococonut from the moulds, place them on the sauce, dust with the reserved coconut and decorate with the mint and the chocolate shavings.

Fulvio Pierangelini

Fulvio Pierangelini's passion for cooking began at the age of fifteen. It was then he became convinved that he should study cooking techniques so that when he grew up he would be able to start work on solid foundations. He was pressured by his family to stay at school and then go to university to obtain a degree in political science, but he did not give up easily and spent his summer holidays working with high-calibre chefs to learn the techniques and culinary secrets that were later to create his distinctive style. His dishes show some affinity with nouvelle cuisine, but the ingredients are typically local, albeit being interpreted without being limited by tradition. In 1981 he opened Il Gambero Rosso, a restaurant on the San Vincenzo waterfront and, within a few years, became the most imitated chef in the whole of Tuscany. This imitation reached such a level that he felt compelled to put up a notice at the entrance to his restaurant controversially banning entry by fellow chefs. The cuisine of Fulvio Pierangelini, time after time sanctioned by Michelin stars, is part passion and part instinct, although he maintains that most of the results of his recipes are inspired by the quality of the raw ingredients which he checks and selects carefully and thoroughly each day. The most often discussed and applauded dishes on his menu include scallops à la coque with oil and lemon, ravioli with tomato and pecorino cheese with green garlic and pigeon casserole.

Il Gambero Rosso
piazza della Vittoria 13
S. Vincenzo (LI)
Italy

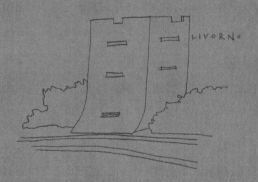

MENUS

PASSATINA DI CECI CON GAMBERI

RAVIOLI DI PESCE AI FRUTTI DI MARE

PICCIONI AL VINO ROSSO

SEMIFREDDO AI FRUTTI DI BOSCO

PURÉE OF CHICKPEAS WITH PRAWNS

PASSATINA DI CECI CON GAMBERI

Serves 4

100 g/3¹/₂ oz chickpeas, soaked overnight and drained

1 garlic clove

1 fresh rosemary sprig

800 g/1³/₄ lb raw prawns, peeled and deveined

extra virgin olive oil, for drizzling

salt and pepper

Put the chickpeas, garlic and rosemary in a saucepan, add water to cover and bring to the boil, then lower the heat and simmer gently for about 2¹/₂ hours until the chickpeas are tender. Drain well, discard the garlic and rosemary and pass the chickpeas through a sieve into a bowl. Steam the prawns for a few minutes until they change colour. Spoon a pool of chickpea purée on to each of four warm dishes and top with the prawns. Drizzle with olive oil and season with salt and pepper to taste.

FISH RAVIOLI WITH SHELLFISH

RAVIOLI DI PESCE AI FRUTTI DI MARE

Serves 4

For the pasta dough

200 g/7 oz plain flour, plus extra for dusting

2 eggs

2 tablespoons chopped fresh flat-leaf parsley

For the filling

1-kg/2¹/₄-lb skate, cleaned and skinned

1 litre/1³/₄ pints Fish Stock (see page 208–9)

For the sauce

5 tablespoons olive oil

2 garlic cloves

1 medium cuttlefish, skinned, cleaned and cut into small pieces

1 small octopus, skinned, cleaned and cut into small pieces

5 tablespoons dry white wine

200 g/7 oz tomatoes, peeled and coarsely chopped

20 raw prawns, peeled and deveined

10 mussels, shelled

salt and pepper

To make the filling, place the skate in a pan, add the stock and bring just to the boil, then lower the heat and simmer for about 20 minutes. Remove the skate with a fish slice and leave to cool. Reserve the vegetables from the stock. When the fish is cold, remove the flesh from the cartilage and place in a food processor with the reserved vegetables. Process until thoroughly combined. Make the pasta dough (see page 268) with the flour and eggs and roll out on a lightly floured surface to a very thin sheet, then cut it into strips. Place cherry-size mounds of the filling on the long side of the strips at 2.5-cm/1-inch intervals. Fold the pasta over them, pressing out the air, and seal the edges. Cut out the ravioli with a wheel and place on a lightly floured tea towel. To make the sauce, heat the oil in a shallow saucepan, add the garlic and cook for a few minutes, then remove and discard them. Add the cuttlefish and octopus and cook over a medium-high heat, stirring frequently, until golden brown. Add the wine and cook until it has evaporated. Add the tomatoes, season with salt and pepper and cook for a few minutes, then add the prawns and mussels and cook for a further 10 minutes. Cook the ravioli in a large pan of salted, boiling water, then drain well, dress with the shellfish sauce and sprinkle with the parsley.

PIGEONS IN RED WINE

Heat half the olive oil in a frying pan, add the garlic cloves and cook for a few minutes, then remove and discard, Add the pigeons and cook, turning occasionally, until golden brown all over and cooked through. Season with salt and pepper and remove them from the pan. Remove the breasts and legs from the pigeons, set aside and keep warm. Carefully bone the rest of the pigeons, reserving the carcasses. Heat the remaining oil in a frying pan, add the shallots and carrots and cook over a low heat, stirring occasionally, until softened. Place the pigeon carcasses in a shallow saucepan and heat gently. Add the wine and cook until it has reduced, then strain into a jug. Place the pigeon breasts on a warm serving dish, drizzle with the wine sauce and garnish with the shallots and carrots. Serve the legs separately.

PICCIONI AL VINO ROSSO

Serves 4

4 tablespoons olive oil

3 garlic cloves

4 x 400-g/14-oz pigeons

2 shallots, chopped

2 carrots, chopped

375 ml/13 fl oz full-bodied red wine

salt and pepper

FROZEN MOUSSE WITH FRUITS OF THE FOREST

Melt the butter in a non-stick pan, stir in the sugar and cook over a medium heat until lightly caramelized. Add the berries to the pan and toss them in the caramel for a few minutes, then remove from the heat and leave to cool. To make the meringue, stiffly whisk the egg whites in a grease-free bowl, then gradually whisk in the sugar. Gently fold the berries into the meringue. Stiffly whip the cream in another bowl and fold into the meringue. Divide the mixture among four small moulds and chill in the refrigerator for at least 6 hours until set. To make the custard, blanch the pistachios in boiling water for 1 minute, drain, rub off the skins and chop very finely. Pour the milk into a saucepan, add the pistachios and bring just to the boil, then remove the pan from the heat. Beat the egg yolks with the sugar in another saucepan until pale and fluffy. Gradually add the warm milk in a thin stream, stirring constantly. Cook the custard over a low heat, stirring constantly, until thick enough to coat the back of the spoon. Do not allow the custard to boil. Remove the pan from the heat and place in a bowl of iced water. Meanwhile, melt the chocolate in a heatproof bowl set over a pan of barely simmering water. Divide the custard among four dishes, turn out the frozen mousses and place them in the centre of each dish and decorate with wild strawberries and drizzled chocolate.

SEMIFREDDO AI FRUTTI DI BOSCO

Serves 4

50 g/2 oz unsalted butter

2 tablespoons caster sugar

400 g/14 oz mixed berries, such as raspberries, strawberries, blueberries and blackberries

200 ml/7 fl oz double cream

For the meringue

2 egg whites

100 g/3½ oz caster sugar

For the custard

1 tablespoon pistachio nuts

400 ml/14 fl oz milk

3 egg yolks

100 g/3½ oz caster sugar

To decorate

100 g/3½ oz dark or plain chocolate, broken into pieces

100 g/3½ oz wild strawberries

Stefano de Pieri

Stefano's
Mildura Grand Hotel
Seventh Street
Mildura, Victoria
Australia

The food of Stefano de Pieri comes straight from the heart. Raised on a tiny farm in Treviso near Venice, his family sold their produce at the local food market. Surrounded by superb regional cuisine, his palette received a fine education. As a young man, his sense of adventure turned him to Australia, and ultimately to the town of Mildura by the mighty Murray River in north-west Victoria, where he has settled. Here he has embraced wholeheartedly the local food and wine, establishing a series of renowned eateries that showcase the traditional cuisine of his native Veneto through the fabulous ingredients he finds in his new locality. Stefano de Pieri is largely self-taught, having undertaken only the briefest of formal culinary training. However, his real mentor was his mother, from whom he has inherited the unfailing instinct and expertise for which he is now recognised. Memories of the flavours of his childhood have gone on to inspire the hearty cuisine of Stefano's, his flagship restaurant, located in the atmospheric cantina cellar of the Mildura Grand Hotel. There, he serves five-course Northern Italian banquets using only the finest and freshest of local produce. As an enthusiastic proponent of the Slow Food movement, Stefano de Pieri's menu changes daily, presenting a parade of exciting seasonal dishes and buoyant combinations of tastes and aromas. Regular stars of his menus include Murray cod, silver perch, yabbies and scallops. Stefano de Pieri, and the food of his multi-award-winning restaurant, are enthusiastic ambassadors for his beloved region. He is an active campaigner for the care of the ecology of the Murray River, has founded a lively arts festival and, of course, has put his particular part of Australia firmly on the international culinary map.

MENUS

COZZE AL VAPORE CON ERBE AROMATICHE

ZUPPA DI PICCIONE

GUANCE DI MANZO BRASATE AL VINO

PANNA COTTA CARAMELLATA

MUSSELS WITH AROMATIC HERBS

Discard any mussels with broken shells or that do not shut immediately when sharply tapped. Chop the garlic, chilli, ginger, coriander and lime leaves, lemon rind or lemon grass. Heat the oil in a large saucepan and add all the herbs and flavourings. Add the mussels, cover and cook over a high heat for 3–5 minutes until the mussels have opened. Discard any mussels that remain closed, tip the remainder into a bowl and serve.

COZZE AL VAPORE CON ERBE AROMATICHE

Serves 4

40 live mussels, scrubbed and beards removed

1 garlic clove, crushed with the back of a knife

$^1/_4$–$^1/_2$ fresh chilli

6 thin slices of fresh root ginger

6 large fresh coriander sprigs

3–4 kaffir lime leaves or thinly pared rind

of $^1/_4$ lemon or 2 lemon grass stalks

1 tablespoon olive oil

8 tablespoons coarsely chopped fresh flat-leaf parsley

PIGEON AND BREAD SOUP

Heat the oil in a saucepan, add the carrots, celery, onions and sage leaves and cook over a low heat, stirring occasionally, for about 10 minutes or until lightly browned. Increase the heat to medium, add the pigeons and cook, turning frequently, until browned on all sides. Add the wine, season with salt and pepper, lower the heat and simmer for about 1 hour or until the pigeons are cooked through. If the mixture seems to be drying out during cooking, add a little hot water to the pan. Remove the pigeons from the pan and leave to cool. Pass the cooking juices and vegetables through a fine sieve into a bowl, leave to cool and then chill in the refrigerator until the fat has set on top. Remove and discard the fat. Using your fingers, pull the pigeon meat off the bones, including the legs, chop and set aside. Put the pigeon carcasses in a pan, add water to cover and cook over a very low heat for about 2 hours. (Alternatively, use chicken stock instead of water for a stronger flavour.) Strain the pigeon stock into a bowl and discard the carcasses. Preheat the oven to 150°C/300°F/Gas Mark 2. Make a layer of bread slices in the base of an ovenproof dish, ladle over enough stock to soak, sprinkle with a layer of the chopped pigeon meat, add spoonfuls of the de-fatted cooking juices and sprinkle generously with Parmesan. Continue making layers until all the ingredients are used. Cover the dish with greaseproof paper and bake for 1 hour. Remove and discard the paper, increase the oven temperature to 180°C/350°F/Gas Mark 4 and bake until piping hot. Reheat the remaining stock. Divide the pigeon mixture among hot serving bowls with a little extra stock on the side, not the top, and serve.

ZUPPA DI PICCIONE

Serves 4

4 tablespoons olive oil

120 g/4 oz carrots, coarsely chopped

80 g/3 oz celery, coarsely chopped

175 g/6 oz onions, coarsely chopped

3–4 fresh sage leaves

4 pigeons, plucked and drawn

250 ml/8 fl oz red wine

16–20 slices of day-old bread,

preferably sourdough, crusts removed

175 g/6 oz Parmesan cheese, freshly grated

salt and pepper

BRAISED BEEF CHEEKS

GUANCE DI MANZO BRASATE AL VINO

Serves 4

6 beef cheeks

175 g/6 oz plum tomatoes, peeled

3 tablespoons olive oil

40 g/1½ oz celery, coarsely chopped

50 g/2 oz carrots, coarsely chopped

80 g/3 oz onions, coarsely chopped

2 garlic cloves, chopped

2 bay leaves

250–275 ml/8–9 fl oz strong red wine

salt and pepper

polenta or mashed potatoes, to serve

Preheat the oven to 180°C/350°F/Gas Mark 4. Line a baking tray, roasting tin or shallow ovenproof dish with greaseproof paper. Trim off the excess fat from the beef cheeks but do not cut off all the fat. Coarsely chop the tomatoes, reserving their juices. Place the tomato flesh and juices in a food processor and process to a purée. Heat the oil in a heavy-based saucepan, add the celery, carrots, onions and garlic and cook over a low heat, stirring occasionally, for about 10 minutes until lightly browned. Increase the heat to medium, add the beef cheeks and cook, turning frequently, until browned all over. Season, add the bay leaves and wine and cook until the liquid has reduced. Add the puréed tomatoes and cook for a few minutes more, then transfer the mixture to the prepared tray, tin or dish, cover with greaseproof paper and foil and bake for 2½ hours until the beef is very tender. Transfer the beef cheeks to another dish and pour the cooking juices into a jug or bowl. When cold, chill in the refrigerator. Remove the fat from the top of the cooking juices, pour the juices over the beef and reheat in a preheated oven at 180°C/350°F/Gas Mark 4. Serve with polenta or mashed potatoes.

CARAMELIZED PANNA COTTA

PANNA COTTA CARAMELLATA

Serves 4

1 litre/1¾ pints double cream

1 vanilla pod

1 cinnamon stick

pinch of coffee grains

thinly pared rind of 1 orange, 1 lemon or both

120 g/4 oz sugar, plus extra to taste

10 small egg whites or 8 medium egg whites

fruit, to serve

Pour the cream into a saucepan, add the vanilla, cinnamon, coffee and citrus rind and bring just to the boil. Stir in sugar to taste until it has dissolved, then remove from the heat and leave to cool. Meanwhile, put the sugar in a saucepan, add about 3 tablespoons water and bring to the boil, swirling the pan to dissolve the sugar, then cook for 4–5 minutes until caramelized, but not burnt. Pour the caramel into four dariole moulds to make a 3–5-mm/⅛–¼-inch thick layer. When the cream is cold, remove and discard the flavourings. Preheat the oven to 140°C/275°F/Gas Mark 1. Line a roasting tin with a tea towel. Whisk the egg whites until soft peaks form, then fold them into the cream. Divide the mixture among the moulds, place them in the roasting tin and add boiling water to halfway up the sides. Bake for 35–40 minutes until slightly risen. Remove from the oven and leave to cool. Do not worry if the creams fall slightly and appear unset. Chill in the refrigerator overnight, when they will acquire a soft creamy texture. To serve, place the moulds in a bath of warm water to dissolve the caramel slightly or remove from the refrigerator well in advance. Serve with fruit of your choice.

Ruth Rogers and Rose Gray

In 1987, Ruth Rogers and Rose Gray opened The River Café in converted 19th-century warehouses on the banks of the Thames, at Hammersmith, London. Neither were following a traditional route: Ruth Rogers' mother-in-law had imbued her with a passion for good food; Rose Gray briefly cooked in the kitchen at Nell's Club in New York and had researched Italian recipes in Tuscany. From these unorthodox beginnings, The River Café has become one of the best known Italian restaurants, both in the United Kingdom and beyond. As firm exponents of seasonal and well sourced ingredients, both are at the forefront of the fresh-produce revolution. 'Good cooking is about fresh seasonal ingredients, used thoughtfully.' Rogers and Gray routinely journey to Italy, and have a flourishing vegetable and herb garden adjacent to the restaurant. Complimenting their respect for regional ingredients, they have introduced classic Italian cooking methods to diners at The River Café, and share their joy for rustic Italian cooking through their cookbooks and television projects. At The River Café, regional dishes, both robust and subtle, are served in a modern atmosphere, using sophisticated skill and materials in the kitchen, heralding Rose and Ruth's pleasure and excitement in cooking.

The River Café
Thames Wharf
Rainville Road
London
United Kingdom

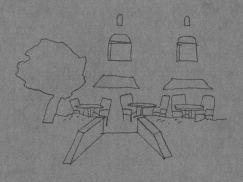

MENUS

PUNTARELLE ALLE ROMANA

TAGLIATELLE CON RUCOLA E CREMA DI LIMONE

TETRAONE CON BRUSCHETTA E CAVOLO NERO

NEMESIS

PUNTARELLE ALLA ROMANA

PUNTARELLE ALLA ROMANA

Serves 6

2 puntarelle heads

5 salted anchovies, heads removed, cleaned and filleted (see page 596)

2 tablespoons red wine vinegar

1 garlic clove, very finely chopped

1 teaspoon black pepper

2 dried chillies • 4 tablespoons extra virgin olive oil

1 lemon, cut into wedges

Fill a bowl with cold water and ice cubes. Pull the hollow buds from the puntarelle heads and thinly slice them lengthways with a small knife. Put the sliced buds in the iced water for 1 hour or until crisped and curled up. Cut the anchovy fillets into 1-cm/ $^1/_2$-inch pieces. Place in a bowl, add the vinegar and stir until disintegrated. Add the garlic and pepper to the anchovies and crumble in the chillies. Leave to stand for 15 minutes, then stir in the olive oil. Drain the puntarelle and spin dry. Place in a bowl and spoon the sauce over it. Serve with the lemon wedges.

TAGLIATELLE WITH CRÈME FRAÎCHE AND ROCKET

TAGLIATELLE CON RUCOLA E CREMA DI LIMONE

Serves 6

250 ml/8 fl oz crème fraîche

finely grated rind and juice of 2 lemons

320 g/11$^1/_2$ oz egg tagliatelle

150 g/5 oz rocket leaves, coarsely chopped

150 g/5 oz Parmesan cheese, freshly grated

salt and pepper

Pour the crème fraîche into a bowl, stir in the lemon rind and juice and season with salt and pepper. Bring a large pan of salted water to the boil, add the tagliatelle and cook until al dente, then drain and return to the pan. Pour the lemon and cream sauce over the pasta, add the rocket and half the Parmesan and toss to combine. Serve with the remaining Parmesan.

GROUSE WITH BRUSCHETTA AND CAVOLO NERO

TETRAONE CON BRUSCHETTA E CAVOLO NERO

Serves 6

For the grouse with bruschetta

4 plucked and drawn grouse • 16 fresh thyme sprigs

200 g/7 oz unsalted butter

1 tablespoon extra virgin olive oil

350 ml/12 fl oz red wine

$^1/_4$ sourdough loaf, thickly sliced

1 garlic clove, peeled

For the cavolo nero

4 heads cavolo nero (Tuscan cabbage), cored

3 tablespoons olive oil

2 garlic cloves, finely chopped

extra virgin olive oil, for drizzling

sea salt and pepper

For the grouse, preheat the oven to 220°C/425°F/Gas Mark 7. Divide the thyme sprigs among the cavities and add a knob of butter to each. Season and place on an oven tray, breast side down. Drizzle the olive oil over the birds and pour over 150 ml/$^1/_4$ pint of the wine. Roast for 10 minutes, then turn them breast side up, pour 150 ml/$^1/_4$ pint of the remaining wine over them and roast, basting occasionally, for a further 10 minutes. Add the rest of the wine and the remaining butter and roast for 5 minutes more. Remove from the oven. Toast the bread slices on both sides. Lightly rub one side of the toast with the garlic. Press the garlic side of each piece of toast into the grouse cooking juices and then invert on to warm plates. Place the grouse on top and pour the remaining cooking juices over the birds. Blanch the cavolo nero in salted, boiling water for 3 minutes, then drain. Heat the olive oil in a heavy-based saucepan, add the garlic and cook over a low heat for a few minutes until it begins to colour. Add the cavolo nero and season generously. Cook for about 5 minutes, then remove from the heat, drizzle with the olive oil and serve with the grouse.

NEMESIS

Preheat the oven to 120°C/250°F/Gas Mark ½. Grease a 25-cm/10-inch cake tin with butter and line with baking parchment. Put the chocolate and butter in a heatproof bowl and melt over a pan of barely simmering water, then remove from the heat. Using an electric mixer beat the eggs with 70 g/2¾ oz of the sugar until quadrupled in volume. Heat the remaining sugar with 100 ml/3½ fl oz water, stirring until the sugar has dissolved, then cook until a light syrup forms. Pour the hot syrup into the melted chocolate mixture and leave to cool slightly, then add the mixture to the egg mixture and beat slowly until combined. Pour the mixture into the prepared tin. Put a folded kitchen cloth on the base of a roasting tin, place the cake tin on top and pour in boiling water to come three-quarters of the way up the side. Bake for 50 minutes until set. Leave the cake to cool in the water bath before turning out.

NEMESIS

Serves 6

225 g/8 oz unsalted butter, plus extra for greasing

340 g/11¾ oz 70% chocolate, broken into pieces

5 eggs

210 g/7¼ oz caster sugar

Ezio Santin

Antica Osteria del Ponte
Cassinetta di Lugagnano (MI)
Italy

Colombina – or Bina – Santin, has a natural gift for cooking which her son Ezio has inherited. Sooner or later, these skills were bound to have been destined to find their rightful setting in the form of a restaurant. In 1976, a lovingly restored, charming and remote country house in Cassinetta di Lugagnano near Milan was reincarnated as the Antica Osteria del Ponte. Within a short time, it became a focus for gourmets, and won many coveted awards – a shower of Michelin stars from 1978 onwards. These were the prize for Ezio Santin's true passion for cooking. Santin turned professional at the age of forty, having previously cooked only as a hobby. He loves the regional cooking of Lombardy and seeks out local produce, carefully judging the optimal cooking of Italian vegetables, 'in order not to eradicate their magnificent original flavour.' He also has a happy knack with fish, allowing him to explore such interesting ideas as red mullet in an orange sauce with candied onions and julienne rind. As far as desserts are concerned, Santin is very fond of chocolate, although he hands over this type of cooking to his son Maurizio who, after studying with the most celebrated maîtres pâtissiers in France, has become an excellent, creative maître pâtissier himself.

MENUS

INSALATA TIEPIDA DI GAMBERI, VERZE E LENTICCHIE

LASAGNETTE AI PORRI, CIPOLLOTTI E TARTUFI NERI

CREPINETTE DI CAPRETTO ALLE MANDORLE

TERRINA DI CIOCCOLATO E MANDORLE

SORBETTO CAFFÈ E CACAO

WARM SALAD OF PRAWNS, SAVOY CABBAGE AND LENTILS

Blanch the cabbage leaves in salted, boiling water until al dente, then drain and keep warm. Heat 1 tablespoon of the oil in a non-stick pan, add the prawns and cook over a medium-high heat for 2 minutes on each side, then season to taste with salt and pepper. Whisk together the remaining oil, the vinegar and the lentil cooking water in a small frying pan, add the lentils and heat through. Cut the cabbage leaves in large pieces and place them in the centre of four warm plates, arrange the prawns on top of them and drizzle with the lentil vinaigrette.

INSALATA TIEPIDA DI GAMBERI, VERZE E LENTICCHIE

Serves 4

8 Savoy cabbage leaves

4 tablespoons olive oil

600 g/1 lb 5 oz raw prawns, peeled and deveined

1 tablespoon red wine vinegar

4 tablespoons cooked lentils,

plus 3 tablespoons of the cooking water

salt and pepper

LASAGNETTE WITH LEEKS, SPRING ONIONS AND BLACK TRUFFLES

Cook the lasagnette in salted, boiling water, then drain and refresh in iced water. Heat the butter and oil in a frying pan, add the spring onions and leeks and cook over a low heat, stirring frequently, for 15 minutes. Season to taste with salt and pepper. Blanch the guanciale or pancetta in boiling water for 2 minutes, then drain and cook in a heated non-stick pan for a further 2 minutes until the fat runs. Remove from the pan, add to the spring onion mixture with the truffles and cream and cook over a medium heat, stirring constantly, for 6 minutes. Remove from the heat and leave to cool. Sandwich together the lasagnette in threes with the cooled filling, then steam for a few minutes to heat through. Meanwhile, make the dressing. Gently warm the oil, truffle juice and vinegar in a small pan. Serve the lasagnette with the warm dressing.

LASAGNETTE AI PORRI, CIPOLLOTTI E TARTUFI NERI

Serves 6

18 lasagnette (6 x 10-cm/2¹/₂ x 4-inch pasta sheets)

50 g/2 oz butter

4 tablespoons olive oil

400 g/14 oz spring onions, thinly sliced

200 g/7 oz leeks, white parts only, thinly sliced

50 g/2 oz guanciale or pancetta, cut into strips

150 g/5 oz black truffles, finely chopped

175 ml/6 fl oz single cream

salt and pepper

For the dressing

6 tablespoons extra virgin olive oil

2 tablespoons black truffle juice

1 tablespoon balsamic vinegar

KID CRÉPINETTES WITH ALMONDS

CREPINETTE DI CAPRETTO ALLE MANDORLE

Serves 4

1 leg and fillet of a small kid

1 sheet caul fat, preferably from a kid

20 g/³/₄ oz blanched almonds, chopped

50 g/2 oz butter

2 tablespoons olive oil

3 tablespoons Chicken Stock (see page 209)

¹/₂ teaspoon Dijon mustard

salt and pepper

roasted new potatoes, to serve

Ask the butcher to fillet the kid leg completely. Soak the caul fat in warm water until it has softened, then drain. Cut the leg meat into medium pieces and cut the fillet into cubes. Put all of the meat into a bowl, add the almonds, season with salt and pepper and mix well. Divide the mixture into eight and roll each piece into a small ball. Cut the caul fat into eight pieces and use it to wrap the balls. Melt half the butter and the oil in a frying pan, add the crépinettes and cook over a medium-high heat for 6 minutes, then turn over and cook for a further 4 minutes. Meanwhile, bring the stock to the boil in a small pan, then remove from the heat. Stir in the mustard, whisk in the remaining butter and season to taste with salt and pepper. Place the crépinettes on a warm serving dish and spoon the sauce over them. Serve them with roasted new potatoes.

ALMOND AND CHOCOLATE LAYERS

TERRINA DI CIOCCOLATO E MANDORLE

Serves 6

unsalted butter, for greasing

plain flour, for dusting

6 egg whites

175 g/6 oz caster sugar

175 g/6 oz ground almonds

light chocolate sauce or coffee and cocoa sorbet (see below), to serve

For the chocolate ganache

250 ml/8 fl oz double cream

300 g/11 oz dark or plain chocolate, broken into small pieces

2 tablespoons rum

Preheat the oven to 180°C/350°F/Gas Mark 4. Lightly grease a Swiss roll tin with butter and dust with flour. Stiffly whisk the egg whites in a grease-free bowl, then gradually whisk in the sugar, followed by the almonds. Spread out the mixture in the prepared tin to a depth of 2 cm/³/₄ inch and bake for 15–20 minutes until golden brown and just firm to the touch, then leave to cool. Meanwhile, prepare the ganache. Bring the cream to the boil in a small saucepan over a medium heat. Put the chocolate in a heat-proof bowl, pour the warm cream over it in a steady stream and leave it to melt, then stir in the rum. Cut the almond biscuit to fit a terrine or loaf tin in layers, then make alternating layers of biscuit and chocolate ganache until all the ingredients are used, ending with a layer of chocolate. To serve, turn out on to a plate, cut into slices and serve with a light chocolate sauce on the side or with a coffee and cocoa sorbet.

COFFEE AND COCOA SORBET

SORBETTO CAFFÉ E CACAO

Makes 500 g/1 lb 2 oz sorbet

135 ml/4¹/₂ fl oz still mineral water

175 g/6 oz caster sugar

2 tablespoons cocoa powder

250 ml/8 fl oz freshly brewed extra-strong coffee

Pour the mineral water into a small saucepan, add the sugar and bring to the boil, stirring constantly, then stir in the cocoa powder. Mix well and pour in the coffee. Strain the mixture into a bowl and leave to cool, then pour into an ice-cream maker and freeze for about 20 minutes or according to the manufacturer's instructions.

Nadia Santini

Nadia Santini is the first Italian female chef of renown and, currently, the only one to boast three Michelin stars. This is truly a record founded on the heritage of her culinary family. A small area of the countryside around Mantua, with its reeds and ponds, duck, geese and lush meadows – Canneto sull'Oglio – is the location for their Dal Pescatore restaurant, which opened in 1920. Antonio Santini comes from the third generation of a family of restaurant owners who have always applied the same management technique – husbands at the tables and wives in the kitchen. Antonio studied economics and business, Nadia political science, and they met at university in Milan. However, one day in 1974, they decided that their paths lay in another direction – that of haute cuisine. They sought advice from Franco Colombani, the great chef at Il Sole in Maleo and a valiant defender of regional cooking in the era of nouvelle cuisine. So, in the elegant rooms of their refurbished restaurant, they serve traditional dishes from the Padania region: pigs' trotters with Savoy cabbage and pulses, duckling in balsamic vinegar and pecorino, ricotta and Parmesan tortelli. Nadia explains her work in the following simple terms, 'I feel drawn towards traditional, even lowly, cuisine, just for the pleasure of making it great.'

Dal Pescatore
Canneto sull'Oglio (MN)
Italy

MENUS

TINCA IN CARPIONE

TORTELLI DI PECORINA, RICOTTA E PARMIGIANO AL TARTUFO BIANCO

ANATRA ALL'ACETO BALSAMICO

PIPASENER E ZABAIONE

TINCA IN CARPIONE

Serves 4

3 tablespoons olive oil, plus extra for drizzling

2 x 600-g/1 lb 5-oz tench, cleaned and filleted

1 litre/1¾ pints white wine vinegar

500 ml/18 fl oz sweet white wine

120 g/4 oz sugar

2 onions, thinly sliced

pinch of ground cinnamon

2–3 cloves

pinch of freshly grated nutmeg

2 tablespoons chopped fresh flat-leaf parsley

balsamic vinegar, for drizzling

salt and pepper

SWEET–AND–SOUR TENCH

Heat the oil in a frying pan, add the fish fillets and cook for about 10 minutes. Remove the fish from the pan with a fish slice and drain on kitchen paper. Add the white wine vinegar, white wine, sugar, onions, cinnamon, cloves, nutmeg and a pinch each of salt and pepper to the pan and cook, stirring occasionally, for about 15 minutes. Place the fish fillets in a heatproof dish, sprinkle with the parsley and pour the sauce over them. Cover the dish and leave to cool. Serve warm or cold, drizzled with olive oil and a few drops of balsamic vinegar.

TORTELLI DI PECORINA, RICOTTA E PARMIGIANO AL TARTUFO BIANCO

Serves 6

350 g/12 oz plain flour, plus extra for dusting

2 eggs

salt

For the filling

80 g/3 oz ricotta cheese

2 eggs, lightly beaten

80 g/3 oz pecorino cheese, freshly grated

80 g/3 oz Parmesan cheese, freshly grated

For the sauce

50 g/2 oz butter, melted

50 g/2 oz Parmesan cheese, freshly grated

50 g/2 oz white truffle, thinly shaved

TUSCAN PECORINO, RICOTTA AND PARMESAN TORTELLI WITH WHITE TRUFFLE

First make the filling. Pass the ricotta through a sieve, then stir in the eggs, pecorino and Parmesan. Set aside and keep cool. Prepare the pasta dough with the flour, eggs and a pinch of salt (see page 268). Halve the dough and roll out one piece on a lightly floured surface into a thin sheet. Place small spoonfuls of the filling on it, spaced evenly apart. Roll out the second piece of dough and place it on top of the first, pressing down gently around the mounds of filling. Cut out tortelli with a small round, square or half-moon cutter, according to taste. Cook the tortelli in salted, boiling water for about 5 minutes, then drain and dress with the melted butter, grated Parmesan cheese and slivers of white truffle.

DUCKLING IN BALSAMIC VINEGAR

Preheat the oven to 150°C/300°F/Gas Mark 2. Place the duckling in an oven-proof dish and spread the butter over it. Add the lemon juice, brandy, white wine, stock, 200 ml/7 fl oz water, the rosemary and sage and season with salt and pepper. Place the dish in the oven and cook for 1–1½ hours or until the duckling is golden brown. Remove the duckling from the dish and strain the cooking liquid into a saucepan. Pour in the red wine and reduce over a low heat. Add the balsamic vinegar and cook until thickened. Cut the duck into quarters, place on individual dishes and pour the hot sauce over them.

ANATRA ALL'ACETO BALSAMICO

Serves 4

2-kg/4½-lb duckling

150 g/5 oz butter

juice of ½ lemon, strained

5 tablespoons brandy

175 ml/6 fl oz white wine

300 ml/½ pint Meat Stock (see page 208)

1 fresh rosemary sprig

1 fresh sage sprig

175 ml/6 fl oz full-bodied red wine

2 tablespoons balsamic vinegar

salt and pepper

PIPASENER PASTRY WITH ZABAGLIONE

Put the sultanas in a bowl, add warm water to cover and leave to soak for 15 minutes, then drain and squeeze out. Pass the ricotta through a sieve. Mix together the flour, sugar, eggs and ricotta in a bowl, then add the sultanas, chocolate, rum and butter and knead lightly. Knead in the yeast. Grease a copper pan with butter and dust with flour, place the dough in the pan and cover with a copper lid. Cook over an open fire, placing the pan on the ashes and covering it with the embers and more ash. The dessert will be cooked after 1 hour. Prepare the zabaglione and serve it warm with the pastry.

PIPASENER E ZABAIONE

Serves 4

50 g/2 oz sultanas

200 g/7 oz ricotta cheese

200 g/7 oz plain flour, plus extra for dusting

200 g/7 oz caster sugar

3 eggs

40 g/1½ oz dark or plain chocolate, broken into pieces

1 tablespoon rum

40 g/1½ oz unsalted butter, plus extra for greasing

1 sachet easy-blend yeast

Zabaglione made with 5 egg yolks (see page 1039)

Gianfranco Vissani

Gianfranco Vissani
Civitella del Lago
Baschi (TR)
Italy

When he was still only thirteen years old, Gianfranco Vissani's catering college already considered him to be promising, although it is unusual for chefs to display outstanding talent before their twentieth birthday. As an adult, the fact remains that Gianfranco Vissani has taken his rightful place in the history of cooking as one of the greatest chefs in Italy. Although penalized by the remote location of his restaurant, almost hidden in a corner of 'dolce Umbria', Vissani has succeeded in achieving world-wide fame. He never repeats his recipes – today the sea bass may be served with tomato, but tomorrow it will be accompanied by asparagus, and next month with artichokes and then with oranges. This is dictated by his creative sensitivity, a style that is capable of instantly grasping the potential of whatever ingredient he has before him. Vissani's was never nouvelle cuisine; his elegant and stylized dishes are solely the fruit of natural talent, one that tries out daring, yet always interesting flavours. Today, his cuisine is recognized as being typically Italian. Even if some recipes include foie gras or Belon oysters or basmati rice, Vissani always includes extra virgin olive oil and other typical local products, such as aromatic Norcia truffles or lentils from the hill area of Castelluccio.

MENUS

FILETTI DI SOGLIOLA CON SEDANO, SALSA AURORA E CAVIALE

ORZO PERLATO CON QUAGLIE E TIMO, SALSA DI PATATE E ARANCIA CON BRUNOISE D'OLIVE

SELLA DI DAINO CON TIMBALLO DI TARTUFI NERI

BABÀ CON SALSA D'ARANCIA

FILLETS OF SOLE WITH CELERY JULIENNE, AURORA SAUCE AND CAVIAR

Make a stock using the fish bones and herbs (see page 208–9). Heat 2 tablespoons of the oil in a frying pan, add the celery and one garlic clove and cook over a low heat for a few minutes. Remove the pan from the heat, drain the celery and discard the garlic. Divide the celery batons among the fish fillets, roll up and steam them until cooked through. Meanwhile, prepare the sauce. Coarsely chop the remaining garlic clove. Heat the remaining oil in a frying pan, add the chopped garlic, tomatoes, shallot and chervil and cook over a low heat, stirring occasionally, for about 10 minutes. Ladle the mixture into a food processor and process until smooth and thoroughly combined. Strain in enough stock to produce the desired consistency and season to taste with salt and white pepper. Pour a pool of sauce on to individual dishes, place the sole parcels on top and garnish with the caviar. Serve immediately.

FILETTI DI SOGLIOLA CON SEDANO, SALSA AURORA E CAVIALE

Serves 4

3 small sole, filleted with bones reserved

bunch of fresh mixed herbs

100 ml/3¹/₂ fl oz extra virgin olive oil

4 tender celery sticks, cut into thin batons

2 garlic cloves

400 g/14 oz cherry tomatoes, peeled and seeded

1 shallot, thinly sliced

2 fresh chervil sprigs, chopped

100 g/3¹/₂ oz caviar

salt and ground white pepper

PEARL BARLEY WITH QUAIL, THYME, POTATO AND ORANGE SAUCE WITH OLIVE BRUNOISE

Make a fairly light stock with the quail carcasses (see page 208), then strain. Dice the meat. Preheat the oven to 180°C/350°F/Gas Mark 4. Heat 3 tablespoons of the oil in a saucepan, add three-quarters of the garlic, one bay leaf, one shallot, the quail meat, and cook over a low heat, stirring occasionally, for about 5 minutes. Add the barley and cook briefly, then pour in a ladleful of the stock and cook, stirring constantly, until the liquid has been absorbed. Continue adding the stock, a ladleful at a time. When the mixture is cooked through and tender, remove from the heat and stir in the Parmesan and thyme. Remove and discard the bay leaf. Line four individual moulds with the spinach, divide the barley mixture among them and bake for 10–15 minutes. Prepare the sauce. Heat 1 tablespoon of the remaining oil in a pan, add the remaining shallot and bay leaf, together with the pork rind, leek, potatoes and orange segments and cook over a low heat, stirring occasionally, for 10 minutes or until the potatoes are tender. Transfer to a food processor and process until smooth, adding orange juice if necessary. Heat the remaining oil, add the olives and remaining garlic and cook over a low heat for a few minutes. Pour a pool of the sauce on to individual dishes, turn out the barley cakes and place in the centre and garnish with the black olives.

ORZO PERLATO CON QUAGLIE E TIMO, SALSA DI PATATE E ARANCIA CON BRUNOISE D'OLIVE

Serves 4

2 quail, boned and with carcasses reserved

4 tablespoons olive oil

3 garlic cloves, finely chopped

2 bay leaves

2 shallots, finely chopped

400 g/14 oz pearl barley

50 g/2 oz Parmesan cheese, freshly grated

1 fresh thyme sprig

50 g/2 oz spinach

1 piece of pork rind, chopped

1 leek, white part only sliced

2 potatoes, par-boiled and sliced

2 oranges, cut into segments

juice of ¹/₂ orange, strained (optional)

100 g/3¹/₂ oz black olives, stoned and finely diced

SELLA DI DAINO CON TIMBALLO
DI TARTUFI NERI

Serves 4

1 saddle of venison

100 g/3¹/₂ oz pork fat or streaky bacon,
cut into strips

4 tablespoons olive oil

1 garlic clove

1 fresh thyme sprig

1 bay leaf

1 quantity Béchamel Sauce (see page 50)

4 egg yolks

50 g/2 oz butter

150 g/5 oz black truffle, thinly shaved

3 potatoes, boiled and sliced

salt and pepper

SADDLE OF VENISON WITH BLACK TRUFFLE TIMBALE

Place the strips of pork fat or bacon over the saddle of venison and tie in place with kitchen string. Heat the oil in a large pan, add the venison, garlic, thyme and bay leaf and season with salt and pepper. Cook, turning frequently to make sure that the meat stays moist, until tender and cooked through. Meanwhile, make the béchamel sauce and, while it is still warm, beat in the egg yolks one at a time. Make layers of the butter, truffle potatoes, alternating with the béchamel sauce in a timbale mould. Place the saddle of venison on a platter. Discard the garlic and herbs and drizzle the cooking liquid over it. Turn out the truffle timbale next to it.

BABÁ CON SALSA D'ARANCIA

Serves 4

1 quantity Babà Dough (see page 1055)

1 quantity Confectioner's Custard (see page 1039),
flavoured with orange juice

thinly pared rind of ¹/₂ orange

100 g/3¹/₂ oz orange marmalade

juice of 2 oranges, strained

100 ml/3¹/₂ fl oz double cream

BABÀ WITH ORANGE SAUCE

Prepare the babà and fill it with the orange-flavoured confectioner's custard. Preheat the oven to 180°C/350°F/Gas Mark 4. Meanwhile, prepare the orange sauce. Cut the orange rind into thin batons. Mix together the marmalade, orange juice and orange rind in a saucepan, add the cream and simmer three times. Wrap the babà in foil and heat through in the oven for a few minutes. Remove the babà from the foil and pour the sauce over it.

Aldo Zilli

Aldo Zilli grew up in the idyllic seaside township of Alba Adriatica, in the central Italian region of Abruzzo. The family's overflowing fruit and vegetable garden contained fifteen rosemary bushes. His father was a farmer and fishmonger. Surrounded by this fine harvest of the land and sea, and nurtured by his mother's magnificent cooking, Aldo Zilli's greatest ambition was to open a fish restaurant. Happily, his childhood dreams have been handsomely realised: Zilli is founder and chef patron of an award-winning group of London restaurants that bear his name. The Zilli establishments have become a magnet for people from the media and entertainment world seeking his modern Italian cuisine of traditional sauces, fresh pastas and superb seafood. After attending catering college in Pescara, Aldo Zilli set out to seek fame and fortune abroad. Settling in London, he initially ran Il Siciliano in Soho. Then in 1987 he opened his flagship restaurant, Signor Zilli, in the same neighbourhood. To suit English sensibilities he initially served fillets instead of the unfamiliar bones and heads of whole fish. The famous lobster spaghetti and the acclaimed skewered tiger prawns with rosemary, garlic and chilli are now his signature dishes. Zilli is fiercely proud of the provenance of his dishes and ingredients and divulges his culinary wisdom and skills at his cookery school, in cookbooks and in television appearances. His vision is to showcase the food of Abruzzo: whether by the mozzarella, olive oil and other produce he imports from his home region, or the new renditions of enduring recipes originally gleaned from his mother.

Signor Zilli
41 Dean Street
London
United Kingdom

MENUS

FUNGHI DI BOSCO GRATINATI AL CAPRINO

LE CRESPELLE DI MIA COGNATA

SPIGOLA AL FINOCCHIO

SEMIFREDDO AI PINOLI

FUNGHI DI BOSCO GRATINATI
AL CAPRINO

Serves 4

8 field mushrooms

2 tablespoons extra virgin olive oil,
plus extra for drizzling

8 x 1-cm/¹/₂-inch thick slices of goats' cheese

40 g/1¹/₂ oz Parmesan cheese, freshly grated

1 garlic clove, finely chopped (optional)

1 teaspoon ground black pepper

juice of 1 lemon, strained

balsamic vinegar, for drizzling

2 tablespoons chopped fresh flat-leaf parsley

FIELD MUSHROOMS WITH GOATS' CHEESE GRATIN

Preheat the grill. Remove the stalks from the mushrooms, place the caps on a grill rack, gill sides uppermost, brush with the oil and grill for 8 minutes. Place a slice of goats' cheese over each mushroom, sprinkle with the Parmesan, garlic, pepper and lemon juice and grill for a further 5 minutes until golden and bubbling. Drizzle with balsamic vinegar and olive oil just before serving and garnish with the parsley.

LE CRESPELLE DI MIA COGNATA

Serves 4

For the stock

1.5-kg/3¹/₄-lb chicken

1 celery stick

2 carrots

4 bay leaves

1 onion, studded with 2 cloves

1 bunch of fresh flat-leaf parsley

4 garlic cloves

2.25–3.5 litres/4–6 pints water

4 tablespoons Parmesan cheese, freshly grated

For the pancakes

4 eggs

300 ml/¹/₂ pint milk

200 g/7 oz plain flour

2 tablespoons chopped fresh flat-leaf parsley

1 large potato, halved

250 ml/8 fl oz sunflower oil

salt and pepper

MARISA'S PANCAKE AND CHICKEN BROTH

To make the pancakes, whisk together the eggs, milk, flour and parsley to a lump-free batter and add salt and pepper to taste. Heat a non-stick pan or pancake pan until very hot, then insert a fork in the potato half and soak it in the sunflower oil. When the pan is hot, rub with the soaked potato and add a small ladleful of the batter. Cover the pan and leave until the pancake starts to move when you move the pan, turn the pancake with a spatula and cook the other side. Continue oiling the pan with the potato half and adding small ladlefuls of the batter until you have a stack of pancakes. To make the stock, put the chicken in a large pan with all the vegetables and herbs, pour in the water and bring to the boil. Lower the heat and simmer, occasionally skimming off the fat with a slotted spoon, for 1¹/₂ hours. Remove the chicken, strain the stock into a soup tureen and place in the middle of the table with a ladle. Place the pancakes, cut into strips if you like, in individual soup bowls, ladle the stock over them and sprinkle the Parmesan. You can then serve the chicken with a good salad to complete the meal.

ROASTED SEA BASS & FENNEL

Preheat the oven to 190°C/375°F/Gas Mark 5. Par-boil the sliced potatoes for 2 minutes, then drain. Make several diagonal slashes across each side of the fish without cutting through to the bone. Place a small sprig of rosemary and a slice of garlic in each slash and put the remaining garlic, the lemon and the remaining rosemary inside the cavity. Rub the fish with 4 tablespoons of the olive oil and sprinkle with sea salt, half the fennel seeds and pepper. Slice the fennel lengthways into 1-cm/^{1}/$_2$-inch thick pieces and place on a baking sheet with the potatoes. Sprinkle with the remaining fennel seeds and season. Place the fish on top, drizzle with the remaining olive oil, cover the baking sheet with foil and bake for about 35 minutes until cooked through. Surround with the potatoes and fennel and garnish with rosemary.

SPIGOLA AL FINOCCHIO

Serves 6

2 baking potatoes, cut into 1-cm/^{1}/$_2$-inch thick slices

1.5-kg/3^1/$_4$-lb sea bass, scaled and cleaned

2–4 fresh rosemary sprigs, plus extra to garnish

2 garlic cloves, lightly crushed

^{1}/$_2$ lemon, thinly sliced

6 tablespoons olive oil

20 g/^{3}/$_4$ oz fennel seeds

2 fennel bulbs

sea salt and pepper

PINE NUT SEMIFREDDO

Preheat the oven to 180°C/350°F/Gas Mark 4. Lightly brush a baking sheet with oil. Spread out the pine nuts on another and roast for 8 minutes until golden, but be very careful not to overcook them. Meanwhile, put the sugar and water into a heavy-based saucepan and set over a medium-high heat. This mixture will first start bubbling and then turn to a clear syrup. When it starts to change colour in parts, carefully shake the pan to mix. When it has become golden brown, tip the pan away from you and carefully pour in the pine nuts. Lower the heat to a simmer and stir gently to coat the nuts. When the caramel becomes a dark golden colour, remove the pan from the heat and spread the mixture on the oiled baking sheet. Let it cool. Break up the cold praline and put half in a food processor, then pulse until quite fine. Set aside. Put the remaining praline in the food processor and pulse until crushed but not powdery, then set aside. To make the semifreddo, halve the vanilla pod lengthways and scrape out the seeds into a bowl. Add the egg yolks and sugar and whisk until the mixture turns pale. Whisk the cream in another bowl until soft peaks form. Whisk the egg whites with a pinch of salt in another, grease-free bowl until they form firm peaks. Fold the cream into the egg yolk mixture, then fold in the egg whites. Finally, fold in only the finely crushed praline. Pour the mixture into a freezerproof container and freeze for 3 hours until firm. Serve in scoops, decorated with the remaining praline.

SEMIFREDDO AI PINOLI

Serves 8

For the praline

sunflower oil, for brushing

150 g/5 oz pine nuts

200 g/7 oz caster sugar

4 tablespoons water

For the semifreddo

1 vanilla pod

4 eggs, separated

4 tablespoons caster sugar

300 ml/^{1}/$_2$ pint double or whipping cream

salt

LIST OF RECIPES AND INDEX

LIST OF RECIPES

SAUCES, MARINADES AND FLAVOURED BUTTERS

HOT SAUCES

49 Bagna Cauda
50 Béchamel Sauce (Basic Recipe)
50 Mushroom Béchamel
50 Maître d'Hôtel Béchamel
50 Béchamel with Cream
51 Paprika Béchamel
51 Mustard Béchamel
51 Yogurt Béchamel
51 Mornay Sauce
52 Soubise Sauce
52 Bolognese Meat Sauce
52 White Meat Sauce
53 Chicken Liver Sauce
53 Spinach Sauce
53 Leek Sauce
54 Butter Sauce
54 Curry Sauce
54 Onion Sauce
54 Apple Sauce
55 Saffron Sauce
55 Marsala Sauce
55 Béarnaise Sauce (Basic Recipe)
56 Easy Béarnaise Sauce
56 Chinese Sauce
56 Anchovy Sauce
56 Marchand de Vin Sauce
57 Brain Sauce
57 Walnut Sauce
57 Red Pepper Sauce
57 Tomato Sauce
59 Quick Tomato Sauce

59 Horseradish Sauce
59 Normandy Sauce
59 Hollandaise Sauce
60 Piquant Sauce
60 Royal Sauce
60 Espagnole Sauce
61 Special Sauce
61 Spicy Sauce
61 Velouté Sauce (Basic Recipe)
61 Sauce Aurore
62 Seafood Sauce
62 Tuna Sauce

COLD SAUCES AND STOCKS

64 Aïoli
64 Redcurrant and Apple Chutney
65 Onion Chutney
65 Mayonnaise (Basic Recipe)
67 Curry and Cream Mayonnaise
67 Gorgonzola Mayonnaise
67 Whipped Cream Mayonnaise
67 Avocado Mayonnaise
67 Herb Mayonnaise
68 Horseradish Mayonnaise
68 Andalusian Mayonnaise
68 Maltese Mayonnaise
68 Pesto
68 Rémoulade Sauce
69 Pine Nut Sauce
69 Gorgonzola Sauce
69 Balsamic Vinegar Sauce
69 Paprika Sauce
70 Ricotta Sauce
70 Yogurt Sauce
70 Grapefruit Sauce

70 Black Truffle Sauce
70 Barbecue Sauce
72 Cocktail Sauce
72 Caper Sauce
72 Mint Sauce
72 Whipped Cream and Radish Sauce
73 Gribiche Sauce
73 Mediterranean Sauce
73 Russian Garlic Sauce
73 Tartare Sauce
74 Tuna Sauce
74 Green Sauce
74 Tapénade
76 Vinaigrette
76 Roux
76 Stocks

MARINADES

77 Brandy Marinade
77 Juniper Marinade
78 Vinegar Marinade
78 Yogurt Marinade
78 White Wine Marinade
78 Red Wine Marinade
80 Herb Marinade
80 Cooked Marinade
80 Spicy Marinade
80 Quick Lemon Marinade

FLAVOURED BUTTERS

82 Spinach Butter
82 Mushroom Butter
83 Shrimp Butter
83 Basil Butter

83	Caviar Butter	109	Mediterranean Prawns with Rocket	137	Tuna Tartines
83	Curry Butter	111	Oysters	138	Two-colour Omelette Tartines
83	Fennel Butter	111	Raw Sole with Chilli	138	Anchovy and Egg Sauce Tartines
83	Butter with Cheese and Almonds			138	Crab and Apple Tartines

VEGETABLE ANTIPASTI

85	Gorgonzola Butter	112	Sweet-and-Sour Caponata	138	Jellied Tongue Tartines
85	Butter with Dried Salted Roe	113	Artichokes Jardinière	139	Jellied Mustard Tartines
85	Burgundy Butter	113	Stuffed Artichokes Jardinière	139	Jellied Russian Salad Tartines
85	Anchovy Butter	114	Stuffed Onion Gratin		
85	Garlic Butter	114	Onions in Orange Mustard		**BARQUETTES AND TARTLETS**
85	Maître d'Hôtel Butter	114	Spinach Hearts	140	Pâte Brisée
87	Butter Sauce	115	Mushroom Salad	141	Prawn Barquettes
87	Lobster Butter	115	Chicory with Ham	141	Four-cheese Barquettes
87	Sage Butter	115	Cauliflower Salad (1)	141	Anchovy Barquettes
87	Mustard Butter	115	Cauliflower Salad (2)	143	Crab Barquettes
87	Sardine Butter	116	Cucumber and Prawn Salad	143	Cheese Tartlets
88	Horseradish Butter	116	Russian Salad	143	Gorgonzola Tartlets
88	Smoked Salmon Butter	116	Stuffed Aubergines	144	Avocado Tartlets
88	Tuna Butter	116	Rolled Peppers	144	Chicken Tartlets
88	Clarified Butter	119	Tomato Flowers		
88	Melted Butter	119	Stuffed Porcini Mushrooms		**SAVOURY PUFFS**
88	Beurre Manié	120	Greengrocer's Bag	146	Mushroom Puffs
		120	Vegetable-Garden Strudel	146	Creamy Cheese Puffs
		121	Pepper Pie	148	Salmon Puffs

ANTIPASTI, APPETIZERS AND PIZZAS

		121	Courgette Pie	148	Bacon Fritters
		122	Nest Eggs	148	Tomato Fritters
		122	Stuffed Courgettes		

ITALIAN ANTIPASTI

			CANAPÉS		**BOUCHÉES AND PUFF PASTRY**
95	Tomato Bruschetta	123	Chicken Liver Canapés	149	Ricotta Morsels
95	Piedmontese Tartare	124	Cheese Canapés	150	Country Bouchées
95	Semolina Baskets	124	Niçoise Canapés	150	Parisian Brioches
97	Ham Moulds	124	Lobster Canapés	150	Country Bonbons
97	Vine Leaf Parcels	124	Hot Canapés with Mozzarella	151	Radicchio Bundles
98	Mortadella Parcels	126	Avocado and Tomato Canapés	151	Small Cheese Crackers
98	Russian Salad Roulades	126	Carrot Canapés	151	Roman Crescents
98	Soused Boiled Beef	126	Ham Canapés	153	Piconcini from Marche
98	Boiled Beef Tortino			153	Curried Chicken Puffs
99	Sweet-and-Sour Tongue		**CROSTINI**	154	Mushroom Puffs
99	Nervetti with Onions	127	Tuscan Anchovy Crostini	154	Horseradish and Sausage Puffs
99	Spicy Quails' Eggs	128	Chicken Liver Crostini	154	Curried Langoustine Puffs
100	Rosemary and Cheese Rolls	128	Chicken Liver and Prosciutto Crostini		
100	Pineapple Kebabs	128	Mushroom and Caper Crostini		**CRÊPES**
102	Sage Appetizer	130	Crostini with Mushrooms in a Light Sauce	155	Crêpe Batter (Basic Recipe)
102	Scherrer's Tartare			156	Asparagus Crêpes
102	Truffle, Chicken and Lamb's Lettuce	130	Grapefruit Crostini	156	Mushroom Crêpes
		130	Sausage Crostini	156	Anchovy Crêpes
	FISH ANTIPASTI	132	Sweet-and-Sour Crostini	156	Ham and Fontina Crêpes
103	Fresh Anchovies with Lemon	132	Seafood Crostini		
104	Prawn Bites	132	Mountain Crostini with Speck and Apple Cream		**PÂTÉS AND TERRINES**
104	Cherry Tomato and Crab Bites			158	Pineapple Bavarois
104	Tuna Bites			159	Florentine Mould
104	Stuffed Squid		**TARTINES**	159	Gorgonzola Mousse
105	Fish Carpaccio	133	Prawn Butter Tartines	160	Pigeon Mousse with Truffle Vinaigrette
105	Baby Squid in Baskets	134	Caviar Tartines	160	Meadow Flower Mousse
105	Langoustine Cocktail	134	Cucumber Tartines	160	Ham and Kiwi Fruit Mousse
106	Smoked Trout in Pink Cream	134	Watercress Tartines	161	Salmon Mousse with Prawn Cream
106	Spider Crab au Gratin	134	Cheese and Brandy Tartines	161	Cold Tomato Mousse
107	Crab and Langoustine Cups	135	Rustic Tartines	162	Chicken Liver Pâté
107	Baby Octopus and Green Bean Salad	135	Grappa and Pear Tartines	162	Delicate Chicken Pâté
107	Whitebait Salad	135	Pizzaiola Tartines	164	Delicate Calf's Liver Pâté
109	Octopus and Rocket Salad	137	Avocado Tartines	164	Smoked Salmon Pâté
109	Langoustine and Fig Salad	137	Roquefort Tartines	164	Tuna Pâté
				166	Duck Terrine

MOULDS AND SOUFFLÉS

168 Tuna Mould with Leek Sauce
168 Leek Moulds
168 Courgette Moulds
169 Two-colour Mould
169 Artichoke Heart Mould
170 Carrot Mould
170 Carrot and Fennel Mould
171 Cauliflower Mould
171 Chicory Mould
171 Fennel Mould
172 Pea and Amaretti Mould
172 Celery and Ham Mould
172 Spinach Mould
173 Sea Trout Mould
173 Clam and Mussel Mould
174 Pumpkin Mould
174 Chestnut Soufflé
174 Onion Soufflé
176 French Bean Soufflé
176 Cheese Soufflé
176 Mushroom Soufflé
177 Crab Soufflé
177 Spicy Corn Soufflé
177 Potato Soufflé
178 Tomato Soufflé
178 Ham Soufflé

SAVOURY TARTS, QUICHES AND PIES

179 Asparagus Quiche
180 Smoked Salmon Quiche
180 Quiche Lorraine
181 Mushroom Tart with Walnut Cream
181 Broccoli Tart
182 Seafood Tart
182 Rocket and Taleggio Pie
183 Cod and Mushroom Tart
183 Savoury Cabbage Pie
184 Old-fashioned Onion Tart
184 Wild Greens and Artichoke Pie
185 Chicken and Chervil Tart
185 Leek Tart
186 Ham and Tarragon Tart
186 Spinach and Salmon Tart
187 Rustic Vegetable Pie
187 Pumpkin Pie
188 Easter Pie
188 Farmhouse Rainbow Pie
190 Aunt Maria's Farmhouse Pie

VOL-AU-VENT

191 Valle d'Aosta Vol-au-vents
192 Chicken Vol-au-vents
192 Ham in Vol-au-vents
192 Prawn in Vol-au-vents

PIZZAS

193 Pizza Dough (Basic Recipe)
194 Calzone
194 Mushroom Pizza
194 Pizza Napoletana
196 Fisherman's Pizza
196 Potato Pizza
196 'White' Pizza
198 Sausage Pizza
198 Chicory Pizza
198 Margherita Pizza
199 Four Seasons Pizza

FIRST COURSES

BROTHS

206 Ricotta Dumplings in Broth
206 Watercress Broth
206 Spiced Wine Broth
206 Small Cheese Gnocchi in Clear Broth
207 Bread Gnocchi in Broth
207 Broth à la Royale
207 Home-made Broth à la Royale
208 Broth with Crêpe Strips
208 Meat Stock
208 Fish Stock (1)
209 Fish Stock (2)
209 Chicken Stock
209 Vegetable Stock
210 Aromatic Cold Broth
210 Consommé
210 Concentrated Fish Stock
211 Aspic

CREAM SOUPS

213 Cream of Porcini Soup
213 Cream of Jerusalem Artichoke Soup
214 Cream of Truffle Soup
214 Cream of Asparagus Soup
214 Cream of Artichoke Soup
215 Cream of Carrot Soup
215 Cream of Carrot and Mussel Soup
217 Cream of Cauliflower Soup with Mussels
217 Cream of Chickpeas au Gratin
217 Cream of Bean Soup
218 Cream of Fennel Soup with Smoked Salmon
218 Cream of Prawn and Bean Soup
219 Cream of Prawn and Tomato Soup
219 Cream of Chicory Soup
219 Cream of Lettuce Soup
220 Cream of Dried Pulses Soup
220 Cream of Potato Soup
220 Cream of Pea and Potato Soup
221 Cream of Tomato Soup
221 Cream of Leek Soup
221 Cream of Celery Soup
222 Cream of Spinach Soup
222 Cream of Pumpkin Soup au Gratin
222 Cream of Courgette Soup
222 Cold Cucumber Cream Soup
224 Velvety Lentil Soup
224 Green Cream Soup Vichyssoise

VARIOUS SOUPS

225 Farfalline with Pesto
226 Gazpacho
226 Simple Gazpacho
226 Lentil and Squid Soup
227 Mesc-iuá
227 Courgette Flower Soup
227 Wheat Germ Soup
229 Herb Soup
229 Corn Soup
229 Leek Soup
229 Soup with Meatballs
230 Barley and Pulse Soup
230 Whitebait Soup
230 Chickpea and Spinach Soup
231 Swiss Chard and Lentil Soup
231 Farro and Leek Soup
231 Millet Soup
232 Nettle Soup
232 Barley and Chicken Soup
232 Caesar's Mushroom Soup
233 Leek and Potato Soup
233 Flemish Soup
233 Three-colour Soup
233 Green Soup
234 Bread Soup
234 Bread Soup with Tomato
234 Passatelli
235 Pasta and Chickpeas
235 Pasta and White Bean
235 Pasta, Potatoes and Celery
236 Porridge
236 Pot-au-feu
236 Quadrucci with Vegetables
236 Rice and Peas
238 Rice and Potatoes
238 Semolina
238 Stracciatella
238 Tapioca

MINESTRONES

239 Genoese Pesto Minestrone
241 Milanese Minestrone
241 Minestrone Napoletana
242 Puglian Minestrone
242 Borsch
243 Tuscan Minestrone
243 Farro and Bean Minestrone
243 Winter Minestrone
245 Seasonal Minestrone
245 Savoy Cabbage and Rice Minestrone

THICK SOUPS

246 Ribollita
248 Pavian Soup
248 Barley Soup al Verde
248 Barley and Pea Soup
249 Cabbage Soup
249 Escarole Soup
249 Milk and Onion Soup
250 Onion Soup au Gratin
250 Mussel Soup

250	Bean and Barley Soup
251	Oatmeal Soup
251	Cheese and Leek Soup
251	Bean and Mushroom Soup
252	Crab Soup
252	Lettuce Soup au Gratin
254	Thick Bread Soup
254	Bread and Lentil Soup
254	Potato Soup
255	Potato and Clam Soup
255	Leek and Lentil Soup
255	Radicchio Soup
256	Frog Soup
256	Pumpkin Soup
256	Courgette Soup

GNOCCHI

257	Parisian Gnocchi
258	Roman Gnocchi
258	Bread Gnocchi
259	Bread and Spinach Gnocchi
259	Parmesan Gnocchi
260	Potato Gnocchi (Basic Recipe)
260	Gnocchi alla Bava
260	Walnut Gnocchi
262	Potato and Nettle Gnocchi
262	Potato Gnocchi with Langoustines
263	Potato Gnocchi filled with Fondue
263	Triestian Potato Gnocchi with Prunes
264	Potato and Spinach Gnocchi
264	Ricotta and Spinach Gnocchi
264	Rice Gnocchi
266	Semolina and Ham Gnocchi
266	Pumpkin and Amaretti Gnocchi
266	Wholemeal Gnocchi

FRESH PASTA

268	Fresh Pasta Dough (Basic Recipe)
268	Green Pasta Dough (Basic Recipe)
268	Agnolotti Piedmontese
269	Bigoli with Anchovies
269	Cannelloni with Béchamel Sauce
269	Italian Cheese and Prosciutto Crêpes
270	Fettuccine in Brown Butter
270	Fettuccine in White Sauce
270	Lasagne Bolognese
272	Lasagne Napoletana
272	Aubergine and Ricotta Lasagne
273	Radicchio Lasagne
273	Maccheroni alla Chitarra
273	Maccheroni alla Chitarra with Chicken Livers
274	Maltagliati with Pumpkin
274	Orecchiette (Basic Recipe)
274	Orecchiette with Broccoli
274	Orecchiette with Turnip Tops
276	Orecchiette with Tomato and Ricotta
276	Genoese Pansotti
277	Valtellina Pizzoccheri
277	Ravioli Napoletana
279	Vegetable and Cheese filled Ravioli
279	Stracci with Lobster
279	Tagliatelle with Mushrooms

280	Tagliatelle with Aubergine
280	Cuttlefish Ink Tagliatelle
280	Tagliatelle with Salmon
281	Tagliatelle with Artichokes
281	Tagliatelle with Spinach
281	Tagliatelle with Cream, Peas and Ham
282	Tagliatelline with Onions
282	Tagliolini with Langoustines
282	Tagliolini with Butter and Truffle
282	Tagliolini with Scallops and Lettuce
283	Pumpkin Tortelli
283	Curried Tortellini
283	Tortellini Bolognese
285	Mushroom Tortelloni
285	Pesto Tortelloni with Squid

DRIED PASTA

288	Bavette with Clams and Courgettes
288	Bucatini with Green Tomatoes
288	Bucatini with Mushroom Sauce
289	Bucatini with Pepper Sauce
289	Farfalle with Smoked Pancetta
289	Fusilli with Mushrooms
290	Fusilli in Cuttlefish Ink
290	Fusilli Salad
290	Linguine with Genoese Pesto
292	Macaroni with Mushrooms
292	Macaroni with Cuttlefish
292	Macaroni au Gratin
293	Pasta with Sardines
293	Penne with Lettuce
295	Penne Arrabbiata
295	Penne with Black Olives
295	Penne with Turnip Tops
295	Penne with Saffron
296	Curried Penne Salad
296	Fried Penne
296	Penne Rigate with Artichokes
298	Penne Rigate in Vodka
298	Rigatoni with Meatballs
298	Baked Wholewheat Rigatoni
299	Rigatoni with Cream, Pesto and Tomatoes
299	Spaghetti with Garlic and Chilli Oil
299	Spaghetti with Broccoli
299	Spaghetti with Capers
300	Spaghetti Carbonara
300	Spaghetti Americana
300	Spaghetti with Raw Tomato
302	Spaghetti with Rosemary
302	Spaghetti with Anchovies
302	Spaghetti with Tuna
303	Spaghetti with Breadcrumbs
303	Spaghetti with Courgettes
303	Spaghetti with Bottarga
304	Tortiglioni with Mushroom and Aubergine
304	Vermicelli with Clams

POLENTA

306	Polenta Gnocchi
306	Polenta Soup

306	Polenta with Gorgonzola
307	Polenta with Langoustines and Radicchio
307	Polenta with Cod
307	Polenta with Meat Sauce
308	Polenta with Fondue
308	Polenta with Ricotta
308	Polenta with Sausage
309	Polenta with Eggs
309	Valle d'Aosta Polenta Pasticciata
309	Polenta Pasticciata with Mushrooms
311	Polenta Pasticciata with Anchovies
311	Polenta Taragna

RICE

313	Baked Rice (Basic Recipe)
313	Creole Rice (Basic Recipe)
313	Rice cooked in Milk (Basic Recipe)
314	Indian Rice (Basic Recipe)
314	Boiled Rice (Basic Recipe)
314	Wholegrain Rice (Basic Recipe)
314	Pilaf Rice (Basic Recipe)
315	Sicilian Croquettes
315	Rice with Curry Sauce and Prawns
315	Cantonese Rice
317	Rice with Mint
317	Rice with Carrots and Walnuts
318	Indonesian Rice
318	Rice with Raw Egg
318	Curried Rice and Lentils
318	Rice with Spinach
320	Seasoned Boiled Rice
320	Moulded Rice with Ham and Peas
320	Baked Rice with Parsley
321	Mini Rice Croquettes with Mozzarella
321	Paella

RICE SALADS

322	Rice and Prawn Salad
324	Curried Rice Salad
324	Rice Salad with Cheese
324	Seafood Rice Salad
325	Rice and Beetroot Salad
325	Rice Salad with Pickled Peppers
325	Rice and Crab Meat Salad
327	Low-fat Rice Salad
327	Smoked Fish and Rice Salad
327	Summer Rice Salad

RISOTTOS

328	Seafood Risotto
329	Blueberry Risotto
329	Jerusalem Artichoke Risotto
329	Barolo and Mushroom Risotto
330	Caviar Risotto
330	Milanese Risotto
330	Salmon and Wine Risotto
332	Carrot Risotto
332	Strawberry Risotto
333	Aubergine Risotto
333	Nettle Risotto

333 Radicchio Risotto
335 Prawn Risotto
335 Apple Risotto
336 Cream and Rocket Risotto
336 Pepper Risotto
336 Asparagus Risotto
337 Risotto with Sausages
337 Pumpkin and Artichoke Risotto
337 Four Cheese Risotto
339 Black Risotto with Cuttlefish
339 Cream and Leek Risotto
339 Green Risotto

TIMBALES
342 Pheasant Pie
342 Pumpkin Pie
343 Penne and Mushroom Pie
343 Tagliatelle Pie
344 Sartù
346 Fusilli Timbale
346 Macaroni Napoletana Timbale
347 Rice Timbale
347 Cheese Pie
348 Vincisgrassi
348 Raviolini Vol-au-vents
349 Seafood Vol-au-vents

■ EGGS AND FRITATTA

POACHED
354 Poached Eggs with Artichoke Hearts
356 Poached Eggs with Cheese
356 Poached Eggs with Asparagus Croquettes
357 Poached Eggs with Mixed Vegetables
357 Poached Eggs in Gelatine

SOFT BOILED
358 Eggs with Asparagus
358 Eggs with Ketchup

SHIRRED
359 Eggs with Mushrooms
359 Eggs with Parsley
360 Eggs with Truffle
360 Eggs with Asparagus
360 Eggs with Fennel and Mozzarella
361 Eggs with Aubergines
361 Eggs with Polenta
361 Eggs with Tomatoes
363 Eggs with Sausage
363 Eggs on Milk Soaked Bread

FRIED
364 Eggs with Anchovy Butter
364 Eggs in Red Wine
365 Eggs with Vinegar
365 American-style Eggs
365 Eggs Rossini
365 Eggs with Brussels Sprouts

EN COCOTTE
366 Eggs en Cocotte with Leeks
366 Fisherman's Eggs en Cocotte
368 Eggs en Cocotte with Bacon Fat
368 Eggs en Cocotte with Bolognese Meat Sauce
368 Fragrant Eggs en Cocotte

MEDIUM BOILED
369 Boiled Eggs with Spinach
370 Boiled Eggs with Mushrooms
370 Boiled Eggs with Herbed Mustard
370 Boiled Eggs with Tomato
371 Boiled Eggs with Broccoli
371 Boiled Eggs with Artichoke Hearts

HARD BOILED
372 Hard-boiled Eggs in Aspic
374 Hard-boiled Eggs in Curry Sauce
374 Hard-boiled Eggs Napoletana
374 Hard-boiled Eggs with Walnuts
375 Hard-boiled Eggs with Hats
375 Hard-boiled Eggs with Prawns
375 Hard-boiled Eggs with Smoked Salmon
375 Hard-boiled Eggs with Oysters
376 Hard-boiled Eggs and Ham in Aspic
376 Fried Stuffed Hard-boiled Eggs

SCRAMBLED
377 Scrambled Eggs with Artichokes
378 Abruzzo Scrambled Eggs
378 Scrambled Eggs with Fontina
378 Scrambled Eggs with Truffle
379 Scrambled Eggs with Spinach
379 Scrambled Eggs with Beans
379 Scrambled Eggs with Chicken Livers
379 Scrambled Eggs with Sausage
381 Scrambled Eggs in their Nests

SAVOURY CRÊPES
383 Smoked Salmon Crêpes
383 Pickled Salmon Crêpes
384 Cheese and Walnut Crêpes
384 Cardoon Crêpes
384 Spinach and Ricotta Crêpes

FRITTATA
386 Pepper Frittata
386 Cheese Frittata
387 Borage Frittata
387 Ham Frittata
387 Ham and Sage Frittata
387 Celery and Sausage Frittata
388 Tuna Frittata
388 Onion and Thyme Frittata
388 Bread Frittata
388 Olive Frittata
389 Courgette Frittata
389 Potato and Cinnamon Frittata
389 Meat Frittata
390 Filled Frittata
390 Frittata Cake

OMELETTES
392 Pepper Omelette
392 Crab Meat Omelette
392 Provençal Omelette
393 Omelette with Snails
393 Courgette Omelette
393 Radicchio Omelette
393 Aromatic Omelette
395 Curried Mushroom Omelette
395 Four Cheese Omelette
395 Ricotta Omelette

■ VEGETABLES

ASPARAGUS
401 Asparagus au Gratin
401 Asparagus Bella Elena
401 Asparagus with Pancetta
402 Parmesan Asparagus
402 Asparagus with Orange
402 Valley d'Aosta Asparagus
402 Asparagus Mimosa
404 Asparagus Mousse
404 Asparagus Rolls

BEETROOT
406 Beetroot with Béchamel Sauce
406 Beetroot with Anchovies
406 Beetroot with Onions

BUCK'S HORN PLANTAIN
409 Buck's Horn Plantain with Pancetta
409 Tasty Buck's Horn Plantain

SWISS CHARD
411 Swiss Chard with Parmesan
411 Swiss Chard with Anchovies
411 Swiss Chard au Gratin

BROCCOLI
412 Broccoli with Bottarga
414 Broccoli with Anchovies
414 Spicy Broccoli with Yogurt
414 Braised Broccoli
414 Fabulous Broccoli

GLOBE ARTICHOKES
416 Artichokes in Garlic and Olive Oil
416 Artichokes with Cheese
416 Jewish Artichokes
418 Artichokes with Chicken Liver Mousse
418 Artichokes Napoletana
419 Provençal Artichokes
419 Roman Artichokes
419 Sardinian Artichokes
420 Artichokes with Pecorino
420 Artichokes with Tuna
420 Fried Artichokes
421 Artichokes in Hollandaise Sauce
421 Artichokes stuffed with Sausage
421 Artichokes stuffed with Peppers

422 Artichoke Clafoutis
422 Artichoke Moulds
422 Savoury Artichoke and Potato Pie
422 Artichoke Pie

CARDOONS
424 Cardoons with Cheese
424 Cardoons with Bagna Cauda
424 Delicate Cardoons
425 Fried Cardoons
425 Cardoon Salad
426 Cardoon Moulds with Mushrooms

CARROTS
428 Carrots with Roquefort
428 Carrots with Rosemary
428 Surprise Raw Carrots
428 Glazed Carrots with Lemon
430 Carrots in French Sauce
430 Marinated Carrots
430 Baby Carrots in Cream
431 Surprise Carrot Croquettes

CHESTNUTS
432 Roast Chestnuts
433 Roast Chestnuts with Brussels Sprouts
433 Braised Chestnuts
433 Chestnut Purée

DANDELION
435 Dandelion with Garlic and Olive Oil
435 Dandelion with Parmesan
435 Dandelion Tip Salad

CAULIFLOWER
437 Cauliflower with Gorgonzola
437 Cauliflower with Ham
437 Two-colour Cauliflower with Pepper
439 Cauliflower Croquettes
439 French-style Croquettes
439 Cauliflower Salad
440 Cauliflower in Egg Sauce
440 Cauliflower in Green Sauce
440 Spiced Cauliflower

CABBAGE
442 Cabbage with Paprika
442 Baked Savoy Cabbage
442 Capuchin Savoy Cabbage
443 Pan-cooked Savoy Cabbage
443 Sauerkraut with Mushroom and Potatoes
443 Braised Sauerkraut
444 Ricotta and Savoy Cabbage Rolls

BRUSSELS SPROUTS
446 Parmesan Brussels Sprouts
448 Brussels Sprouts with Almonds
448 Brussels Sprouts au Gratin
448 Velouté Brussels Sprouts

CHICKPEAS
449 Chickpeas with Anchovies
450 Chickpeas with Tuna
450 Ligurian Pancakes
450 Ligurian Polenta

CUCUMBERS
451 Cucumbers in Mayonnaise
452 Cucumbers with Cream
452 Parisian Cucumbers
452 Cucumbers with Olives

CHICORY FAMILY
454 Chicory with Béchamel Sauce
454 Chicory with Chilli
454 Chicory Purée

TURNIP TOPS
456 Turnip Tops Baked in a Parcel
456 Parmesan Turnip Tops
456 Turnip Tops with Ham
456 Spicy Turnip Tops

ONIONS
459 Fried Onion Rings
459 Baby Onion Omelette
459 Grosseto Onions
461 Stuffed Onions
461 Baby Onions with Sage
461 The Sultan's Onions
462 Glazed Baby Onions
462 Braised Baby Onions

BEANS
464 Three Pulse Salad
464 Beans Pizzaiola
464 Beans Uccelletto
466 Beans with Sausages
466 Exotic Beans
466 Summer Cannellini Beans
467 Mixed Bean Salad
467 Bean Purée

GREEN BEANS
469 French Beans in Egg Cream
469 Polish Beans
469 Green Beans with Parmesan
469 French Beans with Tomato
470 Frosted Green Beans with Sesame
470 Runner Beans au Gratin
470 French Beans in Béchamel Sauce au Gratin
472 French Bean Salad
472 Beans in Garlic Sauce
472 French Beans in Egg Sauce

BROAD BEANS
474 Piedmontese Broad Beans
474 Broad Beans with Ham
474 Fresh Broad Bean Purée

FENNEL
477 Devil's Fennel
477 Fennel with Mozzarella
477 Fennel with White Wine
477 Fennel with Walnuts and Oranges
478 Fried Fennel
478 Fennel en Croûte
478 Fennel Pie

MUSHROOMS
481 Mushrooms with Cream
482 Mushrooms with Tomato
482 Mushrooms with Pumpkin
482 Melting Baked Porcini
483 Mushrooms au Gratin
483 Warm Mushroom Salad
483 Mushrooms with Aïoli
484 Porcini with Tarragon
484 Porcini with Prosciutto
484 Fried Porcini
484 Stuffed Mushrooms
486 Porcini Trifolati
486 Mushroom Caps Montanara
486 Mushroom and Potato Pie

BEANSPROUTS
488 Beansprouts with Prawns
488 Beansprouts with Parmesan
488 Spicy Beansprouts

ENDIVE
489 Curly Endives in Batter
490 Escarole stuffed with Olives and Capers
490 Curly Endive Purée

CHICORY
491 Chicory with Prague Ham
493 Baked Chicory
493 Baked Chicory with Nutmeg

SALADS
494 Salmon Salad with 'Beads'
496 Mixed Salad with Pomegranate
496 Avocado Salad
496 Bresaola with Lamb's Lettuce
498 White Cabbage Salad
498 Cucumber Salad
498 Sweetcorn and Radicchio Salad
498 Caesar's Mushroom Salad with Marjoram
499 Spinach and Scallop Salad
499 Spinach and Mushroom Salad
499 Turkey and Bean Salad
500 Treviso Radicchio Salad with Mushrooms
500 Treviso Radicchio and Prawn Salad
500 Yellow Salad with Sweetcorn
501 Hawaiian Salad
501 Mixed Tuna Salad
501 Rich Salad
502 Sicilian Salad
502 Caper Salad

LETTUCE
504 Lettuce Hearts with Herbs
504 Braised Lettuce with Pancetta Coppata
504 Stuffed Lettuce

LENTILS
506 Lentils with Sausages
508 Lentils in Tomato Sauce
508 Lentils with Bacon
508 Lentil Purée

AUBERGINES
509 Aubergine Caviar
510 Aubergine Fricassée
510 Aubergines with Cream
510 Aubergines with Anchovies
512 Grilled Aubergines
512 Grandmother's Aubergines
512 Aubergines stuffed with Mozzarella
513 Aubergines au Gratin
513 Surprise Aubergines in Breadcrumbs
514 Festive Aubergines
514 Roast Aubergines with Ricotta
515 Marinated Aubergines
515 Parmesan Aubergines
517 Aubergine Terrine
517 Cold Aubergine Tower

POTATOES
519 Potato and Cauliflower Ring
519 Potato Brioches
520 Potato Croquettes with Fontina
520 Delice of Potato Vegetable Sauce
521 Spicy Potato Salad
521 Ham and Potato Rolls
521 Potato Nests with Eggs
522 Potatoes Baked in Foil with Yogurt
522 Fontina Potato Bake
522 Baked Potatoes with Salmon
523 Potatoes in Béchamel Sauce
523 Normandy Potatoes
523 Potatoes with Scamorza
524 Duchess Potatoes
524 Potatoes in White Butter Sauce
524 Potatoes and Onions baked
    in an Earthenware Dish
525 Sausage Stuffed Potatoes
525 Provençal Sautéed Potatoes
525 Stewed Potatoes with Tomato
526 New Potatoes with Rosemary
526 Creamy Mashed Potato

PEPPERS
528 Pepper and Farro Salad
530 Pepper and Tuna Rolls
530 Delicate Peperonata
530 Roast Peppers
532 Fancy Peppers
532 Sweet and Sour Peppers
532 Summer Stuffed Peppers

PEAS
534 Triple-colour Terrine

534 Peas with Mint
534 Peas with Pancetta
536 Peas with Parsley
536 Peas with Carrots
536 Peas with Lettuce
536 Home-cooked Mangetouts

TOMATOES
539 Tomato Jelly Ring
539 Tomato and Mozzarella Parcels
539 Tomato and Gruyère Mould
540 Red Tomato Frittata
540 Tomato Fritters
540 Baked Tomatoes
541 Tomatoes au Gratin
541 Tomatoes with Cucumber Mousse
541 Tomatoes with Aubergines
542 Tomatoes with Courgettes
542 Tomatoes with Robiola
542 Tomatoes with Bacon au Gratin
543 Tomatoes stuffed with Pecorino
543 Tomatoes stuffed with Russian Salad
543 Tomatoes stuffed with Rice
545 Tomatoes stuffed with Tuna
545 Rustic Tomato Pie

LEEKS
546 Leeks with Tomato
548 Leeks with Ham
548 Leeks au Gratin
548 Leeks in Hollandaise Sauce

RADICCHIO
549 Radicchio and Walnut Rolls
550 Baked Radicchio
550 Radicchio with Parmesan
550 Radicchio Mimosa
550 Treviso Radicchio Salad with Orange
553 Fried Radicchio
553 Radicchio en Croûte

TURNIPS
555 Turnips with Bacon
555 Turnips with Cream
555 Stuffed Turnips
556 Roast Turnips with Potatoes
556 Roast Turnips with Leeks and Pumpkins

RADISHES
558 Radishes with Cheese
558 Glazed Radishes
560 Radish Salad with Olives
560 Radish Salad with Yogurt

SCORZONERA
562 Scorzonera with Horseradish
562 Scorzonera with Anchovies
562 Scorzonera Fricassée

CELERY
563 Celeriac Carpaccio with Anchovies
563 Celery with Gorgonzola
564 Celery in Béchamel Sauce

564 Greek-style Celery
564 Molise Celery
564 Celery and Walnut Salad
566 Celery in Tomato Sauce
566 Fried Celeriac
566 Celeriac au Gratin

SPINACH
568 Spinach Croquettes
568 Spinach in Cream
568 Genoese Spinach
570 Spinach and Mushroom Salad
570 Spinach in White Butter Sauce

TRUFFLES
572 Classic Truffle Frittata
572 Roast Truffles with Potatoes
572 Parmesan Truffles

JERUSALEM ARTICHOKES
574 Jerusalem Artichoke Salad
574 Jerusalem Artichoke and Potato Purée
574 Jerusalem Artichokes in Cream

PUMPKIN
577 Mozarella Pumpkin Sandwich
577 Baked Pumpkin with Potatoes
577 Parmesan Pumpkin
578 Pumpkin with Rosemary

COURGETTES
580 Stuffed Courgette Barquettes
580 Courgette and Potato Charlotte
580 Fried Courgette Flowers
582 Stuffed Courgette Flowers
582 Fried Stuffed Courgette Flowers
582 Baby Courgette Salad
583 Sweet and Sour Courgettes
583 Courgettes with Lemon
583 Roast Courgettes
584 Surprise Courgettes
584 Fancy Courgettes
585 Fancy Courgettes with Salmon and Leeks
585 Courgette Salad with Thyme
585 Courgettes in Egg Sauce

FISH, CRUSTACEANS AND SHELLFISH

ANCHOVIES
596 Fried Anchovies
598 Anchovies au Gratin
598 Anchovies with Truffles
598 Mixed Fish Fry
598 Layered Anchovies and Potatoes

SHAD
599 Shad with Sage
600 Shad with Tomato Sauce
600 Fried Shad
600 Soused Shad

HERRINGS
601 Kippers with Grapefruit
601 Herring and Cauliflower Salad

SALT COD AND STOCKFISH
603 Salt Cod au Gratin
603 Salt Cod Livorno-style
603 Salt Cod with Olives and Capers
604 Salt Cod with Potatoes and Peppers
604 Fried Salt Cod
604 Mediterranean Stockfish
605 Veneto-style Creamed Stockfish

WHITEBAIT
606 Whitebait in Egg Cream
606 Whitebait with Olive Oil and Lemon

SEA BASS
607 Sea Bass Baked in a Parcel
609 Sea Bass with Fennel
609 Jellied Sea Bass
609 Baked Marinated Sea Bass

GREY MULLET
610 Grey Mullet in Vinegar
611 Grey Mullet with Parsley
611 Grey Mullet and Dill Parcels
611 Stuffed Grey Mullet in Olive Sauce

GROUPER
612 Baked Grouper
614 Grouper with Avocado
614 Grouper with Olives

MONKFISH
615 Monkfish with Lemon
616 Monkfish in Red Wine
616 Monkfish with Cauliflower
    and Spring Onions
617 Monkfish with Anchovy Sauce
617 Monkfish and Prawn Roulades
619 Monkfish Stew with Tumeric Rice

SEA BREAM
622 Sea Bream baked in a Salt Crust
622 Braised Sea Bream
622 Jellied Sea Bream
623 Grilled Sea Bream
623 Sea Bream with Fennel Bulbs
623 Baked Sea Bream
624 Sea Bream with Olives
624 Sea Bream with Courgettes
624 Aromatic Sea Bream
625 Roast Sea Bream
625 Sea Bream with Mushrooms
625 Fish Tartare with Kiwi Fruit
626 Marinated Sea Bream

COD
627 Cod with Leeks
627 Cod in Curry Sauce
628 Baked Cod with Vegetables
628 Provençal Cod
628 Sicilian Cod
629 Cod Stew with Olives and Capers
629 Cod and Walnut Terrine

HAKE
630 Hake with Potatoes
630 Hake in Green Sauce
632 Hake in Shallot Sauce
632 Fried Hake

HUSS
633 Huss with Vegetables
634 Huss with Celery
634 Huss with Potatoes au Gratin
634 Huss with Green Tomatoes

SWORDFISH
635 Fabulous Smoked Swordfish
635 Baked Swordfish
636 Swordfish Parcels
636 Braised Swordfish
638 Marinated Swordfish
638 Swordfish Steaks in Balsamic Vinegar

SKATE
639 Skate with Capers
639 Skate Niçoise

TURBOT
640 Turbot Fillets with Vegetables
641 Turbot Fillets with a Potato Topping
641 Baked Turbot with Lentil Sauce
642 Turbot in Orange
642 Turbot in Sparkling Wine
643 Turbot with Saffron in Clam Sauce
643 Turbot with Olive Sauce

SALMON
644 Salmon and Bacon Bites
644 Salmon and Chicory Parcels
646 Salmon Fishcakes
646 Salmon Tartare
646 Smoked Salmon Terrine

JOHN DORY
647 John Dory Fillets in Sauce
648 John Dory Fillets in Béchamel Sauce
648 Baked John Dory Roulades
648 John Dory with Mangetouts

SARDINES
649 Sardine Rolls
649 Grilled Sardines
650 Sardines Marinara
650 Sardines with Shallots
650 Sardines in Breadcrumbs
652 Sardines Bellavista
652 Stuffed Sardines
652 Succulent Sardines

SCORPION FISH
654 Genoese Salad
655 Scorpion Fish with Mushrooms
655 Scorpion Fish with Thyme
655 Scorpion Fish in White Wine
    and Saffron

MACKEREL
656 Mackerel with French Beans
656 Mackerel with Sage Butter
658 Greek Mackerel
658 Mackerel with Currants
658 Mackerel and White Wine Terrine

SOLE
659 Almond-coated Sole Fillets
661 Sole Salad
661 Sole and Prawn Roulades
661 Sole with Mushrooms
662 Grilled Sole
662 Sole in Cider
662 Sole with Thyme
663 Sole in Melted Butter
663 Sole in Piquant Sauce

STURGEON
664 Sturgeon in Sweet-and-Sour Sauce
665 Sturgeon in Anchovy Sauce
665 Sturgeon in Balsamic Vinegar
665 Grilled Sturgeon
666 Sturgeon with Artichokes
666 Sturgeon with Red Pepper Sauce

TUNA
667 Tuna in Vinegar
668 Tuna with Celery
668 Tuna and Bean Salad
668 Slow-cooked Tuna

RED MULLET
669 Red Mullet with Fennel
670 Red Mullet Livorno-style
670 Red Mullet with Herbs
670 Red Mullet with Beans

EEL
671 Breton Eel
672 Roast Eel
672 Eel with Savoy Cabbage
672 Eel in Green Sauce
673 Braised Eel
673 Eel Kebabs

CARP
674 Carp with Maître
    d'Hôtel Butter
675 Carp with Olives
675 Oriental Carp
675 Carp in Wine

CHAR
676 Char with Herbs
677 Fried Char
677 Poached Char
    with Horseradish Sauce
677 Char and Potato Pie

PIKE

678 Pike in Beurre Blanc
679 Old-fashioned Pike
679 Pike Blanquette

PERCH

680 Perch Baked in
    Creamy Herb Sauce
681 Milanese Perch
681 Perch with Sage
681 Perch with Anchovies

TENCH

682 Tench with Herbs
683 Soused Tench with Herbs
683 Tench in a Salt Crust
683 Stuffed Tench

TROUT

684 Sea Trout Roll
685 Smoked Trout with Melon
685 Sea Trout with Juniper Berries
685 Provençal Trout
686 Trout with Mushrooms
    and Mussels
686 Smoked Sea Trout
    and Vegetable Casserole
686 Sea Trout Roe with Potatoes

LOBSTER

689 Creole Spiny Lobster
690 Spicy Lobster
690 Lobster in Tarragon
690 Armorican Lobster
692 Lobster and Prawn Salad
692 Magnificent Medallions
    of Lobster

PRAWNS

693 Asparagus and Prawns
694 Fried Prawns in Pink Sauce
694 Prawns with Salmon Mousse
694 Prawn Salad with Beans
696 Prawns in Strong Sweet Sauce
696 Courgettes with Prawns

SPIDER CRAB

697 Spider Crab in Olive Oil and Lemon
699 Spider Crab with Mayonnaise
699 Spider Crab Mimosa

CRAB

700 Cherry Tomatoes stuffed
    with Crab
702 Crab with Avocado
702 Crab Salad
702 Crab Rolls

LANGOUSTINES

703 Langoustines with Tomatoes
705 Langoustines with Curry Sauce
705 Langoustines with Sage
705 Grilled Langoustines

SQUID

707 Marche-style Squid
708 Fried Squid
708 Squid stuffed with Prawns
708 Grilled Stuffed Squid

SCALLOPS

710 Baked Scallops
712 Scallop Salad
712 Scallops in Saffron Sauce

MUSSELS

713 Creamy Mussels
714 Mussels Marinara
714 Mussels with Green Peppers
714 Mussels au Gratin
714 Peppered Mussels

OYSTERS

717 Greek Oysters
717 American Oysters
717 Hot Oysters in Beurre Blanc
718 Curried Oysters
718 Oysters in Salted
    Sabayon Sauce

OCTOPUS

719 Octopus and Potato Salad
721 Ligurian Musky Octopus
721 Musky Octopus Napoletana
721 Braised Musky Octopus
722 Poached Octopus
722 Octopus in Red Wine
722 Mariner's Octopus

CUTTLEFISH

723 Warm Cuttlefish Salad
    with Green Asparagus
723 Cuttlefish with Spinach
724 Cuttlefish with Peas
724 Cuttlefish with Artichokes
724 Stuffed Cuttlefish
724 Cuttlefish au Gratin

FISH SOUPS

726 Marche-style Fish Soup
726 Livorno-style Fish Soup
728 Fisherman's Soup
728 Pirate's Fish Soup
729 Mixed Fish Soup with Orange
729 Mixed Shellfish Soup

SNAILS

731 Bourguignonne Snails
731 Ligurian Snails
731 Lombard Snails

FROGS

732 Genoese Frogs' Legs
732 Frogs' Legs in White Wine
733 Fried Frogs' Legs in Tomato Sauce
733 Frogs' Legs in Breadcrumbs
733 Frogs in Batter

MEAT AND OFFAL

LAMB

742 Roman Spring Lamb
742 Lamb with Mushrooms
744 Arabian Lamb
744 Leg of Lamb à la Périgourdine
745 Roast Leg of Lamb
745 Roast Leg of Lamb in a Herb Crust
745 Lamb Cutlets with Anchovy Butter
747 Lamb Cutlets Cooked in Vinegar
747 Lamb Cutlets with Mint
747 Lamb Cutlets Scottadito
748 Lamb Fricassée with Onions
748 Lamb Meatballs with Aubergine
748 Shoulder of Lamb in a Parcel
750 Shoulder of Lamb à la Boulangère
750 Shoulder of Lamb with Mirto
752 Chopped Lamb and Carrots

KID

753 Leg of Kid with Truffle Cream
754 Piedmontese Leg of Kid
754 Easter Leg of Kid
754 Kid Cutlets with Cream

PORK, BACON, HAM

760 Roast Loin of Pork
760 Roast Pork with Orange
760 Roast Port in Grape Juice
760 Braised Pork with Rosemary
762 Roast Pork with Apples
762 Roast Pork with Lemon
764 Pan-fried Pork Fillet
764 Cassoeula
764 Pork Chops with Blueberries
766 Curried Pork Chops
766 Pork Chops in Gorgonzola
766 Pork Chops in Cream
766 Pork Shoulder with Prunes
767 Pork Shoulder with Cardoons
767 Spare Ribs with Polenta
767 Pork Chops in Butter and Sage
768 Pork Chops with Tuscan Cabbage
768 Pork Chops with Yellow Peppers
768 Croûtes with Pork Fillet
    and Pâté de Foie Gras
769 Pork en Croûte
769 Pork Roulades with Apricots
770 Loin of Pork with Tuna Sauce
770 Loin of Pork with Juniper
771 Bacon and Potato Pie
771 Baked Ham
772 Smoked Ham with Marsala
772 Ham in White Wine
772 Spare Ribs in White Wine
774 Sweet-and-Sour Spare Ribs
774 Chopped Pork with Prunes
774 Pork Stew with Smoked Sausages
775 Sweet-and-Sour Pork Stew
775 Pork Stew with Peas
775 Spicy Pork Stew
776 Pork Kebabs with Prunes

776 Pork Hock with Vegetables
776 Pork Tenerelle

BEEF

782 Pot-roast Beef
with Brandy and Grapefruit
782 Pot-roast Beef in Cream
782 Pot-roast Beef with Anchovies
and Tomato
783 Roast Beef with Carrots
783 Pot-roast Marinated Beef
783 Steak with Mushrooms
784 Steak in Balsamic Vinegar
784 Steak Pizzaiola
784 Steak with Mustard
785 Beef Patties with Cream
and Mushroom
785 Piedmontese Boiled Meat
785 Milanese Mixed Boiled Meat
786 Braised Beef
786 Braised Beef with Barolo
788 Beef Stroganoff
788 Braised Beef with Onions
788 Carpaccio
790 Florentine T-bone Steak
790 Salted T-bone Steak in Sauce
791 Beef Wellington
791 Fondue Bourguignonne
791 Goulash
792 Hamburgers American-style
792 Hamburgers with Ham
792 Beef and Spinach Roulades
793 Beef and Bresaola Roulades
793 Tasty Roulades
793 Simple Poached Beef
795 Simple Poached Beef Salad
795 Simple Poached Beef
with Rosemary
795 Steak with Sage
795 Steak in White Wine
796 Meatballs in Brandy
796 Meatballs with Anchovies
796 Meatballs with Potato
798 Meatballs with Lemon
798 Meatballs with Spinach
798 Meatballs
with a Tasty Onion Garnish
799 Roast Beef
799 Roast Beef with Chestnuts
799 Rapid Roast with Rocket
800 Beef Stew
800 Beef Stew with Coffee
800 Beef Stew with Wine and Onions
801 Florentine Beef Stew
801 Beef Stew with White Wine
801 Beefburgers
802 Steak Tartare
802 Tournedos Rossini

MUTTON

805 Leg of Mutton in Vodka
805 Leg of Mutton with Turnips
805 English Mutton Chops

807 Irish Stew
807 Mutton stewed in Citrus Juice
807 Mutton and Bean Stew
808 Mutton and Potato Stew
808 Chopped Mutton with Prunes
808 Marinated Mutton Kebabs

VEAL

814 Milk Pot-roast
814 Veal Braised in Milk
with Prosciutto
814 Pot-roast Veal with Walnuts
815 Braised Veal with Olives
815 Braised Veal with Lemon
815 Pot-roast Veal with Kidney
816 Braised Veal Topside
816 Simple Roast Veal
816 Braised Veal with Truffle
817 Veal Cutlets with Artichokes
817 Braised Veal
817 Summer Veal
818 Genoese Stuffed Breast of Veal
818 Pot-roast of Codino of Veal
819 Milanese Veal Chops
819 Valley d'Aosta Veal Chops
819 Villeroy Veal Cutlets
821 Veal in 'Reduced Stock'
821 Veal Bolognese
821 Veal Steak in Vinegar
822 Veal Steaks with Egg and Lemon
822 Veal Knots
822 Veal Steaks in Olive Sauce
823 Veal Ribbons
823 Fillet of Veal in Conza
823 Meat Mould
824 Veal Bundles with Truffles
824 Veal Roulades with Vegetables
824 Simple Poached Veal
824 Veal Roulades in Aspic
825 Veal Noisettes in Butter,
Sage and Rosemary
825 Veal Noisettes à la Financière
825 Milanese Osso Buco
827 Veal Osso Buco with Peas
827 Meat Pie
827 Roast Breast of Veal
828 Breast of Veal with Mayonnaise
828 Breast of Veal with Herbs
828 Breast of Veal with Sausages
829 Braised Breast of Veal
829 Veal Escalopes in Lemon
829 Veal Escalopes with Marsala
831 Veal Meatloaf
831 Roman Saltimbocca
831 Veal Escalopes with Mushrooms
833 Veal Escalopes with Pizzaiola
833 Veal Escalopes with Mustard
833 Veal Escalopes with Milk
834 Veal Escalopes with Herbs
834 Veal Escalopes with Grapefruit
834 Veal Fritters
835 Six-aroma Veal Stew
835 Curried Veal

835 Veal and Vegetable Stew
836 Breast of Veal with
Artichoke Hearts
836 Shin of Veal in Cider
838 Roast Shin of Veal
838 Hot Veal in Tuna Sauce
838 Cold Veal in Tuna Sauce

SAUSAGES

839 Cappello del Prete en Croûte
840 Cotechino
840 Wrapped Cotechino
840 Cotechino with Lentils
842 Cotechino with Mushroom Sauce
842 Cotechino in a Jacket
842 Ten-herb Sausages
844 Sausages in Tomato
844 Sausages with Carrots
844 Sausages with Leeks au Gratin
844 Sausages with Potato Tart
845 Sausages and Turnips
845 Fried Sausages
845 Frankfurters with Savoy Cabbage
845 Zampone

SWEETBREADS

848 Sweetbreads with Watercress
849 Sweetbreads au Gratin with Peas
849 Sweetbreads with Cream
and Mushrooms
850 Sweetbreads with Madeira
850 Sweetbreads in White Wine
850 Sweetbreads with Globe Artichokes
851 Sweetbreads with Jerusalem Artichokes
851 Sweetbreads in Breadcrumbs

BRAINS

853 Brain with Tomato Sauce
853 Brains with Capers
853 Brains with Butter and Sage
853 Brains au Gratin
854 Milanese-style Brains
854 Brains and Bone Marrow
in Curry Sauce
854 Brains in Anchovy Sauce
855 Brain Roulades with Truffle
855 Small Brain Moulds with Herbs

OXTAIL

857 Oxtail with Pancetta
857 Oxtail Vaccinara

PLUCK

858 Roman Lamb's Lights
859 Lights in Marsala
859 Greengrocer's Lights
859 Fried Lights

HEART

861 Heart Kebabs
861 Heart with Herbs
861 Grilled Heart
861 Heart with Anchovies

LIVER

862 Pig's Liver in a Net
863 Liver with Shallots
863 Liver with Butter and Sage
863 Veneto-style Liver
863 Liver with Lemon
864 Liver Uccelletto
864 Liver in Merlot
864 Liver with Globe Artichokes
864 Sweet-and-Sour Liver

TONGUE

865 Boiled Smoked Tongue
866 Tongue with Green Olives
866 Braised Tongue
866 Tongue in Tartare Sauce
866 Spicy Tongue

KIDNEYS

868 Kidneys with Mustard
868 Kidneys in Madeira
868 Kidneys in Bordeaux
869 Kidneys with Raw Spring Onions
869 Kidneys, Sausage and
   Mushrooms

CALF'S HEAD

871 Boiled Calf's Head
871 Fried Calf's Head
871 Calf's Head Salad

TRIPE

872 Tripe with Mushrooms
873 Milanese Tripe
873 Tripe with Herbs
873 Simple Tripe

POULTRY

DUCK

878 Duck à l'Orange
878 Duck Cooked in Beer
879 Duck in Almond Sauce
879 Duck with Peaches
880 Duck with Green Peppercorns
880 Stuffed Duck with Honey
882 Sweet-and-Sour Duck
882 Duck in Herb Sauce
884 Stuffed Duck in Turnip Sauce
884 Jugged Duck Legs
886 Duck Fillets with Figs
886 Breast of Duck with
   Grapefruit

CAPON

887 Capon Roast in a Parcel
888 Capon in Cardoon Sauce
888 Poached Capon
888 Stuffed Capon
889 Truffled Capon
889 Simple Capon Galantine

GUINEA FOWL

890 Pot-roast Guinea Fowl
891 Guinea Fowl with Artichoke Hearts
891 Guinea Fowl with Pineapple
892 Guinea Fowl with Sage
892 Guinea Fowl Ortolana
892 Guinea Fowl with Mascarpone
895 Guinea Fowl with Red Wine
895 Guinea Fowl with Cream and Lemon
895 Stuffed Guinea Fowl with Mushrooms
896 Guinea Fowl stuffed with Sultanas
896 Guinea Fowl with Truffles
   Baked in a Parcel

CHICKEN-BOILERS

898 Chicken with Pomegranate
898 Rustic Chicken
900 Chicken with Carrots and Onions
900 Chicken in Pink Sauce

GOOSE

902 Roast Goose
   with Sweet-and-Sour Peppers
902 Sweet-and-Sour Goose Legs
903 German Goose with Apples
903 Braised Goose
904 Goose stuffed with Potatoes
904 Breast of Goose in Balsamic Vinegar
906 Goose Stew

PIGEON

908 Roast Pigeons
908 Grilled Pigeons
910 Piquant Pigeons
910 Pigeons with Olives
910 Stuffed Pigeons

CHICKEN

913 Chicken Pie
913 Chicken Legs in Red Wine
913 American Chicken Salad
914 Chicken and Celeriac Salad
914 Chicken Roulades with Sage
914 Chicken, Anchovy and
   Caper Roulades
916 Chicken Roulades with Chives
916 Poached Stuffed Chicken
916 Chicken Breasts in Vinegar
918 Chicken Breasts and
   Fennel au Gratin
918 Chicken Breasts Stuffed
   with Mascarpone
919 Soused Chicken Breasts
919 Chicken Breasts in
   Almond Sauce
919 Chicken with Mushrooms
920 Chicken Roasted in a Parcel
920 Chicken Curry
920 Chicken Babi
922 Chicken Cacciatore
922 Devilled Chicken
922 Philippines Chicken
924 Chicken with Garlic

924 Greek Chicken
924 Chicken with Cream
924 Stuffed Chicken
924 Chicken Ratatouille
926 Chicken with Onions
926 Chicken with Apples
926 Chicken with Olives
928 Chicken with Lemon (1)
928 Chicken with Lemon (2)
928 Chicken on a Spit
929 Chicken with Sparkling Wine
929 Chicken with Tuna
929 Chicken in White Wine
930 Chicken in Red Wine
930 Pot-roast Chicken
930 Stuffed Chicken
931 Chicken with Yellow Peppers
931 Chicken with Green Peppers
931 Fried Marinated Chicken
932 Fried Chicken in Breadcrumbs
932 Chicken in Salt Crust
932 Chicken in a Brick
934 Spicy Indian Meatballs
934 Chopped Chicken with
   Lemon Balm
934 Chicken Stew with Olives
934 Chopped Chicken with Almonds

OSTRICH

935 Ostrich Eggs
936 Conte Rosso Ostrich Fillet
936 Ostrich Stew

TURKEY

938 Pot-roast Turkey
938 Turkey à l'Orange
939 Turkey Leg with Spinach
939 Turkey Leg with Herbs
940 Turkey Breast with Cheese
940 Turkey Breast with Almonds
940 Turkey Fricassée with Porcini
941 Tasty Turkey Roulades
941 Turkey Roll with Olives
942 Turkey Stew with Mustard
942 Glazed Turkey
943 Christmas Turkey
943 Turkey stuffed with Chestnuts
945 Turkey stuffed with Brussels Sprouts

GAME

WOODCOCK

949 Curried Woodcock
950 Woodcock with Juniper
950 Woodcock with Truffle
950 Woodcock with Green Apples

PHEASANT

951 Pheasant with Fruit
953 Pheasant in Cream Sauce
953 Pheasant with Olives

953 Stuffed Pot-roast Pheasant
954 Pheasant with Mushrooms
954 Pheasant with Orange

PARTRIDGE
956 Partridge with Mustard
958 Stuffed Partridge
958 Marinated Partridge

QUAIL
959 Quail with Yogurt
959 Quail in White Wine
960 Quail Risotto
960 Quail on the Spit

CHAMOIS
962 Alsace Chamois
963 Chamois In Red Wine
963 Chamois Chops with Mushrooms
    and Dried Fruit

VENISON
964 Roast Venison
966 Venison Stew
966 Roast Saddle of Venison
    with Cranberries

WILD BOAR
967 Wild Boar with Apples
969 Wild Boar with Olives
969 Wild Boar in Sauce

RABBIT
970 Roast Rabbit
971 Rabbit Cacciatore
971 Rabbit in Vinegar
971 Rabbit in Olive Oil and Lemon
973 Rabbit with Bay Leaves
973 Rabbit with Mustard
973 Rabbit in Milk
974 Rabbit with Honey and Vegetables
974 Rabbit in Cider
974 Rabbit in Red Wine
976 Braised Rabbit with Rosemary
976 Rabbit with Peperonata
976 Fried Rabbit
977 Stewed Rabbit
977 Marinated Rabbit
977 Stuffed Rabbit
978 Rabbit and Tuna Roll
978 Rabbit Stew with Anchovies
979 Rabbit Stew with Walnuts
979 Rabbit Stew with Tomatoes and Basil
979 Rabbit 'Tuna'

HARE
980 Hare Cacciatore
981 Hare with Wine
981 Hare with Juniper Berries
983 Sweet and Strong Hare

WILD GAME DISHES
984 Wild Duck with Figs

985 Venison with Cream
985 Mushroom and Game Pie

CHEESE
991 Caprino Bavarois
991 Buffalo Milk Mozzarella Caprese
    Salad
991 Scamorza Carpaccio
992 Cheese Rings
992 Mascarpone and Anchovy Cream
992 Cream of Ricotta and
    Vegetable Soup
993 Poppy-seed Croquettes
993 Taleggio Toasts
993 Aubergine and Mozzarella Rounds
994 Spicy Bundles
994 Puff Pastry Flowers with Toma
994 Savoyard Fondue
995 Piedmontese Fondue
995 Gruyère Gourgère
996 Chicory, Cheese and Walnuts
996 Bresaola Rolls with Ricotta
996 Mixed Green Salad with Caprino
997 Toasted Mozzarella
997 Fried Mozzarella Sandwiches
997 Cheese and Ham Pâté
998 Fontina and Ham Roll
998 Potato and Cheese Roll
999 Cheese Pie
999 Robiola Triangles

DESSERTS AND BAKING

PASTRY AND DOUGH
1007 Pâte Brisée
1007 Almond Paste 1
1008 Almond Paste 2
1008 Shortcrust Pastry 1
1008 Shortcrust Pastry 2
1010 Eggless Shortcrust Pastry
1010 Genoese Pastry
1010 Margherita Sponge
1011 Choux Paste
1011 Savoury Choux Paste
1012 Brioche
1012 Yeast Cake
1013 Tart Case
1013 Sponge Cake
1013 Sablé Dough
1014 Speedy Puff Pastry
1014 Easy Pâte Brisée

SWEET SAUCES AND DECORATIONS
1015 Melted Chocolate
1015 Cold Icing

1016 Butter Icing
1016 Coffee Icing
1016 Chocolate Icing
1016 Decorative Icing
1016 Meringues
1017 Whipped Cream
1017 Batter for Frying
1017 Chocolate Sauce
1017 Cold Chocolate Sauce
1018 Orange Sauce
1018 Apricot Sauce
1018 Cherry Sauce
1018 Strawberry Sauce
1019 Hazelnut Sauce
1019 Thick Syrup
1019 Caramel

BAVAROIS
1020 Orange Bavarois
1021 Vanilla Bavarois
1021 Plum Bavarois
1022 Wine Bavarois

MOULDS AND PUDDINGS
1023 Piedmont Pudding
1024 Chocolate Mould
1024 Lime Mould
1024 Honey Pudding
1025 Chestnut Mould
1025 Fruit Jelly
1026 Rice Pudding
1026 Almond Pudding
1027 English Bread and
     Butter Pudding
1027 Semolina Pudding
1027 Semolina Pudding with
     Black Cherries
1028 Crème Caramel
1028 Chocolate Delight
1028 Rice Pudding
1030 Milk Brûlée
1030 Panna Cotta

CHARLOTTES
1031 Amaretti Charlotte
1032 Fruits of the Forest Charlotte
1032 Plum and Pear Charlotte
1034 Blackcurrant Charlotte
1034 Charlotte Delight
1035 Black Grape Charlotte

CUSTARDS AND CREAMS
1036 Chestnut Cream
1038 Blueberry Cream
1038 Apricot Cream
1038 Banana Cream
1038 Mascarpone Cream
1039 Custard
1039 Confectioner's Custard
1039 Old-fashioned Crème Brûlée
1039 Zabaglione

SOUFFLÉS

1040 Chocolate Soufflé
1042 Vanilla Soufflé (Basic Recipe)
1042 Rhubarb Soufflé
1042 Rum Soufflé
1043 Torrone Soufflé
1043 Zabaglione Soufflé

TEA-TIME CAKES

1045 Carrot Ring Cake
1046 Easy Ring Cake
1046 Marbled Ring Cake
1046 Velvety Ring Cake
1048 Kugelhopf
1048 Muffins
1049 Fruit Cake
1049 Scones

PETITS FOURS AND BISCUITS

1050 Cinnamon Biscuits
1050 Yogurt Biscuits
1051 Ugly-but-Good Biscuits
1051 English Biscuits
1051 Sablés
1052 Date and Walnut Bonbons
1052 Rolled Wafers
1052 Praline
1054 Meringues with Whipped Cream
1054 Caramel Tartlets

DESSERT CAKES

1055 Coffee Baba
1056 Chestnut Cake
1056 Apricot Clafoutis
1056 Cherry Clafoutis
1058 Pear Crown
1058 Rhubarb Tart
1059 Fig Tart
1059 Blackberry Tart
1060 Tutti Frutti Tart
1060 Walnut and Coffee Cake
1061 Cherry Tart
1061 Strawberry Dessert
1062 Mascarpone Dessert
1062 Three-chocolate Millefeuille
1063 Mocha Cake
1063 Italian Bread and Butter Pudding
1064 Fruits of the Forest Crumble
1064 Splendid Maria-cake
1064 Apricot Strudel
1065 Ricotta Strudel
1065 Simple Strudel
1066 Tarte Tatin
1066 Chocolate Cake
1066 Chocolate Cake with Jam
1067 Chocolate and Pear Tart
1067 Cake with Orange Icing
1069 Lemon Tart
1069 Yogurt Cake
1069 Yogurt and Ricotta Cake
1070 Alsace Tart
1070 Apple Cake

1070 Almond Cake
1072 Apple and Pear Tart
1072 Hazelnut Cake
1072 Walnut Cake
1074 Walnut and Honey Tart
1074 Peach Pie
1074 Ricotta Cake
1076 Ricotta and Sultana Tart
1076 Ricotta and Sour Cherry Tart
1076 Pumpkin Cake
1077 Sachertorte
1077 Viennese Apple Pie

FRUIT DESSERTS

1078 Summer Pineapple
1079 Watermelon with Rum
1079 Caramelised Oranges
1079 Cherries in Alcohol
1079 Strawberry and Rhubarb Compete
1080 Spiced Figs
1080 Strawberries with Orange
1080 Fresh Fruit Jelly
1080 Fruit Salad
1082 Exotic Fruit Salad
1082 Melon Fruit Salad
1082 Apple Dumplings
1084 Apples in their Nests
1084 Spiced Apples with Sultanas
1084 Melon Surprise
1084 Blueberries in Syrup
1085 Pears in Chocolate
1085 Cinnamon Pears
1085 Pears with Lemon
1085 Spicy Candied Pears
1087 Peaches with Chocolate
1087 Peaches with Strawberries
1087 Peaches in Red Wine
1088 Stuffed Peaches
1088 Plums in Wine

SWEET CRÊPES

1089 Chocolate Crêpes
1090 Jam Crêpes
1090 Apple Crêpes
1090 Sugar Crêpes
1090 Crêpes Suzette
1091 Pancakes
1091 Blueberry Pancakes

SWEET OMELETTES

1092 Sweet Omelette (Basic Recipe)
1093 Apricot Jam and Cream Omelette
1093 Rasberry Omelette
1093 Omelette with Dried Fruit and Almonds

FRITTERS

1094 Amaretti Fritters
1094 Sweet Fritters
1096 Fruit and Champagne Fritters
1096 Apple Fritters
1097 Doughnuts
1097 Fritters

ICE CREAMS

1098 Fruits of the Forest Ice Cream
1098 Marron Glacé Ice Cream
1100 Coffee Ice Cream
1100 Caramel Ice Cream
1100 Chocolate Ice Cream
1101 Vanilla Ice Cream
1101 Strawberry Ice Cream
1101 Lemon Ice Cream
1101 Hazelnut Ice Cream
1102 Yogurt Ice Cream
1102 Raspberry Semifreddo
1102 Cream Semifreddo
1102 Torrone Semifreddo
1104 Cream and Chocolate Semifreddo
1104 Marron Glace Semifreddo
1104 Kiwi Sorbet
1106 Banana Sorbet
1106 Lemon Sorbet

OTHER DESSERTS

1107 Baked Citrus Fruit with Mint
1108 Gratin Fruits of the Forest with Zabaglione
1108 Chocolate Marquise
1108 Plum Meringue
1109 Grape Meringue Pie
1109 Montebianco
1109 Chocolate Profiteroles
1110 Semolina with Cherries
1110 Tiramisu
1110 Zuccotto
1112 Italian Trifle

JELLIES AND JAMS

1114 Strawberry Jelly
1115 Quince Jelly
1115 Redcurrant Jelly
1115 Grape Jelly
1116 Apricot Jam
1116 Orange Marmalade
1116 Chestnut Jam
1117 Cherry Jam
1117 Fig Jam
1117 Strawberry Jam
1117 Berry Jam
1118 Kiwi Jam
1118 Apple Jam
1118 Pear Jam
1118 Peach Jam
1119 Green Tomato Jam
1119 Plum Jam
1119 Rhubarb Jam
1119 Grape Jam

MENUS BY CELEBRATED CHEFS

AIMO & NADIA

1124 Seafood Stew with Lentils
1124 Spaghetti with Spring Onions and Red Chilli

1125 Shoulder of Veal with Uva Fragola
1125 Chestnut Flour Pie with Pears

LIDIA BASTIANICH
1127 Prawns in the Scampi Style
1128 Zite with Sausage, Onions and Fennel
1129 Erminia's Chicken and Potatoes
1130 Crostata with Chocolate, Hazelnuts and Orange

MARIO BATALI
1132 Sweet Pea Flan with Carrot Vinaigrette
1133 Beef Cheek Ravioli
1134 Barbecued Pigeon Al Mattone with Porcini Mustard
1135 Semolina Budino with Rhubarb and Mint Marmellata

NINO BERGESE
1137 Creamed Risotto
1137 Saddle of Veal Alla Bergese
1137 Florentine Tart

GIANFRANCO BOLOGNESI
1139 Tagliatelle All'Antica with Truffles
1139 Partridges with Savoy Cabbage, Fried Sage and Vegetables
1140 Panna Cotta, Almond Tart and Zabaglione

CARLO BROVELLI
1142 Scallops and Fried Celery
1142 Ravioli with Eggs and Asparagus
1143 Sturgeon Steaks in Gremolata
1143 Orange and Grand Marnier Mousse

ARRIGO CIPRIANI
1145 Carpaccio Cipriani
1145 Spring Risotto
1146 Baked Langoustines
1146 Italian Crêpes with Custard Cream

FRANCO COLOMBANI
1148 Capon Salad
1148 Braised Beef
1148 Pound Cake with Mascarpone Cream

ENZO DEPRÀ
1150 Chicken Liver Pâté with Herbs and Truffle
1150 Casunzjei Pasta with Potatoes and Seasoned Ricotta
1151 Ragù of Snails with Celeriac
1151 Bread Pudding with Vanilla Sauce

MARIA PIA DE RAZZA–KLEIN
1153 Marinated Octopus and Fennel Salad with Mature Pecorino Cheese
1154 Fresh 'Guitar String' Spaghetti with Mussels, Cherry Tomatoes and Olives
1155 Roast Lamb with Radicchio

Trevisano, Quince and Pancetta
1155 Radicchio Trevisano with Quince and Pancetta
1156 Cooked Saffron Milk Puddings with Blood Orange and Vincotto Sauce

ALFONSO E LIVIA JACCARINO
1158 Mussel Purses with Courgette Flowers
1158 Caciotta Ravioli with Tomato and Basil
1159 Scorpion Fish in White Wine
1159 Aubergine Pie with Chocolate

GIORGIO LOCATELLI
1161 Pan-Fried Scallops with Saffron Vinaigrette
1162 Pheasant Ravioli with Rosemary Jus
1162 Rabbit with Prosciutto and Polenta
1164 Amedei Chocolate Tasters

STEFANO MANFREDI
1166 Crostini with Peppers and Onions in Agrodolce
1166 Tagliatelli with Yabbies, Butter and Sesame Seeds
1167 Roast Pheasant with Savoy Cabbage, Chestnuts and Red Wine
1168 Torta Sbrisolona with Quince, Mascarpone Cream and Vincotto

GUALTIERO MARCHESI
1170 Sturgeon Salad with Caviar
1170 Open Raviolo
1171 Fillet of Veal alla Rossini
1171 Panettone Pudding

KAREN MARTINI
1173 Yellow Fin Tuna Carpaccio with Shaved Fennel and Lemon and Bottarga
1173 Seared Prawns with Cannellini Bean Salad and Tartufo Dressing
1174 Chargrilled Lamb Cutlets with Oregano and Hot Feta Dressing
1175 Choux Pastry Crest with Almond Cream, Praline, Chocolate Sauce and Gold Leaf

GIANLUIGI MORINI
1177 Tortellini with Goose Liver Cream
1177 Quail Stuffed with Green Vegetables and Peas
1178 Chocococonut

FULVIO PIERANGELINI
1180 Purée of Chickpeas with Prawns
1180 Fish Ravioli with Shellfish
1181 Pigeons in Red Wine
1181 Frozen Mousse with Fruits of the Forest

STEFANO DE PIERI
1183 Mussels with Aromatic Herbs
1183 Pigeon and Bread Soup
1184 Braised Beef Cheeks
1184 Caramelized Panna Cotta

RUTH ROGERS AND ROSE GRAY
1186 Puntarelle alla Romana
1186 Tagliatelle with Crème Fraîche and Rocket
1186 Grouse with Bruschetta and Cavolo Nero
1187 Nemesis

EZIO SANTIN
1189 Warm Salad of Prawns, Savoy Cabbage and Lentils
1189 Lasagnette with Leeks, Spring Onions and Black Truffles
1190 Kid Crépinettes with Almonds
1190 Almond and Chocolate Layers
1190 Coffee and Cocoa Sorbet

NADIA SANTINI
1192 Sweet-and-Sour Tench
1192 Tuscan Pecorino, Ricotta and Parmesan Tortelli with White Truffle
1193 Duckling in Balsamic Vinegar
1193 Pipasener Pastry with Zabaglione

GIANFRANCO VISSANI
1195 Fillets of Sole with Celery Julienne, Aurora Sauce and Caviar
1195 Pearl Barley with Quail, Thyme, Potato and Orange Sauce with Olive Brunoise
1196 Saddle of Vension with Black Truffle Timbale
1196 Babá with Orange Sauce

ALDO ZILLI
1198 Field Mushrooms with Goats' Cheese Gratin
1198 Marisa's Pancake and Chicken Broth
1199 Roasted Sea Bass & Fennel
1199 Pine Nut Semifreddo

1216

INDEX

Page numbers in *italic* refer to the illustrations

A

abbacchio alla Romana 742, *743*
Abruzzo scrambled eggs 378
acciughe al limone 103
acciughe fritte 596
acciughe gratinate 596
acciughe tartufate 598
agnello ai funghi 742
*agnello al forno con cotorno di
    radicchio trevisano alle mele cotogne
    e pancetta* 1155
agnello all'Araba 744
agnolotti alla Piemontese 268
agnolotti Piemontese 268
agoni al pomodoro 600
agoni alla salvia 599
agoni fritti 600
agoni in carpione 600
aïoli 64
    mushrooms with aïoli 483
alcohol, cherries in 1079
    see also wine
almonds
    almond and chocolate layers 1190
    almond cake 1070
    almond-coated sole fillets 659, *660*
    almond paste (1) 1007
    almond paste (2) 1008
    almond pudding 1025
    apple and pear tart 1072
    apricot jam and cream omelette 1093
    Arabian lamb 744
    Brussels sprouts with almonds *447*, 448
    butter with cheese and almonds 83
    chestnut mould 1025, *1026*
    chicken breasts in almond sauce 919
    chopped chicken with almonds 934
    choux pastry crest with almond cream,
        praline, chocolate sauce and
        gold leaf 1175
    date and walnut bonbons 1052
    duck in almond sauce 879
    kid crepinettes with almonds 1190
    omelette with dried fruit and
        almonds 1093
    praline 1052, *1053*
    sablé dough 1013
    turkey breast with almonds 940

splendid Maria-cake 1064
zuccotto 1110
Alsace chamois 962
Alsace tart 1070
amaretti
    amaretti charlotte 1031
    amaretti fritters 1094
    pea and amaretti mould 172
    peach pie 1074, *1075*
    Piedmont pudding 1023
    pumpkin and amaretti gnocchi 266
    pumpkin cake 1076
    stuffed peaches 1088
amaretti fritti 1094
American chicken salad 913
American oysters 717
American-style eggs 365
ananas d'estate 1078
anatra al pepe verde 880, *881*
anatra all'aceto balsamico 1193
anatra alla birra 878
anatra alla salsa di mandorle 880
anatra all'arancia 878
anatra alle pesche 879
anatra farcita al miele 880
anatra in agrodolce 882
anatra in salsa aromatica 882
anatra ripiena in salsa di rape 884
anatra selvatica con i fichi 984
anchovies 596–8
    anchovies au gratin 596
    anchovy and egg sauce tartines 138
    anchovies with truffles 598
    anchovy barquettes 141
    anchovy butter *84*, 85
    anchovy crêpes 156
    anchovy sauce 56
    aubergines with anchovies 510
    bagna cauda *48*, 49
    beetroot with anchovies 406
    bigoli with anchovies 269
    black truffle sauce 70
    brains in anchovy sauce 854
    broccoli with anchovies *413*, 414
    calf's head salad 871
    cardoons with bagna cauda 424
    cauliflower salad 439
    cauliflower salad (1) 115

cauliflower salad (2) 115
celeriac carpaccio with anchovies 563
chicken, anchovy and caper
    roulades 914
chickpeas with anchovies 449
cold veal in tuna sauce *837*, 838
dandelion tip salad 435
Devil's fennel 477
eggs with anchovy butter 364
fancy peppers 532
four seasons pizza 199
fresh anchovies with lemon 103
fried anchovies 596
fried stuffed courgette flowers 582
Genoese salad 654
Genoese spinach 568
green sauce 74, *75*
hard-boiled eggs Napoletana 374
heart with anchovies 861
hot veal in tuna sauce 838
jellied mustard tartines 139
lamb cutlets with anchovy butter 745
layered anchovies and potatoes 598
loin of pork with tuna sauce 770
mascarpone and anchovy cream 992
meatballs with anchovies 796
monkfish with anchovy sauce 617
nest eggs 122
pepper pie 121
perch with anchovies 681
pine nut sauce 69
pizza Napoletana 194, *197*
polenta pasticciata with anchovies 311
pot-roast beef with anchovies and
    tomato 782
rabbit stew with anchovies 978
sardines bellavista 652
scorzonera with anchovies 562
seafood sauce 62, *63*
Sicilian cod 628
spaghetti with anchovies 30
spicy turnip tops 456, *457*
steak tartare 802
stuffed artichokes jardiniere 113
stuffed porcini mushrooms 119
sturgeon in anchovy sauce 665
Swiss chard with anchovies 411
tapénade 74

tasty buck's horn plantain 409
tasty turkey roulades 941
toasted mozzarella 997
tuna pâté 164
tuna sauce 74
Tuscan anchovy crostini 127
Andalusian mayonnaise 68
anelli fritti 459
anello di gelatina al pomodoro 539
anello di patate e cavolfiore 519
anguille alla Bretone 671
anguille arrosto 672
anguille con le verze 672
anguille in salsa verde 672
anguille in umido 673
anguria al rum 1079
animelle al crescione 848
animelle al gratin con piselli 849
animelle al Madera 850
animelle al vino bianco 850
animelle alla panna e funghi 849
animelle con i carciofi 850
animelle con i topinambur 851
animelle impanate 851

apples
Alsace tart 1070
apple and pear tart 1072
apple cake 1070, *1071*
apple crêpes 1090
apple dumplings 1082, *1083*
apple fritters 1096
apple jam 1118
apple risotto 335
apple sauce 54
apples in their nests 1084
baked ham 771
cabbage with paprika 442
chamois in red wine 963
chicken curry 920
chicken with apples 926
Christmas turkey 943
crab and apple tartines 138
fruit and champagne fritters 1096
German goose with apples 903
lemon ice cream 1101
mountain crostini with speck and
   apple cream 132
radish salad with yogurt 560

redcurrant and apple chutney 64
roast pork with apples 762
Scherrer's tartare 102
shin of veal in cider 836
spiced apples with sultanas 1084
tarte Tatin 1066
Viennese apple pie 1077
wild boar with apples 967, *968*
woodcock with green apples 950

apricot jam
apricot jam and cream omelette 1093
chocolate cake with jam 1066
doughnuts 1097

apricots
apricot clafoutis 1056
apricot cream 1038
apricot jam 1116
apricot sauce 1018
apricot strudel 1064
chamois chops with mushrooms and
   dried fruit 963
omelette with dried fruit and
   almonds 1093
pork roulades with apricots 769
tutti frutti tart 1060
Arabian lamb 744
aragosta alla Creola 689
aragosta alle spezie 690
aragosta in salsa di dragoncello 690, *691*
arance caramellate 1079
arancini alla Siciliana 315, *316*
aringhe al pompelmo 601
arista al forno *757*, 760
aromatic cold broth 210
aromatic omelette 393
aromatic sea bream 624
arrosto al brandy e pompelmo 782
arrosto al latte 814
arrosto al latte e prosciutto 814
arrosto al limone 815
arrosto alla panna 782
arrosto all'arancia 760
arrosto alle acciughe e pomodoro 782
arrosto alle carote 783
arrosto alle noci 814
arrosto alle olive 815
arrosto all'uva 760
arrosto con il rosmarino 760

arrosto con le mele 762
arrosto con limone caramellato *761*, 762
arrosto con rognone 815
arrosto di faraona 890
arrosto di girello 816
*arrosto di oca con pepperoni in
   agrodolce* 902
arrosto di piccioni 908
arrosto di tacchinella 938
arrosto di tacchino all'arancia 938
arrosto marinato 783
arrosto semplice 816
arrosto tartufato 816

artichoke hearts
boiled eggs with artichoke hearts 371
guinea fowl with artichoke hearts 891
poached eggs with artichoke
   hearts 354, *355*

artichokes, globe 415–22, *417*
artichoke clafoutis 422
artichoke heart mould 169
artichoke moulds 422
artichoke pie 422
artichokes in garlic and olive oil 416
artichokes in hollandaise sauce 421
artichokes jardiniere 113
artichokes Napoletana 418
artichokes stuffed with peppers 421
artichokes stuffed with sausage 421
artichokes with cheese 416
artichokes with chicken liver mousse 418
artichokes with pecorino 420
artichokes with tuna 420
breast of veal with artichoke hearts 836
cream of artichoke soup 214
cuttlefish with artichokes 724
delicate cardoons 424
four seasons pizza 199
fried artichokes 420
Genoese salad 654
ham canapés 126
Jerusalem artichoke salad 574
Jewish artichokes 416
liver with globe artichokes 864
nest eggs 122
penne rigate with artichokes
296, *297*
Provençal artichokes 419

pumpkin and artichoke risotto 337
Roman artichokes 419
Roman lamb's lights 858
Sardinian artichokes 419
savoury artichoke and potato pie 422
scrambled eggs with artichokes 377
stuffed artichokes jardiniere 113
sturgeon with artichokes 666
sweetbreads with globe artichokes 850
tagliatelle with artichokes 281
veal cutlets with artichokes 817
wild greens and artichoke pie 184
artichokes, Jerusalem see Jerusalem
    artichokes
asparagi al gratin 401
asparagi alla Bella Elena 401
asparagi alla pancetta 401
asparagi alla parmigiana 402, *403*
asparagi alla Valdostana 402
asparagi all'arancia 402
asparagi e gamberi 693
asparagi mimosa 402
asparagus 400–4
    asparagus and prawns 693
    asparagus au gratin 401
    asparagus Bella Elena 401
    asparagus crêpes 156, *157*
    asparagus mimosa 402
    asparagus mousse 404
    asparagus quiche 179
    asparagus risotto 336
    asparagus rolls 404
    asparagus with orange 402
    asparagus with pancetta 401
    cream of asparagus soup 214
    eggs with asparagus 358, 360
    Parmesan asparagus 402, *403*
    poached eggs with asparagus
        croquettes 356
    ravioli with eggs and asparagus 1142
    Valle d'Aosta asparagus 402
    warm cuttlefish salad with green
        asparagus 723
aspic 211
    hard-boiled eggs and ham in aspic 376
    hard-boiled eggs in aspic 372, *373*
    veal roulades in aspic 824
    see also gelatine
aspic di uova sode 372, *373*
astici all'armoricana 690
astici in insalata con mazzancolle 692
aubergines 509–17
    aubergine and mozzarella rounds 993
    aubergine and ricotta lasagne 272
    aubergine caviar 509
    aubergine fricassée 510, *511*
    aubergine pie with chocolate 1159
    aubergine risotto 333
    aubergine terrine 517
    aubergines au gratin 513
    aubergines stuffed with mozzarella 512
    aubergines with anchovies 510
    aubergines with cream 510

chicken ratatouille 924, *925*
cold aubergine tower 517
crab rolls 702
eggs with aubergines 361
festive aubergines 514
frittata cake 390, *391*
Grandmother's aubergines 512
greengrocer's bag 120
grilled aubergines 512
Gruyère gourgère 995
lamb meatballs with aubergine 748
marinated aubergines 515, *516*
monkfish and prawn roulades 617, *618*
Parmesan aubergines 515
roast aubergines with ricotta 514
stuffed aubergines 116, *118*
summer cannellini beans 466
summer stuffed peppers 532
surprise aubergines in breadcrumbs 513
sweet-and-sour caponata 112
tagliatelle with aubergine 280
Taleggio toasts 993
tomatoes with aubergines 541
tortiglioni with mushroom and
    aubergine 304
Aunt Maria's farmhouse pie 190
avocados
    avocado and tomato canapés 126
    avocado mayonnaise 67
    avocado salad 496
    avocado tartines 137
    avocado tartlets 144
    crab with avocado 702
    exotic beans 466
    grouper with avocado 614
    rich salad 501

B

babá al caffé 1055
babá, con salsa d'arancia 1196
babá with orange sauce 1196
baby octopus and green bean salad 107
baby squid in baskets 105
baccalà al gratin 603
baccalà alla Livornese 603
baccalà con olive e capperi 603
baccalà con patate e peperoni 604
baccalà fritto 604
bacini di cozze con fiori di zucca 1158
bacon 756
    bacon and potato pie 771
    bacon fritters 148
    chicken pie 913
    grilled heart 861
    lentils with bacon 508
    onions in orange mustard 114
    quiche Lorraine 180
    salmon and bacon bites 644
    tomatoes with bacon au gratin 542
    turnips with bacon 555
    see also pancetta
bacon fat, eggs en cocotte with 368

bagna cauda *48*, 49
    cardoons with bagna cauda 424
balsamic vinegar
    balsamic vinegar sauce 69
    breast of goose in balsamic
        vinegar 904, *905*
    steak in balsamic vinegar 784
    sturgeon in balsamic vinegar 665
    sturgeon in sweet-and-sour sauce 664
    sweet-and-sour goose legs 902
    swordfish steaks in balsamic vinegar 638
bananas
    banana cream 1038
    banana sorbet 1106
    fruit and champagne fritters 1096
    summer pineapple 1078
barba di frate alla pancetta 409
barba di frate saporita 409
barbabietole alla besciamella 406
barbabietole alle acciughe 406
barbabietole alle cipolle 406
barchette ai gamberetti 141, *142*
barchette ai quattro formaggi 141
barchette di acciughe 141
barchette di polpa di granchio 143
barchette di zucchine ripiene 580
barley
    barley and chicken soup 232
    barley and pea soup 248
    barley and pulse soup 230
    bean and barley soup 250
    barley soup al verde 248
Barolo
    Barolo and mushroom risotto 329
    braised beef with Barolo 786, *787*
barquettes 140–3
    anchovy barquettes 141
    crab barquettes 143
    four-cheese barquettes 141
    pâte brisée 140
    prawn barquettes 141, *142*
basil
    aromatic omelette 393
    basil butter 83
    fragrant eggs en cocotte 368
    linguine with Genoese pesto 290, *291*
    pesto 68
    pesto tortelloni with squid 285
    rabbit stew with tomatoes and basil 979
batter
    batter for frying 1017
    crêpe batter 155
bavarese al vino 1022
bavarese alla vaniglia 1021
bavarese all'arancia 1020
bavarese alle prugne 1021
bavarese d'ananas 158
bavarese di caprini 991
bavaresi 1020–2
Bavarian cream *see* bavarois
bavarois 1020–2
    caprino bavarois 991
    orange bavarois 1020

pineapple bavarois 158
plum bavarois 1021
vanilla bavarois 1021
wine bavarois 1022
bavette alle vongole e zucchine 288
bavette with clams and courgettes 288
beans 463–7
bean purée 467
beans pizzaiola 464
beans Uccelletto 464, *465*
beans with sausages 466
exotic beans 466
mixed bean salad 467
mutton and bean stew 807
scrambled eggs with beans 379
summer cannellini beans 466
three pulse salad 464
see also pulses *and individual types of bean*
beansprouts 487–8
beansprouts with Parmesan 488
beansprouts with prawns 488
spicy beansprouts 488
yellow salad with sweetcorn 500
béarnaise sauce 55
beccaccia al curry 949
beccaccia al ginepro 950
beccaccia al tartufo 950
beccaccia con mele verdi 950
béchamel sauce 50
baked wholewheat rigatoni 298
beetroot with béchamel sauce 406
cannelloni with béchamel sauce 269
celery in béchamel sauce 564
chicken breasts and fennel au gratin 918
chicory with béchamel sauce 454
chicory with Prague ham 491, *492*
French beans in béchamel sauce au gratin 470
huss with potatoes au gratin 634
John Dory fillets in béchamel sauce 648
lasagne Bolognese 270, *271*
macaroni au gratin 292
meat mould 823
mushroom béchamel 50
potatoes in béchamel sauce 523
Villeroy veal cutlets 819
yogurt béchamel 51
beef 777–802
agnolotti Piedmontese 268
aspic 211
beef and bresaola roulades 793
beef and spinach roulades 792
beef cheek ravioli 1133
beef patties with cream and mushrooms 785
beef stew 800
beef stew with coffee 800
beef stew with white wine 801
beef stew with wine and onions 800
beef Stroganoff 788
beef Wellington 791
beefburgers 801

boiled beef tortino 98
Bolognese meat sauce 52
borsch 242
braised beef 786, 1148
braised beef cheeks 1184
braised beef with Barolo 786, *787*
braised beef with onions 788
carpaccio 788, *789*
consommé 210
country bonbons 150
Florentine beef stew 801
Florentine mould 159
Florentine T-bone steak 790
fondue Bourguignonne 791
goulash 791
hamburgers American-style 792
hamburgers with ham 792
lasagne Napoletana 272
meat stock 208
meatballs in brandy 796, *797*
meatballs in lemon 798
meatballs with a tasty onion garnish 798
meatballs with anchovies 796
meatballs with potato 796
meatballs with spinach 798
Milanese mixed boiled meat 785
Piedmontese boiled meat 785
polenta with meat sauce 307
pot-au-feu 236
pot-roast beef in cream 782
pot-roast beef with anchovies and tomato 782
pot-roast beef with brandy and grapefruit 782
pot-roast marinated beef 783
rapid roast with rocket 799
roast beef 799
roast beef with carrots 783
roast beef with chestnuts 799
salted T-bone steak in sauce 790
sartù 344, *345*
Sicilian croquettes 315, *316*
simple poached beef 793, *794*
simple poached beef salad 795
simple poached beef with rosemary 795
soused boiled beef 98
special sauce 61
steak in balsamic vinegar 784
steak in white wine 795
steak pizzaiola 784
steak tartare 802
steak with mushrooms 783
steak with mustard 784
steak with sage 795
stuffed courgette barquettes 580
tasty roulades 793
tournedos Rossini 802
veal roulades in aspic 824
white meat sauce 52
see also oxtail
beer
chicken in beer *921*, 922
duck cooked in beer 878

beetroot 405–7
beetroot with anchovies 406
beetroot with béchamel sauce 406
beetroot with onions 406
borsch 242
Genoese salad 654
rice and beetroot salad 325
beetroot tops
cappello del prete en croûte 839
berry jam 1117
besciamella 50
besciamella ai funghi 50
besciamella alla panna 50
besciamella alla paprica 51
besciamella alla senape 51
besciamella allo yogurt 51
besciamella maître d'hôtel 50
besciamella mornay 51
besciamella soubise 52
beurre blanc, hot oysters in 717
beurre manié 88
bianchetti alla crema d'uova 606
bianchetti all'olio e limone 606
bietole al parmigiano 411
bietole con le acciughe 411
bietole gratinate 411
bigné ai funghi 146
bigné al salmone 148
bigné alla crema di formaggio 146
bigoli alle acciughe 269
bigoli with anchovies 269
blueberries
blueberries in syrup 1084
blueberry cream 1038
blueberry pancakes 1091
blueberry risotto 329
fruits of the forest charlotte 1032, *1033*
fruits of the forest crumble 1064
gratin fruits of the forest with zabaglione 1108
pork chops with blueberries 764, *765*
tutti frutti tart 1060
biscotti alla cannella 1050
biscotti allo yogurt 1050
biscotti brutti ma buoni 1051
biscotti inglesi 1051
biscotti sablé 1051
biscuits 1050–4
cinnamon biscuits 1050
date and walnut bonbons 1052
English biscuits 1051
rolled wafers 1052
sablés 1051
ugly-but-good biscuits 1051
yogurt biscuits 1050
bistecche ai funghi 783
bistecche alla pizzaiola 784
bistecche alla senape 784
bistecche all'aceto balsamico 784
bistecche di filetto 764
bistecche tritate con panna e funghi 785
black grape charlotte 1035
black risotto with cuttlefish *338*, 339

black sea bream 620
black truffle sauce 70
blackberries
    blackberry tart 1059
    fruits of the forest crumble 1064
    fruits of the forest ice cream 1098
    gratin fruits of the forest with
      zabaglione 1108
blackcurrants
    blackcurrant charlotte 1034
    fruits of the forest charlotte 1032, *1033*
    tutti frutti tart 1060
boar, wild *see* wild boar
bocconcini di cervella 853
bocconcini di gamberetti 104
bocconcini di pomodori e granchio 104
bocconcini di ricotta 149
bocconcini di salmone con bacon 644
bocconcini di tonno 104
bocconcini rustici 150
boiled beef tortino 98
bollito alla Piemontese 785
bollito misto alla Milanese 785
Bolognese lasagne 270, *271*
Bolognese meat sauce 52
    eggs en cocotte with Bolognese meat
      sauce 368
    tortellini Bolognese 283
bomboline di ricotta in brodo 206
bonbon di datteri e noci 1052
bone marrow
    brains and bone marrow in curry
      sauce 854
    kidneys in Bordeaux 868
    old-fashioned onion tart 184
    veal noisettes à la financière 825
bonet 1023
borage
    borage frittata 387
    Genoese pansotti 276
borlotti beans
    barley and pulse soup 230
    scrambled eggs with beans 379
    turkey and bean salad 499
borsch 242
bottaggio alla Milanese 764, *763*
bottarga
    broccoli with bottarga 412
    spaghettini with bottarga 303
    yellow fin tuna carpaccio with shaved
      fennel, lemon and bottarga 1173
bouchées 149–54
    country bonbons 150
    country bouchées 150
    curried chicken puffs 153
    curried langoustine puffs 154
    horseradish and sausage puffs 154
    mushroom puffs 154
    Parisian brioches 150
    piconcini from Marche 153
    radicchio bundles 151, *152*
    ricotta morsels 149
    Roman crescents 151

small cheese crackers 151
bouillon cubes 205
Bourguignonne 791
Bourguignonne snails 731
braciole ai mirtilli 764, *765*
braciole al curry 766
braciole al Gorgonzola 766
braciole alla panna 766
bracioline con carciofi 817
brains 852–5
    brain roulades with truffle 855
    brain sauce 57
    brains and bone marrow in curry
      sauce 854
    brains au gratin 853
    brains in anchovy sauce 854
    brains with butter and sage 853
    brains with capers 853
    brains with tomato sauce 853
    Genoese stuffed breast of veal *811, 818*
    Milanese-style brains 854
    small brain moulds with herbs 855
brandy
    brandy marinade 77
    cheese and brandy tartines 134
    guinea fowl with mascarpone 892, *894*
    hazelnut sauce 1019
    jam crêpes 1090
    meatballs in brandy 796, *797*
    mocha cake 1063
    pork roulades with apricots 769
    pot-roast beef with brandy and
      grapefruit 782
    special sauce 61
    spicy sauce 61
    stuffed duck with honey 880
    watermelon with rum 1079
branzino al cartoccio 607, *608*
branzino al finocchio 609
branzino in gelatina 609
branzino marinato al forno 609
brasato 786, 817
brasato al Barolo 786, *787*
brasato alle cipolle 788
bread
    bread and lentil soup 254
    bread and spinach gnocchi 259
    bread frittata 388
    bread gnocchi 258
    bread gnocchi in broth 207
    bread pudding with vanilla sauce 1151
    bread soup 234
    bread soup with tomato 234
    cotechino with mushroom sauce 842
    croûtes with pork fillet and pâté de
      foie gras 768
    eel kebabs 673
    eggs on milk soaked bread 363
    English bread and butter pudding 1027
    fennel pie 478
    fried chicken in breadcrumbs 932
    fried mozzarella sandwiches 997
    gazpacho 226

Italian bread and butter pudding 1063
passatelli 234
Pavian soup 248
pigeon and bread soup 1183
robiola triangles 999
rosemary and cheese rolls 100, *101*
royal sauce 60
rustic tomato pie 545
salmon fishcakes 646
sardines in breadcrumbs 650
Scherrer's tartare 102
spaghetti with breadcrumbs 303
sweetbreads in breadcrumbs 851
Taleggio toasts 993
tomato bruschetta 95, *96*
see also canapés; crostini; tartines
bresaola
    beef and bresaola roulades 793
    bresaola and grapefruit 94
    bresaola with lamb's lettuce 496, *497*
    bresaola with oil and lemon 94
    bresaola rolls with ricotta 996
Breton eel 671
brill 640-3
    see also turbot
brioche 1012
    Parisian brioches 150
    potato brioches 519
brioche di patate 519
brioches alla Parigina 150
broad beans 473–5
    broad beans with ham 474
    cream of bean soup 217
    fresh broad bean purée 474, *475*
    Piedmontese broad beans 474
broccoletti alla bottarga 412
broccoletti alle acciughe 414
broccoletti piccanti allo yogurt 414
broccoletti stufati 414
broccoli 412–14
    boiled eggs with broccoli 371
    braised broccoli 414
    broccoli tart 181
    broccoli with anchovies *413*, 414
    broccoli with bottarga 412
    fabulous broccoli 414
    orecchiette with broccoli 274, *275*
    spaghetti with broccoli 299
    spicy broccoli with yogurt 414
broccoli fantasia 414
brodetto marchigiano 726
brodo al crescione 206
brodo al vino aromatizzato 206
brodo con gnocchetti di formaggio 206
brodo con gnocchetti di pane 207
brodo con royale 207
brodo con royale alla casalinga 207
brodo con tagliolini di crêpes 208
brodo di carne 208
brodo di pesce (1) 208
brood di pesce (2) 209
brodo di pollo 209
brodo di verdure 209

brodo freddo aromatico 210
broths 202, 204–11
  aromatic cold broth 210
  bread gnocchi in broth 207
  broth à la royale 207
  broth with crêpe strips 208
  chicken stock 209
  concentrated fish stock 210
  consommé 210
  fish stock (1) 208
  fish stock (2) 209
  home-made broth à la royale 207
  Marisa's pancake and chicken
    broth 1198
  meat stock 208
  ricotta dumplings in broth 206
  small cheese gnocchi in clear broth 206
  spiced wine broth 206
  vegetable stock 209
  watercress broth 206
bruschetta, tomato 95, *96*
bruschetta al pomodoro 95, *96*
Brussels sprouts 446–8
  Brussels sprouts au gratin 448
  Brussels sprouts with almonds *447*, 448
  eggs with Brussels sprouts 365
  Parmesan Brussels sprouts 446
  roast chestnuts with Brussels
    sprouts 433
  turkey stuffed with Brussels sprouts 945
  velouté Brussels sprouts 448
bucatini
  bucatini with mushroom sauce 288
  bucatini with pepper sauce 289
  bucatini ai pomodori verdi 288
  bucatini alla salsa di funghi 288
  bucatini con salsa ai peperoni 289
  bucatini with green tomatoes 288
buck's horn plantain 408–9
  buck's horn plantain with pancetta 409
  tasty buck's horn plantain 409
buckwheat flour
  polenta taragna 311
budino al cioccolato 1024
budino al lime 1024
budino al miele 1024
budino di castagne 1025, *1026*
budino di frutta in gelatina 1025
budino di mandorle 1025
budino di pane all'inglese 1027
budino di riso 1028
*budino di semolina con rabarbaro e
  sciroppo di mentuccia* 1135
budino di semolino 1027
budino di semolino alle amarene 1027
bue alla strogonoff 788
buffalo milk mozzarella Capri salad 991
burgers
  beefburgers 801
  hamburgers American-style 792
  hamburgers with ham 792
Burgundy butter 85
burro agli spinaci 82

burro ai funghi 82
burro ai gamberetti 83
burro al basilico 83
burro al caviale 83
burro al finocchio 83
burro al formaggio e mandorle 83
burro al gorgonzola 85
burro al rafano 88
burro al salmone affumicato 88, *89*
burro al tonno 88
burro alla bottarga 85
burro alla bourguignonne 85
burro alla maître d'hôtel 85
burro alla mugnaia 87
burro alla polpa d'aragosta 87
burro alla salvia 86, 87
burro alla senape 87
burro all'acciuga 84, 85
burro all'aglio 85
burro alle sardine 87
burro chiarificato 88
burro fuso 88
burro 'infarinato' 88
butter 1003
  beurre manié 88
  brains with butter and sage 853
  butter icing 1016
  butter sauce 54
  carp with maître d'hôtel butter 674
  clarified butter 88
  hot oysters in beurre blanc 717
  liver with butter and sage 863
  melted butter 88
  pike in beurre blanc 678
  pork chops in butter and sage 767
  prawn butter tartines 133
  roux 76
  sole in melted butter 663
  veal noisettes in butter, sage and
    rosemary 825
butters, flavoured 46, 82–9
  anchovy butter *84*, 85
  basil butter 83
  Burgundy butter 85
  butter sauce 87
  butter with cheese and almonds 83
  butter with dried salted roe 85
  caviar butter 83
  curry butter 83
  fennel butter 83
  garlic butter 85
  Gorgonzola butter 85
  horseradish butter 88
  lobster butter 87
  maître d'hôtel butter 85
  mushroom butter 82
  mustard butter 87
  sage butter 86, 87
  sardine butter 87
  shrimp butter 83
  smoked salmon butter 88, *89*
  spinach butter 82
  tuna butter 88

C

cabbage 441–5
  baked Savoy cabbage 442
  braised sauerkraut 443
  cabbage soup 249
  cabbage with paprika 442
  Capuchin Savoy cabbage 442
  cassoeula *763*, 764
  eel with Savoy cabbage 672
  frankfurters with Savoy cabbage 845
  pan-cooked Savoy cabbage 443
  pork chops with Tuscan cabbage 768
  pork hock with vegetables 776
  pork stew with smoked sausages 774
  ricotta and Savoy cabbage rolls 444, *445*
  sauerkraut with mushrooms and
    potatoes 443
  savoury cabbage pie 183
  Savoy cabbage and rice minestrone 245
  Valtellina pizzoccheri 277, *278*
  white cabbage salad 498
  see also red cabbage
cacciucco 726, *727*
Caesar's mushroom salad with
  marjoram 498
Caesar's mushroom soup 232
cakes 1044–9
  almond cake 1070
  Alsace tart 1070
  apple and pear tart 1072
  apple cake 1070, *1071*
  apricot clafoutis 1056
  apricot strudel 1064
  blackberry tart 1059
  cake with orange icing 1067, *1068*
  carrot ring cake 1045
  cherry clafoutis 1056
  cherry tart 1061
  chestnut cake 1056, *1057*
  chocolate and pear tart 1067
  chocolate cake 1066
  chocolate cake with jam 1066
  coffee baba 1055
  easy ring cake 1046
  fig tart 1059
  fruit cake 1049
  fruits of the forest crumble 1064
  hazelnut cake 1072, *1073*
  Italian bread and butter pudding 1063
  kugelhopf 1048
  lemon tart 1069
  marbled ring cake 1046, *1047*
  Margherita sponge 1010
  mocha cake 1063
  peach pie 1074, *1075*
  pear crown 1058
  pound cake with mascarpone cream 1148
  pumpkin cake 1076
  rhubarb tart 1058
  ricotta and sour cherry tart 1076
  ricotta and sultana tart 1076
  ricotta cake 1074
  ricotta strudel 1065

Sachertorte 1077
simple strudel 1065
splendid Maria-cake 1064
sponge cake 1013
strawberry dessert 1061
tarte Tatin 1066
three-chocolate millefeuille 1062
tutti frutti tart 1060
velvety ring cake 1046
Viennese apple pie 1077
walnut and coffee cake 1060
walnut and honey tart 1074
walnut cake 1072
yeast cake 1012
yogurt and ricotta cake 1069
yogurt cake 1069

calabrese broccoli
fabulous broccoli 414
calamari alla marchigiana 707
calamari fritti 708
calamari ripieni 104
calamari ripieni ai gamberetti 708
calamari ripieni alla griglia 708, *709*

calf's brains
brains and bone marrow in
    curry sauce 854

calf's feet
nervetti with onions 99

calf's head 870–1
boiled calf's head 871
calf's head salad 871
fried calf's head 871
Milanese mixed boiled meat 785
Piedmontese boiled meat 785

calf's liver
delicate calf's liver pâté *163*, 164

calf's tongue
sweet-and-sour tongue 99
calzone 194, *195*
camoscio al vino rosso 963
camoscio Alsaziano 962
canapé ai fegatini 123
canapé al formaggio 124
canapé alla nizzarda 124
canapé all'aragosta 124
canapé caldi con le ovoline 124, *125*
canapé di avocado e pomodori 126
canapé di carote 126
canapé di prosciutto 126

canapés 123–6
avocado and tomato canapés 126
carrot canapés 126
cheese canapés 124
chicken liver canapés 123
ham canapés 126
hot canapés with mozzarella 124, *125*
lobster canapés 124
Niçoise canapés 124
candied pears, spicy 1085

candied peel
chocolate marquise 1108
fruit cake 1049
rice pudding 1028

cannellini beans
bean and mushroom soup 251
cream of prawn and bean soup 218
mesc-iuà 227
mixed tuna salad 501
Polish beans 469
prawn salad with beans 694
red mullet with beans 670
summer cannellini beans 466
thick bread soup 254
cannellini estivi 466
cannelloni alla besciamella 269
cannelloni with béchamel sauce 269
Cantonese rice 317
capello di vitello sanato all'uva
    fragola 1125

capers
American chicken salad 913
balsamic vinegar sauce 69
brains with capers 853
caper salad 502
caper sauce 72
chicken with tuna 929
chicken, anchovy and caper
    roulades 914
cod stew with olives and capers 629
escarole stuffed with olives and
    capers 490
gribiche sauce 73
hard-boiled eggs and ham in aspic 376
loin of pork with tuna sauce 770
mushroom and caper crostini 128
rabbit in vinegar 971
salt cod with olives and capers 603
skate with capers 639
sole in piquant sauce 663
spaghetti with capers 299
spicy turnip tops 456, *457*
steak tartare 802
summer veal 817
sweet-and-sour crostini 132
tapénade 74
tuna sauce 74
veal escalopes pizzaiola 833
cappesante all'aspretto di zafferano 1161
cappesante e sedano fritto 1142

capon 887–9
capon in cardoon sauce 888
capon roast in a parcel 887
capon salad 1148
poached capon 888
simple capon galantine 889
stuffed capon 888
truffled capon 889
caponata, sweet-and-sour 112
caponata in agrodolce 112
cappello del prete in crosta 839
cappesante al forno 710
cappesante in insalata 712
cappesante in salsa di zafferano *711*, 712
cappon magro 654
cappone al cartoccio 887
cappone in salsa di cardi 888

cappone lessato 888
cappone ripieno 888
cappone tartufato 889
caprese di mozzarella di bufala 991
Capri salad, buffalo milk mozzarella 991
caprino bavarois 991
capriolo arrosto 964, *965*
capriolo in salmì 966
Capuchin Savoy cabbage 442

caramel 1019
caramel ice cream 1100
caramel tartlets 1054
crème caramel 1028
lime mould 1024
milk brulée 1030
old-fashioned crème brûlée 1038
praline 1052, *1053*
tarte Tatin 1066
caramelized oranges 1079
caramelle rustiche 150
carciofi aglio e olio 416
carciofi al formaggio 416
carciofi al pecorino 420
carciofi al tonno 420
carciofi alla giardiniera 113
carciofi alla giudia 416
carciofi alla mousse di fegatini 418
carciofi alla Napoletana 418
carciofi alla provenzale 419
carciofi alla Romana 419
carciofi alla sarda 419
carciofi fritti 420
carciofi giardiniera saporiti 113
carciofi in salsa olandese 421
carciofi ripieni alla salsiccia 421
carciofi ripieni con peperoni 421
cardi ai formaggi 424
cardi alla bagna cauda 424
cardi delicati 424
cardi fritti 425
cardi in insalata 425

cardoons 423–6
capon in cardoon sauce 888
cardoon crêpes 384
cardoon moulds with mushrooms 426
cardoon salad 425
cardoons with bagna cauda 424
cardoons with cheese 424
fried cardoons 425
pork shoulder with cardoons 767
carne cruda alla piemontese 95
carne estiva 817
carote al roquefort 428
carote al rosmarino 428
carote crude al rafano 428
carote glassate al limone 428, *429*
carote in salsa francese 430
carote marinate 430
carotine novelle alla panna 430

carp 674–5
carp in wine 675
carp with maître d'hôtel butter 674
carp with olives 675

oriental carp 675
carpa al vino 675
carpa alla maître d'hôtel 674
carpa alle olive 675
carpa all'orientale 675
carpaccio 788, *789*
  carpaccio Cipriani 1145
  celeriac carpaccio with anchovies 563
  fish carpaccio 105
  scamorza carpaccio 991
  yellow fin tuna carpaccio with shaved
    fennel, lemon and bottarga 1173
carpaccio Cipriani 1145
carpaccio di pesce 105
carpaccio di scamorza 991
carpaccio di sedano alle acciughe 563
*carpaccio di tonno con finocchio e
    bottarga* 1173
carré alle prugne 766
carré con i cardi 767
carrots 427–31
  baby carrots in cream 430
  beef stew with white wine 801
  carrot and fennel mould 170
  carrot canapés 126
  carrot mould 170
  carrot ring cake 1045
  carrot risotto 332
  carrots in French sauce 430
  carrots with Roquefort 428
  carrots with rosemary 428
  chicken with carrots and onions 900
  chopped lamb and carrots 752
  crab and langoustine cups 107
  cream of carrot and mussel
    soup 215, *216*
  cream of carrot soup 215
  Easter leg of kid 754, *755*
  Florentine mould 159
  glazed carrots with lemon 428, *429*
  marinated carrots 430
  onions in orange mustard 114
  peas with carrots 536
  pork hock with vegetables 776
  potatoes and onions baked in an
    earthenware dish 524
  rice with carrots and walnuts 317
  roast beef with carrots 783
  sausages with carrots 844
  surprise carrot croquettes 431
  surprise raw carrots 428
  sweet pea flan with carrot
    vinaigrette 1132
  three-colour terrine 534
  two-colour mould 169
  veal and vegetable stew 835
cassoeula 763, *764*
castagnaccio 1056, *1057*
castagne arrostite 432
castagne con cavolini al forno 433
casunziei di patate e ricotta forte 1150
catalonga al parmigiano 435
catalonga all'aglio e olio 435

caul 756
  pig's liver in a net 862
cauliflower 436–40
  cauliflower croquettes 439
  cauliflower in egg sauce 440
  cauliflower in green sauce 440
  cauliflower mould 171
  cauliflower salad 115, 439
  cauliflower with Gorgonzola 437
  cauliflower with ham 437
  cream of cauliflower soup with
    mussels 217
  French-style cauliflower 439
  Genoese salad 654
  herring and cauliflower salad 601
  monkfish with cauliflower and spring
    onions 616
  potato and cauliflower ring 519
  savoury cabbage pie 183
  spiced cauliflower 440
  two-colour cauliflower with
    pepper 437, *438*
caviale di melanzane 509
caviar
  caviar butter 83
  caviar risotto 330
  caviar tartines 134
  fillets of sole with celery julienne, aurora
    sauce and caviar 1195
  sturgeon salad with caviar 1170
cavolfiore al gorgonzola 437
cavolfiore al prosciutto 437
cavolfiore bicolore al peperone 437, *438*
cavolfiore fritto alla francese 439
cavolfiore in insalata 439
cavolfiore in salsa d'uova 440
cavolfiore in salsa verde 440
cavolfiore speziato 440
cavolini di bruxelles alla parmigiana 446
*cavolini di bruxelles con le
    mandorle* 447, *448*
cavolini di bruxelles gratinati 448
cavolini di bruxelles vellutati 448
cavolo alla paprica 442
cavolo nero
  pork chops with Tuscan cabbage 768
cavolo verza al forno 442
cavolo verza alla cappucina 442
cavolo verza in padella 443
ceci alle acciughe 449
ceci con il tonno 450
cecina (o farinata) 450
cefalo all'aceto 610
cefalo all'prezzemolo 611
cefalo in cartoccio all'aneto 611
cefalo ripieno in salsa d'olive 611
celeriac
  celeriac au gratin 566
  celeriac carpaccio with anchovies 563
  chicken and celeriac salad 914
  fried celeriac 566
  marinated partridge 958
  ragù of snails with celeriac 1151

celery 563–6
  American chicken salad 913
  celery and ham mould 172
  celery and sausage frittata 387
  celery and walnut salad 564, *565*
  celery in béchamel sauce 564
  celery in tomato sauce 566
  celery with Gorgonzola 563
  cream of celery soup 221
  fabulous smoked swordfish 635
  fillets of sole witth celery julienne, aurora
    sauce and caviar 1195
  Genoese salad 654
  Greek-style celery 564
  huss with celery 634
  Molise celery 564
  pasta, potatoes and celery 235
  scallops and fried celery 1142
  tuna with celery 668
  vichyssoise 224
cernia al forno 614
cernia all'avocado 614
cernia alle olive 613, 614
cervella ai capperi 853
cervella al burro e salvia 853
cervella al gratin 853
cervella alla Milanese 854
cervella con filoni al curry 854
cervella in salsa di acciughe 854
cervo alla panna 985
cestini di calamaretti 105
cestini di semolino 95
cetrioli alla maionese 451
cetrioli alla panna 452
cetrioli alla parigina 452
cetrioli alle olive 452
chamois 962–3
  Alsace chamois 962
  chamois chops with mushrooms and
    dried fruit 963
  chamois in red wine 963
champagne
  fruit and champagne fritters 1096
  summer pineapple 1078
chanterelle mushrooms
  fusilli with mushrooms 289
  pheasant with mushrooms 954, *955*
char 676–7
  char and potato pie 677
  char with herbs 676
  fried char 677
  poached char with horseradish sauce 677
chard *see* Swiss chard
charlotte agli amaretti 1031
charlotte ai frutti di bosco 1032, *1033*
charlotte al ribes 1034
charlotte alle prugne e alle pere 1032
charlotte delizia 1034
charlotte di uva nera 1035
charlotte di zucchine e patate 580
charlottes 1031–5
  amaretti charlotte 1031
  black grape charlotte 1035

blackcurrant charlotte 1034
charlotte delight 1034
fruits of the forest charlotte 1032, *1033*
plum and pear charlotte 1032
cheese 988–99
'white' pizza 196
artichokes with cheese 416
artichokes with pecorino 420
asparagus au gratin 401
asparagus mousse 404
asparagus quiche 179
asparagus rolls 404
aubergine and mozzarella rounds 993
aubergine and ricotta lasagne 272
aubergine risotto 333
aubergine terrine 517
aubergines au gratin 513
aubergines stuffed with mozzarella 512
Aunt Maria's farmhouse pie 190
avocado tartines 137
baked Savoy cabbage 442
baked wholewheat rigatoni 298
banana cream 1038
beansprouts with Parmesan 488
beef and spinach roulades 792
bresaola rolls with ricotta 996
broccoli tart 181
Brussels sprouts au gratin 448
buffalo milk mozzarella Capri salad 991
butter with cheese and almonds 83
calzone 194, *195*
caprino bavarois 991
cardoons with cheese 424
carrot mould 170
carrots with Roquefort 428
cauliflower mould 171
cauliflower with Gorgonzola 437
celery and walnut salad 564, *565*
celery with Gorgonzola 563
charlotte delight 1034
cheese and brandy tartines 134
cheese and ham pâté 997
cheese and leek soup 251
cheese and prosciutto crêpes 269
cheese and walnut crêpes 384
cheese canapés 124
cheese frittata 386
cheese pie 347
cheese pie 999
cheese rings 992
cheese soufflé 176
cheese tartlets 143
chicken and chervil tart 185
chicken breasts stuffed with
    mascarpone 918
chicory with ham 115
chicory, cheese and walnuts 996
cold aubergine tower 517
courgette pie 121
courgettes capricciose 584
cream of ricotta and vegetable soup 992
creamy cheese puffs 146
creamy mashed potato 526

cucumber salad 498
dandelion with Parmesan 435
Easter pie 188, *189*
eggs with fennel and mozzarella 360
fabulous smoked swordfish 635
fancy peppers 532
farmhouse rainbow pie 188
fennel en croûte 478, *479*
fennel pie 478
fennel with mozzarella 477
festive aubergines 514
fontina and ham roll 998
fontina potato bake 522
four cheese omelette 395
four seasons pizza 199
four-cheese barquettes 141
four-cheese risotto 337
fried mozzarella sandwiches 997
fried stuffed courgette flowers 582
fried stuffed hard-boiled eggs 376
frittata cake 390, *391*
fusilli salad 290
Genoese pansotti 276
gnocchi alla bava 260
Gorgonzola butter 85
Gorgonzola mayonaise 67
Gorgonzola mousse 159
Gorgonzola sauce 69, *71*
Gorgonzola tartlets 143
grapefruit crostini 130
grapefruit sauce 70
grappa and pear tartines 135
green beans with Parmesan 469
greengrocer's bag 120
Gruyère gougère 995
guinea fowl with mascarpone 892, *894*
ham and fontina crêpes 156
ham and kiwi fruit mousse 160
ham and potato rolls 521
ham and tarragon tart 186
ham soufflé 178
hot canapés with mozzarella 124, *125*
lasagne Napoletana 272
leeks au gratin *547,* 548
leeks with ham 548
lettuce soup au gratin 252
macaroni Napoletana timbale 346
Margherita pizza 198
mascarpone and anchovy cream 992
mascarpone cream 1038
mascarpone dessert 1062
meadow flower mousse 160
mini rice croquettes with mozzarella 321
mixed green with caprino 996
mornay sauce 51
mortadella parcels 98
moulded rice with ham and peas 320
mozzarella pumpkin sandwich 577
mushroom and potato pie 486
mushroom caps Montanara 486
mushroom puffs 154
mushroom soufflé 176
mushroom tortelloni 285

mutton stewed in citrus juice 807
onion soufflé 174
onion soup au gratin 250
orecchiette with tomato and ricotta 276
Parisian brioches 150
Parmesan asparagus 402, *403*
Parmesan aubergines 515
Parmesan Brussels sprouts 446
Parmesan gnocchi 259
Parmesan pumpkin 577
Parmesan truffles 572
Parmesan turnip tops 456
passatelli 234
pesto 68
pesto tortelloni with squid 285
piconcini from Marche 153
Piedmontese fondue 995
pineapple kebabs 100
pizza Napoletana 194, *196*
pizzaiola tartines 135, *136*
poached eggs with cheese 356
polenta taragna 311
polenta with Gorgonzola 306
polenta with ricotta 308
poppy-seed croquettes 993
pork chops in Gorgonzola sauce 766
potato and cauliflower ring 519
potato and cheese roll 998
potato brioches 519
potato croquettes with fontina 520
potato gnocchi filled with fondue 263
potato pizza 196
potatoes with scamorza 523
puff pastry flowers with toma 994
pumpkin soup 256
pumpkin tortelli 283, *284*
radicchio and walnut rolls 549
radicchio bundles 151, *152*
radicchio with Parmesan 550
radishes with cheese 558
ravioli Napoletana 277
rice gnocchi 264
rice salad with cheese 324
rice with raw egg 318
ricotta and Savoy cabbage rolls 444, *445*
ricotta and sour cherry tart 1076
ricotta and spinach crêpes 384, *385*
ricotta and spinach gnocchi 264, *265*
ricotta and sultana tart 1076
ricotta cake 1074
ricotta dumplings in broth 206
ricotta morsels 149
ricotta omelette 395
ricotta sauce 70
ricotta strudel 1065
roast aubergines with ricotta 514
roast turnips with potatoes 556
robiola triangles 999
rocket and taleggio pie 182
Roman crescents 151
Roman gnocchi 258
Roquefort tartines 137
rosemary and cheese rolls 100, *101*

rustic tartines 135
salmon puffs 148
sausage crostini 130, *131*
savoury cabbage pie 183
Savoyard fondue 994
scamorza carpaccio 991
scrambled eggs with fontina 378
seafood tart 182
Sicilian croquettes 315, *316*
simple tripe 873
small cheese crackers 151
small cheese gnocchi in clear broth 206
smoked salmon quiche 180
spaghetti carbonara 300
spaghetti with courgettes 303
spicy bundles 994
spicy corn soufflé 177
spider crab au gratin 106
spinach and salmon tart 186
spinach croquettes 568
spinach mould 172
stuffed courgette flowers 582
stuffed onion gratin 114
stuffed onions 461
summer rice salad 327
summer stuffed peppers 532
surprise aubergines in breadcrumbs 513
surprise courgettes 584
Swiss chard au gratin 411
Swiss chard with Parmesan 411
Taleggio toasts 993
tiramisu 1110, *1111*
toasted mozzarella 997
tomato and Gruyère mould 539
tomato and mozzarella parcels 539
tomato fritters *147*, 148
tomato soufflé 178
tomatoes stuffed with pecorino 543, *544*
tomatoes with courgettes 542
tomatoes with cucumber mousse 541
tomatoes with robiola 542
tuna bites 104
turkey breast with cheese 940
Valle d'Aosta asparagus 402
Valle d'Aosta polenta pasticciata 309
Valle d'Aosta veal chops 819
Valle d'Aosta vol-au-vents 191
Valtellina pizzoccheri 277, *278*
veal Bolognese 821
vegetable and cheese filled ravioli 279
walnut gnocchi 260
wholemeal gnocchi 266
wild greens and artichoke pie 184
yogurt and ricotta cake 1069

cherries
cherries in alcohol 1079
cherry clafoutis 1056
cherry jam 1117
cherry sauce 1018
cherry tart 1061
ricotta and sour cherry tart 1076
semolina pudding with black
   cherries 1027

semolina with cherries 1110
cherry tomato and crab bites 104
chervil
chicken and chervil tart 185
chestnuts 432–3
braised chestnuts 433
chestnut cake 1056, *1057*
chestnut cream 1036
chestnut flour pie with pears 1125
chestnut jam 1116
chestnut mould 1025, *1026*
chestnut purée 433
chestnut soufflé 174
Christmas turkey 943
glazed turkey 942
Montebianco 1109
roast beef with chestnuts 799
roast pheasant with Savoy cabbage,
   chestnuts and red wine 1167
roast chestnuts 432
roast chestnuts with Brussels
   sprouts 433
roast goose with sweet-and-sour
   peppers 902
turkey stuffed with chestnuts 943, *944*
chiacchiere 1094, *1095*
chicken 876, 911–34
American chicken salad 913
barley and chicken soup 232
beansprouts with prawns 488
Cantonese rice 317
chicken and celeriac salad 914
chicken and chervil tart 185
chicken babi 920
chicken breasts and fennel au gratin 918
chicken breasts in almond sauce 919
chicken breasts in vinegar 916
chicken breasts stuffed with
   mascarpone 918
chicken cacciatore 922
chicken curry 920
chicken in a brick 932
chicken in a salt crust 932, *933*
chicken in beer *921,* 922
chicken in pink sauce 900
chicken in red wine 930
chicken in white wine 929
chicken legs in red wine 913
chicken on the spit 928
chicken pie 913
chicken ratatouille 924, *925*
chicken roasted in a parcel 920
chicken roulades with chives 916
chicken roulades with sage 914, *915*
chicken stew with olives 934
chicken stock 209
chicken tartlets 144, *145*
chicken vol-au-vents 192
chicken with apples 926
chicken with carrots and onions 900
chicken with cream 924
chicken with garlic 924
chicken with green peppers 931

chicken with lemon (1) 928
chicken with lemon (2) 928
chicken with mushrooms 919
chicken with olives 926
chicken with onions 926, *927*
chicken with pomegranate 898, *899*
chicken with sparkling wine 929
chicken with tuna 929
chicken with yellow peppers 931
chicken, anchovy and caper
   roulades 914
chopped chicken with almonds 934
chopped chicken with lemon balm 934
cream of porcini soup 213
curried chicken puffs 153
delicate chicken pâté 162
devilled chicken 922, *923*
Erminia's chicken and potatoes 1129
Flemish soup 233
Florentine mould 159
fried chicken in breadcrumbs 932
fried marinated chicken 931
Greek chicken 924
hard-boiled eggs in aspic 372, *373*
Indonesian rice 318
Marisa's pancake and chicken
   broth 1198
Philippines chicken 922
Piedmontese boiled meat 785
poached stuffed chicken 916, *917*
pot-roast chicken 930
rustic chicken 898
sausage stuffed potatoes 525
soused chicken breasts 919
spicy Indian meatballs 934
stuffed chicken 930
stuffed turnips 555
truffle, chicken and lamb's lettuce 102
vincisgrassi 348
see also capon
chicken giblets
macaroni Napoletana timbale 346
rice timbale 347
vincisgrassi 348
chicken livers
artichokes with chicken liver
   mousse 418
chicken liver and prosciutto
   crostini 128, *129*
chicken liver canapés 123
chicken liver crostini 128
chicken liver pâté 162
chicken liver pâté with herbs and
   truffle 1150
chicken liver sauce 53
country bouchées 150
maccheroni alla chitarra 273
pigeon mousse with truffle
   vinaigrette 160
sartù 344, *345*
scrambled eggs with chicken
   livers 379
semolina baskets 95

chickpea flour
Ligurian pancakes 450
Ligurian polenta 450
chickpeas 449–50
barley and pulse soup 230
chickpea and spinach soup 230
chickpeas with anchovies 449
chickpeas with tuna 450
cream of chickpeas au gratin 217
mesc-iuà 227
pasta and chickpeas 235
purée of chickpeas with prawns 1180
three pulse salad 464
chicory 453–4, 491–3
baked chicory 493
baked chicory with nutmeg 493
chicory, cheese and walnuts 996
chicory mould 171
chicory pizza 198
chicory purée 454
chicory with béchamel sauce 454
chicory with chilli 454
chicory with ham 115
chicory with Prague ham 491, *492*
courgette salad with thyme 585
cream of chicory soup 219
Flemish soup 233
salmon and chicory parcels 644
chilli powder
devilled chicken 922, *923*
raw sole with chilli 110
chillies
Abruzzo scrambled eggs 378
chicory with chilli 454
rustic tartines 135
spaghetti with garlic and chilli oil 299
spaghetti with rosemary 302
spaghetti with spring onions and red
chilli 1124
spicy Indian meatballs 934
Chinese sauce 56
chives, chicken roulades with 930
chocolate
almond and chocolate layers 1190
amaretti charlotte 1031
amedei chocolate tasters 1164
aubergine pie with chocolate 1159
charlotte delight 1034
chocococonut 1178
chocolate and pear tart 1067
chocolate cake 1066
chocolate cake with jam 1066
chocolate crêpes 1089
chocolate delight 1028
chocolate ice cream *1099,* 1100
chocolate icing 1016
chocolate marquise 1108
chocolate mould 1024
chocolate profiteroles 1109
chocolate soufflé 1040, *1041*
choux pastry crest with almond cream,
praline, chocolate sauce and
gold leaf 1175

cold chocolate sauce 1017
cream and chocolate semifreddo 1104
cream semifreddo 1102
crostata with chocolate. hazelnuts and
orange 1130
English biscuits 1051
hot chocolate sauce 1017
marbled ring cake 1046, *1047*
melted chocolate 1015
peaches with chocolate 1087
pears in chocolate 1085, *1086*
Piedmont pudding 1023
Sachertorte 1077
splendid Maria-cake 1064
sweet-and-sour tongue 99
three-chocolate millefeuille 1062
tiramisu 1110, *1111*
zuccotto 1110
chops
lamb 739
mutton 804
choux paste 1011
savoury choux paste 1011
choux pastry crest with almond cream,
praline, chocolate sauce and
gold leaf 1175
Christmas turkey 943
chutney al ribes e mele 64
chutney di cipolline 65
chutneys
onion chutney 65
redcurrant and apple chutney 64
cialde arrotolate 1052
ciambella alle carote 1045
ciambella facile 1046
ciambella marmorizzata 1046, *1047*
ciambella vellutata 1046
ciambelline di formaggio 992
cicoria al peperoncino 454
cicoria alla besciamella 454
cider
rabbit in cider 974
shin of veal in cider 836
sole in cider 662
cider vinegar
swordfish steaks in balsamic
vinegar 638
ciliege sotto spirito 1079
ciliegine ripiene di granchio 700
cima alla Genovese 811, 818
cime di rapa al cartoccio 456
cime di rapa al prosciutto 456
cime di rapa alla parmigiana 456
cime di rapa piccantine 456, *457*
cinghiale alle mele 967, *968*
cinghiale alle olive 969
cinghiale in salsa 969
cinnamon
cinnamon biscuits 1050
cinnamon pears 1085
potato and cinnamon frittata 389
cioccococco 1178
cioccolata fusa 1015

cipollata 459
cipolle alla grossetana 459, *460*
cipolle gratinate 114
cipolle ripiene 461
cipolline alla salvia 461
cipolline alla senape arancione 114
cipolline del sultano 461
cipolline glassate 462
cipolline stufate 462
citrons
Sicilian salad 502
citrus fruit
baked citrus fruit with mint 1107
see also lemon, orange *etc.*
clafoutis
apricot clafoutis 1056
artichoke clafoutis 422
cherry clafoutis 1056
clafoutis alle albicocche 1056
clafoutis alle ciliege 1056
clafoutis di carciofi 422
clams
bavette with clams and
courgettes 288
clam and mussel mould 173
fisherman's pizza 196
Marche-style fish soup 726
mixed fish soup with orange 729
mixed shellfish soup 729
paella 321
pirate's fish soup 728
potato and clam soup 255
seafood rice salad 324
seafood tart 182
swordfish parcels 636, *637*
turbot with saffron in clam sauce 643
vermicelli with clams 304
clarified butter 88
clear stock 205
cockles
mixed shellfish soup 729
cocktail di scampi 105
cocktail sauce 72
cod 627–9
baked cod with vegetables 628
cod and mushroom tart 183
cod and walnut terrine 629
cod in curry sauce 627
cod stew with olives and capers 629
cod with leeks 627
mixed fish soup with orange 729
polenta with cod 307
Provençal cod 628
Sicilian cod 628
see also salt cod; stockfish
coda di manzo alla pancetta 857
coda di manzo alla vaccinara 857
coda di rospo al limone 615
coda di rospo al vino rosso 616
coda di rospo con cavolfiore e cipolle 616
coda di rospo con salsa d'acciughe 617
code di gamberi fritte in salsa rosa 694
codino arrosto 818

coffee
beef stew with coffee 800
coffee and cocoa sorbet 1190
coffee baba 1055
coffee ice cream 1100
coffee icing 1016
mocha cake 1063
tiramisu 1110, *1111*
walnut and coffee cake 1060
cold chocolate sauce 1017
cold icing 1015
composta di fragole al rabarbaro 1079
compote, strawberry and rhubarb 1079
concentrated stock 205
confectioner's custard 1039
blackberry tart 1059
hazelnut sauce 1019
Italian trifle 1112, *1113*
coniglio al forno 970
*coniglio al forno con prosciutto crudo e
polenta* 1163
coniglio al latte 973
coniglio al miele con verdure 974, *975*
coniglio al sidro 974
coniglio al vino rosso 974
coniglio alla cacciatora 971, *972*
coniglio alla senape 973
coniglio all'aceto 971
coniglio all'agro 971
coniglio all'alloro 973
coniglio arrosto al rosmarino 976
coniglio con peperonata 976
coniglio fritto 976
coniglio in umido 977
coniglio marinato 977
coniglio ripieno 977
consommé 205, 210
Conte Rosso ostrich fillet 936
cooked marinade 80
coratella d'agnello al Marsala 859
coratella d'agnello alla Romana 859
coratella d'agnello dell'ortolano 859
coratella d'agnello in tegame 859
coriander
Arabian lamb 744
corn *see* sweetcorn
corn soup 229
cornichons
cauliflower in green sauce 440
rice salad with pickled peppers 325
cornmeal
yogurt cake 1069
corona alle pere 1058
cosce di oca in agrodolce 902
cosce in salmì 884
coscia agli spinaci 939
coscia alle erbe aromatiche 939
cosciotto alla crema tartufata 753
cosciotto alla Perigordina 744
cosciotto alla Piemontese 754
cosciotto alla vodka 805
cosciotto arrosto 745
cosciotto con le rape 805, *806*

cosciotto in crosta d'erbe 745, *746*
cosciotto pasquale 754, *755*
costata alla Fiorentina 790
costata di bue al sale con salsa 790
costine con polenta 767
costolette al burro d'acciuga 745
costolette al burro e salvia 767
costolette al cavolo nero 768
costolette alla menta 747
costolette alla Milanese 819, *820*
costolette alla panna 754
costolette alla Valdostana 819
costolette alla Villeroy 819
costolette all'aceto 747
costolette all'Inglese 805
costolette con peperoni 768
*costolette di camoscio ai funghi e frutta
secca* 963
costolette a scottadito 747
cotechino 840
cotechino in a jacket 842
cotechino with lentils 840, *841*
cotechino with mushroom sauce 842
cotechino arrotolato 840
cotechino con lenticchie 840, *841*
cotechino con salsa di funghi 842
cotechino vestito 842
cotolette al 'consumato di brodo' 821
cotolette alla Bolognese 821
*costolettine di agnello con patate e condito
con feta e origano* 1174
country bonbons 150
country bouchées 150
courgette flowers
corn soup 229
courgette flower soup 227, *228*
fried courgette flowers 580, *581*
fried stuffed courgette flowers 582
mussel purses with courgette
flowers 1158
stuffed courgette flowers 582
courgettes 579–85
baby courgette salad 582
bavette with clams and courgettes 288
chicken ratatouille 924, *925*
cod stew with olives and capers 629
corn soup 229
courgette and potato charlotte 580
courgette frittata 389
courgette moulds 168
courgette omelette 393, *394*
courgette pie 121
courgette salad with thyme 585
courgette soup 256
courgettes capricciose 584
courgettes capricciose with salmon
and leeks 585
courgettes in egg sauce 585
courgettes with lemon 583
courgettes with prawns 696
cream of courgette soup 222
Greek-style celery 564
Gruyère gourgère 995

oysters in salted sabayon sauce 718
roast courgettes 583
sea bream with courgettes 624
spaghetti with courgettes 303
stuffed courgette barquettes 580
stuffed courgettes 122
surprise courgettes 584
sweet-and-sour courgettes 583
Taleggio toasts 993
tomatoes with courgettes 542
veal and vegetable stew 835
court-bouillon 591
cozze al vapore con erbe aromatiche 1183
cozze alla crema 713
cozze alla marinara 714
cozze con peperoni verdi 714, *715*
cozze gratinate 714
crab 688, 700–2
cherry tomato and crab bites 104
cherry tomatoes stuffed with crab 700
crab and apple tartines 138
crab and langoustine cups 107
crab barquettes 143
crab meat omelette 392
crab rolls 702
crab salad *701*, 702
crab soufflé 177
crab soup 252, *253*
crab with avocado 702
rice and crab meat salad 325
see also spider crab
cranberries
roast saddle of venison with
cranberries 966
crauti con funghi e patate 443
crauti in umido 443
cream
apricot jam and cream omelette 1093
aubergines with cream 510
baby carrots in cream 430
beef patties with cream and
mushrooms 785
black grape charlotte 1035
caprino bavarois 991
chicken with cream 924
chocolate profiteroles 1109
cocktail sauce 72
cream and leek risotto 339
cream and rocket risotto 336
cucumbers with cream 452
curry and cream mayonnaise 67
grape meringue pie 1109
guinea fowl with cream and lemon 895
guinea fowl with truffles baked in a
parcel 896
Italian trifle 1112, *1113*
Jerusalem artichokes in cream 574
kid cutlets with cream 754
leg of kid with truffle cream 753
meringues with whipped cream 1054
Montebianco 1109
mushrooms with cream 481
Normandy sauce 59

panna cotta *1029,* 1030
pheasant in cream sauce 953
pineapple bavarois 158
plum and pear charlotte 1032
plum bavarois 1021
pork chops in cream 766
pot-roast beef in cream 782
rigatoni with cream, pesto and
   tomatoes 299
spinach in cream 568
steak with mustard 784
sweetbreads with cream and
   mushrooms 849
tagliatelle with cream, peas and ham 281
turnips in cream 555
vanilla bavarois 1021
venison with cream 985
whipped cream 1017
whipped cream and radish sauce 72
whipped cream mayonnaise 67
wine bavarois 1022
zuccotto 1110
see also ice creams
cream cheese
   avocado tartines 137
   rocket and taleggio pie 182
   Roquefort tartines 137
cream of artichoke soup 214
cream of asparagus soup 214
cream of bean soup 217
cream of carrot and mussel soup 215, *216*
cream of carrot soup 215
cream of cauliflower soup with
   mussels 217
cream of celery soup 221
cream of chickpeas au gratin 217
cream of chicory soup 219
cream of courgette soup 222
cream of dried pulses soup 219
cream of fennel soup with smoked
   salmon 218
cream of Jerusalem artichoke soup 213
cream of leek soup 221
cream of lettuce soup 219
cream of pea and potato soup 220
cream of porcini soup 213
cream of potato soup 220
cream of prawn and bean soup 218
cream of prawn and tomato soup 218
cream of pumpkin soup au gratin 222
cream of ricotta and vegetable soup 992
cream of spinach soup 221
cream of tomato soup 220
cream of truffle soup 214
cream soups 212–24
creams 1036–9
   apricot cream 1038
   banana cream 1038
   bluberry cream 1038
   chestnut cream 1036
   mascarpone cream 1038
   old-fashioned crème brûlée 1038
creamy cheese puffs 146

creamy mussels 713
crema ai marroni 1036
crema ai mirtilli 1038
crema ai porcini 213
crema ai topinambur 213
crema al tartufo 214
crema di albicocche 1038
crema di asparagi 214
crema di banane 1038
crema di carciofi 214
crema di carote 215
crema di carote con le cozze 215, *216*
crema di cavolfiore con le cozze 217
crema di ceci al gratin 217
crema di fave 217
crema di finocchi al salmone
   affumicato 218
crema di gamberetti e fagioli 218
crema di gamberi e pomodori 218
crema di indivia belga 219
crema di lattuga 219
crema di legumi 219
crema di mascarpone 1038
crema di mascarpone e pasta
   d'acciughe 992
crema di patate 220
crema di piselli e patate 220
crema di pomodoro 220
crema di porri 221
crema di ricotta e verdure 992
crema di sedano 221
crema di spinaci 221
crema di zucca gratinata 222
crema di zucchine 222
crema fredda di cetrioli 222
crema inglese 1039
crema pasticciera 1039
crema verde 223, *224*
crème brûlée, old-fashioned 1039
crème brûlée d'altri tempi 1038
crème caramel 1028
Creole rice 313
Creole spiny lobster 689
crêpes
   anchovy crêpes 156
   apple crêpes 1090
   asparagus crêpes 156, *157*
   batter 155
   broth with crêpe strips 208
   cardoon crêpes 384
   cheese and prosciutto crêpes 269
   cheese and walnut crêpes 384
   chocolate crêpes 1089
   crêpes Suzette 1090
   ham and fontina crêpes 156
   Italian crêpes with custard cream 1146
   jam crêpes 1090
   Marissa's pancake and chicken
     broth 1198
   mushroom crêpes 156
   pancakes 1091
   pickled salmon crêpes 383
   ricotta and spinach crêpes 384, *385*

smoked salmon crêpes 383
   sugar crêpes 1090
crêpes agli asparagi 156, *157*
crêpes ai funghi 156
crêpes al cioccolato 1089
crêpes al prosciutto e fontina 156
crêpes al salmone affumicato 383
crêpes al salmone marinato 383
crêpes alla marmellata 1090
crêpes alle acciughe 156
crêpes alle mele 1090
crêpes allo zucchero 1090
crêpes con formaggio e noci 384
crêpes con i cardi 384
crêpes con ricotta e spinaci 384, *385*
crepinette di capretto alle mandorle 1190
crespelle alla crema pasticciera 1151
crespelle di formaggio e prosciutto 269
crespelle di mia cognata 1198
croccantini 1052, *1053*
crocchette ai semi di papavero 993
crocchette di cavolfiore 439
crocchette di patate alla fontina 520
crocchette di spinaci 568
crocchette a sorpresa 431
croquettes
   cauliflower croquettes 439
   mini rice croquettes with mozzarella 321
   poppy-seed croquettes 993
   potato croquettes with fontina 520
   Sicilian croquettes 315, *316*
   spinach croquettes 568
   surprise carrot croquettes 431
crostata al rabarbaro 1058
crostata di cioccolato, nocciole e
   arancia 1130
crostata di farina di castagne farcita
   con pere 1125
crostata di fichi 1059
crostata di more 1059
crostata tutti frutti 1060
crostata with chocolate, hazelnuts and
   orange 1130
crostini 127–32
   chicken liver and prosciutto
     crostini 128, *129*
   chicken liver crostini 128
   crostini with mushrooms in a light
     sauce 130
   crostini with peppers and onions in
     agrodolce 1166
   grapefruit crostini 130
   mountain crostini with speck and apple
     cream 132
   mushroom and caper crostini 128
   sausage crostini 130, *131*
   seafood crostini 132
   sweet-and-sour crostini 132
   Tuscan anchovy crostini 127
crostini alla toscana 127
crostini con fegatini di pollo 128
crostini con fegatini di pollo e
   prosciutto 128, *129*

crostini con funghi e capperi 128
crostini con funghi in guazzetto 130
crostini con peperoni e cipolle al agrodolce 1166
crostini con pompelmo 130
crostini con salsiccia 130, 131
crostini in agrodolce 132
crostini marinari 132
crostini montanari con speck e crema di mele 132
crostoni al taleggio 993
crostoni di filetto al foie gras 768
croûtes with pork fillet and pâté de foie gras 768
crumble, fruits of the forest 1064
crystallized fruit
Italian trifle 1112, *1113*
cubetti di cuore allo spiedo 861
cucumber 451–2
cold cucumber cream soup 222
cucumber and prawn salad 116
cucumber salad 498
cucumber tartines 134
cucumbers in mayonnaise 451
cucumbers with cream 452
cucumbers with olives 452
curried penne salad 296
gazpacho 226
Parisian cucumbers 452
scamorza carpaccio 991
simple gazpacho 226
smoked trout with melon 685
tomatoes with cucumber mousse 541
cuore agli aromi 861
cuore alla griglia 861
cuore alle acciughe 861
cuori di lattuga alle erbe 504, *505*
cuoricini di spinaci 114
cupolette di prosciutto 97
curly endive in batter 489
curly endive purée 490
currants
fruit cake 1049
mackerel with currants 658
curry
brains and bone marrow in curry sauce 854
chicken curry 920
cod in curry sauce 627
curried chicken puffs 153
curried langoustine puffs 154
curried mushroom omelette 395
curried oysters 718
curried penne salad 296
curried pork chops 766
curried rice and lentils 318
curried rice salad 324
curried tortellini 283
curried veal 835
curried woodcock 949
curry and cream mayonnaise 67
curry butter 83
curry sauce 54

hard-boiled eggs in curry sauce 374
lamb curry 741
langoustines with curry sauce 705
rice with curry sauce and prawns 315
custards 1036–9
blackcurrant charlotte 1034
blueberry cream 1038
cold chocolate sauce 1017
confectioner's custard 1039
custard 1039
plum bavarois 1021
cuttlefish 723–4
black risotto with cuttlefish *338, 339*
cuttlefish au gratin 724
cuttlefish with artichokes 724
cuttlefish with peas 724
cuttlefish with spinach 723
macaroni with cuttlefish 292
Marche-style fish soup 726
mixed fish soup with orange 729
pirate's fish soup 728
stuffed cuttlefish 724
warm cuttlefish salad with green asparagus 723
cuttlefish ink
cuttlefish ink tagliatelle 280
fusilli in cuttlefish ink 290

D

dandelion 434–5
caper salad 502
dandelion tip salad 435
dandelion with garlic and olive oil 435
dandelion with Parmesan 435
salmon salad with 'beads' 494
dark stock 204
date and walnut bonbons 1052
daurade 620
degustazione di cioccolato Amedei 1164
delicate calf's liver pâté *163, 164*
delicate chicken pâté 162
delicate peperonata *529,* 530
delicate stock 205
delizia al cioccolato 1028
delizia al riso 1028
delizia di patate alla crema dell'orto 520
delizie di trota in crema rosa 106
dentex 620
see also sea bream
dentice al sale 621, 622
dentice brasato 622
dentice in gelatina 622
devilled chicken 922, *923*
Devil's fennel 477
dill
grey mullet and dill parcels 611
dischetti di melanzane e mozzarella 993
dolce alle noci e al caffé 1060
dolce di ciliege 1061
dolce di fragole 1061
dolce di mascarpone 1062
dolce di pane con salsa alla vaniglia 1151

dough
easy pâte brisée 1014
for desserts 1002, 1007
fresh pasta dough 268
green pasta dough 268
pizza dough 193
sablé dough 1013
doughnuts 1097
dried fruit
chamois chops with mushrooms and dried fruit 963
fruit cake 1049
omelette with dried fruit and almonds 1093
see also currants, sultanas *etc.*
Dublin Bay prawns 703
grilled langoustines 705
langoustines with curry sauce 705
langoustines with sage 705
langoustines with tomatoes 703
mixed fish soup with orange 729
polenta with langoustines and radicchio 307
potato gnocchi with langoustines 262
tagliolini with langoustines 282
duchesse potatoes 524
duck 876-86
breast of duck with grapefruit *885,* 886
duck à l'orange 878
duck cooked in beer 878
duck fillets with figs *883,* 886
duck in almond sauce 879
duck in herb sauce 882
duckling in balsamic vinegar 1193
duck terrine *165,* 166
duck with green peppercorns 880, *881*
duck with peaches 879
jugged duck legs 884
stuffed duck in turnip sauce 884
stuffed duck with honey 880
sweet-and-sour duck 882
wild duck with figs 984
dumplings
apple dumplings 1082, *1083*
ricotta dumplings in broth 206

E

Easter leg of kid 754, *755*
Easter pie 188, *189*
easy béarnaise sauce 56
easy pâte brisée 1014
easy ring cake 1046
eau-de-vie
cherries in alcohol 1079
eel 671–3
braised eel 673
Breton eel 671
eel in green sauce 672
eel kebabs 673
eel with Savoy cabbage 672
roast eel 672
eggless shortcrust pastry 1010

eggs 352–95
  Abruzzo scrambled eggs 378
  American chicken salad 913
  American-style eggs 365
  anchovy and egg sauce tartines 138
  aromatic omelette 393
  artichoke pie 422
  asparagus mimosa 402
  baby onion omelette 459
  boiled eggs with artichoke hearts 371
  boiled eggs with broccoli 371
  boiled eggs with herbed mustard 370
  boiled eggs with mushrooms 370
  boiled eggs with spinach 369
  boiled eggs with tomato 370
  borage frittata 387
  bread frittata 388
  cauliflower in egg sauce 440
  cauliflower salad 439
  celery and sausage frittata 387
  cheese frittata 386
  chicken pie 913
  chicken tartlets 144, *145*
  classic truffle frittata 572
  confectioner's custard 1039
  courgette frittata 389
  courgette omelette 393, *394*
  courgette pie 121
  courgettes in egg sauce 585
  crab meat omelette 392
  curried mushroom omelette 395
  custard 1039
  Easter pie 188, *189*
  eggs en cocotte with bacon fat 368
  eggs en cocotte with Bolognese meat
    sauce 368
  eggs en cocotte with leeks 366, *367*
  eggs in red wine 364
  eggs on milk soaked bread 363
  eggs Rossini 365
  eggs with anchovy butter 364
  eggs with asparagus 358
  eggs with asparagus 360
  eggs with aubergines 361
  eggs with Brussels sprouts 365
  eggs with fennel and mozzarella 360
  eggs with ketchup 358
  eggs with mushrooms 359
  eggs with parsley 359
  eggs with polenta 361
  eggs with sausage 363
  eggs with tomatoes 361, *362*
  eggs with truffle 360
  eggs with vinegar 365
  filled frittata 390
  fisherman's eggs en cocotte 366
  four cheese omelette 395
  fragrant eggs en cocotte 368
  French beans in egg cream 469
  French beans in egg sauce 472
  fried stuffed hard-boiled eggs 376
  frittata cake 390, *391*
  Genoese salad 654

  green sauce 74, *75*
  gribiche sauce 73
  ham and sage frittata 387
  ham frittata 387
  hard-boiled eggs and ham in aspic 376
  hard-boiled eggs in aspic 372, *373*
  hard-boiled eggs in curry sauce 374
  hard-boiled eggs Napoletana 374
  hard-boiled eggs with hats 375
  hard-boiled eggs with oysters 375
  hard-boiled eggs with prawns 375
  hard-boiled eggs with smoked
    salmon 375
  hard-boiled eggs with walnuts 374
  jellied mustard tartines 139
  jellied Russian salad tartines 139
  mayonnaise 65, *66*
  meat frittata 389
  nest eggs 122
  Niçoise canapés 124
  olive frittata 388
  omelette with snails 393
  onion and thyme frittata 388
  paprika sauce 69
  Pavian soup 248
  pepper frittata 386
  pepper omelette 392
  piquant sauce 60
  poached eggs in gelatine 357
  poached eggs with artichoke
    hearts 354, *355*
  poached eggs with asparagus
    croquettes 356
  poached eggs with cheese 356
  poached eggs with mixed
    vegetables 357
  polenta with eggs 309, *310*
  potato and cinnamon frittata 389
  potato nests with eggs 521
  Provençal omelette 392
  radicchio mimosa 550
  radicchio omelette 393
  ravioli with eggs and asparagus 1142
  red tomato frittata 540
  rice with raw egg 318
  ricotta omelette 395
  scrambled eggs in their nests *380,* 381
  scrambled eggs with artichokes 377
  scrambled eggs with beans 379
  scrambled eggs with chicken livers 379
  scrambled eggs with fontina 378
  scrambled eggs with sausage 379
  scrambled eggs with spinach 379
  scrambled eggs with truffle 378
  spaghetti carbonara 300
  spider crab mimosa 699
  stracciatella *237,* 238
  stuffed aubergines 116, *118*
  tartare sauce 73
  tomato flowers 119
  tuna bites 104
  tuna frittata 388
  tuna tartines 137

  two-colour omelette tartines 138
  veal steaks with egg and lemon 822
  watercress tartines 134
  whitebait in egg cream 606
  zabaglione *1037,* 1039
  see also crêpes; omelettes; quails' eggs;
    quiches; soufflés
eggs, ostrich 935
endive 489–90
  curly endive in batter 489
  curly endive purée 490
English biscuits 1051
English bread and butter pudding 1027
English mutton chops 805
escarole
  escarole soup 249
  escarole stuffed with olives and
    capers 490
  Genoese pansotti 276
  hard-boiled eggs with hats 375
  marinated swordfish 638
espagnole sauce 60
exotic beans 466
exotic fruit salad 1082

F

fabulous smoked swordfish 635
fagiano alla frutta 951, *952*
fagiano alla panna 953
fagiano alle olive 953
*fagiano arrosto con verza, castagne e salsa
  al vino rosso* 1167
fagiano arrosto ripieno 953
fagiano con i funghi 954, *955*
fagioli ai tre legumi 464
fagioli alla pizzaiola 464
fagioli all'Uccelletto 464, *465*
fagioli con salsiccia 466
fagioli esotici 466
fagioli in puré 467
fagioli misti in insalata 467
fagiolini al parmigiano 469
fagiolini al pomodoro 469
fagiolini alla crema d'uova 469
fagiolini alla polacca 469
fagiolini glassati al sesamo 470, *471*
fagiolini gratinati 470
fagiolini gratinati alla besciamella 470
fagiolini in insalata 472
fagiolini in salsa d'aglio 472
fagiolini in salsa d'uova 472
fagottini di foglie di vite 97
fagottini di mortadella 98
fagottini di pomodori e mozzarella 539
fagottini di radicchio 151, *152*
fagottini di salmone con indivia 644
fagottini piccanti 994
faraona ai carciofi 891
faraona al mascarpone 892, *894*
faraona al vino rosso 895
faraona alla salvia 892
faraona all'ananas 891

faraona all'ortolana 892, *893*
faraona con panna e limone 895
faraona farcita con i funghi 895
faraona ripiena con uvetta 896
faraona tartufata al cartoccio 896
farfalle alla pancetta affumicata 289
farfalle with smoked pancetta 289
farfalline al pesto 225
farfalline with pesto 225
farmhouse rainbow pie 188

farro
farro and bean minestrone 243, *244*
farro and leek soup 231
mesc-iuà 227
pepper and farro salad 528
fave al prosciutto 474
fave alla piemontese 474
feathered game 949–61

feet, calf's
nervetti with onions 99
feet, pig's *see* trotters
fegatelli nella rete 862
fegato agli scalogni 863
fegato al burro e salvia 863
fegato al limone 863
fegato al Merlot 864
fegato alla Veneta 847, *863*
fegato all'uccelletto 864
fegato con carciofi 864
fegato in agrodolce 864

fennel 476–9
bresaola with lamb's lettuce 496, *497*
carrot and fennel mould 170
chicken breasts and fennel
au gratin 918
cream of fennel soup with smoked
salmon 218
Devil's fennel 477
eggs with fennel and mozzarella 360
fennel en croûte 478, *479*
fennel mould 171
fennel pie 478
fennel with mozzarella 477
fennel with walnuts and orange 477
fennel with white wine 477
fried fennel 478
marinated octopus and fennel salad with
mature pecorino 1153
pasta with sardines 293, *294*
red mullet with fennel 669
roasted sea bass with fennel 1199
sea bass with fennel 609
sea bream with fennel bulbs 623
yellow fin tuna carpaccio with shaved
fennel, lemon and bottarga 1173
zite with sausage, onions and
fennel 1128

fennel seeds
fennel butter 83
fesa al formaggio 940
fesa alle mandorle 940
festive aubergines 514
fettine all'aceto 821

fettine all'uovo e limone 822
fettine annodate 822
fettine in salsa d'olive 822

fettuccine
fettuccine in brown butter 270
fettuccine in white sauce 270
fettuccine al burro bruno 270
'fettuccine' di carne 823
fettuccine in salsa bianca 270
fichi alle spezie 1080, *1081*

figs
duck fillets with figs *883,* 886
fig jam 1117
fig tart 1059
langoustine and fig salad 109, *110*
prosciutto and figs 94
spiced figs 1080, *1081*
wild duck with figs 984
filetti di anatra ai fichi 883, 886
filetti di fagiano all'arancia 954
filetti di San Pietro in salsa 647
*filetti di San Pietro in salsa
besciamella* 648
*filetti di sogliola con sedano, salsa aurora e
caviale* 1195
filetti di sogliole alle mandorle 659, *660*
filetti di sogliole in insalata 661
filetto di struzzo alla Conte Rosso 936
filetto in conza 823
filetto in crosta al pâté 791
filetto di rombo con verdure 640
filetto di rombo vestito di patate 641
filetto di vitello alla Rossini 1171
filetto farcito in crosta 769
finocchi al vino bianco 477
finocchi alla diavola 477
finocchi alla mozzarella 477
finocchi con noci e arance 477
finocchi in crosta 478, *479*
finocchi fritti 478
fiore di sfoglia con toma 994
*fiori di latte alla zafferano con salsa alle
aranche rosse e vincotto* 1156
fiori di zucchine fritti 580, *581*
fiori di zucchine ripieni 582
fiori di zucchine ripieni e fritti 582
fishcakes, salmon 646
fisherman's eggs en cocotte 366
fisherman's pizza 196
fisherman's soup 728
fish ravioli with shellfish 1180
flan di carne 823
flan di pomodori alla groviera 539
flan di tonno con salsa ai porri 168
Flemish soup 233
Florentine beef stew 801
Florentine mould 159
Florentine T-bone steak 790

flour 1002
beurre manié 88
roux 76

flowers
meadow flower mousse 160

foie gras
croûtes with pork fillet and pâté de foie
gras 768
jellied tongue tartines 138

fondue
Piedmontese fondue 995
polenta with fondue 308
Savoyard fondue 994
fonduta alla Savoiarda 994
fonduta Piemontese 995
fontina and ham roll 998
four-cheese barquettes 141
four-cheese omelette 395
four-cheese risotto 337
four seasons pizza 199
fragole all'arancia 1080
fragrant eggs en cocotte 368

frankfurters
baked tomatoes 540
frankfurters with Savoy cabbage 845
horseradish and sausage puffs 154
Parisian brioches 150
Polish beans 469

French beans
beans in garlic sauce 472
French bean salad 472
French bean soufflé 176
French beans in béchamel sauce au
gratin 470
French beans in egg cream 469
French beans in egg sauce 472
French beans with tomato 469
frosted green beans with
sesame 470, *471*
Genoese salad 654
green beans with Parmesan 469
mackerel with French beans 656, *657*
Polish beans 469
see also green beans
French sauce, carrots in 430
French-style cauliflower 439
fresh pasta dough 268
freshwater fish, poaching 592
fricassea ai porcini 940
fricassea con cipolline 748, *749*
fricassea di melanzane 510, *511*

fricassée
beef 779
turkey fricassée with porcini 940

frittata 353, 382, 386–91
borage frittata 387
bread frittata 388
celery and sausage frittata 387
cheese frittata 386
classic truffle frittata 572
courgette frittata 389
filled frittata 390
frittata cake 390, *391*
ham and sage frittata 387
ham frittata 387
meat frittata 389
olive frittata 388
onion and thyme frittata 388

pepper frittata 386
potato and cinnamon frittata 389
red tomato frittata 540
tuna frittata 388
frittata ai peperoni 386
frittata al formaggio 386
frittata al prosciutto cotto 387
frittata al prosciutto cotto e salvia 387
frittata al sedano e salsiccia 387
frittata al tonno 388
frittata alla borragine 387
frittata classica di tartufi 572
frittata con cipolle e timo 388
frittata con il pane 388
frittata con le olive 388
frittata con le zucchine 389
frittata con patate e cannella 389
frittata di carne 389
frittata ripiena 390
frittata rossa di pomodori 540
frittelle al bacon 148
frittelle di frutta allo champagne 1096
frittelle di mele 1096
frittelline rosa di pomodoro 540
fritters 1094-7
amaretti fritters 1094
apple fritters 1096
asparagus Bella Elena 401
bacon fritters 148
curly endive in batter 489
doughnuts 1097
fried celeriac 566
fried courgette flowers 580, *581*
fried onion rings 459
fried stuffed courgette flowers 582
fritters 1097
fruit and champagne fritters 1096
sage appetizer 102
sweet fritters 1094, *1095*
tomato fritters *147*, 148, 540
veal fritters 834
fritto misto di pesci azzurri 598
frogs 732–3
fried frogs' legs in tomato sauce 733
frog soup 256
frogs in batter 733
frogs' legs in breadcrumbs 733
frogs' legs in white wine 732
Genoese frogs' legs 732
fromage frais
avocado tartlets 144
grappa and pear tartines 135
frozen mousse with fruits of the forest 1181
fruit
berry jam 1117
desserts 1078–88
fresh fruit jelly 1080
fruit and champagne fritters 1096
fruit jelly 1025
fruits of the forest charlotte 1032, *1033*
fruits of the forest crumble 1064
fruits of the forest ice cream 1098
gratin fruits of the forest with

zabaglione 1108
see also apples, strawberries *etc.*
fruit cake 1049
fruit salads
exotic fruit salad 1082
fruit salad 1080
melon fruit salad 1082
frutta fresca in gelatina 1080
fumet 592
fumetto di pesce 210
funghi al pomodoro 482
funghi alla crema 481
funghi con la zucca 482
funghi crogiolati al forno 482
funghi di bosco gratinati al caprino 1198
funghi gratinati 483
funghi in insalata 115
funghi in insalata tiepida 483
funghi in salsa aïoli 483
funghi porcini al dragoncello 484
funghi porcini al prosciutto 484
funghi porcini fritti 484
funghi ripieni 484
funghi trifolati 485, *486*
furred game 962–85
fusilli
fusilli in cuttlefish ink 290
fusilli salad 290
fusilli timbale 346
fusilli with mushrooms 289
fusilli ai funghi 289
fusilli al nero di seppia 290
fusilli in insalata 290

G

galantina semplice di cappone 889
galantine, simple capon 889
gallettine al formaggio 151
gallina alla melagrana 898, *899*
gallina campagnola 898
gallina con carote e cipolle 900
gallina in salsa rosa 900
gamberi di spuma di salmone 694
gamberi in insalata con fagioli 694
gamberi in salsa dolceforte 695, *696*
gamberi 'stile scampi' 1127
garlic
aïoli 64
beans in garlic sauce 472
chicken with garlic 924
garlic butter 85
leg of lamb à la Périgourdine 744
mushrooms with aïoli 483
Provençal sautéed potatoes 525
rémoulade sauce 68
Russian garlic sauce 73
spaghetti with garlic and chilli oil 299
gazpacho 226
simple gazpacho 226
gazpacho semplice 226
gelatina 211
gelatina di fragole 1114

gelatina di mele cotogne 1115
gelatina di ribes 1115
gelatina d'uva 1115
gelatine
apricot cream 1038
blackcurrant charlotte 1034
fresh fruit jelly 1080
fruits of the forest charlotte 1032, *1033*
jellied mustard tartines 139
jellied Russian salad tartines 139
jellied sea bass 609
jellied sea bream 622
jellied tongue tartines 138
magnificent medallions of lobster 692
panna cotta *1029*, 1030
pineapple bavarois 158
poached eggs in gelatine 357
prawns with salmon mousse 694
tomato jelly ring 539
see also aspic
gelato ai frutti di bosco 1098
gelato ai marron glacé 1098
gelato al caffè 1100
gelato al caramello 1100
gelato al cioccolato 1100
gelato di crema alla vaniglia 1101
gelato di fragole 1101
gelato di limone 1101
gelato di nocciole 1101
gelato di yogurt 1102
Genoese frogs' legs 732
Genoese pansotti 276
Genoese pastry 1010
plum bavarois 1021
Genoese pesto minestrone 239, *240*
Genoese salad 654
Genoese spinach 568
Genoese stuffed breast of veal *811,* 818
German goose with apples 903
germogli di soia ai gamberetti 488
germogli di soia al parmigiano 488
germogli di soia piccanti 488
gherkins
breast of veal with mayonnaise 828
green sauce 74, *75*
hot veal in tuna sauce 838
jellied tongue tartines 138
rice salad with pickled peppers 325
spicy potato salad 521
yogurt sauce 70
giambonetti di pollo al vino rosso 913
giblets
macaroni Napoletana timbale 346
rice timbale 347
vincisgrassi 348
gilthead sea bream 620
glassa a freddo 1015
glassa al burro 1016
glassa al caffè 1016
glassa al cioccolato 1016
glassa per decorare 1016
glazed turkey 942
globe artichokes *see* artichokes

gnocchi 257–66
  bread and spinach gnocchi 259
  bread gnocchi 258
  bread gnocchi in broth 207
  gnocchi alla bava 260
  Parisian gnocchi 257
  Parmesan gnocchi 259
  polenta gnocchi 306
  potato and nettle gnocchi 262
  potato and spinach gnocchi 264
  potato gnocchi 260, *261*
  potato gnocchi filled with fondue 263
  potato gnocchi with langoustines 262
  pumpkin and amaretti gnocchi 266
  rice gnocchi 264
  ricotta and spinach gnocchi 264, *265*
  Roman gnocchi 258
  semolina and ham gnocchi 266
  small cheese gnocchi in clear broth 206
  Triestian potato gnocchi
    with prunes 263
  walnut gnocchi 260
  wholemeal gnocchi 266
gnocchi alla Parigina 257
gnocchi alla Romana 258
gnocchi di pane 258
gnocchi di pane e spinaci 259
gnocchi di parmigiano 259
gnocchi di patate 260, *261*
gnocchi di patate alla bava 260
gnocchi di patate alle noci 260
gnocchi di patate alle ortiche 262
gnocchi di patate con gli scampi 262
*gnocchi di patate con ripieno di
  fonduta* 263
*gnocchi di patate con susine alla
  Triestina* 263
gnocchi di patate e spinaci 264
gnocchi di polenta 306
gnocchi di ricotta e spinaci 264, *265*
gnocchi di riso 264
gnocchi di semolino al prosciutto 266
gnocchi di zucca e amaretti 266
gnocchi integrali 266
goats' cheese
  caprino bavarois 991
  field mushrooms with goats' cheese
    gratin 1198
  mixed greens with caprino 996
  rustic tartines 135
goose 876, 901–7
  braised goose 903
  breast of goose in balsamic
    vinegar 904, *905*
  German goose with apples 903
  goose stew 906, *907*
  goose stuffed with potatoes 904
  roast goose with sweet-and-sour
    peppers 902
  sweet-and-sour goose legs 902
goose liver
  pigeon mousse with truffle
    vinaigrette 160

Gorgonzola butter 85
Gorgonzola mayonaise 67
Gorgonzola mousse 159
Gorgonzola sauce 69, *71*
Gorgonzola tartlets 143
gourgère, Gruyère 995
goulash 791
gran zuccotto di pâté 159
granceola all'olio e limone 697
granceola con maionese 699
granceola gratinata 106
granceola mimosa 699
granchio con avocado 702
granchi e scampi in coppette 107
granchio in insalata 701, *702*
Grand Marnier
  chocolate and pear tart 1067
  gratin fruits of the forest with
    zabaglione 1108
  zuccotto 1110
Grandmother's aubergines 512
grape juice, roast pork in 760
grapefruit
  baked citrus fruit with mint 1107
  breast of duck with grapefruit *885*, 886
  bresaola and grapefruit 94
  crab and langoustine cups 107
  grapefruit crostini 130
  grapefruit sauce 70
  kippers with grapefruit 601
  pot-roast beef with brandy and
    grapefruit 782
  stuffed artichokes jardiniere 113
  veal escalopes with grapefruit 834
grapes
  black grape charlotte 1035
  grape jam 1119
  grape jelly 1115
  grape meringue pie 1109
  melon surprise 1084
  pheasant with fruit 951, *952*
  simple strudel 1065
  wine bavarois 1022
grappa
  blueberries in syrup 1084
  grappa and pear tartines 135
gratin di agrumi alla menta 1107
*gratin di frutti di bosco allo
  zabaione* 1108
gratins
  anchovies au gratin 596
  asparagus au gratin 401
  aubergines au gratin 513
  brains au gratin 853
  Brussels sprouts au gratin 448
  celeriac au gratin 566
  chicken breasts and fennel
    au gratin 918
  cuttlefish au gratin 724
  French beans in béchamel sauce
    au gratin 470
  huss with potatoes au gratin 634
  leeks au gratin *547*, 548

macaroni au gratin 292
mushrooms au gratin 483
mussels au gratin 714
runner beans au gratin 470
salt cod au gratin 603
sausages with leeks au gratin 844
spider crab au gratin 106
stuffed onion gratin 114
sweetbreads au gratin with peas 849
Swiss chard au gratin 411
tomatoes au gratin 541
tomatoes with bacon au gratin 542
Greek chicken 924
Greek mackerel 658
Greek oysters 717
Greek-style celery 564
green beans 468–72
  baby octopus and green bean
    salad 107
  see also French beans
green cream soup *223*, 224
green pasta dough 268
green risotto 339
green sauce 74, *75*
green soup 233
green tomato jam 1119
greengrocer's bag 120
greengrocer's lights 859
grey mullet 610–11
  grey mullet and dill parcels 611
  grey mullet in vinegar 610
  grey mullet with parsley 611
  mixed fish soup with orange 729
  stuffed grey mullet in olive
    sauce 611
gribiche sauce 73
Grosseto onions 459, *460*
grougère alla groviera 995
grouper 612–14
  baked grouper 614
  grouper with avocado 614
  grouper with olives *613*, 614
grouse with bruschetta and cavolo
  nero 1186
Gruyère gourgère 995
guance di manzo brasate al vino 1184
guinea fowl 876, 890–6
  guinea fowl ortolana 892, *893*
  guinea fowl stuffed with sultanas 896
  guinea fowl with artichoke hearts 891
  guinea fowl with cream and lemon 895
  guinea fowl with mascarpone 892, *894*
  guinea fowl with pineapple 891
  guinea fowl with red wine 895
  guinea fowl with sage 892
  guinea fowl with truffles baked in a
    parcel 896
  pot-roast guinea fowl 890
  stuffed guinea fowl with
    mushrooms 895
gulasch 791
gurnard
  fisherman's soup 728

H

hake 630–2
  fried hake 632
  hake in green sauce 630, *631*
  hake in shallot sauce 632
  hake with potatoes 630
  mixed fish soup with orange 729
  seafood vol-au-vent 349

ham 756
  agnolotti Piedmontese 268
  Aunt Maria's farmhouse pie 190
  baked ham 771
  boiled eggs with artichoke hearts 371
  breast of veal with herbs 828
  broad beans with ham 474
  calzone 194, *195*
  cauliflower with ham 437
  celery and ham mould 172
  cheese and ham pâté 997
  chicken breasts stuffed with
    mascarpone 918
  chicken with cream 924
  chicory with béchamel sauce 454
  chicory with ham 115
  chicory with Prague ham 491, *492*
  cooked ham and kiwi fruit 94
  delicate chicken pâté 162
  eggs with Brussels sprouts 365
  exotic beans 466
  farmhouse rainbow pie 188
  Florentine mould 159
  fontina and ham roll 998
  fontina potato bake 522
  four seasons pizza 199
  French beans in béchamel sauce au
    gratin 470
  ham and fontina crêpes 156
  ham and kiwi fruit mousse 160
  ham and potato rolls 521
  ham and sage frittata 387
  ham and tarragon tart 186
  ham canapés 126
  ham frittata 387
  ham in white wine 772, *773*
  ham moulds 97
  ham soufflé 178
  ham vol-au-vents 192
  hamburgers with ham 792
  hard-boiled eggs and ham in aspic 376
  hard-boiled eggs in aspic 372, *373*
  leeks with ham 548
  meat pie 827
  moulded rice with ham and peas 320
  Parisian brioches 150
  penne rigate in vodka 298
  poached eggs in gelatine 357
  porcini with prosciutto 484
  potato soufflé 177
  ravioli Napoletana 277
  ricotta morsels 149
  Roman crescents 151
  Russian salad roulades 98
  semolina and ham gnocchi 266

simple capon galantine 889
smoked ham with Marsala 772
stuffed capon 888
stuffed courgette barquettes 580
stuffed duck with honey 880
stuffed onion gratin 114
stuffed rabbit 977
stuffed turnips 555
sweetcorn and radicchio salad 498
tagliatelle pie 343
tagliatelle with cream, peas and
  ham 281
turkey roll with olives 941
turkey stuffed with Brussels sprouts 945
turnip tops with ham 456
Valle d'Aosta asparagus 402
hamburger all'Americana 792
hamburger con prosciutto 792
hamburgers American-style 792
hamburgers with ham 792

hare 980–3
  hare cacciatore 980
  hare with juniper berries 981
  hare with wine 981, *982*
  sweet and strong hare 983
Hawaiian salad 501

hazelnuts
  crostata with chocolate, hazelnuts and
    orange 1130
  English biscuits 1051
  hazelnut cake 1072, *1073*
  hazelnut ice cream 1101
  hazelnut sauce 1019
  peaches with chocolate 1087
  ugly-but-good biscuits 1051
head, calf's *see* calf's head

heart 860–1
  grilled heart 861
  heart kebabs 861
  heart with anchovies 861
  heart with herbs 861

herbs
  heart with herbs 861
  herb marinade 80, *81*
  herb mayonnaise 67
  herb soup 229
  roast leg of lamb in a herb
    crust 745, *746*
  small brain moulds with herbs 855
  ten-herb sausages 842, *843*
  tripe with herbs 873
  veal escalopes with herbs 834
  see also parsley, sage *etc.*

herrings 601
  herring and cauliflower salad 601
  Scherrer's tartare 102

hollandaise sauce 59
  artichokes in hollandaise sauce 421
  leeks in hollandaise sauce 548

honey
  banana cream 1038
  caramel tartlets 1054
  honey pudding 1024

pork chops with blueberries 764, *765*
rabbit with honey and
  vegetables 974, *975*
stuffed duck with honey 880
walnut and honey tart 1074

horseradish
  horseradish and sausage puffs 154
  horseradish butter 88
  horseradish mayonnaise 68
  horseradish sauce 59
  poached char with horseradish
    sauce 677
  scorzonera with horseradish 562
  surprise raw carrots 428
hot canapés with mozzarella 124, *125*

huss 633–4
  huss with celery 634
  huss with green tomatoes 634
  huss with potatoes au gratin 634
  huss with vegetables 633

I

ice creams 1098–104
  caramel ice cream 1100
  chocolate ice cream *1099,* 1100
  coffee ice cream 1100
  cream and chocolate semifreddo 1104
  cream semifreddo 1102
  fruits of the forest ice cream 1098
  hazelnut ice cream 1101
  lemon ice cream 1101
  marron glacé ice cream 1098
  marron glacé semifreddo 1104
  raspberry semifreddo 1102, *1103*
  strawberry ice cream *1099,* 1101
  torrone semifreddo 1102
  vanilla ice cream *1099,* 1101
  yogurt ice cream 1102
icings 1015-16
impasto per la pizza 193
impepata di cozze 714
Indian rice 314
indivia al prosciutto 115
indivia belga al prosciutto di praga 491, *492*
indivia belga, formaggio e noci 996
indivia belga in teglia 493
*indivia belga in teglia alla noce
  moscata* 493
indivia fritta in pastella 489
indivia ripiena di olive e capperi 490
Indonesian rice 318
insalata al salmone e 'perline' 494
insalata con melagrana 495, *496*
insalata d'aringhe con cavolfiori 601
insalata di avocado 496
insalata di bianchetti 107, *108*
insalata di bresaola e songino 496, *497*
insalata di capone 1148
insalata di cavolfiore (1) 115
insalata di cavolfiore (2) 115
insalata di cavolo capuccio 498
insalata di cetrioli 498

insalata di cetrioli e gamberi 116
insalata di gamberetti e fagioli bianchi,
    condita con olio di tartufo 1173
insalata di mais e radicchio 498
insalata di moscardini e fagiolini 107
insalata di ovoli crudi alla maggiorana 498
insalata di peperoni e farro 528
insalata di polipo su letto di finocchietti e
    scaglie di pecorino stagionato 1153
insalata di pollo all'Americana 913
insalata di pollo con sedano-rapa 914
insalata di polpi e patate 719, 720
insalata di polpo e rucola 109
insalata di scampi e fichi 109, 110
insalata di spinaci e cappesante 499
insalata di spinaci e funghi 499
insalata di storione con le sue uova 1170
insalata di tacchino e fagioli 499
insalata di topinambur con carciofi 574
insalata di trevisana ai funghi 500
insalata di trevisana ai gamberetti 500
insalata di zucchine novelle 582
insalata gialla al mais 500
insalata hawaiana 501
insalata mista al tonno 501
insalata piccante di patate 521
insalata ricca 501
insalata russa 116, 117
insalata siciliana 502
insalata tiepida di gamberi, verze e
    lenticchie 1189
insalata tiepida di seppie con asparagi
    verdi 723
insalatina ai capperi 502
intingolo di chiocciole al sedano rapa e
    dadolata di polenta 1151
involtini agli spinaci 792
involtini ai tartufi 824
involtini alle albicocche 769
involtini alle verdure 824
involtini con bresaola 793
involtini di bresaola alla ricotta 996
involtini di cavolo alla ricotta 444, 445
involtini di cervella al tartufo 855
involtini di coda di rospo con
    gamberetti 617, 618
involtini di granchio ripieni 702
involtini di insalata russa 98
involtini di patate al prosciutto 521
involtini di peperoni al tonno 530
involtini di pollo alla salvia 914, 915
involtini di pollo alle acciughe e
    capperi 914
involtini di pollo all'erba cipollina 916
involtini di radicchio alle noci 549
involtini di San Pietro al forno 648
involtini di sardine 649
involtini di sogliole con i gamberi 661
involtini gustosi 793
involtini saporiti 941
Irish stew 807
Italian bread and butter pudding 1063
Italian trifle 1112, 1113

J

jam
    apples in their nests 1084
    apricot jam and cream
        omelette 1093
    blackberry tart 1059
    chocolate cake with jam 1066
    doughnuts 1097
    jam crêpes 1090
    raspberry omelette 1093
jams and jellies 1114–19
    apple jam 1118
    apricot jam 1116
    berry jam 1117
    cherry jam 1117
    chestnut jam 1116
    fig jam 1117
    grape jam 1119
    grape jelly 1115
    green tomato jam 1119
    kiwi jam 1118
    orange marmalade 1116
    peach jam 1118
    pear jam 1118
    plum jam 1119
    quince jelly 1115
    redcurrant jelly 1115
    rhubarb jam 1119
    strawberry jam 1117
    strawberry jelly 1114
jellied mustard tartines 139
jellied Russian salad tartines 139
jellied sea bass 609
jellied sea bream 622
jellied tongue tartines 138
jellies see jams and jellies
jelly
    fresh fruit jelly 1080
    fruit jelly 1025
Jerusalem artichokes 573–4
    cream of Jerusalem artichoke
        soup 213
    Jerusalem artichoke and potato
        purée 574
    Jerusalem artichoke risotto 329
    Jerusalem artichoke salad 574
    Jerusalem artichokes in cream 574
    sweetbreads with Jerusalem
        artichokes 851
Jewish artichokes 416, 417
John Dory 647–8
    baked John Dory roulades 648
    John Dory fillets in béchamel
        sauce 648
    John Dory fillets in sauce 647
    John Dory with mangetouts 648
jugged duck legs 884
juniper berries
    hare with juniper berries 981
    juniper marinade 77
    loin of pork with juniper 770
    sea trout with juniper berries 685
    woodcock with juniper 950

K

kebabs
    eel kebabs 673
    heart kebabs 861
    marinated mutton kebabs 808
    pineapple kebabs 100
    pork kebabs with prunes 776
ketchup, eggs with 358
kid 753–5
    Easter leg of kid 754, 755
    kid crepinettes with almonds 1190
    kid cutlets with cream 754
    leg of kid with truffle cream 753
    Piedmontese leg of kid 754
kidney beans see red kidney beans
kidneys 867–9
    kidneys in Bordeaux 868
    kidneys in Madeira 868
    kidneys, sausage and mushrooms 869
    kidneys with mustard 868
    kidneys with raw spring onions 869
    pot-roast veal with kidney 815
kippers with grapefruit 601
kirsch
    cherry sauce 1018
    raspberry omelette 1093
    strawberry sauce 1018
kiwi fruit
    cooked ham and kiwi fruit 94
    exotic fruit salad 1082
    fish tartare with kiwi fruit 625
    ham and kiwi fruit mousse 160
    kiwi jam 1118
    kiwi sorbet 1104
    tutti frutti tart 1060
krapfen 1097
kugelhopf 1048
kugelhupf 1048

L

lamb 738–52
    Arabian lamb 744
    chargrilled lamb cutlets with oregano and
        hot feta dressing 1174
    chopped lamb and carrots 752
    lamb cutlets cooked in vinegar 747
    lamb cutlets scottadito 747
    lamb cutlets with anchovy butter 745
    lamb cutlets with mint 747
    lamb fricassée with onions 748, 749
    lamb meatballs with aubergine 748
    lamb with mushrooms 742
    leg of lamb à la Périgourdine 744
    roast lamb with Treviso radicchio, quince
        and pancetta 1155
    roast leg of lamb 745
    roast leg of lamb in a herb
        crust 745, 746
    Roman spring lamb 742, 743
    shoulder of lamb à la
        boulangère 750, 751
    shoulder of lamb in a parcel 748

shoulder of lamb with mirto 750
see also lights; mutton

lambs' brains
brain sauce 57
brains and bone marrow in curry
sauce 854
brains with tomato sauce 853

lamb's lettuce
bresaola with lamb's lettuce 496, *497*
truffle, chicken and lamb's lettuce 102
warm mushroom salad 483

langoustines 703–5
baked langoustines 1146
crab and langoustine cups 107
curried langoustine puffs 154
grilled langoustines 705
langoustine and fig salad 109, *110*
langoustine cocktail 105
langoustines with curry sauce 705
langoustines with sage 705
langoustines with tomatoes 703
mixed fish soup with orange 729
polenta with langoustines and
radicchio 307
potato gnocchi with langoustines 262
seafood sauce 62, *63*
tagliolini with langoustines 282

lasagne
aubergine and ricotta lasagne 272
lasagne Bolognese 270, *271*
lasagne Napoletana 272
lasagnette with leeks, spring onions and
black truffles 1189
radicchio lasagne 273
lasagne alla Bolognese 270, *271*
lasagne alla Napoletana 272
lasagne con melanzane e ricotta 272
lasagne di radicchio 273
lasagnette ai porri, cipollotti e tartufi
neri 1189
latte brûlée 1030
lattuga brasata con pancetta 504
lattuga ripiena 504
lavarelli alle erbe 676
lavarelli fritti 677
lavarelli lessati con salsa al rafano 677
layered anchovies and potatoes 598

leeks 546–8
cheese and leek soup 251
cheese tartlets 143
chicken vol-au-vents 192
cod with leeks 627
courgettes capricciose with salmon and
leeks 585
cream and leek risotto 339
cream of leek soup 221
eggs en cocotte with leeks 366, *367*
farro and leek soup 231
fusilli timbale 346
green cream soup *223*, 224
leek and lentil soup 255
leek and potato soup 233
leek moulds 168

leek sauce 53
leek soup 229
leek tart 185
leeks au gratin *547*, 548
leeks in hollandaise sauce 548
leeks with ham 548
leeks with tomatoes 546
Normandy potatoes 523
roast turnips with leeks and
pumpkin 556, *557*
sausages with leeks au gratin 844
tuna mould with leek sauce 168
vichyssoise 224

lemon
apple fritters 1096
baked citrus fruit with mint 1107
banana sorbet 1106
braised veal with lemon 815
bresaola with oil and lemon 94
chicken with lemon (1) 928
chicken with lemon (2) 928
courgettes with lemon 583
fillet of veal in conza 823
fish tartare with kiwi fruit 625
fresh anchovies with lemon 103
glazed carrots with lemon 428, *429*
Greek chicken 924
Greek oysters 717
grilled pigeons 908
guinea fowl with cream and lemon 895
lemon ice cream 1101
lemon sorbet *1105*, 1106
lemon tart 1069
liver with lemon 863
marinated sea bream 626
marinated swordfish 638
meatballs in lemon 798
monkfish with lemon 615
mutton stewed in citrus juice 807
pears with lemon 1085
piquant pigeons 910
quick lemon marinade 80
rabbit in olive oil and lemon 971
roast pork with lemon *761*, 762
salmon tartare *645*, 646
sole in piquant sauce 663
spider crab in olive oil and lemon 697
summer veal 817
veal escalopes in lemon *829*, 830
veal steaks with egg and lemon 822
whitebait with olive oil and lemon 606
lemon balm, chopped chicken with 934
lenticchie con salsiccia 506
lenticchie e calameretti 226
lenticchie stufate al bacon 508
lenticchie in umido 508

lentils 506–8
baked turbot with lentil sauce 641
barley and pulse soup 230
bread and lentil soup 254
cotechino with lentils 840, *841*
curried rice and lentils 318
leek and lentil soup 255

lentil and squid soup 226
lentil purée 508
lentils in tomato sauce 508
lentils with bacon 508
lentils with sausages 506
seafood stew with lentils 1124
Swiss chard and lentil soup 231
three pulse salad 464
velvety lentil soup 224
warm salad of prawns, Savoy cabbage
and lentils 1189
lepre al vino 981, *982*
lepre alla cacciatora 980
lepre con il ginepro 981
lepre dolce forte 983
lesso casalingo 793, *794*
lesso di manzo in carpione 98
lesso di manzo in tortino 98
lesso in insalata 795
lesso insaporito al rosmarino 795
lesso ripieno 916, *917*
lesso semplice 824

lettuce 503–5
artichokes jardiniere 113
braised lettuce with pancetta
coppata 504
cream of lettuce soup 219
cream of ricotta and vegetable soup 992
lettuce hearts with herbs 504, *505*
lettuce soup au gratin 252
peas with lettuce 536
penne with lettuce 293
spicy quails' eggs 99
stuffed lettuce 504
tagliolini with scallops and lettuce 282

lights 858–9
fried lights 859
greengrocer's lights 859
lights in Marsala 859
Roman lamb's lights 858
Ligurian musky octopus 721
Ligurian pancakes 450
Ligurian polenta 450
Ligurian snails 731

limes
fish tartare with kiwi fruit 625
lime mould 1024
lingua affumicata e lessata 865
lingua alle olive verdi 866
lingua brasata 866
lingua in dolceforte 99
lingua in salsa tartara 866
lingua piccante 866
linguine al pesto genovese 290, *291*
linguine with Genoese pesto 290, *291*

liver 862–4
delicate calf's liver pâté *163*, 164
liver in Merlot 864
liver uccelletto 864
liver with butter and sage 863
liver with globe artichokes 864
liver with lemon 863
liver with shallots 863

pigeon mousse with truffle
vinaigrette 160
pig's liver in a net 862
sweet-and-sour liver 864
Veneto-style liver *847*, 863
see also chicken livers; foie gras

lobster 688-92
American lobster 690
Creole spiny lobster 689
Genoese salad 654
lobster and prawn salad 692
lobster butter 87
lobster canapés 124
lobster in tarragon sauce 690, *691*
magnificent medallions of lobster 692
spicy lobster 690
stracci with lobster 279

loganberries
fruits of the forest ice cream 1098
Lombard snails 731
lombate al vino bianco 795
lombate alla salvia 795
lombo tonnato 770
lonza al ginepro 770
low-fat rice salad 327
luccio al burro bianco 678
luccio all'antica 679
luccio in blanquette 679
lumache alla bourguignonne 731
lumache alla Ligure 731
lumache alla Lombarda 731

lumpfish roe
smoked salmon terrine 646

lychees
exotic fruit salad 1082

M

macaroni
macaroni au gratin 292
macaroni Napoletana timbale 346
macaroni with cuttlefish 292
macaroni with mushrooms 292
maccheroni ai funghi porcini 292
maccheroni alla chitarra 273
*maccheroni alla chitarra con
fegatini* 273
maccheroni alla chitarra with chicken
livers 273
maccheroni con le seppioline 292
maccheroni gratinati 292
macedonia 1080
macedonia di frutta esotica 1082
macedonia di meloni 1082

mackerel 656-8
Greek mackerel 658
mackerel and white wine terrine 658
mackerel with currants 658
mackerel with French beans 656, *657*
mackerel with sage butter 656

Madeira
kidneys in Madeira 868
sweetbreads with Madeira 850

sweetbreads with watercress 848
tournedos Rossini 802
magnificent medallions of
lobster 692
maionese 65, *66*
maionese al curry e panna 67
maionese al Gorgonzola 67
maionese al rafano 68
maionese alla panna montata 67
maionese all'avocado 67
maionese alle erbe 67
maionese Andalusa 68
maionese Maltese 68

maître d'hôtel butter 85
carp with maître d'hôtel butter 674
maltagliati with pumpkin 274
maltagliati con la zucca 274
Maltese mayonnaise 68

mandarins
crêpes Suzette 1090

mangetouts
home-cooked mangetouts 536, *537*
John Dory with mangetouts 648
mixed greens with caprino 996

mangoes
exotic fruit salad 1082
mazzancolle alla rucola 109

maraschino liqueur
fruit salad 1080
melon surprise 1084
marbled ring cake 1046, *1047*
marchand de vin sauce 56
Marche-style fish soup 726
Marche-style squid 707
Margherita pizza 198
Margherita sponge 1010
Margherite alle uova e asparagi 1142

marinades 46, 77–81
brandy marinade 77
cooked marinade 80
herb marinade 80, *81*
juniper marinade 77
quick lemon marinade 80
red wine marinade 78
spicy marinade 80
vinegar marinade 78
white wine marinade 78, *79*
yogurt marinade 78
marinata al brandy 77
marinata al ginepro 77
marinata al vino bianco 78, *79*
marinata al vino rosso 78
marinata all'aceto 78
marinata allo yogurt 78
marinata aromatico 80, *81*
marinata cotta 80
marinata piccante 80
marinata veloce al limone 80
marinated partridge 958
marinated rabbit 977
marinated sea bream 626
marinated swordfish 638
mariner's octopus 722

marjoram
Caesar's mushroom salad with
marjoram 498
marmalade, orange 1116
marmellata d'albicocche 1116
marmellata d'arance 1116
marmellata di castagne 1116
marmellata di ciliege 1117
marmellata di fichi 1117
marmellata di fragole 1117
marmellata di frutti di bosco 1117
marmellata di kiwi 1118
marmellata di mele 1118
marmellata di pere 1118
marmellata di pesche 1118
marmellata di pomodori verdi 1119
marmellata di prugne 1119
marmellata di rabarbaro 1119
marmellata d'uva 1119
marquise al cioccolato 1108

marron glacés
marron glacé ice cream 1098
marron glacé semifreddo 1104
marroni brasati 433
marrow, bone *see* bone marrow

Marsala
braised breast of veal 829
capon roast in a parcel 887
croûtes with pork fillet and pâté de foie
gras 768
lights in Marsala 859
Marsala sauce 55
ricotta and sultana tart 1076
smoked ham with Marsala 772
sweetbreads with Jerusalem
artichokes 851
veal escalopes with Marsala 829
veal knots 822
veal noisettes à la financière 825
veal ribbons 823
zabaglione *1037,* 1039
zabaglione soufflé 1043

mascarpone cheese
chicken breasts stuffed with
mascarpone 918
Gorgonzola tartlets 143
grapefruit sauce 70
grappa and pear tartines 135
guinea fowl with mascarpone 892, *894*
mascarpone and anchovy cream 992
mascarpone cream 1038
mascarpone dessert 1062
pound cake with mascarpone
cream 1148
tiramisu 1110, *1111*
torta sbrisolona with quince, mascarpone
cream and vincotto 1168
mattonella tricolore 534

mayonnaise 65, *66*
American chicken salad 913
Andalusian mayonnaise 68
asparagus with orange 402
avocado mayonnaise 67

breast of veal with mayonnaise 828
carpaccio 788, *789*
chicken and celeriac salad 914
chicken tartlets 144, *145*
chicken with tuna 929
courgettes with prawns 696
cucumbers in mayonnaise 451
curry and cream mayonnaise 67
Gorgonzola mayonaise 67
herb mayonnaise 67
horseradish mayonnaise 68
langoustine cocktail 105
lobster canapés 124
Maltese mayonnaise 68
poached char with horseradish
  sauce 677
rémoulade sauce 68
spicy quails' eggs 99
spider crab with mayonnaise 699
watercress tartines 134
whipped cream mayonnaise 67
white cabbage salad 498
meadow flower mousse 160
meatballs
lamb meatballs with aubergine 748
meatballs in brandy 796, *797*
meatballs in lemon 798
meatballs with anchovies 796
meatballs with potato 796
meatballs with spinach 798
meatballs with a tasty onion garnish 798
pork tenerelle 776
rigatoni with meatballs 298
soup with meatballs 229
spicy Indian meatballs 934
meatloaf, veal 831
medaglioni di aragosta in bellavista 692
Mediterranean prawns with rocket 109
Mediterranean sauce 73
Mediterranean stockfish 604
melanzane alla panna 510
melanzane alle acciughe 510
melanzane arrosto 512
melanzane della nonna 512
melanzane farcite alla mozzarella 512
melanzane in festa 514
melanzane in forno alla ricotta 514
melanzane gratinate 513
melanzane impanate a sorpresa 513
melanzane marinate 515, *516*
melanzane ripiene 116, *118*
mele in crosta 1082, *1083*
mele nel nido 1084
mele speziate con uvetta 1084
melon
fruit jelly 1025
langoustine and fig salad 109, *110*
melon fruit salad 1082
melon surprise 1084
prosciutto and melon 94
smoked trout with melon 685
spicy bundles 994
watermelon with rum 1079

melone sorpresa 1084
melted butter 88
melted chocolate 1015
meringa 1016
meringata alle prugne 1108
meringata all'uva 1109
meringhe alla panna montata 1054
meringues 1016
  meringues with whipped cream 1054
  plum meringue 1108
Merlot, liver in 864
merluzzo ai porri 627
merluzzo al curry 627
merluzzo al forno con verdure 628
merluzzo alla provenzale 628
merluzzo alla Siciliana 628
mesc-iuà 227
messicani in gelatina 824
mezzelune alla Romana 151
Milanese minestrone 241
Milanese mixed boiled meat 785
Milanese osso buco 825, *826*
Milanese perch 681
Milanese risotto 330, *331*
Milanese-style brains 854
Milanese tripe 873
Milanese veal chops 819, *820*
milk 1003
  chestnut mould 1025, *1026*
  confectioner's custard 1039
  crème caramel 1028
  custard 1039
  English bread and butter pudding 1027
  fruits of the forest charlotte 1032, *1033*
  Italian bread and butter pudding 1063
  milk and onion soup 249
  milk brulée 1030
  milk pot-roast 814
  old-fashioned crème brûlée 1038
  panna cotta *1029,* 1030
  Piedmont pudding 1023
  polenta soup 306
  rabbit in milk 973
  rice cooked in milk 313
  rice pudding 1028
  semolina pudding 1027
  semolina pudding with black
    cherries 1027
  veal braised in milk with prosciutto 814
  veal escalopes with milk 833
millefeuille, three-chocolate 1062
millefoglie ai tre cioccolati 1062
millet soup 231
minestra ai fiori di zucchine 227, *228*
minestra al germe di grano 227
minestra aromatica 229
minestra con i porri 229
minestra con il mais 229
minestra con noccioline di carne 229
minestra con orzo e legumi 230
minestra di bianchetti 230
minestra di ceci e spinaci 230
minestra di coste e lenticchie 231

minestra di farro e porri 231
minestra di miglio 231
minestra di ortiche 232
minestra di orzo e pollo 232
minestra di ovoli 232
minestra di polenta 306
minestra di porri e patate 233
minestra fiamminga 233
minestra tricolore 233
minestra verde 233
minestrone alla Genovese col pesto 239
minestrone alla Milanese 241
minestrone alla Napoletana 241
minestrone alla Pugliese 242
minestrone alla Russa 242
minestrone alla Toscana 243
minestrone di farro e fagioli 243, *244*
minestrone di stagione 245
minestrone di verza e riso 245
minestrone d'inverno 243
minestrones 239–45
  borsch 242
  farro and bean minestrone 243, *244*
  Genoese pesto minestrone 239, *240*
  Milanese minestrone 241
  minestrone Napoletana 241
  Puglian minestrone 242
  Savoy cabbage and rice
    minestrone 245
  seasonal minestrone 245
  Tuscan minestrone 243
  winter minestrone 243
mini rice croquettes with mozzarella 321
mini supplì di riso con mozzarella 321
mint
  baked citrus fruit with mint 1107
  lamb cutlets with mint 747
  mint sauce 72
  peas with mint 534
  rice with mint 317
  yogurt sauce 70
mirtilli sciroppati 1084
mirto (myrtle liqueur)
  shoulder of lamb with mirto 750
misto verde al caprino 996
mixed fish fry 598
mixed greens with caprino 996
mixed salad with pomegranate *495,* 496
mixed tuna salad 501
mocha cake 1063
moka 1063
Molise celery 564
monkfish 615–19
  fisherman's soup 728
  monkfish and prawn roulades 617, *618*
  monkfish in red wine 616
  monkfish stew with turmeric rice 619
  monkfish with anchovy sauce 617
  monkfish with cauliflower and spring
    onions 616
  monkfish with lemon 615
Montebianco 1109
mornay sauce 51

mortadella
Aunt Maria's farmhouse pie 190
country bonbons 150
meat pie 827
mortadella parcels 98
moscardini alla Ligure 721
moscardini alla Napoletana 721
moscardini in umido 721
moulded rice with ham and peas 320
moulds
artichoke heart mould 169
carrot and fennel mould 170
carrot mould 170
cauliflower mould 171
celery and ham mould 172
chestnut mould 1025, *1026*
chicory mould 171
chocolate mould 1024
clam and mussel mould 173
courgette moulds 168
fennel mould 171
Florentine mould 159
honey pudding 1024
leek moulds 168
lime mould 1024
meat pie 827
pea and amaretti mould 172
pumpkin mould 174, *175*
sea trout mould 173
small brain moulds with herbs 855
spinach mould 172
tomato and Gruyère mould 539
tuna mould with leek sauce 168
two-colour mould 169
see also mousses (savoury); pâtés;
  terrines
mountain crostini with speck and apple
  cream 132
mousse di asparagi 404
mousse di gorgonzola 159
*mousse di piccione con vinaigrette al
  tartufo* 160
mousse di pratoline 160
mousse di prosciutto e kiwi 160
mousse di salmone con crema 161
mousse fredda di pomodori 161
mousses
artichokes with chicken liver mousse 418
asparagus mousse 404
cold tomato mousse 161
frozen mousse with fruits of the
  forest 1181
Gorgonzola mousse 159
ham and kiwi fruit mousse 160
meadow flower mousse 160
pigeon mousse with truffle
  vinaigrette 160
prawns with salmon mousse 694
salmon mousse with prawn cream 161
tomatoes with cucumber mousse 541
see also moulds; pâtés; terrines
mozzarella alla piastra 997
mozzarella in carrozza 997

mozzarella cheese
aubergine and mozzarella rounds 993
buffalo milk mozzarella Capri salad 991
fried mozzarella sandwiches 997
hot canapés with mozzarella 124, *125*
mini rice croquettes with mozzarella 321
mozzarella pumpkin sandwich 577
pizzaiola tartines 135, *136*
toasted mozzarella 997
tomato and mozzarella parcels 539
tomatoes with courgettes 542
fennel with mozzarella 477
muffins 1048
mullet *see* grey mullet; red mullet
mushrooms 480–6
Barolo and mushroom risotto 329
bean and mushroom soup 251
beef patties with cream and
  mushrooms 785
beef Stroganoff 788
boiled eggs with mushrooms 370
Breton eel 671
bucatini with mushroom sauce 288
Caesar's mushroom salad with
  marjoram 498
Caesar's mushroom soup 232
capon roast in a parcel 887
cardoon moulds with mushrooms 426
chamois chops with mushrooms and
  dried fruit 963
chicken breasts stuffed with
  mascarpone 918
chicken in red wine 930
chicken pie 913
chicken with mushrooms 919
cod and mushroom tart 183
corn soup 229
cotechino with mushroom sauce 842
cream of porcini soup 213
crostini with mushrooms in a light
  sauce 130
curried mushroom omelette 395
eggs with mushrooms 359
field mushrooms with goats' cheese
  gratin 1198
filled frittata 390
Flemish soup 233
French beans in béchamel sauce au
  gratin 470
fried porcini 484
fusilli with mushrooms 289
ham in white wine 772, *773*
kidneys in Bordeaux 868
kidneys, sausage and mushrooms 869
lamb with mushrooms 742
macaroni with mushrooms 292
melting baked porcini 482
mushroom and caper crostini 128
mushroom and game pie 985
mushroom and potato pie 486
mushroom béchamel 50
mushroom butter 82
mushroom caps Montanara 486

mushroom crêpes 156
mushroom pizza 194
mushroom puffs 146, 154
mushroom salad 115
mushroom soufflé 176
mushroom tart with walnut cream 181
mushroom tortelloni 285
mushroom trifolati 485, *486*
mushrooms au gratin 483
mushrooms with aïoli 483
mushrooms with cream 481
mushrooms with pumpkin 482
mushrooms with tomato 482
penne and mushroom pie 343
pheasant with mushrooms 954, *955*
Piedmontese tartare 95
pike blanquette 679
polenta pasticciata with mushrooms 309
porcini with prosciutto 484
porcini with tarragon 484
pork en croûte 769
rabbit in cider 974
sardines bellavista 652
sauerkraut with mushrooms and
  potatoes 443
scorpion fish with mushrooms 655
sea bream with mushrooms 625
sole with mushrooms 661
spinach and mushroom salad
  499, *569*, 570
steak with mushrooms 783
steamed turbot fillets with
  vegetables 640
stuffed guinea fowl with mushrooms 895
stuffed mushrooms 484
stuffed partridge 957, *958*
stuffed porcini mushrooms 119
sweetbreads with cream and
  mushrooms 849
tagliatelle with mushrooms 279
tomatoes with bacon au gratin 542
tortiglioni with mushroom and
  aubergine 304
Treviso radicchio salad with
  mushrooms 500
tripe with mushrooms 872
trout with mushrooms and
  mussels 686, *687*
turkey fricassée with porcini 940
veal escalopes with mushrooms 831
veal noisettes à la financière 825
warm mushroom salad 483
musky octopus Napoletana 721
mussels 713–15
baby squid in baskets 105
clam and mussel mould 173
cream of carrot and mussel
  soup 215, *216*
cream of cauliflower soup with
  mussels 217
creamy mussels 713
fisherman's pizza 196
fisherman's soup 728

four seasons pizza 199
fresh 'guitar string' spaghetti with mussels, cherry tomatoes and olives 1154
Livorno-style fish soup 726, *727*
Marche-style fish soup 726
mixed shellfish soup 729
mussel purses with courgette flowers 1158
mussel soup 250
mussels au gratin 714
mussels marinara 714
mussels with aromatic herbs 1183
mussels with green peppers 714, *715*
paella 321
peppered mussels 714
pirate's fish soup 728
seafood rice salad 324
seafood risotto 328
swordfish parcels 636, *637*
trout with mushrooms and mussels 686, *687*

mustard
boiled eggs with herbed mustard 370
jellied mustard tartines 139
kidneys with mustard 868
mustard béchamel 51
mustard butter 87
onions in orange mustard 114
partridge with mustard 956
rabbit with mustard 973
steak with mustard 784
turkey stew with mustard 942
veal escalopes with mustard 833

mutton 803–9
chopped mutton with prunes 808, *809*
English mutton chops 805
Irish stew 807
leg of mutton in vodka 805
leg of mutton with turnips 805, *806*
marinated mutton kebabs 808
mutton and bean stew 807
mutton and potato stew 808
mutton stewed in citrus juice 807
see also lamb

N

nasello con patate 630
nasello in salsa verde 630, *631*
nasello in tegame 632
nasello insaporito agli scalogni 632
Nemesis 1187
nervetti e cipolle 99
nervetti with onions 99
nest eggs 122

nettles
nettle risotto 333
nettle soup 232
potato and nettle gnocchi 262
Niçoise canapés 124
nidi di patate con le uova 521
nodini al burro, salvia e rosmarino 825

nodini alla finanziera 825
Normandy potatoes 523
Normandy sauce 59
Norwegian lobster *see* langoustines

nougat
torrone semifreddo 1102
torrone soufflé 1043
nutmeg, baked chicory with 493

O

oats
oatmeal soup 251
porridge 236
wholemeal gnocchi 266
oca alla tedesca con le mele 903
oca brasata 903
oca ripiena di patate 904

octopus 719–22
baby octopus and green bean salad 107
braised musky octopus 721
fisherman's pizza 196
Ligurian musky octopus 721
marinated octopus and fennel salad with mature pecorino 1153
mariner's octopus 722
musky octopus Napoletana 721
octopus and potato salad 719, *720*
octopus and rocket salad 109
octopus in red wine 722
pirate's fish soup 728
poached octopus 722
seafood rice salad 324
oil *see* olive oil
old-fashioned crème brûlée 1038
old-fashioned onion tart 184
old-fashioned pike 679

olive oil
bresaola with oil and lemon 94
fillet of veal in conza 823
quick lemon marinade 80
rabbit in olive oil and lemon 971
rabbit 'tuna' 979
red wine marinade 78
spicy marinade 80
white wine marinade 78, *79*
whitebait with olive oil and lemon 606

olives
Abruzzo scrambled eggs 378
American chicken salad 913
Arabian lamb 744
artichokes jardiniere 113
artichokes Napoletana 418
brains with capers 853
braised veal with olives 815
breast of veal with mayonnaise 828
carp with olives 675
cauliflower salad 439
chicken stew with olives 934
chicken with olives 926
cod stew with olives and capers 629
courgettes capricciose 584
crab and langoustine cups 107

cucumbers with olives 452
escarole stuffed with olives and capers 490
fancy peppers 532
four seasons pizza 199
fresh 'guitar string' spaghetti with mussels, cherry tomatoes and olives 1154
Genoese salad 654
Greek mackerel 658
grouper with olives *613*, 614
hard-boiled eggs and ham in aspic 376
Molise celery 564
Niçoise canapés 124
olive frittata 388
penne with black olives 295
pheasant with mushrooms 954, *955*
pheasant with olives 953
pigeons with olives 910
pizzaiola tartines 135, *136*
Provençal trout 685
rabbit in vinegar 971
radish salad with olives *559*, 560
rolled peppers 119
rustic tartines 135
salt cod with olives and capers 603
sea bream with olives 624
Sicilian cod 628
smoked salmon pâté 164
spicy beansprouts 488
stuffed grey mullet in olive sauce 611
sweet-and-sour caponata 112
tapénade 74
tongue with green olives 866
tuna tartines 137
turbot with olive sauce 643
turkey roll with olives 941
turkey stuffed with chestnuts *943*, 944
veal escalopes pizzaiola 833
veal fritters 834
veal steaks in olive sauce 822
wild boar with olives 969
omelette ai peperoni 392
omelette al radicchio 393
omelette alla marmellata di albicocche e panna 1093
omelette alla polpa di granchio 392
omelette alla provenzale 392
omelette alle lumache 393
omelette alle zucchine 393, *394*
omelette aromatica 393
omelette base dolce 1093
omelette con frutta secca alla fiamma 1093
omelette con funghi al curry 395
omelette di lamponi 1093
omelette variante ai quattro formaggi 395
omelette variante alla ricotta 395

omelettes
apricot jam and cream omelette 1093
aromatic omelette 393
baby onion omelette 459
courgette omelette 393, *394*

crab meat omelette 392
curried mushroom omelette 395
four cheese omelette 395
omelette with dried fruit and
    almonds 1093
omelette with snails 393
Provençal omelette 392
radicchio omelette 393
raspberry omelette 1093
ricotta omelette 395
sweet omelette 1092
two-colour omelette tartines 138
see also frittata

onions 458–62
baby onion omelette 459
baby onions with sage 461
beef stew with white wine 801
beef stew with wine and onions 800
beetroot with onions 406
braised baby onions 462
braised beef with onions 788
cabbage with paprika 442
chicken ratatouille 924, *925*
chicken roasted in a parcel 920
chicken with carrots and onions 900
chicken with onions 926, *927*
crostini with peppers and onions
    in agrodolce 1166
Easter leg of kid 754, *755*
fried onion rings 459
glazed baby onions 462
goulash 791
Greek-style celery 564
Grosseto onions 459, *460*
Irish stew 807
lamb fricassée with onions 748, *749*
meatballs with a tasty onion garnish 798
milk and onion soup 249
nervetti with onions 99
old-fashioned onion tart 184
onion and thyme frittata 388
onion chutney 65
onion sauce 54
onion soufflé 174
onion soup au gratin 250
onions in orange mustard 114
oriental carp 675
potatoes and onions baked in an
    earthenware dish 524
shin of veal in cider 836
shoulder of lamb à la
    boulangère 750, *751*
soubise sauce 52
spicy Indian meatballs 934
stuffed onion gratin 114
stuffed onions 461
tagliatelline with onions 282
the sultan's onions 461
Veneto-style liver 847, *863*
see also spring onions

orange
asparagus with orange 402
babá with orange sauce 1196
baked citrus fruit with mint 1107
banana sorbet 1106
cake with orange icing 1067, *1068*
caramelized oranges 1079
cooked saffron milk puddings with blood
    orange and vincotto sauce 1156
crostata with chocolate, hazelnuts and
    orange 1130
duck à l'orange 878
fennel with walnuts and orange 477
fruit jelly 1025
Maltese mayonnaise 68
mixed fish soup with orange 729
mutton stewed in citrus juice 807
orange and Grand Marnier mousse 1143
orange bavarois 1020
orange marmalade 1116
orange sauce 1018
pearl barley with quail, thyme, potato and
    orange sauce with olive brunoise 1195
pheasant with fruit 951, *952*
pheasant with orange 954
roast pork with orange 760
strawberries with orange 1080
summer pineapple 1078
Treviso radicchio salad with
    orange 550, *552*
turbot in orange sauce 642
turkey à l'orange 938
orata ai ferri 623
orata ai finocchi 623
orata al forno 623
orata alle olive 624

orecchiette
orecchiette 274
orecchiette with broccoli 274, *275*
orecchiette with tomato and ricotta 276
orecchiette with turnip tops 274
orecchiette con broccoli 274, *275*
orecchiette con cime di rapa 274
orecchiette con pomodoro e ricotta 276
oriental carp 675
*orzo perlato con quaglie e timo, salsa di
    patate e arancia con brunoise
    d'olive* 1195
ossibuchi alla Milanese 825, *826*
ossibuchi con piselli 826
ossobuco di storione in gremolata 1143

osso buco
Milanese osso buco 825, *826*
veal osso buco with peas 827

ostrich 935–6
Conte Rosso ostrich fillet 936
ostrich stew 936
ostrich eggs 935
ostriche alla Greca 717
ostriche all'americana 717
ostriche calde al burro bianco 717
ostriche calde al curry 718
ostriche con lo zabaione salato 718
ovetti di quaglia piccanti 99

oxtail 856–7
oxtail vaccinara 857

oxtail with pancetta 857
oysters 111, 716–18
American oysters 717
curried oysters 718
Genoese salad 654
Greek oysters 717
hard-boiled eggs with oysters 375
hot oysters in beurre blanc 717
oysters in salted sabayon sauce 718

P

paella 321
palm hearts
crab salad *701*, 702
rich salad 501
palombo al sedano 634
palombo alle verdure 633
palombo con patate al gratin 634
palombo con pomodori verdi 634
pan dolce 1063
pancakes 1091
blueberry pancakes 1091
Ligurian pancakes 450
pancakes ai mirtilli 1091
pancetta
American-style eggs 365
artichokes stuffed with sausage 421
asparagus with pancetta 401
beef stew with white wine 801
beef stew with wine and onions 800
beef Wellington 791
braised lettuce with pancetta
    coppata 504
braised sauerkraut 443
braised veal with truffle 816
Breton eel 671
Brussels sprouts au gratin 448
buck's horn plantain with pancetta 409
chicken in red wine 930
chicken legs in red wine 913
chicken roulades with sage 914, *915*
Christmas turkey 943
duck à l'orange 878
farfalle with smoked pancetta 289
hare with juniper berries 981
kidneys in Bordeaux 868
langoustines with sage 705
liver uccelletto 864
loin of pork with juniper 770
Milanese tripe 873
Normandy potatoes 523
old-fashioned pike 679
olive frittata 388
oxtail with pancetta 857
Parisian brioches 150
peas with pancetta 534, *535*
pheasant in cream sauce 953
Piedmontese leg of kid 754
pork roulades with apricots 769
potato pizza 196
pot-roast turkey 938
Provençal artichokes 419

quail on the spit 960, *961*
roast beef with carrots 783
roast lamb with Treviso radicchio, quince
    and pancetta 1155
roast leg of lamb 745
roast pigeons 908
sardine rolls 649
sausage pizza 198
spaghetti amatriciana 300, *301*
spaghetti carbonara 300
stuffed partridge *957, 958*
tasty turkey roulades 941
tomato and mozzarella parcels 539
turkey stuffed with chestnuts *943, 944*
wild boar in sauce 969
see also bacon
pancotto 234
panini al rosmarino e formaggio 100
panissa 450
panna cotta *1029,* 1030
    caramelized panna cotta 1184
    panna cotta, almond tart and
        zabaglione 1140
panna cotta caramellata 1184
panna cotta, torta di mandorle e zabaione
    artusiano 1140
panna montata 1017
pansotti, Genoese 276
pansotti alla Genovese 276
papaya
    exotic fruit salad 1082
pappa al pomodoro 234
paprika
    cabbage with paprika 442
    goulash 791
    paprika béchamel 51
    paprika sauce 69
Parisian brioches 150
Parisian cucumbers 452
Parisian gnocchi 257
Parmesan asparagus 402, *403*
Parmesan aubergines 515
Parmesan Brussels sprouts 446
Parmesan gnocchi 259
Parmesan pumpkin 577
Parmesan truffles 572
Parmesan turnip tops 456
parmigiana di melanzane 515
parsley
    baked rice with parsley 320
    eggs with parsley 359
    grey mullet with parsley 611
    herb marinade 80, *81*
    maître d'hôtel butter 85
    peas with parsley 536
    tartare sauce 73
partridge 956–8
    marinated partridge 958
    mushroom and game pie 985
    partridge with mustard 956
    partridges with Savoy cabbage, fried sage
        and vegetables 1139
    stuffed partridge *957,* 958

passatelli 234
passatina di ceci con gamberi 1180
pasta all'uovo 268
pasta brisée 140, 1007
pasta con le sarde 293, *294*
pasta di choux con crema pasticciera di
    mandorle e salsa cioccolato e mandorle
    croccanti 1175
pasta di mandorle (1) 1007
pasta di mandorle (2) 1008
pasta e ceci alla Toscana 235
pasta e fagioli 235
pasta frolla (1) 1008
pasta frolla (2) 1008
pasta frolla senza uova 1010
pasta Genovese 1010
pasta Margherita 1010
pasta, patate e sedano 235
pasta per bignè 1011
pasta per bignè salata 1011
pasta per brioche 1012
pasta per dolci lievitata 1012
pasta per fondo torta 1013
pasta per pan di spagna 1013
pasta per sablé 1013
pasta sfoglia rapida 1014
pasta tipo brisée 1014
pasta verde 268
pastella per crêpes 155
pastella per friggere 1017
pasticcio di bacon e patate 771
pasticcio di carne 827
pasticcio di fagiano 342
pasticcio di melanzane con cioccolato 1159
pasticcio di pasta di zucca 342
pasticcio di penne ai funghi 343
pasticcio di tagliatelle 343
pastries
    apple dumplings 1082, *1083*
    apricot strudel 1064
    baby squid in baskets 105
    bouchées 149–54
    pork en croûte 769
    puff pastry flowers with toma 994
    radicchio en croûte 553
    ricotta strudel 1065
    salmon and chicory parcels 644
    simple strudel 1065
    three-chocolate millefeuille 1062
    tomato and mozzarella parcels 539
    veal fritters 834
    vegetable-garden strudel 120
    vol-au-vents 191–2
    see also barquettes; pies; tartlets; tarts
pastry 1007–14
    choux paste 1011
    easy pâte brisée 1014
    eggless shortcrust pastry 1010
    Genoese pastry 1010
    pâte brisée 140, 1007
    savoury choux paste 1011
    shortcrust pastry (1) 1008
    shortcrust pastry (2) 1008, *1009*

speedy puff pastry 1014
tart case 1013
patate al cartoccio con lo yogurt 522
patate al forno al salmone 522
patate al forno alla fontina 522
patate alla besciamella 523
patate alla Normanna 523
patate alla scamorza 523
patate duchessa 524
patate in salsa bianca 524
patate in terracotta con cipolle 524
patate ripiene alla salsiccia 525
patate saltate alla provenzale 525
patate stufate al pomodoro 525
patatine novelle al rosmarino 526, *527*
pâté ai fegatini 162
pâte brisée 140, 1007
pâté de foie gras 846
    eggs Rossini 365
pâté delicato di pollo 162
pâté delicato di vitello 163, 164
pâté di formaggio e prosciutto cotto 997
pâté di salmone 164
pâté di tonno 164
pâtés 158–64
    cheese and ham pâté 997
    chicken liver pâté 162
    chicken liver pâté with herbs and
        truffle 1150
    cold tomato mousse 161
    delicate calf's liver pâté *163,* 164
    delicate chicken pâté 162
    Gorgonzola mousse 159
    ham and kiwi fruit mousse 160
    meadow flower mousse 160
    pigeon mousse with truffle
        vinaigrette 160
    salmon mousse with prawn cream 161
    smoked salmon pâté 164
    tuna pâté 164
    see also moulds; mousses (savoury);
        terrines
Pavian soup 248
peaches
    duck with peaches 879
    melon surprise 1084
    peach jam 1118
    peach pie 1074, *1075*
    peaches in red wine 1087
    peaches with chocolate 1087
    peaches with strawberries 1087
    stuffed peaches 1088
    zabaglione soufflé 1043
pear brandy
    pears in chocolate 1085, *1086*
pears
    apple and pear tart 1072
    chestnut flour pie with pears 1125
    chocolate and pear tart 1067
    cinnamon pears 1085
    grappa and pear tartines 135
    pear crown 1058
    pear jam 1118

pears in chocolate 1085, *1086*
pears with lemon 1085
plum and pear charlotte 1032
spicy candied pears 1085
peas 533–7
barley and pea soup 248
cheese tartlets 143
cream of pea and potato soup 220
curried tortellini 283
cuttlefish with peas 724
Florentine mould 159
ham vol-au-vents 192
Indonesian rice 318
moulded rice with ham and peas 320
pea and amaretti mould 172
peas with carrots 536
peas with lettuce 536
peas with mint 534
peas with pancetta 534, *535*
peas with parsley 536
pork stew with peas 775
quail stuffed with green vegetables and
peas 1177
rice and crab meat salad 325
rice and peas 236
sweetbreads au gratin with peas 849
sweet pea flan with carrot
vinaigrette 1132
tagliatelle with cream, peas and
ham 281
three-colour soup 233
three-colour terrine 534
veal osso buco with peas 827
see also petits pois
peel, candied *see* candied peel
penne
curried penne salad 296
fried penne 296
penne and mushroom pie 343
penne arrabbiata 295
penne rigate in vodka 298
penne rigate with artichokes 296, *297*
penne with black olives 295
penne with lettuce 293
penne with turnip tops 295
penne with saffron 295
penne alla lattuga 293
penne all'arrabbiata 295
penne alle olive nere 295
penne con cime di rapa 295
penne gialle 295
penne in insalata al curry 296
penne in tegame 296
penne rigate ai carciofi 296, *297*
penne rigate alla vodka 298
peperonata delicata 529, 530
peperoni arrosto 530, *531*
peperoni arrotolati 119
peperoni capricciosi 532
peperoni in agrodolce 532
peperoni ripieni d'estate 532
peppercorns
duck with green peppercorns 880, *881*

peppered mussels 714
peppers 528–32
Andalusian mayonnaise 68
artichokes stuffed with peppers 421
aubergine terrine 517
beef stew with coffee 800
bucatini with pepper sauce 289
chicken ratatouille 924, *925*
chicken with green peppers 931
chicken with yellow peppers 931
crostini with peppers and onions in
agrodolce 1166
crab soufflé 177
delicate peperonata *529*, 530
fancy peppers 532
farmhouse rainbow pie 188
frittata cake 390, *391*
gazpacho 226
greengrocer's bag 120
Hawaiian salad 501
heart kebabs 861
marinated partridge 958
mixed greens with caprino 996
mortadella parcels 98
mussels with green peppers 714, *715*
paella 321
pepper and farro salad 528
pepper and tuna rolls 530
pepper frittata 386
pepper omelette 392
pepper pie 121
pepper risotto 336
pineapple kebabs 100
pirate's fish soup 728
pork chops with yellow peppers 768
rabbit with peperonata 976
red pepper sauce 57
rice salad with pickled peppers 325
roast goose with sweet-and-sour
peppers 902
roast peppers 530, *531*
rolled peppers 119
salmon tartare *645*, 646
salt cod with potatoes and peppers 604
sardines bellavista 652
smoked trout in pink cream 106
sole salad 661
stuffed aubergines 116, *118*
sturgeon with red pepper sauce 666
summer cannellini beans 466
summer stuffed peppers 532
sweet-and-sour peppers 532
sweet-and-sour pork stew 775
sweet-and-sour spare ribs 774
tasty turkey roulades 941
two-colour cauliflower with
pepper 437, *438*
perch 680–1
Milanese perch 681
perch baked in creamy herb sauce 680
perch with anchovies 681
perch with sage 681
pere al cioccolato 1085, *1086*

pere al limone 1085
pere alla cannella 1085
pere pralinate alle spezie 1085
pernice alla senape 956
*pernice con verze, salvia fritta e
verdure* 1139
pernice farcita 957, 958
pernice marinata 958
pesce persico alla Milanese 681
pesce persico alla salvia 681
pesce persico alle acciughe 681
*pesce persico in teglia alla crema
verde* 680
pesce spada affumicato in fantasia 635
pesce spada al forno 635
pesce spada in cartoccio 636, *637*
pesce spada in umido 636
pesce spada marinato 638
pesche al cioccolato 1087
pesche al vino rosso 1087
pesche alle fragoline 1087
pesche ripiene 1088
pesto 68
farfalline with pesto 225
Genoese pesto minestrone 239, *240*
linguine with Genoese pesto 290, *291*
pesto tortelloni with squid 285
rigatoni with cream, pesto and
tomatoes 299
petits fours 1050–4
petits pois
macaroni with cuttlefish 292
see also peas
petti all'aceto 916
petti con finocchi al gratin 918
petti farciti al mascarpone 918
petti in carpione 919
petti in salsa di mandorle 919
petto al forno 827
petto alla maionese 828
petto alle erbe 828
petto alle salsicce 828
petto arrosto 829
petto di anatra al pompelmo 885, *886*
petto d'oca all'aceto balsamico 904, 905
pheasant 951–5
pheasant in cream sauce 953
pheasant pie 342
pheasant ravioli with rosemary jus 1162
pheasant with fruit 951, 952
pheasant with mushrooms 954, 955
pheasant with olives 953
pheasant with orange 954
roast pheasant with Savoy cabbage,
chestnuts and red wine 1167
stuffed pot-roast pheasant 953
Philippines chicken 922
piccata al limone 829, 830
piccata al Marsala 829
*piccione 'al mattone' con mostarda di
porcini* 1134
piccioni al vino rosso 1181
piccioni alla griglia 908

piccioni all'agro 910
piccioni alle olive 910
piccioni farciti 909, *910*
pickled salmon crêpes 383
pickles
  barbecue sauce 70
piconcini from Marche 153
piconcini marchigiani 153
Piedmont pudding 1023
Piedmontese boiled meat 785
Piedmontese broad beans 474
Piedmontese fondue 995
Piedmontese leg of kid 754
Piedmontese tartare 95
pies 182–90
  artichoke pie 422
  Aunt Maria's farmhouse pie 190
  bacon and potato pie 771
  beef Wellington 791
  cappello del prete en croûte 839
  cheese pie 999
  chicken pie 913
  Easter pie 188, *189*
  farmhouse rainbow pie 188
  grape meringue pie 1109
  mushroom and game pie 985
  mushroom and potato pie 486
  peach pie 1074, *1075*
  pheasant pie 342
  pumpkin pie 187, 342
  rocket and taleggio pie 182
  rustic tomato pie 545
  rustic vegetable pie 187
  savoury artichoke and potato pie 422
  savoury cabbage pie 183
  tagliatelle pie 343
  timbales 340–9
  Viennese apple pie 1077
  wild greens and artichoke pie 184
pigeon 876, 908–10
  barbecued pigeon al mattone with porcini
    mustard 1134
  grilled pigeons 908
  pigeon and bread soup 1183
  pigeon mousse with truffle
    vinaigrette 160
  pigeons in red wine 1181
  pigeons with olives 910
  piquant pigeons 910
  roast pigeons 908
  stuffed pigeons 909, 910
pig's liver
  pig's liver in a net 862
  sweet-and-sour liver 864
pig's trotters *see* trotters
pike 678–9
  old-fashioned pike 679
  pike blanquette 679
  pike in beurre blanc 678
pilaf rice 314
pine nuts
  leek moulds 168
  pesto 68

pine nut sauce 69
pine nut semifreddo 1199
pineapple
  exotic beans 466
  exotic fruit salad 1082
  fruit and champagne fritters 1096
  guinea fowl with pineapple 891
  Hawaiian salad 501
  pineapple bavarois 158
  pineapple kebabs 100
  prosciutto and pineapple 94
  summer pineapple 1078
  sweet-and-sour spare ribs 774
pipasener e zabaione 1193
Pipasener pastry with zabaglione 1193
piquant pigeons 910
piquant sauce 60
pirate's fish soup 728
piselli al prezzemolo 536
piselli alla menta 534
piselli alla pancetta 534, *535*
piselli con carote 536
piselli con lattuga 536
pizza ai funghi 194
pizza alla Napoletana 194, *196*
pizza alla pescatora 196
pizza alle patate 196
pizza bianca 196
pizza calzone 194, *195*
pizza con le salsicce 198
pizza d'indivia 198
pizza margherita 198
pizza quattro stagioni 199
pizzaiola tartines 135, *136*
pizzas 93, 193–9
  calzone 194, *195*
  chicory pizza 198
  dough 193
  fisherman's pizza 196
  four seasons pizza 199
  Margherita pizza 198
  mushroom pizza 194
  pizza Napoletana 194, *196*
  potato pizza 196
  sausage pizza 198
  'white' pizza 196
pizzoccheri, Valtellina 277, *278*
pizzoccheri della Valtellina 277, *278*
plantain *see* buck's horn plantain
pluck 858–9
plum-cake 1049
plums
  plum and pear charlotte 1032
  plum bavarois 1021
  plum jam 1119
  plum meringue 1108
  plums in wine 1088
polenta 305–11
  eggs with polenta 361
  Ligurian polenta 450
  mushroom caps Montanara 486
  polenta gnocchi 306
  polenta pasticciata with anchovies 311

polenta pasticciata with mushrooms 309
polenta soup 306
polenta taragna 311
polenta with cod 307
polenta with eggs 309, *310*
polenta with fondue 308
polenta with Gorgonzola 306
polenta with langoustines and
  radicchio 307
polenta with meat sauce 307
polenta with ricotta 308
polenta with sausage 308
rabbit with prosciutto and polenta 1163
spare ribs with polenta 767
Valle d'Aosta polenta pasticciata 309
woodcock with truffle 950
polenta al Gorgonzola 306
polenta con gli scampi e la cicoria 307
polenta con il merluzzo 307
polenta con il ragù 307
polenta con la fonduta 308
polenta con la ricotta 308
polenta con la salciccia 308
polenta con le uova 309, 310
polenta pasticciata alla Valdostana 309
polenta pasticciata con i funghi 309
polenta pasticciata con le acciughe 311
Polish beans 469
pollo ai funghi 919
pollo al cartoccio 920
pollo al curry 920
pollo al limone (1) 928
pollo al limone (2) 928
pollo al tonno 929
pollo al vino bianco 929
pollo al vino rosso 930
pollo alla babi 920
pollo alla birra 921, 922
pollo alla cacciatora 922
pollo alla diavola 922, *923*
pollo alla Filippina 922
pollo alla Greca 924
pollo alla panna 924
pollo alla ratatouille 924, *925*
pollo all'aglio 924
pollo alle cipolle 926, *927*
pollo alle mele 926
pollo alle olive 926
pollo allo spiedo 928
pollo allo spumante 929
pollo arrosto ripieno 930
pollo e patate di Nonna Erminia 1129
pollo con peperoni gialli 931
pollo con peperoni verdi 931
pollo fritto marinato 931
pollo impanato e fritto 932
pollo in crosta di sale 932, *933*
pollo in terracotta 932
pollo ripieno 930
polpette al brandy 796, *797*
polpette al limone 798
polpette alle acciughe 796
polpette alle melanzane 748

1246

polpette alle patate 796
polpette con spinaci 798
polpette piccanti all'Indiana 934
polpette saporite 798
polpettone casalingo 831
polpi affogati 722
polpi al vino rosso 722
polpi del marinaio 722

pomegranate
chicken with pomegranate 898, *899*
exotic fruit salad 1082
mixed salad with pomegranate *495*, 496
pomodori al forno 540
pomodori al gratin 541
pomodori alla mousse di cetrioli 541
pomodori alle melanzane 541
pomodori alle zucchine 542
pomodori con robiola 542
pomodori fioriti 119
pomodori gratinati al bacon 542
pomodori ripieni al pecorino 543, *544*
pomodori ripieni d'insalata russa 543
pomodori ripieni di riso 543
pomodori ripieni di tonno 545
poppy-seed croquettes 993

porcini mushrooms
barbecued pigeon al mattone with
    porcini mushrooms 1134
bean and mushroom soup 251
boiled eggs with mushrooms 370
bucatini with mushroom sauce 288
cream of porcini soup 213
fried porcini 484
lamb with mushrooms 742
macaroni with mushrooms 292
melting baked porcini 482
mushroom and caper crostini 128
mushroom and game pie 985
mushroom caps Montanara 486
mushroom trifolati *485*, 486
porcini with prosciutto 484
porcini with tarragon 484
sardines bellavista 652
sole with mushrooms 661
stuffed porcini mushrooms 119
turkey fricassée with porcini 940
porcini ripieni 119

pork 756–76
braised pork with rosemary 760
cassoeula *763*, 764
chopped pork with prunes 774
croûtes with pork fillet and pâté de foie
    gras 768
curried pork chops 766
duck terrine *165*, 166
loin of pork with juniper 770
loin of pork with tuna sauce 770
pan-fried pork fillet 764
pork chops in butter and sage 767
pork chops in cream 766
pork chops in Gorgonzola sauce 766
pork chops with blueberries 764, *765*
pork chops with Tuscan cabbage 768

pork chops with yellow peppers 768
pork en croûte 769
pork hock with vegetables 776
pork kebabs with prunes 776
pork roulades with apricots 769
pork shoulder with cardoons 767
pork shoulder with prunes 766
pork stew with peas 775
pork stew with smoked sausages 774
pork tenerelle 776
roast loin of pork *757*, 760
roast pork in grape juice 760
roast pork with apples 762
roast pork with lemon *761*, 762
roast pork with orange 760
spare ribs in white wine 772
spare ribs with polenta 767
spicy pork stew 775
sweet-and-sour pork stew 775
sweet-and-sour spare ribs 774
white meat sauce 52
porri al pomodoro 546
porri al prosciutto 548
porri gratinati *547*, 548
porri in salsa olandese 548
porridge 236

port
chopped pork with prunes 774
melon fruit salad 1082
pork chops in cream 766
pot-au-feu 236
pot-roast beef in cream 782
pot-roast beef with anchovies and
    tomato 782
pot-roast beef with brandy and
    grapefruit 782
pot-roast chicken 930
pot-roast guinea fowl 890
pot-roast marinated beef 783

potato flour
easy ring cake 1046

potatoes 518–27
bacon and potato pie 771
baked potatoes with salmon 522
baked pumpkin with potatoes 577
balsamic vinegar sauce 69
casunzjei pasta with potatoes and
    seasoned vegetables 1150
char and potato pie 677
courgette and potato charlotte 580
cream of pea and potato soup 220
cream of potato soup 220
cream of truffle soup 214
creamy mashed potato 526
delice of potato with vegetable
    sauce 520
duchesse potatoes 524
Easter leg of kid 754, *755*
Erminia's chicken and potatoes 1129
fontina potato bake 522
goose stuffed with potatoes 904
goulash 791
hake with potatoes 630

ham and potato rolls 521
herb soup 229
huss with potatoes au gratin 634
Irish stew 807
Jerusalem artichoke and potato
    purée 574
layered anchovies and potatoes 598
leek and potato soup 233
meatballs with potato 796
mixed greens with caprino 996
mushroom and potato pie 486
mutton and potato stew 808
mutton stewed in citrus juice 807
new potatoes with rosemary 526, *527*
Normandy potatoes 523
oatmeal soup 251
octopus and potato salad 719, *720*
pan-cooked Savoy cabbage 443
pasta, potatoes and celery 235
pepper pie 121
poppy-seed croquettes 993
pork hock with vegetables 776
potato and cauliflower ring 519
potato and cheese roll 998
potato and cinnamon frittata 389
potato and clam soup 255
potato and nettle gnocchi 262
potato and spinach gnocchi 264
potato brioches 519
potato croquettes with fontina 520
potato gnocchi 260, *261*
potato gnocchi filled with fondue 263
potato gnocchi with langoustines 262
potato nests with eggs 521
potato pizza 196
potato soufflé 177
potato soup 254
potatoes and onions baked in an
    earthenware dish 524
potatoes baked in foil with yogurt 522
potatoes in béchamel sauce 523
potatoes in white butter sauce 524
potatoes with scamorza 523
prawn barquettes 141, *142*
Provençal sautéed potatoes 525
rice and potatoes 238
roast truffles with potatoes 572
roast turnips with potatoes 556
Roman spring lamb 742, *743*
salt cod with potatoes and peppers 604
Sardinian artichokes 419
sauerkraut with mushrooms and
    potatoes 443
sausage stuffed potatoes 525
sausages with potato tart 844
savoury artichoke and potato pie 422
scrambled eggs in their nests *380*, 381
sea trout roe with potatoes 686
shoulder of lamb à la
    boulangère 750, *751*
small cheese crackers 151
smoked salmon pâté 164
spicy potato salad 521

stewed potatoes with tomato 525
Triestian potato gnocchi with prunes 263
turbot fillets with a potato topping 641
vichyssoise 224
walnut gnocchi 260
praline 1052, *1053*
prawns 693–6
  asparagus and prawns 693
  baby squid in baskets 105
  beansprouts with prawns 488
  courgettes with prawns 696
  cream of prawn and bean soup 218
  cream of prawn and tomato soup 218
  cucumber and prawn salad 116
  fisherman's pizza 196
  fried prawns in pink sauce 694
  Genoese salad 654
  hard-boiled eggs with prawns 375
  Hawaiian salad 501
  jellied Russian salad tartines 139
  lobster and prawn salad 692
  low-fat rice salad 327
  Mediterranean prawns with rocket 109
  monkfish and prawn roulades 617, *618*
  mushroom salad 115
  prawn barquettes 141, *142*
  prawn bites 104
  prawn butter tartines 133
  prawn risotto 335
  prawn salad with beans 694
  prawn vol-au-vents 192
  prawns in strong sweet sauce *695,* 696
  prawns prepared in scampi style 1127
  prawns with salmon mousse 694
  purée of chickpeas with prawns 1180
  rice and prawn salad *322,* 323
  rice with curry sauce and prawns 315
  salmon mousse with prawn cream 161
  seafood crostini 132
  seafood tart 182
  seafood vol-au-vent 349
  seared prawns with cannellini bean salad
    and tartufo dressing 1173
  sole and prawn roulades 661
  spider crab with mayonnaise 699
  squid stuffed with prawns 708
  stuffed squid 104
  Treviso radicchio and prawn salad 500
  warm salad of prawns, Savoy cabbage
    and lentils 1189
profiteroles, chocolate 1109
profiteroles al cioccolato 1109
prosciutto
  cheese and prosciutto crêpes 269
  chicken liver and prosciutto
    crostini 128, *129*
  chicory pizza 198
  chicory with ham 115
  delicate calf's liver pâté *163,* 164
  duck terrine *165, 166*
  espagnole sauce 60
  ham vol-au-vents 192
  liver uccelletto 864

pineapple kebabs 100
prosciutto and figs 94
prosciutto and melon 94
prosciutto and pineapple 94
rabbit with prosciutto and polenta 1163
roast breast of veal 827
Roman saltimbocca 831, *832*
spicy bundles 994
surprise aubergines in breadcrumbs 513
sweet-and-sour crostini 132
tortellini Bolognese 283
veal Bolognese 821
veal braised in milk with prosciutto 814
vine leaf parcels 97
  see also ham
prosciutto al forno 771
prosciutto al marsala 772
prosciutto al vino bianco 772, *773*
Provençal artichokes 419
Provençal cod 628
Provençal omelette 392
Provençal sautéed potatoes 525
Provençal trout 685
prugne al vino 1088
prunes
  chamois chops with mushrooms and
    dried fruit 963
  chopped mutton with prunes 808, *809*
  chopped pork with prunes 774
  country bouchées 150
  leg of mutton in vodka 805
  omelette with dried fruit and
    almonds 1093
  pork kebabs with prunes 776
  pork shoulder with prunes 766
  Triestian potato gnocchi with prunes 263
puddings 1023–30
  almond pudding 1025
  bread pudding with vanilla sauce 1151
  cooked saffron milk puddings with blood
    orange and vincotto sauce 1156
  English bread and butter pudding 1027
  panettone pudding 1171
  Piedmont pudding 1023
  rice pudding 1028
  semolina pudding 1027
  semolina pudding with black
    cherries 1027
puff pastry
  bouchées 149–54
  puff pastry flowers with toma 994
  speedy puff pastry 1014
puffs, savoury 146–8
pulses
  cream of dried pulses soup 219
  see also beans
pumpkin 575–8
  baked pumpkin with potatoes 577
  cream of pumpkin soup au gratin 222
  guinea fowl ortolana 892, *893*
  maltagliati with pumpkin 274
  mozzarella pumpkin sandwich 577
  mushrooms with pumpkin 482

Parmesan pumpkin 577
pumpkin and amaretti gnocchi 266
pumpkin and artichoke risotto 337
pumpkin cake 1076
pumpkin mould 174, *175*
pumpkin pie 187, 342
pumpkin soup 256
pumpkin tortelli 283, *284*
pumpkin with rosemary 578
roast turnips with leeks and
  pumpkin 556, *557*
puntarelle alla Romana 1186
punte di catalonga in insalata 435
puntine al vino bianco 772
puntine in agrodolce 774
puré di cicoria 454
puré di fave fresche 474, *475*
puré di indivia 490
puré di lenticchie 508
puré di marroni 433
puré di patate cremoso 526
puré di topinambur e patate 574

Q

quadrucci con verdure 236
quadrucci with vegetables 236
quaglie al vino bianco 959
quaglie allo yogurt 959
quaglie con risotto 960
quaglie farcite con verdure e piselli 1177
quail 959–61
  pearl barley with quail, thyme, potato and
    orange sauce with olive brunoise 1195
  quail in white wine 959
  quail on the spit 960, *961*
  quail stuffed with green vegetables and
    peas 1177
  quail with risotto 960
  quail with yogurt 959
quails' eggs, spicy 99
quiche agli asparagi 179
quiche al salmone affumicato 180
quiches 179–80
  asparagus quiche 179
  quiche Lorraine 180
  smoked salmon quiche 180
quince jelly 1115

R

rabbit 970–9
  braised rabbit with rosemary 976
  fried rabbit 976
  marinated rabbit 977
  rabbit 'tuna' 979
  rabbit and tuna roll 978
  rabbit cacciatore 971, *972*
  rabbit in cider 974
  rabbit in milk 973
  rabbit in olive oil and lemon 971
  rabbit in red wine 974
  rabbit in vinegar 971

rabbit stew with anchovies 978
rabbit stew with tomatoes and basil 979
rabbit stew with walnuts 979
rabbit with bay leaves 973
rabbit with honey and
    vegetables 974, *975*
rabbit with mustard 973
rabbit with peperonata 976
rabbit with prosciutto and polenta 1163
roast rabbit 970
stewed rabbit 977
stuffed rabbit 977
radicchio 549–53
baked radicchio 550, *551*
crab salad *701, 702*
fabulous smoked swordfish 635
fried radicchio 553
polenta with langoustines and
    radicchio 307
radicchio and walnut rolls 549
radicchio bundles 151, *152*
radicchio en croûte 553
radicchio lasagne 273
radicchio mimosa 550
radicchio omelette 393
radicchio risotto 333, *334*
radicchio soup 255
radicchio with Parmesan 550
sweetcorn and radicchio salad 498
Treviso radicchio and prawn salad 500
Treviso radicchio salad with
    mushrooms 500
Treviso radicchio salad with
    orange 550, *552*
radicchio al forno 550, *551*
radicchio al parmigiano 550
radicchio mimosa 550
radicchio rosso all'arancia 550, *552*
radicchio rosso fritto 553
radicchio rosso in crosta 553
radishes 558–60
glazed radishes 558
radish salad with olives *559,* 560
radish salad with yogurt 560
radishes with cheese 558
whipped cream and radish sauce 72
ragù alla bolognese 52
ragù bianco 52
ragù con fegatini 53
raisins
carrot ring cake 1045
English bread and butter pudding 1027
fruit cake 1049
Italian bread and butter pudding 1063
kugelhopf 1048
omelette with dried fruit and
    almonds 1093
ricotta strudel 1065
simple strudel 1065
rane al vino bianco 732
rane alla Genovese 732
rane fritte in salsa 733
rane impanate 733

rane in pastella 733
rape al bacon 555
rape alla panna 555
rape farcite 555
rape in teglia con patate 556
rape in teglia con porri e zucca 556, *557*
rascasse *see* scorpion fish
raspberries
fruit and champagne fritters 1096
fruits of the forest charlotte 1032, *1033*
fruits of the forest crumble 1064
fruits of the forest ice cream 1098
melon surprise 1084
raspberry semifreddo 1102, *1103*
summer pineapple 1078
tutti frutti tart 1060
raspberry jam
apples in their nests 1084
blackberry tart 1059
raspberry omelette 1093
raspberry jelly
strawberry dessert 1061
ratatouille, chicken 924, *925*
ravanelli con formaggio 558
ravanelli glassati 558
ravanelli in insalata con le olive 559, 560
ravanelli in insalata con lo yogurt 560
ravioli
beef cheek ravioli 1133
caciotta ravioli with tomato and
    basil 1158
fish ravioli with shellfish 1180
open raviolo 1170
pheasant ravioli with rosemary jus 1162
ravioli Napoletana 277
ravioli with eggs and asparagus 1142
vegetable and cheese filled ravioli 279
ravioli alla Napoletana 277
ravioli alle uova e asparagi 1142
*ravioli di cacciota al pomodorino e
    basilico* 1158
ravioli di fagiano 1168
*ravioli di guancia di vitello con fegatini e
tartufo nero* 1133
ravioli di magro 279
ravioli di pesce ai frutti di mare 1180
raviolini vol-au-vent 348
raviolo aperto 1170
ray 639
razza ai capperi 639
razza alla nizzarda 639
red cabbage
baked ham 771
red kidney beans
bean and barley soup 250
red mullet 669–70
red mullet Livorno-style 670
red mullet with beans 670
red mullet with fennel 669
red mullet with herbs 670
red sea bream 620
red tomato frittata 540
red wine marinade 78

redcurrants
fruits of the forest charlotte 1032, *1033*
redcurrant and apple chutney 64
redcurrant jelly 1115
rémoulade sauce 68
rhubarb
rhubarb jam 1119
rhubarb soufflé 1042
rhubarb tart 1058
strawberry and rhubarb compote 1079
ribollita 246, *247*
rice 312–21
baked rice 313
baked rice with parsley 320
boiled rice 314
Cantonese rice 317
Creole rice 313
curried rice and lentils 318
curried rice salad 324
Indian rice 314
Indonesian rice 318
low-fat rice salad 327
mini rice croquettes with mozzarella 321
monkfish stew with turmeric rice 619
moulded rice with ham and peas 320
nettle soup 232
paella 321
pilaf rice 314
rice and beetroot salad 325
rice and crab meat salad 325
rice and peas 236
rice and potatoes 238
rice and prawn salad 322, *323*
rice cooked in milk 313
rice gnocchi 264
rice pudding 1028
rice salad with cheese 324
rice salad with pickled peppers 325
rice salads 322–7
rice timbale 347
rice with carrots and walnuts 317
rice with curry sauce and prawns 315
rice with mint 317
rice with raw egg 318
rice with spinach 318, *319*
Savoy cabbage and rice minestrone 245
seafood rice salad 324
seasoned boiled rice 320
Sicilian croquettes 315, *316*
smoked fish and rice salad 327
summer rice salad 327
tomatoes stuffed with rice 543
wholegrain rice 314
see also risottos
rich salad 501
ricotta
bresaola rolls with ricotta 996
calzone 194, *195*
casunzjei pasta with potatoes and
    seasoned ricotta 1150
charlotte delight 1034
cheese and ham pâté 997
cheese pie 999

cream of ricotta and vegetable soup 992
Easter pie 188, *189*
polenta with ricotta 308
ricotta and Savoy cabbage
  rolls 444, *445*
ricotta and sour cherry tart 1076
ricotta and spinach crêpes 384, *385*
ricotta and spinach gnocchi 264, *265*
ricotta and sultana tart 1076
ricotta cake 1074
ricotta morsels 149
ricotta omelette 395
ricotta sauce 70
ricotta strudel 1065
salmon puffs 148
seafood tart 182
spicy bundles 994
tuna bites 104
Tuscan pecorino, ricotta and Parmesan
  tortelli with white truffle 1192
yogurt and ricotta cake 1069

rigatoni
baked wholewheat rigatoni 298
rigatoni with cream, pesto and
  tomatoes 299
rigatoni with meatballs 298
rigatoni con polpettine 298
rigatoni integrali al forno 298
rigatoni panna, pesto e pomodoro 299

ring cakes
carrot ring cake 1045
easy ring cake 1046
marbled ring cake 1046, *1047*
velvety ring cake 1046
risi e bisi 236
riso al curry con gamberi 315
riso alla Cantonese 317
riso alla menta 317
riso alle carote e noci 317
riso all'Indonesiana 318
riso all'uovo crudo 318
riso con lenticchie al curry 318
riso con spinaci 318, *319*
riso e patate 238
riso in cagnone 320
riso in forma con prosciutto e piselli 320
riso in forno al prezzemolo 320
riso in insalata ai gamberetti 322, *323*
riso in insalata al curry 324
riso in insalata al formaggio 324
riso in insalata alla marinara 324
riso in insalata con barbabietole 325
riso in insalata con peperoni sottaceto 325
riso in insalata con polpa di granchio 325
riso in insalata di magro 327
riso in insalata di pesce affumicato 327
riso in insalata estivo 327
riso mantecato 1137

risottos 328–39
apple risotto 335
asparagus risotto 336
aubergine risotto 333
Barolo and mushroom risotto 329

black risotto with cuttlefish *338,* 339
blueberry risotto 329
carrot risotto 332
caviar risotto 330
cream and leek risotto 339
cream and rocket risotto 336
creamed risotto 1137
four-cheese risotto 337
green risotto 339
Jerusalem artichoke risotto 329
Milanese risotto 330, *331*
nettle risotto 333
pepper risotto 336
prawn risotto 335
pumpkin and artichoke risotto 337
quail with risotto 960
radicchio risotto 333, *334*
risotto with sausages 337
salmon and wine risotto 330
seafood risotto 328
spring risotto 1145
strawberry risotto 332
risotto ai frutti di mare 328
risotto ai mirtilli 329
risotto ai topinambur 329
risotto al Barolo con funghi 329
risotto al caviale 330
risotto al radicchio Trevigiano 333, *334*
risotto alla Milanese 330, *331*
risotto alla primavera 1145
risotto alla salsa di salmone e
  spumante 330
risotto alle carote 332
risotto alle fragole 332
risotto alle melanzane 333
risotto alle ortiche 333
risotto con i gamberi 335
risotto con le mele 335
risotto con panna e rucola 336
risotto con peperoni 336
risotto con punte di asparagi 336
risotto con salsiccia 337
risotto con zucca e carciofi 337
risotto mantecato ai quattro
  formaggi 337
risotto nero con le seppie *338,* 339
risotto panna e porri 339
risotto verde 339
roast-beef con le castagne 799
robiola triangles 999

rocket
bresaola rolls with ricotta 996
cream and rocket risotto 336
hard-boiled eggs with hats 375
magnificent medallions of lobster 692
marinated swordfish 638
Mediterranean prawns with rocket 109
octopus and rocket salad 109
rapid roast with rocket 799
rocket and taleggio pie 182
tagliatelle with crème fraîche and
  rocket 1186
Sicilian salad 502

roe
butter with dried salted roe 85
caviar butter 83
caviar risotto 330
caviar tartines 134
sea trout roe with potatoes 686
smoked salmon terrine 646
rognone al Madera 868
rognone al vino di Bordeaux 868
rognone alla senape 868
rognone con cipolline crude 869
rognone con salsiccia e funghi 869
rolled peppers 119
rolled wafers 1052
rolls, rosemary and cheese 100
Roman artichokes 419
Roman crescents 151
Roman gnocchi 258
Roman lamb's lights 858
Roman saltimbocca 831, *832*
Roman spring lamb 742, *743*
rombo al forno con sugo di lenticchie 641
rombo all'arancia 642
rombo allo spumante 642
rombo allo zafferano con sugo di
  vongole 643
rombo con salsa di olive 643
Roquefort tartines 137

rosemary
braised pork with rosemary 760
braised rabbit with rosemary 976
carrots with rosemary 428
new potatoes with rosemary 526, *527*
pumpkin with rosemary 578
rosemary and cheese rolls 100, *101*
simple poached beef with rosemary 795
spaghetti with rosemary 302
veal noisettes in butter, sage and
  rosemary 825
rotolini di asparagi 404
rotolo alle olive 941
rotolo di coniglio con il tonno 978
rotolo di fontina e prosciutto 998
rotolo di patate e formaggio 998
rotolo di trota salmonata 684

roulades
baked John Dory roulades 648
beef and bresaola roulades 793
beef and spinach roulades 792
brain roulades with truffle 855
chicken, anchovy and caper roulades 914
chicken roulades with chives 916
chicken roulades with sage 914, *915*
monkfish and prawn roulades 617, *618*
pork roulades with apricots 769
Russian salad roulades 98
sole and prawn roulades 661
tasty roulades 793
tasty turkey roulades 941
veal roulades in aspic 824
veal roulades with vegetables 824
roux 76
royal sauce 60

rum
amaretti fritters 1094
apple fritters 1096
apricot jam and cream omelette 1093
chestnut jam 1116
chocolate cake with jam 1066
chocolate marquise 1108
coffee baba 1055
fig tart 1059
Italian trifle 1112, *1113*
mascarpone cream 1038
Montebianco 1109
omelette with dried fruit and
  almonds 1093
Piedmont pudding 1023
rum soufflé 1042
watermelon with rum 1079

runner beans
runner beans au gratin 470
see also green beans; French beans
Russian garlic sauce 73

Russian salad 116, *117*
jellied Russian salad tartines 139
Russian salad roulades 98
tomatoes stuffed with Russian salad 543
rustic chicken 898
rustic tartines 135
rustic tomato pie 545
rustic vegetable pie 187

S

sabayon sauce, oysters in salted 718
sabbiosa con crema di mascarpone 1148
sablé dough 1013
sablés 1051
sacchetti dell'ortolano 120
Sachertorte 1077

saffron
penne with saffron 295
saffron sauce 55
scallops in saffron sauce 711, *712*
scorpion fish in white wine and
  saffron 655
turbot with saffron in clam sauce 643

sage
baby onions with sage 461
brains with butter and sage 853
chicken roulades with sage 914, *915*
guinea fowl with sage 892
ham and sage frittata 387
langoustines with sage 705
liver uccelletto 864
liver with butter and sage 863
mackerel with sage butter 656
perch with sage 681
pork chops in butter and sage 767
Roman saltimbocca 831, *832*
sage appetizer 102
sage butter *86*, 87
shad with sage 599
steak with sage 795
veal noisettes in butter, sage and

rosemary 825
salads 494–502
American chicken salad 913
avocado salad 496
baby courgette salad 582
baby octopus and green bean salad 107
bresaola with lamb's lettuce 496, *497*
buffalo milk mozzarella Capri salad 991
Caesar's mushroom salad with
  marjoram 498
calf's head salad 871
caper salad 502
capon salad 1148
cardoon salad 425
cauliflower salad 439
cauliflower salad (1) 115
cauliflower salad (2) 115
celery and walnut salad 564, *565*
chicken and celeriac salad 914
courgette salad with thyme 585
crab salad *701*, 702
cucumber salad 498
curried penne salad 296
curried rice salad 324
dandelion tip salad 435
French bean salad 472
fusilli salad 290
Genoese salad 654
Hawaiian salad 501
herring and cauliflower salad 601
jellied Russian salad tartines 139
Jerusalem artichoke salad 574
langoustine and fig salad 109, *110*
lettuce hearts with herbs 504, *505*
lobster and prawn salad 692
low-fat rice salad 327
mixed bean salad 467
mixed greens with caprino 996
mixed salad with pomegranate *495*, 496
mixed tuna salad 501
mushroom salad 115
octopus and potato salad 719, *720*
octopus and rocket salad 109
pepper and farro salad 528
prawn salad with beans 694
radish salad with olives *559*, 560
radish salad with yogurt 560
rice and beetroot salad 325
rice and crab meat salad 325
rice and prawn salad 322, *323*
rice salad with cheese 324
rice salad with pickled peppers 325
rice salads 322–7
rich salad 501
Russian salad 116, *117*
Russian salad roulades 98
salmon salad with 'beads' 494
scallop salad 712
seafood rice salad 324
Sicilian salad 502
simple poached beef salad 795
smoked fish and rice salad 327
sole salad 661

spicy potato salad 521
spinach and mushroom
  salad 499, 569, 570
spinach and scallop salad 499
sturgeon salad with caviar 1170
summer rice salad 327
sweetcorn and radicchio salad 498
three pulse salad 464
tomatoes stuffed with Russian salad 543
Treviso radicchio and prawn salad 500
Treviso radicchio salad with
  mushrooms 500
Treviso radicchio salad with
  orange 550, *552*
tuna and bean salad 668
turkey and bean salad 499
warm cuttlefish salad with green
  asparagus 723
warm mushroom salad 483
warm salad of prawns, Savoy cabbage
  and lentils 1189
white cabbage salad 498
whitebait salad 107, 108
yellow salad with sweetcorn 500
salmon 644–6
fish carpaccio 105
prawns with salmon mousse 694
salmon and bacon bites 644
salmon and chicory parcels 644
salmon fishcakes 646
salmon mousse with prawn cream 161
salmon puffs 148
salmon salad with 'beads' 494
salmon tartare *645*, 646
spinach and salmon tart 186
see also smoked salmon
salsa agli spinaci 53
salsa ai pinoli 69
salsa ai porri 53
salsa al burro 54
salsa al cioccolato 1017
salsa al cioccolato fredda 1017
salsa al curry 54
salsa al gorgonzola 69, *71*
salsa al marsala 55
salsa al pompelmo 70
salsa al tartufo nero 70
salsa alla paprica 69
salsa alla ricotta 70
salsa alla vaniglia 1151
salsa all'aceto balsamico 69
salsa all'arancia 1018
salsa alle cipolline 54
salsa alle mele 54
salsa allo yogurt 70
salsa allo zafferano 55
salsa barbecue 70
salsa bearnese 55
salsa bearnese semplificata 56
salsa cinese 56
salsa cocktail 72
salsa d'acciughe 56
salsa del vinaio 56

salsa di albicocche 1018
salsa di capperi 72
salsa di cervella 57
salsa di ciliege 1018
salsa di fragole 1018
salsa di menta 72
salsa di nocciole 1019
salsa di noci 57
salsa di panna montata e ravanelli 72
salsa di peperoni 57
salsa di pomodoro 57, *58*
salsa di pomodoro veloce 59
salsa di rafano o cren 59
salsa gribiche 73
salsa mediterranea 73
salsa normanna 59
salsa olandese 59
salsa piccante 60
salsa reale 60
salsa russa all'aglio 73
salsa spagnola 60
salsa speciale 61
salsa superpiccante 61
salsa tartara 73
salsa tonnata 74
salsa vellutata 61
salsa vellutata aurora 61
salsicce al pomodoro 844
salsicce alle dieci erbe 842, *843*
salsicce con carote 844
salsicce con porri al gratin 844
salsicce con torta di patate 844
salsicce e rape 845
salsicce in tegame 845
salt cod 602–5
  fried salt cod 604
  salt cod au gratin 603
  salt cod Livorno-style 603
  salt cod with olives and capers 603
  salt cod with potatoes and peppers 604
  see also stockfish
salt crust
  chicken in a salt crust 932, *933*
  sea bream baked in a salt
    crust *621, 622*
  tench in a salt crust 683
salted T-bone steak in sauce 790
saltimbocca alla Romana 831, *832*
San Pietro con taccole 648
sandwich di zucca alla mozzarella 577
sarago alle zucchine 624
sarago aromatico 624
sarago arrosto 625
sarago con funghi 625
sardine alla griglia 649
sardine alla marinara 650
sardine allo scalogno 650
sardine impanate 650
sardine in bellavista 652
sardine ripiene 652
sardine saporite 651, 652
sardines 649–52
  fisherman's eggs en cocotte 366

grilled sardines 649
pasta with sardines 293, *294*
sardine butter 87
sardine rolls 649
sardines bellavista 652
sardines in breadcrumbs 650
sardines marinara 650
sardines with shallots 650
stuffed sardines 652
succulent sardines *651*, 652
Sardinian artichokes 419
sartù 344, *345*
sauces 47
  aïoli 64
  anchovy sauce 56
  apple sauce 54
  apricot sauce 1018
  bagna cauda *48*, 49
  balsamic vinegar sauce 69
  barbecue sauce 70
  béarnaise sauce 55
  béchamel sauce 50
  béchamel with cream 50
  black truffle sauce 70
  Bolognese meat sauce 52
  brain sauce 57
  butter sauce 54
  caper sauce 72
  cherry sauce 1018
  chicken liver sauce 53
  Chinese sauce 56
  cocktail sauce 72
  cold chocolate sauce 1017
  curry sauce 54
  custard 1039
  easy béarnaise sauce 56
  espagnole sauce 60
  Gorgonzola sauce 69, *71*
  grapefruit sauce 70
  green sauce 74, *75*
  gribiche sauce 73
  hazelnut sauce 1019
  hollandaise sauce 59
  horseradish sauce 59
  hot chocolate sauce 1017
  leek sauce 53
  maître d'hôtel béchamel 50
  marchand de vin sauce 56
  Marsala sauce 55
  mayonnaise 65, *66*
  Mediterranean sauce 73
  mint sauce 72
  mornay sauce 51
  mushroom béchamel 50
  mustard béchamel 51
  Normandy sauce 59
  onion sauce 54
  orange sauce 1018
  paprika béchamel 51
  paprika sauce 69
  pesto 68
  pine nut sauce 69
  piquant sauce 60

quick tomato sauce 59
red pepper sauce 57
rémoulade sauce 68
ricotta sauce 70
royal sauce 60
Russian garlic sauce 73
saffron sauce 55
sauce aurore 61
seafood sauce 62, *63*
soubise sauce 52
special sauce 61
spicy sauce 61
spinach sauce 53
strawberry sauce 1018
tapénade 74
tartare sauce 73
tomato sauce 57, *58*
tuna sauce 62
tuna sauce 74
vanilla sauce 1151
velouté sauce 61
vinaigrette 76
walnut sauce 57
whipped cream and radish sauce 72
white meat sauce 52
yogurt béchamel 51
yogurt sauce 70
see also butters, flavoured; chutneys;
  mayonnaise
sauerkraut
  braised sauerkraut 443
  sauerkraut with mushrooms and
    potatoes 443
sausage meat
  stuffed lettuce 504
sausages 736, 839–45
  artichokes stuffed with sausage 421
  baked Savoy cabbage 442
  baked tomatoes 540
  baked tomatoes 540
  beans with sausages 466
  breast of veal with sausages 828
  cappello del prete en croûte 839
  celery and sausage frittata 387
  Christmas turkey 943
  cotechino 840
  cotechino in a jacket 842
  cotechino with lentils 840, *841*
  cotechino with mushroom sauce 842
  crostini with mushrooms in a light
    sauce 130
  eggs with sausage 363
  frankfurters with Savoy cabbage 845
  fried sausages 845
  Grosseto onions 459, *460*
  guinea fowl with red wine 895
  horseradish and sausage puffs 154
  horseradish and sausage puffs 154
  kidneys, sausage and mushrooms 869
  lentils with sausages 506
  Parisian brioches 150
  Parisian brioches 150
  polenta with sausage 308

Polish beans 469
Polish beans 469
pork stew with smoked sausages 774
pot-roast beef with anchovies and
   tomato 782
Provençal omelette 392
risotto with sausages 337
sausage crostini 130, *131*
sausage pizza 198
sausage stuffed potatoes 525
sausages and turnips 845
sausages in tomato 844
sausages with carrots 844
sausages with leeks au gratin 844
sausages with potato tart 844
scrambled eggs with sausage 379
stuffed guinea fowl with mushrooms 895
stuffed rabbit 977
ten-herb sausages 842, *843*
turkey stuffed with chestnuts *943*, 944
wrapped cotechino 840
savarin di cardi ai funghi 426
savoury artichoke and potato pie 422
savoury cabbage pie 183
savoury choux paste 1011
savoury puffs 146–8
   creamy cheese puffs 146
   mushroom puffs 146
   salmon puffs 148
Savoy cabbage
   eel with Savoy cabbage 672
   frankfurters with Savoy cabbage 845
   Partridge with Savoy cabbage, fried sage
      and vegetables 1139
   roast pheasant with Savoy cabbage,
      chestnuts and red wine 1167
   Savoy cabbage and rice minestrone 245
   warm salad of prawns, Savoy cabbage
      and lentils 1189
Savoyard fondue 994
sbriciolata ai frutti di bosco 1064
scallops 710–12
   baked scallops 710
   mixed shellfish soup 729
   pan-fried scallops with saffron
      vinaigrette 1161
   scallop salad 712
   scallops and fried celery 1142
   scallops in saffron sauce *711*, 712
   seafood sauce 62, *63*
   spinach and scallop salad 499
   tagliolini with scallops and lettuce 282
scaloppe di storione agrodolci 664
scaloppe di storione alle acciughe 665
scaloppine ai funghi 831
scaloppine al latte 833
scaloppine al pompelmo 834
scaloppine alla pizzaiola 833
scaloppine alla senape 833
scaloppine alle erbe 834
scamorza carpaccio 991
scampi ai pomodori 703
scampi al forno 1146

scampi alla salsa di curry 705
scampi alla salvia 705
scampi grigliati 705
Scherrer's tartare 102
sciroppo di zucchero denso 1019
scones 1049
scorfano ai funghi 655
scorfano al vino bianco 1159
scorfano al timo 655
scorfano al vino bianco e zafferano 655
scorpion fish 653–5
   Genoese salad 654
   mixed fish soup with orange 729
   scorpion fish in white wine 1159
   scorpion fish in white wine and
      saffron 655
   scorpion fish with mushrooms 655
   scorpion fish with thyme 655
scorzonera 561–2
   Genoese salad 654
   scorzonera fricassée 562
   scorzonera with anchovies 562
   scorzonera with horseradish 562
scorzonera al cren 562
scorzonera alle acciughe 562
scorzonera in fricassea 562
'scottata' alla rucola 799
sea bass 607–9
   baked marinated sea bass 609
   fisherman's soup 728
   jellied sea bass 609
   paella 321
   roasted sea bass with fennel 1199
   sea bass baked in a parcel 607, *608*
   sea bass with fennel 609
sea bream 620–6
   aromatic sea bream 624
   baked sea bream 623
   braised sea bream 622
   fish tartare with kiwi fruit 625
   grilled sea bream 623
   jellied sea bream 622
   marinated sea bream 626
   roast sea bream 625
   sea bream baked in a salt
      crust *621*, 622
   sea bream with courgettes 624
   sea bream with fennel bulbs 623
   sea bream with mushrooms 625
   sea bream with olives 624
sea trout
   sea trout mould 173
   sea trout roll 684
   sea trout with juniper berries 685
sea trout roe with potatoes 686
seafood tart 182
seafood crostini 132
seafood rice salad 324
seafood risotto 328
seafood sauce 62, *63*
seafood stew with lentils 1124
seafood vol-au-vent 349
seasonal minestrone 245

sedano al gorgonzola 563
sedano al pomodoro 566
sedano alla besciamella 564
sedano alla greca 564
sedano alla molisana 564
sedano alle noci 564, *565*
sedano fritto 566
sedano gratinato 566
sella di capriolo arrosto ai mirtilli rossi 966
*sella di daino con timbalo di tartufo
   neri* 1196
sella di vitello alla Bergese 1137
semifreddo ai frutti di bosco 1181
semifreddo ai pinoli 1199
semifreddo al lampone 1102, *1103*
semifreddo al torrone 1102
semifreddo alla panna 1102
semifreddo di crema di cioccolato 1104
semifreddo di marron glacé 1104
semolina 238
   Roman gnocchi 258
   semolina and ham gnocchi 266
   semolina baskets 95
   semolina pudding 1027
   semolina pudding with black
      cherries 1027
   semolina budino with rhubarb and mint
      marmellata 1135
   semolina with cherries 1110
   vincisgrassi 348
semolino 238
semolino alle ciliege 1110
seppie agli spinaci 723
seppie ai piselli 724
seppie con i carciofi 724
seppie farcite 724
seppie gratinate 724
sesame seeds
   frosted green beans with
      sesame 470, *471*
sfoglia di funghi alla crema di noci 181
sfogliatine al pollo e curry 153
sfogliatine con funghi 154
sfogliatine con rafano e würstel 154
sfogliatine con scampi al curry 154
sformatini alle erbe 855
sformatini di carciofi 422
sformatini di porri 168
sformatini di zucchine 168
sformato bicolore 169
sformato di carciofi 169
sformato di carote 170
sformato di carote e finocchi 170
sformato di cavolfiore 171
sformato di cicoria 171
sformato di finocchi 171
sformato di panettone 1162
sformato di piselli dolci 172
*sformato di piselli in vinaigrette di
   carota* 1132
sformato di sedano al prosciutto 172
sformato di spinaci 172
sformato di trota salmonata 173

sformato di vongole e cozze 173
sformato di zucca 174, *175*
sgombri ai fagiolini 656, *657*
sgombri al burro 656
sgombri al ribes 658
sgombri alla Greca 658
sgonfiotti 1097
sgonfiotti di carne 834
sgonfiotti di pomodori *147,* 148
shad 599–600
  fried shad 600
  shad with sage 599
  shad with tomato sauce 600
  soused shad 600
shallots
  hake in shallot sauce 632
  liver with shallots 863
  sardines with shallots 650
shortcrust pastry (1) 1008
shortcrust pastry (2) 1008, *1009*
shortcrust pastry, eggless 1010
shrimp butter 83
Sicilian cod 628
Sicilian croquettes 315, *316*
Sicilian salad 502
simple strudel 1065
six-aroma veal stew 835
skate 639
  skate Niçoise 639
  skate with capers 639
small cheese crackers 151
smoked ham with Marsala 772
smoked salmon
  baked potatoes with salmon 522
  courgettes capricciose with salmon and
    leeks 585
  cream of fennel soup with smoked
    salmon 218
  fish tartare with kiwi fruit 625
  hard-boiled eggs with smoked
    salmon 375
  low-fat rice salad 327
  salmon and wine risotto 330
  smoked fish and rice salad 327
  smoked salmon butter 88, *89*
  smoked salmon crêpes 383
  smoked salmon pâté 164
  smoked salmon quiche 180
  smoked salmon terrine 646
  tagliatelle with salmon 280
smoked swordfish
  fabulous smoked swordfish 635
  smoked fish and rice salad 327
smoked trout
  smoked salmon terrine 646
  smoked sea trout and vegetable
    casserole 686
  smoked trout in pink cream 106
  smoked trout with melon 685
snails 730–1
  bourguignonne snails 731
  Ligurian snails 731
  Lombard snails 731

omelette with snails 393
ragù of snails with celeriac 1151
snipe 949-50
  curried snipe 949
  snipe with green apples 950
  snipe with juniper 950
  snipe with truffle 950
sogliole ai funghi 661
sogliole al sidro 662
sogliole al timo 662
sogliole alla griglia 662
sogliole con burro fuso 663
sogliole in salsa piccante 663
sogliolette crude al peperoncino 110
sole 659–63
  almond-coated sole fillets 659, *660*
  fillets of sole with celery julienne, aurora
    sauce and caviar 1195
  grilled sole 662
  mixed fish soup with orange 729
  raw sole with chilli 110
  sole and prawn roulades 661
  sole in cider 662
  sole in melted butter 663
  sole in piquant sauce 663
  sole salad 661
  sole with mushrooms 661
  sole with thyme 662
sorbets 1098
  banana sorbet 1106
  coffee and cocoa sorbet 1190
  kiwi sorbet 1104
  lemon sorbet *1105,* 1106
sorbetto al kiwi 1104
sorbetto al limone 1105, 1106
sorbetto alla banana 1106
sorbetto caffé e cacao 1190
sorrel
  smoked sea trout and vegetable
    casserole 686
soubise sauce 52
soufflé al cioccolato 1040, *1041*
soufflé al rabarbaro 1042
soufflé al rum 1042
soufflé al torrone 1043
soufflé alla vaniglia 1042
soufflé con zabaione 1043
soufflé di castagne 174
soufflé di cipolle 174
soufflé di fagiolini 176
soufflé di formaggio 176
soufflé di funghi 176
soufflé di granchio 177
soufflé di mais piccante 177
soufflé di patate 177
soufflé di pomodori 178
soufflé di prosciutto 178
soufflés
  cheese soufflé 176
  chestnut soufflé 174
  chocolate soufflé 1040, *1041*
  crab soufflé 177
  French bean soufflé 176

ham soufflé 178
mushroom soufflé 176
onion soufflé 174
potato soufflé 177
rhubarb soufflé 1042
rum soufflé 1042
spicy corn soufflé 177
tomato soufflé 178
torrone soufflé 1043
vanilla soufflé 1042
zabaglione soufflé 1043
soups
  barley and chicken soup 232
  barley and pea soup 248
  barley and pulse soup 230
  barley soup al verde 248
  bean and barley soup 250
  bean and mushroom soup 251
  borsch 242
  bread and lentil soup 254
  bread soup 234
  bread soup with tomato 234
  cabbage soup 249
  Caesar's mushroom soup 232
  cheese and leek soup 251
  chickpea and spinach soup 230
  cold cucumber cream soup 222
  corn soup 229
  courgette flower soup 227, *228*
  courgette soup 256
  crab soup 252, *253*
  cream of artichoke soup 214
  cream of asparagus soup 214
  cream of bean soup 217
  cream of carrot and mussel
    soup 215, *216*
  cream of carrot soup 215
  cream of cauliflower soup with
    mussels 217
  cream of celery soup 221
  cream of chickpeas au gratin 217
  cream of chicory soup 219
  cream of courgette soup 222
  cream of dried pulses soup 219
  cream of fennel soup with smoked
    salmon 218
  cream of Jerusalem artichoke soup 213
  cream of leek soup 221
  cream of lettuce soup 219
  cream of pea and potato soup 220
  cream of porcini soup 213
  cream of potato soup 220
  cream of prawn and bean soup 218
  cream of prawn and tomato soup 218
  cream of pumpkin soup au gratin 222
  cream of ricotta and vegetable soup 992
  cream of spinach soup 221
  cream of tomato soup 220
  cream of truffle soup 214
  escarole soup 249
  farfalline with pesto 225
  farro and bean minestrone 243, *244*
  farro and leek soup 231

fisherman's soup 728
Flemish soup 233
frog soup 256
gazpacho 226
Genoese pesto minestrone 239, *240*
green cream soup *223*, 224
green soup 233
herb soup 229
leek and lentil soup 255
leek and potato soup 233
leek soup 229
lentil and squid soup 226
lettuce soup au gratin 252
Livorno-style fish soup 726, *727*
Marche-style fish soup 726
mesc-iuà 227
Milanese minestrone 241
milk and onion soup 249
millet soup 231
minestrone Napoletana 241
mixed fish soup with orange 729
mixed shellfish soup 729
mussel soup 250
nettle soup 232
oatmeal soup 251
onion soup au gratin 250
passatelli 234
pasta and chickpeas 235
pasta and white bean 235
pasta, potatoes and celery 235
Pavian soup 248
pigeon and bread soup 1183
pirate's fish soup 728
polenta soup 306
potato and clam soup 255
potato soup 254
pot-au-feu 236
Puglian minestrone 242
pumpkin soup 256
quadrucci with vegetables 236
radicchio soup 255
ribollita 246, *247*
rice and peas 236
rice and potatoes 238
Savoy cabbage and rice minestrone 245
seasonal minestrone 245
semolina 238
simple gazpacho 226
soup with meatballs 229
stracciatella *237*, 238
Swiss chard and lentil soup 231
tapioca 238
thick bread soup 254
three-colour soup 233
Tuscan minestrone 243
velvety lentil soup 224
vichyssoise 224
wheat germ soup 227
whitebait soup 230
winter minestrone 243
see also broths
soused boiled beef 98
soused chicken breasts 919

soused shad 600
soused tench with herbs 683
soy sauce
chopped chicken with almonds 934
chopped chicken with lemon balm 934
sweet-and-sour pork stew 775
soya beans
barley and pulse soup 230
spaghetti
fresh 'guitar string' spaghetti with
mussels, cherry tomatoes and
olives 1154
spaghetti amatriciana 300, *301*
spaghetti carbonara 300
spaghetti with anchovies 302
spaghetti with breadcrumbs 303
spaghetti with broccoli 299
spaghetti with capers 299
spaghetti with courgettes 303
spaghetti with garlic and chilli oil 299
spaghetti with raw tomato 300
spaghetti with rosemary 302
spaghetti with spring onions and red
chilli 1124
spaghetti with tuna 302
spaghetti aglio, olio e peperoncino 299
spaghetti ai broccoletti 299
spaghetti ai capperi 299
spaghetti al cipollotto e peperoncino 1124
spaghetti al pomodoro crudo 300
spaghetti al rosmarino 302
spaghetti alla carbonara 300
*spaghetti alla chitarra verdi e bianchi con
sughetto di cozze, pomodorini ed olive* 1154
spaghetti all'amatriciana 300, *301*
spaghetti con acciughe 302
spaghetti con il tonno 302
spaghetti con la mollica 303
spaghetti con le zucchine 303
spaghettini alla bottarga 303
spaghettini with bottarga 303
spalla al cartoccio 748
spalla al mirto 750
spalla alla fornaia 750, *751*
spare ribs
spare ribs in white wine 772
spare ribs with polenta 767
sweet-and-sour spare ribs 774
special sauce 61
speck
mountain crostini with speck and apple
cream 132
stuffed turnips 555
speedy puff pastry 1014
spezzatino ai sei profumi 835
spezzatino al caffè 800
spezzatino al curry 835
spezzatino al pomodoro e basilico 979
spezzatino al succo di agrumi 807
spezzatino al vino e cipolle 800
spezzatino alla melissa 934
spezzatino alla senape 942
spezzatino alle acciughe 978

spezzatino alle carote 752
spezzatino alle noci 979
spezzatino alle olive 934
spezzatino all'Irlandese 807
spezzatino con fagioli 807
spezzatino con le mandorle 934
spezzatino con le prugne 774
spezzatino con patate 808
spezzatino con piselli 775
spezzatino con prugne 808, *809*
spezzatino con salsiccia affumicata 774
spezzatino con verdure 835
*spezzatino di coda di rospo con riso alla
curcuma* 619
spezzatino di manzo 800
*spezzatino di merluzzo con olive e
capperi* 629
spezzatino in agrodolce 775
spezzatino speziato 775
spiced apples with sultanas 1084
spiced cauliflower 440
spiced figs 1080, *1081*
spiced wine broth 206
spicy beansprouts 488
spicy broccoli with yogurt 414
spicy bundles 994
spicy candied pears 1085
spicy corn soufflé 177
spicy Indian meatballs 934
spicy lobster 690
spicy marinade 80
spicy pork stew 775
spicy potato salad 521
spicy quails' eggs 99
spicy sauce 61
spicy tongue 866
spider crab 697–9
spider crab au gratin 106
spider crab in olive oil and lemon 697
spider crab mimosa 699
spider crab with mayonnaise 699
spiedini all'ananas 100
spiedini alle prugne 776
spiedini d'anguille 673
spiedini marinati 808
spiedo di quaglie 960, *961*
spigola al finocchio 1199
spinach 567–70
agnolotti Piedmontese 268
barley soup al verde 248
beef and spinach roulades 792
boiled eggs with spinach 369
bread and spinach gnocchi 259
cannelloni with béchamel sauce 269
chickpea and spinach soup 230
cream of spinach soup 221
curried oysters 718
cuttlefish with spinach 723
farmhouse rainbow pie 188
Genoese spinach 568
green pasta dough 268
green risotto 339
herb mayonnaise 67

meatballs with spinach 798
potato and spinach gnocchi 264
rice with spinach 318, *319*
ricotta and spinach crêpes 384, *385*
ricotta and spinach gnocchi 264, *265*
rustic vegetable pie 187
scrambled eggs with spinach 379
smoked sea trout and vegetable
   casserole 686
spinach and mushroom
   salad 499, *569,* 570
spinach and salmon tart 186
spinach and scallop salad 499
spinach butter 82
spinach croquettes 568
spinach hearts 114
spinach in cream 568
spinach in white butter sauce 570
spinach mould 172
spinach sauce 53
stuffed capon 888
tagliatelle pie 343
tagliatelle with spinach 281
three-colour terrine 534
turkey leg with spinach 939
two-colour mould 169
vegetable and cheese filled ravioli 279
wrapped cotechino 840
spinaci alla crema 568
spinaci alla genovese 568
spinaci in insalata con
   champignon 569, 570
spinaci in salsa bianca 570
spinacino ai carciofi 836
spiny lobster, Creole 689
splendid Maria-cake 1064
splendida torta Maria 1064
sponge cake 1013
   fruits of the forest charlotte 1032, *1033*
   Italian trifle 1112, *1113*
   Margherita sponge 1010
sponge fingers
   black grape charlotte 1035
   charlotte delight 1034
   marron glacé semifreddo 1104
   plum and pear charlotte 1032
   tiramisu 1110, *1111*
   zabaglione soufflé 1043
   zuccotto 1110
spring onions
   kidneys with raw spring onions 869
   monkfish with cauliflower and spring
      onions 616
spuome d'arancia e Grand Marnier 1143
squid 707–9
   baby squid in baskets 105
   fried squid 708
   grilled stuffed squid 708, *709*
   lentil and squid soup 226
   Marche-style squid 707
   mixed fish soup with orange 729
   pesto tortelloni with squid 285
   seafood crostini 132

squid stuffed with prawns 708
stuffed cuttlefish 724
stuffed squid 104
star fruits
   exotic fruit salad 1082
steak in balsamic vinegar 784
steak in white wine 795
steak pizzaiola 784
steak tartare 802
steak with mushrooms 783
steak with mustard 784
steak with sage 795
stews
   beef stew 800
   beef stew with coffee 800
   beef stew with white wine 801
   beef stew with wine and onions 800
   cassoeula *763,* 764
   chicken cacciatore 922
   chicken stew with olives 934
   cod stew with olives and capers 629
   Florentine beef stew 801
   goose stew 906, *907*
   goulash 791
   Irish stew 807
   marinated rabbit 977
   Milanese mixed boiled meat 785
   Milanese osso buco 825, *826*
   monkfish stew with turmeric rice 619
   mutton and bean stew 807
   mutton and potato stew 808
   mutton stewed in citrus juice 807
   ostrich stew 936
   oxtail vaccinara 857
   Piedmontese boiled meat 785
   pork stew with peas 775
   pork stew with smoked sausages 774
   rabbit cacciatore 971, *972*
   rabbit in cider 974
   rabbit in milk 973
   rabbit in olive oil and lemon 971
   rabbit in red wine 974
   rabbit in vinegar 971
   rabbit stew with anchovies 978
   rabbit stew with tomatoes and basil 979
   rabbit stew with walnuts 979
   rabbit with honey and
      vegetables 974, *975*
   rabbit with mustard 973
   rabbit with peperonata 976
   shin of veal in cider 836
   six-aroma veal stew 835
   spicy pork stew 775
   seafood stew with lentils 1124
   stewed rabbit 977
   stracotto stew 779
   sweet-and-sour pork stew 775
   turkey stew with mustard 942
   veal and vegetable stew 835
   veal osso buco with peas 827
   venison stew *965,* 966
   wild boar with apples 967, *968*
   wild boar with olives 969

stinco al sidro 836
stinco arrosto 838
stinco con verdure 776
stoccafisso alla Mediterranea 604
stoccafisso mantecato alla veneta 605
stockfish 602
   Mediterranean stockfish 604
   Veneto-style creamed stockfish 605
   see also salt cod
stocks 76
   for broths 204–5
   chicken stock 209
   clear or delicate stock 205
   concentrated fish stock 210, 592
   concentrated stock 205
   court-bouillon 591
   dark stock 204
   fish stock 208–9, 591
   meat stock 208
   stock cubes 205
   vegetable stock 205, 209
storione alla griglia 665
storione all'aceto balsamico 665
storione con carciofi 666
storione con salsa ai peperoni 666
'stracci' agli astici 279
stracci with lobster 279
stracciatella 237, 238
stracotto 779, 1148
stracotto al vino bianco 801
stracotto alla fiorentina 801
stracotto di struzzo 936
strawberries
   fruit jelly 1025
   fruits of the forest charlotte 1032, *1033*
   gratin fruits of the forest with
      zabaglione 1108
   peaches with strawberries 1087
   strawberries with orange 1080
   strawberry and rhubarb compote 1079
   strawberry dessert 1061
   strawberry ice cream *1099,* 1101
   strawberry jam 1117
   strawberry jelly 1114
   strawberry risotto 332
   strawberry sauce 1018
   summer pineapple 1078
strudels
   apricot strudel 1064
   ricotta strudel 1065
   simple strudel 1065
   vegetable-garden strudel 120
strudel dell'orto 120
strudel di albicocche 1064
strudel di ricotta 1065
strudel semplice 1065
stuffed chicken 930
stuffed cuttlefish 724
stuffed peaches 1088
stuffed tench 683
sturgeon 664–6
   grilled sturgeon 665
   sturgeon in anchovy sauce 665

sturgeon in balsamic vinegar 665
sturgeon in sweet-and-sour sauce 664
sturgeon salad with caviar 1170
sturgeon steaks in gremolata 1143
sturgeon with artichokes 666
sturgeon with red pepper sauce 666
stuzzichini di salvia 102
succulent sardines *651, 652*

sugar 1003
caramelized oranges 1079
sugar crêpes 1090
thick syrup 1019
see also caramel
sugo agli scampi e cappesante 62, *63*
sugo al tonno 62

sultanas
English bread and butter pudding 1027
fruit cake 1049
Genoese spinach 568
Greek-style celery 564
guinea fowl stuffed with sultanas 896
old-fashioned onion tart 184
ricotta and sultana tart 1076
semolina pudding 1027
spiced apples with sultanas 1084
spinach croquettes 568
the sultan's onions 461
sweet-and-sour crostini 132
sweet-and-sour liver 864
sweet-and-sour tongue 99
sweet and strong hare 983
veal fritters 834
Viennese apple pie 1077
summer cannellini beans 466
summer pineapple 1078
summer rice salad 327
summer veal 817
surprise aubergines in breadcrumbs 513
surprise carrot croquettes 431
surprise courgettes 584
surprise raw carrots 428
svizzere 801
svizzere di salmone 646
sweet-and-sour caponata 112
sweet-and-sour courgettes 583
sweet-and-sour crostini 132
sweet-and-sour duck 882
sweet-and-sour goose legs 902
sweet-and-sour liver 864
sweet-and-sour peppers 532
sweet-and-sour pork stew 775
sweet-and-sour sauce, sturgeon in 664
sweet-and-sour spare ribs 774
sweet-and-sour tongue 99
sweet and strong hare 983

sweetbreads 848–51
Genoese stuffed breast of veal *811,* 818
rice timbale 347
sweetbreads au gratin with peas 849
sweetbreads in breadcrumbs 851
sweetbreads in white wine 850
sweetbreads with cream and
mushrooms 849
sweetbreads with globe artichokes 850
sweetbreads with Jerusalem
artichokes 851
sweetbreads with Madeira 850
sweetbreads with watercress 848
veal noisettes à la financière 825
vincisgrassi 348

sweetcorn
corn soup 229
Hawaiian salad 501
low-fat rice salad 327
spicy corn soufflé 177
sweetcorn and radicchio salad 498
yellow salad with sweetcorn 500

Swiss chard 410–11
breast of veal with herbs 828
Easter pie 188, *189*
Genoese stuffed breast of veal *811,* 818
green soup 233
ricotta and Savoy cabbage rolls 444, *445*
rustic vegetable pie 187
Swiss chard au gratin 411
Swiss chard and lentil soup 231
Swiss chard with anchovies 411
Swiss chard with Parmesan 411

swordfish 635–8
baked swordfish 635
braised swordfish 636
fish carpaccio 105
marinated swordfish 638
swordfish parcels 636, *637*
swordfish steaks in balsamic vinegar 638
see also smoked swordfish

syrup
blueberries in syrup 1084
thick syrups 1019

T

tacchinella glassata 942
tacchino di natale 943
tacchino ripieno di castagne 943, 944
tacchino ripieno di cavolini di Bruxelles 945
taccole alla casalinga 536, *537*

tagliatelle
cheese pie 347
cuttlefish ink tagliatelle 280
pasta and chickpeas 235
tagliatelle all'antica with truffles 1139
tagliatelle pie 343
tagliatelle with artichokes 281
tagliatelle with aubergine 280
tagliatelle with cream, peas and
ham 281
tagliatelle with crème fraîche and
rocket 1186
tagliatelle with mushrooms 279
tagliatelle with salmon 280
tagliatelle with spinach 281
tagliatelle with yabbies, butter and
sesame seeds 1166
tagliatelle ai funghi 279
tagliatelle al nero di seppia 280
tagliatelle al salmone 280
tagliatelle all'antica con tartufi 1139
tagliatelle alle melanzane 280
tagliatelle con carciofi 281
*tagliatelle con gamberi di fiume, burro e
sesamo* 1166
*tagliatelle con rucola e crema di
limone* 1186
tagliatelle con spinaci 281
tagliatelle panna, piselli e prosciutto 281
tagliatelline alle cipolle 282
tagliatelline with onions 282

tagliolini
tagliolini with butter and truffle 282
tagliolini with langoustines 282
tagliolini with scallops and lettuce 282
tagliolini agli scampi 282
tagliolini al burro e tartufo 282
tagliolini alle cappesante e lattuga 282
Taleggio toasts 993
tapénade 74
tapioca 238
taragna 310

tarragon
ham and tarragon tart 186
lobster in tarragon sauce 690, *691*
porcini with tarragon 484
tartara alla Scherrer 102
tartara di manzo 802
tartara di pesci ai kiwi 625
tartara di salmone 645, 646

tartare sauce 73
tongue in tartare sauce 866
tartelette al caramello 1054
tartelette al formaggio 143
tartelette al gorgonzola 143
tartelette di avocado 144
tartelette di pollo 144, *145*
tartine al burro di gamberetti 133
tartine al caviale 134
tartine al cetriolo 134
tartine al crescione 134
tartine al formaggio e brandy 134
tartine al Roquefort 137
tartine al tonno 137
tartine alla campagnola 135
tartine alla grappa con le pere 135
tartine alla pizzaiola 135, *136*
tartine all'avocado 137
tartine bicolore di frittatine 138
tartine con acciughe in salsa 138
tartine di granchio alle mele 138
tartine gelatinate alla lingua 138
tartine gelatinate alla senape 139
tartine gelatinate all'insalata russa 139

tartines 133–9
anchovy and egg sauce tartines 138
avocado tartines 137
caviar tartines 134
cheese and brandy tartines 134
crab and apple tartines 138
cucumber tartines 134
grappa and pear tartines 135

jellied mustard tartines 139
jellied Russian salad tartines 139
jellied tongue tartines 138
pizzaiola tartines 135, *136*
prawn butter tartines 133
Roquefort tartines 137
rustic tartines 135
tuna tartines 137
two-colour omelette tartines 138
watercress tartines 134
tartlets 143–5
avocado tartlets 144
cheese tartlets 143
chicken tartlets 144, *145*
Gorgonzola tartlets 143
pâte brisée 140
tarts
Alsace tart 1070
apple and pear tart 1072
blackberry tart 1059
broccoli tart 181
caramel tartlets 1054
cherry tart 1061
chicken and chervil tart 185
chocolate and pear tart 1067
cod and mushroom tart 183
fig tart 1059
Florentine tart 1137
ham and tarragon tart 186
leek tart 185
lemon tart 1069
mushroom tart with walnut cream 181
old-fashioned onion tart 184
rhubarb tart 1058
ricotta and sour cherry tart 1076
ricotta and sultana tart 1076
sausages with potato tart 844
seafood tart 182
spinach and salmon tart 186
strawberry dessert 1061
tart case 1013
tarte Tatin 1066
tutti frutti tart 1060
walnut and honey tart 1074
tartufi al forno con patate 572
tartufi alla parmigiana 572
tartufo, pollo e songino 102
tasty roulades 793
tasty turkey roulades 941
teglia d'acciughe e patate 598
ten-herb sausages 842, *843*
tench 682–3
soused tench with herbs 683
stuffed tench 683
sweet-and-sour tench 1192
tench in a salt crust 683
tench with herbs 682
tenerelle 776
terrina d'anatra 165, 166
terrina di cioccolato e mandorle 1190
terrina di fegatini alle erbe e tartufo 1150
terrina di melanzane 517
terrina di merluzzo con le noci 629

terrina di salmone affumicato 646
terrina di sgombri al vino bianco 658
terrines 158
aubergine terrine 517
cod and walnut terrine 629
duck terrine 165, 166
Florentine mould 159
ham moulds 97
mackerel and white wine terrine 658
smoked salmon terrine 646
three-colour terrine 534
see also moulds; mousses (savoury);
pâtés
teste di funghi alla montanara 486
testina di vitello bollita 871
testina di vitello fritta 871
testina di vitello in insalata 871
tetraone con bruschetta e cavolo nero 1186
thick syrup 1019
three-chocolate millefeuille 1062
three-colour soup 233
three-colour terrine 534
thyme
courgette salad with thyme 585
onion and thyme frittata 388
scorpion fish with thyme 655
sole with thyme 662
timbales 340–9
cheese pie 347
fusilli timbale 346
macaroni Napoletana timbale 346
penne and mushroom pie 343
pheasant pie 342
pumpkin pie 342
raviolini vol-au-vent 348
rice timbale 347
sartù 344, *345*
seafood vol-au-vent 349
tagliatelle pie 343
vincisgrassi 348
timballo di fusilli 346
timballo di maccheroni alla Napoletana 346
timballo di riso 347
tinca alle erbe 682
tinca in carpione 1192
tinca in carpione alle erbe 683
tinca in crosta di sale 683
tinca ripiena 683
tiramisu 1110, *1111*
toasts, Taleggio 993
tomatoes 538–45
Abruzzo scrambled eggs 378
Andalusian mayonnaise 68
aubergine fricassée 510, *511*
aubergines au gratin 513
avocado and tomato canapés 126
avocado tartines 137
avocado tartlets 144
baked tomatoes 540
beans Uccelletto 464, *465*
boiled eggs with tomato 370
braised goose 903

bread soup 234
bread soup with tomato 234
bucatini with green tomatoes 288
buffalo milk mozzarella Capri salad 991
celeriac au gratin 566
celery in tomato sauce 566
cherry tomato and crab bites 104
cherry tomatoes stuffed with crab 700
chicken in pink sauce 900
chicken ratatouille 924, *925*
chicken stew with olives 934
chicken with yellow peppers 931
cold tomato mousse 161
courgette soup 256
cream of prawn and tomato soup 218
cream of tomato soup 220
crostini with mushrooms in a light
sauce 130
eggs with tomatoes 361, *362*
fancy peppers 532
fisherman's pizza 196
Florentine beef stew 801
four seasons pizza 199
fragrant eggs en cocotte 368
French beans with tomato 469
French-style cauliflower 439
fried frogs' legs in tomato sauce 733
gazpacho 226
goulash 791
Gradmother's aubergines 512
green tomato jam 1119
grouper with olives *613,* 614
hard-boiled eggs Napoletana 374
huss with green tomatoes 634
langoustines with tomatoes 703
leeks with tomatoes 546
lentils in tomato sauce 508
maccheroni alla chitarra 273
Margherita pizza 198
Milanese tripe 873
mushrooms with tomato 482
Niçoise canapés 124
orecchiette with tomato and ricotta 276
Parmesan aubergines 515
Parmesan pumpkin 577
pasta and chickpeas 235
penne arrabbiata 295
piquant sauce 60
pizza Napoletana 194, *196*
pizzaiola tartines 135, *136*
poached octopus 722
pot-roast beef with anchovies and
tomato 782
Provençal artichokes 419
Provençal omelette 392
quick tomato sauce 59
rabbit cacciatore 971, *972*
rabbit stew with tomatoes and
basil 979
red tomato frittata 540
rigatoni with cream, pesto and
tomatoes 299
rustic tomato pie 545

salt cod Livorno-style 603
sauce aurore 61
sausage pizza 198
sausages in tomato 844
seafood sauce 62, 63
shad with tomato sauce 600
simple gazpacho 226
skate with capers 639
spaghetti amatriciana 300, *301*
spaghetti with raw tomato 300
steak pizzaiola 784
stewed potatoes with tomato 525
stuffed aubergines 116, *118*
sweet-and-sour caponata 112
tasty turkey roulades 941
tomato and Gruyère mould 539
tomato and mozzarella parcels 539
tomato bruschetta 95, 96
tomato flowers 119
tomato fritters 147, 148, 540
tomato jelly ring 539
tomato sauce 57, *58*
tomato soufflé 178
tomatoes au gratin 541
tomatoes stuffed with pecorino 543, *544*
tomatoes stuffed with rice 543
tomatoes stuffed with Russian salad 543
tomatoes stuffed with tuna 545
tomatoes with aubergines 541
tomatoes with bacon au gratin 542
tomatoes with courgettes 542
tomatoes with cucumber mousse 541
tomatoes with robiola 542
tripe with herbs 873
tripe with mushrooms 872
tuna sauce 62
veal escalopes pizzaiola 833
tongue 865–6
 boiled smoked tongue 865
 braised tongue 866
 hard-boiled eggs in aspic 372, *373*
 jellied tongue tartines 138
 spicy tongue 866
 stuffed capon 888
 sweet-and-sour tongue 99
 three-colour soup 233
 tongue in tartare sauce 866
 tongue with green olives 866
tonno al sedano 668
tonno all'aceto 667
'tonno' di coniglio 979
tonno in insalata con fagiolini 668
tonno stufato 668
topinambur alla panna 574
torre fredda di melanzane 517
torrone
 torrone semifreddo 1102
 torrone soufflé 1043
torta ai broccoletti 181
torta ai formaggi 347
torta al cioccolato 1066
torta al cioccolato con marmellata 1066
torta al cioccolato e alle pere 1067

torta al limone 1069
torta alla glassa d'arancia 1067, *1068*
torta alla marinara 182
torta alla rucole e taleggio 182
torta allo yogurt 1069
torta allo yogurt e ricotta 1069
torta Alsaziana 1070
torta con le mele 1070, *1071*
torta delicata di merluzzo agli
 champignon 183
torta di cavoli 183
torta di cipolle all'antica 184
torta di erbette e carciofi 184
torta di formaggio 999
torta di frittate 390, *391*
torta di funghi e selvaggina 985
torta di mandorle 1070
torta di mele e pere 1072
torta di nocciole 1072, *1073*
torta di noci 1072
torta di noci e miele 1074
torta di pesche 1074, *1075*
torta di pollo al cerfoglio 185
torta di porri 185
torta di prosciutto al dragoncello 186
torta di ricotta 1074
torta di ricotta e uvetta 1076
torta di ricotta e visciole 1076
torta di spinaci al salmone 186
torta di verdure della lunigiana 187
torta di zucca 187, 1076
torta Fiorentina 1137
torta pasqualina 188, *189*
torta rustica arcobaleno 188
torta rustica di carciofi e patate 422
torta rustica Zia Maria 190
torta sbrisolona with quince, mascarpone
 cream and vincotto 1168
torta sbrisolona con mela cotogna, crema di
 mascarpone e vincotto 1168
torta tipo Sacher 1077
torta Viennese alle mele 1077
tortelli, pumpkin 283, 284
tortelli di pecorina, ricotta e parmigiano al
 tartufo bianco 1192
tortelli di zucca 283, *284*
tortellini
 curried tortellini 283
 tortellini Bolognese 283
 tortellini with goose liver cream 1177
tortellini al curry 283
tortellini alla bolognese 283
tortellini con crema di fegato d'oca 1177
tortelloni
 mushroom tortelloni 285
 pesto tortelloni with squid 285
tortelloni di funghi 285
tortelloni di pesto con calamaretti 285
tortiglioni con funghi e melanzane 304
tortiglioni with mushroom and
 aubergine 304
tortino ai carciofi 422
tortino di finocchi 478

tortino di funghi e patate 486
tortino di lavarelli con patate 677
tortino di peperoni 121
tortino di zucchine 121
tortino rustico di pomodori 545
tournedos alla Rossini 802
tournedos Rossini 802
trance di dentice marinate 626
trance di pesce spada all'aceto
 balsamico 638
Treviso radicchio
 baked radicchio 550, *551*
 fried radicchio 553
 radicchio en croûte 553
 Treviso radicchio and prawn salad 500
 Treviso radicchio salad with
  mushrooms 500
 Treviso radicchio salad with
  orange 550, *552*
triangolini alla robiola 999
Triestian potato gnocchi with
 prunes 263
trifle, Italian 1112, *1113*
triglie al finocchio 669
triglie alla Livornese 670
triglie alle erbe aromatiche 670
triglie con fagioli 670
tripe 872–3
 Milanese tripe 873
 simple tripe 873
 tripe with herbs 873
 tripe with mushrooms 872
trippa ai funghi 872
trippa alla Milanese 873
trippa aromatica 873
trippa in bianco 873
trota affumicata al melone 685
trota al ginepro 685
trota alla Provenzale 685
trota con funghi e cozze 686, *687*
trota con verdure 686
trotters
 cassoeula *763, 764*
 zampone 845
trout 684–7
 Provençal trout 685
 trout with mushrooms and
  mussels 686, *687*
 see also sea trout; smoked trout
truffle pâté
 beef Wellington 791
 tournedos Rossini 802
truffles 571–2
 anchovies with truffles 598
 bagna cauda *48,* 49
 black truffle sauce 70
 brain roulades with truffle 855
 braised veal with truffle 816
 classic truffle frittata 572
 chicken liver pâté with herbs and
  truffle 1150
 cream of truffle soup 214
 eggs with truffle 360

guinea fowl with truffles baked in a parcel 896

lasagnette with leeks, spring onions and black truffles 1189

leg of kid with truffle cream 753

Parmesan truffles 572

Piedmontese fondue 995

Piedmontese tartare 95

pigeon mousse with truffle vinaigrette 160

radicchio bundles 151, *152*

roast truffles with potatoes 572

saddle of venison with black truffle timbale 1196

scrambled eggs with truffle 378

seared prawns with cannellini bean salad and tartufo dressing 1173

stuffed pot-roast pheasant 953

tagliatelle all'antica with truffles 1139

tagliolini with butter and truffle 282

truffle, chicken and lamb's lettuce 102

truffled capon 889

Tuscan pecorino, ricotta and Parmesan tortelli with white truffle 1192

Valle d'Aosta veal chops 819

veal Bolognese 821

veal bundles with truffles 824

woodcock with truffle 950

tuna 667–8

artichokes with tuna 420

baby octopus and green bean salad 107

bucatini with green tomatoes 288

calf's head salad 871

cauliflower salad (1) 115

cauliflower salad (2) 115

chicken with tuna 929

chickpeas with tuna 450

cold veal in tuna sauce *837*, 838

cuttlefish ink tagliatelle 280

fusilli salad 290

Genoese salad 654

hot veal in tuna sauce 838

loin of pork with tuna sauce 770

low-fat rice salad 327

mixed tuna salad 501

pepper and tuna rolls 530

rabbit and tuna roll 978

rolled peppers 119

rustic tartines 135

slow-cooked tuna 668

spaghetti with tuna 302

stuffed courgettes 122

summer rice salad 327

tapénade 74

tomato flowers 119

tomato jelly ring 539

tomatoes stuffed with tuna 545

tuna and bean salad 668

tuna bites 104

tuna butter 88

tuna frittata 388

tuna in vinegar 667

tuna mould with leek sauce 168

tuna pâté 164

tuna sauce (cold) 74

tuna sauce (hot) 62

tuna tartines 137

tuna with celery 668

yellow fin tuna carpaccio with shaved fennel, lemon and bottarga 1173

turbot 640–3

baked turbot with lentil sauce 641

steamed turbot fillets with vegetables 640

turbot fillets with a potato topping 641

turbot in orange sauce 642

turbot in sparkling wine 642

turbot with olive sauce 643

turbot with saffron in clam sauce 643

turkey 876, 937–45

Christmas turkey 943

glazed turkey 942

pot-roast turkey 938

tasty turkey roulades 941

turkey à l'orange 938

turkey and bean salad 499

turkey breast with almonds 940

turkey breast with cheese 940

turkey fricassée with porcini 940

turkey leg with herbs 939

turkey leg with spinach 939

turkey roll with olives 941

turkey stew with mustard 942

turkey stuffed with Brussels sprouts 945

turkey stuffed with chestnuts *943, 944*

turmeric

monkfish stew with turmeric rice 619

turnip tops 455–7

orecchiette with turnip tops 274

Parmesan turnip tops 456

penne with turnip tops 295

Puglian minestrone 242

spicy turnip tops 456, *457*

turnip tops baked in a parcel 456

turnip tops with ham 456

turnips 554–7

leg of mutton with turnips 805, *806*

roast turnips with leeks and pumpkin 556, *557*

roast turnips with potatoes 556

sausages and turnips 845

stuffed duck in turnip sauce 884

stuffed turnips 555

turnips in cream 555

turnips with bacon 555

Tuscan anchovy crostini 127

Tuscan minestrone 243

Tuscan pecorino, ricotta and Parmesan tortelli with white truffle 1192

tutti frutti tart 1060

two-colour cauliflower with pepper 437, *438*

two-colour omelette tartines 138

two-colour mould 169

U

ugly-but-good biscuits 1051

uova affogate ai carciofi 354, *355*

uova affogate al formaggio 356

uova affogate con crocchette di asparagi 356

uova affogate con verdure miste 357

uova affogate in gelatina 357

uova al piatto ai funghi 359

uova al piatto al prezzemolo 359

uova al piatto al tartufo 360

uova al piatto con asparagi 360

uova al piatto con finocchi e mozzarella 360

uova al piatto con melanzane 361

uova al piatto con polenta 361

uova al piatto con pomodori 361, *362*

uova al piatto con salsiccia 363

uova al piatto sui crostoni al latte 363

uova alla coque con asparagi 358

uova alla coque con ketchup 358

uova in cocotte ai porri 366, *367*

uova in cocotte al lardo 368

uova in cocotte al ragù 368

uova in cocotte alla pestatora 366

uova in cocotte aromatiche 368

uova di struzzo 935

uova di trota e patate 686

uova fritte al burro d'acciuga 364

uova fritte al civet 364

uova fritte alla Rossini 365

uova fritte all'aceto 365

uova fritte all'americana 365

uova fritte con cavolini di Bruxelles 365

uova mollette agli spinaci 369

uova mollette ai funghi 370

uova mollette al pomodoro 370

uova mollette alla senape aromatica 370

uova mollette con i broccoli 371

uova mollette con i carciofi 371

uova nel nido 122

uova sode al curry 374

uova sode alla Napoletana 374

uova sode alle noci 374

uova sode col capello 375

uova sode con i gamberetti 375

uova sode con il salmone 375

uova sode con le ostriche 375

uova sode in gelatina 376

uova sode ripiene e fritte 376

uova strapazzate ai carciofi 377

uova strapazzate al tartufo 378

uova strapazzate al verde 379

uova strapazzate alla fontina 378

uova strapazzate all'abruzzese 378

uova strapazzate con i fagioli 379

uova strapazzate con i fegatini 379

uova strapazzate con la salsiccia 379

uova strapazzate nel nido 380, 381

V

Valle d'Aosta polenta pasticciata 309
Valle d'Aosta vol-au-vents 191
Valle d'Aosta asparagus 402
Valle d'Aosta veal chops 819
Valtellina pizzoccheri 277, *278*

vanilla
bread pudding with vanilla sauce 1151
vanilla bavarois 1021
vanilla ice cream *1099,* 1101
vanilla soufflé 1042

veal 810–38
braised breast of veal 829
braised veal 817
braised veal topside 816
braised veal with lemon 815
braised veal with olives 815
braised veal with truffle 816
breast of veal with artichoke hearts 836
breast of veal with herbs 828
breast of veal with mayonnaise 828
breast of veal with sausages 828
cannelloni with béchamel sauce 269
cold veal in tuna sauce *837,* 838
cotechino in a jacket 842
country bonbons 150
curried veal 835
duck terrine *165,* 166
fillet of veal alla Rossini 1171
fillet of veal in conza 823
Genoese stuffed breast of veal *811,* 818
Grosseto onions 459, *460*
guinea fowl with truffles baked in a
    parcel 896
hot veal in tuna sauce 838
meat mould 823
meat pie 827
meat stock 208
Milanese mixed boiled meat 785
Milanese osso buco 825, *826*
Milanese veal chops 819, *820*
milk pot-roast 814
Piedmontese boiled meat 785
Piedmontese tartare 95
poached stuffed chicken 916, *917*
pot-au-feu 236
pot-roast codino of veal 818
pot-roast veal with kidney 815
pot-roast veal with walnuts 814
roast breast of veal 827
roast shin of veal 838
Roman saltimbocca 831, *832*
saddle of veal alla Bergese 1137
shin of veal in cider 836
shoulder of veal with uva fragola 1125
simple capon galantine 889
simple poached veal 824
simple roast veal 816
six-aroma veal stew 835
soup with meatballs 229
summer veal 817
tortellini Bolognese 283
Valle d'Aosta veal chops 819

veal and vegetable stew 835
veal Bolognese 821
veal braised in milk with prosciutto 814
veal bundles with truffles 824
veal cutlets with artichokes 817
veal escalopes in lemon *829,* 830
veal escalopes pizzaiola 833
veal escalopes with grapefruit 834
veal escalopes with herbs 834
veal escalopes with Marsala 829
veal escalopes with milk 833
veal escalopes with mushrooms 831
veal escalopes with mustard 833
veal fritters 834
veal in 'reduced stock' 821
veal knots 822
veal meatloaf 831
veal noisettes à la financière 825
veal noisettes in butter, sage and
    rosemary 825
veal osso buco with peas 827
veal ribbons 823
veal roulades in aspic 824
veal roulades with vegetables 824
veal steaks in olive sauce 822
veal steaks in vinegar 821
veal steaks with egg and lemon 822
Villeroy veal cutlets 819
vine leaf parcels 97
wrapped cotechino 840
vellutata di lenticchie 224
velouté Brussels sprouts 448

velouté sauce 61
sauce aurore 61
velvety lentil soup 224
velvety ring cake 1046
Veneto-style creamed stockfish 605
Veneto-style liver *847,* 863

venison 964–6
mushroom and game pie 985
roast saddle of venison with
    cranberries 966
roast venison 964, *965*
saddle of venison with black truffle
    timbale 1196
venison stew 966
venison with cream 985
vermicelli con le vongole 304
vermicelli with clams 304
vichyssoise 224
Viennese apple pie 1077
Villeroy veal cutlets 819

vinaigrette 76
truffle vinaigrette 160
vincisgrassi 348
vine leaf parcels 97

vinegar
balsamic vinegar sauce 69
béarnaise sauce 55
breast of goose in balsamic
    vinegar 904, 905
chicken breasts in vinegar 916
Chinese sauce 56

cooked marinade 80
eggs with vinegar 365
frogs in batter 733
grey mullet in vinegar 610
lamb cutlets cooked in vinegar 747
Ligurian musky octopus 721
marinated partridge 958
mint sauce 72
onion chutney 65
Philippines chicken 922
rabbit in vinegar 971
red wine marinade 78
redcurrant and apple chutney 64
sea trout with juniper berries 685
soused chicken breasts 919
soused shad 600
soused tench with herbs 683
steak in balsamic vinegar 784
sturgeon in balsamic vinegar 665
sturgeon in sweet-and-sour sauce 664
sweet-and-sour goose legs 902
sweet-and-sour liver 864
sweet-and-sour peppers 532
sweet-and-sour tongue 99
swordfish steaks in balsamic
    vinegar 638
tongue in tartare sauce 866
tuna in vinegar 667
veal steaks in vinegar 821
vinaigrette 76
vinegar marinade 78
wild boar in sauce 969
vitello tonnato caldo 838
vitello tonnato freddo 837, 838

vodka
cherries in alcohol 1079
leg of mutton in vodka 805
lemon sorbet *1105,* 1106
penne rigate in vodka 298
vol-au-vent al pollo 192
vol-au-vent al prosciutto 192
vol-au-vent alla valdostana 191
vol-au-vent con gli scampi 192
vol-au-vent con raviolini 348
vol-au-vent di mare 349
vol-au-vents 191–2
chicken vol-au-vents 192
ham vol-au-vents 192
prawn vol-au-vents 192
raviolini vol-au-vent 348
seafood vol-au-vent 349
Valle d'Aosta vol-au-vents 191

W

wafers, rolled 1052
walnuts
caramel tartlets 1054
celery and walnut salad 564, *565*
cheese and walnut crêpes 384
chicory, cheese and walnuts 996
cod and walnut terrine 629
date and walnut bonbons 1052

fennel with walnuts and orange 477
Genoese pansotti 276
hard-boiled eggs with walnuts 374
mushroom tart with walnut cream 181
pheasant with fruit 951, *952*
pot-roast veal with walnuts 814
rabbit stew with walnuts 979
radicchio and walnut rolls 549
rice with carrots and walnuts 317
small cheese crackers 151
Viennese apple pie 1077
walnut and coffee cake 1060
walnut and honey tart 1074
walnut cake 1072
walnut gnocchi 260
walnut sauce 57

watercress
green cream soup *223*, 224
herb mayonnaise 67
sweetbreads with watercress 848
watercress broth 206
watercress tartines 134

watermelon
melon fruit salad 1082
watermelon with rum 1079
wheat germ soup 227
whipped cream 1017
whipped cream mayonnaise 67

white beans
farro and bean minestrone 243, *244*
Milanese tripe 873
pasta and white bean 235
ribollita 246, *247*
tuna and bean salad 668
white cabbage salad 498
white meat sauce 52
'white' pizza 196
white sea bream 620
white wine marinade 78, *79*

whitebait 606
whitebait in egg cream 606
whitebait salad 107, *108*
whitebait soup 230
whitebait with olive oil and
  lemon 606
wholegrain rice 314
wholemeal gnocchi 266

wild boar 967–9
wild boar in sauce 969
wild boar with apples 967, *968*
wild boar with olives 969
wild duck with figs 984
wild game 984–5
wild greens and artichoke pie 184

wine
Alsace chamois 962
Barolo and mushroom risotto 329
beef stew with white wine 801
beef stew with wine and
  onions 800
black grape charlotte 1035
braised beef with Barolo 786, *787*
braised breast of veal 829

braised goose 903
braised veal 817
capon roast in a parcel 887
caramelized oranges 1079
carp in wine 675
caviar risotto 330
chamois in red wine 963
chicken in red wine 930
chicken in white wine 929
chicken legs in red wine 913
chicken with carrots and
  onions 900
chicken with olives 926
chicken with sparkling wine 929
chicken with tuna 929
chicken with yellow peppers 931
cinnamon pears 1085
cod and mushroom tart 183
cooked marinade 80
croûtes with pork fillet and pâté de
  foie gras 768
curried woodcock 949
eggs in red wine 364
eggs with sausage 363
exotic fruit salad 1082
fennel with white wine 477
fresh fruit jelly 1080
frogs' legs in white wine 732
fruit and champagne fritters 1096
goose stew 906, *907*
Greek-style celery 564
guinea fowl with red wine 895
ham in white wine 772, *773*
hare cacciatore 980
hare with juniper berries 981
hare with wine 981, *982*
honey pudding 1024
jugged duck legs 884
juniper marinade 77
kidneys in Bordeaux 868
kidneys in Madeira 868
lamb fricassée with onions 748, *749*
leg of lamb à la Périgourdine 744
lights in Marsala 859
liver in Merlot 864
Livorno-style fish soup 726, *727*
mackerel and white wine
  terrine 658
marchand de vin sauce 56
marinated partridge 958
marinated rabbit 977
Marsala sauce 55
monkfish in red wine 616
mushroom and game pie 985
octopus in red wine 722
old-fashioned onion tart 184
onions in orange mustard 114
ostrich stew 936
oysters in salted sabayon sauce 718
peaches in red wine 1087
peaches with strawberries 1087
pear crown 1058
Piedmontese leg of kid 754

pigeons in red wine 1181
plum and pear charlotte 1032
plum bavarois 1021
plum meringue 1108
plums in wine 1088
polenta pasticciata with
  anchovies 311
quail in white wine 959
rabbit in red wine 974
red wine marinade 78
ricotta and sultana tart 1076
roast pheasant with Savoy cabbage,
  chestnuts and red wine 1167
roast venison 964
salmon and wine risotto 330
Savoyard fondue 994
scorpion fish in white wine 1159
scorpion fish in white wine and
  saffron 655
sea trout with juniper berries 685
semolina with cherries 1110
smoked ham with Marsala 772
spare ribs in white wine 772
spiced apples with sultanas 1084
spiced wine broth 206
spicy pork stew 775
steak in white wine 795
strawberry risotto 332
stuffed squid 104
summer pineapple 1078
sweet fritters 1094, *1095*
sweetbreads in white wine 850
sweetbreads with Jerusalem
  artichokes 851
sweetbreads with Madeira 850
sweetbreads with watercress 848
tournedos Rossini 802
trout with mushrooms and
  mussels 686, *687*
turbot in sparkling wine 642
veal escalopes with Marsala 829
veal knots 822
veal noisettes à la financière 825
veal ribbons 823
venison stew *965*, 966
venison with cream 985
white wine marinade 78, 79
wild boar in sauce 969
wild boar with apples 967, *968*
wild boar with olives 969
wild duck with figs 984
wine bavarois 1022
winter minestrone 243

woodcock 949–50
woodcock with green apples 950
woodcock with juniper 950
woodcock with truffle 950
woodcock with truffle 950
zabaglione 1037, 1039
zabaglione soufflé 1043

Worcestershire sauce
spicy marinade 80
würstel con verza 845

Y

yeast 1004
  coffee babá 1055
  kugelhopf 1048
  velvety ring cake 1046
  yeast cake 1012
yellow salad with sweetcorn 500
yogurt
  potatoes baked in foil with yogurt 522
  quail with yogurt 959
  radish salad with yogurt 560
  spicy broccoli with yogurt 414
  yogurt and ricotta cake 1069
  yogurt béchamel 51
  yogurt biscuits 1050
  yogurt cake 1069
  yogurt ice cream 1102
  yogurt marinade 78
  yogurt sauce 70

Z

zabaglione *1037,* 1039
  gratin fruits of the forest with zabaglione 1108
  panna cotta, almond tart and zabaglione 1140
  Pipasener pastry with zabaglione 1193
  zabaglione soufflé 1043
zabaione 1037, 1039
zampone 845
zite
  pasta with sardines 293, *294*
  zite with sausage, onions and fennel 1128
zite con salsiccia, cipolle e finocchio 1128
zucca al forno con patate 577
zucca al rosmarino 578
zucca alla parmigiana 577
zucchero caramellato 1019
zucchine a sorpresa 584
zucchine agrodolci 583
zucchine ai gamberetti 696
zucchine al limone 583
zucchine arrosto 583
zucchine capricciose 584
zucchine capricciose al salmone e porri 585
zucchine con insalata belga al timo 585
zucchine in crema d'uova 585
zucchine ripiene 122
zuccotto 1110
zuppa alla Pavese 248
zuppa con orzo al verde 248
zuppa con orzo e piselli 248
zuppa di cavoli 249
zuppa di cicoria 249
zuppa di cipolle al latte 249
zuppa di cipolle gratinata 250
zuppa di cozze 250
zuppa di fagioli e orzo 250

zuppa di fiocchi d'avena 251
zuppa di formaggi e porri 251
zuppa di funghi e fagioli 251
zuppa di granchi 252, *253*
zuppa di lattughe gratinata 252
zuppa di pane 254
zuppa di pane e lenticchie 254
zuppa di patate 254
zuppa di patate e vongole 255
zuppa di piccione 1183
zuppa di pesce del pescatore 728
zuppa di pesce del pirata 728
zuppa di pesce misto all'arancia 729
zuppa di pesce misto di conchiglie 729
zuppa di porri e lenticchie 255
zuppa di radicchio 255
zuppa di rane 256
zuppa di zucca 256
zuppa di zucchine 256
zuppa Inglese 1112, *1113*
zuppetta di mare con lenticchie 1124